Hoisington

D1567570

BUSINESS ORGANIZATIONS

Statutes, Problems and Cases

First Edition

BUSINESS ORGANIZATIONS

Statutes, Problems and Cases

First Edition

Michael K. Molitor

Associate Professor
Thomas M. Cooley Law School
Grand Rapids, Michigan

Vandeplas Publishing

United States of America

Business Organizations: Statutes, Problems and Cases
First Edition

Molitor, Michael K.

Published by:

Vandeplas Publishing – December 2011

801 International Parkway, 5th Floor
Lake Mary, FL. 32746
USA

www.vandeplaspublishing.com

ISBN: 978-1-60042-157-0

PREFACE

The order of items in the subtitle of this book, *Statutes, Problems, and Cases*, was chosen for a reason: the law of business organizations is primarily statute-based. While cases certainly are important, in my opinion they usually play a supporting role. True, cases help us interpret statutes and provide many important rules governing business organizations. But they are secondary to statutes. In researching an issue concerning business organizations, lawyers almost invariably begin with the applicable statute and then look to see how courts have interpreted the statute.

This is different from the experience that many students have in their first-year law school courses such as Torts, Property, Criminal Law, and most notably, Constitutional Law. In those courses, "famous" cases often are given star treatment and statutes appear as "bit players." Moreover, cases often seem more "fun" than statutes; they tell the story of a plaintiff who was (allegedly) harmed by a defendant or of a person who committed a violent crime. Supreme Court opinions interpreting the Constitution can be even more interesting; they address many issues about which people have passionate opinions, such as religion, abortion, privacy, free speech, race and gender discrimination, gun control, and governmental power. Some Supreme Court opinions rival great literature in their eloquence. By contrast, statutes seem dry, wordy, complex, and far removed from everyday experience. And statutes concerning business organizations seem to many people to be even worse. After all, who cares about some rich business-people arguing over money?

Well, *you* should. Businesses are extremely important to our economy and way of life, because businesses—from tiny sole proprietorships to massive multinational corporations—employ the majority of workers in the United States. The success or failure of businesses will affect millions of persons' livelihood and their ability to save for retirement or put their children through college. In short, businesses create wealth through their products and services. The laws governing business entities thus have enormous societal implications. Contrary to the impression that some may have of business organization law being—ahem—less than thrilling, business organizations law is *important*. It also can be exciting. And I don't say that just because I teach a course on business organizations. Even lawyers who don't consider themselves "business" attorneys need to know the basics.

Statutes are important, not only in the law of business organizations, but in nearly every other area of law. In fact, statutes are increasingly *more* important than case law. Even if you decide that you dislike business organizations law and want nothing further to do with it, as a future lawyer you will need to know how to read, interpret, and—most importantly—*apply* statutes. There's just no avoiding them. The structure of this book will, hopefully, sharpen your statutory interpretation skills. To that end, there are a myriad of problems in each chapter that are designed to ensure that students have read the applicable statute and can apply the statute to a fact pattern. When reading this textbook, it is vitally important that you work on these problems. Don't skip over the problems and wonder what the answers are and/or wait for your professor to explain them in class. Try them! This will certainly entail more work, but you will be a better student—and a better lawyer—for the effort that you expend. In addition, each chapter ends with a series of multiple choice questions concerning the concepts discussed in that chapter. Because my intent was not to "hide the ball" (as some law students are fond of accusing professors), detailed explanations to each multiple choice question appear in the appendix. Hopefully, these problems will allow you to test your mastery of the subject matter.

That said, it is not as if there are no cases in this textbook. On the contrary, there *are* a great many "famous" business organizations cases here, particularly opinions from Delaware courts concerning the duty of care (see Chapter 6), the duties of the board of directors of a corporation that is involved in a takeover battle (see Chapter 12), and many other topics. However, I have tried to be judicious in the treatment of cases in this textbook, avoiding "throwing in" a case simply to illustrate a point that could be easily explained or illustrated in a problem. In addition, I have tried to edit the cases to remove or simplify "unnecessary" details without losing the aspects of the case that I considered important for this textbook. (Omitted portions of cases are indicated with asterisks for those who wish to look up the full opinions. Also, most citations to other cases have been replaced with "[Citation omitted.].")

Business organizations can be a sprawling topic and there are many ways to organize it, each of them with cogent supporting arguments. But I chose what I believe to be a logical way to present the material. Furthermore, due to space limitations there are many details that have been omitted, which you may explore in advanced courses on business organizations, securities regulation, and taxation. In addition, you will undoubtedly learn more in practice if you decide to become a business attorney. But in the end, this textbook should give all future lawyers, not just business attorneys, a solid grounding in the applicable law. Hopefully, this book is comprehensive but not overwhelming.

I am very fortunate to work at The Thomas M. Cooley Law School and to have had the opportunity to take a sabbatical during which I wrote the bulk of this textbook. In particular, I would like to thank President Don LeDuc and Associate Dean Nelson Miller for their support and encouragement and my colleagues Ronald Trosty, Joni Larson, James Carey, Paul Sorensen, David Tarrien, and Byron Babbish for their many helpful comments and observations and for use of some multiple choice questions. Many students at Thomas M. Cooley Law School during the summer and fall of 2011 also provided helpful comments on a preliminary version of this textbook. Amy Ash provided valuable research assistance. And one certainly cannot forget Lindsey Burns, who provided great proofreading and computer assistance.

Last but certainly not least, I would like to thank my long-suffering wife, Jennifer. She had to listen to me constantly update her on the progress of this book for many months and even slogged through a chapter or two. She did so with grace and good humor.

But enough of my rambling. Let's learn some Biz Orgs!

—Mike Molitor, November 2011

TABLE OF CONTENTS

CHAPTER 4: PARTNER DISSOCIATION AND PARTNERSHIP DISSOLUTION

CHAPTER 5: INTRODUCTION TO CORPORATE LAW

CHAPTER 6: THE DUTY OF CARE

CHAPTER 7: THE DUTY OF LOYALTY

CHAPTER 8: DERIVATIVE LAWSUITS

CHAPTER 9: CLOSELY HELD CORPORATIONS

CHAPTER 12: MAJOR CORPORATE TRANSACTIONS

CHAPTER 13: THE SECURITIES ACT OF 1933

CHAPTER 14: INSIDER TRADING

TABLE OF CASES

R

S

T

U

V

W

Z

CHAPTER 1

INTRODUCTION TO BUSINESS ORGANIZATIONS

Welcome to the wonderful world of business organizations. This chapter begins with an overview of the many different forms that may be used to operate a for-profit business in the United States. Next, it discusses the primary sources of law that govern business organizations and introduces you to the role played by business attorneys. Finally, it introduces you to the basics of financial statements.

§ 1.01   THE MAIN FORMS OF BUSINESS ORGANIZATION IN AMERICA

Objectives: After reading the following material, you should be able to describe the basic characteristics of the different forms of business organization used in the United States (sole proprietorships, partnerships, limited liability partnerships, corporations, limited liability companies, limited partnerships, and limited liability limited partnerships). You should also be able to explain to a client who wants to start a business how the selection of a form of business organization affects (1) whether the owner(s) of the business is (are) liable for the business's debts and obligations and (2) whether the business is a "flow through" tax entity.

Subsidiary Objectives: You should be able to explain to a client who wants to start a business:

•   Limited Liability. Why it may be desirable to select a business organization form that shields the owner(s) of the business from personal liability for the debts and obligations of the business; and

•   "Flow Through" Tax Treatment. Why it may be desirable to select a business organization form that provides for "flow through" tax treatment.

Choosing a form of organization for a new business has never been an easy task, but it has become considerably more difficult in recent years. Traditionally, the founder of a business who intended to be the sole owner of the business had two choices: a sole proprietorship or a corporation. If there were to be multiple owners, the choices were between a partnership and a corporation. Limited partnerships were also available but tended to be used only in somewhat specialized situations. These traditional choices remain, but today there is a veritable alphabet soup of other choices available: the limited liability company ("LLC"), the limited liability partnership ("LLP"), and even the limited liability limited partnership ("LLLP"). Although there are many factors that a lawyer and her[*] client should consider when choosing a form of business organization, for now it's important to understand the basic characteristics of each. Keep in mind that the following discussion is relatively basic; many exceptions to the following statements exist. In particular, the tax effects of forming, operating, and dissolving a business are much more complex than what is presented below. *If you plan to be a business lawyer, you should also take Taxation of Business Entities or a similar course.*

TERMINOLOGY

An *LLC* is a limited liability company. An *LLP* is a limited liability partnership. An *LP* is a limited partnership. An *LLLP* is a limited liability limited partnership.

The Sole Proprietorship. The sole proprietorship is the simplest form of business organization. In fact, it is so simple that it is not really accurate to call it an "organization" at all. Instead, a sole proprietorship results when a person has decided to run a business, but without incorporating the business or forming it as an LLC or some other type of entity. In a sole proprietorship, there is no legal distinction between the business and the owner (who, of course, is called the ***sole proprietor***). Nonetheless, it is almost always a wise idea for the sole proprietor to separate her personal finances from the business's finances, such as by having separate bank accounts and accounting records.

There is both good news and bad news in the sole proprietorship. The good news is that the business, not being a separate entity from the owner, does not pay taxes. Of course, this is not to say that the *owner* avoids taxes. Instead, if the business generates taxable income, the owner must report this income on her personal tax return and pay taxes on it. The sole proprietor's obligation to pay

---

[*]   Throughout this book, I typically will use "her" instead of the more cumbersome "his or her" and "she" instead of "he or she."

taxes based on the business's income hardly sounds like "good news." However, as will become clear when you read about corporations later in this chapter, this can result in a smaller amount of taxes being paid overall.

The bad news about the sole proprietorship is that the owner is personally liable for all of the business's debts and obligations. This is because there is no legal separation between the sole proprietorship and the sole proprietor. Thus, if there are, say, $10,000 worth of assets associated with the business, but the business has $100,000 worth of debts, a creditor of the sole proprietorship may collect the $90,000 shortfall from the sole proprietor's personal assets (e.g., her home, car, bank account, etc.),* unless the creditor had previously agreed to limit its recovery to business-related assets. In fact, there is no requirement that the creditor levy on business-related assets first.

One way to manage such personal liability is through insurance. If the sole proprietorship has insurance against a particular event, such as a slip and fall accident on the business's premises, then the insurance company will pay the damages. Nonetheless, as a legal matter, the sole proprietor will remain personally liable for unpaid liabilities. Indeed, if the business fails, leaving huge unpaid debts, the sole proprietor's personal finances may be ruined.

The Partnership (also known as the General Partnership). The key distinction between a partnership and a sole proprietorship is that the partnership has two or more owners, whereas the sole proprietorship has only one owner. Another distinction is that, at least under modern law, a partnership is considered a separate entity from its owners (called the partners). Thus, if A and B form the AB Partnership, there are actually three legal "persons": A, B, and the AB Partnership. Being a legal "person" means that the AB Partnership may own property, enter into contracts, and sue and be sued (among other things).

With regard to taxes and liability issues, the partnership and the sole proprietorship are very similar. A partnership is not a tax-paying entity (outside of rare situations far outside the scope of this book), although it must file an "informational" return with the Internal Revenue Service and applicable state taxing authorities. For example, assume that A and B have formed the AB Partnership. Unless they have agreed otherwise, any profits and losses generated by the AB Partnership will be shared equally between the partners. So if the AB Partnership generates $100,000 of profits (that is, income) in 2012, each of the two partners must report $50,000 of income on her personal tax return for 2012 and pay taxes on it. For this reason, partnerships are sometimes referred to as having "flow through" or "pass through" tax treatment: they do not pay taxes, but their income (or loss) flows through to the partners.

---

*   Some states exempt certain personal assets from seizure by creditors.

> **TERMINOLOGY**
> A *distribution* occurs when a business pays out some of its assets—typically cash—to its owners according to their percentage ownership interest in the business. In a corporation, a distribution is commonly called a *dividend*.

Importantly, Partner A and Partner B must pay taxes on their share of the AB Partnership's income even if the partnership does not pay any *distributions* to either partner. Keep in mind that the AB Partnership is a separate entity, which means that it may own property, including cash. The partnership need not pay any distributions to its partners—although the partners typically will cause the partnership to pay distributions. But again, even if a partner receives no distributions, or receives distributions that are less than the amounts of partnership income that have been allocated to her, she must still report her share of that income on her personal tax return. In this example, both Partner A and Partner B will report $50,000 of income on their respective personal income tax returns—even if they do not receive a dime of distributions from the AB Partnership. (Again, keep in mind that the tax effects of running a business are much more complex than what is discussed in this book.)

In terms of liability, the general rule is that partners in a partnership are jointly and severally liable for the debts and obligations of the partnership. It is worth pausing here to consider how serious joint and several liability is for defendants. If defendants are jointly and severally liable for a claim, the creditor may recover the full amount owed from any single defendant. Consider again Partner A and Partner B and their AB Partnership. Assume that a plaintiff is owed $10,000, but the partnership has no assets with which to pay the claim. Further, Partner A has disappeared and cannot be found. The plaintiff in this situation would be able to recover the entire $10,000 debt from Partner B (assuming that the plaintiff follows the procedural rules described in Chapter 3). Partner B would not be able to claim that she is liable to the plaintiff for only $5,000 because she is only a "half owner" of the partnership. While it is true in this example that if Partner B pays the entire $10,000 debt, she would have a right of contribution from Partner A for $5,000, the plaintiff is unlikely to be concerned about that. Instead, that is a matter for the partners to work out among themselves afterwards.

Forming a partnership does not require that any filing be made with the state government. In this sense, the partnership form is referred to as a "default" form for a business with more than one owner: the business has to be *something*, and if it wasn't incorporated or formed as an LLC or some other type of entity (which would require a filing with the appropriate state government), it has to be a partnership. Similarly, a one-owner business that wasn't incorporated or formed as an LLC or some other type of entity will be a sole proprietorship.

The Limited Liability Partnership (LLP). In 1991, Texas became the first state to adopt an LLP statute. The idea behind this was very simple: change the undesirable characteristic of partnerships (the personal, joint and several liability of the partners), but leave the other characteristics of the partnership intact. In the partnership statute that this book addresses, the Uniform Partnership Act (1997), or *RUPA*, the LLP concept is found in Section 306(c), which provides in part that:

> An obligation of a partnership incurred while the partnership is a limited liability partnership [LLP], whether arising in contract, tort, or otherwise, is solely the obligation of the partnership. A partner is not personally liable … for such an obligation solely by reason of being or so acting as a partner.

Thus, in nearly all respects other than liability issues, the LLP is the same as a general partnership.[*] In the previous example where the AB Partnership owed $10,000 to the plaintiff but the partnership had no assets with which to pay the claim, neither Partner A nor Partner B would be liable for the claim if the partnership were an LLP (unless one of them had been personally responsible for the claim, such as by committing a tort). While the partnership would of course be liable for its own debts and obligations, if it has no assets with which to pay these claims, creditors will go unpaid if it is an LLP.

> **TERMINOLOGY**
>
> *RUPA* is an acronym for "Revised Uniform Partnership Act." The current version of RUPA was adopted by the National Conference of Commissioners on Uniform State Laws in 1997. An earlier version was adopted in 1992, but amended in 1993, 1994 and 1996. The "RUPA" that this book uses is the Uniform Partnership Act (1997). Approximately 35 states now use some version of RUPA. Most of the remaining states use an earlier statute, the Uniform Partnership Act (1914), sometimes referred to as "UPA."

Today, every state recognizes some form of LLP. However, some state statutes only provide for a "partial shield" LLP. In a partial shield LLP, partners are not personally liable for the wrongful acts of other partners or employees (e.g., torts or malpractice), but *are* personally liable for other liabilities of the partnership. For example, assume that the AB Partnership LLP described above has two debts: rent owed to its landlord, and an injury claim resulting from Partner A's negligence. Both Partner A and Partner B would be personally liable for the rent owed the landlord, but Partner B would not be personally liable for the tort committed by Partner A. In contrast, Section 306(c) of RUPA, quoted above, creates a "full shield" LLP in which partners are not liable for any of the partnership's debts or obligations (unless they personally caused them).

---

[*]   There are a few other differences. For example, Section 1001 of RUPA requires a partnership to file a statement of qualification with the state government in order to be an LLP.

One may wonder why, at least in "full shield" states, LLPs[*] are not more prevalent. One reason is bad timing: Texas didn't create LLPs until 1991. LLCs, which also provide for "flow through" taxation and limited liability for their owners, were already popular by then. Indeed, had LLPs been invented before LLCs, the LLC form may never have gained its current popularity.

The Corporation. Like partnerships, corporations have been around for centuries. Unlike a partnership, which has partners and perhaps employees, the "cast of characters" in a corporation is relatively crowded: there are shareholders; directors; and officers and other employees. Sometimes these different roles are a bit blurry, such as where a person is the sole shareholder, serves as the sole director, and also works for the corporation, drawing a salary. However, it is important to consider the different roles separately. The shareholders are called the "owners" of the

> **TERMINOLOGY**
> As a group, the directors of a corporation are called the **board of directors.** Students with previous work experience sometimes confuse directors with officers, particularly if they worked at a corporation as the "Director of Purchasing" or the "Director of Marketing" or a similar (unfortunately named) officer position. Officers are considered employees of the corporation. Members of the board of directors, on the other hand, are not employees.

corporation but have surprisingly little control over it in their shareholder role. Instead, the shareholders annually elect the directors, who are given general authority to run the business. Although the directors *could* make nearly every business decision that the corporation must make, typically it is more efficient to delegate some decision-making power to officers (and other employees).

We will spend several chapters discussing the corporate form in great detail, but here we must be concerned with liability issues and tax issues. The great advantage of the corporate form is limited liability: shareholders of a corporation are not personally liable for the corporation's debts and obligations. While there are exceptions to this general rule that are discussed further in Chapter 5, typically the worst possible outcome for a shareholder is that her stock will become worthless, such as where the corporation files bankruptcy. Thus, she will have lost whatever she spent to acquire the stock.

> **TERMINOLOGY**
> **Shareholders** (or "stockholders" in some states) are the owners of a corporation. A shareholder owns stock, which is considered an **equity** interest in the corporation, as opposed to a **debt** interest. The difference between equity and debt is considered further in Chapter 5.

But that is the extent of the damage—the shareholder's personal assets are not at risk of being seized to pay the

---

[*]   The proper punctuation of LLPs (or LLP's) and LLCs (or LLC's) is apparently disputed. This book will punctuate such acronyms without apostrophes. Some may disagree.

corporation's debts and obligations. Contrast this to a partnership, where partners would remain personally liable for the partnership's unpaid debts.

QUESTION
If shareholders have virtually no power to operate the corporation, what should they do if they are unhappy with the performance of the directors?

The "C Corporation."   This limited liability for shareholders comes with a tradeoff, however: a "double layer" of taxation.   "C corporations" are taxpayers.   Thus, if a corporation earns income, it must pay taxes on that income at the corporate tax rates then in effect. Obviously, the corporation will be left with less cash on hand after paying these taxes. If the corporation then pays dividends to its shareholders, the shareholders must report those dividends as income on their personal income tax returns. Although dividend income is currently taxed at lower rates than earned income, this "double layer" of taxation associated with the corporation often is less desirable than the "flow through" tax treatment of partnerships. Note that dividends that the corporation pays are not deductible from its taxable income.

A few techniques can be used to lessen the effect of this double layer of taxation. Consider a corporation that has a few shareholders, who also work for the corporation and are paid salaries. In this situation, it may be advantageous to pay the employees high salaries. Businesses are entitled to a deduction for "reasonable" salaries under Section 162 of the Internal Revenue Code. The salary amounts paid to employees will reduce the corporation's taxable income—and thus its tax burden. While the employees will obviously be taxed on the amount of salary compensation they receive, if the salaries are roughly equal to what the corporation's taxable income would have been (without paying the salaries), then the effect of the "double layer" of taxation can be reduced. There are many other tax-planning techniques that you may learn about if you take Taxation of Business Entities or a similar course.

The "S Corporation."   Another technique to avoid the "double layer" of taxation is to elect to be an "S corporation."   It is important to note that C corporations and S corporations *are identical in all respects other than tax treatment.* Generally speaking, S corporations are not taxed on their income. Instead, their income is passed through to the shareholders, who report their share of that income on their tax returns. In other words, an S corporation is a flow-though tax entity, much like a partnership. (Although there are some important tax

EXAMPLE
Both "C corporations" and "S corporations" are formed by filing *articles of incorporation* with the state government. Both "C corporations" and "S corporations" will have *bylaws, shareholders*, a *board of directors*, and *officers.*

differences between partnerships and S corporations, they are beyond the scope of this textbook.)

One may then wonder why more corporations aren't clamoring to become S corporations. The problem is that many corporations will not qualify. This is because Section 1361 of the Internal Revenue Code imposes the following restrictions (among others):

- S corporations may not have more than 100 shareholders (subject to certain "counting" rules; for example, a husband and wife will count as only one shareholder);

- S corporations may only have individuals, estates, certain trusts, and certain nonprofit organizations as shareholders;

- S corporations may only have U.S. citizens and resident aliens as shareholders;

- S corporations may not have more than one class of stock (although certain variations in voting rights are permitted); and

- S corporations must be incorporated in the United States.

Thus, a publicly traded corporation will not qualify to be an S corporation. ("Publicly traded" corporations either (1) are listed on a national securities exchange such as the New York Stock Exchange or (2) have 500 or more shareholders, as discussed in more detail in Chapter 10.) Not only will a publicly traded corporation have too many shareholders, but many of those shareholders won't be individuals or other qualified shareholders, and many of them won't be U.S. citizens or resident aliens. But if a corporation qualifies for S corporation status, it generally would be well-advised to do so and obtain the benefits of flow-though tax treatment.

__The Limited Liability Company (LLC).__ LLCs are relatively new on the scene. In 1977, Wyoming became the first state to adopt an LLC statute. Unfortunately, due to historical factors described further in Chapter 16, LLC statutes vary widely from state to state. But it is possible to describe a few universal characteristics of the LLC form, which is a hybrid between a partnership and a corporation.

LLCs are sometimes called the "best of both worlds" because they combine the desirable aspect of corporate status (limited liability for owners) with the desirable aspect of partnership status (flow-though tax treatment). Thus, as a general rule, the owners of an LLC (called the ***members***) will not be personally liable for the debts and obligations of the LLC. If the LLC files bankruptcy, then the worst that will happen to a member is that the value of her interest in the LLC will dwindle to zero. Meanwhile, the LLC will be treated as a partnership for tax purposes if there are multiple members, and treated as a "disregarded entity" if there is only one member. In other words, the LLC gets flow-through tax treatment. Of course, this "best of both worlds" status may also be obtained in an S corporation. However, the LLC form is not subject to the restrictions on S corporations under the Internal Revenue Code described above.

Another way in which an LLC can be considered a hybrid between a partnership and a corporation is in terms of management structure. Generally, a person (or persons) forming an LLC must choose between a ***member-managed*** LLC and a ***manager-managed*** LLC. A member-managed LLC is one in which all of the members have power to make business decisions. In this way, it resembles a partnership, in which all partners have power to make business decisions. Alternatively, a manager-managed LLC is one in which one or more "managers" (who may or may not also be members) are given decision-making authority to the extent specified in the LLC's ***operating agreement***. In this way, a manager-managed LLC resembles a corporation, with centralized decision-making (a corporation's board of directors).

> **TERMINOLOGY**
>
> An ***operating agreement*** is an agreement among the members of an LLC. It is similar to the ***bylaws*** of a corporation. To form an LLC, one must file ***articles of organization*** with the appropriate state government.

The Limited Partnership (LP). LPs are similar to general partnerships in that they have flow-through tax treatment.[*] But in an LP there are two different types of partners: ***general partners*** and ***limited partners***. Typically in an LP there will be one general partner (or perhaps a few) and several limited partners. The advantage of being a general partner is control: except to the extent otherwise provided in the limited partnership agreement, the general partner has full decision-making authority over the LP. The disadvantage of being a general partner is liability: much like partners in a general partnership, the general partner in an LP will be personally liable for the LP's debts and obligations. On the other hand, limited partners have no control over the LP (except to the extent the agreement grants them voting rights), but will not be personally liable for the LP's debts and obligations except in unusual circumstances discussed in Chapter 15.

---

[*] In some situations, however, limited partnerships will be taxed as "C corporations," such as if they are publicly traded. *See* Section 7704(a) of the Internal Revenue Code.

The Limited Liability Limited Partnership (LLLP).   Recently, approximately twenty states have adopted statutes creating LLLPs. An LLLP is really just an LP with a twist: general partners will not be personally liable for the LLLP's obligations. (Limited partners, of course, would remain shielded from personal liability in most situations.) Thus, the LLLP is to the LP as the LLP is to the general partnership.

QUESTIONS
What are the differences between an LP, an LLP, and an LLLP? What about an LLC?

Other Forms of Business Organization.   There are a few other, but relatively rarely used, ways to run a business in the United States. One is the business trust. Also, because this is a book about "business" organizations, nonprofit entities will not be covered although in many ways they are similar to for-profit organizations. However, a few words about "professional" entities are in order here.

Many states permit persons who are licensed in various "learned professions" such as medicine and law to form corporations or LLCs under some circumstances. For example, a law firm could be formed as a partnership, or a sole proprietorship if there is only one lawyer/partner. Alternatively, the law firm could be formed as a "professional" corporation (often referred to as a *PC*) or a "professional" LLC (often referred to as a *PLLC* or perhaps a *PLC*). These statutes typically require that all of the owners must be licensed in the applicable field. Thus, only licensed attorneys may be shareholders of a law firm that is organized as a PC. The types of professions allowed to organize as a PC or PLLC vary from state to state, but often include not only doctors and lawyers, but also accountants, dentists, optometrists, veterinarians, architects, and engineers.

As discussed above, a chief benefit of running a business as a corporation or an LLC is that the owners generally escape personal liability for the debts and obligations of the business. Does this mean that the shareholders of a PC or the members of a PLLC may escape personal liability for malpractice? No. First, most of these statutes prohibit professionals from organizing as a "regular" corporation or LLC, instead requiring them to form as a PC or PLLC (if not a partnership or sole proprietorship).[*] Second, most statutes specifically provide that an owner of a PC or PLLC will be personally liable for her own wrongful acts

---

[*]   Keep in mind, however, that even a shareholder of a "regular" corporation will be personally liable for torts that she commits (and malpractice is simply negligence committed by a professional).

such as malpractice, as well as the wrongful acts of persons under her supervision or control. Thus, there is no way to avoid liability for one's own malpractice or the malpractice of someone under your supervision or control. Using a PC or a PLLC (or an LLP, for that matter) can, however, shield an owner from liability for malpractice committed by *other* owners. Using a PC or a PLLC will also usually shield an owner from personal liability for other debts and obligations of the business, such as rent due to a landlord.

PRACTICE QUESTIONS[*]

Multiple Choice Question 1-1: Belinda and Tina want to open a new business selling tents and other camping gear. Belinda and Tina will each be a 50% owner of the business. In addition, they want to make sure that (1) each owner will have an "equal say" in all business decisions, (2) the owners will not have personal liability for the debts and obligations of the business, and (3) the business will be taxed on a "flow-through" basis. Belinda and Tina have asked for your legal advice as to which form of business organization they should choose. *Which of the following is the best advice you could give them?*

A.   They should form a limited partnership with one owner (either Belinda or Tina) as the general partner and the other owner as the limited partner.
B.   They should form a general partnership.
C.   They should form an S corporation.
D   They should form a C corporation.

Multiple Choice Question 1-2: Tim and Jim are the members of Tim-Jim, LLC. Todd and Rod are the partners of Todd-Rod, a general partnership. Ike and Mike are the shareholders of Ike-Mike Corp., an S corporation. One day, three cars being driven by employees of these three respective businesses were involved in three separate car accidents. The court in each case determined that each business was liable for the accident in which its employee was involved. However, none of the three businesses has enough assets to pay its liability. *Assuming no other facts, which of the following statements concerning liability is correct?*

A.   Tim and Jim are personally responsible for Tim-Jim's liability.
B.   Todd and Rod are personally responsible for Todd-Rod's liability.
C.   Ike and Mike are personally responsible for Ike-Mike's liability.
D.   Both A and B are correct.
E.   Both B and C are correct.

---

[*]   Answers to and explanations of the multiple choice questions appear in the Appendix.

Multiple Choice Question 1-3: Miriam and Chloe are partners in a business that performs lawn care and other landscaping services. One day while mowing a lawn, Miriam negligently injured a customer. *Assuming no other facts, which of the following statements concerning the partners' liabilities is correct?*

A.   If the business is an LP, then neither Miriam nor Chloe will be personally liable for this tort.

B.   If the business is an LLP formed under RUPA, then neither Miriam nor Chloe will be personally liable for this tort.

C.   If the business is an LLP formed under RUPA, then Miriam will be personally liable for this tort but Chloe will not be.

D.   If the business is a general partnership, then both Miriam and Chloe will be personally liable for this tort.

E.   Both C and D are correct.

§ 1.02   SOURCES OF BUSINESS ORGANIZATION LAW

State Law. Business law is primarily state law. Perhaps surprisingly, when forming a business such as a corporation, you can choose any state's law to use to form the entity, even if you never go to that state or do any business there. Generally, the law of the state where the entity is formed will govern the "internal affairs" of the entity, that is, the relations between the owners of the entity and the managers of the entity. For example, assume that a corporation is incorporated under Delaware law but is physically located in and does all of its business in Texas. Delaware law will control its "corporate governance," as well as any disputes between the corporation's shareholders, directors and officers. Thus, if the shareholders sue the directors claiming that the directors breached the fiduciary duties that they owe to the corporation, then Delaware law will apply in that lawsuit. One does not have to litigate the matter in a Delaware court, but the court in which the lawsuit is filed must apply Delaware law to the case.[*]

> **TERMINOLOGY**
> The ***internal affairs doctrine*** means that the rules for how a business entity is governed, and for resolving disputes between the business's owners and its managers, are found in the law where the business is incorporated or organized, not where it is physically located.

---

[*]   As discussed above, the formation of a partnership does not require any filing with a state government. However, Section 106(b) of RUPA provides that a partnership's internal affairs generally will be governed by the law of the state where the partnership has its chief office.

On the other hand, if a customer sues the corporation for an injury, or an employee sues the corporation because she believes she has been wrongfully terminated from her employment, then Texas law would apply to those disputes in this example.   In addition, businesses are subject to other generally applicable laws, and businesses in certain industries are subject to laws regulating those industries.   For example, businesses that produce hazardous waste are subject to a panoply of state and federal environmental-protection laws; however, these or similar laws are not really considered to be "business entity" laws and will not be discussed in this textbook.

Within any jurisdiction, there is generally a hierarchy of laws: the constitution, statutes, and case law.[*]   State constitutions rarely have anything to say about business organizations.   Instead, business organization law is primarily statutory.   Certainly, cases are also important, both to help interpret the meanings of statutes and to provide additional rules in some situations.   However, cases are "inferior" to statutes in the sense that a judge may not overturn a statute simply because she believes the statute to be unwise.   Generally, judges may overturn a statute only if it is unconstitutional.

In this textbook, you will study RUPA (see above) with respect to partnerships; the Model Business Corporation Act ("MBCA") and parts of the Delaware General Corporation Law with respect to corporations; the Uniform Limited Partnership Act (2001) with respect to LPs; and the Revised Uniform Limited Liability Company Act with respect to LLCs.   With the exception of the Delaware statute, each of these statutes is a model statute.   This means that a private entity, as opposed to an actual legislature, has drafted the model statute and recommended that states adopt it.   In other words, these statutes are not "real."   However, most states have adopted these statutes in whole or in part and many other states have statutes that are modeled on these statutes.   Thus, wherever you end up practicing law in the United States, chances are that your state's statutes will closely resemble the statutes you will study in this book.   Delaware is also covered because, as discussed in Chapter 5, Delaware is considered the leading state for corporate law and many big, "important" corporations are incorporated in Delaware.

Agency law, which is covered in Chapter 2, is primarily common law, that is, developed through case law rather than being statute-based.   In Chapter 2, you will study the *Restatement (Third) of Agency* and a few portions of the *Restatement (Second) of Agency*.   The *Restatements*, which are published by the American Law Institute, are not statutes.   Instead, they are largely a reflection of what the law, as previously developed by the courts, is.   However, the

---

[*] The administrative rules of a governmental agency may also apply.   However, in this textbook the only administrative rules that we will discuss are SEC rules under the Securities Act of 1933 and the Securities Exchange Act of 1934.

Restatements resemble statutes in that they comprehensively address a given area of law and are organized into different sections.

Federal Law and Stock Exchange Rules. Federal law will also play a part in this textbook, albeit a small one. Primarily, the federal law affecting business organizations has to do with publicly traded corporations and securities law. For example, in Chapter 10, you will learn about the federal proxy rules under Section 14 of the Securities Exchange Act, which apply to publicly traded corporations. Insider trading under Rule 10b-5 and short-swing profits under Section 16(b) of the Securities Exchange Act are discussed in Chapter 14. Also, Chapter 13 discusses the federal Securities Act of 1933, which generally provides that when a business (or any other person, for that matter) wants to offer and sell "securities," such as shares of stock or bonds, it must either register those securities with the Securities and Exchange Commission ("SEC") or comply with an exemption from the registration requirement. In addition, if a company has stock or other securities listed on an exchange such as the New York Stock Exchange or Nasdaq, it must abide by the rules of that exchange. Typically, these rules are covered in a Securities Regulation course in law school, but they are discussed in some detail in Chapter 10.

Charter Documents. Another important source of the rules governing a particular business entity will be its **charter documents**. In the case of a partnership, this will be the partnership agreement (if the partnership has one). For a corporation, this will be the corporation's articles of incorporation and its bylaws. For an LLC, the charter documents consist of its articles of organization and its operating agreement, and for an LP, the charter documents are the certificate of limited partnership and the limited partnership agreement. Each of these charter documents may contain rules that are different from those found in the applicable statute. For example, several sections of the MBCA begin with the phrase "Unless the corporation's articles or bylaws provide otherwise ..." before going on to state a "rule" governing a particular topic. In a situation like this, the statute section would only apply if the corporation's articles or bylaws (as the case may be) did not specify a different rule. Thus, the MBCA and other statutes give business owners and their lawyers many opportunities to modify rules that they do not consider appropriate for their organization.

However, note that a business entity's charter documents may only address "internal" affairs; third parties generally will not be bound by such documents because they are not parties to them and did not approve them. For example, Section 103(b)(10) of RUPA provides that a partnership agreement may not restrict the rights of third parties (i.e., people who are not partners in that partnership).

How to Read Statutes. It has been my experience that many law students approach statutes with something bordering on fear, maybe even panic. Statutes appear dense, complicated, wordy, and difficult. As a result, some students, I'm sure, don't bother reading them and instead rely on class sessions or other sources to get the "gist" of the statutes. (Obviously, this is not true of most students.) In addition, a class like Business Organizations is often the first time that students are heavily exposed to statutes in law school, other than perhaps the Uniform Commercial Code in the Contracts course. Because the first-year classes, which are considered the core curriculum, tend to emphasize case law, one may come away with the impression that cases are the only law that matters.

This is unfortunate in many respects. Statutes should be welcomed, not feared. The primary benefit of statutes is that they *comprehensively* address a given topic. Unlike case law, which arises haphazardly as actual disputes between parties are litigated, statutes provide nearly all of the rules for a given topic in one place. True, there may be "gaps" in statutes (i.e., issues the legislature did not address), but statutes are almost always more complete than case law. Moreover, statutes are *all in one place*, unlike the rules from case law, which are scattered around in opinions from different courts at different points in time, and may not even be consistent with one another. Finally, in the real world statutes are often much more important than case law. As time goes on, more and more areas of the law are addressed primarily through statutes rather than case law.

With that said, the fact remains that statutes can be difficult reading. Further, what a professor or anyone else may tell you about a statute is no substitute your own careful reading of that statute. So here are some tips in reading statutes.

First, go slowly. There are few extraneous or irrelevant words in statutes. Read the statute slowly, then read it again. And then a third time. Read it a fourth time on the following day to make sure that your understanding of it is still accurate. While you may also want to spend a little time looking through the statute's table of contents or index to get an idea of where the section you're reading fits into the whole statute, the cardinal rule when reading a particular statute section is to slow down and take your time.

Second, focus on how the statute section is structured. If there are several subsections, focus on whether they are separated by an "and" or an "or." This can make all the difference in the world as to the statute's meaning. If the subsections are separated by neither an "and" nor an "or," consider how the different subsections relate to one another. Similarly, the statute's punctuation is likely also important.

Third, pay close attention to the words used in the statute. For example, if a statute says you "shall" do something, then you are required to do so. On the other hand, if the statute says that you "may" do something, then it is optional but not required. The word "such" usually means that the noun following "such" was previously defined or described. If there are any words or phrases that you don't understand, consult the "definitions" section of the statute, which is likely to be at the beginning of the statute. You should always look at the definitions section anyway, as you may be surprised to find that certain words and phrases that you thought you understood have a particular, maybe even unique, meaning within the statute.

Fourth, if the section you are reading contains a cross-reference to another statute section, go read the other section. Don't just think "I wonder what Section X says."

Fifth, consider whether the statute makes sense. If the statute doesn't make sense, or if it seems to lead to a ridiculous result, that is a strong indication that you have misunderstood the statute.

Finally, if all of the foregoing fails, consult your professor. Despite your best efforts to understand them, there will always be some statutes that are simply poorly written or ambiguous. But note that there is a difference between being vague (not having a meaning that is precise) and being ambiguous (having more than one possible meaning). Statute must, to some degree, be vague because they provide rules that will be applied to a multitude of fact patterns.

§ 1.03   RESPONSIBILITIES OF BUSINESS ATTORNEYS

The phrase "business attorney" could mean many different things. Some people may use that phrase to refer to attorneys who work as "in house" counsel rather than at an outside law firm. It could also refer to attorneys that primarily represent businesses, as opposed to individuals, in law suits. However, such attorneys are more properly thought of as litigators.

Instead, the phrase "business attorneys" usually means "deal lawyers"— attorneys who represent businesses or business people in negotiating and drafting contracts or completing transactions such as mergers or asset purchases. Business attorneys also frequently assist business people in forming entities, such as drafting articles of incorporation and bylaws for a new corporation. Another common task of business attorneys is compliance. For example, securities lawyers typically assist publicly traded corporations in drafting and filing their periodic reports to the SEC under the Securities Exchange Act of 1934 and in drafting their proxy statements for their annual meetings of shareholders. Securities lawyers also help companies navigate the thicket of securities regulation when they want to issue and sell securities, such as in an initial public offering. Very rarely does a "business attorney" go to court. Instead, the usual goal of a business attorney is to keep her client *out* of court, such as by drafting clear agreements that won't lead to litigable issues, or helping assure that the client complies with applicable laws and regulations, for example.

So, if the business attorney doesn't go to court to win a case (or at least settle the case on acceptable terms), how should we judge her performance? Are business attorneys simply a nuisance, exacting a "transaction tax" on businesses that want to engage in transactions, or a "cost of doing business" on companies that must comply with burdensome government regulation? Whatever one's view on the merits of a particular law or governmental rule (i.e., whether it is onerous, or whether more or different regulation would be beneficial to society), the fact remains that if a company is subject to a law or rule, it must observe that law or rule. Obviously, attorneys will play an important part in assuring such compliance. So, perhaps the way to judge a "compliance" attorney is by whether the company achieves compliance, or at least avoids any fines or other penalties associated with noncompliance.

As for the transaction attorney, perhaps the way to judge her is by whether her client is better off as a result of her involvement in the transaction (net of her attorney fees). In other words, did the attorney help the client negotiate a "good deal" or avoid hidden pitfalls that business people, without legal training, would not have seen? Is the deal worth more to the client as a result of the attorney's involvement? On the other hand, while simply achieving legal compliance or making your client better off may comply with the bare minimum requirements of the rules of professional ethics, it may not be enough for you personally. It may not be good for your client in the long run, either. The fallout from the Enron and other scandals of the early 2000s left many people wondering why the lawyers didn't do more to prevent such catastrophes. Similarly, the 2008-2009 financial crisis has provided many examples of companies that, while not technically breaking the law in most instances, were doing incredibly unwise and risky things that led to their demise or the need for a "bailout." Witness Lehman Brothers and AIG.

Ethical issues are confronted by business attorneys as frequently as attorneys in any other type of practice. While this book from time to time discusses ethical issues, one that should be considered at this point is the *identity* of the client. If you are engaged as the attorney for a business entity, you must remember that you represent the *entity*, not its owners or managers. For example, consider Rule 1.13 of the Model Rules of Professional Conduct, which is entitled "Organization As Client." Subsection (a) of this rule provides that a "lawyer employed or retained by an organization represents the organization acting through its duly authorized constituents."

A problem that may arise is that the interests of the entity may diverge from the interests of the persons with whom you are dealing. For example, if you represent ABC Corp., a large corporation, you are likely frequently to work with the officers or other employees of ABC Corp. in performing your legal services. After all, a corporation can't pick up the telephone and ask you to do something, only an individual can. After many years of dealing with particular individuals who work for ABC Corp., it may be easy to forget that they are not your client—ABC Corp. is your client.

A problem may arise if the interests or motives of one of these individuals will conflict with ABC Corp.'s interests. For example, an officer of ABC Corp. may not want to comply with a given law because it will make the company less profitable and thus reduce her performance-based bonus compensation. To this end, consider subsection (b) of Rule 1.13, which provides:

> If a lawyer for an organization knows that an officer, employee or other person associated with the organization is engaged in action, intends to act or refuses to act in a matter related to the representation that is a violation of a legal obligation to the organization, or a violation of law that reasonably might be imputed to the organization, and that is likely to result in substantial injury to the organization, then the lawyer shall proceed as is reasonably necessary in the best interest of the organization. Unless the lawyer reasonably believes that it is not necessary in the best interest of the organization to do so, the lawyer shall refer the matter to higher authority in the organization, including, if warranted by the circumstances to the highest authority that can act on behalf of the organization as determined by applicable law.

In other words, sometimes you may need to go "over the head" of the officers of ABC Corp. Doing so may result in some hard feelings, but may be ethically necessary. *See also* Model Rule of Professional Conduct 1.6(c), (f), and (g). In particular, subsection (f) is important. It provides:

> In dealing with an organization's directors, officers, employees, members, shareholders or other constituents, a lawyer shall explain the identity of the client when the lawyer knows or reasonably should know that the organization's interests are adverse to those of the constituents with whom the lawyer is dealing.

§ 1.04   THE BASICS OF FINANCIAL STATEMENTS

Objectives: *After reading the following material, you should be able to:*

* ***GAAP.*** *Describe the source of the rules known as generally accepted accounting principles, or GAAP, and explain which businesses are required to follow GAAP.*

* ***Balance Sheets.*** *List and describe the three categories of items that appear on a business's balance sheet. Explain why the balance sheet is called the "balance" sheet. Describe generally how the dollar values of the various assets that appear on the balance sheet are determined.*

* ***Income Statements.*** *List and describe the three categories of items that appear on a business's income statement.*

* ***Cash Flows Statements.*** *Explain the purpose of a cash flows statement. Explain some reasons why a business's net income for a period may differ from its cash flows for that period.*

Given that running a business involves money, one needs a method to measure the amount of money (and other assets) that the business generates and has on hand. This method is called ***accounting*** and the primary documents produced by a business's accountants and its accounting system are called ***financial statements***. While accounting is a profession distinct from law, some familiarity with financial statements is vitally important for attorneys representing businesses. Moreover, some of these concepts will reappear from time to time throughout the remainder of this book. One cannot completely avoid math by going to law school.

The three main financial statements that every business has are a ***balance sheet***, an ***income statement***, and a ***cash flows statement***. But before you examine these financial statements and what they mean, a few words about how they are prepared are in order.

GAAP. The rules governing accounting and the preparation of financial statements are called generally accepted accounting principles, or ***GAAP***. A private organization, the Financial Accounting Standards Board, or FASB, is the designated organization in the United States[*] for developing financial accounting standards. Although the SEC has authority under the Securities Exchange Act of 1934 to determine the accounting standards used by publicly traded companies, it has for the most part deferred to the FASB in developing accounting rules.

> **TERMINOLGY**
> *GAAP* means generally accepted accounting principles, which are accounting rules issued by the Financial Accounting Standards Board. Not all companies are required to use GAAP in their financial statements.

GAAP consists of a series of "standards" developed by the FASB in its *Statements of Financial Accounting Standards*, each one dealing with a specific topic, as well as several other sources, all of which have been "codified" in the *FASB Accounting Standards Codification* project. To the extent that GAAP does not cover a particular topic, accountants are free to treat the topic in whatever way they believe best.[**] The main importance of GAAP is consistency. If a company follows GAAP, then a person examining its financial statements can be relatively confident that she knows how the financial statements were prepared. Similarly, if a person is comparing the financial statements of two companies, both of which follow GAAP, then she knows that she is comparing "apples to apples."

The SEC requires publicly traded companies to follow GAAP through its Regulation S-X and other rules. Although most other companies are not legally required to follow GAAP, there may be some pressure for them to follow GAAP anyway. For example, a company may have a substantial bank loan and the bank may require the company to follow GAAP so that it can adequately monitor the company's financial performance. In addition, if the company's financial statements are audited by an accounting firm that is a member of the American Institute of Certified Public Accountants (AICPA), the notes to the financial statements will disclose the differences between the company's methods and GAAP. Rather than disclose such differences, the company may simply choose to follow GAAP. On the other hand, private companies are generally not required to make their financial statements available to the public.

But enough about GAAP—this book will not turn readers into certified public accountants. On to the actual financial statements.

---

[*]   In addition, the FASB is currently working with the International Accounting Standards Board toward the possible adoption of international reporting standards for U.S.-based companies.

[**]   Conversely, if an auditing firm believes that following GAAP in a given situation would produce materially misleading financial statements, it must depart from GAAP. *See* Rule 203 of the AICPA's *Code of Professional Ethics.*

The Balance Sheet. A balance sheet measures, on a given day, three categories of items: (1) ***assets***, which are things that the business owns; (2) ***liabilities***, which are amounts that the business owes to third parties such as banks; and (3) the difference between these two items, which is called ***owners' equity*** (or, if the business is a corporation, ***shareholders' equity***). The balance sheet is called the balance sheet because its two sides will balance. In other words, the equation for the balance sheet is:

$$\text{Assets} = \text{Liabilities} + \text{Owners' Equity}$$

To take a simple example, let's assume that two minutes ago Bob incorporated a new corporation,[*] Bob's Groceries, Inc. As of right now, the balance sheet of Bob's Groceries would look like this:

Bob's Groceries, Inc.
Balance Sheet as of [Date]

Assets			Liabilities		
Cash:	$	0	Bank loans:	$	0
Other assets:	$	0	Other liabilities:	$	0
			Owners' Equity		
			Paid-in capital:	$	0
			Retained earnings:	$	0
Total Assets:	$	0	Total Liabilities and Owners' Equity:	$	0

Obviously, Bob's Groceries is never going to become a viable business without some capital. So, let's assume that Bob decides to invest $30,000 in the corporation, in exchange for shares of stock. Thus, the corporation now owns $30,000 of cash. Immediately after that event, the balance sheet would look like:

---

[*] All of the concepts discussed in this section are also applicable if the business were some other type of entity, such as a partnership, LLC, etc.

Bob's Groceries, Inc.
Balance Sheet as of [Date]

Assets		Liabilities	
Cash:	$30,000	Bank loan:	$ 0
Other assets:	$ 0	Other liabilities:	$ 0
		Owners' Equity	
		Paid-in capital:	$30,000
		Retained earnings:	$ 0
Total Assets:	$30,000	Total Liabilities and Owners' Equity:	$30,000

Alternatively, assume that Bob's Groceries obtained a $30,000 loan from the bank as "seed money" instead of $30,000 from Bob. In that case, the balance sheet would look like this:

Bob's Groceries, Inc.
Balance Sheet as of [Date]

Assets		Liabilities	
Cash:	$30,000	Bank loan:	$30,000
Other assets:	$ 0	Other liabilities:	$ 0
		Owners' Equity	
		Paid-in capital:	$ 0
		Retained earnings:	$ 0
Total Assets:	$30,000	Total Liabilities and Owners' Equity:	$30,000

Because $30,000 doesn't sound like enough money to open a grocery store, a more realistic scenario would be that Bob invests $30,000 in the corporation in exchange for stock *and* the corporation obtains a $30,000 bank loan. At that point, the balance sheet would look like this:

Bob's Groceries, Inc.
Balance Sheet as of [Date]

Assets		*Liabilities*	
Cash:	$60,000	Bank loan:	$30,000
Other assets:	$ 0	Other liabilities:	$ 0
		Owners' Equity	
		Paid-in capital:	$30,000
		Retained earnings:	$ 0

Total Assets:	$60,000	Total Liabilities and Owners' Equity:	$60,000

Note that in all of these examples the balance sheet balances: the bottom line number on the left side (the side consisting of assets) is the same as the bottom line number on the right side (the side consisting of liabilities and owners' equity). Also note that the balance sheet is only accurate for a particular day. If tomorrow Bob's Groceries uses some of its cash to buy grocery inventories, the balance sheet will obviously change: the amount of cash on hand will be smaller, but a new category of assets for inventories will be needed.

The foregoing examples of balance sheets are very simple; a balance sheet for a large, well-established company is likely to be quite complicated. Thus, you should examine some of the common categories and types of items that appear on a business's balance sheets. In terms of assets, there are generally three categories: *current assets*, which are assets that will be converted into cash or used or consumed in the near future (typically one year); *property, plant and equipment*, which are tangible and relatively long-lived assets; and *other assets*, which (not surprisingly) are assets that don't fit into the other two categories.

Current assets typically consist of *cash and cash equivalents*, such as certificates of deposit (CDs) and money market accounts; *marketable securities* (securities, such as stocks or bonds, that may be sold easily and are expected to be converted into cash within a year); *accounts receivable* (amounts owed to the business by customers or clients, minus a deduction for amounts that are not likely to be collected); *inventories*, which may include raw materials, partially completed goods, and completed goods; and certain *prepaid expenses*. The category of property, plant and equipment typically consists of *land, buildings*, and *equipment*. (Buildings and equipment are subject to depreciation, which is discussed below.) The category of *other assets* may include intangible items such as patents or trademarks, among other things.

One common mistake made by persons who are unfamiliar with financial statements is to assume that the dollar value of a given item on the balance sheet is

> **TIP**
> The value of an asset on the balance sheet is probably not the asset's fair market value. Instead, most tangible assets are valued on the balance sheet at the lower of cost (the amount the business paid for the item) or market value.

that item's fair market value (that is, the amount for which you would be able to sell the item to a third party). This is not necessarily so. Obviously, if a balance sheet reports that a business had $10,000 of cash as of the date of the balance sheet, then you can be comfortable that the company had $10,000 of cash that day. After all, cash is cash. But assume that the balance sheet shows that the company had $50,000 of land. Does this mean that the land had a fair market value of $50,000 on that day? Probably not. Most non-cash balance sheet assets are valued at their acquisition cost. In accounting lingo, the value of an asset on the balance sheet will be the lower of cost or fair market value. If the company acquired the land in 1943 for $50,000 but today it is worth millions of dollars, the value of the land on the balance sheet will still be $50,000.

Thus, the dollar values of assets on balance sheets may be quite misleading to the uninitiated reader. There are at least two reasons for this approach. First, it is much easier to determine the acquisition cost of an item than its fair market value because an appraisal would often be necessary to determine fair market value. Second, if fair market value were used, then a new appraisal or other estimate would be necessary every time the company prepared a new balance sheet, which might entail a great deal of additional work and expense.

Tangible items with a long, but not infinite life, are subject to *depreciation*. (Intangible items are subject to *amortization*.) For example, assume that Bob's Groceries purchases a new machine for $10,000 and this machine has an expected useful life of five years. As you will see when you read about the income statement and the cash flows statement later in this chapter, if the company uses "straight line" depreciation, then $2,000 of depreciation expense will appear in the

> **TERMINOLOGY**
> *Depreciation* spreads the cost of a long-lived asset over its expected useful life, rather than just the accounting period in which it was purchased.

company's income statement for five consecutive years (because the $10,000 cost of the machine divided by five years is $2,000 per year). This perhaps gives a more accurate picture of the company's expenses; it is as if Bob's Groceries would be using one-fifth of the machine in each year, rather than all of the machine in the first year and none of it in later years. On the balance sheet, depreciable items usually appear with two figures: the original acquisition cost, as well as "accumulated" depreciation, that is, the amount of depreciation expense that has been charged against this asset so far. For example, if one year has passed since the acquisition of the machine, its value would be represented on the balance sheet as $10,000 less $2,000 of accumulated depreciation.[*] Land and cash are not depreciated because they theoretically last forever.

Liabilities are amounts that the business must pay to third parties, or services that the business must perform for them. The two broad categories of liabilities are *current liabilities*, which are those that are expected to be paid or otherwise satisfied in the near future (typically one year); and *other liabilities*, which is sometimes called *long-term liabilities*. Within the category of current liabilities, one may find such line items as *accounts payable*, which are amounts owed to suppliers and vendors that have not yet been paid; *notes payable* or *bank loans*, which are owed to financial institutions rather than suppliers or vendors; *taxes payable*; and *current portion of long-term debt*, which is the amount of a long-term loan that is due within one year.

Owners' equity consists of two items: *paid-in capital*, which is the amount that the owners of the business have invested in the business in exchange for ownership interests such as shares of stock if the business is a corporation; and *retained earnings*, which is the difference between the total amount of earnings of the business since it was formed and the amount that the business has paid out in distributions to its owners since it was formed. One may thus think of retained earnings as the earnings that have been reinvested in the business instead of being paid out to the owners. Paid-in capital may be subdivided into *capital stock* and *additional paid-in capital* if the business is a corporation that has a "par value" for its stock. Par value is discussed further in Chapter 5.

> **TIP**
> Whenever a business is dissolved, its assets must be used to pay creditors first. Secured creditors (those will a perfected security interest in collateral) generally will have a higher priority to that collateral than will unsecured creditors. The owners of the business are the "last in line."

When a business is dissolved, typically its assets first will be used to pay creditors. In other words, creditors have "first dibs" on a company's assets. If some assets are left over after the creditors have been fully paid, then these amounts will be distributed to the business's owners. On the other hand, if there are no assets left after the business has paid its creditors, then the owners will get nothing. (If the business is a partnership, the partners would also have to pay any liabilities that the business was unable to pay. See Chapter 3.) As such, because creditors' claims appear as liabilities on the balance sheet and creditors' claims have priority to the company's assets over the company's owners, it may be helpful to think of owners' equity as the amount of assets that "belong" to the company's owners. For example, assume that you have a house that is worth $100,000, but you have a mortgage on the house with a $70,000 balance. If you default on your mortgage and the bank forecloses on the house and sells it for $100,000, the bank would get

---

[*] Of course, each machine will not appear as a separate line item on the balance sheet.

the first $70,000 (plus, of course, various fees and expenses) and you would get whatever is left over. In this example, you might say that your equity in the house—that is, the part that you "own"—is $30,000. Looking at a balance sheet gives a similar impression, although you must keep in mind that the values of some assets on the balance sheet may be different from their fair market values, as discussed above. Also, owners of a company generally do not have a legal claim to its assets before dissolution.

The Income Statement. Unlike the balance sheet, which reports information as of a given date, an income statement measures a period of time, such as a month, a quarter (three months), or a year. The income statement will report three categories of information for this period of time: the business's *revenues* during the period; its *expenses* during the period; and its *income* (if revenues were greater than expenses) or *loss* (if expenses were greater than revenues) during the period.

Revenues are fairly self-explanatory. If a business sells widgets (a popular, but hypothetical, product used in many business school textbooks), then its revenues will consist of the sales price of the widgets that it has sold during the period. If the company is, say, a law firm, its revenues will be the amounts billed to clients for services rendered during that period. Most businesses use what is known as *accrual accounting*, in which revenues are "booked" in the period in which they are recognized, even if the company does not receive actual cash payment until a later period.[*] In general, to "count" as a revenue under GAAP, an amount must be reasonably certain of being collected.

Depending on the business, there may be only a few categories of expenses or there may be several. One category, at least in the case of a business that sells products (as opposed to one that provides services) is *cost of sales*, sometimes called *cost of goods sold*. While the calculation of this amount can actually be quite complicated for many companies, a simple example may suffice. If a company were solely in the business of acquiring widgets from a third-party supplier for $10 and reselling them to customers for $15, then for every widget it sells during the period its revenues would be $15 and its cost of sales would be $10. Other common categories of expenses include *salaries* or *wages*, which are amounts paid to employees; *research and development expenses*; *general and administrative expenses*; and *interest expenses*. Depreciation (discussed above) may also be an expense during the period. Deducting the various expenses from the company's revenues will yield *income (or loss) before taxes*. Thus, taxes are

---

[*]   By contrast, if a company used *cash-basis accounting*, revenues would not be "booked" until they were actually received in cash.

typically set forth as a separate line item on the income statement, and the final line item will be *net income (or loss)*.

Assume that during its first year of existence Bob's Groceries (1) sold $100,000 worth of groceries to customers; (2) paid $60,000 to the suppliers of those groceries; (3) paid Bob a salary of $20,000; (4) paid $1,000 in utility bills and other similar expenses; (5) paid $2,000 of interest on a bank loan; (6) paid $10,000 for a machine that has an expected useful life of five years; (7) had $2,000 of depreciation expense on the machine; and (8) generated a tax liability of $6,000. Its income statement for the year would look like this:

Bob's Groceries, Inc.
Income Statement for Year Ended [Date]

Revenues (sales):	$100,000
Cost of good sold:	$ 60,000
Salaries:	$ 20,000
General and administrative expenses:	$ 1,000
Interest expense:	$ 2,000
Depreciation expense:	$ 2,000
Net income before taxes:	$ 15,000
Taxes:	$ 6,000
Net income:	$ 9,000

Depending on the complexity of a business, its income statement may include other line items or categories of revenues, expenses or income. For example, the term *gross margin* means the difference between the company's revenues and its cost of sales. Subtracting *operating expenses* (those expenses that aren't part of cost of goods sold) from gross margin results in *operating income*. And adding *other income* (e.g., interest earned on bank accounts or other investments) to operating income yields *total income*.

The Cash Flows Statement. The purpose of the cash flows statement is to determine, for the same period covered by the income statement, how much cash the business generated or used. Typically, one of the line items on the cash flows statement will be "Cash, beginning of period," which is the amount of cash or cash equivalents that the business had on the first day of the period. Another line will be "Cash, end of period."

You may wonder why a cash flows statement is necessary. In the example above, Bob's Groceries generated $9,000 of net income during the year. Therefore, it will have had $9,000 more cash in the bank at the end of the year than it did at the beginning of the year, right? No. The careful reader will have noticed a few things about Bob's Groceries' income statement. First, the facts on the previous page state that the business paid $10,000 for a machine but the income statement does not reflect this cash payment. Second, the income statement reflects $2,000 of depreciation expenses, but that is not a cash payment—Bob's Groceries did not pay the $2,000 of depreciation expense to anyone.

Thus, because the income statement (1) may reflect expenses (such as depreciation) that don't require cash payments to third parties and (2) may not reflect expenditures (such as the $10,000 investment in the machine in this example) that do require cash payments to third parties, the income statement will typically give an inaccurate picture of how much cash the business is generating or using. In this example, Bob Groceries will actually have only $1,000 more cash on hand at the end of the year than it did at the beginning of the year. This is because, starting with the $9,000 net income figure, you must (1) subtract the $10,000 cost of the machine because it cost the business cash but didn't appear as an expense on the income statement and (2) add back the $2,000 depreciation expense because it appeared as an expense on the income statement but didn't actually "cost" Bob's Groceries anything. In other words, $9,000 minus $10,000 plus $2,000 equals $1,000.

There obviously are many more things that can cause a business's cash flow amount for a given period to be different from its net income for that period. For example, changes in balance sheet items from the beginning of the period to the end of the period may affect the cash flows statement. The company may have paid distributions (which would reduce cash) or may have obtained a loan (which would increase cash). Generally, any increase in the value of a non-cash item on the balance sheet will reduce the amount of cash, whereas any increase in liabilities will increase cash. But it is enough to say for our purposes that one needs the cash flows statement, along with the balance sheet and the income statement, of course, to get a full picture of a business's financial health. A business may be, according to its income statement, very profitable yet be "bleeding" cash. Conversely, an unprofitable business may actually be generating a great deal of cash.

Preparation and Frequency of Financial Statements. If a business is publicly traded, it must file with the SEC four financial statements for every year: unaudited financial statements for each of the first three quarters of the year, and audited financial statements covering the entire year. These financial statements are made publicly available. An *audit* is performed by an accounting firm consisting of certified public accountants. Privately held businesses typically are not required to have audited annual financial statements, but may be required to do so by their lenders or other third parties.

Financial Statements As a Tool For Valuing a Business. Putting a value on a business is not an exact science. Different people, even experts, may disagree about what a business is worth. Moreover, they may use different methods or measures to arrive at their conclusions. These techniques are taught in great depth in business schools. Because this is a textbook for law school and not business school and lawyers are rarely asked to determine the value of a business, only a few words about the valuation of companies are in order here. A bit more information appears in Chapter 5.

If a business is a publicly traded corporation, the stock market usually will do a decent job determining the value of a share of the company's stock. As discussed in more detail in Chapter 10, publicly traded corporations are required to disclose a great deal of information about themselves, including financial statements, to the public on a continuous, ongoing basis. Because everyone will have equal access to this information (as well as general information about the economy), some economists argue that the price of a share of publicly traded stock reflects all publicly known information about that company. For example, if the current market price of ABC Corp. common stock is $10, and ABC Corp. announces some positive news such as increased sales or that it entered into a major new contract, then the trading price of ABC Corp. is almost certain to rise above $10 per share very quickly after this announcement. Although this theory has been subject to intense academic criticism in recent years and stock markets often do get it wrong (witness the 2001 "dot com" crash or the 2008-2009 financial crisis), so far no one seems to have developed a better way of valuing stock than subjecting it to market trading.[*]

If a business is privately held, valuation is much more difficult. Typically, to determine what a private business is worth, a professional, independent appraiser will be needed. Many accounting firms and investment banking firms

---

[*]   Keep in mind that the market price of a share of a company's stock reflects the price of *one share*. If a buyer wants to buy an entire company or a controlling interest in it, the buyer will likely need to pay a "premium" far above the current market price of the company's stock.

provide such services. Clearly, the appraiser is going to examine the company's financial statements but, as you have seen, financial statements alone (particularly the balance sheet) may not give a complete picture of the business's health or worth. More information will be needed. For example, what are the future prospects of the business in which the company is engaged? All other things being equal, a typewriter company is probably not as valuable as a software company. Also, if a similar company was recently sold in another transaction between sophisticated parties, the price paid in that transaction will provide a valuable comparison to this company's worth.

In addition to such "market" information, information about the company itself is obviously important. For example, what are the trends in the company's earnings? All other things being equal, a company with a recent history of increasing sales will be more valuable than one with a trend of declining sales. Further, a number of sophisticated financial formulas and models can be applied to the financial statements of a company to estimate the company's worth (or at least the price that a buyer should offer for it). Some of these formulas are discussed in Chapter 5. But many other techniques are used and the appraisal industry from time to time develops a new "state of the art" approach.

Again, this is law school, not business school. However, if you do decide to become a business attorney, more than a passing familiarity with some of the valuation techniques used by appraisers will be useful.

CHAPTER 2
AGENCY

Agency law involves the relationship between at least two, but usually three, persons: the *principal*, which is the person on whose behalf work or some task is being done; the *agent*, which is the person doing the work or performing the task; and the *third party*, which is the person with whom the agent deals on behalf of the principal. When you understand that the word "person" in the prior sentence means not just an individual but any legal entity such as a partnership, a corporation, or an LLC, then you can see why agency issues will recur throughout the book. After all, a non-individual "person" must act through agents. (But of course, any of the three persons in an agency situation could be an individual.)

Although agency issues are addressed to some degree in partnership, corporate, and LLC statutes, to the extent that those statutes do not answer an agency-law question, the common law will step in to supply the answer. In this chapter, the primary source of common law rules that you will study is the *Restatement (Third) of Agency.*[*] However, this is not to say that the *Restatement*'s rules will be followed precisely in every jurisdiction. When you are studying for the bar examination in a given state, you may find that its agency-law rules are somewhat different.

§ 2.01   FORMING AN AGENCY RELATIONSHIP

Objectives: You should be able to list and describe the roles of the three persons in an agency relationship, and list and describe the elements necessary to create an agency relationship between a principal and an agent. Given a fact pattern, you should be able to determine whether two persons have formed a principal-agent relationship or have instead formed some other type of relationship.

In studying agency law, it may be best to start at the beginning. Section 1.01 of the *Restatement (Third) of Agency* provides as follows:

---

[*]   The *Restatement (Third) of Agency* was published by the American Law Institute in 2006. The prior version, the *Restatement (Second) of Agency*, was published in 1958. Two notable differences between these two versions are that the *Restatement (Third)* deletes the concept of inherent authority, and replaces the terminology of "master" and "servant" in *respondeat superior* with "employer" and "employee." Unless otherwise indicated, references to the "*Restatement*" in this book are to the *Restatement (Third)*.

Agency is the fiduciary relation that arises when one person (a "principal") manifests assent to another person (an "agent") that the agent shall act on the principal's behalf and subject to the principal's control, and the agent manifests assent or otherwise consents so to act.

Many issues appear in this deceptively short, simple section. First, note that agency is a fiduciary relationship. The word "fiduciary" is one that you will hear a lot in law school. While it may mean different things in different contexts, generally speaking, a person who is a fiduciary for another person owes that person very strict duties, usually consisting two broad categories: a duty of loyalty and a duty of care. In the context of agency law, this means that the agent owes fiduciary duties to the principal. While it is true that the principal owes some duties to the agent, these duties are much less demanding than those that the agent owes to the principal. Thus, the principal is not a "fiduciary," but the agent is.

Second, each party must "manifest assent" to the relationship (or, in the case of the agent, otherwise consent to act). In other words, agency is a consensual relationship. Neither party can be forced into it.[*] Note here that Section 1.03 of the *Restatement* defines a "manifestation" as "written or spoken words or other conduct." A simple nod of one's head may be enough to "manifest assent." Third, the agent must act on behalf of the principal (as opposed to furthering the agent's own interests) and the principal is in control of the agent's actions.

Agency relationships are present in many different contexts. See if you think any of the following situations involve an agency relationship.

Problems

Problem 2-1: Your wealthy uncle recently died. In his will, he established a testamentary trust for your benefit and funded it with $1 million. The will directs the trustee of the trust to prudently invest this money on your behalf, to use it to pay your educational expenses and, when you have completed your education or reached the age of 30 (whichever occurs first), distribute any remaining amounts to you. Big National Bank was designated as the trustee of this trust and has accepted this position. You are currently in law school and are 24 years old. *Is Big National Bank your agent?*

---

[*]   As discussed in comment d to Section 1.01 of the *Restatement*, some "relationships that are less than fully consensual and, therefore, not common-law agency relations trigger legal consequences equivalent to those of agency." This comment later gives court-appointed counsel as an example of such a relationship.

Problem 2-2: John is an adult who suffers from mental delusions, which greatly worry his relatives and friends. John's father, Bill, petitioned the probate court to have a guardian and conservator appointed for John. The court appointed Bill as John's guardian and conservator. *Is Bill an agent for John?*

Problem 2-3: Kate needed to order a birthday cake for her son's birthday, so she went to Cakes 'n' Stuff, a sole proprietorship owned by Kenny. Kate told Kenny what kind of cake she wanted and how it should be decorated. Kenny promised Kate that the cake would be ready by the following day. *Is Kenny an agent for Kate?*

Problem 2-4: ABC Catering hired Jessica to work as an office manager. *Is Jessica an agent for ABC Catering?*

Problem 2-5: Yesterday, your roommate mentioned that she was going to go to the hardware store today. Before you left the apartment this morning, you put a note and a $10 bill on the kitchen table. The note said: "Use this money to buy me a good screwdriver." After she awoke and read the note, your roommate took the money and went to the hardware store. *Is your roommate your agent? If so, for what purpose? Does it matter that she is not being paid for her actions?*

§ 2.02 THE PRINCIPAL'S CONTRACTUAL LIABILITY TO THE THIRD PARTY

Objectives: You should understand the ways in which a principal will become bound contractually to a third party because of the acts of an agent (or purported agent). Given a fact pattern, you should be able to determine whether the principal is bound contractually to the third party and (1) which theory (or theories) of agency law support(s) that conclusion and (2) the facts that are relevant to that conclusion.

    Subsidiary Objectives: *You should also be able to:*

    •   ***Ways the Agent Can Bind the Principal to a Contract With the Third Party.*** *List the four primary methods by which a principal will be bound contractually to a third party because of the acts of an agent (or purported agent). Given a fact* *pattern, determine whether the principal is bound to a third party under any one or more of the four theories listed below.*

- *Actual Authority. List and describe the elements necessary for an agent to have actual authority to accomplish a particular task or to enter into a particular transaction on behalf of the principal. Explain the difference between actual express authority and actual implied authority.*

- *Apparent Authority. List and describe the elements necessary for an agent to have apparent authority to accomplish a particular task or enter into a particular transaction on behalf of the principal.*

- *Estoppel. Explain how a person may be estopped from denying liability on a contract or other transaction with a third party due to the actions of a purported agent.*

- *Ratification. Explain how a person may ratify an unauthorized contract or other transaction.*

> **TERMINOLOGY**
> An agent or other person may bind a principal to a contract with a third party in four different ways: **actual authority**, **apparent authority**, **estoppel** and **ratification**.

One of the main issues in agency law is determining whether the principal is contractually bound to the third party due to the agent's actions. In general, there are four ways that this may happen: (1) if the agent acted with **actual authority**; (2) if the agent acted with **apparent authority**; (3) if a person is **estopped** from denying liability; and (4) if a person *ratifies* an unauthorized act. Strictly speaking, only the first two categories involve a "true" agency relationship (and even apparent authority may be held by a person who is not an agent). In other words, a "principal" may be estopped from denying liability resulting from the acts of a person who was technically not her "agent." Similarly, a "principal" may ratify the unauthorized actions of a non-agent (or an agent), in which case the actions will be treated as if they *had been* authorized. Although it is possible for these different categories to overlap in a given situation, each will be examined separately below.

Before we continue, note that another type of authority, *inherent authority*, appears in the *Restatement (Second)* but was omitted from the *Restatement (Third)*. It will not be discussed in this chapter, although it may continue to "live on" in some states.

A.   ACTUAL AUTHORITY

Section 2.01 of the *Restatement* provides that:

An agent acts with actual authority when, at the time of taking action that has legal consequences for the principal, the agent reasonably believes, in accordance with the principal's manifestations to the agent, that the principal wishes the agent so to act.

Based on this, as well as Section 3.01, it is clear that the creation of actual authority requires a few steps.[*] First, the principal must make a "manifestation." As noted above, a manifestation consists of words or other conduct. However, it is possible that, at least in some situations, *inaction* could constitute the required manifestation, such as where the principal fails to object to or try to stop events that it knows is occurring.

Second, the agent must become aware of the manifestation. The communication of the manifestation could come directly from the principal or indirectly, such as through some other source. For example, if the principal tells A to tell B something and A does so, then that information has reached B from the principal. Third, the manifestation must cause the agent to reasonably believe that the principal wants her to do something or has authorized her to do something.

So far, so good; the concept of actual authority doesn't seem terribly difficult or surprising, although it is possible that the phrase "reasonably believes" may result in some interpretive problems from time to time. Comment c to Section 2.02 of the *Restatement* notes that agent's belief must be reasonable, which is an objective standard. However, the agent must also actually believe that she is authorized to act, which is a subjective standard. *See also* Section 2.02(2) of the *Restatement.*

But how far does actual authority extend—does it only give the agent the authority to do things that the principal has actually stated, or is it broader than that? Read Section 2.02 of the *Restatement* and consider the following problem:

Problem

Problem 2-6: Johann was planning to sell his car, but didn't get around to doing so before he left for a vacation in the Bahamas. Before he left, Johann asked his friend Rhonda if she would be

---

[*]   Also, note that in some situations, a writing or other record may be required to create actual authority. See Section 3.02 of the *Restatement.*

willing (for a $100 fee) to help him sell his car. Rhonda nodded her head, and Johann handed her the keys to his car, telling her that she should negotiate the best price she could, but not less than $8,000. When Rhonda went to pick up the car from Johann's house, she discovered it was covered with mud and full of fast food wrappers and other garbage. Thus, Rhonda decided to take the car to the car wash, where she got the "super wash," which cost $15. Instead of paying the $15, Rhonda convinced the car wash to bill Johann for it upon his return from vacation. Rhonda also decided that the car would look nicer with flames painted on its sides. Thus, Rhonda agreed with Tom, the owner of Local Auto Garage and Detailing, that he would paint flames on the car, at a cost of $1,000. Rhonda gave Tom a $50 deposit and told him that Johann would pay the rest of the bill. Tom agreed to paint the flames by the next week. *Under the theory of actual authority, is Johann obligated to pay for the car wash? Is he obligated to pay for the painted flames? (If not, what happens to the $50 deposit?)*

While the precise scope of an agent's *actual implied* authority under Section 2.02 may be subject to debate in a given situation, the reason for it is clear: in many cases it would be very difficult and time-consuming, or perhaps even impossible, for the principal to anticipate every step that an agent may need to take to accomplish her "big picture" goal and then tell the agent what those steps may be. Thus, as a gap filler, actual implied authority promotes economic efficiency.

Another issue that may arise is whether the agent's actual authority depends on the third party's knowledge of the agent's instructions, or the identity or existence of the principal. Re-read Sections 2.01 and 2.02 of the *Restatement* and consider the following problems. In answering Problems 2-8 and 2-9 below, it may also be helpful to consider Sections 6.02, 6.03, and 8.09 of the *Restatement*.

Problems

Problem 2-7: Maynard Moneybags is a wealthy and successful businessman who collects historical artifacts. Maynard was thus very excited when he heard that Suzanne Franklin, the great-great-great-great granddaughter of Benjamin Franklin, wanted to sell Ben's famous kite. However, Maynard did not want to have his purchase reported in the news media. Thus, Maynard contacted a famous museum director, Pam Pretentious, and asked her to approach Suzanne about purchasing the kite on his behalf, but without revealing his identity to Suzanne. He told Pam that he would pay her $5,000 for her services, and that she could pay any price up to $1 million for the kite. Pam informed Suzanne that she wanted to purchase the kite on behalf of a "wealthy friend." After some negotiations, Suzanne agreed to sell the kite for $875,000. In the meantime, however, Maynard began to wonder whether he should be spending his money on historical artifacts. *Is Maynard obligated to purchase the kite from Suzanne?*

Problem 2-8: Does your answer to Problem 2-7 change if the purchase price had been $1.1 million rather than $875,000?

Problem 2-9: Does your answer to Problem 2-7 change if Pam had told Suzanne that she wanted to buy the kite for herself rather than on behalf of a "wealthy friend"?

B.   APPARENT AUTHORITY

Section 2.03 of the *Restatement* provides that:

Apparent authority is the power held by an agent or other actor to affect a principal's legal relations with third parties when a third party reasonably believes the actor has authority to act on behalf of the principal and that belief is traceable to the principal's manifestations.

> **QUESTION**
> Both actual authority and apparent authority require that someone have a reasonable belief that the agent is authorized. Whose belief is it?

Based on this, as well as Section 3.03, there are a few requirements to the creation of apparent authority. First, the principal must make a "manifestation." Second, the third party must become aware of the manifestation. As with actual authority, this could occur directly or indirectly. Third, the third party must reasonably believe, based on the principal's manifestation, that the agent is authorized to act on the principal's behalf in some way. In the following problems, consider whether the agent had apparent authority to bind the principal to a contract:

Problems

Problem 2-10: Recall Johann and Rhonda from Problem 2-6 above. Assume that Rhonda's friend Samantha was present when Johann asked Rhonda to help him sell his car and handed her the keys. A few days later, however, Johann called Rhonda from the

Bahamas and told her that he had changed his mind and that she should not sell the car.   Nonetheless, when Samantha asked Rhonda later that day whether the car was still for sale, Rhonda said yes. Samantha then offered Rhonda $8,000 for the car, and Rhonda accepted her offer. *Is Johann obligated to sell the car to Samantha? If so, is Rhonda liable to Johann? See* Section 8.09 of the *Restatement.*

Problem 2-11:   ABC Caterers hired Sam to work as an office assistant, answering the telephone and performing other clerical tasks. One day, while Sam was alone at the office, Maggie walked in and said that she needed a caterer for her wedding, which was to take place two days later. (Maggie's prior caterer had suddenly gone out of business.) She then proceeded to explain to Sam the very elaborate menu that was needed. Sam told Maggie that ABC Caterers would be happy to cater her wedding and they each signed ABC's "standard" contract, which Sam retrieved from a drawer in his desk. *Is ABC Caterers obligated to cater Maggie's wedding?*

Problem 2-12:   Would your answer change if the owner of ABC Catering had explicitly forbidden Sam from agreeing to catering contracts, but Maggie did not know that? What if Maggie knew that?

Problem 2-13:   International Conglomo Inc. ("ICI") is a very large, multi-national corporation. The President of ICI, Wendy Wilson, has negotiated for ICI to obtain a $2 million loan from Big National Bank. Big National Bank has agreed to make the loan. *Does Wendy have authority to sign the loan agreement on behalf of ICI? If you were legal counsel to the bank, what would you do? Would your answer change if ICI were a very small company?*

Problem 2-14:   Section 2.03 of the *Restatement* refers to apparent authority as a "power" held by an agent. Is there a difference between a "power" and a "right"? Again, consider Section 8.09 of the *Restatement.*

Problem 2-15:   Can an agent for an undisclosed principal have apparent authority?

Actual authority and apparent authority could overlap in a given situation. For example, if you went to a florist shop and ordered a dozen roses to be delivered to your spouse or significant other for his or her birthday, the florist shop employee with whom you arranged the order would almost certainly have actual authority to agree to that transaction. Most likely, that is what the employee had been hired to do—make sales! Simultaneously, because it would be reasonable for you to believe that someone working at a florist shop has the authority to agree to sell roses, that employee would also have apparent authority to bind the florist shop to complete the transaction. (This type of apparent authority is sometimes called the "power of position.") Of course, to enforce the contract against the florist shop, it would only be necessary to show that the employee has *either* actual or apparent authority.

The following case considers whether the third party has a duty to inquire whether a representative of the principal has authority to agree to resolve a dispute.

Truck Crane Service Co. v. Barr-Nelson, Inc.
Supreme Court of Minnesota
329 N.W.2d 824 (1983)

AMDAHL, Chief Justice. Defendant Barr-Nelson, Inc. appeals from a decision holding it liable under a payment guarantee agreement signed by an employee, Victor Barr, without its knowledge and against its express denial of liability. We reverse, holding that the employee lacked apparent authority sufficient to bind the principal as a matter of law.

The respondent Truck Crane Service Co. supplied cranes for several job sites where Barr-Nelson was the general contractor. Barr-Nelson ordered these services directly in some instances, and the amount due under these orders is undisputed. However, Barr-Nelson's subcontractor, Associated Builders, also ordered crane services for a Barr-Nelson project. Under the subcontract, Associated Builders was directly liable for these services, and was initially billed for them. Associated Builders then disappeared or became insolvent in mid-performance of this contract and failed to pay for services rendered by Truck Crane at a Barr-Nelson job site.

Truck Crane then billed Barr-Nelson for the services ordered by Associated Builders, but Barr-Nelson denied liability and refused to pay. On November 29, 1979, George Barr, president of Barr-Nelson, memorialized his objections to these billings in a letter to Truck Crane, and asserted the liability of Associated Builders. Truck Crane's chief executive officer, who was aware of the letter from George Barr, nevertheless called the Barr-Nelson offices and attempted to negotiate a payment guarantee agreement with an employee, Victor Barr.

Victor, brother of George Barr, had been the secretary-treasurer of Barr-Nelson until June of 1978. He had once had the authority to sign checks, and his name had been printed on company checks with the title "Secretary-Treasurer" until this dispute arose in 1979. Truck Crane had received one of the checks bearing this imprint on October 18, 1979, but that check was signed by another Barr-Nelson officer, Dave Nelson. There was no evidence that any personnel at Truck Crane had noticed or remembered this check or its imprint prior to the time the guarantee was signed.

When Truck Crane reached him at Barr-Nelson's offices, Victor was there to help open mail and answer phones on a voluntary basis; George Barr was aware of this activity. Victor also worked on a paid basis as a construction laborer for the company.

During their telephone conversation, Victor Barr and the Truck Crane officer discussed the disputed invoices, and Victor admitted they were all related to Barr-Nelson projects and that Truck Crane "had the money coming." In response to Truck Crane's threat of legal action, Victor agreed to sign a guarantee agreement. He was not informed of George Barr's earlier letter to Truck Crane, nor did Truck Crane inquire as to Victor's authority to override the position taken by George Barr.

The sole issue raised in this appeal is whether Victor Barr was clothed with apparent authority sufficient to bind the principal, Barr-Nelson, Inc.

Apparent authority to contract for the principal consists of the following elements:

> The principal must have held the agent out as having authority, or must have knowingly permitted the agent to act on its behalf; furthermore, the party dealing with the agent must have actual knowledge that the agent was held out by the principal as having such authority or had been permitted by the principal to act on its behalf; and the proof of the agent's apparent authority must be found in the conduct of the principal, not the agent [citation omitted].

The trial court found that several factors reasonably interpreted by Truck Crane caused them to believe that Victor Barr was acting as Barr-Nelson's agent: Victor had been secretary-treasurer for Barr-Nelson and no steps were taken to inform Truck Crane that Victor no longer held that office; Victor's name appeared on company checks as secretary-treasurer; Victor was an employee who answered telephones and did other general office work for the company; and Barr-Nelson knew or should have known of, and acquiesced in such conduct by Victor.

These factors are insufficient as a matter of law to support a finding of apparent authority sufficient to bind the principal. They do not clearly establish an affirmative course of conduct by the principal that would constitute holding out or even knowingly permitting Victor to contract for the company. Even less do they establish reliance by the plaintiff on any such acts of the principal.[*]   The appearance of Victor's name and title on company checks would be the strongest factor in the plaintiff's case, but for the fact that plaintiff failed to establish any awareness of or reliance on it at the time the agreement was reached. Apparent authority "exists only as to those third persons who learn of the manifestation from words or conduct for which the principal is responsible." [Citation omitted.] Victor's presence in the company offices and conduct of opening mail and answering phones was similar to that of any clerical employee; when he stepped out of his permitted role and presumed to contract for the company, the law of agency became effective and shielded the principal from liability for acts of the employee of which the principal neither knew nor approved.[**]

Further, one who deals with an agent is put to a certain burden of reasonableness and diligence. "Every person who undertakes to deal with an agent is put on inquiry and must discover whether the agent has the authority to complete the proposed act." [Citation omitted.] We have previously held that as a matter of law, a general manager of a retail store was without apparent authority to contract for a new line of goods, where the store owner had first told the plaintiff that he did not desire to put in that line of goods. [Citation omitted.] The fact that the plaintiff in this case had been notified in writing by Barr-Nelson's president that Barr-Nelson denied liability for these services put the plaintiff on inquiry as to the authority of any other Barr-Nelson employee to countermand such a position.

***

Finally, note that a person may have apparent authority to bind another person to a contract even though she is technically not that person's agent. Thus, reading Section 2.03 of the *Restatement* closely, you will note that it defines apparent authority as being held by an agent "or other actor."

---

[*]   [Footnote by author]: Most courts do not require detrimental reliance for apparent authority.

[**]   [Footnote by court]: The result has been different where members of the public were dealing over the telephone with employees of an insurance provider, for example, since recovery in those cases was premised on the fact that the public was invited to conduct such business over the telephone and had no reasonable basis for questioning the authority of the employee to speak for the company. [Citation omitted].

C.   ESTOPPEL

Section 2.05 of the *Restatement* provides that:

A person who has not made a manifestation that an actor has authority as an agent and who is not otherwise liable as a party to a transaction purportedly done by the actor on that person's account is subject to liability to a third party who justifiably is induced to make a detrimental change in position because the transaction is believed to be on the person's account, if (1) the person intentionally or carelessly caused such belief, or (2) having notice of such belief and that it might induce others to change their positions, the person did not take reasonable steps to notify them of the facts.

In the typical estoppel situation, the purported "principal" has not hired a person as her agent (hence the use of the word "actor" in Section 2.05 rather than "agent") and thus has not given the "actor" any actual or apparent authority. Normally, this would mean that the purported "principal" is not liable on the contract. For example, it would hardly be a fair world in which to live if someone, completely unbeknownst to you, could go around convincing other people that she was your agent and then subject you to contractual liability.

On the other hand, sometimes it may be your "fault" that the third party has changed its position because it believed the actor was your agent. Thus, Section 2.05 requires, among other things, that the purported "principal" either intentionally caused people to think that the "actor" was authorized, or had notice of that belief but did not then take reasonable steps to notify them that the actor lacked authority. Consider Section 2.05 in the following problems:

Problems

Problem 2-16:   The Bigville Broncos football team plays in a stadium in downtown Bigville. Next to the stadium is a large parking lot owned by Rutherford. There are four entrances to the parking lot, and near each entrance is a large sign that states: "Public Parking $12." A few times in the past two months, a well-dressed neighborhood resident (Rutherford thinks that his name is Tim) has approached cars entering the parking lot, acted as if he was the parking lot attendant, directed persons to parking places, collected $12 from them, and then promptly fled the scene. Rutherford has not been able to catch Tim (or whatever his name is) in the act, due to the large size of the parking lot. This Sunday, Nellie drove into Rutherford's parking lot, was approached by

Tim, and paid him $12 to park in the lot. While Nellie was walking from her car to the stadium, Rutherford shouted at her: "Hey, you owe me $12 for parking. Pay or I'll have your car towed." *Must Nellie pay Rutherford the $12?*

Problem 2-17: Rutherford is tired of losing money to Tim. *Other than calling the police, what would you advise Rutherford to do?*

Problem 2-18: Would your answer to Problem 2-17 change if Tim had been dressed in filthy rags and could not give Nellie correct change for the $20 bill that she gave him?

In some cases, it may be difficult to tell where apparent authority ends and estoppel begins. Consider the following problem:

Problem 2-19: Patty is the sole proprietor of Patty's Restaurant. For many years, Alex was the purchasing manager for the restaurant and routinely ordered food on behalf of the restaurant from Food Vendors, Inc. Typically, Alex ordered about $5,000 of food from Food Vendors each week, usually on Wednesdays. One Tuesday, Patty and Alex got into an argument and Patty fired Alex. The following day, Alex, who was very upset at being fired, called Food Vendors, Inc. and ordered $5,000 worth of food items. *Is PRI obligated to pay for this food under the doctrines of apparent authority and/or estoppel?*

D.   RATIFICATION

Chapter 4 of the *Restatement*, which consists of Sections 4.01 through 4.08, concerns ratification. Ratification turns what was previously an unauthorized act into an authorized act. *See* Sections 4.01(1) and 4.02(1) of the *Restatement*. Essentially, if a party ratifies a contract or other transaction, it is agreeing to be bound by it. In this sense, the decision whether to ratify a contract or transaction is volitional. The purported "principal" is free to reject the contract or transaction (assuming she is not bound under the doctrines of actual authority, apparent authority, or estoppel). On the other hand, if the purported "principal" *likes* the deal, she may want to agree to it. Ratification would have the same effect as if the purported "agent" had had actual authority to agree to the contract or transaction.

But of course, ratification is more complicated than that. One question that must be considered is *how* a person may ratify an act. Section 4.01(2) of the *Restatement* sets forth two ways: *express ratification* and *implied ratification*. For example, assume that Sally signs a lease on behalf of ABC Corp. (as the tenant) but lacks any actual or apparent authority to bind ABC Corp. to the lease and that there are no circumstances that would indicate that ABC Corp. is estopped from denying liability on the lease. Currently, ABC Corp. will not be a party to the lease. However, if its board of directors later passes a resolution ratifying the lease (which the directors might do if they think the lease is favorable to ABC Corp.) then obviously the corporation has expressly ratified the lease. On the other hand, in the absence of such a board resolution, if ABC Corp. moved into the premises and began paying rent, this would likely be considered implied ratification of the lease within the meaning of Section 4.01(2)(b) of the *Restatement.*

Another important issue is that ratification must be done knowingly. That is, Section 4.06 requires that the person ratifying the transaction must know the "material facts" of the transaction (or be aware that she lacks knowledge of the material facts). Further, Section 4.07 requires that ratification be on an "all or nothing" basis. That is, one cannot ratify certain aspects of an act, contract, or transaction but not other aspects of it.

Finally, Sections 4.03, 4.04, and 4.05 of the *Restatement* impose some limits on the effectiveness of a ratification. For example, Section 4.04 requires that the person making the ratification must have existed at the time of the act, and must have capacity at the time of the ratification. Section 4.05 provides that a ratification may not be effective if it occurs after a change in circumstances that would result in "adverse and inequitable" effects on the third party.

Consider whether a ratification did or may occur in the following problem:

Problem

Problem 2-20: Casey Counselor recently graduated from law school and joined a large law firm. Around the same time, she bought a house. Because she had very few items of furniture and was too busy to buy more, Casey's house was largely empty, other than a futon, an old couch, a dresser, and a few tables and chairs. Knowing of Casey's situation, Casey's mother, Beth, decided to order some furniture for her from the Lazy Shopper catalog. Beth convinced Lazy Shopper that she was acting at Casey's request (which was not true), and that they should deliver the furniture to Casey "C.O.D.," meaning that payment would be due upon delivery. Four to six weeks later, Casey was relaxing on the old couch in her living room when the doorbell rang. Two deliverymen were there with several cardboard boxes containing furniture from Lazy Shopper. *Is Casey obligated to purchase this furniture? What facts would she need to know before she may ratify this transaction?*

§ 2.03   WHICH PARTIES ARE BOUND ON THE CONTRACT?

Objectives: *Given a fact pattern in which the principal is bound to a contract with a third party due to the actions of the agent, you should be able to determine (1) whether the third party is bound to the principal, (2) whether the agent is bound to the third party when the principal is disclosed, unidentified, or undisclosed, and (3) whether the agent will incur liability to the principal. Given a fact pattern in which the principal is* not *bound to a contract with a third party, determine what recourse, if any, the third party has against the agent or purported agent.*

A.   LIABILTY OF THE THIRD PARTY ON THE CONTRACT

Assuming that the actions of an agent or purported agent have resulted in the principal being bound to the third party under any of the theories described in the previous section, it probably will not surprise you to know that this will almost always mean that the third party is likewise bound to the principal on the contract. After all, it takes at least two people to form a contract.

However, there are a few minor exceptions to this general rule. First, if the principal were undisclosed (see Section 1.04 of the *Restatement* for definitions of **disclosed**, **unidentified**, and **undisclosed** principals), the third party may refuse to render performance to the principal—and instead render performance to the agent—if doing so would materially increase the third party's costs or other burdens.

The second exception also concerns a situation where the principal was undisclosed. If the third party would not have dealt directly with the principal or entered into a contract with the principal (such as where the third party dislikes the principal or disapproves of the principal in some way), and the principal or agent know or have reason to know this, then the third party may avoid performing the contract if the agent makes a misrepresentation about the *lack* of an agency relationship.* Consider these requirements in the context of the following problems:

Problems

Problem 2-21: Mrs. Hatfield is known far and wide as making the best wedding cakes east of the Mississippi River. Julia McCoy wanted to order one of Mrs. Hatfield's cakes for her upcoming wedding but knew that, if she were to walk into Mrs. Hatfield's shop she would be turned away, due to a longstanding feud between the Hatfield and McCoy families. Instead, Julia asked her friend Wendy Mullins to order a cake from Mrs. Hatfield for delivery in two weeks, specifying the type of cake that she wanted. Wendy went to Mrs. Hatfield's shop and ordered the cake and Mrs. Hatfield agreed to prepare and deliver the cake to the address that Wendy gave her. When asked by Mrs. Hatfield, Wendy stated that the cake was for her own wedding. *If Mrs. Hatfield discovers that the cake is really for Julia's wedding, may she refuse to perform the contract? What if she finds out after the cake has been delivered (and eaten)?*

Problem 2-22: Would your answer to Problem 2-21 change if Wendy had instead stated that she was ordering the cake for "a friend's wedding"?

B.   LIABILITY OF THE AGENT ON THE CONTRACT (AND OUTSIDE THE CONTRACT)

Assuming that the principal is bound to the third party but the principal does not or cannot perform the contract, may the third party look to the agent for performance? Read *Restatement* Sections 6.01, 6.02, and 6.03 and consider the following problems:

Problems

Problem 2-23: Recall Maynard Moneybags, Suzanne Franklin, and Pam Pretentious from Problem 2-7. Assume that Pam had explained to Suzanne that she was acting on Maynard's behalf and

---

* See, e.g., WILLIAM A. GREGORY, THE LAW OF AGENCY AND PARTNERSHIP 193 (3d ed. 2001) ("[I]t is not fraudulent if the agent represents that he is acting on behalf of himself alone, unless he has reason to believe that the identity of the principal is important to the [third] party. The contract will not be avoided simply because the [third] party would not have dealt with the principal.") (citation omitted).

that Suzanne agreed to sell the famous kite to Maynard for $875,000. However, although the kite was delivered to him, Maynard never paid the purchase price and has now disappeared, taking the kite with him. *May Suzanne recover the purchase price from Pam?*

Problem 2-24: Would your answer to Problem 2-23 change if Pam had not told Suzanne that she was acting on Maynard's behalf, but had only told her that she was acting on behalf of a "wealthy friend"?

Problem 2-25: Would your answer to Problem 2-23 change if Pam had simply told Suzanne that she was buying the kite for her own personal collection?

Problem 2-26: If there are different results in the prior three problems, what is the policy reason for these differences? If you were acting as an agent, what steps should you or would you take to minimize your chances of being held liable on the contract?

Note that in Problems 2-23 through 2-26 the principal (Maynard) was in fact bound to the third party (Suzanne). After all, the agent (Pam) was acting within the scope of her actual authority when she purchased the kite for $875,000. (At this point, also reconsider your answer to Problem 2-8 above.)

But what if the principal was not in fact bound on the contract? Read Section 6.10 of the *Restatement* and consider the following problem:

Problem

Problem 2-27: Recall Casey Counselor and her mother, Beth, from Problem 2-20 above. Assume that Casey decides to reject the furniture and send it back to Lazy Shopper. *May Lazy Shopper recover any damages from Beth?*

§ 2.04   ATTRIBUTION OF INFORMATION FROM THE AGENT TO THE PRINCIPAL

Another important topic in agency law concerns the attribution to the principal of information in the agent's possession. For example, if the third party gives a required notice to the agent, will that notice be considered to be notice to the principal? Similarly, if the agent knows a particular fact, is that the same as if the principal knew that fact? Chapter 5 of the *Restatement* (consisting of Sections 5.01 through 5.04) addresses these issues. Of course, the *Restatement* does not tell us what *effect* this attribution will have; it only tells us whether the attribution of information will be deemed to occur. For example, if a contract requires that Party A give notice to Party B at least ten days before Party A may knock down a building, the *Restatement* will help us determine whether Party B "received" notice (and, if so, when) if Party A notifies Party B's agent of its intent to knock down the building. But it is the contract that will tell us what the effect of that notice is. In this example, once the required ten days have passed, the contract allows Party A to knock down the building

Read Chapter 5 of the *Restatement* and consider the following problems:

Problems

Problem 2-28: Ivy Skilton lives in a neighborhood that is next to a golf course owned by Greens 'n Tees, Inc. ("GTI"). A few years ago, in exchange for a $1,000 payment, Ivy granted GTI a right of first refusal on her house. The right of first refusal provides that, if Ivy wishes to sell her house and receives a bona fide offer from a third party to purchase her house, she must give GTI at least forty-eight hours notice. During that time, GTI may exercise its right of first refusal and purchase Ivy's house at the same price offered by the third party. Today, Tom Suarez offered Ivy $300,000 for her house (an offer that Ivy found too good to pass up). Ivy telephoned GTI and informed one of the caddies who was working that day that she had received an offer for $300,000 for her house. *Has Ivy properly notified GTI?*

Problem 2-29: Assume that GTI received proper notice and decided not to exercise its right of first refusal and purchase Ivy's house. When he decided to begin looking to buy a house a few months ago, Tom had hired Maggie Mayer as his real estate agent (also known as a realtor). During the inspection of the house, Ivy disclosed to Maggie that there was leak in the basement, but offered her $500 to "keep it quiet." Maggie accepted. Tom later purchased the house from Ivy, not knowing about the leak in the basement. *If Tom later sues Ivy for not disclosing the leak, will Ivy be able to claim that Tom had knowledge of the leak?*

Problem 2-30: GTI (from the two problems above) decided to sell its golf course to Pennington Golf Corp. ("PGC"). In the real estate purchase agreement, GTI made a "representation and warranty" to PGC that, to its knowledge and belief, there were no sinkholes or other hazards present on the golf course. Before signing the agreement on behalf of the company, GTI's President carefully interviewed all of its employees to determine if they were aware of any sinkholes or other hazards on the golf course. None of them were. However, Greenskeeper Billy was on vacation when these interviews took place. Billy had observed that the ground near the 17th hole seemed "spongy" and he was suspicious that it was a sinkhole. Billy had meant to mention this to his supervisors, but did not do so before leaving for vacation. After PGC purchased the golf course, it found that there was a sinkhole near the 17th hole. *Did GTI make a false representation and warranty to PGC?*

§ 2.05   DUTIES OF THE AGENT AND THE PRINCIPAL TO EACH OTHER

Section 1.01 of the *Restatement* provides that agency is a "fiduciary" relationship. As discussed above, this means that the agent owes fiduciary duties to the principal. While the principal does owe some duties to the agent, they are much less demanding than those owed by the agent to the principal. The duties owed by both parties are set forth in Chapter 8 of the *Restatement*.

A.   DUTIES OF THE AGENT TO THE PRINCIPAL

Although this is not a precisely accurate statement, the duties that the agent owes to the principal roughly fall into two categories: a *duty of loyalty* and a *duty of care*. Throughout this textbook, you will see other situations where one party owes another party a duty of care and/or a duty of loyalty. For example, a partner in a partnership owes a duty of care and a duty of loyalty to her partners and to the partnership. A director of a corporation owes a duty of care and a duty of loyalty to the corporation. Other examples will appear as well.

Generally speaking, a duty of loyalty is concerned with conflicts of interest. If an agent is acting to further her own interest and not the interest of the principal, then she may be violating her duty of loyalty. The duty of care, on the other hand, is concerned whether the agent is doing a "good job." If an agent is lazy or makes careless decisions, then she may be violating her duty of care to the principal. But more precision is needed than merely to say that the agent has violated her "duty of loyalty" or her "duty of care." Let's examine exactly what these duties entail. Sections 8.02, 8.03, 8.04, 8.05, and 8.06 are examples of the agent's duty of loyalty. Sections 8.08 through 8.12 concern the various aspects of an agent's duty of care.[*]

Section 8.02 of the *Restatement* provides that an agent may not "acquire a material benefit from a third party in connection with transactions conducted or other actions taken on behalf of the principal or otherwise through the agent's use of the agent's position." Thus, in Problem 2-29 above, Maggie breached this duty when she accepted the $500 from Ivy. Similarly, an officer of a corporation that accepts a bribe from a third party in exchange for signing a contract on behalf of the corporation would violate this duty. Section 8.02 recognizes that receiving such benefits creates an inherent conflict of interest; because the agent owes fiduciary duties to the principal, her only compensation for serving as an agent should come from the principal. Query whether a corporate officer would violate this duty when she is "wined and dined" by a third party hoping to get business from the corporation. Section 8.03 is somewhat similar, providing that an agent may not "deal with the principal as or on behalf of an adverse party in a transaction connected with the agency relationship."

Problem

Problem 2-31: Assume that an agent happens to own a piece of real estate that her principal is interested in purchasing. *May the agent sell the real estate to the principal? What problems or issues may arise in the course of this transaction?*

Section 8.04, which concerns competition, is fairly straightforward: an agent "has a duty to refrain from competing with the principal and from taking action on behalf of or otherwise assisting the principal's competitors." However, the agent may "take action, not otherwise wrongful, to *prepare* for competition following termination of the agency relationship" (emphasis added). Competition by corporate officers and directors is discussed in some detail in Chapter 7. However, in the meantime, consider the following problems:

Problems

Problem 2-32: You are an employee of ABC Advertising, Inc. ("ABC"), which is located in the Midwest of the United States. One day, your best friend from college calls you to ask you to invest in an ice cream parlor in Miami. *May you do so without violating Section 8.04 of the Restatement?*

---

[*]   Depending on the facts, Section 8.10 could implicate the duty of loyalty as well. This section provides that an "agent has a duty, within the scope of the agency relationship, to act reasonably and to refrain from conduct that is likely to damage the principal's enterprise."

Problems 2-33: You are an employee of ABC from Problem 2-32. You are dissatisfied with your job, and wish to move to New York City to open an advertising agency there. *May you file articles of incorporation for your new company before quitting your job at ABC? May you ask some of ABC's clients whether they would want to become clients of your new company, before quitting your job at ABC? May you do any or all of these things after you quit ABC?*

Section 8.05(2) provides that an agent may not communicate the principal's confidential information for her own purposes or a third party's purposes. Thus, an agent could not serve as a "mole" for one of the principal's competitors. What is considered "confidential information"—as opposed to information that is generally known or can be learned or determined from legitimate sources—is often a murky issue that can result in litigation.[*]

Obviously, if the above rules were always applicable, certain actions that may be mutually beneficial to the principal and the agent would not be possible (or at least not possible if the agent wanted to avoid the risk of later being sued by the principal). Thus, Section 8.06 allows the principal to consent to any actions that would otherwise violate the agent's duties under Sections 8.01 through 8.05. In obtaining the principal's consent, the agent must act in good faith; disclose all material facts that the agent knows (or has reason to know or *should* know) "would affect the principal's judgment," subject to a few exceptions; and deal "fairly" with the principal. If the principal's consent is properly obtained in this manner, then the agent's conduct will be deemed not to be a breach of its fiduciary duties under Sections 8.01 through 8.05.

However, note that subsection (b) of Section 8.06 also requires that the consent from the principal "concerns either a specific act or transaction, or acts or transactions of a specified type that could reasonably be expected to occur in the ordinary course of the agency relationship." In other words, an agent who attempts to obtain a "blanket" waiver from the principal of all of the agent's fiduciary duties is not likely to be successful in this regard. Instead, the principal's consent ordinarily must be obtained on a "case by case" basis. This rule may seem to some as overly protective, and to limit the rights of competent parties to contract with each other as they wish. However, you must not forget that agent is, at its heart, a *fiduciary* relationship. Harsh dealing or "boilerplate" provisions that would be perfectly acceptable in arms' length transactions are not usually acceptable in the agency context.

---

[*] Comment c to Section 8.05 notes that the agent *may* reveal confidential information "to protect a superior interest of the agent or a third party." Without such an exception, most "whistleblower" statutes would be of little use.

The primary section concerning an agent's duty of care is Section 8.08, which provides in part that (subject to any contrary provision in an agreement between the principal and the agent) the agent must "act with the care, competence, and diligence normally exercised by agents in similar circumstances." However, these "circumstances" include any "special skills or knowledge" that the agent possesses. Further, if the agent *claims* to have special skills or knowledge (maybe that is why the principal hired her in the first place), then she must "act with the care, competence, and diligence normally exercised by agents with such skills or knowledge." Textbooks usually are of little use in helping evaluate whether an agent's conduct fell short of, or complied with, this duty of care, beyond stating the legal rules. Instead, the determination of whether an agent has breached her duty of care is an issue for the fact finder in a trial: the judge if it is a bench trial or the jury if it is a jury trial.

On a related note, Section 8.09(1) provides that an agent has a duty to act only within the scope or her actual authority. We considered this section in connection with Problems 2-8, 2-9, and 2-14 above. Further, Section 8.09(2) provides that the agent must "comply with all lawful instructions" that she receives from the principal (or other designated persons). This of course recognizes, as stated in Section 1.01, that the principal is in control of how the agent conducts her work.

Section 8.11 concerns when an agent must disclose information that the agent knows (or has reason to know or *should* know) to the principal. According to this section, the agent is under a "reasonable duty" to disclose such information if the "agent knows or has reason to know that the principal would wish to have the facts or the facts are material to the agent's duties to the principal." However, the agent must only make this disclosure where it can be done without violating a "superior duty" that the agent owes to someone else.

Finally, Section 8.12 sets forth certain duties the agent owes with respect to the safekeeping of the principal's property.

B.   DUTIES OF THE PRINCIPAL TO THE AGENT

As noted above, the principal's duties to the agent are very slight, consisting only of three sections in the *Restatement*: Sections 8.13, 8.14, and 8.15.

Section 8.13 merely states that the principal must comply with the terms of any contract that it has with the agent. To be fair, Section 8.07 states that the agent owes similar contractual duties to the principal. At first, these sections hardly seem necessary. However, they remind us that in many cases there may be a contract between the principal and agent that modifies some of the rules set forth above and/or provides additional rules for the parties' relationship. Similarly, as discussed above, a principal may consent to certain acts that would otherwise be a breach of the agent's duties under Sections 8.01 through 8.05. One place to document or memorialize that consent would be in a written contract between the principal and agent.

Section 8.14 provides that the principal must indemnify the agent (that is, make the agent whole, or "hold her harmless" by paying the agent an amount of money) in certain circumstances. Generally, if an agent incurs an expense or suffers a loss as a result of her work for the principal, she should be entitled to indemnification. The first such situation in Section 8.14 is where the contract between the principal and agent provides for indemnification of a particular expense. If the contract calls for indemnification then obviously the principal must comply with the terms of the contract.

Even in the absence of a contract, however, the principal must indemnify the agent for payments made by the agent that were in the scope of her actual authority or that were "beneficial to the principal, unless the agent acts officiously in making the payment." In this context, "officiously" means that the agent volunteered to make a payment where none was required. Further, the principal must indemnify the agent for any losses that the agent suffered that "fairly should be borne by the principal in light of their relationship." Obviously then, the principal will not be liable for expenses that the agent incurs that were outside the scope of her actual authority. Nor will the principal be liable for the agent's losses associated with her negligence or knowing commission of a tort (although, as discussed in the next section, the principal may be liable to a *third party* as a result of an agent's tort).

Finally, under Section 8.15 the principal's dealings with the agent must be done "fairly and in good faith." This includes a duty on the principal's part to give the agent "information about risks of physical harm or pecuniary loss that the principal knows, has reason to know, or should know are present in the agent's work but unknown to the agent." Thus, an employer who hires an employee to work in a dangerous workplace generally would be obligated to disclose the dangers to the employee.

§ 2.06   *RESPONDEAT SUPERIOR*

Objectives: You should be able to describe how an employer (or master) can be liable to a third party for torts committed by an employee (or servant) that result in physical harm to a third party. Given a fact pattern, you should also be able to determine whether the employer (or master) is liable for a tort committed by the employee (or servant) that results in physical harm to a third party.

Much can be said about *respondeat superior*. However, this textbook is not the place to present an exhaustive discussion of that doctrine. Instead, I will assume that readers have taken the Torts course (or courses) in law school and spent several weeks learning about *respondeat superior* then. Nonetheless, no treatment of agency law would be complete without some discussion of when an employer/master is liable for torts committed by its employee/servant. As comment b to Section 2.04 of the *Restatement* puts it: "Functionally tied though the doctrine is to tort law, it has long been classified as an element of agency doctrine."

First, a note about terminology. The *Restatement (Third) of Agency* represents a departure from the *Restatement (Second) of Agency*, which used the terminology of "master" and "servant." *Respondeat superior* was described in Section 219(1) of the *Restatement (Second)* as follows: "A master is subject to liability for the torts of his servants committed while acting in the scope of their employment." By contrast, the *Restatement (Third)* uses the terminology "employer" and "employee" and thus describes

> **TERMINOLOGY**
> The *Restatement (Third)* uses the terms "employer" and "employee" for *respondeat superior* issues. The *Restatement (Second)* uses the terms "master" and "servant." If a person is performing work for you but is neither an employee nor a servant, what is she?

respondeat superior as follows in Section 2.04: "An employer is subject to liability for torts committed by employees while acting within the scope of their employment." One reason for this change is that the word "servant" may conjure up in one's mind images of persons performing menial tasks; thus, one may (mistakenly) conclude that *respondeat superior* would not apply if the tortfeasor were in a position that required a high degree of skill. However, this is not the case. Even persons in high-skill positions can be considered "servants." Thus, although using the word "employee" presents problems of its own, it was thought to be an improvement over "servant." (How quickly courts will adopt this new terminology remains to be seen, however.)

Nonetheless, the different terminology probably doesn't often lead to different conclusions as to whether the tortfeasor was an "employee" or a "servant." This is because Section 220(1) of the *Restatement (Second)* defines a servant as a "person employed to perform services in the affairs of [the master] and who with respect to the physical conduct in the performance of the services is subject to the [master's] control or right to control." Similarly, Section 7.07(3) of the *Restatement (Third)* defines an employee as "an agent whose principal controls or has the right to control the manner and means of the agent's performance of work." Note that this definition presupposes that an employee is an agent. Also note that non-individuals can be agents and therefore "employees," and that even persons that serve gratuitously (without pay) can be considered "employees."

Comment f to Section 7.07 of the *Restatement (Third)* sets forth many factors to be considered in deciding whether a person is an "employee." These factors are largely the same as the factors listed in Section 220(2) of the *Restatement (Second)* to be used in deciding whether a person is a "servant." Because it is thus not likely that the choice between the terminology used in the two *Restatements* will often lead to different results, the following discussion will focus on the terms "employer" and "employee" rather than "master" and "servant," for the sake of simplicity. Nonetheless, Section 220(2) remains a good source of factors to use in deciding whether someone is an "employee." You should now review that section in your statutory supplement.

Section 7.07(1) of the *Restatement (Third)* states the rule for *respondeat superior* as follows: "An employer is subject to vicarious liability for a tort committed by its employee acting within the scope of employment." Thus, once it is determined that a person is an employee (and thus employed by an "employer"), the next question is whether the employee was acting in the scope of her employment when the tort occurred.

Section 7.07(2) helps to answer this question by stating that an employee is within the scope of her employment "when performing work assigned by the employer or engaging in a course of conduct subject to the employer's control." However, this section also provides that an employee is acting outside the scope of her employment when the act "occurs within an independent course of conduct not intended by the employee to serve any purpose of the employer." Beyond this, Section 7.07(2) gives no guidance for determining whether an act occurred in the scope of employment, unlike the detailed Sections 228 and 229 of the *Restatement (Second)*.* Nonetheless, try your hand at the following problems after also reading Sections 7.01 and 7.07 of the *Restatement (Third)*:

---

* Under Section 228(1) of the *Restatement (Second)*, one of the requirements for finding that an act occurred in the scope of employment is that it "occurs substantially within

Problems

Problem 2-34: Dr. Payne is a brain surgeon who is employed by Community Hospital. One day, Dr. Payne negligently performs a surgery on a patient. *Is the hospital liable for this tort? Is Dr. Payne?*

Problems 2-35: After moving into the house he purchased from Ivy Skilton in Problem 2-29, Tom Suarez decided that he wanted to replace the front porch. Tom hired Basic Construction, Inc. ("BCI"), a local construction firm, to tear out the old porch and build a new one. Tom and representatives of BCI talked for several weeks to decide on the design and materials for the new porch. On the first day of the construction project, Billy Simmons, a full-time employee of BCI, began dismantling Tom's porch. While Billy was working, a brick flew through the air and struck a passing pedestrian on the head. The court determined that this accident was due to Billy's negligence. *Is Tom liable for this tort? Is BCI liable for this tort? Is Billy liable for this tort?*

Problems 2-36: Jeff Stiles is a "runner" for Smith, Johnson and Perkins, a law firm. Jeff's duties include taking pleadings and other documents to the local courthouse for filing. One day, while on his way to file a complaint at the courthouse, Jeff negligently injured a pedestrian. The law firm's employee handbook specifically prohibits employees from committing negligence. *Is the law firm liable for this tort? Is Jeff liable for this tort?*

Problems 2-37: One day, while Jeff Stiles from Problem 2-36 was on his way to work, he negligently injured a pedestrian. (Jeff is not a very good driver.) *Is the law firm liable for this tort? Is Jeff liable for this tort?*

Problems 2-38: Juan Tillman is a lawyer with Smith, Johnson and Perkins, the law firm from Problems 2-36 and 2-37. While driving to a deposition at another law firm for a lawsuit involving the firm's client Perfect Pet Foods Inc. ("PPFI"), Juan negligently injured a pedestrian. *Is the law firm liable for this tort? Is Juan liable for this tort? Is PPFI liable for this tort?*

---

the authorized time and space limits." Perhaps due to the growth of "telecommuting" and other nontraditional forms of work, the *Restatement (Third)* does not contain this requirement.

<u>Problems 2-39</u>: While driving back to the office following the deposition described in Problem 2-38, Juan decided to stop at Pete's Drycleaners to drop off a suit that needed to be dry-cleaned. While he was walking out the door of Pete's Drycleaners, Juan negligently slammed the door into another customer, breaking her nose. *Is the law firm liable for this tort? Is Juan liable for this tort?*

Although negligence-based torts are more common, intentional torts may result in *respondeat superior* liability as well. Unfortunately, the *Restatement (Third)* is not terribly helpful on this point, apparently content with the terse description of whether an act is in the "scope of employment" set forth in Section 7.07(2).

The *Restatement (Second)* is more helpful, noting in Section 228 that, to be considered in the scope of employment, a servant's conduct must (1) be of the kind she is employed to perform; (2) occur "substantially within the authorized time and space limits"; (3) be "actuated, at least in part, by a purpose to serve the master," and (4) "if force is intentionally used by the servant against another, the use of force is not unexpectable by the master." (Section 228 contains *prerequisites* for determining whether an act is in the scope of employment; Section 229 lists additional factors to consider in making this determination.) The classic example of an intentional tort resulting in *respondeat superior* liability is the nightclub "bouncer" who removes an intoxicated and rowdy customer from the premises and, in the process, commits an intentional tort such as assault or battery. In such a case, it is likely that the four factors of Section 228 will be met. On the other hand, if the next day the bouncer sees the (formerly) rowdy customer on the street and punches him in the face because he's still mad at him, the nightclub's owner will not be liable under *respondeat superior* for that tort.

For the most part, *respondeat superior* applies to torts committed by an employee (or servant) that result in physical harm to a third party. But what if an agent commits a tort that harms the third party's reputation or results in financial loss? That is one of the issues considered in the following section.

§ 2.07   OTHER TORT LIABILITY OF THE PRINCIPAL

Respondeat superior does not exhaust the situations where one may be liable for torts committed by another person. Indeed, there are many such situations, some of which are discussed below.

First, a principal may owe a *direct* duty (as opposed to vicarious[*] liability as in *respondeat superior*) to third parties to properly select, train, and supervise its agents. On this issue, Section 7.05(1) of the *Restatement* provides that the principal can be liable for an agent's conduct that harms a third party if the principal's negligence in selecting, training (or retraining), supervising, or controlling the agent caused harm to the third party. Note that this applies even if the agent is not considered an "employee" or a "servant." For example, if a principal owns a building and hires a security firm to provide security guards who are stationed at the front desk of the building, the security firm may very well be considered an independent contractor. Thus, if one of the security guards is negligent and injures a third party, it will *not* be relevant to ask whether the building owner is liable under *respondeat superior*. However, it is possible that the security guards will be considered agents of the building owner (i.e., nonemployee agents). Thus, one argument that the injured third party may make is that the building owner was negligent in not properly selecting, training, supervising, or controlling the security guards. To make things more complex, note that the principal could be liable even if the security guard was not negligent. For example, if the injury would not have happened if the guard had been properly trained by building owner, then the building owner may be liable under Section 7.05, but the security guard may not have been negligent in this example.

Further, if the principal has a "special relationship" with a third party, the principal must act with reasonable care as to risks arising out of that relationship, including the risk that the principal's agents will harm the third party. *See* Section 7.05(2) of the *Restatement*. Comment e to this section gives some examples of these relationships: "a common carrier with its passengers, an innkeeper with its guests, [and] a school with its students," among others. Thus, for example, an owner of a day care center should use great caution to prevent any of the employees of the center from abusing children. Although such conduct is outside the employee's scope of employment, the owner of the day care facility could face liability under Section 7.05(2) if it did not act with reasonable care to prevent it from occurring, such as by conducting background checks of employees and preventing employees from being alone with children.

Section 7.06 of the *Restatement* provides that if the principal has a duty to protect a third party, the principal cannot avoid liability by delegating performance of that duty to an agent. For example, business owners have a duty to use reasonable care to provide safe premises for their customers. If the owner of a restaurant delegates this duty to the manager of the restaurant but the manager does not adequately perform this duty, then the restaurant owner would be liable

---

[*]   See Section 7.08 of the *Restatement* for another example of vicarious liability. This section provides in part that a "principal is subject to vicarious liability for a tort committed by an agent in dealing or communicating with a third party on or purportedly on behalf of the principal when actions taken by the agent with apparent authority constitute the tort ...."

to an injured customer. The only way for the owner to avoid liability for its duty to use reasonable care in this situation is for the restaurant manager to perform the duty adequately.

An agent may also make statements to third parties. These statements could be unintentionally inaccurate, intentionally inaccurate (i.e., misrepresentations), or defamatory. Will the principal be subject to liability as a result of such statements? It depends on whether the agent had actual or apparent authority to make statements about the subject matter. *See* Sections 7.04 and 7.08 of the *Restatement*. For example, Section 7.04 provides that a principal is liable for an agent's act that is within the scope of the agent's actual authority or that is ratified by the principal if (1) the agent's act was tortious or (2) the act, if it had been done by the principal, would have made the principal liable. Thus, if an agent makes a misrepresentation it would be necessary to show that the misrepresentation was within the agent's actual authority or was ratified by the principal. Ratification (or lack thereof) would be easy to determine. But is a misstatement outside an agent's actual authority if the principal did not authorize the agent to make *false* statements?[*] Not necessarily. If the agent has actual authority to make a statement about *a subject* and makes an intentional misstatement about that subject, then the principal may well be liable.

Finally, you should not forget that the principal owes its agents duties just as it owes duties to anyone else. Thus, if a principal negligently injures an agent, the principal will be liable. Often, however, injuries that occur "on the job" will be covered by workers' compensation laws, which are the subject of a different course in law school.

But before this turns into a Torts textbook, let's return to more "traditional" agency law.

§ 2.08   TERMINATION OF THE AGENCY RELATIONSHIP

Like all good things, the relationship between a principal and an agent will someday come to an end. There are many ways that this could happen.

First, remember that, according to Section 1.01 of the *Restatement*, agency is a consensual relationship; both the principal and the agent must agree to it. A consequence of this rule is that, in the absence of a different contract provision or unusual circumstances, either party may freely terminate the relationship at any time by "express will," that is, by informing or otherwise making the other party

---

[*]   After all, it hopefully is rare that principals actually *tell* their agents to lie.

aware of the termination. For example, the great majority of employees of private companies in the United States are "at-will" employees. This means that the employer may terminate their employment (i.e., "fire" them) at any time, for any reason or even no reason at all simply by telling the employee, so long as doing so does not violate anti-discrimination, "whistleblower," or other employment-related laws. While there are some exceptions to this rule, such as with employees who have employment contracts that specify that they may only be fired for "cause," or employees who are members of a union that has a collective bargaining agreement with the employer, these are not terribly prevalent. Thus, it is usually easy for the employer (principal) to terminate the relationship. Similarly, the employee (agent) may freely quit her employment at any time as well.

The above paragraph describes situations in which either party has both the power *and* the right to terminate the agency relationship. In other words, not only may the party terminate the relationship, but she will not be liable to the other party for damages as a result of doing so. The principal always has the power to terminate the relationship. So does the agent. But there may be situations in which a party has the power—but not the right—to terminate the relationship. For example, if you hire a realtor to help you sell your house, the contract that you sign with the realtor will likely provide that the realtor will receive a commission when your house is sold, typically around 6% or 7% of the sales price. The contract will also probably specify a duration, say, six months. Anticipating this commission, the realtor will do a great deal of work to try to sell your house, such as listing it on various websites, listing services or other publications, holding "open houses," etc. Because an unscrupulous homeowner may try to take advantage of this work without paying the commission (such as by firing the agent and then trying to sell the house by herself once a potential buyer has been found), the contract likely will provide that if the house is sold within some period of time following termination or expiration of the agreement, the homeowner must still pay the commission to the realtor. Thus, although the homeowner still has the *power* to terminate the agreement, she does not have an absolute, unfettered right to do so without incurring an obligation or other liability.

Another example of where a party has the power but not the right to terminate an agency relationship is an employment contract. If the employment contract provides that the employee will be employed for a set period of time (provided she performs her employment duties and does not commit an act that would constitute "cause" for firing), the employer may still terminate the contract at any time. However, doing so will make the employer liable for damages. The usual measure of damages in this situation is the employee's lost wages for the remainder of the contract's term, subject to a duty on the employee's part to mitigate damages by looking for other employment.

Beyond a termination by the express will of either party, there are many other ways in which an agency relationship may end. For example, the parties may have agreed, either expressly (whether in a written contract or otherwise) or impliedly, that the relationship would end upon the expiration of a set period of time, or when a particular task is accomplished, or when some other event occurs. When the period of time is over, the task is completed, or the event occurs, then the agency relationship would automatically end by its own terms. *See* Sections 3.09 and 3.10 of the *Restatement*.

An agent's actual authority will also end if an agent who is an individual dies. If the agent were a non-individual entity, its actual authority will end when it ceases to exist or begins to dissolve or its powers are suspended (as may happen by statute). *See* Sections 3.07(1) and (3) of the *Restatement*. If the principal is an individual and dies, the agent's actual authority is also terminated. However, the termination is effective only when the agent, or the third party with whom the agent is dealing, has notice that the principal has died. If the principal is not an individual, then the agent's actual authority will end if the principal ceases to exist or begins to dissolve or its powers are suspended. *See* Sections 3.07(2) and (4) of the *Restatement*.

Similarly, if the principal loses legal capacity[*] to do an act, then the agent will no longer have actual authority to do that act. However, the termination of the agent's actual authority is effective only when the agent, or the third party with whom the agent is dealing, has notice that the principal has permanently lost capacity or has been found by a court to lack capacity. *See* Section 3.08(1) of the *Restatement*. Nonetheless, subsection (2) of Section 3.08 allows an agent's actual authority to continue in this situation if a written document made the agent's authority effective only upon the principal's loss of capacity, or the written document provided that the agent's authority would continue notwithstanding the principal's incapacity. As you may have learned in your Wills, Estates and Trusts and/or Estate Planning courses, many states allow for "durable" powers of attorney that continue in effect even if the principal becomes incompetent; section 3.08(2) reflects this practice.[**] However, such a durable power of attorney is only possible where the principal is an individual. *See* Section 3.08(3).

Note that the termination of an agent's *actual* authority may not necessarily terminate its apparent authority. Instead, the agent's apparent

---

[*]   A principal who is an individual could lose capacity if she is found by a court to be mentally incompetent. A principal that is a business entity could lose capacity to do an act if there is a change in the law or if its charter documents are amended to prohibit the act.

[**]   In a somewhat similar vein, Section 3.12 provides that powers given as security and irrevocable proxies to exercise voting rights in a business may only be terminated as provided in Section 3.13.

authority will terminate only when it is no longer reasonable for a third party to believe that the agent has actual authority. *See* Section 3.11 of the *Restatement.* However, once an agent has notice that her actual authority has terminated in one of the ways described above, she will be under a duty *not* to act for the principal. Revisit Problem 2-10 above in light of this rule.

Generally speaking, once the agency relationship has been terminated, the parties will no longer owe duties to one another, except with respect to events that arose before the termination. Thus, if the principal is obligated to indemnify the agent for losses or other expenses as described above, the mere fact that the agency relationship has been terminated will not forgive the principal of this obligation. Also, the general rule is that an agent is free to compete with the principal after termination of the agency relationship. However, there are some exceptions to this general rule, as discussed in Chapter 7.

PRACTICE QUESTIONS

Multiple Choice Question 2-1: Suzy is the sole proprietor of Suzy's Electronics Sales and Repair ("Suzy's Electronics"). Arthur is an employee of Suzy's Electronics. When he was hired, Suzy told Arthur that he could quote prices for repair work to customers only for television sets. Matthew came into the shop one day, and Arthur agreed that Suzy's Electronics would fix Matthew's DVD player for $50. Unfortunately, to fix the DVD player Arthur needed to order a part from China which cost more than $50. Together with labor, the actual repair work cost $200. *Which of the following statements is correct?*

A.   Suzy's Electronics does not have to repair Matthew's DVD player for $50 because Arthur only had authority to agree to repair television sets.

B.   Suzy's Electronics does not have to repair Matthew's DVD player for $50 because Arthur was acting outside the scope of his employment.

C.   Suzy's Electronics does not have to repair Matthew's DVD player for $50 unless Matthew can prove that he detrimentally relied on Arthur's promise. If he cannot, Suzy's Electronics can charge Matthew the full $200 repair fee.

D.   Suzy's Electronics must repair Matthew's DVD player for $50.

Multiple Choice Question 2-2: Katherine decided to sell her "mint condition" 1965 Ford Mustang. Although Katherine had previously received several offers for the Mustang, she decided to auction it to get a higher price. Katherine placed an advertisement in the newspaper stating that she would auction off the Mustang on November 20th. Mark saw the advertisement and thought: "Wow, I want that car. But Katherine would never sell that car to me. She hates me." Mark then called his assistant, Ned, and said to him: "Katherine is going to auction off her 1964 Mustang. I want you to go to the auction and bid for the car on my behalf. I want you to go because Katherine would never the sell the car to me directly. You can bid up to $125,000. If she asks, say that you're bidding on behalf of someone else, but don't say who." Ned attended the auction. Beforehand, Katherine asked Ned if he was bidding for himself. Ned said: "I'm here representing a bidder who wishes to remain anonymous. But he has authorized me to bid up to $125,000." Ned was the winning bidder at the auction, bidding $110,000. *Which of the following statements is NOT correct?*

A.   Mark is obligated to purchase the Mustang from Katherine for $110,000 because Ned had actual authority.

B.   Mark is not obligated to purchase the Mustang from Katherine because Mark was an unidentified principal.

C.   Mark is obligated to purchase the Mustang from Katherine for $110,000, but if Mark does not pay, Katherine can recover $110,000 from Ned.

D.   Even if Katherine finds out that Mark was the actual purchaser of the Mustang, she is still obligated to sell the Mustang to Mark.

Multiple Choice Question 2-3: Same facts as in Question 2-2, except that before the auction Ned revealed to Katherine that Mark was the buyer and Katherine agreed to sell the Mustang even though she did not like Mark. In addition, Katherine explained to Ned that the Mustang was not exactly in mint condition; instead, it needed new brakes and some major repairs to its transmission. Ned, who was annoyed at Mark for constantly insulting him and treating him badly, did not tell this information to Mark before Ned won the auction. When Mark found out about the needed repairs to the Mustang, he tried to rescind the purchase, arguing that he would not have bought the Mustang if he had known about the needed repairs. *Which of the following is correct? Assume that Mark would have a legal right to rescind the contract if Katherine had only revealed the needed repairs to Ned or Mark* <u>*after*</u> *the auction.*

A.   Mark may not rescind the contract because a fact known by an agent is always considered to be known by the principal.

B.   Mark may rescind the contract because his agent Ned has breached his fiduciary duties to him.

C.   Mark may not rescind the contract, but he does have a cause of action against Ned for the cost of the repairs.

D.   Mark may rescind the purchase because he did not have actual knowledge of the needed repairs.

Multiple Choice Question 2-4: Hank Yankee was the sole proprietor of Hank's Groceries. Hank hired Frank Jones as an employee to stock groceries on shelves and perform other odd jobs at the store. One day, after Frank had stocked several dozen cans of soup on shelves, a customer, Wanda, was severely injured after soup cans crashed down on her as she was reaching for a can of cream of broccoli soup. Wanda sued for her injuries on a negligence theory, seeking $1 million in damages. *If Hank can prove that (1) he had instructed Frank to be extremely careful in stocking soup cans but that Frank had ignored Hank's instructions and (2) the assets of Hank's Groceries are far less than $1 million, will Hank be personally liable for all or part of Wanda's claim?*

A.   No, because Frank ignored Hank's instructions and therefore was outside the scope of his employment.

B.   No, because Hank is not liable for any debts of the business beyond the assets of the business.

C.   Yes.

D.   Yes, but only if Wanda can prove that Hank negligently trained Frank.

Multiple Choice Question 2-5:   Garth is a clerk in the shipping department of Empire, Inc. ("Empire"), which manufactures machine guns and other military products. Garth's job description in Empire's employee handbook provides that he is responsible for arranging transportation of Empire's products to customers. A large sign on the wall in Empire's shipping department states that "Shipping clerk may not approve shipping contracts in excess of $3,000 without supervisor approval."   However, the sign is incorrect—Empire's employee handbook was recently revised to state that Garth may not enter into any shipping contracts in excess of $2,000 without approval from his supervisor. Garth has read the new employee handbook. One day, Mr. Rumsfeld, an employee of Axis, Inc. ("Axis"), visited Empire's shipping department and met with Garth. After a long discussion with Mr. Rumsfeld, Garth signed two contracts with Axis on Empire's behalf, on forms supplied by Mr. Rumsfeld. Contract #1 obligated Empire to purchase ten copy/fax machines from Axis for $4,000. Contract #2 provided that Axis would transport a shipment of 5,000 of Empire's machine guns to an Army base in Iowa for a fee of $2,500. When Garth's manager learned of these contracts, she wanted to cancel both of them. *Which of the following statements is most likely correct?*

A.   Empire is bound on both contracts.
B.   Empire is bound on neither contract.
C.   Empire is bound on Contract #1 but not Contract #2.
D.   Empire is bound on Contract #2 but not Contract #1.

Multiple Choice Question 2-6:   Brett is a purchasing agent for Harvey's Restaurant, a sole proprietorship. Because he tends to exceed his authority, Brett was expressly forbidden by the owner of the restaurant, Nell, to ever deal with Drew, a beer distributor.   The prohibition, however, did not deter Brett; he continued to buy beer from Drew anyway. When Nell found out about Brett's insubordination, she fired him and then promptly informed Drew that all sales were off and that Drew would not be paid since Brett had no authority to buy beer from Drew.   *In determining the scope of Brett's apparent authority to bind Harvey's Restaurant to Drew, which of the following would not be important?*

A.   Nell's description to Drew of Brett's position in Harvey's Restaurant.
B.   A reaction of silence by Nell when Brett had made similar agreements in the past with Drew.
C.   The express limitation placed on Brett's authority which Drew did not know about.
D.   None of the above.

Multiple Choice Question 2-7: Samantha, a rich antique collector, hired Zelda to buy for her a very rare and expensive portrait of Winston Churchill from Clive. Zelda and Samantha did not execute a written agreement since they had worked with each other in the past and they trusted each other. Clive was not to be told that Zelda was an agent for Samantha or anybody else since that would greatly increase the portrait's price. *Which of the following is most correct?*

A.   If Zelda makes a contract to buy the portrait, Clive may, if he wishes, void the contract once he learns that Samantha is the principal.

B.   Zelda's contract is void since an agency agreement with an undisclosed principal must be in writing.

C.   Since Zelda did not tell Clive for whom he was buying the portrait, Samantha cannot be liable.

D.   If Zelda executes a contract with Clive and neither Zelda nor Samantha pay Clive the agreed upon price after Clive tenders the portrait, Clive may sue Zelda even though Zelda was acting on Samantha's instructions.

Multiple Choice Question 2-8: In which of the following circumstances will an agent not be personally liable to the third party with whom the agent deals?

A.   If an agent with actual authority enters into a contract with the third party on behalf of an undisclosed principal.

B.   If an agent with actual authority enters into a contract with the third party on behalf of an unidentified principal.

C.   If an agent with actual authority enters into a contract with the third party on behalf of a disclosed principal.

D.   If an agent commits a negligence-based tort while engaged in the principal's business.

Multiple Choice Question 2-9: Pete is the sole proprietor of Pete's Exotic Wines and Cheeses, a specialty food store. Previously, Pete often traveled around the world, looking for new wines and cheeses to sell at his store. However, Pete had a heart attack last year, and his doctor advised him not to travel any longer. Afterwards, Pete hired Annie to work at his store and to assist him in ordering products. One day, Pete asked Annie if she would like to travel to the Bordeaux region of France to "scout out" new products for the store and order them from merchants. Annie, who had never been to France, was delighted to go. Unfortunately, when she got to France on May 15th, Annie realized that very few of the wine and cheese merchants there spoke English and that the French that she had learned in high school didn't help her much. Thus, Annie hired Marcel, an interpreter, to assist her in negotiating with various French merchants. *Will Pete be liable to pay Marcel's fees?*

A.   Yes, because Pete will be estopped from denying liability.
B.   Yes, because Annie had apparent authority.
C.   Yes, because Annie had actual express authority.
D.   Yes, because Annie had actual implied authority.
E.   No.

Multiple Choice Question 2-10: Same facts as in Question 2-9. On May 20th, Annie signed a contract with Claude, a French winery owner, to purchase 300 cases of Claude's wine. Annie did not reveal to Claude that she was acting on behalf of Pete (or anyone else, for that matter). Unfortunately, Pete had died from another heart attack on May 19th. Annie did not learn of Pete's death until May 21. *Is Pete's estate bound to purchase these cases of wine from Claude?*

A.   No, because Pete died before the contract was signed.
B.   No, because Pete was an undisclosed principal.
C.   Yes, but Pete's estate will be able to recover damages from Annie.
D.   Yes.

Multiple Choice Question 2-11: Alex was authorized by Peter to purchase five rare books for a maximum of $50,000. Alex purchased six books for $75,000. *Which of the following is correct?*

A.   Peter cannot ratify the contract since Alex's actions clearly exceeded his authority.
B.   The express limitation on Alex's authority negates any apparent authority.
C.   Neither Peter nor Alex is liable on the contract since the seller is always obligated to ascertain the Agent's authority.
D.   If Peter refuses to perform the contract, Alex is liable to the seller.

Multiple Choice Question 2-12: Jack authorized Joan to solicit orders on behalf of Jack, but without authority to grant discounts or to collect payments on orders which she solicited. Joan then granted to Frank a 10 percent discount based on Frank's agreement to make immediate payment on his $10,000 order. Frank had previously dealt with Jack through Joan, but this was the first time he had been offered a discount. Frank gave Joan a check for $9,000. Joan then gave Jack the check and the order which clearly reflected the 10 percent discount. Jack shipped the order and cashed Frank's check. Jack then attempted to collect $1,000, which Jack alleged is the balance due on Frank's order. *Which of the following is correct?*

A.   Jack can collect $1,000 from Frank because Joan contracted outside the scope of her authority.

B.   Jack cannot collect the $1,000 from Frank because Jack ratified the discount given by Joan.

C.   Jack cannot collect the $1,000 from Frank because Joan will be held to have had implied authority to provide discounts and collect payment.

D.   None of the above are correct.

CHAPTER 3
THE BIRTH AND LIFE OF A PARTNERSHIP

The partnership (or "general partnership") is one of the oldest forms of business organization in the United States. At its core, a partnership is an "association" (that is, a group) of two or more persons who, as owners, run a for-profit business. As discussed in Chapter 1, there are advantages and disadvantages to operating a business as a partnership. The primary advantage is that the partnership is a "flow through" tax entity—the partnership itself does not pay taxes on the income that it earns (although it must file an informational return with the IRS). Instead, the partners pay taxes on their respective shares of the income that the partnership generates. The primary downside of operating a business as a partnership is that the partners will be jointly and severally liable for the partnership's debts and other obligations. These issues are explored in more detail in this chapter. So too are many issues relating to the formation of a partnership and issues that arise while it is in existence, such as the management and voting rights that partners have and the fiduciary duties that partners owe to each other and to the partnership.

Given the unlimited personal liability that partners are exposed to for the business's debts, today it is rare for an attorney to advise clients to operate a business as a partnership. In most cases, a business form that shields owners from liability, such as a corporation or a limited liability company (LLC), will be preferable. A law student may legitimately ask why a course on business organizations will devote a fairly substantial amount of time to studying a business form that may be becoming obsolete. There are several answers to this objection. First, there are many partnerships still in existence. Similarly, oftentimes people run a business without realizing that it is a partnership. Second, as discussed in Chapter 1, many businesses, such as law firms, that provide professional services cannot be organized in a way that would shield the owners from malpractice liability. Thus, the partnership remains a viable choice for these sorts of businesses. Third, many concepts that you will learn about in this chapter and Chapter 4 will reappear (in somewhat different form) in later chapters. Finally, partnership law provides a good basis for understanding the LLC, which is a hybrid between a partnership and a corporation. In other words, one cannot really understand LLCs without first understanding partnerships and corporations.

§ 3.01   HAS A PARTNERSHIP BEEN FORMED?

Objectives: *You should be able to analyze a fact pattern to determine whether two or more persons have formed a partnership. You should also be able to identify the arguments that will be made for, and against, finding that a partnership was created.*

Subsidiary Objectives: *Given a fact pattern in which A receives a portion of the profits of B's unincorporated business, you should be able to determine whether A and B will be presumed to be partners (see RUPA § 202). You should also be able to identify the factors that are relevant to determining whether two or more persons have formed a partnership.*

A partnership is sometimes called a "default" form of business. This is because it is not necessary to take any formal steps to form a partnership. All that is required is that the business meets the statutory definition of a "partnership."[*] Contrast this to a corporation: a business technically does not exist as a corporation until someone files the articles of incorporation for that corporation. The persons associated with this "corporation" may believe that they have formed a corporation and may act as if they have, but unless the articles of incorporation are filed with the relevant state government, no corporation actually exists. Instead, until the articles of incorporation are filed, it is likely that the business would be characterized as a partnership. (The same is true of an LLC: an LLC is not formed until its articles of organization are filed with the state.)

> **RUPA**
> As noted in Chapter 1, **RUPA** is an acronym for "Revised Uniform Partnership Act." The current version of RUPA was adopted by the National Conference of Commissioners on Uniform State Laws in 1997 and a majority of states have statutes modeled on RUPA. Other states have statutes that are modeled on the Uniform Partnership Act (1914), referred to as "*UPA*." To a large degree RUPA is consistent with UPA; however, the drafters of RUPA had a great deal of time to improve upon UPA.

Usually, it will be clear whether two or more persons who are running a business have formed a partnership. For example, they may have signed a partnership agreement. (Section 3.02 below concerns the role of the partnership agreement in governing disputes that arise in a partnership.)

---

[*]   Some states have statutes that require partnerships to file a form with a local government stating their name and the identities of their partners. However, a failure to do so typically only results in a monetary fine; it would not affect the actual *existence* of the partnership.

Nonetheless, sometimes it may be ambiguous whether two or more persons are partners. This issue can become important because, if they *are* partners, then they will be jointly and severally liable for the debts and obligations of the business.

Section 202 of RUPA partially answers some of the questions that may arise in this context. Read Section 202 and consider the following problems:

Problems

Problem 3-1:   *May ABC Corp. and DEF Corp. form a partnership?*

Problem 3-2: *If Amir, Bob, and Catrina form a partnership but later decide to incorporate their business, will the business be both a corporation and a partnership?*

Problem 3-3: *Is intent necessary to form a partnership?*

Problem 3-4: *What is the difference between the "gross returns" of a business and the "profits" of a business? See RUPA §§ 202(c)(2) and (c)(3).*

Problem 3-5: Joe's Asbestos, a sole proprietorship owned by Joe Smith, has been manufacturing asbestos and selling it throughout the United States for the past twenty years. Joe only learned that asbestos was dangerous when his business was named as a defendant in a multi-billion dollar class action lawsuit filed by several thousand lung cancer victims. Unfortunately, Joe has nowhere close to enough money to pay any potential judgment if he loses the case (that is, he is "uncollectible"). But the plaintiffs have also sued (1) Landlord Corp., which owns the premises where Joe conducts his business, and (2) Neil Smedly, one of Joe's employees. The plaintiffs argued that Landlord Corp. and Neil are partners with Joe. *Why are the plaintiffs arguing that Landlord Corp. and Neil are partners in Joe's business?*

Problem 3-6: Same facts as in Problem 3-5. Under its lease with Joe's Asbestos, Landlord Corp. is entitled to be paid monthly rent of $1,000, plus 10% of Joe's profits for that month. In a typical month, the total rent that Joe pays to Landlord Corp. is $3,000. Also, the lease provides that if Joe's Asbestos wishes to change the products that it manufactures or hire more than three new employees, it must first seek approval from Landlord Corp. Neil works as the plant manager of Joe's Asbestos, where he oversees hiring and firing employees, payroll, and ensuring that suppliers and utility bills are paid.   Neil has also been instrumental in improving the quality of Joe's products and opening new markets (i.e., finding new customers). A few years ago, Joe changed Neil's compensation from a fixed $50,000 per year annual salary to a $30,000 annual salary plus 5% of Joe's revenues for the year. Joe only agreed to do this if Neil would contribute $10,000 to the business, which he did. At the time, Neil specifically asked Joe whether he (Neil) would be liable for any losses of the business. Joe replied: "No."   On a few occasions, Joe introduced Neil to customers by calling him "my partner Neil."

Landlord Corp. and Neil have both filed motions to dismiss the case against them, arguing that they are not partners with Joe and that, even if they were, the plaintiffs cannot hold them liable because they did not even learn of the existence of Landlord Corp. and Neil until after the case was filed. *How should the court rule on these motions?* In answering this question, study RUPA § 202 as well as the following two cases.

MacArthur Co. v. Stein
Supreme Court of Montana
934 P.2d 214 (1997)

TRIEWEILER, Justice.   MacArthur Company filed a complaint *** in which it alleged that Karl Stein, Midland Roofing, Midland Roofing and Gutters, and John Does 1 and 2 were jointly and severally liable for an outstanding debt for roofing materials supplied by MacArthur to Midland Roofing and Gutters. *** [T]he District Court concluded that Stein was a partner in Midland Roofing and Gutters at the time the debt to MacArthur was incurred. The District Court therefore concluded that *** Stein was liable to MacArthur for the amount of $39,875.27, plus interest and attorney fees. Stein appeals from the judgment of the District Court. We affirm the District Court.

***

FACTUAL BACKGROUND

Karl Stein has operated Midland Roofing in Billings[, Montana] since 1974. Prior to July 1991, Midland Roofing was a sole proprietorship owned solely by Stein.

In the summer of 1991, several hail storms occurred in the Billings area. As a result, the demand for roofing services increased significantly in the late summer and fall of 1991. Stein recognized an opportunity to increase his profits because of the sudden demand for roofing services. He sought to take advantage of the business opportunity by seeking a line of credit at a local financial institution, but was unable to secure financing.

John L. Potter and Jesse Beebe approached Stein in late June or early July 1991 with the idea of expanding Stein's business to take advantage of the increase in roofing demand. Both Potter and Beebe were out-of-state businessmen who engaged in "storm tracking"—the business of traveling to areas where there was increased roofing activity due to storm damage. In early negotiations, Potter asserted that he could handle the general operation of a roofing business and that a third party, Bill Evans, could handle sales and material acquisition. In addition, Beebe represented that he had the ability to secure credit for the expanded business.

In early July, the parties entered into an agreement ***. Pursuant to the agreement, Stein, Beebe, and Potter agreed to create a new entity which would operate under the name of Midland Roofing and Gutters. The parties expressly intended that the business name would be so similar to Stein's business name, Midland Roofing, that the public and customers would be unable to distinguish between the two businesses. In addition, both Midland Roofing and the new entity, Midland Roofing and Gutters, were to use the same telephone number and all calls to that number were to be answered by employees of Midland Roofing and Gutters. The parties agreed that a record would be made of all telephone calls and that Stein would be given a first right to accept any potential roofing job. Midland Roofing and Gutters had the option to complete any other jobs.

As part of the parties' initial written agreement, Stein's compensation was equal to three percent of total gross charges for all "nail-on roofing" jobs and ten percent of gross charges for "hot roofing" jobs performed by Midland Roofing and Gutters. Midland Roofing and Gutters also agreed to pay one of Stein's employees a portion of his salary for inspection work and to set aside $.50 per roofing square to be set up in a two-signature account, which would bear the signatures of Stein and Beebe, to cover any warranty work necessary after Midland Roofing and Gutters ceased operation.

In August 1991, Jesse Beebe arranged a line of credit for Midland Roofing and Gutters from MacArthur Company. Stein had previously been denied credit by the company. His purchases from MacArthur were on a "cash only" basis. On the credit application, Beebe listed Midland Roofing and Gutters as the company seeking credit, and named himself as the "principal or officer." Neither Stein nor Midland Roofing was mentioned on the credit application, and MacArthur was not advised of Stein's association with Midland Roofing and Gutters. Based solely on Beebe's credit references, MacArthur granted Midland Roofing and Gutters a line of credit and supplied the company with materials from August 1991 through January 1992.

In January 1992, Jesse Beebe, John Potter, and Bill Evans departed the Billings area without notice, and left an unpaid balance to MacArthur Company in the amount of $39,875.27. [MacArthur Company then sued Stein, Midland Roofing, Midland Roofing and Gutters, and John Does 1 and 2, alleging that] each of the defendants, as partners in Midland Roofing and Gutters, was jointly and severally liable for the outstanding debt to MacArthur. [The trial court found that Stein was a partner in Midland Roofing and Gutters and that he was jointly and severally liable for the debt to MacArthur.] ***

DISCUSSION

The issue in this case is whether the District Court erred when it concluded that Karl Stein was a partner in Midland Roofing and Gutters and was therefore liable for the partnership's debt to MacArthur Company.

***

[Section 35-10-201 of the Montana Code] defines a partnership as "an association of two or more persons to carry on as co-owners a business for profit." [Here, the court also recounts Section 25-10-202 of the Montana Code, which is very similar to RUPA § 202.]

This Court established the elements for the determination of the existence of a partnership in *Bender v. Bender*[, 397 P.2d 957, 962 (Mont. 1965)]: (1) the parties must clearly manifest their intent to associate themselves as a partnership; (2) each party must contribute something that promotes the enterprise; (3) each party must have a right of mutual control over the subject matter of the enterprise; and (4) the parties must agree to share the profits of the enterprise. We have consistently held that each of the four *Bender* requirements must be established in order to prove the existence of a partnership. [Citations omitted.]

In this case, the District Court analyzed the alleged partnership of Stein, Beebe, Potter, and Evans pursuant to both [Section 35-10-202] and the elements of partnership set forth in *Bender*. The court found that the parties' actions and conduct were sufficient to establish their intent to associate themselves as a partnership. In addition, the court found that each party had contributed something that promoted Midland Roofing and Gutters, that each had a joint proprietary interest and a right of mutual control over the enterprise, and that each had received a share of the profits of the enterprise. Based on its findings, the court concluded that Stein, Beebe, Potter, and Evans had created a partnership and that that partnership was in existence at the time the debt to MacArthur Company was incurred. The court therefore concluded that, as a partner in Midland Roofing and Gutters, Stein was [jointly and severally liable for the debt].

1. The initial test for the determination of whether a partnership exists is the intent of the parties. [Citation omitted.] At trial, Stein testified that he did not intend to create a partnership through his negotiations with Beebe and Potter. However, as this Court noted in *Trick Insurance Exchange v. Industrial Indemnity Co.*[, 688 P.2d 1243, 1244-45 (Mont. 1984)]:

> [I]f the facts bring the arrangement within the definition of a partnership, the parties cannot escape liability incident to that relationship merely by saying that no such thing exists. If the intended action of the parties creates a partnership in fact, what the parties call their arrangement or intend their arrangement to be is irrelevant.

(Citation omitted.) Therefore, where intent cannot be directly ascertained, it must be established from all the facts, circumstances, actions, and conduct of the parties. [Citation omitted.] In this case, then, it is not necessary that Stein intended to be a partner in Midland Roofing and Gutters; it is only necessary that he intended his actions and that his actions created a partnership in fact.

In this case, the District Court found that, regardless of Stein's intentions, the parties had created a partnership in fact through their actions and conduct. Specifically, the court found that the remaining three elements of *Bender*—contribution, joint interest and control, and the right to share profits—had been proven and were indicative of the parties' intent to establish a partnership.

2. Pursuant to *Bender,* in addition to the requirement of intent, each of the purported partners must contribute something that promotes the enterprise. [Citation omitted.] In this case, the District Court found that each of the parties had made a contribution to Midland Roofing and Gutters sufficient to indicate the creation of a partnership. Specifically, the court found that Stein had contributed to Midland Roofing and Gutters the name of his business, his business license, and his goodwill in the community. In addition, the court noted that Stein had agreed to warrant work completed by Midland Roofing and Gutters. The other parties, the court found, had contributed roofing skills, start-up revenue, and sales skills. Based on the substantial contributions of each of the parties, the District Court found that the element of contribution had been established.

The uncontroverted evidence at trial established that Stein lent his business name, his telephone number, his business leads, his [goodwill], his business license, and his expertise to Midland Roofing and Gutters. We hold that such contribution was promotive of the enterprise of Midland Roofing and Gutters. We therefore conclude that the District Court's finding that the element of contribution had been established is supported by substantial, credible evidence and is not clearly erroneous.

A further requirement of *Bender* is that each party to an enterprise have a joint proprietary interest in, and right of control over the subject matter of the enterprise. [Citation omitted.] In this case, the District Court found that Stein did have such interest and control. Specifically, the court found that, pursuant to the parties' agreement, Stein had the right to exercise quality control over the work performed by Midland Roofing and Gutters and, after inspection, could have required that the work conform with his standards. In addition, the court found that Stein had agreed to perform future warranty work for Midland Roofing and Gutters and had established a joint account for the payment for that work. Finally, the court found that Stein had reserved the right to discontinue the parties' arrangement and prohibit Midland Roofing and Gutters from using his telephone number and business license. Although the court noted that Stein did not specifically hire the employees of Midland Roofing and Gutters or arrange for their work schedule or payment, the court found that "there are sufficient indices of control and proprietary interest to determine that he was in fact a partner."

In addition to the District Court's specific findings regarding Stein's proprietary interest and right of control, the record reflects that Stein was involved in the oversight of the day-to-day workings of Midland Roofing and Gutters. Stein testified at trial that he visited Midland Roofing and Gutter job sites and gave advice on local building code requirements. In addition, Stein testified that he was in the offices of Midland Roofing and Gutters on a daily basis and answered the phones for that entity. Moreover, the evidence presented at trial established that Stein and Midland Roofing and Gutters worked together to contact the general public. This evidence was clearly indicative of Stein's interest in and control of Midland Roofing and Gutters. We therefore hold that the District Court's finding of Stein's right of mutual control and joint proprietary interest is supported by substantial credible evidence and is not clearly erroneous.

The final element of *Bender* requires that there must be an agreement to share profits in order to establish a partnership. [Citation omitted.] In this case, the District Court found that Stein was entitled to receive a percentage of Midland Roofing and Gutters' profit. Specifically, the court noted that both the written agreement formalizing the parties' arrangement and its subsequent modification entitled Stein to a percentage of the gross revenue[*] on all work done by Midland Roofing and Gutters. In addition, the court noted that, according to testimony at trial, Stein earned between $75,000 and $92,000 in both cash and materials from

---

[*]   [Footnote by author]: Are profits the same as revenues?

his agreement with Midland Roofing and Gutters. As the District Court correctly stated, "[t]he receipt by a person of a share of the profits of a business is prima facie evidence that such person is a partner in the business." [Section 35-10-202(4) of the Montana Code.] Based on the evidence at trial, which clearly established that Stein was entitled to share the profits of Midland Roofing and Gutters, we hold that the District Court's finding that the final element of *Bender* had been satisfied is not clearly erroneous.

Because we uphold the District Court's findings regarding the establishment of the four elements of a partnership, we hold that the court's conclusion that Stein, Beebe, Potter, and Evans had created a partnership is correct. [Therefore, Stein is liable for the debt of Midland Roofing and Gutters to MacArthur Company.] *** Furthermore, we reject Stein's contention that he is not liable to MacArthur because MacArthur was not aware of his relationship with Midland Roofing and Gutters when it extended credit to the company. Reliance is an element of partnership by estoppel; it is not necessary to the establishment of liability of a partner in fact. ***

In reading the following case, note that it applies a Texas statute that in many respects differs from RUPA § 202. Nonetheless, this case contains a good discussion of the factors that courts typically examine to determine whether two or more persons are partners.

Ingram v. Deere
Supreme Court of Texas
288 S.W.3d 886 (2009)

Justice WAINWRIGHT. In this case, we review a court of appeals judgment reinstating a jury verdict finding that Louis Deere, D.O. and Jesse C. Ingram, Ph.D. formed a partnership pursuant to the Texas Revised Partnership Act (TRPA).

TRPA lists five factors to be considered in determining whether a partnership has been formed. This determination should be made by examining the totality of the circumstances in each case, with no single factor being either necessary or sufficient to prove the existence of a partnership. Here, the evidence is legally insufficient to establish that a partnership existed between Ingram and Deere. ***

[I.] Ingram, a licensed psychologist, and Deere, a board certified psychiatrist, entered into an oral agreement in 1997, which provided that Deere would serve as the medical director for a multidisciplinary pain clinic. Deere contends that they agreed he would receive one-third of the clinic's revenues, Ingram would receive one-third, and the remaining one-third would be used to pay the clinic's expenses. Deere also claims that when he and Ingram began working together, Ingram told him their work "was a joint venture, or [they] were partners, or [they] were doing this together." Ingram contends that they only agreed Deere would receive one-third of the clinic's revenues and that there was no agreement as to the other two-thirds. Deere acknowledges that, during his time at the clinic, he never contributed money to the clinic, he did not participate in the hiring of any employees, he did not know any of the clinic staff's names, he never purchased any of the clinic's equipment, his name was not on the clinic's bank account, and his name was not on the lease agreement for the clinic space.

Fourteen months after Deere began working at the clinic, Ingram prepared a written agreement to memorialize their arrangement. The document was entitled "Physician Contractual Employment Agreement" and stated that Ingram was the "sole owner" of the clinic. Deere refused to sign the document, claiming that it contradicted their initial arrangement. Immediately after Deere received the document, he ceased working at the clinic.

Deere later sued Ingram, asserting claims of common law fraud, statutory fraud, fraudulent inducement, breach of contract, breach of fiduciary duty, and declaratory judgment and seeking specific performance, damages, and attorneys' fees. The jury found that Deere and Ingram entered into a partnership agreement and that Ingram breached the agreement and his fiduciary duty to Deere. [Although the jury awarded Deere damages, the trial judge "signed a judgment n.o.v. and rendered a take-nothing judgment in Ingram's favor" on other grounds.]

***

[II.C.1—Texas Common Law.]   Under the common law, [this] Court recognized that a partnership or joint enterprise "presupposes an agreement to that end," which could be either express or implied. [Citation omitted.] We explained that the "intention of the parties to a contract is a prime element in determining whether or not a partnership or joint venture exists." [Citation omitted.]. The common law also considered that profit sharing was the most important factor shedding light on the intention to establish a partnership. [Citation omitted.] These two elements were incorporated into a five-factor test that developed under the common law for partnership formation: (1) intent to form a partnership, (2) a community of interest in the venture, (3) an agreement to share profits, (4) an agreement to share losses, and (5) a mutual right of control or management of the enterprise. [Citations omitted.] These factors continued to guide the question of partnership formation when Texas promulgated and later amended statutory regimes governing partnerships.

[II.C.2—Texas Statutory Law.]   The Texas Uniform Partnership Act (TUPA) was passed in 1961 and substantially adopted the major provisions of the Uniform Partnership Act (UPA), which itself was adopted in every state except Louisiana after it was approved by the National Conference of Commissioners on Uniform State Laws in 1914. [Citation omitted.] TUPA was replaced by TRPA, effective January 1, 1994, ***. It is uncontested that TRPA governs this dispute; rather, the parties contest whether Deere has proven the existence of a partnership under TRPA.

TRPA provides that "an association of two or more persons to carry on a business for profit as owners creates a partnership." Tex. Rev. Civ. Stat. art. 6132b-2.02(a).   Unlike TUPA, TRPA articulates five factors, similar to the common law factors, that indicate the creation of a partnership. They are:

(1)   receipt or right to receive a share of profits of the business;

(2)   expression of an intent to be partners in the business;

(3)   participation or right to participate in control of the business;

(4)   sharing or agreeing to share:
       (A)   losses of the business; or
       (B)   liability for claims by third parties against the business; and

(5)   contributing or agreeing to contribute money or property to the business.

Id. art. 6132b-2.03(a).   The common law required proof of all five factors to establish the existence of a partnership. [Citation omitted.]   However, TRPA contemplates a less formalistic and more practical approach to recognizing the formation of a partnership.

First, TRPA does not require direct proof of the parties' intent to form a partnership.   ***   Instead, TRPA lists the "expression of intent" to form a partnership as a factor to consider. Tex. Rev. Civ. Stat. art. 6132b-2.03(a)(2). Second, unlike the common law, TRPA does not require proof of *all* of the listed factors in order for a partnership to exist.   Third, sharing of profits—deemed essential for establishing a partnership under the common law—is treated differently under TRPA because sharing of profits is not required. [Citation omitted.] Still, TRPA comments note that the traditional import of sharing profits as well as control over the business will probably continue to be the most important factors. [Citation omitted.] Additionally, TRPA recognizes that sharing of losses may be indicative of a partnership arrangement but states that such an arrangement is "not necessary to create a partnership." *Id.* art. 6132b-2.03(c).

TRPA also restates and extends the list of circumstances in TUPA that do not by themselves indicate that a person is a partner. *Id.* art. 6132b-2.03(b).

The question of how many of the TRPA factors are required to form a partnership is a matter of first impression for this Court. The TRPA factors seem to serve as a proxy for the common law requirement of intent to form a partnership by identifying conduct that logically suggests a collaboration of a business's purpose and resources to make a profit as partners. After examining the statutory language and considering that TRPA abrogated the common law's requirement of proof of all five factors, we determine that the issue of whether a partnership exists should be decided considering all of the evidence bearing on the TRPA partnership factors.   ***   Many states apply this totality-of-the-circumstances test.

We note the difficulty of uniformly applying a totality-of-the-circumstances test, [citation omitted], but we cannot ignore the Legislature's decision to codify the essential common law partnership factors in TRPA without specifying that proof of all or some of the factors is required to establish a partnership. *See* Tex. Rev. Civ. Stat. art. 6132b-2.03; [citation omitted]. Yet, we can provide additional guidelines for this analysis. Of course, an absence of any evidence of the factors will preclude the recognition of a partnership under Texas law. [Citation omitted.] Even conclusive evidence of only one factor normally will be insufficient to establish the existence of a partnership. To hold otherwise would create a probability that some business owners would be legally required to share profits with individuals or be held liable for the actions of individuals who were neither treated as nor intended to be partners. [Citation omitted.] The Legislature does not indicate that it intended to spring surprise or accidental partnerships on independent business persons, if, for example, an employee is paid out of business profits with no other indicia of a de facto partnership under TRPA. On the other end of the spectrum, conclusive evidence of all of the TRPA factors will establish the existence of a partnership as a matter of law. The challenge of the totality-of-the-circumstances test will be its application between these two points on the continuum.

[II.D.—Existence of a Partnership.] In this case, we consider whether more than a scintilla of evidence of any of the factors indicative of a partnership was introduced at trial.

1.   Profit Sharing

Deere argues that he received or had the right to receive a share of the clinic's profits because he and Ingram had an agreement in which each of them would receive one-third of the clinic's "gross revenue" and the remainder would be used for expenses. It is true that the "receipt or right to receive a share of profits of the business" may be indicative of the existence of a partnership under TRPA, but a share of profits paid as "wages or other compensation to an employee or independent contractor" is not indicative of a partnership interest in the business. [Citation omitted.]

The evidence does not establish that Deere received a share of profits as contemplated under TRPA for two reasons. First, the agreement between Ingram and Deere cannot constitute Deere's receipt of "profits," but rather of gross revenue. *** Simply put, Deere's share depended on the clinic's receipts, not its excess of revenues over expenditures. Therefore, the evidence in this case leads to one conclusion: Deere did not share the clinic's profits but agreed to and received a percentage of the clinic's gross revenues.

Second, Ingram wrote twenty checks to Deere as compensation from January 1997 until March 1999. These checks referred to Deere as a "medical consultant" and the payments as "contract labor." Therefore, they contradict his argument that he received profits as a partner in the clinic. Under TRPA, receipt of profits as compensation for an employee's services or an independent contractor's work is not evidence that parties were partners. [Citation omitted.] Because Deere cashed the checks without challenging the characterizations, this fact also does not support his argument.

2.   Expression of Intent to Be Partners

"[E]xpression of an intent to be partners in the business" is one of five factors courts use in determining whether a partnership exists. Tex. Rev. Civ. Stat. art. 6132b-2.03(a)(2). This is different from the common law definition of a partnership that required proof that the parties intended to form a partnership at the outset of their agreement. [Citations omitted.] Conversely, TRPA evaluates the parties' *expression* of intent to be partners as one factor, Tex. Rev. Civ. Stat. art. 6132b-2.03(a)(2), and it does not by its terms give the parties' intent or expression of intent any greater weight than the other factors, *see* Tex. Rev. Civ. Stat. art. 6132b-2.03(a).

***

Evidence of expressions of intent could include, for example, the parties' statements that they are partners, one party holding the other party out as a partner on the business's letterhead or name plate, or in a signed partnership agreement. [Citations omitted.]

The terms used by the parties in referring to the arrangement do not control, [citation omitted], and merely referring to another person as "partner" in a situation where the recipient of the message would not expect the declarant to make a statement of legal significance is not enough. [Citation omitted.] The term "partner" is regularly used in common vernacular and may be used in a variety of ways. [Citation omitted.] Referring to a friend, employee, spouse, teammate, or fishing companion as a "partner" in a colloquial sense is not legally sufficient evidence of expression of intent to form a business partnership. [Citation omitted.] However, the same terms could constitute legally significant evidence of expression of intent when made in a circumstance that indicates significance to the business endeavor. Thus, courts should look to the terminology used by the putative partners, the context in which the statements were made, and the identity of the speaker and listener.

Deere argues that he expressed his intent to be a partner with Ingram by sharing the clinic's profits and losses and having access to the clinic's records. His evidence of other factors, sharing of profits and losses and control of the business, is insufficient to establish expression of intent. Deere's evidence is also insufficient because there must be evidence that both parties expressed their intent to be partners. [Citation omitted.] Because Ingram is the party denying the existence of a partnership, an expression of intent to be partners by Ingram would be of particular interest.

The evidence of Ingram's expression of intent to be business partners is the following exchange during Deere's trial testimony:

Q.   What representations did [Ingram] make to you when you were forming this idea that later turned out to be not true?

A.   [Deere] Well, that number one, that this was a joint venture, or that we were partners, or we were doing this together.

Deere's testimony is unclear and gives the alleged arrangement with Ingram three different characterizations—that they were joint venturers, partners, or "were doing this together." It is unclear from this testimony what Ingram believed to be the nature of their relationship. Any significance of Deere's testimony is further obviated because he testified that partner "means some people working together." Accordingly, Deere called the employees he supervised at his clinic "partners." After Deere's counsel explained to him the legal definition of a partnership during his testimony, Deere referred to his trial attorney as his "partner" because he was "depending on [him]."

Deere also testified that the clinic kept its established name after he joined as the medical director, and he and Ingram never discussed a name change. He never signed a lease agreement for the building owned by Ingram where the clinic was housed, was not named on the clinic's bank account, never signed a signature card for the clinic's bank account, and never filed taxes representing that he was co-owner of the clinic. Additionally, Deere paid his own medical malpractice insurance, which he acknowledged was his common practice when he did contract work. Deere cannot provide the content, context, or circumstances to give any of the alleged expressions of intent legal significance as evidence of a partnership.

3.   Control

Deere argues he had an equal right to control and manage the clinic's business because, although he was never allowed to see the books and records, he repeatedly requested to see them. He also points to Ingram's testimony that "maybe" Deere viewed the clinic's books on one occasion. Furthermore, Deere argues that he had control because Ingram discussed with him how much the clinic made, the amounts paid to the staff, and the need to hire Ingram's wife as personnel director. No other evidence supports these statements and proves he participated in or had the right to control the clinic's business.

The right to control a business is the right to make executive decisions. [Citations omitted.] However, being sporadically provided information regarding the business does not indicate that Deere had control of or the right to control the business. At most, Deere's evidence demonstrates that Ingram talked with Deere about the business. But owners talk with consultants, employees, accountants, attorneys, spouses, and many others about their businesses, and these conversations do not establish that these people have control of the businesses. Likewise, those same classes of people may have the opportunity to look at the businesses' books, but once again, a review of the books itself is not evidence of control. Deere submitted no evidence that he made executive decisions or had the right to make executive decisions and has shown no evidence of this factor.

4.   Sharing of Losses and Liability for Third Party Claims

***

According to Deere, he and Ingram agreed that Deere would receive one-third of the clinic's gross revenue, Ingram would receive one-third of the clinic's gross revenue, and the remainder would be used to pay clinic expenses. Deere argues that this agreement determined how losses would be shared, but he testified that there was never a discussion of how expenses in excess of one-third of the clinic's gross revenue would be divided between him and Ingram. The meaning of "net operating losses" is "the excess of operating expenses over revenues, the amount of which can be deducted from gross income if other deductions do not exceed gross income." Black's Law Dictionary 963 (8th ed. 2004). Here, Ingram and Deere never discussed what would happen to the allocation if expenses exceeded one-third of the revenue or gross income. They never discussed losses, only expenses. There is no legally cognizable evidence to support the contention that Ingram and Deere agreed to share losses.

5.   Contribution of Money or Property

Finally, there is no evidence that Deere "contribut[ed] or agree[d] to contribute money or property" to the clinic as a partner. Tex. Rev. Civ. Stat. art. 6132b-2.03(a)(5). Deere does not argue that there was any *agreement* that he contribute either money or property to the enterprise. *See Id.* Furthermore, Deere does not contend that he actually contributed money to the clinic. In fact, Deere acknowledged at trial that he did not contribute to clinic renovations or the purchase of medical equipment and supplies and that he did not agree to use his personal resources to pay for any expenses in the operation of the clinic. Rather, Deere's only argument regarding this factor is that he contributed his reputation as property to the alleged partnership.

TRPA defines "property" as "all property, real, personal, or mixed, tangible or intangible, or an interest in that property." *Id.* art. 6132b-1.01(15). Reputation is a type of goodwill and may be valuable intangible property. [Citation omitted.] Therefore, an individual's reputation can be property that is contributed to the partnership. However, even if a person lends her good name to a business, she does not automatically become a de facto partner. At a minimum, the putative partner would have to prove that any such value can be distinguished from services rendered or property given as an employee.

a.   Contribution of Valuable Property

Although Deere claims his reputation was a valuable contribution to the alleged partnership, the evidence does not support this assertion. ***

b.   Contribution as a Partner

Furthermore, there is no evidence that Deere added value to the clinic as a partner and not an employee. Even if we were to assume that Deere contributed quantifiable value and enjoyed a good reputation in the psychiatric or pain management fields, he cannot establish this factor without evidence that the contribution is distinguishable from the contributions of an employee. Employees may contribute to business endeavors by lending their time and reputation, but that is not a contribution to the venture indicative of a partnership interest. Even assuming Deere's reputation was impeccable, nothing indicates that Deere contributed or agreed to contribute to the clinic as a partner and not as an employee. In sum, there is no legally sufficient evidence that Deere contributed property to the multidisciplinary pain clinic that would establish a partnership interest.

[III.] Whether a partnership exists must be determined by an examination of the totality of the circumstances. Evidence of none of the factors under the Texas Revised Partnership Act will preclude the recognition of a partnership, and even conclusive evidence of only one factor will also normally be insufficient to establish the existence of a partnership under TRPA. However, conclusive evidence of all five factors establishes a partnership as a matter of law. In this case, Deere has not provided legally sufficient evidence of any of the five TRPA factors to prove the existence of a partnership. Accordingly, we reverse the court of appeals' judgment and reinstate the trial court's take-nothing judgment.

Justice JOHNSON filed a concurring opinion. [Omitted]

---

§ 3.02   FORMING A PARTNERSHIP AND DRAFTING A PARTNERSHIP AGREEMENT

Objectives: You should be able to explain to a client who wants to start a business as a partnership (1) what steps (if any) are necessary to form a partnership and (2) what issues the client should consider in drafting a partnership agreement.

Subsidiary Objectives: You should also be able to:

• *Actions Necessary to Form a Partnership. Explain to your client whether she (1) needs any other owners and/or (2) must file any documents with the state government to operate her business as a partnership.*

• *Partnership Agreement. Advise your client whether she should have a written partnership agreement with the other partner(s). Are the partners required to have a partnership agreement? Even if not, would you advise having a partnership agreement? Must a partnership agreement be in writing?*

• *"Default" Partnership Rules. Explain why RUPA is described as supplying "default" rules governing partnerships. (See RUPA § 103(a).) List and describe some of the "default" provisions of RUPA that your client may want to modify in her partnership agreement. Given a fact pattern, determine whether a provision in a partnership agreement is permitted under RUPA § 103(b). If a provision is not permitted under RUPA § 103(b), what happens to it? What, if anything, happens to the portions of the partnership agreement that are permissible under RUPA § 103?*

RUPA § 101(6) defines a "partnership" as "an association of two or more persons to carry on as co-owners a business for profit formed under Section 202, predecessor law, or comparable law of another jurisdiction." Thus, if an association is formed under RUPA § 202, a predecessor to RUPA such as the Uniform Partnership Act (UPA), or the partnership statute of another state, it will be considered a partnership. Meanwhile, RUPA § 202(a) provides in part that that "the association of two or more persons to carry on as co-owners a business for profit forms a partnership, whether or not the persons intend to form a partnership." As discussed in the previous section, no filing is required with the state government to form a partnership.

As discussed in Section 3.01 above, it sometimes may be difficult to determine whether the relationship between two or more persons is a partnership. However, let us assume in this section that it is clear that a partnership has been, or will be, formed. One issue that should be considered at this point is whether to create a partnership agreement. This is because RUPA is largely a set of "default" rules that will apply to a partnership only if that partnership has not adopted different rules in its partnership agreement. In other words, RUPA takes the position that partners should be largely free to structure their relationship as they see fit, with

> ***"Joint Ventures"***
> It is sometimes difficult to distinguish partnerships from "joint ventures." Generally speaking, joint ventures usually have more limited business purposes than partnerships. But this does not mean that the two are mutually exclusive. Comment 2 to RUPA § 202 notes that "[r]elationships that are called 'joint ventures' are partnerships if they otherwise fit the definition of a partnership." However, an "association is not ... a partnership ... simply because it is called a 'joint venture.'"

minimal interference from the government in the form of mandatory rules that all partnerships must follow. On the other hand, a partnership agreement may address some issues but remain silent on others. With respect to these latter issues, RUPA will "step in" and supply the rules. Further, partners may not even be aware that they have formed a partnership—as noted above, intent is not necessary to form a partnership. In such a case, the chances that these partners would have a partnership agreement, even a partial one, is virtually nonexistent. Here, RUPA would supply a comprehensive set of rules governing that partnership.

This approach is embodied in RUPA § 103(a), which provides that:

Except as otherwise provided in subsection (b), relations among the partners and between the partners and the partnership are governed by the partnership agreement. To the extent the partnership agreement does not otherwise provide, [RUPA] governs relations among the partners and between the partners and the partnership.

Thus, if two parties want to form a partnership but they do not "like" a particular provision of RUPA, they are free to change that rule by putting a different rule in their partnership agreement. Note here that RUPA § 101(7) defines a "partnership agreement" as "the agreement, whether written, oral, or implied, among the partners concerning the partnership ...."   While it may be difficult in a court proceeding to prove the existence or contents of an oral agreement, there is no "statute of frauds" in RUPA.

> ***Approaching a Partnership Law Issue***
> When analyzing a partnership law issue, you should first ask whether the partnership agreement addresses the issue. If not, find the applicable rule in RUPA. If the agreement does address the issue, ask whether the partnership agreement violates RUPA § 103(b). If not, apply the rule from the partnership agreement. If so, find the applicable rule in RUPA.

RUPA does not give the partners complete *carte blanche* to do whatever they want to do in their partnership agreement, however. Section 103(b) sets forth a list of "forbidden" topics. Study RUPA § 103(b) and consider whether the partnership agreements in the following problems are valid under RUPA.

Problems

Problem 3-7: Amy, Betty, and Claude formed a partnership. One section of their partnership agreement provided: "Under no circumstances shall any partner be personally liable to a third party for any debts or other obligations of the partnership." *Is this provision enforceable under RUPA?*

Problem 3-8: Nadia, Omar, Peter, and Quincy went into business as partners to open an art gallery. Their partnership agreement contained the following provisions: (1) a new partner may be admitted to the partnership if 75% of the current partners vote yes; (2) ordinary negligence will be considered to be a breach of a partner's duty of care to the partnership; and (3) no partner will be deemed to owe a duty of loyalty to the partnership. *Which, if any, of these provisions are enforceable under RUPA? See* RUPA §§ 103(b), 401(i), 404(b), and 404(c).

Problem 3-9:   The Big Law Firm is a partnership with 100 partners. It has a partnership agreement, but the agreement does not address how it may be amended. *What vote is needed to amend the partnership agreement of the Big Law Firm? See* RUPA § 401(j).

Problem 3-10: *Would it be permissible for the Big Law Firm's partnership agreement to provide that it may be amended if at least 75% of the partners vote in favor of a proposed amendment?*

Keep in mind as you work your way through the remainder of this chapter, as well as Chapter 4, that nearly all of the provisions of RUPA may be "changed" with respect to a given partnership. In fact, you may want to keep a running list of provisions of RUPA that your future clients may not find desirable. RUPA's rules are, by and large, perfectly reasonable for a partnership that has a small number of partners. However, in many cases RUPA's default rules would be a disaster for a partnership that has many partners.

§ 3.03   OWNERSHIP OF PROPERTY BY A PARTNERSHIP

Objectives:

●   ***Does the Partnership Own an Asset?*** *Given a fact pattern, you should be able to determine whether a partnership owns a particular asset.*

●   ***Titling an Asset to the Partnership.*** *Assume that Joe Smith and Bob Smith form a partnership called the "Smith Brothers Partnership" and that the partnership acquires Blackacre, a piece of real estate, from John Jones. You should be able to complete the following deed for Blackacre in a way that will indicate that the Smith Brothers Partnership owns Blackacre (see RUPA § 204).*

DEED

Know by all these persons present, that on this 15ᵗʰ day of June, 2012, John Jones (hereinafter the "Seller"), for good and valuable consideration, the sufficiency of which is hereby acknowledged, has bargained, assigned and conveyed Blackacre to:

_____

(hereinafter the "Buyer").

• ***Permissible Uses of Partnership Property.*** *Assuming the Smith Brothers Partnership owns Blackacre, explain to Joe and Bob what they (as partners and as individuals) may—and what they may not—do with Blackacre. See RUPA §§ 203, 401(g) and 501.*

In addition to being an association of two or more persons who carry on as co-owners of a for-profit business, a partnership is something else: a "person" in the eyes of the law. RUPA § 201(a), which reflects the "entity theory" of the partnership,[*] states that a "partnership is an entity distinct from its partners." Thus, if A, B, and C form a partnership, there are actually four "persons" present: A, B, C, and the ABC partnership. This means that a partnership may do the things that any other "person" may legally do: it may sign contracts, sue and be sued, and hire employees. It may also own property, which is the subject of this section.

RUPA § 203 states that property that is "acquired" by a partnership is the partnership's property (as opposed to being the property of any *partner*). At first, this seems straightforward; using the example above, if the ABC partnership acquires a widget, then that widget belongs to the ABC partnership and not any of A, B, or C. This result is confirmed by RUPA § 501, which specifically states that a partner is not a co-owner of any partnership property. Further, RUPA § 401(g) states that a "partner may use or possess partnership property only on behalf of the partnership." For example, if a partnership owned, say, a copy machine, a partner is not legally entitled to use the copy machine for her personal copies (although this surely is something that happens every day without legal objections being raised).

---

[*]   By contrast, UPA did not treat a partnership as an entity that is separate from the partners.

But when exactly is property "acquired" by a partnership? This is where the somewhat confusing section 204 comes in. When studying RUPA § 204, note its structure. Subsections (a) and (b) concern the situation where an item of property (whether personal property or real property) is acquired in the name of the partnership or the name(s) of one or more of the partners. It would seem that these subsections only concern situations whether the item of property has a title document, such as a deed for a piece of real estate or a certificate of title for a vehicle.[*] Also, note that subsections (b)(1) and (b)(2) simply elaborate on subsection (a)(1), clarifying exactly when an item of property was acquired "in the name of the partnership."

Subsections (c) and (d), on the other hand, seem to deal with any type of property, whether or not it has a title document. Subsection (c) sets forth a commonsensical rule, essentially providing that an item is presumed to belong to the partnership if partnership funds were used to purchase it. Subsection (d) reminds us that partners can still own separate property from the partnership; simply because one joins a partnership does not mean that one turns over all of one's property to the partnership. However, note that subsections (c) and (d) are rebuttable presumptions; the partners' intent ultimately controls. Study section 204 and apply it to the following problems:

Problems

Problem 3-11: Mike, Nick, and Omar, three auto mechanics, decided to form a partnership to "run their own shop." Before forming this partnership with Mike and Nick, Omar had owned a great many tools and other pieces of equipment. The three partners then began using these items in connection with their auto repair business. *Who now owns Omar's tools and equipment? What if Omar claims that he was merely loaning the tools and equipment to the partnership? How would you have addressed this issue if you had been the partnership's lawyer?*

Problem 3-12: Same facts as in Problem 3-11. The partnership did very well, in fact, so well that "overflow" space was needed and the partnership began using the garage at the house that Mike shared with his wife Sue as additional space in which to repair cars. Mike and Sue had purchased their house shortly after the partnership was formed, but the deed simply states that Mike and Sue are the owners of the house. *Does the partnership have any*

---

[*]   Comment 2 to RUPA § 204 states in part that the "concept of record title is emphasized, although the term itself is not used. Titled personal property, as well as all transferable interests in real property acquired in the name of the partnership, are covered by [subsection (a)]."

ownership interest in Mike's garage? Does the partnership owe Mike rent for using this space?

Problem 3-13: Several months after the partnership was formed, Mike went to an auto supply store and purchased several cases of motor oil, charging the purchase price to the partnership's credit card. *Who owns these cases of oil?*

§ 3.04   MANAGEMENT AND AGENCY ISSUES IN A PARTNERSHIP

Objectives:

•   *How Partnership Decisions Are Made.* *You should be able to explain to the partners of a partnership (1) how many votes each partner has under RUPA with respect to partnership decisions and whether the partnership agreement may vary this number or give one partner authority to make certain decisions without the approval of the other partners, (2) what decisions relating to the partnership may be made by a majority vote, and (3) what decisions require unanimous approval. In addition, given a fact pattern, you should be able to determine whether a particular decision involves a matter that is in the ordinary course of the partnership's business.*

•   *When Is a Partnership Bound to a Third Party?* *Given a fact pattern in which a partner has been dealing with a third party on behalf of the partnership, you should be able to determine whether the partner's actions have resulted in the partnership being bound to a contract with the third party.*

Under ideal circumstances, a partnership will be harmonious; the partners may usually, if not always, agree on what the business should do, making actual voting on disputes rare or even nonexistent. Alternatively, a partnership agreement could delegate to one or more partners the power to make certain business decisions. Such "managing partners" are relatively commonplace and their presence would eliminate the necessity of partners having to vote on many matters. Nonetheless, as in any human institution, disputes are bound to arise between the partners. Thus, either RUPA or the partnership agreement must give us rules to resolve these disputes. The primary sections of RUPA that deal with these issues are sections 401(f) and 401(j).

On a related note, Chapter 2 of this book promised that agency law issues would recur throughout this book and here they are again: RUPA § 301 reminds us that partners can be agents of the partnership and therefore can bind the partnership to transactions or other contracts with third parties. Of course, partners are not the only persons who may be considered agents of the partnership. For example, if the partnership hired an employee, that employee may, depending on the facts, have actual or apparent authority to bind the partnership to a contract with a third party.

Study the foregoing sections of RUPA and apply them to the following problems:

Problems

Problem 3-14: Recall Mike, Nick, and Omar from Problems 3-11 through 3-13. One day, Nick told the other two partners that he thought that the partnership needed to buy a new auto repair diagnostic computer, at a cost of $20,000. Mike agreed, but Omar said that he thought that the partnership did not need to buy it. *Have the partners approved the purchase of this computer?*

Problem 3-15: Same facts as in Problem 3-14, except that both Mike and Omar decided that the partnership should not buy the computer. Undeterred, Nick went to Diagnostic Equipment Suppliers, Inc. ("DESI"), and told them he was a partner in an auto repair business with Mike and Omar. He then signed a contract with DESI to buy the Auto Diagnosis 3000 computer for $20,000. When Mike and Omar found out about this, they were furious. *Is the partnership obligated to purchase this computer from DESI? If so, how could Mike or Omar have prevented this from happening?*

Problem 3-16: Nick also decided (on his own) that the partnership should go into the business of running a coffee shop in a vacant space next to the garage where the partnership ran its auto repair business. To that end, Nick ordered several coffee and espresso machines and several hundred pounds of coffee beans from Caffeinemaniacs, Inc., a catalog supply firm. When Mike and Omar found out about this, they were furious. *Is the partnership obligated to purchase these items from Caffeinemaniacs?*

Problem 3-17:   Tam and Pam are the only partners in a partnership. Tam voted that the partnership should buy a new copy machine. Pam voted no. *Will the partnership be buying a new copy machine?*

§ 3.05   FIDUCIARY DUTIES OF PARTNERS

> *Objectives: You should be able to explain to a client who is a partner in a partnership what fiduciary duties she owes to the partnership and the other partners (see RUPA § 404). Given a fact pattern, you should also be able to determine whether she has breached her fiduciary duties to the partnership. You should also be able to explain whether it is permissible under RUPA § 103(b) to eliminate or modify any of these duties in the partnership agreement.*

It is axiomatic that partners owe strict fiduciary duties to each other and (at least under RUPA's entity theory) to the partnership. The rationale behind this rule is that, if a partnership's business is to prosper, there must be a high degree of trust between the partners; imposing fiduciary duties on the partners is the way to enforce this trust. Thus, a person who joins a partnership should be aware that she is entering into a relationship that is the opposite of the arm's length relationship that one typically has with the rest of the world.

It is one thing to say that a person owes a "fiduciary" duty to another person or persons but quite another to describe the contours of that duty or decide whether that duty has been breached. The following is one of the most famous cases to address this issue. You will find it in nearly every law textbook that discusses partnerships.

Meinhard v. Salmon
New York Court of Appeals
164 N.E. 545 (1928)

CARDOZO, C. J. On April 10, 1902, Louisa M. Gerry leased to the defendant Walter J. Salmon the premises known as the Hotel Bristol at the northwest corner of Forty-Second street and Fifth avenue in the city of New York. The lease was for a term of 20 years, commencing May 1, 1902, and ending April 30, 1922. The lessee undertook to change the hotel building for use as shops and offices at a cost of $200,000. Alterations and additions were to be accretions to the land.

Salmon, while in [contract] with the lessor as to the execution of the lease, was in [contract] with Meinhard, the plaintiff, for the necessary funds. The result was a joint venture with terms embodied in a writing. Meinhard was to pay to Salmon half of the moneys requisite to reconstruct, alter, manage, and operate the property. Salmon was to pay to Meinhard 40 [percent] of the net profits for the first five years of the lease and 50 [percent] for the years thereafter. If there were losses, each party was to bear them equally. Salmon, however, was to have sole power to "manage, lease, underlet and operate" the building. There were to be certain pre-emptive rights for each in the contingency of death.

They were coadventurers, subject to fiduciary duties akin to those of partners. [Citation omitted.] As to this we are all agreed. The heavier weight of duty rested, however, upon Salmon. He was a coadventurer with Meinhard, but he was manager as well. During the early years of the enterprise, the building, reconstructed, was operated at a loss. If the relation had then ended, Meinhard as well as Salmon would have carried a heavy burden. Later the profits became large with the result that for each of the investors there came a rich return. For each the venture had its phases of fair weather and of foul. The two were in it jointly, for better or for worse.

When the lease was near its end, Elbridge T. Gerry had become the owner of the reversion. He owned much other property in the neighborhood, one lot adjoining the Bristol building on Fifth avenue and four lots on Forty-Second street. He had a plan to lease the entire tract for a long term to some one who would destroy the buildings then existing and put up another in their place. In the latter part of 1921, he submitted such a project to several capitalists and dealers. He was unable to carry it through with any of them. Then, in January, 1922, with less than four months of the lease to run, he approached the defendant Salmon. The result was a new lease to the Midpoint Realty Company, which is owned and controlled by Salmon, a lease covering the whole tract, and involving a huge outlay. The term is to be 20 years, but successive covenants for renewal will extend it to a maximum of 80 years at the will of either party. The existing buildings may remain unchanged for seven years. They are then to be torn down, and a new building to cost $3,000,000 is to be placed upon the site. The rental, which under the Bristol lease was only $55,000, is to be from $350,000 to $475,000 for the properties so combined. Salmon personally guaranteed the performance by the lessee of the covenants of the new lease until such time as the new building had been completed and fully paid for.

The lease between Gerry and the Midpoint Realty Company was signed and delivered on January 25, 1922. Salmon had not told Meinhard anything about it. Whatever his motive may have been, he had kept the negotiations to himself. Meinhard was not informed even of the bare existence of a project. The first that he knew of it was in February, when the lease was an accomplished fact. He then made demand on the defendants that the lease be held in trust as an asset of the venture, making offer upon the trial to share the personal obligations incidental to the guaranty. The demand was followed by refusal, and later by this suit. A referee gave judgment for the plaintiff ***. The case is now here on an appeal by the defendants.

Joint adventurers, like copartners, owe to one another, while the enterprise continues, the duty of the finest loyalty. Many forms of conduct permissible in a workaday world for those acting at arm's length, are forbidden to those bound by fiduciary ties. A trustee is held to something stricter than the morals of the market place. Not honesty alone, but the punctilio of an honor the most sensitive, is then the standard of behavior. As to this there has developed a tradition that is unbending and inveterate. Uncompromising rigidity has been the attitude of courts of equity when petitioned to undermine the rule of undivided loyalty by the "disintegrating erosion" of particular exceptions. [Citation omitted.] Only thus has the level of conduct for fiduciaries been kept at a level higher than that trodden by the crowd. It will not consciously be lowered by any judgment of this court.

The owner of the reversion, Mr. Gerry, had vainly striven to find a tenant who would favor his ambitious scheme of demolition and construction. Baffled in the search, he turned to the defendant Salmon in possession of the Bristol, the keystone of the project. He figured to himself beyond a doubt that the man in possession would prove a likely customer. To the eye of an observer, Salmon held the lease as owner in his own right, for himself and no one else. In fact he held it as a fiduciary, for himself and another, sharers in a common venture. If this fact had been proclaimed, if the lease by its terms had run in favor of a partnership, Mr. Gerry, we may fairly assume, would have laid before the partners, and not merely before one of them, his plan of reconstruction. The pre-emptive privilege, or, better, the pre-emptive opportunity, that was thus an incident of the enterprise, Salmon appropriated to himself in secrecy and silence. He might have warned Meinhard that the plan had been submitted, and that either would be free to compete for the award. If he had done this, we do not need to say whether he would have been under a duty, if successful in the competition, to hold the lease so acquired for the benefit of a venture than about to end, and thus prolong by indirection its responsibilities and duties. The trouble about his conduct is that he excluded his coadventurer from any chance to compete, from any chance to enjoy the opportunity for benefit that had come to him alone by virtue of his agency. This chance, if nothing more, he was under a duty to concede. The price of its denial is an extension of the trust at the option and for the benefit of the one whom he excluded.

No answer is it to say that the chance would have been of little value even if seasonably offered. Such a calculus of probabilities is beyond the science of the [courts of] chancery. Salmon, the real estate operator, might have been preferred to Meinhard, the woolen merchant. On the other hand, Meinhard might have offered better terms, or reinforced his offer by alliance with the wealth of others.

Perhaps he might even have persuaded the lessor to renew the Bristol lease alone, postponing for a time, in return for higher rentals, the improvement of adjoining lots. We know that even under the lease as made the time for the enlargement of the building was delayed for seven years. All these opportunities were cut away from him through another's intervention. *** The very fact that Salmon was in control with exclusive powers of direction charged him the more obviously with the duty of disclosure, since only through disclosure could opportunity be equalized. If he might cut off renewal by a purchase for his own benefit when four months were to pass before the lease would have an end, he might do so with equal right while there remained as many years. [Citation omitted.] He might steal a march on his comrade under cover of the darkness, and then hold the captured ground. Loyalty and comradeship are not so easily abjured.

Little profit will come from a dissection of the precedents. None precisely similar is cited in the briefs of counsel. What is similar in many, or so it seems to us, is the animating principle. Authority is, of course, abundant that one partner may not appropriate to his own use a renewal of a lease, though its term is to begin at the expiration of the partnership. [Citation omitted.] The lease at hand with its many changes is not strictly a renewal. Even so, the standard of loyalty for those in trust relations is without the fixed divisions of a graduated scale. ***

We have no thought to hold that Salmon was guilty of a conscious purpose to defraud. Very likely he assumed in all good faith that with the approaching end of the venture he might ignore his coadventurer and take the extension for himself. *** [However,] Salmon had put himself in a position in which thought of self was to be renounced, however hard the abnegation. He was much more than a coadventurer. He was a managing coadventurer. For him and for those like him the rule of undivided loyalty is relentless and supreme. [Citations omitted.] A different question would be here if there were lacking any nexus of relation between the business conducted by the manager and the opportunity brought to him as an incident of management. [Citations omitted.] For this problem, as for most, there are distinctions of degree. If Salmon had received from Gerry a proposition to lease a building at a location far removed, he might have held for himself the privilege thus acquired, or so we shall assume. Here the subject-matter of the new lease was an extension and enlargement of the subject-matter of the old one. A managing coadventurer appropriating the benefit of such a lease without warning to his partner might fairly expect to be reproached with conduct that was underhand[ed], or lacking, to say the least, in reasonable candor, if the partner were to surprise him in the act of signing the new instrument. Conduct subject to that reproach does not receive from equity a healing benediction.

A question remains as to the form and extent of the equitable interest to be allotted to the plaintiff. ***

ANDREWS, J. (dissenting). ***

***

Were this a general partnership between Mr. Salmon and Mr. Meinhard, I should have little doubt as to the correctness of [the majority's opinion], assuming the new lease to be an offshoot of the old. ***

We have here a different situation governed by less drastic principles. I assume that where parties engage in a joint enterprise each owes to the other the duty of the utmost good faith in all that relates to their common venture. Within its scope they stand in a fiduciary relationship. I assume prima facie that even as between joint adventurers one may not secretly obtain a renewal of the lease of property actually used in the joint adventure where the possibility of renewal is expressly or impliedly involved in the enterprise. I assume also that Mr. Meinhard had an equitable interest in the Bristol Hotel lease. Further, that an expectancy of renewal inhered in that lease. Two questions then arise. Under his contract did he share in that expectancy? And if so, did that expectancy mature into a graft of the original lease? To both questions my answer is "No."

The one complaint made is that Mr. Salmon obtained the new lease without informing Mr. Meinhard of his intention. Nothing else. There is no claim of actual fraud. No claim of misrepresentation to any one. ***

***

It seems to me that the venture so inaugurated had in view a limited object and was to end at a limited time. There was no intent to expand it into a far greater undertaking lasting for many years. The design was to exploit a particular lease. Doubtless in it Mr. Meinhard had an equitable interest, but in it alone. This interest terminated when the joint adventure terminated. There was no intent that for the benefit of both any advantage should be taken of the chance of renewal— that the adventure should be continued beyond that date. Mr. Salmon has done all he promised to do in return for Mr. Meinhard's undertaking when he distributed profits up to May 1, 1922. Suppose this lease, nonassignable without the consent of the lessor, had contained a renewal option. Could Mr. Meinhard have exercised it? Could he have insisted that Mr. Salmon do so? Had Mr. Salmon done so could he insist that the agreement to share losses still existed, or could Mr. Meinhard have claimed that the joint adventure was still to continue for 20 or 80 years? I do not think so. The adventure by its express terms ended on May 1, 1922. The contract by its language and by its whole import excluded the idea that the tenant's expectancy was to subsist for the benefit of the plaintiff. On that date whatever there was left of value in the lease reverted to Mr. Salmon, as it would had the lease been for thirty years instead of twenty. Any equity which Mr.

Meinhard possessed was in the particular lease itself, not in any possibility of renewal. There was nothing unfair in Mr. Salmon's conduct.

***

So far I have treated the new lease as if it were a renewal of the old. As already indicated, I do not take that view. Such a renewal could not be obtained. Any expectancy that it might be had vanished. What Mr. Salmon obtained was not a graft springing from the Bristol lease, but something distinct and different— as distinct as if for a building across Fifth avenue. I think also that in the absence of some fraudulent or unfair act the secret purchase of the reversion even by one partner is rightful. Substantially this is such a purchase. Because of the mere label of a transaction we do not place it on one side of the line or the other. Here is involved the possession of a large and most valuable unit of property for 80 years, the destruction of all existing structures and the erection of a new and expensive building covering the whole. No fraud, no deceit, no calculated secrecy is found. Simply that the arrangement was made without the knowledge of Mr. Meinhard. I think this not enough.

The judgment of the courts below should be reversed ***.

POUND, CRANE, and LEHMAN, JJ., concur with CARDOZO, C. J., for modification of the judgment appealed from and affirmance as modified. ANDREWS, J., dissents in opinion in which KELLOGG and O'BRIEN, JJ., concur.

In *Meinhard*, Judge (later Justice) Cardozo states that "joint adventurers" (this also applies to partners) owe each other "the duty of the finest loyalty" and that this duty involves "[n]ot honesty alone, but the punctilio of an honor the most sensitive …." This is eloquent, memorable language. But what exactly does it *mean*? Apparently, the only way to advise a client what she may do without violating *Meinhard*'s duty of finest loyalty is to read cases that have applied *Meinhard* and then compare the facts in those cases to your client's situation. Obviously, this is not precise, and a great many gray areas will remain. It is hard to give solid legal advice using only *Meinhard* as a guide. Lawyers tend to err on the side of caution when the rules are murky.

> ### The Obligation of "Good Faith and Fair Dealing"
>
> RUPA § 404(d) states that a partner must discharge her duties, and exercise her rights, "consistently with the obligation of good faith and fair dealing." According to comment 4 to this section, this is not a "separate and independent obligation," nor is it a fiduciary duty. Instead, it is a "contract concept, imposed on the partners because of the consensual nature of a partnership." Unfortunately, the exact meaning of this obligation "is not firmly fixed under present law," leaving it to future courts to develop its contours.

RUPA § 404 tries to do better. While a full description of a partner's fiduciary duties certainly could not be expected in a statute, RUPA § 404 does take significant steps toward that goal. First, subsection (a) states that the only two "fiduciary" duties that a partner owes are the duties of loyalty and care. Second, subsections (b) and (c), which describe a partner's duty of loyalty and duty of care, respectively, do so not by stating what a partner is *required* to do, but stating what a partner must *refrain* from doing. In other words, as long as a partner avoids the types of conduct described in those subsections, then she would not be breaching her duty of care or duty of loyalty. Third, subsection (b) states that a partner's duty of loyalty is "limited to" refraining from the three types of actions described in subsections (b)(1), (2), and (3). This is good news in the sense that it provides a "limit" on the duty of loyalty. Finally, subsection (c) describes a partner's duty of care. The remaining subsections add more detail.

Study RUPA § 404, as well as RUPA § 405(a), and apply it to the following problems:

Problems

<u>Problem 3-18</u>:   *If the events in* Meinhard v. Salmon *took place today, would Salmon be found to have violated RUPA § 404?*

<u>Problem 3-19</u>:   You represent Greg Jones, a wealthy real estate developer in Big City.   Greg is considering entering into a partnership with two other real estate tycoons to build and operate a large shopping mall.   However, Greg is concerned that if he joins this partnership, the other partners will try to prevent him from continuing to operate and invest in other real estate projects, particularly those that feature retail outlets.   *What provisions would you suggest adding to the partnership agreement to alleviate Greg's concerns?   See RUPA § 103(b)(3).*

<u>Problem 3-20</u>:   Doctors Alpha, Beta, and Gamma formed a partnership to run a medical practice which will perform cosmetic (i.e., "plastic") surgery.   One day, while performing surgery on a

patient, Dr. Gamma committed malpractice, injuring the patient. *Has Dr. Gamma violated her duty of care to the partnership? If so, may the partnership recover damages from Dr. Gamma? What would the amount of those damages be?*

Problem 3-21: *Would your answer to Problem 3-20 change if the partnership agreement had provided that a partner's duty of care is to avoid engaging in negligence, gross negligence, reckless conduct, intentional misconduct, or a knowing violation of law? See RUPA § 103(b)(4).*

Problem 3-22: *Would your answer to Problem 3-20 change if the partnership agreement had provided that a partner's only duty of care is to avoid engaging in intentional or reckless homicide? See RUPA § 103(b)(4).*

Problem 3-23: Continuing with the partnership of Doctors Alpha, Beta, and Gamma, one day a patient saw Dr. Alpha in a coffee shop and paid an outstanding bill that the patient owed the partnership, in cash. Dr. Alpha, who felt that his other partners did not appreciate him or adequately compensate him for his medical genius, decided to keep the cash and not tell the other partners about it. *Which subsection of RUPA § 404(b) tells you that Dr. Alpha has violated his duty of loyalty to the partnership?*

Problem 3-24: *May a partner loan money to the partnership or would this mean that she is acting as "a party having an interest adverse to the partnership" within the meaning of RUPA § 404(b)(2)?*

Problem 3-25: *If you represented a partner who wanted to sell a piece of real estate to the partnership (and the partnership is willing to buy it), what advice would you give your client?*

§ 3.06   LIABILITY ISSUES IN A PARTNERSHIP

Objectives: *Given a fact pattern in which a partnership incurs a liability to a third party, either contractually (such as in a loan from a bank) or by a tort (such as where one of the partners or an employee of the partnership commits negligence in the course of partnership business), you should be able to (1) determine which person(s) is (are) liable for this obligation and (2) explain how the* *creditor may recover against the assets that belong to the person(s) who is (are) liable.*

Subsidiary Objectives: *You should also be able to:*

•   ***Partnership Liability for Actions of a Partner or Employee.*** *Given a fact pattern, determine whether a partnership is bound to a third party by the actions of a partner or by the actions of an employee.*

•   ***Partner Liability.*** *Given a fact pattern, determine whether a partner is personally liable for a partnership liability (see RUPA § 306).*

•   ***Recovery From a Partner's Personal Assets.*** *Given a fact pattern, determine whether a plaintiff may collect money damages from the partnership and/or the individual partners.*

Like any other business, a partnership will generate liabilities, such as debts owed to a bank or suppliers, rent that is owed to a landlord, or liabilities for torts committed by partners or partnership employees. This section concerns how a creditor that is owed a debt relating to the partnership's business may go about suing for, and collecting, that debt from the partnership and/or the partners. The primary sections of RUPA that you will examine are Sections 305, 306, and 307.

RUPA §§ 305 and 306 are relatively straightforward. Section 305 sets forth the circumstances when a partnership is liable for the acts of a partner. (Of course, the partnership could also be liable for the acts an employee who is not a partner, but that issue is not directly addressed by Section 305.) Section 306(a) provides a familiar general rule: partners are jointly and severally liable for the partnership's debts and obligations (unless the creditor agrees otherwise or unless otherwise provided by law). It is worth pausing here to consider how scary joint and several liability may be. Assume that there are two partners, A and B, and each of them has a 50% ownership interest in the partnership. If the partnership is unable to pay a debt, the creditor could recover the full amount owed from either A *or* B (subject to the procedural rules discussed below). It is *not* the case that the creditor would have to recover 50% of the unpaid debt from A and the other 50% from B. While a partner who pays more than her "fair share" of a debt is entitled to contribution from the other partner(s), this is not something about which the plaintiff must be concerned. Section 306(b) gives us an exception to this rule, providing that a "new" partner is not liable for partnership obligations that were incurred before the new partner was admitted to the partnership. Subsection (c) deals with limited liability partnerships (LLPs), which are discussed in Chapter 1.

Sections 305 and 306 are not terribly difficult to understand, but Section 307 does have a few surprises in store, particularly in subsections (c) and (d). Rather than discussing Section 307 in detail here, perhaps the best way to understand it is to apply it (and Sections 305 and 306) to the following problems:

Problems

Problem 3-26: Same facts as Problem 3-20: Doctors Alpha, Beta, and Gamma formed a partnership to run a medical practice, which will perform plastic surgery. One day, while performing surgery on a patient, Dr. Gamma committed malpractice, injuring the patient. *Is the partnership liable to the patient? Is Dr. Gamma liable to the patient? Are Doctors Alpha and Beta liable to the patient?*

Problem 3-27: Suppose that the patient from Problem 3-26 files suit against the partnership, but does not name Doctor Alpha, Doctor Beta, or Doctor Gamma as a defendant in the lawsuit. *If the patient wins the lawsuit, from whose assets may she collect the judgment?*

Problem 3-28: Suppose instead that the patient from Problem 3-26 filed suit only against Doctor Gamma. *If the patient wins the lawsuit, from whose assets may she collect the judgment? If Doctor Gamma pays the judgment from her own assets, will she have a right of indemnity from the partnership?*

Problem 3-29: The DEF partnership consists of three partners: Doug, Eugene, and Frieda. Last year, DEF obtained a loan from Smalltown Bank, but was unable to repay the loan in full. The bank filed suit against DEF and each of the three partners, and won a judgment for $100,000. The only asset of DEF is $10,000 in cash. *Explain how the bank may go about satisfying its judgment from the various defendants' assets.*

Problem 3-30: *Would your answer to Problem 3-29 change if the bank had required each of the three partners to sign a personal guaranty pursuant to which they promised to repay any debts that the partnership was unable to repay?*

Problem 3-31: In January, the HIJ Partnership (which consists of three partners: Helen, Ivan, and Juan) signed a one-year lease of office space with Realty Corp. The lease requires that HIJ pay $1,000 of rent to Realty Corp. on or before the first day of every month. In June, Kelly was admitted to the HIJ Partnership (which was then renamed the HIJK Partnership). However, in August, the HIJK Partnership was unable to pay the rent it owed to Realty Corp. *Is Kelly liable for all or any part of the remaining rental payments due to Realty Corp. under the lease?*

Problem 3-32: Same facts as Problem 3-31. *What vote was necessary to admit Kelly as a new partner in the partnership? See RUPA § 401(i). Would this rule be a good idea for a law firm with 100 partners?*

As noted above, Section 305 deals with whether the partnership may be liable for the actions of a partner. This will be the case if the partner's actions were either in the "ordinary course of business of the partnership" or if the actions were done "with authority of the partnership." The following case considers whether a partner's actions were done in the "ordinary course." You may also find this case useful in deciding whether a partner's actions can bind the partnership under RUPA § 301 (which is discussed above in § 3.04).

Moren ex rel. Moren v. Jax Restaurant
Court of Appeals of Minnesota
679 N.W.2d 165 (2004)

Crippen, Judge. Remington Moren, through his father, commenced a negligence action against appellant Jax Restaurant for injures he sustained while on appellant's premises. The district court granted a summary judgment, dismissing appellant's third-party negligence complaint against respondent Nicole Moren, a partner in Jax Restaurant and the mother of Remington Moren. Because the court correctly determined that liability for Nicole Moren's negligence rested with the partnership, even if the partner's conduct partly served her personal interests, we affirm.

FACTS

Jax Restaurant, the partnership, operates its business in Foley, Minnesota. One afternoon in October 2000, Nicole Moren, one of the Jax partners, completed her day shift at Jax at 4:00 p.m. and left to pick up her two-year-old son Remington from day care. At about 5:30, Moren returned to the restaurant with Remington after learning that her sister and partner, Amy Benedetti, needed help.

Moren called her husband who told her that he would pick Remington up in about 20 minutes.

Crushed Hand

Because Nicole Moren did not want Remington running around the restaurant, she brought him into the kitchen with her, set him on top of the counter, and began rolling out pizza dough using the dough-pressing machine. As she was making pizzas, Remington reached his hand into the dough press. His hand was crushed, and he sustained permanent injuries.

Through his father, Remington commenced a negligence action against the partnership. The partnership served a third-party complaint on Nicole Moren, arguing that, in the event it was obligated to compensate Remington, the partnership was entitled to indemnity or contribution from Moren for her negligence. The district court's summary judgment was premised on a legal conclusion that Moren has no obligation to indemnify Jax Restaurant so long as the injury occurred while she was engaged in ordinary business conduct. The district court rejected the partnership's argument that its obligation to compensate Remington is diminished in proportion to the predominating negligence of Moren as a mother, although it is responsible for her conduct as a business owner. This appeal followed.

ISSUE

Does Jax Restaurant have an indemnity right against Nicole Moren in the circumstances of this case?

ANALYSIS

***

Under Minnesota's Uniform Partnership Act of 1994 (UPA), a partnership is an entity distinct from its partners, and as such, a partnership may sue and be sued in the name of the partnership. Minn. Stat. §§ 323A.2-10, 323A.3-07 and 323A.12-01 (2002). "A partnership is liable for loss or injury caused to a person ... as a result of a wrongful act or omission, or other actionable conduct, of a partner acting in the ordinary course of business of the partnership or with authority of the partnership." Minn. Stat. § 323A.3-05(a) (2002); [citation omitted]. Accordingly, a "partnership shall ... indemnify a partner for liabilities incurred by the partner in the ordinary course of the business of the partnership ...." Minn. Stat. § 323A.4-01(c) (2002). Stated conversely, an "act of a partner which is not apparently for carrying on in the ordinary course the partnership business or business of the kind carried on by the partnership binds the partnership only if the act was authorized by the other partners." Minn. Stat. § 323A.3-01(2) (2002). Thus, under the plain language of the UPA, a partner has a right to indemnity from the partnership, but the partnership's claim of indemnity from a partner is not authorized or required.

The district court correctly concluded that Nicole Moren's conduct was in the ordinary course of business of the partnership and, as a result, indemnity by the partner to the partnership was inappropriate. It is undisputed that one of the cooks scheduled to work that evening did not come in, and that Moren's partner asked her to help in the kitchen. It also is undisputed that Moren was making pizzas for the partnership when her son was injured. Because her conduct at the time of the injury was in the ordinary course of business of the partnership, under the UPA, her conduct bound the partnership and it owes indemnity to her for her negligence. Minn. Stat. §§ 323A.3-05(a) and 323A.4-01(c).

Appellant heavily relies on one foreign case for the proposition that a partnership is entitled to a contribution or indemnity from a partner who is negligent. *See Flynn v. Reaves,* 135 Ga. App. 651, 218 S.E.2d 661 (1975). In *Flynn,* the Georgia Court of Appeals held that "where a partner is sued individually by a plaintiff injured by the partner's sole negligence, the partner cannot seek contribution from his co-partners even though the negligent act occurred in the course of the partnership business." *Id.* at 663. But this case is inapplicable because the Georgia court applied common law partnership and agency principles and, like appellant, makes no mention of the UPA, which is the law in Minnesota.

Appellant also claims that because Nicole Moren's action of bringing Remington into the kitchen was partly motivated by personal reasons, her conduct was outside the ordinary course of business. Because it has not been previously addressed, there is no Minnesota authority regarding this issue. But there are two cases from outside of Minnesota that address the issue in a persuasive fashion. *Grotelueschen v. Am. Family Ins. Co.,* 171 Wis.2d 437, 492 N.W.2d 131, 137 (1992) (An "act can further part personal and part business purposes and still occur in the ordinary course of the partnership."); *Wolfe v. Harms,* 413 S.W.2d 204, 215 (Mo. 1967) ("[E]ven if the predominant motive of the partner was to benefit himself or third persons, such does not prevent the concurrent business purpose from being within the scope of the partnership."). Adopting this rationale, we conclude that the conduct of Nicole Moren was no less in the ordinary course of business because it also served personal purposes. It is undisputed that Moren was acting for the benefit of the partnership by making pizzas when her son was injured, and even though she was simultaneously acting in her role as a mother, her conduct remained in the ordinary course of the partnership business.

***

DECISION

Because Minnesota law requires a partnership to indemnify its partners for the result of their negligence, the district court properly granted summary judgment to respondent Nicole Moren. In addition, we conclude that the conduct of a partner may be partly motivated by personal reasons and still occur in the ordinary course of business of the partnership.

Affirmed.

---

§ 3.07   FINANCIAL ISSUES IN A PARTNERSHIP

Objectives: You should be able to explain how the profits and losses of a partnership are allocated among the partners, and how a partner's "partnership account" will change over time, depending on various events.

Subsidiary Objectives: You should also be able to:

● *Partner Salaries. Explain to a client who wants to start a business as a partnership whether partners are entitled to receive a salary for the work that they perform for the partnership.*

● *Allocation of Partnership Profits and Losses. Describe to your client how partnership profits, as well as losses, are allocated among the partners.*

● *Can You Change the Default Rules? Explain to your client whether it is permissible under RUPA § 103(b) to change the default rules governing how profits and losses are allocated among the partners.*

● *Does Allocation of Profits Result in Cash in Hand? Explain the difference between a partner receiving an allocation of profits and a partner receiving a distribution.*

● *Partnership Accounts. List the events that will cause a partner's partnership account to increase. List the events that will cause a partner's partnership account to decrease. Given a fact pattern, determine the current value of a partner's partnership account.*

Obviously, partners hope that their partnership will make money, that is, be profitable. This section concerns the many ways in which a partner may "make money" from the fact that she is a partner in a (profitable) partnership.

Most working people earn a living by being paid for their work, whether on an hourly basis or through a flat salary (where the employee receives the same pay regardless of the number of hours worked). But partners are not employees; instead, they are the owners of the business. Further, RUPA § 401(h) provides that a partner is "not entitled to remuneration [i.e., compensation] for services performed for the partnership," except in connection with winding up the partnership (a topic that we will defer until Chapter 4).

So, if partners cannot expect to be paid for their work through a salary, what is to motivate them to actually do any work? In a word, profits. If none of the partners invest any time or effort in the partnership's business, then the partnership is almost certain to fail. On the other hand, while hard work is no guarantee of actual success, the harder the partners work the more likely it is that the partnership will be profitable, all other things being equal.

Unless the partners agree otherwise, profits are divided equally; otherwise, endless disputes would erupt over which partner was working harder than the others. RUPA § 401(b) reflects this, providing that "[e]ach partner is entitled to an equal share of the partnership profits and is chargeable with a share of the partnership losses in proportion to the partner's share of the profits." Note here that both "profits" and "losses" are determined *annually*, in connection with the preparation of the partnership's income statement for the year.

RUPA § 401(a) also creates something called a partnership account. In other words, every partner is deemed to have an "account" during the time that she is a partner. Note that this account is not a separate fund that the partnership must keep segregated from its other assets or that is not available to the partnership's creditors. It is simply a bookkeeping entry, a number on a piece of paper or computer screen. However, this account will become tremendously important in Chapter 4, when you learn about what must be done when a partner leaves the partnership but the partnership continues in existence, as well as what must be done if a partnership dissolves. Thus, we will revisit the partnership account in Chapter 4.

For the time being, however, you should understand that the partnership account is not a fixed number; it is always changing. RUPA § 401(a)(1) specifies two events that will "credit" (that is, increase) one's partnership account balance and RUPA § 401(a)(2) specifies two events that will "charge" (that is, decrease) one's partnership account balance.

Examine RUPA §§ 401(a), (b) and (h) (and don't forget RUPA § 103) and apply them to the following problems:

Problems

Problem 3-33: Tina, Amy, and Abby formed a partnership that sells t-shirts over the Internet. The partners did not have a partnership agreement. Tina contributed $1,000 to get the business "up and running," Amy contributed $4,000, and Abby contributed $2,000. Tina worked at the partnership (often for sixty hours per week) but the other two partners did not. In its first year, the partnership earned a profit of $3,000. *How will this profit be allocated among the partners?*

Problem 3-34: *Would your answer to Problem 3-33 change if the partners had a partnership agreement that provided that Tina would be allocated 50% of the profits and that Amy and Abby would each be allocated 25% of the profits?*

Problem 3-35:   Assume that Tina, Amy, and Abby had a partnership agreement that provided that Tina would be allocated 50% of the profits and that Amy and Abby would each be allocated 25% of the profits, but did not address how losses would be allocated. In its first year, the partnership experienced a $3,000 loss. *How will this loss be allocated among the partners?*

Problem 3-36: Assume that Tina, Amy, and Abby did not have a partnership agreement that addressed the allocation of profits or losses. In its first year, the partnership earned a $300,000 profit. (Its t-shirts were apparently very popular.) Tina votes that the partnership should distribute at least half of this money to the partners, but Amy and Abby vote that the partnership should keep the money. *What will happen to this $300,000? Who owns this money?*

Problem 3-37: Assume in Problem 3-36 that the partnership does not distribute any of the $300,000 to the partners. *How much will each of the partners need to report as income on their income tax returns for this year?*

Problem 3-38: Tina, who is tired of working sixty hours a week while her partners do not work at all, asks you whether she could earn a salary from the partnership (in addition to her right to share in its profits). *Is there any way that Tina may earn a salary from the partnership? If so, how?*

Problem 3-39: In Year 1, Brad and Jennifer decided to go into business as partners to manufacture hair dye. Because they were good friends, they did not consult an attorney to prepare a written partnership agreement. However, Brad and Jennifer did orally agree that (1) Brad and Jennifer would each contribute $10,000 to the partnership to get it "up and running" and (2) Brad would be allocated 60% of the profits and Jennifer would be allocated 40% of the profits.

After the two partners made their initial contributions to the partnership, the partnership began operating. Year 1 was a very bad year for the partnership; it incurred a $10,000 loss that year. However, Year 2 was much better; the partnership made a profit of $20,000 in Year 2. The partners then caused the partnership to distribute $6,000 to Brad and $6,000 to Jennifer. *What are the current balances in the respective partnership accounts of Brad and Jennifer?*

As you should now understand, the way that partners make money is by (1) having a partnership that generates profits, (2) being allocated a share of those profits, and then (3) causing the partnership to distribute some or all of those profits to the partner. As you might imagine, in a large partnership (for example, a big law firm), the provisions concerning partner compensation are usually among the most detailed parts of the partnership agreement. But, as with anything, RUPA supplies the rules if the partners do not have different rules in their partnership agreement.

What if a partner has money troubles and needs cash quickly? May he sell his partnership interest to someone else, assuming that he can find someone who wants to buy it and that the parties can negotiate a mutually acceptable price? If you were a *shareholder* in a corporation, you could sell your stock—and *all* of the rights associated with it—to someone else unless you had contractually agreed not to do so. (More on that in Chapters 5 and 9.) Partnership interests are a bit different. Study RUPA §§ 502 and 503 and consider the following problem:

Problem

Problem 3-40:   Hans, Johann, and Greg decided to form a partnership to manufacture and sell pretzels, called Pretzels To Go. The partners did not prepare a written partnership agreement, nor did they orally agree on anything other than that they would be "equal partners." Three years later, Johan's daughter got engaged to marry Stephan and decided that she was going to have the biggest, most expensive wedding ever. Worried about how to pay for the wedding, Johann entered into an agreement with Madeline, whereby Madeline paid Johann $50,000 and Johann transferred his entire interest in the Pretzels To Go partnership to Madeline. The next day, Madeline showed up at the partnership's offices and told Hans and Greg that she was their "new partner." *Has Johann violated his duty of loyalty to the partnership? What rights does Madeline have? What rights, if any, has Johann retained? Was the consent of Hans and Greg necessary for this transfer?*

Finally, although it is difficult to justify putting this issue in a section discussing how partners "make money," one should consider the concept of the charging order under RUPA § 504, which is very similar to the garnishment of an employee's wages by a judgment creditor. Study RUPA § 504 and apply it to the following problem:

Problem

Problem 3-41: One Saturday, Hans from Problem 3-40 was out driving on a personal errand (nothing pretzel-related) when he struck and injured Eva. Eva sued Hans and obtained a judgment for $500,000. Unfortunately, Hans does not have $500,000. His only significant asset is his interest in the partnership with Johann and Greg. *Explain to Eva whether she may reach the partnership's assets to satisfy this $500,000 judgment. If not, what can she do to satisfy her judgment? What should she do if the partnership stops paying distributions to the partners?*

The foregoing are some of the major issues that are likely to arise during the "birth" and the "life" of a partnership. Chapter 4 concerns what could be called the "death" of a partnership, that is, what happens if a partner leaves the partnership and what happens if the partnership dissolves. In the meantime, however, try your hand at the multiple choice questions that begin on the following page.

PRACTICE QUESTIONS

Multiple Choice Question 3-1: DFP Dentists is a general partnership with three partners: Dr. Drill, Dr. Fill, and Dr. Pain. Dr. Drill and Dr. Pain have been partners in the partnership since 2000. Dr. Fill joined the partnership in 2010. One day, Pam the Patient filed a lawsuit against DFP Dentists and the three dentists individually. Pam claims that Dr. Pain negligently performed a root canal on her in 2008 and that, as a result, Pam now cannot chew food. The following motions were later filed in court:

Motion #1: DFP Dentists filed a motion to dismiss Pam's lawsuit on the basis that DFP Dentists is not responsible for torts that are committed by its partners.

Motion #2: Dr. Drill filed a motion to dismiss the lawsuit against him individually because he was not responsible for Pam's injury and therefore will never have any liability to Pam.

Motion #3: Dr. Fill filed a motion to dismiss the lawsuit against him individually because he is not personally liable for an event that took place before he joined the partnership.

What is the likely disposition of these motions?

A.   All three motions will be denied.
B.   All three motions will be granted.
C.   Motion #1 will be granted; the other two motions will be denied.
D.   Motion #2 will be granted; the other two motions will be denied.
E.   Motion #3 will be granted; the other two motions will be denied.

Multiple Choice Question 3-2: Cheryl and Lance formed a partnership to run a clothing store. Some time later, Lance sold his partnership interest to Alex. *Which of the following is correct?*

A.   Lance may not sell any part of his partnership interest unless Cheryl consents.
B.   Lance is still a partner, but Alex now has the right to share in the profits and losses of the partnership and to receive distributions that Lance otherwise would have received.
C.   Alex is now a partner, but he cannot vote on any partnership matters.
D.   Lance's attempted sale of his partnership interest is an act of dissociation or withdrawal; thus, Lance is no longer a partner.

Multiple Choice Question 3-3:   Jason and Denard are partners and have a partnership agreement that states: "No partner shall be personally liable for the debts or obligations of the partnership." The partnership borrowed money from National Bank. Jason signed the loan agreement on behalf of the partnership. The partnership later defaulted on its obligation to repay the loan. *Upon obtaining judgment(s) against the partnership, Jason, and Denard, which of the following best describes how the bank may proceed?*

A.   The bank may only collect from the partnership because the partnership agreement provides that Jason and Denard are not personally liable.

B.   The bank has the choice of collecting either from Jason, because he signed for the loan, or from the partnership.

C.   The bank has the choice of collecting from Jason and/or Denard provided that the partnership's assets are not sufficient to repay the loan.

D.   The bank has the choice of collecting from any of Jason, Denard, or the partnership.

E.   The bank may only collect from Jason, because the loan was not approved by Denard and therefore was not binding on Denard or the partnership.

Multiple Choice Question 3-4:   Tara, Pepe, and Avey are partners, but do not have a partnership agreement. For the most recent year, the partnership had a profit of $18,000. Tara and Pepe want the partnership to distribute $5,000 to each of the three partners and retain $3,000 in the partnership for future growth. Avey wants the partnership to distribute $6,000 to each of the partners. *What will be the result?*

A.   No distributions will be made.

B. $5,000 will be distributed to each of the partners.

C. $6,000 will be distributed to each of the partners.

D. $5,000 will be distributed to each of Tara and Pepe, and $6,000 will be distributed to Avey.

Multiple Choice Question 3-5: Yogi and Zelda are partners. Their partnership is currently insolvent, as is Yogi individually. However, Zelda has enough assets to pay all of Yogi's personal debts as well as the partnership's debts. *Which of the following statements is correct?*

A.   Zelda is jointly liable with Yogi for Yogi's personal debts.
B.   Zelda is jointly liable with Yogi to partnership creditors to the extent that their claims exceed the remaining partnership assets.
C.   Partnership creditors cannot recover against Zelda's personal assets beyond the amount that she contributed to the partnership.
D.   None of the above is correct.

Multiple Choice Question 3-6: Stan, Kishna, Eric and James orally decided to form a partnership called "SKEJ" to produce videogames. Because Eric was wealthy, he contributed $990,000 of "seed money" to SKEJ. Stan, Kishna and James did not have much cash, but they were all computer experts and agreed to work full time at SKEJ designing videogames. Eric was hesitant about being the only owner to contribute cash to the business, so he persuaded Stan, Kishna and James each to contribute $3,333.33 (for a total of almost $10,000) in "seed money" to SKEJ (which they did). In its second year of operations, SKEJ made a profit of $100,000. Eric, eager to get some of his seed money contribution back, wanted SKEJ to distribute that money to the four owners. Stan, Kishna and James opposed the distribution because they believed that SKEJ should re-invest its profits in additional computer equipment to produce a new videogame that they wanted to design, called "Football on Crutches." Outraged, Eric yelled "I put in almost all the money! I can do what I want and force the business to distribute the money to me." *Is Eric correct?*

A.   Yes, because the voting power of the four owners is determined by the amount of money that they contributed to SKEJ; thus, Eric can outvote the others 99 to 1.
B.   Yes, because the profits of the business are shared by the four owners based on the amount of money that they contributed to SKEJ; thus, Eric will receive 99% of the profits and the others will receive 1%.
C.   Both A and B are correct.
D.   No, Eric is not correct.

Multiple Choice Question 3-7: In January 2010, Stu, George, and Pete went into business as partners to run a nightclub, but did not have a partnership agreement. When the partnership was formed, Stu contributed $5,000, George contributed $5,000, and Pete contributed $10,000. The partnership incurred a $15,000 loss during 2010. It made a profit of $90,000 in 2011, and a profit of $120,000 in 2012. In 2010 and 2011, no partner took a distribution from the partnership. In 2012, Stu took a $50,000 distribution, George took a $40,000 distribution, and Pete took a $50,000 distribution. *As of the end of 2012, what are the balances in the partners' respective partnership accounts?*

A.   Stu's account is $65,000; George's account is $65,000; and Pete's account is $65,000.

B.   Stu's account is $20,000; George's account is $30,000; and Pete's account is $25,000.

C.   Stu's account is $25,000; George's account is $35,000; and Pete's account is $30,000.

D.   Stu's account is $20,000; George's account is $30,000; and Pete's account is $20,000.

Multiple Choice Question 3-8: In January 2010, Keith and Sally went into business as partners to run a grocery store. Keith and Sally did not have a written partnership agreement, but they did orally agree that Keith would be allocated 2/3 (66.7%) of the profits and that Sally would be allocated 1/3 (33.3%) of the profits. When the partnership was formed, Keith contributed $20,000 and Sally contributed $10,000. The partnership incurred a $15,000 loss during 2010. It made a profit of $90,000 in 2011, and a profit of $120,000 in 2012. In 2010 and 2011, no partner took a distribution from the partnership. In 2012, Keith took a $50,000 distribution and Sally took a $30,000 distribution. *As of the end of 2012, what are the balances in the partners' respective partnership accounts?*

A.   Keith's account is $150,000; and Sally's account is $75,000.

B.   Keith's account is $97,500; and Sally's account is $97,500.

C.   Keith's account is $67,500; and Sally's account is $77,500.

D.   Keith's account is $100,000; and Sally's account is $45,000.

Multiple Choice Question 3-9: Mr. Brown, Mr. Blue, and Mr. Pink formed a partnership to manufacture coffee mugs. Mr. Brown, who was a multi-millionaire and contributed most of the "start up money" to the business, insisted that the three partners enter into a written partnership agreement that included the following provisions (among others):

I.   On all matters in the ordinary course of business which require a vote of the partners, Mr. Brown shall have 10 votes and Mr. Blue and Mr. Pink shall have 1 vote each.

II.   The admission of a new partner to the partnership shall require the unanimous consent of all of the partners.

III.   No partner shall be liable to any third party for any obligation of the partnership arising in the ordinary course of business unless and until that partner has at least $1 million of personal assets.

IV.   No partner may withdraw (dissociate) from the partnership without the consent of all of the partners.

V.   The partnership shall continue until the partners vote to dissolve it.

Which of the above provisions of the partnership agreement (if any) are not permissible under RUPA?

A.   I, III, IV and V only.
B.   I, II, III and IV only.
C.   II and IV only.
D.   III and IV only.
E.   III only.

Multiple Choice Question 3-10: Under RUPA, the primary test to determine whether a partnership exists is:

A.   whether the partnership's profits are allocated equally among the partners.
B.   whether the partners have equal rights to manage the partnership.
C.   whether the partners are sharing profits.
D.   whether the partners own the partnership's assets.
E.   whether the partnership is profitable.

Multiple Choice Question 3-11: Betty, Tammy, and Sue orally decided to form a partnership to operate a hair salon. Betty specialized in a haircut called the "Mohawk," Tammy specialized in a haircut called the "Mullet," and Sue specialized in a haircut called the "Comb Over." Things went well for several years until Sue became ill from inhaling harmful fumes from hair dye. Unable to pay enormous medical bills, Sue sold her interest in the partnership to Bill, who also specialized in "Comb Over" haircuts. Bill arrived at the hair salon the following day, informed Betty and Tammy that he was their new partner because he bought Sue's interest in the partnership, and started cutting a client's hair. Betty and Tammy then called you for advice, because they immediately disliked Bill and did not want to be partners with him. *Which of the following would be correct advice you could give Betty and Tammy?*

A.   As a transferee of Sue's partnership interest, Bill has no right to participate in the partnership business without the consent of Betty and Tammy.

B.   Bill cannot be admitted as a new partner in the partnership without the consent of Betty and Tammy.

C.   Bill is entitled to Sue's share of the profits of the business, even if Betty and Tammy do not consent.

D.   All of the above are correct.

QUESTIONS 3-12 TO 3-15 ARE BASED ON THE FOLLOWING FACTS

Multiple Choice Question 3-12: The Downtown Rockers is a rock band that has been formed as a partnership. The members are Mick (vocals), Rocco (Guitar), Little Joe (bass), Big Steve (keyboards), Brutus (drums), and Jeremy (manager). There is no partnership agreement, except that the partners have agreed that Jeremy will be allocated 10% of the profits and the other five partners will each be allocated 18% of the profits. The partnership owns a van and various amplifiers, equipment, and musical instruments. *Which of the following statements is correct?*

A.   When the partners must vote on something, Jeremy will have 10 votes and each of the other partners will have 18 votes.

B.   If Jeremy signs a contract to have the partnership play at Madison Square Garden, the partnership can refuse to perform if the contract wasn't approved by the other partners.

C.   Rocco has the right to use the partnership's van to help his mother move into a new house.

D.   Little Joe must obtain approval from the partnership to sell the bass guitar that he plays.

Multiple Choice Question 3-13: Same facts as Question 3-12. *Which of the following statements is true about Little Joe's rights with respect to the partnership?*

A.   Little Joe's approval would not be needed to admit a new partner to the partnership, assuming that a majority of the current partners vote to admit the new partner.

B.   Little Joe's creditors cannot seize partnership property to satisfy Little Joe's personal debts.

C.   Each of the partners will be allocated an equal share of partnership losses.

D.   Little Joe will be liable for partnership debts only to the extent that he has made contributions to the partnership.

Multiple Choice Question 3-14: Same facts as Question 3-12. One day, Brutus was driving the partnership's van after having imbibed too many alcoholic beverages and ingested certain other substances. The police and the court system found that Brutus's driving was reckless. *Which of the following statements is true?*

A.   Brutus has breached his fiduciary duty of loyalty to the partnership.

B.   Brutus has breached his fiduciary duty of care to the partnership.

C.   Both A and B are correct.

D.   Brutus did not breach his fiduciary duties to the partnership unless he is found to have engaged in a knowing violation of law.

Multiple Choice Question 3-15: Same facts as Question 3-12. Rocco wants to start a "side project," that is, a new rock band with some of his other friends, while remaining a member of the Downtown Rockers. The other partners are opposed to this idea because they are worried that Rocco's new band would result in the Downtown Rockers getting fewer "gigs." *Which of the following statements is true?*

A.   Rocco is free to start a new band while remaining a member of the Downtown Rockers because partners are not required to devote their full-time efforts to the partnership.

B.   Rocco is free to start a new band while remaining a member of the Downtown Rockers as long as he is still available to play at any gigs that the Downtown Rockers have.

C.   If Rocco writes a new song, he must give the Downtown Rockers a right of first refusal to use it.

D.   If Rocco quits the Downtown Rockers, then he may join the other band.

Multiple Choice Question 3-16: Kate has for many years been a "silent partner" in a partnership, which does not have a partnership agreement under RUPA. Recently, however, Kate has decided she wants to take a more active role in the partnership's affairs. *Which of the following is correct?*

A.   Kate's vote will be proportional to her capital contribution to the partnership.

B.   Kate has an equal voice in the partnership management regardless of her capital contribution.

C.   Even ordinary partnership decisions require unanimous agreement by the partners.

D.   All of the above are correct.

Multiple Choice Question 3-17: Clark and Helen opened a restaurant as partners and together managed the day-by-day operations of their restaurant. One day, Clark, while driving to work, was severely injured in an accident and was unable to work for six months. Meanwhile, to save money, Helen performed Clark's normal duties at the restaurant. Since they had been friends for years and trusted each other, Clark and Helen did not have a partnership agreement under RUPA. *Can Helen receive a salary for performing Clarks job?*

A.   She may receive a salary based on a fair market value of Clark's services.

B.   She may not receive a salary for filling in for Clark.

C.   She may receive a salary if she can prove she is devoting substantial time to the business and that Clark's inactivity was unexpected.

D.   She may not receive a salary unless her capital contribution exceeds one-half the total of all contributions to the partnership.

Multiple Choice Question 3-18: Allen, Beth, and Carol are partners in a hardware store. The three partners have previously discussed selling the business, but have not made a final decision. One day, Carol received an offer for all of the partnership's inventory from Dave. Carol thought that the offer was excellent, but could not contact her partners to inform them. Fearing Dave would revoke the offer, Carol signed the contract conveying the partnership's inventory to Dave. Upon hearing of the deal later, Beth and Allen are angry and do not wish to sell the inventory to Dave. *Under RUPA, the partnership:*

A.   is not bound by Carol's actions.

B.   is bound by Carol's actions.

C.   is bound if an appraiser determines that the price is reasonable.

D.   is bound unless Dave knew Carol had not contracted Allen and Beth before signing the contract.

CHAPTER 4
PARTNER DISSOCIATION
AND PARTNERSHIP DISSOLUTION

Chapter 3 covered many of the issues that may arise while a person is a partner in a partnership. In this chapter, you will learn what causes a person to cease being a partner, that is, events that cause a partner's *dissociation* from the partnership. Many of these events of dissociation probably will not be surprising, such as where a partner dies (or a non-individual partner dissolves) or simply decides to "quit." But some of the other events of dissociation may surprise you, and the sections of RUPA that concern these issues demand careful reading.

If a partner has dissociated, all you know is that that partner is no longer a partner. However, you do not know whether the partnership will continue to exist without that partner or whether the partnership will end. Thus, this chapter will also discuss the many events that cause a partnership to go into *dissolution.* As with dissociation, some of the things that cause a partnership to dissolve will not surprise you but others may. Further, when a partnership dissolves, you will need to figure out how to wind up its business, pay creditors, and then, if there are partnership funds or other assets remaining, determine how to distribute them to the partners. Once that process is complete, the story of the partnership is more or less over.

Before continuing, it is worth remembering that RUPA is largely a series of "default" rules that apply only in the absence of different provisions in the partnership agreement. The same is almost entirely true of the information that you will see in this chapter; that is, nearly all of RUPA's provisions on dissociation and dissolution may be modified in the partnership agreement. The only two exceptions to this are found in RUPA §§ 103(b)(6) and (7) (which you should go look at now).

§ 4.01   DISSOCIATION OF A PARTNER

Objectives: You should be able to list the events that cause a partner to be dissociated from a partnership. Given a fact pattern, you should be able to determine whether a partner has dissociated from the partnership and, if so, the consequences of the dissociation.

Subsidiary Objectives: You should be able to determine whether a partnership is an "at will" partnership, or a partnership for a term or undertaking. Given a fact pattern involving a partner dissociating from a partnership, you should be able to determine whether the dissociation was "wrongful" and, if so, list and describe the consequences of the wrongful dissociation. Further, you should be able to list and describe the consequences of all dissociations (whether rightful or wrongful).

Dissociation refers to an event that causes a particular partner to cease being a partner. Section 601 of RUPA contains a complete list of these events of dissociation. Obviously, if an event occurs and that event is on the "list" in Section 601, then you know that a partner has dissociated; conversely, if an event

---

TERMINOLOGY

There is just no getting around the fact that dissociation and dissolution *sound* very similar and therefore may be easy to confuse with one another. But they refer to very different concepts. When a partner *dissociates* the only thing that has happened is that *that* partner is no longer a partner. On the other hand, if a partnership *dissolves*, the *whole partnership* will begin coming to an end.

---

happens and it's not on the list, then you know that a partner has not dissociated from the partnership. Although you should go read RUPA § 601 carefully right now, a few words about it are in order here.

Section 601(1) is probably the most commonsensical subsection in Section 601, basically providing that a partner may "quit" being a partner by express will, either immediately or as of a date in the future. Note that this subsection applies even if the partnership agreement is silent on this issue. In fact, RUPA § 103(b)(6) states that a partnership may not deny a partner the power (as opposed to the right) to dissociate from a partnership by express will; the most that the partnership agreement could do to restrict this right is to require that any notice be in writing. Subsections (2) and (3), however, are different in that they are operative only to the extent that the partnership agreement "uses" these sections. Subsection (2) provides that the partnership agreement could specify a list of events that would cause a partner to be dissociated. Subsection (3) provides that the partnership agreement could set forth a method of expelling a partner; typically, this would be done by requiring the other partners to vote on whether to expel a partner, but note that the statute does not require that there be any reason for expelling the partner pursuant to this subsection (although the partnership agreement could require a reason).

Speaking of voting to expel a partner, RUPA § 601(4) allows a partner to be expelled by the unanimous vote of the *other* partners in four specified situations (subsections (4)(i) through (iv)), even if the partnership agreement does not specifically provide for this situation. Somewhat similarly, subsection (5) allows either the partnership itself or one of the partners to seek a court order expelling a partner from the partnership if the partner has committed one or more of the "bad acts" specified in subsections (5)(i) through (iii). If the partner to be expelled disputes the facts, then a trial would likely be required to determine whether grounds for the dissociation exist.

Subsection (6) provides that a partner will be dissociated from any partnership in which he or she (or it) is a partner if certain debt-related events occur. Subsection (7) provides that an individual partner will be dissociated if she dies or certain events occur which indicate that she has lost mental capacity. Finally, subsections (8) through (10), concern partners that are not individuals; these subsections essentially provide that such partners will be dissociated when they themselves dissolve or otherwise cease to exist.

Again, you should read RUPA § 601 carefully. It would also be advisable to read RUPA § 102. After doing so, work on the following problems:

Problems

Problem 4-1: The XYZ Partnership has three partners: Xavier, Yolanda, and Zeke. For the past several months, Zeke has been unhappy with the behavior of his partners and has been considering quitting and moving to Hawaii. One day, while sitting at home alone watching television, Zeke shouted: "That's it, I quit the XYZ Partnership." *Has Zeke dissociated from the XYZ Partnership?*

Problem 4-2: Same facts as in Problem 4-1, except that on his way into the office, Zeke was hit by an automobile and died. *Has Zeke dissociated from the XYZ Partnership?*

Problem 4-3: Same facts as in Problem 4-2, except that Zeke did not die. Instead, he is currently in a coma on life support machines. All of the doctors who have examined Zeke have determined that it is extremely unlikely that he will ever regain consciousness. *Is Zeke still a partner in the XYZ Partnership?*

Problem 4-4: A group of twenty doctors has approached you about drafting a partnership agreement for a partnership that they wish to form. *What sorts of provisions would you suggest including in the partnership pursuant to RUPA § 601(2)?*

Problem 4-5:   A group of twenty doctors has approached you about drafting a partnership agreement for a partnership that they wish to form.   *What sorts of provisions would you suggest including in the partnership pursuant to RUPA § 601(3)?*

Problem 4-6: RUPA § 601(6) provides, among other things, that a partner will be dissociated from a partnership if the partner files for bankruptcy. *Why would RUPA have such a provision? Is this just adding insult to injury?*

Another issue that must be considered if a partner has dissociated from a partnership is whether the dissociation was **wrongful.** As noted above, a partner always has the *power* to dissociate from a partnership by express will. This does not necessarily mean that a partner always has the *right* to do so. If a partner dissociates but did not have the right to do so, then the law may attach some consequences to that wrongful dissociation. Subsections (b) and (c) of RUPA § 602 concern wrongful dissociations and their consequences. Read those sections, along with RUPA §§ 101(8) and 603, and consider the following problems:

Problems

Problem 4-7:   The TUV Partnership has three partners: Tom, Ulrich, and Vivian. When they formed the partnership three years ago, they agreed that the purpose of the partnership would be to operate a coffee shop.   However, recently Ulrich and Vivian proposed that the partnership should open a seafood restaurant. Tom, who doesn't like this idea, told Ulrich that he was quitting the partnership. *Has Tom dissociated from the TUV Partnership? If so, was his dissociation wrongful? If Tom has dissociated, does he have any further right to participate in the management of the partnership?*

Problem 4-8: Same facts as Problem 4-7, except that Tom, Ulrich, and Vivian had agreed that the partnership would continue for seven years. *Has Tom dissociated from the TUV Partnership? If so, was his dissociation wrongful?*

Problem 4-9: Same facts as Problem 4-7, except that Tom, Ulrich, and Vivian had agreed that the partnership would continue until it had served one million cups of coffee (which it has yet to do). *Has Tom dissociated from the TUV Partnership? If so, was his dissociation wrongful? If so, what are the consequences of a wrongful dissociation?*

Problem 4-10: Same facts as Problem 4-7, except that you may assume that the TUV Partnership (now renamed the UV Partnership) continues in existence. *May Tom open his own coffee shop next door to the coffee shop operated by the UV Partnership?*

Problem 4-11: As in Problems 4-4 and 4-5, a group of twenty doctors has approached you about drafting a partnership agreement for a partnership that they wish to form. *Will this likely be an at-will partnership or a partnership for a term or undertaking?*

Again, dissociation concerns whether a partner continues to be a partner. An event of dissociation may or may not cause the partnership to dissolve. (In addition, as you will see in the next section, other events may cause a partnership to dissolve.) Section 603(a) recognizes that there are only two paths that a partnership could follow after a partner dissociates from it: either the partnership will continue on, with one fewer partner (in which case Article 7 of RUPA will apply), or the partnership will dissolve (in which case Article 8 of RUPA will apply). We now turn our attention to the events that will cause a partnership to dissolve.

§ 4.02 WHAT CAUSES A PARTNERSHIP TO DISSOLVE?

Objectives: You should be able to list the events that will cause a partnership to be dissolved. Given a fact pattern, you should be able to determine whether an event has caused the partnership to dissolve.

§ 801

RUPA § 801 is very complex and demands careful reading. But before you go read it, note a few things. First, subsection (1) only applies if the partnership is an at-will partnership, and subsection (2) only applies if the partnership is for a term or undertaking. Obviously, these are mutually exclusive categories; thus, subsection (1) and (2) will not both apply to a particular partnership. Subsections (3) through (6), however, apply to all partnerships.

At-will vs For a term

Second, subsection (1) has a clause in the middle that begins with the words "other than ...." This clause demands that you cross-reference back to RUPA § 601, because it essentially means that some types of dissociation under RUPA § 601 will result in the dissolution of the partnership and others won't. Figuring out which are which will require you to go back and read RUPA § 601.

Finally, subsection (2), which only concerns partnerships for a term or undertaking, has three subsections. Unfortunately, these subsections don't appear in a "logical" order. For example, probably most obvious event that will cause a partnership for a term or an undertaking to dissolve is the completion of the term or undertaking. Nonetheless, this event appears in RUPA § 801(2)(iii) rather than section 801(2)(i).

Now, go read RUPA § 801 and then come back and work on these problems:

Problems

Problem 4-12: The QRS Partnership has three partners: Quentin, Renee, and Sully. The partnership was formed four years ago, at which time the partners agreed that the partnership would continue in existence for ten years. Earlier today, Renee walked into Quentin's office and told him that she was quitting the partnership, effective two weeks from today. *Will the QRS Partnership dissolve in two weeks?*

Problem 4-13: Same facts as Problem 4-12, except that the partners never agreed that the partnership would last for a particular period of time. *Will the QRS Partnership dissolve in two weeks? If so, is there any way to stop this from happening?*

Problem 4-14: Same facts as Problem 4-12, except that the partners never agreed that the partnership would last for a particular period of time and Renee dies instead of telling Quentin that she is quitting. *Will the QRS Partnership dissolve?*

Problem 4-15: Seven years ago, Partners A, B, C, D, and E formed the (unimaginatively named) ABCDE Partnership, which they agreed would have a ten-year term. Yesterday, Partner A told the other partners that she was quitting the partnership. Today, Partners B, C, D, and E had a meeting to discuss what to do. At the meeting, Partner B said: "Things just aren't the same around here without Partner A. I quit." Partner B then left the room. Partners C, D, and E then voted on whether to dissolve the partnership. Partner C voted yes (i.e., to dissolve the partnership) and Partners D and E voted no. *Will the ABCDE Partnership dissolve?*

Problem 4-16: *In Problem 4-15, did Partner A wrongfully dissociate from the partnership? Did Partner B?*

Similarly to RUPA § 601 (which gives us a complete list of things that cause a partner to dissociate), RUPA § 801 gives us a complete list of things that cause a partnership to dissolve. If something happens that's on the "list," then the partnership will dissolve. If something happens but that event is not on the list, then the partnership will not dissolve. Section 4.04 below concerns what will happen when the partnership dissolves. Before then, however, let's consider what happens when a partner dissociates from a partnership, but the partnership does *not* dissolve.

§ 4.03   "MERE DISSOCIATION" UNDER ARTICLE 7

Objectives: Given a fact pattern in which a partner dissociates from a partnership but the partnership does not dissolve, you should be able to determine (1) how to calculate the amount that the dissociated partner will be paid for her interest in the partnership; (2) when the dissociated partner will be paid for her interest; (3) whether the dissociated partner will continue to be personally liable for partnership obligations incurred before her dissociation and partnership obligations incurred after her dissociation; and (4) whether the dissociated partner retains the ability to bind the partnership to a third party after her dissociation.

As noted above, RUPA § 603(a) provides that if a partner dissociates from the partnership *without* causing the partnership to dissolve, then Article 7 of RUPA (that is, Sections 701 through 705) will apply.

Probably the most obvious thing that will happen when a partner dissociates but the partnership continues on without her is that you will need to figure out how much to pay the dissociated partner for her interest. RUPA § 701(a) requires this payment, and other subsections of section 701 give us the "mechanics" as to when and how payment will be made. But *how much* will the dissociated partner be paid for her interest? Obviously, a statute could not give us a dollar amount with which to answer that question. Instead, RUPA § 701(b) gives us a formula:

> The buyout price of a dissociated partner's interest is the amount that would have been distributable to the dissociating partner under Section 807(b) if, on the date of dissociation, the assets of the partnership were sold at a price equal to the greater of the liquidation value or the value based on a sale of the entire business

as a going concern without the dissociated partner and the partnership were wound up as of that date. ***

So, what does this mean? Basically, it requires us to conduct a "hypothetical" sale and dissolution of the partnership, and figure out the amounts that *each* of the partners would receive if the partnership were sold and dissolved. (Of course, the partnership is not actually dissolving in this scenario; you are merely conducting this exercise to figure out how much to pay the dissociated partner.) There are a few complications, however. First, as a starting point for our calculations, you must use the higher of (1) the "liquidation" value of the partnership's assets and (2) the "going concern" value of the partnership. Liquidation value basically means the amount that would be received if the partnership's assets were sold off piece by piece. Sometimes this is colloquially referred to as "fire sale" value.[*] On the other hand, "going concern" value refers to the amount that would be received if the *entire partnership* were sold to a *single buyer* who intended to continue running the business. In a given situation, these two values could differ greatly.

Second, the bigger problem we have in applying RUPA § 701(b) at this point is that we don't yet know how to apply RUPA § 807(b), which is discussed below in Section 4.05. For this reason, we will defer further discussion of RUPA § 701(b) until then.

Several other consequences follow from a partner dissociating without causing the partnership to dissolve. These are set forth in the remaining subsections of Section 701, as well as Sections 702, 703, and 704. (Section 705 is relatively straight-forward and will not be discussed below.) Carefully read those sections and then test your knowledge on the following problems:

Problems

Problem 4-17: The LMNOP Partnership, which runs a bakery, has five partners: Lydia, Mike, Nelly, Opie, and Peng. Although the partnership is an at-will partnership, there is a clause in the partnership agreement which provides that the dissociation of any partner will not cause the partnership to dissolve. Last week, Peng informed Nelly that she quit the partnership, effective immediately. Today, Nelly ordered $500 worth of supplies from Dough Brothers, Inc., a long-time supplier of LMNOP. *If the partnership does not pay for these supplies, may Dough Brothers seek recovery from Peng? If so, how do you reconcile this result with RUPA § 701(d)?*

---

[*]   However, comment 3 to RUPA § 701 notes that "[l]iquidation value is not intended to mean distress sale value."

Problem 4-18: Same facts as Problem 4-17, except that Peng (not Nelly) ordered the supplies from Dough Brothers, Inc. (Perhaps Peng was in a vindictive mood that day.) *Is the partnership obligated to pay for the supplies? If so, may it seek recovery from Peng?*

Problem 4-19: Same facts as Problem 4-17. Three weeks after Peng quit the partnership, the partnership (now renamed the LMNO Partnership) placed its first order with Bread Sisters, Inc., a new supplier, for $500 worth of supplies. *If the partnership does not pay for these supplies, may Bread Sisters seek recovery from Peng?*

Problem 4-20: Same facts as Problem 4-17. Seven weeks after Peng quit the partnership, a customer became ill after eating a toxic doughnut that the partnership had produced. *May the customer name Peng as a defendant in the resulting products liability lawsuit?*

Problem 4-21: Two years before Peng quit the partnership, the partnership signed a five-year lease with Landlord, Inc. *If the partnership stops paying its monthly rent, may Landlord Inc. name Peng as a defendant in the resulting lawsuit? What if Landlord Inc. knows that Peng has quit the partnership but it and the partnership agree to a substantial increase in the rental amount?*

Problem 4-22: *What advice would you give Peng to minimize her "lingering" liability under RUPA § 703 after she leaves the partnership? What if the partnership had several dozen suppliers? What advice would you give the LMNO Partnership to minimize Peng's "lingering" authority to bind the partnership under RUPA § 702?*

Problem 4-23: Same facts as Problem 4-17, except that the partnership had a ten-year term and was formed four years ago. *When will Peng be paid the value of her partnership interest under RUPA § 701? What if you "run the numbers" and determine that Peng is entitled to receive only $27 for her interest in the partnership?*

§ 4.04   THE DISSOLUTION PROCESS UNDER ARTICLE 8

Objectives: Given a fact pattern, you should be able to determine whether an event has caused a partnership to dissolve and, if so, determine how the partnership's assets will be distributed to creditors and partners.

> *Subsidiary Objectives: You should also be able to:*
>
> • *explain what a partnership must do when it dissolves;*
>
> • *explain the order of priority of claims against the partnership's assets when it dissolves;*
>
> • *describe the various ways in which a partnership may "liquidate" its assets and how to choose from among these alternatives;*
>
> • *given a fact pattern, determine if a partner's act during the winding up process will bind the partnership; and*
> • *given a fact pattern where a dissolved partnership has wound up its business, liquidated its assets, paid its creditors, and has some cash "left over," calculate how the remaining cash will be distributed to the partners.*

RUPA § 801, discussed above, concerned whether a dissolution has occurred. If one of the events listed in Section 801 has occurred, you may be tempted to think: well, that's it, the partnership is over. It was fun while it lasted.

Not so fast. First, even though RUPA may say that a given event resulted in a partnership's dissolution, don't forget that nearly everything in RUPA is a "default" rule that can be modified by agreement of the partners. For example, assume that one of three partners dissociated from an at-will partnership by express will (which, according to RUPA, would trigger a dissolution of such a partnership), but the remaining two partners want to continue the business. Further, the dissociated partner does not want to insist on a liquidation of the partnership. In such a case, the parties may agree that the partnership will continue in existence but "buy out" the dissociated partner's interest.

Second, if dissolution does in fact occur, it is merely the beginning of the end, not the end itself. There is a lot more work to do. RUPA § 802(a) states that a partnership remains in existence following dissolution, but only for the purpose of "winding up." Once winding up is over, that is when the partnership is "terminated."

The winding up process could take a day or two in the case of a small, simple partnership or literally years in the case of a large, complex partnership. But we can list with some confidence the tasks that must be completed during the winding up process. Section 803(c) has a good summary, stating in part that the persons winding up a partnership may continue the partnership "as a going concern for a reasonable time"; pursue, defend, settle, mediate or arbitrate civil and criminal lawsuits; "settle and close the partnership's business"; sell or transfer partnership assets; pay or discharge partnership liabilities; distribute the partnership's assets to the partners under RUPA § 807; and "perform other necessary acts."

> **THE "SWITCHING PROVISION"**
> RUPA Section 603(a) states that if a partner dissociates without causing the partnership to dissolve, Article 7 of RUPA applies. If dissolution occurs, then Article 8 of RUPA applies. In this section, we are discussing Article 8, which consists of Sections 801 through 807.

Put more simply, the usual process is to complete work that remains uncompleted, liquidate the partnership's assets, use the funds from that liquidation to pay partnership creditors, and then, if funds remain, figure out how to distribute those funds to the partners. Before you delve further into the complexities of this process, consider the following problems:

Problems

Problem 4-24: Partners A, B, and C have decided to dissolve and wind up the ABC Partnership. The partnership's only asset is a bank account with $60,000 in it, but it owes its creditors $100,000. *Will A, B, and C remain jointly and severally liable for the unpaid $40,000 of creditors' claims following dissolution of the partnership?*

Problem 4-25: Same facts as Problem 4-24. One of the debts that the partnership owes is $10,000 for a loan that Partner C had made to the partnership. *If the partnership's assets are not sufficient to pay all of its liabilities, should the debt owed to Partner C be given lower priority than debts owed to persons who are not partners?*

Let's assume a financially happier situation than in the prior two problems: following the liquidation process, the partnership was able to pay all of its creditors in full, and even has some money left over. For example, assume that the ABC Partnership (which of course consists of Partners A, B, and C) has fully paid all of its creditors and has $30,000 left over. Further, assume that the partnership agreement for the ABC Partnership did *not* change the default rule from RUPA § 401(b) that partners share profits equally. At this point, you will likely be very tempted to conclude that you have a very simple situation on your hands: each partner gets $10,000, and the winding process is now complete.

Doing things this way could result in injustice to the partner who contributed more capital to the partnership (and/or took fewer distributions) than did the other partners. Similarly, it could result in a windfall to the partner who contributed less capital to the partnership (and/or took greater distributions). For this reason, RUPA § 807(b) provides that, upon dissolution of a partnership, each partner is entitled to a "settlement" of her partnership account. RUPA § 807(a) states that partners are entitled to this amount "in cash."

Hopefully, someone has been keeping track of the partners' respective partnership accounts. If not, you may need to examine the partnership's history to determine what the partners' accounts currently are, by reference to RUPA § 401(a). This issue was introduced in Chapter 3, but it becomes very important here. RUPA § 401(a)(1) specifies two events that will "credit" (that is, increase) one's partnership account balance and RUPA § 401(a)(2) specifies events that will "charge" (that is, decrease) one's partnership account balance. The two events that will increase a partner's partnership account are (1) any contributions made by the partner and (2) any share of profits allocated to that partner. The two events that cause a partnership account to decrease are the opposite: (1) any distributions taken by the partner and (2) any share of losses allocated to that partner

To make sure that you can correctly calculate these amounts, let's revisit Problem 3-39 from Chapter 3. In that problem, Brad and Jennifer decided to go into business as partners, agreeing that they each would contribute $10,000 to the partnership and that Brad would be allocated 60% of the profits and Jennifer would be allocated 40% of the profits.

Immediately following these contributions, Brad's partnership account is $10,000, as is Jennifer's. In 2011, the partnership incurred a $10,000 loss.[*] Because Brad and Jennifer agreed to share profits on a 60/40 basis, they also impliedly agreed to share losses on a 60/40 basis. (*See* RUPA § 401(b).) Thus, $6,000 of this loss will be charged to Brad's partnership account, and $4,000 will be charged to Jennifer's. Their current balances are thus $4,000 for Brad's

---

[*] Note that profits and losses are determined *annually*, not on an "as they occur" basis.

account ($10,000 minus $6,000) and $6,000 for Jennifer's account ($10,000 minus $4,000).

In 2012, the partnership made a profit of $20,000. Of this profit, sixty percent ($12,000) will be allocated to Brad, raising his partnership account balance to $16,000, and forty percent ($8,000) will be allocated to Jennifer, raising her partnership account balance to $14,000. Finally, the partners then caused the partnership to distribute $6,000 to Brad and $6,000 to Jennifer. These distributions will reduce their account balances, with an end result of a $10,000 balance for Brad, and an $8,000 balance for Jennifer.

Why is this important? Again, RUPA § 807(b) provides that each partner is entitled to a "settlement" of her partnership account balance when the partnership dissolves. In other words, the partnership (after fully paying creditors, of course) must pay each partner an amount equal to her partnership account balance. If there is *still* more money left over, this excess will be considered a profit that will be divided equally among the partners (unless the partnership agreement contains a different profit-sharing formula). If there is not enough to "zero out" each partner's partnership account balance, then that shortfall will be considered a loss that will be divided equally among the partners (unless otherwise agreed).

Simple enough, right? (Maybe not.) Now apply these rules to the following problems. To make them somewhat easier, the first two problems specify the partners' respective account balances. The third and fourth require you to "recreate" the balances using RUPA § 401(a).

Problems

Problem 4-26: Partners Alpha, Beta, and Omega have decided to dissolve and wind up the ABO Partnership. After fully paying all creditors, the partnership has $21,000 of cash left over. As of the date of dissolution, Partner Alpha's partnership account balance was $8,000; Partner Beta's balance was $3,000; and Partner Omega's balance was $1,000. *How will this $21,000 be distributed to the partners?*

Problem 4-27: Same facts as Problem 4-26, except that the partnership only had $6,000 after fully paying its creditors. *How will this $6,000 be distributed to the partners?*

Problem 4-28: Harry, Igor, and Janice formed a partnership, but decided that they did not need to have a partnership agreement. Upon formation, Harry contributed $10,000; Igor contributed $5,000; and Janice contributed $20,000. In the first year of the partnership's existence, it earned a $63,000 profit. In the second year, the partnership earned a $33,000 profit. At that point, Harry took a $10,000 distribution and Igor took a $5,000 distribution, but Janice decided not to take a distribution. In the third year, the partnership incurred a $9,000 loss. The partners have dissolved the partnership, liquidated its assets, and fully paid its creditors. There is now $110,000 remaining. *How will this $110,000 be distributed to the partners?*

Problem 4-29: Same facts as Problem 4-28, except that the partnership only has $101,000 remaining. *How will this $101,000 be distributed to the partners?*

As noted above, RUPA § 803(c) contains a good summary of what happens during the winding up process. You should note a few additional things. First, the people who are entitled to participate in the winding up process are all of the partners, except for any partner that wrongfully dissociated. *See* RUPA § 803(a). Second, two major tasks during winding up are paying debts or completing obligations owed *to* third parties, and receiving payments or other performance due *from* third parties. In theory, this sounds easy, but in practice it may be very complex. For example, an amount that is owed to the partnership by a third party may not be due for several years; simply dissolving the partnership will not accelerate the time that payment is due. In such a situation, the partnership may end up selling to someone else its right to receive payment, unless it wants the winding up process to take a very long time. As for amounts or other performances owed to third parties, obviously the partnership could simply pay the amounts or perform the obligations. Alternatively, it could delegate its obligations to someone else (which may require the consent of the person to whom performance is owed, as you learned in your Contracts course in law school).

During the winding up process, another issue that may arise is whether the partnership's assets must be sold for cash or whether they could instead be distributed "in kind" to the partners. If they must be sold, must a public auction be held or may the assets be sold in some other way? If a public auction is held, may one of the partners bid on the assets at the auction? Of course, if the parties agree as to what should be done, then these legal issues are more or less moot. However, if the partners cannot agree, then a court may be called on to resolve the matter.

The following case, *Horne v. Aune*, involved a situation where the former partners clearly despised one another and could not reach an amicable resolution. The facts can be quickly summarized. In 2002, Steven Aune and Cecilia Horne purchased a $303,500 house as tenants in common after they decided to "pursue a family life together." Each party paid an equal amount of the down payment, and they obtained a joint mortgage for the balance. However, "Horne and Aune experienced relationship troubles almost immediately." In November 2002, they signed an agreement which provided in part that Horne and Aune "are equal partners in said property sharing equally in ownership, care, upkeep and title and mortgage obligations including property taxes and property insurance costs." In addition, the agreement contained this clause:

> [Section 6.] If either party is lawfully, but unwillingly removed from the property by law enforcement or by invoking a restraining order or any other method, the party remaining in residence will be solely financially responsible for upholding all expense obligations pertaining to the mortgage, taxes, insurance and care and upkeep of the property until the removed party returns and peaceable co-habitation resumes. Upon return, both parties will resume the equally shared obligations ....

In December 2002, there was an altercation, which resulted in Aune being arrested and receiving a deferred sentence. One condition of his sentence was that he have no contact with Horne. Horne stayed in the house, paying all expenses. Aune refused to pay his half of the expenses because of section 6 of the partnership agreement.

In September 2003, Horne sued Aune, seeking (among other things) a dissolution and winding up the partnership. She also asked that the house be sold, but that "she be permitted to purchase Aune's interest in the property at a reasonable sum to be determined by the court." During mediation, the parties "agreed that it would be better for one or the other to buy the house rather than publicly sell it in order to avoid the transaction costs of a public sale. But they were unable to agree on who would buy out whom, or at what price." An appraisal valued the house at $335,000; both parties agreed this was accurate.

Because the balance of the mortgage on the house was $235,000, the trial court found that the partnership had $100,000 in equity. The court "ordered that the partnership was dissolved and should be wound up and that the property should be sold, with each party receiving 50 percent of the net proceeds. The court further ordered that, in lieu of a public sale, the partnership could be wound up by either party buying out the other's interest for $50,000 within 45 days." But if the parties were "deadlocked," then the house would be sold through a real estate agent.

Not surprisingly, more disagreement ensued. Each party tendered $50,000 to the other. Following another hearing, the trial court "determined that the property would not be sold to wind up the partnership. Instead, the court ordered Horne to buy Aune's partnership interest for $50,000. The court ordered Aune to quitclaim his interest to Horne in exchange for the cash payment and a release from his mortgage obligation." Aune then appealed.

Portions of the opinion in the case appear below.

Horne v. Aune
Court of Appeals of Washington
121 P.3d 1227 (2005)

Houghton, Judge. In this appeal, we are asked to decide whether in winding up a partnership, the Revised Uniform Partnership Act (RUPA), chapter 25.05 RCW [Revised Code of Washington], requires a public sale of partnership property; or whether the court may instead allow a partner to purchase the property for its agreed value with cash payment to the other partner of his partnership interest?

Steven Aune appeals a court order requiring him to sell his one-half partnership interest in real property to Cecilia Horne. He demands a public sale of the property, with cash distribution of the proceeds.

Because RUPA's winding-up provision [RUPA Section 807], does not mandate a public sale of partnership property as the only means of liquidating partnership assets, we affirm. And given the facts of this case, we hold the trial court did not abuse its discretion by allowing Horne to purchase the property instead of listing her home with a real estate agent.

***

Aune first contends that the court impermissibly ordered a distribution in kind by requiring him to quitclaim his interest in the property to Horne in exchange for a cash payment. He asserts that, in the absence of agreement, a court must order a public sale of partnership property to wind up a partnership.

The question raised is whether RUPA requires a public sale of partnership property to wind up a partnership. ***

Under UPA, the departure of any partner resulted in dissolution and winding up, absent agreement to the contrary. It had been unclear under the common law whether, on winding up, partners were entitled to cash distribution of their partnership interest, as opposed to physical partition of the surplus property.

[Citation omitted.]   UPA resolved the ambiguity by providing that each partner was entitled to cash distribution.

In 1998, Washington adopted RUPA.   RUPA limits the circumstances under which a partnership must dissolve and be wound up following the departure of a partner. When a partner dissociates from a partnership, remaining partners generally may elect to either buy out the exiting partner's interest and continue the partnership business, or else dissolve and wind up the partnership.   [RUPA Section 603.*] But when partners choose the path of dissolution and winding up, the procedures are substantially the same under RUPA as they were under UPA.

[RUPA Section 807] governs winding up of partnership business.   It provides in part:

> (1)   In winding up a partnership's business, *the assets of the partnership*, including the contributions of the partners required by this section, *must be applied to discharge its obligations to creditors,* including, to the extent permitted by law, partners who are creditors. *Any surplus must be applied to pay in cash the net amount distributable to partners* in accordance with their right to distributions under subsection (2) of this section.

> (2)   *Each partner is entitled to a settlement of all partnership accounts* on winding up the partnership business. *In settling accounts* among the partners, profits and losses that result from the *liquidation of the partnership assets* must be credited and charged to the partners' accounts.   The partnership shall make a distribution to a partner in an amount equal to any excess of the credits over the charges in the partner's account.

(emphasis added.)

No Washington court has construed this statute.   But in *Guntle [v. Barnett,* 871 P.2d 627 (Wash. Ct. App. 1994)], we considered UPA's analogous winding-up statute, former [Revised Code of Washington Section] 25.04.320 (1997) (Each partner is entitled to have "the partnership property applied to discharge its liabilities, and the surplus applied to pay in cash the net amount owing to the respective partners."). [In *Guntle,* the court held that the trial court improperly ordered an in-kind distribution of the partnership's assets without the consent of all of the partners.]

***

---

*   [Footnote by author]: The court cited RUPA Section 603; however, Section 603 does not directly support this statement.

*** *Guntle* does not hold that the phrase have "the partnership property applied to discharge its liabilities" means that the court must order a public sale of partnership property. It merely holds that, in winding up a partnership, the court cannot distribute partnership assets and debts in kind, as it would in a marital dissolution, but must have "the partnership property applied to discharge its liabilities, and the surplus applied to pay in cash the net amount owing to the respective partners." [Citation omitted.]

Guntle did not resolve the central issue here: whether the winding-up statute necessarily requires a forced sale of partnership assets, as opposed to permitting a partner to purchase the property, with cash payment to the other partner of his interest. This issue is one of first impression. Other jurisdictions are split.

Aune urges us to follow Montana's Supreme Court where it held that RUPA's winding-up provision requires liquidation of partnership assets through a forced sale. *McCormick v. Brevig*, [96 P.3d 697 (Mont. 2004)]. *McCormick* involved a family farm, held in partnership by a brother and sister. The sister sued for an accounting, dissolution, and winding up. The trial court ordered the partnership dissolved and wound up. But the trial court ordered that the brother could purchase his sister's share, according to its appraised value, instead of liquidating the partnership assets by selling the ranch and distributing the proceeds. In so ruling, the trial court relied on a dictionary definition of "liquidation" to conclude that it can mean something other than a forced sale of partnership property, i.e., a judicially ordered buy out of a partner's interest. [Citation omitted.]

In reversing, the Montana Supreme Court rejected the trial court's resort to the dictionary, reasoning that the plain meaning of "liquidation of the partnership assets" is to reduce the partnership assets to cash, pay creditors, and distribute the cash surplus to partners. [Citation omitted.] The court suggests that, because RUPA provides one track for buy out and another for dissolution and winding up, the legislature did not intend to permit a buy out where partners opt for dissolution.

Horne urges us to follow Alaska, Maryland, Oregon, and other states that have permitted a broader interpretation of the winding-up provision.

These jurisdictions hold that, while winding up generally has been equated with the forced sale of partnership assets, the statute does not strictly require such a result. Historically, the purpose of forced sale was to accurately determine the value of partnership assets. In reality, forced sale often results in economic waste. Thus, courts have accepted alternatives to forced sale as a means of winding up partnership business. Some courts have permitted distribution in kind. [Citations omitted.] Others have permitted a buy out. [Citation omitted.]

In *Disotell [v. Stiltner*, 100 P.3d 890 (Alaska 2004)], the Alaska Supreme Court affirmed a trial court's order permitting a partner to buy out another's partnership interest in lieu of compelled liquidation. *Disotell* involved a partnership between a contractor and a real estate agent, Stiltner, to develop a hotel on property Stiltner owned. Disagreements arose and Stiltner sued for dissolution and winding up. Instead of ordering a forced sale of the property, the trial court gave Stiltner the option of purchasing Disotell's partnership interest as a means of winding up the partnership.

The Alaska Supreme Court affirmed, holding that the statute does not absolutely compel liquidation and forbid a buy out. "Under appropriate, although perhaps limited, circumstances, a buyout [sic] seems a justifiable way of winding up a partnership." [Citation omitted.] A buy-out option reduced economic waste by avoiding the transaction costs of a forced sale; it also guaranteed Disotell a fair value for his partnership interest. Moreover, the property was also Stiltner's residence: the court deemed it inequitable to force him out.

In *Creel v. Lilly*, [729 A.2d 385 (Md. 1999)], the Maryland Supreme Court held that neither UPA nor RUPA absolutely requires, on winding up, a forced sale of partnership assets. *Creel* involved a partnership that dissolved because of a partner's death [under UPA]. The deceased's estate demanded forced sale of the partnership, invoking UPA's winding-up provision. After finding that there was no dispute concerning the value of the partnership assets, the trial court permitted the surviving partners to continue the business on cash payment of the deceased partner's interest.

The Maryland Supreme Court affirmed, siding with the line of cases holding that winding up does not equal forced sale. The court construed UPA's winding-up provision, while expressly noting that the result would be same under RUPA. The court noted that RUPA's reforms primarily target the economic waste of compelled liquidation. In the court's view, where partnership assets can accurately be valued by means other than forced sale, judicial alternatives to forced sale, including buy out, may be an acceptable means of winding up the partnership.

We decline Aune's invitation to follow the Montana Supreme Court's reasoning in *McCormick*. Instead, we adopt Maryland's approach in *Creel*. Contrary to *McCormick*, the winding-up statute does not plainly mean forced sale. Thus, in our view, the trial court's resort to the dictionary in *McCormick* was appropriate. According to Black's Law Dictionary, "liquidate" means:

1. To settle (an obligation) by payment or other adjustment; to extinguish (a debt). 2. To ascertain the precise amount of (debt, damages, etc) by litigation or agreement. 3. To determine the liabilities and distribute the assets of (an entity), esp. in bankruptcy or dissolution. 4. To convert (a non-liquid asset) into cash. 5. To wind up the affairs of (a corporation, business, etc.).

[Citation omitted.]

As used in [RUPA Section 807], the phrase "liquidation of the partnership assets," guarantees partners the right to receive, in cash, the fair value of their property interest upon winding up and dissolution of the partnership. But that result may be achieved by means other than forced sale. Historically, liquidation equaled forced sale because that was deemed the most accurate method of valuing partnership assets. But where, as here, the parties stipulate to the partnership assets' value, there is no reason to equate liquidation with forced sale.

A key factual distinction between *Guntle* and this case is that Aune is not being forced to accept property in lieu of cash; he is receiving the full cash value of his partnership interest. Absent a valid dispute concerning the value of the partnership property, he has no legal right, under the winding-up statute, to force the public sale of partnership assets. [Affirmed.] ***

There are a few other issues to cover before we finish our discussion of dissolution. First, note that RUPA § 802(b) allows the partnership to "undo" its dissolution before its winding up is complete, assuming that certain conditions are met.

Second, RUPA § 804 provides that, after dissolution, a partnership will be bound by a partner's act, if the act is either (1) "appropriate for winding up the partnership's business" or (2) the type of act that, before dissolution, would have bound the partnership to a third party under RUPA § 301 (discussed in Chapter 3), assuming the third party "did not have notice of the dissolution." (See also RUPA § 806, which would make a partner liable to the partnership for acts that bind the partnership but were not appropriate for winding up the partnership.) However, note that RUPA § 805 allows a partner (other than a wrongfully dissociating one) to file a "statement of dissolution" which could act to curtail partners' authority. This is because the entire world is deemed to have constructive notice of the contents of the statement of dissolution ninety days after it is filed. (In addition, such a statement can immediately curtail the power to transfer real authority if the statement is filed in the applicable "office for recording transfers of real property," i.e., the register of deeds.) Thus, once ninety days have passed, the only acts of a partner that could bind the dissolving partnership would be those that are "appropriate for winding up the partnership's business."

Third, some courts have recognized that the dissolution process may result in unfairness to "services" partners, as opposed to "capital" partners. To illustrate this, consider the following situation. Partners A and B form a partnership. Partner A contributes $100,000. Partner B does not contribute anything, but agrees to work for the partnership (without drawing a salary) for a year. The fair value of Partner B's services for a year is $100,000. The partnership is dissolved after a year, without having any profits or losses, but the value of its assets remaining after fully paying creditors is $50,000. Applying RUPA's dissolution provisions, this will mean that the partnership has a $50,000 loss. Each partner must bear half of this loss, but Partner B must "kick in" another $25,000 because her partnership account was zero before the loss, whereas Partner A's partnership account was $100,000 before the loss. Thus, Partner A will receive $75,000, and. Partner B will receive nothing upon dissolution of the partnership. In the grand scheme of things, Partner A lost $25,000 of her initial $100,000 investment. However, Partner B lost $125,000 if you take the value of her services into account. Unfortunately, as you saw in Chapter 3, RUPA § 401(h) provides that Partner B was not entitled to remuneration for her services (unless the partnership agreement provided otherwise).

To remedy this situation, some older decisions have held that the value of a partner's services should increase her capital account if she has not been compensated for them. See, e.g., *Schymanski v. Conventz*, 674 P.2d 281 (Alaska 1983); *Parker v. Northern Mixing Co.*, 756 P.2d 881 (Alaska 1988); *Kovackik v. Reed*, 315 P.2d 314 (Cal. 1957). However, comment 3 to RUPA § 401 takes the opposite position:

> It may seem unfair that the contributor of services, who contributes little or no capital, should be obligated to contribute toward the capital loss of the large contributor who contributed no services. In entering a partnership with such a capital structure, the partners should foresee that application of the default rule may bring about unusual results and take advantage of their power to vary by agreement the allocation of capital losses.

Finally, you should not forget to figure out what to do if a partner dissociates but the partnership does *not* dissolve. As noted in Section 4.03 above, in this situation you must conduct a "hypothetical" sale and dissolution of the partnership, using the higher of (1) the "liquidation" value of the partnership's assets and (2) the "going concern" value of the partnership as the hypothetical sales price. Back in Section 4.03, you did not know how to do this; now you do.

§ 4.05   FIDUCIARY DUTY ISSUES IN DISSOLUTION (OR, "FREEZE OUTS")

If you are a clever and devious person, the following thought may have occurred to you: Suppose that I am a partner in a partnership that has struggled for many years, but that now looks like a promising business. If it is an at-will partnership, I may easily dissolve it; all I need to do is dissociate by express will under RUPA § 601(1). This dissociation will not be wrongful under RUPA § 602(b)(1) unless the partnership agreement were to make it wrongful (which is unlikely). Therefore, I will not be liable for any damages as a result of my dissociation. Furthermore, upon my dissociation, I am free to compete with my partners pursuant to RUPA § 603(b)(2), meaning that I can now pursue the same business that the partnership was conducting. Finally, my express-will dissociation under RUPA § 601(1) will cause the partnership to dissolve under RUPA § 801(1). This means that, after the partnership pays off its creditors, I will get some portion of the remaining amounts, which I may use in furtherance of my new business.

Before you decide to do this, it may be wise to consider the following case. After reading it, consider whether RUPA § 602(b) would lead to a different result.

Page v. Page
Supreme Court of California
359 P.2d 41 (1961)

Traynor, Justice. Plaintiff and defendant are partners in a linen supply business in Santa Maria, California. Plaintiff appeals from a judgment declaring the partnership to be for a term rather than at will.

The partners entered into an oral partnership agreement in 1949. Within the first two years each partner contributed approximately $43,000 for the purchase of land, machinery, and linen needed to begin the business. From 1949 to 1957 the enterprise was unprofitable, losing approximately $62,000. The partnership's major creditor is a corporation, wholly owned by plaintiff, that supplies the linen and machinery necessary for the day-to-day operation of the business. This corporation holds a $47,000 demand note of the partnership. The partnership operations began to improve in 1958. The partnership earned $3,824.41 in that year and $2,282.30 in the first three months of 1959. Despite this improvement plaintiff wishes to terminate the partnership.

The Uniform Partnership Act provides that a partnership may be dissolved "By the express will of any partner when no definite term or particular undertaking is specified." [California Corporations Code § 15031(1)(b)]. The trial court found that the partnership is for a term, namely, "such reasonable time as is necessary to enable said partnership to repay from partnership profits, indebtedness incurred for the purchase of land, buildings, laundry and delivery equipment and linen for the operation of such business." Plaintiff correctly contends that this finding is without support in the evidence.

Defendant testified that the terms of the partnership were to be similar to former partnerships of plaintiff and defendant, and that the understanding of these partnerships was that "we went into partnership to start the business and let the business operation pay for itself, put in so much money, and let the business pay itself out." There was also testimony that one of the former partnership agreements provided in writing that the profits were to be retained until all obligations were paid.

Upon cross-examination defendant admitted that the former partnership in which the earnings were to be retained until the obligations were repaid was substantially different from the present partnership. The former partnership *** provided for a definite term of five years and a partnership at will thereafter. Defendant insists, however, that the method of operation of the former partnership showed an understanding that all obligations were to be repaid from profits. He nevertheless concedes that there was no understanding as to the term of the present partnership in the event of losses. He was asked: "(W)as there any discussion with reference to the continuation of the business in the event of losses?" He replied, "Not that I can remember." He was then asked, "Did you have any understanding with Mr. Page, your brother, the plaintiff in this action, as to how the obligations were to be paid if there were losses?" He replied, "Not that I can remember. I can't remember discussing that at all. We never figured on losing, I guess."

Viewing this evidence most favorably for defendant, it proves only that the partners expected to meet current expenses from current income and to recoup their investment if the business were successful.

Defendant contends that such an expectation is sufficient to create a partnership for a term under the rule of [*Owen v. Cohen*, 119 P.2d 713 (Cal. 1941)]. In that case we held that when a partner advances a sum of money to a partnership with the understanding that the amount contributed was to be a loan to the partnership and was to be repaid as soon as feasible from the prospective profits of the business, the partnership is for the term reasonably required to repay the loan. It is true that *Owen v. Cohen, supra*, and other cases hold that partners may impliedly agree to continue in business until a certain sum of money is earned [citation omitted], or one or more partners recoup their investments [citation omitted], or until certain debts are paid [citing *Owen v. Cohen*], or until certain property could be disposed of on favorable terms [citation omitted]. In each of these cases, however, the implied agreement found support in the evidence.

In *Owen v. Cohen, supra,* the partners borrowed substantial amounts of money to launch the enterprise and there was an understanding that the loans would be repaid from partnership profits. *** In each of these cases the court properly held that the partners impliedly promised to continue the partnership for a term reasonably required to allow the partnership to earn sufficient money to accomplish the understood objective. ***

In the instant case, however, defendant failed to prove any facts from which an agreement to continue the partnership for a term may be implied. The understanding to which defendant testified was no more than a common hope that the partnership earnings would pay for all the necessary expenses. Such a hope does not establish even by implication a "definite term or particular undertaking" as required by [California Corporations Code, § 15031(1)(b)]. All partnerships are ordinarily entered into with the hope that they will be profitable, but that alone does not make them all partnerships for a term and obligate the partners to continue in the partnerships until all of the losses over a period of many years have been recovered.

Defendant contends that plaintiff is acting in bad faith and is attempting to use his superior financial position to appropriate the now profitable business of the partnership. Defendant has invested $43,000 in the firm, and owing to the long period of losses his interest in the partnership assets is very small. The fact that plaintiff's wholly-owned corporation holds a $47,000 demand note of the partnership may make it difficult to sell the business as a going concern. Defendant fears that upon dissolution he will receive very little and that plaintiff, who is the managing partner and knows how to conduct the operations of the partnership, will receive a business that has become very profitable because of the establishment of Vandenberg Air Force Base in its vicinity. Defendant charges that plaintiff has been content to share the losses but now that the business has become profitable he wishes to keep all the gains.

There is no showing in the record of bad faith or that the improved profit situation is more than temporary. In any event these contentions are irrelevant to the issue whether the partnership is for a term or at will. Since, however, this action is for a declaratory judgment and will be the basis for future action by the parties, it is appropriate to point out that defendant is amply protected by the fiduciary duties of co-partners.

Even though the Uniform Partnership Act provides that a partnership at will may be dissolved by the express will of any partner [California Corporations

Code, § 15031(1)(b)], this power, like any other power held by a fiduciary, must be exercised in good faith.

We have often stated that "partners are trustees for each other, and in all proceedings connected with the conduct of the partnership every partner is bound to act in the highest good faith to his copartner, and may not obtain any advantage over him in the partnership affairs by the slightest misrepresentation, concealment, threat, or adverse pressure of any kind." [Citations omitted.] ***

A partner at will is not bound to remain in a partnership, regardless of whether the business is profitable or unprofitable. A partner may not, however, by use of adverse pressure "freeze out" a co-partner and appropriate the business to his own use. A partner may not dissolve a partnership to gain the benefits of the business for himself, unless he fully compensates his co-partner for his share of the prospective business opportunity. In this regard his fiduciary duties are at least as great as those of a shareholder of a corporation.

***

*** [I]n the instant case, plaintiff has the power to dissolve the partnership by express notice to defendant. If, however, it is proved that plaintiff acted in bad faith and violated his fiduciary duties by attempting to appropriate to his own use the new prosperity of the partnership without adequate compensation to his co-partner, the dissolution would be wrongful and the plaintiff would be liable as provided by [California Corporations Code, § 15038(a)(2)] (rights of partners upon wrongful dissolution) for violation of the implied agreement not to exclude defendant wrongfully from the partnership business opportunity.

The judgment is reversed.

Page v. Page foreshadows much of the material that you will see in Chapter 9, which concerns closely held businesses. Suffice it to say for now that the many ways in which small business owners may seek to take advantage of their fellow owners is limited only by their imagination. Fortunately, the law provides ways to fight back.

§ 4.06   A BRIEF NOTE ON DISSOLUTION UNDER UPA

Both Chapter 3 and this chapter have discussed RUPA almost exclusively; UPA was mentioned only tangentially a few times. For the most part, this should not concern you, even if you intend to practice in a state that has not yet adopted RUPA because RUPA is largely consistent with UPA. However, UPA's dissolution provisions differ *dramatically* from RUPA's.

As you know from the above discussion of RUPA, there are many situations in which a partner may dissociate from a partnership without resulting in a dissolution of the partnership. UPA, however, treats the partnership as much more "fragile." In other words, nearly every time a partner ceases being a partner (UPA does not use the word "dissociation") a dissolution of the partnership will result under UPA. In part, this is because UPA subscribes to the "aggregate theory," which treats the partnership as a collection of individuals, whereas RUPA treats the partnership as an entity that is separate from the partners (*see* RUPA § 201). In this sense, UPA essentially provides that any time a partner leaves the partnership for any reason, it is no longer the same partnership and therefore will be dissolved. Of course, UPA's dissolution provisions are much more complicated than this, but we will not discuss them further here. However, if you take the bar examination in a state that follows UPA, be prepared to learn a few new things.

Now that you are an expert on partnership law, you should try the following multiple choice questions, applying RUPA.

PRACTICE QUESTIONS

Multiple Choice Question 4-1: Robert, Sam, and Joni formed a partnership to build and manage a health club, but did not have a partnership agreement. After construction started but before the health club was finished, Robert told Joni he quit the partnership. *Which of the following is correct?*

A.   Robert may not dissociate until the health club is completed; thus, he is still a partner.

B.   Robert's dissociation is wrongful because this is a partnership for a term or undertaking, but the partnership will continue in existence.

C.   Robert's dissociation is wrongful because this is a partnership for a term or undertaking, but the partnership will dissolve.

D.   Robert's dissociation will cause the partnership to dissolve.

Multiple Choice Question 4-2:   After many years as a partner, Partner A has decided to retire and leave the ABC partnership (which until now had consisted of Partners A, B, and C). Assume that this dissociation did not cause the dissolution of the partnership. *As a former partner, Partner A:*

A.   Remains liable for the partnership's debts that were incurred before her dissociation, unless her former partners agree to release her.

B.   Remains liable for the partnership debts that were incurred before her dissociation, unless the creditors agree to release her.

C.   Remains liable for the partnership debts that were incurred before her dissociation, unless both her former partners and the creditors agree to release him.

D.   None of the above.

Multiple Choice Question 4-3:   In 2010, Rich, Devin, Peter, and Roxanne formed a partnership to run a nightclub. The partners agreed that the partnership would have a six-year term, but did not otherwise have a partnership agreement. In 2011, Devin filed bankruptcy. Also in 2011, the partners obtained a court order expelling Peter from the partnership because he was sexually harassing nightclub employees, many of whom had either quit working for the nightclub or threatened to sue. *Which of the following is correct?*

A.   Devin has not dissociated; Peter's dissociation is wrongful.

B.   Both Devin's dissociation and Peter's dissociation are wrongful.

C.   Neither Devin's dissociation nor Peter's dissociation is wrongful.

D.   Devin's dissociation is wrongful, but Peter's dissociation is not wrongful.

E.   Peter's dissociation is wrongful, but Devin's dissociation is not wrongful.

Multiple Choice Question 4-4:   Same facts as the previous question, except that the partnership was an at-will partnership. *Which of the following is correct?*

A.   Devin has not dissociated; Peter's dissociation is wrongful.

B.   Both Devin's dissociation and Peter's dissociation are wrongful.

C.   Neither Devin's dissociation nor Peter's dissociation is wrongful.

D.   Devin's dissociation is wrongful, but Peter's dissociation is not wrongful.

E.   Peter's dissociation is wrongful, but Devin's dissociation is not wrongful.

QUESTIONS 4-5 TO 4-6 ARE BASED ON THE FOLLOWING FACTS

In 2009, Larry, Mary, Nancy, Otis, and Paul formed a partnership to operate a hotel. Because the partners were good friends, they did not hire an attorney to draft a partnership agreement. However, Paul, who had attended law school for a year, thought it would be a good idea to write down two issues that the partners had discussed. To that end, Paul wrote the following on a piece of paper, which was an accurate reflection of what all the partners had orally agreed.

> *El-Em-En-Oh-P Partnership Agreement: The partners agree that the partnership shall operate a hotel for 10 years. The partnership may not hire an employee or make an expenditure of more than $1,000 without the consent of all the partners.*

Only Paul signed this piece of paper.

The partnership incurred a loss of $100,000 in 2009. It had a profit of $150,000 in 2010, and a profit of $200,000 in 2011. No partner made any contributions to, or received any distributions from, the partnership, except that Paul had made a $100,000 contribution in 2009.

In early January 2012, four of the partners wished to hire an employee, Bob, to be the hotel's manager. However, at a meeting to consider hiring Bob, Nancy strongly objected and told the other partners that if they hired Bob, she would quit the partnership. The next day, the other partners hired Bob to be the manager of the hotel. Later that day, Nancy told Otis: "I quit."

Multiple Choice Question 4-5: *Which of the following statements is correct? You may assume that the decision whether to hire an employee is a matter in the "ordinary course of business."*

A.   The partners validly hired Bob by a majority vote.
B.   By informing Otis that she was quitting the partnership, Nancy dissociated from the partnership, but her dissociation will not cause a dissolution of the partnership.
C.   By informing Otis that she was quitting the partnership, Nancy dissociated from the partnership, and her dissociation will cause a dissolution of the partnership unless at least two of the remaining partners decide to continue the business within 90 days.
D.   By informing Otis that she was quitting the partnership, Nancy dissociated from the partnership, and her dissociation will cause a dissolution of the partnership unless at least three of the remaining partners decide to continue the business within 90 days.

Multiple Choice Question 4-6: Same facts as the previous question. Regardless of how you answered the previous question, assume for purposes of this question that the partnership dissolved when Nancy dissociated from it. Assume further that during the winding up process, the partnership discovered that it had $500,000 in assets, but owed $100,000 to Big Bank. Assume for purposes of this question that Nancy's dissociation was not wrongful under RUPA.

A.   Each partner gets $80,000.
B.   Paul gets $100,000 and the other four partners each get $75,000.
C.   Paul gets $160,000 and the other four partners each get $60,000.
D.   Paul gets $130,000 and the other four partners each get $67,500.

QUESTIONS 4-7 TO 4-9 ARE BASED ON THE FOLLOWING FACTS

In January 2009, Don, Paul, and John went into business as partners to run an automobile repair business. The three partners did not have a partnership agreement, nor did they agree that the partnership would exist only for a specific period of time. In January 2009, the partnership obtained a $100,000 loan from Last National Bank (the "Bank") which it used to buy equipment. Don, Paul, and John each signed documents personally guaranteeing the repayment of this loan. The loan agreement required the partnership to make monthly payments of interest, and fully pay off the loan in October 2015. The partnership also signed a lease with Slumlord Corp. ("Slumlord"). The lease required monthly rent payments from January 2009 to November 2013. No partner signed a guaranty of the lease.

When the partnership was formed, Don contributed $5,000, Paul contributed $5,000, and John contributed $10,000 to the partnership. The partnership incurred a $15,000 loss during 2009, but made a profit of $90,000 in 2010, and a profit of $120,000 in 2011. In 2009 and 2010, no partner took a distribution. In 2011, Don took a $50,000 distribution, Paul took a $40,000 distribution, and John took a $50,000 distribution. In early January 2012, Paul was involved in a serious automobile accident. Although he did not die, doctors determined that Paul would never regain consciousness, and would remain in a coma. A short time later, the probate court appointed Paul's wife Marie as Paul's guardian and conservator. Paul currently remains alive, but in a coma on life support machines.

Questions appear on the following page

Multiple Choice Question 4-7: *Which of the following statements is correct?*

A.   The appointment of Marie as Paul's guardian/conservator dissolved the partnership.

B.   The appointment of Marie as Paul's guardian/conservator dissolved the partnership, <u>unless</u> both Don and John vote to continue the partnership within 90 days.

C.   The appointment of Marie as Paul's guardian/conservator did not dissolve the partnership, but it did result in Paul's dissociation from the partnership.

D.   The appointment of Marie as Paul's guardian/conservator did not dissolve the partnership, but it does mean that Marie replaces Paul as a partner.

Multiple Choice Question 4-8:   Regardless of how you answered the previous question (Question 4-7), assume that the appointment of Marie as Paul's guardian/conservator dissolved the partnership. *In that case, which of the following statements would be correct if the partnership does not have enough assets to pay its liabilities?*

A.   The three partners will be liable to repay the loan to the Bank, but not the remaining rent payments to Slumlord.

B.   The three partners will be liable to repay both the loan to the Bank and the remaining rent payments to Slumlord.

C.   The three partners will not be liable to repay either the loan to the Bank or the remaining rent payments to Slumlord.

D.   Don and John will be liable to repay both the loan to the Bank and the remaining rental payments to Slumlord, but Paul will only be liable for payments that would be due within the next three years.

Multiple Choice Question 4-9:   Regardless of how you answered the previous questions (Questions 4-7 and 4-8), assume that the appointment of Marie as Paul's guardian/ conservator dissolved the partnership and that the partnership had $90,000 left over after fully paying all of its liabilities. *As to how much will each partner receive upon dissolution of the partnership, which of the following is correct?*

A.   Don will receive $25,000, Paul will receive $35,000, and John will receive $30,000.

B.   Don will receive $7,500, Paul will receive $17,500, and John will receive $65,000.

C.   Don will receive $30,000, Paul will receive $30,000, and John will receive $30,000.

D.   None of the above is correct.

QUESTIONS 4-10 TO 4-12 ARE BASED ON THE FOLLOWING FACTS

Green, Cash, and Loot is a large law firm that has 300 partners, including Sally. It has a detailed partnership agreement, but the agreement does not contain any provisions concerning dissociation or dissolution. One day, Sally went into the managing partner's office and said: "I quit."

Multiple Choice Question 4-10: Which of the following is correct?

A.   Sally has dissociated, but the partnership will not dissolve because her notice was not in writing.

B.   Sally has dissociated, but the partnership will not dissolve if it pays her cash equal to that amount she would get if the partnership were liquidated and its assets were sold at a price equal to the greater of liquidation value or the value based on a sale of the entire business as a going concern without her as a partner, minus any damages caused by her dissociation. The deadline for payment is within 120 days.

C.   Same as Answer B, except that the deadline for payment is within one year.

D.   Sally has dissociated, and her dissociation will cause the partnership to dissolve unless she and all of the others partners agree that it will not dissolve.

Multiple Choice Question 4-11: Same facts as the previous question. Regardless of how you answered the previous question, assume for purposes of this question that the partnership did not dissolve when Sally dissociated from it. Four months later, Sally was walking down the street when she saw Sam, who was the owner of a sole proprietorship that supplies the law firm's paper and office supplies. Sam and Sally had known each other for several years, but Sam did not know that she had quit the partnership. Sam asked Sally whether the partnership wanted to continue its supply contract with Sam's business for an additional year. She replied: "Sure, if you give us a five percent discount." Sam agreed. *Assuming no other facts, and that there are no statutes of frauds issues in this problem, is the partnership bound on this contract?*

A.   The partnership is not bound, because Sally was not a partner at the time of this contract.

B.   The partnership is not bound, because Sally did not have actual authority to agree to this contract.

C.   The partnership is not bound, because this conversation took place more than 90 days after Sally dissociated from the partnership.

D.   The partnership is bound.

Multiple Choice Question 4-12: Same facts as the previous question, except that the partnership filed a statement of dissociation with the proper state governmental agency immediately after Sally quit the partnership. *Assuming no other facts, and that there are no statutes of frauds issues in this problem, is the partnership bound on this contract?*

A.   The partnership is not bound, because Sally was not a partner at the time of this contract.
B.   The partnership is not bound, because Sally did not have actual authority to agree to this contract.
C.   The partnership is not bound, because this conversation took place more than 90 days after Sally dissociated from the partnership.
D.   The partnership is bound.

Multiple Choice Question 4-13: Glenn, Ben, Pam, and Sam formed a partnership to run a farm. They did not have a written partnership agreement, but they did agree that the partnership would have a five-year term. After one year, Glenn quit the partnership. The remaining partners decided to continue running the farm. Glenn then demanded that the partnership pay him the value of his interest in the partnership. *Which of the following is correct?*

A.   Glenn's dissociation was wrongful; thus, he is not entitled to anything.
B.   Glenn is entitled to the fair market value of his partnership interest, minus any damages caused by his dissociation. The partnership must pay this amount to Glenn within 120 days.
C.   Glenn is entitled to cash equal to that amount he would get if the partnership were liquidated and its assets were sold at a price equal to the greater of liquidation value or the value based on a sale of the entire business as a going concern without Glenn as a partner, minus any damages caused by Glenn's dissociation. The partnership must pay this amount to Glenn within 120 days.
D.   Same as Answer C, except that the partnership is not obligated to pay this amount to Glenn until the end of the five-year term unless Glenn can show that earlier payment would not cause the partnership undue hardship.

CHAPTER 5
INTRODUCTION TO CORPORATE LAW

You should consider this chapter to be a clean break from Chapters 3 and 4 because a corporation is very different from a partnership; very little of the material from those chapters will be relevant here (although Chapters 1 and 2 remain important). To illustrate, what is the primary advantage and what is the primary disadvantage of operating a business as a partnership? That's easy, you may say to yourself: the primary advantage is that the partnership is a "flow through" tax entity and the primary disadvantage is that partners are personally liable, jointly and severally, for the partnership's debts and other obligations. But the corporation is precisely the opposite. Unless it is an "S" corporation as discussed in Chapter 1, it pays taxes on its income and shareholders pay taxes on any dividends that they receive. However, as a general rule, shareholders are not personally liable for the corporation's debts and other obligations. Barring some unusual circumstances, even if the corporation goes bankrupt, the worst case outcome for a shareholder is that the value of her stock in the company plummets to zero.

Another difference is that corporations are more complicated. With a partnership, there were essentially two categories of people: partners and non-partners. With a corporation, however, there are (1) *shareholders*, (2) *directors*, and (3) *officers and employees*. Further muddying this situation is that a given person can be more than one of these "types" of people simultaneously: a director may also be an officer and may also be a shareholder. When considering a problem involving corporate law, it will be vitally important for you to determine in what capacity a person is acting. Things that are permissible for one group of these people to do may be impermissible for another group. The manner in which one group may take action may be different from the manner in which another group may act.

The title of this chapter is "Introduction to Corporate Law," but in one sense that is misleading: we are going to cover a lot of ground in this chapter. We will begin with an overview of corporations, then proceed to discuss what actions and documents are needed to form a corporation. We will consider the strange case of "promoters," the somewhat perplexing concept of stock (and the many varieties thereof), and why and how a corporation may pay dividends to its shareholders. We will examine the board of directors and ask how the board may take action when it needs to do something. We will look at shareholders, asking what matters must be approved by them and how the shareholders may go about voting on something.

Hopefully, at the end of this chapter you will have a pretty good sense of how a corporation "works."   Later chapters will consider what happens if people (primarily the directors or officers) do their tasks sloppily or are motivated by dishonesty or a conflict of interest.

§ 5.01   OVERVIEW OF CORPORATIONS

Objectives: You should be able to explain to a potential client who wants to start a business the primary advantages and disadvantages of operating the business as a corporation. You should also be able to identify the different groups of "players" that typically are associated with a corporation, such as the corporation's shareholders. You should also be able to answer the following questions:

- *Which of these groups are employed by the corporation?*
- *Which of these groups are agents of the corporation?*
- *Which of these groups are the owners of the corporation?*
- *Which of these groups has power to make decisions for the corporation?*
- *What basic rights and responsibilities do members of these groups have?*

To begin with the basics, you should note that a corporation is a legal "person." It may own property, enter into contracts, hire employees, sue and be sued, etc. So far, this sounds much like a partnership. But there are some key differences. First, as you saw in Chapter 3, a partnership can exist even if the partners don't realize that they have formed a partnership. The same cannot be said of the corporation: as discussed in Section 5.02 below, several steps need to be taken to successfully form a corporation. It is thus impossible to "accidentally" form a corporation. Second, as discussed above, a corporation is a tax-paying entity unless it is an "S" corporation, and shareholders usually are not personally liable for the corporation's debts and other obligations.

There are also many more "players." When reading about the roles and responsibilities of these various types of persons, keep in mind that a person may simultaneously be more than one type.

Shareholders. The shareholders collectively "own" the corporation. I put the word "own" in quotation marks, however, because this can be a misleading statement. Thinking back to your Property class(es), you probably think of ownership as bringing with it a "bundle of rights." In other words, if you own something, you can pretty much do whatever you want to do with that item (although there may be some laws governing your use of it and you generally cannot inflict harm on someone else with it). If you own something, you can use it, destroy it, sell it, give it away, etc. You have a lot of power over things that you own.

Shareholders' ownership of the corporation is different. Perhaps surprisingly, shareholders have almost no control over the corporation. If you own shares of stock in, say, The Coca-Cola Company, you are a part-owner of that corporation, but you cannot walk into Coca-Cola's offices and start giving orders about developing new beverages. As a shareholder you do not have any right to make business decisions for the corporation, nor are you an agent of the corporation. While it is true that the shareholders must approve certain "fundamental" transactions such as mergers and major asset sales, they do so only after such transactions have been initiated by the board of directors (discussed below).

At this point, some of you may object, thinking something along these lines: my uncle owns a company, which means that he's a shareholder, and he's the "boss." He can do whatever he wants with the company. True, but if your uncle is the sole owner of the corporation (or a co-owner with one or a few other people) he is almost certainly *more than a shareholder*. He is very likely to be a director of the company and an officer and employee of the company. It is in these latter categories that he has power to make decisions and otherwise act for the corporation, as discussed in more detail below.

So, if shareholders cannot control the company, why do we call them the "owners"? There are a few reasons. First, once a year shareholders will elect some or all of the members of the board of directors. The directors are the ones that really "call the shots" for the corporation. As you will learn in greater detail in later chapters, generally speaking directors owe fiduciary duties to the corporation. However, the "traditional" view of corporate law is that the purpose of a corporation is to benefit the shareholders (as opposed to employees or other "stakeholders"). Therefore, directors usually perform their duties by asking first whether their actions will, or are likely to, benefit the shareholders.

Second, shareholders are considered the "residual" owners of the corporation. Recall our discussion of partnership dissolution in Chapter 4. When a partnership dissolves, it must pay its creditors (i.e., those to which it owes money or other obligations) first. If it is able to pay its creditors fully, any excess funds will go to the owners—the partners. A corporation is similar. As discussed in more detail in Chapter 12 of this book, when a corporation is dissolved, it must first pay its creditors. If it is able to do so in full, any excess funds will go to its owners—the shareholders.*

Again, shareholders don't make business decisions for the corporation, but they periodically elect the people who do—the directors.

Directors. Section 8.01 of the Model Business Corporation Act (the "**MBCA**") and the statutes of most states provide that the corporation's business and affairs are managed by, or under the direction of, the board. This means that the board of directors has the power to make virtually all of the decisions that a corporation needs to make (subject to needing shareholder approval for some really important decisions like mergers, as noted above). If the board of directors of Wal-Mart wanted to, it could reserve the power to decide whether the corporation should sell groceries to you the next time that you shop at a Wal-Mart store. Of course, this would be an incredibly inefficient way to run a large corporation like Wal-Mart. But notice the phrase "or under the direction of" in MBCA § 8.01. This means that the board can delegate some of its decision-making power. Typically it delegates power to ***officers*** and other ***employees***.

Officers and Employees. Officers and employees "work" for the corporation, that is, they are employed by the corporation and typically earn a living through the salary or other wages that the corporation pays them. You should note that officers are a subcategory of employees: all officers are employees, but not all employees are officers. Where should one draw the line between who is considered an officer and who is considered a "mere" employee? Different corporations will answer this question differently because most statutes require little in the way of officers. For example, the MBCA does not specifically require that a corporation have any particular list of officers. *See* MBCA § 8.40. The Michigan corporate statute, like those of many other states, only specifically requires that a corporation have a president, a treasurer, and a secretary.** A large, complicated corporation like Wal-Mart will likely have a very long list of officers, many of whom will have titles beginning with "Vice President of ...", not to mention literally tens of thousands of employees. In contrast, your uncle's company may only have the statutory minimum of officers, and he may

---

* However, one big distinction between corporations and partnerships on this issue is that if a corporation *cannot* fully pay its creditors, generally speaking the shareholders simply get nothing; they are not personally liable for unpaid business debts, as partners would be.

** When you first hear the phrase "corporate secretary," you may think of someone who does a lot of typing and filing. Instead, a corporate secretary is typically in charge of keeping minutes of board and shareholder meetings, sending out required notices, and performing other "corporate" tasks.

simultaneously hold all of those titles and be the only employee. One of the things that can be confusing about corporations is that they range in size from tiny to absolutely huge, but corporate statutes rarely make such a distinction. In the eyes of most statutes, a corporation is a corporation is a corporation.

But the important point here is not to decide whether someone is an officer or not. Both officers and employees are *agents* of the corporation—unlike directors. This means that an officer or employee of the corporation may bind the corporation to a contract with a third party through any of the methods that you learned about in Chapter 2. An individual director, on the other hand, is not an agent of the corporation. (Moreover, directors act as a *group* rather than on a individual basis, although a given corporation may only have one person on its board of directors.) True, a particular director may *also* be an employee of the corporation, but in her capacity as a *director* she is not an agent of the corporation.

What authority do officers or other employees have? They may have actual authority. Typically, at least with respect to officers, a corporation's bylaws will describe the powers and responsibilities of the person holding a particular officer position. Another source of actual authority could be a board resolution. For example, if the board of directors has just passed a resolution (something that you will learn more about in Section 5.07 below) approving a major loan from a bank, part of its resolution may say something to the effect of "… and the president of the corporation is hereby authorized to sign and deliver the loan agreement on the corporation's behalf." In this situation, the president would clearly have actual authority to sign the loan agreement. Other sources of actual authority could include employment contracts or employee manuals. And don't forget that officers and employees may of course have apparent authority, depending on the circumstances.

Other "Players." Although much, if not most, of corporate law concerns the interactions between shareholders, directors, and officers/employees, there are a few other groups that deserve mention. First, as with any type of entity, there will be *third parties*, which probably don't require much explanation. Second, to form a corporation one needs one or more *incorporators.* The only real function served by incorporators is to sign the corporation's articles of incorporation and deliver that document to the appropriate governmental agency, such as the secretary of state, for filing. Once this task is completed, there really isn't anything more that an incorporator must do. In the case of your uncle's company, it is very likely that he or his attorney was the incorporator. A corporation may also have *bondholders*, that is, people who own debt securities that the corporation has issued. (Shareholders own stock, which is considered an equity interest in the corporation.)

A corporation may have one or more **subsidiaries.** A subsidiary is a corporation with more than half of its outstanding stock owned by another corporation, which is called the *parent* corporation. If the parent owns all of the stock of the subsidiary, then the subsidiary is a *wholly owned subsidiary*.

Finally, another person who may (or may not) appear is a *promoter*. Promoters are persons who sign a contract on behalf of a corporation before it exists; thus, such contracts are called *pre-incorporation contracts*. After reading Section 5.03 below, you will understand why it is not very wise to be a promoter, particularly because it is usually quite easy to form a corporation, which is a subject that we will now consider.

§ 5.02   HOW TO FORM A CORPORATION

Objectives: You should be able to explain to a potential client the steps that are necessary to form (incorporate) a corporation and start its business operations. Given a fact pattern, you should be able to determine whether the formation of a corporation has been completed.

Subsidiary Objectives: You should also be able to:

●   *Describe some of the factors that your client should consider in choosing a state of incorporation.*

●   *Explain to your client what must be done if the corporation is incorporated under the law of one state, but "does business" in one or more other states.*

●   *List the two charter documents that the MBCA requires all corporations to have and describe the mandatory and some of the optional provisions of those documents. Explain to your client whether it is advisable for the corporation's articles of incorporation to include a provision describing the corporation's purpose(s).*

●   *Explain to your client what else must be done to complete the formation of the corporation after its articles have been filed.*

A.   CHOOSING A STATE OF INCORPORATION

In order to form a corporation and achieve its primary benefit—limited liability for shareholders, directors, and officers—it is necessary to file the *articles of incorporation* for the corporation. Setting aside the somewhat arcane *de facto* corporation and corporation by estoppel doctrines (see box below), a corporation simply does not exist until this document is filed with the appropriate state government. Before considering what you need to include in the articles, you have a more fundamental consideration: which state should you choose?

THE *DE FACTO* CORPORATION AND CORPORATION BY ESTOPPEL DOCTRINES
Under the *de facto* corporation doctrine, a defectively formed corporation will still be considered a "real" corporation (a *de jure* corporation) in the eyes of everyone except the state government. Typically, this doctrine requires that the incorporators of the corporation were acting in good faith and conducted some business in the corporation's name. By contrast, the corporation by estoppel doctrine merely prevents *one particular person* from arguing that a corporation was not properly formed. Typically, this doctrine requires that this person dealt with the "corporation" on the assumption that it was properly formed. This doctrine would not stop other persons from asserting that the "corporation" was not properly formed. This is important, because if a corporation was not properly formed, then its owners may be liable for its debts.

This may seem like a strange question at first, and you may wonder why you don't simply choose the state where the corporation plans to have its main office or conduct most or all of its business activities. For example, if you're working for a client that wants to start a small business in say, Michigan, why don't you simply incorporate under Michigan law? Well, you certainly could. But you are not *required* to.

A corporation may be formed under any state's law, even if it never plans to have an office in that state or otherwise conduct any business in that state. Because every state has a corporate statute, you could tell this client that she may incorporate her business in Wyoming, or Oregon, or Alabama, or, well, you get the idea. And in each case, she could still have the corporation's headquarters in Michigan and have it conduct its business in Michigan.

No offense to the other states, but in a situation like this, it will usually boil down to a choice between incorporation under the law of Michigan (the state where your client's corporation will be headquartered and do most of its business) or the law of Delaware. Michigan would be an obvious choice in this situation, if only because the client will likely live in Michigan and hire an attorney who practices in Michigan and who is more familiar with the Michigan corporate statute than those of other states. (Feel free to substitute some other state for Michigan if you live in another state. I'm just using Michigan because the client in this example lives there.)

But why Delaware? It may surprise you, but the great majority of large, publicly traded or otherwise "important" corporations are incorporated in Delaware. For example, The Coca Cola Company is incorporated under Delaware law but has its headquarters in Atlanta, Georgia. There are hundreds or even thousands of similar examples. Delaware is an attractive choice for such companies because its statute is widely viewed as being on the forefront or cutting edge of corporate law (and has been for quite some time, which gives Delaware a great deal of historical "momentum" as well). Moreover, its legislature closely monitors the statute and amends it frequently in response to developments in the corporate world. Further, Delaware has a specialized court system for business law and judges who have a great deal of experience in corporate law. Coupled with the fact that a great many large corporations (which tend to generate a fair amount of litigation) are incorporated in Delaware, this has resulted in a large, well-considered body of case law interpreting the Delaware statute, which adds an amount of certainty for lawyers advising corporations.

In the example above, your client forming a small business probably won't actually choose Delaware; Michigan law would be just fine for a small business that is located there (and will also be less expensive). But let's assume that your client, needlessly, says "Nothing but the best for me. I want to incorporate in Delaware." Under the *internal affairs doctrine*, this will mean that any matters that are "internal" to the corporation, such as disputes between the shareholders and the directors, would be governed by Delaware law. (However, note that even if a corporation is incorporated in Delaware, you would not need to actually litigate any disputes involving the corporation in Delaware courts.) Also, incorporating in a state other than the state in which the corporation will conduct its business will present some potential issues for your client under MBCA §§ 15.01 and 15.02. Read those sections and consider the following problems.

Problems

Problem 5-1:   Your long-time client, Fred Mulligan, is the majority shareholder of Fred Mulligan Corp. ("FMC"), which manufactures widgets and sells them to retail stores. Fred is also the sole director and officer of FMC. FMC is incorporated under the law of the state of Winterland, but has its headquarters and all of its employees, and conducts nearly all of its business, in the state of Summerland. *Which of these states considers FMC to be a "foreign" corporation?*

Problem 5-2:   Same facts as in Problem 5-1. *As a foreign corporation with respect to one of these states, what must FMC do?*

Problem 5-3:   Assume that FMC does not comply with the obligations you told it that it must observe in response to Problem 5-2. *Will FMC encounter any problems if it attempts to sue a customer located in Summerland for an unpaid debt? What if a customer sues FMC on a products liability claim in a court in Summerland?*

Problem 5-4: *In the two lawsuits described in Problem 5-3, which state's law will apply: the law of Winterland or the law of Summerland?*

Problem 5-5:   Under Winterland law, a corporation must give shareholders at least 20 days advance notice of a shareholder meeting.   Under Summerland law, a corporation must give shareholders at least 10 days advance notice of a shareholder meeting. *What is the minimum amount of advance notice that FMC must give its shareholders for a shareholder meeting—10 days or 20 days?*

Problem 5-6: FMC recently began selling widgets to a retail chain in the state of Springland. *Is FMC considered a foreign corporation with respect to Springland? If so, what must it do?*

B.   THE INCORPORATION PROCESS

Now that you've chosen the state in which you want to incorporate, what do you need to do? To make things easy, let's assume that the state you've chosen has a corporate statute that is identical to the MBCA. To form your corporation, you need to file its articles of incorporation with the secretary of state, according to MBCA §§ 2.01 and 2.03. Fortunately, drafting a "plain vanilla" set of articles of incorporation could be done quickly; there are only four required pieces of information that must appear in the articles, according to MBCA § 2.02(a). However, note that subsection (b) contains a list of some provisions that you could, but are not required to, include in the articles. Some of these "optional" provisions will become very important later in this book.

For now though, carefully read MBCA § 2.02, along with MBCA §§ 3.01 and 3.04, and work on these problems:

Problems

Problem 5-7:   Your client, Pam McGillicutty, wants to form a corporation that will run a restaurant and has hired you to draft the articles of incorporation. Pam plans to own 50% of the stock, with her husband owning the other 50%. Pam plans to name her corporation "The McGillicutty Restaurant." *Is this a proper name to appear in the corporation's articles of incorporation?*

Problem 5-8:   MBCA § 2.02(a)(2) requires the articles to state the number of shares that the corporation is "authorized to issue." *What does this mean? What number of shares would you suggest that the corporation should be authorized to issue: 1,000 or 1 million?*

Problem 5-9:   *Would you suggest that the corporation's articles state that the "purpose of the corporation is to operate a restaurant" (or similar words)? Why or why not?*

Problem 5-10:   *Why does MBCA § 2.02(a)(3) require the articles to include the address of the corporation's "registered office" and the name of its "registered agent"?*

Once the articles of incorporation are filed with the state and the corporation's existence begins, there is more to be done. MBCA § 2.05 explains that an organizational meeting must be held. If the initial members of the board were actually named in the articles of incorporation, then the board will simply hold the meeting. If the initial directors were not named in the articles, then the incorporators must first appoint them. In any event, some of the tasks that must be completed at this meeting are to appoint the corporation's officers[*] and adopt the corporation's bylaws. Although MBCA § 2.05 does not specifically mention it, the corporation must also issue at least one share of stock to someone (who will thereupon become a shareholder). *See* MBCA § 6.03(c).

MBCA § 2.06 reminds us that a corporation must also have bylaws. (Although many state statutes do not actually require bylaws, it is extremely rare to find a corporation that does not have bylaws.) That section does not require that the bylaws contain any particular provisions, nor does it give us any suggestions as to provisions that should appear in the bylaws. However, if you

---

[*]   The board appoints the officers. Although the board has the power to hire and fire any employee, typically the board delegates at least some of this authority to the officers. If The Coca-Cola Company hires you to work in a bottling plant, for example, it is doubtful that its board of directors even knows your name.

have ever examined the bylaws for a corporation, you will know that bylaws typically concern matters such as the corporation's officer positions and the duties and responsibilities of those positions; rules for the conduct of board meetings; rules for the conduct of shareholder meetings; provisions authorizing the corporation to indemnify directors and officers for certain expenses; etc. Bylaws need not be filed with the state government; thus, they are not available for public inspection like a corporation's articles of incorporation, unless the corporation happens to be publicly traded, in which case its bylaws must be publicly available pursuant to rules of the Securities and Exchange Commission (the "SEC").

Problem

> Problem 5-11: The articles of incorporation of ABC Corp. provide that its board shall consist of ten persons. The bylaws of ABC Corp. provide that its board shall consist of twelve persons. (ABC Corp. apparently had a sloppy lawyer.) *What is the size of ABC Corp.'s board of directors?*

§ 5.03   PRE-INCORPORATION TRANSACTIONS AND "PROMOTERS"

> *Objectives: You should be able to explain what (or who) a "promoter" is. Given a fact pattern where a promoter (P) makes a contract with a third party (TP) on behalf of a corporation that has not yet been formed (C), determine whether P and/or C are liable on the contract in the following situations: (1) C is never formed; (2) C is formed, but does not adopt the contract with TP; and (3) C is formed and adopts the contract with TP. If a promoter (against your legal advice) insists that she must act now to enter into a contract with a third party on behalf of a corporation that has not yet been formed, give her advice to make sure that she will not be personally liable on the contract.*

It's pretty easy to incorporate a new corporation, particularly if there will only be one or a few owners and they don't need to negotiate extensively about the provisions that will appear in the articles and bylaws. It's certainly not rocket science. So usually the best course of action will simply be to form a corporation and then have the corporation enter into a contract. But let's assume that you have a very impatient client (or one who has not yet received legal advice because she's been too busy working on business issues) who signs a contract and *then* comes to you for legal advice. Is she personally liable on that contract?

Before you tackle any problems, you should read MBCA § 2.04, as well as Section 6.04 of the *Restatement (Third) of Agency*. (By the way, do you notice any differences between these two sections, beyond the fact that the MBCA talks about corporations and the *Restatement* talks about principals and agents?) Also read the following case:

RKO-Stanley Warner Theatres, Inc. v. Graziano
Supreme Court of Pennsylvania
355 A.2d 830 (1976)

EAGEN, Justice. On April 30, 1970, RKO-Stanley Warner Theatres, Inc., (RKO), as seller, entered into an agreement of sale with Jack Jenofsky and Ralph Graziano, as purchasers. This agreement contemplated the sale of the Kent Theatre, a parcel of improved commercial real estate located at Cumberland and Kensington Avenues in Philadelphia, for a total purchase price of $70,000. Settlement was originally scheduled for September 30, 1970, and, at the request of Jenofsky and Graziano, continued twice, first to October 16, 1970 and then to October 21, 1970. However, Jenofsky and Graziano failed to complete settlement on the last scheduled date.

Subsequently, on November 13, 1970, RKO filed a complaint in equity seeking judicial enforcement of the agreement of sale. Although Jenofsky, in his answer to the complaint, denied personal liability for the performance of the agreement, the chancellor, after a hearing, entered [an order] granting the requested relief sought by RKO. *** This appeal ensued.

At the time of the execution of this agreement, Jenofsky and Graziano were engaged in promoting the formation of a corporation to be known as Kent Enterprises, Inc. Reflecting these efforts, Paragraph 19 of the agreement, added by counsel for Jenofsky and Graziano, recited:

> "It is understood by the parties hereto that it is the intention of the Purchaser to incorporate. Upon condition that such incorporation be completed by closing, all agreements, covenants, and warranties contained herein shall be construed to have been made between Seller and the resultant corporation and all documents shall reflect same."

In fact, Jenofsky and Graziano did file Articles of Incorporation for Kent Enterprises, Inc., with the State Corporation Bureau on October 9, [1970]; twelve days prior to the scheduled settlement date. Jenofsky now contends the inclusion of Paragraph 19 in the agreement and the subsequent filing of incorporation papers, released him from any personal liability resulting from the non-performance of the agreement.

The legal relationship of Jenofsky to Kent Enterprises, Inc., at the date of the execution of the agreement of sale was that of promoter. [Citation omitted.] As such, he is subject to the general rule that a promoter, although he may assume to act on behalf of a projected corporation and not for himself, will be held personally liable on contracts made by him for the benefit of a corporation he intends to organize. [Citations omitted.] This personal liability will continue even after the contemplated corporation is formed and has received the benefits of the contract, unless there is a novation or other agreement to release liability. [Citations omitted.]

The imposition of personal liability upon a promoter where that promoter has contracted on behalf of a corporation is based upon the principle that one who assumes to act for a nonexistent principal is himself liable on the contract in the absence of an agreement to the contrary. [Citation omitted.] As stated in Comment (a) under [Section 326 of the *Restatement (Second) of Agency*]: "there is an inference that a person intends to make a present contract with an existing person. If, therefore, the other party knows that there is no principal capable of entering into such a contract, there is a rebuttable inference that, although the contract is nominally in the name of the nonexistent person, the parties intend that the person signing as agent should be a party, unless there is some indication to the contrary."*

However, even though a contract is executed by a promoter on behalf of a proposed corporation, where the person with whom the contract is made agrees to look to the corporation alone for responsibility, the promoter incurs no personal liability with respect to the contract. [Citations omitted.]

In *O'Rorke v. Geary*, [56 A. 541 (Pa. 1903)], wherein this Court affirmed on the basis of the opinion of the court below, there is set forth the three possible understandings that parties may have when an agreement is executed by a promoter on behalf of a proposed corporation. It is stated therein:

> "When a party is acting for a proposed corporation, he cannot, of course, bind it by anything he does, at the time, but he may (1) take on its behalf an offer from the other which, being accepted after the formation of the company, becomes a contract; (2) make a contract at the time binding himself, with the stipulation or understanding, that if a company is formed it will take his place and that then he shall be relieved of responsibility; or (3) bind

---

* [Footnote by court]: Although Comment (a) speaks in terms of a principal-agent relationship, it is clear that this proposition is also particularly applicable to promoters. Comment (b) of Section 326 provides: "The classic illustration of the rule stated in this Section is the *promoter*." (Emphasis supplied.)

himself personally without more and look to the proposed company, when formed, for indemnity."

[Citations omitted.]

Both RKO and Jenofsky concede the applicability of alternative No. 2 to the instant case. That is, they both recognize that Jenofsky (and Graziano) was [were] to be initially personally responsible with this personal responsibility subsequently being released. Jenofsky contends the parties, by their inclusion of Paragraph 19 in the agreement, manifested an intention to release him from personal responsibility upon the mere formation of the proposed corporation, provided the incorporation was consummated prior to the scheduled closing date. However, while Paragraph 19 does make provision for recognition of the resultant corporation as to the closing documents, it makes no mention of any release of personal liability. Indeed, the entire agreement is silent as to the effect the formation of the projected corporation would have upon the personal liability of Jenofsky and Graziano. Because the agreement fails to provide expressly for the release of personal liability, it is, therefore, subject to more than one possible construction. [Citation omitted.]

In *Consolidated Tile and Slate Co. v. Fox*, [189 A.2d 228, 229 (Pa. 1963)], we stated that where an agreement is ambiguous and reasonably susceptible of two interpretations, "it must be construed most strongly against those who drew it." We further stated, "if the language of the contract is ambiguous and susceptible of two interpretations, one of which makes it fair, customary and such as prudent men would naturally execute, while the other makes it inequitable, unusual, or such as reasonable men would not likely enter into, the construction which makes it rational and probable must be preferred." [Citation omitted.] Instantly, the chancellor determined that the intent of the parties to the agreement was to hold Jenofsky personally responsible until such time as a corporate entity was formed and until such time as that corporate entity adopted the agreement. We believe this construction represents the only rational and prudent interpretation of the parties' intent.

As found by the court below, this agreement was entered into on the financial strength of Jenofsky and Graziano, alone as individuals. Therefore, it would have been illogical for RKO to have consented to the release of their personal liability upon the mere formation of a resultant corporation prior to closing. For it is a well-settled rule that a contract made by a promoter, even though made for and in the name of a proposed corporation, in the absence of a subsequent adoption (either expressly or impliedly) by the corporation, will not be binding upon the corporation. [Citation omitted.] If, as Jenofsky contends, the intent was to release personal responsibility upon the mere incorporation prior to closing, the effect of the agreement would have been to create the possibility that

RKO, in the event of non-performance, would be able to hold no party accountable; there being no guarantee that the resultant corporation would ratify the agreement. Without express language in the agreement indicating that such was the intention of the parties, we may not attribute this intention to them.

Therefore, we hold that the intent of the parties in entering into this agreement was to have Jenofsky and Graziano personally liable until such time as the intended corporation was formed and ratified the agreement. [Affirmed]

[Concurring opinion omitted.]

MANDERINO, Justice (dissenting): I dissent. Contrary to the majority's finding that the agreement was ambiguous because of its failure to provide expressly for the release of appellant Jenofsky from personal liability, I find clear on the face of paragraph 19 of the agreement an intention to release Jenofsky from personal liability upon the mere formation of the proposed corporation, provided the incorporation was completed prior to the scheduled closing date. According to paragraph 19, once the incorporation was completed, "all agreements ... (would) be construed to have been made between the seller and the resultant corporation ...."

It is inconceivable to me how the majority can agree with the Chancellor's finding that Jenofsky was to be personally responsible until the new corporation in some way adopted the agreement. There is no language anywhere in the agreement to suggest such a far-fetched interpretation. Paragraph 19 clearly states that Jenofsky was to be released from personal liability as soon as the corporation was formed.

Nor is it our duty to decide the logic, or lack of logic, of the parties in entering into this agreement. This was not a contract of adhesion, and, just because we might not have entered into the same contract, we nevertheless cannot read beyond its clearly intended meaning. I would therefore reverse ***.

Question:

The court states: "[W]hile Paragraph 19 does make provision for recognition of the resultant corporation as to the closing documents, it makes no mention of any release of personal liability." Do you agree? The dissent did not. How should Jenofsky's attorney have drafted this provision?

While some of us may disagree with the outcome under the majority opinion in the *Graziano* case, it does tell us some general rules about promoter liability which are consistent with MBCA § 2.04 and Section 6.04 of the *Restatement (Third) of Agency* (and its predecessor Section 326 of the *Restatement (Second) of Agency*). First, the general rule is that a promoter will be liable on a preincorporation contract, assuming she is aware that the corporation has not yet been formed. However, an equally important rule is that the parties may "contract around" this rule. In other words, if a promoter is in a situation where being a promoter is unavoidable, she could avoid being personally liable on the contract by stating in the contract that she is not personally liable. Thus, in this situation the parties' intent could trump the general rule. Nonetheless, this must be done very carefully. If there is any ambiguity, a court will likely resolve the issue in favor of the general rule. Thus, to avoid promoter liability, the promoter must be very, very clear in the contract that she is not liable. (And this clarity may alert the other party to this issue. The other party may then be unwilling to let the promoter "off the hook" and not agree to the contract language that the promoter wants!)

What about the corporation? So far, it doesn't exist, so it couldn't possibly be liable on a contract that predates its existence. However, if the corporation is later incorporated, that alone does not make it liable on the contract. The *Graziano* court referenced this rule when it wrote: "[I]t is a well-settled rule that a contract made by a promoter, even though made for and in the name of a proposed corporation, in the absence of a subsequent adoption (either expressly or impliedly) by the corporation, will not be binding upon the corporation." Of course, there is no law saying that corporations must adopt preincorporation contracts; they may choose not to do so. (Note here that "adopt" is a better word than "ratify" in this situation because ratification technically requires that the corporation was in existence at the time of the contract.)

But let's assume that the corporation (1) is incorporated after the contract was entered into and (2) adopts the contract (which it may do either expressly or impliedly). What happens to the promoter—is she released from further liability? Again, it depends on the intent of the parties, as expressed in the language of the contract. But if that language is missing or ambiguous, the general rule is that the promoter is not released of liability unless there is a *novation* (which you learned about in your Contracts course). The lucky third party now has two parties (the promoter and the corporation) to look to for performance under the contract.

Now that you know the general rules, consider what would happen in the following problem.

Problem

Problem 5-12: During October 2010, Steve, Clarissa, and Jennifer were in the process of forming a corporation to be called The Snazzy Cafe, Inc. ("SCI"). Although they agreed that the corporation would run a restaurant, they had some disagreements about what should be included in SCI's articles of incorporation and bylaws. Thus, negotiations continued during the entire month of October. On October 22, Steve learned that Stanley planned to offer a location for lease. Because Steve thought this location would be the perfect place for the restaurant and was worried that other people would want to lease it, he offered to lease the location from Stanley. After some discussions, Steve and Stanley entered into a five-year lease on October 25th. On the line for the tenant's signature in the lease, Steve signed: "Steve Jones, as agent for The Snazzy Cafe, Inc."

The articles of incorporation for SCI were filed on November 1. The articles stated that Steve, Clarissa, and Jennifer were the initial directors of the corporation. On November 9, the three directors properly held a board meeting. During the meeting, Steve proposed that SCI approve the lease that he had signed with Stanley. After discussions, Steve, Clarissa, and Jennifer unanimously approved the following resolution: "RESOLVED, that the directors of The Snazzy Cafe, Inc. hereby approve the corporation's adoption of a lease dated October 25, 2010 between the corporation and Stanley Smith, and hereby relieve and release Steve Jones of all personal liability on this lease."

The Snazzy Cafe restaurant opened for business in early 2011 but went out of business after only a few months (but SCI did not dissolve). Afterwards, SCI stopped paying rent that was due to Stanley, although it does have some cash remaining in its bank account. Stanley has properly performed all of his obligations as landlord under the lease. *Does Stanley have a valid cause of action against SCI for unpaid rent? Does he have a valid cause of action against Steve?*

§ 5.04   STOCK, BONDS, VALUATION, AND RELATED ISSUES

Objectives: You should be able to explain to a client who is considering forming a corporation the nature and characteristics of stock, what rights shareholders have and do not have, how a corporation issues stock, how the value of a business and its stock is determined, the nature and typical characteristics of debt, and the basic operations of stock markets.

Subsidiary Objectives: You should also be able to:

• *Explain the difference between a corporation's authorized shares and its outstanding shares and, given a fact pattern, determine how many shares of stock a corporation is authorized to issue and how many shares are currently outstanding.*

• *Describe the rights that are typically associated with common stock. Describe some rights that are* not *associated with common stock.*

• *Describe some of the rights that are often associated with preferred stock.*

• *Describe some of the rights that are often associated with bonds and other types of debt.*

• *Explain some of the basic principles used in determining the value of stock and other financial assets both for privately held and publicly traded corporations.*

A.   HOW CORPORATIONS ISSUE STOCK

When one first encounters "stock," it can be a somewhat perplexing concept. Essentially, shares of stock are the units into which ownership, also called *equity*, of the corporation is divided. But before turning to a discussion of the different types of stock, such as common stock and preferred stock, it's useful to understand the difference between *authorized* stock and *outstanding* stock. Recall MBCA § 2.02(a). One of the items that must appear in the corporation's articles of incorporation is the number of shares that the corporation is "authorized to issue." *See also* MBCA § 6.01. Of course, being "authorized" to do something merely means that you *may* do it, not that you are required to do it. Thus, this means that the number of authorized shares is the number that the corporation may—but need not—"issue." However, note that MBCA § 6.03(c) requires the corporation to issue at least one share of stock; you really can't have a corporation without having at least one person who is a shareholder.[*]

What does it mean to "issue" shares of stock? A stock issuance occurs when the corporation sells, either for cash or some other type of consideration, some of its authorized-but-unissued shares to one or more persons. After the issuance is completed, these persons will, of course, become shareholders (or, as Delaware calls them, stockholders). Shares that have been issued and that are currently owned by a shareholder are called outstanding shares.

Not surprisingly, the board of directors must approve any stock issuances by the corporation (unless MBCA § 6.21(a) applies, which is unlikely). The corporation's current shareholders are not required to approve any stock issuances by the corporation, unless MBCA § 6.21(f) applies. Read MBCA §§ 6.01, 6.03, 6.21, and 6.30, puzzle over them, and then apply them to the following problems:

Problems

Problem 5-13:   You have been hired to draft the articles of incorporation of LJ Corp., a "start up" (i.e., new) corporation that plans to run a hardware store and have two 50% shareholders, Linda and Juan, who will work for the corporation. *How many shares of authorized common stock should LJ Corp. have in its articles?*

Problem 5-14:   Same facts as Problem 5-13, but assume that you decided that LJ Corp. should have 100,000 shares of authorized common stock. *How many shares should LJ Corp. issue to Linda and Juan? How much money should Linda and Juan pay for these shares? Who decides? Must they pay in cash, or can they pay with some other type of consideration? Following the issuance of shares to Linda and Juan (in whatever amount you chose), how many authorized-but-unissued shares will LJ Corp. have?*

Problem 5-15:   The articles of incorporation of Conglomo Corp. state that the corporation is authorized to issue 200,000 shares of common stock. There currently are 100,000 shares of Conglomo Corp. common stock outstanding, owned by approximately 75 people. Conglomo wants to issue more shares to raise money to expand its business. Therefore, its board has approved a stock offering of 30,000 shares for $20 per share. *Must Conglomo's*

---

[*]   Also, some states impose taxes on the number of shares of authorized stock that corporations have, although there is nothing to this effect in the MBCA.

current shareholders approve this stock offering before it may take place? Must Conglomo offer some or all of these "new" shares to its current shareholders?

Problem 5-16:   Same facts as Problem 5-15, except that Conglomo's articles state that the corporation is authorized to issue 100,000 shares of common stock. *Is there any way that Conglomo can conduct this proposed stock offering?*

Problem 5-17:   Same facts as Problem 5-15, except that Conglomo's articles state that it is authorized to issue 10,000,000 shares of common stock, and there are already 5,000,000 shares outstanding, which are traded on the New York Stock Exchange (NYSE).   Yesterday, the closing price of a share of Conglomo common stock on the NYSE was $17 per share. *What should be the offering price per share in Conglomo's proposed stock offering?*

Problem 5-18: *What is a stock split? If Conglomo determines that the trading price of its 5 million outstanding shares of common stock is too high and declares a two-for-one stock split, how many outstanding shares will there be afterwards?   If you owned 100,000 shares before the stock split, how many shares will you own after the stock split?   Will your percentage ownership of Conglomo change?   What is the difference between a stock split and a stock dividend?*

Stock, whether it be common or preferred, is considered a "security" under both federal and state securities laws. (Many debt instruments, such as bonds, are also considered securities.) Therefore, before a corporation, even a newly formed one, offers stock to any potential investors it must either register the stock with the SEC or find an exemption from this registration requirement. (The same is generally true with respect to each state in which the corporation will offer the stock for sale.) We will defer further discussion of these requirements until Chapter 13.

To sum up, authorized shares may be thought of as "potential" shares, whereas outstanding shares are those that are currently owned by shareholders. If you own a share of stock, that share is outstanding and you are a shareholder. But you should next ask: what *kind* of stock is it?

B.   COMMON STOCK

Every corporation has common stock, so it is fairly easy to describe the characteristics that common stock has (and doesn't have) and then be pretty confident that this description will hold true from company to company to company. In other words, if you have shares of common stock in Corporation A and I have shares of common stock in Corporation B, I can confidently describe the rights we have (and don't have) with respect to these companies. True, the companies themselves might be radically different in terms of their value or the type of businesses that they operate, but the *legal* rights that common shareholders have are more or less the same regardless of the corporation.[*]

First, even though the common shareholders "own" the corporation, they don't have much control over it. Instead, they elect the people who run the corporation (the directors). Typically, this is done annually, as explained in more detail in Section 5.07 below. Shareholders may also from time to time be called on to vote on certain major transactions such as mergers. In addition, if the corporation's stock is publicly traded, stock exchange rules (but not state law) may require shareholder approval of certain compensation plans. In any event, when counting votes on things that shareholders vote on, each share of common stock generally has one vote. Thus, if you own 100 shares and I own 50 shares of common stock in the same corporation, you have twice as much voting power as I do. Note that this is fundamentally different than in a partnership. The default rule under RUPA is that each partner has equal voting power.

Another important attribute of common stock is that it is freely transferable. (This is also true of preferred stock.) If you own shares of common stock, you may sell them, give them to charity, leave them to someone in your will or through the laws of intestacy, etc. The only times that this would not be true are where the corporation's articles or bylaws impose restrictions on the transferability of shares, or if you are a party to an agreement (either with the corporation or one or more other shareholders) that restricts the transferability of your shares. *See* MBCA § 6.27. The free transferability of shares is sort of the whole point of investing; one makes money in the stock market by buying shares at one price and then selling them later at a higher price (hopefully). Similarly, if you own your

> **QUESTIONS TO PONDER**
> Why would an "S" corporation want to restrict the transferability of its stock? Why would a closely held corporation (one that is owned by a small number of shareholders who also work for the corporation) want to restrict the transferability of its stock?

---

[*]   This assumes that Corporation A and Corporation B are incorporated in the same state and that neither has included any "unusual" provisions in its articles of incorporation. If either of these statements is not true, then shareholders' legal rights with respect to these corporations could differ substantially.

"own" corporation, either alone or with a few other shareholders, and you want to retire, you may sell the company to someone else. One way to do this is to sell your stock in the company.

Common stock may also receive **dividends**. Section 5.05 below discusses dividends in detail, but suffice it to say here that dividends (also known as "distributions") are payments that the corporation makes with respect to its stock. In a sense, the corporation is giving away its money (or other assets) to the shareholders. The amount of dividends that you will receive depends on how many shares you own, because each share will be paid the same amount. Thus, using the above example, if you own 100 shares and I own 50 shares of common stock in the same corporation, and the corporation's board declares a dividend on the common stock, you will receive twice as much as I will receive. Note, however, that the board decides whether dividends will be paid. Outside of some unusual situations, common shareholders have no right to demand that they be paid dividends.

Finally, the other important attribute of common stock is that it is last in line to receive the corporation's assets upon dissolution. To take a simple example, assume that the ever-popular ABC Corp. has 10,000 shares of common stock outstanding, which is its only class of stock. Assume further that ABC Corp. has $100,000 in cash when it dissolves, but owes $70,000 to creditors. Obviously, the creditors will be paid first. (This is a recurring theme in this book.) The remaining $30,000 will be divided equally among the 10,000 outstanding shares of common stock, with the result that each share will be paid $3.

There are some important rights that are missing from common stock, though. For one thing, you have already seen that, as a shareholder, you have almost no control over the corporation despite the fact that you are one of the "owners." In addition, being a shareholder does not entitle you to a job with the corporation or otherwise guarantee you any financial return on your investment. In fact, the corporation may never pay dividends and may file bankruptcy, in which case whatever you paid for your stock has now gone up in smoke. Of course, if you are the *only* shareholder, or you own a very significant percentage of the stock, then you likely also decide who will be on the board of directors (such as yourself) and then can essentially cause the corporation to hire you, but note that this did not directly result from the fact that you are a *shareholder*.

In addition, a very important right that is missing from common stock is any right to force the corporation to repurchase the shares from you. As noted above, common stock is nearly always freely transferable. The flip side of this is that the corporation is under no obligation to buy it back from you. If you are unable to find someone who will buy the stock from you (or one who will buy it at a decent price), then in a sense you are "stuck." This presents a danger of being locked in to your investment, particularly in a closely held corporation. For this reason, if you are at all concerned about your ability to find a buyer for your stock, it may be wise to ask the corporation to sign an agreement, commonly called a *buy-sell agreement*, whereby it agrees to purchase your stock from you under certain circumstances.

Modern corporation statutes do not automatically give shareholders *preemptive rights*, that is, a right of first refusal to purchase any additional shares of stock that the corporation issues in the future so that you can maintain your percentage ownership in the company. For example, say that you own 2,500 shares of the 10,000 outstanding shares of ABC Corp. common stock. This, of course, makes you a 25% shareholder of ABC Corp. But then suppose that ABC Corp.'s board decides to issue and sell an additional 10,000 shares, and that it does not allow you to buy any of them. You still own your 2,500 shares, but because there would now be 20,000 shares outstanding, you went from being a 25% shareholder to a 12.5% shareholder. This is because you did not have preemptive rights in this example. *See* MBCA § 6.30. Of course, ABC Corp.'s articles of incorporation could have a provision granting shareholders preemptive rights. In that case, you would have had an opportunity to purchase 2,500 of the 10,000 shares that ABC Corp. was issuing in this example, so that you could maintain your 25% ownership level. Historically, most corporate statutes provided that shareholders had preemptive rights unless the corporation's articles denied such rights. Today, the situation is exactly the opposite. Again, see MBCA § 6.30.

A few more words are in order about common stock. Although the MBCA does not do so, some corporate statutes require that stock have a *par value*. The par value of a share of stock is the minimum amount of money that the corporation must receive when it issues a share. For example, if the par value of ABC Corp. common stock is $1 per share, then ABC Corp. must receive at least $1 per share when it issues shares to someone. Of course, ABC Corp. will want to receive more; par value is a "floor" rather than a "ceiling." But even if ABC Corp. stock has par value, there is no guarantee that you will receive at least $1 per share when you, a shareholder, resell it to someone else. If that person is unwilling to pay that high a price, you cannot force her to do so. (Also, note that ABC Corp. does not get any of the money when a shareholder resells her shares to someone else.)

> **TERMINOLOGY**
>
> A *stock option* is the right to buy shares of stock. The *exercise price*, sometimes called the *strike price*, is the per-share price at which you can buy shares if you decide to *exercise* the option. Also, typically you must hold a stock option for a stated period of time before they *vest* and may be exercised.

Finally, you may have heard the phrase *stock option* before. A stock option is well named: if you have a stock option, you have an option (but not an obligation) to purchase the shares of stock that are subject to the option. For example, you may have an option to purchase, say, 500 shares of ABC Corp. common stock, for $10 per share, exercisable at any point during the next five years. If the current value of ABC Corp. common stock is $10 per share, then it probably doesn't make economic sense for you to exercise your option now. But if next year the value of ABC Corp. stock has risen to, say, $12 per share, then it probably does make economic sense for you to exercise your option to purchase new shares from ABC Corp. for $10. Conversely, if the value of ABC Corp. stock has fallen to $8 per share, then only a fool would exercise her options to purchase it for $10 per share.

Why would ABC Corp. agree to such an arrangement? At first, it seems to be a lose-lose proposition for the corporation. However, the people who typically are granted stock options are those who are in a position, if they are motivated to work hard, to affect the company's performance and thus the value of its stock. For this reason, the people who usually receive stock options are directors, officers, and other "key" employees. By aligning their personal financial interests with the interests of the corporation and its shareholders, everyone is better off. Or at least that's the theory.[*]

C.   PREFERRED STOCK

When one first encounters preferred stock, it is tempting to conclude that it is somehow "better" than common stock. After all, one would rather be "preferred" over those ordinary people who own common stock. But before you jump to the conclusion that it is better to own a particular company's preferred stock than its common stock, it would be wise to ask what the terms of the preferred stock actually are.

First, keep in mind that relatively few companies have preferred stock. There certainly is no requirement that corporations issue preferred stock, let alone have preferred stock authorized for issuance in their articles of incorporation. In

---

[*] To be clear, it should be noted that preferred stock may also have a par value and that there may be stock options to buy preferred stock. These are not concepts that are unique to common stock. Further, options can be purchased from third parties; they need not be issued by the corporation itself.

other words, preferred stock is relatively rare.   Second, if you know that a particular corporation has a class of preferred stock, you actually know very little information—you know that it has common stock and that it has preferred stock, but you don't actually know *why* the preferred stock has preferential rights over the common stock. To find that out, you need to go read the corporation's articles of incorporation; the rights and other characteristics of the preferred stock will be found in the articles.[*] And preferred stock in Corporation A could vary dramatically from preferred stock in Corporation B, which in turn could vary dramatically from preferred stock in Corporation C. In sum, there's not really a "normal" kind of preferred stock.

That said, here are some things that shouldn't surprise you if you encounter preferred stock. (Note that MBCA § 6.01(c) gives us some "ideas" for preferred stock, but subsection (f) reminds us that these are not the only possibilities.) Preferred stock may have a ***dividend preference***. For example, shares of ABC Corp. preferred stock may be entitled to receive, say, $5 per share in dividends annually before ABC Corp. may pay any dividends on its common stock. But keep in mind that ABC Corp. may be unable to pay dividends in a given year if business is bad and it doesn't have a lot of cash on hand. For that reason, it is typically the case that dividend preferences will be ***cumulative***. In this example, that would mean that if ABC Corp. were unable to pay any dividends on the preferred stock in a given year, then it would have to pay $10 ($5 plus $5) per share in dividends on the preferred stock in the following year before it could pay any dividends on the common stock in that year. To further complicate things, the preferred stock's dividend preference could then be ***participating*** or ***non-participating***. In this example, if it were non-participating, this would mean that the preferred stock would get $5 per share in dividends annually *and no more*. If it were participating, then the preferred stock would get $5 per share in dividends annually *plus* whatever dividends are declared on the common stock. (However, note that the precise meaning of "participating" and "non-participating" may vary from one corporation to another. As with anything having to do with preferred stock, a very careful reading of the corporation's articles of incorporation will *always* be necessary.)

It is also fairly typical for preferred stock to have a ***liquidation preference***. For example, ABC Corp. preferred stock may be entitled to receive, say, $10 per share upon the dissolution of ABC Corp. before any amounts could be paid to the common shareholders. (Of course, note that creditors must be fully paid before *any* shareholders will get anything upon the corporation's dissolution.) Following

---

[*]   However, the corporation could have "blank check" preferred, in which case the precise terms of a class of preferred stock would be determined by the board and set forth in any amendment to the corporation's articles that would not require approval by the current shareholders. This allows the board to quickly react to market conditions when issuing and selling preferred stock.

that payment, the preferred stock could then either be participating or non-participating, as discussed in the prior paragraph.

Problem

Problem 5-19: ABC Corp. has two classes of stock: (1) common stock, of which there are 10,000 shares outstanding, and (2) preferred stock, of which there are 5,000 shares outstanding. The preferred stock has a $10 per share liquidation preference. ABC Corp. has dissolved. After liquidating its assets, it had $200,000 in cash. However, it owes creditors $50,000. *How will this money be divided among (1) creditors, (2) holders of preferred stock, and (3) holders of common stock, if the preferred stock's liquidation preference is non-participating? How does your answer change if the preferred stock's liquidation preference is participating?*

Preferred stock may also have **conversion rights**, that is, the right to convert into shares of common stock, either at the option of the shareholder or upon some predetermined event. If it is convertible, a conversion ratio must be determined, because you would obviously need to know how many shares of common stock a share of preferred stock would become upon its conversion. Conversely, preferred stock may be **redeemable** at the corporation's or the holder's option at a fixed price or a price determined by some formula, or may be convertible into another class of stock at the corporation's or the holder's option.

Although this is not universally true, preferred stock is usually nonvoting. However, it may be given voting rights in some circumstances. For example, the preferred shareholders may have the right to elect a designated number of directors to the company's board of directors if dividends were not paid for a specified period of time.

All of this may leave you a bit bewildered the first time you encounter it. Don't worry though—if your professor wants to test you on preferred stock, she will need to tell you what the terms of the corporation's preferred stock are. As you now know, there is no universal meaning to the phrase preferred stock. In fact, in many cases it more resembles debt (such as bonds) than equity (such as common stock).

D.   DIVIDING STOCK INTO CLASSES AND SERIES

As if things weren't complicated enough, stock (either common stock or preferred stock) could be divided into different classes and even further divided into different series. MBCA § 6.01(a) is the primary section of the MBCA dealing with this issue. Go read it now. Then see if you can answer the following problem:

Problem

Problem 5-20: Stef, Pete, and Fred want to form a corporation. They have agreed on a capital structure that will only involve common stock, but they want it arranged so that (1) each shareholder will have equal voting power but (2) when dividends are paid or the company is sold, Stef will receive 50% of the money and Pete and Fred will each receive 25%. *Can you think of an idea that would accomplish their goals?*

Because this is an introductory level textbook about business organizations, we generally will keep things relatively simple from here on and assume that the corporation has only a single class of common stock, unless otherwise stated.

E.   DEBT

As a law student, it is very likely that you are familiar with the concept of *debt*, but a discussion of it in the corporate context is necessary here. Because debt is essentially contractual, it could take an almost unlimited variety of forms. Nonetheless, it is possible to describe some of its basic attributes, or at least terms that are relatively customary. Debt, of course, involves two parties: a *creditor* or *lender*, and a *debtor*. The creditor lends money to the debtor, and the debtor promises to repay this amount, called the *principal*, at a later specified date, called the *maturity date*. (Note that stock does not have a maturity date. Therefore, stock is never "paid back.") In addition, the debtor agrees to pay *interest* to the lender. To take an extremely simple example, if I borrow $100 from you at 10% interest and agree to repay it to you in one year, in one year I will owe you $110. Interest compensates creditors for the *time value of money*, which is a concept explained in a bit more detail in Section G below. Interest may either be fixed, which means that the interest rate remains the same during the duration of the debt, or variable, which means that the interest rate may fluctuate according to market rates of interest or other measures.

In other context of a corporation, there are two primary ways in which it can borrow funds: from a bank or other financial institution, or by issuing and selling bonds. (As with the decision to issue stock, the decision to obtain a major loan or issue bonds rests with the board of directors.) The first is a relatively simple contractual transaction: the bank agrees to lend money to the corporation and the corporation agrees to repay it at the maturity date, together with interest, or perhaps the principal must be repaid in installments. No bank, of course, would lend money unless it is reasonably sure that the borrower will be able to repay it; in other words, the loan must not be unduly risky. (Loans that carry a higher risk of nonpayment will likely be made, if at all, at interest rates that are higher than less risky loans to compensate the lender for the greater risk.) In addition, the bank will certainly take additional steps to protect itself, such as insisting on having a first-priority security interest in some or all of the borrower-corporation's assets as collateral, which the bank may seize if the debtor **defaults** on its payment obligations, as you have learned or will learn about in your Secured Transactions course. In addition, the bank will likely require the company to abide by certain **covenants**, such as not paying dividends to shareholders until the loan is repaid. Typically, if the debtor defaults on any of its obligations under the loan agreement, the bank may **accelerate** the debt, that is, declare the principal and unpaid interest to be immediately due.

For our purposes, the bond market is more interesting. The loan described in the preceding paragraph was made by one bank (or maybe a "syndicate" of banks), whereas bonds[*] are typically sold to several lenders, perhaps hundreds or even thousands. In a sense, you can think of a bond offering by a corporation as the corporation simultaneously obtaining multiple loans from many lenders, but on identical terms. But the premise is the same: the corporation issuing the bonds owes money to the people who purchase the bonds, who are called **bondholders**. Bonds have a principal amount, sometimes called the **face value**. Bonds pay interest, sometimes called the **coupon rate** because in days long past bonds had actual paper coupons that the bondholder would detach and return to the corporation when an interest payment was due.[**] And of course bonds are repayable by the corporation on their maturity date. But unlike most "regular" loans (other than those involved in the terribly complex transactions involving mortgage loans that occur on Wall Street in the modern world), bonds typically can be and indeed are resold by the initial purchasers to other persons. In other

---

[*]   **Bonds** typically are secured by the corporation's assets as collateral, whereas **debentures** are typically unsecured. Both bonds and debentures tend to have a longer duration than do **notes**. For ease of reading, however, we will refer to all of these types of debt simply as "bonds."

[**]   **Zero coupon** bonds do not pay interest. However, upon maturity the issuer must repay a higher amount than the face value of the bond. In effect, it is as if the bond had paid interest.

words, there is a "secondary" bond market. For example, if I purchased a corporate bond that has a $1,000 face value, a 6% coupon rate, and a maturity date that is in five years, I certainly could hold the bond for the next five years, collect $60 of interest every year ($1,000 multiplied by 6%), and then be repaid the $1,000 principal amount at the end of five years by the debtor-corporation. Alternatively, I could sell the bond to someone else. Particularly for the bonds of well-established companies, there is a very active, "liquid" trading market in which to resell bonds.

What will the price be when the bond is resold? A major factor will be the prevailing market interest rates at the time of the resale.[**] In the above example, a 6% interest rate may have been typical for this type of bond at the time it was issued by the corporation, but what if interest rates have changed since then? If interest rates have gone up, then this bond, paying a now-paltry 6% of interest, is less valuable. If rates have gone down, then this bond will seem more valuable. If I want to sell it to someone else, however, I can't expect the issuer to reset the interest rate; the rate on this bond remains fixed. But the price at which I sell it to someone else is always a matter of negotiation or market forces. If market interest rates have gone up and made the bond less valuable, then I will sell it to someone else for less than the $1,000 face value; if market interest rates have gone down, then I will likely be able to sell the bond for more than $1,000. In this way, the **effective interest rate** on the bond is adjusted by market forces, even if the "real" interest rate remains the same.

From the corporation's perspective, one attractive thing about debt, whether it be a "regular" loan or a bond, is that the interest payments are tax deductible. To take a simple example (nearly always a bad idea when talking about tax issues), if the corporation is subject to a tax rate of 25%, the 6% interest rate that it pays on the bonds in the above paragraph works out to a "real" interest rate of only 4.5% (6% multiplied by 75%). In other words, for every dollar of interest that it pays, it saves twenty-five cents in taxes. In contrast, dividends that the corporation pays are not tax-deductible. For this reason, the Internal Revenue Service has very complicated regulations designed to ferret out situations where a company calls something debt that really should be characterized as equity. More on that in your Taxation of Business Entities course.

From the lender's perspective, one attractive thing about debt as compared to equity is that it is less risky—there is a greater likelihood that a lender will earn

---

[**]   How interest rates fluctuate depends on complex market forces, as well as actions of the Federal Reserve System and other governmental agencies. Luckily for you, these forces are beyond the scope of this textbook. In addition, ratings agencies, such as Moody's and Standard and Poor's "rate" the debt of various bond issuers. A bond with a "AAA" rating is perceived as very safe and therefore will generally pay a lower interest rate than lower-rated bonds.

some return on its investment (the loan) than will a common shareholder on her investment (the amount that she paid for the stock). For one thing, the interest rate, maturity date and other terms of the debt are fixed by contract. If the borrower defaults, then the creditor may sue to enforce these terms or may even force the company into bankruptcy in some situations. In contrast, holders of common stock rarely may sue if they are disappointed in the returns that their stock has generated. In addition, if the company were dissolved, then creditors are paid before owners, as discussed above. Thus, if the corporation's assets are somewhat limited, debt holders stand a much better chance of being paid than do shareholders. On the other hand, shareholders may become *very* rich if the corporation's business performs very well. Even in that case, however, creditors only get what they are entitled to by contract (principal and interest). In sum, there is usually a much greater range of possible outcomes with stock than with bonds and other types of debt. But this goes with the territory of being an "owner."

In this textbook, we will mainly focus on stock and shareholders, as opposed to bondholders, if only because shareholders have voting and other rights provided by statute, whereas the rights of bondholders are largely fixed by contract. Nonetheless, you should realize that bonds and other forms of debt are an incredibly important source of financing for many corporations. Particularly for large corporations, it often is more common to see them issuing bonds than issuing new shares of stock.

F.   CHOOSING A CAPITAL STRUCTURE

A corporation (as well as any other type of business entity, for that matter) needs money to run its business. One major source of these funds will be the profits that the company generates by running its business. Of course, to get from being a start-up company to an established, profitable company may be a long road. Two other sources of funds are selling stock and issuing debt, as discussed above. So what is the optimal mix of equity and debt for a corporation? What types of stock should there be? There are courses on this very subject taught in business schools and many experts vehemently disagree with one another, so you obviously are not going to become an expert on this topic by reading this textbook. But a few things should be said about *leverage*.

> **REMINDER**
> Don't forget when planning the formation of a corporation that, if it plans to be an "S" corporation, it may not have more than one class of stock (although certain variations in voting rights are permitted). See Chapter 1.

Debt is almost always a vital part of a corporation's capital structure. To understand why, let's assume that a business has $10,000 and an opportunity to invest in two different investments, each of which requires a $10,000 minimum investment and will result in a 10% rate of return (e.g., interest). Sounds like the business can only invest in one of them, right? Clearly, if the business took its $10,000 and invested it in either option, it would have $11,000 at the end of the year (the original $10,000 investment plus the 10% return, ignoring tax effects). But how about this: why not borrow $10,000 from a bank at 5% interest and then invest $10,000 in *both* investments? This will cost $500 in interest expenses (5% of $10,000), but the total return will thus be $1,500 ($1,000 from each investment, minus $500). Interestingly, the business's ***return on equity***, that is, the return on the portion of the investment that wasn't borrowed, went from 10% in the first example, to 15% in the second example ($1,500 divided by $10,000). A similar effect occurs when a corporation uses debt as part of its capital structure—once interest on the debt is paid, any earnings that the corporation has would be divided among a smaller amount of equity, resulting in a higher per-share return on equity than if the corporation had no debt. This can provide a powerful incentive to rely on debt, or leverage, to "lever up" returns on equity.

But in the prior example, the 10% return was assumed to be guaranteed. Real life is obviously not so safe. The 10% return may never materialize, or may even turn negative. Meanwhile, the obligation to pay interest on borrowed funds remains. Let's change the prior examples, and assume that the 10% expected return ends up being 0%. In the first example where the corporation used only its own $10,000 and did not borrow any funds, it still has its original $10,000 but its return on equity was 0%. In the second example, the business still has its original $10,000, as well as the $10,000 that it borrowed, but it had to pay $500 in interest. Its return on equity in this example was thus *negative* 5%. To put it simply, leverage may result in superior returns on equity when times are good, but can rapidly make things *dramatically worse* when times are bad. Keeping an "equity cushion" is highly advisable.

In the end, for these and other reasons that would be explored in much more depth if this were business school, some amount of debt will be an important part of a corporation's capital structure. On the other hand, too much debt can get the corporation into serious trouble when there's a downturn in its business or asset prices fall. (Remember Lehman Brothers?) This is simply because debt must be repaid with interest, whereas equity is never repaid. Finding the proper mix of debt and equity is one of the most important tasks of the corporation's financial advisors. Further, this mix will likely evolve over the course of the company's lifetime.

G.   VALUATION OF PRIVATELY HELD BUSINESSES

None of the above discussion actually told us what the stock of a corporation is *worth*, that is, what its **valuation** is. Obviously, the value of a share of stock depends in the first instance on the value of the company. To take an exceedingly simple example, assume that we have a privately held corporation. Because the company is privately held, its stock obviously is not traded on any sort of stock market, so you cannot look in the *Wall Street Journal* to see what a share of its stock is "going for." In addition, you may not have any "comparables," that is, information about similar companies that were sold in the recent past in transactions involving sophisticated parties, to give us an idea of what this business is worth. Thus, to figure out what this company and its stock are worth you need an appraiser, hopefully one with a lot of training and experience. Fortunately, many accounting firms, investment banking firms, and others provide appraisal services. The appraiser will examine the company's financial statements and a great deal of other information (both internal and external to the company) in an effort to estimate what the company is worth. But it is important to understand that each business is unique, and there is no "scientific" or "right" answer to deciding what a business is worth. Different experts may come to different conclusions.[*]

As noted briefly in Chapter 1, there are a variety of techniques and measures that may be used to make this determination, most of which are beyond the scope of this textbook. But, just for fun, let's say that you are an appraiser and you learn the following information about a privately held company that your client wants to buy or sell. First, the company's only physical asset is a machine that manufactures widgets. However, the business owns a patent for these particular widgets. The patent has another ten years before it expires, at which point competitors will be allowed to manufacture the widgets and the business will likely "go under" due to all of this competition. The company purchased the machine for $50,000 one year ago, and the machine had an expected useful life of ten years. Thus, the current book value of the machine on the company's balance sheet is $45,000 (the $50,000 cost, minus one year of depreciation under "straight line" depreciation). The company's balance sheet shows no long-term debt or other liabilities. If the company were to sell the machine for scrap metal and spare parts today, it would likely receive $10,000.

The income statement reveals that the business has revenues of $100,000 per year and net income of $45,000 per year. The cash flows statement shows that

---

[*]   One must also be careful of the motivations involved. Not to be cynical, but you shouldn't be surprised to find that an appraiser hired by a seller would be more likely to find a high value for the business than would an appraiser hired by a buyer.

the company generates $50,000 of cash per year (the $45,000 of net income, with the $5,000 depreciation expense added back). These numbers have been more or less the same for the past several years. The market for the company's widgets appears stable, but is not growing greatly. Moreover, there do not appear to be many cost savings that a buyer would be able to impose if it bought the business; the current owners have been running it fairly efficiently.

With these admittedly basic facts, what do you think such a business would be worth? Because you are a lawyer rather than a financial advisor, it is probably unfair to ask you this question. On the other hand, it often is useful for a lawyer to be familiar with some basic concepts of valuation. You won't learn how to become an appraiser by reading a textbook like this, but let's first look at some ideas that may have occurred to you and understand why they would be *wrong* answers to the question of what the business is worth. One idea is simply that the business is worth the *scrap value* of its assets, which in this case would be $10,000, or

> **When Do Lawyers Get Involved in Valuation Issues?**
> While expert appraisers usually will tell the lawyers what something is worth, lawyers may need to cross-examine valuation experts in litigation; advise clients who are buying or selling businesses or other assets; and give advice on the value of a business or other asset for estate tax purposes. Other examples abound.

perhaps its *book value*, which in this case would be $45,000. It is easy to see why these figures would be well below what this business is "worth." Keep in mind that, in a single year, this business will generate $50,000 of cash, well above both of these values. (Also, we forgot that the company owns a patent. Intangible assets also have value, not just tangible ones.)

Thus, it becomes clear that one primary inquiry in valuing a business is not what its assets are worth, but the income or cash flows that are generated by those assets. Generally speaking, most valuation experts will focus on cash flows rather than net income, due to the many non-cash expenses that appear on the income statement and the many out-of-pocket expenses that do not. So, let's focus on this company's cash flows. What if we say that the company is worth $50,000 because that is the amount of cash that it generates in a year? Hopefully, you immediately understood why this is too low a figure: the company appears likely to generate this amount of cash for more than one year.

Well then, how about $500,000, which is the $50,000 multiplied by the remaining ten years on the patent's life? After all, this company has the exclusive rights to manufacture these widgets, it's been earning this amount of money for the past several years, and the widget market appears stable. In other words, there doesn't appear to be a great deal of *risk* involved; it is pretty much a sure thing that, during the next ten years, this company will generate $500,000 of cash flows. Would this be a bad idea? Yes, because we neglected the concept of *present value*, sometimes referred to as the ***time value of money***. A dollar that you will receive one year from now (or at some other point in the future) is worth *less* than a dollar in your hand today because, if you had that dollar today you could earn interest on it during the coming year or otherwise invest it productively.

Determining the present value of something can be a very complicated undertaking, and in this textbook we won't get close to understanding many of the details involved.   But one factor that will be important is deciding what the ***discount rate*** should be (which itself is a very complex process).   Generally speaking, the riskier something is, the greater the discount rate should be, and thus the smaller its present value should be. Conversely, the less risky something is, then the smaller its discount rate should be and the greater its present value should be. To determine the present value of something that will be received in a year, we could use the relatively simple formula: $PV = FV / (1 + R)$. In this formula, PV is the present value, FV is the future value, and R is the discount rate. In this example, the present value of $50,000 one year from now, using a 10% discount rate, is $45,454.55 because that is the result of dividing $50,000 (the future value) by 1.1 (which is 1 plus the 10% discount rate). Calculating the present value of amounts that we will receive more than one year from now, or amounts that we will receive for more than one year, is more complicated.

This brings us to something called the ***discounted cash flow method***. While its application can be extremely complex, the overall goal of the discounted cash flow method is to determine the sum of all future cash flows that a business may generate and then discount that amount to present value. Now, this is not to say that the discounted cash flow approach is the "correct" method of business valuation, or that it will result in an "accurate" valuation of the widget business, or that there aren't other ways to value a business, but hopefully you understand the basic idea: future cash flows must be discounted to present value. Beyond these basic concepts of valuation, things rapidly get complicated but those issues are outside the scope of this textbook. Further, advising a client who is buying or selling a business involves many issues besides money. Nonetheless, let's explore a few more issues before concluding this brief introduction to valuation issues.

Suppose that you represent a client that wants to purchase some—but not all—of the shares of a ABC Corp., a privately held corporation. Because you wanted to get a very good understanding of what ABC Corp. is worth, you hired *three* appraisers, but all three appraisers came back and said that ABC Corp. is worth exactly $1 million, and no one in the world has any reason to disagree with these conclusions. What is a share of ABC Corp. stock worth? Obviously, it depends on how many shares there are. If there are 1 million shares of common stock outstanding, then each share *should* be worth $1. (If there were 500,000 shares of common stock outstanding, then each share should be worth $2 in this example. And so on.)

But does that mean that your client should pay that price for the stock? It depends. Let's say that currently there are two shareholders of this company: Shareholder A, who owns 510,000 (51%) of the shares, and Shareholder B, who owns 490,000 (49%) of the shares. If your client were offering to buy Shareholder B's shares from her, what would be a good price? If you answered $490,000 ($1 million multiplied by 49%), then your client probably would be paying too much. For one thing, note that Shareholder B is a minority shareholder. Shareholder A has a majority of the stock and therefore has control of the board of directors (as you will learn in later sections in this chapter). This means that Shareholder A is in a position to control the company and Shareholder B is not.* Thus, Shareholder B's stock probably isn't really worth $490,000. In addition, note that there are only two shareholders in this example; obviously, the company's stock is not traded on any stock exchange. Thus, if your client does decide to purchase Shareholder B's stock (or, for that matter, Shareholder A's stock) and then wants to resell it to someone else, doing so will be difficult (even though your client is legally free to do so). Your client would have to find a buyer, negotiate a price and other terms, etc. For this reason, your client may also want to reduce the amount that she is willing to pay for the stock. Following application of this *minority discount* and this *marketability discount*, it looks like Shareholder B's stock is worth far less than $490,000 in an arm's length transaction like this.

H.   A NOTE ABOUT PUBLICLY TRADED COMPANIES

Now let's change gears and assume that the corporation is publicly traded, that is, its stock is listed on a national securities exchange such as the New York Stock Exchange or Nasdaq. (These and other stock markets are discussed in more detail in Chapter 10.) If a corporation has a class of securities listed on a national securities exchange, then it is a "reporting company" under the Securities Exchange Act of 1934. As a reporting company, the corporation continually files various documents with the SEC (which are also publicly available), such as its annual report on Form 10-K, its quarterly reports on Form 10-Q, and other reports. In sum, the goal of this disclosure regime is to ensure that the public—the "market"—is continually updated as to the corporation's financial and business performance. If the corporation is performing well, then (all other things being equal) the price of its stock should rise; if it is performing poorly or if some

---

*   We learned earlier in this chapter that shareholders have little or no direct control over the corporation. However, if you own 51% of the outstanding stock of a corporation, then you will certainly only elect people to the board (such as yourself) who do things of which you approve.

adverse event happens to it, the price of its stock should fall.* In fact, the "efficient capital markets hypothesis" holds that the price of a share of publicly traded stock reflects all publicly known information about that company and that the market is thus "efficient" at pricing the value of shares of publicly traded stock. (Nonetheless, many academic commentators question the accuracy of this hypothesis.)

The key point for our purposes in this chapter is to understand that, if the company is publicly traded, then it's relatively simple to figure out what a share of its stock is worth on a given day. As you know from the discussion above about determining the value of a *privately* held corporation, valuation is more of an art than a science. Different experts may come to very different conclusions. But there's probably no better way of figuring out what a share of stock is worth than to put it to a "market test." For a class of stock that is actively traded (what is called "liquid"), hundreds

> **TERMINOLOGY**
>
> If the market for a company's stock is very active, and a high number of shares regularly are traded, we say that the market for that company's stock is "liquid." On the other hand, if a company's stock is infrequently traded, we say that the market for it is "thin" or that the stock is "thinly traded."

or even thousands of people buy and sell that stock every day and the market price likely won't be greatly affected by any particular transaction. Because all of these are transactions are resales (that is, the company is not issuing any new shares on an ordinary day), then the number of shares that are sold will be exactly equal to the number of shares that are purchased. Given the laws of supply and demand, if there are more people who want to sell than to buy, perhaps because a piece of bad news about the company was just disclosed, then the price will fall. If there are more buyers than sellers on a given day, then the price will rise. But one of the key drivers of the stock price will be the information about the company that is continually being made public. Using that information, all of the hundreds and thousands of buyers and sellers will come to their own rational decisions about the price for which they are willing to buy or sell the stock. And that should be a pretty good indication of what the stock is "really" worth.

This is not to say that the stock market is never wrong—one need look no further than the major stock market crashes during the first decade of this century to realize that the many professional "stock pickers" out there can get things wrong, and get them wrong very badly. Nor does buying a publicly traded stock at today's price give you any guarantee that the price will "hold" in the future. But it remains true that one of the best ways of figuring out what a share of stock is worth is to have it be traded on a stock market and have its valuation be determined by the "wisdom of the crowd."

---

* "Macro" events will also drive the value of stocks that are publicly traded. For example, if World War III breaks out tomorrow, it is a pretty safe bet that the trading prices of nearly every publicly traded stock will fall.

Problem

Problem 5-21:   You represent Banana Corp. Banana wants to acquire Tangerine Corp. in a merger, which would require approval by a majority of the Tangerine common shares. Tangerine common stock is listed on the New York Stock Exchange.   There are 20 million shares of Tangerine stock outstanding, owned by several thousand shareholders, none of whom owns more than 1% of the stock. For the past year, the trading price of Tangerine stock has been remarkably stable, always around $10 per share. *If Banana offers to pay $10 for each share of Tangerine stock in the merger, do you think that Tangerine's shareholders will approve the merger? Why or why not? If not, what price should Banana offer?*

§ 5.05   DISTRIBUTIONS AND DIVIDENDS

Objectives: You should be able to:

• *Explain what a corporate "distribution" is and some reasons why a corporation may approve a distribution such as a cash dividend.*

• *Given (1) the aggregate amount of a cash dividend approved by a corporation's board of directors to be paid to the common shareholders and (2) the number of outstanding shares of each class of the corporation's stock (and, if there are shares of preferred stock, the rights and preferences of the preferred stock), determine how much will be paid to a holder of one share of common stock.*

• *Given (1) the corporation's balance sheet and (2) information about whether the corporation has any outstanding shares of preferred stock that have liquidation preferences, determine the maximum amount of cash dividends that the corporation legally may pay.*

• *Explain to a member of the corporation's board of directors what adverse consequences may result for her if she approves a dividend in excess of what may legally be paid.*

A *distribution*, commonly but somewhat imprecisely referred to as a *dividend*, involves a payment by the corporation, either in the form of cash or something else, to the shareholders with respect to their shares. In other words, shares of the same class share (pun intended) in dividends on a pro rata basis. To take a simple example, if a corporation has only common stock, of which there are 100 shares outstanding, and declares an aggregate dividend of $1,000, then $10 will be paid with respect to each share of common stock. If you own two shares, you will receive $20; if I own four shares, I will receive $40; and so on. You can then use your $20 for whatever you wish (although it is taxable income): the money no longer belongs to the corporation.

Wait a minute, you may be thinking, why would a corporation essentially give away its money? Wouldn't it be better off using the money to pay down its debts, invest in new lines of business, or even simply keep the money in the bank to earn interest? Well, keep in mind that the traditional view of corporate law is that the purpose of a corporation is to benefit its shareholders financially. If the corporation has "excess" funds on hand, the board thus has a decision to make: should the corporation keep these funds and reinvest them in its business, or should the corporation give some or all of these funds to the shareholders? This essentially boils down to a business decision; the board must decide what is the best use of the money.

It is difficult to make generalizations here, as every corporation will have to consider its own circumstances in deciding whether to pay dividends and, if so, what amount. Nonetheless, it is common for new, growing corporations not to pay any dividends at all, instead using earnings and other funds to "grow" the business. In doing so, the hope is that the shareholders will be better off in the long run due to the growth in the value of their stock as the company expands. On the other hand, many established, profitable companies regularly pay dividends to their shareholders and many shareholders buy stock in such corporations in part because of their expectations that they will receive dividends. But there is no guarantee that dividends will continue. As noted above, this is a decision that the board must make. In addition, there are some legal issues that must be addressed, to which we will now turn.

A.   THE MODERN APPROACH UNDER THE MBCA

In Section 5.04(B) above, you saw that the MBCA does not require that there be a par value for a corporation's stock. Fortunately, this simplifies the legal analysis of dividends greatly. MBCA § 6.40(c) contains *two* tests that the corporation must be able to pass in order legally to pay a dividend. First, *after* paying a dividend, the corporation must remain able to "pay its debts as they become due in the usual course of business." Setting aside the fact that there doesn't seem to be any difference between the "usual" course of business and the "ordinary" course of business, the point is this: the corporation can't pay so much in dividends that it would be unable to pay its bills. Making this determination will obviously be very fact-intensive, and you would need a great deal of information about what expenses the corporation incurs in the "usual" course.

But, even if it can pass this "insolvency" text, there is another test. MBCA § 6.40(c)(2) states that a dividend may not be paid if, *afterwards*, the corporation's total assets would be less than the sum of (1) its total liabilities and (2) "the amount that would be needed, if the corporation were to be dissolved at the time of the distribution, to satisfy the preferential rights upon dissolution of shareholders whose preferential rights are superior to those receiving the distribution." This is sometimes called the "balance sheet test," because it obviously will require us to look at the company's balance sheet and the effect that a dividend will have on it.

What will that effect be? If a dividend involves the corporation giving money away, then clearly its assets will decrease. Keeping in mind that a balance sheet must always balance, we obviously need something on the other side of the balance sheet to decrease by the same amount. Will it be liabilities or will it be shareholders' equity? Hopefully, when you remember that shareholders are owners and not creditors, you will understand why "liabilities" is the wrong answer to this question.

That leaves us to decipher the meaning of clause (2) above, which talks about shareholders who have "preferential rights" to those who are receiving the distribution. If the dividend is being paid to the common shareholders, what shareholders might have such "preferential rights"? That's right, the preferred stock. Thus, if a corporation doesn't actually have any preferred stock, then clause (2) is irrelevant. If it does have preferred stock, then you must figure out how much you would need to pay—if the corporation were to be dissolved today—to the preferred stock to satisfy their liquidation preferences. That amount, plus the amount of the corporation's liabilities, must always be "kept back" in the form of assets. Although the corporation isn't being dissolved, when it pays a dividend it must always make sure that its assets[*] remain sufficient to pay the claims of people who are "superior" to the people receiving the dividend. Assuming that that made sense, see if you can solve the following problems.

---

[*]   Note that "assets" in this context means the total amount of assets that appear on the company's balance sheet, whether they consist of cash, land, or anything else.

Problems

Problem 5-22: The only outstanding shares of Grape Corp. stock are 2,000 shares of common stock. Grape's most recent balance sheet shows that it has $100,000 of assets, $70,000 of liabilities, and shareholders' equity of $30,000. *What is the maximum amount of dividends that Grape Corp. could pay on its common stock and pass the "balance sheet test" of MBCA § 6.40(c)(2)? What is the per-share amount of that dividend?*

Problem 5-23: Same facts as Problem 5-22, except that Grape Corp. also has 1,000 shares of preferred stock outstanding, which have a $5 per share liquidation preference. *What is the maximum amount of dividends that Grape Corp. could pay on its common stock and pass the "balance sheet test" of MBCA § 6.40(c)(2)?*

Problem 5-24: The only outstanding shares of Orange Corp. stock are 7,000 shares of common stock. Orange's most recent balance sheet shows that it has $160,000 of assets and $70,000 of liabilities. *What is the maximum amount of dividends that Orange Corp. could pay on its common stock and pass the "balance sheet test" of MBCA § 6.40(c)(2)?*

Problem 5-25: Same facts as Problem 5-24, except that Orange Corp. also has 3,000 shares of preferred stock outstanding, which have a $7 per share liquidation preference. *What is the maximum amount of dividends that Orange Corp. could pay on its common stock and pass the "balance sheet test" of MBCA § 6.40(c)(2)?*

Problem 5-26: Same facts as Problem 5-24. *What is the maximum amount of dividends that Orange Corp. could pay on its <u>preferred</u> stock and still pass the "balance sheet test" of MBCA § 6.40(c)(2)?*

B.   OTHER APPROACHES (INCLUDING DELAWARE)

Although your professor may only expect you to know the MBCA approach to dividends for exam purposes, it is still useful to understand that many other states, including the important state of Delaware, take a very different approach to dividends. This approach is more complicated because of par value. Recall that par value is the minimum per-share amount that the corporation must receive when it issues new shares of stock. If the corporation has

> **PAR VALUE**
>
> As noted in the text, ***par value*** is the minimum amount that the corporation must receive when it issues shares of stock. The MBCA, as well as several states, no longer require par value. However, even in states that require par value, it could be set very low, even $0.01

common stock with a par value of $10 per share, it must receive at least $10 per share when it issues and sells new shares of common stock. Of course, the corporation will want to sell shares for the highest price that it can (and that purchasers are willing to pay).

Assume that a newly formed corporation issues 1,000 shares of common stock (which have a $10 par value per share) for $50 per share, for a total of $50,000. This will result in the shareholder's equity portion of the balance sheet being a bit more detailed than you encountered in Chapter 1. In this example, the par value amount of $10,000 (1,000 shares multiplied by $10 per share) will be allocated to "stated capital," sometimes called "paid-in capital," and the remaining $40,000 of the aggregate issuance price will be allocated to "capital surplus." Thereafter, if the company is profitable and its assets increase more than its liabilities, this excess will appear in the shareholders' equity portion of the balance sheet as "earned surplus." (Conversely, if the company's liabilities increase more than its assets, then it would have an "accumulated deficit.") The importance of these figures is that in states that follow such a "legal capital" system, the amount of dividends that the company may pay is determined by referring to these figures. Basically, corporations are allowed to pay dividends out of their surplus (whether capital surplus or earned surplus), but not out of their stated capital. It's as if the stated capital acts as a "cushion" that the corporation must always retain, in case it needs to use it to pay creditors (but not to pay dividends to shareholders).

For example, consider Section 170(a)(1) of the Delaware General Corporation Law. This statute, which of course applies to any corporation that is incorporated under Delaware law, provides that the directors may pay dividends either (1) out of the corporation's surplus or (2) if there is no surplus, "out of its net profits for the fiscal year in which the dividend is declared and/or the preceding fiscal year."[*]   Delaware defines "surplus" as the excess of the corporation's net assets (i.e., the difference between its total assets and its total liabilities) over the amount of its capital. Meanwhile, if the corporation's shares have a par value,[**] then "capital" is defined as the par value of the shares multiplied by the number of outstanding shares plus, if the board so chooses, any additional part of the consideration the company received when the shares were sold. Thus, for example, assume that 123 Corp., a new corporation, sold 1,000 shares of $10 par value stock for an issuance price of $25 per share. Assume further that a year later, its total assets are $31,000, its total liabilities are $5,000, and that the shareholders' equity portion of its balance sheet is made up of (1) stated capital of $10,000, (2) capital surplus of $15,000, and (3) earned surplus of $1,000. (Do you see why?) Here, the corporation's net assets would be $26,000 (which is $31,000 minus $5,000). The amount of its "capital" under the Delaware statute is $10,000. It could pay the difference between these two amounts, $16,000, as dividends. In effect, the maximum amount of dividends that it could pay is the sum of its capital surplus and its earned surplus.

Again, the MBCA does away with the notion of par value and all of these resulting complications for dividend payments. This likely makes life somewhat easier for law students, as well as lawyers advising corporations that are incorporated in states that follow the MBCA approach.

C.   OTHER ISSUES WITH DIVIDENDS

Let's say that the board of directors, while understanding these tests, chooses to ignore them and pay a greater amount of dividends than the statute would permit. This sounds foolish of course, but people have done worse things and maybe these directors also own shares of the corporation's stock and want to be paid high dividends. Who enforces the statute? Examine MBCA § 8.33 and solve the following problem.

Problem

Problem 5-27: The board of directors of Strawberry Corp. was advised by the company's accountants and lawyers that the maximum amount of dividends that the corporation could pay was $10,000. Nonetheless, the board declared total dividends of

---

[*]   Clause (2) is sometimes referred as "nimble dividends" and won't be discussed further.

[**]   Even for shares that don't have a par value, the board must designate part of the issuance price of the shares as capital. If the board fails to do so, then the full issuance price is considered to be capital. Again, though, the MBCA does away with these concepts.

$15,000 and the corporation paid this amount to its shareholders. *What is the board's liability, if any? If the board members are liable, to whom are they liable? Will any of the shareholders who received the dividend be liable to repay it?*

A careful reader may have noticed that the statute does not require that corporations follow GAAP (see Chapter 1) when preparing their financial statements (although subsection (d) of MBCA § 6.40 does state that the board may base its determination that a dividend is legal either on "financial statements prepared on the basis of accounting practices and principles that are reasonable in the circumstances or on a fair valuation or other method that is reasonable in the circumstances"). Aware of this, many sophisticated creditors will insist on protections beyond what MBCA § 6.40(c) or other applicable statutes provide. For example, it is very common for banks, when making a loan to a corporation, to prohibit the corporation from paying *any* dividends until the loan is fully repaid.

Finally, a careful reader will also have noticed that MBCA § 6.40(c) uses the word "distribution" rather than "dividend." MBCA § 1.40(6) defines a distribution as:

> a direct or indirect transfer of money or other property (except its own shares) ... to or for the benefit of its shareholders in respect of any of its shares. A distribution may be in the form of a declaration or payment of a dividend; a purchase, redemption, or other acquisition of shares; a distribution of indebtedness; or otherwise.

One effect of this statute is that if a corporation wishes to repurchase shares, the statute treats the repurchase as a dividend, which means that the corporation must ensure that it will "pass" the two tests of MBCA § 6.40(c) when doing so. However, note that stock splits and stock dividends are not considered to be distributions under this definition.

§ 5.06 PIERCING THE CORPORATE VEIL AND ENTERPRISE LIABILITY

insolvency

Objectives: *Given a fact pattern involving an insolvent corporation, you should be able to (1) identify the arguments that a corporate creditor will make to convince the court to "pierce the corporate veil" (i.e., impose personal liability on the corporation's shareholder(s) for the debt), (2) identify the arguments that the shareholder(s) will make to convince the court <u>not</u> to pierce the* *corporate veil, and (3) evaluate whether the court should pierce the corporate veil.*

Subsidiary Objectives: *You should also be able to:*

●	*Identify the factors used by courts to justify piercing the corporate veil and why these factors are important to that decision.*

●	*Explain to a client who is a shareholder (1) some things that she should do, and (2) some things that she should avoid, with the goal of making a future veil-piercing claim less likely to be successful.*

●	*Explain to a client (a bank) that is considering making a loan to a closely held corporation some steps to take to make the repayment of the loan more likely.*

●	*Explain to a client that is a parent corporation with two or more subsidiaries some steps to take to help ensure that (1) the parent corporation will not be held liable for the obligations of a subsidiary, and (2) no subsidiary will be held liable for the obligations of any other subsidiary.*

As you have seen repeatedly so far in this textbook, one of the chief benefits of running a business as a corporation, as opposed to a partnership or sole proprietorship, is that the shareholders enjoy limited liability. If the corporation's debts exceed its assets, then the general rule is that the corporation's creditors may not recover the unpaid amounts from the shareholders. From the shareholder's perspective, the worst thing that could happen is that the corporation files for bankruptcy protection and the common stock is "wiped out." But that's as bad as it gets—the shareholder's personal assets are not at risk of being seized to pay corporate debts.

When one first encounters this rule, it seems a bit unfair because it may allow business owners to shift some costs from themselves onto outsiders if the company is unable to pay. (Economists call these costs "externalities.") For example, imagine a manufacturing company that produces dangerous products that injure several hundred consumers. These victims then sue the corporation for their injuries, but the corporation's assets are woefully inadequate to pay the plaintiffs' claimed damages. As they say, you can't get blood from a stone. If the manufacturing company's shareholders, who may have been enriched through dividends during the corporation's existence, do not have to pay for the amount of the damages that the corporation cannot pay, then the plaintiffs will not be fully compensated for their injuries. Business risks and costs have thus been shifted from the owners to outsiders.

Of course, there must be offsetting benefits to the corporate form; otherwise, the law would not permit corporations to exist. One of the main arguments in favor of limited liability is that it encourages large-scale enterprises that can attract capital from investors who can rest assured that they only risk their investment, not any of their other assets. Following the industrial revolution, the scale of business greatly increased compared to earlier times. The extensive financing needs of large industrial corporations meant that they needed to seek capital (that is, investments) from dozens, hundreds, or even thousands of investors. These investments would not be forthcoming if potential investors, the great majority of whom did not expect to be involved in managing the business and therefore could not oversee it, feared that the business's failure would expose them to personal liability. Obviously, a partnership is not a viable way to operate such an enterprise. If the law had never developed beyond partnerships and sole proprietorships, many of the marvels of the modern age would likely never have seen the light of day. Instead, we'd all still be using horses and buggies.

There are, of course, several other policy reasons supporting the general rule that shareholders are not personally liable for the corporation's debts, but let's now look at some exceptions to this general rule. First, note MBCA § 6.22(b), which provides that "[u]nless otherwise provided in the articles of incorporation, a shareholder of a corporation is not personally liable for the acts or debts of the corporation except that he may become personally liable by reason of his own acts or conduct." Now, it should be obvious that it would be exceedingly rare to find a corporation whose articles of incorporation make the shareholders liable for some or all its debts. But the last phrase is intriguing. How do you think that phrase affects the following problems?

Problems

Problem 5-28:   Simmons Landscaping, Inc. is a brand new corporation that is wholly owned by Bob Simmons. Bob also serves as the corporation's sole director, its sole officer, and its sole employee although if the business does well he plans to hire other employees some day. Although Bob invested $1,000 to get the company started, the company needs to borrow $10,000 to purchase equipment. *If you represent a bank that is considering making this loan, what would you recommend that the bank do to increase its chances of having the loan fully repaid?*

<u>Problem 5-29</u>:   One day, Bob was out mowing lawns when he negligently ran over the foot of a customer, who was horribly injured. *Is Simmons Landscaping, Inc. liable for this tort? Is Bob personally liable to this customer/victim if the assets of Simmons Landscaping, Inc. are not sufficient to compensate her fully for her injuries?*

Piercing the Corporate Veil.   In addition, there is another situation in which a shareholder of a corporation may end up being personally liable for one or more of the debts of the corporation, a doctrine known as ***piercing the corporate veil.*** Think of the "corporate veil" as the general rule of shareholder non-liability; it protects shareholders from the corporation's debts. If a court allows a creditor to pierce the corporate veil, then what has happened is that one or more of the shareholders[*] will be personally liable for what is otherwise a corporate debt.

Well, you may ask, why doesn't the corporation simply pay its debts? After all, a corporation is a legal "person," which means it is liable for its debts and may be sued if it doesn't pay them (assuming the debts are valid and the corporation doesn't have any defenses to payment). Why do we have to drag the shareholders into this? The obvious answer is that in a veil-piercing situation the corporation *can't* pay its debts—it doesn't have the money. As stated above, you can't get blood from a stone. When you reflect that there are a great many insolvent corporations out there, it probably shouldn't surprise you to learn that there are literally thousands of reported court decisions involving veil-piercing.

Which presents another problem. How can you possibly learn about all of these decisions in a textbook such as this? You can't. Chances are, when you go to practice law in the state of your choice, the law of that state will be different, perhaps slightly but perhaps greatly, from what you will learn here. But the following case is as good an example of veil-piercing as you are likely to find. When reading it, be sure to ask yourself *which* of the debtor-corporation's shareholders end up being personally liable for its debts.

---

[*]   Some courts and other authorities note that veil piercing may be used to impose liability for a corporation's debts on its directors or officers as well. However, as will become clear as you read the following materials, these are often the same people in a closely held corporation.

DeWitt Truck Brokers, Inc. v. W. Ray Flemming Fruit Co.
United States Court of Appeals, Fourth Circuit
540 F.2d 681 (1976)

[Author's note: As stated in more detail below, the plaintiff, DeWitt Truck Brokers, Inc., provided transportation services to the defendant corporation, W. Ray Flemming Fruit Company. The defendant corporation sold fruit for farmers. It did not purchase the fruit from the farmers; instead, it sold the produce as the farmers' agent in return for a sales commission. When the fruit was sold, the W. Ray Flemming Fruit Company remitted to the farmer the sales price of the fruit, minus transportation costs and its sales commission. Plaintiff sued both the defendant corporation and its majority shareholder, W. Ray Flemming, when they failed to pay for approximately $15,000 of transportation services provided by the plaintiff.]

RUSSELL, Circuit Judge: In this action on debt, the plaintiff seeks, by piercing the corporate veil under the law of South Carolina, to impose individual liability on the president [and majority shareholder] of the indebted corporation individually [because the corporation is insolvent].   The District Court, making findings of fact which may be overturned only if clearly erroneous, pierced the corporate veil and imposed individual liability.   The individual defendant appeals. We affirm.

At the outset, it is recognized that a corporation is an entity, separate and distinct from its officers and stockholders, and that its debts are not the individual indebtedness of its stockholders.   This is expressed in the presumption that the corporation and its stockholders are separate and distinct.   [Citations omitted.] And this oft-stated principle is equally applicable, whether the corporation has many or only one stockholder.   But this concept of separate entity is merely a legal theory, "introduced for purposes of convenience and to subserve the ends of justice," and the courts "decline to recognize (it) whenever recognition of the corporate form would extend the principle of incorporation 'beyond its legitimate purposes and (would) produce injustices or inequitable consequences.'" [Citations omitted.]   Accordingly, "in an appropriate case and in furtherance of the ends of justice," the corporate veil will be pierced and the corporation and its stockholders "will be treated as identical." [Citation omitted.]

This power to pierce the corporate veil, though, is to be exercised "reluctantly" and "cautiously" and the burden of establishing a basis for the disregard of the corporate fiction rests on the party asserting such claim. [Citation omitted.]

The circumstances which have been considered significant by the courts in actions to disregard the corporate fiction have been "rarely articulated with any clarity." [Citation omitted.] Perhaps this is true because the circumstances "necessarily vary according to the circumstances of each case," and every case where the issue is raised is to be regarded as "sui generis (to) * * * be decided in accordance with its own underlying facts." Since the issue is thus one of fact, its resolution "is particularly within the province of the trial court" and such resolution will be regarded as "presumptively correct and (will) be left undisturbed on appeal unless it is clearly erroneous." [Citations omitted.]

Contrary to the basic contention of the defendant, however, proof of plain fraud is not a necessary element in a finding to disregard the corporate entity. This was made clear in Anderson v. Abbott, [321 U.S. 349 (1944)], where the Court, after stating that "fraud" has often been found to be a ground for disregarding the principle of limited liability based on the corporate fiction, declared:

> *** The cases of fraud make up part of that exception (which allow the corporate veil to be pierced, citing cases). But they do not exhaust it. An obvious inadequacy of capital, measured by the nature and magnitude of the corporate undertaking, has frequently been an important factor in cases denying stockholders their defense of limited liability." (Italics added.)

***

On the other hand, equally as well settled as is the principle that plain fraud is not a necessary prerequisite for piercing the corporate veil is the rule that the mere fact that all or almost all of the corporate stock is owned by one individual or a few individuals, will not afford sufficient grounds for disregarding corporateness. [Citations omitted.] But when substantial ownership of all the stock of a corporation in a single individual is combined with other factors clearly supporting disregard of the corporate fiction on grounds of fundamental equity and fairness, courts have experienced "little difficulty" and have shown no hesitancy in applying what is described as the "alter ego" or "instrumentality" theory in order to cast aside the corporate shield and to fasten liability on the individual stockholder. [Citation omitted.]

But, in applying the "instrumentality" or "alter ego" doctrine, the courts are concerned with reality and not form, with how the corporation operated and the individual defendant's relationship to that operation. [Citation omitted.] *** And the authorities have indicated certain facts which are to be given substantial weight in this connection. One fact which all the authorities consider significant in the inquiry, and particularly so in the case of the one-man or closely-held corporation, is whether the corporation was grossly undercapitalized for the purposes of the corporate undertaking. [Citations omitted.] And, "(t)he obligation

Concentration of ownership

FACTORS

to provide adequate capital begins with incorporation and is a continuing obligation thereafter *** during the corporation's operations." [Citation omitted.] Other factors that are emphasized in the application of the doctrine are failure to observe corporate formalities, non-payment of dividends, the insolvency of the debtor corporation at the time, siphoning of funds of the corporation by the dominant stockholder, non-functioning of other officers or directors, absence of corporate records, and the fact that the corporation is merely a facade for the operations of the dominant stockholder or stockholders.   The conclusion to disregard the corporate entity may not, however, rest on a single factor, whether undercapitalization, disregard of corporation's formalities, or what-not, but must involve a number of such factors; in addition, it must present an element of injustice or fundamental unfairness.   But undercapitalization, coupled with disregard of corporate formalities, lack of participation on the part of the other stockholders, and the failure to pay dividends while paying substantial sums, whether by way of salary or otherwise, to the dominant stockholder, all fitting into a picture of basic unfairness, has been regarded fairly uniformly to constitute a basis for an imposition of individual liability under the doctrine.   [Citations omitted.]

undercapital.

***

If these factors, which were deemed significant in other cases concerned with this same issue, are given consideration here, the finding of the District Court that the corporate entity should be disregarded was not clearly erroneous. Certainly the corporation was, in practice at least, a close, one-man corporation from the very beginning. Its incorporators were the defendant Flemming, his wife and his attorney. It began in 1962 with a capitalization of 5,000 shares, issued for a consideration of one dollar each. In some manner which Flemming never made entirely clear, approximately 2,000 shares were retired. At the times involved here Flemming owned approximately 90% of the corporation's outstanding stock, according to his own testimony, though this was not verified by any stock records. Flemming was obscure on who the other stockholders were and how much stock these other stockholders owned, giving at different times conflicting statements as to who owned stock and how much. His testimony on who were the officers and directors was hardly more direct. He testified that the corporation did have one other director, Ed Bernstein, a resident of New York. It is significant, however, that, whether Bernstein was nominally a director or not, there were no corporate records of a real directors' meeting in all the years of the corporation's existence and Flemming conceded this to be true. Flemming countered this by testifying that Bernstein traveled a great deal and that his contacts with Bernstein were generally by telephone. The evidence indicates rather clearly that Bernstein was "nothing more than (a) figurehead(s)," who had "attended no directors meeting," and even more crucial, never received any fee or reimbursement of expenses or salary of any kind from the corporation.

The District Court found, also, that the corporation never had a stockholders' meeting. *** It is thus clear that corporate formalities, even rudimentary formalities, were not observed by the defendant.

Beyond the absence of any observance of corporate formalities is the purely personal matter in which the corporation was operated. No stockholder or officer of the corporation other than Flemming ever received any salary, dividend, or fee from the corporation, or, for that matter, apparently exercised any voice in its operation or decisions. In all the years of the corporation's existence, Flemming was the sole beneficiary of its operations and its continued existence was for his exclusive benefit. During these years he was receiving from $15,000 to $25,000 each year from a corporation, which, during most of the time, was showing no profit and apparently had no working capital. Moreover, the payments to Flemming were authorized under no resolution of the board of directors of the corporation, as recorded in any minutes of a board meeting. Actually, it would seem that Flemming's withdrawals varied with what could be taken out of the corporation at the moment: If this amount were $15,000, that was Flemming's withdrawal; if it were $25,000, that was his withdrawal.

To summarize: The District Court found, and there was evidence to sustain the findings, that there was here a complete disregard of "corporate formalities" in the operation of the corporation, which functioned, not for the benefit of all stockholders, but only for the financial advantage of Flemming, who was the sole stockholder to receive one penny of profit from the corporation in the decade or more that it operated, and who made during that period all the corporate decisions and dominated the corporation's operations.

That the corporation was undercapitalized, if indeed it were not without any real capital, seems obvious. Its original stated "risk capital" had long since been reduced to approximately $3,000[*] by a reduction in the outstanding capital, or at least this would seem to be inferable from the record, and even this, it seems fair to conclude, had been seemingly exhausted by a long succession of years when the corporation operated at no profit. The inability of the corporation to pay a dividend is persuasive proof of this want of capital. In fact, the defendant Flemming makes no effort to refute the evidence of want of any capital reserves on the part of the corporation. It appears patent that the corporation was actually operating at all times involved here on someone else's capital. This conclusion follows from a consideration of the manner in which Flemming operated in the name of the corporation during the year when plaintiff's indebtedness was incurred.

---

[*]   [Footnote by author]: As the court stated, when the corporation was formed, it issued 5,000 shares of stock for $1 each. However, the corporation later redeemed 2,000 shares, presumably for a $2,000 payment. Thus, it appears that Mr. Flemming had only invested a total of $3,000 in the company which he stood to lose if the company were to dissolve.

***

The corporation was engaged in the business of a commission agent, selling fruit produce for the account of growers of farm products such as peaches and watermelons in the Edgefield, South Carolina, area. It never purported to own such products; to repeat, it (always acting through Flemming) sold the products as agent for the growers. Under the arrangement with the growers, it was to remit to the grower the full sale price, less any transportation costs incurred in transporting the products from the growers' farm or warehouse to the purchaser and its sales commission. An integral part of these collections was, as stated, represented by the plaintiff's transportation charges. Accordingly, during the period involved here, the corporation had as operating funds seemingly only its commissions and the amount of the plaintiff's transportation charges, for which the corporation had claimed credit in its settlement with its growers. At the time, however, Flemming was withdrawing funds from the corporation at the rate of at least $15,000 per year; and doing this, even though he must have known that the corporation could only do this by withholding payment of the transportation charges due the plaintiff, which in the accounting [i.e., invoice or account statement] with the growers Flemming represented had been paid the plaintiff. And, it is of some interest that the amount due the plaintiff for transportation costs was approximately the same as the $15,000 minimum annual salary the defendant testified he was paid by the corporation. Were the opinion of the District Court herein to be reversed, Flemming would be permitted to retain substantial sums from the operations of the corporation without having any real capital in the undertaking, risking nothing of his own and using as operating capital what he had collected as due the plaintiff. Certainly, equity and fundamental justice support individual liability of Flemming for plaintiff's charges, payment for which he asserted in his accounting with the growers that he had paid and for which he took credit on such accounting. This case patently presents a blending of the very factors which courts have regarded as justifying a disregard of the corporate entity in furtherance of basic and fundamental fairness.

Finally, it should not be overlooked that at some point during the period when this indebtedness was being incurred *** the plaintiff became concerned about former delays in receipt of payment for its charges and, to allay that concern, Flemming stated to the plaintiff, *** that "he (i.e., Flemming) would take care of (the charges) personally, if the corporation failed to do so ***." On this assurance, the plaintiff contended that it continued to haul for the defendant. *** This assurance was given for the obvious purpose of promoting the individual advantage of Flemming. This follows because the only person who could profit from the continued operation of the corporation was Flemming. When one, who is the sole beneficiary of a corporation's operations and who dominates it, as did Flemming in this case, induces a creditor to extend credit to the corporation on such an assurance as given here, that fact has been considered by many authorities sufficient basis for piercing the corporate veil. [Citations omitted.] The only argument against this view is bottomed on the statute of frauds. [Citation omitted.] But reliance on such statute is often regarded as without merit in a case where the promise or assurance is given "at the time or before the debt is created," for in that case the promise is original and without the statute. [Citation omitted.] A number of courts, including South Carolina, however, have gone further and have held that, where the promisor owns substantially all the stock of the corporation and seeks by his promise to serve his personal pecuniary advantage, the question whether such promise is "within the statute of frauds" is a fact question to be resolved by the trial court and this is true whether the promise was made before the debt was incurred or during the time it was being incurred. [Citations omitted.] This is that type of case and may well have been resolved on this issue.

For the reasons stated, we conclude that the findings of the District Court herein are not clearly erroneous and the judgment of the District Court is [affirmed].

Questions About *DeWitt Truck Brokers*

1.   Beside Ray Flemming, who were the other shareholders of W. Ray Flemming Fruit Co.? Were they liable for the unpaid $15,000 debt?

2.   What are "corporate formalities"? What were the corporate formalities that Mr. Flemming and the corporation did not observe? Did this failure make it less likely that the corporation could pay the debt?

3.   Would DeWitt Truck Brokers have been a more "sympathetic" plaintiff if it had been a tort creditor instead of a contract creditor? For example, would the case have been more readily decided in the plaintiff's favor if an employee of the W. Ray Flemming Fruit Co. had negligently damaged some property owned by DeWitt Truck Brokers?

4.   Why does the court care about the fact that W. Ray Flemming Fruit Co. didn't pay dividends? Wouldn't *not* paying dividends make it more likely that it would have been able to pay the money it owed to DeWitt Truck Brokers?

5.   Traditionally, the board of directors must set the salaries of corporate officers. How was Mr. Flemming's salary determined?

6.   Was the W. Ray Flemming Fruit Co. "adequately capitalized"? How do you know whether a corporation is adequately capitalized? At what time do we decide whether a corporation is adequately capitalized?

7.   Is fraud necessary to pierce the corporate veil?

8.   What could DeWitt Truck Brokers have done differently to make it more likely it would be paid, without having to sue?

9.   What could Mr. Flemming have done differently to make it less likely the corporate veil would be pierced?

As you might gather from reading *DeWitt Truck Brokers* and thinking about the above questions, veil-piercing is a "messy" topic. Courts (not just this one) love to use phrases like "alter ego" and words like "instrumentality" and they really love to use lists of factors. *DeWitt Truck Brokers* gives us a rather lengthy list of factors to consider (and, depending on one's reading of the case, also requires that there be an "element of injustice or fundamental unfairness") in order to pierce the veil.

Other courts use longer lists. For example, in *Laya v. Erin Homes, Inc.*, 352 S.E.2d 93 (W. Va. 1986), the court wrote:

"Piercing the corporate veil" is an equitable remedy, the propriety of which must be examined on an ad hoc basis. [Citation omitted.] Some of the factors to be considered in deciding whether to pierce the corporate veil are:

(1)   commingling of funds and other assets of the corporation with those of the individual shareholders;

(2)   diversion of the corporation's funds or assets to noncorporate uses (to the personal uses of the corporation's shareholders);

(3)   failure to maintain the corporate formalities necessary for the issuance of or subscription to the corporation's stock, such as formal approval of the stock issue by the board of directors;

(4)   an individual shareholder representing to persons outside the corporation that he or she is personally liable for the debts or other obligations of the corporation;

(5)   failure to maintain corporate minutes or adequate corporate records;

(6)   identical equitable ownership in two entities;

(7)   identity of the directors and officers of two entities who are responsible for supervision and management ***;

(8)   failure to adequately capitalize a corporation for the reasonable risks of the corporate undertaking;

(9)   absence of separately held corporate assets;

(10)   use of a corporation as a mere shell or conduit to operate a single venture or some particular aspect of the business of an individual or another corporation;

(11)   sole ownership of all the stock by one individual or members of a single family;

(12)   use of the same office or business location by the corporation and its individual shareholder(s);

(13)   employment of the same employees or attorney by the corporation and its shareholder(s);

(14)   concealment or misrepresentation of the identity of the ownership, management or financial interests in the corporation, and concealment of personal business activities of the shareholders (sole shareholders do not reveal the association with a corporation, which makes loans to them without adequate security);

(15)   disregard of legal formalities and failure to maintain proper arm's length relationships among related entities;

(16)   use of a corporate entity as a conduit to procure labor, services or merchandise for another person or entity;

(17)   diversion of corporate assets from the corporation by or to a stockholder or other person or entity to the detriment

of creditors, or the manipulation of assets and liabilities between entities to concentrate the assets in one and the liabilities in another;

(18)   contracting by the corporation with another person with the intent to avoid the risk of nonperformance by use of the corporate entity; or the use of a corporation as a subterfuge for illegal transactions; [and]

(19)   the formation and use of the corporation to assume the existing liabilities of another person or entity. [Citation omitted.]

There are many problems with "list" cases beyond the fact that law students fear the possibility of having to remember them on an exam. For one thing, many of the factors seem to overlap. Also, it often is unclear how many factors on the list are needed to pierce the corporate veil (one? several? a majority?) and whether some factors on the list are more important than others. Using a list also raises the possibility that it might be applied mechanically, with little thought given to the *purpose* behind the list or *why* a given factor is important. In a perfect world, courts would be more explicit about the policy reasons behind some of these factors.

Professor Franklin Gevurtz of McGeorge School of Law tries to step into this breach in his treatise *Corporation Law* (2nd ed. 2010). At the risk of oversimplifying his arguments, Professor Gevurtz points out that contract creditors are much better equipped than tort victims to protect themselves when dealing with a corporation. For example, before agreeing to a contract or other transaction with a corporation, they could ask to see its financial statements, ask its shareholders to personally guarantee performance of the contract, or charge higher fees to compensate them for the risk of nonperformance. If they fail to do these things, then one could argue that they have impliedly agreed to look *only* to the corporation for performance and should not be allowed to pierce the veil. On the other hand, if they have been misled by the corporation or the corporation has engaged in fraud or the shareholders improperly use corporate resources (thus lessening the corporation's ability to pay), then veil-piercing should be appropriate. Tort victims, on the other hand, do not have the same luxury of being able to plan ahead; one can hardly say "wait, don't hit me with that truck until I check out your financial ability to pay my medical bills!" So, in an effort to encourage corporations to "internalize" risks, Professor Gevurtz argues that a primary inquiry in these types of veil-piercing cases should be whether the corporation was adequately capitalized, including liability insurance, for its reasonably foreseeable risks.

Nonetheless, courts remain fond of lists in veil-piercing cases. They are perhaps a bit less fond of giving us a principled way of deciding whether the veil should be pierced and often don't tailor the lists for whether the case involves a contract creditor or a tort victim. Accordingly, veil-piercing litigation is an area where your skills as a lawyer will be exceedingly important. But how will the case turn out? In all but the clearest cases, one can only guess.

That said, there are a few things that can definitely be said about veil piercing. First, this is a doctrine that only applies if the debtor corporation is closely held. In Chapter 9, you will learn about closely held corporations, but here it is sufficient to define them as corporations that have a small number (e.g., three or four) of shareholders. In fact, there apparently is no reported decision in which a plaintiff-creditor successfully argued to pierce the veil of a corporation that had more than nine shareholders. *See* Robert B. Thompson, *Piercing the Corporate Veil Within Corporate Groups: Corporate Shareholders as Mere Investors*, 3 CONN. J. INT'L L. 379, 383 (1999); *see also* Robert B. Thompson, *Piercing the Corporate Veil: An Empirical Study*, 76 CORNELL L. REV. 1036 (1991) (examining 1,600 reported veil-piercing decisions).

Second, some states have begun to deemphasize the importance of whether the corporation observed "corporate formalities" in veil-piercing cases. There are statutes in some states, particularly with respect to LLCs rather than corporations, that provide that disregarding formalities should not be considered in veil-piercing cases. *See* Revised Uniform Limited Liability Company Act § 304(b). *Cf.* MBCA § 7.32(f). Third, Professor Thompson's study (cited above) reports that veil-piercing occurred in approximately 40% of the many cases that he examined, but that it was actually *less* likely in tort cases than in contract cases.

What if the shareholder of the debtor corporation isn't an individual like W. Ray Flemming in the *DeWitt Truck Brokers* case, but is itself a corporation? As noted at the beginning of this chapter, if a majority of a corporation's stock is owned by another corporation, then the first corporation a "subsidiary" and the second corporation is a "parent." But just because the parent is a corporation doesn't mean it's not a shareholder like anyone else. Accordingly, if the subsidiary is insolvent, creditors of the subsidiary may attempt to pierce the subsidiary's veil and make the parent liable for the subsidiary's debts. Should this situation be treated differently than where the shareholder(s) is (are) an individual(s)? Arguments can be made either way. Some commentators argue that this should be treated as a variant of "enterprise liability" (discussed below) and call for different rules. Others argue that it is not substantially different than a "regular" veil-piercing situation.

In re Silicone Gel Breast Implants Products Liability Litigation, 887 F. Supp. 1447 (N.D. Ala. 1995), is another "list case," albeit one involving whether to pierce the veil of a subsidiary and make the parent corporation liable for products liability claims against the subsidiary. In the case, the parent corporation moved for summary judgment, claiming that it could not be liable for the debts of its wholly owned subsidiary. The court wrote:

> The potential for abuse of the corporate form is greatest when, as here, the corporation is owned by a single shareholder. The evaluation of corporate control claims cannot, however, disregard the fact that, no different from other stockholders, a parent corporation is expected—indeed, required—to exert some control over its subsidiary. Limited liability is the rule, not the exception. [Citation omitted.] However, when a corporation is so controlled as to be the alter ego or mere instrumentality of its stockholder, the corporate form may be disregarded in the interests of justice. So far as this court has been able to determine, some variation of this theory of liability is recognized in all jurisdictions.

> An initial question is whether veil-piercing may ever be resolved by summary judgment. Ordinarily the fact-intensive nature of the issue will require that it be resolved only through a trial. Summary judgment, however, can be proper if *** the evidence presented could lead to but one result. Because [this] court concludes that a jury (or in some jurisdictions, the judge acting in equity) could—and, under the laws of many states, probably should—find that [the subsidiary] was but the alter ego of [the parent], summary judgment must be denied [in this case].

> The totality of circumstances must be evaluated in determining whether a subsidiary may be found to be the alter ego or mere instrumentality of the parent corporation. Although the standards are not identical in each state, all jurisdictions require a showing of substantial domination. Among the factors to be considered are whether:

> • the parent and the subsidiary have common directors or officers

> • the parent and the subsidiary have common business departments

> • the parent and the subsidiary file consolidated financial statements and tax returns

- the parent finances the subsidiary

- the parent caused the incorporation of the subsidiary

- the subsidiary operates with grossly inadequate capital

- the parent pays the salaries and other expenses of the subsidiary

- the subsidiary receives no business except that given to it by the parent

- the parent uses the subsidiary's property as its own

- the daily operations of the two corporations are not kept separate

- the subsidiary does not observe the basic corporate formalities, such as keeping separate books and records and holding shareholder and board meetings.

Id. at 1452.

While some of these factors are similar to those used in *DeWitt Truck Brokers*, query whether all of them "make sense."

Enterprise Liability. A doctrine that is similar to piercing the corporate veil is called *enterprise liability*. Although this term can mean different things in different contexts, you may think of it in the context of this book as "horizontal" veil-piercing. For example, let's assume that you are a pedestrian who is hit by a taxi cab in New York City and suffer serious injuries. But when you sue the corporation that owns the cab that hit you (let's call it Corp. One), you discover that that corporation has very little in the way of assets: mainly just two taxi cabs which haven't been very well maintained. However, you also learn that the corporation is owed by a single shareholder, Mr. Carlton. And—get this—Mr. Carlton also owns *nine* other corporations, each of which owns two taxi cabs, the license to operate the cabs in New York City, and the minimum amount of insurance allowed by law. Moreover, they all operate out of the same garage in New York City using the same dispatching system.

A chart of the organization might look like this:

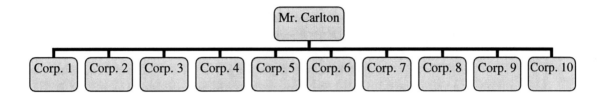

Who will you sue, beyond Corp. One? Why not sue Mr. Carlton? This is what might be called an example of "vertical" veil-piercing, which really just means ordinary veil-piercing. But, while you're at it, why not also sue Corps. Two through Ten, which could be called "brother-sister" corporations to Corp. One? This would be an example of arguing for "horizontal" veil-piercing or, as actual courts call it, enterprise liability. That's exactly what the plaintiff argued in *Walkovsky v. Carlton*, 223 N.E.2d 6 (N.Y. 1966); *see also Walkovsky v. Carlton*, 244 N.E.2d 55 (N.Y. 1968). Unfortunately, while it has great facts, *Walkovsky* isn't entirely clear on the issue of enterprise liability, if only because Corps. Two through Ten didn't move to dismiss the case against them like Mr. Carlton did. But here's how another court dealt with this issue.

Pan Pacific Sash & Door Co. v. Greendale Park, Inc.
California Court of Appeals, Second District, Division 3
333 P.2d 802 (1958)

PATROSSO, Justice pro tem. This is an appeal by the defendants Greendale Park, Inc., and Ralmor Corporation from a judgment in favor of plaintiff in the principal sum of $12,535.96 plus interest on the sum of $16,271.41 from September 1, 1955.

The complaint is in two counts. The first seeks to foreclose a mechanic's lien for the value of sash doors, frames and jambs furnished by plaintiff pursuant to an agreement with defendant Ralmor and used in the construction of residences upon 100 lots in a tract of land owned by the defendant Greendale. The second cause of action is in the form of a common count for goods, wares and merchandise sold and delivered to the appellants. Prior to the trial the first count was dismissed and the case went to trial upon the second cause of action alone. Defendants filed separate answers to the second count. Defendant Greendale denied that it was indebted to the plaintiff in any sum. Ralmor, while admitting that it was indebted to plaintiff, pleaded a counterclaim in the sum of $3,735.45 for damage alleged to have been sustained by it as a result of defective material furnished by the plaintiff.

At the pretrial hearing which was held on May 16, 1957, plaintiff stated that, while not pleaded, plaintiff upon the trial would contend "that the ownership of stock in Ralmor Corporation and Greendale Park, Inc. is the same or substantially the same so as to constitute one corporation the alter ego of the other." [Counsel for the defendant objected but was overruled.] ***

As its first ground for reversal of the judgment Greendale contends that the trial court erred in admitting over its objection evidence designed to establish that it and Ralmor were the alter ego of each other upon the ground that such evidence was outside of the issues made by the pleadings. [This court rejected this argument because, *inter alia*, the defendants were given sufficient advance warning that plaintiff intended to raise this issue.]

***

Greendale next contends that the evidence is insufficient to support the trial court's findings *** to the effect that Ralmor was the alter ego of Greendale. The evidence upon this score may be epitomized as follows:

Ralmor was incorporated in 1951, its sole stockholders being R. L. Blink and his wife and M. S. Hoffberg and his wife, each owning 50 shares of stock which had been issued at its par value of $1 per share. The same parties composed its board of directors. Mr. Blink was at all times its president and treasurer and Mr. Hoffberg was at all times its vice-president and secretary. Greendale was incorporated in August 1954. Its sole stockholders consisted of Mr. Hoffberg and Mr. Blink each owning 250 shares of stock which had been issued at its par value of $1 per share. Its board of directors consisted of Mr. Hoffberg and Mr. Blink and their attorney. The minutes disclose, however, that the latter [the attorney] was not present and did not participate in any meetings of the board of directors subsequent to September 13, 1954. Mr. Hoffberg was at all times its president and Mr. Blink was at all times its vice-president and secretary. The evidence justified the inference that Greendale was organized for the purpose of acquiring a tract of land in the Antelope Valley and building homes thereon. The property in question had been purchased by Messrs. Hoffberg and Blink and it was conveyed to the corporation subject to an encumbrance in the sum of $100,000 in consideration of the issuance by the corporation to Messrs. Hoffberg and Blink of its promissory note in the sum of $45,000. Both corporations' offices were located in the same premises and they had at least some employees in common.

After the transfer to Greendale of the tract of land previously mentioned and on January 20, 1955, Greendale entered into a building construction contract with Ralmor whereby the latter agreed to construct houses on the 100 lots in the tract at cost plus a fee of $500 per house. On the following day Greendale borrowed from the Bank of America $1,194,000 upon its note secured by a trust deed upon the land which sum, under the agreement with the bank, was to be disbursed through an escrow as the construction of the houses on the property progressed. In connection with this loan Greendale, Ralmor, Mr. and Mrs. Blink and Mr. and Mrs. Hoffberg executed an agreement with the bank whereby they jointly and severally guaranteed the construction and completion of each house and the full and complete performance of all work required to be done by the plans and specifications and the payment in full for all labor and materials used in connection with said construction work and the completion of each of said houses free and clear of any and all mechanics' liens. Contemporaneous with the execution of the last mentioned agreement another agreement was executed between the bank and the same parties whereby the latter jointly and severally guaranteed to purchase from the bank for the unpaid principal balance plus accrued interest the loan upon any and all houses which had not been paid in full within nine months from the date thereof. Simultaneously *** Greendale and Ralmor executed a written order to the bank wherein and whereby they authorized the bank to pay to Ralmor *or* Greendale the proceeds of the bank loan as the same was disbursed by it under the loan agreement.

Insofar as the record discloses the only business of the corporations during the period with which we are concerned was the construction of the houses upon the tract in question and the sale thereof. The financial records which were introduced in evidence disclosed numerous loans from Greendale to Ralmor and from Ralmor to Greendale. Both corporations appear to have operated largely on money borrowed from Messrs. Blink and Hoffberg and others including one Greendale who purchased $50,000 of Greendale debentures but under an agreement whereby Blink, Hoffberg and Ralmor agreed to repurchase the same for the principal amount upon Mr. Greendale's demand and they were later so purchased by Blink and Hoffberg. Each corporation was heavily indebted and unable to pay its obligations.

Upon the basis of the foregoing evidence the trial court was warranted in concluding, as it did, that each corporation was but an instrumentality or conduit of the other in the prosecution of a single venture, namely, the construction and sale of houses upon the tract in question. Both corporations had the same stockholders, directors and officers, occupied the same premises as their offices and had common employees. Each was without substantial capital. [Citation omitted.] When Greendale was without funds required for its operation and Ralmor had funds available a loan was made from the latter to the former and vice versa. Each corporation received the benefit of the materials supplied by the plaintiff and incorporated in the houses which were under construction upon the tract. There was such unity of interest and ownership that the separateness of the two corporations had in effect ceased and an adherence to the fiction of a separate existence of the two corporations would, under the circumstances here present, promote injustice and make it inequitable for Greendale to escape liability for an obligation incurred as much for its benefit as for Ralmor. As said in [citation omitted]: "Where injustice would result from a strict adherence to the doctrine of separate corporate existence, a court will look behind the corporate structure to determine the identity of the party who should be charged with a corporation's liability.["] [Citation omitted.] Since the separate personality of a corporation is but a statutory privilege it must not be employed as a cloak for the evasion of obligations. The conditions which must be present before the corporate veil will be pierced are outlined in *Minifie v. Rowley*, [202 P. 673, 676 (Cal. 1921)], where the court points out that before the obligations of a corporation can be regarded as those of another person, the following circumstances must appear:

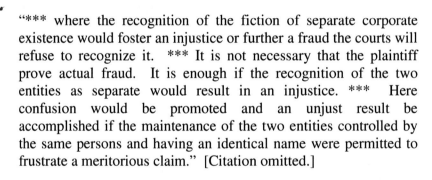

> "First, that the corporation is not only influenced and governed by that person, but that there is such a unity of interest and ownership that the individuality, or separateness, of the said person and corporation has ceased; second, that the facts are such that an adherence to the fiction of the separate existence of the corporation would, under the particular circumstances, sanction a fraud or promote injustice."

The second requirement suggested in *Minifie v. Rowley, supra,* is further refined in the following expression:

> "*** where the recognition of the fiction of separate corporate existence would foster an injustice or further a fraud the courts will refuse to recognize it. *** It is not necessary that the plaintiff prove actual fraud. It is enough if the recognition of the two entities as separate would result in an injustice. *** Here confusion would be promoted and an unjust result be accomplished if the maintenance of the two entities controlled by the same persons and having an identical name were permitted to frustrate a meritorious claim." [Citation omitted.]

***

---

§ 5.07   THE BOARD OF DIRECTORS

Objectives: *You should be able to determine whether a decision affecting the corporation must be made by the board of directors, or whether the decision may be made by other actors in the corporation, such as officers or employees. You should also be able to determine whether action ostensibly taken by the board at a meeting, or through unanimous written consent, was properly taken.*

A.   IN GENERAL

The board of directors is the ultimate source of decision-making authority in the corporation. MBCA § 8.01(b) provides that "[a]ll corporate powers shall be exercised by or under the authority of" the board. Stop and think about that for a minute: *all* corporate powers is an extraordinarily broad grant of power to the board. Further, Section 8.01(b) provides that corporation's "business and affairs" shall be "managed by or under the direction of" the board. This also is an extremely broad grant of power. Theoretically at least, the means that the board has the power to make *every* decision affecting the corporation's business. While it is true that later in this book you will run into a few major decisions that also require shareholder approval, even in these situations the shareholders are only voting on things that the board has proposed beforehand. Moreover, the list of these major transactions that require shareholder approval is pretty short.

Thus, on a day-to-day or even year-to-year basis, the board has full power to run the company and make decisions for it. However, by using the phrases "under the authority of" and "under the direction of," MBCA § 8.01(b) also contemplates that the board may delegate the power to make decisions to other entities in the corporation. These delegations typically are to one of two different groups: (1) board committees or (2) officers and other employees.

Board Committees.   MBCA § 8.25 concerns board committees (sometimes called "subcommittees," to remind us that they the consist of a portion of the overall board). This section provides that a committee must be created by a vote of a majority of the total number of directors on the board, or whatever other number is required to take action under the company's articles or bylaws. It also tells us that committee meetings are governed by the same rules that you will learn about below concerning the conduct of board meetings.

MBCA § 8.25 also provides that a committee could exercise any power that the full board could exercise except for the matters listed in subsection (e), which are powers that only the full board may exercise. Nonetheless, it is customary for a board to create a committee (if it creates any at all) only to complete a specific task or for certain ongoing, but specialized, matters. For example, assume that our corporation has outgrown its current facilities; employees simply do not have enough room to work, so the corporation will need to either expand its current facilities or move to a new location. Obviously, this is a pretty important decision, one that ought to be made by the full board of directors after a great deal of study. But what if there are, say, twenty members of the board? It might not be a terribly efficient way to make this decision to have all twenty board members review architectural plans, visit proposed new locations, etc. In a situation like this, it probably would be a better idea for the board to select three or four of its members (hopefully those who have a keen interest in the matter at hand and/or some degree of expertise in it) and designate them as a committee to make the decision about the corporation's headquarters location. Or, instead of giving the committee the power to actually make the decision, the board could instruct the committee to study the matter and then make a recommendation that the full board could consider.

State law has very little to say about board committees other than MBCA § 8.25. State law does not require that the board have a specific list of committees, or that the board must have any committees at all. Instead, it simply allows the board to create committees if it wishes to do so, and then puts a few limits on what authority may be delegated to the committee. Thus, it should not surprise you to see many privately held corporations with boards of directors that have never formed a committee. This would be particularly so if the corporation has a small number of directors. (A corporation could have only a single director, which would obviously makes the idea of committees silly.)

However, if the corporation has a class of securities listed on a stock exchange, things are very different: certain committees are *required* by stock exchange rules. For example, rules of the New York Stock Exchange require the board of directors of every listed company to have at least three committees: a compensation committee, an audit committee, and a nominating/corporate governance committee. The first of these generally evaluates officer performance and recommends officer compensation levels to the full board for approval. The audit committee generally exists to review the company's financial statements and accounting procedures and gauge their integrity. The nominating/corporate governance committee evaluates board candidates and recommends the nomination of persons for election as directors at the annual shareholders' meeting. This committee also ensures that the corporation is in compliance with other "corporate governance" requirements such as SEC rules and stock exchange requirements.

Each of these committees must consist only of "independent" directors within the meaning of New York Stock Exchange rules. (Nasdaq and other stock markets have similar rules.) The definition of "independent" is very demanding; most business relationships between a director and the corporation would prevent that director from being considered independent. A director who is employed as an officer by the corporation obviously is not independent. Further, the audit committee must consist only of persons who are "financially literate" (or who become financially literate within a reasonable period of time), and at least one member of the audit committee must have accounting or financial management expertise. In part, these requirements were driven by the Sarbanes-Oxley Act of 2002, one requirement of which is that listed companies may only have independent directors on their audit committees and must periodically disclose whether they have at least one "audit committee financial expert" (as defined in SEC regulations).[*] Again, though, keep in mind that these requirements only apply to listed companies.

Delegating Authority to Officers and Employees. As you know from our discussion in Section 5.01, the "line up" of officers will vary greatly from corporation to corporation to corporation. Nonetheless, we can say with confidence that the board has the power to hire and fire officers (although if an officer has an employment contract and is fired without "cause," the corporation could be liable for money damages). We can also say with confidence that officers and employees are agents of the corporation. In this sense, it may be helpful to think of the board as making the decisions, but the officers and directors being given the task of carrying out those decisions.

However, the board may also delegate the authority to make a particular decision, or a specified class of recurring decisions, to one or more officers. It is extremely difficult to make generalizations about the extent to which boards will do so, due to the fact that corporations vary so much in size and in complexity. In the case of your uncle's corporation, where he is the only director and the only officer, he may simply "do things" without any explicit authority granted by the board (himself). On the other hand, in the case of a multinational corporation with 30,000 employees in twenty different countries, it is very likely that the authority given to various officers has been carefully crafted and demarcated by the board.

The above paragraph generally assumes that the board has delegated to an officer or other employee the actual authority to do something. This could occur either through a description of an officer's position in the corporation's bylaws, through a board resolution explicitly delegating authority to an officer, or some other manner. But a third party could also argue that an officer's or employee's

---

[*]   Note that the audit committee is not actually required to have a financial expert. However, it would be pretty embarrassing for it to disclose that it doesn't have one!

authority, even if it wasn't explicitly delegated from the board, arose simply from the fact that she held a particular title. As noted above, since officers and employees are agents, this means that they also may have apparent authority to bind the corporation, which is a topic you saw in some depth in Chapter 2. In fact, there is a line of cases holding that the president or Chief Executive Officer (CEO) of a corporation has apparent authority to bind the corporation to decisions that are in the ordinary course of business. (Although these decisions often state this as a general rule, they often differ as to whether certain types of contracts or other transactions are in the ordinary course of business.) In this sense, because one requirement of apparent authority is that the third party must have a reasonable belief that the agent is authorized, these cases may be telling us that it is reasonable to assume that a corporation's president or CEO has the authority to agree to things that are in the ordinary course of business. But as with anything concerning apparent authority, much will depend on the circumstances. In particular, business "custom" will be important in deciding whether an officer has apparent authority.

But what sorts of things *must* the board do? The MBCA is somewhat coy on this issue. As you have seen, MBCA § 8.01 provides the board with more or less full control over the corporation, but contemplates that the board could delegate authority to officers (*see* MBCA § 8.41) and committees (*see* MBCA § 8.25). In addition, there are a few sections in the MBCA that require board action. See, e.g., MBCA § 8.40 (board appoints officers, unless otherwise provided in bylaws); MBCA § 10.03 (board must approve amendments to corporation's articles of incorporation; shareholder approval usually required as well); MBCA § 11.04 (board must approve mergers involving the corporation; shareholder approval usually required as well); MBCA § 14.02 (to dissolve corporation, the board must recommend dissolution to the shareholders, with some exceptions). Cf. MBCA § 8.25(e) (powers that may not be delegated to board committees).

But this still is a far cry from giving us a full list of required board decisions or even some standard to make this determination ourselves. About the best that the MBCA does is Section 8.01(c), which lists eight items that are included in a board's "oversight responsibilities," but this only applies to publicly traded corporations. But perhaps the most one can say is that the line between things that *must* be approved by the board and things that officers or even lower employees may be able to do without board approval is a murky one. Different corporations will answer this question differently. The board of a large, complex corporation may only be involved in important, "big picture" decisions. The board of a smaller or simpler corporation may be more "hands on." There are, however, many sources of guidance as to what boards *should* do, particularly for large corporations. See, e.g., AMERICAN LAW INSTITUTE, PRINCIPLES OF CORPORATE GOVERNANCE: ANALYSIS AND RECOMMENDATIONS § 3.02 (1992);

AMERICAN BAR ASSOCIATION, COMMITTEE ON CORPORATE LAWS, CORPORATE DIRECTOR'S GUIDEBOOK (5th ed. 2007).

Regardless of the corporation, it seems safe to say that the more important a decision is, either in terms of the amount of money involved or its effect on the company's business policies, the more likely it is that that decision may only be made by the corporation's board of directors. If you are ever in any doubt as to whether a particular person has the authority to agree to a contract or other transaction on behalf of the corporation, then it couldn't hurt to ask that the board specifically approve the transaction. If it does, then any trace of doubt would be removed.

One thing should be mentioned before moving on to discuss the mechanics of board action. The model described above, where the shareholders elect the directors, the directors determine the corporation's business policies and strategies, and then the officers carry out the board's directions, may not be an accurate description of how many corporations actually operate in "real life." As you will see in Chapter 9, in closely held corporations the line between the board and the officers is often somewhat blurry, due to the fact that the same people often occupy both roles. And as you will see in Chapter 10, executive officers in public corporations often have a much more active role in making business decisions than the above discussion would lead you to believe. But we will defer further discussion of those issues until later.

B.   BOARD MEETINGS AND OTHER ACTIONS

In this section, we will assume that there is an action that calls for board approval and will try to figure out how to go about obtaining that approval in a manner that is procedurally proper, that is, a manner that satisfies the applicable requirements of the statute (and, if different, the corporation's articles and bylaws).

Rather than describing those requirements in this book, the best way for a student to learn them is to try some problems. Carefully read MBCA §§ 8.20 through 8.24 before you try the problems concerning board action below. Assume in the problems that the corporation does not have any provisions in its articles of incorporation or bylaws that would change the rules that are set forth in the statute, unless otherwise noted. Also, before trying your hand at these problems, let me give you a few hints. First, there are three methods by which a board may act: through a unanimous written consent resolution, at a regular meeting, or at a special meeting. Second, if a meeting is held, notice may (or may not) be required beforehand. If notice is required, every director must receive the notice, but a director may in some situations waive notice. Third, if a meeting is held, a quorum of directors must be "present," and the requisite vote of the directors must be obtained. If that didn't make sense (or even if it did), go read MBCA §§ 8.20 through 8.24 and then do these problems:

Problems

Problem 5-30:   The board of directors of Broccoli and Carrots Corp. ("BCC") consists of ten persons. BCC's bylaws provide that the board shall have meetings on the first business day of every month. You are counsel to BCC and on March 30 learned from BCC's president that BCC needs to sign a major loan agreement with Fourth National Bank (the "Bank") immediately. The loan agreement will require approval by BCC's board. It appears that all of BCC's directors are in town and available. *What would you recommend to get the loan agreement approved as quickly as possible?*

Problem 5-31: Same facts as in Problem 5-30, except that these events took place on March 13. *What would you recommend to get the loan agreement approved as quickly as possible?*

Problem 5-32: Same facts as in Problem 5-31, except that you learned that one of BCC's directors is currently climbing Mount Everest and is not expected back for three weeks. *What would you recommend to get the loan agreement approved as quickly as possible?*

Problem 5-33: The board of directors of Peas and Beans Corp. ("PBC") consists of five persons. PBC's bylaws provide that notice of director meetings shall be sent by facsimile (fax) machine to each director's fax number on file with the corporation, and that notice is effective when the fax is received.[*] On July 17, the president of PBC faxed to each of the five directors the following notice: "Please join us for a special meeting of the board of PBC, to be held at 1 p.m. on July 18, at the company's offices at 111 Vegetable Way, Anytown, USA." *Was this notice proper? Would your answer be different if the meeting was a regular meeting? By the way, what is a "regular" meeting?*

---

[*]   MBCA § 1.41 concerns notice requirements. In this problem, it would be permissible for PBC's bylaws to provide that notice by fax is effective when received.

Problem 5-34: Same facts as Problem 5-33, except that the notice was sent on July 2 and contained all information required by the statute. At the meeting, three of the directors attended. PBC's president announced that the purpose of the meeting was to decide whether PBC should acquire the assets of Cauliflower Corp. After a great deal of discussion, two directors voted to acquire the assets of Cauliflower Corp., and the other director voted no. *Did PBC's board properly approve this transaction? Would your answer change if one of the directors left the meeting before the vote was taken and the two remaining directors both voted yes?*

Problem 5-35: *Would your answer to Problem 5-34 change if one of the directors was not physically present at the meeting but instead was listening to it on a conference call?*

Problem 5-36: *By the way, how would you know whether the president of PBC has the power to call a special meeting of the directors?*

§ 5.08   SHAREHOLDERS AND SHAREHOLDER VOTING

Objectives: You should be able to determine whether a proposed decision affecting the corporation must be approved by the shareholders. You should also be able to determine whether action ostensibly taken by the shareholders at a meeting, or through unanimous written consent, was properly taken.

Subsidiary Objectives: You should also be able to:

•   *Given a fact pattern involving shareholder voting, whether on the election or removal of directors or some other matter, determine whether the shareholders have properly approved a particular action, whether at a meeting or through a written consent resolution.*

•   *Explain the difference between a staggered board of directors and a non-staggered board, and explain how often directors (and how many of them) are elected to the board and how long their terms of office last in both situations.*

•   *For a plurality voting system, given a fact pattern that specifies the number of open board positions, the names of each of the candidates, and the number of shares voted for each candidate, determine which person(s) were elected to the board.*

• *For a cumulative voting system, given a fact pattern that specifies the number of open board positions, the names of each of the candidates, and the number of votes voted for each candidate, determine which person(s) were elected to the board. In addition, for a cumulative voting system, you should be able to determine how many shares a shareholder must own in order to be guaranteed of electing a given number of candidates to the board.*

• *Explain how directors may be removed from office before their terms expires, both under a plurality voting system and under a cumulative voting system.*

• *Determine whether an agreement between two or more shareholders that specifies how they will vote their shares on certain matters (1) is valid and (2) if so, how it may be enforced if one of the parties to the agreement does not comply with it.*

• *Describe what information that corporations are required to provide to shareholders under state law. Describe any additional information that shareholders are entitled to inspect and the procedures for exercising the right to such inspection.*

A.   MECHANICS OF SHAREHOLDER ACTION

Before discussing what matters require shareholder approval and how one counts votes on those matters, it may be best to begin with a discussion of *how* shareholders act, that is, how they go about voting on something, whatever it may be. There are three different methods: a written consent resolution, an annual meeting, and a special meeting.

Written Consent Resolutions. As for the written consent resolution, MBCA § 7.04 is actually quite complicated, but only subsections (a) and (b) need concern us here. Subsection (a) provides that the shareholders may take action if *all* of them sign one or more documents describing the action. Taking action through a written consent resolution is just as good as if the shareholders took action at a meeting (discussed below). For example, if you needed shareholder approval of, say, a merger, you could type up a document that describes the merger and states that the shareholders have approved it. If every single shareholder signs this document (or a counterpart copy of it), then the shareholders have approved the merger.

Subsection (b), on the other hand, provides that you could have a less-than-unanimous consent resolution, if the corporation's articles of incorporation so allow. Specifically, it provides that the corporation's articles may allow shareholder action to be taken without a meeting "if consents in writing setting forth the action so taken are signed by the holders of outstanding shares having not less than the minimum number of votes that would be required to authorize or take action at a meeting at which all shares entitled to vote on the action were present and voted." Huh?

Let's say that there are 1,000,000 shares of stock outstanding. If all of these shares were present at a meeting and voted, then one would need at least 500,001 shares to vote yes to approve an action other than electing directors (as you will see below). Thus, MBCA § 7.04(b) provides that—if permitted by the corporation's articles—the action would be approved if you get the holders of at least 500,001 shares to sign a document stating that the shareholders have approved the action.

Note that MBCA § 7.04 itself does not put a limit on the number of shares or shareholders that a corporation may have to use written consent resolutions. However, this option is most often used by corporations that have a very small number of shareholders—if unanimous consent is required, it becomes less and less likely to be obtained as the number of shareholders grows. Could you imagine Coca-Cola's shareholders taking action through a written consent resolution? Me neither. If that's the case, shareholder action will need to be taken at a meeting.

Shareholder Meetings. There are two types of shareholder meetings: annual and special.[*] Obviously, the annual meeting is held once a year; typically, the corporation's bylaws specify when the annual meeting is to be held. Special meetings are held on an "as needed" basis. For example, if the annual meeting is typically held in March and it is now June and you want the shareholders to vote on something, you should probably call a special meeting instead of waiting until next March.

Regardless of the type of shareholder meeting involved, proper notice must be given to the shareholders who are "entitled to vote." However, note that shareholders can waive notice either expressly or impliedly pursuant to MBCA § 7.06. The shareholders who are entitled to vote are those who owned shares on

---

[*]   MBCA § 7.03 provides for a court-ordered meeting, but we will omit a discussion of that here.

the *record date*. Note that the record date will be *before* the date of the meeting. At first, you may find this puzzling and may wonder why you just don't figure out, right before the shareholder meeting begins, who owns shares (and how many shares they own) and then let those people vote at the meeting. But keep in mind that because stock is freely transferable, shares of the corporation's stock may be being furiously bought and sold among shareholders all the time. Maybe the corporation is publicly traded, in which case it may have thousands of shareholders and millions of shares may change hands every day. In such a case, the list of who the shareholders are, and how many shares they own, could radically change from day to day. If you had to figure out, on the morning of the shareholder meeting, who owned shares and how many they owned this could be an impossible task. Thus, the concept of the record date was invented. It may be helpful to think of the record date as a rule of convenience for the corporate secretary.

MBCA §§ 7.05 through 7.07 concern notices of shareholder meetings and record dates. Read those sections, as well as MBCA § 1.41(c), and then apply them to the following problems:

Problems

Problem 5-37: Grape Corp. has 1,000 shares of common stock outstanding, owned by five shareholders. On March 1, the secretary of Grape Corp. mailed the following notice to each shareholder: "Please join us for the annual meeting of Grape Corp. to be held at 1 p.m. on March 16, at the corporation's offices located at 111 Fruit Way, Anytown, USA." At the meeting, the corporate secretary announced that the purpose of the meeting was to vote on the election of four directors to the board. *Was proper notice of this shareholder meeting given?*

Problem 5-38: Same facts as Problem 5-37, except that the notice was mailed on March 8. *Was proper notice of this shareholder meeting given?*

Problem 5-39: Same facts as Problem 5-37, except that at the meeting the corporate secretary announced that the purposes of the meeting were to vote on the election of four directors to the board. *Was proper notice of this shareholder meeting given?*

Problem 5-40: Same facts as Problem 5-37. *What is the earliest date that could have been chosen as the record date? What is the latest date that could have been chosen as the record date? By the way, who chooses the record date?*

> **"VOTING GROUPS"**
> In MBCA § 7.25, you will notice references to "voting groups" of shareholders. This refers to the situation where there are different classes of voting stock that may vote separately as a class. In this part of this book, we are keeping things simple; there is only one voting group—the common stock.

To take action at a shareholder meeting, a *quorum* of the voting shares must be present. A quorum at a shareholder meeting generally requires a majority of the outstanding voting *shares* to be present. MBCA § 7.25. How, you may ask, can a *share* be considered present? There are two ways: the owner of the shares could attend the meeting in person or the shares could be represented by *proxy*. Obviously, if a person who owns, say, 100 shares attend the meeting, then her shares will be considered present at the meeting.

A proxy involves an agency relationship: the shareholder who signs a proxy card[*] can be considered the principal and the person who is designated as the shareholder's proxy (which in this context is really just another word for representative) can be considered the shareholder's agent. By signing a proxy card, the shareholder authorizes the proxy to attend the shareholder meeting on her behalf and vote her shares. For example, the shareholder can specify, on the proxy card, how she wishes her shares to be voted and the proxy is bound to follow those instructions.

MBCA § 7.22 concerns proxies. Read that section, along with MBCA § 7.07 (which you encountered above) and MBCA § 7.25, and work on the following problems:

Problems

Problem 5-41: Lettuce Corp. has 10,000 shares of common stock outstanding. The stock is owned by five shareholders: Adam (who owns 1,000 shares), Belinda (who owns 1,000 shares), Carmen (who owns 2,000 shares), Duffy (who owns 3,000) shares, and Eunice (who owns 3,000 shares). Lettuce Corp.'s annual shareholder meeting will be held on May 1 and proper notice was mailed to all five shareholders on April 16. The record date for voting at the meeting is April 15. On April 18, Adam sold his 1,000 shares to Zeke. *Who is entitled to vote these shares at the meeting?*

---

[*]   Proxies no longer need to be on paper—they may be electronic. See MBCA § 7.22(b). As discussed in Chapter 10, much shareholder voting in public companies is now done on the Internet.

Problem 5-42: Same facts as Problem 5-41, except that Adam sold his 1,000 shares to Zeke on April 10. *Who is entitled to vote these shares at the meeting?*

Problem 5-43: Same facts as Problem 5-41, except that when Adam sold his 1,000 shares to Zeke on April 16 he told Zeke: "Don't worry, I hereby give you my proxy to vote my shares at the upcoming shareholder meeting in any way that you wish." Nonetheless, Adam attended the meeting and wanted to vote the shares. *Who is entitled to vote these shares at the meeting? Would your answer change if Adam had written these words on a piece of paper and then signed it?*

Problem 5-44: *If the only shareholders who attend the meeting, in person or by proxy, are Duffy and Eunice, would a quorum be present?*

Problem 5-45: *If all five shareholders attend the meeting, but Duffy and Eunice leave the meeting after five minutes, can the meeting continue?*

Having the ability for shares to be considered present for quorum purposes through a proxy is absolutely critical for a publicly traded corporation. To understand why, let's imagine that there is a public corporation which is headquartered in Juno, Alaska and has 10 million shares of common stock outstanding. Further, the corporation's shares are owned by 10,000 people, each of whom owns exactly 1,000 shares, or 0.01% of the outstanding shares. (How's that for round numbers?) If you are one of these shareholders, would you travel to Alaska to attend the shareholder meeting—which will be held on January 15—in person? Probably not, unless you happened to live in Alaska. If most or all of the other shareholders are like you, then this corporation would never be able to conduct any business at a shareholder meeting because a quorum would never be present. But if the holders of a majority of the shares sign proxy cards authorizing someone who's already in Alaska, say, the company's president, to attend the meeting and vote their shares, then business may be conducted at the meeting.

Although you will consider this in more detail in Chapter 10, if a publicly traded company solicits proxies from shareholders, it must follow complex SEC rules under Section 14 of the Securities Exchange Act of 1934. One of the primary requirements in these rules is that each shareholder from whom a proxy is solicited must be furnished with a very detailed proxy statement explaining not only the matters that shareholders will vote on at the meeting, but a great deal of information about the company as well. Further, these rules apply not only if the company itself is soliciting proxies, but if anyone else (for example, a dissatisfied shareholder) is soliciting proxies from shareholders.   But we will defer further discussion of the SEC proxy rules until Chapter 10.   Now that you understand *how* shareholders vote, it's time to understand (1) what matters they vote on and (2) how to count votes to determine if those matters have been approved by the shareholders.

B.   ELECTION OF DIRECTORS BY SHAREHOLDERS

As has been pointed out repeatedly above, the shareholders are the owners of the corporation, but have little control over it.   Instead, the shareholders periodically elect the directors.   In this section, you will learn exactly how that occurs.

Number of Directors and Staggered Boards.   First, how many directors does the corporation have?   MBCA § 8.03(a) tells us that you must look to the corporation's articles of incorporation or bylaws to answer that question.   A corporation must have at least one director, but there is no maximum number. Second, how frequently are the directors elected?   MBCA § 8.03(c) tells us that if the corporation does not have a "staggered" board, then directors are elected annually.   If you were elected to such a corporation's board today, then you would have a one-year term of office as a director.   (Technically, your term of office would be until the next annual shareholder meeting.)   At the next shareholder meeting, maybe you will be re-elected to the board, but maybe you won't.   This also applies to every other director.   So if the corporation had, say, eighty-two directors, it's possible that none of the eighty-two directors might be re-elected next year.   Instead, the directors might be replaced by eighty-two different people. Such a result could be very disruptive: the "institutional memory" of the directors would be lost and the new directors might adopt radically different corporate policies.

One of the common justifications for having a "staggered" board is that it may prevent such disruption from occurring.   MBCA § 8.06 allows the board to be classified (i.e., staggered) into two or three classes.   To see how this would work, read MBCA § 8.06 and then consider the following problem:

Problem

Problem 5-46:   It is January 1, 2000, and you were just elected to the board of directors of Staggered Corp.   The board of directors of Staggered Corp. consists of nine people (including you), and is staggered into three classes. You are in "Class 1." *How long is your term as a director? When would you next stand for re-election to the board? How many other directors are in Class 1 with you? How many directors are in Class 2 and Class 3? When do those directors next stand for re-election? Why do you think Staggered Corp. has a staggered board?*

Election of Directors Under Plurality Voting. Once you know how many directors the corporation has and how frequently they are elected, it is time to consider how to count votes in an election of directors by the shareholders. To keep things simple, let's assume that the corporation hasn't done anything "fancy" with its stock. Instead, it has only one class of stock: good old common stock, which as you know has one vote per share. *See* MBCA § 7.21(a).

There are two common methods of electing directors: ***plurality voting*** (which is also known as ***straight voting***) and ***cumulative voting***. To be elected as a director under a plurality voting system, you merely need more votes cast for you than anyone else who is running for that position. A majority of the votes is not necessary. Further, each shareholder can vote each of her shares for the number of open board positions that will be filled at the shareholder meeting. To take a simple example, if there are five open positions on the board of directors, each shareholder will be able to vote *each of her shares for five candidates.* Thus, if you own 100 shares, you can cast 100 votes for Amy, 100 votes for Bob, 100 votes for Cindy, 100 votes for Diego, and 100 votes for Emily.

But you should note a couple of things here. First, you can't really vote "against" anyone in plurality voting. With respect to any particular candidate, you either vote for her or you vote for someone else, but you don't have a choice between voting "for" or "against" candidates in plurality voting. Second, note that you didn't need to "break up" your votes in this example; instead, you were able to vote *each share* for a number of candidates equal to the number of open board positions. Here, since there were five open board positions, you were able to vote each of your shares for five different candidates.

> **MAJORITY VOTING**
> Many public companies recently have moved to a majority voting system in director elections, due to the perceived unfairness of plurality voting. In such a system, shareholders may vote "for" or "against" board candidates. But this is much more complicated than it sounds. See Chapter 10 for more details.

Third, in this example, the five candidates who receive the most votes (whether they be Amy, Bob, Cindy, Diego, and Emily, or other candidates) will be elected to the board.

Plurality voting is somewhat counterintuitive when one first encounters it. But see if you can correctly apply it to the following problems:

Problems

Problem 5-47:   Carrot Corp. has 1,000,000 shares of common stock outstanding. Its board of directors consists of five directors. Mr. A, Ms. B, Mr. C, Mr. D, and Ms. E currently serve as directors of Carrot Corp. Each of the directors owns 10 shares of stock. The directors are widely hated by the shareholders, who think that they are idiots and thieves. At this year's annual meeting of shareholders, the only candidates for the five board positions are Mr. A, Ms. B, Mr. C, Mr. D, and Ms. E. *How many votes do these candidates need to be elected to the board under plurality voting? If you are one of the candidates and you cast 10 votes for yourself, will you be elected even if no one else votes for you?*

Problem 5-48:   Kale Corp. has two shareholders: Shareholder A, who owns 51 shares of common stock, and Shareholder B, who owns 49 shares. The board of directors of Kale Corp. consists of 82 persons. Shareholder A and Shareholder B do not like each other and neither one would ever vote for a board candidate selected by the other. *How many directors will Shareholder A be able to elect under plurality voting? How many directors will Shareholder B be able to elect?*

Here's the answer to Problem 5-48: Shareholder A gets to elect all 82 director candidates! This is because each shareholder gets to vote each of her shares for 82 candidates (which is the number of board positions in this example). The 82 people that Shareholder A wants to elect to the board will each get 51 votes. The 82 people that Shareholder B wants to elect to the board will each get 49 votes. The top 82 "vote getters" will thus be the candidates for which Shareholder A voted. In other words, for each of the 82 board positions to be filled in this example, Shareholder A's candidate will receive more votes than Shareholder B's candidate and thus will be elected to that position. Even though Shareholder B owns nearly half of the company, she was not able to elect a single director in this example.

If you were Shareholder B, would you be upset about this? Absolutely. Fortunately, there are a few things that you could try so that you would be able to elect some of the directors. You could enter into a voting agreement with Shareholder A that provides that you will each vote your shares so that, say, 42 candidates chosen by Shareholder A and 40 candidates chosen by you are elected to the board every year. (Shareholder voting agreements are discussed in Section D below.) Of course, you can't force Shareholder A to sign such an agreement against her will. Another idea would be to use something called cumulative voting in the election of directors.

Election of Directors Under Cumulative Voting. Cumulative voting is tricky and it is possible that you might not believe the following paragraphs the first time that you read them. For one thing, cumulative voting changes the normal "one share, one vote rule." *See* MBCA §§ 7.21(a), 7.28. In cumulative voting, the number of *votes* you have is equal to the number of shares that you own multiplied by the number of director open positions at this election. For example, if you own 10 shares and there will be 5 persons elected to the board at this shareholder meeting, then you would have 50 votes under cumulative voting. Second, you can cast *all* of your votes for a single candidate, or you could spread them around as you wish among different candidates.

Third, there is a formula for cumulative voting. It is:

$$\frac{N \times S}{D + 1} + \text{"1"} = X$$

In this formula, "N" is the number of directors that you wish to elect to the board; "S" is the number of shares that will be voted at the shareholder meeting (but because shareholders aren't under any obligation to vote their shares, when applying this formula you can assume that all of the outstanding shares will be voted); and "D" is the *total* number of directors that will be elected to the board at the shareholder meeting. Generally, 1 is simply 1, but the "1" that is in quotation marks means either of two things. If the result of dividing (N x S) by (D + 1) is a whole number, then "1" means that you should simply add 1. On the other hand, if the result of dividing (N x S) by (D + 1) is a fraction, then "1" means that you must round up to the next whole number. For example, if (N x S) divided by (D + 1) was 33.33, then you would round up to 34. Finally, "X" is the number of shares that a shareholder would need to own to be *guaranteed* of being able to elect "N" number of directors. If the shareholder has that many shares, then great. If not, too bad.[*]

What do you think "X" will be? Assume there are 3 board positions and 100 outstanding shares of common stock. Common sense would tell you that because 100 divided by 3 is 33.33, then you would need 34 shares to elect

---

[*] However, two or more shareholders, none of whom has the requisite "X" number of shares, could "pool" their shares to get to "X" and thus be able to elect a director of their choosing to the board.

someone of your choosing to this three-person board. *But common sense would lead you astray.* Applying the formula, you should see that "N" is 1 because the question is asking how many shares it would take to elect one director; "S" is 100 because there are 100 outstanding shares and you may assume that they will all be voted; and "D" is 3. Here, (1 x 100) divided by (3 + 1) is 25, which is a whole number, so you would add 1 to get 26. Thus, if you owned at least 26 of the 100 outstanding shares and you cast all of your votes for a candidate, that candidate *will* be elected to the board.

Assume that, completely by coincidence, you owned 26 shares in this example and that there was one other shareholder who owned the other 74 shares. (Remember, in this example, there are a total of 100 outstanding shares.) How many votes would you have? The answer is 78 (the 26 shares that you own, multiplied by the 3 board positions to be filled at this election). This means that the other shareholder would have 222 votes (74 shares multiplied by 3 board positions). Assuming that you cast all 78 of your votes for a single candidate, can the other shareholder allocate her 222 votes so as to "beat" your candidate 3 times? No. This is because if the other shareholder cast 79 votes for one candidate and another 79 votes for another candidate, she would only have 64 votes left to cast for a third candidate. Your candidate (who received 78 votes), will thus be one of the top three "vote getters."

It is easy to disbelieve cumulative voting. But apply your knowledge to the following problems. In each problem, once you know what "X" is, ask yourself how many *votes* a shareholder who owns "X" number of shares would have.

Problems

Problem 5-49: Squash Corp. has 1,000 shares of common stock outstanding. Its board of directors, which consists of four persons, is elected through cumulative voting. *How many shares must you own to be able to elect one director to Squash Corp.'s board?*

Problem 5-50: Same facts as Problem 5-49. *How many shares must you own to be able to elect two directors to Squash Corp.'s board?*

Problem 5-51: Same facts as Problem 5-49, except that there are seven persons on Squash Corp.'s board. *How many shares must you own to be able to elect one director to Squash Corp.'s board?*

Problem 5-52: *If a corporation went from having a non-staggered board to having a staggered board, would that increase or decrease the number of shares that a shareholder would need to own to be able to elect a director under cumulative voting?*

Removal of Directors; Filling Vacancies. Shareholders may always remove a director before her term as a director expires. (Think of this as a "recall.") MBCA § 8.08 provides that directors may be removed with or without "cause," unless the articles of incorporation require cause, however that may be defined in the articles, to remove a director. MBCA § 8.08 then goes on to specify how many votes are needed to remove a director. If plurality voting is used, then the director would be removed if the number of shares voted in favor of removing the director exceeds the number of shares voted against removing the director. But what if the corporation had cumulative voting? Take a close look at MBCA § 8.08(c) and decide what would happen in the following problem.

Problem

Problem 5-53: Pepper Corp. has 100 shares of common stock outstanding and a three-person board of directors that is elected using cumulative voting. Shareholder A owns 26 shares and Shareholder B owns 74 shares. Three weeks ago, at the annual shareholder meeting, Shareholder A elected herself to the board. However, Shareholder B then had the corporation call a special shareholder meeting for the sole purpose of voting to remove Shareholder A from the board. At the meeting, Shareholder A voted all 26 of her shares *not* to remove herself from the board, whereas Shareholder B voted all 74 of his shares to remove her from the board. *Will Shareholder A be removed from the board?*

If a director is removed before the end of her term, that obviously will create a vacancy on the board. MBCA § 8.10 provides alternative ways in which the vacancy may be filled; however, the corporation's articles of incorporation may provide a different rule for filling vacancies on the board of directors.

Who Nominates the Director Candidates? As you learned above in the discussion of plurality voting, if the number of persons running for election to the board is equal to the number of director positions that will be filled at the shareholder meeting, then each candidate is virtually guaranteed of being elected to the board. If ten people were running for ten spots on the board, then it would only take a single share to vote in favor of a candidate to elect that candidate to the board. Thus, it's crucially important to decide how directors are nominated, because nomination is often akin to actual election. Unfortunately, the MBCA and the laws of most states don't directly answer this question. In the context of a closely held corporation, it would be common for the shareholders to have a voting agreement specifying that they will each vote their shares so that mutually acceptable candidates would be elected. (Again, voting agreements are discussed in Section D below.)

Alternatively, a shareholder could make a nomination "from the floor" at a shareholder meeting. With a publicly traded corporation, however, this strategy wouldn't work because the vast majority of shares would have previously been voted by proxy, as you saw above. While you could solicit proxies from other shareholders to vote in favor of your nominees, this is a very expensive and complicated endeavor if the company is publicly traded. Nonetheless, some recent developments may make it easier for shareholders of publicly traded corporations to have an influence in the director nomination process. These are discussed in Chapter 10.

C.   SHAREHOLDER VOTING ON OTHER MATTERS

Shareholders *do* get to vote on matters other than electing directors, just not that many. For example, in Chapter 12 you will see that shareholders (usually) must vote to approve any merger in which the corporation will be involved and that certain major sales of the corporation's assets require shareholder approval. In addition, generally speaking the shareholders must vote to approve any amendments to the corporation's articles of incorporation (with certain exceptions). *See* MBCA § 10.03. Further, there may be non-corporate law reasons to seek shareholder approval of certain matters. For example, if the corporation has shares listed on a stock exchange, the rules of the stock exchange may require it to seek shareholder approval of certain items, most notably certain compensation plans where company stock or stock options would be granted to officers or directors.

Nonetheless, the list of things that require shareholder approval is short. Fortunately, counting votes on these matters is much simpler than it is when counting votes on the election of directors. One thing that you should know is that, when voting on a matter other than the election of directors, shareholders are usually given three choices: (1) yes or for, (2) no or against, or (3) abstain. Read MBCA §§ 7.25(a) and (c) and consider the following problems:

Problems

Problem 5-54: Pumpkin Corp. has 10 million shares outstanding. Proper notice was given of a special shareholders meeting, the purpose of which was to vote on a matter other than the election of directors. At the meeting, 8 million shares were present. Of these shares, 4 million voted in favor of the proposal, 3.5 million voted against it, and 500,000 shares abstained. *Did the shareholders of Pumpkin Corp. properly approve the proposal?*

Problem 5-55: Same facts as Problem 5-54, except that Pumpkin Corp. is incorporated in Delaware. *Did the shareholders of Pumpkin Corp. properly approve the proposal?* (The Delaware statute is set forth below.)

As you may have guessed from the nature of the previous question, Delaware takes a different approach. Its statute provides in part as follows:[*]

§ 216. Quorum and required vote for stock corporations.

***   In the absence of [a different] specification in the certificate of incorporation or bylaws of the corporation:

(1)   A majority of the shares entitled to vote, present in person or represented by proxy, shall constitute a quorum at a meeting of stockholders;

(2)   In all matters other than the election of directors, the affirmative vote of the majority of shares present in person or represented by proxy at the meeting and entitled to vote on the subject matter shall be the act of the stockholders;

***

But let's go back to the MBCA. One last thing to address in this section is MBCA § 7.27, which provides that a corporation may increase the quorum and/or voting requirements that would otherwise apply to shareholder action. Read that section carefully and do this problem. Thankfully, this is the last problem in this chapter.

---

[*]   However, for mergers and certain other "major" transactions, Delaware requires approval by a majority of the outstanding shares, as discussed in Chapter 12.

Problem

Problem 5-56:   Tomato Corp. is owned by two shareholders: Angel, who owns 51 shares of common stock, and Ziggy, who owns 49 shares. When they formed the corporation, Ziggy insisted on the following provision being included in the articles of incorporation: "No merger involving the corporation may be approved unless the holders of not less than sixty percent of the outstanding shares of common stock vote in favor thereof." At the most recent shareholder meeting, Angel voted to remove this provision from the articles. Ziggy voted against this proposal. *Have the shareholders of Tomato Corp. removed this provision from the articles of incorporation?*

D.   SHAREHOLDER VOTING AGREEMENTS

Shareholders are under no obligation to vote their shares. Many shareholders, particularly in publicly traded corporations that have millions and millions of outstanding shares, do not vote their shares. For example, if you own 100 shares of Coca-Cola stock, and there are 1 billion shares outstanding, should you bother to vote your shares? Many shareholders would answer no to this question because their 100 votes on any given matter have virtually no chance of swaying the outcome. Commentators describe these shareholders as "rationally apathetic."

But if shareholders are not obligated to vote their shares, should we be concerned if they enter into agreements with other shareholders governing how they will vote on certain matters? The following case considers this issue. The holding of this case is relatively simple, but you should also use the case as an occasion to revisit cumulative voting and make sure that you understand it.

Ringling Bros.-Barnum & Bailey Combined Shows, Inc. v. Ringling
Supreme Court of Delaware
53 A.2d 441 (1947)

PEARSON, Judge. The Court of Chancery was called upon to review an attempted election of directors at the 1946 annual stockholders meeting of the corporate defendant. The pivotal questions concern an agreement between two of the three present stockholders, and particularly the effect of this agreement with relation to the exercise of voting rights by these two stockholders. At the time of the meeting, the corporation had outstanding 1000 shares of capital stock held as follows: 315 by petitioner Edith Conway Ringling; 315 by defendant Aubrey B. Ringling Haley (individually or as executrix and legatee of a deceased husband);

and 370 by defendant John Ringling North. The purpose of the meeting was to elect the entire board of seven directors. The shares could be voted cumulatively. Mrs. Ringling asserts that by virtue of the operation of an agreement between her and Mrs. Haley, the latter was bound to vote her shares for an adjournment of the meeting, or in the alternative, for a certain slate of directors. Mrs. Haley contends that she was not so bound for reason that the agreement was invalid, or at least revocable.

The two ladies entered into the agreement in 1941. *** The agreement then provides as follows:

> Now, [t]herefore, in consideration of the mutual covenants and agreements hereinafter contained the parties hereto agree as follows:
>
> ***
>
> 2.   In exercising any voting rights to which either party may be entitled by virtue of ownership of stock or voting trust certificates held by them in [the] corporation, each party will consult and confer with the other and the parties will act jointly in exercising such voting rights in accordance with such agreement as they may reach with respect to any matter calling for the exercise of such voting rights.
>
> 3.   In the event the parties fail to agree with respect to any matter covered by paragraph 2 above, the question in disagreement shall be submitted for arbitration to Karl D. Loos, of Washington, D. C. as arbitrator and his decision thereon shall be binding upon the parties hereto.
>
> ***

The Mr. Loos mentioned in the agreement is an attorney and has represented both parties since 1937, and, before and after the voting trust was terminated in late 1942, advised them with respect to the exercise of their voting rights. At the annual meetings in 1943 and the two following years, the parties voted their shares in accordance with mutual understandings arrived at as a result of discussions. In each of these years, they elected five of the seven directors. Mrs. Ringling and Mrs. Haley each had sufficient votes, independently of the other, to elect two of the seven directors. By both voting for an additional candidate, they could be sure of his election regardless of how Mr. North, the remaining stockholder, might vote.[*]

Some weeks before the 1946 meeting, they discussed with Mr. Loos the matter of voting for directors. They were in accord that Mrs. Ringling should cast sufficient votes to elect herself and her son; and that Mrs. Haley should elect herself and her husband; but they did not agree upon a fifth director. The day before the meeting, the discussions were continued, Mrs. Haley being represented by her husband since she could not be present because of illness. In a conversation with Mr. Loos, Mr. Haley indicated that he would make a motion for an adjournment of the meeting for sixty days, in order to give the ladies additional time to come to an agreement about their voting. On the morning of the meeting, however, he stated that because of something Mrs. Ringling had done, he would not consent to a postponement. Mrs. Ringling then made a demand upon Mr. Loos to act under the third paragraph of the agreement "to arbitrate the disagreement" between her and Mrs. Haley in connection with the manner in which the stock of the two ladies should be voted. At the opening of the meeting, Mr. Loos read the written demand and stated that he determined and directed that the stock of both ladies be voted for an adjournment of sixty days. Mrs. Ringling then made a motion for adjournment and voted for it. Mr. Haley, as proxy for his wife, and Mr. North voted against the motion. Mrs. Ringling ... objected to the voting of Mrs. Haley's stock in any manner other than in accordance with Mr. Loos' direction. The chairman ruled that the stock could not be voted contrary to such direction, and declared the motion for adjournment had carried. Nevertheless, the meeting proceeded to the election of directors. Mrs. Ringling stated that she would continue in the meeting "but without prejudice to her position with respect to the voting of the stock and the fact that adjournment had not been taken." Mr. Loos directed Mrs. Ringling to cast her votes

> 882 for Mrs. Ringling,
> 882 for her son, Robert, and
> 441 for a Mr. Dunn,

who had been a member of the board for several years. She complied. Mr. Loos directed that Mrs. Haley's votes be cast

---

[*]   [Footnote by court]: Each lady was entitled to cast 2205 votes (since each had the cumulative voting rights of 315 shares, and there were 7 vacancies in the directorate). The sum of the votes of both is 4410, which is sufficient to allow 882 votes for each of 5 persons. Mr. North, holding 370 shares, was entitled to cast 2590 votes, which obviously cannot be divided so as to give to more than two candidates as many as 882 votes each. It will be observed that in order for Mrs. Ringling and Mrs. Haley to be sure to elect five directors (regardless of how Mr. North might vote) they must act together in the sense that their combined votes must be divided among five different candidates and at least one of the five must be voted for by both Mrs. Ringling and Mrs. Haley.

882 for Mrs. Haley,
882 for Mr. Haley, and
441 for Mr. Dunn.

Instead of complying, Mr. Haley attempted to vote his wife's shares

1103 for Mrs. Haley, and
1102 for Mr. Haley.

Mr. North voted his shares

864 for a Mr. Woods,
863 for a Mr. Griffin, and
863 for Mr. North.

The chairman ruled that the five candidates proposed by Mr. Loos, together with Messrs. Woods and North, were elected. The Haley-North group disputed this ruling insofar as it declared the election of Mr. Dunn; and insisted that Mr. Griffin, instead, had been elected. A director's meeting followed in which Mrs. Ringling participated after stating that she would do so "without prejudice to her position that the stockholders' meeting had been adjourned and that the directors' meeting was not properly held." Mr. Dunn and Mr. Griffin, although each was challenged by an opposing faction, attempted to join in voting as directors for different slates of officers. Soon after the meeting, Mrs. Ringling instituted this proceeding.

The [trial judge] determined that the agreement to vote in accordance with the direction of Mr. Loos was valid as a "stock pooling agreement" with lawful objects and purposes, and that it was not in violation of any public policy of this state. He held that where the arbitrator acts under the agreement and one party refuses to comply with his direction, "the Agreement constitutes the willing party * * * an implied agent possessing the irrevocable proxy of the recalcitrant party for the purpose of casting the particular vote". It was ordered that a new election be held before a master, with the direction that the master should recognize and give effect to the agreement if its terms were properly invoked.

***

*** [Defendants contend] that the voting provisions are illegal and revocable. They say that the courts of this state have definitely established the doctrine "that there can be no agreement, or any device whatsoever, by which the voting power of stock of a Delaware corporation may be irrevocably separated from the ownership of the stock, except by an agreement which complies with Section 18" of the Corporation Law ... and except by a proxy coupled with an interest. They rely on [prior cases] and contend that the doctrine is derived from Section 18 itself ****. The statute reads, in part, as follows:

> Sec. 18. Fiduciary Stockholders; Voting Power of; Voting Trusts: *** One or more stockholders may by agreement in writing deposit capital stock of an original issue with or transfer capital stock to any person or persons, or corporation or corporations authorized to act as trustee, for the purpose of vesting in said person or persons, corporation or corporations, who may be designated Voting Trustee or Voting Trustees, the right to vote thereon for any period of time determined by such agreement, not exceeding ten years, upon the terms and conditions stated in such agreement. Such agreement may contain any other lawful provisions not inconsistent with said purpose. * * * Said Voting Trustees may vote upon the stock so issued or transferred during the period in such agreement specified; stock standing in the names of such Voting Trustees may be voted either in person or by proxy, and in voting said stock, such Voting Trustees shall incur no responsibility as stockholder, trustee or otherwise, except for their own individual malfeasance.

In our view, neither the cases nor the statute sustain the rule for which the defendants contend. Their sweeping formulation would impugn well-recognized means by which a shareholder may effectively confer his voting rights upon others while retaining various other rights. For example, defendants' rule would apparently not permit holders of voting stock to confer upon stockholders of another class, by the device of an amendment of the certificate of incorporation, the exclusive right to vote during periods when dividends are not paid on stock of the latter class. The broad prohibitory meaning which defendants find in Section 18 seems inconsistent with their concession that proxies coupled with an interest may be irrevocable, for the statute contains nothing about such proxies. The statute authorizes, among other things, the deposit or transfer of stock in trust for a specified purpose, namely, "vesting" in the transferee "the right to vote thereon" for a limited period; and prescribes numerous requirements in this connection. Accordingly, it seems reasonable to infer that to establish the relationship and accomplish the purpose which the statute authorizes, its requirements must be complied with. But the statute does not purport to deal with agreements whereby shareholders attempt to bind each other as to how they shall vote their shares. Various forms of such pooling agreements, as they are sometimes called, have been held valid and have been distinguished from voting trusts.

We think the particular agreement before us does not violate Section 18 or constitute an attempted evasion of its requirements, and is not illegal for any other reason. Generally speaking, a shareholder may exercise wide liberality of judgment in the matter of voting, and it is not objectionable that his motives may be for personal profit, or determined by whims or caprice, so long as he violates no duty owed his fellow shareholders. The ownership of voting stock imposes no legal duty to vote at all. A group of shareholders may, without impropriety, vote their respective shares so as to obtain advantages of concerted action. They may lawfully contract with each other to vote in the future in such way as they, or a majority of their group, from time to time determine. Reasonable provisions for cases of failure of the group to reach a determination because of an even division in their ranks seem unobjectionable. The provision here for submission to the arbitrator is plainly designed as a deadlock-breaking measure, and the arbitrator's decision cannot be enforced unless at least one of the parties (entitled to cast one-half of their combined votes) is willing that it be enforced. We find the provision reasonable. It does not appear that the agreement enables the parties to take any unlawful advantage of the [other] shareholder, or of any other person. It offends no rule of law or public policy of this state of which we are aware.

***

*** The Court of Chancery may, in a review of an election, reject votes of a registered shareholder where his voting of them is found to be in violation of rights of another person. It seems to us that upon the application of Mrs. Ringling, the injured party, the votes representing Mrs. Haley's shares should not be counted. Since no infirmity in Mr. North's voting has been demonstrated, his right to recognition of what he did at the meeting should be considered in granting any relief to Mrs. Ringling; for her rights arose under a contract to which Mr. North was not a party. With this in mind, we have concluded that the election should not be declared invalid, but that effect should be given to a rejection of the votes representing Mrs. Haley's shares. No other relief seems appropriate in this proceeding. Mr. North's vote against the motion for adjournment was sufficient to defeat it. With respect to the election of directors, the return of the inspectors should be corrected to show a rejection of Mrs. Haley's votes, and to declare the election of the six persons for whom Mr. North and Mrs. Ringling voted.

This leaves one vacancy in the directorate The question of what to do about such a vacancy was not considered by the court below and has not been argued here. For this reason, and because an election of directors at the 1947 annual meeting (which presumably will be held in the near future) may make a determination of the question unimportant, we shall not decide it on this appeal. If a decision of the point appears important to the parties, any of them may apply to raise it in the Court of Chancery, after the mandate of this court is received there.

An order should be entered directing a modification of the order of the Court of Chancery in accordance with this opinion.

Questions About *Ringling Brothers*

1.   If this case arose today, would the outcome be different under MBCA § 7.31?

2.   The court in *Ringling Brothers* examines the Delaware statute concerning voting trusts and concludes that it did not apply. What is the difference between a voting agreement under MBCA § 7.31 and a voting trust under MBCA § 7.30?

MBCA § 7.31 is pretty straightforward: shareholder voting agreements are permissible. Because shareholders don't really vote on a great variety of issues, shareholder voting agreements typically concern only one topic: how the shareholders will vote their shares for director candidates. After all, this is the only topic that shareholders will reliably vote on year after year. If shareholders want to do something more "interesting" then MBCA § 7.32 would be the more appropriate section. But we will wait until Chapter 9 to discuss that section.

E.   SHAREHOLDERS INSPECTION OF CORPORATE BOOKS AND RECORDS

To round out our discussion of basic shareholder rights, we need to look at one last topic: shareholders' rights to inspect corporate books and records. MBCA § 16.02 is the primary section of the MBCA concerning this topic. When reading it, note that the shareholder is entitled by right to inspect the items referred to in subsection (a). By contrast, if the shareholder wants to inspect the books and records specified in subsection (b), she must (among other things) show that she has a "proper purpose." Courts typically require that the shareholder's purpose be economic in nature, that is, related to her investment in the company. For example, *State ex rel. Pillsbury v. Honeywell, Inc.*, 191 N.W.2d 406 (Minn. 1971), concerned a shareholder who purchased Honeywell stock after learning that it was involved in manufacturing weapons and munitions for the Vietnam war. The court denied the shareholder the right to inspect Honeywell's shareholder list for the purpose of communicating his anti-Vietnam war views to other shareholders and to convince them to pressure the corporation to stop making weapons and munitions.

The following is a recent case from the Supreme Court of Delaware concerning the evidence required from a shareholder who wishes to inspect corporate books and records relating to possible wrongdoing at the corporation.

Seinfeld v. Verizon Communications, Inc.
Supreme Court of Delaware
909 A.2d 117 (2006)

HOLLAND, Justice. The plaintiff-appellant, Frank D. Seinfeld ("Seinfeld"), brought suit under section 220 of the Delaware General Corporation Law to compel the defendant-appellee, Verizon Communications, Inc. ("Verizon"), to produce, for his inspection, its books and records related to the compensation of Verizon's three highest corporate officers from 2000 to 2002. Seinfeld claimed that their executive compensation, individually and collectively, was excessive and wasteful. On cross-motions for summary judgment, the Court of Chancery applied well-established Delaware law and held that Seinfeld had not met his evidentiary burden to demonstrate a proper purpose to justify the inspection of Verizon's records.

The settled law of Delaware required Seinfeld to present some evidence that established a credible basis from which the Court of Chancery could infer there were legitimate issues of possible waste, mismanagement or wrongdoing that warranted further investigation. [Citations omitted.] Seinfeld argues that burden of proof "erects an insurmountable barrier for the minority shareholder of a public company." We have concluded that Seinfeld's argument is without merit.

We reaffirm the well-established law of Delaware that stockholders seeking inspection under section 220 must present "some evidence" to suggest a "credible basis" from which a court can infer that mismanagement, waste or wrongdoing may have occurred. The "credible basis" standard achieves an appropriate balance between providing stockholders who can offer some evidence of possible wrongdoing with access to corporate records and safeguarding the right of the corporation to deny requests for inspections that are based only upon suspicion or curiosity. [Citation omitted.] Accordingly, the judgment of the Court of Chancery must be affirmed.

Facts

Seinfeld asserts that he is the beneficial owner of approximately 3,884 shares of Verizon, held in street name through a brokerage firm. His stated purpose for seeking Verizon's books and records was to investigate mismanagement and corporate waste regarding the executive compensations of Ivan G. Seidenberg, Lawrence T. Babbio, Jr. and Charles R. Lee. Seinfeld alleges that the three executives were all performing in the same job and were paid amounts, including stock options, above the compensation provided for in their employment contracts. Seinfeld's section 220 claim for inspection is further premised on various computations he performed which indicate that the three executives' compensation totaled $205 million over three years and was, therefore, excessive, given their responsibilities to the corporation.

During his deposition, Seinfeld acknowledged he had no factual support for his claim that mismanagement had taken place. He admitted that the three executives did not perform any duplicative work. Seinfeld conceded he had no factual basis to allege the executives "did not earn" the amounts paid to them under their respective employment agreements. Seinfeld also admitted "there is a possibility" that the $205 million executive compensation amount he calculated was wrong.

The issue before us is quite narrow: should a stockholder seeking inspection under section 220 be entitled to relief without being required to show some evidence to suggest a credible basis for wrongdoing? We conclude that the answer must be no.

Stockholder Inspection Rights

Delaware corporate law provides for a separation of legal control and ownership. [Citation omitted.] The legal responsibility to manage the business of the corporation for the benefit of the stockholder owners is conferred on the board of directors by statute. [Citation omitted.] The common law imposes fiduciary duties upon the directors of Delaware corporations to constrain their conduct when discharging that statutory responsibility. [Citation omitted.]

Stockholders' rights to inspect the corporation's books and records were recognized at common law because "[a]s a matter of self-protection, the stockholder was entitled to know how his agents were conducting the affairs of the corporation of which he or she was a part owner." [Citation omitted.] The qualified inspection rights that originated at common law are now codified in Title 8, section 220 of the Delaware Code, which provides, in part:

> (b)   Any stockholder, in person or by attorney or other agent, shall, upon written demand under oath stating the purpose thereof, have the right during the usual hours for business to inspect for any proper purpose [certain books and records of the corporation].

Section 220 provides stockholders of Delaware corporations with a "powerful right." [Citation omitted.] By properly asserting that right under section 220, stockholders are able to obtain information that can be used in a variety of contexts. Stockholders may use information about corporate mismanagement, waste or wrongdoing in several ways. For example, they may: institute derivative litigation; "seek an audience with the board [of directors] to discuss proposed reform or, failing in that, they may prepare a stockholder resolution for the next annual meeting, or mount a proxy fight to elect new directors." [Citation omitted.]

Inspection Litigation Increases

More than a decade ago, we noted that "[s]urprisingly, little use has been made of section 220 as an information-gathering tool in the derivative [suit] context." [Citation omitted.] Today, however, stockholders who have concerns about corporate governance are increasingly making a broad array of section 220 demands. [Citation omitted.] The rise in books and records litigation is directly attributable to this Court's encouragement of stockholders, who can show a proper purpose, to use the "tools at hand" to obtain the necessary information before filing a derivative action. [Citation omitted.] Section 220 is now recognized as "an important part of the corporate governance landscape." [Citation omitted.]

Seinfeld Denied Inspection

The Court of Chancery determined that Seinfeld's deposition testimony established only that he was concerned about the large amount of compensation paid to the three executives. That court concluded that Seinfeld offered "no evidence from which [it] could evaluate whether there is a reasonable ground for suspicion that the executive's compensation rises to the level of waste." It also concluded that Seinfeld did not "submit any evidence showing that the executives were not entitled to [the stock] options." The Court of Chancery properly noted that a disagreement with the business judgment of Verizon's board of directors or its compensation committee is not evidence of wrongdoing and did not satisfy Seinfeld's burden under section 220. The Court of Chancery held:

> viewing the evidence in the light most favorable to Seinfeld, the court must conclude that he has not carried his burden of showing that there is a credible basis from which the court can infer that the Verizon board of directors committed waste or mismanagement in compensating these three executives during the relevant period of time. Instead, the record clearly establishes that Seinfeld's Section 220 demand was made merely on the basis of suspicion or curiosity.

***

Credible Basis From Some Evidence

In a section 220 action, a stockholder has the burden of proof to demonstrate a proper purpose by a preponderance of the evidence. [Citation omitted.] It is well established that a stockholder's desire to investigate wrongdoing or mismanagement is a "proper purpose." [Citation omitted.] Such investigations are proper, because where the allegations of mismanagement prove meritorious, investigation furthers the interest of all stockholders and should increase stockholder return. [Citation omitted.]

The evolution of Delaware's jurisprudence in section 220 actions reflects judicial efforts to maintain a proper balance between the rights of shareholders to obtain information based upon credible allegations of corporation mismanagement and the rights of directors to manage the business of the corporation without undue interference from stockholders. In [*Thomas & Betts Corp. v. Leviton Mfg. Co.*, 681 A.2d 1026 (Del. 1996)], this Court held that, to meet its "burden of proof, a stockholder must present *some credible* basis from which the court can infer that waste or mismanagement may have occurred." [Citation omitted.] Six months later, in [*Security First Corp. v. U.S. Die Casting & Dev. Co.*, 687 A.2d 563 (Del. 1997)], this Court held "[t]here must be *some evidence* of possible mismanagement as would warrant further investigation of the matter." [Citation omitted.]

Our holdings in *Thomas & Betts* and *Security First* were contemporaneous with our decisions that initially encouraged stockholders to make greater use of section 220. In [*Grimes v. Donald*, 673 A.2d 1207 (Del. 1996)], decided just months before *Thomas & Betts*, this Court reaffirmed the salutary use of section 220 as one of the "tools at hand" for stockholders to use to obtain information. [Citation omitted.] When the plaintiff in *Thomas & Betts* suggested that the burden of demonstrating a proper purpose had been attenuated by our encouragement for stockholders to use section 220, we rejected that argument:

> Contrary to plaintiff's assertion in the instant case, this Court in *Grimes* did not suggest that its reference to a Section 220 demand as one of the "tools at hand" was intended to eviscerate or modify the need for a stockholder to show a proper purpose under Section 220. [Citation omitted.]

In *Security First* and *Thomas & Betts*, we adhered to the Court of Chancery's holding in [an earlier case] that:

> A mere statement of a purpose to investigate possible general mismanagement, without more, will not entitle a shareholder to broad [Section 220] inspection relief.   There must be some

evidence of possible mismanagement as would warrant further investigation of the matter. [Citation omitted.]

Standard Achieves Balance

Investigations of meritorious allegations of possible mismanagement, waste or wrongdoing, benefit the corporation, but investigations that are "indiscriminate fishing expeditions" do not. "At some point, the costs of generating more information fall short of the benefits of having more information. At that point, compelling production of information would be wealth-reducing, and so shareholders would not want it produced." [Citation omitted.] Accordingly, this Court has held [in *Security First*] that an inspection to investigate possible wrongdoing where there is no "credible basis," is a license for "fishing expeditions" and thus adverse to the interests of the corporation:

> Stockholders have a right to at least a limited inquiry into books and records when they have established some credible basis to believe that there has been wrongdoing .... Yet it would invite mischief to open corporate management to indiscriminate fishing expeditions. [Citation omitted.]

A stockholder is "not required to prove by a preponderance of the evidence that waste and [mis]management are actually occurring." [Citation omitted.] Stockholders need only show, by a preponderance of the evidence, a credible basis from which the Court of Chancery can infer there is possible mismanagement that would warrant further investigation—a showing that "may ultimately fall well short of demonstrating that anything wrong occurred." [Citation omitted.] That "threshold may be satisfied by a credible showing, through documents, logic, testimony or otherwise, that there are legitimate issues of wrongdoing." [Citation omitted.]

Although the threshold for a stockholder in a section 220 proceeding is not insubstantial, the "credible basis" standard sets the lowest possible burden of proof. The only way to reduce the burden of proof further would be to eliminate any requirement that a stockholder show *some evidence* of possible wrongdoing. That would be tantamount to permitting inspection based on the "mere suspicion" standard that Seinfeld advances in this appeal. However, such a standard has been repeatedly rejected as a basis to justify the enterprise cost of an inspection. [Citation omitted.]

***

We remain convinced that the rights of stockholders and the interests of the corporation in a section 220 proceeding are properly balanced by requiring a stockholder to show "some evidence of *possible* mismanagement as would warrant further investigation." The "credible basis" standard maximizes stockholder value by limiting the range of permitted stockholder inspections to those that might have merit. [Citation omitted.] Accordingly, our holdings in *Security First* and *Thomas & Betts* are ratified and reaffirmed. [Affirmed.]

***

Now that you understand the basics of corporate law, you should try the multiple choice questions that appear below.

PRACTICE QUESTIONS

Multiple Choice Question 5-1: Mattress Corp. has three shareholders: Mr. Sleep, Ms. Slumber, and Mr. Dream. Each shareholder owns 100 shares of common stock, and also serves as one of the three directors of the corporation. Last year, Mr. Sleep and Ms. Slumber signed an agreement that provided that they would each vote their shares so that each of them would be elected to the board of directors every year. This year, Mr. Sleep and Ms. Slumber had a serious argument, resulting in a "falling out." As a result, Mr. Sleep orally agreed with Mr. Dream that they would each vote their shares at this year's shareholder meeting so that Ms. Slumber would not be re-elected to the board. At the shareholders meeting, Ms. Slumber demanded that Mr. Sleep vote his shares as he had agreed with her. Meanwhile, Mr. Dream demanded that Mr. Sleep vote his shares as he had agreed with him. *What will be the result of this dispute?*

A. Mr. Sleep is not bound by his agreement with Mr. Dream because it was not in writing.
B. Mr. Sleep is not bound by his agreement with Ms. Slumber <u>or</u> his agreement with Ms. Slumber because fewer than all of the shareholders signed those agreements and they were not included in the bylaws.
C. Mr. Sleep must vote his shares in accordance with his agreement with Ms. Slumber.
D. Mr. Sleep must vote his shares in accordance with his agreement with Mr. Dream.
E. Both A and C are correct.

Multiple Choice Question 5-2:   Builder Corp., which is in the business of building and remodeling homes, has 125 shareholders. One of the shareholders is Joe Smith, who owns approximately 0.5% of the outstanding shares. Joe is currently in the process of forming his own corporation that will be in the construction business. Joe is seeking to inspect and copy the following two items relating to Builder Corp.: (1) its bylaws and (2) its list of shareholders. Joe plans to use the bylaws as a "model" for the bylaws for his corporation and to use the shareholder list to send advertising flyers concerning his new company to the other 124 shareholders. *Assuming that Joe follows any applicable procedures to seek inspection of these documents, which of the following is correct?*

A.   Joe will be entitled by right to inspect and copy both the bylaws and the shareholder list.

B.   Joe will be entitled by right to inspect and copy the bylaws, but likely will not be permitted to inspect the shareholder list because he does not have a proper purpose for doing so.

C.   Joe will be entitled by right to inspect and copy the shareholder list, but likely will not be permitted to inspect the bylaws because he does not have a proper purpose for doing so.

D.   Joe likely will not be permitted to inspect either the bylaws or the shareholder list because he does not have a proper purpose for doing so.

Multiple Choice Question 5-3:   The board of directors of Union Corp. ("Union") consists of nine directors, all of whom are elected annually by the shareholders. The only outstanding shares of Union stock are 10,000 shares of common stock. Union's articles of incorporation provide that directors are elected by cumulative voting.   Under cumulative voting, how many shares of Union common stock would a shareholder need to own to make sure that she is able to elect at least one member of the board of directors? Assume that all 10,000 shares will be voted.

A.   1,000 shares.
B.   1,001 shares.
C.   1,111 shares.
D.   1,112 shares.

Multiple Choice Question 5-4: BBQ Sauce, Inc. ("BBQSI") is a corporation that has 100,000 shares of common stock outstanding, owned by five individuals (each of whom owns 20,000 shares). On August 1, the corporate secretary of BBQSI personally delivered to all five shareholders written notice of a special shareholder meeting to be held on August 13. The notice did not state the purpose of the meeting, but did state the date, time, and place of the meeting. All five shareholders attended the meeting and were asked to vote on a proposal to sell all of BBQSI's assets, including its factory, to another company. Three of the shareholders present at the meeting voted yes, and the other two voted no. *Was the shareholder approval of the sale of BBQSI's assets valid?*

A. Yes.
B. No. The action was invalid because notice of the meeting was not given at least sixty days before the meeting.
C. No. The action was invalid because the notice of the meeting did not specify the purpose of the meeting.
D. Yes, because any defect in the notice was cured by the fact that a majority of the shares were voted in favor of the proposal.

Multiple Choice Question 5-5:   On April 1, the corporate secretary of Bug Control, Inc. ("Bug Control") personally delivered to all nine members of Bug Control's board of directors written notice of a special board meeting to be held on April 2. The notice did not state the purpose of the meeting, but did state the date, time, and place of the meeting. Five directors attended the meeting and were asked to vote on a proposal to sell all of Bug Control's assets to Bug Zapper, Inc. Three of the directors present at the meeting voted yes, and the other two directors voted no. *Was the board's action valid?*

A. No. The board's action was invalid because the notice was not given at least two days before the meeting.
B. No. The board's action was invalid because the notice was not given at least ten days before the meeting.
C. No. The board's action was invalid because the notice did not specify the purpose of the meeting.
D. Yes. The board's action was valid because the five directors who attended the meeting were a quorum, they waived any defect in notice by attending the meeting, and a majority of the directors present at the meeting voted to approve the asset sale.

Multiple Choice Question 5-6: The board of directors of Square Corp. consists of seven directors. Neither Square Corp.'s articles of incorporation nor its bylaws contain any provisions concerning director meetings, except that its bylaws provide that regular meetings of the board shall be held at 10:00 a.m. on the first business day of each month at the company's offices and that the President of the Corporation has the power to call special meetings of the board. Because Square Corp. needed quickly to approve a loan agreement with Moneybags Bank, Mr. Triangle, Square Corp.'s President, sent the following notice to each of the directors on June 7 via facsimile (fax), in each case to the fax number that the director had previously provided to the corporation:

June 7, [year]
Notice of Special Meeting of the Board of Directors of Square Corp.

Dear [Director's Name]: Please be advised that the board of directors of Square Corp. will hold a special meeting on June 13 at 8:00 a.m. at the company's offices. Please let me know as soon as possible if you will not be able to attend.

Very Truly Yours, Mr. Triangle, President

At the June 13, board meeting, three directors and Mr. Triangle (who was not a director) appeared in person. At the meeting, all three directors present voted to approve the loan agreement. Mr. Triangle then presented a written proxy signed by Mr. Octagon (who was a director) which said that Mr. Octagon delegated authority to vote in favor of the loan agreement to Mr. Triangle. Mr. Triangle then said to the other directors, "Your three votes, plus this proxy from Mr. Octagon, means that the loan agreement is approved." You represent Moneybags Bank, which has asked for your opinion as to whether the loan agreement was properly approved by the board of directors of Square Corp. *You correctly tell the bank:*

A.   The loan agreement was not properly approved because a quorum of directors was not present at the meeting and because the notice of the directors' meeting was sent fewer than 10 days before the meeting.

B.   The loan agreement was not properly approved because a quorum of directors was not present at the meeting.

C.   The loan agreement was not properly approved because, even though a quorum of directors was present at the meeting, the notice of the directors' meeting did not state what the purpose of the meeting was.

D.   The loan agreement was properly approved.

Multiple Choice Question 5-7: The board of directors of Yellow Corp. consists of eleven directors. Neither Yellow Corp.'s articles of incorporation nor its bylaws contain any provisions concerning director meetings, except that its bylaws provide that regular board meetings shall be held at 9:00 a.m. on the first business day of January, April, July and October each year at the company's offices. No notice of the October 1, meeting was given to the directors. At the October 1 board meeting, five directors appeared in person, and called another director from the conference telephone and put him on speakerphone so that he could hear what was being discussed at the meeting and speak to the other directors. At the meeting, four directors voted to approve a new employment agreement with Yellow Corp.'s president. Shortly after the vote was taken, another director, Mr. White, burst through the doors of the room where the meeting was being held and yelled: "I object to this meeting. The approval of that employment agreement is invalid because I didn't receive notice of this meeting, there's no valid quorum and only four directors voted for it!" *Is Mr. White correct?*

A. Yes, because he didn't receive notice of the board meeting.
B. Yes, because a quorum of directors wasn't present at the meeting.
C. Yes, because only four directors out of eleven voted to approve the employment agreement.
D. No.

Multiple Choice Question 5-8: Regular Corp.'s annual shareholder meeting will be held on December 1 and proper notice was mailed to all of its shareholders on November 3. The record date for voting at the meeting is November 1. On November 25, a shareholder named Allie signed a proxy card that stated that it was "irrevocable" and that authorized Buffy to vote Allie's shares at the meeting. Buffy is also a shareholder of Regular Corp. Nonetheless, Allie attended the meeting and wanted to revoke the proxy and vote the shares. *May Allie revoke this proxy?*

A. No, because the proxy stated that it was irrevocable.
B. No, because the proxy stated that it was irrevocable and Buffy, as a shareholder in Regular Corp., has an interest in the shares subject to the proxy.
C. Yes, because the proxy was signed after the record date.
D. Yes, because the proxy was signed fewer than ten days before the meeting.
E. Yes, because Buffy has no interest in the shares subject to the proxy.

Multiple Choice Question 5-9: Desert Corporation has the following balance sheet:

Assets		Liabilities	
Cash	$ 70,000	Note	$ 30,000
Equipment	$ 50,000	Line of Credit	$ 40,000
Real Estate	$ 250,000		
Total	$ 370,000	Total	$ 70,000
		Shareholder's Equity	
		Paid-in Capital	$ 50,000
		Capital Surplus	$ 150,000
		Earned Surplus	$ 100,000
		Total	$ 300,000

What is the maximum amount of distribution that the board may lawfully declare under the MBCA and pay to the common stockholders? You may assume that Desert Corporation will be able to pay its debts as they become due in the usual course of business after the distribution and that it has no preferred stock.

A. $100,000
B. $250,000
C. $300,000
D. $370,000

Multiple Choice Question 5-10: Same facts as Multiple Choice Question 5-9, except that Desert Corporation also has 10,000 shares of preferred stock outstanding, each of which has a $5 per-share liquidation preference. *What is the maximum amount of distribution that the board may lawfully declare under the MBCA and pay to the common stockholders?* You may assume that Desert Corporation will be able to pay its debts as they become due in the usual course of business after the distribution.

A. $100,000
B. $250,000
C. $300,000
D. $370,000

Multiple Choice Question 5-11: The board of directors of Pink Corp. consists of nine directors, all of whom are elected annually by the shareholders. Pink corporate has 1,000 authorized shares and 300 outstanding shares of common stock. Pink Corp.'s articles of incorporation provide for cumulative voting. *How many shares of Pink Corp. common stock would a shareholder need to own to ensure that she is able to elect at least two members of the board if all shares are voted?*

A.   31 shares
B.   61 shares
C.   101 shares
D.   202 shares

Multiple Choice Question 5-12: Same facts as Multiple Choice Question 5-11, except that Pink Corp.'s board of directors consists of ten directors. *How many shares of Pink Corp. common stock would a shareholder need to own to ensure that she is able to elect at least two members of the board if all shares are voted?*

A.   60 shares
B.   40 shares
C.   28 shares
D.   55 shares

Multiple Choice Question 5-13: The board of directors of Grey Corp. consists of five directors, all of whom are elected annually. On April 1, the only outstanding shares of Grey Corp. stock were 1,000 shares of common stock. On that date, Mr. Black owned 501 of these shares and Mr. White owned the other 499 shares. However, on April 3, Mr. Black sold one share of Grey Corp. common stock to Mr. White. Grey Corp.'s articles of incorporation provide that shareholders elect directors by a plurality vote. Both Mr. Black and Mr. White attended Grey Corp.'s annual shareholders' meeting to vote for their choices for election to the board of directors. The record date for the meeting was April 2. The meeting was held on May 3. *Assuming that both shareholders vote all of the shares that they can vote for the election of director candidates, which of the following is correct?*

A.   Mr. Black will be able to elect his choices to all five open director positions.
B.   Mr. Black will be able to elect his choices to only four of the five open director positions.
C.   Mr. Black will be able to elect his choices to only three of the five open director positions
D.   Each of Mr. Black and Mr. White will elect two directors and they must agree upon the fifth director because they each own the same number of shares.

Multiple Choice Question 5-14: The only outstanding stock of Stereo Corp. ("Stereo") is 100,000 shares of common stock. In April, Stereo's board of directors approved resolutions calling a special meeting of shareholders to be held on May 28, and setting May 7 as the record date for the meeting. On May 10, Stereo's corporate secretary mailed a notice to all of the persons who were Stereo shareholders on May 7. The notice stated the date, time, and place of the meeting, and also described the purposes of the meeting, which were to consider and vote on (1) selling a factory that Stereo owned in China and (2) amending Stereo's articles of incorporation to require that at least 66.67% of the outstanding shares of Stereo stock must vote in favor of a merger in order for any merger to occur. Shareholders that owned a total of 67,000 shares attended the meeting in person or by valid proxies. At the meeting, Proposal 1 (Sale of Factory) received 8,000 "yes" votes, 3,000 "no" votes, and 56,000 abstentions. Proposal 2 (Articles Amendment) received 51,000 "yes" votes, 11,000 "no" votes, and 5,000 abstentions. ***Did Stereo's shareholders properly approve Proposal 1 (Sale of Factory)?***

A.   Yes.

B.   No. Proposal 1 failed because Stereo's shareholders did not receive proper notice of the meeting; therefore, the meeting was invalid.

C.   No. Proposal 1 failed because there were only 8,000 yes votes, which is less than a majority of the 100,000 outstanding shares.

D.   No. Proposal 1 failed because there were only 8,000 yes votes, which is less than a majority of the 67,000 shares represented at the meeting.

Multiple Choice Question 5-15: Same facts as Multiple Choice Question 5-14. Regardless of how you answered that question, assume that proper notice of the shareholder meeting was given. ***Did Stereo's shareholders properly approve Proposal 2 (Articles Amendment)?***

A.   Yes. Proposal 2 passed because the 51,000 yes votes were more than the required 66.67% of the 67,000 shares represented at the meeting.

B.   Yes. Proposal 2 passed because the 51,000 yes votes were more than the required 66.67% of the 62,000 votes cast on Proposal 2.

C.   No. Proposal 2 failed because the yes votes fell short of the required 66.67% of the 100,000 outstanding shares.

D.   Yes. Proposal 2 passed because the 51,000 yes votes were a majority of the 100,000 outstanding shares.

Multiple Choice Question 5-16:   Mexican Restaurant Corp. ("MRC") owns and operates a chain of seventeen restaurants that serve Mexican food. MRC's articles of incorporation contain only the items that are required by MBCA § 2.02(a). Janice is a majority shareholder of MRC but is not a director or officer of MRC. Janice was horrified when she learned that MRC's board of directors approved a resolution to stop serving Mexican food at each of the restaurants and to serve Norwegian food instead. Janice thinks this a terrible decision that will be disastrous for the company and has come to you for advice on the best course of action to have the board's decision be changed as quickly as possible. *Which of the following would be the best advice for Janice?* You may assume that Janice has the power to call a special meeting of MRC's shareholders.

A.   Janice should call a special meeting of shareholders for the purpose of overturning the board's decision.
B.   Janice should sue for an injunction because the shareholders did not approve this fundamental change in MRC's business.
C.   Janice should call a special meeting of shareholders for the purpose of removing the current directors and replacing them with different directors.
D.   Janice should force the corporation to repurchase her stock because she did not approve this fundamental change in MRC's business.

Multiple Choice Question 5-17:   In August, Hassan and Pete were discussing their idea to form a corporation to run a coffee shop, but had not taken any steps to start the business. On September 1, Hassan saw that an ideal location for the coffee shop was for rent. Unbeknownst to Pete, Hassan then signed a two-year lease with the landlord, but insisted that the following clause be included in the lease: "Landlord understands and agrees that this lease will be adopted by Two Friends Coffee, Inc. upon formation of that corporation and that Two Friends Coffee, Inc. will thereafter be liable for rental payments under this lease." Two Friends Coffee, Inc. was incorporated on September 18. Hassan and Pete, who became the sole shareholders and the sole directors of the corporation, then unanimously passed a board resolution that provided that the corporation agreed to adopt the lease. Unfortunately, Two Friends Coffee, Inc. went bankrupt six months later. The landlord has sued both Hassan and Pete for money damages under the lease. *What is the likely outcome of this lawsuit?*

A.   Neither Hassan nor Pete will be liable unless the landlord can convince the court to "pierce the corporate veil."
B.   Neither Hassan nor Pete will be liable because the terms of the lease contemplate that only Two Friends Coffee, Inc. will be liable.
C.   Hassan will likely be liable but Pete will not be.
D.   Both Hassan and Pete will be liable because they were partners at the time that the lease was signed.

Multiple Choice Question 5-18:   Your client was a subcontractor on a construction project and is owned $10,000 by General Contractor Corp. ("GCC"). However, GCC is insolvent and unable to pay its bills. Roosevelt Smith, a local businessman, is the sole shareholder and director of GCC. *Which of the following facts, if true, would help your client to convince a court to pierce the corporate veil and hold Mr. Smith liable for this debt?*

  I. Mr. Smith owns several other businesses, including a restaurant, a movie theatre, and a concrete manufacturing business.

  II. Mr. Smith showed your client a balance sheet for GSS that misrepresented its financial condition by inaccurately indicating it had $270,000 in assets.

  III. GSS has several other unpaid creditors.

  IV. Mr. Smith is a multimillionaire.

  V. Mr. Smith used GSS funds to pay the mortgage payments on his house.

A. All of the above.
B. I, II, and V only.
C. II and V only.
D. II, III, IV and V only.
E. II, III, and V only.

Multiple Choice Question 5-19: Your client, Rich Spoiled, just inherited 25% of the outstanding shares of Scion Corp. from his father Anthony, who died last week. Anthony was one of the founders of Scion Corp., served as one of its four directors, and was the president, earning a salary of $250,000 per year. Rich has come to you for advice concerning his rights as a 25% shareholder of Scion Corp. *Assuming no other facts, which of the following is correct advice for Rich?*

I.   If Scion Corp. issues new shares of stock in the future, it must offer Rich the opportunity to purchase at least 25% of the new shares.

II.   Because he owns 25% of the stock, Rich will be entitled to select one of the four directors at the next annual shareholder meeting.

III.   Before Rich may sell any of his shares of Scion Corp. stock, he must offer the other shareholders a right of first refusal to purchase the shares.

IV.   Rich may require Scion Corp. to repurchase his shares if he no longer wants them.

A. None of the above.
B. I, II, and III only.
C. I, II, and IV only.
D. II only.
E. III only.

Multiple Choice Question 5-20: Alpha Corp. produces automobile parts. Alpha Corp. has two shareholders: Mr. Alpha owns 99% of the outstanding common stock (for which he paid $990 when the corporation was formed ten years ago), and Mr. Beta owns the remaining 1% (for which he paid $10). When the corporation was formed, the two shareholders elected Mr. Alpha as the sole director of the corporation. Mr. Alpha, in his capacity as a director, then appointed himself as the President, Secretary and Treasurer of the corporation and approved his salary, which is $300,000 per year. No director or shareholder meetings have been held since that time. Mr. Beta does not work for Alpha Corp.; instead, he has a full-time job with another company. Following payment of its expenses (including Mr. Alpha's salary), Alpha Corp.'s annual after-tax profits average about $1,000. One year ago, Mr. Alpha borrowed $8,000 from Alpha Corp. As a result, Alpha Corp. has only approximately $1,000 in cash on hand. Metal Corp., one of Alpha Corp.'s suppliers, claimed that Alpha Corp. owes it approximately $250,000 in unpaid bills and that Mr. Alpha promised that he would "stand behind" these bills. Mr. Alpha informed Metal Corp. that Alpha Corp. does not have enough assets to repay this debt. Metal Corp. then sued Mr. Alpha and Mr. Beta, claiming that they should be personally liable for this debt. *Which of the following is the most likely result in this lawsuit?*

A.   Mr. Alpha will be personally liable for this debt because the court will "pierce the corporate veil," but Mr. Beta will not likely be personally liable for this debt.

B.   Neither Mr. Alpha nor Mr. Beta will be personally liable for this debt because shareholders are not liable for the corporation's debts.

C.   Both Mr. Alpha and Mr. Beta will be personally liable for this debt because Alpha Corp. is a closely held corporation.

D.   Neither Mr. Alpha nor Mr. Beta will be personally liable for this debt because Alpha Corp. is a closely held corporation.

Multiple Choice Question 5-21: Fish Corp. ("Fish") has 3,000 outstanding shares of common stock. Twelve people own these 3,000 shares, including Ms. Bass (who owns 300 shares), Mr. Perch (who owns 300 shares), and Mr. Trout (who owns 301 shares). Twelve years ago, Ms. Bass, Mr. Perch, and Mr. Trout signed a shareholder voting agreement that provides that they will always vote their shares of Fish stock so that the three of them are always directors of Fish. Including Ms. Bass, Mr. Perch, and Mr. Trout, there are nine persons on the Fish board of directors, and the corporation's articles of incorporation provide that directors are elected by cumulative voting. The annual meeting of Fish shareholders is scheduled for tomorrow. However, earlier today Ms. Bass had a bitter argument with Mr. Perch and Mr. Trout. As a result, Mr. Perch and Mr. Trout are refusing to comply with the shareholder voting agreement. *Which of the following is correct?*

A.   The shareholder voting agreement is no longer valid, because it was signed more than ten years ago.

B.   The shareholder voting agreement is not valid because only three out of the twelve shareholders signed it.

C.   Even if the agreement is no longer valid and no other shareholders vote for her, Ms. Bass has enough shares to elect herself to the board under cumulative voting.

D.   None of the above is correct.

Multiple Choice Question 5-22: X Corp. will be holding its annual shareholder meeting next month and the board has sent out a notice of the meeting to its shareholders and also set a record date. As of the record date set by the board, Frank Jones was shown on the corporation's stock ledger book as the owner of 10,000 shares of the corporation's common stock. However, after the record date but shortly before the meeting, he sold his shares to Ralph Smith. Thinking that he might be unable to personally attend the meeting, Frank gave a proxy to vote his shares to his brother, Arthur Jones, who was also an X Corp. shareholder and who told Frank that he would be personally attending the meeting. Frank has now changed his mind and has appeared at the meeting demanding the right to vote the shares. Also at the meeting are Ralph and Arthur, who are likewise demanding the right to vote the same shares. *Which of the following statements is most correct:*

A.   The corporation should permit Frank to vote.

B.   The corporation should permit Ralph to vote.

C.   The corporation should permit Arthur to vote.

D.   The corporation must adjourn the meeting until the issue can be resolved.

Multiple Choice Question 5-23: Forty-eight percent of the stock of Widget Corp. ("WC") is owned in equal amounts by four individuals, with the remaining 52% of the stock owned by Y Corporation. The four WC shareholders are also the officers and directors of WC, as well as being directors of Y Corporation. WC was incorporated originally to engage in the purchase and sale of widgets and was adequately capitalized. Although it was initially profitable, when widgets lost favor in the eyes of the public, the board changed its direction and the corporation began to engage in the purchase and sale of wassits. Unfortunately, wassits sold poorly and WC is virtually bankrupt. A number of suits have now been started by creditors, one of whom is asking the court to "pierce the corporate veil" and to impose liability personally on the WC's shareholders. *Which one of the following factors would the court consider to be most significant in ruling on the plaintiff's request to pierce the corporate veil:*

A.   That WC is currently insolvent.
B.   That the shareholders of WC have consistently intermingled the corporation's assets with their own.
C.   That the shareholders of WC are also directors of Y Corporation, thus dominating WC's affairs.
D.   That a majority of WC's stock is owned by another corporation.

Multiple Choice Question 5-24:   A corporation's registered agent has the authority to:

A.   Accept service of process on behalf of the corporation.
B.   Bind the corporation to loan agreements with major banks.
C.   Hire and fire employees for the incorporation.
D.   All of the above.

Multiple Choice Question 5-25: Which of the following is correct?

A.   An individual can be an officer or director of a corporation, but not both.
B.   Each director must own at least one share of stock in the corporation.
C.   Directors usually cannot be removed from the board except for "cause."
D.   None of the above is correct.

Multiple Choice Question 5-26: *The officers of a corporation:*

A.   Are appointed by the board of directors.
B.   May have actual, express and actual, implied authority, but cannot have apparent authority to act on behalf of the corporation.
C.   Can be dismissed by the shareholders at an annual or special meeting.
D.   None of the above is correct.

Multiple Choice Question 5-27: Melina was one of several persons interested in organizing a book publishing company to be incorporated as Interesting Books Corp. Melina entered into an employment contract for the editorial services of Marcus. It was mutually understood that Marcus would perform certain duties and that these might be performed on behalf of a corporation yet to be formed. Melina, purporting on behalf of Interesting Books Corp., also entered into an agreement with Anton Printing Company for printing services to be rendered by it at a future date. Interesting Books Corp. was later properly incorporated under the MBCA, after execution of these contracts. Marcus then performed services for the corporation in accordance with his agreement with Melina. *If Marcus seeks to recover the compensation agreed upon in his agreement with Melina.*

A.   The corporation is liable to Marcus for the salary under the agreement if it adopted the agreement.
B.   The corporation is automatically bound by the pre-incorporation agreement of Melina as its agent.
C.   Absent express adoption of the agreement by the corporation's board of directors, Marcus may recover for his services only from Melina.
D.   Any personal obligation Melina undertook under the agreement is terminated if Marcus assumes a position with the corporation at the salary specified in the agreement.

Multiple Choice Question 5-28: Assume that Melina did not disclose the fact that Interesting Books Corp. had not yet been incorporated to Anton Printing Company when the two parties executed the contract for printing services. *Melina will not have any liability on the contract:*

A.   because she made it in the name of Interesting Books Corp.
B.   if Interesting Books Corp. subsequently adopts the contract.
C.   if Interesting Books Corp. and Anton Printing Company enter into a novation regarding the contract.
D.   if Interesting Books Corp. is incorporated but its board then rejects the contract.

CHAPTER 6
THE DUTY OF CARE

Directors owe two primary fiduciary duties: the duty of care and the duty of loyalty. This chapter concerns the duty of care, as well as the so-called duty of good faith. Chapter 7 concerns the duty of loyalty. In addition, Chapter 8 discusses one of the primary means to enforce these duties: the derivative action, which is a lawsuit brought by a shareholder on behalf of the corporation.

Conceptually, the duty of care and the duty of loyalty should be easily distinguishable. At the risk of oversimplification, if the allegation is that the directors (or some of them) have made an incredibly unwise decision that led to losses for the corporation, or that the directors were "asleep at the switch" while something damaging was occurring that they could have prevented, the duty of care is the underlying basis for the claim. The basic problem in duty-of-care cases is that the directors made bad decisions or were lazy in their supervision of the corporation.

On the other hand, if the allegation is that a director(s) was (were) motivated by *personal* interests that conflicted with the corporation's interests, the duty of loyalty is involved. In other words, the hallmark of a duty-of-loyalty problem is the presence of a conflict of interest on the part of one or more of the directors. Or at least this is how things used to be; as you will see in Section 6.07 below, recent Delaware decisions indicate that the duty of good faith—which may or may not involve a conflict of interest—should be characterized as an aspect of the duty of loyalty. Thus, one could make a credible argument that a discussion of the duty of good faith belongs in Chapter 7 rather than this chapter. But it is in this chapter for reasons that hopefully will become clear as you read on.

Prior chapters featured a lot of hypothetical problems, many of which were designed to require close attention to the relevant statutes. This chapter will be different. While this chapter does discuss the complex MBCA provisions concerning the duty of care, case law is much more important here than it was in prior chapters. For one thing, there are many "classic" duty-of-care cases that all law students should read. No one should take a course on Business Organizations without being exposed to *Smith v. Van Gorkom* (and many others). Also, many of these cases raise important policy issues and involve conclusions as to which reasonable minds may disagree. While the "black letter law" of the duty of care can usually be easily stated, its application often is difficult.

§ 6.01   FIDUCIARY DUTIES IN GENERAL

Before delving into the details of the duty of care, it might be helpful to address a few "big picture" issues. First, who owes the fiduciary duties of care and loyalty? Clearly members of the board of directors do. You will see several statutes and cases that explicitly provide that directors owe fiduciary duties. There is absolutely no doubt on this point. However, directors are not the only "players" in a corporation. What about shareholders? What about officers and other employees? Corporate statutes (usually) do not address the duties that these groups may or may not owe.

Generally, shareholders do not owe fiduciary duties to anyone. (However, you will see some exceptions to this statement in Chapters 9 and 11.) As for officers and employees, recall from Chapter 5 that these persons are considered agents of the corporation for many purposes. As you saw in Chapter 2, agents owe a duty of care and a duty of loyalty, both as described in various sections of the *Restatement (Third) of Agency*. For example, Section 8.08 of the *Restatement* provides in part that "an agent has a duty to the principal to act with the care, competence, and diligence normally exercised by agents in similar circumstances." Thus, if a warehouse worker negligently damages the corporation's merchandise, the corporation theoretically has a cause of action against the worker. Such lawsuits are not typical, however. Many employees are "judgment proof" in the sense that they are not collectible. Insurance is usually a better solution than suing one's employees.

As you should remember, officers are a subset of employees, so they also owe the duties of care and loyalty that are described in the *Restatement*. However, the MBCA perhaps can be said to elevate the duties that officers owe beyond those of "regular" employees; MBCA § 8.42, entitled "Standards of Conduct for Officers," uses identical language to MBCA § 8.30, which is entitled "Standards of Conduct for Directors." Moreover, the Delaware Supreme Court recently addressed the nature of officers' duties:

> The [Delaware] Court of Chancery has held, and the parties do not dispute, that corporate officers owe fiduciary duties that are identical to those owed by corporate directors. That issue— whether or not officers owe fiduciary duties identical to those of directors—has been characterized as a matter of first impression for this Court. In the past, we have implied that officers of Delaware corporations, like directors, owe fiduciary duties of care and loyalty, and that the fiduciary duties of officers are the same as those of directors. We now explicitly so hold.

Gantler v. Stephens, 965 A.2d 695, 708-09 (Del. 2009) (citations omitted throughout).   While the remainder of this chapter will consider the duties that *directors* owe, it would be a mistake for you to come away thinking that these are the only persons who owe duties.

Second, to *whom* do directors owe duties?   There is less clarity on this issue that one would desire.   The traditional answer is that the directors owe their duties to the *corporation* and that their main goal should be to maximize the corporation's profits (legally, of course).   This sounds like a simple statement and it usually works well, but there are times when it isn't appropriate.   For example, later in this chapter you will read the case of *Smith v. Van Gorkom*, which involves the directors of Trans Union deciding whether to approve a merger of Trans Union into another company.   If the merger occurs, the shareholders of Trans Union would be paid cash for their shares and Trans Union would cease to exist.   In a situation like that, it seems silly to talk about the directors owing duties to Trans Union—Trans Union won't be around anymore if the merger happens! Instead, the directors' goal should be to enrich the shareholders in the merger because this is their "last shot."   Indeed, to oversimplify things a bit, there is a line of Delaware cases that basically hold that directors must get the best price reasonably available for the shareholders' stock when the corporation will be sold. You will see some of these cases in Chapter 12.

An alternative statement of directors' duties, found in many authorities, is that directors owe duties to the corporation *and* its shareholders.   However, this statement is somewhat misleading because it could give one the impression that shareholders may have a *direct* cause of action against the directors for any breach of those duties.   Instead, the usual method of enforcing directors' duties (if the corporation itself does not take steps to do so) is through a *derivative* lawsuit.   See Chapter 8.   But as stated above, what this statement really means is that the directors' primary goal should be to maximize the corporation's profits.   Although there is a great deal of debate on this issue, many view this norm as being economically efficient.   One reason is that, compared to other "constituencies," the shareholders are better incentivized to monitor the directors' performance because they can be dramatically affected by the corporation's financial performance.   As you saw in Chapter 5, creditors either will be fully paid or they won't be, but this is a narrower range of outcomes than for shareholders, who may either lose their investment entirely if the corporation goes bankrupt or become extremely rich if the corporation does extremely well.   Another reason is that shareholders' goals and interests are relatively homogenous compared to other groups such as employees, making it easier for directors to decide their goals.

In any event, corporate law traditionally has held that directors do not owe duties to anyone other than the shareholders.   But there are even a few caveats to this statement.   First, a few cases have recognized that directors may owe duties to creditors when the corporation is insolvent or close to it. Second, in the *Francis v. United Jersey Bank* case that appears later in this chapter, the court discusses situations in which directors may owe duties to the clients or customers of the corporation. This is particularly so when the corporation is a bank or financial institution. Further, about twenty-nine states have "constituency" statutes that allow directors to consider the interests of persons other than shareholders, such as employees and the communities in which the corporation operates, when making decisions. However, these statutes do not create any cause of action on the part of these groups if the directors do not do so.

In the end, the question of to *whom* directors owe duties is a complicated one. Nonetheless, in this textbook we will usually follow the general rule and say that directors owe fiduciary duties to the corporation and—indirectly—to the shareholders.

§ 6.02   THE STATUTES

As with anything in the law, if there's a statute that addresses an issue, it's probably a good idea to begin there. So before turning to the many cases in this chapter, let's examine MBCA §§ 8.30 and 8.31.

MBCA § 8.30 has six subsections. Subsection (a) tells us that a director must act in good faith, and in a manner that she reasonably believes to be in the best interests of the corporation. The meaning of "good faith" is considered in detail in Section 6.07 below. As for the second clause, note the phrase "reasonably believes." Students sometimes miss this phrase, and come away from reading the statute thinking that directors have a duty to *act* in the best interests of the corporation. If that were the standard, then it would be pretty easy to sue the directors every time a decision turned out poorly. But as you will see, it actually is quite difficult to successfully sue directors for a breach of the duty of care.

Subsection (b) identifies the standard of care: when performing their duties, directors must use "the care that a person in a like position would reasonably believe appropriate under similar circumstances." Although this sounds like a negligence-based standard and courts in many states have held that the standard of care is to avoid negligent behavior, this is not the case under the MBCA—probably. Earlier versions of the MBCA stated that directors must use "the care an ordinarily prudent person in a like position would exercise under similar circumstances." In discussing the change to the current language, the official comment to MBCA § 8.30 notes that the former language "has long been problematic" and "had a familiar resonance long associated with the field of tort law." Thus, the language of MBCA § 8.30(b) was modified. As you read the cases in this chapter, you will see that different courts use different language to discuss the applicable standard of care, but one thing that is clear is that it is the fact-finder in litigation who will make the determination of whether the director-defendant(s) complied with the applicable standard of care.

Subsection (c) requires directors to disclose to other directors information that is relevant to their decision-making process or oversight function, unless a confidentiality obligation applies. Subsection (d), together with subsections (f)(1) and (f)(3), allows the board to delegate tasks to other persons within the corporation. Subsection (e), together with subsections (f)(1) through (f)(3), allows directors to rely on certain opinions and reports from other persons. These subsections will be considered in more detail later in this chapter.

Suppose that a director has breached her duty of care under MBCA § 8.30(b). Does that mean that she will be liable for damages to the corporation? Not necessarily. In order to hold a director liable, the plaintiff has to run a gauntlet of obstacles in MBCA § 8.31, which is entitled "Standards of Liability for Directors." First, subsection (a)(1)(i) recognizes that some—but not all—corporations have provisions in their articles of incorporation that shield directors from monetary liability for all acts or omissions other than the four exceptions set forth in MBCA § 2.02(b)(4). These articles provisions are considered in more detail in Section 6.05(A) below, but it should be obvious that their presence will make the plaintiff's case much more difficult. In addition, MBCA § 8.31(a)(1)(ii) may provide a director with protection if she is being sued with respect to a "director's conflicting interest transaction." We will defer further discussion of these sorts of transactions until Chapter 7.

Assuming that the plaintiff has made it this far, subsection (a)(2) requires her to establish that the director's (or directors') conduct met any one or more of the five types of "bad" conduct described in that section. Finally, subsection (b) imposes even more requirements on the plaintiff.

All in all, MBCA § 8.31 presents a pretty tough test for plaintiffs suing directors. The rest of this chapter presents additional obstacles.

§ 6.03   DIRECTOR DECISION-MAKING

Objectives: *In a situation where the directors of a corporation are being sued for a breach of their duty of care as a result of a decision they have made, you should be able to (1) identify the arguments the plaintiff will make to impose personal liability on the directors, (2) identify the arguments the defendant directors will make that they have not breached their duty of care or* *otherwise should not be held liable, and (3) evaluate how a court should decide the case.*

Subsidiary Objectives For Plaintiffs: *For a client who wishes to sue the directors for a business decision that they have made, you should also be able to:*

- *explain the standard for a director's duty of care and evaluate whether your client will be able to show that the defendant-directors breached their duty of care;*

- *explain the various "hoops" that your client must overcome to win her case, both under statutes, case law, and (if applicable) provisions in the corporation's articles of incorporation, and evaluate whether your client will be able to meet these requirements;*

- *explain what will happen if your client* cannot *rebut the business judgment rule or meet any other applicable requirement; and*

- *explain what will happen if your client* can *rebut the business judgment rule and meet the other applicable requirements.*

Subsidiary Objectives For Defendants: *In addition to the above, for a client who is a director and is being sued for a business decision made by the board, you should also be able to explain her potential liability in the following situations: (1) there were several other people on the board and the other directors were fully informed of all material information before they made the challenged business decision, but your client paid no attention whatsoever at the board meeting; and (2) your client voted against the challenged business decision, but enough other directors voted in favor of it for the decision to be approved.*

As you saw in Chapter 5, MBCA § 8.01 gives the board the power to make virtually all of the corporation's business decisions and even though the board may delegate some authority to officers and other employees, the "big" decisions must be made by the board. Boards may need to make decisions quickly in response to rapidly changing circumstances and with less-than-perfect information. Moreover, in business there often isn't a "standard" approach to a problem like there would be if you, say, went to the doctor to have a symptom diagnosed. Thus, you should not be surprised that, like anything in life, a decision by the board may turn out badly—like New Coke, or the Pontiac Aztek, or the decision to get involved in the subprime mortgage market.

Here is a case where a board decided *not* to do something that a shareholder thought would surely earn more money for the corporation.

Shlensky v. Wrigley
Appellate Court of Illinois, First District, Third Division
237 N.E.2d 776 (1968)

SULLIVAN, Justice.   This is an appeal from a dismissal of plaintiff's amended complaint on motion of the defendants. The action was a stockholders' derivative suit against the directors for negligence and mismanagement. The corporation was also made a defendant. Plaintiff sought damages and an order that defendants cause the installation of lights in Wrigley Field and the scheduling of night baseball games.

Plaintiff is a minority stockholder of defendant corporation, Chicago National League Ball Club (Inc.), a Delaware corporation with its principal place of business in Chicago, Illinois. Defendant corporation owns and operates the major league professional baseball team known as the Chicago Cubs. The corporation also engages in the operation of Wrigley Field, the Cubs' home park, the concessionaire sales during Cubs' home games, television and radio broadcasts of Cubs' home games, the leasing of the field for football games and other events and receives its share, as visiting team, of admission moneys from games played in other National League stadia. The individual defendants are directors of the Cubs and have served for varying periods of years. Defendant Philip K. Wrigley is also president of the corporation and owner of approximately 80% of the stock therein.

Plaintiff alleges that since night baseball was first played in 1935 nineteen of the twenty major league teams have scheduled night games. In 1966, out of a total of 1,620 games in the major leagues, 932 were played at night. Plaintiff alleges that every member of the major leagues, other than the Cubs, scheduled substantially all of its home games in 1966 at night, exclusive of opening days, Saturdays, Sundays, holidays and days prohibited by league rules. Allegedly this has been done for the specific purpose of maximizing attendance and thereby maximizing revenue and income.

The Cubs, in the years 1961-65, sustained operating losses from its direct baseball operations. Plaintiff attributes those losses to inadequate attendance at Cubs' home games. He concludes that if the directors continue to refuse to install lights at Wrigley Field and schedule night baseball games, the Cubs will continue to sustain comparable losses and its financial condition will continue to deteriorate.

Plaintiff alleges that, except for the year 1963, attendance at Cubs' home games has been substantially below that at their road games, many of which were played at night.

Plaintiff compares attendance at Cubs' games with that of the Chicago White Sox, an American League club, whose weekday games were generally played at night. The weekend attendance figures for the two teams was similar; however, the White Sox week-night games drew many more patrons than did the Cubs' weekday games.

Plaintiff alleges that the funds for the installation of lights can be readily obtained through financing and the cost of installation would be far more than offset and recaptured by increased revenues and incomes resulting from the increased attendance.

Plaintiff further alleges that defendant Wrigley has refused to install lights, not because of interest in the welfare of the corporation but because of his personal opinions "that baseball is a 'daytime sport' and that the installation of lights and night baseball games will have a deteriorating effect upon the surrounding neighborhood." It is alleged that he has admitted that he is not interested in whether the Cubs would benefit financially from such action because of his concern for the neighborhood, and that he would be willing for the team to play night games if a new stadium were built in Chicago.

Plaintiff alleges that the other defendant directors, with full knowledge of the foregoing matters, have acquiesced in the policy laid down by Wrigley and have permitted him to dominate the board of directors in matters involving the installation of lights and scheduling of night games, even though they knew he was not motivated by a good faith concern as to the best interests of defendant corporation, but solely by his personal views set forth above. It is charged that the directors are acting for a reason or reasons contrary and wholly unrelated to the business interests of the corporation; that such arbitrary and capricious acts constitute mismanagement and waste of corporate assets, and that the directors have been negligent in failing to exercise reasonable care and prudence in the management of the corporate affairs.

The question on appeal is whether plaintiff's amended complaint states a cause of action. It is plaintiff's position that fraud, illegality and conflict of interest are not the only bases for a stockholder's derivative action against the directors. Contrariwise, defendants argue that the courts will not step in and interfere with honest business judgment of the directors unless there is a showing of fraud, illegality or conflict of interest.

The cases in this area are numerous and each differs from the others on a factual basis. However, the courts have pronounced certain ground rules which appear in all cases and which are then applied to the given factual situation. The court in *Wheeler v. Pullman Iron & Steel Co.*, [32 N.E. 420 (Ill. 1892)], said:

> ***   Every one purchasing or subscribing for stock in a corporation impliedly agrees that he will be bound by the acts and proceedings done or sanctioned by a majority of the shareholders, or by the [directors] of the corporation duly chosen by such majority, within the scope of the powers conferred by the charter, and courts of equity will not undertake to control the policy or business methods of a corporation, although it may be seen that a wiser policy might be adopted and the business more successful if other methods were pursued. The *** [directors] must be permitted to control the business of the corporation in their discretion, when not in violation of its charter or some public law, or corruptly and fraudulently subversive of the rights and interests of the corporation or of a shareholder.

The standards set in Delaware are also clearly stated in the cases. In *Davis v. Louisville Gas & Electric Co.*, [142 A. 654 (Del. Ct. Ch. 1928)], a minority shareholder sought to have the directors enjoined from amending the certificate of incorporation. The court said on page 659:

> We have then a conflict in view between the responsible managers of a corporation and an overwhelming majority of its stockholders on the one hand and a dissenting minority on the other—a conflict touching matters of business policy, such as has occasioned innumerable applications to courts to intervene and determine which of the two conflicting views should prevail. The response which courts make to such applications is that it is not their function to resolve for corporations questions of policy and business management. The directors are chosen to pass upon such questions and their judgment *unless shown to be tainted with fraud* is accepted as final. The judgment of the directors of corporations enjoys the benefit of a presumption that it was formed in good faith and was designed to promote the best interests of the corporation they serve. (Emphasis supplied)

Similarly, the court in *Toebelman v. Missouri-Kansas Pipe Line Co.*, [41 F. Supp. 334 (D. Del. 1941)], said at page 339:

***   "In a purely business corporation *** the authority of the directors in the conduct of the business of the corporation must be regarded as absolute when they act within the law, and the court is without authority to substitute its judgment for that of the directors." [Citation omitted.]

***

Plaintiff in the instant case argues that the directors are acting for reasons unrelated to the financial interest and welfare of the Cubs. However, we are not satisfied that the motives assigned to Philip K. Wrigley, and through him to the other directors, are contrary to the best interests of the corporation and the stockholders. For example, it appears to us that the effect on the surrounding neighborhood might well be considered by a director who was considering the patrons who would or would not attend the games if the park were in a poor neighborhood. Furthermore, the long run interest of the corporation in its property value at Wrigley Field might demand all efforts to keep the neighborhood from deteriorating. By these thoughts we do not mean to say that we have decided that the decision of the directors was a correct one. That is beyond our jurisdiction and ability. We are merely saying that the decision is one properly before directors and the motives alleged in the amended complaint showed no fraud, illegality or conflict of interest in their making of that decision.

While all the courts do not insist that one or more of the three elements must be present for a stockholder's derivative action to lie, nevertheless we feel that unless the conduct of the defendants at least borders on one of the elements, the courts should not interfere. The trial court in the instant case acted properly in dismissing plaintiff's amended complaint.

***

Finally, we do not agree with plaintiff's contention that failure to follow the example of the other major league clubs in scheduling night games constituted negligence. Plaintiff made no allegation that these teams' night schedules were profitable or that the purpose for which night baseball had been undertaken was fulfilled. Furthermore, it cannot be said that directors, even those of corporations that are losing money, must follow the lead of the other corporations in the field. Directors are elected for their business capabilities and judgment and the courts cannot require them to forego their judgment because of the decisions of directors of other companies. Courts may not decide these questions in the absence of a clear showing of dereliction of duty on the part of the specific directors and mere failure to "follow the crowd" is not such a dereliction. [Affirmed.] ***

> **WRIGLEY FIELD**
> The Cubs tried to install lights at Wrigley Field in
> the early 1980s, but it was not until 1988 that they
> reached a compromise with upset neighbors.
> Today, the Cubs may only play a limited number of
> night games per season at Wrigley Field, under an
> agreement with the Chicago city council.

Questions about *Shlensky v. Wrigley*

1.   If the purpose of the corporation is to make as much money as possible within the bounds of the law, then who had the better argument from a business perspective: the plaintiff or the defendants?

2.   Did the court need to consider whether the directors' conduct was negligent (which it did in the last paragraph of the opinion)?

3.   Shlensky lost the case. He still owns stock in a company that isn't making as much money as it could. What should he do now?

Shlensky v. Wrigley is a famous example of the **business judgment rule**. Although this rule has been phrased in different ways by different courts and engenders a lot of arguing among academics, it basically boils down to a judicial "hands off" philosophy. Unless the plaintiff can overcome the business judgment rule, the court will not second-guess the directors, even if their decision appears foolish. This will mean that the decision itself will not be overturned by the court and that the directors will not incur any liability for the consequences of their decision, such as lost revenues.

This deference to director decisions seems far greater than the deference that courts show to other professionals, such as doctors or lawyers. Why? As the court in *Joy v. North*, 692 F.2d 880 (2d Cir. 1982), explained:

> While it is often stated that corporate directors and officers will be liable for negligence in carrying out their corporate duties, all seem agreed that such a statement is misleading. Whereas an automobile driver who makes a mistake in judgment as to speed or distance injuring a pedestrian will likely be called upon to respond in damages, a corporate officer [or director] who makes a mistake in judgment as to economic conditions, consumer tastes or

production line efficiency will rarely, if ever, be found liable for damages suffered by the corporation. Whatever the terminology, the fact is that liability is rarely imposed upon corporate directors or officers simply for bad judgment and this reluctance to impose liability for unsuccessful business decisions has been doctrinally labeled the business judgment rule. Although the rule has suffered under academic criticism, it is not without rational basis.

First, shareholders to a very real degree voluntarily undertake the risk of bad business judgment. Investors need not buy stock, for investment markets offer an array of opportunities less vulnerable to mistakes in judgment by corporate officers. Nor need investors buy stock in particular corporations. In the exercise of what is genuinely a free choice, the quality of a firm's management is often decisive and information is available from professional advisors. Since shareholders can and do select among investments partly on the basis of management, the business judgment rule merely recognizes a certain voluntariness in undertaking the risk of bad business decisions.

Second, courts recognize that after-the-fact litigation is a most imperfect device to evaluate corporate business decisions. The circumstances surrounding a corporate decision are not easily reconstructed in a courtroom years later, since business imperatives often call for quick decisions, inevitably based on less than perfect information. The entrepreneur's function is to encounter risks and to confront uncertainty, and a reasoned decision at the time made may seem a wild hunch viewed years later against a background of perfect knowledge.

Third, because potential profit often corresponds to the potential risk, it is very much in the interest of shareholders that the law not create incentives for overly cautious corporate decisions. Some opportunities offer great profits at the risk of very substantial losses, while the alternatives offer less risk of loss but also less potential profit. Shareholders can reduce the volatility of risk by diversifying their holdings. In the case of the diversified shareholder, the seemingly more risky alternatives may well be the best choice since great losses in some stocks will over time be offset by even greater gains in others. Given mutual funds and similar forms of diversified investment, courts need not bend over backwards to give special protection to shareholders who refuse to reduce the volatility of risk by not diversifying. A rule which penalizes the choice of seemingly riskier alternatives thus may not be in the interest of shareholders generally.

Id. at 885-86 (citations and footnotes omitted throughout).

Questions about *Joy v. North*

1.   The court notes that shareholders undertake the risk of bad management by buying stock in a corporation. Is this just blaming the victim? Should patients be blamed for choosing negligent doctors?

2.   The court notes that "after-the-fact litigation" is not a good way to evaluate business decisions. In other words, "hindsight is 20/20," as the saying goes. But can't this rationale also be used to support a "medical judgment rule" that would shield doctors from liability? Why are corporate directors more deserving of protection than doctors?

3.   The court notes that it may be in society's best interests to encourage directors to take risks. Why?

4.   Another frequently-stated justification for the business judgment rule (which is noted in some of the cases cited in *Shlensky*) is that courts are not business experts and therefore should not be called on to judge business decisions. Do you find this rationale persuasive?

Joy v. North went on to note that the business judgment rule is not absolute; it can be overcome by a plaintiff. *Shlensky* gave us some ideas how to do so. The next case, *Smith v. Van Gorkom*, does as well.

It is probably helpful to summarize the facts of *Smith v. Van Gorkom* because they are very complex. The case involved a proposed merger between Trans Union Corp. and a new corporation controlled by Jay Pritzker. We will study mergers in depth in Chapter 12, but a few words about them are in order here. In this merger, Trans Union would be the "target" or "disappearing" corporation, which means that it would no longer exist after the merger. Instead, all of its assets and all of its liabilities would become assets and liabilities of the acquiring, or "surviving," corporation. This also means that Trans Union stock would disappear; the merger agreement provided that each share of Trans Union stock that was outstanding immediately before the merger would become $55 in cash. But a lot of things happened before the merger agreement was approved.

Jerome Van Gorkom was the Chief Executive Officer (CEO) of Trans Union, which was a publicly traded company. He was also one of the ten members of the board. Four of the other nine board members were Trans Union officers, sometimes called "inside" directors, and the other five were "outside" directors, all of whom had very impressive credentials. For some time, Trans Union and its board had been considering what to do about the company's investment tax credits (ITCs). Basically, because it was not generating enough income, Trans Union was not able to fully deduct its ITCs from its taxable income.

In August 1985, Van Gorkom met with some of the officers of Trans Union, including Donald Romans, the Chief Financial Officer, to discuss this issue. One idea that was "floated" at the meeting was selling Trans Union to a company that had enough income to use the ITCs fully. Another idea was a leveraged buyout (LBO), which is a transaction in which a group of investors borrow a great deal of money, secured by the company's assets, and use that money to "buy out" Trans Union's shareholders. An LBO would result in Trans Union going from being publicly traded to being closely held. In early September, Trans Union's officers met again to discuss the LBO idea. Romans presented some calculations he had done that assumed a buy-out price of between $50 and $60 per share. However, the court's opinion noted that "[t]his work did not purport to establish a fair price for either [Trans Union] or 100% of the stock. It was intended to determine the cash flow needed to service the debt that would 'probably' be incurred in a leveraged buy-out, based on 'rough calculations'."

Here the story gets interesting. Van Gorkom (who owned a great deal of Trans Union stock and was seriously thinking about retiring after having worked at Trans Union for twenty-four years) then began meeting with Jay Pritzker—without telling any other directors or officers. At a meeting on September 13, Van Gorkom suggested selling Trans Union to Pritzker at $55 per share in a merger. As the court's opinion noted, "[a]lthough Pritzker mentioned $50 as a more attractive figure, no other price was mentioned." Two days later, Pritzker indicated that he was interested. A few more meetings were held over the next few days, attended by two other Trans Union officers. Pritzker also asked for an option to buy one million shares of Trans Union stock for $38 per share (the market price at the time was $37.25 per share). Importantly, Pritzker gave Trans Union a short deadline: he wanted the board to decide on the merger proposal by late Sunday, September 21.

On Friday, September 19, Van Gorkom called for a special board meeting to be held at noon the next day. Only he and the two officers who had met with

Pritzker knew what the subject of the meeting would be. Nine of the ten directors attended the board meeting, which lasted two hours. At the board meeting, Van Gorkom gave a twenty-minute oral presentation about the proposed merger, but did not have copies of the merger agreement that Pritzker's lawyers had drafted. As the court noted, "Van Gorkom did not disclose to the Board ... the methodology by which he alone had arrived at the $55 figure, or the fact that he first proposed the $55 price in his negotiations with Pritzker." Van Gorkom told the board that Trans Union would have ninety days in which it could receive—but not solicit—competing offers to buy the company. He also informed the board of the September 21 deadline and Pritzker's demand for an option to purchase one million shares for $38 per share. An outside lawyer advising the board stated that the board could be sued if they did not accept the proposal. The lawyer also said that it was not necessary to get a "fairness opinion" from an investment banking firm concerning the proposed price of $55 per share. Romans, the Chief Financial Officer, stated that $55 per share was "at the beginning of the range" of a fair price, but that his prior studies weren't meant to determine what a fair price for stock would be.

At the end of the two-hour meeting, the board approved the merger, but one condition that the board imposed on its acceptance was that Trans Union would be able to accept any better offer that it received during the next ninety days. Van Gorkom signed the merger agreement later that day, but "[n]either he nor any other director read the agreement prior to its signing and delivery to Pritzker."

Due to some resistance from Trans Union officers, Pritzker later agreed to amend the merger agreement to allow Trans Union to solicit (as opposed to merely receive) competing offers to buy the company. These amendments were approved by Trans Union's board on October 8, and Trans Union then hired an investment banking firm to solicit competing offers from

> **PRITZKER'S OPTION**
> Note that Pritzker bought 1 million shares of Trans Union stock for $38 per share when he was offering to buy the company for $55 per share. If a competing offer came along for, say, $58 per share and Trans Union accepted the offer, Pritzker would get a "consolation prize" of $20 million ($58 minus $38 per share, multiplied by 1 million

interested buyers. However, shortly thereafter Pritzker had exercised his option to buy one million shares of Trans Union stock for $38 per share. Also, the amended merger agreement only gave Trans Union until February 1, 1981 (a little less than four months) to receive a better offer. Ultimately, Trans Union received two other offers, but both fell through for various reasons.

On February 10, 1981, Trans Union's shareholders approved the merger with Pritzker's company. The vote was 69.9% in favor and 7.25% against; 22.85% of the shares were not voted. The plaintiffs in this lawsuit had tried to enjoin the merger before it could occur, but the Delaware Court of Chancery denied an injunction. Nonetheless, the lawsuit continued and eventually reached the Delaware Supreme Court.

Smith v. Van Gorkom
Supreme Court of Delaware
488 A.2d 858 (1985)

HORSEY, Justice (for the majority): This appeal from the Court of Chancery involves a class action brought by shareholders of the defendant Trans Union Corporation ("Trans Union" or "the Company"), originally seeking rescission of a cash-out merger of Trans Union into the defendant New T Company ("New T"), a wholly-owned subsidiary of the defendant, Marmon Group, Inc. ("Marmon"). Alternate relief in the form of damages is sought against the defendant members of the Board of Directors of Trans Union, New T, and Jay A. Pritzker and Robert A. Pritzker, owners of Marmon.

Following trial, the former Chancellor granted judgment for the defendant directors by unreported letter opinion dated July 6, 1982. Judgment was based on [a finding that] the Board of Directors had acted in an informed manner so as to be entitled to protection of the business judgment rule in approving the cash-out merger ***. The plaintiffs appeal.

Speaking for the majority of the Court, we conclude that [the ruling] of the Court of Chancery [is] clearly erroneous. Therefore, we reverse and direct that judgment be entered in favor of the plaintiffs and against the defendant directors for the fair value of the plaintiffs' stockholdings in Trans Union ***.

***

*** [W]e conclude that the [Trial] Court's ultimate finding that the Board's conduct was not "reckless or imprudent" is contrary to the record and not the product of a logical and deductive reasoning process.

The plaintiffs contend that the Court of Chancery erred as a matter of law by exonerating the defendant directors under the business judgment rule without first determining whether the rule's threshold condition of "due care and prudence" was satisfied. The plaintiffs assert that the Trial Court found the defendant directors to have reached an informed business judgment on the basis of "extraneous considerations and events that occurred after September 20, 1980." The defendants deny that the Trial Court committed legal error in relying upon post-September 20, 1980 events and the directors' later acquired knowledge. The defendants further submit that their decision to accept $55 per share was informed because: (1) they were "highly qualified;" (2) they were "well-informed;" and (3) they deliberated over the "proposal" not once but three times. On essentially this evidence and under our standard of review, the defendants assert that affirmance is required. We must disagree.

Under Delaware law, the business judgment rule is the offspring of the fundamental principle, codified in [Section 141(a) of the Delaware General Corporation Law] that the business and affairs of a Delaware corporation are managed by or under its board of directors. In carrying out their managerial roles, directors are charged with an unyielding fiduciary duty to the corporation and its shareholders. The business judgment rule exists to protect and promote the full and free exercise of the managerial power granted to Delaware directors. The rule itself "is a presumption that in making a business decision, the directors of a corporation acted on an informed basis, in good faith and in the honest belief that the action taken was in the best interests of the company." Thus, the party attacking a board decision as uninformed must rebut the presumption that its business judgment was an informed one. [Citations omitted throughout this paragraph.]

The determination of whether a business judgment is an informed one turns on whether the directors have informed themselves "prior to making a business decision, of all material information reasonably available to them." [Citation omitted.] ***

Under the business judgment rule there is no protection for directors who have made "an unintelligent or unadvised judgment." A director's duty to inform himself in preparation for a decision derives from the fiduciary capacity in which he serves the corporation and its stockholders. Since a director is vested with the responsibility for the management of the affairs of the corporation, he must execute that duty with the recognition that he acts on behalf of others. Such obligation does not tolerate faithlessness or self-dealing. But fulfillment of the fiduciary function requires more than the mere absence of bad faith or fraud. Representation of the financial interests of others imposes on a director an affirmative duty to protect those interests and to proceed with a critical eye in assessing information of the type and under the circumstances present here. [Citations omitted throughout this paragraph.]

Thus, a director's duty to exercise an informed business judgment is in the nature of a duty of care, as distinguished from a duty of loyalty. Here, there were no allegations of fraud, bad faith, or self-dealing, or proof thereof. ***

***

*** We think the concept of gross negligence is also the proper standard for determining whether a business judgment reached by a board of directors was an informed one.

In the specific context of a proposed merger of domestic corporations, a director has a duty *** along with his fellow directors, to act in an informed and deliberate manner in determining whether to approve an agreement of merger before submitting the proposal to the stockholders. Certainly in the merger context, a director may not abdicate that duty by leaving to the shareholders alone the decision to approve or disapprove the agreement. ***

It is against those standards that the conduct of the directors of Trans Union must be tested, as a matter of law and as a matter of fact, regarding their exercise of an informed business judgment in voting to approve the Pritzker merger proposal.

***

The defendants argue that the determination of whether their decision to accept $55 per share for Trans Union represented an informed business judgment requires consideration, not only of that which they knew and learned on September 20, but also of that which they subsequently learned and did over the following four-month period before the shareholders met to vote on the proposal in February, 1981. *** Thus, the defendants contend that what the directors did and learned subsequent to September 20 and through January 26, 1981, was properly taken into account by the Trial Court in determining whether the Board's judgment was an informed one. We disagree with this *post hoc* approach.

[III]   The issue of whether the directors reached an informed decision to "sell" the Company on September 20, 1980 must be determined only upon the basis of the information then reasonably available to the directors and relevant to their decision to accept the Pritzker merger proposal. This is not to say that the directors were precluded from altering their original plan of action, had they done so in an informed manner. What we do say is that the question of whether the directors reached an informed business judgment in agreeing to sell the Company, pursuant to the terms of the September 20 Agreement presents, in reality, two questions: (A) whether the directors reached an informed business judgment on September 20, 1980; and (B) if they did not, whether the directors' actions taken subsequent to September 20 were adequate to cure any infirmity in their action taken on September 20. We first consider the directors' September 20 action in terms of their reaching an informed business judgment.

[III.A]   On the record before us, we must conclude that the Board of Directors did not reach an informed business judgment on September 20, 1980 in voting to "sell" the Company for $55 per share pursuant to the Pritzker cash-out merger proposal. Our reasons, in summary, are as follows:

The directors (1) did not adequately inform themselves as to Van Gorkom's role in forcing the "sale" of the Company and in establishing the per share purchase price; (2) were uninformed as to the intrinsic value of the Company; and (3) given these circumstances, at a minimum, were grossly negligent in approving the "sale" of the Company upon two hours' consideration, without prior notice, and without the exigency of a crisis or emergency.

As has been noted, the Board based its September 20 decision to approve the cash-out merger primarily on Van Gorkom's representations. None of the directors, other than Van Gorkom and Chelberg [who was also Trans Union's President and Chief Operating Officer], had any prior knowledge that the purpose of the meeting was to propose a cash-out merger of Trans Union. No members of Senior Management were present, other than Chelberg, Romans and Peterson; and the latter two had only learned of the proposed sale an hour earlier. Both general counsel Moore and former general counsel Browder attended the meeting, but were equally uninformed as to the purpose of the meeting and the documents to be acted upon.

Without any documents before them concerning the proposed transaction, the members of the Board were required to rely entirely upon Van Gorkom's 20-minute oral presentation of the proposal. No written summary of the terms of the merger was presented; the directors were given no documentation to support the adequacy of $55 price per share for sale of the Company; and the Board had before it nothing more than Van Gorkom's statement of his understanding of the substance of an agreement which he admittedly had never read, nor which any member of the Board had ever seen.

Under [Section 141(e) of the Delaware General Corporation Law] "directors are fully protected in relying in good faith on reports made by officers." [Citations omitted.] The term "report" has been liberally construed to include reports of informal personal investigations by corporate officers. [Citation omitted.] However, there is no evidence that any "report," as defined under § 141(e), concerning the Pritzker proposal, was presented to the Board on September 20. Van Gorkom's oral presentation of his understanding of the terms of the proposed Merger Agreement, which he had not seen, and Romans' brief oral statement of his preliminary study regarding the feasibility of a leveraged buy-out of Trans Union do not qualify as § 141(e) "reports" for these reasons: The former lacked substance because Van Gorkom was basically uninformed as to the essential provisions of the very document about which he was talking. Romans' statement was irrelevant to the issues before the Board since it did not purport to be a valuation study. At a minimum for a report to enjoy the status conferred by § 141(e), it must be pertinent to the subject matter upon which a board is called to act, and otherwise be entitled to good faith, not blind, reliance. Considering all of the surrounding circumstances—hastily calling the meeting without prior notice of its subject matter, the proposed sale of the Company without any prior consideration of the issue or necessity therefor, the urgent time constraints imposed by Pritzker, and the total absence of any documentation whatsoever—the directors were duty bound to make reasonable inquiry of Van Gorkom and Romans, and if they had done so, the inadequacy of that upon which they now claim to have relied would have been apparent.

***

The defendants rely on the following factors to sustain the Trial Court's finding that the Board's decision was an informed one: (1) the magnitude of the premium or spread between the $55 Pritzker offering price and Trans Union's current market price of $38 per share; (2) the amendment of the Agreement as submitted on September 20 to permit the Board to accept any better offer during the "market test" period; (3) the collective experience and expertise of the Board's "inside" and "outside" directors; and (4) their reliance on Brennan's legal advice that the directors might be sued if they rejected the Pritzker proposal. We discuss each of these grounds *seriatim:*

(1)   A substantial premium may provide one reason to recommend a merger, but in the absence of other sound valuation information, the fact of a premium alone does not provide an adequate basis upon which to assess the fairness of an offering price. Here, the judgment reached as to the adequacy of the premium was based on a comparison between the historically depressed Trans Union market price and the amount of the Pritzker offer. Using market price as a basis for concluding that the premium adequately reflected the true value of the Company was a clearly faulty, indeed fallacious, premise, as the defendants' own evidence demonstrates.

The record is clear that before September 20, Van Gorkom and other members of Trans Union's Board knew that the market had consistently undervalued the worth of Trans Union's stock, despite steady increases in the Company's operating income in the seven years preceding the merger. ***

***

The parties do not dispute that a publicly-traded stock price is solely a measure of the value of a minority position and, thus, market price represents only the value of a single share. Nevertheless, on September 20, the Board assessed the adequacy of the premium over market, offered by Pritzker, solely by comparing it with Trans Union's current and historical stock price.

Indeed, as of September 20, the Board had no other information on which to base a determination of the intrinsic value of Trans Union as a going concern.

As of September 20, the Board had made no evaluation of the Company designed to value the entire enterprise, nor had the Board ever previously considered selling the Company or consenting to a buy-out merger. Thus, the adequacy of a premium is indeterminate unless it is assessed in terms of other competent and sound valuation information that reflects the value of the particular business.

Despite the foregoing facts and circumstances, there was no call by the Board, either on September 20 or thereafter, for any valuation study or documentation of the $55 price per share as a measure of the fair value of the Company in a cash-out context. It is undisputed that the major asset of Trans Union was its cash flow. Yet, at no time did the Board call for a valuation study taking into account that highly significant element of the Company's assets.

We do not imply that an outside valuation study is essential to support an informed business judgment; nor do we state that fairness opinions by independent investment bankers are required as a matter of law. Often insiders familiar with the business of a going concern are in a better position than are outsiders to gather relevant information; and under appropriate circumstances, such directors may be fully protected in relying in good faith upon the valuation reports of their management. [Citation omitted.]

Here, the record establishes that the Board did not request its Chief Financial Officer, Romans, to make any valuation study or review of the proposal to determine the adequacy of $55 per share for sale of the Company. On the record before us: The Board rested on Romans' elicited response that the $55 figure was within a "fair price range" within the context of a leveraged buy-out. No director sought any further information from Romans. No director asked him why he put $55 at the bottom of his range. No director asked Romans for any details as to his study, the reason why it had been undertaken or its depth. No director asked to see the study; and no director asked Romans whether Trans Union's finance department could do a fairness study within the remaining 36-hour period available under the Pritzker offer.

***

The record also establishes that the Board accepted without scrutiny Van Gorkom's representation as to the fairness of the $55 price per share for sale of the Company—a subject that the Board had never previously considered. The Board thereby failed to discover that Van Gorkom had suggested the $55 price to Pritzker and, most crucially, that Van Gorkom had arrived at the $55 figure based on calculations designed solely to determine the feasibility of a leveraged buy-out. No questions were raised either as to the tax implications of a cash-out merger or how the price for the one million share option granted Pritzker was calculated.

We do not say that the Board of Directors was not entitled to give some credence to Van Gorkom's representation that $55 was an adequate or fair price. Under § 141(e), the directors were entitled to rely upon their chairman's opinion of value and adequacy, provided that such opinion was reached on a sound basis. Here, the issue is whether the directors informed themselves as to all information that was reasonably available to them. Had they done so, they would have learned of the source and derivation of the $55 price and could not reasonably have relied thereupon in good faith.

None of the directors, Management or outside, were investment bankers or financial analysts. Yet the Board did not consider recessing the meeting until a later hour that day (or requesting an extension of Pritzker's Sunday evening deadline) to give it time to elicit more information as to the sufficiency of the offer, either from inside Management (in particular Romans) or from Trans Union's own investment banker, Salomon Brothers, whose Chicago specialist in merger and acquisitions was known to the Board and familiar with Trans Union's affairs.

Thus, the record compels the conclusion that on September 20 the Board lacked valuation information adequate to reach an informed business judgment as to the fairness of $55 per share for sale of the Company.

(2)   This brings us to the post-September 20 "market test" upon which the defendants ultimately rely to confirm the reasonableness of their September 20 decision to accept the Pritzker proposal. In this connection, the directors present a two-part argument: (a) that by making a "market test" of Pritzker's $55 per share offer a condition of their September 20 decision to accept his offer, they cannot be found to have acted impulsively or in an uninformed manner on September 20; and (b) that the adequacy of the $17 premium for sale of the Company was conclusively established over the following 90 to 120 days by the most reliable evidence available—the marketplace. Thus, the defendants impliedly contend that the "market test" eliminated the need for the Board to perform any other form of fairness test either on September 20, or thereafter.

Again, the facts of record do not support the defendants' argument. There is no evidence: (a) that the Merger Agreement was effectively amended to give the Board freedom to put Trans Union up for auction sale to the highest bidder; or (b) that a public auction was in fact permitted to occur. ***

***

(3)   The directors' unfounded reliance on both the premium and the market test as the basis for accepting the Pritzker proposal undermines the defendants' remaining contention that the Board's collective experience and

sophistication was a sufficient basis for finding that it reached its September 20 decision with informed, reasonable deliberation. ***

(4)   Part of the defense is based on a claim that the directors relied on legal advice rendered at the September 20 meeting by James Brennan, Esquire, who was present at Van Gorkom's request. ***

Several defendants testified that Brennan advised them that Delaware law did not require a fairness opinion or an outside valuation of the Company before the Board could act on the Pritzker proposal. If given, the advice was correct. However, that did not end the matter. Unless the directors had before them adequate information regarding the intrinsic value of the Company, upon which a proper exercise of business judgment could be made, mere advice of this type is meaningless; and, given this record of the defendants' failures, it constitutes no defense here.[22]

We conclude that Trans Union's Board was grossly negligent in that it failed to act with informed reasonable deliberation in agreeing to the Pritzker merger proposal on September 20; and we further conclude that the Trial Court erred as a matter of law in failing to address that question before determining whether the directors' later conduct was sufficient to cure its initial error.

A second claim is that counsel advised the Board it would be subject to lawsuits if it rejected the $55 per share offer. It is, of course, a fact of corporate life that today when faced with difficult or sensitive issues, directors often are subject to suit, irrespective of the decisions they make. However, counsel's mere acknowledgement of this circumstance cannot be rationally translated into a justification for a board permitting itself to be stampeded into a patently unadvised act. While suit might result from the rejection of a merger or tender offer, Delaware law makes clear that a board acting within the ambit of the business judgment rule faces no ultimate liability. [Citation omitted.] Thus, we cannot conclude that the mere threat of litigation, acknowledged by counsel, constitutes either legal advice or any valid basis upon which to pursue an uninformed course.

***

[In Part III.B of the opinion, the court concluded that the board's actions after the September 20 board meeting did not "cure" its grossly negligent conduct at the meeting. "[A]ccordingly, the Trial Court erred in according to the

---

[22]   Nonetheless, we are satisfied that in an appropriate factual context a proper exercise of business judgment may include, as one of its aspects, reasonable reliance upon the advice of counsel. This is wholly outside the statutory protections of § 141(e) involving reliance upon reports of officers, certain experts and books and records of the company.

defendants the benefits of the business judgment rule." Part IV of the opinion is omitted.]

[V] *** The defendants contend that the stockholders' "over-whelming" vote approving the Pritzker Merger Agreement had the legal effect of curing any failure of the Board to reach an informed business judgment in its approval of the merger.

The parties tacitly agree that a discovered failure of the Board to reach an informed business judgment in approving the merger constitutes a voidable, rather than a void, act. Hence, the merger can be sustained, notwithstanding the infirmity of the Board's action, if its approval by majority vote of the shareholders is found to have been based on an informed electorate. [Citation omitted.] The disagreement between the parties arises over: (1) the Board's burden of disclosing to the shareholders all relevant and material information; and (2) the sufficiency of the evidence as to whether the Board satisfied that burden.

***

The burden must fall on defendants who claim ratification based on shareholder vote to establish that the shareholder approval resulted from a fully informed electorate. On the record before us, it is clear that the Board failed to meet that burden. [Citations omitted.]

***

[VI] To summarize: we hold that the directors of Trans Union breached their fiduciary duty to their stockholders (1) by their failure to inform themselves of all information reasonably available to them and relevant to their decision to recommend the Pritzker merger; and (2) by their failure to disclose all material information such as a reasonable stockholder would consider important in deciding whether to approve the Pritzker offer.

We hold, therefore, that the Trial Court committed reversible error in applying the business judgment rule in favor of the director defendants in this case.

On remand, the Court of Chancery shall conduct an evidentiary hearing to determine the fair value of the shares represented by the plaintiffs' class, based on the intrinsic value of Trans Union on September 20, 1980. *** Thereafter, an award of damages may be entered to the extent that the fair value of Trans Union exceeds $55 per share. [Reversed and remanded.]

McNEILLY, Justice, dissenting: The majority opinion reads like an advocate's closing address to a hostile jury. And I say that not lightly. Throughout the opinion great emphasis is directed only to the negative, with nothing more than lip service granted the positive aspects of this case. ***

*** The majority has spoken and has effectively said that Trans Union's Directors have been the victims of a "fast shuffle" by Van Gorkom and Pritzker. That is the beginning of the majority's comedy of errors. The first and most important error made is the majority's assessment of the directors' knowledge of the affairs of Trans Union and their combined ability to act in this situation under the protection of the business judgment rule.

Trans Union's Board of Directors consisted of ten men, five of whom were "inside" directors and five of whom were "outside" directors. The "inside" directors were Van Gorkom, Chelberg, Bonser, William B. Browder, Senior Vice-President-Law, and Thomas P. O'Boyle, Senior Vice-President-Administration. At the time the merger was proposed the inside five directors had collectively been employed by the Company for 116 years and had 68 years of combined experience as directors. The "outside" directors were A.W. Wallis, William B. Johnson, Joseph B. Lanterman, Graham J. Morgan and Robert W. Reneker. With the exception of Wallis, these were all chief executive officers of Chicago based corporations that were at least as large as Trans Union. The five "outside" directors had 78 years of combined experience as chief executive officers, and 53 years cumulative service as Trans Union directors.

The inside directors wear their badge of expertise in the corporate affairs of Trans Union on their sleeves. But what about the outsiders? [Here the dissenting opinion described the impressive backgrounds and experience of the outside directors.]

Directors of this caliber are not ordinarily taken in by a "fast shuffle". I submit they were not taken into this multi-million dollar corporate transaction without being fully informed and aware of the state of the art as it pertained to the entire corporate panorama of Trans Union. True, even directors such as these, with their business acumen, interest and expertise, can go astray. I do not believe that to be the case here. These men knew Trans Union like the back of their hands and were more than well qualified to make on the spot informed business judgments concerning the affairs of Trans Union including a 100% sale of the corporation. Lest we forget, the corporate world of then and now operates on what is so aptly referred to as "the fast track". These men were at the time an integral part of that world, all professional business men, not intellectual figureheads.

***

I have no quarrel with the majority's analysis of the business judgment rule. It is the application of that rule to these facts which is wrong. An overview of the entire record, rather than the limited view of bits and pieces which the majority has exploded like popcorn, convinces me that the directors made an informed business judgment which was buttressed by their test of the market.

***

[One other dissenting opinion is omitted. Three justices were in the majority in *Smith v. Van Gorkom*; two dissented.]

Questions about *Smith v. Van Gorkom*

1.   The court criticizes the Trans Union directors for, among other things, having a short meeting and not having read the merger agreement before approving it. If you represented the board of a corporation that was considering a merger, what would you recommend to lessen the chance that the directors would be sued by unhappy shareholders?

2.   Speaking of shareholders, why didn't the fact that the shareholders overwhelmingly approved the merger shield the directors from liability?

3.   Van Gorkom owned a great deal of Trans Union stock and made a great deal of money when Trans Union was acquired by Pritzker. Does this mean that he had a conflict of interest in approving the merger? If so, why didn't the plaintiff argue, using *Shlensky* as support, that this conflict of interest was sufficient to rebut the business judgment rule?

4.   How is gross negligence different from "regular" negligence?

5.   The plaintiffs won in *Smith v. Van Gorkom*. What were the damages? *See Smith v. Van Gorkom*, 1985 WL 22040 (Del. Ct. Ch., Oct. 11, 1985).

Smith v. Van Gorkom was widely viewed as a bad decision. Some commentators have even referred to it as one of the worst corporate law decisions of all time. Nonetheless, whether you agree with the dissent or the majority opinion, the case does provide another idea for overcoming the business judgment rule if you are representing the plaintiff in a lawsuit against the directors.

There is another possible way for a plaintiff to overcome the business judgment rule, which is found in a handful of decisions: argue that the directors made an irrational or wasteful decision. (Technically, these are two different arguments, but they are often lumped together in this context.) This is more difficult than it sounds. First, note that this focuses on the *substance* of the decision, rather than the directors' motives (e.g., conflict of interest) or the *process* in which the decision was made (e.g., *Van Gorkom*'s focus on whether the directors were grossly negligent by not being sufficiently informed before making the decision). As you have seen, the business judgment rule can be seen as a judicial "hands off" approach. Therefore, you shouldn't be surprised if it takes an *extremely* bad decision by the directors to lose the benefit of the business judgment rule if other grounds are not present.

ILLEGALITY

In *Shlensky*, the court noted that one way to rebut the business judgment rule involves "illegality." There are many decisions in which corporate directors were found liable to the corporation for knowingly approving or condoning illegal acts by the corporation (at least where it was clear that the acts were illegal). This is true even if the illegality benefited the company, such as by saving more money than any fines that were imposed. Also, a director or officer who causes the corporation to break the law may herself be criminally liable under the relevant statute.

Nonetheless, there are a few cases that (arguably) accepted irrationality or waste as a basis for rebutting the business judgment rule. (See Chapter 7 for a definition of "waste.") For example, simplifying the facts in *Litwin v. Allen*, 25 N.Y.S.2d 667 (N.Y. Sup. Ct. 1940), the board approved a transaction in which the corporation purchased debentures. However, the seller had the option to repurchase the debentures—at the same price—in the next six months. Thus, if the debentures went up in value you could expect the seller to repurchase them; if they went down in value, you would not expect the seller to repurchase them. In other words, there did not appear to be any possible way that the corporation would "come out ahead" on this transaction.

Litwin is one of the rare cases where directors were liable for bad decisions without a showing that they were uninformed or were acting in bad faith (e.g., fraud, illegality, or a conflict of interest). *Cf.* AMERICAN LAW INSTITUTE, PRINCIPLES OF CORPORATE GOVERNANCE: ANALYSIS AND RECOMMENDATIONS § 4.01(c) (1992). This section of the *ALI Principles* provides that a director fulfils her duty of care if she is not interested (as defined in the *ALI Principles*) in the subject of the decision; is informed to the extent she "reasonably believes appropriate under the circumstances"; and "rationally believes that the business judgment is in the best interest of the corporation." Note that the last clause specifies a "rational" belief. It is much easier to demonstrate[*] that a decision was "rational" (i.e., not crazy) than that it was "reasonable." A comment to the section elaborates: "[t]here is no reason to insulate an objectively irrational business decision—one so removed from the realm of reason that it should not be sustained ...."

What happens if a plaintiff successfully rebuts the business judgment rule? Consider the following passage from *Cede & Co. v. Technicolor, Inc.,* 634 A.2d 345 (Del. 1994):

> The [business judgment] rule posits a powerful presumption in favor of actions taken by the directors in that a decision made by a loyal and informed board will not be overturned by the courts unless it cannot be "attributed to any rational business purpose." Thus, a shareholder plaintiff challenging a board decision has the burden at the outset to rebut the rule's presumption. To rebut the rule, a shareholder plaintiff assumes the burden of providing evidence that directors, in reaching their challenged decision, breached any one of the *triads* of their fiduciary duty—good faith, loyalty or due care. If a shareholder plaintiff fails to meet this evidentiary burden, the business judgment rule attaches to protect corporate officers and directors and the decisions they make, and our courts will not second-guess these business judgments. If the rule is rebutted, the burden shifts to the defendant directors, the proponents of the challenged transaction, to prove to the trier of fact the "entire fairness" of the transaction to the shareholder plaintiff.

Id. at 361 (citations omitted throughout). Like *Van Gorkom, Technicolor* involved a "cash out" merger where the plaintiff-shareholders' stock was converted into cash. In such a situation, it may make sense to require the defendant-directors to show entire fairness which, as you will learn in Chapter 7, requires that they show both "fair dealing" and "fair price."

However, in a case where a plaintiff is suing because of a more routine decision made by the board and overcomes the business judgment rule, it may not make sense to ask whether the corporation received a "fair price" or whether the transaction was accomplished through "fair dealing." For one thing, the decision may not have involved a "price" or any "dealing" at all. For example, one presumes that if the plaintiff had somehow won in *Shlensky,* the court would have ordered the Cubs to begin playing night games as soon as possible, and made the directors liable for the difference between what the Cubs could have earned

---

[*]   To be clear, do not forget that the plaintiff has the burden of overcoming the business judgment rule.

playing night games and what they actually did earn during the period at issue. (Of course, proving the amount of these damages would be difficult.)

But perhaps a more basic problem with the *Technicolor* approach is that it seems to do away with part of the plaintiff's prima facie case. If this were a tort case, the plaintiff would be required to prove damages (among other things). Why then should the directors be required essentially to prove the *absence* of damages by showing that the transaction was fair? Perhaps recognizing this problem, MBCA § 8.31 reminds us that plaintiffs have the burden of proving causation and damages in suits where they are seeking money damages from the directors.

Another question to consider is *which* directors should be liable. To that end, the following portion of the comment to MBCA § 8.30 may be helpful:

> If the observance of the directors' conduct is called into question, courts will typically evaluate the conduct of the entire board (or committee). Deficient performance of section 8.30 duties on the part of a particular director may be overcome, absent unusual circumstances, by acceptable conduct (meeting, for example, subsection (b)'s standard of care) on the part of other directors sufficient in number to perform the function or discharge the duty in question. While not thereby remedied, the deficient performance becomes irrelevant in any evaluation of the action taken. (This contrasts with a director's duties of loyalty, fair dealing and disclosure which will be evaluated on an individual basis ....)

On the other hand, what if a director voted *against* a decision that gave rise to a lawsuit? In thinking about this question, you may also want to consider when a director is deemed to have voted *for* a decision or at least to have "assented" to it. *See* MBCA § 8.24(d).

§ 6.04   BOARD OVERSIGHT

> ***Objectives:*** *In a situation where the directors of a corporation are being sued due to allegedly insufficient oversight of the corporation, you should be able to (1) identify the arguments the plaintiff will make to impose personal liability on the directors, (2) identify the arguments the defendant directors will make that they have not breached their duty of care or otherwise should not be held liable, and (3) evaluate how a court should decide the case.*

Subsidiary Objectives For Plaintiffs: *For a client who wishes to sue the directors for allegedly insufficient oversight of the corporation, you should also be able to:*

- *explain the standard for a director's duty of care and evaluate whether your client will be able to show that the defendant-directors breached their duty of care;*

- *explain the various "hoops" that your client must overcome to win her case, both under statutes, case law, and (if applicable) provisions in the corporation's articles of incorporation, and evaluate whether your client will be able to meet these requirements;*

- *explain what will happen if she can't meet these requirements; and*

- *explain what will happen if she can meet these requirements.*

Subsidiary Objectives For Defendants: *In addition to the above, for a client who is a director, explain what the director must do to properly discharge her duty of oversight.*

Obviously, directors need to make decisions. But many decisions are made by others in the corporation, such as officers and employees. (And of course a decision by anyone could end up getting the corporation into a lot of trouble.) As such, part of a director's duty of care is to devote sufficient *oversight* to the corporation and its business. Cf. MBCA § 8.31(a)(2)(iv) (possible director liability for "a sustained failure ... to devote attention to ongoing oversight of the business and affairs of the corporation, or a failure to devote timely attention, by making ... appropriate inquiry, when particular facts and circumstances of significant concern materialize that would alert a reasonably attentive director to the need therefor.").

The following is a famous case in which a director was found not to have devoted sufficient attention to oversight of the corporation. During the time the director was "asleep at the switch," so to speak, some bad things happened.

Francis v. United Jersey Bank
Supreme Court of New Jersey
432 A.2d 814 (1981)

POLLOCK, J. The primary issue on this appeal is whether a corporate director is personally liable in negligence for the failure to prevent the misappropriation of trust funds by other directors who were also officers and shareholders of the corporation.

Plaintiffs are trustees in bankruptcy of Pritchard & Baird Intermediaries Corp. (Pritchard & Baird), a reinsurance broker or intermediary. Defendant Lillian P. Overcash is the daughter of Lillian G. Pritchard and the executrix of her estate. At the time of her death, Mrs. Pritchard was a director and the largest single shareholder of Pritchard & Baird. Because Mrs. Pritchard died after the institution of suit but before trial, her executrix was substituted as a defendant. United Jersey Bank is joined as the administrator of the estate of Charles Pritchard, Sr., who had been president, director and majority shareholder of Pritchard & Baird.

This litigation focuses on payments made by Pritchard & Baird to Charles Pritchard, Jr. and William Pritchard, who were sons of Mr. and Mrs. Charles Pritchard, Sr., as well as officers, directors and shareholders of the corporation. Claims against Charles, Jr. and William are being pursued in bankruptcy proceedings against them.

The trial court, sitting without a jury, characterized the payments as fraudulent conveyances within [the relevant New Jersey statute] and entered judgment of $10,355,736.91 plus interest against the estate of Mrs. Pritchard. [Citation omitted.] The judgment includes damages from her negligence in permitting payments from the corporation of $4,391,133.21 to Charles, Jr. and $5,483,799.02 to William. ***

*** [T]he critical question is not whether the misconduct of Charles, Jr. and William should be characterized as fraudulent conveyances or acts of conversion. Rather, the initial question is whether Mrs. Pritchard was negligent in not noticing and trying to prevent the misappropriation of funds held by the corporation in an implied trust. A further question is whether her negligence was the proximate cause of the plaintiffs' losses. Both lower courts found that she was liable in negligence for the losses caused by the wrongdoing of Charles, Jr. and William. We affirm.

[I]   The matrix for our decision is the customs and practices of the reinsurance industry and the role of Pritchard & Baird as a reinsurance broker. Reinsurance involves a contract under which one insurer agrees to indemnify another [insurance company] for loss sustained under the latter's policy of insurance. Insurance companies that insure against losses arising out of fire or other casualty seek at times to minimize their exposure by sharing risks with other insurance companies. Thus, when the face amount of a policy is comparatively large, the company may enlist one or more insurers to participate in that risk. Similarly, an insurance company's loss potential and overall exposure may be reduced by reinsuring a part of an entire class of policies (e.g., 25% of all of its fire insurance policies). The selling insurance company is known as a ceding company. The entity that assumes the obligation is designated as the reinsurer.

The reinsurance broker arranges the contract between the ceding company and the reinsurer. In accordance with industry custom before the Pritchard & Baird bankruptcy, the reinsurance contract or treaty did not specify the rights and duties of the broker. Typically, the ceding company communicates to the broker the details concerning the risk. The broker negotiates the sale of portions of the risk to the reinsurers. In most instances, the ceding company and the reinsurer do not communicate with each other, but rely upon the reinsurance broker. The ceding company pays premiums due a reinsurer to the broker, who deducts his commission and transmits the balance to the appropriate reinsurer. When a loss occurs, a reinsurer pays money due a ceding company to the broker, who then transmits it to the ceding company.

***

***   [When it was incorporated] in 1959, Pritchard & Baird had five directors: Charles Pritchard, Sr., his wife Lillian Pritchard, their son Charles Pritchard, Jr., George Baird and his wife Marjorie. William Pritchard, another son, became director in 1960. *** The corporation issued 200 shares of common stock. Charles Pritchard, Sr. acquired 120 shares, his sons Charles Pritchard, Jr., 15 and William, 15; Mr. and Mrs. Baird owned the remaining 50. In June 1964, Baird and his wife resigned as directors and sold their stock to the corporation. From that time on the corporation operated as a close family corporation with Mr. and Mrs. Pritchard and their two sons as the only directors. After the death of Charles, Sr. in 1973, only the remaining three directors continued to operate as the board. Lillian Pritchard inherited 72 of her husband's 120 shares in Pritchard & Baird, thereby becoming the largest shareholder in the corporation with 48% of the stock.

The corporate minute books reflect only perfunctory activities by the directors, related almost exclusively to the election of officers and adoption of banking resolutions and a retirement plan. None of the minutes for any of the meetings contain a discussion of the loans to Charles, Jr. and William or of the financial condition of the corporation. Moreover, upon instructions of Charles, Jr. that financial statements were not to be circulated to anyone else, the company's statements for the fiscal years beginning February 1, 1970, were delivered only to him.

Charles Pritchard, Sr. was the chief executive and controlled the business in the years following Baird's withdrawal. Beginning in 1966, he gradually relinquished control over the operations of the corporation. In 1968, Charles, Jr. became president and William became executive vice president. Charles, Sr. apparently became ill in 1971 and during the last year and a half of his life was not involved in the affairs of the business. He continued, however, to serve as a director until his death on December 10, 1973. Notwithstanding the presence of Charles, Sr. on the board until his death in 1973, Charles, Jr. dominated the management of the corporation and the board from 1968 until the bankruptcy in 1975.

Contrary to the industry custom of segregating [client] funds, Pritchard & Baird commingled the funds of reinsurers and ceding companies with its own funds. All monies (including commissions, premiums and loss monies) were deposited in a single account. Charles, Sr. began the practice of withdrawing funds from the commingled account in transactions identified on the corporate books as "loans." As long as Charles, Sr. controlled the corporation, the "loans" correlated with corporate profits and were repaid at the end of each year. Starting in 1970, however, Charles, Jr. and William begin to siphon ever-increasing sums from the corporation under the guise of loans. As of January 31, 1970, the "loans" to Charles, Jr. were $230,932 and to William were $207,329. At least by January 31, 1973, the annual increase in the loans exceeded annual corporate revenues. By October 1975, the year of bankruptcy, the "shareholders' loans" had metastasized to a total of $12,333,514.47.

The trial court rejected the characterization of the payments as "loans." [Citation omitted.] No corporate resolution authorized the "loans," and no note or other instrument evidenced the debt. Charles, Jr. and William paid no interest on the amounts received. The "loans" were not repaid or reduced from one year to the next; rather, they increased annually. The designation of "shareholders' loans" on the balance sheet was an entry to account for the distribution of the premium and loss money to Charles, Sr., Charles, Jr. and William. As the trial court found, the entry was part of a "woefully inadequate and highly dangerous bookkeeping system." [Citation omitted.]

The "loans" to Charles, Jr. and William far exceeded their salaries and financial resources. If the payments to Charles, Jr. and William had been treated as dividends or compensation, then the balance sheets would have shown an excess of liabilities over assets. If the "loans" had been eliminated, the balance sheets would have depicted a corporation not only with a working capital deficit, but also with assets having a fair market value less than its liabilities. ***

***

The pattern that emerges from these figures is the substantial increase in the monies appropriated by Charles Pritchard, Jr. and William Pritchard after their father's withdrawal from the business and the sharp decline in the profitability of the operation after his death. This led ultimately to the filing in December, 1975, of an involuntary petition in bankruptcy and the appointments of the plaintiffs as trustees in bankruptcy of Pritchard & Baird.

Mrs. Pritchard was not active in the business of Pritchard & Baird and knew virtually nothing of its corporate affairs. She briefly visited the corporate offices in Morristown on only one occasion, and she never read or obtained the annual financial statements. She was unfamiliar with the rudiments of reinsurance and made no effort to assure that the policies and practices of the corporation, particularly pertaining to the withdrawal of funds, complied with industry custom or relevant law. Although her husband had warned her that Charles, Jr. would "take the shirt off my back," Mrs. Pritchard did not pay any attention to her duties as a director or to the affairs of the corporation. [Citation omitted.]

After her husband died in December 1973, Mrs. Pritchard became incapacitated and was bedridden for a six-month period. She became listless at this time and started to drink rather heavily. Her physical condition deteriorated, and in 1978 she died. The trial court rejected testimony seeking to exonerate her because she "was old, was grief-stricken at the loss of her husband, sometimes consumed too much alcohol and was psychologically overborne by her sons." [Citation omitted.] That court found that she was competent to act and that the reason Mrs. Pritchard never knew what her sons "were doing was because she never made the slightest effort to discharge any of her responsibilities as a director of Pritchard & Baird." [Citation omitted.]

***

[III]   *** Generally directors are accorded broad immunity and are not insurers of corporate activities. The problem is particularly nettlesome when a third party asserts that a director, because of nonfeasance, is liable for losses caused by acts of insiders, who in this case were officers, directors and shareholders. Determination of the liability of Mrs. Pritchard requires findings that she had a duty to the clients of Pritchard & Baird, that she breached that duty and that her breach was a proximate cause of their losses.

The New Jersey Business Corporation Act *** makes it incumbent upon directors to ["]discharge their duties in good faith and with that degree of diligence, care and skill which ordinarily prudent men would exercise under similar circumstances in like positions.["] ***

***

Because [the New Jersey Business Corporation Act] is modeled in part upon section 717 of the New York statute, we consider also the law of New York in interpreting the New Jersey statute. ***

Prior to the enactment of section 717, the New York courts, like those of New Jersey, had espoused the principle that directors owed that degree of care that a businessman of ordinary prudence would exercise in the management of his own affairs. [Citations omitted.] In addition to requiring that directors act honestly and in good faith, the New York courts recognized that the nature and extent of reasonable care depended upon the type of corporation, its size and financial resources. Thus, a bank director was held to stricter accountability than the director of an ordinary business. [Citation omitted.]

In determining the limits of a director's duty, section 717 continued to recognize the individual characteristics of the corporation involved as well as the particular circumstances and corporate role of the director. ***

*** [D]irectors must discharge their duties in good faith and act as ordinarily prudent persons would under similar circumstances in like positions. Although specific duties in a given case can be determined only after consideration of all of the circumstances, the standard of ordinary care is the wellspring from which those more specific duties flow.

As a general rule, a director should acquire at least a rudimentary understanding of the business of the corporation. Accordingly, a director should become familiar with the fundamentals of the business in which the corporation is engaged. [Citation omitted.] Because directors are bound to exercise ordinary care, they cannot set up as a defense lack of the knowledge needed to exercise the requisite degree of care. If one "feels that he has not had sufficient business experience to qualify him to perform the duties of a director, he should either acquire the knowledge by inquiry, or refuse to act." [Citation omitted.]

Directors are under a continuing obligation to keep informed about the activities of the corporation. Otherwise, they may not be able to participate in the overall management of corporate affairs. *Barnes v. Andrews*, 298 F. 614 (S.D.N.Y. 1924); [other citations omitted]. Directors may not shut their eyes to corporate misconduct and then claim that because they did not see the misconduct, they did not have a duty to look. The sentinel asleep at his post contributes nothing to the enterprise he is charged to protect. [Citation omitted.]

Directorial management does not require a detailed inspection of day-to-day activities, but rather a general monitoring of corporate affairs and policies.

[Citation omitted.]   Accordingly, a director is well advised to attend board meetings regularly. ***

While directors are not required to audit corporate books, they should maintain familiarity with the financial status of the corporation by a regular review of financial statements. [Citations omitted.] *** The extent of review, as well as the nature and frequency of financial statements, depends not only on the customs of the industry, but also on the nature of the corporation and the business in which it is engaged. *** Adequate financial review normally would be more informal in a private corporation than in a publicly held corporation.

***

The review of financial statements, however, may give rise to a duty to inquire further into matters revealed by those statements. [Citations omitted.] Upon discovery of an illegal course of action, a director has a duty to object and, if the corporation does not correct the conduct, to resign. [Citations omitted.]

In certain circumstances, the fulfillment of the duty of a director may call for more than mere objection and resignation. Sometimes a director may be required to seek the advice of counsel. *** [In addition, a] director may have a duty to take reasonable means to prevent illegal conduct by co-directors; in any appropriate case, this may include threat of suit. [Citation omitted.]

A director is not an ornament, but an essential component of corporate governance. Consequently, a director cannot protect himself behind a paper shield bearing the motto, "dummy director." [Citation omitted.] *** Thus, all directors are responsible for managing the business and affairs of the corporation. [Citations omitted.]

***

A director's duty of care does not exist in the abstract, but must be considered in relation to specific obligees. In general, the relationship of a corporate director to the corporation and its stockholders is that of a fiduciary. [Citation omitted.] ***

While directors may owe a fiduciary duty to creditors also, that obligation generally has not been recognized in the absence of insolvency. [Citation omitted.] With certain corporations, however, directors are [deemed] to owe a duty to creditors and other third parties even when the corporation is solvent. Although depositors of a bank are considered in some respects to be creditors, courts have recognized that directors may owe them a fiduciary duty. [Citation omitted.] Directors of nonbanking corporations may owe a similar duty when the corporation holds funds of others in trust. [Citations omitted.]

***

The most striking circumstances affecting Mrs. Pritchard's duty as a director are the character of the reinsurance industry, the nature of the misappropriated funds and the financial condition of Pritchard & Baird. The hallmark of the reinsurance industry has been the unqualified trust and confidence reposed by ceding companies and reinsurers in reinsurance brokers. Those companies entrust money to reinsurance intermediaries with the justifiable expectation that the funds will be transmitted to the appropriate parties. Consequently, the companies could have assumed rightfully that Mrs. Pritchard, as a director of a reinsurance brokerage corporation, would not sanction the [commingling] and the conversion of loss and premium funds for the personal use of the principals of Pritchard & Baird.

As a reinsurance broker, Pritchard & Baird received annually as a fiduciary millions of dollars of clients' money which it was under a duty to segregate. To this extent, it resembled a bank rather than a small family business. Accordingly, Mrs. Pritchard's relationship to the clientele of Pritchard & Baird was akin to that of a director of a bank to its depositors. All parties agree that Pritchard & Baird held the misappropriated funds in an implied trust. That trust relationship gave rise to a fiduciary duty to guard the funds with fidelity and good faith. [Citations omitted.]

As a director of a substantial reinsurance brokerage corporation, she should have known that it received annually millions of dollars of loss and premium funds which it held in trust for ceding and reinsurance companies. Mrs. Pritchard should have obtained and read the annual statements of financial condition of Pritchard & Baird. Although she had a right to rely upon financial statements prepared in accordance with [the statute], such reliance would not excuse her conduct. The reason is that those statements disclosed on their face the misappropriation of trust funds.

From those statements, she should have realized that, as of January 31, 1970, her sons were withdrawing substantial trust funds under the guise of "Shareholders' Loans." The financial statements for each fiscal year commencing with that of January 31, 1970, disclosed that the working capital deficits and the "loans" were escalating in tandem. Detecting a misappropriation of funds would not have required special expertise or extraordinary diligence; a cursory reading of the financial statements would have revealed the pillage. Thus, if Mrs. Pritchard had read the financial statements, she would have known that her sons were converting trust funds. When financial statements demonstrate that insiders are bleeding a corporation to death, a director should notice and try to stanch the flow of blood.

In summary, Mrs. Pritchard was charged with the obligation of basic knowledge and supervision of the business of Pritchard & Baird. Under the circumstances, this obligation included reading and understanding financial statements, and making reasonable attempts at detection and prevention of the illegal conduct of other officers and directors. She had a duty to protect the clients of Pritchard & Baird against policies and practices that would result in the misappropriation of money they had entrusted to the corporation. She breached that duty.

[IV]   Nonetheless, the negligence of Mrs. Pritchard does not result in liability unless it is a proximate cause of the loss. [Citation omitted.] Analysis of proximate cause requires an initial determination of cause-in-fact. Causation-in-fact calls for a finding that the defendant's act or omission was a necessary antecedent of the loss, i.e., that if the defendant had observed his or her duty of care, the loss would not have occurred. [Citations omitted.] Further, the plaintiff has the burden of establishing the amount of the loss or damages caused by the negligence of the defendant. [Citation omitted.] ***

Cases involving nonfeasance present a much more difficult causation question than those in which the director has committed an affirmative act of negligence leading to the loss. Analysis in cases of negligent omissions calls for determination of the reasonable steps a director should have taken and whether that course of action would have averted the loss.

Usually a director can absolve himself from liability by informing the other directors of the impropriety and voting for a proper course of action. [Citation omitted.] Conversely, a director who votes for or concurs in certain actions may be "liable to the corporation for the benefit of its creditors or shareholders, to the extent of any injuries suffered by such persons, respectively, as a result of any such action." [Citation omitted.] ***

Even accepting the hypothesis that Mrs. Pritchard might not be liable if she had objected and resigned, there are two significant reasons for holding her liable. First, she did not resign until just before the bankruptcy. Consequently, there is no factual basis for the speculation that the losses would have occurred even if she had objected and resigned. Indeed, the trial court reached the opposite conclusion: "The actions of the sons were so blatantly wrongful that it is hard to see how they could have resisted any moderately firm objection to what they were doing." [Citation omitted.] Second, the nature of the reinsurance business distinguishes it from most other commercial activities in that reinsurance brokers are encumbered by fiduciary duties owed to third parties. In other corporations, a director's duty normally does not extend beyond the shareholders to third parties.

***

Within Pritchard & Baird, several factors contributed to the loss of the funds: [commingling] of corporate and client monies, conversion of funds by Charles, Jr. and William and dereliction of her duties by Mrs. Pritchard. The wrongdoing of her sons, although the immediate cause of the loss, should not excuse Mrs. Pritchard from her negligence which also was a substantial factor contributing to the loss. [Citation omitted.] Her sons knew that she, the only other director, was not reviewing their conduct; they spawned their fraud in the backwater of her neglect. Her neglect of duty contributed to the climate of corruption; her failure to act contributed to the continuation of that corruption. Consequently, her conduct was a substantial factor contributing to the loss.

*** We conclude that even if Mrs. Pritchard's mere objection had not stopped the depredations of her sons, her consultation with an attorney and the threat of suit would have deterred them. That conclusion flows as a matter of common sense and logic from the record. Whether in other situations a director has a duty to do more than protest and resign is best left to case-by-case determinations. In this case, we are satisfied that there was a duty to do more than object and resign. Consequently, we find that Mrs. Pritchard's negligence was a proximate cause of the misappropriations.

To conclude, by virtue of her office, Mrs. Pritchard had the power to prevent the losses sustained by the clients of Pritchard & Baird. With power comes responsibility. She had a duty to deter the depredation of the other insiders, her sons. She breached that duty and caused plaintiffs to sustain damages.

The judgment of the Appellate Division is affirmed.

It may be instructive to contrast *Francis* with another famous case involving a director who was found not to have devoted sufficient oversight to the corporation, *Barnes v. Andrews*, 298 F. 614 (S.D.N.Y. 1928). *Barnes* involved Liberty Starters Corporation, which had been formed to make starters for Ford engines and "aeroplanes." Although the business looked promising and the corporation raised more than $500,000 through stock sales shortly after it was formed, it failed within three years. One of the reasons was the fact that the company's engineer could not get along with the factory manager (who was probably incompetent). The business managed to make many component parts, but it never actually produced any finished products. Meanwhile, the money steadily ran out until it was essentially gone. Barnes, the plaintiff in the case, was then appointed as a receiver, charged with the task of rounding up the corporation's assets and using them to pay creditors to the extent possible. One of the assets that Barnes believed that the corporation had was a lawsuit against Andrews, who had been one of the directors.

Andrews had served as a director from October 9, 1919, until he resigned on June 21, 1920. During that time, there were only two board meetings; Andrews attended one but missed the other due to his mother's death. As Judge Learned Hand observed of Andrews: "He was a friend of the [company's] president, who had induced him as the largest stockholder to become a director, and his only attention to the affairs of the company consisted of talks with the president as they met from time to time." Judge Hand found that Andrews had failed in his obligation to "give reasonable attention to the corporate business." In other words, Andrews has breached his duty of care to the corporation; he should have been much more diligent in overseeing the company's business. However, Andrews avoided liability.

As Judge Hand wrote:

> The plaintiff must, however, go further than to show that [Andrews] should have been more active in his duties. This cause of action rests upon a tort, as much though it be a tort of omission as though it had rested upon a positive act. The plaintiff must accept the burden of showing that the performance of the defendant's duties would have avoided loss, and what loss it would have avoided. ***

> ***   [W]hen a business fails from general mis-management, business incapacity, or bad judgment, how is it possible to say that a single director could have made the company successful, or how much in dollars he could have saved? *** [T]he plaintiff must show that, had Andrews done his full duty, he could have made the company prosper, or at least could have broken its fall. He must show what sum he could have saved the company. Neither of these has he made any effort to do.

> The defendant is not subject to the burden of proving that the loss would have happened, whether he had done his duty or not. If he were, it would come to this: That, if a director were once shown slack in his duties, he would stand charged prima facie with the difference between the corporate treasury as it was, and as it would be, judged by a hypothetical standard of success. How

could such a standard be determined? How could [anyone] guess how far a director's skill and judgment would have prevailed upon his fellows, and what would have been the ultimate fate of the business, if they had? How is it possible to set any measure of liability, or to tell what he would have contributed to the event? Men's fortunes may not be subjected to such uncertain and speculative conjectures. It is hard to see how there can be any remedy, except one can put one's finger on a definite loss and say with reasonable assurance that protest would have deterred, or counsel persuaded, the managers who caused it. No men of sense would take the office, if the law imposed upon them a guaranty of the general success of their companies as a penalty for any negligence.

***

True, [Andrews] was not very well-suited by experience for the job he had undertaken, but I cannot hold him on that account. After all, it is the same corporation that chose him which now seeks to charge him. I cannot agree with the language of [citation omitted] that in effect he gave an implied warranty of any special fitness. Directors are not specialists, like lawyers or doctors. They must have good sense, perhaps they must have acquaintance with affairs; but they need not—indeed, perhaps they should not—have any technical talent. They are the general advisers of the business, and if they faithfully give such ability as they have to their charge, it would not be lawful to hold them liable. Must a director guarantee that his judgment is good? Can shareholders call him to account for deficiencies which their votes assured him did not disqualify him for his office? While he may not have been the Cromwell for that Civil War, Andrews did not engage to play any such role.

Id. at 616-18.

Question about *Barnes v. Andrews*

Why didn't Andrews have the business judgment rule as a defense in this case?

Delaware has a line of important cases on the issue of directorial oversight. The first case is *Graham v. Allis-Chalmers Mfg. Co.*, 188 A.2d 125 (Del. 1963), which involved a derivative action by the shareholders against the directors to recover damages that the corporation had sustained due to anti-trust law violations. The violations had been committed by employees. Although the directors were not aware of the violations or of any "red flags" that should have alerted them to the possibility that violations were occurring, the plaintiffs argued that the directors should be liable as a result of "their failure to take action designed to learn of and prevent anti-trust activity on the part of any employees of Allis-Chalmers."

The Delaware Supreme Court rejected this theory in the following passage:

> [D]irectors are entitled to rely on the honesty and integrity of their subordinates until something occurs to put them on suspicion that something is wrong. If such occurs and goes unheeded, then liability of the directors might well follow, but absent cause for suspicion there is no duty upon the directors to install and operate a corporate system of espionage to ferret out wrongdoing which they have no reason to suspect exists.

> The duties of the Allis-Chalmers Directors were fixed by the nature of the enterprise which employed in excess of 30,000 persons, and extended over a large geographical area. By force of necessity, the company's Directors could not know personally all the company's employees. The very magnitude of the enterprise required them to confine their control to the broad policy decisions. That they did this is clear from the record. At the meetings of the Board in which all Directors participated, these questions were considered and decided on the basis of summaries, reports and corporate records. These they were entitled to rely on
> ***.

> In the last analysis, the question of whether a corporate director has become liable for losses to the corporation through neglect of duty is determined by the circumstances. If he has recklessly reposed confidence in an obviously untrustworthy employee, has refused or neglected cavalierly to perform his duty as a director, or has ignored either willfully or through inattention obvious danger signs of employee wrongdoing, the law will cast the burden of liability upon him. This is not the case at bar, however, for as soon as it became evident that there were grounds

for suspicion, the Board acted promptly to end it and prevent its recurrence.

Id. at 130.

A little over thirty years later, the Delaware Court of Chancery (which is a lower court than the Delaware Supreme Court) had an opportunity to interpret *Graham* in *In re Caremark International Inc. Derivative Litigation*, 698 A.2d 959 (Del. Ch. 1996). In *Caremark* the corporation was alleged to have engaged, though acts of its employees, in many violations of Medicare and other laws. The corporation eventually pleaded guilty to one charge of mail fraud and paid fines of $250 million. A derivative suit was then filed on behalf of the corporation against its directors, seeking reimbursement of this amount. As in *Graham*, the plaintiffs did not allege that the directors approved the acts that violated the law, nor even that the directors were aware of the violations while they were occurring. Instead, the essence of the plaintiffs' claim was that the directors *should have* known—the directors should have had a better monitoring system in place that would have prevented these violations (and the massive fines that resulted from them) from occurring.

The precise issue in the *Caremark* opinion was whether the court should approve a settlement agreement. (As you will learn in Chapter 8, settlements in derivative lawsuits require court approval, unlike most "regular" litigation.) The settlement agreement, while providing for substantial fees for the plaintiffs' attorneys, did not involve any payment by the defendant directors. Instead, the settlement agreement essentially gave the plaintiffs "express assurances that Caremark will have a more centralized, active supervisory system in the future. Specifically, the settlement mandate[d] duties to be performed by the ... Compliance and Ethics Committee on an ongoing basis and increases the responsibility for monitoring compliance with the law at the lower levels of management." Basically, Caremark agreed to improve its internal systems for monitoring legal compliance.

To approve a settlement agreement in a derivative lawsuit, the court must find that it is fair to the corporation and the shareholders. The court in *Caremark* found that the settlement agreement was fair, mainly because, if there were a trial it was very unlikely that the plaintiffs would win. Instead, the "record tends to show an active consideration by Caremark management and its Board of the Caremark structures and programs that ultimately led to the company's indictment and to the large financial losses incurred in the settlement of those claims." Nonetheless, the nature of the claim—which the court described as "possibly the most difficult theory in corporation law upon which a plaintiff might hope to win a judgment"—required the court to confront the earlier *Graham* opinion. Set forth below are some important parts of Chancellor Allen's opinion in *Caremark*.

In re **Caremark International Inc. Derivative Litigation**
Court of Chancery of Delaware
698 A.2d. 959 (1996)

***   [A] class of cases in which director liability for inattention is theoretically possible entail circumstances in which a loss eventuates not from a decision but, from unconsidered inaction. Most of the decisions that a corporation, acting through its human agents, makes are, of course, not the subject of director attention. Legally, the board itself will be required only to authorize the most significant corporate acts or transactions: mergers, changes in capital structure, fundamental changes in business, appointment and compensation of the CEO, etc. As the facts of this case graphically demonstrate, ordinary business decisions that are made by officers and employees deeper in the interior of the organization can, however, vitally affect the welfare of the corporation and its ability to achieve its various strategic and financial goals. *** [This raises the] question, what is the board's responsibility with respect to the organization and monitoring of the enterprise to assure that the corporation functions within the law to achieve its purposes?

***

In 1963, the Delaware Supreme Court in *Graham v. Allis-Chalmers Mfg. Co.*, [citation omitted], addressed the question of potential liability of board members for losses experienced by the corporation as a result of the corporation having violated the anti-trust laws of the United States. There was no claim in that case that the directors knew about the behavior of subordinate employees of the corporation that had resulted in the liability. Rather, as in this case, the claim asserted was that the directors *ought to have known* of it and if they had known they would have been under a duty to bring the corporation into compliance with the law and thus save the corporation from the loss. The Delaware Supreme Court concluded that, under the facts as they appeared, there was no basis to find that the directors had breached a duty to be informed of the ongoing operations of the firm. In notably colorful terms, the court stated that "absent cause for suspicion there is no duty upon the directors to install and operate a corporate system of espionage to ferret out wrongdoing which they have no reason to suspect exists." The Court found that there were no grounds for suspicion in that case and, thus, concluded that the directors were blamelessly unaware of the conduct leading to the corporate liability.

How does one generalize this holding today? Can it be said today that, absent some ground giving rise to suspicion of violation of law, that corporate directors have no duty to assure that a corporate information gathering and reporting systems exists which represents a good faith attempt to provide senior management and the Board with information respecting material acts, events or conditions within the corporation, including compliance with applicable statutes and regulations?   I certainly do not believe so.   I doubt that such a broad generalization of the *Graham* holding would have been accepted by the Supreme Court in 1963.   The case can be more narrowly interpreted as standing for the proposition that, absent grounds to suspect deception, neither corporate boards nor senior officers can be charged with wrongdoing simply for assuming the integrity of employees and the honesty of their dealings on the company's behalf.   [Citation omitted.]

A broader interpretation of *Graham v. Allis-Chalmers*—that it means that a corporate board has no responsibility to assure that appropriate information and reporting systems are established by management—would not, in any event, be accepted by the Delaware Supreme Court in 1996, in my opinion.   In stating the basis for this view, I start with the recognition that in recent years the Delaware Supreme Court has made it clear—especially in its jurisprudence concerning takeovers, from *Smith v. Van Gorkom* through *Paramount Communications v. QVC* [which appears in Chapter 12]—the seriousness with which the corporation law views the role of the corporate board.   Secondly, I note the elementary fact that relevant and timely *information* is an essential predicate for satisfaction of the board's supervisory and monitoring role ***.   Thirdly, I note the potential impact of the [recently adopted] federal organizational sentencing guidelines on any business organization.   Any rational person attempting in good faith to meet an organizational governance responsibility would be bound to take into account this development and the enhanced penalties and the opportunities for reduced sanctions that it offers.

In light of these developments, it would, in my opinion, be a mistake to conclude that our Supreme Court's statement in *Graham* concerning "espionage" means that corporate boards may satisfy their obligation to be reasonably informed concerning the corporation, without assuring themselves that information and reporting systems exist in the organization that are reasonably designed to provide to senior management and to the board itself timely, accurate information sufficient to allow management and the board, each within its scope, to reach informed judgments concerning both the corporation's compliance with law and its business performance.

Obviously the level of detail that is appropriate for such an information system is a question of business judgment.   And obviously too, no rationally designed information and reporting system will remove the possibility that the corporation will violate laws or regulations, or that senior officers or directors may nevertheless sometimes be misled or otherwise fail reasonably to detect acts material to the corporation's compliance with the law.   But it is important that the board exercise a good faith judgment that the corporation's information and reporting system is in concept and design adequate to assure the board that appropriate information will come to its attention in a timely manner as a matter of ordinary operations, so that it may satisfy its responsibility.

Thus, I am of the view that a director's obligation includes a duty to attempt in good faith to assure that a corporate information and reporting system, which the board concludes is adequate, exists, and that failure to do so under some circumstances may, in theory at least, render a director liable for losses caused by non-compliance with applicable legal standards. I now turn to an analysis of the claims asserted with this concept of the directors duty of care, as a duty satisfied in part by assurance of adequate information flows to the board, in mind.

***

*** Since it does appear that the Board was to some extent unaware of the activities that led to liability, I turn to a consideration of the other potential avenue to director liability that the pleadings take: director inattention or "negligence". Generally where a claim of directorial liability for corporate loss is predicated upon ignorance of liability creating activities within the corporation, as in *Graham* or in this case, in my opinion only a sustained or systematic failure of the board to exercise oversight—such as an utter failure to attempt to assure a reasonable information and reporting system exists—will establish the lack of good faith that is a necessary condition to liability. Such a test of liability—lack of good faith as evidenced by sustained or systematic failure of a director to exercise reasonable oversight—is quite high. But, a demanding test of liability in the oversight context is probably beneficial to corporate shareholders as a class, as it is in the board decision context, since it makes board service by qualified persons more likely, while continuing to act as a stimulus to *good faith performance of duty* by such directors.

Here the record supplies essentially no evidence that the director defendants were guilty of a sustained failure to exercise their oversight function. To the contrary, insofar as I am able to tell on this record, the corporation's information systems appear to have represented a good faith attempt to be informed of relevant facts. If the directors did not know the specifics of the activities that lead to the indictments, they cannot be faulted.

The liability that eventuated in this instance was huge. But the fact that it resulted from a violation of criminal law alone does not create a breach of fiduciary duty by directors. The record at this stage does not support the conclusion that the defendants either lacked good faith in the exercise of their monitoring responsibilities or conscientiously permitted a known violation of law by the corporation to occur. The claims asserted against them must be viewed at this stage as extremely weak.

***

The *Caremark* standard was later approved by the Delaware Supreme Court in *Stone v. Ritter*, which is discussed in Section 6.07 below.

§ 6.05   EXCULPATION AND INDEMNIFICATION

Beyond the business judgment rule and the many hurdles for plaintiffs that are presented by MBCA § 8.31, there are a few additional reasons why a director who has breached her duty of care may not actually pay any damages.

A.   EXCULPATION PROVISIONS IN ARTICLES

As noted above, *Smith v. Van Gorkom* was widely viewed as a bad decision by academics. But beyond law professors complaining about the case, it also had real-world consequences. Most notably, Delaware—which as you know is the state of incorporation for most publicly traded companies—amended its statute to add Section 102(b)(7), which allows (but does not require) a corporation's certificate of incorporation to contain:

> A provision eliminating or limiting the personal liability of a director to the corporation or its stockholders for monetary damages for breach of fiduciary duty as a director, provided that such provision shall not eliminate or limit the liability of a director: (i) for any breach of the director's duty of loyalty to the corporation or its stockholders; (ii) for acts or omissions not in good faith or which involve intentional misconduct or a knowing violation of law; (iii) under § 174 of this title [which concerns illegal dividends]; or (iv) for any transaction from which the director derived an improper personal benefit. ***

The MBCA was similarly amended to add Section 2.02(b)(4), which allows (but does not require) a corporation's articles to include:

> a provision eliminating or limiting the liability of a director to the corporation or its shareholders for money damages for any action taken, or any failure to take any action, as a director, except liability for (A) the amount of a financial benefit received by a director to which he is not entitled; (B) an intentional infliction of harm on the corporation or the shareholders; (C) a violation of

section 8.33 [which concerns illegal dividends]; or (D) an intentional violation of criminal law.

Stop and think about these provisions for a minute. If you were a director, you obviously would *love* these provisions, because they "shield" you from monetary liability (but not equitable remedies such as injunctions) for any action or inaction other than the four exceptions noted in each statute. Some of these exceptions implicate your duty of loyalty (e.g., subsections (i) and (iv) of the Delaware statute and subsection (A) of the MBCA), which you will learn about in Chapter 7. Beyond that, the other exceptions seem pretty easy to avoid. Who, after all, would intentionally inflict harm on the corporation or the shareholders within the meaning of MBCA § 2.02(b)(4)(B)? (Note that the Delaware section also does not shield directors for "acts or omissions not in good faith." This issue is considered in Section 6.07 below.)

Keep in mind that both of these statutory sections represent *optional* provisions to put in a corporation's articles. A given corporation may or may not have such a provision. (If it does, then obviously the plaintiff's case, at least if she is seeking monetary damages from the directors, will be much more difficult.) If you were to form a corporation today, then you could simply decide, in your role as the incorporator, whether to include such a provision in the articles. But for a preexisting corporation, if you wish to amend the articles of incorporation, then shareholder approval is ordinarily required. So in the wake of *Smith v. Van Gorkom* and the passage of Section 102(b)(7) of the Delaware statute and MBCA § 2.02(b)(4), many corporations asked their shareholders to vote on proposals to add such director-shielding provisions to their articles. How would you vote on such a proposal if you were a shareholder? How do you think that most shareholders presented with these proposals actually voted?

B.   INDEMNIFICATION

Another reason why directors may not end up paying any damages is *indemnification*. Indemnification refers to a situation where one person agrees to reimburse another person for any expenses and/or liabilities that she incurs. Given the widespread panic following *Smith v. Van Gorkom*, indemnification of directors for lawsuits arising from their service as directors took on a new urgency.

The MBCA provisions concerning indemnification (MBCA §§ 8.50 to 8.59) are long and detailed, and I will attempt only a short summary here. There are two types of indemnification under the statute: permissible and mandatory.

Under MBCA § 8.51, a corporation *may* indemnify a director[*] against liability in a "proceeding" (which includes not only civil lawsuits, but criminal suits, administrative proceedings, arbitration, and other types of proceedings) if certain conditions are met. One condition is that the director conducted herself in "good faith." In addition, depending on the nature of the suit, the director must have either reasonably believed that her conduct was in the "best interests of the corporation" or that it was "not opposed to the best interests of the corporation." In a criminal proceeding, the director must also have "had no reasonable cause to believe ... her conduct was unlawful." Alternatively, MBCA § 8.51 permits indemnification where it is permitted or required by a provision in the corporation's articles, as allowed by MBCA § 2.02(b)(5). As used in this section and others, the term "liability" includes judgments, settlements, penalties, and fines, as well as "reasonable expenses incurred with respect to a proceeding," such as attorney fees. However, there are some situations in which indemnification is not allowed, such as in connection with a proceeding where the director was "adjudged liable on the basis of receiving a financial benefit to which ... she was not entitled ...." Further, generally the director may not be indemnified (other than for expenses) if she was found liable, either through a judgment or a settlement, to the corporation itself. *See* MBCA § 8.51(d)(1).

MBCA § 8.52 concerns mandatory (as opposed to permissible) indemnification. Basically, the corporation *must* indemnify a director "who was wholly successful, on the merits or otherwise, in the defense of any proceeding ... against expenses incurred by the director in connection with the proceeding." A comment to this section notes that "wholly successful" means that the "entire proceeding [was] disposed of on a basis which does not involve a finding of liability." The phrase "on the merits or otherwise" could include situations where the proceeding was dismissed on a "technicality" such as the statute of limitations.

A careful reader will have noted that indemnification under MBCA § 8.51 is optional (unless required by the corporation's articles) and indemnification under MBCA § 8.52 is only mandatory when the proceeding is completed or dismissed. As a law student, you surely know that litigation in America is anything but quick and easy, and that attorney fees could really add up in the meantime. Luckily for a director facing such a situation, MBCA § 8.53 allows (but does not require) the corporation to "advance" expenses to a director while a proceeding is pending. One condition of making an advance is that the director must agree in writing to return any advances if it is later found that she was not entitled to mandatory indemnification under MBCA § 8.52.

There is a great deal more that could be said about indemnification, such as discussing when a court may order indemnification or the advancement of

---

[*]   See MBCA § 8.50 for the definition of "director." It is somewhat broader than you would think. See also MBCA § 8.56, which concerns indemnification of officers.

expenses under MBCA § 8.54, and who must determine whether the director met the conditions required for indemnification. You can learn more about this topic in an advanced course on Corporations. In addition, you should note that many corporations, particularly publicly traded corporations, have very generous[*] indemnification provisions in their articles or bylaws (or contracts with directors), the reason being that few smart people would want to serve as directors without them, particularly if other corporations have them. After all, being a director is very risky.

Before we leave this section, a few words about *insurance* are in order. MBCA § 8.57 specifically states that corporations may maintain insurance for officers and directors against liabilities arising out of their service as directors and/or officers. This insurance is often called "D&O insurance." The statute contains no restrictions on what sort of insurance the corporation may maintain; indeed, it states that the corporation may maintain *insurance* even if it could not *indemnify* the director under the sections discussed above. However, the private insurance market (as well as applicable insurance laws) will regulate the availability—and cost—of insurance. For example, a common maxim of insurance law is that you can't purchase insurance against intentional misconduct. What rational insurance company would issue such a policy?

§ 6.06   OTHER ISSUES

In the complex world that we live in, many board decisions will involve technical issues, such as whether a given course of action will run afoul of laws or regulations or whether it is scientifically or technically feasible. Yet, as Judge Hand observed in *Barnes v. Andrews*, "[d]irectors are not specialists, like lawyers or doctors. They must have good sense, perhaps they must have acquaintance with affairs; but they need not ... have any technical talent." Recognizing that it would be an inefficient way to run a business to have the directors fully educate themselves about every technical or legal issue that may arise, the MBCA allows directors to rely on opinions and reports from others. In other words, directors may "call in the experts" to advise them on such issues. If the expert's advice turns out to be incorrect, then perhaps the corporation may have a malpractice action against the expert, but the directors can hardly be faulted for relying on such advice in good faith.

---

[*]   What I mean by "generous" is that permissible indemnification under MBCA § 8.51 often becomes more or less mandatory under a corporation's articles or bylaws or a contract with a director. However, under MBCA §8.59 a "corporation may provide indemnification or advance expenses to a director or an officer only as permitted by" MBCA §§ 8.50 through 8.59. For example, a corporation would not be permitted to indemnify a director with respect to a proceeding in which she was unsuccessful and was found to have acted in bad faith (unless ordered by a court under MBCA § 8.54).

Further, as you saw in Chapter 5, directors generally may delegate certain tasks to others in the corporation, such as board committees or officers or employees. What should happen if the board delegates a task to someone and that person "screws it up"? Again, if the directors made the delegation in good faith, it hardly seems fair to make them the guarantors of adequate performance by the person to whom the task was delegated. Read MBCA §§ 8.30(d), (e), and (f) and consider the following problems. The answers to these problems are probably obvious, but be sure to look at the specific language of the statute to support your analysis.

Problems

Problem 6-1: The board of directors of ABC Corp., which consists of seventeen persons, has two pressing matters to address. First, the CEO of the corporation had announced her retirement, and the board must choose a successor CEO. A nationwide search may be necessary. *May the board delegate to ABC Corp.'s night watchman the task of reviewing the résumés of CEO candidates, interviewing them, and recommending the next CEO to the board? Why or why not?*

Problem 6-2: Suppose that ABC's board forms a three-person subcommittee that will review the résumés of CEO candidates, interview them, and make a recommendation to the board. After several weeks, the committee recommends that Jane Jones, who has very impressive education and work credentials, be hired. The board agrees and unanimously hires Jane Jones as the new CEO. Unfortunately, it turns out that Jane is a heroin addict who proceeds to steal millions of dollars from the company. *If the shareholders sue all of the board members for breaching their duty of care by hiring Jane, what should be the result?*

Problem 6-3: The second pressing matter for ABC's board is that the corporation has to decide whether to enter into an agreement under which it will supply certain computer and other technical equipment to companies in China. One director wondered whether this contract would violate national security laws. *How should the board go about deciding whether to enter into this contract?*

Problem 6-4: Suppose that ABC's board engages outside counsel to decide whether the contract would be legal. After three weeks of intensive research, outside counsel tells the board that the contract is legal. Unfortunately, it is not, and ABC Corp. ends up paying $5 million in fines to the U.S. government. *If the shareholders sue all of the board members for breaching their duty of care by approving the contract, what should be the result?*

Problem 6-5: Same facts as Problem 6-4, except that you are one of the directors and, shortly before the board voted on the contract, you read a summary of U.S. v. Johnson Corp., which held that a similar contract was illegal. This decision, however, was from a federal district court in a district in which ABC Corp. does not do business. *If the shareholders sue all of the board members for breaching their duty of care by approving the contract, what should be the result?*

Problem 6-6: Why weren't the other directors in *Smith v. Van Gorkom* able to defend the case by arguing that they relied on Van Gorkom's opinion that $55 per share was a good price for Trans Union?

Another issue that may arise when the board members are sued for breaching their duty of care is whether they should all be treated similarly. And as noted above, Judge Hand observed that directors are not "specialists." But what if one of them actually is? Should that person be held to a higher standard than the other, "mere mortal," directors? On this issue, consider the following passage from *In re Emerging Communications Shareholder Litigation*, 2004 WL 1305745 (Del. Ct. Ch. 2004):

> Muoio is culpable because he voted to approve the transaction even though he knew, or at the very least had strong reasons to believe, that the $10.25 per share merger price was unfair. Muoio was in a unique position to know that. He was a principal and general partner of an investment advising firm, with significant experience in finance and the telecommunications sector. From 1995 to 1996, Muoio had been a securities analyst for, and a vice president of, Lazard Freres & Co. in the telecommunications and media sector. From 1985 to 1995, he was a securities analyst for Gabelli & Co., Inc., in the communications sector, and from 1993 to 1995, he was a portfolio manager for Gabelli Global Communications Fund, Inc.
>
> Hence, Muoio possessed a specialized financial expertise, and an ability to understand ECM's intrinsic value, that was unique to the ECM board members (other than, perhaps, Prosser). Informed by his specialized expertise and knowledge, Muoio conceded that the $10.25 price was "at the low end of any kind of

fair value you would put," and expressed to Goodwin his view that the Special Committee might be able to get up to $20 per share from Prosser. In these circumstances, it was incumbent upon Muoio, as a fiduciary, to advocate that the board reject the $10.25 price that the Special Committee was recommending. As a fiduciary knowledgeable of ECM's intrinsic value, Muoio should also have gone on record as voting against the proposed transaction at the $10.25 per share merger price. Muoio did neither. Instead he joined the other directors in voting, without objection, to approve the transaction.

At the other end of the spectrum, however, the *Francis* court did not treat Mrs. Pritchard leniently because she had an alcohol problem and was depressed.

Two other observations are in order before we conclude our discussion of the duty of care. First, as noted earlier in this chapter, MBCA § 8.42, entitled "Standards of Conduct for Officers," uses identical language to MBCA § 8.30 and the Delaware Supreme Court recently held that officers' duties to the corporation are identical to directors' duties. Does this mean that officers should also get the benefit of the business judgment rule like directors do? So far, a clear majority answer to this question has not emerged from the case law, although Section 4.01 of the *ALI Principles of Corporate Governance* takes the position that officers should be so protected. But if most courts eventually do answer this question affirmatively, the next question will be how far down this rule should extend: should "regular" employees also get the benefit of the business judgment rule if they are sued for poor decisions that they made?

Finally, you have probably come away from reading the preceding pages of this chapter with the impression that it is very, very difficult to sue directors for breaching their duty of care, at least successfully. This is true. But one nonetheless constantly hears about lawsuits by shareholders against the boards of underperforming corporations, and often the shareholders win these cases. Keep in mind that many of these cases arise under federal securities laws and involve publicly traded corporations. Federal securities laws also impose additional duties on corporate directors. We will briefly consider some of these issues in Chapter 10. But suffice it to say here that the rules in such cases sometimes differ greatly from what we have seen in this chapter.

§ 6.07   IS THERE A DUTY OF GOOD FAITH?

Is there a duty of good faith? No, at least not a *separate* fiduciary duty that stands shoulder-to-shoulder with the fiduciary duties of care and loyalty. Is the concept of good faith nonetheless important? Absolutely. Allow me to explain. As noted above, Section 102(b)(7) of the Delaware General Corporation Law allows corporations to include a provision in their articles of incorporation[*] that shields directors from monetary liability for any actions or inactions except for, among other things, "acts or omissions not in good faith." Because many corporations have added such provisions to their articles, as a practical matter directors in these corporations are immune from liability for breaching their duty of care, so long as they act in good faith (and avoid the other exceptions of Section 102(b)(7)). While MBCA § 2.02(b)(4) does not exclude acts or omissions not in good faith from the liability "shield," MBCA § 8.30(a)(1) requires directors to discharge their duties in good faith, and that MBCA § 8.31(a)(2)(i) provides that one possible basis for director liability is where the "challenged conduct consisted of or was the result of ... action not in good faith." In addition, permissible indemnification generally is not available if the director did not act in good faith, as discussed in Section 6.05(B) above.

Thus, "good faith" is an important concept. But what does it *mean*? The recent derivative litigation involving The Walt Disney Company and the later case of *Stone v. Ritter* shed some light on the meaning of good faith. Interested readers may wish to read the full opinions, as the following is a relatively short summary.

In *Disney*, the company hired Michael Ovitz (previously considered the most powerful man in Hollywood) to be its president. However, only fourteen months later, Disney fired Ovitz. Because he was fired without cause under his employment contract, Ovitz was entitled to severance pay of more than $130 million. While Ovitz was probably pleased with this payout, several Disney shareholders were not—they filed a derivative lawsuit alleging (among other things) that Disney's directors had breached their fiduciary duties by approving an employment agreement with Ovitz that could result in such an astronomical payout if he was fired without cause, and by later approving his firing without cause. Not surprisingly, however, Disney had a Section 102(b)(7) provision in its certificate of incorporation. (Disney is incorporated in Delaware.) Thus, the plaintiffs essentially had to argue that the Disney board had not acted in good faith when approving the employment contract or Ovitz's firing without cause.

Initially, the Delaware Chancery Court dismissed the plaintiff's claims for breach of fiduciary duty because the plaintiffs had not made a "demand" on the board before filing the suit. (This is something that you will learn about in

---

[*]   Delaware calls it the certificate of incorporation.

Chapter 8.)   In addition, the plaintiff's other claims were dismissed for other reasons. *In re The Walt Disney Co,. Derivative Litigation,* 731 A.2d 342 (Del. Ch. 1998).   However, the Delaware Supreme Court granted the plaintiffs leave to amend their complaint. *Brehm v. Eisner,* 746 A.2d 244 (Del. 2000).   The court also advised the plaintiffs to seek more facts by exercising their statutory right to inspect Disney's books and records. (See Section 5.08(E) of Chapter 5.)

The plaintiffs did so and filed an amended complaint which portrayed Disney's board as almost completely indifferent to the Ovitz contract.   The defendants moved to dismiss the amended complaint, but the Court of Chancery denied the motion. *In re The Walt Disney Co. Derivative Litig.,* 825 A.2d 275 (Del. Ch. 2003).   The court concluded that the directors' conduct may not have been in good faith:

> A fair reading of the new complaint, in my opinion, gives rise to a reason to doubt whether the board's actions were taken honestly and in good faith ***.   Since acts or omissions not undertaken honestly and in good faith, or which involve intentional misconduct, do not fall within the protective ambit of § 102(b)(7), I cannot dismiss the complaint based on the exculpatory Disney charter provision.

Id. at 286.   The court also noted that if the facts alleged in the complaint were true, the directors would not be entitled to the business judgment rule.   Thus, the case went to trial, which lasted for thirty-seven days.

In the end, the Delaware Chancery Court found for the defendants. *In re The Walt Disney Co. Derivative Litig.,* 907 A.2d 693 (Del. Ch. 2005). Specifically, to oversimplify an eighty-three page opinion, the court concluded that the defendant-directors were, at worst, ordinarily negligent.   Thus, they had not breached their duty of care and also were entitled to the business judgment rule, even though they had fallen far short of "best practices" and that "many lessons of what not to do can be learned from" their conduct.   Alternatively, the court found that plaintiffs had not shown that the directors had not acted in good faith.[*]

On appeal, the Delaware Supreme Court affirmed. *In re The Walt Disney Co. Derivative Litig.,* 906 A.2d 27 (Del. 2006).   Although a discussion of the issue of whether the directors had acted in good faith was not necessary because the trial court found that the directors had acted with due care, the Delaware Supreme

---

[*]   As the Delaware Supreme Court summarized it: "The Court of Chancery held that the business judgment rule [presumed to be] protected the decisions of the compensation committee [of Disney's board] and the remaining Disney directors, not only because they had acted with due care but also because they had not acted in bad faith." 906 A.2d at 61.

Court nonetheless attempted to explain the meaning of "good faith" in the following (heavily edited) passage:

> The first category involves so-called "subjective bad faith," that is, fiduciary conduct motivated by an actual intent to do harm. That such conduct constitutes classic, quintessential bad faith is a proposition so well accepted in the liturgy of fiduciary law that it borders on axiomatic. ***

> The second category of conduct, which is at the opposite end of the spectrum, involves lack of due care—that is, fiduciary action taken solely by reason of gross negligence and without any malevolent intent. In this case, appellants assert claims of gross negligence to establish breaches not only of director due care but also of the directors' duty to act in good faith. Although the Chancellor found, and we agree, that the appellants failed to establish gross negligence, to afford guidance we address the issue of whether gross negligence (including a failure to inform one's self of available material facts), without more, can also constitute bad faith. The answer is clearly no.

> ***

> That leaves the third category of fiduciary conduct, which falls in between the first two categories of (1) conduct motivated by subjective bad intent and (2) conduct resulting from gross negligence. This third category is what the Chancellor's definition of bad faith—intentional dereliction of duty, a conscious disregard for one's responsibilities—is intended to capture. The question is whether such misconduct is properly treated as a non-exculpable, nonindemnifiable violation of the fiduciary duty to act in good faith. In our view it must be ***.

> *** [In his post-trial opinion, the Chancellor] identified different examples of bad faith as follows:

>> The good faith required of a corporate fiduciary includes not simply the duties of care and loyalty *** but all actions required by a true faithfulness and devotion to the interests of the corporation and its shareholders. A failure to act in good faith may be shown, for instance, where the fiduciary intentionally acts with a purpose other than that of advancing the best interests of the corporation, where the fiduciary acts with the intent to violate applicable positive

law [i.e., laws that apply to the corporation itself], or where the fiduciary intentionally fails to act in the face of a known duty to act, demonstrating a conscious disregard for his duties. There may be other examples of bad faith yet to be proven or alleged, but these three are the most salient.

***

For these reasons, we uphold the Court of Chancery's definition as a legally appropriate, although not the exclusive, definition of fiduciary bad faith. ***

Id. at 64-67 (footnotes and citations omitted throughout).

Stone v. Ritter, 911 A.2d 362 (Del. 2006), is helpful for us in two respects. First, it clarified some language in the *Disney* opinions about whether there was a separate duty of good faith. The *Stone* court wrote:

although good faith may be described colloquially as part of a "triad" of fiduciary duties that includes the duties of care and loyalty, the obligation to act in good faith does not establish an independent fiduciary duty that stands on the same footing as the duties of care and loyalty. Only the latter two duties, where violated, may directly result in liability, whereas a failure to act in good faith may do so, but indirectly.

Id. at 369.

Second, *Stone* approved the *Caremark* standard. (Recall that *Caremark* was a decision of the Delaware Court of Chancery, whereas *Stone* was the Delaware Supreme Court.) In context of the case, which involved allegations of inadequate oversight by the board that were very similar to the facts in *Caremark* itself and also involved a Section 102(b)(7) articles provisions that would shield directors from liability unless they were not acting in good faith, the *Stone* court held that

Caremark articulates the necessary conditions predicate for director oversight liability: (a) the directors utterly failed to implement any reporting or information system or controls; *or* (b) having implemented such a system or controls, consciously failed to monitor or oversee its operations thus disabling themselves from being informed of risks or problems requiring their attention. In either case, imposition of liability requires a showing that the directors knew that they were not discharging their fiduciary obligations. Where directors fail to act in the face of a known duty to act, thereby demonstrating a conscious disregard for their responsibilities, they breach their duty of loyalty by failing to discharge that fiduciary obligation in good faith.

Id. at 370 (citations omitted throughout). Note that if the plaintiff made either of the above-described showings, the directors would not be shielded from liability by a Section 102(b)(7) provision in the corporation's articles. However, in *Stone* the plaintiffs failed to make either required showing because they essentially admitted that the board had a complex reporting system (even if it hadn't worked properly).

Confused yet? Don't worry too much if you are; these cases have engendered a great deal of debate and disagreement (and probably confusion) among judges, lawyers, and academics. One thing that *is* certain, though, is that the future will bring more cases elaborating on the meaning of "good faith."

One last note: the careful reader will note that the *Stone* opinion characterized good faith as involving a director's duty of loyalty, rather than the duty of care. The duty of loyalty is considered in the following chapter. But before then, try your hand at some practice multiple choice questions concerning the duty of care.

PRACTICE QUESTIONS

Multiple Choice Question 6-1: *Which of the following statements concerning a director's duty of care is correct?*

A.   Directors have a duty to act in the best interests of the corporation.

B.   The person suing the directors for a breach of the duty of care and seeking money damages of behalf of the corporation has the burden of proving causation and damages.

C.   Under Delaware law, directors need not implement a "monitoring system" over the corporation's legal compliance unless and until they know, or should know, that the company's employees are engaged in illegal activities.

D.   When discharging their duty of care, directors may rely on the opinions and reports of other people, as long as those other people are professionals (such as lawyers or accountants).

Multiple Choice Question 6-2: *Which of the following statements concerning a director's duty of care is correct?*

A.   A finding of negligence is ordinarily sufficient to prove that the directors breached their duty of care.
B.   Directors are never liable for harm resulting from the illegal actions of employees, unless the directors knew about the illegal actions before they occurred.
C.   Directors may successfully defend any duty-of-care lawsuit by proving that a majority of them were disinterested in the challenged transaction.
D.   None of the above is correct.

Multiple Choice Question 6-3:   Tripleday Books Corp. ("TBC") is a book-publishing company that has a very successful history of publishing self-help books, including several by famous celebrities. In March, TBC's board of directors unanimously approved a contract for a new book: "How to Be A Good Husband" by Bob Jennings, a famous baseball player. At the time of the contract, TBC's board was aware that Mr. Jennings had admitted to several extra-marital affairs. However, TBC's directors believed that Mr. Jennings's book was well-written and would be successful because he is a major celebrity.

The book was a disaster, selling fewer than 100 copies. A shareholder has properly brought a derivative lawsuit against TBC's board of directors alleging that the directors breached their duty of care and seeking to recover from the directors the $5 million advance payment that TBC made to Mr. Jennings. *Which of the following statements is correct?*

A.   The board of directors will lose the case because the contract with Mr. Jennings was a terrible decision and thus was not in the best interests of the corporation.
B.   To win the case, the board of directors will have the burden of proving that the contract with Mr. Jennings was fair to TBC.
C.   The board of directors will have the business judgment rule as a defense in the case, provided that the directors first prove that they were sufficiently informed of all material information reasonably available to them before they approved the contract and that they acted in good faith.
D.   None of the above is correct.

Multiple Choice Question 6-4: Shelia was asked by Helicopter Corp., a Delaware corporation which does not have any "special" provisions in its certificate (articles) of incorporation, to serve as a director. *If Shelia accepts this position, which of the following cannot result in her being personally liable for damages?*

A.   Diverting corporate opportunities to herself.
B.   Gross negligence in the performance of her duties as a director.
C.   Honest errors of judgment that are made with due diligence.
D.   All of the above could result in personal liability for Shelia.

Multiple Choice Question 6-5: Several employees of BSI Inc. ("<u>BSI</u>"), none of whom were directors of BSI, pleaded guilty to criminal charges that they engaged in illegal bribery of various governmental officials. In connection with these pleas, BSI agreed to pay a $50 million fine to the federal government and to terminate the employment of the employees involved in the bribery. Despite having a corporate monitoring system in place, the members of BSI's board of directors did not know about the bribery until the Federal Bureau of Investigation (FBI) began an investigation several months after the bribery had taken place. A group of BSI shareholders has approached you about the possibility of filing a derivative action against BSI's directors for breach of their duty of care. The shareholders want BSI to recover from the directors the fine that the company paid to the federal government. *Which one of the following statements would be correct advice to these shareholders?*

A.   The case will be very difficult to win if BSI's articles of incorporation contain a provision limiting director liability in accordance with Section 2.02(b)(4) of the MBCA.
B.   Although the BSI directors will have the "business judgment rule" available as a defense in the case, it will be easy to overcome the "business judgment rule" because the directors will be defendants in the lawsuit and thus have a conflict of interest.
C.   Although the BSI directors will have the "business judgment rule" available as a defense in the case, it will be easy to overcome the "business judgment rule" by showing that the directors were grossly negligent in not reasonably informing themselves about the bribery at a board meeting.
D.   The case will be difficult to win because the plaintiffs must prove that the directors made a decision that was not in good faith.

Multiple Choice Question 6-6:   Assume that a director is grossly negligent in performing her oversight duties as a director and the corporation thereafter become insolvent and files for bankruptcy protection. *If the bankruptcy trustee sues the director on behalf of the corporation, which of the following would be correct?*

A.   The plaintiff will have the burden of proving that the director breached her duty of loyalty to the corporation.
B.   The director will be liable for breaching the business judgment rule.
C.   The director will not be liable unless the plaintiff proves that the director's gross negligence caused damage to the corporation.
D.   None of the above.

Multiple Choice Question 6-7:   Jeb Smothers ("Smothers") was the CEO and a director of Sunnybrook Corporation ("Sunnybrook"). Sunnybrook was formed to manufacture parts for various airplanes as well as NASA spacecraft. In January 2011, Smothers asked his good friend Bobucar Jensen ("Jensen") to serve on Sunnybrook's board of directors. Jensen agreed and was elected as one of Sunnybrook's twelve directors at the annual shareholders' meeting on March 15, 2011. At that time, Sunnybrook owned a factory to produce the parts, but had not yet actually produced any. It had also hired several executives and managers to run the business, each of whom received a substantial salary. Jensen served as a director of Sunnybrook until his resignation on September 1, 2011. Jensen attended only one of the three board meetings held during his time as a director. Jensen learned much of what he knew about Sunnybrook's business from informal conversations with Smothers. A few months later, the corporation filed bankruptcy. Thereafter, a shareholder filed a derivative action on behalf of Sunnybrook against Jensen, alleging that he breached his fiduciary duties to Sunnybrook. *What is the likely outcome of this lawsuit?*

A.   Jensen will prevail, because the business judgment rule will shield him from liability.
B.   Jensen will prevail, provided his inaction was not a proximate cause of harm to Sunnybrook.
C.   The plaintiff will prevail, because Jensen breached his duty of care to Sunnybrook.
D.   The plaintiff will prevail because Jensen had a duty to monitor the business and make sure that the parts were being produced.

MULTIPLE CHOICE QUESTIONS 6-8 TO 6-11 ARE BASED ON THE FOLLOWING FACT PATTERN

Big Oil Corp. ("BOC") is in the oil drilling and production business. In 2009, BOC's board of directors approved the construction of an offshore well in the Gulf of Mexico called the Really Deep Well. Because this well was 6,000 feet below the ocean surface, the board held four lengthy meetings to discuss safety and other issues before approving the well. Two different designs for the well were discussed at these meetings. The first design was presented by Eureka, Inc. ("Eureka"). The second, more expensive, design was presented by Drilling Safety, Inc. ("DSI"). Eureka's design featured two shut-off valves near the top of the drilling platform above the ocean surface. DSI's design was similar, but also included two emergency shut-off valves near the ocean floor. At these meetings, the board listened to several independent oil industry experts discuss the two well designs. Some of these experts believed that Eureka's well design was not sufficiently safe. However, several other experts believed that Eureka's design was sufficiently safe, because it had two shut-off valves on the drilling platform. In the end, the choice between the two different designs boiled down to cost: Eureka's design cost much less than DSI's design. When the series of meetings was done, BOC's board chose the Eureka design and authorized the construction of the Really Deep Well using that design. The director who argued most strenuously in favor of the Eureka design was Dave Drum. Mr. Drum did not inform the other BOC directors that his daughter, Bertha Barrel, is the majority shareholder of Eureka.

In April 2010, there was an explosion at the Really Deep Well. Eleven BOC employees were killed, and several million barrels of oil leaked from a rupture in the well near the ocean floor for more than three months. Eventually, the leak was stopped, but not before billions of dollars of damage had been done. Among the persons submitting damage claims to BOC were fishermen who fished in the Gulf of Mexico and several state and local governments that had spent billions of dollars cleaning up oil. BOC agreed that it was liable for these costs, and set aside $20 billion to be used to pay these claims. In addition, the federal government fined BOC several million dollars for safety violations.

A group of shareholders wants to bring a derivative suit on behalf of BOC against the directors. In addition to Mr. Drum, there are nine other people on BOC's board, including Camilla Crude and Dave Drill. Ms. Crude was absent from the series of meetings because she was on a four-week vacation. Dave Drill, who is the grandson of the founder of BOC and owns 5% of its stock, flunked out of high school. He is also known to attend board meetings while intoxicated and it is believed that he smokes crack cocaine.

BOC is incorporated in an MBCA state that also follows Delaware case law. BOC does not have any "unusual" provisions in its articles of incorporation.

Multiple Choice Question 6-8:   *If Mr. Drum is sued for breaching his fiduciary duties to BOC, what is the likely outcome of the lawsuit?*

A.   Mr. Drum will likely win the case—he will be entitled to the protection of the business judgment rule because the board as a whole was well-informed before it chose the Eureka well design.
B.   Mr. Drum will likely lose the case unless he can show that the transaction was entirely fair to BOC.
C.   Mr. Drum will likely lose the case because BOC was fined by the government, which means it engaged in illegal activities.
D.   Mr. Drum will likely win the case because he acted in good faith.

Multiple Choice Question 6-9:   *If Ms. Crude is sued for breaching her fiduciary duties to BOC, what is the likely outcome of the lawsuit?*

A.   Ms. Crude will likely win the case because she did not vote in favor of the Eureka well design.
B.   Ms. Crude will likely lose the case because she did not attend the board meeting at which the Eureka well design was approved.
C.   Ms. Crude will likely win the case because she will be entitled the protection of the business judgment rule.
D.   Ms. Crude will likely lose the case if the plaintiffs can show causation and damages.

Multiple Choice Question 6-10:   *If Mr. Drill is sued for breaching his fiduciary duties to BOC, what is the likely outcome of the lawsuit?*

A.   Mr. Drill will likely win the case because he did not violate his duty of loyalty.
B.   Mr. Drill will likely win the case by proving that he has below-average intelligence and is addicted to drugs.
C.   Mr. Drill will likely lose the case because two experts told the board that the Eureka well design was not safe.
D.   Mr. Drill will likely win the case—he will be entitled to the protection of the business judgment rule because the board as a whole was well-informed before it decided to choose the Eureka well design.
E.   Mr. Drill will likely lose the case because BOC was fined by the government, which means it engaged in illegal activities.

Multiple Choice Question 6-11:   *If the directors other than Mr. Drum, Ms. Crude, and Mr. Drill are sued for breaching their fiduciary duties to BOC, what is the likely outcome of the lawsuit?*

A.   The directors will likely win the case—they will be entitled to the protection of the business judgment rule because the board was well-informed before it decided to choose the Eureka well design.

B.   The directors will likely lose the case because two experts told the board that the Eureka well design was not safe.

C.   The directors will likely win the case because they chose the cheapest well design and therefore reasonably believed they were acting in the best interests of BOC.

D.   The directors will likely win the case because the only way the plaintiffs could win the case is if they showed that the directors intentionally tried to harm the corporation or approved illegal dividends, none of which happened here.

E.   The directors will likely lose the case because BOC was fined by the government, which means it engaged in illegal activities.

CHAPTER 7
THE DUTY OF LOYALTY

As noted at the beginning of Chapter 6, directors owe two primary fiduciary duties: the duty of care and the duty of loyalty. This chapter concerns the duty of loyalty. (However, Delaware courts have stated that the duty to act in good faith, which was discussed in Chapter 6, is an aspect of the duty of loyalty.)

Fundamentally, the duty of loyalty involves a conflict of interest, that is, a conflict between a director's (or officer's) personal interests and the corporation's interests. As you know, directors owe fiduciary duties to the corporation. MBCA § 8.30(a), for example, provides that directors must act in good faith and in a manner that they reasonably believe is in the best interests of the corporation. But directors are human beings too; just because a person is a director does not mean that she does not have other aspects of her life, particularly if she is an "outside" director who does not work as an officer or employee of the corporation. Because human nature is human nature—to use an ugly word, greed has a long history—there is always a risk that a director may seek to favor her personal interests at the corporation's expense. This is particularly dangerous because, as you saw in Chapter 5, directors (as a group) have the power to cause the corporation to take actions that would enrich them. Thus, the duty of loyalty largely exists to "police" these conflicts of interest so that the corporation is not harmed by potentially selfish actions by its fiduciaries.

At the same time, just because a director has a personal interest in a given transaction should not mean that such a transaction is completely off-limits. For example, if a director owns a piece of land that the corporation needs to expand its facilities, and the director is willing to sell the land for a fair price, why should the corporation be forbidden from purchasing the land from that director? (On the other hand, how likely is this scenario?) For this reason, the law has developed some methods to allow such transactions to take place if safeguards are met. As this chapter unfolds, you will see these safeguards take shape in similar patterns in different contexts.

This chapter concerns three major aspects of the duty of loyalty (interested director transactions, usurpations of corporation opportunities, and competition with the corporation), as well as the "special" case of director compensation. But do not go into the "real world" thinking that these are the *only* ways in which a director may breach her duty of loyalty. Whenever a conflict of interest is involved, the duty of loyalty may be implicated.

Finally, as you read this chapter, keep a sharp eye out for the business judgment rule that you learned about in Chapter 6. Does it apply? If so, how?

§ 7.01   INTERESTED DIRECTOR TRANSACTIONS

Objectives: You should be able to:

• *Given a fact pattern involving a transaction between (1) a director or a related person or entity and the (2) corporation or a subsidiary, determine whether the transaction is a "director's conflicting interest transaction." In making this determination, you will need to understand and apply statutory defined terms such as "related person" and "material financial interest."*

• *Given a fact pattern involving a transaction that is a director's conflicting interest transaction, explain how the transaction may be "sanitized." To this end,*

• *Approval by Qualified Directors: Given a fact pattern where the directors of the corporation vote on a director's conflicting interest transaction, determine whether the requirements of MBCA § 8.62 have been met.*

• *Approval by Qualified Shares: Given a fact pattern where the shareholders vote on a director's conflicting interest transaction, determine whether the requirements of MBCA § 8.63 have been met.*

• *Effects of Approval by Qualified Directors or Qualified Shares: Given a fact pattern where either the directors or the shareholders properly approve a director's conflicting interest transaction, explain the effects of this approval (that is, whether the transaction may still be challenged and, if so, on what grounds).*

• *"Fair" to the Corporation. Given a fact pattern where neither the directors nor the shareholders properly approve a director's conflicting interest transaction, determine whether the requirements of MBCA § 8.61(b)(3) have been met.*

• *Given a fact pattern in which a director's conflicting interest transaction is not properly approved by the qualified directors or the qualified shareholders and was not fair to the corporation, explain what remedies would be available to the corporation.*

The rules for director's conflicting interest transactions (which I will abbreviate as "*DCITs*" but will also sometimes call "interested director transactions") are intuitively easy to grasp—but also easy to misunderstand or misapply when it comes to details. Basically, a DCIT involves a director (or perhaps a relative or related entity) engaging in a transaction with the corporation (or perhaps a subsidiary or related entity). The danger here should be obvious. If the director is, say, selling something to the corporation such as a piece of land, the worry is that the corporation will pay too much. If the director is buying something from the corporation, the worry is that the director will pay too little. In either event, it is as if the director is simply stealing from the corporation.

Although there is a bit of an academic debate about whether this was really the case, the common law's answer to this problem was basically to provide that any transaction in which a director had a direct or indirect personal interest was void (that is, void from the outset) or voidable (that is, it would be set aside by a court if a shareholder challenged it). The benefit of that rule was simplicity: it is clear and easy to apply. The chief downside is that it's too inflexible: why should a beneficial transaction be prohibited just because a director is on the other side? Thus, the common law in many states evolved to provide that an interested director's transaction would be upheld if the interested director could show that the transaction was "fair." Later, legislatures entered the fray and enacted statutes that represent an uneasy solution that you will learn about in this section.

Let's begin with some definitions. Read MBCA §§ 8.60(1), (4), and (5) and apply them to the following problems:

Problems

Problem 7-1: Amy Holland, a billionaire, wants to sell her 1993 used car (the market value of which is $100) to ABC Corp. Amy is a director of ABC Corp. *Is this transaction a DCIT under the MBCA?*[*]

Problem 7-2: Same facts as Problem 7-1, except that the car is owned by Amy's husband, Tom. *Is this transaction a DCIT?*

Problem 7-3: Same facts as Problem 7-1, except that the car is owned by Amy's nephew, Caleb. *Is this transaction a DCIT?*

---

[*]   Yes, it is doubtful that such a transaction would actually happen or that, if it did, anyone would bother suing over it. But focus on the question that is being asked and read the statute closely.

Problem 7-4: Same facts as Problem 7-1, except that the car is owned by Bob McFarlane, who rents the "pool house" on Amy's estate but is not related to Amy. *Is this transaction a DCIT?*

Problem 7-5: Same facts as Problem 7-1, except that the car is owned by Amy Corp. Amy owns 51% of the outstanding stock of Amy Corp. *Is this transaction a DCIT?*

Problem 7-6: Same facts as Problem 7-1, except that the car is owned by Public Corp., a publicly traded company. Amy owns 0.1% of the outstanding stock of Public Corp. She is not a director or officer of Public Corp. *Is this transaction a DCIT?*

Problem 7-7: Same facts as Problem 7-6, except that the instead of a car, Public Corp. is selling $100 billion worth of equipment to ABC Corp. *Is this transaction a DCIT? If not, what facts would you need to change to make it so? Does the fact that Amy is a billionaire matter in deciding whether she has a "material" financial interest?*

These problems were designed to help us understand what is—and what is not—a DCIT.[*] Next you must understand the implications of this determination. To do so, look at MBCA § 8.61(b). This section says that a transaction that is *not* a DCIT may not be challenged "on the ground that the director has an interest respecting the transaction." In other words, even if a director has some sort of personal interest in a transaction, if it does not meet the definition of a DCIT, then it cannot be challenged *because of* that interest. But are there any other grounds for challenging the transaction?

Problem

Problem 7-8: The directors of DEF Corp. recently approved the corporation's purchase of an office building from GHI Corp. One of DEF Corp.'s directors owns 0.5% of the stock of GHI Corp. You are a shareholder of DEF Corp. and are upset because you think the corporation paid far too much for this office building. *Are there any grounds on which you could sue the board for approving this transaction? If so, what is (are) the obstacle(s) to winning your lawsuit?*

---

[*]   In contrast to the MBCA's detailed definition of a DCIT, many state statutes refer only to transactions in which a director has an "interest." Obviously, this leaves open many interpretive issues.

Another issue to consider is what a director should do if she is the director that has an interest in a DCIT. After all, who wouldn't want to take steps to minimize the possibility of being sued? MBCA § 8.61(b) provides three alternatives:

- the transaction can be approved, at any time, by the "qualified" directors pursuant to MBCA § 8.62; or

- the transaction can be approved, at any time, by the "qualified" shares pursuant to MBCA § 8.63; or

- the transaction can be shown to have been "fair" (a defined term) to the corporation at the "relevant time" (another defined term).

While these three alternatives *sound* fairly straightforward, one complication is the fact that both MBCA § 8.62 (if that is the chosen "route") and MBCA § 8.63 (if that is chosen) are very complex. (For that matter, deciding whether the transaction was "fair" is a bit complicated as well, as you will see below.) When reading these sections, make sure that you know what the defined terms mean.

> **TERMINOLOGY**
> Although the MBCA uses the word "qualified" in Sections 8.60 through 8.63, this chapter will use the words "qualified" and "disinterested" interchangeably.

For example, MBCA § 8.62 uses the phrase "qualified directors," which is defined in MBCA § 1.43. Similarly, MBCA § 8.63 uses the phrase "qualified shares." Study MBCA §§ 1.43, 8.62, and 8.63 and consider these problems:

Problems

Problem 7-9: Big Time Corp. ("BTC") has six directors: Allen, Bobbi, Cindy, Domingo, Eunice, and Fred. Although Cindy, Domingo, Eunice, and Fred work as officers of BTC, Allen and Bobbi do not. Instead, Allen is a senior partner at a medium-sized accounting firm. Bobbi is an associate at the same firm. BTC would like to purchase an airplane that Allen owns. Allen has agreed to sell the airplane to BTC, but wants to take steps to prevent a shareholder of BTC from challenging the transaction. *What course of action would you recommend to Allen?*

Problem 7-10: Same facts as Problem 7-9. In addition, BTC's board unanimously approved the airplane purchase at a regular board meeting attended by all six directors. *Did this board approval meet the requirements of MBCA § 8.62? Why or why not?*

Problem 7-11: Same facts as Problem 7-9. In addition, BTC's board unanimously approved the airplane purchase at a regular board meeting attended by Bobbi, Cindy, Domingo, Eunice, and Fred. *Did this board approval meet the requirements of MBCA § 8.62? Why or why not?*

Problem 7-12: Same facts as Problem 7-9. In addition, BTC's board unanimously approved the airplane purchase at a regular board meeting attended by Cindy, Domingo, Eunice, and Fred. *Did this board approval meet the requirements of MBCA § 8.62? Why or why not?*

Problem 7-13: Same facts as Problem 7-9. In addition, BTC's board approved the airplane purchase at a regular board meeting attended by Domingo, Eunice, and Fred (three of the six directors). Domingo and Eunice voted yes on the transaction, but Fred voted no. *Did this board approval meet the requirements of MBCA § 8.62? Why or why not?*

Problem 7-14: Same facts as Problem 7-9. In addition, there are 200,000 shares of BTC common stock outstanding. Each director owns 10,000 shares. The remaining 140,000 shares are owned by several dozen other people. Instead of seeking board approval of the transaction, BTC called a special shareholders meeting for the purpose of voting on it. At the meeting, 150,000 shares were present in person or by proxy, including the shares owned by the six directors. Also, 80,000 shares (including the shares owned by all six directors) were voted in favor of the transaction and 70,000 shares were voted against it. *Did this shareholder approval meet the requirements of MBCA § 8.63? Why or why not? Would your answer change if the shareholders approved the transaction after it took place?*

Problem 7-15: *Would your answers to any of the foregoing questions change if Allen had not disclosed to BTC that (1) he desperately needed cash and (2) there was a mechanical problem with one of the engines on the airplane? What if BTC had had a mechanic inspect the airplane before purchasing it?*

What happens if the director(s) who is (are) interested in a DCIT does (do) not seek approval by the disinterested/qualified directors or the disinterested/qualified shareholders? MBCA § 8.61(b) contemplates that the transaction must be established (by who?) to have been "fair" to the corporation. That doesn't sound too difficult, does it?

The next case considers this issue. Before reading it, it may be a good idea to read Section 144 of the Delaware General Corporation Law, which is similar—but not identical—to MBCA § 8.61.

Section 144 provides in part that:

(a)   No contract or transaction between a corporation and 1 or more of its directors or officers, or between a corporation and any other [entity] in which 1 or more of its directors or officers, are directors or officers, or have a financial interest, shall be void or voidable solely for this reason, *** if:

    (1)   The material facts as to the director's or officer's relationship or interest and as to the contract or transaction are disclosed or are known to the board of directors or the committee, and the board or committee in good faith authorizes the contract or transaction by the affirmative votes of a majority of the disinterested directors, even though the disinterested directors be less than a quorum; or

    (2)   The material facts as to the director's or officer's relationship or interest and as to the contract or transaction are disclosed or are known to the stockholders entitled to vote thereon, and the contract or transaction is specifically approved in good faith by vote of the stockholders; or

    (3)   The contract or transaction is fair as to the corporation as of the time it is authorized, approved or ratified, by the board of directors, a committee or the stockholders.

HMG/Courtland Properties, Inc. v. Gray
Delaware Chancery Court
749 A.2d 94 (1999)

STRINE, Vice Chancellor. This case involves thirteen year old real estate sales transactions between HMG/Courtland Properties, Inc. as seller and two of HMG's directors, Lee Gray and Norman Fieber as buyers. While Fieber's self-interest in the transactions was properly disclosed, neither he nor Gray informed their fellow directors that Gray—who took the lead in negotiating the sales for HMG—had a buy-side interest. Gray's interest was concealed from HMG for a decade and was only discovered inadvertently by the company in 1996.

***

Since 1983, Maurice Wiener has served as HMG's Chairman of the Board and Chief Executive Officer ("CEO"). ***

Defendant Lee Gray was at all relevant times a director, President, and Treasurer of HMG. ***

Defendant Norman A. Fieber ("Fieber") was a director of HMG and a member of HMG's Audit Committee from 1985 until 1997. ***

***

Like many [real estate companies], HMG relies heavily upon its investment adviser. HMG has no employees of its own, and [a separate company referred to in this opinion as the "Adviser"] operates as the management of HMG, subject to the oversight and control of HMG's Board of Directors. All recommendations regarding HMG's real estate investments flow through the Adviser and are presented by the Adviser to the HMG Board. ***

During the period relevant to this litigation, Wiener and Gray were the key decision-makers at the Adviser. Although Wiener was the CEO of HMG and the Adviser and Gray was the President of each, Wiener and Gray operated less as superior and subordinate, and more as the long-standing colleagues and friends they were. ***

***

During 1984 and 1985, Wiener and Gray began to give serious consideration to undertaking a major transaction to generate additional return from the Grossman's Portfolio [a portfolio of properties that HMG had purchased with a company called SBA], which by then had been downsized to 34 properties. As part of their consideration of how to maximize value from the Grossman's

Portfolio, SBA commissioned appraisals of the Portfolio in 1984 (the "1984 Appraisals" or "Appraisals"). ***

***

In late 1985 or early 1986, Gray suggested to Wiener that they approach Norman Fieber about entering into a joint venture as to the Grossman's Portfolio. The rationale for such a venture was that Fieber could help HMG maximize the development potential of the Portfolio. ***

At the time Gray suggested this idea, Norman Fieber was a member of the HMG Board. He had gained his entrée to that position through Gray, whom he had known for many years and who had introduced Fieber to Wiener in the 1970s. Although Gray and Fieber were not close, personal friends, they had a lasting and deep business friendship that involved investing in each other's projects on a thinly-documented basis reflective of substantial mutual trust. ***

[Author's note: To summarize and greatly simplify what happened next, Grey and Fieber negotiated the sale by HMG of the properties in the Grossman's Portfolio (or portions of them) to a joint venture called "NAF Associates," which was controlled by Fieber. Gray was the lead negotiator for HMG, and the negotiations took a long time. At some point in the process, Fieber agreed that an entity called "Martine"—in which Gray and one his relatives had an interest—could be an investor in NAF. Although Fieber argued that he did not know until late in the process that Martine (and therefore Gray) would be an investor in NAF, the court found that he "knew that it was likely that he would take in co-investors and that *** Gray would be invited to [invest]." Thus, Gray ended up with a "buy side" interest in the transactions. Fieber's interest in the transactions was obviously known to the other HMG directors, but Gray did not disclose his interest to the other directors of HMG. The court also accepted allegations that Gray intentionally misled HMG's other directors about the identities of the investors in NAF and that Fieber helped him do so. In any event, Fieber—who knew of Gray's interest in NAF—did not disclose it to HMG's board. HMG's board, including Gray, eventually approved the transactions, although Fieber abstained from voting. About ten years later, HMG learned that Gray had an interest in NAF. HMG then sued both Gray and Fieber.]

***

HMG contends that Gray and Norman Fieber engaged in self-dealing and therefore they bear the burden to demonstrate the entire fairness of the Transactions [as the court defined that term]. For his part, Fieber claims that Gray's interest in the Transactions was immaterial and therefore the HMG Board's decision to ratify the Transactions was a proper exercise of discretion subject to protection by the business judgment rule. Gray concedes that the defendants had the initial burden to demonstrate fairness and claims that they have done so without rebuttal from HMG.

Both HMG and Fieber initially [focused] their attention on the business judgment rule, with much less emphasis on [Section 144 of the Delaware General Corporation Law]. But this case directly implicates both the business judgment rule and § 144. Even though the business judgment rule and § 144 serve somewhat different purposes and cannot be interpreted identically, they are closely related.

*** [I]n a case where § 144 is directly applicable, compliance with its terms should be a minimum requirement to retain the protection of the business judgment rule. [Citation omitted.] The desirability of doctrinal and statutory coherence, where that can be accomplished without sacrificing public policy interests, also counsels that conclusion. In this case, both the business judgment rule as traditionally interpreted and § 144 point toward the entire fairness standard as the appropriate form of review.

***

*** [A] plaintiff wishing to rebut the presumption of the business judgment rule [must] produce evidence that a director had a non-disclosed, material interest in the challenged transaction and "a reasonable [director] would have regarded the existence of the material interest as a significant fact in the evaluation of the proposed transaction." [Citation omitted.]

Fieber argues that Gray's percentage interest in the overall Transactions was so minimal that Gray's interest does not rise to the level of a material interest that would have been considered significant by a reasonable, disinterested director in voting on the Transactions. This contention misconceives the appropriate legal standard.

As [prior cases] demonstrate, Gray's interest in the Wallingford and NAF Transactions implicates both the primary rationale for the entire fairness standard of review and the core concern of § 144—"self-dealing." [Citation omitted.] ***

***

Gray's undisclosed, buy-side interest in the Transactions is a classic case of self-dealing. Under [prior cases], proof of such *undisclosed self-dealing*, in itself, is sufficient to rebut the presumption of the business judgment rule and invoke entire fairness review. [Citation omitted.]

Section 144 of the Delaware General Corporation Law dictates this conclusion. That statute is implicated whenever a corporation and "1 or more of its directors or officers ... or other organization in which 1 or more of its directors or officers ... have a financial interest" engage in a transaction.

The interests of Gray and Fieber in the Wallingford and NAF Transactions trigger the statute. Section 144 provides that a self-dealing transaction will not be "void or voidable solely for this reason" if the transaction is ratified by a majority of the disinterested directors or by a shareholder vote. [Citation omitted.] Such ratification is valid, however, only if the "material facts as [to the director's] relationship or interest and as to the contract or transaction are disclosed or are known to the [relevant ratifying authority] ...." Neither Fieber nor Gray disclosed Gray's "interest" in the "[T]ransaction[s]" to the HMG Board. In the absence of such disclosure, [Section 144(a)(1)], the Transactions can only be rendered non-voidable if they were "fair as to [HMG] as of the time [they were] authorized." [Section 144(a)(3); other citations omitted.]

***

[Quoting a prior case, the court stated the rule as follows:]

> The concept of entire fairness has two components: fair dealing and fair price. [Citation omitted.] Fair dealing "embraces questions of when the transaction was timed, how it was initiated, structured, negotiated, disclosed to the directors, and how the approvals of the directors and the stockholders were obtained." [Citation omitted.] Fair price "relates to the economic and financial considerations of the proposed merger, including all relevant factors: assets, market value, earnings, future prospects, and any other elements that affect the intrinsic or inherent value of a company's stock." [Citation omitted.] *In making a determination as to the entire fairness of a transaction, the Court does not focus on one component over the other, but examines all aspects of the issue as a whole.* [Citation omitted.]

[*Fair Dealing*]   The defendants have failed to convince me that the Wallingford and NAF Transactions were fairly negotiated or ratified. From the beginning of the negotiations, Gray, the primary negotiator for the seller in the Transactions, was interested in taking a position on the buyer's side. As such, Gray lacked the pure seller-side incentive that should have been applied on behalf of HMG—particularly in Transactions in which one director was already on the other side.

Given the intrinsically unique nature of real estate, the bargaining skills and incentives of HMG's negotiator were likely to be more important than if the negotiator was arranging for the sale of a financial asset. As the defendants' own expert conceded, in the context of a real estate sales transaction negotiation skills are "exceedingly important."

Gray took the lead in discussing these Transactions with the Fiebers. His colleagues Wiener and Rothstein relied on his depiction of the bargaining in determining whether to agree to the Fiebers' proposed terms. They did so in ignorance of Gray's conflict. Similarly, HMG's Executive Committee and Board were deprived of information about Gray's conflict.

The process was thus anything but fair. Because neither Gray nor Fieber disclosed Gray's interest, the HMG Board unwittingly ratified Transactions in which a conflicted negotiator was relied upon by the Adviser to negotiate already conflicted Transactions.

[*Fair Price*]   The defendants attempt to meet their burden of demonstrating fair price by trying to convince me that the prices used in the Transactions were in a range of fairness, as proven by the 1984 Appraisals. ***

Once again, I believe the defendants misconceive their burden. On the record before me, I obviously cannot conclude that HMG received a shockingly low price in the Transactions or that the prices paid were not within the low end of the range of possible prices that might have been paid in negotiated arms-length deals. In that narrow sense, the defendants have proven that the price was "fair." But that proof does not necessarily satisfy their burden under the entire fairness standard. As the [American Law Institute *Principles of Corporate Governance*] point out:

> A contract price might be fair in the sense that it corresponds to market price, and yet the corporation might have refused to make the contract if a given material fact had been disclosed .... Furthermore, fairness is often a range, rather than a point, so that a transaction involving a payment by the corporation may be fair even though it is consummated at the high end of the range. *If an undisclosed material fact had been disclosed, however, the corporation might have declined to transact at that high price, or might have bargained the price down lower in the range.*

***

The defendants have failed to persuade me that HMG would not have gotten a materially higher value for Wallingford and the Grossman's Portfolio had

Gray and Fieber come clean about Gray's interest. That is, they have not convinced me that their misconduct did not taint the price to HMG's disadvantage. I base this conclusion on several factors.

First, the defendants' own expert on value, James Nolan, testified that his opinion that the prices paid in the Transactions were fair was premised on his assumption that Gray was not the leading negotiator from HMG's side. To the extent that Gray was a principal player in discussing terms with Fieber, Nolan said that his conclusion about the fairness of the price might well be different.

Second, the 1984 Appraisals understated the values of the Wallingford Property and the Portfolio as of early 1986. The Leased Fee Values in the 1984 Appraisals were generated through a discounted cash flow analysis utilizing 1983 actual rents and projected rents for 1984-1986. By 1986, it was clear that the Grossman's stores operating at Portfolio sites were performing better, and thereby generating higher lease payments (because a portion of the lease payments was tied to store sales) than estimated by the appraisers who conducted the 1984 Appraisals. If an update had been done in 1986, it would have produced values well in excess of the 1984 Appraisals. ***

Third, a skilled and properly motivated negotiator could have done better than Leased Fee Value in price negotiations. As the defendants' expert Nolan testified, the skills of a negotiator are "exceedingly important" in a real estate transaction. Even without an updated appraisal, a properly motivated negotiator could have argued from the actual rents in 1984 and 1985 that the Leased Fee Value understated the value of the Portfolio. *** I have no confidence that Gray negotiated with the Fiebers in any vigorous or skillful way. Since he wanted to participate on the buy-side, he had less than a satisfactory incentive to do so. Since the outcome of a real estate negotiation is often heavily influenced by the skills of the negotiators, this factor undercuts the claim that the price was fair to HMG. [Citation omitted.]

Finally, had Gray disclosed his interest, I believe that HMG would have terminated his involvement in the negotiations and have taken a much more traditional approach to selling the affected properties. To the extent that HMG continued to consider a sales transaction, I believe it would have commissioned new appraisals and would have sought purchasers other than Fieber. ***

Taken together, these factors lead me to conclude that the defendants have not demonstrated that they paid a fair price in the sense inherent in the entire fairness standard. ***

***

For the foregoing reasons, judgment shall be entered for HMG against [the defendants]. The parties shall report back to me in three weeks. If an agreed upon order is not presented, each party shall submit its position regarding the outstanding issues and an accompanying form of order.

Questions About *HMG v. Gray* and "Fairness"

1.   Why couldn't Gray and Fieber prove "fair dealing" in the transaction? What if Gray had not been the main negotiator for HMG? What are some other things that would prevent a finding of fair dealing?

2.   What would have happened if Gray and Fieber had failed to prove "fair dealing" but *were* able to prove that NAF paid a "fair price" to HMG?

3.   Is the definition of "fairness" in this case consistent with the MBCA? *See* MBCA § 8.60(6). *See also* numbered paragraph 6 of the Official Comment to MBCA § 8.60.

4.   At what point in time is "fairness" measured?

HMG involved a situation where the interested directors did not properly seek approval by the disinterested directors or the disinterested shareholders and thus were stuck attempting to prove that the transaction was entirely fair. *See also Marciano v. Nakash*, 535 A.2d 400 (Del. 1987) (where director and shareholder approval of an interested director was not possible because shareholders and directors were evenly divided, court applied an "intrinsic fairness" or "full fairness" test*). But let's now consider various different scenarios.

---

*   A "wrinkle" in the *Marciano* case was that neither the directors nor the shareholders had actually approved the transaction, and the third prong of Section 144 of the Delaware statute provides that the transaction must have been fair "as of the time it [was] authorized, approved or ratified, by the board of directors, a committee [of the board] or the stockholders." Thus, the court assumed that the *statute* could not apply, but nonetheless applied the intrinsic fairness test as a matter of common law.

Effects of Disinterested/Qualified Director Approval. First, what would happen if the disinterested directors properly approve a DCIT pursuant to MBCA § 8.62 (or whatever other statute may be applicable, such as Section 144 of the Delaware statute)? Looking at the text of MBCA § 8.61(b), this would seem to be the end of the inquiry, at least insofar as the duty of loyalty is concerned. After all, that section provides that a DCIT may not be challenged on the ground that a director had an interest if the DCIT was properly approved by the qualified directors or properly approved by the qualified shares or was fair to the corporation. The official comment to MBCA § 8.62(b) is consistent with this conclusion, providing in part that:

> a challenge to the effectiveness of board action for purposes of [MBCA § 8.61(b)(1)] might also assert that, while the conflicted director's conduct in connection with the process of approval by qualified directors may have been consistent with the statute's expectations, the qualified directors dealing with the matter did not act in good faith or on reasonable inquiry.

In other words, the business judgment rule applies (or, more properly, MBCA §§ 8.30 and 8.31 apply) when the DCIT has been properly "sanitized" through qualified director approval. The Delaware Supreme Court came to a similar conclusion with respect to Section 144 of the Delaware statute in *Benihana of Tokyo, Inc. v. Benihana, Inc.*, 906 A.2d 114 (Del. 2006) (business judgment rule applies when transaction was approved by disinterested directors pursuant to Section 144).

But should you be worried about group dynamics? Will supposedly "disinterested" directors face psychological pressure—or even more explicit pressure—to make the decision that the interested director wants them to make? Does it depend on whether the interested director is also a major shareholder who could "boot" the disinterested directors off the board? One court that may have been concerned about this possibility was the Iowa Supreme Court in the frequently cited case of *Cookies Food Products, Inc. v. Lakes Warehouse Distributing, Inc.*, 430 N.W2d. 447 (Iowa 1988). In Cookie's, Duane "Speed" Herrig began as a minority shareholder of a small corporation that manufactured barbeque sauce. When it started, the company struggled mightily. However, due to a distribution agreement between Cookie's and a company owned by Mr. Herrig, Cookie's "turned the corner" and became quite profitable. Mr. Herrig also did quite well under the distribution agreement, and used his newfound wealth to buy enough shares from other shareholders to become the majority shareholder. Not surprisingly, Mr. Herrig then elected himself to the board, along with four other directors of his choosing. Also not surprising, the contracts between Cookie's and Mr. Herrig became more and more favorable to him.

The other shareholders challenged these contracts as a breach of Mr. Herrig's duty of loyalty to Cookie's. However, Iowa had a statute that is very similar to MBCA § 8.61(b); the Iowa statute provided that an interested director transaction "shall not be void or voidable because of [the director's interest] ... if any of the following occur" and then listed what by now should be three familiar options to you: (1) disinterested director approval after full disclosure; (2) disinterested shareholder approval after full disclosure; or (3) to quote the Iowa statute again, "the contract or transaction is fair and reasonable to the corporation." Because the transactions between Cookie's and Mr. Herrig had been approved by the disinterested directors after full disclosure, that would seem to be the end of the matter.

Nonetheless, despite what seems to be clear language in the statute, the Iowa Supreme Court added an "extra" requirement in the following passage:

> Some commentators have supported the view that satisfaction of any *one* of the foregoing statutory alternatives, in and of itself, would prove that a director has fully met the duty of loyalty. We are obliged, however, to interpret statutes in conformity with the common law wherever statutory language does not directly negate it. Because the common law and [the Iowa statute] require directors to show "good faith, honesty, and fairness"[*] in self-dealing, we are persuaded that satisfaction of any one of these three alternatives under the statute would merely preclude us from rendering the transaction void or voidable *outright* solely on the basis "of such [director's] relationship or interest." To the contrary, we are convinced that the legislature did not intend by this statute to enable a court *** to rubber stamp *any* transaction to which a board of directors or the shareholders of a corporation have consented. Such an interpretation would invite those who stand to gain from such transactions to engage in improprieties to obtain consent. We thus require directors who engage in self-dealing to establish the additional element that they have acted in good faith, honesty, and fairness.

Id. at 452-53 (citations omitted throughout).

---

[*]   [Footnote by author]: The closest thing to this language in the relevant Iowa statute in effect at the time was a statement that a "director shall perform the duties of a director, *** in good faith, in a manner such director reasonably believes to be in the best interests of the corporation, and with such care as an ordinarily prudent person in a like position would use under similar circumstances." There was no explicit reference to honesty, and the only reference to fairness was in the portion concerning interested director transactions.

Other cases have followed a similar approach, requiring that all interested-director transactions pass a fairness test. *See Rivercity v. American Can Co.*, 600 F. Supp. 908 (E.D. La.), aff'd, 753 F.2d 1300 (5th Cir. 1985); *Scott v. Multi-Amp Corp.*, 386 F. Supp. 44 (D.N.J. 1974). While these cases depended in part on the language of the relevant statute, they do seem to indicate some judicial skepticism of interested director transactions, even those that were approved by disinterested directors. Again, "group dynamics" may pressure disinterested directors to approve a transaction that one of their colleagues wants. Requiring fairness even after disinterested director approval may be an appropriate "safety valve" that gives more protection than the business judgment rule.

Effects of Disinterested/Qualified Shareholder Approval. What if interested directors were to seek approval of a director's conflicting interest transaction from the disinterested *shareholders* instead of the disinterested directors? Perhaps we should be a bit worried about having shareholders approve a transaction—after all, shareholders generally do not owe fiduciary duties like directors do. Also, shareholders, particularly small shareholders, may not have much of an incentive to inform themselves about the transaction before approving it. The following case, another one interpreting Delaware's Section 144, addresses this scenario.

Lewis v. Vogelstein
Delaware Court of Chancery
699 A.2d 327 (1997)

ALLEN, Chancellor. This shareholders' suit challenges a stock option compensation plan for the directors of Mattel, Inc., which was approved or ratified by the shareholders of the company at its 1996 Annual Meeting of Shareholders. Two claims are asserted.

First, and most interestingly, plaintiff asserts that the proxy statement that solicited shareholder proxies to vote in favor of the adoption of the 1996 Mattel Stock Option Plan ("1996 Plan" or "Plan") was materially incomplete and misleading, because it did not include an estimated present value of the stock option grants to which directors might become entitled under the Plan. ***

Second, it is asserted that the grants of options actually made under the 1996 Plan did not offer reasonable assurance to the corporation that it would receive adequate value in exchange for such grants, and that such grants represent excessively large compensation for the directors in relation to the value of their service to Mattel. For these reasons, the granting of the option is said to constitute a breach of fiduciary duty.

*** Plaintiff maintains that because the Plan constitutes a self-interested transaction by the incumbent directors, all of whom qualify for grants under the 1996 Plan, they must justify it as entirely fair in order to avoid liability for breach of loyalty, which it is said they cannot do. As shown below, this approach does not constitute a different claim than that stated above.

Pending is defendants' motion to dismiss the complaint for failure to state a claim upon which relief may be granted. ***

***

[I] The facts as they appear in the pleading are as follows. The Plan was adopted in 1996 and ratified by the company's shareholders at the 1996 annual meeting. It contemplates two forms of stock option grants to the company's directors: a one-time grant of options on a block of stock and subsequent, smaller annual grants of further options.

With respect to the one-time grant, the Plan provides that each outside director will qualify for a grant of options on 15,000 shares of Mattel common stock at the market price on the day such options are granted (the "one-time options"). The one-time options are alleged to be exercisable immediately upon being granted although they will achieve economic value, if ever, only with the passage of time. It is alleged that if not exercised, they remain valid for ten years.

With respect to the second type of option grant, the Plan qualifies each director for a grant of options upon his or her re-election to the board each year (the "Annual Options"). The maximum number of options grantable to a director pursuant to the annual options provision depends on the number of years the director has served on the Mattel board. Those outside directors with five or fewer years of service will qualify to receive options on no more than 5,000 shares, while those with more than five years service will qualify for options to purchase up to 10,000 shares. Once granted, these options vest over a four year period, at a rate of 25% per year. When exercisable, they entitle the holder to buy stock at the market price on the day of the grant.

According to the complaint, options granted pursuant to the annual options provision also expire ten years from their grant date, whether or not the holder has remained on the board.

When the shareholders were asked to ratify the adoption of the Plan, as is typically true, no estimated present value of options that were authorized to be granted under the Plan was stated in the proxy solicitation materials.

[Author's note: In Part II of the opinion, the court concluded that "the allegations of failure to disclose estimated present value calculations [for the stock options] fails to state a claim upon which relief may be granted. Where shareholder ratification of a plan of option compensation is involved, the duty of disclosure is satisfied by the disclosure or fair summary of all of the relevant terms and conditions of the proposed plan of compensation, together with any material extrinsic fact within the board's knowledge bearing on the issue."]

[III]   Thus, concluding that the complaint does not state a claim for breach of any duty to fully disclose material facts to shareholders in connection with the board's request that the shareholders ratify the board's act of creating a directors' stock option plan, I turn to the motion to dismiss the complaint's allegation to the effect that the Plan, or grants under it, constitute a breach of the directors' fiduciary duty of loyalty. As the Plan contemplates grants to the directors that approved the Plan and who recommended it to the shareholders, we start by observing that it constitutes self-dealing that would ordinarily require that the directors prove that the grants involved were, in the circumstances, entirely fair to the corporation. [Citation omitted.]   However, it is the case that the shareholders have ratified the directors' action. *** The question then becomes what is the effect of informed shareholder ratification on a transaction of this type (i.e., officer or director pay).

A.   Shareholder Ratification Under Delaware Law:

What is the effect under Delaware corporation law of shareholder ratification of an interested transaction? The answer to this apparently simple question appears less clear than one would hope or indeed expect. Four possible effects of shareholder ratification appear logically available: First, one might conclude that an effective shareholder ratification acts as a complete defense to any charge of breach of duty. Second, one might conclude that the effect of such ratification is to shift the substantive test on judicial review of the act from one of fairness that would otherwise be obtained (because the transaction is an interested one) to one of waste. Third, one might conclude that the ratification shifts the burden of proof of unfairness to plaintiff, but leaves that shareholder-protective test in place. Fourth, one might conclude (perhaps because of great respect for the collective action disabilities that attend shareholder action in public corporations) that shareholder ratification offers no assurance of assent of a character that deserves judicial recognition. Thus, under this approach, ratification on full information would be afforded no effect. Excepting the fourth of these effects, there are cases in [Delaware] that reflect each of these approaches to the effect of shareholder voting to approve a transaction. [Citations omitted.]

***

    1.   *Ratification generally:* I start with principles broader than those of corporation law. Ratification is a concept deriving from the law of agency which contemplates the *ex post* conferring upon or confirming of the legal authority of an agent in circumstances in which the agent had no authority or arguably had no authority. [Citation omitted.] To be effective, of course, the agent must fully disclose all relevant circumstances with respect to the transaction to the principal prior to the ratification. [Citation omitted.] ***

     *** [T]he effect of informed ratification is to validate or affirm the act of the agent as the act of the principal. [Citation omitted.]

     Application of these general ratification principles to shareholder ratification is complicated by three other factors. First, most generally, in the case of shareholder ratification there is of course no single individual acting as principal, but rather a class or group of divergent individuals—the class of shareholders. This aggregate quality of the principal means that decisions to affirm or ratify an act will be subject to collective action disabilities; that some portion of the body doing the ratifying may in fact have conflicting interests in the transaction; and some dissenting members of the class may be able to assert more or less convincingly that the "will" of the principal is wrong, or even corrupt and ought not to be binding on the class. In the case of individual ratification these issues won't arise, assuming that the principal does not suffer from multiple personality disorder. Thus the collective nature of shareholder ratification makes it more likely that following a claimed shareholder ratification, nevertheless, there is a litigated claim on behalf of the principal that the agent lacked authority or breached its duty. The second, mildly complicating factor present in shareholder ratification is the fact that in corporation law the "ratification" that shareholders provide will often not be directed to lack of legal authority of an agent but will relate to the consistency of some authorized director action with the equitable duty of loyalty. Thus shareholder ratification sometimes acts not to confer legal authority—but as in this case—to affirm that action taken is consistent with shareholder interests. Third, when what is "ratified" is a director conflict transaction, the statutory law—in Delaware Section 144 of the Delaware General Corporation Law—may bear on the effect.[*]

---

[*]   [Footnote by court]: Most jurisdictions have enacted statutes that appear to offer a procedural technique for removing courts from a fairness evaluation of the terms of director conflict transactions. Generally courts have given them a very narrow interpretation, however. In Delaware that statute *** is Section 144 of the DGCL. Early on it was narrowly held that compliance with that section simply removed the automatic taint of a director conflict transaction, but nevertheless left the transaction subject to substantive judicial review for fairness. *See Fliegler v. Lawrence,* [361 A.2d 218, 222 (Del. 1976)] (involving claimed independent board action, not ratification by shareholders). This interpretation tended to be the general judicial response to these "safe-harbor" statutes. *See Cookies Food Prod., Inc. v. Lakes Warehouse Distrib., Inc.,* 430 N.W.2d 447, 452-453 (Iowa 1988) (requiring directors who engage in self-dealing to prove that they have acted in good faith). ***

2.   *Shareholder ratification:*   These differences between shareholder ratification of director action and classic ratification by a single principal, do lead to a difference in the effect of a valid ratification in the shareholder context. The principal novelty added to ratification law generally by the shareholder context, is the idea *** that, in addition to a claim that ratification was defective because of incomplete information or coercion, shareholder ratification is subject to a claim by a member of the class that the ratification is ineffectual (1) because a majority of those affirming the transaction had a conflicting interest with respect to it or (2) because the transaction that is ratified constituted a corporate waste. As to the second of these, it has long been held that shareholders may not ratify a waste except by a unanimous vote. [Citation omitted.] The idea behind this rule is apparently that a transaction that satisfies the high standard of waste constitutes a *gift* of corporate property and no one should be forced against their will to make a gift of their property. In all events, informed, uncoerced, disinterested shareholder ratification of a transaction in which corporate directors have a material conflict of interest has the effect of protecting the transaction from judicial review except on the basis of waste. [Citations omitted.]

B.   The Waste Standard:

The judicial standard for determination of corporate waste is well developed. Roughly, a waste entails an exchange of corporate assets for consideration so disproportionately small as to lie beyond the range at which any reasonable person might be willing to trade. [Citation omitted.] Most often the claim is associated with a transfer of corporate assets that serves no corporate purpose; or for which no consideration at all is received. Such a transfer is in effect a gift. If, however, there is *any substantial* consideration received by the corporation, and if there is a *good faith judgment* that in the circumstances the transaction is worthwhile, there should be no finding of waste, even if the fact finder would conclude *ex post* that the transaction was unreasonably risky. Any other rule would deter corporate boards from the optimal rational acceptance of risk, for reasons explained elsewhere. [Citation omitted.] Courts are ill-fitted to attempt to weigh the "adequacy" of consideration under the waste standard or, *ex post,* to judge appropriate degrees of business risk.

C.   Ratification of Officer or Director Option Grants:

Let me turn now to the history of the Delaware law treating shareholder ratification of corporate plans that authorize the granting of stock options to corporate officers and directors. What is interesting about this law is that while it is consistent with the foregoing general treatment of shareholder ratification—*i.e.,* it appears to hold that informed, non-coerced ratification validates any such plan or grant, unless the plan is wasteful —in its earlier expressions, the waste standard used by the courts in fact was not a waste standard at all, but was a form of "reasonableness" or proportionality review.

      1.   Development of Delaware law of option compensation: It is fair to say I think that Delaware law took a skeptical or suspicious stance towards the innovation of stock option compensation as it developed in a major way following World War II. Such skepticism is a fairly natural consequence of the common law of director compensation and of the experience that corporate law judges had over the decades with schemes to water stock or to divert investors' funds into the hands of promoters or management.

***

      [But in] *Beard v. Elster,* [160 A.2d 731 (Del. 1960)], the Delaware Supreme Court relaxed slightly the general formulation of [prior cases] and rejected the reading of [a prior case] to the effect that the corporation had to have (or insure receipt of) *legally cognizable* consideration in order to make an option grant valid. The court also emphasized the effect that approval by an independent board or committee might have. It held that what was necessary to validate an officer or director stock option grant was a finding that a reasonable board could conclude from the circumstances that the corporation may reasonably expect to receive a proportionate benefit. A good faith determination by a disinterested board or committee to that effect, at least when ratified by a disinterested shareholder vote, entitled such a grant to business judgment protection (*i.e.,* classic waste standard). [Citation omitted.] After *Beard,* judicial review of officer and director option grants sensibly focused in practice less on attempting independently to assess whether the corporation in fact would receive proportionate value, and more on the procedures used to authorize and ratify such grants. But *Beard* addressed only a situation in which an independent committee of the board functioned on the question.

      2.   Current law on ratification effect on option grants: A substantive question that remains however is whether in practice the waste standard that is utilized where informed shareholders ratify a grant of options adopted and recommended by a self-interested board *is* the classical waste test (*i.e.,* no consideration; gift; no person of ordinary prudence could possibly agree, etc.) or whether, in fact, it *is a species of intermediate review* in which the court assesses reasonableness in relationship to perceived benefits.

      The Supreme Court has not expressly deviated from the "proportionality" approach to waste of its earlier decision, although in recent decades it has had few occasions to address the subject. In *Michelson v. Duncan,* [407 A.2d 211 (Del. 1979)], a stock option case in which ratification had occurred, however, the court repeatedly referred to the relevant test where ratification had occurred as that of

"gift or waste" and plainly meant by waste, the absence of *any consideration* ("...
when there are issues of fact as to the *existence of consideration,* a full hearing is
required regardless of shareholder ratification." [Citation omitted.] Issues of
"sufficiency" of consideration or adequacy of assurance that a benefit or
proportionate benefit would be achieved were not referenced.

The Court of Chancery has interpreted the waste standard in the ratified
option context as invoking not a proportionality or reasonableness test *** but the
traditional waste standard referred to in *Michelson.* [Citations omitted.]

In according substantial effect to shareholder ratification these more recent
cases are not unmindful of the collective action problem faced by shareholders in
public corporations. These problems do render the assent that ratification can
afford very different in character from the assent that a single individual may give.
In this age in which institutional shareholders have grown strong and can more
easily communicate, however, that assent, is, I think, a more rational means to
monitor compensation than judicial determinations of the "fairness," or
sufficiency of consideration, which seems a useful technique principally, I
suppose, to those unfamiliar with the limitations of courts and their litigation
processes. In all events, the classic waste standard does afford some protection
against egregious cases or "constructive fraud."

Before ruling on the pending motion to dismiss the substantive claim of
breach of fiduciary duty, under a waste standard, I should make one other
observation. The standard for determination of motions to dismiss is of course
well established and understood. Where under any state of facts consistent with
the factual allegations of the complaint the plaintiff would be entitled to a
judgment, the complaint may not be dismissed as legally defective. It is also the
case that in some instances "mere conclusions" may be held to be insufficient to
withstand an otherwise well made motion. Since what is a "well pleaded" fact and
what is a "mere conclusion" is not always clear, there is often and inevitably some
small room for the exercise of informed judgment by courts in determining
motions to dismiss under the appropriate test. Consider for example allegations
that an arm's-length corporate transaction constitutes a waste of assets. Such an
allegation is inherently factual and not easily amenable to determination on a
motion to dismiss and indeed often not on a motion for summary judgment.
[Citation omitted.] Yet it cannot be the case that allegations of the facts of any (or
every) transaction coupled with a statement that the transaction constitutes a waste
of assets, necessarily states a claim upon which discovery may be had; such a rule
would, in this area, constitute an undue encouragement to strike suits. Certainly
some set of facts, if true, may be said as a matter of law not to constitute waste.
*** In some instances the facts alleged, if true, will be so far from satisfying the
waste standard that dismissal is appropriate.

This is not such a case in my opinion.   Giving the pleader the presumptions to which he is entitled on this motion, I cannot conclude that no set of facts could be shown that would permit the court to conclude that the grant of these options, particularly focusing upon the one-time options, constituted an exchange to which no reasonable person not acting under compulsion and in good faith could agree.   In so concluding, I do not mean to suggest a view that these grants are suspect, only that one time option grants to directors of this size seem at this point sufficiently unusual to require the court to refer to evidence before making an adjudication of their validity and consistency with fiduciary duty. Thus, for that reason the motion to dismiss will be denied.   It is so Ordered.

Questions about *Lewis v. Vogelstein*

1.   The court mentioned in its opinion the "collective action problem faced by shareholders in public corporations."   What did it mean by this?

2.   Can shareholders *ever* properly approve a "wasteful" transaction between the corporation and one of its directors?

One case cited in *Lewis v. Vogelstein* is *Fliegler v. Lawrence*, 361 A.2d 218 (Del. 1976).   In *Fliegler*, the court suggested that if an interested director transaction had been approved by a majority of the disinterested shares, an objecting shareholder would need to prove that the "terms are so unequal as to amount to a gift or waste of corporate assets" to successfully challenge the transaction.   However, under the facts of the case, the shares owned by the interested directors were needed to approve the transaction; because a majority of the *disinterested* shares had not approved the transaction, the court still required a showing of fairness. *See also In re Wheelabrator Technologies*, 663 A.2d 1194 (Del. Ch. 1995) (informed approval by disinterested shareholders extinguishes duty-of-care claim against directors and also "invokes 'the business judgment rule and limits judicial review [of a duty-of-loyalty claim] to issues of gift or waste with the burden of proof upon the party attacking the transaction'") (citation omitted).   Is this any different than what the court concluded in the *Benihana of Tokyo* case above?

Finally, what should the remedy be for an interested director transaction that was not properly "sanitized" through disinterested director or shareholder approval and that was not shown to have been fair?   Typically, courts will rescind the transaction, if possible.   Perhaps this rather modest remedy is a reason that it seems reasonable to require an interested director to prove that a DCIT that was not "sanitized" was "fair."

§ 7.02   USURPING "CORPORATE OPPORTUNITIES"

Objectives: You should be able to:

•   *Determine whether an opportunity that a director or officer wishes to pursue is a "corporate opportunity," as defined in both (1) the American Law Institute Principles of Corporate Governance and (2) Delaware (common) law.*
•   *Explain to a director or officer who wishes to pursue a "corporate opportunity" what steps she should take so that she will not later be sued for usurping a corporate opportunity, under both the American Law Institute Principles of Corporate Governance and the common law (whichever is applicable).*

•   *Explain what remedies are available to the corporation when a director or officer usurps a "corporate opportunity" and does not have a valid defense to this claim.*

A "corporate opportunity" involves a situation where a director or officer learns of some sort of business opportunity from a third party and, instead of letting the corporation take the opportunity, pursues it on her own. This is fundamentally different than the interested director transaction that you learned about in Section 7.01 because the director or officer is pursuing the opportunity on her own (or perhaps together with a third party) rather than engaging in a transaction with the corporation itself. But if we decide that an opportunity is a "corporate opportunity" (that is, it meets the applicable definition of this term), then it is as if the director or officer has stolen something that rightfully belonged to the corporation. For this reason, the term that is used is not "business" opportunity but "corporate" opportunity which indicates that it belonged to the corporation.

The two primary issues that you must consider are (1) what is a "corporate opportunity"? and (2) what steps can an officer or director who wishes to pursue the corporate opportunity take to "sanitize" her taking of the opportunity? Interestingly, the MBCA has largely "punted" on the issue of whether something is a corporate opportunity. *See* MBCA § 8.70. Thus, we will look at other sources of law. Two major sources of guidance on this issue are Delaware law and the *ALI Principles of Corporate Governance*, which are applied in the following two cases, respectively. In reading these cases, see if they remind you at all of the *Meinhard v. Salmon* case from Chapter 2.

Broz v. Cellular Information Systems, Inc.
Supreme Court of Delaware
673 A.2d 148 (1996)

VEASEY, Chief Justice: In this appeal, we consider the application of the doctrine of corporate opportunity. The Court of Chancery decided that the defendant, a corporate director, breached his fiduciary duty by not formally presenting to the corporation an opportunity which had come to the director individually and independent of the director's relationship with the corporation. Here the opportunity was not one in which the corporation in its current mode had an interest or which it had the financial ability to acquire, but, under the unique circumstances here, that mode was subject to change by virtue of the impending acquisition of the corporation by another entity.

We conclude that, although a corporate director may be shielded from liability by offering to the corporation an opportunity which has come to the director independently and individually, the failure of the director to present the opportunity does not necessarily result in the improper usurpation of a corporate opportunity. We further conclude that, if the corporation is a target or potential target of an acquisition by another company which has an interest and ability to entertain the opportunity, the director of the target company does not have a fiduciary duty to present the opportunity to the target company. Accordingly, the judgment of the Court of Chancery is [reversed].

[I.]   Robert F. Broz ("Broz") is the President and sole stockholder of RFB Cellular, Inc. ("RFBC"), a Delaware corporation engaged in the business of providing cellular telephone service in the Midwestern United States. At the time of the conduct at issue in this appeal, Broz was also a member of the board of directors of plaintiff below-appellee, Cellular Information Systems, Inc. ("CIS"). CIS is a publicly held Delaware corporation and a competitor of RFBC.

The conduct before the Court involves the purchase by Broz of a cellular telephone service license for the benefit of RFBC.* The license in question, known as the Michigan-2 Rural Service Area Cellular License ("Michigan-2"), is

---

* [Footnote by court]: The Court recognizes that the actual purchase of the Michigan-2 license was consummated by RFBC as a corporate entity, rather than by Broz acting as an individual for his own benefit. Broz is, however, the sole party in interest in RFBC and all actions taken by RFBC, including the acquisition of Michigan-2, are accomplished at the behest of Broz. Therefore, insofar as the purchase of Michigan-2 is concerned, the Court will not distinguish between the actions of Broz and those of RFBC in analyzing Broz' alleged breach of fiduciary duty.

issued by the Federal Communications Commission ("FCC") and entitles its holder to provide cellular telephone service to a portion of northern Michigan. CIS brought an action against Broz and RFBC for equitable relief, contending that the purchase of this license by Broz constituted a usurpation of a corporate opportunity properly belonging to CIS, irrespective of whether or not CIS was interested in the Michigan-2 opportunity at the time it was offered to Broz.

The principal basis for the contention of CIS is that PriCellular, Inc. ("PriCellular"), another cellular communications company which was contemporaneously engaged in an acquisition of CIS, was interested in the Michigan-2 opportunity. CIS contends that, in determining whether the Michigan-2 opportunity rightfully belonged to CIS, Broz was required to consider the interests of PriCellular insofar as those interests would come into alignment with those of CIS as a result of PriCellular's acquisition plans.

After trial, the Court of Chancery agreed with the contentions of CIS and entered judgment against Broz and RFBC.   ***   The trial court imposed a constructive trust on the agreement to purchase Michigan-2 and directed that the right to purchase the license be transferred to CIS. From this judgment, Broz and RFBC appeal.

[II. Facts]   Broz has been the President and sole stockholder of RFBC since 1992. RFBC owns and operates an FCC license area, known as the Michigan-4 Rural Service Area Cellular License ("Michigan-4"). The license entitles RFBC to provide cellular telephone service to a portion of rural Michigan. Although Broz' efforts have been devoted primarily to the business operations of RFBC, he also served as an outside director of CIS at the time of the events at issue in this case. CIS was at all times fully aware of Broz' relationship with RFBC and the obligations incumbent upon him by virtue of that relationship.

In April of 1994, Mackinac Cellular Corp. ("Mackinac") sought to divest itself of Michigan-2, the license area immediately adjacent to Michigan-4. To this end, Mackinac contacted Daniels & Associates ("Daniels") and arranged for the brokerage firm to seek potential purchasers for Michigan-2. In compiling a list of prospects, Daniels included RFBC as a likely candidate. ***

Michigan-2 was not, however, offered to CIS. Apparently, Daniels did not consider CIS to be a viable purchaser for Michigan-2 in light of CIS' recent financial difficulties. The record shows that, at the time Michigan-2 was offered to Broz, CIS had recently emerged from lengthy and contentious Chapter 11 proceedings. Pursuant to the Chapter 11 Plan of Reorganization, CIS entered into a loan agreement that substantially impaired the company's ability to undertake new acquisitions or to incur new debt. In fact, CIS would have been unable to purchase Michigan-2 without the approval of its creditors.

*** During the period from early 1992 until the time of CIS' emergence from bankruptcy in 1994, CIS divested itself of some fifteen separate cellular license systems. CIS contracted to sell four additional license areas on May 27, 1994, leaving CIS with only five remaining license areas, all of which were outside of the Midwest.

On June 13, 1994, following a meeting of the CIS board, Broz spoke with CIS' Chief Executive Officer, Richard Treibick ("Treibick"), concerning his interest in acquiring Michigan-2. Treibick communicated to Broz that CIS was not interested in Michigan-2. Treibick further stated that he had been made aware of the Michigan-2 opportunity prior to the conversation with Broz, and that any offer to acquire Michigan-2 was rejected. After the commencement of the PriCellular tender offer, in August of 1994, Broz contacted another CIS director, Peter Schiff ("Schiff"), to discuss the possible acquisition of Michigan-2 by RFBC. Schiff, like Treibick, indicated that CIS had neither the wherewithal nor the inclination to purchase Michigan-2. In late September of 1994, Broz also contacted Stanley Bloch ("Bloch"), a director and counsel for CIS, to request that Bloch represent RFBC in its dealings with Mackinac. Bloch agreed to represent RFBC, and, like Schiff and Treibick, expressed his belief that CIS was not at all interested in the transaction. Ultimately, all the CIS directors testified at trial that, had Broz inquired at that time, they each would have expressed the opinion that CIS was not interested in Michigan-2.

[A few months later, PriCellular began a tender offer for CIS's stock. Due to some financing issues, the closing of the tender offer was delayed until November.]

On August 6, September 6 and September 21, 1994, Broz submitted written offers to Mackinac for the purchase of Michigan-2. During this time period, PriCellular also began negotiations with Mackinac to arrange an option for the purchase of Michigan-2. ***

In late September of 1994, PriCellular reached agreement with Mackinac on an option to purchase Michigan-2. The exercise price of the option agreement was set at $6.7 million, with the option remaining in force until December 15, 1994. *** The agreement further provided that Mackinac was free to sell Michigan-2 to any party who was willing to exceed the exercise price of the Mackinac-PriCellular option contract by at least $500,000. On November 14, 1994, Broz agreed to pay Mackinac $7.2 million for the Michigan-2 license, thereby meeting the terms of the option agreement. An asset purchase agreement was thereafter executed by Mackinac and RFBC.

Nine days later, on November 23, 1994, PriCellular completed its financing and closed its tender offer for CIS. Prior to that point, PriCellular owned no equity interest in CIS. Subsequent to the consummation of the PriCellular tender offer for CIS, members of the CIS board of directors, including Broz, were discharged and replaced with a slate of PriCellular nominees. On March 2, 1995, this action was commenced by CIS in the Court of Chancery.

At trial in the Court of Chancery, CIS contended that the purchase of Michigan-2 by Broz constituted the impermissible usurpation of a corporate opportunity properly belonging to CIS. ***

***

[IV. Application of the Corporate Opportunity Doctrine.] The doctrine of corporate opportunity represents but one species of the broad fiduciary duties assumed by a corporate director or officer. A corporate fiduciary agrees to place the interests of the corporation before his or her own in appropriate circumstances. In light of the diverse and often competing obligations faced by directors and officers, however, the corporate opportunity doctrine arose as a means of defining the parameters of fiduciary duty in instances of potential conflict. The classic statement of the doctrine is derived from the venerable case of *Guth v. Loft, Inc.*, [5 A.2d 503 (Del. 1939)]. In *Guth*, this Court held that:

> if there is presented to a corporate officer or director a business opportunity which the corporation is financially able to undertake, is, from its nature, in the line of the corporation's business and is of practical advantage to it, is one in which the corporation has an interest or a reasonable expectancy, and, by embracing the opportunity, the self-interest of the officer or director will be brought into conflict with that of the corporation, the law will not permit him to seize the opportunity for himself.

[*Id.* at 510-11.]

The corporate opportunity doctrine, as delineated by *Guth* and its progeny, holds that a corporate officer or director may not take a business opportunity for his own if: (1) the corporation is financially able to exploit the opportunity; (2) the opportunity is within the corporation's line of business; (3) the corporation has an interest or expectancy in the opportunity; and (4) by taking the opportunity for his own, the corporate fiduciary will thereby be placed in a position inimicable to his duties to the corporation. The Court in *Guth* also derived a corollary which states that a director or officer *may* take a corporate opportunity if: (1) the opportunity is presented to the director or officer in his individual and not his corporate capacity; (2) the opportunity is not essential to the corporation; (3) the corporation holds no interest or expectancy in the opportunity; and (4) the director or officer has not wrongfully employed the resources of the corporation in pursuing or exploiting the opportunity. [Citation omitted.]

Thus, the contours of this doctrine are well established. It is important to note, however, that the tests enunciated in *Guth* and subsequent cases provide guidelines to be considered by a reviewing court in balancing the equities of an individual case. No one factor is dispositive and all factors must be taken into account insofar as they are applicable. Cases involving a claim of usurpation of a corporate opportunity range over a multitude of factual settings. Hard and fast rules are not easily crafted to deal with such an array of complex situations. *** In the instant case, we find that the facts do not support the conclusion that Broz misappropriated a corporate opportunity.

We note at the outset that Broz became aware of the Michigan-2 opportunity in his individual and not his corporate capacity. As the Court of Chancery found, "Broz did not misuse proprietary information that came to him in a corporate capacity nor did he otherwise use any power he might have over the governance of the corporation to advance his own interests." [Citation omitted.] This fact is not the subject of serious dispute. In fact, it is clear from the record that Mackinac did not consider CIS a viable candidate for the acquisition of Michigan-2. Accordingly, Mackinac did not offer the property to CIS. In this factual posture, many of the fundamental concerns undergirding the law of corporate opportunity are not present (e.g., misappropriation of the corporation's proprietary information). The burden imposed upon Broz to show adherence to his fiduciary duties to CIS is thus lessened to some extent. [Citation omitted.] Nevertheless, this fact is not dispositive. The determination of whether a particular fiduciary has usurped a corporate opportunity necessitates a careful examination of the circumstances, giving due credence to the factors enunciated in *Guth* and subsequent cases.

We turn now to an analysis of the factors relied on by the trial court. First, we find that CIS was not financially capable of exploiting the Michigan-2 opportunity. Although the Court of Chancery concluded otherwise, we hold that this finding was not supported by the evidence. [Citation omitted.] The record shows that CIS was in a precarious financial position at the time Mackinac presented the Michigan-2 opportunity to Broz. Having recently emerged from lengthy and contentious bankruptcy proceedings, CIS was not in a position to commit capital to the acquisition of new assets. Further, the loan agreement entered into by CIS and its creditors severely limited the discretion of CIS as to the acquisition of new assets and substantially restricted the ability of CIS to incur new debt.

The Court of Chancery based its contrary finding on the fact that PriCellular had purchased an option to acquire CIS' bank debt. Thus, the court reasoned, PriCellular was in a position to exercise that option and then waive any unfavorable restrictions that would stand in the way of a CIS acquisition of Michigan-2. The trial court, however, disregarded the fact that PriCellular's own financial situation was not particularly stable. PriCellular was unable to finance the acquisition of CIS through conventional bank loans and was forced to use the more risky mechanism of a junk bond offering to raise the required capital. Thus, the court's statement that "PriCellular had other sources of financing to permit the funding of that purchase" is clearly not free from dispute. Moreover, as discussed [below], the fact that PriCellular had available sources of financing is immaterial to the analysis. At the time that Broz was required to decide whether to accept the Michigan-2 opportunity, PriCellular had not yet acquired CIS, and any plans to do so were wholly speculative. Thus, contrary to the Court of Chancery's finding, Broz was not obligated to consider the contingency of a PriCellular acquisition of CIS and the related contingency of PriCellular thereafter waiving restrictions on the CIS bank debt. Broz was required to consider the facts only as they existed at the time he determined to accept the Mackinac offer and embark on his efforts to bring the transaction to fruition. [Citation omitted.]

Second, while it may be said with some certainty that the Michigan-2 opportunity was within CIS' line of business, it is not equally clear that CIS had a cognizable interest or expectancy in the license.* Under the third factor laid down by this Court in *Guth*, for an opportunity to be deemed to belong to the fiduciary's corporation, the corporation must have an interest or expectancy in that opportunity. As this Court stated in [a prior case] "[f]or the corporation to have an actual or expectant interest in any specific property, there must be some tie between that property and the nature of the corporate business." Despite the fact that the nature of the Michigan-2 opportunity was historically close to the core operations of CIS, changes were in process. At the time the opportunity was

---

*   [Footnote by court]: The language in the *Guth* opinion relating to "line of business" is less than clear:

> Where a corporation is engaged in a certain business, and an opportunity is presented to it embracing an activity as to which it has fundamental knowledge, practical experience and *ability to pursue,* which, logically and naturally, is adaptable to its business *having regard for its financial position,* and *is consonant with its reasonable needs and aspirations for expansion,* it may properly be said that the opportunity is within the corporation's line of business.

[Citation omitted (emphasis added).] This formulation of the definition of the term "line of business" suggests that the business strategy and financial well-being of the corporation are also relevant to a determination of whether the opportunity is within the corporation's line of business. Since we find that these considerations are decisive under the other factors enunciated by the Court in *Guth,* we do not reach the question of whether they are here relevant to a determination of the corporation's line of business.

presented, CIS was actively engaged in the process of divesting its cellular license holdings. CIS' articulated business plan did not involve any new acquisitions. Further, as indicated by the testimony of the entire CIS board, the Michigan-2 license would not have been of interest to CIS even absent CIS' financial difficulties and CIS' then current desire to liquidate its cellular license holdings. Thus, CIS had no interest or expectancy in the Michigan-2 opportunity. [Citation omitted.]

Finally, the corporate opportunity doctrine is implicated only in cases where the fiduciary's seizure of an opportunity results in a conflict between the fiduciary's duties to the corporation and the self-interest of the director as actualized by the exploitation of the opportunity. In the instant case, Broz' interest in acquiring and profiting from Michigan-2 created no duties that were inimicable to his obligations to CIS. Broz, at all times relevant to the instant appeal, was the sole party in interest in RFBC, a competitor of CIS. CIS was fully aware of Broz' potentially conflicting duties. Broz, however, comported himself in a manner that was wholly in accord with his obligations to CIS. Broz took care not to usurp any opportunity which CIS was willing and able to pursue. Broz sought only to compete with an outside entity, PriCellular, for acquisition of an opportunity which both sought to possess. Broz was not obligated to refrain from competition with PriCellular. Therefore, the totality of the circumstances indicates that Broz did not usurp an opportunity that properly belonged to CIS.

[IV.A—Presentation to the Board] In concluding that Broz had usurped a corporate opportunity, the Court of Chancery placed great emphasis on the fact that Broz had not formally presented the matter to the CIS board. *** In so holding, the trial court erroneously grafted a new requirement onto the law of corporate opportunity, viz., the requirement of formal presentation under circumstances where the corporation does not have an interest, expectancy or financial ability.

The teaching of *Guth* and its progeny is that the director or officer must analyze the situation *ex ante* to determine whether the opportunity is one rightfully belonging to the corporation. If the director or officer believes, based on one of the factors articulated above, that the corporation is not entitled to the opportunity, then he may take it for himself. Of course, presenting the opportunity to the board creates a kind of "safe harbor" for the director, which removes the specter of a *post hoc* judicial determination that the director or officer has improperly usurped a corporate opportunity. Thus, presentation avoids the possibility that an error in the fiduciary's assessment of the situation will create future liability for breach of fiduciary duty. It is not the law of Delaware that presentation to the board is a necessary prerequisite to a finding that a corporate opportunity has not been usurped.

***

[V.   Conclusion]   The corporate opportunity doctrine represents a judicially crafted effort to harmonize the competing demands placed on corporate fiduciaries in a modern business environment.   The doctrine seeks to reduce the possibility of conflict between a director's duties to the corporation and interests unrelated to that role.   In the instant case, Broz adhered to his obligations to CIS. We hold that the Court of Chancery erred as a matter of law in concluding that Broz had a duty formally to present the Michigan-2 opportunity to the CIS board. We also hold that the trial court erred in its application of the corporate opportunity doctrine under the unusual facts of this case, where CIS had no interest or financial ability to acquire the opportunity, but the impending acquisition of CIS by PriCellular would or could have caused a change in those circumstances.

Therefore, we hold that Broz did not breach his fiduciary duties to CIS. Accordingly, we [reverse] the judgment of the Court of Chancery holding that Broz diverted a corporate opportunity properly belonging to CIS and imposing a constructive trust.

Northeast Harbor Golf Club, Inc. v. Harris
Supreme Judicial Court of Maine
661 A.2d 1146 (1995)

ROBERTS, Justice.   Northeast Harbor Golf Club, Inc., appeals from a judgment *** following a nonjury trial.   The Club maintains that the trial court erred in finding that Nancy Harris did not breach her fiduciary duty as president of the Club by purchasing and developing property abutting the golf course.   Because we today adopt principles different from those applied by the trial court in determining that Harris's activities did not constitute a breach of the corporate opportunity doctrine, we vacate the judgment.

[I.   Facts]   Nancy Harris was the president of the Northeast Harbor Golf Club, a Maine corporation, from 1971 until she was asked to resign in 1990.   The Club also had a board of directors that was responsible for making or approving significant policy decisions.   The Club's only major asset was a golf course in Mount Desert.   During Harris's tenure as president, the board occasionally discussed the possibility of developing some of the Club's real estate in order to raise money.   Although Harris was generally in favor of tasteful development, the board always "shied away" from that type of activity.

In 1979, Robert Suminsby informed Harris that he was the listing broker for the Gilpin property, which comprised three noncontiguous parcels located among the fairways of the golf course. The property included an unused right-of-way on which the Club's parking lot and clubhouse were located. It was also encumbered by an easement in favor of the Club allowing foot traffic from the green of one hole to the next tee. Suminsby testified that he contacted Harris because she was the president of the Club and he believed that the Club would be interested in buying the property in order to prevent development.

Harris immediately agreed to purchase the Gilpin property in her own name for the asking price of $45,000. She did not disclose her plans to purchase the property to the Club's board prior to the purchase. She informed the board at its annual August meeting that she had purchased the property, that she intended to hold it in her own name, and that the Club would be "protected." The board took no action in response to the Harris purchase. She testified that at the time of the purchase she had no plans to develop the property and that no such plans took shape until 1988.

In 1984, while playing golf with the postmaster of Northeast Harbor, Harris learned that a parcel of land owned by the heirs of the Smallidge family might be available for purchase. The Smallidge parcel was surrounded on three sides by the golf course and on the fourth side by a house lot. It had no access to the road. With the ultimate goal of acquiring the property, Harris instructed her lawyer to locate the Smallidge heirs. Harris testified that she told a number of individual board members about her attempt to acquire the Smallidge parcel. At a board meeting in August 1985, Harris formally disclosed to the board that she had purchased the Smallidge property. The minutes of that meeting show that she told the board she had no present plans to develop the Smallidge parcel. Harris testified that at the time of the purchase of the Smallidge property she nonetheless thought it might be nice to have some houses there. Again, the board took no formal action as a result of Harris's purchase. Harris acquired the Smallidge property from ten heirs, paying a total of $60,000. In 1990, Harris paid $275,000 for the lot and building separating the Smallidge parcel from the road in order to gain access to the otherwise landlocked parcel.

The trial court expressly found that the Club would have been unable to purchase either the Gilpin or Smallidge properties for itself, relying on testimony that the Club continually experienced financial difficulties, operated annually at a deficit, and depended on contributions from the directors to pay its bills. On the other hand, there was evidence that the Club had occasionally engaged in successful fund-raising, including a two-year period shortly after the Gilpin purchase during which the Club raised $115,000. The Club had $90,000 in a capital investment fund at the time of the Smallidge purchase.

In 1987 or 1988, Harris divided the real estate into 41 small lots, 14 on the Smallidge property and 27 on the Gilpin property. Apparently as part of her estate plan, Harris conveyed noncontiguous lots among the 41 to her children and retained others for herself. In 1991, Harris and her children exchanged deeds to reassemble the small lots into larger parcels. At the time the Club filed this suit, the property was divided into 11 lots, some owned by Harris and others by her children who are also defendants in this case. Harris estimated the value of all the real estate at the time of the trial to be $1,550,000.

In 1988, Harris, who was still president of the Club, and her children began the process of obtaining approval for a five-lot subdivision known as Bushwood on the lower Gilpin property. Even when the board learned of the proposed subdivision, a majority failed to take any action. A group of directors formed a separate organization in order to oppose the subdivision on the basis that it violated the local zoning ordinance. After Harris's resignation as president, the Club also sought unsuccessfully to challenge the subdivision. [Citation omitted.] Plans of Harris and her family for development of the other parcels are unclear, but the local zoning ordinance would permit construction of up to 11 houses on the land as currently divided.

After Harris's plans to develop Bushwood became apparent, the board grew increasingly divided concerning the propriety of development near the golf course. At least two directors, Henri Agnese and Nick Ludington, testified that they trusted Harris to act in the best interests of the Club and that they had no problem with the development plans for Bushwood. Other directors disagreed.

In particular, John Schafer, a Washington, D.C., lawyer and long-time member of the board, took issue with Harris's conduct. He testified that he had relied on Harris's representations at the time she acquired the properties that she would not develop them. According to Schafer, matters came to a head in August 1990 when a number of directors concluded that Harris's development plans irreconcilably conflicted with the Club's interests. As a result, Schafer and two other directors asked Harris to resign as president. In April 1991, after a substantial change in the board's membership, the board authorized the instant lawsuit against Harris for the breach of her fiduciary duty to act in the best interests of the corporation. The board simultaneously resolved that the proposed housing development was contrary to the best interests of the corporation.

The Club filed a complaint against Harris, her sons John and Shepard, and her daughter-in-law Melissa Harris. As amended, the complaint alleged that during her term as president Harris breached her fiduciary duty by purchasing the lots without providing notice and an opportunity for the Club to purchase the property and by subdividing the lots for future development. The Club sought an injunction to prevent development and also sought to impose a constructive trust on the property in question for the benefit of the Club.

The trial court found that Harris had not usurped a corporate opportunity because the acquisition of real estate was not in the Club's line of business. Moreover, it found that the corporation lacked the financial ability to purchase the real estate at issue. Finally, the court placed great emphasis on Harris's good faith. It noted her long and dedicated history of service to the Club, her personal oversight of the Club's growth, and her frequent financial contributions to the Club. The court found that her development activities were "generally ... compatible with the corporation's business." This appeal followed.

[II. The Corporate Opportunity Doctrine.] ***

*** Corporate fiduciaries in Maine must discharge their duties in good faith with a view toward furthering the interests of the corporation. They must disclose and not withhold relevant information concerning any potential conflict of interest with the corporation, and they must refrain from using their position, influence, or knowledge of the affairs of the corporation to gain personal advantage. [Citation omitted.]

Despite the general acceptance of the proposition that corporate fiduciaries owe a duty of loyalty to their corporations, there has been much confusion about the specific extent of that duty when, as here, it is contended that a fiduciary takes for herself a corporate opportunity. [Citation omitted.] This case requires us for the first time to define the scope of the corporate opportunity doctrine in Maine.

Various courts have embraced different versions of the corporate opportunity doctrine. The test applied by the trial court and embraced by Harris is generally known as the "line of business" test. The seminal case applying the line of business test is *Guth v. Loft, Inc.,* 5 A.2d 503 (Del. 1939). In *Guth,* the Delaware Supreme Court adopted an intensely factual test stated in general terms as follows:

> [I]f there is presented to a corporate officer or director a business opportunity which the corporation is financially able to undertake, is, from its nature, in the line of the corporation's business and is of practical advantage to it, is one in which the corporation has an interest or a reasonable expectancy, and, by embracing the opportunity, the self-interest of the officer or director will be brought into conflict with that of his corporation, the law will not permit him to seize the opportunity for himself.

Id. at 511. The "real issue" under this test is whether the opportunity "was so closely associated with the existing business activities ... as to bring the transaction within that class of cases where the acquisition of the property would throw the corporate officer purchasing it into competition with his company." *Id.* at 513. The Delaware court described that inquiry as "a factual question to be decided by reasonable inferences from objective facts." *Id.*

The line of business test suffers from some significant weaknesses. First, the question whether a particular activity is within a corporation's line of business is conceptually difficult to answer. The facts of the instant case demonstrate that difficulty. The Club is in the business of running a golf course. It is not in the business of developing real estate. In the traditional sense, therefore, the trial court correctly observed that the opportunity in this case was not a corporate opportunity within the meaning of the *Guth* test. Nevertheless, the record would support a finding that the Club had made the policy judgment that development of surrounding real estate was detrimental to the best interests of the Club. The acquisition of land adjacent to the golf course for the purpose of preventing future development would have enhanced the ability of the Club to implement that policy. The record also shows that the Club had occasionally considered reversing that policy and expanding its operations to include the development of surrounding real estate. Harris's activities effectively foreclosed the Club from pursuing that option with respect to prime locations adjacent to the golf course.

Second, the *Guth* test includes as an element the financial ability of the corporation to take advantage of the opportunity. The court in this case relied on the Club's supposed financial incapacity as a basis for excusing Harris's conduct. Often, the injection of financial ability into the equation will unduly favor the inside director or executive who has command of the facts relating to the finances of the corporation. Reliance on financial ability will also act as a disincentive to corporate executives to solve corporate financing and other problems. In addition, the Club could have prevented development without spending $275,000 to acquire the property Harris needed to obtain access to the road.

The Massachusetts Supreme Judicial Court adopted a different test in *Durfee v. Durfee & Canning, Inc.,* [80 N.E.2d 522 (Mass. 1948)]. The *Durfee* test has since come to be known as the "fairness test." According to *Durfee,* the

> true basis of governing doctrine rests on the unfairness in the particular circumstances of a director, whose relation to the corporation is fiduciary, taking advantage of an opportunity [for her personal profit] when the interest of the corporation justly call[s] for protection. This calls for application of ethical standards of what is fair and equitable ... in particular sets of facts.

Id. at 529 [quotation omitted]. As with the *Guth* test, the *Durfee* test calls for a broad-ranging, intensely factual inquiry. The *Durfee* test suffers even more than the *Guth* test from a lack of principled content. It provides little or no practical guidance to the corporate officer or director seeking to measure her obligations.

The Minnesota Supreme Court elected "to combine the 'line of business' test with the 'fairness' test." *Miller v. Miller,* [222 N.W.2d 71, 81 (Minn. 1974)]. It engaged in a two-step analysis, first determining whether a particular opportunity was within the corporation's line of business, then scrutinizing "the equitable considerations existing prior to, at the time of, and following the officer's acquisition." *Id.* The *Miller* court hoped by adopting this approach "to ameliorate the often-expressed criticism that the [corporate opportunity] doctrine is vague and subjects today's corporate management to the danger of unpredictable liability." *Id.* In fact, the test adopted in *Miller* merely piles the uncertainty and vagueness of the fairness test on top of the weaknesses in the line of business test.

Despite the weaknesses of each of these approaches to the corporate opportunity doctrine, they nonetheless rest on a single fundamental policy. At bottom, the corporate opportunity doctrine recognizes that a corporate fiduciary should not serve both corporate and personal interests at the same time. *** The various formulations of the test are merely attempts to moderate the potentially harsh consequences of strict adherence to that policy. It is important to preserve some ability for corporate fiduciaries to pursue personal business interests that present no real threat to their duty of loyalty.

[III.   The American Law Institute Approach.] In an attempt to protect the duty of loyalty while at the same time providing long-needed clarity and guidance for corporate decisionmakers, the American Law Institute has offered the most recently developed version of the corporate opportunity doctrine. [Section 5.05 of the ALI's *Principles of Corporate Governance*] provides as follows:

> § 505   Taking of Corporate Opportunities by Directors or Senior Executives
>
> (a)   *General Rule.* A director [§ 1.13] or senior executive [§ 1.33] may not take advantage of a corporate opportunity unless:
>
> (1)   The director or senior executive first offers the corporate opportunity to the corporation and makes disclosure concerning the conflict of interest [§ 1.14(a)] and the corporate opportunity [§ 1.14(b)];

(2)   The corporate opportunity is rejected by the corporation; and

(3)   Either:

    (A)   The rejection of the opportunity is fair to the corporation;

    (B)   The opportunity is rejected in advance, following such disclosure, by disinterested directors [§ 1.15], or, in the case of a senior executive who is not a director, by a disinterested superior, in a manner that satisfies the standards of the business judgment rule [§ 4.01(c)]; or

    (C)   The rejection is authorized in advance or ratified, following such disclosure, by disinterested shareholders [§ 1.16], and the rejection is not equivalent to a waste of corporate assets [§ 1.42].

(b)   *Definition of a Corporate Opportunity.* For purposes of this Section, a corporate opportunity means:

(1)   Any opportunity to engage in a business activity of which a director or senior executive becomes aware, either:

    (A)   In connection with the performance of functions as a director or senior executive, or under circumstances that should reasonably lead the director or senior executive to believe that the person offering the opportunity expects it to be offered to the corporation; or

    (B)   Through the use of corporate information or property, if the resulting opportunity is one that the director or senior executive should reasonably be expected to believe would be of interest to the corporation; or

(2)   Any opportunity to engage in a business activity of which a senior executive becomes aware and knows is closely related to a business in which the corporation is engaged or expects to engage.

(c)   *Burden of Proof.* A party who challenges the taking of a corporate opportunity has the burden of proof, except that if such party establishes that the requirements of Subsection (a)(3)(B) or (C) are not met, the director or the senior executive has the burden of proving that the rejection and the taking of the opportunity were fair to the corporation.

(d)   *Ratification of Defective Disclosure.*   A good faith but defective disclosure of the facts concerning the corporate opportunity may be cured if at any time (but no later than a reasonable time after suit is filed challenging the taking of the corporate opportunity) the original rejection of the corporate opportunity is ratified, following the required disclosure, by the board, the shareholders, or the corporate decisionmaker who initially approved the rejection of the corporate opportunity, or such decisionmaker's successor.

(e)   *Special Rule Concerning Delayed Offering of Corporate Opportunities.*   Relief based solely on failure to first offer an opportunity to the corporation under Subsection (a)(1) is not available if: (1) such failure resulted from a good faith belief that the business activity did not constitute a corporate opportunity, and (2) not later than a reasonable time after suit is filed challenging the taking of the corporate opportunity, the corporate opportunity is to the extent possible offered to the corporation and rejected in a manner that satisfies the standards of Subsection (a).

The central feature of the ALI test is the strict requirement of full disclosure prior to taking advantage of any corporate opportunity.   *Id.,* § 5.05(a)(1).   "If the opportunity is not offered to the corporation, the director or senior executive will not have satisfied § 5.05(a)."   *Id.,* cmt. to § 5.05(a).   The corporation must then formally reject the opportunity.   *Id.,* § 505(a)(2).   The ALI test is discussed at length and ultimately applied by the Oregon Supreme Court in *Klinicki v. Lundgren,* [695 P.2d 906 (Ore. 1985)].   As *Klinicki* describes the test, "full disclosure to the appropriate corporate body is ... an absolute condition precedent to the validity of any forthcoming rejection as well as to the availability to the director or principal senior executive of the defense of fairness."   *Id.* at 920. A "good faith but defective disclosure" by the corporate officer may be ratified after the fact only by an affirmative vote of the disinterested directors or shareholders. [ALI Principles] § 5.05(d).

The ALI test defines "corporate opportunity" broadly.   It includes opportunities "closely related to a business in which the corporation is engaged."   *Id.,* § 5.05(b).   It also encompasses any opportunities that accrue to the fiduciary as a result of her position within the corporation.   *Id.*   This concept is most clearly illustrated by the testimony of Suminsby, the listing broker for the Gilpin property, which, if believed by the factfinder, would support a finding that the Gilpin property was offered to Harris specifically in her capacity as president of the Club.

If the factfinder reached that conclusion, then at least the opportunity to acquire the Gilpin property would be a corporate opportunity. The state of the record concerning the Smallidge purchase precludes us from intimating any opinion whether that too would be a corporate opportunity.

Under the ALI standard, once the Club shows that the opportunity is a corporate opportunity, it must show either that Harris did not offer the opportunity to the Club or that the Club did not reject it properly. If the Club shows that the board did not reject the opportunity by a vote of the disinterested directors after full disclosure, then Harris may defend her actions on the basis that the taking of the opportunity was fair to the corporation. *Id.,* § 5.05(c). If Harris failed to offer the opportunity at all, however, then she may not defend on the basis that the failure to offer the opportunity was fair. *Id.,* cmt. to § 5.05(c).

*** [T]oday we follow the ALI test. The disclosure-oriented approach provides a clear procedure whereby a corporate officer may insulate herself through prompt and complete disclosure from the possibility of a legal challenge. The requirement of disclosure recognizes the paramount importance of the corporate fiduciary's duty of loyalty. At the same time it protects the fiduciary's ability pursuant to the proper procedure to pursue her own business ventures free from the possibility of a lawsuit.

***

[IV. Conclusion.] The question remains how our adoption of the rule affects the result in the instant case. The trial court made a number of factual findings based on an extensive record.[*] The court made those findings, however, in the light of legal principles that are different from the principles that we today announce. Similarly, the parties did not have the opportunity to develop the record in this case with knowledge of the applicable legal standard. In these circumstances, fairness requires that we remand the case for further proceedings. Those further proceedings may include, at the trial court's discretion, the taking of further evidence.

[Vacated and remanded for further proceedings consistent with this opinion.]

---

[*]   [Footnote by court]: Harris raised the defense of laches and the statute of limitations but the court made no findings on those issues. ***

Questions About *Broz, Harris*, and Corporate Opportunities

1.   What would have been the outcome of the *Broz* case if the *ALI Principles* had applied?

2.   Under the *ALI Principles*, when is the corporation's financial ability to pursue the opportunity relevant?

3.   Under both the *ALI Principles* and Delaware law, what should a director or officer do if she wants to pursue an opportunity that might be considered a "corporate opportunity"?

4.   What should be the remedy if a director or officer usurped a corporate opportunity? What remedy did the trial court impose in *Broz*? What remedy was the corporation seeking in *Harris*?

5.   What is an "interest or expectancy" for purposes of the Delaware approach to corporate opportunities?

6.   What would have been the outcome of *Meinhard v. Salmon* under the *ALI Principles* and Delaware law?

To understand how flexible the "line of business" portion of corporate opportunity tests may be, consider the following portions of *In re eBay, Inc. Shareholders Litigation*, 2004 Del Ch. LEXIS 4; 2004 WL 253521 (Del. Ch., Jan. 23, 2004), an unpublished opinion in which the court denied the defendants' motion to dismiss:

> In 1998, eBay retained Goldman Sachs and other investment banks to underwrite an initial public offering ["IPO"] of common stock. Goldman Sachs was the lead underwriter. The stock was priced at $18 per share. Goldman Sachs purchased about 1.2 million shares. Shares of eBay stock became immensely valuable during 1998 and 1999, rising to $175 per share in early April 1999. Around that time, eBay made a [second public] offering, issuing 6.5 million shares of common stock at $170 per share for a total of $1.1 billion.   Goldman Sachs again served as lead underwriter. Goldman Sachs was asked in 2001 to serve as eBay's financial advisor in connection with an acquisition by eBay of PayPal, Inc. For these services, eBay has paid Goldman Sachs over $8 million.

> During this same time period, Goldman Sachs "rewarded" the individual defendants [who were directors and officers of

eBay] by allocating to them thousands of [different companies']
IPO shares, managed by Goldman Sachs, at the initial offering
price. Because the IPO market during this particular period of
time was extremely active, prices of initial stock offerings often
doubled or tripled in a single day. Investors who were well
connected, either to Goldman Sachs or to similarly situated
investment banks serving as IPO underwriters, were able to flip
these investments into instant profit by selling the equities in a few
days or even in a few hours after they were initially purchased.

The essential allegation of the complaint is that Goldman
Sachs provided these IPO share allocations to the individual
defendants to show appreciation for eBay's business and to
enhance Goldman Sachs' chances of obtaining future eBay
business. *** Defendant [Meg] Whitman owns 3.3% of eBay
stock and has been President, CEO and a director since early 1998.
Whitman also has been a director of Goldman Sachs since 2001.
Goldman Sachs allocated Whitman shares in over a [sic] 100 IPOs
at the initial offering price. Whitman sold these equities in the
open market and reaped millions of dollars in profit. *** [Similar
allegations were made against other eBay directors.]

***

Plaintiffs have stated a claim that defendants usurped a
corporate opportunity of eBay [sufficient to survive a motion to
dismiss]. Defendants insist that Goldman Sachs' IPO allocations
to eBay's insider directors were "collateral investments
opportunities" that arose by virtue of the inside directors status as
wealthy individuals. They argue that this is not a corporate
opportunity within the corporation's line of business or an
opportunity in which the corporation had an interest or expectancy.
These arguments are unavailing.

First, no one disputes that eBay financially was able to
exploit the opportunities in question. Second, eBay was in the
business of investing in securities. The complaint alleges that
eBay "consistently invested a portion of its cash on hand in
marketable securities." According to eBay's 1999 [Annual Report
on Form] 10-K, for example, eBay had more than $550 million
invested in equity and debt securities. eBay invested more than
$181 million in "short-term investments" and $373 million in
"long-term investments." Thus, investing was "a line of business"
of eBay. Third, the facts alleged in the complaint suggest that

investing was integral to eBay's cash management strategies and a significant part of its business. Finally, it is no answer to say, as do defendants, that IPOs are risky investments. It is undisputed that eBay was never given an opportunity to turn down the IPO allocations as too risky.

Defendants also argue that to view the IPO allocations in question as corporate opportunities will mean that every advantageous investment opportunity that comes to an officer or director will be considered a corporate opportunity. On the contrary, the allegations in the complaint in this case indicate that unique, below-market price investment opportunities were offered by Goldman Sachs to the insider defendants as financial inducements to maintain and secure corporate business. This was not an instance where a broker offered advice to a director about an investment in a marketable security. The conduct challenged here involved a large investment bank that regularly did business with a company steering highly lucrative IPO allocations to select insider directors and officers at that company, allegedly both to reward them for past business and to induce them to direct future business to that investment bank. This is a far cry from the defendants' characterization of the conduct in question as merely "a broker's investment recommendations" to a wealthy client.

Nor can one seriously argue that this conduct did not place the insider defendants in a position of conflict with their duties to the corporation. One can realistically characterize these IPO allocations as a form of commercial discount or rebate for past or future investment banking services. Viewed pragmatically, it is easy to understand how steering such commercial rebates to certain insider directors places those directors in an obvious conflict between their self-interest and the corporation's interest. ***

Finally, even if one assumes that IPO allocations like those in question here do not constitute a corporate opportunity, a cognizable claim is nevertheless stated on the common law ground that an agent is under a duty to account for profits obtained personally in connection with transactions related to his or her company. ***

§ 7.03   COMPETING WITH THE CORPORATION

Objectives: You should be able to:

•   *Explain to a corporate client that has learned that an officer or employee may be competing with its business what legal remedies it may have.*

•   *Explain to a corporate client that has learned that a director may be competing with its business what legal remedies it may have.*

•   *Explain to a corporate client that has learned that a* <u>former</u> *officer/employee or director may be competing with its business what legal remedies it may have.*

•   *Explain to a corporate client that is concerned that certain of its officers/employees or directors (or others) may engage in competing businesses in the future what steps it can take now to diminish their ability to compete in the future.*

Closely related to the corporate opportunity doctrine is the concept of competition. If an officer or director usurps a corporate opportunity, then it may lead to her competing with the corporation. On the other hand, maybe the officer or director simply began competing with the company on her own or was even doing so before joining the corporation. In any event, this section will examine competition as an issue separate from usurpation of corporation opportunities.

The first issue is to decide *who* is competing. In other words, if the person who is competing is an officer or employee, that person is an agent of the corporation as you learned in Chapter 5. This makes it fairly easy to prevent that person from competing with the corporation: Section 8.04 of the *Restatement (Third) of Agency* provides that during the agency relationship, agents have a "duty to refrain from competing with the principal and from taking action on behalf of or otherwise assisting the principal's competitors." While it may be ambiguous in a given situation whether a person's activities are truly "competition," at least the existence of the duty not to compete is clear. (Section 8.04 also provides an additional helpful rule by providing that, even while she is employed by the principal, "an agent may take action, not otherwise wrongful, to prepare for competition following termination of the agency relationship.")

But employees, including officers, change jobs or "strike out on their own" all the time. Given that the whole basis of our capitalistic economy is competition, you should not be surprised to find that the law favors competition. Thus, if you want someone to be prevented from competing with you in the future, you will need that person to sign a **noncompetition agreement**, sometimes called a **covenant not to compete**. Of course, if that person is *already* competing with you, the chances that she will sign a noncompetition agreement are obviously pretty slim.[*] Generally, you can't prevent someone from competing with you unless they are infringing on your intellectual property (patents, copyrights, etc.) or trade secrets or engaging in some other form of unfair competition.

Again, the law favors competition. Thus, courts will not simply enforce any old noncompetition agreement. Instead, to be enforceable a noncompetition agreement must be "reasonable." Consider this rule in the context of the following problem:

Problem

Problem 7-16: Horace Tillman was a highly paid executive of a medical supply company in Lansing, Michigan. As a condition to being hired by this company, Horace signed a noncompetition agreement in which he agreed that, during his employment and for a period of fifteen years afterwards, he would not compete in the medical supply business, or be employed by a company that is in the medical supply business, anywhere east of the Mississippi River. *Is a court likely to uphold this noncompetition agreement? If not, should the entire agreement be invalidated?*

If the person who is competing with the company is a director—but not an officer or employee—then the analysis is a bit more opaque. For one thing, because directors are not agents, the *Restatement (Third) of Agency* will not apply. Thus, you will need some other source of law. Unfortunately, there do not seem to be a great deal of cases concerning whether directors may compete with a corporation and corporate statutes do not often directly address this issue. However, the introductory comment to Subchapter F of the MBCA (i.e., MBCA §§ 8.60 to 8.63, which was discussed in Section 7.01 above) observes that "[i]f a director decides to engage in business activity that directly competes with the corporation's own business, the economic interest in that competing activity ordinarily will conflict with the best interests of the corporation and put in issue the breach of the director's duties to the corporation."

> **WHAT WOULD YOU DO?**
> What would you recommend that a corporation do if one of its directors is competing with it?

---

[*]   Of course, you could try to pay for the noncompetition agreement, but may then run afoul of antitrust and unfair competition laws, which you may learn about in another course.

But this statement is hardly definitive, particularly because it is in a comment rather than the actual statute. Perhaps in an effort to bring some more clarity to this issue, Section 5.06(a) of the *ALI Principles of Corporate Governance* provides that:

> Directors and senior executives may not advance their pecuniary interests by engaging in competition with the corporation unless either:

> (1)   Any reasonably foreseeable harm to the corporation by such competition is outweighed by the benefit that the corporation may reasonably be expected to derive from allowing the competition to take place, or there is no reasonably foreseeable harm to the corporation from such competition;

> (2)   The competition is authorized in advance or ratified, following disclosure concerning the conflict of interest and the competition, by disinterested directors, or in the case of a senior executive who is not a director, is authorized in advance by a disinterested superior, in a manner that satisfies the standards of the business judgment rule; or

> (3)   The competition is authorized in advance or ratified, following such disclosure, by disinterested shareholders, and the shareholders' action is not equivalent to a waste of corporate assets.

Does this approach remind you of anything else that was discussed in this chapter?

§ 7.04   DIRECTOR COMPENSATION

Even though directors historically were not expected to be compensated for their service (being motivated to increase the value of their stock was enough), that is not the case today. Moreover, query whether a for-profit corporation would be able to attract highly qualified directors if they did not compensate them in some way. But who decides what these salaries should be? There's no "higher up" decision-maker than the board.

Would you like to decide your own salary? Of course. And if you're anything like most other people, you'd probably be pretty generous. On its face, this is exactly the position in which MBCA § 8.11 put directors, providing simply that, unless the articles of bylaws provide otherwise, "the board of directors may fix the compensation of directors." However, the official comment to MBCA §

8.61 provides in part that "it must be kept in mind that board action on directors' compensation and benefits would be subject to judicial sanction if they are not favorably acted upon shareholders pursuant to section 8.63 or if they are not in the circumstances fair to the corporation pursuant to section 8.61(b)(3)." In other words, directors don't really have *carte blance* to set their own compensation. (On the other hand, be sure to pay close attention to the opinion in *Marx v. Akers* in Chapter 8, a case in which a plaintiff claimed that the directors of IBM were paying themselves excessive compensation.) In addition, for public companies, there are some additional considerations that will be discussed in Chapter 10.

Executive (as opposed to director) compensation has been an extremely "hot button" issue in recent years. In a nutshell, executives of large corporations in American get paid gobs of money. And these amounts seem to be getting bigger all of the time. For example, in 1980 chief executive officers of the largest companies in the United States earned, on average, forty-two times as much as these companies' average workers. By 2001, this ratio had risen to 531 to one. Because much of the public ire at executive compensation is directed at publicly traded companies (if only because private companies are not required to disclose how much they pay their executives), we will consider this issue further in Chapter 10. In the meantime, here are some multiple choice questions concerning the material that we covered in this chapter.

PRACTICE QUESTIONS

NOTE: IN THE FOLLOWING QUESTIONS, THE WORD "DISINTERESTED" IS SYNONYMOUS WITH "QUALIFIED"

Multiple Choice Question 7-1: *If a corporation purchases property owned by one of its directors, which of the following statements is most correct?*

A.   The purchase contract is automatically voidable because of the director's conflict of interest.

B.   The contract will be upheld, as long as the director does not participate in the board meeting when the board approves the purchase.

C.   The contract will be upheld if it is established to be fair to the corporation.

D.   None of the above.

Multiple Choice Question 7-2: Duane is a director of Machine Corp. ("MC") and owns 45% of the outstanding MC stock. Because MC needed a machine that Duane owned, Duane caused MC to buy the machine from him, signing on behalf of MC as its president. He then called a special meeting of shareholders to vote on approving this purchase. At the meeting, after having disclosed all of the material facts about the transaction to the other shareholders, Duane voted all of his shares in favor of the transaction. However, all of the other shareholders present (who collectively owned 30% of outstanding stock of MC) voted against the transaction. *Which of the following is correct?*

A.   The transaction may not be challenged due to Duane's interest because a majority of the shares present at the meeting approved it.

B.   Because this is a director's conflicting interest transaction, all of the disinterested shares present at the meeting would have to approve the transaction to protect it against challenges based on Duane's interest in the transaction.

C.   Because this is a director's conflicting interest transaction, Duane's shares may be counted for purposes of establishing a quorum, but they may not be voted.

D.   None of the above.

Multiple Choice Question 7-3:   There are 10,000,000 shares of Vaccine Corporation ("VC") common stock outstanding. There are five people on VC's board of directors, none of whom are related: Mr. Flu, Ms. Smallpox, Ms. Polio, Mr. Hepatitis, and Ms. H1N1. Each director owns 1,000,000 shares of VC common stock. VC wanted to buy a piece of property that is jointly owned by Ms. Polio, Mr. Hepatitis, and Ms. H1N1 (the "Sellers"). The fair market value of the property, as determined by a recent expert appraisal, is $25,000. However, after negotiations with Ms. Smallpox (who was acting on behalf of VC), the Sellers agreed to sell the property to VC for $20,000. Ms. Smallpox and Mr. Flu then unanimously approved VC's purchase of the property at a board meeting which none of the Sellers attended. The shareholders of VC also voted on the transaction at a shareholder meeting by the following margins: 3,000,000 shares were voted in favor of the transaction; 2,000,000 shares were voted against the transaction; and 5,000,000 shares (which were the 5,000,000 shares owned by VC's directors) abstained from voting. You may assume that full disclosure of the material terms of the transaction was made to the directors and the shareholders of VC. *If a shareholder of VC challenges this transaction as a breach of the duty of loyalty of the Sellers, what is the most likely result?*

A.   The Sellers will lose, unless they prove that the transaction was "fair" to VC.

B.   The Sellers will win, unless the shareholder proves that the transaction was not "fair" to VC.

C.   The Sellers will win, because the transaction was properly approved by the disinterested directors of VC.

D.   The Sellers will win, because the transaction was properly approved by the disinterested shareholders of VC.

E.   Both C and D are correct.

Multiple Choice Question 7-4:   The directors of Metal Corp. unanimously approved a resolution that provided that the corporation would pay them each $50,000 per year for serving as directors. *Which of the following is correct?*

A.   Director compensation amounts may only be determined by the shareholders.

B.   Although directors can establish their own compensation amounts, the amounts must later be approved by the disinterested shareholders.

C.   Directors are not permitted to receive compensation for their services as directors other than stock options.

D.   None of the above.

Multiple Choice Question 7-5:   The board of directors of Zoo Corp. ("Zoo") consists of five persons: Mr. Gorilla, Mr. Monkey, Mr. Elephant, Mr. Tiger, and Mr. Lion. There are 800,000 shares of Zoo common stock outstanding. Oddly enough, each of the five directors of Zoo owns exactly 50,000 shares of Zoo common stock and each of the spouses of the five directors owns exactly 10,000 shares of Zoo common stock. (All five Zoo directors are married.) Four of the five directors (Mr. Gorilla, Mr. Monkey, Mr. Elephant, and Mr. Tiger) wish to purchase a valuable piece of real estate from Zoo. Realizing that this transaction would be a "directors' conflicting interest transaction" (also known as an "interested director transaction"), they have asked you for legal advice about how to "sanitize" this transaction against a claim that it would violate their duty of loyalty to Zoo. *Which of the following would be the best advice you could give them? Assume the transaction would not constitute "waste."*

A.   They should have Mr. Lion approve the transaction because he is the only "disinterested" director (also known as a "qualified" director) with respect to this transaction.

B.   They should submit the transaction for approval by Zoo's shareholders; as long as at least a majority of the 600,000 shares of Zoo common stock not owned by the four interested directors are voted in favor of the transaction after full disclosure, they will have "sanitized" the transaction.

C.   They should submit the transaction for approval by Zoo's shareholders; as long as a majority of the 560,000 qualified shares of Zoo common stock that are cast are voted in favor of the transaction after full disclosure, they will have "sanitized" the transaction.

D.   They should submit the transaction for approval by Zoo's shareholders; as long as at least 400,001 shares of Zoo common stock (regardless of who owns those shares) are voted in favor of the transaction after full disclosure, they will have "sanitized" the transaction.

Multiple Choice Question 7-6: Sam Phillips is a director of Conglomo Records Corp. ("CRC"). Several years ago, long before he was in any way associated with CRC, Sam bought the rights ("Rights") to all of the recordings of Steelbelly Perkins, an obscure blues singer, for $25,000. Due to a recent, highly popular, documentary about blues music, interest in Steelbelly Perkins has increased. CRC would like to release all of Steelbelly's old records, and Sam is willing to sell the Rights to the recordings to CRC for $300,000, which is the estimated fair market value of the Rights. *If Sam sells the Rights to CRC after full disclosure, which of the following would be correct?*

A.   If the sale was approved by a majority of the disinterested directors, the sale would be proper and Sam would not have to show his $275,000 profit was fair.

B.   If Sam sells the Rights to CRC for more than he paid for them, he would be breaching his duty of loyalty to CRC.

C.   Sam could sell the Rights to CRC for $300,000 even without full disclosure of the circumstances of the sale because he is acting in good faith.

D.   Sam could not sell the Rights to CRC without the unanimous approval of all of the disinterested directors.

E.   None of the above is correct.

Multiple Choice Question 7-7: Dave is a director, but not an officer, of Bomb Corp., a manufacturer of bombs and other military items. One day, Dave was playing golf with his former college roommate, Jeff, when Jeff told Dave that he had discovered a way to convert lead into gold. Although Dave did not believe Jeff's claim at first, he eventually came to believe that Jeff was telling the truth, especially when he examined the results of Jeff's laboratory experiments. Dave then asked Jeff why he had told him about this discovery. Jeff said: "Well, to make any money off of this discovery, I need either a ton of money or I need to partner with a company that has some heavy-duty manufacturing or industrial operations. I thought that, with your manufacturing experience with Bomb Corp., maybe you would know what companies might be interested in this idea." Dave replied: "I know that Bomb Corp. is short on cash right now and that its factory is obsolete. But I know several wealthy people who would be interested in investing in this idea. We can form a new company in which you and I will be the controlling shareholders, have those people invest a bunch of money, and then use the money to develop your lead-into-gold process." Later, Dave and Jeff formed Gold Corp. and became the majority shareholders in it. Gold Corp. subsequently began turning lead into gold, earning enormous profits. Bomb Corp. later sued Dave, claiming that the opportunity to develop the lead-into-gold process was a "corporate opportunity" that belonged to Bomb Corp. *Which of the following facts would be helpful to Dave to argue that the opportunity to develop the lead-into-gold process was not a "corporate opportunity" under the American Law Institute (ALI) Principles of Corporate Governance?*

> I.   *Dave and Jeff had been friends in college.*

> II.   *Turning lead into gold is not the same "line of business" as manufacturing military items.*

> III.   *Bomb Corp. was not financially able to take advantage of this opportunity.*

> IV.   *Dave did not use any of Bomb Corp.'s information or resources to learn of the opportunity.*

A.   All of the above.
B.   I and IV only.
C.   I, II, and IV only.
D.   III and IV only.

Multiple Choice Question 7-8: Same facts as the previous question. *Which of the following facts would be helpful to Dave to argue that the opportunity to develop the lead-into-gold process was <u>not</u> a "corporate opportunity" under the common-law (Delaware) Guth test?*

> *I.   Dave and Jeff had been friends in college.*

> *II.   Turning lead into gold is not the same "line of business" as manufacturing military items.*

> *III.   Bomb Corp. was not financially able to take advantage of this opportunity.*

> *IV.   Dave did not use any of Bomb Corp.'s information or resources to learn of the opportunity.*

A.   All of the above.
B.   I and IV only.
C.   I, II, and IV only.
D.   III and IV only.

Multiple Choice Question 7-9: Sixty percent of the stock of H&M Corp. ("H&M") is owned by the Hatfield family and the other forty percent is owned by the McCoy family. H&M's board of directors consists of seven people; four of the directors are members of the Hatfield family and the other three directors are members of the McCoy family. Because the company needed funds and was unable to obtain a bank loan, the four Hatfield directors loaned $50,000 to H&M at the prime interest rate. The three McCoy directors voted against the loan. *If the McCoy shareholders sue the Hatfield directors for breaching their duty of loyalty to H&M as a result of this loan, what is the likely result?*

A.   The Hatfields will win because the loan appears to have been fair to the corporation.
B.   The McCoys will win because a majority of disinterested directors did not approve the loan.
C.   The McCoys will win because a majority of disinterested shares were not voted in favor of the loan.
D.   The Hatfields will win because they did not engage in self-dealing.

Multiple Choice Question 7-10:   Joe and Steve formed an advertising agency called Madison Ave. Corp. ("MAC") and both of them became directors of MAC. Soon after MAC was formed, MAC approached Fashionista Corp. about becoming an advertising client of MAC.   Meanwhile, however, Steve formed another advertising agency with Henrietta called S&H Advertising Inc. ("S&H"). Steve then obtained the advertising contract with Fashionista Corp. for S&H.   Joe was not aware of Steve's actions until Fashionista Corp. has already contracted with S&H.   *MAC may have a cause of action against Steve for:*

A.   A director's conflicting interest transaction.
B.   Breach of the duty of care.
C.   Taking a corporate opportunity.
D.   None of the above.

Multiple Choice Question 7-11:   Land Corp. has five directors: A, B, C, D, and E. Directors A and B wish to sell a piece of real estate that they own to Land Corp., and the company wishes to buy it.   Directors A and B fully disclose their conflict of interest to the other three directors and abstain from voting on the transaction. Directors C, D, and E, after several weeks of negotiations with a lawyer representing Directors A and B, approve the transaction.   Some shareholders of Land Corp. who are upset that the company paid what they think is too high a price for the land, have brought suit against all five directors.   *What is the most likely result in this lawsuit?   Assume that the plaintiffs would be able to show causation and damages.*

A.   All five directors will win the case because (1) Directors A and B properly "sanitized" the transaction and (2) the Directors C, D, and E will be protected by the business judgment rule.
B.   Directors A and B will win the case because they properly "sanitized" the transaction, but Directors C, D, and E will lose the case because they will not be protected by the business judgment rule.
C.   Directors A and B will lose the case because they did not properly "sanitize" the transaction, but Directors C, D, and E will win the case because they will be protected by the business judgment rule.
D.   All five directors will lose the case because (1) Directors A and B did not properly "sanitize" the transaction and (2) Directors C, D, and E will not be protected by the business judgment rule.
E.   None of the above is correct.

Multiple Choice Question 7-12: Vince Lutz is a director of Minnesota Mining, Inc. ("MMI"), a corporation that owns several rock quarries, but that is considering selling all of its assets and dissolving. One day, Vince received a telephone call from his high school friend, Julius Smithers. Julius told Vince that he would like to buy one of MMI's rock quarries. However, Vince convinced Julius that it would be a better idea for Julius to buy a parcel of land that Vince's wife owned. This land does not have a rock quarry on it, but it is near one of MMI's rock quarries and Vince told Julius that he thought that it would be perfect for rock mining. Julius eventually agreed, and purchased the land from Vince's wife. *If MMI sues Vince, what is the likely result?*

A.   Vince will win because this was not a director's conflicting interest transaction.

B.   Vince will lose because this was a director's conflicting interest transaction and he did not have it approved by the disinterested directors or shareholders.

C.   Vince will win, because the land belonged to his wife, not Vince himself.

D.   Vince will lose, because he was required to tell MMI's board about Julius's interest in purchasing one of its rock quarries and did not.

Multiple Choice Question 7-13: *Under Delaware law, which of the following statements concerning interested director transactions is correct? Assume in each answer that approval of the interested director transaction was made after full disclosure.*

A.   Disinterested shareholder approval of an interested director transaction means that the transaction may not be successfully challenged unless the plaintiff shows the transaction was wasteful.

B.   Disinterested shareholder approval of an interested director transaction means that the transaction may not be successfully challenged unless the defendant fails to show that the transaction was not wasteful.

C.   Disinterested director approval of an interested director transaction means that the transaction may not be successfully challenged unless the plaintiff shows the transaction was unfair.

D.   Disinterested director approval of an interested director transaction means that the transaction may not be successfully challenged unless the defendant fails to show that the transaction was fair.

E.   None of the above is correct.

Multiple Choice Question 7-14: The board of directors of Plastics Corp. ("PC") consisted of eleven directors, one of whom, Jon, was an "inside director" (i.e., he worked for PC as its President) and ten of whom were "outside directors" (i.e., their only relationship to PC was serving as directors). In the fall of one year, PC's board of directors held a meeting to discuss Jon's compensation for the following year. Jon did not attend this meeting. At the meeting, the directors heard a presentation by Executive Metrics, Inc., a well-known consulting firm that the board had previously hired to make a recommendation as to Jon's compensation. Executive Metrics recommended that Jon be paid a base salary of $1.2 million, and granted options to purchase 20,000 shares of PC common stock at the current market price. The board then unanimously approved this compensation package. However, PC lost more than $20 million during the following year and the price of its stock declined by more than 50%. *If a shareholder validly sued the outside directors, alleging that Jon's compensation package violates the board's fiduciary duties, which of the following is most likely correct?*

A.   The shareholder will win if he proves that Jon's compensation was not "fair" to PC.

B.   The outside directors will win, but only if they can prove that Jon's compensation was "fair" to PC.

C.   The outside directors will win if the shareholder cannot overcome the business judgment rule.

D.   The outside directors will win, but only if the disinterested shareholders of PC had approved Jon's compensation package.

CHAPTER 8
DERIVATIVE LAWSUITS

A careful reader may have noticed a dilemma when thinking about the directors' duties of care and loyalty, coupled with the fact that MBCA § 8.01 gives the board of directors control over most of the corporation's decisions. If the directors have breached their fiduciary duties and harmed the corporation, what would stop the directors from refusing to allow the corporation to sue them? To put it in perhaps more familiar terms, it would be as if a prosecutor who has committed a crime could refuse to file charges against herself. If that were the case, wrongs would go unpunished, and everything that you learned in Chapters 6 and 7 would be of academic interest but meaningless in the real world.

Corporate law's answer to this dilemma is the derivative lawsuit, which allows a shareholder who meets certain standing requirements to force the corporation to sue those who have harmed it. In a derivative lawsuit, a shareholder sues *on behalf of* the corporation. A consequence of this is that, generally, any recovery in a derivative lawsuit goes to the *corporation* rather than the shareholder-plaintiff. Instead, the benefit that the shareholder may receive if the suit is successful is only indirect: the value of her stock may increase if the harm that had been visited on the corporation is remedied.

But one should have serious concerns about putting a shareholder in charge of making a business (litigation) decision for the corporation. Shareholders generally do not owe fiduciary duties to the corporation, so should you trust them? How do you know that a shareholder will pursue the case vigorously or competently? What if the shareholder is bringing a "strike suit," hoping to force a quick settlement that will handsomely reward the shareholder's attorney with fees (or perhaps the shareholder herself in an "under the table" arrangement)? What if the shareholder is bringing the suit in an effort to gain an advantage in some unrelated dispute with the corporation?

These concerns are further exacerbated by the fact that oftentimes in a derivative lawsuit the shareholder-plaintiff owns a rather small amount of stock. Thus, because any recovery will go to the corporation rather than the shareholder, even if she is successful and her stock increases in value, this is probably not a big incentive to bring a derivative lawsuit. To address this disincentive, corporate law provides that the court may order the corporation to pay the shareholder-plaintiff's costs and attorney fees if the case is successful. (If the case is not successful, the plaintiff is also not likely to pay any fees, because her attorney probably took the case on a contingency-fee basis.)

So, who really has the economic incentive to bring a derivative lawsuit? That's right: the plaintiff's attorney, who probably will be more concerned with getting paid large fees than with the actual result in the case. Further, if the defendants in the case are directors, they will want to settle the case quickly because a settlement that does not involve a finding of culpability may allow them to be indemnified by the corporation (as discussed in Section 6.05(B) of Chapter 6). This would probably be acceptable to the plaintiff's attorney, so long as the settlement will allow her to collect her fees. The shareholder-plaintiff probably doesn't care much, because she is more or less a figurehead with little economic interest in the suit.

This should set off alarm bells. In most litigation, the plaintiff and the defendants are the real parties in interest. If they negotiate a settlement of the case, then that is probably a good measure of the "value" of the case. But in a derivative lawsuit, one has to be suspicious of the motives of the parties involved. On the other hand, derivative lawsuits are necessary to make sure that the directors' fiduciary duties can actually be enforced. The law's solution to these issues is to impose several additional procedural requirements on derivative lawsuits that are not found in "regular" litigation. You might think of this chapter as "Civil Procedure Plus."

One final note before we get started: don't fall into the trap of thinking that *every* derivative lawsuit involves an underlying claim against some or all of the directors. True, many, if not most, of them actually do. But a derivative lawsuit may be appropriate any time that a corporation has a cause of action against someone who has harmed it, even a third party, but has not sued that person.

§ 8.01   DISTINGUISHING BETWEEN DIRECT AND DERIVATIVE LAWSUITS

Objectives: Given a fact pattern, you should be able to determine whether a cause of action may be brought as a direct action by a shareholder, or must instead be brought as a derivative action on behalf of the corporation. In addition, you should be able to explain the public policy reasons why the law provides a way for a shareholder—who normally is not entitled to make business decisions for the corporation—to sue on behalf of the corporation when the board of directors has not caused the corporation to do so itself.

> **TERMINOLOGY**
> A *derivative* lawsuit is one brought by a shareholder-plaintiff on behalf of the corporation, to remedy harm that the corporation has suffered. A *direct* lawsuit is one brought by a plaintiff in her own right, to remedy harm that the shareholder herself has suffered.

Again, derivative lawsuits involve not only everything that you learned in your Civil Procedure course, but other rules as well. While you will study those rules later in this chapter, suffice it to say for now that they can be very cumbersome for plaintiffs. Thus, generally speaking a plaintiff would prefer to bring a suit as a *direct* lawsuit, i.e., a "normal" lawsuit, rather than a derivative lawsuit. So our first issue will be trying to decide whether a given lawsuit may be brought as a direct lawsuit or instead must be brought as a derivative lawsuit.

MBCA § 7.40(1) defines a derivative lawsuit as a "civil suit in the right of a domestic corporation." Perhaps the following case will be more helpful.

Tooley v. Donaldson, Lufkin & Jenrette, Inc.
Supreme Court of Delaware
845 A.2d 1031(2004)

VEASEY, Chief Justice: Plaintiff-stockholders brought a purported class action in the Court of Chancery, alleging that the members of the board of directors of their corporation breached their fiduciary duties by agreeing to a 22-day delay in closing a proposed merger. Plaintiffs contend that the delay harmed them due to the lost time-value of the cash paid for their shares. The Court of Chancery granted the defendants' motion to dismiss on the sole ground that the claims were, "at most," claims of the corporation being asserted derivatively. They were, thus, held not to be direct claims of the stockholders, individually. Thereupon, the Court held that the plaintiffs lost their standing to bring this action when they tendered their shares in connection with the merger.

Although the trial court's legal analysis of whether the complaint alleges a direct or derivative claim reflects some concepts in our prior jurisprudence, we believe those concepts are not helpful and should be regarded as erroneous. We set forth in this Opinion the law to be applied henceforth in determining whether a stockholder's claim is derivative or direct. That issue must turn *solely* on the following questions: (1) who suffered the alleged harm (the corporation or the suing stockholders, individually); and (2) who would receive the benefit of any recovery or other remedy (the corporation or the stockholders, individually)?

To the extent we have concluded that the trial court's analysis of the direct vs. derivative dichotomy should be regarded as erroneous, we view the error as harmless in this case because the complaint does not set forth *any* claim upon which relief can be granted. In its opinion, the Court of Chancery properly found on the facts pleaded that the plaintiffs have no separate contractual right to the alleged lost time-value of money arising out of extensions in the closing of a tender offer. These extensions were made in connection with a merger where the plaintiffs' right to any payment of the merger consideration had not ripened at the time the extensions were granted. No other individual right of these stockholders having been asserted in the complaint, it was correctly dismissed.

***

Facts

Patrick Tooley and Kevin Lewis are former minority stockholders of Donaldson, Lufkin & Jenrette, Inc. (DLJ), a Delaware corporation engaged in investment banking. DLJ was acquired by Credit Suisse Group (Credit Suisse) in the Fall of 2000. Before that acquisition, AXA Financial, Inc. (AXA), which owned 71% of DLJ stock, controlled DLJ. Pursuant to a stockholder agreement between AXA and Credit Suisse, AXA agreed to exchange with Credit Suisse its DLJ stockholdings for a mix of stock and cash. The consideration received by AXA consisted primarily of stock. Cash made up one-third of the purchase price. Credit Suisse intended to acquire the remaining minority interests of publicly-held DLJ stock through a cash tender offer, followed by a merger of DLJ into a Credit Suisse subsidiary.

The tender offer price was set at $90 per share in cash. The tender offer was to expire 20 days after its commencement. The merger agreement, however, authorized two types of extensions. First, Credit Suisse could unilaterally extend the tender offer if certain conditions were not met, such as [Securities and Exchange Commission] regulatory approvals or certain payment obligations. Alternatively, DLJ and Credit Suisse could agree to postpone acceptance by Credit Suisse of DLJ stock tendered by the minority stockholders.

Credit Suisse availed itself of both types of extensions to postpone the closing of the tender offer. The tender offer was initially set to expire on October 5, 2000, but Credit Suisse invoked the five-day unilateral extension provided in the agreement. Later, by agreement between DLJ and Credit Suisse, it postponed the merger a second time so that it was then set to close on November 2, 2000.

Plaintiffs challenge the second extension that resulted in a 22-day delay. They contend that this delay was not properly authorized and harmed minority stockholders while improperly benefiting AXA. They claim damages representing the time-value of money lost through the delay.

The Decision of the Court of Chancery

The order of the Court of Chancery dismissing the complaint, and the Memorandum Opinion upon which it is based, state that the dismissal is based on the plaintiffs' lack of standing to bring the claims asserted therein. Thus, when plaintiffs tendered their shares, they lost standing under Court of Chancery Rule 23.1, the contemporaneous holding rule. The ruling before us on appeal is that the plaintiffs' claim is derivative, purportedly brought on behalf of DLJ. The Court of Chancery, relying upon our confusing jurisprudence on the direct/derivative dichotomy, based its dismissal on the following ground: "Because this delay affected all DLJ shareholders equally, plaintiffs' injury was not a special injury, and this action is, thus, a derivative action, at most."

Plaintiffs argue that they have suffered a "special injury" because they had an alleged contractual right to receive the merger consideration of $90 per share without suffering the 22-day delay arising out of the extensions under the merger agreement. But the trial court's opinion convincingly demonstrates that plaintiffs had no such contractual right that had ripened at the time the extensions were entered into: *** [Examining the merger agreement, the Court of Chancery had found that DLJ's stockholders "had no individual contractual right to payment until November 3, 2000," which is the day that their shares were accepted for payment. As a result, they had "no contractual basis to challenge a delay in the closing of the tender offer up until November 3." In fact, the merger agreement had not been breached. (Emphasis deleted.)] Moreover, no other individual right of these stockholder-plaintiffs was alleged to have been violated by the extensions.

That conclusion could have ended the case because it portended a definitive ruling that plaintiffs have no claim whatsoever on the facts alleged. But the defendants chose to argue, and the trial court chose to decide, the standing issue, which is predicated on an assertion that this claim is a derivative one asserted on behalf of the corporation, DLJ.

*** The trial court's analysis was hindered, however, because it focused on the confusing concept of "special injury" as the test for determining whether a claim is derivative or direct. The trial court's premise was as follows:

> In order to bring a *direct* claim, a plaintiff must have experienced some "special injury." [Citation omitted]. A special injury is a wrong that "is separate and distinct from that suffered by other shareholders, ... or a wrong involving a contractual right of a shareholder, such as the right to vote, or to assert majority control, which exists independently of any right of the corporation." [Citation omitted.]

In our view, the concept of "special injury" that appears in some Supreme Court and Court of Chancery cases is not helpful to a proper analytical distinction between direct and derivative actions. We now disapprove the use of the concept of "special injury" as a tool in that analysis.

The Proper Analysis to Distinguish Between Direct and Derivative Actions

The analysis must be based solely on the following questions: Who suffered the alleged harm—the corporation or the suing stockholder individually—and who would receive the benefit of the recovery or other remedy? This simple analysis is well imbedded in our jurisprudence, but some cases have complicated it by injection of the amorphous and confusing concept of "special injury."

The Chancellor, in the very recent *Agostino* case [citation omitted], correctly points this out and strongly suggests that we should disavow the concept of "special injury." In a scholarly analysis of this area of the law, he also suggests that the inquiry should be whether the stockholder has demonstrated that he or she has suffered an injury that is not dependent on an injury to the corporation. In the context of a claim for breach of fiduciary duty, the Chancellor articulated the inquiry as follows: "Looking at the body of the complaint and considering the nature of the wrong alleged and the relief requested, has the plaintiff demonstrated that he or she can prevail without showing an injury to the corporation?"* We believe that this approach is helpful in analyzing the first prong of the analysis: what person or entity has suffered the alleged harm? The second prong of the analysis should logically follow.

A Brief History of Our Jurisprudence

The derivative suit has been generally described as "one of the most interesting and ingenious of accountability mechanisms for large formal organizations." [Citation omitted.] It enables a stockholder to bring suit on behalf of the corporation for harm done to the corporation. Because a derivative suit is

---

*   [Footnote by court]: *** The Chancellor further explains that the focus should be on the person or entity to whom the relevant duty is owed.   *** [T]his test is similar to that articulated by the American Law Institute (ALI), a test that we cited with approval in Grimes v. Donald, 673 A.2d 1207 (Del. 1996). The ALI test is as follows:

> A direct action may be brought in the name and right of a holder to redress an injury sustained by, or enforce a duty owed to, the holder. An action in which the holder can prevail without showing an injury or breach of duty to the corporation should be treated as a direct action ***.

[Citation omitted].

being brought on behalf of the corporation, the recovery, if any, must go to the corporation. A stockholder who is directly injured, however, does retain the right to bring an individual action for injuries affecting his or her legal rights as a stockholder. Such a claim is distinct from an injury caused to the corporation alone. In such individual suits, the recovery or other relief flows directly to the stockholders, not to the corporation.

Determining whether an action is derivative or direct is sometimes difficult and has many legal consequences, some of which may have an expensive impact on the parties to the action. For example, if an action is derivative, the plaintiffs are then required to comply with the requirements of Court of Chancery Rule 23.1, that the stockholder: (a) retain ownership of the shares throughout the litigation; (b) make [pre-suit] demand on the board; and (c) obtain court approval of any settlement. Further, the recovery, if any, flows only to the corporation. The decision whether a suit is direct or derivative may be outcome-determinative. Therefore, it is necessary that a standard to distinguish such actions be clear, simple and consistently articulated and applied by our courts.

***

*** [T]wo confusing propositions have encumbered our caselaw governing the direct/derivative distinction. The "special injury" concept *** can be confusing in identifying the nature of the action. The same is true of the prop-osition that *** an action cannot be direct if all stockholders are equally affected or unless the stockholder's injury is separate and distinct from that suffered by other stockholders. The proper analysis has been and should remain that *** a court should look to the nature of the wrong and to whom the relief should go. The stockholder's claimed direct injury must be independent of any alleged injury to the corporation. [To bring a direct action, the] stockholder must demonstrate that the duty breached was owed to the stockholder and that he or she can prevail without showing an injury to the corporation.

Standard to Be Applied in This Case

In this case it cannot be concluded that the complaint alleges a derivative claim. There is no derivative claim asserting injury to the corporate entity. There is no relief that would go the corporation. Accordingly, there is no basis to hold that the complaint states a derivative claim.

But, it does not necessarily follow that the complaint states a direct, individual claim. While the complaint purports to set forth a direct claim, in reality, it states no claim at all. The trial court analyzed the complaint and correctly concluded that it does not claim that the plaintiffs have any rights that have been injured. Their rights have not yet ripened. The contractual claim is nonexistent until it is ripe, and that claim will not be ripe until the terms of the merger are fulfilled, including the extensions of the closing at issue here. Therefore, there is no direct claim stated in the complaint before us.

Accordingly, the complaint was properly dismissed. But, due to the reliance on the concept of "special injury" by the Court of Chancery, the ground set forth for the dismissal is erroneous, there being no derivative claim. That error is harmless, however, because, in our view, there is no direct claim either.

Conclusion

For purposes of distinguishing between derivative and direct claims, we expressly disapprove both the concept of "special injury" and the concept that a claim is necessarily derivative if it affects all stockholders equally. In our view, the tests going forward should rest on those set forth in this opinion.

We affirm the judgment of the Court of Chancery dismissing the complaint, although on a different ground from that decided by the Court of Chancery. ***

***

Now that you know how to decide whether a lawsuit may be brought as a direct action by a shareholder or whether it must be brought as a derivative lawsuit, consider the following problems. In each problem, the question is the same: *direct or derivative?*

Problems

Problem 8-1:   Jonesy, a shareholder of Seaside Resorts, Inc. ("SRI"), wishes to sue the board for refusing to allow him to inspect the minutes (records) of board and shareholder meetings.

Problem 8-2:   Smitty, a shareholder of SRI, wishes to sue the board of directors for breaching their duty of care by allegedly causing SRI to pay too much for land that SRI recently purchased.

Problem 8-3:   SRI's articles of incorporation provide that the purpose of the corporation is to run a resort hotel. Rufus, a shareholder of SRI, has learned that the board of directors is considering purchasing a paint factory and wants to sue for an injunction. (*See* MBCA § 3.04.)

Problem 8-4: Clyde, a shareholder of SRI, wishes to sue one of SRI's directors for allegedly usurping a "corporate opportunity" to purchase a hotel in a neighboring town.

Problem 8-5: Buford, a shareholder and employee of SRI, wants to sue because he believes he was fired from his job for illegal discrimination.

Problem 8-6: SRI has not held an annual shareholders meeting in more than fifteen months. Reese, a shareholder of SRI, wants to sue to compel SRI to hold a shareholders meeting. (*See* MBCA § 7.03.)

Problem 8-7: Patty, a shareholder of SRI, has learned that the board of directors is considering selling all of SRI's assets without first seeking shareholder approval[*] and wants to sue for an injunction.

Problem 8-8: Bart, a shareholder of SRI, is upset that the board of directors recently approved a stock offering (1) at a price per share that Bart believes was far too low and (2) without observing shareholders' preemptive rights to purchase more shares of SRI stock, as set forth in SRI's articles of incorporation.

Problem 8-9: SRI's business has not been performing well lately and Clem, a shareholder of SRI, thinks it's because SRI's board has been doing a poor job overseeing the corporation. Clem would like to sue the directors for breaching their duty of care because he is upset that the value of his SRI stock has greatly declined.

Problem 8-10: The shareholders in *Smith v. Van Gorkom* sued the (now former) directors of Trans Union for violating their duty of care by approving, and recommending that the shareholders approve, a merger. The shareholder-plaintiffs believe that they should have received more money for their Trans Union stock.

---

[*] As will be discussed in Chapter 12, shareholder approval is necessary for a corporation to sell all or substantially all of its assets outside the ordinary course of business.

Problem 8-11: What's the difference between a derivative lawsuit and a class action lawsuit?

One other note before moving on: in closely held corporations, which you will consider in more detail in Chapter 9, courts often are willing to characterize as direct a lawsuit that would probably be considered derivative in the context of a non-closely held corporation. But more on that in Chapter 9.

§ 8.02   PLAINTIFF STANDING REQUIREMENTS IN DERIVATIVE LAWSUITS

Objectives: Given a fact pattern in which a person wishes to bring a derivative action on behalf of a corporation, you should be able to determine whether that person has the requisite standing under MBCA § 7.41. At what point(s) in time do you make this determination?

As noted at the beginning of this chapter, the person who typically has the most to gain from a derivative lawsuit is the plaintiff's attorney rather than the shareholder-plaintiff herself. Nonetheless, not just any shareholder will do. A shareholder must have proper *standing* to be a plaintiff in a derivative lawsuit.

On the issue of standing, MBCA § 7.41 provides that:

A shareholder may not commence or maintain a derivative proceeding unless the shareholder:

      (1)   was a shareholder of the corporation at the time of the act or omission complained of or became a shareholder through transfer by operation of law from one who was a shareholder at that time; and

      (2)   fairly and adequately represents the interests of the corporation in enforcing the right of the corporation.[*]

---

[*]   Cases and statutes in other jurisdictions sometimes impose additional standing requirements, but we will concern ourselves only with the MBCA here.

Subsection (1) is sometimes referred to as the "contemporaneous ownership" rule. Basically, it means that you may not be a derivative plaintiff unless you owned stock at the time of the "harm," i.e., the "act or omission complained of" (as well as the date that the suit is filed). The usual rationale given for this rule is that it's bad public policy to allow people to "buy a lawsuit" simply by going out and buying a share of stock.[*] (By the way, is there any minimum number, value, or percentage of shares that you must own to be a derivative plaintiff?) While arguments can be made against this rationale and there doesn't seem to be much data that indicate that people who "buy lawsuits" are underhanded or do a worse job pursuing lawsuits than do other people, this is the rule in nearly every jurisdiction. MBCA § 7.41(2) adds the requirement that the shareholder-plaintiff "fairly and adequately" represent the corporation in the lawsuit. After all, the purpose of the lawsuit is to remedy a wrong that has been visited on the corporation, not to enrich the shareholder-plaintiff. Read MBCA § 7.41 (and the official comments thereto) and try the following problems:

Problems

Problem 8-12: In order to be a shareholder-plaintiff in a derivative lawsuit, must you own a physical stock certificate, or is it sufficient to own stock in "street name" through a bank or brokerage firm? *See* MBCA § 7.40(2).

Problem 8-13: May bondholders be derivative plaintiffs? What if the bonds are convertible into common stock? May holders of stock options be derivative plaintiffs?

Problem 8-14: Can a director who is not a shareholder but believes that that the other board members have breached their duty of loyalty to the corporation become a derivative plaintiff?

Problem 8-15: What if the shareholder-plaintiff sells all of her shares during the lawsuit? What if the shares are converted into cash when the corporation merges into a different corporation? *See Lewis v. Anderson*, 477 A.2d 1040 (Del. 1984).

---

[*]   Expanding this idea a bit, the argument continues that a person who bought stock at a price that was depressed by the harm—assuming the harm has become public knowledge—would receive a "windfall" if the harm is remedied and the value of the stock returns to its pre-harm level. If you think about this rationale for a while, however, you will see that it doesn't entirely hold up to scrutiny.

Problem 8-16: Al owns one share of stock in each of 12,000 or so publicly traded corporations in the United States, including ABC Corp. Every morning, Al scans the headlines in the *Wall Street Journal* hoping to find some wrongdoing by a board of directors, so that he can then call his brother Frank (an attorney) and be the first person to file a derivative lawsuit against the wrongdoers. Last year, Al filed fifty-seven derivative lawsuits. *Does Al have standing to be the plaintiff in a derivative lawsuit involving ABC Corp.? If not, why not?* See *Davis v. Comed, Inc.,* 619 F.2d 588 (6th Cir. 1980) (listing factors to consider in deciding whether plaintiff has standing).

Problem 8-17: Sarah is a director of DEF Corp., and is accused of violating her duty of loyalty by embezzling funds from the company. Sarah's husband Tom is a shareholder of DEF Corp. and wishes to bring a derivative lawsuit against Sarah on behalf of DEF Corp. *Does Tom have standing?*

Problem 8-18: Edna is the shareholder-plaintiff in a derivative lawsuit involving GHI Corp. Edna's friend Sam (an attorney) told her about the facts in the case and convinced her to file the lawsuit (with Sam as her attorney), but since then Edna has done little to keep informed about the case. *Does Edna still have standing to maintain this lawsuit?* See *Lewis v. Curtis,* 671 F.2d 779 (3d Cir. 1982). *Compare Mills v. Esmark, Inc.,* 573 F. Supp. 169 (N.D. Ill. 1983).

Problem 8-19: What are some of the ways that you could acquire stock "by operation of law" so as to satisfy the contemporaneous ownership requirement of MBCA § 7.41(1)?

Problem 8-20: Exactly *when* does the plaintiff need to own stock to satisfy the contemporaneous ownership rule? What if the "wrong" occurred over the course of several months, but the plaintiff did not own stock the entire time? See, e.g., *Valle v. North Jersey Auto Club,* 376 A.2d 1192 (N.J. 1977); *Palmer v. Morris,* 316 F.2d 649 (5th Cir. 1963).

§ 8.03   THE DEMAND REQUIREMENT

Objectives: You should be able to:

•   *Given a fact pattern, determine whether the prospective shareholder-plaintiff must make a "demand" on the corporation's board of directors that they cause the corporation to sue the alleged wrongdoer, under each of (1) the MBCA, (2) New York law, and (3) Delaware law, whichever is applicable, before the plaintiff may file suit.*

•   *Determine what happens if the board of directors accepts the prospective shareholder-plaintiff's demand.*
•   *Given a fact pattern in which the board of directors rejects the prospective shareholder-plaintiff's demand but the plaintiff still wishes to bring the derivative action, (1) explain what showing the plaintiff must make in her complaint to be able to bring suit and (2) determine whether a court would find that the plaintiff has made the required showing.*

A.   IN GENERAL

As you have seen repeatedly up to this point, the board of directors is basically in charge of making the corporation's business decisions, including litigation decisions. In a derivative action, of course, the directors have not (yet) caused the corporation to sue whoever harmed it. (If they had, then that would simply be a "normal" lawsuit by the corporation against the alleged wrongdoer.) But this does not mean that we should not give the board one last chance to decide whether to have the corporation file suit before we allow a shareholder to file a derivative lawsuit. Read MBCA § 7.42 and consider the following problem.

Problem

Problem 8-21:   A shareholder of IJK Corp., a corporation incorporated under the MBCA, wishes to sue the board of directors breaching their duty of loyalty by approving director fees of $1 million for each meeting that a director attends. *Must the shareholder make a demand on the board before filing this derivative lawsuit? If so, what do you think the board's response will be? How long will the board take to respond?*

As you probably gathered by reading MBCA § 7.42, the MBCA imposes what is called a "universal demand" requirement. However, while the universal demand requirement is certainly easy to understand, only a minority of states have taken a similar approach. Instead, many states recognize that it sometimes would be "futile" to make a demand and therefore excuse shareholder-plaintiffs from the demand requirement in some situations. (Of course, doing so means that the parties may have something else to litigate about: whether a demand was required or excused.) The following case considers how both Delaware (obviously an important state for corporate law) and New York (also important) approach this issue.

Marx v. Akers
Court of Appeals of New York
666 N.E.2d 1034 (1996)

SMITH, Judge. Plaintiff commenced this shareholder derivative action against International Business Machines Corporation (IBM) and IBM's board of directors without first demanding that the board initiate a lawsuit. The amended complaint (complaint) alleges that the board wasted corporate assets by awarding excessive compensation to IBM's executives and outside directors. The issues raised on this appeal are whether the Appellate Division abused its discretion by dismissing plaintiff's complaint for failure to make a demand and whether plaintiff's complaint fails to state a cause of action. We affirm the order of the Appellate Division because we conclude that plaintiff was not excused from making a demand with respect to the executive compensation claim and that plaintiff has failed to state a cause of action for corporate waste in connection with the allegations concerning payments to IBM's outside directors.

Facts and Procedural History

The complaint alleges that during a period of declining profitability at IBM the director defendants engaged in self-dealing by awarding excessive compensation to the 15 outside directors on the 18-member board. Although the complaint identifies only one of the three inside directors as an IBM executive (defendant Akers is identified as a former chief executive officer of IBM),* plaintiff also appears to allege that the director defendants violated their fiduciary duties to IBM by voting for unreasonably high compensation for IBM executives.

Defendants moved to dismiss the complaint for (1) failure to state a cause of action, and (2) failure to serve a demand on IBM's board to initiate a lawsuit

---

* [Footnote by court]: The other inside directors, although identified as Employee Directors, are never explicitly identified as executive officers in the complaint. However, the names of these directors appear on a chart disclosing "payments to certain executives."

based on the complaint's allegations. The [Trial] Court dismissed, holding that plaintiff failed to establish the futility of a demand. [The Trial] Court concluded that excusing a demand here would render [New York] Business Corporation Law § 626(c) "virtually meaningless in any shareholders' derivative action in which all members of a corporate board are named as defendants." Having decided the demand issue in favor of defendants, the court did not reach the issue of whether plaintiff's complaint stated a cause of action.

The Appellate Division affirmed the dismissal, concluding that the complaint did not contain any details from which the futility of a demand could be inferred. The Appellate Division found that plaintiff's objections to the level of compensation were not stated with sufficient particularity in light of statutory authority permitting directors to set their own compensation.

Background

A shareholder's derivative action is an action "brought in the right of a domestic or foreign corporation to procure a judgment in its favor, by a holder of shares or of voting trust certificates of the corporation or of a beneficial interest in such shares or certificates" ([New York] Business Corporation Law § 626(a)]). "Derivative claims against corporate directors belong to the corporation itself" [citation omitted].

"The remedy sought is for wrong done to the corporation; the primary cause of action belongs to the corporation; recovery must [inure] to the benefit of the corporation. The stockholder brings the action, in behalf of others similarly situated, to vindicate the corporate rights and a judgment on the merits is a binding adjudication of these rights" [citations omitted].

Business Corporation Law § 626(c) provides that in any shareholders' derivative action, "the complaint shall set forth with particularity the efforts of the plaintiff to secure the initiation of such action by the board or the reasons for not making such effort." Enacted in 1961, section 626(c) codified a rule of equity developed in early shareholder derivative actions requiring plaintiffs to demand that the corporation initiate an action, unless such demand was futile, before commencing an action on the corporation's behalf. [Citation omitted.] The purposes of the demand requirement are to (1) relieve courts from deciding matters of internal corporate governance by providing corporate directors with opportunities to correct alleged abuses, (2) provide corporate boards with reasonable protection from harassment by litigation on matters clearly within the discretion of directors, and (3) discourage "strike suits" commenced by shareholders for personal gain rather than for the benefit of the corporation. [Citation omitted.] "[T]he demand is generally designed to weed out unnecessary or illegitimate shareholder derivative suits." [Citation omitted.]

By their very nature, shareholder derivative actions infringe upon the managerial discretion of corporate boards. "As with other questions of corporate policy and management, the decision whether and to what extent to explore and prosecute such [derivative] claims lies within the judgment and control of the corporation's board of directors." [Citation omitted.]   Consequently, we have historically been reluctant to permit shareholder derivative suits, noting that the power of courts to direct the management of a corporation's affairs should be "exercised with restraint." [Citation omitted.]

In permitting a shareholder derivative action to proceed because a demand on the corporation's directors would be futile,

> the object is for the court to chart the course for the corporation which the directors should have selected, and which it is presumed that they would have chosen if they had not been actuated by fraud or bad faith.   Due to their misconduct, the court substitutes its judgment ad hoc for that of the directors in the conduct of its business.

[Citation omitted.]

Achieving a balance between preserving the discretion of directors to manage a corporation without undue interference, through the demand requirement, and permitting shareholders to bring claims on behalf of the corporation when it is evident that directors will wrongfully refuse to bring such claims, through the demand futility exception, has been accomplished by various jurisdictions in different ways.   One widely cited approach to demand futility which attempts to balance these competing concerns has been developed by Delaware courts and applies a two-pronged test to each case to determine whether a failure to serve a demand is justified.   At the other end of the spectrum is a universal demand requirement which would abandon particularized determinations in favor of requiring a demand in every case before a shareholder derivative suit may be filed.

The Delaware Approach

Delaware's demand requirement, codified in Delaware Chancery Court Rule 23.1, provides, in relevant part,

> In a derivative action brought by 1 or more shareholders or members to enforce a right of a corporation *** [the complaint shall allege] with particularity the efforts, if any, made by the plaintiff to obtain the action the plaintiff desires from the directors

or comparable authority and the reasons for the plaintiff's failure to obtain the action or for not making the effort.

Interpreting Rule 23.1, the Delaware Supreme Court in *Aronson v. Lewis*, 472 A.2d 805 [(Del. 1984)] developed a two-prong test for determining the futility of a demand. Plaintiffs must allege particularized facts which create a reasonable doubt that,

> (1) the directors are disinterested and independent and (2) the challenged transaction was otherwise the product of a valid exercise of business judgment. Hence, the Court of Chancery must make two inquiries, one into the independence and disinterestedness of the directors and the other into the substantive nature of the challenged transaction and the board's approval thereof." [Citation omitted.]

The two branches of the *Aronson* test are disjunctive. [Citation omitted.] Once director interest has been established, the business judgment rule becomes inapplicable and the demand excused without further inquiry. [Citation omitted.] Similarly, a director whose independence is compromised by undue influence exerted by an interested party cannot properly exercise business judgment and the loss of independence also justifies the excusal of a demand without further inquiry. [Citation omitted.] Whether a board has validly exercised its business judgment must be evaluated by determining whether the directors exercised procedural (informed decision) and substantive (terms of the transaction) due care. [Citation omitted.]

The reasonable doubt threshold of Delaware's two-fold approach to demand futility has been criticized. The use of a standard of proof which is the heart of a jury's determination in a criminal case has raised questions concerning its applicability in the corporate context. [Citation omitted.] The reasonable doubt standard has also been criticized as overly subjective, thereby permitting a wide variance in the application of Delaware law to similar facts. [Citation omitted.]

Universal Demand

A universal demand requirement would dispense with the necessity of making case-specific determinations and impose an easily applied bright line rule. The Business Law Section of the American Bar Association has proposed requiring a demand in all cases, without exception, and permits the commencement of a derivative proceeding within 90 days of the demand unless the demand is rejected earlier. [MBCA § 7.42(1).] However, plaintiffs may file suit before the expiration of 90 days, even if their demand has not been rejected, if the corporation would suffer irreparable injury as a result. [MBCA § 7.42(2).]

The American Law Institute (ALI) has also proposed a "universal" demand. Section 7.03 of ALI's Principles of Corporate Governance would require shareholder derivative action plaintiffs to serve a written demand on the corporation *unless* a demand is excused because "the plaintiff makes a specific showing that irreparable injury to the corporation would otherwise result." [ALI Principles of Corporate Governance, § 7.03(b).] Once a demand has been made and rejected, however, the ALI would subject the board's decision to "an elaborate set of standards that calibrates the deference afforded the decision of the directors to the character of the claim being asserted." [Citation omitted.]

At least [eleven] States have adopted, by statute, the universal demand requirement proposed in the Model Business Corporation Act. Georgia, Michigan, Wisconsin, Montana, Virginia, New Hampshire, Mississippi, Connecticut, Nebraska and North Carolina require shareholders to wait 90 days after serving a demand before filing a derivative suit unless the demand is rejected before the expiration of the 90 days, or irreparable injury to the corporation would result. [Citations omitted.] ***

New York State has also considered and continues to consider implementing a universal demand requirement. However, even though bills to adopt a universal demand have been presented over three legislative sessions, the Legislature has yet to enact a universal demand requirement. [Citations omitted.]

New York's Approach to Demand Futility

Although instructive, neither the universal demand requirement nor the Delaware approach to demand futility is adopted here. Since New York's demand requirement is codified in [New York] Business Corporation Law § 626(c), a universal demand may only be adopted by the Legislature. Delaware's approach, which resembles New York law in some respects, incorporates a "reasonable doubt" standard which, as we have already pointed out, has provoked criticism as confusing and overly subjective. An analysis of the *Barr* decision compels the conclusion that in New York, a demand would be futile if a complaint alleges with particularity that (1) a majority of the directors are interested in the transaction, or (2) the directors failed to inform themselves to a degree reasonably necessary about the transaction, or (3) the directors failed to exercise their business judgment in approving the transaction.

In *Barr v. Wackman*, [329 N.E.2d 180 (N.Y. 1975)], we considered whether the plaintiff was excused from making a demand where the board of Talcott National Corporation (Talcott), consisting of 13 outside directors, a director affiliated with a related company and four interested inside directors, rejected a merger proposal involving Gulf & Western Industries (Gulf & Western) in favor of another proposal on allegedly less favorable terms for Talcott and its shareholders. The merger proposal, memorialized in a board-approved "agreement in principle," proposed exchanging one share of Talcott common stock for approximately $24 consisting of $17 in cash and 0.6 of a warrant to purchase Gulf & Western stock, worth approximately $7. This proposal was abandoned in favor of a cash tender offer for Talcott shares by Associates First Capital Corporation (a Gulf & Western subsidiary) at $20 per share—$4 less than proposed for the merger.

The plaintiff in *Barr* alleged that Talcott's board discarded the merger proposal after the four "controlling" inside directors received pecuniary and personal benefits from Gulf & Western in exchange for ceding control of Talcott on terms less favorable to Talcott's shareholders. As alleged in the complaint, these benefits included new and favorable employment contracts for nine Talcott officers, including five-year employment contracts for three of the controlling directors. ***

In *Barr*, we held that insofar as the complaint attacked the controlling directors' acts in causing the corporation to enter into a transaction for their own financial benefit, demand was excused because of the self-dealing, or self-interest of those directors in the challenged transaction. Specifically, we pointed to the allegation that the controlling directors "breached their fiduciary obligations to Talcott in return for personal benefits." [Citation omitted.]

We also held in *Barr*, however, that as to the disinterested outside directors, demand could be excused even in the absence of their receiving any financial benefit from the transaction. That was because the complaint alleged that, by approving the terms of the less advantageous offer, those directors were guilty of a "breach of their duties of due care and diligence to the corporation." [Citation omitted.] Their performance of the duty of care would have "put them on notice of the claimed self-dealing of the affiliated directors." [Citation omitted.] The complaint charged that the outside directors failed "to do more than passively rubber-stamp the decisions of the active managers." [Citation omitted.] These allegations, the *Barr* Court concluded, also excused demand as to the charges against the disinterested directors.

Barr also makes clear that "[i]t is not sufficient *** merely to name a majority of the directors as parties defendant with conclusory allegations of wrongdoing or control by wrongdoers" [citation omitted] to justify failure to make a demand. Thus, *Barr* reflects the statutory requirement that the complaint "shall set forth with particularity the *** reasons for not making such effort." [Citing New York Business Corporation Law § 626(c).]

Unfortunately, various courts have overlooked the explicit warning that conclusory allegations of wrongdoing against each member of the board are not sufficient to excuse demand and have misinterpreted *Barr* as excusing demand whenever a majority of the board members who approved the transaction are named as defendants. [Citations omitted.] As stated most recently [in a New York case], "[t]he rule is clear in this State that no demand is necessary if 'the complaint alleges acts for which a majority of the directors may be liable and plaintiff reasonably concluded that the board would not be responsive to a demand'." [Citations omitted.] The problem with such an approach is that it permits plaintiffs to frame their complaint in such a way as to automatically excuse demand, thereby allowing the exception to swallow the rule.

We thus deem it necessary to offer the following elaboration of *Barr's* demand/futility standard. [Thus, the rule in New York is as follows.] (1) Demand is excused because of futility when a complaint alleges with particularity that a majority of the board of directors is interested in the challenged transaction. Director interest may either be self-interest in the transaction at issue [citation omitted] or a loss of independence because a director with no direct interest in a transaction is "controlled" by a self-interested director. (2) Demand is excused because of futility when a complaint alleges with particularity that the board of directors did not fully inform themselves about the challenged transaction to the extent reasonably appropriate under the circumstances. [Citation omitted.] The "long-standing rule" is that a director "does not exempt himself from liability by failing to do more than passively rubber-stamp the decisions of the active managers." [Citation omitted.] (3) Demand is excused because of futility when a complaint alleges with particularity that the challenged transaction was so egregious on its face that it could not have been the product of sound business judgment of the directors.

The Current Appeal

Plaintiff argues that the demand requirement was excused both because the outside directors awarded themselves generous compensation packages and because of the acquiescence of the disinterested directors in the executive compensation schemes. The complaint states:

> Plaintiff has made no demand upon the directors of IBM to institute this lawsuit because such demand would be futile. *** [E]ach of the directors authorized, approved, participated and/or acquiesced in the acts and transactions complained of herein and are liable therefor. Further, each of the Non-Employee [outside] Directors has received and retained the benefit of his excessive compensation and each of the other directors has received and retained the benefit of the incentive compensation described

above. The defendants cannot be expected to vote to prosecute an action against themselves. Demand upon the company to bring action [sic] to redress the wrongs herein is therefore unnecessary.

Defendants argue that neither the [Trial] Court nor the Appellate Division abused its discretion in holding that plaintiff's complaint did not set forth the futility of a demand with particularity.

As in *Barr*, we look to the complaint here to determine whether the allegations are sufficient and establish with particularity that demand would have been futile. Here, the plaintiff alleges that the compensation awarded to IBM's outside directors and certain IBM executives was excessive.

Defendants' motion to dismiss for failure to make a demand as to the allegations concerning the compensation paid to IBM's executive officers [i.e., the three "inside" directors] was properly granted. A board is not interested "in voting compensation for one of its members as an executive or in some other nondirectorial capacity, such as a consultant to the corporation," although "so-called 'back-scratching' arrangements, pursuant to which all directors vote to approve each other's compensation as officers or employees, do not constitute disinterested directors' action." [Citation omitted.] Since only three directors are alleged to have received the benefit of the executive compensation scheme, plaintiff has failed to allege that a majority of the board was interested in setting executive compensation. Nor do the allegations that the board used faulty accounting procedures to calculate executive compensation levels move beyond "conclusory allegations of wrongdoing" [citation omitted] which are insufficient to excuse demand. The complaint does not allege particular facts in contending that the board failed to deliberate or exercise its business judgment in setting those levels. Consequently, the failure to make a demand regarding the fixing of executive compensation was fatal to that portion of the complaint challenging that transaction.

However, a review of the complaint indicates that plaintiff also alleged that a majority of the board was self-interested in setting the compensation of outside directors because the outside directors comprised a majority of the board.

Directors are self-interested in a challenged transaction where they will receive a direct financial benefit from the transaction which is different from the benefit to shareholders generally. [Citations omitted.] A director who votes for a raise in directors' compensation is always "interested" because that person will receive a personal financial benefit from the transaction not shared in by stockholders. [Citations omitted.] Consequently, a demand was excused as to plaintiff's allegations that the compensation set for outside directors was excessive.

Corporate Waste

Our conclusion that demand should have been excused as to the part of the complaint challenging the fixing of [the fifteen "outside"] directors' compensation does not end our inquiry. We must also determine whether plaintiff has stated a cause of action regarding director compensation, i.e., some wrong to the corporation. We conclude that plaintiff has not, and thus dismiss the complaint in its entirety.

Historically, directors did not receive any compensation for their work as directors. [Citation omitted.] Thus, a bare allegation that corporate directors voted themselves excessive compensation was sufficient to state a cause of action. [Citations omitted.] Many jurisdictions, including New York, have since changed the common-law rule by statute providing that a corporation's board of directors has the authority to fix director compensation unless the corporation's charter or bylaws provides otherwise. Thus, the allegation that directors have voted themselves compensation is clearly no longer an allegation which gives rise to a cause of action, as the directors are statutorily entitled to set those levels. Nor does a conclusory allegation that the compensation directors have set for themselves is excessive give rise to a cause of action. [As one authority stated:]

> The courts will not undertake to review the fairness of official salaries, at the suit of a shareholder attacking them as excessive, unless wrongdoing and oppression or possible abuse of a fiduciary position are shown. However, the courts will take a hand in the matter at the instance of the corporation or of shareholders in extreme cases. A case of fraud is presented where directors increase their collective salaries so as to use up nearly the entire earnings of a company; where directors or officers appropriate the income so as to deprive shareholders of reasonable dividends, or perhaps so reduce the assets as to threaten the corporation with insolvency."

[Citation omitted.] Thus, a complaint challenging the excessiveness of director compensation must—to survive a dismissal motion—allege compensation rates excessive on their face or other facts which call into question whether the compensation was fair to the corporation when approved, the good faith of the directors setting those rates, or that the decision to set the compensation could not have been a product of valid business judgment.*

---

*   [Footnote by court]: There is general agreement that the allocation of the burden of proof differs depending on whether the compensation was approved by disinterested directors or shareholders, or by interested directors. Plaintiffs must prove wrongdoing or waste as to compensation arrangements regarding disinterested directors or shareholders, but directors

Applying the foregoing principles to plaintiff's complaint, it is clear that it must be dismissed. The complaint alleges that the directors increased their compensation rates from a base of $20,000 plus $500 for each meeting attended to a retainer of $55,000 plus 100 shares of IBM stock over a five-year period. The complaint also alleges that "[t]his compensation bears little relation to the part-time services rendered by the Non-Employee Directors or to the profitability of IBM. The board's responsibilities have not increased, its performance, measured by the company's earnings and stock price, has been poor yet its compensation has increased far in excess of the cost of living."

These conclusory allegations do not state a cause of action. There are no factually based allegations of wrongdoing or waste which would, if true, sustain a verdict in plaintiff's favor. Plaintiff's bare allegations that the compensation set lacked a relationship to duties performed or to the cost of living are insufficient as a matter of law to state a cause of action. Accordingly, the order of the Appellate Division should be affirmed, with costs.

Marx discusses three different approaches to the demand issue: the universal demand requirement, Delaware law (represented by the unfortunately worded test from the *Aronson v. Lewis* case), and New York law. Despite their facial differences, the Delaware approach and the New York approach may not be that different. For example, the first part of the Delaware test is largely similar to the first part of the New York test, both basically excusing demand if the plaintiff can show that a majority of the board is interested in the challenged transaction. And an argument can be made that the second part of the Delaware test is a summary of the second and third parts of the New York test. The chart on the next page may help you visualize this.

---

who approve their own compensation bear the burden of proving that the transaction was fair to the corporation. [Citations omitted.] ***

Delaware		New York
[For demand to be excused] Plaintiff must allege particularized facts which create a reasonable doubt that		Demand is excused if complaint alleges with particularity that
(1) the directors are disinterested and independent, or	↔	(1) a majority of the board of directors is interested in the challenged transaction, or
(2) the challenged transaction was otherwise the product of a valid exercise of business judgment	↔	(2) the board of directors did not fully inform themselves about the challenged transaction to the extent reasonably appropriate under the circumstances, or
	↔	(3) the challenged transaction was so egregious on its face that it could not have been the product of sound business judgment of the directors.

But let's consider what these tests *mean* in a bit more detail. First, what is the "challenged transaction"? Obviously, this is the transaction underlying the derivative lawsuit. If the plaintiff is arguing, for example, that the directors breached their duty of loyalty by paying themselves large bonuses, then the bonuses are the "challenged transaction."

B.   EXCUSING DEMAND DUE TO DIRECTOR INTEREST

Next, how can one meet the first part of the Delaware *Aronson* test, or the first part of the New York *Marx* test? Citing a prior unpublished opinion, this is how the Delaware Chancery Court described the test in *In re The Limited, Inc. Shareholders Litigation*, 2002 WL 537692 (Del. Ch. Ct., Mar. 27, 2002):

> To meet the first prong of the *Aronson* test and adequately show the futility of a pre-suit demand, a plaintiff must plead particularized facts sufficiently demonstrating that the defendant directors had a financial interest in the challenged transaction, that they were motivated by a desire to retain their positions on the board or within the company (an entrenchment motive), or that

they were dominated or controlled by a person interested in the transaction.

Id. at *3 (citation omitted).

This seems like a better description of the first prong of the *Aronson* test than what was presented by the *Aronson* court itself. Speaking of which, the Delaware Supreme Court described the *Aronson* test somewhat differently in a later case: "Stated obversely, the concept of reasonable doubt is akin to the concept that the stockholder has a "reasonable belief" that the board lacks independence or that the transaction was not protected by the business judgment rule. The concept of reasonable belief is an objective test ...." *Grimes v. Donald*, 673 A.2d 1207, 1217 n.17 (Del. 1996).

How many of the directors must be "interested" to excuse a demand? In New York, *Marx* itself specifically said a majority. In Delaware, cases after *Aronson* have also confirmed that that a plaintiff must create a reasonable doubt about the disinterestedness and independence of a majority of the directors to have demand excused under the first prong of *Aronson*.*

The *Disney* litigation described in Chapter 6 is helpful in showing when directors may not be sufficiently disinterested and independent. In *Disney*, the plaintiffs argued, among other things, that the Disney board had breached its fiduciary duties to Disney when it approved Michael Ovitz's employment agreement (which eventually resulted in him receiving more than $130 million in severance compensation). The plaintiffs filed the case without first making a demand. At the time, there were fifteen Disney board members, including Michael Eisner, who was the CEO and a close friend of Ovitz. (Ovitz was no longer on the board.) As the court observed:

> ***   Plaintiffs concede that they failed to make a demand on the Board regarding this issue, but argue that such demand would have been futile and, therefore, is excused. With respect to the first prong of the *Aronson* test, Plaintiffs offer several reasons for their assertion that the Board is not independent. Chief among them is Plaintiffs' assertion that [Michael] Eisner dominates and controls the Board. Plaintiffs argue that at least twelve of the fifteen members of the Disney Board who would have considered such a demand *** had such strong ties to Eisner that they would not have been able to make an impartial decision with respect to any demand Plaintiffs may have

---

* *See also Untermeyer v. Fidelity Daily Income Trust*, 580 F.2d 22 (1st Cit. 1978) (demand excused when half of the board was shown to be interested).

made. In order to prove domination and control by Eisner, Plaintiffs must demonstrate first that Eisner was personally interested in obtaining the Board's approval of the [Ovitz] Employment Agreement and, second, that a majority of the Board could not exercise business judgment independent of Eisner in deciding whether to approve the [Ovitz] Employment Agreement.

In re The Walt Disney Co,. Derivative Litigation, 731 A.2d 342, 354-55 (Del. Ch. 1998).

Examining the plaintiff's contentions in detail, the Delaware Chancery Court concluded that the plaintiffs' demand was not excused. First, the plaintiffs failed to show how *Eisner* was "personally interested" in *Ovitz's* employment agreement. While the two were good friends, that was not enough to create a reasonable doubt that Eisner was disinterested in how much his friend was paid.* Second, the court found that, even if it were to assume that Eisner was personally interested in Ovitz's compensation, the plaintiffs had shown a reasonable doubt concerning the independence of only four of the Disney directors, which was far less than a majority of them.

One of the four directors who may have been "dominated and controlled" by Eisner (and thus not independent and disinterested) was Irwin Russell. The court's discussion of Mr. Russell may be interesting to you as a future lawyer. As the court found:

> Director Irwin E. Russell is an entertainment lawyer who serves as Eisner's personal counsel and has a long history of personal and business ties to Eisner. As a result, Plaintiffs allege Russell is unable to exercise independent business judgment.

> In addition to being Eisner's personal counsel: Russell's law office is listed as the mailing address for Eisner's primary residence; Russell is the registered agent for several entities in which Eisner is involved; Russell has represented Eisner in connection with Eisner's negotiation of the Eisner Compensation Agreement in 1996 and early 1997 (during which negotiation he recused himself from his Board role); and, Plaintiffs assert, Russell practices in a small firm for which the fees derived from Eisner likely represent a large portion of the total amount of fees received by the firm. Accordingly, it appears Plaintiffs have raised a reasonable doubt as to Russell's independence of Eisner's influence for the purpose of considering a demand

---

*   To be fair, plaintiffs' argument was more sophisticated than this summary. *See id.* at 355-56.

Id. at 360. If you want to read why the other directors may or may not have lost their independence due to Eisner's alleged domination and control over them, see *id.* at 356-61.

C.   OTHER GROUNDS TO EXCUSE DEMAND

What about the second prong of the Delaware *Aronson* test and the second and third prongs of the New York *Marx* test? Hopefully, these should have reminded you of ways to overcome the business judgment rule (other than showing that the directors had a conflict of interest). Basically, the plaintiff must allege—with particularity in her complaint—some reason to think that the board would not be entitled to the protection of the business judgment rule with respect to the challenged transaction, such as where the board was not properly informed before making a decision (think back to *Smith v. Van Gorkom* from Chapter 6) or that the board made an irrational decision (the *Marx* court, in its third prong, referred to this as a decision "so egregious on its face that it could not have been the product of sound business judgment ...."). By the way, at this point, you might want to go back and make sure you understood why the plaintiff in *Marx* was not able to have demand excuse under either the second or third prongs, with respect to the claim that the "inside" directors received excessive compensation.

But what if the plaintiff is suing because the board was "asleep at the switch," as in the *Caremark* case from Chapter 6? In that situation, it doesn't seem that the plaintiff would be able to show that a majority of the board was interested in the challenged transaction (or even that there *was* a "challenged transaction"). Similarly, if the board didn't *decide* anything, then it wouldn't seem possible to show, under *Aronson*, that the "challenged transaction was otherwise the product of a valid exercise of business judgment," or either the second or third prongs of the *Marx* test.

So, what should you do in such a case? In *Rales v. Blasband*, 634 A.2d 927, 934 (Del. 1993), the Delaware Supreme Court set forth the following test for cases in which the plaintiff is not challenging a *decision* made by the *current* board. In such a case, the plaintiff must "create a reasonable doubt that, as of the time the complaint is filed, the board of directors could have properly exercised its independent and disinterested business judgment in responding to a demand." The court also specified three situations in which this rule would apply:

> Consistent with the context and rationale of the *Aronson* decision, a court should not apply the *Aronson* test for demand futility where the board that would be considering the demand did not make a business decision which is being challenged in the derivative suit. This situation would arise in three principal scenarios: (1) where a

business decision was made by the board of a company, but a majority of the directors making the decision have been replaced; (2) where the subject of the derivative suit is not a business decision of the board; and (3) where *** the decision being challenged was made by the board of a different corporation [such as a parent corporation].

Id. at 933-34 (citations omitted).

D.   EFFECTS OF ACCEPTANCE OR REJECTION OF DEMAND

Obviously, if the board accepts the plaintiff's demand, then we no longer need the prospective derivative plaintiff.   ("Thanks for bringing this to our attention, but we'll take it from here!")   At that point, it would become a "normal" lawsuit with the corporation as the plaintiff and the wrongdoer(s) as the defendant(s).   But if the board thought this was such a great lawsuit, the board would have probably already caused the corporation to file it.   Therefore, the likely response when a board is presented with a demand is that the board will reject it.

What effect does this rejection have—is it still possible for the plaintiff to file the derivative lawsuit?   Yes, but it will be more difficult.   Basically, courts treat the decision to reject a demand like any other business decision made by a board.   In other words, the decision will be protected by the business judgment rule and the plaintiff must, in order to file the lawsuit, overcome the business judgment rule such as by showing that a majority of the directors had a conflict of interest.[*]   MBCA § 7.44(d) provides that if the plaintiff files the derivative lawsuit after her demand was rejected (remember, under the MBCA the plaintiff *always* has to make a demand), then her "complaint shall allege with particularity facts establishing either (1) that a majority of the board of directors did not consist of qualified directors [as defined in MBCA § 1.43(a)] at the time the determination was made [that is, when the demand was rejected] or (2) that the requirements of subsection (a) [i.e., MBCA § 7.44(a)] have not been met."   What are these requirements of MBCA § 7.44(a)?   Go read it and see.

---

[*]   Here, Delaware adds a wrinkle: cases in Delaware have held that if the plaintiff *does* make a demand, then she has *conceded* that the directors are disinterested.   *See Levine v. Smith*, 591 A.2d 194 (Del. 1991).   The effect of this rule is that no right-minded plaintiff would ever make a demand.   Why not just file the lawsuit without making a demand and then argue over whether a demand was required?

At least outside the MBCA's universal demand requirement, deciding whether a demand is required or excused can be tricky. Hopefully, the following problems will help you better understand these issues:

Problems

Problem 8-22: *To whom must the plaintiff make a demand (if it is required)? Must a demand be in writing?*

Problem 8-23: *Does being a possible defendant in the lawsuit mean that a director is "interested in the challenged transaction"?*

Problem 8-24: The board of directors of Behemoth Corp. consists of seven persons. Ahmad, a shareholder of Behemoth Corp., wants to bring a derivative action against one of the directors, claiming that she usurped a "corporate opportunity," unbeknownst to the other directors. *Is demand required under (1) the MBCA, (2) Delaware law, and (3) New York law?*

Problem 8-25: Same facts as Problem 8-24. Bethany, a shareholder of Behemoth Corp., wants to bring a derivative action against three of the directors, claiming that they breached their duty of loyalty with respect to certain interested director transactions. *Is demand required under (1) the MBCA, (2) Delaware law, and (3) New York law? What if one of the other four directors is employed by one of the defendant-directors?*

Problem 8-26: Same facts as Problem 8-24. Charles, a shareholder of Behemoth Corp., wants to bring a derivative action against all of the directors, claiming that they breached their duty of care by approving a new product that turned out to be a disaster for Behemoth. Before approving this product, the board had spent months doing market research and determined that it was likely that Behemoth would be able to sell sufficient quantities of the product to make a profit. *Is demand required under (1) the MBCA, (2) Delaware law, and (3) New York law?*

Problem 8-27: Same facts as Problem 8-24. Diego, a shareholder of Behemoth Corp., wants to bring a derivative action against Tiny Corp., a customer of Behemoth Corp. for more than $1 million in unpaid purchases. None of the directors of Behemoth Corp. has any relationship to Tiny Corp. *Is demand required under (1) the MBCA, (2) Delaware law, and (3) New York law?*

Problem 8-28: Same facts as Problem 8-27. In addition, assume
that Diego makes a demand, but Behemoth's board then spends
one hour at a board meeting discussing and debating whether to
accept the demand before deciding to reject the demand. *May
Diego still file his derivative lawsuit? If so, how?*

§ 8.04   MOTIONS TO DISMISS BY BOARDS OR SPECIAL LITIGATION COMMITTEES

*Objectives: Given a fact pattern where a shareholder-plaintiff has
filed a derivative lawsuit, either (1) where no demand was
required or (2) after a demand was made but rejected, you should
be able to determine how a court will rule if either the board, or a
"special litigation committee" of the board, moves to dismiss the
lawsuit. You should be able to make this determination applying
(1) the MBCA, (2) Delaware law, and (3) New York law,
whichever is applicable. In addition, you should be able to
describe the necessary qualifications of members of a special
litigation committee.*

Let's assume now that the derivative lawsuit is pending. If there's one
thing that we know about litigation in the United States, at least if it involves a lot
of money, it's that the case will take a long time. During this period, the board
could do different things. For one, it could simply let the lawsuit "play out," that
is, let the shareholder-plaintiff and the defendant(s) battle it out, with the
corporation not being actively involved. Another possibility is that the board, if it
believes that the case is not meritorious or otherwise in the best interests of the
corporation, could seek to have the lawsuit dismissed.

Can the board do so, or does the fact that the shareholder-plaintiff was able
to file the case mean that the board no longer has any control over a derivative
lawsuit? Few courts have gone so far as to say that the board has lost all control
over the lawsuit simply because it's been properly filed.[*] On the other hand,
perhaps a court should be a bit "suspicious" about a board that seeks to dismiss a
derivative lawsuit, particularly if the lawsuit involves a claim against some of the
directors. Due to a great increase in derivative lawsuits in the 1970s, corporate
lawyers came up with an ingenious solution to this problem: the "special litigation
committee." As you saw in Chapter 5, the board can delegate some of its powers

---

[*]   *But see Miller v. Register & Tribune Syndicate, Inc.*, 336 N.W.2d 709 (Iowa 1983) (if
majority of directors are defendants in derivative lawsuit, court will disregard recommendation
of any committee appointed by the board).

to others in the corporation, such as a committee of the board. So, why not create a committee of directors, and then delegate to that committee the task of deciding whether the derivative lawsuit should continue, or whether the corporation should move to dismiss the case?

Who should be on this committee? Clearly, if the committee consists of the same people who are defendants in the underlying lawsuit, then the court will not respect its decision—would you? Me neither. Thus, the committee will consist of non-defendant directors. To make the committee "look" even better, maybe you should bring in some new directors who weren't even on the board when the wrongdoing took place.

Let's say that you are a brand new director who has been appointed to a special litigation committee and given the task of deciding whether a derivative lawsuit—in which some of your fellow directors are defendants—should continue or whether the corporation should instead move to dismiss the case. Will there be any psychological pressure on you to come to the "correct" decision? Let's take a look at how a few different courts (again, New York and Delaware) treated this situation.

In *Auerbach v. Bennett*, four directors of General Telephone & Electronics Corporation (GTE) were involved in making illegal bribes. (The other eleven directors apparently had not known about these bribes beforehand.) When this news came out, a shareholder filed a derivative lawsuit against these four directors as well as some other employees. Rather than arguing that the shareholder should have made a demand before filing the lawsuit, the board created a "special litigation committee" to, among other things, determine the corporation's position with respect to the lawsuit. The committee consisted of three new directors who joined the board after the illegal bribes had occurred. The following is the portion of the opinion in which the court sets forth New York's approach to special litigation committees.

Auerbach v. Bennett
New York Court of Appeals
393 N.E.2d 994 (1979)

JONES, J. ***

***

In the present case we confront a special instance of the application of the business judgment rule and inquire whether it applies in its full vigor to shield from judicial scrutiny the decision of a three-person minority committee of the board acting on behalf of the full board not to prosecute a shareholder's derivative action. The record in this case reveals that the board is a 15-member board, and that the derivative suit was brought against four of the directors. Nothing suggests that any of the other directors participated in any of the challenged [bribes]. Indeed *** no other directors had any prior knowledge of or were in any way involved in any of these [bribes]. Other directors had, however, been members of the board in the period during which the [bribes]occurred. Each of the three director members of the special litigation committee joined the board thereafter.

The business judgment rule does not foreclose inquiry by the courts into the disinterested independence of those members of the board chosen by it to make the corporate decision on its behalf[,] here the members of the special litigation committee. Indeed the rule shields the deliberations and conclusions of the chosen representatives of the board only if they possess a disinterested independence and do not stand in a dual relation which prevents an unprejudicial exercise of judgment. [Citation omitted.]

We examine then the proof submitted by defendants. It is not disputed that the members of the special litigation committee were not members of the corporation's board of directors at the time of the [bribes] in question. Howard Blauvelt, chairman of the board of Continental Oil Company, had been elected to the corporation's board of directors on October 9, 1975. Dr. John T. Dunlop, Lamont University professor at the Graduate School of Business Administration of Harvard University had been elected to the board on April 21, 1976. James R. Barker, chairman of the board and chief executive officer of Moore McCormack Resources, Inc., was added as the third member of the committee when he was elected to the board on July 19, 1976. None of the three had had any prior affiliation with the corporation. Notwithstanding the vigorous and imaginative hypothesizing and innuendo of counsel there is nothing in this record to raise a triable issue of fact as to the independence and disinterested status of these three directors.

The contention of [the plaintiff] that any committee authorized by the board of which defendant directors were members must be held to be legally infirm and may not be delegated power to terminate a derivative action must be rejected. In the very nature of the corporate organization it was only the existing board of directors which had authority on behalf of the corporation to direct the investigation and to assure the cooperation of corporate employees, and it is only that same board by its own action or as here pursuant to authority duly delegated by it which had authority to decide whether to prosecute the claims against defendant directors. The board in this instance, with slight adaptation, followed prudent practice in observing the general policy that when individual members of a board of directors prove to have personal interests which may conflict with the interests of the corporation, such interested directors must be excluded while the remaining members of the board proceed to consideration and action. [Citation omitted.] Courts have consistently held that the business judgment rule applies where some directors are charged with wrongdoing, so long as the remaining directors making the decision are disinterested and independent. [Citations omitted.]

***

We turn then to the action of the special litigation committee itself which comprised two components. First, there was the selection of procedures appropriate to the pursuit of its charge, and second, there was the ultimate substantive decision, predicated on the procedures chosen and the data produced thereby, not to pursue the claims advanced in the shareholders' derivative actions. The latter, substantive decision falls squarely within the embrace of the business judgment doctrine, involving as it did the weighing and balancing of legal, ethical, commercial, promotional, public relations, fiscal and other factors familiar to the resolution of many if not most corporate problems. To this extent the conclusion reached by the special litigation committee is outside the scope of our review. Thus, the courts cannot inquire as to which factors were considered by that committee or the relative weight accorded them in reaching that substantive decision ***. Inquiry into such matters would go to the very core of the business judgment made by the committee. To permit judicial probing of such issues would be to emasculate the business judgment doctrine as applied to the actions and determinations of the special litigation committee. Its substantive evaluation of the problems posed and its judgment in their resolution are beyond our reach.

As to the other component of the committee's activities, however, the situation is different ***. As to the methodologies and procedures best suited to the conduct of an investigation of facts and the determination of legal liability, the courts are well equipped by long and continuing experience and practice to make determinations. In fact they are better qualified in this regard than are corporate directors in general. Nor do the determinations to be made in the adoption of procedures partake of the nuances or special perceptions or comprehensions of business judgment or corporate activities or interests. The question is solely how appropriately to set about to gather the pertinent data.

While the court may properly inquire as to the adequacy and appropriateness of the committee's investigative procedures and methodologies, it may not under the guise of consideration of such factors trespass in the domain of business judgment. At the same time those responsible for the procedures by which the business judgment is reached may reasonably be required to show that they have pursued their chosen investigative methods in good faith. What evidentiary proof may be required to this end will, of course, depend on the nature of the particular investigation, and the proper reach of disclosure at the instance of the shareholders will in turn relate inversely to the showing made by the corporate representatives themselves. The [committee] may be expected to show that the areas and subjects to be examined are reasonably complete and that there has been a good-faith pursuit of inquiry into such areas and subjects. What has been uncovered and the relative weight accorded in evaluating and balancing the several factors and considerations are beyond the scope of judicial concern. Proof, however, that the investigation has been so restricted in scope, so shallow in execution, or otherwise so *pro forma* or halfhearted as to constitute a pretext or sham, consistent with the principles underlying the application of the business judgment doctrine, would raise questions of good faith or conceivably fraud which would never be shielded by that doctrine.

In addition to the issue of the disinterested independence of the special litigation committee, addressed above, the disposition of the present appeal turns, then, on whether on defendants' motions for summary judgment predicated on the investigation and determination of the special litigation committee, [the plaintiff] by tender of evidentiary proof in admissible form has shown facts sufficient to require a trial of any material issue of fact as to the adequacy or appropriateness of the *modus operandi* of that committee or has demonstrated acceptable excuse for failure to make such tender. [Citations omitted.] We conclude that the requisite showing has not been made on this record.

***

*** [W]e do not find either insufficiency or infirmity as to the procedures and methodologies chosen and pursued by the special litigation committee. That committee promptly engaged eminent special counsel to guide its deliberations and to advise it. The committee reviewed the prior work of the audit committee, testing its completeness, accuracy and thoroughness by interviewing represent-atives of Wilmer, Cutler & Pickering, reviewing transcripts of the testimony of 10 corporate officers and employees before the Securities and Exchange Commission, and studying documents collected by and work papers of the Washington law firm. Individual interviews were conducted with the directors found to have participated in any way in the questioned payments, and with representatives of Arthur Andersen & Co. Questionnaires were sent to and answered by each of the corporation's nonmanagement directors. At the con-clusion of its investigation the special litigation committee sought and obtained pertinent legal advice from its special counsel. The selection of appropriate investigative methods must always turn on the nature and characteristics of the particular subject being investigated, but we find nothing in this record that requires a trial of any material issue of fact concerning the sufficiency or appropriateness of the procedures chosen by this special litigation committee. Nor is there anything in this record to raise a triable issue of fact as to the good-faith pursuit of its examination by that committee.

***

Delaware, at least on its face, seems to take a very different approach from New York, as evidenced by *Zapata Corp. v. Maldonado*, 430 A.2d 779 (Del. 1981). In this case, a shareholder brought a derivative lawsuit in 1975. Each member of the board was a defendant in the case. However, by 1979, four of the defendant-directors were no longer on the board. At that point, the remaining directors appointed two new directors to the board (to fill two of the vacancies) and then "created an 'Independent Investigation Committee' *** composed solely of the two new directors, to investigate [the derivative lawsuit] *** and to determine whether the corporation should continue any or all of the litigation. The Committee's determination was stated to be 'final, ... not ... subject to review by the Board of Directors and ... in all respects ... binding upon the Corporation.'" *Id.* at 781. Not surprisingly, the committee later moved to dismiss the case. The Delaware Chancery Court denied the motion to dismiss, basically holding that the shareholder-plaintiff had a right to continue the case over the committee's objections.

On appeal, the Delaware Supreme Court first reviewed several prior cases and distilled the following rules from them: "A demand, when required and refused (if not wrongful), terminates a stockholder's legal ability to initiate a derivative action. But where demand is properly excused, the stockholder does possess the ability to initiate the action on his corporation's behalf." *Id.* at 784. However, note that these two rules did not answer the question presented in this case. The first rule did not apply because this was a demand-excused case. (Remember, all of the original directors had been accused of wrongdoing.) The second rule did not apply because the plaintiff had already *initiated* the lawsuit.

Thus, the question that remained was: in a demand-excused case, how should a court rule on a motion to dismiss filed by a special litigation committee? In the following portion of the opinion, the Delaware Supreme Court answers that question.

Zapata Corp. v. Maldonado
Supreme Court of Delaware
430 A.2d 779 (1981)

QUILLEN, Justice. ***

***

The question to be decided becomes: When, if at all, should an authorized board committee be permitted to cause litigation, properly initiated by a derivative stockholder in his own right, to be dismissed? As noted above, a board has the power to choose not to pursue litigation when demand is made upon it, so long as the decision is not wrongful. If the board determines that a suit would be detrimental to the company, the board's determination prevails. Even when demand is excusable, circumstances may arise when continuation of the litigation would not be in the corporation's best interests. Our inquiry is whether, under such circumstances, there is a permissible procedure under [Section 141(a) of the Delaware General Corporation Law] by which a corporation can rid itself of detrimental litigation. If there is not, a single stockholder in an extreme case might control the destiny of the entire corporation. This concern was bluntly expressed by the Ninth Circuit in *Lewis v. Anderson*, [615 F.2d 778, 783 (9th Cir. 1979), *cert. denied*, 449 U.S. 869 (1980)]: "To allow one shareholder to incapacitate an entire board of directors merely by leveling charges against them gives too much leverage to dissident shareholders." But, when examining the means, including the committee mechanism examined in this case, potentials for abuse must be recognized. This takes us to the second and third aspects of the issue on appeal.

Before we pass to equitable considerations as to the mechanism at issue here, it must be clear that an independent committee possesses the corporate power to seek the termination of a derivative suit. [Section 141(c) of the Delaware General Corporation Law] allows a board to delegate all of its authority to a committee. Accordingly, a committee with properly delegated authority would have the power to move for dismissal or summary judgment if the entire board did.

Even though demand was not made in this case and the initial decision of whether to litigate was not placed before the board, Zapata's board, it seems to us, retained all of its corporate power concerning litigation decisions. If [the plaintiff] Maldonado had made demand on the board in this case, it could have refused to bring suit. Maldonado could then have asserted that the decision not to sue was wrongful and, if correct, would have been allowed to maintain the suit. The board, however, never would have lost its statutory managerial authority. The demand requirement itself evidences that the managerial power is retained by the board. When a derivative plaintiff is allowed to bring suit after a wrongful refusal, the board's authority to choose whether to pursue the litigation is not challenged although its conclusion reached through the exercise of that authority is not respected since it is wrongful. Similarly, [Delaware Chancery Court] Rule 23.1, by excusing demand in certain instances, does not strip the board of its corporate power. It merely saves the plaintiff the expense and delay of making a futile demand resulting in a probable tainted exercise of that authority in a refusal by the board or in giving control of litigation to the opposing side. But the board entity remains empowered under [Section 141(a)] to make decisions regarding corporate litigation. The problem is one of member disqualification, not the absence of power in the board.

The corporate power inquiry then focuses on whether the board, tainted by the self-interest of a majority of its members, can legally delegate its authority to a committee of two disinterested directors. We find our statute clearly requires an affirmative answer to this question. As has been noted, under an express provision of the statute, [Section 141(c)], a committee can exercise all of the authority of the board to the extent provided in the resolution of the board. Moreover, at least by analogy to our statutory section on interested directors, [Section 144], it seems clear that the Delaware statute is designed to permit disinterested directors to act for the board. [Citations omitted.]

We do not think that the interest taint of the board majority is per se a legal bar to the delegation of the board's power to an independent committee composed of disinterested board members. The committee can properly act for the corporation to move to dismiss derivative litigation that is believed to be detrimental to the corporation's best interest.

Our focus now switches to the Court of Chancery which is faced with a stockholder assertion that a derivative suit, properly instituted, should continue for the benefit of the corporation and a corporate assertion, properly made by a board committee acting with board authority, that the same derivative suit should be dismissed as inimical to the best interests of the corporation.

At the risk of stating the obvious, the problem is relatively simple. If, on the one hand, corporations can consistently wrest *bona fide* derivative actions away from well-meaning derivative plaintiffs through the use of the committee mechanism, the derivative suit will lose much, if not all, of its generally-recognized effectiveness as an intra-corporate means of policing boards of directors. [Citation omitted.] If, on the other hand, corporations are unable to rid themselves of meritless or harmful litigation and strike suits, the derivative action, created to benefit the corporation, will produce the opposite, unintended result. [Citations omitted.] It thus appears desirable to us to find a balancing point where *bona fide* stockholder power to bring corporate causes of action cannot be unfairly trampled on by the board of directors, but the corporation can rid itself of detrimental litigation.

As we noted, the question has been treated by other courts as one of the "business judgment" of the board committee. If a "committee, composed of independent and disinterested directors, conducted a proper review of the matters before it, considered a variety of factors and reached, in good faith, a business judgment that (the) action was not in the best interest of (the corporation)", the action must be dismissed.   [Citation omitted.]   The issues become solely independence, good faith, and reasonable investigation. The ultimate conclusion of the committee, under that view, is not subject to judicial review.

We are not satisfied, however, that acceptance of the "business judgment" rationale at this stage of derivative litigation is a proper balancing point. While we admit an analogy with a normal case respecting board judgment, it seems to us that there is sufficient risk in the realities of a situation like the one presented in this case to justify caution beyond adherence to the theory of business judgment.

The context here is a suit against directors where demand on the board is excused. We think some tribute must be paid to the fact that the lawsuit was properly initiated. It is not a board refusal case. Moreover, this complaint was filed in June of 1975 and, while the parties undoubtedly would take differing views on the degree of litigation activity, we have to be concerned about the creation of an "Independent Investigation Committee" four years later, after the election of two new outside directors. Situations could develop where such motions could be filed after years of vigorous litigation for reasons unconnected with the merits of the lawsuit.

Moreover, notwithstanding our conviction that Delaware law entrusts the corporate power to a properly authorized committee, we must be mindful that directors are passing judgment on fellow directors in the same corporation and fellow directors, in this instance, who designated them to serve both as directors and committee members. The question naturally arises whether a "there but for the grace of God go I" empathy might not play a role. And the further question arises whether inquiry as to independence, good faith and reasonable investigation is sufficient safeguard against abuse, perhaps subconscious abuse.

***

Whether the Court of Chancery will be persuaded by the exercise of a committee power resulting in a summary motion for dismissal of a derivative action, where a demand has not been initially made, should rest, in our judgment, in the independent discretion of the Court of Chancery. We thus steer a middle course between those cases which yield to the independent business judgment of a board committee and this case as determined below which would yield to unbridled plaintiff stockholder control. In pursuit of the course, we recognize that "(t)he final substantive judgment whether a particular lawsuit should be maintained requires a balance of many factors ethical, commercial, promotional, public relations, employee relations, fiscal as well as legal." [Citation omitted.] But we are content that such factors are not "beyond the judicial reach" of the Court of Chancery which regularly and competently deals with fiduciary relationships, disposition of trust property, approval of settlements and scores of similar problems. We recognize the danger of judicial overreaching but the alternatives seem to us to be outweighed by the fresh view of a judicial outsider. Moreover, if we failed to balance all the interests involved, we would in the name of practicality and judicial economy foreclose a judicial decision on the merits. At this point, we are not convinced that is necessary or desirable.

After an objective and thorough investigation of a derivative suit, an independent committee may cause its corporation to file a pretrial motion to dismiss in the Court of Chancery. The basis of the motion is the best interests of the corporation, as determined by the committee. The motion should include a thorough written record of the investigation and its findings and recommendations. Under appropriate Court supervision, akin to proceedings on summary judgment, each side should have an opportunity to make a record on the motion. As to the limited issues presented by the motion noted below, the moving party should be prepared to meet the normal burden under [Delaware Chancery Court] Rule 56 that there is no genuine issue as to any material fact and that the moving party is entitled to dismiss as a matter of law. The Court should apply a two-step test to the motion.

First, the Court should inquire into the independence and good faith of the committee and the bases supporting its conclusions. Limited discovery may be ordered to facilitate such inquiries. The corporation should have the burden of proving independence, good faith and a reasonable investigation, rather than presuming independence, good faith and reasonableness. If the Court determines either that the committee is not independent or has not shown reasonable bases for its conclusions, or, if the Court is not satisfied for other reasons relating to the process, including but not limited to the good faith of the committee, the Court shall deny the corporation's motion. If, however, the Court is satisfied under Rule 56 standards that the committee was independent and showed reasonable bases for good faith findings and recommendations, the Court may proceed, in its discretion, to the next step.

The second step provides, we believe, the essential key in striking the balance between legitimate corporate claims as expressed in a derivative stockholder suit and a corporation's best interests as expressed by an independent investigating committee. The Court should determine, applying its own independent business judgment, whether the motion should be granted. This means, of course, that instances could arise where a committee can establish its independence and sound bases for its good faith decisions and still have the corporation's motion denied. The second step is intended to thwart instances where corporate actions meet the criteria of step one, but the result does not appear to satisfy its spirit, or where corporate actions would simply prematurely terminate a stockholder grievance deserving of further consideration in the corporation's interest. The Court of Chancery of course must carefully consider and weigh how compelling the corporate interest in dismissal is when faced with a non-frivolous lawsuit. The Court of Chancery should, when appropriate, give special consideration to matters of law and public policy in addition to the corporation's best interests.

If the Court's independent business judgment is satisfied, the Court may proceed to grant the motion, subject, of course, to any equitable terms or conditions the Court finds necessary or desirable.

***

Auerbach and *Zapata* seem to lie at opposite ends of a spectrum. *Auerbach* is fairly deferential to the decisions of special litigation committees, whereas *Zapata* represents a fairly intrusive judicial attitude. One might be able to reconcile these differing approaches by remembering that *Auerbach* was a demand-required case, whereas *Zapata* was a demand-excused case. You should also remember that it is more likely that a special litigation committee will appear in a demand-excused case than in a demand-required case. This is because a demand will likely be rejected if the board doesn't believe that the case is meritorious. If that happens then, it will be difficult for the plaintiff to thereafter file the lawsuit, as you saw above.

Cases in other jurisdictions take different approaches to special litigation committees. See, e.g., *Joy v. North*, 692 F.2d 880 (2d Cir. 1982) (largely following the *Zapata* approach in demand-excused cases); *Alford v. Shaw*, 358 S.E.2d 323 (N.C. 1987) (suggesting that an approach similar to *Zapata* should be applied both in demand-excused and demand-required cases). But how does the MBCA deal with motions to dismiss filed on behalf of the corporation? To answer that question, read MBCA § 7.44 very carefully.

Problems

Problem 8-29: The board of directors Shady Corp. consists of ten directors. A shareholder wishes to bring a derivative lawsuit against seven of the directors, alleging that they violated their duty of loyalty with respect to certain interested-director transactions. *Is a demand required under New York law or Delaware law? If not, and the plaintiff files the derivative lawsuit, can the three disinterested directors later become a special litigation committee and move to dismiss the case?*

Problem 8-30:   Assume that a special litigation committee consisting solely of independent directors moves to dismiss a derivative lawsuit. *Who has the burden of proof of showing that the committee met the applicable requirements under New York law? Who has the burden under Delaware law? Who has the burden under the MBCA?*

Problem 8-31: The board of directors of ABC Corp. consists of ten directors. A shareholder of ABC Corp. has properly filed a derivative lawsuit against six of the directors, alleging that they usurped a corporate opportunity. All of the directors believe that the lawsuit is simply a "nuisance" lawsuit and should be dismissed. *Advise the board how the board or a committee may move to dismiss the lawsuit, applying the MBCA.*

Problem 8-32: Same facts as Problem 8-31. *Advise the board how the board or a committee may move to dismiss the lawsuit, applying Delaware law. Would your answer change if New York law applied?*

If at this point you feel overwhelmed by the procedural complexities of derivative lawsuits you are probably not alone. Perhaps the flowchart on the following page will help you sort things out. Note, however, that the flowchart only addresses the MBCA. You might want to try your hand at creating separate flowcharts for Delaware and New York law.

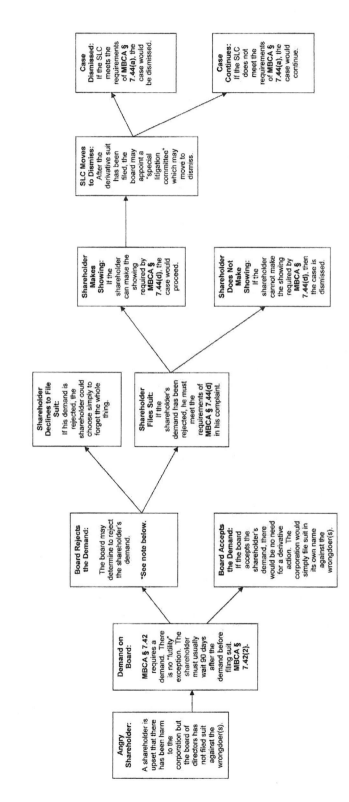

DERIVATIVE ACTION FLOWCHART
CONERNING DEMANDS AND "SPECIAL LITIGATION COMMITTEES"
MODEL BUSINESS CORPORATION ACT

*NOTE: Technically, another possibility (although probably very rare) is that the board of directors could simply do nothing in response to the shareholder's demand (i.e., neither accept it nor reject it within the 90-day period). In that case, the shareholder could file suit after the 90-day period expires, and would not be required to make the showing required by MBCA § 7.44(d).

§ 8.05   OTHER ISSUES IN DERIVATIVE LAWSUITS

There are a few other issues to cover before concluding a study of derivative lawsuits. First, note that just like other lawsuits, derivative lawsuits have a *res judicata* effect. In other words, if a shareholder-plaintiff brings a derivative lawsuit, neither the corporation itself—nor another shareholder—may later sue based on the same claims. Perhaps this is one reason why we want to make sure that a plaintiff is a "fair and adequate" representative of the corporation within the meaning of MBCA § 7.41(2).

Res judicata may also be a reason behind MBCA § 7.45. Unlike a "regular" lawsuit, where the parties are usually free to settle the case upon any terms that they mutually agree, a settlement or dismissal or a derivative lawsuit requires court approval. If you recall *In re Caremark International Inc. Derivative Litigation* from Chapter 6, you will remember that the precise issue before the court was whether it should approve the settlement agreement in a derivative lawsuit.

MBCA § 7.46(1) provides that the court may "order the corporation to pay the plaintiff's reasonable expenses (including counsel fees) ... if it finds that the proceeding has resulted in a substantial benefit to the corporation." Obviously, this is different than the usual rule in the United States that each party must bear its own expenses and attorney fees. But as you saw at the beginning of this chapter, that rule would discourage shareholders from filing derivative lawsuits because even if they win the case they will not directly receive any damages (although the value of their shares may increase). In determining the amount that the plaintiff's attorney should receive as fees, courts generally use either a percentage-of-recovery method or base the fees on the number of hours spent by the attorney, multiplied by an hourly rate determined, at least in part, by reference to what attorneys with similar experience charge for their services.

On the other hand, MBCA § 7.46(2) poses a bit of a danger for potential shareholder-plaintiffs in derivative lawsuits. That section provides that the court may order the plaintiff to pay *any defendant's* reasonable expenses (including attorney fees) if the court "finds that the proceeding was commenced or maintained without reasonable cause or for an improper purpose."

Finally, if the derivative lawsuit is filed in federal court, you should be aware that additional issues may arise. Fortunately or unfortunately for the reader (depending on her perspective), we will not cover those issues in this textbook, other than to note that some requirements imposed in derivative lawsuits by state statutes, such as some statutes that require plaintiffs to post bonds, are considered "substantive" and therefore will be applied by federal courts under the *Erie* doctrine, at least if the underlying claims in the lawsuit involve state, rather than federal, law. *See Cohen v. Beneficial Industrial Loan Corp.*, 337 U.S. 541 (1949); *Erie Railroad Co. v. Tompkins*, 304 U.S. 64 (1938). In cases that allege violations of federal law, Federal Rule of Civil Procedure 23.1 will be applicable. Rule 23.1 will also trump any inconsistent state rules in diversity actions based on state law.

PRACTICE QUESTIONS

QUESTIONS 8-1 TO 8-4 ARE BASED ON THE FOLLOWING FACTS

Engine Parts Corp. ("Engine Parts") manufactures engine parts and sells the parts to automobile manufacturers such as General Motors, Toyota, and Big Car Corp. ("BCC"). In October 2010, Engine Parts shipped a large quantity of engine parts to BCC, which BCC installed in the automobiles that it was manufacturing at that time. Later, it became apparent that these engine parts were defective. As a result, BCC had to recall the automobiles that it had sold that contained the defective engine parts and repair the problems. BCC lost $25 million in 2010 as a result of this recall. However, BCC has not yet sued Engine Parts to recover this loss. Frank Fender is a shareholder of BCC and is upset that BCC's board of directors hasn't sued Engine Parts. Frank owns 100 shares of BCC stock, which he purchased through his stockbroker on April 13, 2011. (BCC is publicly traded and has more than 10 million shares of stock outstanding.)

Multiple Choice Question 8-1: Which of the following statements is correct?

A. Frank does not have proper standing to file this derivative lawsuit on behalf of BCC.

B. Frank may have proper standing to file this derivative lawsuit on behalf of BCC if the court finds that he would be a fair and adequate representative of BCC's interests in the action.

C. Frank may have proper standing to file this derivative lawsuit on behalf of BCC unless the court finds that he would *not* be a fair and adequate representative of BCC's interests in the action.

D. Frank will have proper standing to file this derivative lawsuit on behalf of BCC unless another shareholder, who owns more than the 100 shares that Frank owns, wishes to file the derivative lawsuit.

Multiple Choice Question 8-2: Regardless of how you answered the previous question, assume for purposes of this question that Frank has proper standing to be a proper shareholder-plaintiff. *Is Frank required to make a demand before filing this lawsuit?*

A.   Yes, regardless of whether BCC is incorporated under the MBCA, in Delaware or New York.
B.   Yes, if BCC is incorporated under the MBCA; but no if BCC is incorporated in Delaware or New York.
C.   Yes, if BCC is incorporated in Delaware or New York; but no if BCC is incorporated under the MBCA.
D.   Yes, if BCC is incorporated under the MBCA or in Delaware; but no if BCC is incorporated in New York.
E.   No, regardless of whether BCC is incorporated under the MBCA, in Delaware or New York.

Multiple Choice Question 8-3: Regardless of how you answered the previous question, assume for purposes of this question that Frank was required to make a demand. Therefore, on May 1, 2011, Frank sent a letter to BCC's board of directors, demanding that they sue Engine Parts. On June 1, 2011, the Chairperson of the board of directors of BCC sent the following letter to Frank:

> Dear Mr. Fender: We received your letter to the board of directors demanding that we sue Engine Parts Corp. We carefully considered your request at a lengthy board meeting, but we feel that it would be inappropriate to sue Engine Parts, which has been a long-time supplier of our company. We have discussed the matter with Engine Parts, which has assured us that this problem will never occur again and has offered to sell us engine parts at reduced prices in the future. Thank you for your interest, but we will not be suing Engine Parts.

After he read this letter, Frank decided to file a derivative lawsuit to recover $25 million from Engine Parts for the benefit of BCC. *Which of the following statements is correct? Assume for purposes of this question that BCC is incorporated under the MBCA.*

A.   Frank must wait until 90 days after May 1, 2011 to file this derivative lawsuit.
B.   Frank is now free to file the lawsuit.
C.   Frank is now free to file the lawsuit, but will bear all of the expenses in the lawsuit because the board rejected his demand.
D.   Based on the facts, it is unlikely that Frank may file the lawsuit.

Multiple Choice Question 8-4:   Regardless of how you answered the previous three questions, assume for purposes of this question that Frank had the required standing to be a proper shareholder-plaintiff and that he properly filed the derivative lawsuit. In October 2011, while the lawsuit was still pending, the board of directors of BCC formed a committee which it named the "Special Litigation Committee," and appointed Mr. Jones and Ms. Smith, two directors of BCC, to the committee.   After several lengthy meetings during which they interviewed potential witnesses in the litigation and consulted a lawyer that the committee hired to assist it, the two members of the Special Litigation Committee determined that BCC should move to dismiss the derivative lawsuit because it is not in the best interests of the corporation. *If BCC is incorporated under the MBCA, how will the court likely rule on this motion to dismiss?*

A.   The motion will be denied because the corporation has no right to dismiss a derivative lawsuit after it has been properly filed by a shareholder.

B.   The motion will be denied because Mr. Jones and Ms. Smith, as directors of BCC, are not independent (qualified).

C.   The court will grant the motion only if it finds, using its own business judgment, that dismissing the derivative lawsuit is in the best interests of the corporation.

D.   The court will grant the motion if it finds that the Special Litigation Committee determined in good faith, after conducting a reasonable inquiry, that maintaining the derivative lawsuit is not in the best interests of the corporation.

Multiple Choice Question 8-5:   Which of the following must be brought as derivative lawsuit, and which may be brought as direct lawsuits?

> I.   A shareholder wishes to sue because she wasn't allowed to inspect the corporation's bylaws.

> II.   A shareholder wishes to sue the board for selling some of the corporation's assets for a price that was too low.

> III.   A shareholder wishes to sue the board for approving an excessive salary for the corporation's CEO.

> IV.   A shareholder wishes to sue the former directors for approving a merger in which the shareholders were paid an inadequate price for their shares.

A.   All of the above must be brought as derivative lawsuits.
B.   All of the above may be brought as direct lawsuits.
C.   I, II, and IV may be brought as direct lawsuits; III must be brought as a derivative lawsuit.
D.   I and IV may be brought as direct lawsuits; II and III must be brought as derivative lawsuits.
E.   I may be brought as a direct lawsuit; II, III, and IV must be brought as derivative lawsuits.

QUESTIONS 8-6 TO 8-8 ARE BASED ON THE FOLLOWING FACTS

Bob Benson is the President of Big Bank, Inc. and is also one of the six members of its board of directors. Bob is the only member of the board who is an employee of Big Bank. In January, Big Bank sent Bob and several other employees to a seminar about banking regulation that was held in Las Vegas, Nevada. While in Nevada, Bob and two other employees took a trip to the "Bunny Ranch" (a legal prostitution brothel) and used a company credit card to pay for the services of several prostitutes, which was in violation of company policies (obviously). Also while in Nevada, Bob was arrested for drunk and disorderly conduct. A day later, the *Wall Street Journal* printed a story about Bob's arrest. (The story did not mention the use of the company credit card for prostitutes.) Shep Sullivan, a long-time shareholder of Big Bank, read the story in the *Wall Street Journal* and now wishes to bring a derivative action on behalf of Big Bank against Bob, seeking to recover money damages for harm to Big Bank's reputation.

Multiple Choice Question 8-6: *Which of the following is a correct statement as to whether Shep must make a demand on Big Bank's board of directors before commencing this lawsuit? Choose the best answer.*

A.   If Big Bank is incorporated under Delaware law, Shep will be excused from making a demand on Big Bank's board because he can show that Bob's actions were not the product of a valid exercise of business judgment.

B.   If Big Bank is incorporated under New York law, Shep will be excused from making a demand on Big Bank's board because he can show that Big Bank's board was not fully informed about Bob's actions to the extent reasonably appropriate in the circumstances.

C.   If Big Bank is incorporated under New York law, Shep will be excused from making a demand on Big Bank's board because he can show that Bob's actions were so egregious on their face that they could not have been the product of sound business judgment.

D.   All of the above are correct.

E.   Under either New York or Delaware law, Shep will be required to make a demand.

Multiple Choice Question 8-7: Regardless of how you answered the previous question, assume that Shep made a demand on Big Bank's board of directors. The board then held a three-hour meeting to discuss Shep's demand. At the meeting, Bob told the other directors about his unauthorized use of the company credit card and agreed to pay back the amounts that he had charged on the credit card. The directors other than Bob unanimously voted to reject Shep's demand. (Bob abstained from voting.) The Chairperson of the board then sent Shep a letter that stated that the board had considered his demand but had decided to reject it because "filing the lawsuit against Bob Benson could result in the public disclosure of information that would harm Big Bank's reputation." *Which of the following is a correct statement as to Shep's ability to file the derivative lawsuit after the rejection of his demand? Assume for purposes of this question that Big Bank is incorporated under the MBCA.*

A.   Shep most likely will be unable to file the derivative lawsuit because the directors that rejected his demand were independent (qualified), made a reasonable inquiry, and had a good faith basis for rejecting his demand.

B.   Shep will be able to file the lawsuit because Bob was not independent (qualified) or disinterested.

C.   Shep will be able to file the lawsuit because the board does not have a good faith basis for rejecting his demand.

D.   Shep will be able to file the lawsuit if the court, using its own business judgment, decides that the lawsuit should be brought.

Multiple Choice Question 8-8: Regardless of how you answered the previous two questions, assume that Shep properly filed the derivative action. Two months later, Big Bank's board of directors appointed two of the directors (Mr. Jones and Ms. Smith) as a "Special Litigation Committee" to determine whether Big Bank should move to dismiss the lawsuit. *If the special litigation committee moves to dismiss the lawsuit, which of the following is correct? Assume for purposes of this question that Big Bank is incorporated under the MBCA.*

A.   If Mr. Jones and Ms. Smith were independent (qualified), made a reasonable inquiry, and had a good faith basis for moving to dismiss the lawsuit, the court will dismiss the case.

B.   If Mr. Jones and Ms. Smith were independent (qualified), made a reasonable inquiry, and had a good faith basis for moving to dismiss the lawsuit, the court probably will dismiss the case.

C.   If Mr. Jones and Ms. Smith were independent (qualified), make a reasonable inquiry, and had a good faith basis for moving to dismiss the lawsuit, the court will dismiss the case if the court, using its own business judgment, decides that the lawsuit should be dismissed.

D.   The court will not grant the motion to dismiss because Mr. Jones and Ms. Smith were on Big Bank's board of directors at the time of Bob's wrongdoing.

Multiple Choice Question 8-9: Gator Corp. is in the business of manufacturing athletic uniforms. The board of directors of Gator Corp. consists of eight directors. Five of the directors, Mr. A, Mr. B, Ms. C, Ms. D, and Mr. E, were joint owners of a parcel of worthless land in a swamp in Florida. At a regular meeting of the board of directors held on April 13, the board of Gator Corp., after five minutes of discussion, approved a transaction in which Gator Corp. purchased this land for $3.5 million. No notice of the meeting was given and no agenda for the meeting was sent to the directors before the meeting. Mr. X, a shareholder of Gator Corp. for more than eight years, found out about this transaction and was extremely upset. Mr. X seeks to bring a derivative action against the board of directors for violating their fiduciary duties to the corporation. He would be able to allege all of the facts set forth above "with particularity" in a complaint. Gator Corp. is incorporated in New York. *Must Mr. X first make a demand on the board of directors before commencing his derivative lawsuit?*

A.   No, because a majority of the directors of Gator Corp. were interested in the transaction.

B.   No, if the court agrees that the directors did not sufficiently inform themselves about the transaction before they approved it.

C.   No, if the court agrees that the transaction was so egregious on its face that it could not have been the product of sound business judgment of the directors.

D.   All of the above are correct.

E.   Mr. X must make a demand on the board before filing a derivative lawsuit.

Multiple Choice Question 8-10: Same facts as in the previous question, except that Gator Corp. is incorporated under the MBCA. *Must Mr. X first make a demand on the board of directors before commencing his derivative lawsuit?*

A   No, because a majority of the directors of Gator Corp. were interested in the transaction.

B.   No, if the court agrees that the directors did not sufficiently inform themselves about the transaction before they approved it.

C.   No, if the court agrees that the transaction was so egregious on its face that it could not have been the product of sound business judgment of the directors.

D.   All of the above are correct.

E.   Mr. X must make a demand on the board before filing a derivative lawsuit.

Multiple Choice Question 8-11: *Under Delaware law, if a shareholder wishes to bring a derivative lawsuit to challenge the corporation's purchase of property from one of its directors, the shareholder would have to make a demand for relief on the board of directors, unless she could plead facts that:*

A.   Create a reasonable doubt that the directors were disinterested and independent.

B.   Show it would be inconvenient to make the demand.

C.   Create a reasonable doubt that the challenged transaction was the product of a valid exercise of business judgment.

D.   Either A or C.

Multiple Choice Question 8-12: Assume that the derivative lawsuit referred to in Multiple Question 8-11 is properly commenced because the plaintiff was able to show reasonable doubt that the directors were disinterested and independent. Shortly thereafter, two of the directors resign from the board and two new, independent persons are chosen to fill the vacancies. The board then creates a special litigation committee composed of the two new directors. The committee finds that derivative suit will be extremely costly to the corporation, both in terms of legal fees and potential lost earnings. The committee decides that these costs substantially outweigh any potential benefit to the corporation from maintaining the suit and the committee then files a motion on behalf of the corporation seeking dismissal of the derivative suit. *Which of the following statements is most correct? Keep in mind that this is a Delaware corporation.*

A.   If the court is satisfied that the two new directors were, in fact, independent, acted in good faith and upon a reasonable investigation, the court *may* apply its own business judgment to determine whether the lawsuit should continue.

B.   If the court is satisfied that the two new directors were independent, acted in good faith and upon a reasonable investigation, the court *must* dismiss the lawsuit.

C.   If the court is satisfied that the two new directors were, in fact, independent, acted in good faith and upon a reasonable investigation, the court *must* apply its own business judgment to determine whether the lawsuit should continue.

D.   None of the above.

QUESTIONS 8-13 TO 8-15 ARE BASED ON THE FOLLOWING FACTS

Parker and Shawn incorporated a corporation under the MBCA called Surf Boards, Inc. The corporation was a great success and eventually became a publicly traded company. Thereafter, it was discovered that Parker and Shawn had used corporation assets for what appeared to have been their own personal pursuits, such as extravagant vacations. Parker and Shawn argued that these vacations were legitimate business trips designed to "scout" for new products. At no time before the vacations did Parker or Shawn disclose the vacations or obtain permission from the board of directors. (Neither Parker nor Shawn currently serves on the board of directors.) Since the discovery, the board of directors has taken no action on the issue. Hector, a shareholder who owns 0.05% of the outstanding stock of Surf Boards, Inc., filed a derivative lawsuit on behalf of the corporation seeking damages from Parker and Shawn. Parker, Shawn and the corporation have moved to dismiss the lawsuit on grounds that Hector failed to make a demand on the board of directors. Hector argues that demand is excused.

Multiple Choice Question 8-13: *Which of the following is correct?*

A.   Hector will lose because a demand is required.
B.   Hector will win if he can show that irreparable injury to the corporation would result by waiting for the board to respond to a demand.
C.   Hector will win if he can show that a majority of the directors are interested in the challenged transaction.
D.   Hector will win if he can show that all of the directors are interested in the challenged transaction.

Multiple Choice Question 8-14:   Assume that the demand is excused in the Multiple Choice Question 8-13. The board of directors then appoints a "special litigation committee" consisting of two outside directors, Pamela and Greta. Neither Pamela nor Greta were directors at the time of Parker and Shawn's vacation.   After investigating the charges, Pamela and Greta recommend dismissing Hector's lawsuit. Although Pamela and Greta noted that the lawsuit might be successful, they felt it was in the corporation's best interests to put the matter to rest and avoid all of the bad publicity that the lawsuit is generating. The corporation subsequently moves to dismiss Hector's lawsuit. *For Hector to successfully oppose the motion he must convince the court that:*

A.   Pamela and Greta acted in bad faith.
B.   Pamela and Greta did not conduct a reasonable inquiry.
C.   Pamela and Greta are not disinterested (qualified) directors.
D.   Any of the above.

Multiple Choice Question 8-15: *If Hector is successful in the derivative lawsuit referred to in the preceding two questions, Parker and Shawn will have to pay damages to:*

A.   the corporation.
B.   Hector.
C.   All of the shareholders.
D.   None of the above.

CHAPTER 9
CLOSELY HELD CORPORATIONS

Chapters 5 through 8 discussed rules of law that apply to all corporations, whether they are big or small or somewhere in between. Indeed, much of corporate law is of a "one size fits all" variety, with little or no regard to the size or other characteristics of a given corporation. In fact, many commentators convincingly demonstrate that corporate law rules evolved mainly with large, or even publicly traded, corporations in mind, giving little thought to the needs of small businesses. This makes sense to some degree, because historically most small businesses were operated as partnerships and most large businesses were operated as corporations. But of course there is no reason why a small business can't incorporate. In fact, business lawyers rarely recommend that clients form businesses as partnerships due to the risk of unlimited personal liability. Instead, the more likely candidates are either a corporation or a limited liability company (LLC).

Note, however, that one major characteristic of partnerships that is missing from corporations is that partners owe fiduciary duties to one another. In contrast, the traditional rules of corporate law hold that shareholders do not owe fiduciary duties to each other or the corporation. While it is true that directors and officers owe fiduciary duties, these duties generally run to the corporation, not the shareholders. Moreover, at least outside of situations involving conflicts of interest, fraud, bad faith, or irrationality, the decisions of directors will be protected by the business judgment rule. Thus, most director decisions will be difficult if not impossible to challenge, even if they are less than optimal. Further, "traditional" corporate law is built on the idea of majority rule. In a corporation, there is no requirement of unanimity like there is for some types of partnership decisions. Thus, the person or persons who hold a majority of the stock will be able to elect all of the directors (or a majority of them if cumulative voting applies) and a majority of the directors will be able to make the corporation's business decisions. Thus, a minority shareholder has little power to influence the direction of the business if the majority shareholder(s) disagree with her.

In a publicly traded company, a shareholder who does not like how the corporation is being run has a ready "exit" in that she may quickly and easily sell her shares in the stock market, at a price that is more or less "fair" because it represents what the market thinks a share of the corporation's stock is worth at that time. Not so in a closely held corporation. By definition, a closely held corporation has a small number of shareholders. While shareholders *legally* are free to sell stock, if there is no market for the corporation's stock they will need to go to the trouble of finding a buyer, negotiating a price, etc. In this sense, a shareholder in a closely held corporation is "locked in" to her investment to a much greater degree than a shareholder in a publicly traded corporation (or even one with a lot of shareholders). Further, shareholders of a closely held corporation tend to have much more of their overall personal wealth tied up in the corporation than does a typical shareholder in a publicly traded corporation.

All of this is a recipe for problems if the shareholders of a closely held corporation do not get along. If there are two 50% shareholders (or two groups of 50% shareholders such as two different families), the obvious danger is **deadlock**. If one shareholder votes yes and the other votes no, or if one director votes yes and the other votes no, then nothing happens. Another possibility is that there is a majority shareholder and a minority shareholder. In that case, the traditional rules of corporate law create another danger: the majority may **oppress** or otherwise "squeeze out" the minority.

This chapter concerns ways in which corporate law has evolved to address these dangers. While these ways are helpful, they are "blunt instruments." In other words, they're better than nothing, but not great. Hopefully, when you are done reading this chapter you will realize that a better approach for a client that will be a shareholder in a closely held corporation will be to engage in **advance planning**. Thus, this chapter begins with a discussion of some of the legal issues involved in advance planning, and then returns to that important topic at the end of the chapter.

§ 9.01   OVERVIEW OF CLOSELY HELD CORPORATIONS

Objectives (for Sections 9.01 and 9.02): You should be able to explain to a client that is forming a closely held corporation with some friends or family members some of the major planning issues to consider, as well as some of the primary dangers faced by shareholders in closely held corporations. You should also be able to:

●   *Given a fact pattern, determine whether a corporation is a "closely held" corporation under judicial definitions of that term.*

●   *Explain some of the common reasons why people own stock in closely held corporations.*

●   *Explain some of the things that may "go wrong" for a shareholder in a closely held corporation, particularly a minority shareholder. Further, explain why the traditional rules of corporate law provide little protection for minority shareholders.*

• *Explain some common measures by which a person may protect her interests before she becomes a minority shareholder in a closely held corporation, including but not limited to MBCA § 7.32. (These will be explored in more detail in Section 9.05.)*

• *Briefly explain what causes of action a shareholder in a closely held corporation may have if she is being "abused" in some way. (These will be explored in more detail in Sections 9.03 and 9.04.)*

A.   WHAT IS A "CLOSELY HELD" CORPORATION?

First, a matter of definition: what exactly is a "closely held" corporation? There are very few statutory definitions of this term. Instead, perhaps the most widely followed definition of the term comes from the case *Donahue v. Rodd Electrotype Company of New England, Inc.*, 328 N.E.2d 505 (Mass. 1975), which you will read later in this chapter. The *Donahue* court defined a closely held corporation as "typified by: (1) a small number of stockholders; (2) no ready market for the corporate stock; and (3) substantial majority stockholder participation in the management, direction and operations of the corporation." In other words, a closely held corporation has a small number of shareholders (typically this means fewer than ten) and most of the shareholders also serve as directors and/or are employed by the corporation. However, do not fall into the trap of thinking that a closely held corporation is somehow a completely different type of entity than a "normal" corporation; even a closely held corporation will have articles of incorporation and bylaws, officers and directors, shareholders, etc. Moreover, it is governed by the same statute as any other corporation (in our case, the MBCA).

Why would someone buy stock in a corporation when there will be no ready market in which to sell the stock? Given the many tens of thousands of closely held businesses in America, it is impossible to generalize. However, a prevalent reason is to "create" a job for oneself. "I want to be my own boss," is a common refrain and a lifelong dream for many people. How else to do this than to start your own company? Obviously, however, this is not the only reason. Another common reason is that the shareholder may have inherited the stock from one of the founders of the business. Or, of course, the shareholder may simply have thought that the business was a good investment.

B.   MINORITY ABUSE BY THE MAJORITY

If a person starts a corporation and is the only shareholder of that corporation, then probably the biggest legal risk is veil-piercing. (Of course, given the knowledge that you gained from Chapter 5, you can counsel that person about steps to take to lessen this risk, such as observing corporate formalities, making sure that the corporation is adequately capitalized and has good insurance, etc.) A single shareholder obviously has full control over the business: she will almost certainly elect herself to the board and will most likely be the only director and officer. In such a situation, she can cause the corporation to do whatever she wants it to do (within the bounds of the law, of course).

If there are multiple shareholders, things can get more complicated if conflicts develop, which—human nature being human nature—are bound to occur sooner or later. As you saw above, if there are two equal (50%) shareholders, then the principal risk is deadlock. Deadlock is considered in a bit more detail later in this chapter.

If there is a majority shareholder (or group) and a minority shareholder (or group) then there are many ways that the majority can "beat up" the minority. Let's take a simple example. Suppose that Adam, Betty, and Cindy decide to start a corporation. They have some informal discussions about how the corporation will operate and orally agree that: each of them will own one-third of the stock; they will not permit any other persons to become shareholders unless they all agree; each of the three of them will serve on the board, which will consist only of three members; and, most importantly, they each will work for the company, drawing equal salaries for equal work, assuming the corporation generates enough funds to pay salaries. They also agree that if any of them wants to retire, the company will repurchase his or her stock for a "fair" price. In other words, the plan is that each of the three shareholders/directors/employees will have equal power and responsibilities and will reap an equal financial return, primarily through salary. (Note that there is a tax reason to pay salaries rather than dividends: corporations can deduct reasonable salaries from their taxable income but dividends are not deductible.) But because they want to save money, no one bothers visiting a lawyer to discuss writing these agreements down in some manner. Let's assume further that the three shareholders/ directors/employees work diligently, but the business struggles. However, after a few years of hard work, the business becomes profitable. Meanwhile, Adam has had a "falling out" with Betty and Cindy; arguments become more and more frequent. Eventually, Betty and Cindy decide that they no longer want Adam around.

Assuming that Betty and Cindy are devious characters, what may they do? Keep in mind that they are two of the three directors and that directors make most of the corporation's business decisions. For starters, they could fire Adam from his job. Unless Adam had the foresight to get an employment agreement (which he did not in this example), most states will say that he is an "at will" employee who can be fired for any reason or no reason, assuming that his termination does not violate anti-discrimination or "whistleblower" protection laws (not likely in this example). Firing Adam would of course free up some cash flow that Betty and Cindy may use to increase their own salaries. After all, they are doing more work now that Adam is no longer working. They probably won't use any of this extra money to pay dividends. First, as noted above, dividends are not tax-deductible. Second, if they did pay dividends, then Adam would get one-third of them because he owns one-third of the stock. As you will see in some of the cases in this chapter, there are many other underhanded things that Betty and Cindy could do if they are so inclined.

At this point, Adam is in a quandary: he owns one-third of the stock of a successful corporation but is earning absolutely no financial return on his investment. While he is free to try to sell his stock, doing so will be difficult because this is a closely held corporation. Moreover, what potential buyer in her right mind would pay "top dollar" for Adam's stock when he is being abused by the other shareholders/directors?

Luckily, there are a few ways that Adam can fight back, as you will learn in Sections 9.03 and 9.04 below. But let's first consider what Adam should have done if he could travel back in time to when the corporation was first being formed.

§ 9.02   PLANNING IN CLOSELY HELD CORPORATIONS—A FIRST LOOK

Let's take a closer look at some of Adam's goals. As noted above, Adam, Betty, and Cindy agreed that (1) each of them would own one-third of the stock; (2) they would not permit any other persons to become shareholders unless they all agree; (3) each of them would serve on the board, which will consist only of three members; (4) each of them would work for the company and be paid equal salaries for equal work; and (5) if any of them retires, the company will repurchase his or her stock for a "fair" price. How could Adam have protected these expectations, either contractually or through articles or bylaw provisions? Drawing on your knowledge from Chapter 5, consider the following problems. We will discuss similar problems in more detail in Section 9.05 as well.

Problems

Problem 9-1: *How could Adam, Betty, and Cindy ensure that each of them would own one-third of the stock and that there would be no other shareholders unless they all agreed?*

Problem 9-2: *How could Adam, Betty, and Cindy ensure that each of them would serve on the board and that the board would consist only of three members?*

Problem 9-3: *How could the shareholders ensure that they would be employed by the corporation?*

Problem 9-4: *How could the shareholders ensure that if any of them wants to retire the company will repurchase their stock for a "fair" price?*

A.   COMMON LAW ISSUES

Now let's assume that Adam, Betty, and Cindy had some other ideas in mind. For example, maybe they wanted to ensure that one of them would serve as the President of the company, one of them would be the Vice President, and one would be the Secretary and Treasurer. Or maybe they wanted to make sure that the company would pay dividends to the extent that it legally could.[*] Or maybe they wanted to ensure that certain decisions would be made a certain way. The problem is, if any of these topics are decisions that were ordinarily made by the corporation's board of directors, the common law was often hostile to such agreements, as shown in the following case.

McQuade v. Stoneham
Court of Appeals of New York
189 N.E. 234 (1934)

POUND, Chief Judge.   The action is brought to compel specific performance of an agreement between the parties, entered into to secure the control of National Exhibition Company, also called the Baseball Club (New York Nationals or "Giants"). This was one of Stoneham's enterprises which used the New York polo grounds for its home games. McGraw was manager of the Giants.

---

[*]   As noted above, if Adam, Betty, and Cindy each work for the company, it may be preferable to have the company pay them salaries. However, if one of the shareholders does not intend to work and be paid a salary, she may want to ensure that she will receive some amount of dividends.

McQuade was at the time the contract was entered into a city magistrate. He resigned December 8, 1930.

Defendant Stoneham became the owner of 1,306 shares, or a majority of the stock of National Exhibition Company. Plaintiff and defendant McGraw each purchased 70 shares of his stock. Plaintiff paid Stoneham $50,338.10 for the stock he purchased. As a part of the transaction, the agreement in question was entered into. It was dated May 21, 1919. Some of its pertinent provisions are

> VIII.   The parties hereto will use their best endeavors for the purpose of continuing as directors of said Company and as officers thereof the following:
>
> Directors:
>
> Charles A. Stoneham,
> John J. McGraw,
> Francis X. McQuade
>
> -with the right to [Stoneham] to name all additional directors as he sees fit:
>
> Officers:
>
> Charles A. Stoneham, President,
> John J. McGraw, Vice-President,
> Francis X. McQuade, Treasurer.
>
> IX.   No salaries are to be paid to any of the above officers or directors, except as follows:
>
> President, $45,000,
> Vice President, $7,500,
> Treasurer, $7,500.
>
> X.   There shall be no change in said salaries, no change in the amount of capital, or the number of shares, no change or amendment of the by-laws of the corporation or any matters regarding the policy of the business of the corporation or any matters which may in anywise affect, endanger or interfere with the rights of minority stockholders, excepting upon the mutual and unanimous consent of all of the parties hereto. ***

***

In pursuance of this contract Stoneham became president and McGraw vice president of the corporation. McQuade became treasurer. In June, 1925, his salary was increased to $10,000 a year. He continued to act until May 2, 1928, when Leo J. Bondy was elected to succeed him. The board of directors consisted of seven men. The four outside of the parties hereto were selected by Stoneham and he had complete control over them. At the meeting of May 2, 1928, Stoneham and McGraw refrained from voting, McQuade voted for himself, and the other four voted for Bondy. Defendants did not keep their agreement with McQuade to use their best efforts to continue him as treasurer. On the contrary, he was dropped with their entire acquiescence. At the next stockholders' meeting he was dropped as a director although they might have elected him.

The courts below have refused to order the reinstatement of McQuade, but have given him damages for wrongful discharge, with a right to sue for future damages.

The cause for dropping McQuade was due to the falling out of friends. McQuade and Stoneham had disagreed. The trial court has found in substance that their numerous quarrels and disputes did not affect the orderly and efficient administration of the business of the corporation; that plaintiff was removed because he had antagonized the dominant Stoneham by persisting in challenging his power over the corporate treasury and for no misconduct on his part. The court also finds that plaintiff was removed by Stoneham for protecting the corporation and its minority stockholders. We will assume that Stoneham put him out when he might have retained him, merely in order to get rid of him.

Defendants say that the contract in suit was void because the directors held their office charged with the duty to act for the corporation according to their best judgment and that any contract which compels a director to vote to keep any particular person in office and at a stated salary is illegal. Directors are the exclusive executive representatives of the corporation, charged with administration of its internal affairs and the management and use of its assets. They manage the business of the corporation. [N.Y. General Corporation Law § 27.] ***

Plaintiff contends that the converse of this proposition is true and that an agreement among directors to continue a man as an officer of a corporation is not to be broken so long as such officer is loyal to the interests of the corporation and that, as plaintiff has been found loyal to the corporation, the agreement of defendants is enforceable.

Although it has been held that an agreement among stockholders whereby it is attempted to divest the directors of their power to discharge an unfaithful employee of the corporation is illegal as against public policy *** it must be equally true that the stockholders may not, by agreement among themselves, control the directors in the exercise of the judgment vested in them by virtue of their office to elect officers and fix salaries. Their motives may not be questioned so long as their acts are legal. The bad faith or the improper motives of the parties does not change the rule. *** Directors may not by agreements entered into as stockholders abrogate their independent judgment. ***

Stockholders may, of course, combine to elect directors. That rule is well settled. As Holmes, C. J., pointedly said [citation omitted]: "If stockholders want to make their power felt, they must unite. There is no reason why a majority should not agree to keep together." The power to unite is, however, limited to the election of directors and is not extended to contracts whereby limitations are placed on the power of directors to manage the business of the corporation by the selection of agents at defined salaries.

The minority shareholders whose interests McQuade says he has been punished for protecting, are not, aside from himself, complaining about his discharge. He is not acting for the corporation or for them in this action. It is impossible to see how the corporation has been injured by the substitution of Bondy as treasurer in place of McQuade. ***

It is urged that we should pay heed to the morals and manners of the market place to sustain this agreement and that we should hold that its violation gives rise to a cause of action for damages rather than base our decision on any outworn notions of public policy. Public policy is a dangerous guide in determining the validity of a contract and courts should not interfere lightly with the freedom of competent parties to make their own contracts. We do not close our eyes to the fact that such agreements, tacitly or openly arrived at, are not uncommon, especially in close corporations where the stockholders are doing business for convenience under a corporate organization. We know that majority stockholders, united in voting trusts, effectively manage the business of a corporation by choosing trustworthy directors to reflect their policies in the corporate management. Nor are we unmindful that McQuade has, so the court has found, been shabbily treated as a purchaser of stock from Stoneham. We have said: "A trustee is held to something stricter than the morals of the market place" [citing Meinhard v. Salmon, 164 N.E. 545 (N.Y. 1928)], but Stoneham and McGraw were not trustees for McQuade as an individual. Their duty was to the corporation and its stockholders, to be exercised according to their unrestricted lawful judgment. They were under no legal obligation to deal righteously with McQuade if it was against public policy to do so.

The courts do not enforce mere moral obligations, nor legal ones either, unless some one seeks to establish rights which may be waived by custom and for convenience. We are constrained by authority to hold that a contract is illegal and void so far as it precludes the board of directors, at the risk of incurring legal liability, from changing officers, salaries, or policies or retaining individuals in office, except by consent of the contracting parties. On the whole, such a holding is probably preferable to one which would open the courts to pass on the motives of directors in the lawful exercise of their trust. [Reversed and case dismissed.]

***

Questions About *McQuade v. Stoneham*

1.   Why wasn't the agreement among McQuade, Stoneham, and McGraw enforceable?

2.   Were there other shareholders of National Exhibition Company beside these three gentlemen?

3.   Would the result have been different if McQuade had had an employment agreement with the corporation that provided that he would serve as the corporation's treasurer for five years for $10,000 per year?

While it remains an important part of corporate law today, over time the rule from *McQuade v. Stoneham* eroded a bit. For example, just a few years later, in *Clark v. Dodge*, 199 N.E. 641 (N.Y. 1936), the court upheld an agreement that provided that one shareholder would remain as general manager of the corporation as long as he was "faithful, efficient and competent" and that he would receive one-fourth of the corporation's net income, either as salary or as dividends. Because these are the sorts of decisions that the directors ordinarily make, this agreement would seem to be unenforceable under *McQuade*. However, the court found two factors to be important. First, the agreement was unanimous, that is, all of the shareholders were parties to the agreement. Second, the agreement limited director discretion only with respect to two issues. As the court observed:

> "The business of a corporation shall be managed by its board of directors." [N.Y. Gen. Corp. L. § 27.] That is the statutory norm. Are we committed by the McQuade Case to the doctrine that there may be no variation, however slight or innocuous, from that norm, where salaries or policies or the retention of individuals in office are concerned? There is ample authority supporting that doctrine *** and something may be said

for it, since it furnishes a simple, if arbitrary, test. Apart from its practical administrative convenience, the reasons upon which it is said to rest are more or less nebulous. Public policy, the intention of the Legislature, detriment to the corporation, are phrases which in this connection mean little. Possible harm to bona fide purchasers of stock or to creditors or to stockholding minorities have more substance; but such harms are absent in many instances. If the enforcement of a particular contract damages nobody—not even, in any perceptible degree, the public—one sees no reason for holding it illegal, even though it impinges slightly upon the broad provision of section 27. Damage suffered or threatened is a logical and practical test, and has come to be the one generally adopted by the courts. *** Where the directors are the sole stockholders, there seems to be no objection to enforcing an agreement among them to vote for certain people as officers. ***

***

Except for the broad dicta in the McQuade opinion, we think there can be no doubt that the agreement here in question was legal and that the complaint states a cause of action. There was no attempt to sterilize the board of directors ***. The only restrictions on Dodge were (a) that as a stockholder he should vote for Clark as a director—a perfectly legal contract; (b) that as director he should continue Clark as general manager, so long as he proved faithful, efficient, and competent—an agreement which could harm nobody; (c) that Clark should always receive as salary or dividends one-fourth of the "net income" *** [and] (d) that no salaries to other officers should be paid, unreasonable in amount or incommensurate with services rendered—a beneficial and not a harmful agreement.

If there was any invasion of the powers of the directorate under that agreement, it is so slight as to be negligible; and certainly there is no damage suffered by or threatened to anybody. The broad statements in the McQuade opinion, applicable to the facts there, should be confined to those facts.

Id. at 642-43.

Another important decision came in the 1960s, when the Illinois Supreme Court observed that:

> This court has recognized, albeit *sub silentio*, the significant conceptual differences between the close corporation and its public-issue counterpart *** Where *** no complaining minority interest appears, no fraud or apparent injury to the public or creditors is present, and no clearly prohibitory statutory language is violated, we can see no valid reason for precluding the parties from reaching any arrangements concerning the management of the corporation which are agreeable to all.

Galler v. Galler, 203 N.E.2 577, 585 (Ill. 1964) (citations omitted).

Nonetheless, if shareholders wanted to enter into an "unusual" agreement that went beyond the scope of a mere shareholder voting agreement under MBCA § 7.31 (which you studied in Chapter 5), it was uncertain whether such an agreement would be enforced, even if all of the shareholders had agreed to it, because case law evolves slowly, with different results in different jurisdictions. Fortunately, *legislatures* soon stepped into the gap, enacting statutes such as MBCA § 7.32, which is discussed in the next section.

B.   MBCA § 7.32 AND SIMILAR STATUTES

Although there simply is no substitute for a careful reading of MBCA § 7.32, note a few things about its structure before you go read it. First, subsection (a) is simply a list of "ideas," that is, topics that a Section 7.32 agreement may cover. But note that it is fairly radical in its approach; for example, subsection (a)(1) provides in part that the agreement could restrict the powers of the board, which would seem to directly change the rule from *McQuade*. Subsection (a)(3) provides in part that the agreement could specify who will be the officers of the corporation, which is normally a decision that the board makes periodically. Further, because corporate attorneys are anything if not creative, note that subsection (a)(8) provides that a Section 7.32 agreement could do even stranger things so long as they are "not contrary to public policy." But there is a catch: subsection (b)(1) provides that, to be enforceable,[*] it must meet one of three specified conditions.

---

[*] Note that an agreement that addresses one or more of the topics listed in MBCA § 7.32(a) likely wouldn't be enforceable under the rule from *McQuade v. Stoneham* without a statute to "save" it.

Further, subsections (b)(2) and (b)(3) specify, respectively, how the agreement may be amended and how long it may last (unless the agreement itself provides different answers to these questions). Subsections (c) through (g) provide additional rules. Read MBCA § 7.32 carefully and consider the following problems.

Problems

Problem 9-5: Amir, Barbette, and Constance wish to form a corporation in order to have limited liability but want it to operate much like a partnership. For example, they do not want the corporation to have a board of directors. Instead, they want to put Amir in charge of all marketing decisions, Barbette in charge of all financial decisions, and Constance in charge of all other business decisions. *Could such an agreement be enforceable under MBCA § 7.32?*

Problem 9-6: Same facts as Problem 9-5. In addition, the three shareholders want to agree that the corporation will pay dividends at the end of each year to fullest extent that is legally permitted. *Could such an agreement be enforceable under MBCA § 7.32?*

Problem 9-7: Same facts as Problem 9-5, but you may assume that the agreement is enforceable. *How long will the agreement last? How can it be amended? Is there any way to change the answers to these questions that the statute provides?*

Problem 9-8: Same facts as Problem 9-5, but you may assume that the agreement is enforceable. *Could a creditor in a veil-piercing case argue that the elimination of the board of directors means that the corporation is not observing "corporate formalities"?*

Problem 9-9: Same facts as Problem 9-5, but you may assume that the agreement is enforceable. Assume further than Constance later sells her shares to Dave, who claims that he did not know about the agreement before he bought the shares. *Is the agreement still enforceable? Would your answer change if the corporation's stock certificates did not refer to the Section 7.32 agreement?*

Problem 9-10: Same facts as Problem 9-5, but you may assume that the agreement is enforceable. Assume further that many years later the corporation does an IPO (initial public offering) and its common stock ends up being listed on the New York Stock Exchange. *Is the agreement still enforceable?*

The foregoing was intended to provide you with information about *how* shareholders may engage in advance planning in closely held corporations. We will return to this topic in Section 9.05 below. Before then, Sections 9.03 and 9.04 should convince you of the importance of advance planning.

§ 9.03   FIDUCIARY DUTIES IN CLOSELY HELD CORPORATIONS

Objectives: Given a fact pattern, you should be able to (1) identify the arguments that a plaintiff, who is a shareholder in a closely held corporation, will make to establish that the other shareholder(s) have breached the fiduciary duties that they owe to the plaintiff, (2) identify the counter-arguments that the defendants will make, (3) evaluate whether the court is likely to rule in favor of the plaintiff, including identifying and applying the test that a court would use to determine whether the defendants have breached their fiduciary duties, and (4) if so, determine the forms of relief the court may order. In addition, if the plaintiff is suing because of an action that is not traditionally considered a shareholder right (such as the termination of employment with the corporation), you should be able to identify the factors that courts will evaluate to determine whether the plaintiff nonetheless is entitled to relief.

Before this Chapter, we had assumed that shareholders in corporations did not owe fiduciary duties, either to the corporation or to other shareholders. By contrast, partners in a partnership clearly owe fiduciary duties. And the law agreed with these propositions, at least historically. Thus, the differences between corporations and partnerships were dramatic and clear. However, beginning with the following case, Massachusetts courts began to blur these distinctions.

Donahue v. Rodd Electrotype Company of New England, Inc. concerned a corporation whose stock was owned by two families: Mrs. Donahue and her son owned fifty shares (or about 20.2%) and the Rodd family owned the remaining 198 shares (or about 79.8%). Not surprisingly, the Rodd family controlled the board of directors. In 1970, Harry Rodd decided to retire. The Rodd family (acting in their capacities as directors), then caused the corporation to repurchase 45 of Harry's shares. Harry then sold or gave the rest of his shares to his children, who took over running the company.

As a result of this stock redemption, the number of outstanding shares declined from 248 to 203 and the Donahue family's percentage of ownership increased from 20.2% to 24.6%. So why was Mrs. Donahue upset enough to sue? It wasn't because she thought that the company paid Harry too much for his stock. Instead, she was upset that she didn't get the same chance to sell back her stock. Keep in mind that, under traditional rules of corporate law, the corporation has no obligation to buy back a shareholder's stock unless she has a buy-sell agreement. Also keep in mind that, with respect to stock of a closely held corporation, you can't just call your stockbroker and easily sell your shares. Read on to find out how the court decided the case.

Donahue v. Rodd Electrotype Company of New England, Inc.
Supreme Judicial Court of Massachusetts
328 N.E.2d 505 (1975)

TAURO, Chief Justice. ***

***

In her argument before this court, the plaintiff has characterized the corporate purchase of Harry Rodd's shares as an unlawful distribution of corporate assets to controlling stockholders. She urges that the distribution constitutes a breach of the fiduciary duty owed by the Rodds, as controlling stockholders, to her, a minority stockholder in the enterprise, because the Rodds failed to accord her an equal opportunity to sell her shares to the corporation. The defendants reply that the stock purchase was within the powers of the corporation and met the requirements of good faith and inherent fairness imposed on a fiduciary in his dealings with the corporation. They assert that there is no right to equal opportunity in corporate stock purchases for the corporate treasury. For the reasons hereinafter noted, we agree with the plaintiff and reverse the decree of the Superior Court. However, we limit the applicability of our holding to "close corporations," as hereinafter defined. Whether the holding should apply to other corporations is left for decision in another case, on a proper record.

A.   Close Corporations. In previous opinions, we have alluded to the distinctive nature of the close corporation, but have never defined precisely what is meant by a close corporation. *** We deem a close corporation to be typified by: (1) a small number of stockholders; (2) no ready market for the corporate stock; and (3) substantial majority stockholder participation in the management, direction and operations of the corporation.

As thus defined, the close corporation bears striking resemblance to a partnership. Commentators and courts have noted that the close corporation is often little more than an "incorporated" or "chartered" partnership. *** In essence, though, the enterprise remains one in which ownership is limited to the original parties or transferees of their stock to whom the other stockholders have agreed in which ownership and management are in the same hands, and in which the owners are quite dependent on one another for the success of the enterprise. Many close corporations are "really partnerships, between two or three people who contribute their capital, skills, experience and labor." [Citation omitted.] Just as in a partnership, the relationship among the stockholders must be one of trust, confidence and absolute loyalty if the enterprise is to succeed. Close corporations with substantial assets and with more numerous stockholders are no different from smaller close corporations in this regard. All participants rely on the fidelity and abilities of those stockholders who hold office. Disloyalty and self-seeking conduct on the part of any stockholder will engender bickering, corporate stalemates, and, perhaps, efforts to achieve dissolution.

***

Although the corporate form provides the above-mentioned advantages for the stockholders (limited liability, perpetuity, and so forth), it also supplies an opportunity for the majority stockholders to oppress or disadvantage minority stockholders. The minority is vulnerable to a variety of oppressive devices, termed "freezeouts," which the majority may employ. An authoritative study of such 'freeze-outs' enumerates some of the possibilities: "The squeezers (those who employ the freeze-out techniques) may refuse to declare dividends; they may drain off the corporation's earnings in the form of exorbitant salaries and bonuses to the majority shareholder-officers and perhaps to their relatives, or in the form of high rent by the corporation for property leased from majority shareholders ...; they may deprive minority shareholders of corporate offices and of employment by the company; they may cause the corporation to sell its assets at an inadequate price to the majority shareholders ...." F. H. O'NEAL AND J. DERWIN, EXPULSION OR OPPRESSION OF BUSINESS ASSOCIATES 42 (1961). In particular, the power of the board of directors, controlled by the majority, to declare or withhold dividends and to deny the minority employment is easily converted to a device to disadvantage minority stockholders.

The minority can, of course, initiate suit against the majority and their directors. Self-serving conduct by directors is proscribed by the director's fiduciary obligation to the corporation. However, in practice, the plaintiff will find difficulty in challenging dividend or employment policies. Such policies are considered to be within the judgment of the directors [under the business judgment rule]. *** Judicial reluctance to interfere combines with the difficulty of proof when the standard is "plain abuse of discretion" or bad faith to limit the possibilities for relief. *** [G]enerally, plaintiffs who seek judicial assistance against corporate dividend or employment policies do not prevail.

Thus, when these types of "freeze-outs" are attempted by the majority stockholders, the minority stockholders, cut off from all corporation-related revenues, must either suffer their losses or seek a buyer for their shares. Many minority stockholders will be unwilling or unable to wait for an alteration in majority policy. Typically, the minority stockholder in a close corporation has a substantial percentage of his personal assets invested in the corporation. The stockholder may have anticipated that his salary from his position with the corporation would be his livelihood. Thus, he cannot afford to wait passively. He must liquidate his investment in the close corporation in order to reinvest the funds in income-producing enterprises.

At this point, the true plight of the minority stockholder in a close corporation becomes manifest. He cannot easily reclaim his capital. In a large public corporation, the oppressed or dissident minority stockholder could sell his stock in order to extricate some of his invested capital. By definition, this market is not available for shares in the close corporation. In a partnership, a partner who feels abused by his fellow partners may cause dissolution by [dissociating by express will] *** and recover his share of partnership assets and accumulated profits. *** By contrast, the stockholder in the close corporation or "incorporated partnership" may achieve dissolution and recovery of his share of the enterprise assets only by compliance with the rigorous terms of the [corporate statute, which requires a majority vote]. ***

Thus, in a close corporation, the minority stockholders may be trapped in a disadvantageous situation. No outsider would knowingly assume the position of the disadvantaged minority. The outsider would have the same difficulties. To cut losses, the minority stockholder may be compelled to deal with the majority. This is the capstone of the majority plan. Majority "freeze-out" schemes which withhold dividends are designed to compel the minority to relinquish stock at inadequate prices. When the minority stockholder agrees to sell out at less than fair value, the majority has won.

Because of the fundamental resemblance of the close corporation to the partnership, the trust and confidence which are essential to this scale and manner of enterprise, and the inherent danger to minority interests in the close corporation, we hold that stockholders* in the close corporation owe one another substantially the same fiduciary duty in the operation of the enterprise that partners owe to one another. In our previous decisions, we have defined the standard of duty owed by partners to one another as the "utmost good faith and loyalty." [Citation omitted.] Stockholders in close corporations must discharge their management and stockholder responsibilities in conformity with this strict good faith standard. They may not act out of avarice, expediency or self-interest in derogation of their duty of loyalty to the other stockholders and to the corporation.

---

*   [Footnote by court]: We do not limit our holding to majority stockholders. In the close corporation, the minority may do equal damage through unscrupulous and improper "sharp dealings" with an unsuspecting majority.

We contrast this strict good faith standard with the somewhat less stringent standard of fiduciary duty to which directors and stockholders of all corporations must adhere in the discharge of their corporate responsibilities. Corporate directors are held to a good faith and inherent fairness standard of conduct and are not "permitted to serve two masters whose interests are antagonistic." [Citation omitted.]

[By contrast, the] more rigorous duty of partners and participants in a joint adventure, here extended to stockholders in a close corporation, was described by then Chief Judge Cardozo of the New York Court of Appeals in *Meinhard v. Salmon*, 249 N.Y. 458, 164 N.E. 545 (1928): "Joint adventurers, like copartners, owe to one another, while the enterprise continues, the duty of the finest loyalty. Many forms of conduct permissible in a workaday world for those acting at arm's length, are forbidden to those bound by fiduciary ties. ... Not honesty alone, but the punctilio of an honor the most sensitive, is then the standard of behavior." [Citation omitted.]

***

In [prior cases involving close corporations] we have imposed a duty of loyalty more exacting than that duty owed by a director to his corporation or by a majority stockholder to the minority in a public corporation because of facts particular to the close corporation in the cases. In the instant case, we extend this strict duty of loyalty to all stockholders in close corporations. The circumstances which justified findings of relationships of trust and confidence in these particular cases exist universally in modified form in all close corporations. Statements in other cases which suggest that stockholders of a corporation do not stand in a relationship of trust and confidence to one another will not be followed in the close corporation context.

B.   *Equal Opportunity in a Close Corporation.* Under settled Massachusetts law, a domestic corporation, unless forbidden by statute, has the power to purchase its own shares. *** When the corporation reacquiring its own stock is a close corporation, the purchase is subject to the additional requirement, in the light of our holding in this opinion, that the stockholders, who, as directors or controlling stockholders, caused the corporation to enter into the stock purchase agreement, must have acted with the utmost good faith and loyalty to the other stockholders.

To meet this test, if the stockholder whose shares were purchased was a member of the controlling group, the controlling stockholders must cause the corporation to offer each stockholder an equal opportunity to sell a ratable number of his shares to the corporation at an identical price. Purchase by the corporation confers substantial benefits on the members of the controlling group whose shares were purchased [such as the creation of a purchaser for their shares and access to corporate assets for personal use]. These benefits are not available to the minority stockholders if the corporation does not also offer them an opportunity to sell their shares. The controlling group may not, consistent with its strict duty to the minority, utilize its control of the corporation to obtain special advantages and disproportionate benefit from its share ownership.

*** By definition, there is no ready market for shares of a close corporation. The purchase creates a market for shares which previously had been unmarketable. It transforms a previously illiquid investment into a liquid one. If the close corporation purchases shares only from a member of the controlling group, the controlling stockholder can convert his shares into cash at a time when none of the other stockholders can. Consistent with its strict fiduciary duty, the controlling group may not utilize its control of the corporation to establish an exclusive market in previously unmarketable shares from which the minority stockholders are excluded.

***

The rule of equal opportunity in stock purchases by close corporations provides equal access to these benefits for all stockholders. We hold that, in any case in which the controlling stockholders have exercised their power over the corporation to deny the minority such equal opportunity, the minority shall be entitled to appropriate relief. ***

***

WILKINS, Justice (concurring). I agree with much of what the Chief Justice says in support of granting relief to the plaintiff. However, I do not join in any implication *** that the rule concerning a close corporation's purchase of a controlling stockholder's shares applies to all operations of the corporation as they affect minority stockholders. That broader issue, which is apt to arise in connection with salaries and dividend policy, is not involved in this case. The analogy to partnerships may not be a complete one.

Questions About *Donahue v. Rodd Electrotype Company*

1.   Which shareholders owe fiduciary duties—the majority, the minority, or both?

2.   Would the case have been decided differently if the corporation was publicly traded?   What if it had thirty shareholders?

3.   Was the plaintiff's lawsuit direct or derivative?

4.   Can you explain what the court meant by the phrase "ratable number of his shares" in the following sentence: "[I]f the stockholder whose shares were purchased was a member of the controlling group, the controlling stockholders must cause the corporation to offer each stockholder an equal opportunity to sell a ratable number of his shares to the corporation at an identical price"?

5.   Why were the Rodds considered a controlling group of the corporation?

As you no doubt have gathered, *Donahue* established an "equal opportunity" rule that applies when a closely held corporation redeems stock from a member of a controlling group (such as the Rodd family).   But the more important aspect of the case was its imposition of fiduciary duties on shareholders in closely held corporations, an approach that many other states have since followed.

Unfortunately, the equal opportunity rule, although it is still applicable, doesn't provide us with much guidance in how to resolve *other types* of disputes in closely held corporations.   Fortunately, in the following year the same court got a chance to revise its approach to fiduciary duties in closely held corporations, as seen in the following case.

Wilkes v. Springside Nursing Home, Inc.
Supreme Judicial Court of Massachusetts
353 N.E.2d 657 (1976)

HENNESSEY, Chief Justice.   On August 5, 1971, the plaintiff (Wilkes) filed a bill in equity for declaratory judgment in the Probate Court for Berkshire County, naming as defendants T. Edward Quinn (Quinn), Leon L. Riche (Riche), the First Agricultural National Bank of Berkshire County and Frank Sutherland MacShane as executors under the will of Lawrence R. Connor (Connor), and the Springside Nursing Home, Inc. (Springside or the corporation). Wilkes alleged that he, Quinn, Riche and Dr. Hubert A. Pipkin (Pipkin) entered into a partnership agreement in 1951, prior to the incorporation of Springside, which agreement was breached in 1967 when Wilkes's salary was terminated and he was voted out as an officer and director of the corporation. Wilkes sought, among other forms of relief, damages in the amount of the salary he would have received had he continued as a director and officer of Springside subsequent to March, 1967.

A judge of the Probate Court referred the suit to a master, who, after a lengthy hearing, issued his final report in late 1973. Wilkes's objections to the master's report were overruled after a hearing, and the master's report was confirmed in late 1974. A judgment was entered dismissing Wilkes's action on the merits. We granted direct appellate review. On appeal, Wilkes argued in the alternative that (1) he should recover damages for breach of the alleged partnership agreement; and (2) he should recover damages because the defendants, as majority stockholders in Springside, breached their fiduciary duty to him as a minority stockholder by their action in February and March, 1967.

We conclude that the master's findings were warranted by the evidence and that his report was properly confirmed. However, we reverse so much of the judgment as dismisses Wilkes's complaint and order the entry of a judgment substantially granting the relief sought by Wilkes under the second alternative set forth above.

A summary of the pertinent facts as found by the master is set out in the following pages. It will be seen that, although the issue whether there was a breach of the fiduciary duty owed to Wilkes by the majority stockholders in Springside was not considered by the master, the master's report and the designated portions of the transcript of the evidence before him supply us with a sufficient basis for our conclusion.

In 1951 Wilkes acquired an option to purchase a building and lot located on the corner of Springside Avenue and North Street in Pittsfield, Massachusetts, the building having previously housed the Hillcrest Hospital. Though Wilkes was principally engaged in the roofing and siding business, he had gained a reputation locally for profitable dealings in real estate. Riche, an acquaintance of Wilkes, learned of the option, and interested Quinn (who was known to Wilkes through membership on the draft board in Pittsfield) and Pipkin (an acquaintance of both Wilkes and Riche) in joining Wilkes in his investment. The four men met and decided to participate jointly in the purchase of the building and lot as a real estate investment which, they believed, had good profit potential on resale or rental.

The parties later determined that the property would have its greatest potential for profit if it were operated by them as a nursing home. Wilkes consulted his attorney, who advised him that if the four men were to operate the contemplated nursing home as planned, they would be partners and would be liable for any debts incurred by the partnership and by each other. On the attorney's suggestion, and after consultation among themselves, ownership of the property was vested in Springside, a corporation organized under Massachusetts law.

Each of the four men invested $1,000 and subscribed to ten shares of $100 par value stock in Springside. At the time of incorporation it was understood by all of the parties that each would be a director of Springside and each would participate actively in the management and decision making involved in operating the corporation. It was, further, the understanding and intention of all the parties that, corporate resources permitting, each would receive money from the corporation in equal amounts as long as each assumed an active and ongoing responsibility for carrying a portion of the burdens necessary to operate the business.

The work involved in establishing and operating a nursing home was roughly apportioned, and each of the four men undertook his respective tasks. Initially, Riche was elected president of Springside, Wilkes was elected treasurer, and Quinn was elected clerk. Each of the four was listed in the articles of [incorporation] as a director of the corporation.

At some time in 1952, it became apparent that the operational income and cash flow from the business were sufficient to permit the four stockholders to draw money from the corporation on a regular basis. Each of the four original parties initially received $35 a week from the corporation. As time went on the weekly return to each was increased until, in 1955, it totaled $100.

In 1959, after a long illness, Pipkin sold his shares in the corporation to Connor, who was known to Wilkes, Riche and Quinn through past transactions with Springside in his capacity as president of the First Agricultural National Bank of Berkshire County. Connor received a weekly stipend from the corporation equal to that received by Wilkes, Riche and Quinn. He was elected a director of the corporation but never held any other office. He was assigned no specific area of responsibility in the operation of the nursing home but did participate in business discussions and decisions as a director and served additionally as financial adviser to the corporation.

In 1965 the stockholders decided to sell a portion of the corporate property to Quinn who, in addition to being a stockholder in Springside, possessed an interest in another corporation which desired to operate a rest home on the property. Wilkes was successful in prevailing on the other stockholders of Springside to procure a higher sale price for the property than Quinn apparently anticipated paying or desired to pay. After the sale was consummated, the relationship between Quinn and Wilkes began to deteriorate.

The bad blood between Quinn and Wilkes affected the attitudes of both Riche and Connor. As a consequence of the strained relations among the parties, Wilkes, in January of 1967, gave notice of his intention to sell his shares for an amount based on an appraisal of their value. In February of 1967 a directors' meeting was held and the board exercised its right to establish the salaries of its officers and employees. A schedule of payments was established whereby Quinn was to receive a substantial weekly increase and Riche and Connor were to continue receiving $100 a week. Wilkes, however, was left off the list of those to whom a salary was to be paid. The directors also set the annual meeting of the stockholders for March, 1967.

At the annual meeting in March, Wilkes was not reelected as a director ***. He was further informed that neither his services nor his presence at the nursing home was wanted by his associates.

The meetings of the directors and stockholders in early 1967, the master found, were used as a vehicle to force Wilkes out of active participation in the management and operation of the corporation and to cut off all corporate payments to him. Though the board of directors had the power to dismiss any officers or employees for misconduct or neglect of duties, there was no indication in the minutes of the board of directors' meeting of February, 1967, that the failure to establish a salary for Wilkes was based on either ground. The severance of Wilkes from the payroll resulted not from misconduct or neglect of duties, but because of the personal desire of Quinn, Riche and Connor to prevent him from continuing to receive money from the corporation.   Despite a continuing deterioration in his personal relationship with his associates, Wilkes had consistently endeavored to carry on his responsibilities to the corporation in the same satisfactory manner and with the same degree of competence he had previously shown. Wilkes was at all times willing to carry on his responsibilities and participation if permitted so to do and provided that he receive his weekly stipend.

1.   We turn to Wilkes's claim for damages based on a breach of the fiduciary duty owed to him by the other participants in this venture. In light of the theory underlying this claim, we do not consider it vital to our approach to this case whether the claim is governed by partnership law or the law applicable to business corporations. This is so because, as all the parties agree, Springside was at all times relevant to this action, a close corporation as we have recently defined such an entity in *Donahue v. Rodd Electrotype Co. of New England, Inc.* [citation omitted].

In *Donahue*, we held that "stockholders in the close corporation owe one another substantially the same fiduciary duty in the operation of the enterprise that partners owe to one another." [Citation omitted.] As determined in previous decisions of this court, the standard of duty owed by partners to one another is one of "utmost good faith and loyalty." [Citations omitted.] Thus, we concluded in *Donahue*, with regard to "their actions relative to the operations of the enterprise and the effects of that operation on the rights and investments of other stockholders," "(s)tockholders in close corporations must discharge their management and stockholder responsibilities in conformity with this strict good faith standard. They may not act out of avarice, expediency or self-interest in derogation of their duty of loyalty to the other stockholders and to the corporation." [Citation omitted.]

In the *Donahue* case we recognized that one peculiar aspect of close corporations was the opportunity afforded to majority stockholders to oppress, disadvantage or "freeze out" minority stockholders. In *Donahue* itself, for example, the majority refused the minority an equal opportunity to sell a ratable number of shares to the corporation at the same price available to the majority. The net result of this refusal, we said, was that the minority could be forced to "sell out at less than fair value," [citation omitted] since there is by definition no ready market for minority stock in a close corporation.

"Freeze outs," however, may be accomplished by the use of other devices. One such device which has proved to be particularly effective in accomplishing the purpose of the majority is to deprive minority stockholders of corporate offices and of employment with the corporation. [Citation omitted.] This "freeze-out" technique has been successful because courts fairly consistently have been disinclined to interfere in those facets of internal corporate operations, such as the selection and retention or dismissal of officers, directors and employees, which essentially involve management decisions subject to the principle of majority control. [Citation omitted.] As one authoritative source has said, "(M)any courts apparently feel that there is a legitimate sphere in which the controlling (directors or) shareholders can act in their own interest even if the minority suffers." [Citations omitted.]

The denial of employment to the minority at the hands of the majority is especially pernicious in some instances. A guaranty of employment with the corporation may have been one of the "basic reason(s) why a minority owner has invested capital in the firm." [Citation omitted.] The minority stockholder typically depends on his salary as the principal return on his investment, since the "earnings of a close corporation ... are distributed in major part in salaries, bonuses and retirement benefits." [Citation omitted.] Other noneconomic interests of the minority stockholder are likewise injuriously affected by barring him from corporate office. [Citation omitted.] Such action severely restricts his participation in the management of the enterprise, and he is relegated to enjoying those benefits incident to his status as a stockholder. [Citation omitted.] In sum, by terminating a minority stockholder's employment or by severing him from a position as an officer or director, the majority effectively frustrate the minority stockholder's purposes in entering on the corporate venture and also deny him an equal return on his investment.

The *Donahue* decision acknowledged, as a "natural outgrowth" of the case law of this Commonwealth, a strict obligation on the part of majority stockholders in a close corporation to deal with the minority with the utmost good faith and loyalty. On its face, this strict standard is applicable in the instant case. The distinction between the majority action in *Donahue* and the majority action in this case is more one of form than of substance. Nevertheless, we are concerned that untempered application of the strict good faith standard enunciated in *Donahue* to cases such as the one before us will result in the imposition of limitations on legitimate action by the controlling group in a close corporation which will unduly hamper its effectiveness in managing the corporation in the best interests of all concerned. The majority, concededly, have certain rights to what has been termed "selfish ownership" in the corporation which should be balanced against the concept of their fiduciary obligation to the minority. [Citations omitted.]

Therefore, when minority stockholders in a close corporation bring suit against the majority alleging a breach of the strict good faith duty owed to them by the majority, we must carefully analyze the action taken by the controlling stockholders in the individual case. It must be asked whether the controlling group can demonstrate a legitimate business purpose for its action. [Citations omitted.] In asking this question, we acknowledge the fact that the controlling group in a close corporation must have some room to maneuver in establishing the business policy of the corporation. It must have a large measure of discretion, for example, in declaring or withholding dividends, deciding whether to merge or consolidate, establishing the salaries of corporate officers, dismissing directors with or without cause, and hiring and firing corporate employees.

When an asserted business purpose for their action is advanced by the majority, however, we think it is open to minority stockholders to demonstrate that the same legitimate objective could have been achieved through an alternative course of action less harmful to the minority's interest. [Citations omitted.] If called on to settle a dispute, our courts must weigh the legitimate business purpose, if any, against the practicability of a less harmful alternative.

Applying this approach to the instant case it is apparent that the majority stockholders in Springside have not shown a legitimate business purpose for severing Wilkes from the payroll of the corporation or for refusing to reelect him as a salaried officer and director. The master's subsidiary findings relating to the purpose of the meetings of the directors and stockholders in February and March, 1967, are supported by the evidence. There was no showing of misconduct on Wilkes's part as a director, officer or employee of the corporation which would lead us to approve the majority action as a legitimate response to the disruptive nature of an undesirable individual bent on injuring or destroying the corporation. On the contrary, it appears that Wilkes had always accomplished his assigned share of the duties competently, and that he had never indicated an unwillingness to continue to do so.

It is an inescapable conclusion from all the evidence that the action of the majority stockholders here was a designed "freeze out" for which no legitimate business purpose has been suggested. Furthermore, we may infer that a design to pressure Wilkes into selling his shares to the corporation at a price below their value well may have been at the heart of the majority's plan.

In the context of this case, several factors bear directly on the duty owed to Wilkes by his associates. At a minimum, the duty of utmost good faith and loyalty would demand that the majority consider that their action was in disregard of a long-standing policy of the stockholders that each would be a director of the corporation and that employment with the corporation would go hand in hand with stock ownership; that Wilkes was one of the four originators of the nursing home venture; and that Wilkes, like the others, had invested his capital and time for more than fifteen years with the expectation that he would continue to participate in corporate decisions. Most important is the plain fact that the cutting off of Wilkes's salary, together with the fact that the corporation never declared a dividend ***, assured that Wilkes would receive no return at all from the corporation.

2.   The question of Wilkes's damages at the hands of the majority has not been thoroughly explored on the record before us. Wilkes, in his original complaint, sought damages in the amount of the $100 a week he believed he was entitled to from the time his salary was terminated up until the time this action was commenced. However, the record shows that, after Wilkes was severed from the corporate payroll, the schedule of salaries and payments made to the other stockholders varied from time to time. In addition, the duties assumed by the other stockholders after Wilkes was deprived of his share of the corporate earnings appear to have changed in significant respects. Any resolution of this question must take into account whether the corporation was dissolved during the pendency of this litigation.

Therefore *** [t]he case is remanded *** for further proceedings concerning the issue of damages. Thereafter a judgment shall be entered declaring that Quinn, Riche and Connor breached their fiduciary duty to Wilkes as a minority stockholder in Springside, and awarding money damages therefor. Wilkes shall be allowed to recover from Riche, the estate of T. Edward Quinn and the estate of Lawrence R. Connor, ratably, according to the inequitable enrichment of each, the salary he would have received had he remained an officer and director of Springside. In considering the issue of damages the judge on remand shall take into account the extent to which any remaining corporate funds of Springside may be diverted to satisfy Wilkes's claim.

So ordered.

_____

Questions About *Wilkes v. Springside Nursing Home, Inc.*

1.   Why did the defendants fire Wilkes from his employment? Were the defendants able to demonstrate a legitimate business purpose doing so?

2.   What could Wilkes have argued to show that there was a less harmful alternative?

While the black-letter rule from the *Wilkes* case is easily stated and appears to be a rule that you can apply in a wide range of factual scenarios (unlike the equal opportunity rule from *Donahue*), it often is difficult to predict how a court will decide a given case. For example, consider the following problems:

Problems

Problem 9-11: You are the judge in the *Wilkes* case. However, the defendants have also argued that the reason that Wilkes was fired from his job was that he was a cocaine addict. While using cocaine, Wilkes often was rude to nursing home residents. The defendants also believe that Wilkes may have stolen prescription medicines from residents. Meanwhile, Wilkes argues that he will go to a drug rehabilitation clinic if he can keep his job. *How will you decide the case?*

Problem 9-12: Tom and Matt formed TM Corp. twelve years ago, under Massachusetts law. For years, Tom and Matt each owned 50% of the stock of TM Corp. and worked eighty-hour weeks before the business became successful. For the past three years, Molitor has been working in the mail room at TM Corp. He is not a very competent employee but works very hard. One day, because they feel sorry for Molitor, Tom and Matt decide to give two shares of stock to Molitor as a holiday bonus. As a result, Tom now owns 49% of the stock, Matt owns 49% of the stock, and

Molitor owns 2% of the stock. *If TM Corp. later fires Molitor, must it show a legitimate business purpose for doing so?*

<u>Problem 9-13</u>: *Why weren't the defendants in the* Wilkes *case protected by the business judgment rule?*

A NOTE ON DELAWARE LAW

Although many states have followed Massachusetts law on the issue of fiduciary duties in closely held corporations, one major exception is Delaware. In *Nixon v. Blackwell,* 626 A.2d 1366 (Del. 1993), the Delaware Supreme Court rejected "special, judicially-created rules to 'protect' minority stockholders of closely-held Delaware corporations." Although this statement may be more ambiguous than it seems due to some unique facts in the *Nixon* case, in *Riblet Products Corp. v. Nagy,* 683 A.2d 37, 39 n.2 (Del. 1996), the Delaware Supreme Court rejected the *Wilkes* case, noting that "although majority stockholders have fiduciary duties to minority stockholders [in their capacities as] stockholders, those duties are not implicated when the issue involves the rights of the minority stockholder [in his capacity as an] employee ...." However, there is a chapter of the Delaware General Corporation law that is specially designed for closely held corporations that choose to "opt in" to it. *See* Del. Gen. Corp. L. §§ 341 – 356.

Problem 9-12 is designed to illustrate the difficulties in applying the *Wilkes* test to employment-related decisions. As discussed in Section 9.01, the rule in most (but not all) states is that employees are "at will" and can be freely fired for any reason or no reason unless they have an employment agreement or the firing would violate a law such as an anti- discrimination statute.

Does owning a share of stock in a closely held corporation transform an employee's status from "at will" to "just cause" (that is, the employee cannot be fired without a legitimate business purpose)? It depends. In Massachusetts, the court refused to apply the *Wilkes* test in a case in which a minority shareholder was fired without cause. *Merola v. Exergen Corp.*, 668 N.E.2d 351 (Mass. 1996). One key fact was that the plaintiff had been an employee *before* purchasing stock. Other important facts were that the plaintiff's firing complied with his employment agreement and he made a profit when the corporation redeemed his stock.

Another court that confronted this problem was *Hollis v. Hill*, 232 F.3d 460 (5th Cir. 2000). To greatly summarize the facts in the case, Hill, who was a 50% shareholder (and who was also the president of the company but controlled only half of the board) caused the company to reduce the salary of the other 50% shareholder, Hollis, to zero. In other words, Hill fired Hollis. Meanwhile, however, Hill continued to earn a salary. Naturally, Hollis sued. Here is an important passage in the court's opinion:

> We concede that many of Hill's *** acts, including the diminution and eventual termination of [Hollis's] salary, the failure to deliver financial information, the closing of one of the company's offices, termination of employment, and the cessation of benefits, are classic examples of acts typically shielded from judicial scrutiny under the business judgment rule. Generally, employees who are adversely affected by such officer and director decisions may not claim oppression [or breach of fiduciary duty] by those in control of the corporation, even if they are also shareholders of the corporation. Certain actions by a director, however, receive much different treatment when the corporation only has a few shareholders, including that director.
>
> ***
>
> *** [O]pinions [in other cases] make clear, however, that shareholders do not enjoy fiduciary-rooted entitlements to their jobs. Such a result would clearly interfere with the doctrine of employment [at will]. Rather, the courts have limited relief to instances in which the shareholder has been harmed as a shareholder. The fiduciary duty in the close corporation context, as in the context of public corporations, appropriately is viewed as a protection of the shareholder's investment. The precise nature of an investment in a close corporation often is not clear, particularly when the shareholder is also an employee. It is therefore important to distinguish investors who obtain their return on investment through benefits provided to them as employees from employees who happen also to be investors. To that end, courts may consider the following nonexclusive factors: whether the corporation typically distributes its profits in the form of salaries; whether the shareholder/employee owns a significant percentage of the firm's shares; whether the shareholder/employee is a founder of the business; whether the shares were received as compensation for services; whether the shareholder/employee expects the value of the shares to increase; whether the shareholder/employee has made a significant capital contribution;

whether the shareholder/ employee has otherwise demonstrated a reasonable expectation that the returns from the investment will be obtained through continued employment; and whether stock ownership is a requirement of employment. The minority's shareholder interest is not injured, however, if the corporation redeems shares at a fair price or a price determined by prior contract or the shareholder is otherwise able to obtain a fair price.

Id. at 467, 470-71.

For a recent Texas decision illustrating the difficulty of dealing with the business judgment rule in the context of close-corporation disputes, see *Ritchie v. Rupe*, 339 S.W.3d 275 (Tex. Ct. App. 2011).

§ 9.04   INVOLUNTARY DISSOLUTION

Objectives: Given a fact pattern, you should be able to (1) identify the arguments that a plaintiff, who is a shareholder in a closely held corporation, will make to establish that the other shareholder(s) have "oppressed" her within the meaning of MBCA § 14.30, (2) identify the counter-arguments that the defendants will make, (3) evaluate whether the court is likely to rule in favor of the plaintiff, including identifying and applying the test that a court would use to determine whether "oppression" is present, and (4) if so, determine the forms of relief the court may order. You should also be able to do the same with respect to "deadlock" within the meaning of MBCA § 14.30.

A.   OPPRESSION

As you saw above, fiduciary-duty analysis may provide a shareholder in a closely held corporation who has been "abused" with some form of relief (assuming that she has the resources to litigate the case). Massachusetts started "the ball rolling" on this issue and since then many other states have followed suit. *See generally* Mary Siegel, *Fiduciary Duty Myths in Close Corporate Law*, 29 DEL. J. CORP. L. 377 (2004).

An *alternative* way to provide some relief to an abused shareholder is MBCA § 14.30. That statute (along with somewhat similar statutes in approximately thirty-seven states) provides that a court may order a corporation to be *dissolved* if a plaintiff can establish any of the various grounds for dissolution. One of these grounds, which is set forth in subsection (a)(2)(ii), is that "the directors or those in control of the corporation have acted, are acting, or will act in a manner that is illegal, oppressive, or fraudulent." While the terms "illegal" and "fraudulent" obviously have well-understood meanings, the term "oppressive" is a bit more elusive. Because the statute does not define this term, courts had to do so. The following is one of the leading cases on this issue.

In the Matter of the Judicial Dissolution of Kemp & Beatley, Inc.
Court of Appeals of New York
473 N.E.2d 1173 (1984)

Cooke, Chief Judge. When the majority shareholders of a close corporation award *de facto* dividends to all shareholders except a class of minority shareholders, such a policy may constitute "oppressive actions" and serve as a basis for an order made pursuant to section 1104-a of the [New York] Business Corporation Law dissolving the corporation. In the instant matter, there is sufficient evidence to support the lower courts' conclusion that the majority shareholders had altered a long-standing policy to distribute corporate earnings on the basis of stock ownership, as against petitioners only. Moreover, the courts did not abuse their discretion by concluding that dissolution was the only means by which petitioners could gain a fair return on their investment.

[I.]   The business concern of Kemp & Beatley, incorporated under the laws of New York, designs and manufactures table linens and sundry tabletop items. The company's stock consists of 1,500 outstanding shares held by eight shareholders. Petitioner Dissin had been employed by the company for 42 years when, in June 1979, he resigned. Prior to resignation, Dissin served as vice-president and a director of Kemp & Beatley. Over the course of his employment, Dissin had acquired stock in the company and currently owns 200 shares.

Petitioner Gardstein, like Dissin, had been a long-time employee of the company. Hired in 1944, Gardstein was for the next 35 years involved in various aspects of the business including material procurement, product design, and plant management. His employment was terminated by the company in December 1980. He currently owns 105 shares of Kemp & Beatley stock.

Apparent unhappiness surrounded petitioners' leaving the employ of the company. Of particular concern was that they no longer received any distribution of the company's earnings. Petitioners considered themselves to be "frozen out" of the company; whereas it had been their experience when with the company to receive a distribution of the company's earnings according to their stockholdings, in the form of either dividends or extra compensation, that distribution was no longer forthcoming.

Gardstein and Dissin, together holding 20.33% of the company's outstanding stock, commenced the instant proceeding in June 1981, seeking dissolution of Kemp & Beatley pursuant to section 1104-a of the Business Corporation Law. Their petition alleged "fraudulent and oppressive" conduct by the company's board of directors such as to render petitioners' stock "a virtually worthless asset." Supreme Court referred the matter for a hearing, which was held in March 1982.

Upon considering the testimony of petitioners and the principals of Kemp & Beatley, the referee concluded that "the corporate management has by its policies effectively rendered petitioners' shares worthless, and *** the only way petitioners can expect any return is by dissolution". Petitioners were found to have invested capital in the company expecting, among other things, to receive dividends or "bonuses" based upon their stock holdings. Also found was the company's "established buy-out policy" by which it would purchase the stock of employee shareholders upon their leaving its employ.

The involuntary-dissolution statute ([New York] Business Corporation Law, §1104-a) permits dissolution when a corporation's controlling faction is found guilty of "oppressive action" toward the complaining shareholders. The referee considered oppression to arise when "those in control" of the corporation "have acted in such a manner as to defeat those expectations of the minority stockholders which formed the basis of [their] participation in the venture." The expectations of petitioners that they would not be arbitrarily excluded from gaining a return on their investment and that their stock would be purchased by the corporation upon termination of employment, were deemed defeated by prevailing corporate policies. Dissolution was recommended in the referee's report, subject to giving respondent corporation an opportunity to purchase petitioners' stock.

Supreme Court confirmed the referee's report. It, too, concluded that due to the corporation's new dividend policy petitioners had been prevented from receiving any return on their investments. Liquidation of the corporate assets was found the only means by which petitioners would receive a fair return. The court considered judicial dissolution of a corporation to be "a serious and severe remedy." Consequently, the order of dissolution was conditioned upon the corporation's being permitted to purchase petitioners' stock. The Appellate Division affirmed, without opinion.

At issue in this appeal is the scope of section 1104-a of the Business Corporation Law. Specifically, this court must determine whether the provision for involuntary dissolution when the "directors or those in control of the corporation have been guilty of *** oppressive actions toward the complaining shareholders" was properly applied in the circumstances of this case. We hold that it was, and therefore affirm.

[II.] Judicially ordered dissolution of a corporation at the behest of minority interests is a remedy of relatively recent vintage in New York. Historically, this State's courts were considered divested of equity jurisdiction to order dissolution, as statutory prescriptions were deemed exclusive. [Citation omitted.] Statutes permitting judicial dissolution of corporations either limited the types of corporations under their purview or restricted the parties who could petition for dissolution to the Attorney-General, or the directors, trustees, or majority shareholders of the corporation. [Citations omitted.]

Minority shareholders were granted standing in the absence of statutory authority to seek dissolution of corporations when controlling shareholders engaged in certain egregious conduct. [Citation omitted.] Predicated on the majority shareholders' fiduciary obligation to treat all shareholders fairly and equally, to preserve corporate assets, and to fulfill their responsibilities of corporate management with "scrupulous good faith," the courts' equitable power can be invoked when "it appears that the directors and majority shareholders 'have so palpably breached the fiduciary duty they owe to the minority shareholders that they are disqualified from exercising the exclusive discretion and the dissolution power given to them by statute.'" [Citations omitted.] True to the ancient principle that equity jurisdiction will not lie when there exists a remedy at law, the courts have not entertained a minority's petition in equity when their rights and interests could be adequately protected in a legal action, such as by a shareholder's derivative suit. [Citations omitted.]

Supplementing this principle of judicially ordered equitable dissolution of a corporation, the Legislature has shown a special solicitude toward the rights of minority shareholders of closely held corporations by enacting section 1104-a of the Business Corporation Law.[*] That statute provides a mechanism for the holders

---

[Footnote by court]: The statute provides: ***

"(a) The holders of twenty percent or more of all outstanding shares of a corporation, other than a [publicly traded] corporation ***, who are entitled to vote in an election of directors may present a petition of dissolution on one or more of the following grounds:

"(1)   The directors or those in control of the corporation have been guilty of illegal, fraudulent or oppressive actions toward the complaining shareholders;

"(2)   The property or assets of the corporation are being looted, wasted, or diverted for non-corporate purposes by its directors, officers or those in control of the corporation.

"(b)   The court, in determining whether to proceed with involuntary dissolution pursuant to this section, shall take into account: "(1) Whether liquidation of the corporation is the only feasible means whereby the petitioners may reasonably expect to obtain a fair return on their investment; and "(2) Whether liquidation of the corporation is reasonably necessary

of at least 20% of the outstanding shares of a corporation whose stock is not traded on a securities market to petition for its dissolution "under special circumstances". The circumstances that give rise to dissolution fall into two general classifications: mistreatment of complaining shareholders (subd. [a], par. [1]), or misappropriation of corporate assets (subd. [a], par. [2]) by controlling shareholders, directors or officers.

Section 1104-a (subd. [a], par. [1]) describes three types of proscribed activity: "illegal", "fraudulent", and "oppressive" conduct. The first two terms are familiar words that are commonly understood at law. The last, however, does not enjoy the same certainty gained through long usage. As no definition is provided by the statute, it falls upon the courts to provide guidance. [Citation omitted.]

The statutory concept of "oppressive actions" can, perhaps, best be understood by examining the characteristics of close corporations and the Legislature's general purpose in creating this involuntary-dissolution statute. It is widely understood that, in addition to supplying capital to a contemplated or ongoing enterprise and expecting a fair and equal return, parties comprising the ownership of a close corporation may expect to be actively involved in its management and operation.

As a leading commentator in the field has observed: "Unlike the typical shareholder in a publicly held corporation, who may be simply an investor or a speculator and cares nothing for the responsibilities of management, the shareholder in a close corporation is a co-owner of the business and wants the privileges and powers that go with ownership. His participation in that particular corporation is often his principal or sole source of income. As a matter of fact, providing employment for himself may have been the principal reason why he participated in organizing the corporation. He may or may not anticipate an ultimate profit from the sale of his interest, but he normally draws very little from the corporation as dividends. In his capacity as an officer or employee of the corporation, he looks to his salary for the principal return on his capital investment, because earnings of a close corporation, as is well known, are distributed in major part in salaries, bonuses and retirement benefits." [Citation omitted.]

Shareholders enjoy flexibility in memorializing these expectations through agreements setting forth each party's rights and obligations in corporate governance. [Citation omitted.] In the absence of such an agreement, however, ultimate decision-making power respecting corporate policy will be reposed in the holders of a majority interest in the corporation. [Citation omitted.] A wielding of

---

for the protection of the rights and interests of any substantial number of shareholders or of the petitioners."

this power by any group controlling a corporation may serve to destroy a stockholder's vital interests and expectations.

As the stock of closely held corporations generally is not readily salable, a minority shareholder at odds with management policies may be without either a voice in protecting his or her interests or any reasonable means of withdrawing his or her investment. This predicament may fairly be considered the legislative concern underlying the provision at issue in this case; inclusion of the criteria that the corporation's stock not be traded on securities markets and that the complaining shareholder be subject to oppressive actions supports this conclusion.

Defining oppressive conduct as distinct from illegality in the present context has been considered in other forums. The question has been resolved by considering oppressive actions to refer to conduct that substantially defeats the "reasonable expectations" held by minority shareholders in committing their capital to the particular enterprise. [Citations omitted.] This concept is consistent with the apparent purpose underlying the provision under review. A shareholder who reasonably expected that ownership in the corporation would entitle him or her to a job, a share of corporate earnings, a place in corporate management, or some other form of security, would be oppressed in a very real sense when others in the corporation seek to defeat those expectations and there exists no effective means of salvaging the investment.

Given the nature of close corporations and the remedial purpose of the statute, this court holds that utilizing a complaining shareholder's "reasonable expectations" as a means of identifying and measuring conduct alleged to be oppressive is appropriate. A court considering a petition alleging oppressive conduct must investigate what the majority shareholders knew, or should have known, to be the petitioner's expectations in entering the particular enterprise. Majority conduct should not be deemed oppressive simply because the petitioner's subjective hopes and desires in joining the venture are not fulfilled. Disappointment alone should not necessarily be equated with oppression.

Rather, oppression should be deemed to arise only when the majority conduct substantially defeats expectations that, objectively viewed, were both reasonable under the circumstances and were central to the petitioner's decision to join the venture. It would be inappropriate, however, for us in this case to delineate the contours of the courts' consideration in determining whether directors have been guilty of oppressive conduct. As in other areas of the law, much will depend on the circumstances in the individual case.

The appropriateness of an order of dissolution is in every case vested in the sound discretion of the court considering the application. Under the terms of this statute, courts are instructed to consider both whether "liquidation of the corporation is the only feasible means" to protect the complaining shareholder's expectation of a fair return on his or her investment and whether dissolution "is reasonably necessary" to protect "the rights or interests of any substantial number of shareholders" not limited to those complaining. Implicit in this direction is that once oppressive conduct is found, consideration must be given to the totality of circumstances surrounding the current state of corporate affairs and relations to determine whether some remedy short of or other than dissolution constitutes a feasible means of satisfying both the petitioner's expectations and the rights and interests of any other substantial group of shareholders. [Citations omitted.]

By invoking the statute, a petitioner has manifested his or her belief that dissolution may be the only appropriate remedy. Assuming the petitioner has set forth a prima facie case of oppressive conduct, it should be incumbent upon the parties seeking to forestall dissolution to demonstrate to the court the existence of an adequate, alternative remedy. [Citations omitted.] A court has broad latitude in fashioning alternative relief, but when fulfillment of the oppressed petitioner's expectations by these means is doubtful, such as when there has been a complete deterioration of relations between the parties, a court should not hesitate to order dissolution. Every order of dissolution, however, must be conditioned upon permitting any shareholder of the corporation to elect to purchase the complaining shareholder's stock at fair value. [Citation omitted.]

One further observation is in order. The purpose of this involuntary dissolution statute is to provide protection to the minority shareholder whose reasonable expectations in undertaking the venture have been frustrated and who has no adequate means of recovering his or her investment. It would be contrary to this remedial purpose to permit its use by minority shareholders as merely a coercive tool. [Citation omitted.] Therefore, the minority shareholder whose own acts, made in bad faith and undertaken with a view toward forcing an involuntary dissolution, give rise to the complained-of oppression should be given no quarter in the statutory protection. [Citation omitted.]

[III.] There was sufficient evidence presented at the hearing to support the conclusion that Kemp & Beatley had a long-standing policy of awarding *de facto* dividends based on stock ownership in the form of "extra compensation bonuses." Petitioners, both of whom had extensive experience in the management of the company, testified to this effect. Moreover, both related that receipt of this compensation, whether as true dividends or disguised as "extra compensation", was a known incident to ownership of the company's stock understood by all of the company's principals. Finally, there was uncontroverted proof that this policy was changed either shortly before or shortly after petitioners' employment ended. Extra compensation was still awarded by the company. The only difference was that stock ownership was no longer a basis for the payments; it was asserted that the basis became services rendered to the corporation. It was not unreasonable for the fact finder to have determined that this change in policy amounted to nothing less than an attempt to exclude petitioners from gaining any return on their investment through the mere recharacterization of distributions of corporate income. Under the circumstances of this case, there was no error in determining that this conduct constituted oppressive action within the meaning of section 1104-a of the Business Corporation Law.

Nor may it be said that Supreme Court abused its discretion in ordering Kemp & Beatley's dissolution, subject to an opportunity for a buy-out of petitioners' shares. After the referee had found that the controlling faction of the company was, in effect, attempting to "squeeze-out" petitioners by offering them no return on their investment and increasing other executive compensation, respondents, in opposing the report's confirmation, attempted only to controvert the factual basis of the report. They suggested no feasible, alternative remedy to the forced dissolution. In light of an apparent deterioration in relations between petitioners and the governing shareholders of Kemp & Beatley, it was not unreasonable for the court to have determined that a forced buy-out of petitioners' shares or liquidation of the corporation's assets was the only means by which petitioners could be guaranteed a fair return on their investments.

Accordingly, the order of the Appellate Division should be modified, with costs to petitioners-respondents, by affirming the substantive determination of that court but extending the time for exercising the option to purchase petitioners-respondents' shares to 30 days following this court's determination.

Order modified, with costs to petitioners-respondents, in accordance with the opinion herein and, as so modified, affirmed.

Questions About *Kemp & Beatley*

1.   How would this case have been decided if MBCA §§ 14.30 and 14.34 had applied, rather than the New York statute?

2.   According to *Kemp & Beatley*, how may a defendant prevent dissolution even if the plaintiff proves that she has been oppressed? Would that argument "work" under the MBCA?

3.   Why didn't the plaintiffs in *Kemp & Beatley* argue that the defendants had breached the fiduciary duties that they owe to the plaintiffs as shareholders in a closely held corporation? In other

words, how is oppression analysis different from fiduciary-duty analysis?

4.   Would this litigation have been necessary if Kemp & Beatley were a partnership rather than a corporation?

Problems

Problem 9-14:   Think back to Adam, Betty, and Cindy from Section 9.01 above. They agreed that (1) each of them would own one-third of the stock; (2) they would not permit any other persons to become shareholders unless they all agree; (3) each of them would serve on the board, which will consist only of three members; (4) each of them would work for the company and be paid equal salaries for equal work; and (5) if any of them retires, the company will repurchase his or her stock for a "fair" price. In addition, they agreed that, every Friday, the corporation would pay for their lunches. *If Betty and Cindy cause the corporation to discontinue this free-lunch-on-Friday policy, can Adam successfully argue that he has been oppressed?*

Problem 9-15:   You represent a minority shareholder of Johnson Corp. The majority of the stock of Johnson Corp. is owned by the five members of the Johnson family, who also serve as directors and work for the company. Your client is upset that the Johnson family is causing the company to pay themselves excessive salaries, thereby making the company unable to pay dividends. *Name three different approaches that you could take to suing the Johnson family members. (You may want to go back and look at Chapter 7 for help in answering this question.)*

Although the reasonable expectations test appears to be the most widely followed approach to defining "oppression" for purposes of involuntary dissolution statutes, not all states subscribe to it. For example, in *Kiriakides v. Atlas Food Systems & Services, Inc.*, 541 S.E.2d 257 (S.C. 2001), the South Carolina Supreme Court examined Section 33-14-300(2)(ii) of the South Carolina statute, which permits a court to dissolve a corporation if a shareholder establishes that "the directors or those in control of the corporation have acted, are acting, or will act in a manner that is illegal, fraudulent, oppressive, or unfairly prejudicial either to the corporation or to any shareholder (whether in his capacity as a shareholder, director, or officer of the corporation)."

In *Kiriakides,* the court of appeals adopted several tests for oppression, including a reasonable expectations test, any one of which would be sufficient to find oppression. Examining the statute and its official comments, however, the South Carolina Supreme Court ruled that the definition used by the court of appeals was *too* broad, as shown in the following passage.

> [W]e do not believe the Legislature intended a court to judicially order a corporate dissolution *solely* upon the basis that a party's "reasonable expectations" have been frustrated by majority shareholders. To examine the "reasonable expectations" of minority shareholders would require the courts of this state to microscopically examine the dealings of closely held family corporations, the intentions of majority and minority stockholders in forming the corporation and thereafter, the history of family dealings, and the like. We do not believe the Legislature, in enacting section 33-14-300, intended such judicial interference in the business philosophies and day to day operating practices of family businesses.

Id. at 264. Furthermore, the court found that the South Carolina statute "specifically places the focus upon the *actions* of the majority, i.e., whether they 'have acted, are acting, or will act in a manner that is illegal, fraudulent, oppressive, or unfairly prejudicial either to the corporation or to any shareholder.'" *Id.* at 265. According to the court, this makes a reasonable expectations test (which focuses on the minority's expectations) inconsistent with the statute.

The court also criticized the reasonable expectations test:

> One criticism of the "reasonable expectations" approach is that it "ignores the expectations of the parties other than the dissatisfied shareholder." [Citation omitted.] One recent commentator has suggested that a pure "reasonable expectations" approach overprotects the minority's interests. [Citation omitted.] Similarly, it has been suggested that the reasonable expectations approach is "based on false premises, invites fraud, and is an unnecessary invasion of the rights of the majority." [Citation omitted.]

> We find adoption of the "reasonable expectations" standard is inconsistent with section 33-14-300, which places an emphasis not upon the minority's expectations but, rather, on the actions of the majority. We decline to adopt such an expansive approach to oppressive conduct in the absence of a legislative mandate. We find, consistent with the Legislature's comment to

[South Carolina] section 33-18-400, that the terms "oppressive" and "unfairly prejudicial" are elastic terms whose meaning varies with the circumstances presented in a particular case. *** We find a case-by-case analysis, supplemented by various factors which may be indicative of oppressive behavior, to be the proper inquiry under [the statute]. ***

Id. at 265-66. (So, how does South Carolina define "oppression"?)

Despite cases like *Kiriakides*, the reasonable expectations test remains the most "popular" approach to defining oppression. In addition, at least one court has found that, rather than always being measured at the time that the shareholder became a shareholder, a shareholder's reasonable expectations could evolve over time. *See Meiselman v. Meiselman,* 307 S.E.2d 551 (N.C. 1983).

Finally, note that while fiduciary-duty analysis under *Donahue* and *Wilkes* is technically distinct from oppression analysis, some argue the two different approaches have converged over the years to become quite similar to one another. *See, e.g.*, John H. Matheson & R. Kevin Maler, *A Simple Statutory Solution to Minority Oppression in the Closely Held Business,* 91 MINN. L. REV. 657, 661, 687-89 (2006).

B.   DEADLOCK

Oppression is not the only possible basis for an order of dissolution under MBCA § 14.30. Another important ground is "deadlock." Obviously, the possibility of deadlock is greatest when there are two 50% shareholders or factions (who would be unable to elect directors if they cannot agree on who the directors should be) and/or an evenly divided board. But the mere fact that there are two equal shareholders or factions who from time to time disagree does mean that "deadlock" is present. Nor does the presence of deadlock necessarily mean that the court should order dissolution of the corporation, as shown in the following short—but dense—case.

Wollman v. Littman
Supreme Court, Appellate Division, First Department, New York
316 N.Y.S.2d 526 (1970)

***

The stock of the corporation is held, fifty percent each, by two distinct groups, one of which, the Nierenberg sisters, are plaintiffs, and the other, the Littmans, defendants, each group having equal representation on the board of directors. The corporation's business is the selling of artificial fur fabrics to garment manufacturers. Defendants, the Littmans, allegedly had the idea for the business and developed a market for the fabrics among its manufacturing customers. Plaintiffs are the daughters of Louis Nierenberg, the main stockholder of Louis Nierenberg, Inc., who procures the fabrics and sells them to the corporation. The Littmans, in a separate action in which they are plaintiffs, charge the plaintiffs here (the Nierenberg sisters) and Louis Nierenberg Corporation with seeking to lure away the corporation's customers for Louis Nierenberg Corporation and with doing various acts to affect the corporation's business adversely. The Nierenberg faction countered with this suit, claiming that the bringing of the other action indicates that the corporate management is at such odds among themselves that effective management is impossible. Special Term agreed, but we do not. Irreconcilable differences even among an evenly divided board of directors do not in all cases mandate dissolution. Here, two factors would require further exploration. The first is that the functions of the two disputing interests are distinct, one selling and the other procuring, and each can pursue its own without need for collaboration. The second is that a dissolution which will render nugatory the relief sought in the representative action would actually accomplish the wrongful purpose that defendants (Nierenberg) are charged with in that action. It would not only squeeze the Littmans out of the business but would require the receiver to dispose of the inventory with the Nierenbergs the only interested purchaser financially strong enough to take advantage of the situation. Such a result, if supported by the facts, would be intolerable to a court of equity. A trial of the issues is necessitated.

Questions About *Wollman v. Littman* and Deadlock

1.   Why didn't the court order dissolution of the corporation?

2.   Is a finding of "deadlock" sufficient to order dissolution of the corporation under MBCA § 14.30?

C.   REMEDIES UNDER MBCA § 14.30

The only remedy for oppression or deadlock that is listed in MBCA § 14.30 is the dissolution of the corporation. Dissolution may be beneficial for the plaintiff-shareholder because it would allow her to "extract" some money from the corporation, which she usually cannot do by selling shares if the corporation is closely held.[*] (By the way, note that MBCA § 14.30 technically does not require the corporation to be closely held.)

On the other hand, dissolution could be very disadvantageous, even disastrous, for the other shareholders and the corporation. An otherwise successful and profitable corporation might be shut down—or at least this is what opponents of dissolution statutes often argue. However, this danger is likely a bit exaggerated. For one thing, even if the corporation actually is dissolved, if it had been a successful business it is likely that one or more of the former shareholders will continue running a similar business afterwards, such as by purchasing the corporation's assets during the dissolution process. In other words, it is unlikely that the *business* (as opposed to the precise *corporate entity*) would disappear.

Another likely outcome is that the other shareholders or the corporation will reach an accommodation with the plaintiff whereby they purchase the plaintiff's stock for a mutually agreeable price. This way, everyone is happy: the plaintiff is able to extract some money from the corporation which she can then use to start her own business (free of those obnoxious other shareholders who oppressed her) and the other shareholders are able to continue running the corporation (free of that obnoxious plaintiff). In fact, this is what normally happens even when the court orders dissolution. *See* J.A.C. Hetherington & Michael P. Dooley, *Illiquidity and Exploitation: A Proposed Statutory Solution to the Remaining Close Corporation Problem*, 63 VA. L. REV. 1 (1977) (finding that result in majority of cases in which court ordered dissolution was that the defendant shareholder instead "bought out" the plaintiff shareholder). MBCA § 14.34 recognizes this by providing that the corporation (or one or more of the shareholders) could make an oppression case "go away" by electing to purchase the plaintiff's shares for fair value. Of course, the parties may have differing opinions of what "fair value" is; if they do not agree, the court would need to make that determination.[**]

Nonetheless, dissolution does seem to be a harsh remedy. This would especially seem to be true if the plaintiff-shareholder is alleging a relatively "minor" type of oppression, such as being ousted from the board of directors. In such a case, it seems that the best solution would be simply to order the defendants to let the plaintiff back on the board. For this reason, some state statutes list other

---

[*]   As we will learn in more detail in Chapter 12, upon dissolution of the corporation, creditors are paid first. Assuming that creditors can be fully paid, the remaining funds would be divided among the shareholders according to how many (and what type of) shares they own.

[**]   MBCA § 14.34 has complicated rules concerning how the option to purchase the plaintiff's shares may be exercised. In addition, MBCA § 14.32 allows the court to appoint a receiver (who would wind up and liquidate the corporation) or a custodian (who would manage the corporation) in a section 14.30 proceeding.

possible forms of relief rather than just dissolution. For example, Section 489 of the Michigan Business Corporation, Mich. Comp. Laws Ann. § 450.1489, provides a nonexclusive list of six possible remedies in an oppression case. Further, many courts have interpreted oppression/dissolution statutes as giving them the equitable power to order "lesser" forms of relief (even if not listed in the statute). On the other hand, some courts have taken a more formalistic view. For example, in *Gianotti v. Hamway*, 387 S.E.2d 725, 733 (Va. 1990), the Supreme Court of Virginia interpreted the Virginia oppression/dissolution statute as follows: "The remedy specified by the legislature, while discretionary, is 'exclusive,' and does not permit the trial court to fashion other, apparently equitable remedies."

§ 9.05   PLANNING IN CLOSELY HELD CORPORATIONS—ANOTHER LOOK

Objectives: You should be able to explain to a client who will be a shareholder in a closely held corporation how various agreements or provisions in the corporation's articles of incorporation or bylaws, or in written agreements among the shareholders, may protect her interests and accomplish her objectives. Given information about the client's objectives, you should be able to suggest various forms of such "advance planning" that will implement those objectives.

Let's reconsider Adam, Betty, and Cindy from the beginning of this chapter, who were forming a corporation. They had agreed that (1) each of them would own one-third of the stock; (2) they would not permit any other persons to become shareholders unless they all agree; (3) each of them would serve on the board, which will consist only of three members; (4) each of them would work for the company and be paid equal salaries for equal work; and (5) if any of them retires, the company will repurchase his or her stock for a "fair" price.

If you were representing one of the three shareholders, how would you implement these goals in a manner that would require the other two shareholders to honor them in the future? Consider the following problems. In doing so, you should read or review MBCA §§ 6.27, 6.30, 7.25, 7.27, 7.28, 7.30, 7.31, 7.32, 8.08, and 8.24, some of which you encountered in Chapter 5 or earlier in this chapter. In fact, some of the following problems may serve as useful reviews of some of the things that you learned in Chapter 5.

Problems

Problem 9-16: *What would you recommend to ensure that your client will own one-third of the stock and will <u>continue</u> to own one-third of the stock in the future?*

Problem 9-17: *What would you recommend to ensure that other people could not become shareholders without the approval of all of the shareholders?   Would your answer change if the corporation has <u>already</u> issued shares? (By the way, <u>why</u> would the shareholders want to have such an arrangement?)*

Problem 9-18: *What would you recommend to ensure that your client will serve on the board and that the board will consist only of three persons?*

Problem 9-19: *What would you recommend to ensure that your client will work for the corporation and be paid the same salary as the other shareholder-employees?   What would happen if the corporation refused to honor this arrangement?*

Problem 9-20:   *What would you recommend if the three shareholders want to arrange things such that each of them will have equal voting power, but Adam will receive 50% of any dividends and Betty and Cindy would each receive 25%?*

Problem 9-21: *What would you recommend if your client wanted to make sure that she would have "veto" power over any major transactions?   <u>Where</u> must such a provision or agreement appear—the articles, the bylaws, or somewhere else? How may it be amended? See, e.g., MBCA §§ 7.27 and 8.24.*

Problem 9-22: A typical way to ensure that a shareholder's stock would be repurchased by the corporation or other shareholders is called a "buy-sell" agreement. *What are some of the issues that you should address if you are asked to write a buy-sell agreement?*

Problem 9-23: *Can directors (as opposed to shareholders) use proxies?*

Problem 9-24: Your client is an elderly man who owns one-half of the stock of a successful corporation. He would like to leave the stock to his three grandchildren, but is worried that they will make poor decisions in voting the stock because they currently are all minors. *Do you have any recommendations for your client?* Trust

After working on the above problems and discussing them in class, you should have a pretty good idea of many of the issues involved in "advance planning" for a closely held corporation. In addition, there are many other issues and possible approaches, which you can learn about in an advanced class on Business Organizations. Certainly, advance planning can rarely, if ever, be perfect. But hopefully you understand why advance planning will be preferable to litigating over breaches of fiduciary duties or oppression.

PRACTICE QUESTIONS

Multiple Choice Question 9-1: Ted and Michael wish to incorporate a company called Green Garden, Inc. to make vegetarian food products. Ted plans to invest approximately $600,000 in the business and wants Michael to invest $400,000. Ted has also proposed that: (1) Green Garden, Inc. will have 1,000 shares of common stock authorized in its articles of incorporation and that Ted will own 600 shares and Michael will own 400 shares; (2) the board of directors will consist of Ted, Ted's wife, and Michael; and (3) Ted will be President and earn a salary of $60,000 per year and Michael will be Vice President, Secretary and Treasurer and earn a salary of $40,000 per year. Michael is worried that tensions will develop between him and Ted and that Ted will use his majority ownership position to, as Michael put it, "beat up on me." *Which of the following would help address Michael's concern that Ted may use his majority ownership position to exclude Michael from participating in the business?*

> I. *An employment agreement between Michael (as employee) and the corporation (as employer), terminable only for "cause."*
> II. *A classified board of directors.*
> III. *Cumulative voting for directors.*
> IV. *An agreement under Section 7.32 of the Model Business Corporation Act that would require the directors to annually appoint Michael as the Vice President, Secretary and Treasurer.*

A. All of the above.
B. I, III and IV only.
C. I, II and III only.
D. I, II and IV only.
E. I and IV only.

Multiple Choice Question 9-2: Same facts as in the prior question. Assume that Michael completely ignores your legal advice and instead invests (i.e., becomes a shareholder) in Green Garden, Inc. on the terms proposed by Ted. Assume that you are in a jurisdiction that follows Massachusetts case law but does not have a statute similar to MBCA § 14.30. *If Ted later causes the board of directors to terminate Michael's employment, which of the following best describes Michael's potential remedies (if any)?*

A.   Michael will be able to cause the dissolution of the Green Garden, Inc. if he can convince the court that he has been oppressed by majority actions that have defeated the reasonable expectations that he had when he decided to become a shareholder in the corporation.

B.   Michael has no potential remedy because mere ownership of stock in a corporation does not entitle a shareholder to employment with the corporation.

C.   Michael is entitled to resume his employment with the company because he is a shareholder in a closely held corporation.

D.   Michael will not have a remedy if Ted is able to show that there was a legitimate business purpose for terminating Michael's employment and Michael is unable to show that this purpose could be achieved by other means that are less disruptive to Michael's interests.

Multiple Choice Question 9-3: *All of the following techniques can be used to protect a minority shareholder from abuse by majority shareholders, <u>except</u>:*

A.   Preemptive rights.
B.   Higher quorum requirements than are set by statute.
C.   No par value or low par value stock.
D.   Multiple classes of stock.

Multiple Choice Question 9-4:   Sammy, Dan, Tammy, and Hank are the four shareholders of Stereo Speakers, Inc. ("SSI"), a Massachusetts corporation. There are 1,000 shares of SSI stock outstanding. Sammy owns 400 shares, Dan owns 200, Tammy owns 200, and Hank owns 200. Each of the four shareholders serves on the board of directors, which consists of only those four persons. Sammy, Dan, and Tammy are siblings and almost never disagree on business decisions. Because SSI currently has a great deal of extra cash on hand and Hank has been complaining for some time about the fact that he is having difficulty selling any of this SSI stock to outside investors, Sammy suggested that SSI buy 100 shares from Hank. *Which of the following is correct?*

A.   SSI must offer to buy 25 shares from each of the four shareholders, because each shareholder has an equal right to sell his or her shares back to the corporation if the corporation buy shares back from any shareholder.

B.   SSI must offer to buy 40 shares from Sammy and 20 shares from each of the other three shareholders, because each shareholder has a right to sell a pro rata (ratable) amount of his or her shares back to the corporation if the corporation buys shares back from any shareholder.

C.   This is an interested director's transaction that may only be completed if it is "fair" to the corporation.

D.   SSI may buy 100 shares of Hank's stock.

E.   None of the above is correct since corporations may not purchase their own stock.

Multiple Choice Question 9-5:   AB Corporation has two 50% shareholders: Abe and Ben. The bylaws provide that AB Corporation shall have a two-person board of directors. Both Abe and Ben have served as directors for the past three years. Abe and Ben have now decided that they would like to abolish the board of directors and place the power held by the board in themselves as shareholders. *Which of the following statements is __not__ correct?*

A.   If Abe and Ben approve, a provision to eliminate the board of directors may be placed in the articles of incorporation; it may thereafter be amended only if approved by both Abe and Ben.

B.   Abe and Ben may sign and deliver to the corporation an agreement to eliminate the board of directors; it may thereafter be amended only if approved by both Abe and Ben.

C.   Failure to note the elimination of the board of directors conspicuously on the front or back of both Abe's and Ben's shares renders the provision or agreement void.

D.   If shares of AB Corporation become publicly traded, the provision or agreement ceases to be effective thereafter.

Multiple Choice Question 9-6:   X Corporation has three equal shareholders: Cassy, Richie, and Sven. When the corporation was formed, there were no articles or bylaw provisions or other agreements restricting the transfer of stock. The articles provided that they could be amended only upon a two-thirds vote of the outstanding shares. Three years after forming the corporation, Cassy and Richie became concerned that Sven might sell his shares to an "undesirable" outsider. Cassy and Richie voted to amend the articles so that no shareholder could sell his or her stock without first giving the corporation an opportunity to buy it at book value, which at all times during these facts was 50% of the market value of the stock. Six months later, Ricardo offered to buy Sven's shares at market value. *Which of the following is most correct?*

A.   The amendment to the articles is ineffective with respect to Sven because stock transfer restrictions are illegal under the MBCA.

B.   The amendment to the articles is ineffective with respect to Sven because Sven did not vote in favor of it.

C.   The amendment to the articles is ineffective with respect to Sven because the purchase price is unfair to Sven under these facts.

D.   Both B and C are correct.

QUESTIONS 9-7 TO 9-10 ARE BASED ON THE FOLLOWING FACTS

In 2000, Henry, Dave, and Courtney formed Camera Corporation ("Camera"). Henry, Dave, and Courtney each owned one-third of Camera's outstanding stock. Additionally, Henry, Dave, and Courtney served on Camera's three-member board of directors. Shortly after forming Camera, Henry, Dave, and Courtney signed a written shareholders' agreement which provided that Courtney was assured the position of vice president until she resigned, died, or became incapacitated. Furthermore, under the terms of the shareholders' agreement, Courtney was entitled to a $100,000 annual salary. The agreement provided that it would be valid for fifteen years. The parties filed the shareholders' agreement with Camera's corporate minute book. By the middle of 2011, Henry and Dave had a falling out with Courtney. Henry and Dave then called a special meeting of the board of directors. At the special meeting, Henry and Dave voted to remove Courtney as vice president and stop paying her salary. Courtney attended the meeting and voiced her strong objection to the actions of Henry and Dave. Courtney brought suit against Henry and Dave to enforce her rights under the shareholders' agreement.

Multiple Choice Question 9-7: *What is the most likely result of Courtney's suit against Henry and Dave?*

A.   Courtney will prevail, because the shareholders' agreement is valid and enforceable.
B.   Courtney will prevail, because the board of directors cannot remove an officer without cause.
C.   Henry and Dave will prevail, because the shareholders' agreement unreasonably restricted the discretion of the board of directors.
D.   Henry and Dave will prevail, because the shareholders' agreement automatically expired after 10 years by statute.

Multiple Choice Question 9-8: Same facts as in the previous question. For purposes of this question and the next question only, assume Courtney brought a direct suit against Henry and Dave, individually, for breach of fiduciary duty. At trial, Courtney testified that she worked for Camera full time and depended on her job for her livelihood. Courtney clearly established that she performed her duties well and was instrumental in Camera's success. Furthermore, Courtney proved that Henry and Dave voted to remove her as vice president for personal reasons unrelated to the business. Assume for purposes of this question only that you are in a jurisdiction that follows Massachusetts case law but does not have a statute similar to MBCA § 14.30. *What is the likely result of Courtney's lawsuit against Henry and Dave?*

A.   Henry and Dave will prevail because they had a legitimate business purpose in removing her as vice president.

B.   Henry and Dave will prevail because shareholders of a corporation do not owe a fiduciary duty to each other.

C.   Courtney will prevail, because a "without cause" removal of a minority shareholder from her capacity as an officer is a per se breach of fiduciary duty.

D.   Courtney will prevail, because Henry and Dave had no legitimate business purpose to remove her as vice president.

Multiple Choice Question 9-9: Same facts as in the previous question. For purposes of this question, assume Courtney sued Camera, Henry and Dave, claiming that Henry and Dave's actions were oppressive to her. Assume for purposes of this question only that you are in a jurisdiction that has a statute similar to MBCA § 14.30 but that does not follow Massachusetts case law. *What is the likely result of Courtney's lawsuit against Camera, Henry and Dave?*

A.   Courtney will prevail because her reasonable expectations in investing in Camera were substantially defeated.

B.   Courtney will prevail because a "without cause" removal of a minority shareholder from her capacity as an officer is per se oppressive.

C.   Henry and Dave will prevail because they cannot be held personally liable for oppressive conduct.

D.   Henry and Dave will prevail because Courtney's continued employment is not a protected interest.

Multiple Choice Question 9-10:   Same facts as in the prior question.   For purposes of this question only, assume that Courtney is successful in establishing that Henry and Dave's actions were oppressive. *What is the appropriate statutory remedy under the MBCA?*

A.   The court will order the involuntary dissolution and liquidation of Camera and Camera will be liquidated.

B.   The court will set aside the directors' vote and specifically enforce Courtney's right to serve as vice president and receive a $100,000 annual salary.

C.   The court will order Henry and Dave to pay damages to Courtney for her lost wages.

D.   The court will order involuntary dissolution, unless Henry, Dave or Camera agrees to purchase all of Courtney's shares for fair value.

Multiple Choice Question 9-11:   For many years Tara has made delicious chocolate chip cookies. One day, while nibbling on cookies, she and her three friends (Scarlet, Ashley, and Meg) decided to form Chocolate Chip Express Corporation under the MBCA. To the extent possible, the four friends want to minimize the amount of administrative requirements needed to operate the corporation. Their plan is that each of them will work for the corporation and have an equal voice in making corporate decisions. Since they will be seeing each other every day, they believe they can address problems and make decisions as they come up, rather than have formal (and often time-consuming) meetings. To eliminate such required meetings, they want to eliminate the board of directors. Tara asks you, her attorney, if they can eliminate the board of directors. *What would be correct advice for Tara?*

A.   Under the MBCA, a corporation must always have a board of directors.

B.   Shareholders, by unanimous agreement, can eliminate the board of directors by executing a written shareholder agreement provided that the shareholders make the agreement known to the corporation.

C.   Because a board of directors is one of the attributes that distinguishes a corporation from a partnership, a corporation must always have a board of directors. If the shareholders did eliminate the board, the entity would then be characterized as a partnership, making the shareholders liable for the debts of the corporation.

D.   The shareholders could eliminate the board of directors only if they also agreed to eliminate the officers of the corporation.

Multiple Choice Question 9-12: Ambient Elevator Music Corp. ("AEMC") is owned by four shareholders: Brian, Harold, Reinhard, and Carlos. Each shareholder owns 1,000 shares and serves on the four-person board of directors. Often, the shareholders disagree with one another, with Brian and Harold falling into one "camp" or "faction" and Reinhard and Carlos falling into another. As a result, the shareholders entered into the following two agreements:

I.   Brian and Harold signed a written agreement that they would each use their best efforts to ensure that both of them would be elected to the board of directors. The agreement also provided that Brian and Harold would never vote their shares to approve a merger involving AEMC unless both of them agreed. This agreement was placed in AEMC's corporate minute book.

II.   Reinhard and Carlos signed a written agreement that provided that Carlos had a "proxy" to vote in place of Reinhard at any board meeting at which Reinhard was not present. This agreement was also placed in AEMC's corporate minute book.

Which of the following is most likely correct if a shareholder goes to court to obtain specific performance of either of these agreements?

A.   Agreement I is enforceable. Agreement II is not enforceable because fewer than all shareholders are parties to it.

B.   Agreement II is enforceable. Agreement I is not enforceable because fewer than all shareholders are parties to it.

C.   Both agreements are enforceable.

D.   Neither agreement is enforceable.

CHAPTER 10
PUBLICLY TRADED CORPORATIONS

In Chapter 5, you learned a lot of general information about corporations, such as how they are formed, the respective decision-making spheres of the board and the shareholders, and how the board and shareholders go about making decisions. Then, in Chapter 9, you learned about some "special" problems that apply to closely held corporations. Note that virtually all of the information that you learned in Chapter 5 was still applicable in Chapter 9. Likewise, your knowledge from Chapter 5 will carry over to this chapter. In other words, publicly traded corporations (as that term will be defined below) are still corporations— they have articles and bylaws, directors, shareholders, stock, etc., just like any "regular" corporation. However, Chapter 5 primarily concerned *state* law. By contrast, this chapter will in large part address additional requirements that *federal* law imposes on publicly traded corporations.

The primary federal statute that we will study in this chapter is the Securities Exchange Act of 1934, otherwise known as the "***Exchange Act***" or sometimes the "***1934 Act***." This is one of two federal securities laws that were enacted as part of Franklin Delano Roosevelt's "New Deal" legislative program shortly after the stock market crash of 1929. (The other statute is the Securities Act of 1933, which is the subject of Chapter 13.) The Exchange Act is largely directed at "after-market" trading activity, that is, the functions of securities markets, as well as brokers, dealers, investment banks, and other market participants. In Section 10.02 of this chapter, we will examine some of the basic attributes of the stock markets in the United States.

The Exchange Act imposes complex regulations on publicly traded companies. Thus, this chapter will begin with a discussion of when an issuer must become a "public" or "reporting" company under the Exchange Act. From there, we will examine the periodic reporting requirements of the Exchange Act, the rules governing the solicitation of proxies from shareholders of public companies, and some of the civil liabilities that may result from materially false or misleading proxy statements or other Exchange Act reports. Note, however, that some other portions of the Exchange Act will be covered in other chapters, most notably Chapters 12 and 14.

Finally, Section 10.03 concerns "governance" issues that affect publicly traded corporations. Although one could make a good argument that some (but not all) of these issues should have been addressed in Chapter 5 because they can affect any large corporation, whether or not it is publicly traded, given the great societal importance of these issues with respect to publicly traded corporations, it seemed more appropriate to address them in this chapter than in Chapter 5.

Please note that, given the complex (and constantly changing) nature of much of the material in this chapter, it is somewhat less "interactive" than prior chapters. I have not included learning objectives in this chapter and there are a relatively small number of problems for you to consider.

§ 10.01   THE SECURITIES EXCHANGE ACT OF 1934

As discussed in Chapter 5, for most corporations, *state* law dictates the information that the corporation must provide to its shareholders. For example, Section 5.08(E) of Chapter 5 discusses the corporate information that shareholders are entitled to inspect under the MBCA. However, if the corporation is subject to the reporting requirements of the Exchange Act, the amount of information that it must provide to its shareholders—and the Securities and Exchange Commission ("*SEC*"), and therefore the world at large—dramatically increases. Indeed, as you will see, there is a virtual treasure trove of information about each publicly traded company in its SEC filings, which are easily available online. But before examining the Exchange Act's periodic reporting requirements, we will first examine when registration under the Exchange Act is required. In other words, the first task is to determine when a corporation must become a *reporting company* (also known as a *public company* or *publicly traded company*).[*]

A.   REGISTRATION REQUIREMENTS

There are two main ways whereby a company (also called an "*issuer*") can become subject to the reporting requirements of the Exchange Act: (1) registration under Section 12(b) and (2) registration under Section 12(g). Also, Section 15(d) of the Exchange Act requires issuers who have filed an effective registration statement for a securities offering under the Securities Act of 1933 (which, of course, is a different statute) to comply with the Exchange Act's reporting requirements for some period of time afterward, even if they do not have securities registered under Section 12.

Section 12(b). Section 12(b), along with Section 12(a) of the Exchange Act, essentially provides that any class of securities that is listed on a "national securities exchange" such as the New York Stock Exchange (the "*NYSE*"), must be registered under Section 12(b). The details of how it gets to this result are a bit curious. First, Section 12(a) makes it unlawful:

---

[*]   Technically, a "reporting" company is one that is subject to the Exchange Act's periodic reporting requirements that are discussed in Section 10.01(B), regardless of whether its stock is traded on a national securities exchange. The phrase "publicly traded" usually describes a company who stock is traded on such an exchange or other organized market.

for any member [of a national securities exchange], broker, or dealer to effect any transaction in any security *** on a national securities exchange unless a registration is effective as to such security for such exchange in accordance with the provisions of [the Exchange Act] and the rules and regulations thereunder. ***

Meanwhile, Section 12(b) essentially lists the documents that an issuer must file with the SEC in order to register a class of securities under Section 12(b). (More on this below.) Taken together, these two sections mean that no registered broker-dealer may buy or sell a security over a national securities exchange unless that security is registered pursuant to Section 12(b). Not surprisingly, then, each national securities exchange requires a security to be registered under Section 12(b) before it may be traded on that exchange. In addition, as discussed below, each national securities exchange requires that certain other requirements must be met before a security may be traded on that exchange.

Section 12(g). Section 12(g) is very different from Section 12(b). Under Section 12(g), it does not matter if a security is traded on any sort of securities market. Instead, Section 12(g), along with SEC Rule 12g-1 under the Exchange Act, requires an issuer to register a class of *equity* securities, such as stock, if three conditions are met:

•   the issuer is engaged in interstate commerce or in a business affecting interstate commerce (obviously easy tests to meet), or its securities are traded through the mails or instrumentalities of interstate commerce;

•   the issuer has more than $10 million of assets; and

•   the issuer's equity securities are "held of record" by 500 or more persons.[*]

Whether an issuer must register a class of equity securities under Section 12(g) is determined at the end of its fiscal year. In the case of most companies, this will be December 31. If the issuer meets the requirements of Section 12(g) at the end of its fiscal year, it must register the relevant class of equity securities within the next 120 days. For example, assume that ABC Corp.'s fiscal year ends on December 31 and that ABC Corp. is considered to be engaged in interstate commerce. If, as of December 31, ABC Corp. had more than $10 million of

---

[*]   Section 12(g)(2) excludes eight types of securities from this requirement, including securities that are listed on a national securities exchange (and thus required to be registered under Section 12(b)), and securities issued by certain regulated financial institutions and insurance companies. *See also* Section 36 of the Exchange Act (general exemptive authority of the SEC).

assets, 504 record holders of its common stock, and 125 record holders of its preferred stock, it would be required to register its common stock (but not its preferred stock) under Section 12(g) within 120 days after December 31.

The 500-record holder threshold of Section 12(g) could raise several issues. SEC Rule 12g5-1(a) provides that securities are "held of record" by "each person who is identified as the owner of such securities on records of security holders maintained by or on behalf of the issuer." Thus, each person who has a stock certificate for the issuer's stock will count toward this threshold. But who else "counts" as a holder of record? As discussed below in Section 10.01(C)(1), for many companies whose securities are *already* traded on a stock market, this can be a very difficult question to answer. This is because such corporations may have "street name" or "beneficial" shareholders. In other words, many, if not most, of the shareholders of public companies own their shares through banks or brokerage firms and do not have physical stock certificates. Perhaps surprisingly, most such "beneficial" shareholders do *not* count toward the 500-shareholder threshold of Section 12(g), even though we think of them as the "true" owners of the stock.

Note that a particular class of securities cannot be registered under Section 12(b) and Section 12(g) at the same time. Generally, if an issuer registered a class of equity securities under Section 12(g) but that class was *later* listed on a national securities exchange, the appropriate section for registration would be Section 12(b) rather than Section 12(g). This is true even though the class of securities would still meet the requirements of Section 12(g). *See* Section 12(g)(2)(A).

Registration Forms. If an issuer must register a class of securities under either Section 12(b) or Section 12(g), it usually would use SEC Form 10 to do so. While a discussion of that form is outside the scope of this textbook, suffice it to say that Form 10 calls for very detailed information about the issuer, akin to the information that would be included in a registration statement for a securities offering under the Securities Act of 1933 (which is discussed in Chapter 13) or in a Form 10-K Annual Report (discussed below). In some instances, the somewhat less extensive Form 8-A could be used instead. You may learn more about these, and other, forms in a course on Securities Regulation.

The Meaning of Registering a "Class" of Securities. As you will learn in Chapter 13, when an issuer (or, for that matter, any person) wishes to *offer and sell* securities, Section 5 of the Securities Act provides two choices: (1) register the securities that will be offered and sold or (2) find an exemption from the registration requirement. Thus, for example, if ABC Corp. wanted to offer and sell 10 million shares of its common stock in a registered public offering, it would register *those 10 million shares* with the SEC. If, at some point in the future, ABC Corp. wanted to offer and sell *more* shares of its common stock in another offering, it would again be faced with the choice with registering the shares that it plans to sell at that time or finding an exemption from registration for that offering. The mere fact that ABC Corp. did a registered offering of its common stock in the past would not give it a "pass" from having to register the new offering, although it may be somewhat easier to do a such a secondary offering than an initial public offering (IPO).

By contrast, when an issuer registers under Section 12 of the Exchange Act, the issuer is registering an *entire class* of its securities. By definition, the number of units into which a class may be divided is indeterminate. For example, assume that the above-mentioned ABC Corp., after its registered public offering of common stock under the Securities Act, successfully applies to have its common stock listed on the NYSE. As you know from the above discussion, ABC Corp. would then be required to register its common stock under Section 12(b) of the Exchange Act. Assume further that, at that time, ABC Corp.'s articles of incorporation have 20 million shares of authorized common stock, of which 18 million shares are outstanding. How many of these shares are now registered under Section 12(b)? In a sense, it doesn't really matter. Again, the entire class is registered under the Exchange Act. If in the future ABC Corp. amends its articles of incorporation to create more authorized shares of common stock, the *class* of common stock would still remain registered under Section 12(b).[*]

Thus, registration of a class of securities under Section 12 of the Exchange Act is unrelated to any securities offering or other transaction. If ABC Corp. wants to offer and sell some of these new shares, it would again face the two choices under the *Securities Act*—register the new shares that the company plans to sell in this offering or find an exemption. Again, the fact that the class of securities is registered under the *Exchange Act* does not give ABC Corp. a "pass" to ignore the Securities Act when it wants to offer and sell shares of that class.

Pros and Cons of Being a Publicly Traded Company. That being said, many companies wind up as Section 12 registrants after a public offering of securities under the Securities Act, because they apply to have their securities listed on a national securities exchange immediately after the offering and/or because the offering results in them having 500 or more shareholders and meeting the other requirements of Section 12(g). Thus, the decision to "go public" is voluntary for most companies.

---

[*]   Note that Section 12(g)(5) defines a "class" of securities as "all securities of an issuer which are of substantially similar character and the holders of which enjoy substantially similar rights and privileges."

Is it a good idea to be a public company? It depends on who you ask. Clearly, there are some advantages to being public. For example, a public company (at least one that has securities listed on a national securities exchange) has relatively easy access to the capital markets. That is, if it wishes to raise more money by selling securities, it may (somewhat) easily do so, both because of the name recognition and visibility that comes with being a public company and the fact that many such "established" companies are eligible to use "easier" SEC registration forms than companies that would be conducting an IPO. Such a secondary offering may have lower costs than the company's IPO. Further, the SEC may be more deferential to them than it would be to less well-known companies doing an IPO.

A public company also may be able to use its stock as "acquisition currency," that is, as consideration for the acquisition of other companies. As you will learn in Chapter 12, in a merger the "target" company merges into the "surviving corporation" and the target shareholders receive the agreed-upon "merger consideration" in exchange for their shares. If the surviving corporation is private, the merger consideration most likely will be cash. On the other hand, if the surviving corporation is public, it might be able to use new shares of its own stock as the merger consideration, particularly if it is a well-established company with a stable stock price. To be somewhat flippant, it's almost as if a public company has its own money printing press. Similarly, public companies are better able to use their stock as a compensation device for employees and consultants.

Having shares listed on a national securities exchange can also be beneficial to the company's shareholders. In contrast to a private corporation that does not have an established trading market for its stock, being listed will make it easy for shareholders to sell their shares if they wish to do so. Moreover, the presence of market trading will act to "price" the stock, even for those who do not trade. Thus, you have a better idea of what your stock is worth than you would if it were not publicly traded. Finally, the mere fact that a company is public may give it an advertising and publicity advantage over its private competitors. News outlets tend to focus on public companies over similar, but private, companies.

These advantages come with a heavy cost, however. As you will appreciate more as you read this chapter, it is not easy being a public company. Great quantities of information must be released to the public on an ongoing basis. The SEC forms on which this information must appear are not exactly quickly and easily completed. Not only will these reporting obligations involve a lot of management time that could otherwise be spent on more productive pursuits such as actually running the company, but they will necessitate the use of attorneys and accountants. Such professionals are usually expensive. Moreover, particularly following the Sarbanes-Oxley Act of 2002 the reporting and other obligations under the Exchange Act have gotten significantly more burdensome. Reporting deadlines have sped up and the information that must be reported has become much more extensive.

Also, note that the documents that a public company must continually file with the SEC are *public*. This, of course, is because the Exchange Act and the SEC exist largely to protect investors, including potential investors. But, from the issuer's perspective, this means that not only may current shareholders or prospective shareholders review the issuer's SEC-filed documents but so too may competitors. Due to the detailed disclosure requirements of these forms, competitors will know information about a public company that they probably would not have known otherwise.

Further, officers and directors of a public company are at more of a risk of legal liability than their counterparts at private companies. For example, they could be the targets of lawsuits brought under Rule 10b-5 or other provisions of the Exchange Act that impose liability for materially false or misleading Exchange Act reports or proxy statements. Also, the CEO and Chief Financial Officer of a public company must personally certify the contents of the company's Annual Reports on Form 10-K and Quarterly Reports on Form 10-Q, as discussed below. This could result in significant liability if the reports are materially inaccurate. Further, as you will learn in Chapter 14, officers, directors, and 10% shareholders are subject to potential lawsuits for "short-swing" profits under Section 16(b) of the Exchange Act.

These and other disadvantages of being an Exchange Act registrant have led many public companies in recent years to question whether it is worth it.

De-Registering Under Sections 12(b) and 12(g).   A company that has decided that the "cons" of being a public company outweigh the "pros" may want to de-register from Section 12, which is sometimes called "going dark." A company that goes dark can return to the simpler days of being a private company.

De-registering from Section 12(b) is relatively simple; the issuer would have its securities delisted from whatever national securities exchanged on which they trade. This is done by either the issuer or the exchange filing a Form 25 with the SEC. The removal of the securities from registration under Section 12(b) is typically effective 90 days after the form is filed. See SEC Rule 12d2-2 for more details. Under Section 12(g)(2)(A) of the Exchange Act, if an issuer has a class of securities registered under Section 12(b), then it need not register that class under Section 12(g). However, if the issuer were to deregister the class from Section 12(b), then it would be required to register those securities under Section 12(g) if, at that time, it met the requirements for Section 12(g) registration. Thus, the issuer should ensure that it could, if necessary, deregister its class of securities under Section 12(g).

As you should recall, registration under Section 12(g) is required when the issuer has 500 or more shareholders of record and meets certain other requirements. Does this mean that the issuer could deregister the class of stock under Section 12(g) if it could somehow reduce the number of record shareholders below 500, such as by redeeming stock from some holders? Surprisingly, no. To deregister under Section 12(g), the issuer must reduce the number of record shareholders below *300, not 500.*[*] Some call this rule "500 going up and 300 coming down." (Again, however, don't forget that the determination of which shareholders "count" can be a bit complicated, as discussed in Section 10.01(C)(1) below.) To deregister a class of securities from Section 12(g), the issuer must file a Form 15 with the SEC. See SEC Rule 12g-4 for more details.

As if the above weren't confusing enough, at this point we need to introduce a discussion of Section 15(d) of the Exchange Act.

Section 15(d). A company that is subject to Section 15(d)—but neither Section 12(b) nor Section 12(g)—is sometimes called a "quasi-public" company. This is because Section 15(d) issuers must abide by the periodic reporting requirements discussed in Section 10.01(B) below, but they escape other portions of the Exchange Act, including the proxy rules under Section 14. In other words, Section 15(d) reporting companies are not "full" public companies.

When is a company a "Section 15(d) reporter"? The relevant portion of Section 15(d) is set forth below. When reading it, note that Section 13 of the Exchange Act is the section pursuant to which the SEC requires periodic reports such as Annual Reports on Form 10-K and Quarterly Reports on Form 10-Q.

> Each issuer which has filed a registration statement [for a securities offering] *** which has become effective pursuant to the Securities Act of 1933, as amended, shall file with the [SEC] *** such supplementary and periodic information, documents, and reports as may be required pursuant to section 13 in respect of a security registered pursuant to section 12. The duty to file under this subsection shall be automatically suspended if and so long as any issue of securities of such issuer is registered pursuant to section 12. The duty to file under this subsection shall also be automatically suspended as to any fiscal year, other than the fiscal

---

[*] If the issuer has had fewer than $10 million in assets on the last day of each of its three most recent fiscal years, it could deregister the class of securities from Section 12(g) if there are fewer than 500 record holders of the class. *See* SEC Rule 12g-4.

year within which such registration statement became effective, if, at the beginning of such fiscal year, the securities of each class to which the registration statement relates are held of record by less than three hundred persons. ***

Thus, if an issuer has done a registered offering under the *Securities Act*— which is a different statute—it will become a reporting company under the Exchange Act for some period of time. Whether it will remain so for an indefinite period will depend on whether it has 300 or more shareholders as of the beginning of a fiscal year. However, note that the issuer will always be a reporting company with respect to the year in which its Securities Act registration statement was effective, regardless of how many shareholders it winds up with. It could stop filing period reports with respect to *later years*, however, if it has fewer than 300 record shareholders at the beginning of a fiscal year.

In addition, SEC Rule 12h-3 would allow the issuer to file a Form 15 to suspend its Section 15(d) reporting requirements if at any time (as opposed to the beginning of a fiscal year) it has fewer than 300 record shareholders and meets certain other requirements. However, even if it uses Rule 12h-3, it must still file Exchange Act reports with respect to the year in which its Securities Act registration statement became effective.

Confused yet? Hopefully you won't find the following problems difficult.

Problems

Problem 10-1: Private Co., which is engaged in selling widgets throughout the United States, had 506 shareholders and $11 million of assets as of December 21. Its stock is not listed on a national securities exchange, and its fiscal year ends on December 31. *What, if anything, would you recommend that Private Co. do before the end of the year? What would happen if Private Co. does not take your advice?*

Problem 10-2: Same facts as Problem 10-1, except that Private Co. has only 247 shareholders of record, even after completing a registered stock offering under the Securities Act earlier this year. *Does Private Co. have periodic reporting obligations under the Exchange Act? If so, how long will it continue to have these obligations?*

Problem 10-3: Same facts as Problem 10-2, except that Private Co. stock was admitted for trading on a national securities exchange registered as such with the SEC. *Does Private Co. have periodic reporting obligations under the Exchange Act? If so, how long will it continue to have these obligations?*

Problem 10-4:   *Can you explain the consequences of an issuer being a "Section 15(d) reporter," as opposed to having a class of securities registered under either Section 12(b) or Section 12(g)?*

B.   PERIODIC REPORTING REQUIREMENTS AND REGULATION FD

Section 13(a) of the Exchange Act allows the SEC to specify periodic reports that issuers must file, and issuers that have a class of securities registered under Sections 12(b) or 12(g), or that are subject to Section 15(d), must comply with the SEC's requirements. The SEC requires many different reports, the most important being Annual Reports on Form 10-K, Quarterly Reports on Form 10-Q, and Current Reports on Form 8-K. Section 12 issuers (as well as Section 15(d) issuers) are also subject to Regulation FD, the basic purpose of which is to require such companies to report to the public any previously nonpublic material information that is disclosed to certain third parties. As noted above, the purpose of these reporting requirements is to protect investors by ensuring a steady stream of reliable and current information concerning public companies.

> ***ACCOUNTING AND AUDITOR REQUIREMENTS***
> In addition to the many disclosure requirements that the Exchange Act imposes on issuers (and others), it has many requirements for accounting firms that audit the financial statements of public companies. While this book will not discuss these requirements in any detail, suffice it to say that they are very stringent. Further, in Regulation S-X, the SEC imposes detailed accounting and financial disclosure requirements which are in addition to GAAP (which you encountered in Chapter 1) and GAAS (Generally Accepted Auditing Standards).

Form 10-K.   Once a year, companies with securities registered under Section 12(b) or Section 12(g), as well as Section 15(d) reporting companies, must file an Annual Report on Form 10-K.[*]   A full discussion of the contents of this

---

[*]   Before March 2009, issuers that were "small business issuers" could use the less demanding Form 10-KSB. This form has now been eliminated, as has similar Form 10-QSB. However, issuers that qualify as "smaller reporting companies" are excused from a few of the more "difficult" portions of Form 10-K. In addition, some portions of Regulation S-K specify relaxed disclosure requirements for smaller reporting companies.

form is outside the scope of this textbook; in fact, the only way to really learn how to prepare a Form 10-K is to actually work on one, preferably under the supervision of an experienced securities attorney. Nonetheless, it may be helpful to describe some—but not all—of the various items called for by Form 10-K. (Also, Rule 12b-20 provides that, "[i]n addition to the information expressly required to be included in a statement or report, there shall be added such further material information, if any, as may be necessary to make the required statements, in the light of the circumstances under which they are made, not misleading.") Note that, generally speaking, references to the "issuer" in the following paragraphs include not only the issuer itself but also any subsidiaries that it has.

Item 1—Business. This item requires disclosure of the information called for by Item 101 of Regulation S-K, which is part of the SEC's integrated disclosure system. (This means that many of the items of information required by Exchange Act reports are the same as those that are required in a registration statement for a securities offering under the Securities Act of 1933.) Item 101 is very detailed, requiring the issuer to describe many aspects of its business, in ways too numerous to list here. Interested readers may want to peruse Item 101 to get an idea of its scope.

Item 1A—Risk Factors. This item, which is a relatively new addition to Form 10-K, requires the issuer to describe how the various "risk factors" listed in Item 503(c) of Regulation S-K apply to it, although "smaller reporting companies" are not required to do so. This disclosure must be made in "Plain English," some guidelines for which are listed in Rule 421(d) under the Securities Act. These include using "short sentences," "definite, concrete, everyday words," and bullet points or tables "whenever possible," and refraining from the use of "legal jargon or highly technical business terms" and double negatives. (Surprisingly, this rule has—in my opinion at least—resulted in more readable SEC filings.) The purpose of the risk factors section is to alert investors or potential investors in the issuer's securities to the many ways in which their investment may turn out badly.

Item 3—Legal Proceedings. This item requires the issuer to discuss any material legal proceedings within the meaning of Item 103 of Regulation S-K in which it is involved.

Item 7—Management's Discussion and Analysis of Financial Condition and Results of Operations. This item, which is colloquially referred to as "MD&A," is basically a companion piece to the audited annual financial statements that appear in Item 8. The MD&A, which must be prepared according to the exacting Item 303 of Regulation S-K, should explain the issuer's financial statements and results in sufficient detail to allow investors to make informed investment decisions about the issuer's securities. MD&A is necessary so that investors have a narrative discussion of the issuer's financial statements and the reasons for differences from prior years. Without such a discussion by the issuer, readers would likely be left guessing as to the causes of changes in the issuer's financial results from year to year. MD&A also serves to give readers information about the issuer's future prospects.

Item 8—Financial Statements and Supplementary Data. Item 8 is probably the most important part of Form 10-K. Item 8 requires annual financial statements prepared in accordance with generally accepted accounting principles (GAAP) and additional SEC requirements and audited by an accounting firm that meets stringent independence requirements.

Again, this is not a complete list of the items required by Form 10-K, but hopefully it will suffice to give you a sense of the immense extent of the disclosures that public companies must make on an ongoing basis. The goal is disclosure, disclosure, disclosure. The hope is that this disclosure will allow the markets (that is, investors) to make informed investment decisions. As former Supreme Court Justice Louis Brandeis said of disclosure requirements: "Publicity is justly commended as a remedy for social and industrial diseases. Sunlight is said to be the best of disinfectants; electric light the most efficient policeman." To see whether you agree that the Exchange Act and the SEC are requiring sufficient "sunlight" or "electric light," you might want to read a recent Form 10-K for a public company in which you are interested in some way. All SEC filings are easily available, free of charge, on the SEC's web site (www.sec.gov).

Part III of Form 10-K contains several additional items, many of which relate to the issuer's executive officers and directors and require extensive disclosures about their backgrounds, compensation, ownership of the issuer's stock, and any material business relationships they have with the issuer or its subsidiaries. Because much of this information is required in an issuer's proxy statement on Schedule 14A, we will discuss this information in Section 10.01(C) below. Form 10-K allows most issuers to omit Part III information from the Form 10-K, provided that it is included in a proxy statement that is filed with the SEC within 120 days after the end of the issuer's fiscal year.

Form 10-Q. Public companies must file a Form 10-Q three times a year, following the end of the first, second, and third quarters of their fiscal years. (A Form 10-Q is not required with respect to the fourth quarter because a Form 10-K will be filed to cover the entire year.) Although Form 10-Q requires a great deal of information, its principal purpose is to present quarterly financial statements and MD&A. Unlike Form 10-K, financial statements in a Form 10-Q are not audited.

Form 8-K.   As discussed above, Forms 10-K and 10-Q have a set schedule; issuers know exactly when they must file these forms, quarter after quarter, year after year.   In contrast, Form 8-K must be filed on an "as needed" basis.   In other words, Form 8-K specifies a list of events or conditions that the SEC considers so important that they must be disclosed on a rapid basis, usually within four business days after they occur.   Before the Sarbanes-Oxley Act of 2002 (see Section 10.03 below), Form 8-K specified only a handful of events that were sufficiently important to require prompt disclosure via a Form 8-K filing.   As you may expect, Form 8-K now specifies a much longer list of items that require disclosure.   Although simply listing these items probably gives you little understanding of what the items *mean*, it may be helpful to at least take a quick look at the types of things with which Form 8-K is concerned.   Here is the list:

Item 1.01   Entry into a Material Definitive Agreement

Item 1.02   Termination of a Material Definitive Agreement

Item 1.03   Bankruptcy or Receivership

Item 2.01   Completion of Acquisition or Disposition of Assets

Item 2.02   Results of Operations and Financial Condition

Item 2.03   Creation of a Direct Financial Obligation or an Obligation under an Off-Balance Sheet Arrangement of a Registrant

Item 2.04   Triggering Events That Accelerate or Increase a Direct Financial Obligation or an Obligation under an Off-Balance Sheet Arrangement

Item 2.05   Costs Associated with Exit or Disposal Activities

Item 2.06   Material Impairments

Item 3.01   Notice of Delisting or Failure to Satisfy a Continued Listing Rule or Standard; Transfer of Listing

Item 3.02   Unregistered Sales of Equity Securities

Item 3.03   Material Modification to Rights of Security Holders

Item 4.01   Changes in Registrant's Certifying Accountant

Item 4.02   Non-Reliance on Previously Issued Financial Statements or a Related Audit Report or Completed Interim Review

Item 5.01   Changes in Control of Registrant

Item 5.02   Departure of Directors or Certain Officers; Election of Directors; Appointment of Certain Officers; Compensatory Arrangements of Certain Officers

Item 5.03   Amendments to Articles of Incorporation or Bylaws; Change in Fiscal Year

Item 5.04   Temporary Suspension of Trading Under Registrant's Employee Benefit Plans

Item 5.05   Amendments to the Registrant's Code of Ethics, or Waiver of a Provision of the Code of Ethics.

Item 5.06   Change in Shell Company Status

Item 5.07   Submission of Matters to a Vote of Security Holders

Item 7.01   Regulation FD Disclosure

Item 8.01 of Form 8-K is a catchall entitled "Other Events." Nothing specific is required by this item; instead, it gives issuers the option to disclose events that they deem "of importance to security holders." Finally, Item 9.01 would require the issuer to list any financial statements or exhibits called for by another item of the form.[*]

Filing Deadlines. Before the Sarbanes-Oxley Act, the deadlines for filing Forms 10-K and 10-Q were almost leisurely: Form 10-K was required for all issuers within ninety days after the end of their fiscal year, and Form 10-Q was required within forty-five days after the end of the relevant quarter. Thus, for example, an issuer whose fiscal year coincides with a calendar year would have until approximately March 31 to file its Form 10-K for the prior year.

Of course, the reader will guess correctly that the Sarbanes-Oxley Act and subsequent SEC rule amendments sped these deadlines up, but they did so in a complex way, creating three categories of Exchange Act filers: (1) "large

---

[*]   Also, Form 8-K features Items 6.01 through 6.05. However, these items only apply to asset-backed securities, which are specialized types of securities that you might learn about in an advanced course on Securities Regulation.

accelerated filers" (basically, those whose securities have a market value of $700 million or more, excluding shares held by certain affiliates); (2) "accelerated filers" (these typically have a market value of $75 million or more, calculated in the same manner); and (3) "non-accelerated filers," most of which are also known as "smaller reporting companies." (See Rule 12b-2 under the Exchange Act if you are interested in the precise definitions.) The first group, large accelerated filers, now have only sixty days in which to file Forms 10-K and forty days in which to file Forms 10-Q. Accelerated filers have seventy-five days to file Forms 10-K and forty days for Forms 10-Q. The non-accelerated filers have stayed at the original deadlines of ninety days for Forms 10-K and forty-five days for Forms 10-Q.

Schedule 13D. The Exchange Act imposes many additional reporting requirements with respect to Section 12 registrants, but in some cases *shareholders* of these companies are the ones who must do the reporting. For example, Section 13(d) requires a security holder (or a group acting in concert) to file a report with the SEC once it beneficially owns more than five percent of the outstanding units of a class of Section 12 equity securities. This report, Schedule 13D, requires not only information about the holder (or group) but also information about the holder's (or group's) plans for the issuer. Schedule 13D is discussed further in Chapter 12.

Section 16. Section 16(b), which is a presumed insider trading prohibition, applies to officers, directors, and 10% shareholders of Section 12 registrants. It requires these persons to remit to the issuer any actual or "hypothetical" profit resulting from a matched purchase and sale (or sale and purchase) of the issuer's securities that occur within six months of one another. This is discussed further in Section 14.03 of Chapter 14. To allow the SEC and potential plaintiffs' attorneys to monitor these persons' trading activity, Section 16(a) requires them to file reports with the SEC whenever they buy or sell any of the issuer's securities.

Regulation FD. When the SEC adopted Regulation FD in the year 2000, it stated:

> Regulation FD (Fair Disclosure) is a new issuer disclosure rule that addresses selective disclosure. The regulation provides that when an issuer, or person acting on its behalf, discloses material nonpublic information to certain enumerated persons (in general, securities market professionals and holders of the issuer's securities who may well trade on the basis of the information), it must make public disclosure of that information. The timing of

the required public disclosure depends on whether the selective disclosure was intentional or non-intentional; for an intentional selective disclosure, the issuer must make public disclosure simultaneously; for a non-intentional disclosure, the issuer must make public disclosure promptly. Under the regulation, the required public disclosure may be made by filing or furnishing a Form 8-K, or by another method or combination of methods that is reasonably designed to effect broad, non-exclusionary distribution of the information to the public.

In other words, Regulation FD was designed to level the playing field between securities market participants such as analysts—who are often in a position to receive important, but nonpublic information, from the issuer—and ordinary investors. It may also reduce the incidence of insider trading (see Chapter 14) by requiring simultaneous or prompt *public* disclosure of such information that is given to persons such as analysts. While well-intentioned, Regulation FD can lead to a number of interpretive and compliance issues. You may learn more about it in a course on Securities Regulation.

C.   PROXY RULES UNDER SECTION 14

Section 14(a) of the Exchange Act provides in part that:

It shall be unlawful for any person, by the use of the mails or by any means or instrumentality of interstate commerce or of any facility of a national securities exchange or otherwise, in contravention of such rules and regulations as the [SEC] may prescribe as necessary or appropriate in the public interest or for the protection of investors, to solicit or to permit the use of his name to solicit any proxy or consent or authorization in respect of any security (other than an exempted security) registered pursuant to section 12.

Note a few things about this section. First, it only applies to securities that are registered under Section 12 of the Exchange Act. Thus, if an issuer is only a Section 15(d) reporter, the proxy rules do not apply to it. Second, the statute itself doesn't make anything illegal. Instead, it provides that it would be illegal to solicit proxies *in violation of SEC rules on this topic.* This is a classic example of Congress delegating rulemaking authority to an administrative agency. Third, the phrase "or otherwise" means that there is no requirement that interstate commerce or other "jurisdictional means" be used.

As a practical matter, public companies must solicit proxies for shareholder meetings. Keep in mind that many public companies have thousands upon thousands of "small" shareholders who likely would not want to travel across the country to attend a shareholders meeting at which their shares would represent only a tiny fraction of the total number of outstanding shares. Given this situation, if shares could not be considered "present" at the meeting unless the holders of the shares were physically present, many companies would be unable to muster a quorum for their shareholders meetings, making the conduct of business at such meetings impossible.[*] As you learned in Chapter 5, a shareholder's shares can be represented—and voted—at a shareholders meeting through a proxy.

One of the most important SEC rules under Section 14(a) is Rule 14a-3, which provides that proxy "solicitations" may not occur unless each person solicited is furnished with a proxy statement that contains the information specified in Schedule 14A (which is discussed below). Further, if proxies are solicited by or on behalf of the issuer and the meeting is an annual meeting, each shareholder whose proxy is solicited must be provided with an annual report (often called the "glossy" annual report) that contains much of the information that is included in the issuer's Form 10-K for the prior year. As one might expect, Schedule 14A requires extremely detailed information for even routine annual shareholder meetings.

But before describing those requirements, you should understand when a "solicitation" of a proxy is being made. After all, if there is no "solicitation" being made, then one need not provide a Schedule 14A to the other party to the communication. Note that anyone, not just the issuer of the securities, could be involved in a proxy solicitation. Thus, the proxy rules are important in "proxy contests" and other takeover attempts (which are discussed further in Chapter 12).

What is a "Solicitation"? Rule 14a-1(*l*) provides:

(1)   The terms "solicit' and "solicitation" include:

(i)   Any request for a proxy whether or not accompanied by or included in a form of proxy:

(ii)   Any request to execute or not to execute, or to revoke, a proxy; or

---

[*]   There are some public companies that have majority shareholders, whose physical presence at the meeting would ensure a quorum. While such companies would thus not need to solicit proxies from other shareholders, note that Section 14(c) of the Exchange Act would require them to provide to all shareholders an "information statement" that contains virtually all of the information that would be in a Schedule 14A proxy statement.

> (iii)   The furnishing of a form of proxy or other communication to security holders under circumstances reasonably calculated to result in the procurement, withholding or revocation of a proxy.

***

Pretty clear, isn't it? Well, at least we can be certain that if someone is requesting that a shareholder complete a proxy card for an upcoming shareholders meeting, a "solicitation" is occurring. Other situations may be ambiguous. However, there are some additional rules that may be helpful. For example, Rule 14a-1(*l*) excludes some things from the definition of a "solicitation," including, in subsection (2)(iv):

> A communication by a security holder who does not otherwise engage in a proxy solicitation (other than a solicitation exempt under Rule 14a-2) stating how the security holder intends to vote and the reasons therefor, provided that the communication:

> (A)   Is made by means of speeches in public forums, press releases, published or broadcast opinions, statements, or advertisements appearing in a broadcast media, or newspaper, magazine or other bona fide publication disseminated on a regular basis,

> (B)   Is directed to persons to whom the security holder owes a fiduciary duty in connection with the voting of securities of a registrant held by the security holder, or

> (C)   Is made in response to unsolicited requests for additional information with respect to a prior communication by the security holder made pursuant to this paragraph (l)(2)(iv).

Thus, under current law, if a shareholder wanted to make public statements supporting or opposing proposals that will be voted on by the shareholders, it may do so under this rule without worry that its activities would constitute the "solicitation" of a proxy which would require the filing of a Schedule 14A.[*]

---

[*]   For a case concerning whether advertisements relating to a matter of public interest could be considered proxy solicitations, see Long Island Lighting Company v. Barbash, 779 F.2d 792 (2d Cir. 1985). Note, however, this case was decided before Rule 14a-1(*l*)(2)(iv)(A) was in effect.

In addition, even if something would constitute the "solicitation" of a proxy, Rule 14a-2 specifically excludes some activities from most (but not all) of the proxy rules. For example, under Rule 14a-2(b)(1), a solicitation is exempt from most of the proxy rules if the person making the solicitation is not affiliated with management of the issuer, does not have a personal interest in the matter to be voted upon by the shareholders, and does not directly or indirectly seek the power to act as a proxy or furnish or request a form of revocation, abstention, consent, or authorization (among other requirements).[*] Also, Rule 14a-2(b)(2) excludes from most of the proxy rules "[a]ny solicitation made otherwise than on behalf of the registrant where the total number of persons solicited is not more than ten." This rule is useful for institutional shareholders, allowing them to communicate with one another more easily.

Another notable new SEC rule is Rule 14a-2(b)(6), which provides in part that the following solicitations need not comply with most of the proxy rules:

> Any solicitation by or on behalf of any person who does not seek directly or indirectly, either on its own or another's behalf, the power to act as proxy for a shareholder and does not furnish or otherwise request, or act on behalf of a person who furnishes or requests, a form of revocation, abstention, consent, or authorization in an electronic shareholder forum that is established, maintained or operated pursuant to the provisions of [Rule 14a-17], provided that the solicitation is made more than 60 days prior to the date announced by a registrant for its next annual or special meeting of shareholders.

Under Rule 14a-17, a shareholder or a registrant, or someone acting on their behalf, may operate an "electronic shareholder forum" (e.g., Internet chat rooms or message boards) which "facilitate interaction" among the shareholders, or between the registrant and its shareholders. The rule specifically provides that no shareholder, registrant or person acting on their behalf would be liable for statements made *by other persons* in the forum.

In the end, even though some communications are excluded from the definition of "solicitation" or otherwise exempt from having to comply with most of the proxy rules, the basic fact remains that if a person—whether the registrant or an "insurgent" shareholder—is requesting proxies from other shareholders, that

---

[*]   Under Rule 14a-6(g)(1) a person who engages in a solicitation that is exempt under Rule 14a-2(b)(1) does not need to file a Notice of Exempt Solicitation with the SEC if (1) the solicitation is done orally and not in writing or (2) the soliciting shareholder owns less than $5 million worth of the issuer's stock. Conversely, a person who owns more than $5 million worth of the company's stock and engages in a written proxy solicitation must file this Notice.

person will probably need to comply with the proxy rules. As noted above, the most important requirement of the proxy rules is that the solicitor must furnish a Schedule 14A to each person that is solicited.[*] In addition, Rule 14a-9 imposes civil liability for false or misleading statements made in connection with a proxy solicitation.

Proxy Statement and Proxy Card Requirements. To keep the following discussion relatively simple, we will assume that (1) the proxy solicitation is being made by the registrant (i.e., the issuer), rather than by a shareholder, and (2) the solicitation relates to a meeting at which directors will be elected, such as the annual meeting of shareholders. Further, we will assume that no other matters will be voted on by the shareholders at the meeting. (If the shareholders will vote on other matters then, as you might guess, detailed disclosures about those matters would be required.)

Schedule 14A requires very detailed information. As with the discussion of Form 10-K earlier in this chapter, the goal of the following is not to train readers how to prepare a Schedule 14A proxy statement, but rather to give you a sense of Schedule 14A and the extensive amount of information that it requires.

1. Schedule 14A. Item 1 of Schedule 14A requires information about the date, time, and place of the meeting (among other things) and Item 2 requires disclosure as to whether proxies are revocable. Item 4 requires disclosure about the persons making the solicitation and manner in which solicitations will occur and the costs thereof. Item 6, which is entitled "Voting Securities and Principal Holders Thereof," requires the registrant to:

* state the number of shares outstanding of each class of voting securities that is entitled to vote at the meeting and the record date (if any) with respect to the proxy solicitation;

* make certain disclosures if directors are to be elected at the meeting and the shareholders have cumulative voting rights (which is very rare for a public company);

* furnish the information required by Item 403 of Regulation S-K, which requires detailed information about the securities of the issuer owned by management (i.e., directors and executive officers) and any person or group that the issuer knows owns more than five percent of the issuer's voting securities; and

---

[*]   *See also* Rule 14a-12 (permitting certain written and oral communications before the filing of a proxy statement in some circumstances).

- make certain disclosures if a "change in control" of the issuer has occurred since the beginning of its last fiscal year.

So far, this isn't terribly difficult. But then come Items 7 and 8. Item 7 requires (among other things):

- a disclosure of any material legal proceedings to which any director or officer of the issuer (or any of their affiliates) is a "party adverse to the registrant or any of its subsidiaries or has a material interest adverse to the registrant or any of its subsidiaries," as required by Item 103 of Regulation S-K;

- detailed biographical and other information about the registrant's directors, officers, and "significant employees," as required by Item 401 of Regulation S-K;

- a description of "any transaction, since the beginning of the registrant's last fiscal year, or any currently proposed transaction, in which the registrant was or is to be a participant and the amount involved exceeds $120,000, and in which any related person [as that term is defined] had or will have a direct or indirect material interest," as well as a description of the "registrant's policies and procedures for the review, approval, or ratification of any [such] transaction," as required by Items 404(a) and (b) of Regulation S-K;

- information about compliance by the registrant's officers, directors, and ten-percent shareholders with Section 16(a) of the Exchange Act (which you will learn about in Chapter 14), as required by Item 405 of Regulation S-K;

- information about the audit committee of the registrant's board of directors and whether the audit committee has an "audit committee financial expert," as required by Items 407(d)(4) and (5) of Regulation S-K;

- information about the "leadership structure" of the registrant's board of directors and its "role in risk oversight," as required by Item 407(h) of Regulation S-K; and

- information about the "independence" of the registrant's directors and many other "corporate governance" matters detailed in Item 407 of Regulation S-K (which is very extensive). Notably, Item 407 requires disclosure of information about the issuer's director nomination process, including a description of the "material elements" of any policy that the nominating committee (or, if there isn't one, the board of directors) follows in considering director candidates nominated by shareholders. Further, if "the nominating committee will consider candidates recommended by security holders, [the issuer must] describe the procedures to be followed ... in submitting such recommendations."

Item 8 of Schedule 14A, which is entitled "Compensation of Directors and Executive Officers," requires the information specified in Item 402 of Regulation S-K and portions of Item 407 of Regulation S-K. In turn, these items require incredibly detailed information about the compensation (in just about any conceivable form) received by the registrant's directors and four most highly compensated executive officers, as well as additional information about "compensation committee interlocks and insider participation." In addition, the compensation committee of the registrant's board of directors must include in the Schedule 14A a report containing the information required by Item 407(e)(5) of Regulation S-K. (This report is discussed in the context of the Dodd-Frank Wall Street Reform and Consumer Protection Act in Section 10.03 below.)

Item 9 requires a great deal of information about the registrant's auditors, i.e., the accounting firm that audits the registrant's financial statements, including the fees that that firm earned for audit—and other—services in the past two fiscal years.

The last item of Schedule 14A that we will cover is Item 21, which requires (a thankfully brief) disclosure of the vote that is required for approval of each matter that the shareholders will vote upon, and the method by which votes (including abstentions and "broker nonvotes") will be counted.

2. *"Glossy" Annual Report.* In addition, Rule 14a-3(b) provides that if the solicitation is made on behalf of the registrant and relates to a meeting at which directors will be elected (typically the annual meeting of shareholders), each person whose proxy is solicited must be furnished with an annual report that meets the requirements of this rule. As noted above, this report is often called the "glossy" annual report. This is because many companies try to make it look "flashy" and include lots of attractive photographs and other graphics. However, the rule does not require such "flash" and some companies have recently cut back on this practice due to high printing costs. (Also, as discussed below, electronic delivery is now widely used.) In any event, annual reports must contain a lot of the information that is included in the issuer's Form 10-K for the prior year, such as audited financial statements.

3. *Proxy Card Requirements.* There are separate requirements for the actual proxy *card*, which is the document that a shareholder would sign to authorize a person (typically a member of the registrant's management) to vote the shareholder's shares at the meeting if the shareholder chooses not to attend in

person. Rule 14a-4 requires, that the proxy card must specify who is making the solicitation. Also, the rule requires, among other things, that the proxy card must:

- provide a blank space for dating the proxy card;

- "identify clearly and impartially" each matter upon which shareholders will vote (with some exceptions discussed below);

- with respect to the election of directors, "set forth the names of persons nominated for election as directors [and] *** clearly provide any of [four specified] means for security holders to withhold authority to vote for each nominee ***"; and

- with respect to matters other than the election of directors, provide means whereby the shareholder "is afforded an opportunity to specify by boxes a choice between approval or disapproval of, or abstention."

Provided that certain conditions are met, subsection (c) of Rule 14a-4 allows a proxy to give "discretionary authority" to the holder of the proxy to vote on certain matters as the holder of the proxy thinks best. However, subsection (d) provides that a proxy card may not confer authority to vote on certain matters, including the election of any "office for which a bona fide nominee is not named in the proxy statement" (with some exceptions). In addition, a proxy card may not confer authority to vote at any meeting other than the *upcoming* annual meeting (or any adjournment of that meeting) or to vote with respect to more than one meeting (or any adjournment of that meeting). These last two prohibitions would thus prevent "open ended" proxy cards that could be used for several years.

Keeping with our assumption in this discussion that the Schedule 14A relates to the solicitation of proxies by the registrant (as opposed to an "insurgent" shareholder) and that the only matter that will be voted upon at the annual shareholders meeting is the election of directors, then Rule 14a-6 simply requires the registrant to file the "definitive" Schedule 14A (including a copy of the proxy card) with the SEC no later than the first day that it is sent to any shareholder. (In many other situations, the solicitor, whether the registrant or a shareholder, would be required to file a "preliminary" Schedule 14A with the SEC at least ten days before they are sent to any shareholder. This would give the SEC an opportunity to review these materials. Rule 14a-6 contains additional rules that apply in specialized situations.) Generally speaking, any other "soliciting material" must also be filed.

Again, the above discussion is not meant to teach readers how to prepare a Schedule 14A proxy statement or a proxy card that complies with Rule 14a-4. Indeed, there are many nuances, details, and exceptions that were purposely omitted from this discussion so that it would not become overwhelming. Further, one can expect that the above-described disclosure requirements will continue to change in coming years.

Hopefully though, you understand that complying with these rules is no small task, and that it will almost certainly involve the assistance of an experienced securities lawyer. This, of course, will involve significant costs. Another major cost will be printing and mailing of the proxy statement and proxy card to the shareholders, who many number in the thousands. After all, we need enough of these people to execute and return proxies to ensure that we will have a quorum at the shareholders meeting, which may only be a month or two away.[*]

Delivery Requirements; "Street Names" and Beneficial Owners. So, let's assume that we have our proxy statement and proxy card all ready to go and a printing company standing by to print it in mass quantities. To whom must we mail these materials?

That's easy, you may think to yourself. I remember from Chapter 5 that, under the MBCA, the notice of the meeting (which will be contained in the proxy statement) must be mailed to each shareholder who is "entitled to vote" at the meeting. This means each person who was a shareholder on the record date that the board set for the meeting. So, it should be as simple as looking at the company's stock ledger book, seeing who owned stock certificates on the record date and what their last known addresses are, and then mailing the proxy materials to those persons. We should also include postage-prepaid return envelopes so that people may easily return their proxy cards.

If only life were so simple. The above paragraph assumed that each of the registrant's shareholders was a ***record shareholder***, that is, a person who owned a physical stock certificate representing shares of the registrant's stock. It is true that many shareholders do indeed have stock certificates and therefore count as record shareholders. Today, however, the great majority of shareholders do not have physical stock certificates. Instead, they own stock through a bank or broker-dealer, which in turn holds *a portion of* a stock certificate for a large number of shares. This "big" certificate (which may represent literally millions of shares) often is issued in the name of a large clearing house like Cede & Co.,

---

[*]   As you learned in Chapter 5, the MBCA requires that notice must be given to shareholders at least ten, but not more than sixty days, before the meeting. As you will appreciate from the following discussion, as a practical matter ten days will not be enough time for most public companies.

which we will call the ***depositary***.[*] However, even though the depositary's name appears on the "big" certificate, it does not own that stock for itself. Rather, the depositary maintains constantly updated records of the banks and broker-dealers that hold a position in the shares represented by the certificate and how many of those shares they hold. Further down the line, the banks and broker-dealers are, of course, not the actual owners of the stock—their customers are. When a customer sells some of her shares (or buys more), the issuance of a new physical stock certificate typically is not required. Instead, records are updated electronically, which is a much more efficient way to settle securities trades. For a discussion of the historical evolution of this system, see ROBERT M. HAMILTON ET AL., CASES AND MATERIALS ON CORPORATIONS INCLUDING PARTNERSHIPS AND LIMITED LIABILITY COMPANIES 526-32 (11th. ed. 2010).

For purposes of Section 12(g) of the Exchange Act, institutional custodians such as the depositary are not counted as single holders of record. Instead, each of the depositary's accounts is counted as a record holder. In other words, securities held in street name are held of record only by the banks or brokers—not the ultimate beneficial owners. Thus, under current rules if the depositary held an issuer's stock for the account of two dozen brokerage firms which, in turn, held the stock for several thousand of their customers, only the brokerage firms would be counted toward the 500-record shareholder threshold of Section 12(g)—not the thousands of beneficial owners.

So, how does an issuer that may have thousands of beneficial owners of its stock but has almost no idea who they are (let alone how many shares they own or what their mailing addresses are) go about delivering proxy statements to these shareholders? Obviously, with respect to actual record holders (i.e., those with physical stock certificates), the issuer would mail the proxy statement to the last known addresses of those shareholders in its stock transfer records. With respect to beneficial owners, the process is very complicated, but essentially boils down to the issuer requesting a list from the depositary of the banks and brokers that held a position in its stock as of the record date for the meeting and then asking those banks and brokers how many copies of the proxy materials they will need for their customers. The issuer then delivers the required number of copies to such banks and brokers, who in turn deliver the proxy materials to their customers. You may learn more about this process in an advanced course on Securities Regulation or by reading SEC Rule 14b-1.

---

[*]   The Depository Trust Company, a subsidiary of The Depository Trust & Clearing Corporation, is one of the largest clearing agencies in the world, and helps buyers and sellers of securities "settle" their transactions. Stocks held by DTC are held in the name of its nominee, Cede & Co.

Electronic Delivery and Voting.   As if the above discussion wasn't complex enough, much proxy delivery and voting is now done electronically, rather than solely in paper form.   Under SEC Rule 14a-16, which was adopted in 2007, an issuer must, at least forty calendar days before the date of a shareholders meeting, send its shareholders a paper notice (called a "Notice of Internet Availability of Proxy Materials") stating, among other things, that the issuer's proxy materials are available on a web site, but that shareholders may receive paper copies of proxy materials if they so choose.   If a shareholder does not opt for paper copies, then that shareholder would receive proxy materials, and vote, online.   All of the materials identified in the notice must be publicly accessible, free of charge, at the web site specified in the notice and the materials must remain on the web site until the conclusion of the meeting.   With some exceptions, the notice may not accompany any other document or materials, including the form of proxy (i.e., the proxy card) to be used for the meeting.   Further, the issuer may send a form of proxy to its shareholders only if (1) at least ten days have passed since it sent the notice, and the form of proxy is accompanied by a copy of the notice, or (2) the form of proxy is accompanied or preceded by a copy, via the same "medium," of the proxy statement.   Rule 14a-16 also requires the issuer to send a free, paper or e-mail copy of the proxy materials to any shareholder who requests a copy.   The issuer must keep records of each shareholder who has requested paper or e-mail copies of proxy materials and continue to provide copies to such shareholder in that manner until the shareholder revokes her request to receive paper or e-mail copies.   See Rule 14a-16 for more details.

Shareholder Proposals Under Rule 14a-8.   Printing thousands of copies of a proxy statement and mailing it to thousands of shareholders could easily cost tens of thousands of dollars.   Even with the advent of the "e-proxy" rules described in the previous paragraph, which may reduce printing costs, the *legal* costs involved in preparing a Schedule 14 proxy statement are daunting.   For this reason, no one but the richest and/or most "committed" shareholders would bother soliciting proxies from their fellow shareholders if they wanted the shareholders to vote on something.

Perhaps recognizing this financial barrier to effective "shareholder democracy," SEC Rule 14a-8 provides that a shareholder who meets certain requirements can force the issuer to include a proposal in the issuer's proxy statement and have the shareholders vote on it.   If a shareholder is able to submit a proposal in this way, she obviously avoids the printing and legal costs of preparing and delivering a Schedule 14A proxy statement to the other shareholders. However, Rule 14a-8 also seems to recognize that issuers should not be unduly harassed by their shareholders, many of whom may have motives that differ from promoting the issuer's profitability.   This uneasy balance is reflected in Rule 14a-8's requirements.

Rule 14a-8 may be unique among federal administrative rules in that it is written in a question-and-answer format that was designed to facilitate easy understanding by non-lawyers. In answer to the question "Question 2: Who is eligible to submit a proposal, and how do I demonstrate to the company that I am eligible?," the rule states in part:

> In order to be eligible to submit a proposal, you must have continuously held at least $2,000 in market value, or 1%, of the company's securities entitled to be voted on the proposal at the meeting for at least one year by the date you submit the proposal. You must continue to hold those securities through the date of the meeting.

In addition, a shareholder may only submit one proposal per meeting. The proposal, together with any supporting statement, may not exceed 500 words. Either the shareholder or a legal representative of the shareholder must attend the meeting to present the proposal. The issuer's annual proxy statement must set forth the deadline for submitting shareholder proposals for the following year's annual meeting.

Even if a shareholder meets the requirements of Rule 14a-8 when submitting a proposal, there are several grounds that the issuer could use to exclude a proposal, that is, refuse to include it in its proxy materials. Rule 14a-8(i) (formerly subsection (c)) lists the following grounds:

> 1.   *Improper under state law:* If the proposal is not a proper subject for action by shareholders under the laws of the jurisdiction of the company's organization;
>
> *Note to paragraph (i)(1):* Depending on the subject matter, some proposals are not considered proper under state law if they would be binding on the company if approved by shareholders. In our experience, most proposals that are cast as recommendations or requests that the board of directors take specified action are proper under state law. Accordingly, we will assume that a proposal drafted as a recommendation or suggestion is proper unless the company demonstrates otherwise.
>
> 2.   *Violation of law:* If the proposal would, if implemented, cause the company to violate any state, federal, or foreign law to which it is subject; ***
>
> 3.   *Violation of proxy rules:* If the proposal or supporting statement is contrary to any of the Commission's proxy rules,

including Rule 14a-9, which prohibits materially false or misleading statements in proxy soliciting materials;

4.   *Personal grievance; special interest:* If the proposal relates to the redress of a personal claim or grievance against the company or any other person, or if it is designed to result in a benefit to you, or to further a personal interest, which is not shared by the other shareholders at large;

5.   *Relevance:* If the proposal relates to operations which account for less than 5 percent of the company's total assets at the end of its most recent fiscal year, and for less than 5 percent of its net earnings and gross sales for its most recent fiscal year, and is not otherwise significantly related to the company's business;

6.   *Absence of power/authority:* If the company would lack the power or authority to implement the proposal;

7.   *Management functions:* If the proposal deals with a matter relating to the company's ordinary business operations;

8.   *Director elections:* If the proposal: (i) Would disqualify a nominee who is standing for election; (ii) Would remove a director from office before his or her term expired; (iii) Questions the competence, business judgment, or character of one or more nominees or directors; (iv) Seeks to include a specific individual in the company's proxy materials for election to the board of directors; or (v) Otherwise could affect the outcome of the upcoming election of directors;[*]

9.   *Conflicts with company's proposal:* If the proposal directly conflicts with one of the company's own proposals to be submitted to shareholders at the same meeting; ***

10.   *Substantially implemented:* If the company has already substantially implemented the proposal; ***

11.   *Duplication:* If the proposal substantially duplicates another proposal previously submitted to the company by another proponent that will be included in the company's proxy materials for the same meeting;

---

[*]   This text went into effect in September 2011. This subsection has recently had an interesting history which is discussed below in Section 10.03(B) of this chapter.

12.   *Resubmissions:* If the proposal deals with substantially the same subject matter as another proposal or proposals that has or have been previously included in the company's proxy materials within the preceding 5 calendar years, a company may exclude it from its proxy materials for any meeting held within 3 calendar years of the last time it was included if the proposal received: (i) Less than 3% of the vote if proposed once within the preceding 5 calendar years; (ii) Less than 6% of the vote on its last submission to shareholders if proposed twice previously within the preceding 5 calendar years; or (iii) Less than 10% of the vote on its last submission to shareholders if proposed three times or more previously within the preceding 5 calendar years; and

13.   *Specific amount of dividends:* If the proposal relates to specific amounts of cash or stock dividends.

Not surprisingly, few issuers like to include shareholder proposals—many proposals can be obnoxious or even downright embarrassing to the company. As such, issuers try, if at all possible, to exclude shareholder proposals on one or more of the foregoing grounds. For a determined shareholder, this can lead to litigation, as shown in the following case.

Lovenheim v. Iroquois Brands, Ltd.
United States District Court for the District of Columbia
618 F. Supp. 554 (1985)

GASCH, District Judge.

I.   BACKGROUND

This matter is now before the Court on plaintiff's motion for preliminary injunction.

Plaintiff Peter C. Lovenheim, owner of two hundred shares of common stock in Iroquois Brands, Ltd. (hereinafter "Iroquois/Delaware"), seeks to bar Iroquois/Delaware from excluding from the proxy materials being sent to all shareholders in preparation for an upcoming shareholder meeting information concerning a proposed resolution he intends to offer at the meeting.   Mr. Lovenheim's proposed resolution relates to the procedure used to force-feed geese for production of paté de foie gras in France, a type of paté imported by Iroquois/Delaware.   Specifically, his resolution calls upon the Directors of Iroquois/Delaware to:

form a committee to study the methods by which its French supplier produces paté de foie gras, and report to the shareholders its findings and opinions, based on expert consultation, on whether this production method causes undue distress, pain or suffering to the animals involved and, if so, whether further distribution of this product should be discontinued until a more humane production method is developed.

***

Mr. Lovenheim's right to compel Iroquois/Delaware to insert information concerning his proposal in the proxy materials turns on the applicability of section 14(a) of the Securities Exchange Act of 1934, 15 U.S.C. § 78n(a) ("the Exchange Act"), and the shareholder proposal rule promulgated by the Securities and Exchange Commission ("SEC"), Rule 14a-8. That rule states in pertinent part:

> If any security holder of an issuer notifies the issuer of his intention to present a proposal for action at a forthcoming meeting of the issuer's security holders, the issuer shall set forth the proposal in its proxy statement and identify it in its form of proxy and provide means by which security holders [presenting a proposal may present in the proxy statement a statement of not more than 200 words in support of the proposal].

Iroquois/Delaware has refused to allow information concerning Mr. Lovenheim's proposal to be included in proxy materials being sent in connection with the next annual shareholders meeting. In doing so, Iroquois/Delaware relies on an exception to the general requirement of Rule 14a-8, Rule 14a-8(c)(5). That exception provides that an issuer of securities "may omit a proposal and any statement in support thereof" from its proxy statement and form of proxy:

> if the proposal relates to operations which account for less than 5 percent of the issuer's total assets at the end of its most recent fiscal year, and for less than 5 percent of its net earnings and gross sales for its most recent fiscal year, and is not otherwise significantly related to the issuer's business. [Citation omitted.]

***

II.   LIKELIHOOD OF PLAINTIFF PREVAILING ON MERITS

***

C. *Applicability of Rule 14a-8(c)(5) Exception*

*** [T]he likelihood of plaintiff's prevailing in this litigation turns primarily on the applicability to plaintiff's proposal of the exception to the shareholder proposal rule contained in Rule 14a-8(c)(5).

Iroquois/Delaware's reliance on the argument that this exception applies is based on the following information contained in the affidavit of its president: Iroquois/Delaware has annual revenues of $141 million with $6 million in annual profits and $78 million in assets. In contrast, its paté de foie gras sales were just $79,000 last year, representing a net loss on paté sales of $3,121. Iroquois/Delaware has only $34,000 in assets related to paté. Thus none of the company's net earnings and less than .05 percent of its assets are implicated by plaintiff's proposal. [Citation omitted.] These levels are obviously far below the five percent threshold set forth in the first portion of the exception claimed by Iroquois/Delaware.

Plaintiff does not contest that his proposed resolution relates to a matter of little economic significance to Iroquois/Delaware. Nevertheless he contends that the Rule 14a-8(c)(5) exception is not applicable as it cannot be said that his proposal "is not otherwise significantly related to the issuer's business" as is required by the final portion of that exception. In other words, plaintiff's argument that Rule 14a-8 does not permit omission of his proposal rests on the assertion that the rule and statute on which it is based do not permit omission merely because a proposal is not economically significant where a proposal has "ethical or social significance."

Iroquois/Delaware challenges plaintiff's view that ethical and social proposals cannot be excluded even if they do not meet the economic or five percent test. Instead, Iroquois/Delaware views the exception solely in economic terms as permitting omission of any proposals relating to a de minimis share of assets and profits. Iroquois/Delaware asserts that since corporations are economic entities, only an economic test is appropriate.

The Court would note that the applicability of the Rule 14a-8(c)(5) exception to Mr. Lovenheim's proposal represents a close question given the lack of clarity in the exception itself. In effect, plaintiff relies on the word "otherwise," suggesting that it indicates the drafters of the rule intended that other noneconomic tests of significance be used. Iroquois/Delaware relies on the fact that the rule examines other significance in relation to the issuer's business. Because of the apparent ambiguity of the rule, the Court considers the history of the shareholder proposal rule in determining the proper interpretation of the most recent version of that rule.

Prior to 1983, paragraph 14a-8(c)(5) excluded proposals "not significantly related to the issuer's business" but did not contain an objective economic significance test such as the five percent of sales, assets, and earnings specified in the first part of the current version. Although a series of SEC decisions through 1976 allowing issuers to exclude proposals challenging compliance with the Arab economic boycott of Israel allowed exclusion if the issuer did less than one percent of their business with Arab countries or Israel, the Commission stated later in 1976 that it did "not believe that subparagraph (c)(5) should be hinged solely on the economic relativity of a proposal." [Citation omitted.] Thus the Commission required inclusion "in many situations in which the related business comprised less than one percent" of the company's revenues, profits or assets "where the proposal has raised *policy questions* important enough to be considered `significantly related' to the issuer's business."

As indicated above, the 1983 revision adopted the five percent test of economic significance in an effort to create a more objective standard. Nevertheless, in adopting this standard, the Commission stated that proposals will be includable notwithstanding their "failure to reach the specified economic thresholds if a significant relationship to the issuer's business is demonstrated on the face of the resolution or supporting statement." [Citation omitted.] Thus it seems clear based on the history of the rule that "the meaning of 'significantly related' is not *limited* to economic significance." [Citation omitted.]

The only decision in this Circuit cited by the parties relating to the scope of section 14 and the shareholder proposal rule is *Medical Committee for Human Rights v. SEC*, 432 F.2d 659 (D.C. Cir. 1970). That case concerned an effort by shareholders of Dow Chemical Company to advise other shareholders of their proposal directed at prohibiting Dow's production of napalm. Dow had relied on the counterpart of the 14a-8(c)(5) exemption then in effect to exclude the proposal from proxy materials and the SEC accepted Dow's position without elaborating on its basis for doing so. In remanding the matter back to the SEC for the Commission to provide the basis for its decision, the Court noted what it termed "substantial questions" as to whether an interpretation of the shareholder proposal rule "which permitted omission of [a] proposal as one motivated primarily by *general* political or social concerns would conflict with the congressional intent underlying section 14(a) of the [Exchange] Act."

Iroquois/Delaware attempts to distinguish *Medical Committee for Human Rights* as a case where a company sought to exclude a proposal that, unlike Mr. Lovenheim's proposal, was economically significant merely because the motivation of the proponents was political. The argument is not without appeal given the fact that the *Medical Committee Court* was confronted with a regulation that contained no reference to economic significance. Yet the *Medical Committee* decision contains language suggesting that the Court assumed napalm was not economically significant to Dow:

> The management of Dow Chemical Company is repeatedly quoted in sources which include the company's own publications as proclaiming that the decision to continue manufacturing and marketing napalm was made not *because* of business consider-ations, but *in spite* of them; that management in essence decided to pursue a course of activity which generated little profit for the shareholders.... [Citation omitted.]

This Court need not consider, as the *Medical Committee* decision implied, whether a rule allowing exclusion of all proposals not meeting specified levels of economic significance violates the scope of section 14(a) of the Exchange Act. [Citation omitted.]   Whether or not the Securities and Exchange Commission could properly adopt such a rule, the Court cannot ignore the history of the rule which reveals no decision by the Commission to limit the determination to the economic criteria relied on by Iroquois/Delaware. The Court therefore holds that in light of the ethical and social significance of plaintiff's proposal and the fact that it implicates significant levels of sales, plaintiff has shown a likelihood of prevailing on the merits with regard to the issue of whether his proposal is "otherwise significantly related" to Iroquois/Delaware's business.

***

IV.   CONCLUSION

For the reasons discussed above, the Court concludes that plaintiff's motion for preliminary injunction should be granted.

As you might guess, in addition to case law, there are a great many SEC no-action letters that contain guidance as to when an issuer may use any of the above-described provisions of Rule 14-8 to exclude a shareholder proposal from its proxy materials. In particular, the "ordinary business" exclusion has a long history of no-action letters (and shifting SEC positions on whether various matters concern an issuer's ordinary business operations).

Issuers often are unable to exclude shareholder proposals, particularly those that are submitted by large institutional shareholders or "activist" shareholders that have good legal counsel.* As a result, every year many companies are required to include shareholder proposals in their proxy statements and have shareholders vote on them. Most shareholder proposals do not achieve majority support from other shareholders. However, sometimes activist shareholders view a "good showing" as a public-relations success that may force the issuer to implement reforms out of embarrassment. A good way to keep track of the trends in this area is to read the annual "post-season" reports of Institutional Shareholder Services, a firm that advises many institutional shareholders (e.g., mutual funds and pension plans) on how they should vote their shares of public companies.

"Common Carrier" Requirements. Another shareholder-friendly rule under Section 14 of the Exchange Act is Rule 14a-7. This rule basically provides that if an issuer solicits proxies for a shareholder meeting, any shareholder who is eligible to vote at the meeting may ask the issuer for a list of shareholders, which would allow that shareholder to contact other shareholders and/or mail proxy materials to them. However, if the issuer does not want to provide the list of shareholders (and most issuers do not want to do so), it could instead offer to mail the requesting shareholder's proxy materials to the other shareholders (at the requesting shareholder's expense, of course). Within five business days after receiving the request, the issuer must notify the shareholder as to whether it will provide the list or instead mail the shareholder's materials. Also, the issuer must give the requesting shareholder a statement of the approximate number of shareholders (both record and beneficial) and an estimate of the cost of mailing proxy materials to those shareholders.

D.   EXCHANGE ACT CIVIL LIABILITY

The Exchange Act imposes civil liability for material false or misleading Exchange Act reports and proxy statements. First, Section 18(a) of the Exchange Act provides in part that:

> Any person who shall make or cause to be made any statement in any application, report, or document filed pursuant to [the Exchange Act] or any rule or regulation thereunder ***, which statement was at the time and in the light of the circumstances under which it was made false or misleading with respect to any

---

* Even if an issuer can exclude a shareholder proposal from its proxy statement pursuant to Rule 14a-8, it may still need to describe the proposal in its proxy materials if the shareholder will present the proposal at the meeting. *See* Item 20 of Schedule 14A ("If action is to be taken on any matter not specifically referred to in this Schedule 14A, [the issuer must] describe briefly the substance of each such matter in substantially the same degree of detail as is required by Items 5 to 19, inclusive, of this Schedule ....").

material fact, shall be liable to any person (not knowing that such statement was false or misleading) who, in reliance upon such statement, shall have purchased or sold a security at a price which was affected by such statement, for damages caused by such reliance, unless the person sued shall prove that he acted in good faith and had no knowledge that such statement was false or misleading. *** In any such suit the court may, in its discretion, require an undertaking for the payment of the costs of such suit, and assess reasonable costs, including reasonable attorneys' fees, against either party litigant.

Unlike many provisions of the Securities Act, which tend to be very "plaintiff-friendly," this section imposes some serious hurdles for plaintiffs. First, note that this section requires the plaintiff to show that she purchased or sold securities at a price that was affected by the material misstatement or omission. Thus, someone who decided to *hold* securities that she already owned or who decided *not* to purchase securities could not be a plaintiff under Section 18. Even if the plaintiff did purchase or sell securities, she would be required to show that the price was affected by the false or misleading Exchange Act filing, which could present difficult issues of causation. Second, defendants can defend the lawsuit by establishing that they acted in good faith and did not have knowledge that the Exchange Act filing was materially false or misleading. Finally, the court can require an undertaking for costs, including reasonable attorney fees. Because of these demanding requirements, plaintiffs may opt to sue under Rule 10b-5 instead (which is discussed in Chapter 14).

SEC Rule 14a-9 also imposes civil liability for material false or misleading proxy statements, by providing in subsection (a) that:

> No solicitation subject to this regulation shall be made by means of any proxy statement, form of proxy, notice of meeting or other communication, written or oral, containing any statement which, at the time and in the light of the circumstances under which it is made, is false or misleading with respect to any material fact, or which omits to state any material fact necessary in order to make the statements therein not false or misleading ***.

The note to Rule 14a-9 then gives some examples of items that "may" be misleading.

There have been many cases brought under Rule 14a-9, resulting in important court decisions. In the following case, the Supreme Court discusses the meaning of materiality for purposes of Rule 14a-9.

TSC Industries, Inc. v. Northway, Inc.
Supreme Court of United States
426 U.S. 438 (1976)

MR. JUSTICE MARSHALL delivered the opinion of the Court.

***

[II.A.] As we have noted on more than one occasion, § 14(a) of the Securities Exchange Act "was intended to promote 'the free exercise of the voting rights of stockholders' by ensuring that proxies would be solicited with 'explanation to the stockholder of the real nature of the questions for which authority to cast his vote is sought.'" [Citations omitted.] In [*J.I. Case Co. v. Borak*, 377 U.S. 426 (1964)], the Court held that § 14(a)'s broad remedial purposes required recognition *** of an implied private right of action for violations of the provision. And in [*Mills v. Electric Auto-Lite Co.*, 396 U.S. 375 (1970)], we attempted to clarify to some extent the elements of a private cause of action for violation of § 14(a). In a suit challenging the sufficiency under § 14(a) and Rule 14a-9 of a proxy statement soliciting votes in favor of a merger, we held that there was no need to demonstrate that the alleged defect in the proxy statement actually had a decisive effect on the voting. So long as the misstatement or omission was material, the causal relation between violation and injury is sufficiently established, we concluded, if "the proxy solicitation itself ... was an essential link in the accomplishment of the transaction." [Citation omitted.] After *Mills*, then, the content given to the notion of materiality assumes heightened significance.

[II.B] The question of materiality, it is universally agreed, is an objective one, involving the significance of an omitted or misrepresented fact to a reasonable investor. Variations in the formulation of a general test of materiality occur in the articulation of just how significant a fact must be or, put another way, how certain it must be that the fact would affect a reasonable investor's judgment.

The Court of Appeals in this case concluded that material facts include "all facts which a reasonable shareholder might consider important." [Citation omitted.] This formulation of the test of materiality has been explicitly rejected by at least two courts as setting too low a threshold for the imposition of liability under Rule 14a-9. [Citations omitted.] ***

In arriving at its broad definition of a material fact as one that a reasonable shareholder might consider important, the Court of Appeals in this case relied heavily upon language of this Court in [*Mills*]. That reliance was misplaced. ***

***

[II.C]   In formulating a standard of materiality under Rule 14a-9, we are guided, of course, by the recognition in *Borak* and *Mills* of the Rule's broad remedial purpose. That purpose is not merely to ensure by judicial means that the transaction, when judged by its real terms, is fair and otherwise adequate, but to ensure disclosures by corporate management in order to enable the shareholders to make an informed choice. [Citation omitted.]   As an abstract proposition, the most desirable role for a court in a suit of this sort, coming after the consummation of the proposed transaction, would perhaps be to determine whether in fact the proposal would have been favored by the shareholders and consummated in the absence of any misstatement or omission. But as we recognized in *Mills,* [citation omitted], such matters are not subject to determination with certainty. Doubts as to the critical nature of information misstated or omitted will be commonplace. And particularly in view of the prophylactic purpose of the Rule and the fact that the content of the proxy statement is within management's control, it is appropriate that these doubts be resolved in favor of those the statute is designed to protect. [Citation omitted.]

We are aware, however, that the disclosure policy embodied in the proxy regulations is not without limit. [Citation omitted.]   Some information is of such dubious significance that insistence on its disclosure may accomplish more harm than good. The potential liability for a Rule 14a-9 violation can be great indeed, and if the standard of materiality is unnecessarily low, not only may the corporation and its management be subjected to liability for insignificant omissions or misstatements, but also management's fear of exposing itself to substantial liability may cause it simply to bury the shareholders in an avalanche of trivial information—a result that is hardly conducive to informed decision-making. Precisely these dangers are presented, we think, by the definition of a material fact adopted by the Court of Appeals in this case—a fact which a reasonable shareholder might consider important. We [believe] *** that the "might" formulation is "too suggestive of mere possibility, however unlikely." [Citation omitted.]

The general standard of materiality that we think best comports with the policies of Rule 14a-9 is as follows: An omitted fact is material if there is a substantial likelihood that a reasonable shareholder would consider it important in deciding how to vote. This standard is fully consistent with *Mills*['s] general description of materiality as a requirement that "the defect have a significant propensity to affect the voting process." It does not require proof of a substantial likelihood that disclosure of the omitted fact would have caused the reasonable investor to change his vote. What the standard does contemplate is a showing of a substantial likelihood that, under all the circumstances, the omitted fact would have assumed actual significance in the deliberations of the reasonable shareholder. Put another way, there must be a substantial likelihood that the disclosure of the omitted fact would have been viewed by the reasonable investor as having significantly altered the "total mix" of information made available.

***

A Rule 14a-9 plaintiff must prove causation, i.e., that the misstatement or omission caused harm to the plaintiff. Courts have broken this into two elements; *loss causation*, which is a causal link between the false or misleading proxy statement and economic harm to the plaintiff; and *transaction causation*, which is a causal link between the false or misleading proxy statement and the occurrence of the transaction upon which the shareholders were voting. Set forth below are two important opinions on causation.

Mills v. Electric Auto-Lite Co.
Supreme Court of United States
396 U.S. 375 (1970)

MR. JUSTICE HARLAN delivered the opinion of the Court.

This case requires us to consider a basic aspect of the implied private right of action for violation of § 14 (a) of the Securities Exchange Act of 1934 ***. [T]he asserted wrong is that a corporate merger was accomplished through the use of a proxy statement that was materially false or misleading. The question with which we deal is what causal relationship must be shown between such a statement and the merger to establish a cause of action based on the violation of the Act.

[I]   Petitioners were shareholders of the Electric Auto-Lite Company until 1963, when it was merged into Mergenthaler Linotype Company. They brought suit on the day before the shareholders' meeting at which the vote was to take place on the merger, against Auto-Lite, Mergenthaler, and a third company, American Manufacturing Company, Inc. The complaint sought an injunction against the voting by Auto-Lite's management of all proxies obtained by means of an allegedly misleading proxy solicitation; however, it did not seek a temporary restraining order, and the voting went ahead as scheduled the following day. Several months later petitioners filed an amended complaint, seeking to have the merger set aside and to obtain such other relief as might be proper.

*** [Petitioners] alleged that the proxy statement sent out by the Auto-Lite management to solicit shareholders' votes in favor of the merger was misleading, in violation of § 14(a) of the Act and SEC Rule 14a-9 thereunder.

[Citation omitted.] Petitioners recited that before the merger Mergenthaler owned over 50% of the outstanding shares of Auto-Lite common stock, and had been in control of Auto-Lite for two years. American Manufacturing in turn owned about one-third of the outstanding shares of Mergenthaler, and for two years had been in voting control of Mergenthaler and, through it, of Auto-Lite. Petitioners charged that in light of these circumstances the proxy statement was misleading in that it told Auto-Lite shareholders that their board of directors recommended approval of the merger without also informing them that all 11 of Auto-Lite's directors were nominees of Mergenthaler and were under the "control and domination of Mergenthaler." ***

*** [T]he District Court for the Northern District of Illinois ruled as a matter of law that the claimed defect in the proxy statement was, in light of the circumstances in which the statement was made, a material omission. The District Court concluded *** that it had to hold a hearing on the issue whether there was "a causal connection between the finding that there has been a violation of the disclosure requirements of § 14(a) and the alleged injury to the plaintiffs" before it could consider what remedies would be appropriate. [Citation omitted.]

After holding such a hearing, the court found that under the terms of the merger agreement, an affirmative vote of two-thirds of the Auto-Lite shares was required for approval of the merger, and that the respondent companies owned and controlled about 54% of the outstanding shares. Therefore, to obtain authorization of the merger, respondents had to secure the approval of a substantial number of the minority shareholders. At the stockholders' meeting, approximately 950,000 shares, out of 1,160,000 shares outstanding, were voted in favor of the merger. This included 317,000 votes obtained by proxy from the minority shareholders, votes that were "necessary and indispensable to the approval of the merger." The District Court concluded that a causal relationship had thus been shown, and it granted an interlocutory judgment in favor of petitioners on the issue of liability, referring the case to a master for consideration of appropriate relief. [Citation omitted.]

*** [The Court of Appeals] affirmed the District Court's conclusion that the proxy statement was materially deficient, but reversed on the question of causation. The court acknowledged that, if an injunction had been sought a sufficient time before the stockholders' meeting, "corrective measures would have been appropriate." [Citation omitted.] However, since this suit was brought too late for preventive action, the courts had to determine "whether the misleading statement and omission caused the submission of sufficient proxies," as a prerequisite to a determination of liability under the Act. If the respondents could show, "by a preponderance of probabilities, that the merger would have received a sufficient vote even if the proxy statement had not been misleading in the respect found," petitioners would be entitled to no relief of any kind. [Citation omitted.]

*** [R]ightly concluding that "[r]eliance by thousands of individuals, as here, can scarcely be inquired into" [citation omitted], the court ruled that the issue was to be determined by proof of the fairness of the terms of the merger. If respondents could show that the merger had merit and was fair to the minority shareholders, the trial court would be justified in concluding that a sufficient number of shareholders would have approved the merger had there been no deficiency in the proxy statement. In that case respondents would be entitled to a judgment in their favor.

*** [T]he petitioners then sought review in this Court. We granted certiorari, [citation omitted], believing that resolution of this basic issue should be made at this stage of the litigation and not postponed until after a trial under the Court of Appeals' decision.

[II]   *** [Section] 14(a) stemmed from a congressional belief that "[f]air corporate suffrage is an important right that should attach to every equity security bought on a public exchange." [Citation omitted.] The provision was intended to promote "the free exercise of the voting rights of stockholders" by ensuring that proxies would be solicited with "explanation to the stockholder of the real nature of the questions for which authority to cast his vote is sought." [Citation omitted.] The decision below, by permitting all liability to be foreclosed on the basis of a finding that the merger was fair, would allow the stockholders to be bypassed, at least where the only legal challenge to the merger is a suit for retrospective relief after the meeting has been held. A judicial appraisal of the merger's merits could be substituted for the actual and informed vote of the stockholders.

The result would be to insulate from private redress an entire category of proxy violations—those relating to matters other than the terms of the merger. Even outrageous misrepresentations in a proxy solicitation, if they did not relate to the terms of the transaction, would give rise to no cause of action under § 14(a). Particularly if carried over to enforcement actions by the Securities and Exchange Commission itself, such a result would subvert the congressional purpose of ensuring full and fair disclosure to shareholders. Further, recognition of the fairness of the merger as a complete defense would confront small shareholders with an additional obstacle to making a successful challenge to a proposal recommended through a defective proxy statement. The risk that they would be unable to rebut the corporation's evidence of the fairness of the proposal, and thus to establish their cause of action, would be bound to discourage such shareholders from the private enforcement of the proxy rules that "provides a necessary supplement to Commission action." [Citation omitted.]

*** Use of a solicitation that is materially misleading is itself a violation of law, as the Court of Appeals recognized in stating that injunctive relief would

be available to remedy such a defect if sought prior to the stockholders' meeting.
***

Where the misstatement or omission in a proxy statement has been shown to be "material," as it was found to be here, that determination itself indubitably embodies a conclusion that the defect was of such a character that it might have been considered important by a reasonable shareholder who was in the process of deciding how to vote. This requirement that the defect have a significant *propensity* to affect the voting process is found in the express terms of Rule 14a-9, and it adequately serves the purpose of ensuring that a cause of action cannot be established by proof of a defect so trivial, or so unrelated to the transaction for which approval is sought, that correction of the defect or imposition of liability would not further the interests protected by § 14 (a).

There is no need to supplement this requirement, as did the Court of Appeals, with a requirement of proof of whether the defect actually had a decisive effect on the voting. Where there has been a finding of materiality, a shareholder has made a sufficient showing of causal relationship between the violation and the injury for which he seeks redress if, as here, he proves that the proxy solicitation itself, rather than the particular defect in the solicitation materials, was an essential link in the accomplishment of the transaction. This objective test will avoid the impracticalities of determining how many votes were affected, and, by resolving doubts in favor of those the statute is designed to protect, will effectuate the congressional policy of ensuring that the shareholders are able to make an informed choice when they are consulted on corporate transactions. [Citations omitted.][*]

***

[Opinion of Justice Black, concurring in part and dissenting in part, omitted.]

---

[*] [Footnote by Court]: We need not decide in this case whether causation could be shown where the management controls a sufficient number of shares to approve the transaction without any votes from the minority. Even in that situation, if the management finds it necessary for legal or practical reasons to solicit proxies from minority shareholders, at least one court has held that the proxy solicitation might be sufficiently related to the merger to satisfy the causation requirement, [citations omitted].

Appearing below is another important Rule 14a-9 opinion from the Supreme Court which, in addition to addressing the causation issue discussed in *Mills*, also considers whether a statement of opinion can be materially false or misleading so as to give rise to Rule 14a-9 liability. Before reading it, make sure you read the footnote from the *Mills* opinion appearing at the bottom of the prior page.

Virginia Bankshares, Inc. v. Sandberg
Supreme Court of United States
501 U.S. 1083 (1991)

MR. JUSTICE SOUTER delivered the opinion of the Court.

***

The questions before us are whether a statement couched in conclusory or qualitative terms purporting to explain directors' reasons for recommending certain corporate action can be materially misleading within the meaning of Rule 14a-9, and whether causation of damages compensable under § 14(a) can be shown by a member of a class of minority shareholders whose votes are not required by law or corporate bylaw to authorize the corporate action subject to the proxy solicitation. We hold that knowingly false statements of reasons may be actionable even though conclusory in form, but that respondents have failed to demonstrate the equitable basis required to extend the § 14(a) private action to such shareholders when any indication of congressional intent to do so is lacking.

[I]   In December 1986, First American Bankshares, Inc. (FABI), a bank holding company, began a "freeze-out" merger, in which the First American Bank of Virginia (Bank) eventually merged into Virginia Bankshares, Inc. (VBI), a wholly owned subsidiary of FABI. VBI owned 85% of the Bank's shares, the remaining 15% being in the hands of some 2,000 minority shareholders. FABI hired the investment banking firm of Keefe, Bruyette & Woods (KBW) to give an opinion on the appropriate price for shares of the minority holders, who would lose their interests in the Bank as a result of the merger. Based on market quotations and unverified information from FABI, KBW gave the Bank's executive committee an opinion that $42 a share would be a fair price for the minority stock. The executive committee approved the merger proposal at that price, and the full board followed suit.

Although Virginia law only that such a merger proposal be submitted to a vote at a shareholders' meeting, and that the meeting be preceded by circulation of a statement of information to the shareholders, the directors nevertheless solicited proxies for voting on the proposal at the annual meeting set for April 21, 1987. In their solicitation, the directors urged the proposal's adoption and stated they had approved the plan because of its opportunity for the minority shareholders to achieve a "high" value, which they elsewhere described as a "fair" price, for their stock.

Although most minority shareholders gave the proxies requested, respondent Sandberg did not, and after approval of the merger she sought damages in the United States District Court for the Eastern District of Virginia from VBI, FABI, and the directors of the Bank. She pleaded two counts, one for soliciting proxies in violation of § 14(a) and Rule 14a-9, and the other for breaching fiduciary duties owed to the minority shareholders under state law. Under the first count, Sandberg alleged, among other things, that the directors had not believed that the price offered was high or that the terms of the merger were fair, but had recommended the merger only because they believed they had no alternative if they wished to remain on the board. At trial, Sandberg invoked language from this Court's opinion in *Mills v. Electric Auto-Lite Co.*, 396 U.S. 375, 385 (1970), to obtain an instruction that the jury could find for her without a showing of her own reliance on the alleged misstatements, so long as they were material and the proxy solicitation was an "essential link" in the merger process.

The jury's verdicts were for Sandberg on both counts, after finding violations of Rule 14a-9 by all defendants and a breach of fiduciary duties by the Bank's directors. The jury awarded Sandberg $18 a share, having found that she would have received $60 if her stock had been valued adequately.

***

On appeal, the United States Court of Appeals for the Fourth Circuit affirmed the judgments, holding that certain statements in the proxy solicitation were materially misleading for purposes of the Rule, and that respondents could maintain their action even though their votes had not been needed to effectuate the merger. [Citation omitted.] We granted certiorari because of the importance of the issues presented. [Citation omitted.]

[II]   The Court of Appeals affirmed petitioners' liability for two statements found to have been materially misleading in violation of § 14(a) of the Act, one of which was that "The Plan of Merger has been approved by the Board of Directors because it provides an opportunity for the Bank's public shareholders to achieve a high value for their shares." [Citation omitted.] Petitioners argue that statements of opinion or belief incorporating indefinite and unverifiable expressions cannot be actionable as misstatements of material fact within the meaning of Rule 14a-9, and that such a declaration of opinion or belief should never be actionable when placed in a proxy solicitation incorporating statements of fact sufficient to enable readers to draw their own, independent conclusions.

[II.A]   We consider first the actionability per se of statements of reasons, opinion, or belief.   Because such a statement by definition purports to express what is consciously on the speaker's mind, we interpret the jury verdict as finding that the directors' statements of belief and opinion were made with knowledge that the directors did not hold the beliefs or opinions expressed, and we confine our discussion to statements so made.   That such statements may be materially significant raises no serious question.   The meaning of the materiality requirement for liability under § 14(a) was discussed at some length in *TSC Industries, Inc. v. Northway, Inc.*, 426 U.S. 438 (1976), where we held a fact to be material "if there is a substantial likelihood that a reasonable shareholder would consider it important in deciding how to vote."   [Citation omitted.]   We think there is no room to deny that a statement of belief by corporate directors about a recommended course of action, or an explanation of their reasons for recommending it, can take on just that importance.   Shareholders know that directors usually have knowledge and expertness far exceeding the normal investor's resources, and the directors' perceived superiority is magnified even further by the common knowledge that state law customarily obliges them to exercise their judgment in the shareholders' interest.   [Citation omitted.] Naturally, then, the shareowner faced with a proxy request will think it important to know the directors' beliefs about the course they recommend and their specific reasons for urging the stockholders to embrace it.

[II.B.1]   But, assuming materiality, the question remains whether statements of reasons, opinions, or beliefs are statements "with respect to ... material fact[s]" so as to fall within the strictures of the Rule.   Petitioners argue that we would invite wasteful litigation of amorphous issues outside the readily provable realm of fact if we were to recognize liability here on proof that the directors did not recommend the merger for the stated reason, and they cite the authority of *Blue Chip Stamps v. Manor Drug Stores*, 421 U.S. 723 (1975), in urging us to recognize sound policy grounds for placing such statements outside the scope of the Rule.

We agree that *Blue Chip Stamps* is instructive, as illustrating a line between what is and is not manageable in the litigation of facts, but do not read it as supporting petitioners' position.   The issue in *Blue Chip Stamps* was the scope of the class of plaintiffs entitled to seek relief under an implied private cause of action for violating § 10(b) of the Act, prohibiting manipulation and deception in the purchase or sale of certain securities, contrary to Commission rules.   This Court held against expanding the class from actual buyers and sellers to include those who rely on deceptive sales practices by taking no action, either to sell what they own or to buy what they do not.   We observed that actual sellers and buyers who sue for compensation must identify a specific number of shares bought or sold in order to calculate and limit any ensuing recovery.   [Citation omitted.] Recognizing liability to merely would-be investors, however, would have exposed the courts to litigation unconstrained by any such anchor in demonstrable fact, resting instead on a plaintiff's "subjective hypothesis" about the number of shares he would have sold or purchased. [Citation omitted.] ***

Attacks on the truth of directors' statements of reasons or belief, however, need carry no such threats. Such statements are factual in two senses: [1] as statements that the directors do act for the reasons given or hold the belief stated and [2] as statements about the subject matter of the reason or belief expressed. In neither sense does the proof or disproof of such statements implicate the concerns expressed in *Blue Chip Stamps*. The root of those concerns was a plaintiff's capacity to manufacture claims of hypothetical action, unconstrained by independent evidence. Reasons for directors' recommendations or statements of belief are, in contrast, characteristically matters of corporate record subject to documentation, to be supported or attacked by evidence of historical fact outside a plaintiff's control. Such evidence would include not only corporate minutes and other statements of the directors themselves, but circumstantial evidence bearing on the facts that would reasonably underlie the reasons claimed and the honesty of any statement that those reasons are the basis for a recommendation or other action, a point that becomes especially clear when the reasons or beliefs go to valuations in dollars and cents.

It is no answer to argue, as petitioners do, that the quoted statement on which liability was predicated did not express a reason in dollars and cents, but focused instead on the "indefinite and unverifiable" term, "high" value, much like the similar claim that the merger's terms were "fair" to shareholders. The objection ignores the fact that such conclusory terms in a commercial context are reasonably understood to rest on a factual basis that justifies them as accurate, the absence of which renders them misleading. Provable facts either furnish good reasons to make a conclusory commercial judgment, or they count against it, and expressions of such judgments can be uttered with knowledge of truth or falsity just like more definite statements, and defended or attacked through the orthodox evidentiary process that either substantiates their underlying justifications or tends to disprove their existence. *** In this case, whether $42 was "high," and the proposal "fair" to the minority shareholders, depended on whether provable facts about the Bank's assets, and about actual and potential levels of operation, substantiated a value that was above, below, or more or less at the $42 figure, when assessed in accordance with recognized methods of valuation.

Respondents adduced evidence for just such facts in proving that the statement was misleading about its subject matter and a false expression of the directors' reasons. Whereas the proxy statement described the $42 price as offering a premium above both book value and market price, the evidence indicated that a calculation of the book figure based on the appreciated value of the Bank's real estate holdings eliminated any such premium. The evidence on the significance of market price showed that KBW had conceded that the market was closed, thin, and dominated by FABI, facts omitted from the statement. There was, indeed, evidence of a "going concern" value for the Bank in excess of $60 per share of common stock, another fact never disclosed. However conclusory the directors' statement may have been, then, it was open to attack by garden-variety evidence, subject neither to a plaintiff's control nor ready manufacture, and there was no undue risk of open-ended liability or uncontrollable litigation in allowing respondents the opportunity for recovery on the allegation that it was misleading to call $42 "high."

***

[II.B.2] Under § 14(a), then, a plaintiff is permitted to prove a specific statement of reason knowingly false or misleadingly incomplete, even when stated in conclusory terms. In reaching this conclusion we have considered statements of reasons of the sort exemplified here, which misstate the speaker's reasons and also mislead about the stated subject matter (e.g., the value of the shares). A statement of belief may be open to objection only in the former respect, however, solely as a misstatement of the psychological fact of the speaker's belief in what he says. In this case, for example, the Court of Appeals alluded to just such limited falsity in observing that "the jury was certainly justified in believing that the directors did not believe a merger at $42 per share was in the minority stockholders' interest but, rather, that they voted as they did for other reasons, e.g., retaining their seats on the board." [Citation omitted.]

The question arises, then, whether disbelief, or undisclosed belief or motivation, standing alone, should be a sufficient basis to sustain an action under § 14(a), absent proof by the sort of objective evidence described above that the statement also expressly or impliedly asserted something false or misleading about its subject matter. We think that proof of mere disbelief or belief undisclosed should not suffice for liability under § 14(a), and if nothing more had been required or proven in this case, we would reverse for that reason.

On the one hand, it would be rare to find a case with evidence solely of disbelief or undisclosed motivation without further proof that the statement was defective as to its subject matter. While we certainly would not hold a director's naked admission of disbelief incompetent evidence of a proxy statement's false or misleading character, such an unusual admission will not very often stand alone, and we do not substantially narrow the cause of action by requiring a plaintiff to demonstrate something false or misleading in what the statement expressly or impliedly declared about its subject.

On the other hand, to recognize liability on mere disbelief or undisclosed motive without any demonstration that the proxy statement was false or misleading about its subject would authorize § 14(a) litigation confined solely to what one skeptical court spoke of as the "impurities" of a director's "unclean heart." [Citation omitted.] This, we think, would cross the line that *Blue Chip Stamps* sought to draw. While it is true that the liability, if recognized, would rest on an actual, not hypothetical, psychological fact, the temptation to rest an otherwise nonexistent § 14(a) action on psychological enquiry alone would threaten just the sort of strike suits and attrition by discovery that *Blue Chip Stamps* sought to discourage. We therefore hold disbelief or undisclosed motivation, standing alone, insufficient to satisfy the element of fact that must be established under § 14(a).

[II.C] Petitioners' fall-back position assumes the same relationship between a conclusory judgment and its underlying facts that we described in Part II-B-1, *supra*. Thus, *** petitioners argue that even if conclusory statements of reason or belief can be actionable under § 14(a), we should confine liability to instances where the proxy material fails to disclose the offending statement's factual basis. There would be no justification for holding the shareholders entitled to judicial relief, that is, when they were given evidence that a stated reason for a proxy recommendation was misleading and an opportunity to draw that conclusion themselves.

The answer to this argument rests on the difference between a merely misleading statement and one that is materially so. While a misleading statement will not always lose its deceptive edge simply by joinder with others that are true, the true statements may discredit the other one so obviously that the risk of real deception drops to nil. Since liability under § 14(a) must rest not only on deceptiveness but materiality as well (i.e., it has to be significant enough to be important to a reasonable investor deciding how to vote, [citation omitted]), petitioners are on perfectly firm ground insofar as they argue that publishing accurate facts in a proxy statement can render a misleading proposition too unimportant to ground liability. But not every mixture with the true will neutralize the deceptive. If it would take a financial analyst to spot the tension between the one and the other, whatever is misleading will remain materially so, and liability should follow. [Citations omitted.] The point of a proxy statement, after all, should be to inform, not to challenge the reader's critical wits. Only when the inconsistency would exhaust the misleading conclusion's capacity to influence the reasonable shareholder would a § 14(a) action fail on the element of materiality.

Suffice it to say that the evidence invoked by petitioners in the instant case fell short of compelling the jury to find the facial materiality of the misleading statement neutralized. The directors claim, for example, to have made an explanatory disclosure of further reasons for their recommendation when they said they would keep their seats following the merger, but they failed to mention what at least one of them admitted in testimony, that they would have had no expectation of doing so without supporting the proposal [citation omitted]. And although the proxy statement did speak factually about the merger price in describing it as higher than share prices in recent sales, it failed even to mention the closed market dominated by FABI. None of these disclosures that the directors point to was, then, anything more than a half-truth, and the record shows that another fact statement they invoke was arguably even worse. The claim that the merger price exceeded book value was controverted, as we have seen already, by evidence of a higher book value than the directors conceded, reflecting appreciation in the Bank's real estate portfolio. Finally, the solicitation omitted any mention of the Bank's value as a going concern at more than $60 a share, as against the merger price of $42. There was, in sum, no more of a compelling case for the statement's immateriality than for its accuracy.

[III]   The second issue before us, left open in [the footnote to the *Mills* opinion], is whether causation of damages compensable through the implied private right of action under § 14(a) can be demonstrated by a member of a class of minority shareholders whose votes are not required by law or corporate bylaw to authorize the transaction giving rise to the claim. ***

Although a majority stockholder in *Mills* controlled just over half the corporation's shares, a two-thirds vote was needed to approve the merger proposal. After proxies had been obtained, and the merger had carried, minority shareholders brought a *Borak* action. [Citation omitted.] The question arose whether the plaintiffs' burden to demonstrate causation of their damages traceable to the § 14(a) violation required proof that the defect in the proxy solicitation had had "a decisive effect on the voting." [Citation omitted.] The *Mills* Court avoided the evidentiary morass that would have followed from requiring individualized proof that enough minority shareholders had relied upon the misstatements to swing the vote. Instead, it held that causation of damages by a material proxy misstatement could be established by showing that minority proxies necessary and sufficient to authorize the corporate acts had been given in accordance with the tenor of the solicitation, and the Court described such a causal relationship by calling the proxy solicitation an "essential link in the accomplishment of the transaction." [Citation omitted.] In the case before it, the Court found the solicitation essential, as contrasted with one addressed to a class of minority shareholders without votes required by law or bylaw to authorize the action proposed, and left it for another day to decide whether such a minority shareholder could demonstrate causation. [Citation omitted.]

In this case, respondents address *Mills'* [s] open question by proffering two theories that the proxy solicitation addressed to them was an "essential link" under the *Mills* causation test. They argue, first, that a link existed and was essential simply because VBI and FABI would have been unwilling to proceed with the merger without the approval manifested by the minority shareholders' proxies, which would not have been obtained without the solicitation's express misstatements and misleading omissions. On this reasoning, the causal connection would depend on a desire to avoid bad shareholder or public relations, and the essential character of the causal link would stem not from the enforceable terms of the parties' corporate relationship, but from one party's apprehension of the ill will of the other.

In the alternative, respondents argue that the proxy statement was an essential link between the directors' proposal and the merger because it was the means to satisfy a state statutory requirement of minority shareholder approval, as a condition for saving the merger from voidability resulting from a conflict of interest on the part of one of the Bank's directors, Jack Beddow, who voted in favor of the merger while also serving as a director of FABI. [Citation omitted.] Under the terms of Va. Code Ann. § 13.1-691(A) (1989), minority approval after disclosure of the material facts about the transaction and the director's interest was one of three avenues to insulate the merger from later attack for conflict, the two others being ratification by the Bank's directors after like disclosure and proof that the merger was fair to the corporation. On this theory, causation would depend on the use of the proxy statement for the purpose of obtaining votes sufficient to bar a minority shareholder from commencing proceedings to declare the merger void.

Although respondents have proffered each of these theories as establishing a chain of causal connection in which the proxy statement is claimed to have been an "essential link," neither theory presents the proxy solicitation as essential in the sense of *Mills*'[s] causal sequence, in which the solicitation links a directors' proposal with the votes legally required to authorize the action proposed. As a consequence, each theory would, if adopted, extend the scope of *Borak* actions beyond the ambit of *Mills* and expand the class of plaintiffs entitled to bring *Borak* actions to include shareholders whose initial authorization of the transaction prompting the proxy solicitation is unnecessary.

Assessing the legitimacy of any such extension or expansion calls for the application of some fundamental principles governing recognition of a right of action implied by a federal statute, the first of which was not, in fact, the considered focus of the *Borak* opinion. The rule that has emerged in the years since *Borak* and *Mills* came down is that recognition of any private right of action for violating a federal statute must ultimately rest on congressional intent to provide a private remedy, [citation omitted]. From this the corollary follows that the breadth of the right once recognized should not, as a general matter, grow beyond the scope congressionally intended.

This rule and corollary present respondents with a serious obstacle, for we can find no manifestation of intent to recognize a cause of action (or class of plaintiffs) as broad as respondents' theory of causation would entail. At first blush, it might seem otherwise, for the *Borak* Court certainly did not ignore the matter of intent. Its opinion adverted to the statutory object of "protection of investors" as animating Congress' intent to provide judicial relief where "necessary," [citation omitted], and it quoted evidence for that intent from House and Senate Committee Reports, [citation omitted]. *Borak*'s probe of the congressional mind, however, never focused squarely on private rights of action, as distinct from the substantive objects of the legislation, and one Member of the *Borak* Court later characterized the "implication" of the private right of action as resting modestly on the Act's "'exclusively procedural provision' affording access to a federal forum." [Citations omitted.] In fact, the importance of enquiring specifically into intent to authorize a private cause of action became clear only later, [citation omitted], and only later still, [citation omitted], was this intent accorded primacy among the considerations that might be thought to bear on any decision to recognize a private remedy. There, in dealing with a claimed private right under § 17(a) of the Act, we explained that the "central inquiry remains whether Congress intended to create, either expressly or by implication, a private cause of action." [Citation omitted.]

Looking to the Act's text and legislative history mindful of this heightened concern reveals little that would help toward understanding the intended scope of any private right. According to the House Report, Congress meant to promote the "free exercise" of stockholders' voting rights, [citation omitted], and protect "[f]air corporate suffrage," [citation omitted], from abuses exemplified by proxy solicitations that concealed what the Senate Report called the "real nature" of the issues to be settled by the subsequent votes, [citation omitted]. While it is true that these Reports, like the language of the Act itself, carry the clear message that Congress meant to protect investors from misinformation that rendered them unwitting agents of self-inflicted damage, it is just as true that Congress was reticent with indications of how far this protection might depend on self-help by private action. The response to this reticence may be, of course, to claim that § 14(a) cannot be enforced effectively for the sake of its intended beneficiaries without their participation as private litigants. [Citation omitted.] But the force of this argument for inferred congressional intent depends on the degree of need perceived by Congress, and we would have trouble inferring any congressional urgency to depend on implied private actions to deter violations of § 14(a), when Congress expressly provided private rights of action in §§ 9(e), 16(b), and 18(a) of the same Act. [Citations omitted.]

The congressional silence that is thus a serious obstacle to the expansion of cognizable *Borak* causation is not, however, a necessarily insurmountable barrier. This is not the first effort in recent years to expand the scope of an action originally inferred from the Act without "conclusive guidance" from Congress, [citing *Blue Chip Stamps*], and we may look to that earlier case for the proper response to such a plea for expansion. There, we accepted the proposition that where a legal structure of private statutory rights has developed without clear indications of congressional intent, the contours of that structure need not be frozen absolutely when the result would be demonstrably inequitable to a class of would-be plaintiffs with claims comparable to those previously recognized. Faced in that case with such a claim for equality in rounding out the scope of an implied private statutory right of action, we looked to policy reasons for deciding where the outer limits of the right should lie. We may do no less here, in the face of respondents' pleas for a private remedy to place them on the same footing as shareholders with votes necessary for initial corporate action.

[III.A] *Blue Chip Stamps* set an example worth recalling as a preface to specific policy analysis of the consequences of recognizing respondents' first theory, that a desire to avoid minority shareholders' ill will should suffice to justify recognizing the requisite causality of a proxy statement needed to garner that minority support. It will be recalled that in *Blue Chip Stamps* we raised concerns about the practical consequences of allowing recovery, under § 10(b) of the Act and Rule 10b-5, on evidence of what a merely hypothetical buyer or seller might have done on a set of facts that never occurred, and foresaw that any such expanded liability would turn on "hazy" issues inviting self-serving testimony, strike suits, and protracted discovery, with little chance of reasonable resolution by pretrial process. [Citation omitted.] These were good reasons to deny recognition to such claims in the absence of any apparent contrary congressional intent.

The same threats of speculative claims and procedural intractability are inherent in respondents' theory of causation linked through the directors' desire for a cosmetic vote. Causation would turn on inferences about what the corporate directors would have thought and done without the minority shareholder approval unneeded to authorize action. A subsequently dissatisfied minority shareholder would have virtual license to allege that managerial timidity would have doomed corporate action but for the ostensible approval induced by a misleading statement, and opposing claims of hypothetical diffidence and hypothetical boldness on the part of directors would probably provide enough depositions in the usual case to preclude any judicial resolution short of the credibility judgments that can only come after trial. Reliable evidence would seldom exist. Directors would understand the prudence of making a few statements about plans to proceed even without minority endorsement, and discovery would be a quest for re-collections of oral conversations at odds with the official pronouncements, in hopes of finding support for *ex post facto* guesses about how much heat the directors would have stood in the absence of minority approval. The issues would be hazy, their litigation protracted, and their resolution unreliable. Given a choice, we would reject any theory of causation that raised such prospects, and we reject this one.

[III.B] The theory of causal necessity derived from the requirements of Virginia law dealing with postmerger ratification seeks to identify the essential character of the proxy solicitation from its function in obtaining the minority approval that would preclude a minority suit attacking the merger. Since the link is said to be a step in the process of barring a class of shareholders from resort to a state remedy otherwise available, this theory of causation rests upon the proposition of policy that § 14(a) should provide a federal remedy whenever a false or misleading proxy statement results in the loss under state law of a shareholder plaintiff's state remedy for the enforcement of a state right. Respondents agree with the suggestions of counsel for the SEC and FDIC that causation be recognized, for example, when a minority shareholder has been induced by a misleading proxy statement to forfeit a state-law right to an appraisal remedy by voting to approve a transaction, [citation omitted], or when such a shareholder has been deterred from obtaining an order enjoining a damaging transaction by a proxy solicitation that misrepresents the facts on which an injunction could properly have been issued. [Citations omitted.] Respondents claim that in this case a predicate for recognizing just such a causal link exists in Va. Code Ann. § 13.1-691(A)(2) (1989), which sets the conditions under which the merger may be insulated from suit by a minority shareholder seeking to void it on account of Beddow's conflict.

This case does not, however, require us to decide whether §14(a) provides a cause of action for lost state remedies, since there is no indication in the law or facts before us that the proxy solicitation resulted in any such loss. The contrary appears to be the case. Assuming the soundness of respondents' characterization of the proxy statement as materially misleading, the very terms of the Virginia statute indicate that a favorable minority vote induced by the solicitation would not suffice to render the merger invulnerable to later attack on the ground of the conflict. The statute bars a shareholder from seeking to avoid a transaction tainted by a director's conflict if, *inter alia*, the minority shareholders ratified the transaction following disclosure of the material facts of the transaction and the conflict. Va. Code Ann. § 13.1-691(A)(2) (1989). Assuming that the material facts about the merger and Beddow's interests were not accurately disclosed, the minority votes were inadequate to ratify the merger under state law, and there was no loss of state remedy to connect the proxy solicitation with harm to minority shareholders irredressable under state law. Nor is there a claim here that the statement misled respondents into entertaining a false belief that they had no chance to upset the merger until the time for bringing suit had run out.

[IV]   The judgment of the Court of Appeals is reversed.

[Opinions of other Justices omitted.]

Finally, another important source of civil liability under the Exchange Act is Rule 10b-5. However, we will discuss that rule in Chapter 14 instead of this chapter because (among other reasons), it technically applies to any security, not just those that are publicly traded. Speaking of "publicly traded," how do the stock markets in the United States work? That is the subject of the next section.

§ 10.02   AN OVERVIEW OF STOCK MARKETS

Many thousands of companies have securities (typically, shares of stock) that are traded on securities markets in the United States. Before discussing the various securities markets and their requirements, it is important to note that trading in these markets consists of persons buying and selling shares (or other securities, such as bonds) that are *already outstanding*. Thus, for example, if you decide this morning that you would like to buy some shares of Apple Inc., you would not contact the company itself and ask it to issue some "new" (i.e., authorized-but-unissued) shares to you. Instead, you would most likely call your stockbroker or visit your online trading account and submit a purchase order for a given number of shares of Apple stock at a specified price.[*] Meanwhile, someone else would be deciding to sell her shares of Apple stock. Through a very complicated process, your purchase order eventually would be matched with her sell order and you would end up purchasing her shares of Apple stock. If this is your first purchase of Apple stock, you are now a shareholder of Apple and have all of the rights associated with that status. If the seller has sold all of her shares of Apple stock, she would no longer be an Apple shareholder after this transaction.

Thus, on any given day, the number of outstanding shares of Apple stock does not change, assuming that Apple did not issue more shares or repurchase shares from existing shareholders on that day. Instead, the persons who own those shares, and the numbers of shares that they own, would change. In other words, virtually all of the trading in Apple stock on a given day consists of *resales*. Once you understand this, it should be apparent that Apple Inc. itself does not receive any of the proceeds of these resales. (On the other hand, Apple indirectly benefits by having a strong market for its shares. For example, the existence of a liquid market for a company's shares will likely make it easier for the company to find investors willing to pay "top dollar" for new shares that the company may issue in

---

[*] The price at which a buyer is willing to buy a security is sometimes called the **bid price** and the price at which a seller is willing to sell a security is the **ask** price (which is usually higher than the bid price). The difference between these two amounts is the **spread**. There are different types of orders that a purchaser or seller may submit to a broker, such as **market orders**, which could be filled at the then-prevailing market price, and **limit orders**, which could only be filled at the price specified by the buyer or seller who submitted the order, or a better price. Of course, brokers also earn **commissions** for executing your trades.

the future. Investors in such a "liquid" stock can be relatively assured that, when they want to sell the stock, they will be able to do so easily and at prices that are determined by market forces.)

As the SEC puts it, the "stock market is where buyers and sellers meet to decide on the price to buy or sell securities, usually with the assistance of a broker." The existence of a market for a stock is an enormous benefit for investors, making it relatively easy for them to buy and sell shares at "market prices." As you learned about closely held corporations in Chapter 9, without a market for shares, a shareholder would not easily be able to sell shares as a practical matter even though she is usually legally free to do so. While shareholders of publicly traded companies could, of course, sell their shares to other persons in face-to-face, individually negotiated transactions, this rarely happens unless the shareholder is selling a very large amount of stock. Instead, it is usually more efficient to sell shares into the "market."

You should distinguish market trading from the situation where a company decides to *issue* more shares to new investors. The process by which a company may issue securities is primarily regulated under the Securities Act of 1933, which is discussed in Chapter 13.

There are two categories of stock markets in the United States: *national securities exchanges* and the *over-the-counter (OTC) market*. However, the distinctions between these two types of markets have become a bit blurry in recent years as technology has progressed.

National Securities Exchanges. Generally, on a stock exchange buy and sell orders for a stock are communicated to a centralized location (a "floor") where a "specialist" in that stock matches the orders. Section 5 of the Exchange Act requires that securities exchanges (which the statute defines as any organization, association, or group "which constitutes, maintains, or provides a market place or facilities for bringing together purchasers and sellers of securities or for otherwise performing with respect to securities the functions commonly performed by a stock exchange as that term is generally understood ...."[*]) be registered as such with the SEC, unless the SEC grants the exchange an exemption from the registration requirement. Section 6 of the Exchange Act provides that an exchange may register with the SEC as a "national securities exchange" and details the process for doing so. National securities exchanges, as well as certain other market participants, are known as *self-regulatory organizations*, or "*SROs*," meaning that they are required to adopt rules governing themselves and their members. However, any changes to the rules of an SRO must be approved by the

---

[*]   *See also Board of Trade v. SEC*, 923 F.2d 1270 (7th Cir. 1991).

SEC, and in some cases the SEC can force an SRO to adopt a particular rule. *See* Exchange Act § 19.

There are several securities exchanges registered with the SEC as national securities exchanges, the most prominent being the New York Stock Exchange ("*NYSE*"), now owned by a holding company called NYSE Euronext that operates other securities markets as well. Another important national securities exchange is the Nasdaq Stock Market, which until recently was considered part of the OTC market. There are several other national securities exchanges in the United States (and many securities exchanges that are located in other countries).

Currently, the NYSE Euronext group operates several equities markets, including the NYSE, NYSE Euronext, NYSE Amex,[*] and NYSE Arca (a fully electronic market that includes Nasdaq listings). There are approximately 8,000 issuers that have securities listed on these markets. As of the end of 2010, the combined market capitalization of these companies, in U.S. dollars, was nearly $16 trillion.

Nasdaq, which is owned by the NASDAQ OMX Group, Inc., consists of three different markets: the Global Select Market, the Global Market, and the Capital Market (formerly known as the SmallCap Market).[**] The requirements for listing a security in these markets differ; the Global Select Market is the most demanding. In other words, it is more difficult for a company to qualify for the Global Select Market than the other markets. Currently, Nasdaq has about 3,700 listed companies. At the end of 2010, Nasdaq's listed companies had a combined market capitalization of nearly $5 trillion.

Not every issuer may list its securities on NYSE or Nasdaq. First, because both NYSE and Nasdaq are SEC-registered national securities exchanges, any security listed on either of them must be registered under Section 12(b), which means that the issuer would become an Exchange Act reporting company. Second, both require issuers to meet very detailed quantitative tests for initial listing. These requirements relate to, among other things, the number of "round lot" shareholders (shareholders that own at least 100 shares); the issuer's assets, revenues, earnings and/or cash flows; and the issuer's market capitalization, the number of its outstanding shares, and/or the bid price for its shares. (Afterward, issuers must continue to meet somewhat lesser standards for their securities to remain listed.) Nasdaq also requires that a listed issuer have at least three "market makers," which are firms that must continually stand ready to buy and sell the

---

[*]   In late 2008, NYSE acquired the American Stock Exchange, which is now known as NYSE Amex. As of the end of 2010, more than 550 companies were listed on NYSE Amex.

[**]   Nasdaq also operates a "Portal" market wherein qualified institutional buyers (as defined in Rule 144A under the Securities Act) may buy and sell certain securities.

company's securities for their own accounts at the then-current bid and ask prices, so as to ensure a liquid market. (Market makers profit from the fact that the bid price is higher than the ask price.)

Even if an issuer meets the quantitative tests, it must also meet qualitative standards concerning corporate governance issues. For example, the NYSE *Listed Company Manual* contains detailed requirements relating to shareholder meetings and voting rights, classified boards of directors, and many other corporate governance issues. Nasdaq has detailed qualitative requirements on these topics as well. Moreover, both NYSE and Nasdaq recently implemented extensive changes to their corporate governance requirements to require that a majority of directors be independent; require executive sessions of independent directors; impose new obligations on audit committees, nominating committees, and compensation committees; and require codes of ethics that are applicable to all of an issuer's directors and employees. In general, these new requirements complement, but in many cases they go much further than the requirements of, the Sarbanes-Oxley Act discussed in Section 10.03 below. The Dodd-Frank Wall Street Reform and Consumer Protection Act (also discussed in Section 10.03) will necessitate further changes in these rules.

The Over-the-Counter Market. Unlike securities exchanges, the OTC markets do not have a centralized order-matching system or trading floor. Instead, OTC market trading takes place between brokers and dealers who communicate electronically and (historically, at least) by telephone. Before Nasdaq debuted in 1971, quotations in OTC stocks were reported only in the "Pink Sheets," which formerly was a daily publication of the National Quotations Bureau that was printed on pink paper. Brokers and dealers thus had to call one of the dealers in a particular OTC security to get current quotations for it, resulting in an inefficient market. Today, the two primary OTC markets are the OTCBB Bulletin Board and the Pink Sheets. Generally speaking, stocks traded on OTC markets are much more "thinly" traded than stocks that are listed on national securities exchanges.

1. The OTC Bulletin Board. According to its web site, the OTC Bulletin Board ("***OTCBB***") is a "regulated quotation service that displays real-time quotes, last-sale prices, and volume information in over-the-counter (OTC) equity securities. An OTC equity security generally is any equity that is not listed or traded on [Nasdaq] or a national securities exchange." Issuers whose securities are quoted on the OTCBB need not meet any qualitative or quantitative listing standards, as they must with Nasdaq and the securities exchanges, as discussed above. However, under a rule that became effective in 2000, OTCBB-quoted issuers must either be Exchange Act reporting companies or file financial reports with their banking or insurance regulators. Before this "eligibility rule" took effect, the OTCBB quoted the securities of more than 3,600 non-Exchange Act reporters. After the eligibility rule was approved, more than 3,000 companies were "kicked off" the OTCBB.

2.   *The "Pink Sheets."*   On its web site, OTC Markets Group Inc., which is a privately held company, states that it "operates the world's largest electronic interdealer quotation system for broker-dealers to trade unlisted securities." There are three tiers, which are "based on the level of disclosure companies choose to provide to investors: OTCQX, OTCQB and OTC Pink." Further, the web site explains that "OTCQX is the top tier of the OTC market" and is "[e]xclusively for companies that meet the highest financial standards and undergo a qualitative review." Meanwhile, OTCQB is the "middle tier." OTCQB companies "are reporting with the SEC or a U.S. banking regulator." However, "[t]here are no financial or qualitative standards to be in this tier." Finally, OTC Pink is the "bottom tier" and is a "speculative trading marketplace." Companies traded in this market "may have current, limited or no public disclosure."

Thus, companies whose securities are quoted on the various Pink Sheets markets do not have to be Exchange Act reporters or banking or insurance reporters, although some are. However, note that Exchange Act Rule 15c2-11 requires a broker-dealer to have in its records the "paragraph (a) information" specified in that rule before it publishes any quotation for an issuer's security in any "quotation medium" as defined in the rule (which excludes national securities exchanges). Further, the broker-dealer must, based upon a review of that information along with any other documents and information required by subsection (b) of Rule 15c2-11, have a "reasonable basis under the circumstances" for believing that the information is "accurate in all material respects" and that the sources of the information are reliable.

Electronic Communication Networks.   In addition to the exchange and the OTC markets, recent years have seen the rise of "electronic communication networks," which allow institutional investors and broker-dealer firms to trade securities directly between themselves. A discussion of such ECNs is outside the scope of this textbook, if only because any such discussion would likely become quickly out-of-date. However, note that while ECNs may not be considered "exchanges," they could still be regulated by the SEC as broker-dealers, securities information processors, or clearing agencies.

The Efficient Capital Markets Hypothesis.   As discussed in Chapter 5 and earlier in this chapter, if a company is an Exchange Act reporter, it continually files various documents with the SEC, such as its Forms 10-K and Forms 10-Q.

Information may also be reported more quickly with a Form 8-K or due to the requirements of Regulation FD. Because this information is publicly available, the market is continually updated as to the company's financial and business performance. If it is performing well, then (all other things being equal) the price of its stock should rise; if it is performing poorly or if some adverse event happens, the price of its stock should fall. These price fluctuations are the result of the actions of the many persons who are buying and selling the company's stock on any given day on the basis of this information.

Can you make money in the stock market? Sure. The stock market is prone to wild swings and the value of any given investment could decline over a given period of time or even permanently (for example, if the company goes bankrupt its stock will likely be worthless). However, if you buy shares of a mutual fund that invests in many different companies (i.e., it is diversified), then your investment will likely be worth more at some point in the future. A dollar that was invested decades ago in a broad-based mutual fund is probably worth a lot more today. But can you "beat" the market? In other words, can investors or fund managers outperform the returns of the overall stock market by investing more wisely than others? There is a whole industry of mutual funds and hedge funds that argue that the answer is yes, and try to convince people to invest their money with them so as to earn superior returns. And in fact, many fund managers have impressive records of beating the market for seemingly long periods of time.

However, the "efficient capital markets hypothesis" (the *ECM hypothesis*" or the *"ECM theory"*) holds that the price of a publicly traded company's stock reflects all publicly known information about that company and the overall economy. New information will be quickly digested by the market and reflected in a change in the market price of a security. Thus, the market efficiently "prices" such shares. For example, if new information that is positive becomes publicly known, such as the company announcing better-than-expected earnings, the many hundreds or thousands of market participants will try to exploit that information by buying shares of the company at the current price, which does not—yet—reflect the new information. Of course, in this example, the price will soon rise to reflect this additional demand for the stock. In this way, any price abnormalities are short-lived.

Under the "semi-strong" version of the ECM hypothesis, which is widely accepted by economists and other academics, stock prices reflect all *publicly* known information.[*] Under that theory, if you have "inside" information, i.e., nonpublic information, you can profit from that information before it becomes publicly known. For example, if you know that a "target" company will be acquired by another company at a price much higher than the current trading price of the target's stock, you could make money by buying target stock before this

---

[*] There is also a "weak" form of the ECM hypothesis, but it will not be discussed here.

news is announced. (Of course, you may go to jail for doing so; Chapter 14 discusses insider trading under Exchange Act Rule 10b-5.) However, the "strong" form of the ECM hypothesis posits that stock prices also reflect *non-public* information. One piece of evidence partially supporting this version of the theory (which, by the way, is less accepted than the semi-strong version of the theory), is that the market prices of target company stocks often *do* rise to some degree before takeovers are announced, perhaps because of illegal insider trading.

If the ECM hypothesis (in whichever form) is correct, one implication is that you can't reliably beat the market over a long period of time and you probably shouldn't try to do so. Because the current price of a publicly traded security reflects all public information (and perhaps nonpublic information as well) the only thing that can change the price is *unforeseen* information. Whether that information will be "good" or "bad" is anyone's guess. Unless you have a crystal ball, your guess as to the future changes in the price is only that—a guess. Sometimes you may guess correctly, and you may even go on a "hot steak" where your guesses are often correct. But over time, you will be wrong about as often as you are correct. In that way, your returns will be about the same as the returns of the overall stock market.

Nonetheless, as noted above, there remains an industry of professional "stock pickers" that would like for you to invest your money with them due to their supposed superior intellect or perhaps a great past track record. But as the saying goes, past performance is no guarantee of future results. For this reason, many academics argue that investors are better off investing in "index" mutual funds that attempt to mirror the performance of the entire stock market, as opposed to investing in "actively managed" mutual funds (which typically charge higher fees) or hedge funds (which typically charge even higher fees and are only open to very wealthy investors) or even trying to pick individual stocks. For a great argument in support of this view, see BURTON G. MALKIEL, A RANDOM WALK DOWN WALL STREET (10th ed. 2011).

FINRA. An important SRO in the securities industry is the Financial Industry Regulatory Authority, Inc., or *FINRA*. (Again, an SRO is a self-regulatory organization, not a governmental agency.) FINRA's primary purpose is to regulate brokers and dealers that are members of it and, as its web site explains, its mission is "to protect America's investors by making sure that the securities industry operates fairly and honestly." (Sounds like a tall order!) FINRA was formed by the 2007 merger of the National Association of Securities Dealers, Inc., NASD Regulation, Inc., and the NYSE's regulatory and arbitration divisions. FINRA has more than 3,000 employees and oversees nearly 4,500 brokerage firms, which in turn employ more than 600,000 registered representtatives. You may learn more about FINRA, as well as SEC regulation of broker-dealers, in a course on Securities Regulation.

§ 10.03   PUBLIC COMPANY GOVERNANCE

Although a publicly traded corporation is a corporation like any other corporation formed under a state's corporate statute and therefore is subject to all of the rules that you learned in prior chapters (except Chapter 9), they are subject to some unique concerns. Moreover, *federal* law imposes many additional corporate governance rules on publicly traded companies, as discussed below.

A.   SHAREHOLDER "ACTIVISM" AND THE ROLE OF THE BOARD IN PUBLIC COMPANIES

What is the purpose of a corporation? At first, you may think that is a silly question, and answer that the purpose of a corporation is to benefit its common shareholders by being as profitable as possible within the bounds of the law. Indeed, this is more or less the traditional view. However, for at least as far back as the 1930s,[*] there has been a debate between holders of the "traditional" view, who argue that corporate directors should not owe duties to anyone other than common shareholders, and those who argue that directors should also consider the interests of other "stakeholders" such as preferred shareholders, creditors (e.g., bond holders), employees, the communities in which the corporation operates, and even the public good. Many continue to make this argument and it is reflected to some degree in the "constituency" statutes of many states, which allow corporate directors to consider the interests of such stakeholders in some situations. Further, there are cases that hold that directors may owe duties to preferred shareholders, holders of convertible securities (i.e., securities that may be converted into common or preferred stock), and creditors in some, albeit limited, situations. (Of course, such stakeholders often have *contractual* protections as well.) Nonetheless, the traditional view is much more widely accepted. See, e.g., Section 2.01(a) of the *ALI Principles of Corporate Governance* (with some exceptions, "a corporation should have as its objective the conduct of business activities with a view to enhancing corporate profit and shareholder gain.")

But even if you agree that the traditional view of the corporation's purpose is correct, another question that arises is *who* should make decisions for the corporation. As noted in Chapter 5 and elsewhere in this book, we call the

---

[*]   *See* Adolph A. Berle, Jr., *Corporate Powers as Powers in Trust*, 44 HARV. L. REV. 1049 (1931); E. Merrick Dodd, Jr., *For Whom Are Corporate Managers Trustees?*, 45 HARV. L. REV. 1145 (1932).

shareholders the "owners" of the corporation even though it ends up being sort of a legal fiction. As you know by now, shareholders have very little control over a corporation. Instead, the board of directors is the true decision-maker. Normally, this arrangement works fairly well, because (1) directors usually make decisions by considering whether they will benefit the corporation's shareholders, at least in the long run, (2) if the directors stray too far from these goals, the shareholders could elect different directors at the next annual meeting or possibly remove the current directors before then, and (3) if the directors *really* stray too far from these goals, a shareholder could bring a derivative action against them, alleging a breach of the directors' duty of care and/or the duty of loyalty, as you learned in prior chapters.

Nonetheless, in recent years, many shareholder "activists" and legal scholars have argued for much greater shareholder control, particularly with respect to publicly traded corporations. According to this line of thinking, any change in the rules of corporate governance that increases shareholder power is likely desirable. An underlying premise of this argument is that directors and officers (i.e., "management") often do not act in the shareholders' bests interests. Instead, they may act to benefit or enrich themselves, or may just be plain lazy. Moreover, in many public companies, incumbent management faces no real threat of removal, unless another company wants to acquire the corporation and then clean house. Faced with no real prospect of losing their jobs, management may not perform as well as they would if they were always fighting to stay in office.

Wait a minute, you might say. How can the directors and officers feel so safe in office? If the shareholders truly think that management is not performing well, why don't they just elect different directors, who will then fire the officers and replace them with better ones? After all, you may say to yourself, I learned in Chapter 5 that the shareholders elect at least one-third of the directors every year. If they don't like them, they can "throw the bums out."

That conclusion could well be true if there weren't many shareholders. But think about the nature of many public companies for a minute. Assume that ABC Corp. has 20 million shares of stock outstanding, which are traded on the NYSE and that its board of directors consists of nine persons who have been "staggered" into three classes so that they serve overlapping three-year terms. The 20 million shares of ABC stock are owned by approximately 5,000 shareholders, many of whom own very small numbers of shares. In fact, the only two "big" shareholders are (1) the company's founder, Mr. Bigwig, who owns 500,000 shares and also serves as a director and (2) the Atlantic-Pacific Mutual Fund ("APMF"), an institutional investor that owns 300,000 shares, which it purchased one year ago. You are also an ABC shareholder, but you own only 5,000 shares. Nonetheless, these 5,000 shares represent most of your net worth of $100,000.

As discussed in Chapter 5, typically the board, or perhaps a nominating committee consisting of some board members, nominates candidates for election as directors at the annual meeting of shareholders. Often, the current directors will be re-nominated, year after year after year. Further, assuming that plurality voting is used and that the number of candidates is the same as the number of open board positions to be filled at the meeting, then each candidate would get elected if she receives as little as one vote.

Of course, shareholders could try to nominate their "own" candidates for the board and solicit proxies from their fellow shareholders in favor of these candidates. But even if ABC is not performing well and the fault may lie with management, do you think any of the shareholders will take any steps to nominate their own candidates? Clearly, Mr. Bigwig will not do so, because he is one of the current directors! What about APMF? Although it might do so, the more likely course of action for APMF is to follow the "Wall Street rule" and simply sell its shares of ABC stock and invest the proceeds in some other company. How about you? Again, your 5,000 shares of ABC stock represent most of your personal worth, so this is an important matter for you. Will you nominate one or more of your own candidates for election to ABC's board?

Keeping in mind that (1) ABC is a publicly traded company and thus subject to the Exchange Act's proxy rules that you learned about in Section 10.01(C) above, (2) that there are thousands of ABC shareholders that are probably spread across the country if not the world, the majority of whom have small amounts of shares and thus are "rationally apathetic," that is, not willing to invest much time figuring out how to vote their meager numbers of ABC shares, and (3) soliciting proxies is enormously expensive but the nominees of the incumbent board will not have to bear this expense, you would have to be out of your mind to mount a proxy contest. It simply is not worth your time. Not only would you likely lose (i.e., your candidates would not be elected), you would spend thousands of dollars. Further, in this example, ABC's board is staggered into three classes. Thus, even in the unlikely event that your candidates won, they would only comprise one-third of the board. You would have to repeat the process and win next year to "capture" a majority of the board.

Although the above example paints a somewhat simplistic picture of the nature of shareholdings in public companies, the boards of most public companies end up being self-perpetuating for these and other reasons. Even though the thousands of ABC shareholders collectively "own" ABC, not only do they have virtually no power to make decisions for ABC, they have almost no practical chance of electing their own director candidates. As I wrote elsewhere:

[W]hy don't unhappy shareholders simply solicit proxies in favor of their own candidates? Time and money are the obvious answers. In the typical public corporation with thousands of widely dispersed—and small—shareholders, the solicitation of proxies is a practical necessity, as one would almost certainly be unable to muster a quorum if shareholders were permitted only to vote in person at the meeting. While nominations from the floor of the meeting are possible, they are essentially meaningless because very few shareholders will be at the meeting; the vast majority of shareholders will have previously voted via proxy. The incumbent board can solicit proxies for their nominees at no personal expense. Insurgent shareholders enjoy no such luxury (except in the rare event that they are successful, in which case their nominees, now being elected, would cause the corporation to reimburse them).

Soliciting proxies is difficult and expensive; not only must one go to the expense of printing and mailing the proxy statement and engaging in other solicitation activities, but one must also ensure that any proxy materials comply with the SEC's detailed proxy rules, which almost certainly will require the assistance of expensive attorneys. The shareholder would also face potential liability for any materially false or misleading proxy materials. As a result, only the largest and most determined shareholders would consider mounting a proxy contest in favor of their own nominees, at least outside a takeover battle. Additional problems include the "free rider" problem (i.e., if a shareholder goes to the trouble and expense of soliciting proxies for directors, and those directors are elected and cause the corporation's stock price to increase, most of these gains are reaped by *other* shareholders), overcoming other shareholders' apathy and their possible suspicion of the insurgents, and the risk that new directors would not perform any better than their predecessors. Thus, the rational shareholder who owns a small number of shares and is not interested in gaining control of the board but only wants to nominate a director or two simply will not go to the trouble of soliciting proxies. ***

Molitor, *The Crucial Role of the Nominating Committee,* 11 U.C. DAVIS BUS. L. J. 97, 105-07 (2010) (footnotes omitted).

Nonetheless, in recent years, many developments have occurred that may change this situation. Perhaps.

B.   RECENT DEVELOPMENTS IN PUBLIC COMPANY GOVERNANCE

This section discusses several recent, or at least fairly recent, developments that have affected how public companies are governed. In general, there are two types of such developments. First, there are market developments, that is, changes that have occurred without any formal action by Congress or a regulatory authority such as the SEC. In this category, we will discuss the rise of the power of institutional investors and many corporate-governance reforms that companies voluntarily adopted as a result of shareholder pressure to do so. The second category consists of regulatory developments. In that category, we will briefly discuss the Sarbanes-Oxley Act of 2002, some new SEC rules, and the Dodd-Frank Wall Street Reform and Consumer Protection Act of 2010.

The Growth of Institutional Shareholders.   Historically, the great majority of the shares of public companies were owned by individuals. However, in recent years institutional shareholders, such as mutual funds, pension funds, insurance companies, state and local governments, university endowments, and private foundations, have come to own a very large percentage of publicly traded stocks. In 1950, for example, institutional investors owned only approximately 6.5 percent of the value of all outstanding publicly traded stocks. However, by some measures, approximately 67 percent of all publicly traded stock in the U.S. is now owned by institutions. Other statistics put the percentage even higher, depending on how one defines the terms "institution" or "institutional investor."

Many proponents of "corporate democracy" welcomed this development. Where a public company is owned by thousands of small shareholders, those shareholders will likely be rationally apathetic. And even if they are not rationally apathetic, they would face massive "collective action" problems due to their sheer numbers and the fact that they are likely widely dispersed geographically. But if a significant amount of the company's stock is owned by an institutional shareholder, that shareholder might well be able to press management to adopt shareholder-friendly reforms. Moreover, the fact that the institutional investor owns a lot of the company's stock would make it less able to follow the "Wall Street rule" and sell its stock in the company without seriously depressing the market price. Even if there were several "medium" institutional investors, if they collectively own a large percentage of the company's stock, their small number would make it easy for them to overcome the collective action problems that plague smaller shareholders (who number in the hundreds, thousands or even tens of thousands). Further, the typical institutional investor has a sophisticated manager that monitors its investments and that can easily communicate with management. Thus, it was hoped that institutional investors might prove to be efficient overseers of public companies and that their work may benefit all shareholders. (Of course, some commentators worried that some institutional shareholders would press management to adopt policies that would benefit *them* but not the shareholders generally. The frequent example given in this regard was a labor union that might pressure the board to benefit union members with more favorable contracts.)

Others were skeptical. Mutual funds in particular were viewed as passive investors (as opposed to hedge funds, which are largely seen as more activist[*]), particularly index funds and those that have other relationships with the company that they would not want to jeopardize by antagonizing management. There were also reports over the years that suggested that many institutional investors paid little attention to corporate governance matters and that many mutual funds did not even bother to vote their shares. Further, the Exchange Act has several rules that seem designed to discourage concentrated ownership of public company shares, such as Section 13(d), which is discussed in Chapter 12, and Section 16(b), which is discussed in Chapter 14.

On the other hand, many state and private pension plans have made much use of Rule 14a-8 by submitting shareholder proposals to many companies concerning "social" as well as corporate governance issues. For example, the Cracker Barrel restaurant chain used to have a policy that it would fire any employees that it learned were homosexual. In 1992, a New York-based pension fund that owned shares of Cracker Barrel stock submitted a shareholder proposal that would have recommended that Cracker Barrel end this practice. Cracker Barrel sought a no-action letter from the SEC (which was granted), arguing that the proposal could be excluded on the ground that it related to the company's "ordinary business operations" (*see* Rule 14a-8(i)(7)). The shareholder later sued, but was unsuccessful. However, in 1998 the SEC changed its position, stating that it would return to its prior "case-by-case" approach to shareholder proposals that raise social issues. A few years later, the same pension fund submitted a similar shareholder proposal to Cracker Barrel, and the proposal received 58% shareholder support. Cracker Barrel's board then voted to end its policy of firing homosexual employees.

Other examples abound. But in the end, the evidence remains mixed as to whether institutional shareholders are effective watchdogs and the debate on this issue will likely continue long into the future. However, it seems that we can say at least a few things about institutional investors with relative confidence. First, any given public company is today more likely to have a significant amount of its stock owned by more institutional investors than at any time in the past. Second,

---

[*] Hedge funds are similar to mutual funds in that they pool funds to invest in other companies (or other types of investments). However, most mutual funds are regulated under the federal Investment Company Act, whereas most hedge funds are exempt from such regulation because they restrict ownership to very wealthy and sophisticated investors.

this situation likely changes the dynamic between the board and the shareholders. Although we might have difficulty quantifying this statement, and although it may vary from one company to another, the boards and management of public companies today are often more responsive to, and respectful of, shareholders than in the past.

Developments Affecting the Election of Directors in Public Companies. Even so, it often is difficult for shareholders of public companies to elect directors *of their choosing*. This difficulty is traceable to three primary reasons: (1) the fact that the board itself is in control of the process of nominating directors; (2) the use of plurality voting at most public companies; and (3) the existence of staggered boards at many public companies. While there have been some significant developments on all three of these fronts, it still is an open question whether these developments will result in greater shareholder power over the identities of the persons serving as directors.

1.   Shareholder Nominations of Director Candidates.   As noted above, a publicly traded corporation's proxy statement typically will include only the director candidates who were nominated by the incumbent board. Traditionally, the board nominated candidates who were suggested by the corporation's CEO or other board members. Although shareholders who want to elect a director of their own choosing could solicit proxies from other shareholders in support of that candidate, doing so is rare because it is so expensive. Thus, boards in many public companies are largely self-perpetuating.

However, in 1978 the SEC required public companies to make certain disclosures about their nominating committees (if they had them) and Schedule 14A now requires detailed disclosures about the director nomination process.[*] Also, in the 1970s and 1980s, some influential groups started to recommend that public companies have independent nominating committees that would be receptive to shareholder nominations. Further, after the Sarbanes-Oxley Act of 2002, the stock markets got involved in the director nomination process. For example, the NYSE now requires listed companies to have a nominating and corporate governance committee that consists only of independent directors (as defined). The committee must have a charter that addresses its purposes and responsibilities, which, must include identifying board candidates and selecting, or recommending to the board, director nominees. *See* Section 303A.04 of the

---

[*]   For example, the issuer must describe the "material elements" of any policy its nominating committee (or, if it doesn't have one, the full board) follows in considering director candidates nominated by shareholders. If the issuer does not have such a policy, the proxy statement must state the basis for the board's view that it is "appropriate" not to have one. This is another example of the SEC attempting to "shame" companies into doing something.

NYSE *Listed Company Manual*. As a result of these and other developments, 99 percent of the companies in the S&P 500 had a nominating committee by 2006, although only eight percent of public companies had had one in 1971. Nonetheless, many activist shareholders argue that most nominating committees do not seriously consider board candidates nominated by shareholders.

The SEC has historically been very attentive to these concerns. Its attempts to allow shareholder access to the corporate proxy have a long history, going back as far as 1942. More recently, in 2003, the SEC proposed that public companies be required to include shareholder-nominated candidates in their proxy materials if certain triggering events had occurred. If a triggering event occurred, then for the next two years a shareholder (or group) that had owned more than five percent of the voting stock for at least two years, and that did not seek control of the company, could place nominees in the company's proxy materials. However, this proposal eventually was abandoned.

Then, in *American Federation of State, County and Municipal Employees v. American International Group, Inc.*, 462 F.3d 121 (2d Cir. 2006), the court held that American International Group (AIG) could *not* exclude from its proxy statement a Rule 14a-8 shareholder proposal to amend AIG's bylaws. The proposed amendment to AIG's bylaws would have established a procedure whereby some shareholders could nominate board candidates to appear in the AIG's proxy materials. After *AIG*, the SEC proposed two alternative rules. The first proposed amending Rule 14a-8(i)(8) to make clear that shareholder proposals that might result in an election contest could be excluded. The second proposed amending Rule 14a-8 to allow shareholders (or groups) that had owned more than five percent of the voting stock for at least one year, and that did not seek control of the company, to submit Rule 14a-8 proposals to establish *procedures* for shareholder nominations of directors. The SEC ended up adopting the first release and thus amended Rule 14a-8 to allow the exclusion of shareholder proposals that relate "to a *nomination* or an election for membership on the company's board of directors ... *or a procedure for such nomination or election*." (Emphasis added.) Thus, a company could exclude from its proxy materials director candidates nominated by a shareholder, as well as shareholder proposals that would require the company to adopt procedures for the nomination of board candidates by shareholders.

A little while later, following a change in Presidential administrations, the SEC again proposed a "shareholder access" rule, which was adopted in August 2010. This rule, Rule 14a-11, essentially would have required issuers to include in their proxy materials the names of board candidates nominated by eligible shareholders who followed the rule's procedures. Eligible shareholders (or groups) were those that had owned at least three percent of the issuer's out-standing voting shares for at least three years (among other requirements). If several eligible shareholders properly submitted names of viable nominees under Rule 14a-11, the issuer would have been required to include in its proxy materials a number of such nominees equal to the greater of (1) one or (2) twenty-five percent of the total number of directors on the board (rounded down to the nearest whole number). For example, if the company had ten directors, then it would only be required to include two shareholder-nominated candidates in its proxy materials (subject to some exceptions).

The SEC also amended several other proxy rules to accommodate new Rule 14a-11. For example, the SEC revised Rule 14a-8, which concerns shareholder proposals (as opposed to director nominations). As noted above, after the *AIG* case the SEC amended Rule 14a-8 to allow companies to exclude shareholder proposals that relate "to a nomination or an election for membership on the company's board of directors … or a procedure for such nomination or election." Today, Rule 14a-8 only allows the issuer to exclude a proposal relating to director elections if the proposal: (1) would disqualify a nominee who is standing for election; (2) would remove a director from office before her term expired; (3) questions the competence, business judgment, or character of one or more nominees or directors; (4) seeks to include a specific individual in the company's proxy materials for election to the board of directors; or (5) otherwise could affect the outcome of the upcoming election of directors.[*]

However, in *Business Roundtable, et al. v. SEC* (No. 10-1305, July 22, 2011), the Court of Appeals for the District of Columbia Circuit vacated Rule 14a-11 for noncompliance with the federal Administrative Procedures Act (although the provisions of *Rule 14a-8* described in the forgoing paragraph still apply). This is not to say that SEC cannot implement a proxy-access rule; Section 971 of the Dodd-Frank Wall Street Reform and Consumer Protection Act specifically gives the SEC the authority to promulgate a proxy-access rule. However, the SEC's next move is unclear as of the date of this textbook.

2. Majority Voting. Most publicly traded companies use plurality voting in the election of directors. As noted in Chapter 5, under plurality voting a shareholder typically cannot vote "against" a candidate. Instead, "for" and "withhold" are the only choices. This means that board candidates may be elected with less than a majority of the possible votes cast "for" them; to be elected under plurality voting, all a candidate needs is more votes than any other candidate for

---

[*]   Further, some state laws were amended to facilitate, to some degree at least, shareholder nominations of director candidates. *See* Sections 112 and 113 of the Delaware General Corporation Law and MBCA § 2.06. *See also CA, Inc. v. AFSCME Employees Pension Plan*, 953 A.2d 227 (Del. 2008).

that position, not a majority. If only ten people are running for ten open board positions, those ten candidates are guaranteed to be elected under plurality voting.

Because this seems unfair, in recent years many shareholder activists have submitted Rule 14-8 shareholder proposals to recommend that companies adopt some form of majority voting. (As noted in Section 10.01(C) above, to survive exclusion from the company's proxy materials under Rule 14a-8, shareholder proposals typically must be phrased in the form of recommendations, rather than mandates.) Moreover, unlike many Rule 14a-8 shareholder proposals, these proposals received strong shareholder support at many companies. Due to this shareholder "pressure," the boards of many public companies in recent years have voluntarily adopted majority voting systems for director elections; by 2009, approximately two-thirds of the companies in the S&P 500 had adopted some form of majority voting.

If you think about it for a minute, it should become clear that a potential problem with a majority voting system is that it might result in board vacancies. For example, assume that all of ABC Corp.'s directors are elected annually. If ABC Corp. had a majority voting system and a majority of the shares were cast *against* the board candidates at this year's election, then the current directors' terms would expire, but no one would have been elected to take their places. Because board vacancies could be very damaging to corporations, most states have a "holdover rule" that provides that board members, even those who were not re-elected, maintain their seats until their successors are elected. *See* MBCA § 8.05(3). [*]

Pfizer Inc. was one of the pioneers in majority voting. Under Pfizer's current system, for a candidate to be elected to the board in an uncontested election (that is, an election where the number of candidates is equal to the number of open board positions), more votes must be cast "for" the candidate than "against" her. If an incumbent director has more votes cast against her, she must submit an irrevocable resignation to the board. However, the resignation is effective only if the board accepts it. This means that the board could reject the resignation. This would result in a director who has been "defeated" nonetheless continuing to serve on the board. [**]

---

[*]   The current directors usually fill vacancies on the board with persons of their choosing, even a director candidate who was not reelected to the board. *See* MBCA § 8.10(a).

[**]   *See City of Westland Police and Fire Retirement System v. Axcelis Technologies, Inc.*, No. 594 (Del. Sup. Ct., Aug. 11, 2010) (upholding dismissal of case in which board had refused to accept resignations from directors who received less than a majority of the votes cast).

There are many variations of the majority-voting theme that various public companies have adopted. The Pfizer system described above can be called a "true majority" system because the actual requirement to be elected as a director is a majority vote by the shareholders. In contrast, some majority-voting systems should be called "plurality plus" because they still use plurality voting as the standard for election to the board, but then require directors who receive more "withhold" votes than "yes" votes to submit a resignation (which could then be rejected by the board). Other variations are possible. As the careful reader will have noticed, due to the board's ability to fill vacancies with persons it chooses, none of the systems described above always prevent a director who received more "against" or "withhold" votes than "for" votes from serving on the board. At this point, it seems unlikely that many companies will adopt a majority voting standard that would prohibit a candidate who does not receive majority shareholder support from serving on the board *in all cases*.

Many states, including Delaware (and the MBCA), have recently amended their statutes to facilitate majority voting. *See, e.g.,* MBCA § 10.22 and Sections 141(b) and 216 of the Delaware General Corporation Law. Further, the NYSE recently amended its Rule 452. Previously, that rule had allowed broker-dealers to vote shares owned by customers in the broker-dealers' discretion if the customer did not timely instruct the broker-dealer how to vote the shares and the issue being voted on was a "routine" matter. Now, uncontested director elections are not considered "routine" matters. Because broker-dealers tended to vote in favor of the candidates nominated by the incumbent board, this rule change could eliminate a lot of potential "for" votes.

3.   *De-Staggering Boards of Directors.* Most corporate statutes, including MBCA § 8.06 (which you saw in Chapter 5), allow the board to be staggered into two or three classes. If a board is staggered into three classes, only one-third of the directors will be elected every year and directors will serve three year terms. Historically, most public companies had staggered boards for reasons such as promoting board continuity and making hostile takeovers more difficult.

However, many shareholder activists dislike staggered boards, arguing that because directors would only face election once every two or three years rather than annually, poor performing directors could not be replaced by the shareholders quickly. Thus, in recent years there have been many Rule 14a-8 shareholder proposals asking that boards de-stagger themselves.[*] Many of these proposals

---

[*]   Because most companies with staggered boards have them as a result of a provision in their articles of incorporation, the decision to de-stagger usually rests with the board. As you learned in Chapter 5, although shareholders must vote on articles amendments, they may do so only *after* the board approves the amendment. *See* MBCA § 10.03.

have received high levels of shareholder support, and as a result of this share-holder pressure, today only 35 percent of the companies in the S&P 500 have staggered boards, down from nearly 60 percent in the early 2000s.

The Sarbanes-Oxley Act of 2002. The Sarbanes-Oxley Act of 2002 ("*SOX*") was enacted in the wake of Enron, WorldCom, and other major corporate scandals. While SOX, to a large degree, modifies the Exchange Act to make the reporting requirements imposed on public companies much tougher, it also represents a major federal intrusion into corporate governance matters, which traditionally had been the province of state law.[*] The following discussion is not a comprehensive description of SOX, and interested readers would likely learn more about it in the Securities Regulation course or other courses in law school. Also, given that SOX is nearly ten years old, corporate practitioners have by now gotten "used" to it and accept it as just another part of the corporate governance landscape. Nonetheless, a brief review of some of the more notable provisions of SOX is important to persons taking the introductory Business Organizations course in law school, if only to show the trend of federal regulatory requirements.

  1. Audit Committee Requirements. In section 301 of SOX, Congress directed the SEC to adopt a rule preventing each national securities exchange (e.g., NYSE) and national securities association (at the time of SOX, Nasdaq was not yet an "exchange") from listing the securities of issuers that are not in compliance with certain audit committee requirements. The main rule that the SEC adopted in response is Rule 10A-3 under the Exchange Act. This rule requires that exchange rules must require all audit committee members to be "independent" (as defined) from the issuer, subject to some limited exceptions. Further, the exchange rules must require the audit committee to establish procedures for investigating complaints "regarding accounting, internal accounting controls, or auditing matters" and the "confidential, anonymous submission by employees ... of concerns regarding questionable accounting or auditing matters." Also, pursuant to Section 407 of SOX and related SEC rules, a public issuer must periodically disclose whether its audit committee has at least one member who is a "financial expert" (as discussed in Section 10.01(C) above).

  2. Financial Statement Certification Requirements. Section 906 of SOX provides that each periodic Exchange Act report that contains financial statements must also contain a certification by the issuer's chief executive officer (CEO) and chief financial officer (CFO) that the report "fully complies" with the requirements of Section 13(a) or Section 15(d) of the Exchange Act and that the

---

[*] *Cf. Business Roundtable v. SEC*, 905 F.2d 406 (D.C. Cir. 1990) (invaliding SEC rule that would have regulated voting rights of shareholders).

information in the report "fairly presents, in all material respects, the financial condition and results of operations of the issuer." In addition, Section 302, along with new SEC rules, requires the CEO and CFO to certify in each annual and quarterly Exchange Act report that, among other things, they have reviewed the report and, based on their knowledge, the report does not contain any untrue statements or omit material facts, and that the financial statements and other information fairly present in all material respects the issuer's financial condition and results of operations.

3.   *Internal Controls Report.* Section 404(a) of SOX directed the SEC to adopt rules that would require each annual report (e.g., Form 10-K) to contain an internal controls report (1) stating management's responsibility for establishing and maintaining an "adequate internal control structure and procedures for financial reporting" and (2) containing an assessment of the structure and procedures. Furthermore, Section 404(b) of SOX requires the issuer's independent auditors to attest to and report on the issuer's assessments made under Section 404(a). This section proved to be very controversial because companies found that complying with it was enormously expensive. As a result, although the SEC issued final rules on this topic in 2003 (the main one of which was Exchange Act Rule 13a-15), the rules contained phased-in compliance dates. Also, in the Dodd-Frank Wall Street Reform and Consumer Protection Act, Congress exempted nonaccelerated filers (those with a market capitalization under $75 million) from having to comply with subsection (b) of Section 404. This statute also directed the SEC to study how it could reduce the costs of complying with Section 404(b) for companies with market capitalizations between $75 million and $250 million "while maintaining investor protections for such companies."

4.   *Enhanced Financial Disclosures.* As required by Section 401 of SOX, the SEC amended the MD&A portions of Form 10-K to require issuers to explain any "off-balance sheet" arrangements. It also adopted Regulation G, which provides that if an issuer releases any non-GAAP financial measures it must also present the most directly comparable GAAP financial measure, as well as a reconciliation of the non-GAAP measure to the GAAP measure.

5.   *Auditor Requirements.* Public accounting firms generally may no longer provide non-audit services to public companies contemporaneously with audit services, with some exceptions. SOX also created the Public Company Accounting Oversight Board ("*PCAOB*") and required essentially all public accounting firms to register with the PCAOB. The PCAOB has authority to establish "auditing, quality control, ethics, independence, and other standards

relating to the preparation of audit reports" for public issuers, among other powers.

6.   *Code of Ethics for Senior Financial Officers.* Section 406 of SOX directed the SEC to adopt rules requiring public companies to disclose whether they have a code of ethics for certain senior officers and, if not, why not. The new rule, which is found in Item 406 of Regulation S-K, requires the code to be "reasonably designed to deter wrongdoing" and promote "[h]onest and ethical conduct," "[f]ull, fair, accurate, timely, and understandable disclosure in [Exchange Act] reports," and compliance with laws. This disclosure is required by Item 10 of Form 10-K (but may instead appear in an issuer's proxy statement that is filed with the SEC within 120 days after the end of the issuer's fiscal year).

7.   *Prohibition of Loans to Executives.* Section 402 of SOX added new subsection (k) to Section 13 of the Exchange Act, which makes it illegal for issuers to "extend or maintain credit, to arrange for the extension of credit, or to renew an extension of credit, in the form of a personal loan to or for any director or executive officer," subject to some exceptions.

8.   *Forfeiture of Bonuses.* Section 304(a) of SOX provided that if an issuer had to restate its financial statements "due to the material noncompliance of the issuer, as a result of misconduct, with any financial reporting requirement under the securities laws," the issuer's CEO and its CFO would have to repay any bonus or other incentive or stock-based compensation that they received during the year after the "faulty" financial statements were first filed with the SEC or publicly released, as well as any profits that they realized from selling the issuer's securities during that period. Unfortunately, the term "misconduct" was not defined in the statute, leading to some ambiguities. In recent years, the SEC has used Section 304 in a number of options back-dating cases.

9.   *Attorney Conduct Rules.* Attorneys were not left out of having new requirements imposed under SOX. Section 307 of SOX required the SEC to promulgate new rules applicable to attorneys representing public issuers. The basic purpose of the new rules, which are now found in Rules 1 through 7 of 17 C.F.R. Part 205, is to require "up the ladder" reporting by attorneys who become aware of evidence of a past, pending or imminent "material violation" involving an Exchange Act issuer or certain subsidiaries. "Material violations" include material violations of applicable federal or state securities laws, breaches of fiduciary duties under federal or state law, and "similar" violations of any federal

or state law. An attorney who must report this evidence to the issuer usually must also determine whether the issuer adopts an "appropriate response."

The Dodd-Frank Wall Street Reform and Consumer Protection Act. This sprawling (849 pages in PDF format) statute, which was enacted in 2010, was a response by Congress to the financial crisis that began in 2007 and resulted in, among other things, the "fire sale" of Bear Stearns to JPMorgan Chase in March 2008, the subsequent bankruptcy of Lehman Brothers, the bailout of American International Group (AIG), Congress's passage of the Troubled Asset Relief Program (TARP), and many other dramatic events. This textbook is not the place for a detailed discussion of the many (and extraordinarily complex) causes of the financial crisis or the provisions Dodd-Frank Act and other regulatory responses to the financial crisis, many of which are still evolving. However, a brief discussion of a few of the provisions of this statute are in order. Keep in mind that this statute was adopted during a time of great public outcry over executive compensation, particularly for companies that received "bailouts."

1.   Executive Compensation and "Say on Pay." The Dodd-Frank Act added Section 14A to the Exchange Act. This new section requires that, at least once every three years, public companies must allow their shareholders to have an advisory (i.e., non-binding[*]) vote on executive compensation. In addition, at least once every six years, the issuer must allow its shareholders to vote on whether the advisory vote on executive compensation will take place every year, every two years, or every three years. On a related note, the SEC had earlier amended Items 402 of Regulation S-K to require a "Compensation Discussion and Analysis," which must appear either in the issuer's Form 10-K or its proxy statement (if the proxy statement is filed within 120 days after the end of the issuer's fiscal year). Further, Item 407(e)(5) of Regulation S-K now requires extensive discussion of the activities of the issuer's compensation committee or, if the issuer does not have a compensation committee, the board members who perform equivalent functions.

2.   "Golden Parachutes." New Section 14A also provides that, in any proxy materials in which shareholders are asked to approve a merger or similar change-of-control transaction involving a public company, the company must disclose, in a "clear and simple" manner in accordance with rules to promulgated by the SEC, any so-called "golden parachute" payments (e.g.,

---

[*]   As you know from Chapter 5, the board determines the compensation of the officers. Congress did not want to upset this state-law rule. Thus, the "say on pay" vote by the shareholders could be ignored by the board. On the other hand, the theory is that few boards will want to approve executive compensation that is widely disapproved by the shareholders.

severance payments) that may be received by high-level executives. Further, the shareholders must be allowed to cast an advisory vote on that compensation.

3.   "Clawbacks."   Expanding on Section 304 of SOX (discussed above), Section 954 of the Dodd-Frank Act requires the SEC to pass rules that would prohibit national securities exchanges from listing the securities of issuers that do not develop and implement (and disclose) "clawback" policies. In general, these policies must require that executives, including former executives, repay incentive-based compensation that they earned with respect to the issuer's financial statements, if the financial statements are restated within three years after the compensation was earned. The amount of the repayment would be the difference between what the executive earned and what she "should have" earned, based on the restated financial statements.

4.   Disclosure of "Pay Versus Performance" and Ratio of CEO Pay to Average Worker Pay.   The Dodd-Frank Act added new subsection (i) to Section 14 of the Exchange Act. This subsection requires the SEC to promulgate rules that require issuers to include in their proxy statements information about the "relationship between executive compensation actually paid and the financial performance of the issuer, taking into account any change in the value of the shares of stock and dividends of the issuer ...." The Dodd-Frank Act also directed the SEC to amend Item 402 of Regulation S-K so that public companies must disclose (1) "the median of the annual total compensation of all employees of the issuer, except the [CEO]"; (2) the CEO's annual total compensation; and (3) the ratio between those two amounts.[*]

5.   Independent Compensation Committee Members.   Much like what SOX did with respect to audit committees, Section 952 of the Dodd-Frank Act added new Section 10C to the Exchange Act. This new section directs the SEC to adopt rules preventing national securities exchanges from listing the securities of issuers that do not have "independent" compensation committees, subject to certain exceptions.

Of course, this is just a small sampling of some of the provisions of the Dodd-Frank Act. You may learn more about it in an advanced course on Securities Regulation or Banking Law. In addition, as should be obvious, this is a

---

[*]   However, due to widespread concern about how to comply with this provision, legislation has been introduced to repeal it. As of the date of this textbook, it was unclear whether this provision would remain in effect.

very dynamic area of the law and you should expect continuing changes, some of them major, in the coming years.

Now that you are an expert on the requirements imposed on public companies by the Exchange Act, the SEC, and stock exchange rules, try your hand at the following practice questions.

PRACTICE QUESTIONS

Multiple Choice Question 10-1: *Which of the following is not an accurate statement about liability for materially false or misleading Exchange Act reports under Section 18 of the Securities Exchange Act?*

A.   The plaintiff must show that the defendant acted with scienter (e.g., negligence, recklessness, or intent to defraud).

B.   A defendant may establish a defense by showing that she acted in good faith and had no knowledge that the Exchange Act filing was false or misleading.

C.   The plaintiff must show that she bought or sold securities of the company which filed the false or misleading Exchange Act filing.

D.   The plaintiff must show that she relied on the false or misleading Exchange Act filing.

Multiple Choice Question 10-2: In early 2012, Rental Car Corp. ("RCC") conducted an IPO of its common stock. Immediately after the IPO, RCC had 287 record holders of its common stock. RCC has $30 million in assets and is engaged in interstate commerce but its stock is not listed on any exchange. Its fiscal year ends December 31 and you may assume that it will have the same number of shareholders at the end of 2012. *Which of the following is correct?*

A.   Pursuant to Section 15(d) of the Exchange Act, RCC must comply with the periodic reporting requirements of the Exchange Act with respect to 2012 only.

B.   Pursuant to Section 15(d) of the Exchange Act, RCC must comply with the periodic reporting requirements of the Exchange Act indefinitely (i.e., for the foreseeable future).

C.   RCC must register its common stock under Section 12(g) of the Exchange Act within 120 days after the end of 2012.

D.   RCC must register its common stock under Section 12(b) of the Exchange Act.

Multiple Choice Question 10-3: *The primary purpose of a Form 10-Q filed under the Securities Exchange Act is for a company to report:*

A.   Its annual financial statements.
B.   Its quarterly financial statements.
C.   Material events of an unusual, nonrecurring nature.
D.   Acquisitions of the stock or assets of other companies.
E.   None of the above.

Multiple Choice Question 10-4: *Which of the following is an accurate statement about the proxy rules under Section 14 of the Securities Exchange Act?*

A.   A shareholder who has owned at least $1,000 of stock of a publicly traded company for at least six months may require the company to include a shareholder proposal in its proxy statement under Rule 14a-8.
B.   There is no private cause of action under Rule 14a-9, which prohibits materially false or misleading proxy statements.
C.   A publicly traded company is not required to solicit proxies for an annual meeting of shareholders.
D.   Statements of opinion can never violate Rule 14a-9, which prohibits materially false or misleading proxy statements.

Multiple Choice Question 10-5: *Which of the following is* <u>*not*</u> *an accurate statement about stock markets in the United States?*

A.   Both the NYSE and Nasdaq are national securities exchanges; however, the Pink Sheets is not a national securities exchange.
B.   National securities exchanges are prohibited from adopting rules that are "tougher" than SEC rules.
C.   The SEC has the power to change rules that national exchanges have adopted.
D.   More issuers have securities listed on the NYSE than on Nasdaq.

Multiple Choice Question 10-6: Which of the following is an accurate statement about Section 12(g) of the Securities Exchange Act?

A.   Companies with more than $10 million in assets that had registered a class of securities under Section 12(g) may "deregister" the class once there are fewer than 500 record holders of the class.

B.   Companies with more than $10 million in assets that had registered a class of securities under Section 12(g) may "deregister" the class once there are fewer than 300 record holders of the class.

C.   Banks, insurance companies, and pharmaceutical companies are exempt from having to register securities under Section 12(g).

D.   Registering a class of securities under Section 12(g) requires that the securities are listed on a national securities exchange.

Multiple Choice Question 10-7: Which of the following is an accurate statement about the proxy rules under Section 14 of the Securities Exchange Act?

A.   Under current SEC rules, public companies must include in their proxy materials the name of a director candidate who has been nominated by any shareholder.

B.   Under current SEC rules, public companies must include in their proxy materials the name of a director candidate who has been nominated by a shareholder (or group of shareholders) who owns at least 5% of the company's voting stock.

C.   Under current SEC rules, public companies must reimburse a shareholder who solicits proxies in favor of a director candidate who was not nominated by the "incumbent" board but who ends up being elected to the board.

D.   Both B and C are correct.

E.   None of the above is correct.

Multiple Choice Question 10-8: Which of the following is an accurate statement about the Sarbanes-Oxley Act of 2002 (SOX)?

A.   SOX requires all corporations that have securities registered under Section 12 of the Exchange Act to have an audit committee that is composed entirely of independent directors.
B.   SOX requires that an issuer's Form 10-K must contain a certification by the issuer's CEO and CFO that the report "fully complies" with the requirements of Section 13(a) or Section 15(d) of the Exchange Act.
C.   SOX made it illegal for insiders of a company to buy that company's securities.
D.   SOX requires all corporations that have securities registered under Section 12 of the Exchange Act to have a code of ethics that applies to their directors and officers.
E.   Both A and B are correct.

Multiple Choice Question 10-9: Which of the following are likely consequences of a private company deciding to have its stock listed on a stock exchange and registered under Section 12(b) of the Exchange Act?

I.   In the future, if the company decides to do a registered offering of stock under the Securities Act of 1933, it will be somewhat "easier" than if the company were a private company.

II.   The company will have better access to information about its competitors that are also publicly traded.

III.   The company may be better able to use its stock as "acquisition currency" if it wishes to acquire another company.

IV.   The company will profit from purchases and sales of its securities on the stock market.

A.   All of the above.
B.   I, II, and III only.
C.   I and III only.
D.   II and III only.
E.   I and IV only.

Multiple Choice Question 10-10: *Which of the following is an accurate statement about recent developments in "corporate governance"?*

A.   Many companies have decided to "de-stagger" their boards of directors as a result of shareholder "pressure."

B.   Many companies have decided to "de-stagger" their boards of directors as a result of "pressure" from the SEC.

C.   Many companies have adopted majority voting systems that prohibit a director candidate who receives more "no" votes than "yes" votes from serving on the board under any circumstances.

D.   The new "say on pay" requirements of the Dodd-Frank Wall Street Reform and Consumer Protection Act prohibit companies from paying executives more than the amounts approved by shareholders.

CHAPTER 11
DUTIES OF CONTROLLING SHAREHOLDERS

Until Chapter 9, we assumed that shareholders, in their capacities as shareholders, do not owe fiduciary duties to the corporation or the other shareholders (or anyone else for that matter). Generally speaking, that is true. However, in Chapter 9 you ran into one exception: some courts have held that shareholders in closely held corporations *do* owe fiduciary duties to one another. In this chapter, you will learn about another exception: some courts have imposed fiduciary duties on "controlling" shareholders.

It is very important that you distinguish between this chapter and Chapter 9, which concerned closely held corporations. As you saw in Chapter 9, one characteristic of a closely held corporation is that it has a small number of shareholders. In other words, it's somewhat akin to a partnership and often has as few as two or three owners. By contrast, this chapter concerns *non*-closely held corporations. Note that the previous sentence did not say "publicly traded" corporations. Publicly traded corporations, which tend to have hundreds or thousands (or even tens of thousands) of shareholders, lie at the opposite end of the spectrum from closely held corporations. However, not every corporation is *either* publicly traded or closely held; there are a lot of corporations in between these two extremes. In any event, this chapter does *not* concern closely held corporations.

Also note that there are no statutes to learn about in this chapter. The fiduciary duties of controlling shareholders arise solely out of case law. Nonetheless, this chapter may to some degree remind you of the directors' conflicting interest transactions that you learned about in Chapter 7. After you read this chapter, you may want to ponder whether the absence of statutes helps or hinders your understanding of this topic.

§ 11.01   WHO IS A "CONTROLLING" SHAREHOLDER?

Objectives: Given information about the number of shareholders of a corporation, the number of shares owned by each shareholder, and other relevant information, you should be able to determine if a particular shareholder may be considered a "controlling" shareholder under judicial definitions of that term.

Because this is a chapter about controlling shareholders, it probably would be wise to begin by trying to figure out whether a shareholder is a "controlling" shareholder. Unlike determining whether someone is a director (and therefore owes fiduciary duties), determining whether someone is a controlling shareholder (and therefore owes fiduciary duties, according to some courts) is not always easy.

If a corporation has, say, three equal shareholders, then none of them would be considered a "controlling" shareholder. On the other hand, if two of the shareholders were related to one another and/or made decisions only after consulting with one another, then one might say that they have formed a "group" and that the *group* is a controlling shareholder because the members of the group own two-thirds of the stock in this example. Using a simpler example, if one shareholder owns 51% of the voting stock and the other owns 49%, then the former would be a considered a "controlling" shareholder whereas the latter would not. Of course, in this example this distinction is largely meaningless because courts in states like Massachusetts have held that *all* of the shareholders in a closely held corporation owe fiduciary duties, as you saw in Chapter 9.

What about a publicly traded corporation—or at least a non-closely held corporation? Assume that Mega Corp. has 10,000 shareholders and 1 billion shares of stock outstanding. The "biggest" share-holder is John Jones, who owns 500,000 shares, or 0.05% of the total. Is John a controlling shareholder? The answer should be obvious: no. In fact, there do not appear to be *any* controlling shareholders in this example. Instead, Mega Corp. is owned by thousands of small shareholders, none of whom really has any amount of "control" over Mega Corp. Moreover, given the large number of shareholders, it is likely that the identities of the shareholders are always changing from day to day. In other words, if you were to compile a list of the persons who own Mega Corp. stock today, that list could be very different—even radically different—from yesterday's list of Mega Corp. shareholders. This is because shares in such a publicly traded company are usually subject to a high "turnover" rate. This is one reason why we

> ### THE CONCEPT OF "GROUPS"
> Status as a "controlling" shareholder could arise from one's *own* ownership of shares or from being part of a group whose members *collectively* own a controlling interest. Courts have different approaches to this question, but typically require a showing that the members act in "concert" with one another before they will considered a "group." Also, Section 13(d) of the Securities Exchange Act, discussed in Chapter 12, provides that "[w]hen two or more persons act as a partnership, limited partnership, syndicate, or other group for the purpose of acquiring, holding, or disposing of securities of an issuer, such syndicate or group shall be deemed a 'person' ...." for purposes of determining what percentage of a publicly traded corporation's stock they own.

call such companies "public" companies: it is as if a large swath of the public at large owns them.[*]

Now, if there was a shareholder who happened to own a majority of the outstanding shares of Mega Corp. stock (i.e., 50% plus one share) then that person clearly is a controlling shareholder of Mega Corp. But it may surprise you to find out that one can be considered a controlling shareholder even with far less than a majority of the stock. Lawyers often start to worry about controlling shareholder status at surprisingly small percentages. For example, under Section 16(b) of the Securities Exchange Act of 1934, which you will study in Chapter 14, shareholders who own more than 10% of the outstanding shares of a publicly traded corporation are subject to the same sort of stock trading restrictions as are directors and officers of the corporation. In the context of this chapter, perhaps 20% is a more realistic threshold for controlling shareholder status, however.

But more important than the percentage of shares that a shareholder owns is the amount of influence that the shareholder has on the board of directors and/or the corporation's business decisions. In other words, if a majority of the directors are not really "independent" from a shareholder, then that shareholder is likely a "controlling" shareholder. For example, consider the following Delaware Supreme Court opinion. In this case, Alcatel U.S.A. Corporation ("Alcatel") held more than 43% of the outstanding shares of Lynch Communication Systems, Inc. ("Lynch"). In addition, Alcatel was contractually entitled to designate five of Lynch's eleven directors, including two of the three members of the executive committee of the board. The following portion of the opinion concerns whether Alcatel was a controlling shareholder of Lynch.

Kahn v. Lynch Communication Systems, Inc.
Supreme Court of Delaware
638 A.2d 1110 (1994)

Holland, Justice: ***

***

This Court has held that "a shareholder owes a fiduciary duty only if it owns a majority interest in or exercises control over the business affairs of the corporation." [Citation omitted.] With regard to the exercise of control, this Court has stated:

> [A] shareholder who owns less than 50% of a corporation's outstanding stocks [sic] does not, without more, become a

---

[*]   Of course, as we learned in Chapter 10, there is a much more precise definition of "publicly traded corporation" than this.

controlling shareholder of that corporation, with a concomitant fiduciary status. For a dominating relationship to exist in the absence of controlling stock ownership, a plaintiff must allege domination by a minority shareholder though actual control of corporation conduct. [Citation omitted.]

Alcatel held a 43.3 percent minority share of stock in Lynch. Therefore, the threshold question to be answered by the Court of Chancery was whether, despite its minority ownership, Alcatel exercised control over Lynch's business affairs. Based upon the testimony and the minutes of the August 1, 1986 Lynch board meeting, the Court of Chancery concluded that Alcatel did exercise control over Lynch's business decisions.

***

At the August 1 [board] meeting, Alcatel opposed the renewal of compensation contracts for Lynch's top five managers. According to Dertinger [who was Lynch's CEO and Chairman of the Board], Christian Fayard ("Fayard"), an Alcatel director, told the board members, "you must listen to us. We are [the] 43 percent owner. You have to do what we tell you." The minutes confirm Dertinger's testimony. They recite that Fayard declared, "you are pushing us very much to take control of the company. Our opinion is not taken into consideration."

Although Beringer and Kertz, two of the independent directors, favored renewal of the contracts, according to the minutes, the third independent director, Wineman, admonished the board as follows:

> Mr. Wineman pointed out that the vote on the contracts is a "watershed vote" and the motion, due to Alcatel's "strong feelings," might not carry if taken now. Mr. Wineman clarified that "you [management] might win the battle and lose the war." With Alcatel's opinion so clear, Mr. Wineman questioned "if management wants the contracts renewed under these circumstances." He recommended that management "think twice." Mr. Wineman declared: "I want to keep the management. I can't think of a better management." Mr. Kertz agreed, again advising consideration of the "critical" period the company is entering.

The minutes reflect that the management directors left the room after this statement. The remaining board members then voted not to renew the contracts.

At the same meeting, Alcatel vetoed Lynch's acquisition of the target company, which, according to the minutes, Beringer considered "an immediate fit" for Lynch. Dertinger agreed with Beringer, stating that the "target company is extremely important as they have the products that Lynch needs now." Nonetheless, Alcatel prevailed. The minutes reflect that Fayard advised the board: "Alcatel, with its 44% equity position, would not approve such an acquisition as ... it does not wish to be diluted from being the main shareholder in Lynch." From the foregoing evidence, the Vice Chancellor concluded:

> ... Alcatel did control the Lynch board, at least with respect to the matters under consideration at its August 1, 1986 board meeting. The interplay between the directors was more than vigorous discussion, as suggested by defendants. The management and independent directors disagreed with Alcatel on several important issues. However, when Alcatel made its position clear, and reminded the other directors of its significant stockholdings, Alcatel prevailed. Dertinger testified that Fayard "scared [the non-Alcatel directors] to death." While this statement undoubtedly is an exaggeration, it does represent a first-hand view of how the board operated. I conclude that the non-Alcatel directors deferred to Alcatel because of its position as a significant stockholder and not because they decided in the exercise of their own business judgment that Alcatel's position was correct [citation omitted].

The record supports the Court of Chancery's underlying factual finding that "the non-Alcatel [independent] directors deferred to Alcatel because of its position as a significant stockholder and not because they decided in the exercise of their own business judgment that Alcatel's position was correct." The record also supports the subsequent factual finding that, notwithstanding its 43.3 percent minority shareholder interest, Alcatel did exercise actual control over Lynch by dominating its corporate affairs. The Court of Chancery's legal conclusion that Alcatel owed the fiduciary duties of a controlling shareholder to the other Lynch shareholder followed syllogistically as the logical result of its cogent analysis of the record.

***

Problems

Problem 11-1: Ultra Corp. is a publicly traded company with 100 million shares of stock outstanding. Susan Ultra, the founder of the company, owns 1 million shares of Ultra Corp. stock. No other shareholder owns more than 50,000 shares. Susan recently retired as the president and a director of Ultra Corp. However, the board frequently solicits her advice on important strategic decisions and often has refused to take actions that Susan did not "like." *Is Susan a controlling shareholder of Ultra Corp.? What other facts do you want to know before answering this question?*

Problem 11-2:   Same facts as Problem 11-1, except that Bob Moneybags owns 51% of the outstanding shares of Ultra Corp. stock. Bob despises Susan and is glad that she retired. *Is Susan a controlling shareholder of Ultra Corp.?*

Problem 11-3: *Would it be easier to have a statutory (as opposed to judicial) definition of "controlling" shareholder? How would you write such a definition?*

Before moving on, please note that in this chapter I sometimes use the term "minority" shareholders to refer to the non-controlling shareholders, even though this may not be entirely precise. For example, in *Kahn v. Lynch Communication Systems, Inc.*, Alcatel technically was not a "majority" shareholder because it owned less than a majority of the stock; therefore the other shareholders technically were not "minority" shareholders, when considered as a group. But saying "minority" seems less cumbersome than "non-controlling."

§ 11.02   DUTIES OF CONTROLLING SHAREHOLDERS

Objectives: Given information about a transaction between or involving a corporation and a controlling shareholder of that corporation, you should be able to determine the applicable standard of review that a court will use to evaluate the transaction if it is challenged by a different shareholder. You should also be able to apply that standard of review to predict the likely outcome of such a lawsuit.

Merely saying that a shareholder is a "controlling" shareholder obviously is not the end of our analysis. You will need to consider what fiduciary duties that shareholder has and how to determine whether the shareholder has breached those duties.

The following is one of the leading cases on this issue. It involves a parent corporation (Sinclair Oil Corporation) that owned 97% of the outstanding shares of a subsidiary (Sinclair Venezuelan Oil Company, or "Sinven"). Under any rational definition of "controlling shareholder," Sinclair controlled Sinven. And one shouldn't be too surprised to find that Sinclair elected all of Sinven's directors and thereby dictated Sinven's business policies. After all, it would be a rare parent corporation that would let a subsidiary "run wild" with no oversight or control from the parent. The question becomes, however, whether the parent was causing the subsidiary to do things that favored the parent at the expense of the subsidiary's other shareholders.

Sinclair Oil Corporation v. Levien
Supreme Court of Delaware
280 A.2d 717 (1971)

WOLCOTT, Chief Justice. This is an appeal by the defendant, Sinclair Oil Corporation (hereafter Sinclair), from an order of the Court of Chancery *** requiring Sinclair to account for damages sustained by its subsidiary, Sinclair Venezuelan Oil Company (hereafter Sinven), organized by Sinclair for the purpose of operating in Venezuela, as a result of [1] dividends paid by Sinven, [2] the denial to Sinven of industrial development, and [3] a breach of contract between Sinclair's wholly-owned subsidiary, Sinclair International Oil Company, and Sinven.

Sinclair, operating primarily as a holding company, is in the business of exploring for oil and of producing and marketing crude oil and oil products. *** [It] owned about 97% of Sinven's stock. The plaintiff owns about 3,000 of 120,000 publicly held shares of Sinven. Sinven, incorporated in 1922, has been engaged in petroleum operations primarily in Venezuela and since 1959 has operated exclusively in Venezuela.

Sinclair nominates all members of Sinven's board of directors. The Chancellor found as a fact that the directors were not independent of Sinclair. Almost without exception, they were officers, directors, or employees of corporations in the Sinclair complex. By reason of Sinclair's domination, it is clear that Sinclair owed Sinven a fiduciary duty. *** Sinclair concedes this.

The Chancellor held that because of Sinclair's fiduciary duty and its control over Sinven, its relationship with Sinven must meet the test of intrinsic fairness. The standard of intrinsic fairness involves both a high degree of fairness and a shift in the burden of proof. Under this standard the burden is on Sinclair to prove, subject to careful judicial scrutiny, that its transactions with Sinven were objectively fair. ***

Sinclair argues that the transactions between it and Sinven should [instead] be tested *** by the business judgment rule under which a court will not interfere with the judgment of a board of directors unless there is a showing of gross and palpable overreaching. ***

We think, however, that Sinclair's argument *** is misconceived. When the situation involves a parent and a subsidiary, with the parent controlling the transaction and fixing the terms, the test of intrinsic fairness, with its resulting shifting of the burden of proof, is applied. *** The basic situation for the application of the rule is the one in which the parent has received a benefit to the exclusion and at the expense of the subsidiary.

***

A parent does indeed owe a fiduciary duty to its subsidiary when there are parent-subsidiary dealings. However, this alone will not evoke the intrinsic fairness standard. This standard will be applied only when the fiduciary duty is accompanied by self-dealing—the situation when a parent is on both sides of a transaction with its subsidiary. Self-dealing occurs when the parent, by virtue of its domination of the subsidiary, causes the subsidiary to act in such a way that the parent receives something from the subsidiary to the exclusion of, and detriment to, the minority stockholders of the subsidiary.

[I.] We turn now to the facts. The plaintiff argues that, from 1960 through 1966, Sinclair caused Sinven to pay out such excessive dividends that the industrial development of Sinven was effectively prevented, and it became in reality a corporation in dissolution.

From 1960 through 1966, Sinven paid out $108,000,000 in dividends ($38,000,000 in excess of Sinven's earnings during the same period). The Chancellor held that Sinclair caused these dividends to be paid during a period when it had a need for large amounts of cash. Although the dividends paid exceeded earnings, the plaintiff concedes that the payments were made in compliance with [the applicable statute], authorizing payment of dividends out of surplus or net profits. However, the plaintiff attacks these dividends on the ground that they resulted from an improper motive—Sinclair's need for cash. The Chancellor, applying the intrinsic fairness standard, held that Sinclair did not sustain its burden of proving that these dividends were intrinsically fair to the minority stockholders of Sinven.

Since it is admitted that the dividends were paid in strict compliance with [the statute], the alleged excessiveness of the payments alone would not state a cause of action. Nevertheless, compliance with the applicable statute may not, under all circumstances, justify all dividend payments. If a plaintiff can meet his burden of proving that a dividend cannot be grounded on any reasonable business objective, then the courts can and will interfere with the board's decision to pay the dividend.

Sinclair contends that it is improper to apply the intrinsic fairness standard to dividend payments even when the board which voted for the dividends is completely dominated. ***

We do not accept the argument that the intrinsic fairness test can never be applied to a dividend declaration by a dominated board, although a dividend declaration by a dominated board will not inevitably demand the application of the intrinsic fairness standard. *** If such a dividend is in essence self-dealing by the parent, then the intrinsic fairness standard is the proper standard. For example, suppose a parent dominates a subsidiary and its board of directors. The subsidiary has outstanding two classes of stock, X and Y. Class X is owned by the parent and Class Y is owned by minority stockholders of the subsidiary. If the subsidiary, at the direction of the parent, declares a dividend on its Class X stock only, this might well be self-dealing by the parent. It would be receiving something from the subsidiary to the exclusion of and detrimental to its minority stockholders. This self-dealing, coupled with the parent's fiduciary duty, would make intrinsic fairness the proper standard by which to evaluate the dividend payments.

Consequently it must be determined whether the dividend payments by Sinven were, in essence, self-dealing by Sinclair. The dividends resulted in great sums of money being transferred from Sinven to Sinclair. However, a proportionate share of this money was received by the minority shareholders of Sinven. Sinclair received nothing from Sinven to the exclusion of its minority stockholders. As such, these dividends were not self-dealing. We hold therefore that the Chancellor erred in applying the intrinsic fairness test as to these dividend payments. The business judgment standard should have been applied.

We conclude that the facts demonstrate that the dividend payments complied with the business judgment standard and with [the statute]. The motives for causing the declaration of dividends are immaterial unless the plaintiff can show that the dividend payments resulted from improper motives and amounted to waste. The plaintiff contends only that the dividend payments drained Sinven of cash to such an extent that it was prevented from expanding.

[II.] The plaintiff proved no business opportunities which came to Sinven independently and which Sinclair either took to itself or denied to Sinven. As a matter of fact, with two minor exceptions which resulted in losses, all of Sinven's operations have been conducted in Venezuela, and Sinclair had a policy of exploiting its oil properties located in different countries by subsidiaries located in the particular countries.

***

However, the plaintiff could point to no opportunities which came to Sinven. Therefore, Sinclair usurped no business opportunity belonging to Sinven. Since Sinclair received nothing from Sinven to the exclusion of and detriment to Sinven's minority stockholders, there was no self-dealing. Therefore, business judgment is the proper standard by which to evaluate Sinclair's expansion policies.

Since there is no proof of self-dealing on the part of Sinclair, it follows that the expansion policy of Sinclair and the methods used to achieve the desired result must, as far as Sinclair's treatment of Sinven is concerned, be tested by the standards of the business judgment rule. Accordingly, Sinclair's decision, absent fraud or gross overreaching, to achieve expansion through the medium of its subsidiaries, other than Sinven, must be upheld.

Even if Sinclair was wrong in developing these opportunities as it did, the question arises, with which subsidiaries should these opportunities have been shared? No evidence indicates a unique need or ability of Sinven to develop these opportunities. The decision of which subsidiaries would be used to implement Sinclair's expansion policy was one of business judgment with which a court will not interfere absent a showing of gross and palpable overreaching. *** No such showing has been made here.

[III.] Next, Sinclair argues that the Chancellor committed error when he held it liable to Sinven for breach of contract.

In 1961 Sinclair created Sinclair International Oil Company (hereafter International), a wholly owned subsidiary used for the purpose of coordinating all of Sinclair's foreign operations. All crude [oil] purchases by Sinclair were made thereafter through International.

On September 28, 1961, Sinclair caused Sinven to contract with International whereby Sinven agreed to sell all of its crude oil and refined products to International at specified prices. The contract provided for minimum and maximum quantities and prices. The plaintiff contends that Sinclair caused this contract to be breached in two respects. Although the contract called for payment on receipt, International's payments lagged as much as 30 days after receipt. Also, the contract required International to purchase at least a fixed minimum amount of crude [oil] and refined products from Sinven. International did not comply with this requirement.

Clearly, Sinclair's act of contracting with its dominated subsidiary was self-dealing. Under the contract Sinclair received the products produced by Sinven, and of course the minority shareholders of Sinven were not able to share in the receipt of these products. If the contract was breached, then Sinclair received these products to the detriment of Sinven's minority shareholders. We agree with the Chancellor's finding that the contract was breached by Sinclair, both as to the time of payments and the amounts purchased. Although a parent need not bind itself by a contract with its dominated subsidiary, Sinclair chose to operate in this manner. As Sinclair has received the benefits of this contract, so must it comply with the contractual duties.

Under the intrinsic fairness standard, Sinclair must prove that its causing Sinven not to enforce the contract was intrinsically fair to the minority shareholders of Sinven. Sinclair has failed to meet this burden. Late payments were clearly breaches for which Sinven should have sought and received adequate damages. As to the quantities purchased, Sinclair argues that it purchased all the products produced by Sinven. This, however, does not satisfy the standard of intrinsic fairness. Sinclair has failed to prove that Sinven could not possibly have produced or someway have obtained the contract minimums. As such, Sinclair must account on this claim.

***

We will therefore reverse that part of the Chancellor's order that requires Sinclair to account to Sinven for damages sustained as a result of dividends paid between 1960 and 1966, and by reason of the denial to Sinven of expansion during that period. We will affirm the remaining portion of that order and remand the cause for further proceedings.

Sinclair Oil provides two different standards to choose from in evaluating whether a controlling shareholder breached its fiduciary duties: either (1) intrinsic fairness, which "involves both a high degree of fairness and a shift in the burden of proof" and is similar to the "entire fairness" test that you encountered in earlier chapters, or (2) the business judgment rule.[*] As you know from prior chapters, the choice between these two alternatives probably determines who will win the case. If intrinsic fairness applies, then the controlling shareholder will probably lose. If the business judgment rule applies, then the controlling shareholder will probably win.

---

[*]   As you know, the business judgment rule protects decisions made by directors (and perhaps officers), so it seems strange to see it used in evaluating a *shareholder's* actions. But remember that in the *Sinclair Oil* case Sinven's directors were chosen by Sinclair and presumably would themselves be subject to Sinclair's control. Thus, if the directors would be entitled to the business judgment rule in some situations, then perhaps the shareholder who elected those directors should be as well.

But suppose there is a situation that, under the rules developed in *Sinclair Oil*, calls for application of the intrinsic fairness test. If you represent the controlling shareholder, what might you suggest to bolster its case? Sure, you could suggest conducting the transaction in an extremely "fair" manner. For example, if the controlling shareholder was buying something from the corporation, you might suggest that it pay a very high price. This would obviously lessen then chance of a lawsuit by minority shareholders, but your client probably would not like this idea.

Do you have any other ideas for your client? There is no statute to guide you, but what if you used the director's conflicting interest transaction (DCIT) from Chapter 7 and MBCA §§ 8.60 to 8.63 as a model or analogy? If this were a DCIT rather than a transaction involving a controlling shareholder, it would be wise to seek (1) approval by the minority shareholders (i.e., the disinterested shareholders) and/or (2) approval by the "independent" directors (i.e., the directors who have no financial or other ties to the controlling shareholder).* As you learned in Chapter 7, generally speaking, if a DCIT is approved by disinterested directors or disinterested shareholders after full disclosure in compliance with either MBCA § 8.62 or MBCA § 8.63, it may not be challenged on duty-of-loyalty grounds.

But disinterested directors and disinterested shareholders may have more reason to "fear" a controlling shareholder than a mere interested director. Thus, under Delaware law, if a self-dealing transaction involving a controlling shareholder is approved by disinterested directors or disinterested shareholders after full disclosure, the burden shifts to the plaintiff—but the standard remains entire fairness. In other words, even if the controlling shareholder can demonstrate that the transaction was approved by disinterested shareholders or disinterested/independent directors after full disclosure, the plaintiff could still attempt to prove that the transaction was not entirely fair. The plaintiff could do this by showing that *either* fair dealing or fair price were absent. *See Rosenblatt v. Getty Oil*, 493 A.2d 929 (Del. 1985); *In re Wheelbrator Technologies Shareholder Litigation*, 663 A.2d 1194 (Del. Ch. 1994); *see also In re The Walt Disney Co,. Derivative Litigation*, 731 A.2d 342, 367-68 (Del. Ch. 1998). These issues will also come up in the following section.

---

*   The Official Comment to MBCA § 8.61(b), however, states that the methods of "sanitizing" a DCIT are not relevant to parent-subsidiary relations.

§ 11.03   "SQUEEZE OUT" MERGERS

Objectives: *Given information about a proposed merger between a corporation and its parent corporation (or other controlling shareholder), you should be able to advise the parent corporation of some steps that should be taken to minimize the possibility that a minority shareholder will successfully allege that the merger is a breach of the parent corporation's fiduciary duties.*

Let's say that you are a controlling shareholder or a parent corporation and you want to "get rid of" the minority shareholders. How would you do it? One way would be to offer to purchase their stock from them. If all of the minority shareholders sold their stock to you, then you obviously would become the sole shareholder of the corporation. On the other hand, some shareholders may refuse to sell their stock to you unless you offer them truly astronomical sums.

A merger is a way to force the minority shareholders to surrender their stock. You will study mergers in detail in Chapter 12, but suffice it to say for now that in a merger one corporation, called the "target" corporation, merges into the "surviving" corporation. After the merger, the target corporation no longer exists; all of its assets and liabilities now belong to the surviving corporation. Importantly, shares in the target corporation also no longer exist. Instead, they will be converted into something else like cash (called the "merger consideration"). So a majority shareholder could easily use a merger to eliminate or "cash out" the minority: simply merge the corporation into a different corporation owned by the controlling shareholder, paying the minority shareholders cash for their shares. Or, as in the following case where the controlling shareholder *itself* was a corporation, merge the corporation directly into the controlling shareholder.

Although mergers require shareholder approval, if the controlling shareholder owns a majority of the shares you can easily guess how that vote will turn out. On the other hand, it might "look bad" to have a majority or controlling shareholder force a merger on the other shareholders. For that reason, controlling shareholders sometimes condition mergers on approval by a "majority of the minority," as in the following case.

Weinberger v. UOP, Inc.
Supreme Court of Delaware
457 A.2d 701 (1983)

MOORE, Justice. ***

***

[I.]   Signal is a diversified, technically based company operating through various subsidiaries. Its stock is publicly traded on the New York, Philadelphia and Pacific Stock Exchanges. UOP, formerly known as Universal Oil Products Company, was a diversified industrial company engaged in various lines of business, including petroleum and petro-chemical services and related products, construction, fabricated metal products, transportation equipment products, chemicals and plastics, and other products and services including land development, lumber products and waste disposal. Its stock was publicly held and listed on the New York Stock Exchange. [Through a tender offer, Signal acquired 50.5% of UOP's outstanding stock.]

***

Although UOP's board consisted of thirteen directors, Signal nominated and elected only six. Of these, five were either directors or employees of Signal. The sixth, a partner in the banking firm of Lazard Freres & Co., had been one of Signal's representatives in the negotiations and bargaining with UOP concerning the tender offer and purchase price of the UOP shares.

However, the president and chief executive officer of UOP retired during 1975, and Signal caused him to be replaced by James V. Crawford, a long-time employee and senior executive vice president of one of Signal's wholly-owned subsidiaries. Crawford succeeded his predecessor on UOP's board of directors and also was made a director of Signal.

By the end of 1977 Signal basically was unsuccessful in finding other suitable investment candidates for its excess cash, and by February 1978 considered that it had no other realistic acquisitions available to it on a friendly basis. Once again its attention turned to UOP.

The trial court found that at the instigation of certain Signal management personnel, including William W. Walkup, its board chairman, and Forrest N. Shumway, its president, a feasibility study was made concerning the possible acquisition of the balance of UOP's outstanding shares. This study was performed by two Signal officers, Charles S. Arledge, vice president (director of planning), and Andrew J. Chitiea, senior vice president (chief financial officer). Messrs.

Walkup, Shumway, Arledge and Chitiea were all directors of UOP in addition to their membership on the Signal board.

Arledge and Chitiea concluded that it would be a good investment for Signal to acquire the remaining 49.5% of UOP shares at any price up to $24 each. Their report was discussed between Walkup and Shumway who, along with Arledge, Chitiea and Brewster L. Arms, internal counsel for Signal, constituted Signal's senior management. In particular, they talked about the proper price to be paid if the acquisition was pursued, purportedly keeping in mind that as UOP's majority shareholder, Signal owed a fiduciary responsibility to both its own stockholders as well as to UOP's minority. It was ultimately agreed that a meeting of Signal's Executive Committee [of the board] would be called to propose that Signal acquire the remaining outstanding stock of UOP through a cash-out merger in the range of $20 to $21 per share.

The Executive Committee meeting was set for February 28, 1978. As a courtesy, UOP's president, Crawford, was invited to attend, although he was not a member of Signal's executive committee. On his arrival, and prior to the meeting, Crawford was asked to meet privately with Walkup and Shumway. He was then told of Signal's plan to acquire full ownership of UOP and was asked for his reaction to the proposed price range of $20 to $21 per share. Crawford said he thought such a price would be "generous", and that it was certainly one which should be submitted to UOP's minority shareholders for their ultimate consideration. ***

Thus, Crawford voiced no objection to the $20 to $21 price range, nor did he suggest that Signal should consider paying more than $21 per share for the minority interests. Later, at the Executive Committee meeting the same factors were discussed, with Crawford repeating the position he earlier took with Walkup and Shumway. *** For many reasons, Signal's management concluded that the acquisition of UOP's minority shares provided the solution to a number of its business problems.

Thus, it was the consensus that a price of $20 to $21 per share would be fair to both Signal and the minority shareholders of UOP. Signal's executive committee authorized its management "to negotiate" with UOP "for a cash acquisition of the minority ownership in UOP, Inc., with the intention of presenting a proposal to [Signal's] board of directors ... on March 6, 1978". Immediately after this February 28, 1978 meeting, Signal issued a press release stating:

> The Signal Companies, Inc. and UOP, Inc. are conducting negotiations for the acquisition for cash by Signal of the 49.5 per cent of UOP which it does not presently own, announced Forrest

N. Shumway, president and chief executive officer of Signal, and James V. Crawford, UOP president.

Price and other terms of the proposed transaction have not yet been finalized and would be subject to approval of the boards of directors of Signal and UOP, scheduled to meet early next week, the stockholders of UOP and certain federal agencies.

The announcement also referred to the fact that the closing price of UOP's common stock on that day was $14.50 per share.

Two days later, on March 2, 1978, Signal issued a second press release stating that its management would recommend a price in the range of $20 to $21 per share for UOP's 49.5% minority interest. This announcement referred to Signal's earlier statement that "negotiations" were being conducted for the acquisition of the minority shares.

Between Tuesday, February 28, 1978 and Monday, March 6, 1978, a total of four business days, Crawford spoke by telephone with all of UOP's non-Signal, i.e., outside, directors. Also during that period, Crawford retained Lehman Brothers to render a fairness opinion as to the price offered the minority for its stock. He gave two reasons for this choice. First, the time schedule between the announcement and the board meetings was short (by then only three business days) and since Lehman Brothers had been acting as UOP's investment banker for many years, Crawford felt that it would be in the best position to respond on such brief notice. Second, James W. Glanville, a long-time director of UOP and a partner in Lehman Brothers, had acted as a financial advisor to UOP for many years. Crawford believed that Glanville's familiarity with UOP, as a member of its board, would also be of assistance in enabling Lehman Brothers to render a fairness opinion within the existing time constraints.

***

During this period Crawford also had several telephone contacts with Signal officials. In only one of them, however, was the price of the shares discussed. In a conversation with Walkup, Crawford advised that as a result of his communications with UOP's non-Signal directors, it was his feeling that the price would have to be the top of the proposed range, or $21 per share, if the approval of UOP's outside directors was to be obtained. But again, he did not seek any price higher than $21.

Glanville assembled a three-man Lehman Brothers team to do the work on the fairness opinion. These persons examined relevant documents and information concerning UOP, including its annual reports and its Securities and

Exchange Commission filings from 1973 through 1976, as well as its audited financial statements for 1977, its interim reports to shareholders, and its recent and historical market prices and trading volumes. In addition, on Friday, March 3, 1978, two members of the Lehman Brothers team flew to UOP's headquarters in Des Plaines, Illinois, to perform a "due diligence" visit, during the course of which they interviewed Crawford as well as UOP's general counsel, its chief financial officer, and other key executives and personnel.

As a result, the Lehman Brothers team concluded that "the price of either $20 or $21 would be a fair price for the remaining shares of UOP". ***

***

On March 6, 1978, both the Signal and UOP boards were convened to consider the proposed merger. Telephone communications were maintained between the two meetings. Walkup, Signal's board chairman, and also a UOP director, attended UOP's meeting with Crawford in order to present Signal's position and answer any questions that UOP's non-Signal directors might have. Arledge and Chitiea, along with Signal's other designees on UOP's board, participated by conference telephone. All of UOP's outside directors attended the meeting either in person or by conference telephone.

First, Signal's board unanimously adopted a resolution authorizing Signal to propose to UOP a cash merger of $21 per share as outlined in a certain merger agreement and other supporting documents. This proposal required that the merger be approved by a majority of UOP's outstanding minority shares voting at the stockholders meeting at which the merger would be considered, and that the minority shares voting in favor of the merger, when coupled with Signal's 50.5% interest would have to comprise at least two-thirds of all UOP shares. Otherwise the proposed merger would be deemed disapproved.

UOP's board then considered the proposal. Copies of the agreement were delivered to the directors in attendance, and other copies had been forwarded earlier to the directors participating by telephone. They also had before them UOP financial data for 1974-1977, UOP's most recent financial statements, market price information, and budget projections for 1978. In addition they had Lehman Brothers' hurriedly prepared fairness opinion letter finding the price of $21 to be fair. ***

Signal also suggests that the Arledge-Chitiea feasibility study, indicating that a price of up to $24 per share would be a "good investment" for Signal, was discussed at the UOP directors' meeting. The Chancellor made no such finding, and our independent review of the record, detailed *infra*, satisfies us by a preponderance of the evidence that there was no discussion of this document at

UOP's board meeting. Furthermore, it is clear beyond peradventure that nothing in that report was ever disclosed to UOP's minority shareholders prior to their approval of the merger.

After consideration of Signal's proposal, Walkup and Crawford left the meeting to permit a free and uninhibited exchange between UOP's non-Signal directors. Upon their return a resolution to accept Signal's offer was then proposed and adopted. While Signal's men on UOP's board participated in various aspects of the meeting, they abstained from voting. However, the minutes show that each of them "if voting would have voted yes".

On March 7, 1978, UOP sent a letter to its shareholders advising them of the action taken by UOP's board with respect to Signal's offer. This document pointed out, among other things, that on February 28, 1978 "both companies had announced negotiations were being conducted".

Despite the swift board action of the two companies, the merger was not submitted to UOP's shareholders until their annual meeting on May 26, 1978. In the notice of that meeting and proxy statement sent to shareholders in May, UOP's management and board urged that the merger be approved. The proxy statement also advised:

> The price was determined after discussions between James V. Crawford, a director of Signal and Chief Executive Officer of UOP, and officers of Signal which took place during meetings on February 28, 1978, and in the course of several subsequent telephone conversations. (Emphasis added.)

In the original draft of the proxy statement the word "negotiations" had been used rather than "discussions". However, when the Securities and Exchange Commission sought details of the "negotiations" as part of its review of these materials, the term was deleted and the word "discussions" was substituted. The proxy statement indicated that the vote of UOP's board in approving the merger had been unanimous. It also advised the shareholders that Lehman Brothers had given its opinion that the merger price of $21 per share was fair to UOP's minority. However, it did not disclose the hurried method by which this conclusion was reached.

As of the record date of UOP's annual meeting, there were 11,488,302 shares of UOP common stock outstanding, 5,688,302 of which were owned by the minority. At the meeting only 56%, or 3,208,652, of the minority shares were voted. Of these, 2,953,812, or 51.9% of the total minority, voted for the merger, and 254,840 voted against it. When Signal's stock was added to the minority shares voting in favor, a total of 76.2% of UOP's outstanding shares approved the merger while only 2.2% opposed it.

By its terms the merger became effective on May 26, 1978, and each share of UOP's stock held by the minority was automatically converted into a right to receive $21 cash.

[II.A] A primary issue mandating reversal is the preparation by two UOP directors, Arledge and Chitiea, of their feasibility study for the exclusive use and benefit of Signal. This document was of obvious significance to both Signal and UOP. Using UOP data, it described the advantages to Signal of ousting the minority at a price range of $21-$24 per share. ***

Having written those words, solely for the use of Signal, it is clear from the record that neither Arledge nor Chitiea shared this report with their fellow directors of UOP. We are satisfied that no one else did either. This conduct hardly meets the fiduciary standards applicable to such a transaction. While Mr. Walkup, Signal's chairman of the board and a UOP director, attended the March 6, 1978 UOP board meeting and testified at trial that he had discussed the Arledge-Chitiea report with the UOP directors at this meeting, the record does not support this assertion. Perhaps it is the result of some confusion on Mr. Walkup's part. In any event Mr. Shumway, Signal's president, testified that he made sure the Signal outside directors had this report prior to the March 6, 1978 Signal board meeting, but he did not testify that the Arledge-Chitiea report was also sent to UOP's outside directors. [However, none of UOP's outside directors had seen this report.]

***

The Arledge-Chitiea report speaks for itself in supporting the Chancellor's finding that a price of up to $24 was a "good investment" for Signal. It shows that a return on the investment at $21 would be 15.7% versus 15.5% at $24 per share. This was a difference of only two-tenths of one percent, while it meant over $17,000,000 to the minority. Under such circumstances, paying UOP's minority shareholders $24 would have had relatively little long-term effect on Signal, and the Chancellor's findings concerning the benefit to Signal, even at a price of $24, were obviously correct. [Citation omitted.]

Certainly, this was a matter of material significance to UOP and its shareholders. Since the study was prepared by two UOP directors, using UOP information for the exclusive benefit of Signal, and nothing whatever was done to disclose it to the outside UOP directors or the minority shareholders, a question of breach of fiduciary duty arises. This problem occurs because there were common

Signal-UOP directors participating, at least to some extent, in the UOP board's decision-making processes without full disclosure of the conflicts they faced.*
***

[II.B] Given the absence of any attempt to structure this transaction on an arm's length basis, Signal cannot escape the effects of the conflicts it faced, particularly when its designees on UOP's board did not totally abstain from participation in the matter. There is no "safe harbor" for such divided loyalties in Delaware. When directors of a Delaware corporation are on both sides of a transaction, they are required to demonstrate their utmost good faith and the most scrupulous inherent fairness of the bargain. [Citation omitted.] The requirement of fairness is unflinching in its demand that where one stands on both sides of a transaction, he has the burden of establishing its entire fairness, sufficient to pass the test of careful scrutiny by the courts. [Citations omitted.]

There is no dilution of this obligation where one holds dual or multiple directorships, as in a parent-subsidiary context. [Citation omitted.] Thus, individuals who act in a dual capacity as directors of two corporations, one of whom is parent and the other subsidiary, owe the same duty of good management to both corporations, and in the absence of an independent negotiating structure (see [footnote], *supra*), or the directors' total abstention from any participation in the matter, this duty is to be exercised in light of what is best for both companies. [Citation omitted.] The record demonstrates that Signal has not met this obligation.

[II.C] The concept of fairness has two basic aspects: fair dealing and fair price. The former embraces questions of when the transaction was timed, how it was initiated, structured, negotiated, disclosed to the directors, and how the approvals of the directors and the stockholders were obtained. The latter aspect of fairness relates to the economic and financial considerations of the proposed merger, including all relevant factors: assets, market value, earnings, future prospects, and any other elements that affect the intrinsic or inherent value of a company's stock. [Citations omitted.] However, the test for fairness is not a bifurcated one as between fair dealing and price. All aspects of the issue must be examined as a whole since the question is one of entire fairness. However, in a non-fraudulent transaction we recognize that price may be the preponderant

---

*   [Footnote by court]: Although perfection is not possible, or expected, the result here could have been entirely different if UOP had appointed an independent negotiating committee of its outside directors to deal with Signal at arm's length. [Citation omitted.] Since fairness in this context can be equated to conduct by a theoretical, wholly independent, board of directors acting upon the matter before them, it is unfortunate that this course apparently was neither considered nor pursued. [Citation omitted.] Particularly in a parent-subsidiary context, a showing that the action taken was as though each of the contending parties had in fact exerted its bargaining power against the other at arm's length is strong evidence that the transaction meets the test of fairness. [Citation omitted].

consideration outweighing other features of the merger. Here, we address the two basic aspects of fairness separately because we find reversible error as to both.

[II.D]   Part of fair dealing is the obvious duty of candor required by [a prior case]. Moreover, one possessing superior knowledge may not mislead any stockholder by use of corporate information to which the latter is not privy. [Citation omitted.] Delaware has long imposed this duty even upon persons who are not corporate officers or directors, but who nonetheless are privy to matters of interest or significance to their company. [Citation omitted.] With the well-established Delaware law on the subject, and the Court of Chancery's findings of fact here, it is inevitable that the obvious conflicts posed by Arledge and Chitiea's preparation of their "feasibility study", derived from UOP information, for the sole use and benefit of Signal, cannot pass muster.

The Arledge-Chitiea report is but one aspect of the element of fair dealing. How did this merger evolve? It is clear that it was entirely initiated by Signal. The serious time constraints under which the principals acted were all set by Signal. It had not found a suitable outlet for its excess cash and considered UOP a desirable investment, particularly since it was now in a position to acquire the whole company for itself. For whatever reasons, and they were only Signal's, the entire transaction was presented to and approved by UOP's board within four business days. Standing alone, this is not necessarily indicative of any lack of fairness by a majority shareholder. It was what occurred, or more properly, what did not occur, during this brief period that makes the time constraints imposed by Signal relevant to the issue of fairness.

The structure of the transaction, again, was Signal's doing. So far as negotiations were concerned, it is clear that they were modest at best. Crawford, Signal's man at UOP, never really talked price with Signal, except to accede to its management's statements on the subject, and to convey to Signal the UOP outside directors' view that as between the $20-$21 range under consideration, it would have to be $21. The latter is not a surprising outcome, but hardly arm's length negotiations. Only the protection of benefits for UOP's key employees and the issue of Lehman Brothers' fee approached any concept of bargaining.

As we have noted, the matter of disclosure to the UOP directors was wholly flawed by the conflicts of interest raised by the Arledge-Chitiea report. All of those conflicts were resolved by Signal in its own favor without divulging any aspect of them to UOP.

This cannot but undermine a conclusion that this merger meets any reasonable test of fairness. The outside UOP directors lacked one material piece of information generated by two of their colleagues, but shared only with Signal. True, the UOP board had the Lehman Brothers' fairness opinion, but that firm has been blamed by the plaintiff for the hurried task it performed, when more properly the responsibility for this lies with Signal. There was no disclosure of the circumstances surrounding the rather cursory preparation of the Lehman Brothers' fairness opinion. Instead, the impression was given UOP's minority that a careful study had been made, when in fact speed was the hallmark *** Yet, none of this was disclosed to UOP's minority.

Finally, the minority stockholders were denied the critical information that Signal considered a price of $24 to be a good investment. Since this would have meant over $17,000,000 more to the minority, we cannot conclude that the shareholder vote was an informed one. Under the circumstances, an approval by a majority of the minority was meaningless. [Citation omitted.]

Given these particulars and the Delaware law on the subject, the record does not establish that this transaction satisfies any reasonable concept of fair dealing, and the Chancellor's findings in that regard must be reversed.

[II.E.]   Turning to the matter of price, plaintiff also challenges its fairness. His evidence was that on the date the merger was approved the stock was worth at least $26 per share. In support, he offered the testimony of a chartered investment analyst who used two basic approaches to valuation: a comparative analysis of the premium paid over market in ten other tender offer-merger combinations, and a discounted cash flow analysis.

In this breach of fiduciary duty case, the Chancellor perceived that the approach to valuation was the same as that in an appraisal proceeding. Consistent with precedent, he rejected plaintiff's method of proof and accepted defendants' evidence of value as being in accord with practice under prior case law. This means that the so-called "Delaware block" or weighted average method was employed wherein the elements of value, i.e., assets, market price, earnings, etc., were assigned a particular weight and the resulting amounts added to determine the value per share. This procedure has been in use for decades. [Citation omitted.]   However, to the extent it excludes other generally accepted techniques used in the financial community and the courts, it is now clearly outmoded. It is time we recognize this in appraisal and other stock valuation proceedings and bring our law current on the subject.

[Here, the court determined that "a more liberal approach must include proof of value by any techniques or methods which are generally considered acceptable in the financial community and otherwise admissible in court" and that "all relevant factors" should be considered in determining fair price.]

***

While a plaintiff's monetary remedy ordinarily should be confined to the more liberalized appraisal proceeding herein established, we do not intend any limitation on the historic powers of the Chancellor to grant such other relief as the facts of a particular case may dictate. The appraisal remedy we approve may not be adequate in certain cases, particularly where fraud, misrepresentation, self-dealing, deliberate waste of corporate assets, or gross and palpable overreaching are involved. [Citation omitted.] Under such circumstances, the Chancellor's powers are complete to fashion any form of equitable and monetary relief as may be appropriate, including rescissory damages. Since it is apparent that this long completed transaction is too involved to undo, and in view of the Chancellor's discretion, the award, if any, should be in the form of monetary damages based upon entire fairness standards, i.e., fair dealing and fair price.

Obviously, there are other litigants, like the plaintiff, who abjured an appraisal and whose rights to challenge the element of fair value must be preserved. Accordingly, the quasi-appraisal remedy we grant the plaintiff here will apply only to: (1) this case; (2) any case now pending on appeal to this Court; (3) any case now pending in the Court of Chancery which has not yet been appealed but which may be eligible for direct appeal to this Court; (4) any case challenging a cash-out merger, the effective date of which is on or before February 1, 1983; and (5) any proposed merger to be presented at a shareholders' meeting, the notification of which is mailed to the stockholders on or before February 23, 1983. Thereafter, the provisions of [Section 262 of the Delaware General Corporation Law], as herein construed, respecting the scope of an appraisal and the means for perfecting the same, shall govern the financial remedy available to minority shareholders in a cash-out merger.

***

[III.] Finally, we address the matter of business purpose. The defendants contend that the purpose of this merger was not a proper subject of inquiry by the trial court. The plaintiff says that no valid purpose existed—the entire transaction was a mere subterfuge designed to eliminate the minority. ***

***

In view of the fairness test which has long been applicable to parent-subsidiary mergers, [citation omitted], the expanded appraisal remedy now available to shareholders, and the broad discretion of the Chancellor to fashion such relief as the facts of a given case may dictate, we do not believe that any additional meaningful protection is afforded minority shareholders by the business purpose requirement ***. Accordingly, such requirement shall no longer be of any force or effect.

As the *Weinberger* court observed in a footnote, the result in the case "could have been entirely different if UOP had appointed an independent negotiating committee of its outside directors to deal with Signal at arm's length." Later cases have elaborated on this idea. For example, in *Kahn v. Lynch Communication Systems, Inc.* (a portion of which appears earlier in this chapter), the court held that if a merger with a controlling shareholder is approved by a committee of independent directors, the burden shifts to a shareholder challenging the merger to show that it was not entirely fair. However, courts will scrutinize the committee members and their actions to determine if they truly are independent from the controlling shareholder and if they engaged in arm's length negotiations. *See Kahn v. Tremont Corp.*, 694 A.2d 422 (Del. 1997).[*] There are also many cases that elaborate on the meaning of "fair price," but we will not consider those cases here.

Although *Weinberger* dispensed with this requirement, other courts continue to require a "business purpose" for squeeze-out mergers. *See, e.g., Coggins v. New England Patriots Football Club, Inc.*, 492 N.E.2d 1112 (Mass. 1986). Nonetheless, it is probably not a difficult task for lawyers to point to a business purpose for a merger. In fact, it would be a mistake for you to come away from reading this section with the impression that all squeeze-out mergers are somehow shady or abusive. For example, eliminating minority shareholders could allow a corporation to go private and save the many expenses associated with being a public company.

Another issue that may arise concerns *dissenters' rights*, also known as *appraisal rights*. As you will learn in Chapter 12, many major corporate transactions, including most mergers, give shareholders the right to "dissent" from the transaction and go to court to determine the "fair value" of their shares. Statutes that give shareholders dissenters' rights often provide that these rights are the shareholders' sole remedy, unless the transaction involves fraud or a few other limited exceptions apply. In fact, *Weinberger* and later cases held that dissenters' rights are the exclusive remedy if the plaintiffs challenge the merger on the basis of price alone. We will defer further discussion of this issue until Chapter 12.

Finally, note that if a merger is approved by a majority of the shares, it would force *all* of the shareholders—even those who voted against the merger—to accept cash or the other merger consideration for their shares. By contrast, if the

---

[*]   For example, the *Lynch Communications* court stated that the burden would shift to the plaintiff only if the committee of independent directors had "real bargaining power that it can exercise with the majority shareholder on an [arm's] length basis" and the controlling shareholder did not "dictate the terms of the merger." 638 A.2d at 1117 (citation omitted).

controlling shareholder makes a tender offer (an offer to buy shares) that each minority shareholder is free to accept or reject as she sees fit (in other words, a noncoercive tender offer), then the entire fairness standard does not apply. *See Solomon v. Pathe Communications Corp.*, 672 A.2d 35 (Del. 1996). The court in *In re Pure Resources, Inc. Shareholders Litigation*, 808 A.2d 421 (Del. Ch. 2002), set forth factors to consider in deciding whether a tender offer is noncoercive. You will learn more about tender offers in Chapter 12.

Problems

Problem 11-4: Parent Corp. owns 80% of the outstanding shares of Subsidiary Corp. but would like to acquire the remaining 20% of the shares. *How should Parent Corp. go about doing so? What standard of review will apply to this transaction? Does your answer change if the merger is approved by a majority of the minority shareholders? If so, why didn't that occur in the* Weinberger *case?*

§ 11.04   A NOTE ON "SALES OF CONTROL"

Assume that a corporation is worth $100,000 and that there are two shareholders. Shareholder A owns 51 shares and Shareholder B owns 49 shares. How much is each shareholder's shares worth? You might be tempted to think that each share is worth $1,000 (the $100,000 overall value of the company divided by the 1,000 outstanding shares). However, because Shareholder A has *control* over the company and Shareholder B does not, a third party would probably be willing to pay a higher price for Shareholder A's shares than Shareholder B's shares. (We're assuming that everyone agrees that the entire corporation is worth $100,000.)

If Shareholder A sells her shares to a third party and receives such a *control premium*, must she share that amount with Shareholder B? Generally speaking, the answer is no—a controlling shareholder may freely sell any or all of her shares to a third party on whatever terms she sees fit, with no liability to the other shareholders. However, there is a long (and confusing) line of cases that has created several exceptions to this general rule. For example, if the controlling shareholder is aware of facts that should alert her to the possibility that the buyer will "loot" the company (and thereby harm the minority shareholders), courts have imposed liability. *See DeBaun v. First Western Bank & Trust Co.*, 120 Cal. Rptr. 354 (Cal. Ct. App. 1975); *Gerdes v. Reynolds*, 28 N.Y.S.2d 622 (N.Y. Sup. Ct. 1941). However, the controlling shareholder does not have an obligation to investigate the buyer's plans beforehand.

Another exception concerns situations where it could be shown that the controlling shareholder is also transferring an opportunity or asset that belongs to the *corporation*, rather than merely selling the controlling shareholder's shares. The leading case on this issue, which involved unique facts, is *Perlman v. Feldman*, 219 F.2d 173 (2d Cir. 1955). Finally, there is a line of cases that hold that "sales of office," that is, situations where the selling shareholder also agrees to cause the directors that she had elected to the board to resign, are impermissible. In other words, courts will not enforce contracts whereby directors agree to resign and be replaced by designated other persons. However, if the controlling shareholder truly was selling enough shares to constitute "control" to the buyer, then this is probably permissible. After all, if the buyer now has control over the corporation, she could easily replace the current directors with her own choices, as you learned in Chapter 5.

PRACTICE QUESTIONS

Multiple Choice Question 11-1: Gizmo Corp., a Delaware corporation, is in the consumer electronics business. Gizmo Corp. owns 90% of the stock of Omega Corp., a Delaware corporation which is also in the consumer electronics business. The remaining 10% of the stock of Omega Corp. is held by approximately 1,000 shareholders. The board of directors of Omega Corp. consists of ten persons, all of whom are executives of Gizmo Corp. Last year, Omega Corp. was approached by the inventor of a new hand-held electronic device which combines the features of cell phones, computers, and global positioning systems in a revolutionary way. This inventor was interested in licensing this technology to Omega Corp. The board of directors of Omega Corp. told the inventor that Omega Corp. was not interested in this opportunity, but that he should approach Gizmo Corp. Eventually, Gizmo Corp. and the inventor entered into a licensing agreement that earned millions of dollars for each party. Several shareholders of Omega Corp. have properly brought a derivative lawsuit against Gizmo Corp. for breach of fiduciary duties. *What will likely happen in this case?*

A.   The court will apply the business judgment rule.

B.   The court will apply the intrinsic fairness test. Gizmo Corp. will have the burden of proof.

C.   The court will apply the entire fairness test. The plaintiffs will have the burden of proving that both fair dealing and fair price were lacking.

D.   The court will apply the entire fairness test. The plaintiffs will have the burden of proving either fair dealing or fair price were lacking.

E.   The court will dismiss the case because Gizmo Corp. owes no fiduciary duties.

Multiple Choice Question 11-2: Same facts as the previous question. In addition, Omega Corp. called a special meeting of shareholders to vote on whether to *reject* the opportunity to license the invention. At the meeting, Gizmo Corp. made full disclosure of all material facts about the invention and its desire to license the invention from the inventor. Afterwards, a majority of the shares of Omega Corp. stock owned by persons other than Gizmo Corp. were voted in favor of rejecting the opportunity. Nonetheless, several shareholders of Omega Corp. have properly brought a derivative lawsuit against Gizmo Corp. for breach of fiduciary duties. *What will likely happen in this case?*

A.   The court will apply the business judgment rule.
B.   The court will apply the intrinsic fairness test. Gizmo Corp. will have the burden of proof.
C.   The court will apply the entire fairness test. The plaintiffs will have the burden of proving that both fair dealing and fair price were lacking.
D.   The court will apply the entire fairness test. The plaintiffs will have the burden of proving either fair dealing or fair price were lacking.
E.   The court will dismiss the case because a majority of the shares held by persons other than Gizmo Corp. were voted in favor of rejecting the opportunity.

Multiple Choice Question 11-3: Zoo Corp., a Delaware corporation, has two classes of stock: Class A common stock and Class B common stock. Each share is entitled to one vote on all matters on which shareholders vote; however, the holders of Class A common stock are collectively entitled to elect nine members of the board and the holders of Class B common stock are collectively entitled to elect one member of the board. Monkey Corp. owns all of the Class A common stock. The shares of Class B common stock are owned by approximately 100 persons. Last month, the board of directors of Zoo Corp. caused the corporation to pay dividends on the Class A common stock but did not declare dividends on the Class B common stock. The payment of the dividends complied with all applicable statutes. The holders of Class B common stock have sued Monkey Corp. for breach of fiduciary duties. *What will likely happen in this case?*

A.   The court will apply the business judgment rule.
B.   The court will apply the intrinsic fairness test. Monkey Corp. will have the burden of proof.
C.   The court will apply the entire fairness test. The plaintiffs will have the burden of proving that both fair dealing and fair price were lacking.
D.   The court will apply the entire fairness test. The plaintiffs will have the burden of proving either fair dealing or fair price were lacking.
E.   The court will dismiss the case because Monkey Corp. owes no fiduciary duties.

Multiple Choice Question 11-4: Mr. Fizz founded Soda Pop Corp. ("SPC"), a Delaware corporation, thirty-three years ago. However, for the past twenty years SPC has been a publicly traded corporation. Currently, there are 10 million shares of SPC common stock outstanding. Mr. Fizz owns 370,000 shares and members of his immediate family own an additional 230,000 shares. The other 9.4 million shares are held by approximately 1,200 persons, none of whom owns more than 40,000 shares. Mr. Fizz retired for the board of directors and as an employee of SPC five years ago. Currently, he lives in Bermuda and has very little contact with SPC's board, other than to periodically send the directors angry letters and e-mails complaining about SPC's business performance and the price of its stock. Mr. Fizz recently appeared on a popular business news program and heavily criticized SPC's management. SPC currently has a great deal of extra cash on hand and the board is considering using it to repurchase Mr. Fizz's shares so that he will "shut up and go away." *If SPC repurchases Mr. Fizz's shares and other SPC shareholders sue Mr. Fizz claiming a breach of fiduciary duties, what will likely happen in this case?*

A.   The court will apply the business judgment rule.

B.   The court will apply the intrinsic fairness test. Mr. Fizz will have the burden of proof.

C.   The court will apply the entire fairness test. The plaintiffs will have the burden of proving that both fair dealing and fair price were lacking.

D.   The court will apply the entire fairness test. The plaintiffs will have the burden of proving either fair dealing or fair price were lacking.

E.   The court will dismiss the case because Mr. Fizz owes no fiduciary duties.

CHAPTER 12
MAJOR CORPORATE TRANSACTIONS

A corporation could last forever—at least theoretically. Of course, in reality that is not very likely. Instead, at some point in its "life," a corporation will probably be involved in a major transaction. For example, it could be acquired in a merger or it could acquire another corporation in a merger. Alternatively, it might sell all or substantially all of its assets to another corporation and then dissolve. You will learn about several major corporate transactions (asset sales, dissolutions, mergers, and tender offers) in this chapter, as well as many related issues. While these transactions may not happen very often with respect to a particular corporation, if you are the corporation's lawyer you need to understand the many legal issues involved in these transactions.

§ 12.01   AMENDMENTS TO ARTICLES AND BYLAWS

Objectives: You should be able to explain to a corporate client that wishes to amend its articles of incorporation and/or bylaws whose approval is necessary and what procedures must be followed to do so. Given a fact pattern, you should also be able to determine whether a corporation's articles and/or bylaws have been successfully amended.

We begin this chapter on major corporate transactions with something that isn't a "transaction" at all: amendments to a corporation's articles of incorporation or bylaws. As you learned in Chapter 5, a corporation's articles and bylaws are important sources of rules governing the corporation. We also saw that these documents are not set in stone—they can be amended. But we did not stop in Chapter 5 to ask *how* to amend a corporation's articles or its bylaws.

MBCA §§ 10.01 through 10.09 provide the answers to this question with respect to articles of incorporation. Of those, sections 10.03 and 10.04 are the most important for our purposes.[*] Section 10.03 concerns the general process and approvals that are required to amend articles of incorporation. Section 10.04

---

[*]   This is not to say that the other sections are unimportant. For example, MBCA § 10.01 generally provides that the articles *can* be amended; shareholders do not have a "vested property right" that would prevent the articles from being amended. Also noteworthy is MBCA § 10.05, which sets forth a list of relatively minor amendments that the board of directors can undertake without needing shareholder approval. And MBCA § 10.06 requires the corporation to file a copy of the amendment with its state of incorporation to alert the state to the fact that the articles have been amended.

concerns situations in which different "voting groups" would need to approve articles amendments separately. Read those sections—and refresh your memory of MBCA §§ 7.25(c) and 7.27—before tackling the following problems.

Problems

Problem 12-1:   Articles Corp. has 100,000 shares of common stock outstanding. Articles Corp. wishes to amend its articles of incorporation to provide that directors will be elected pursuant to cumulative voting. After passing a resolution approving such an amendment, Articles Corp.'s board of directors gives proper notice of a shareholders meeting to approve the amendment. At the meeting, the holders of 74,000 shares are present in person or by proxy. Of those shares, 49,000 shares are voted in favor of the amendment, 20,000 shares are voted against it, and 5,000 shares abstain. *Was the amendment properly approved?*

Problem 12-2: Same facts as Problem 12-1. *Would your answer change if Articles Corp. were incorporated in Delaware rather than the MBCA?*[*]

Problem 12-3:   Same facts as Problem 12-3, except that the proposed amendment would add a provision to the articles of incorporation that would require that all mergers involving Articles Corp. must be approved by 60% of the outstanding shares. *Was the amendment properly approved?*

Problem 12-4:   Amendment Corp. has a four-person board of directors and also has two classes of stock: there are 1,000 shares of Class A common stock outstanding and 1,000 shares of Class B common stock outstanding. The two classes of stock are identical in all respects except that the holders of Class A common stock are entitled to elect two directors and the holders of Class B common stock are entitled to elect the other two directors. At a properly held shareholders meeting, 1,000 shares of Class A common stock were voted in favor of an articles amendment that would change

---

[*]   Section 242 of the Delaware General Corporation Law provides in part than an amendment to a corporation's certificate of incorporate requires that:

> a vote of the stockholders entitled to vote thereon shall be taken for and against the proposed amendment. If a majority of the outstanding stock entitled to vote thereon *** has been voted in favor of the amendment, a certificate setting forth the amendment and certifying that such amendment has been duly adopted in accordance with this section shall be *** filed ***.

the name of the corporation to "Change Corp." and 600 shares of Class B common stock were voted *against* the amendment. *Was the amendment properly approved?*

Problem 12-5: Same facts as Problem 12-4, except that the amendment would change the rights of Class B common stock so that its holders would only be entitled to elect one director rather than two directors. *Was the amendment properly approved?*

Problem 12-6: Suppose a shareholder suggests an articles amendment to the board but the board thinks it is a bad idea. *Is there any way for the shareholder to force the board to submit the amendment to a shareholder vote?*

Problem 12-7: *For comparison purposes, what level of partner approval is necessary to approve a partnership agreement?* (Recall Chapter 3.)

With respect to amendments to *bylaws*, MBCA § 10.20 is the main section. (We briefly encountered MBCA § 10.22 in Chapter 10 but will ignore it here. MBCA § 10.21 concerns only bylaw provisions that relate to quorum or voting requirements for director meetings.) MBCA § 10.20(a) provides that the shareholders may amend the bylaws. Thus, bylaws could not deny shareholders the ability to amend them. Presumably, the required shareholder vote for a bylaw amendment would be the same as for an articles amendment.

In addition, subsection (b) provides that the board may amend the bylaws—unless that power is reserved exclusively to the shareholders, either with respect to the bylaws generally or a particular section of the bylaws. But what would happen if the board and the shareholders disagree on a bylaws amendment? Consider the following problem, which is similar to Problem 12-6 above except that it concerns bylaw amendments rather than articles amendments.

Problem

Problem 12-8: Suppose a shareholder suggests a bylaws amendment to the board but the board thinks it is a bad idea. *Is there any way for the shareholder to force the board to submit the amendment to a shareholder vote? If so, what would stop the board from simply changing the bylaw back to the way it was before the shareholders amended it?*

§ 12.02   OVERVIEW OF BUSINESS ACQUISITIONS

The rest of this chapter will concern the methods by which one company (called the *Acquirer* or *Acquiring* corporation) can acquire another company (called the *Target*). Before we consider these methods, it may be helpful to consider *why* the Acquirer would want to acquire the Target. Simply put, it's economics. The capitalistic system that we live in is built on growth. Businesses want to grow, particularly publicly traded companies, who often have a significant faction of impatient shareholders who want to see the company grow as quickly as possible so that price of its stock will rise. Growth could obviously be "organic" in the sense that the company could grow by making better products or performing better services and continually increasing the amount of them that it sells. On the other hand, a company could grow by acquiring another company. Doing so may be a quick way to expand into a new line of business or a new geographical area or even to eliminate a current competitor (although antitrust laws will regulate such motives).

From the Target's perspective, everything's for sale if the price is right, as the saying goes. If the Target is a closely held corporation, the owners of it may be interested in selling it because they are nearing retirement or are simply bored with the business and want to do something different. If the Target is publicly traded, the shareholders may be interested in selling the company if the price that is offered is high enough. In any event, when the board of directors of a potential Target company is presented with a proposal to be acquired, it has a fiduciary duty to consider the offer in good faith (as you will see in more detail below).

One major issue that will need to be negotiated by the Acquirer and the Target is the amount of consideration that the Acquirer will pay to acquire the Target. Obviously, the board of directors of the Acquirer will try to negotiate as low a price as possible, while the board of directors of the Target will seek to get a high price. Many factors will bear on what the price will be, including the characteristics of the Target, its future business prospects, and current economic and market conditions. (Many of those issues are more appropriate for business school than for law school, but you should refresh your memory of valuation issues by re-reading Sections 5.04(G) and (H) of Chapter 5.)

Another major issue that will need to be decided is what *form* the consideration will take. At first, this may seem surprising, because in your personal experience you are accustomed to paying cash for things (or using credit, which obviously will require you to pay cash in the future). However, the Acquirer will likely have a wider range of options. Obviously, the Acquirer may pay cash. But the Acquirer may also be able to use its own authorized-but-unissued stock as consideration to acquire Target, particularly if the Acquirer is publicly traded and thus has a "liquid" market for its stock (which means that the

Target shareholders will be able to easily resell any Acquirer stock that they receive in the transaction). If the Target shareholders end up receiving cash in the transaction then they will have no continuing ownership interest in either Target or Acquirer. On the other hand, if they end up receiving Acquirer stock (or a combination of cash and Acquirer stock), they will have an ownership interest in the Acquirer.

There are a great many other issues that will arise during negotiations for an acquisition and you will learn more about them if you take a course on mergers and acquisitions. However, let's now discuss *how* an acquisition may occur. Generally speaking (and excluding "proxy contests," which are briefly discussed in Section 12.07 below), there are three types of ways for the Acquirer to "buy" the Target.

Mergers. First, the Target could ***merge*** into the Acquirer (or maybe a subsidiary of the Acquirer). In a merger all of the assets and liabilities of the Target become assets and liabilities of the Acquirer by operation of law (that is, automatically) and the Target ceases to exist. Because the Target no longer exists following a merger, no one will continue to own stock in the Target. Thus, the Target's shareholders (other than those who exercise dissenters' rights as explained in Section 12.06 below) will end up with something very different than Target stock following the merger, such as cash or Acquirer stock.[*]

A diagram of a simple merger would look like this:

Asset Purchases. Second, the Acquirer could buy all or substantially all of the Target's assets and then continue running the same business that the Target was running. After all, what *is* a corporation other than a collection of assets? Buy those assets, which would include both tangible and intangible assets, and you've bought "the company."

---

[*]   A related type of transaction is called a ***consolidation***. Unlike a merger, in which the Acquirer will survive and the Target will disappear, in a consolidation two (or more) companies will merge into a *new* company. Further, another type of transaction is a ***share exchange***, in which the shareholders of the Target are all required to sell (for cash or other consideration) their shares to the Acquirer if the transaction is approved. Because they are relatively rare, we will not discuss consolidations or share exchanges further in this textbook.

A diagram of an asset purchase would thus look like this:

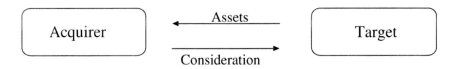

Note than in an asset purchase, the Target remains in existence, and the consideration paid by the Acquirer goes to the Target itself rather than to the Target's shareholders. However, if the Target has sold all or substantially all of its assets, oftentimes it will dissolve shortly afterwards (although it is not required to do so). Thus, you will learn about dissolutions in Section 12.04 below.

One disadvantage of an asset purchase as compared to a merger is that an asset purchase will require a great deal more work in terms of transferring assets, which may need to occur one by one. For example, if the seller owned several pieces of real estate, a deed would be required for each transfer. (By contrast, in a merger the transfer of the Target's assets occurs by operation of law.) On the other hand, one significant advantage of an asset purchase is that—usually—the buyer does not assume the seller's liabilities.

Stock Purchases. The third main way to "buy" a company is to buy all of its outstanding stock. If there is only one or a small number of persons who own this stock, then doing so is not very difficult logistically—simply approach those shareholders, negotiate a price and other terms of the transaction, and then buy the stock from them. At that point, you own the company. On the other hand, if there are hundreds or thousands of shareholders, then other methods may be necessary such as a tender offer.

In any event, a diagram of a stock purchase would thus look like this:

Note that it in a stock purchase, the Target also remains in existence; it simply becomes a subsidiary of the Acquirer (if the Acquirer is another corporation). However, oftentimes the Acquirer will later merge the Target into the Acquirer (or a different subsidiary of the Acquirer). This will be particularly likely if the stock purchase did not result in the Acquirer owning 100% of the outstanding shares of the Target; a merger would be necessary to "eliminate" the other Target shareholders. In this second-step merger, the remaining Target shareholders would likely receive the same consideration that the Acquirer paid in the initial stock purchase.

In the following sections, you will learn about these various methods of buying a business, as well as many other issues. Because asset purchases (or, if you represent the seller, asset *sales*) are probably the easiest of these methods to understand, we will start there.

§ 12.03   ASSET SALES

Objectives: You should be able to explain to a client that wishes to purchase a substantial amount of the assets of a corporation: (1) whether the board of directors and/or the shareholders of the selling corporation must approve the sale and (2) whether your client (the buyer) may, as a result of the transaction, be subject to the debts and liabilities of the selling corporation.

Subsidiary Objectives: You should also be able to:

●   *Board and Shareholder Approval. Given a fact pattern that specifies the assets that a corporation wishes to sell, determine whether the approval of the corporation's board of directors and/or shareholders is necessary before the sale may take place. In addition, given a fact pattern where a corporation's shareholders are required to approve an asset sale, you should be able to determine whether the corporation's shareholders have properly approved the sale.*

●   *Successor Liability. Describe four ways in which a buyer in an asset sale may be found to have assumed the debts and obligations of the selling corporation. Given a fact pattern, you should be able to determine whether a court is likely to find that the buyer has assumed the seller's liabilities, and advise a client company that is considering purchasing the assets of a corporation how to avoid successor liability.*

A.   IS SHAREHOLDER APPROVAL NEEDED TO SELL ASSETS?

If Widget Corp. manufactures widgets, it will probably want to sell those widgets. After all, that it is how it makes money. Technically, every time that Widget Corp. sells a widget that it has manufactured, it is selling one of its assets. Should shareholder approval be required for such sales? The answer to that question is so clear that it hardly bears stating: obviously not. Not only are such sales in the ordinary course of Widget Corp.'s business, but most of them are probably pretty small in terms of dollar value. More-over, if shareholder approval were required to sell widgets, then the shareholders of Widget Corp. would be having meetings twenty-four hours a day, seven days a week, and 365 days a year. On the other hand, some asset sales will be so "big" and/or "unusual" that perhaps shareholder approval should be required. The question becomes: where do we draw the line between asset sales that can be approved by the board without shareholder approval and those asset sales that can only be conducted following shareholder approval?

> ### *The Process of Shareholder Approval*
> In Chapter 5, you learned a lot about the mechanics of shareholder action, such as what notice must be given to hold a shareholders meeting. In addition, in Chapter 10, you learned about the federal proxy rules that apply to publicly traded corporations. Keep in mind as you read these materials that soliciting shareholder approval of a transaction is often difficult and expensive, especially for publicly traded corporations. In addition, there is always the chance that the shareholders might not approve the transaction! Thus, corporations often hope to avoid having to seek shareholder approval, if possible.

MBCA §§ 12.01 and 12.02 address this question. Section 12.01 starts by listing four types of asset sales that do not require prior shareholder approval, including in subsection (1) sales, leases, or other dispositions "of any or all of the corporation's assets [that are] in the usual and regular course of [the corporation's] business." If a particular asset sale or disposition does not fall within one of the four categories listed in Section 12.01, then one would need to examine Section 12.02. Subsection (a) of Section 12.02 informs us that shareholder approval is necessary if—*after* the asset sale—the corporation would not have a "significant continuing business activity." But in reading Section 12.02, ask yourself: does it *define* what a "significant continuing business activity" is? Read MBCA §§ 12.01 and 12.02 carefully and then consider the following problems:

Problems

Problem 12-9: Widget Corp. is in the business of selling widgets. Last year, its revenues were $10 million. Buyer Corp. wants to buy $5 million worth of widgets from Widget Corp., to be delivered one month from now. *Is the approval of Widget Corp.'s shareholders necessary for this sale?*

Problem 12-10: Movie Theatres Corp. ("MTC") owns eighty movie theatres, twenty of which are in each of four states: Michigan, Ohio, Indiana, and Wisconsin. Each theatre owned by MTC is approximately equal to every other theatre in terms of the amount of assets that it represents and the amount of revenues and pre-tax income that it generates for MTC. MTC wishes to sell, in a single transaction, all twenty of its Ohio theatres to a buyer. *Is the approval of MTC's shareholders necessary for this sale? Would your answer be different if these twenty theatres were owned by a subsidiary of MTC, rather than MTC itself?*

Problem 12-11: Same facts as Problem 12-10, except that MTC wishes to sell all forty of its Ohio and Indiana theatres. *Is the approval of MTC's shareholders necessary for this sale?*

Problem 12-12: Same facts as Problem 12-10, except that MTC wishes to sell all sixty of its Ohio, Indiana, and Wisconsin theatres. *Is the approval of MTC's shareholders necessary for this sale?*

Problem 12-13: Hotel Corp. owns two hotels: Hotel A and Hotel B. According to the best information that the company has, the market value of Hotel A is $2.5 million and the market value of Hotel B is $7.5 million. Last year, Hotel A generated revenues of $2.5 million, and Hotel B generated revenues of $7.5 million. Also last year, Hotel A generated pre-tax income of $250,000, and Hotel B generated pre-tax income of $750,000. Hotel Corp. wishes to sell Hotel B to a buyer. *Is the approval of Hotel Corp.'s shareholders necessary for this sale?*

Problem 12-14: Same facts as Problem 12-13, except that Hotel A generated revenues of $2.4 million and pre-tax income of $240,000, and Hotel B generated revenues of $7.6 million and pre-tax income of $760,000. Hotel Corp. wishes to sell Hotel B to a buyer. *Is the approval of Hotel Corp.'s shareholders necessary for this sale? What if Delaware law applied, rather than the MBCA? (See* Katz v. Bregman, *below.)*

In contrast to the precision of the MBCA, many state statutes simply provide that shareholder approval is necessary for a corporation to sell "all or substantially all" of its assets in a transaction (or a series of related transactions). Unfortunately, many of these statutes fail to define the phrase "all or substantially all." While we would probably all agree on what "all" means, "substantially all" may be unclear. Thus, courts could be called on to decide whether a particular transaction is a sale of "substantially all" of a corporation's assets, as seen in the next case.

> ### Is Approval by the _Buyer's_ Shareholders Needed?
>
> Under the MBCA, the shareholders of the buying corporation generally do not have to approve an asset purchase. However, if the buyer will issue _new shares of stock_ as consideration and the new shares would increase the number of outstanding voting shares by more than 20%, shareholder approval is necessary. See MBCA § 6.21(f).

Katz v. Bregman
Delaware Court of Chancery
431 A.2d 1274 (1981)

MARVEL, Chancellor: The complaint herein seeks the entry of an order preliminarily enjoining the proposed sale of the Canadian assets of Plant Industries, Inc. to Vulcan Industrial Packaging, Ltd., the plaintiff Hyman Katz allegedly being the owner of approximately 170,000 shares of common stock of the defendant Plant Industries, Inc., on whose behalf he has brought this action [derivatively]. ***

The complaint alleges that during the last six months of 1980 the board of directors of Plant Industries, Inc., under the guidance of the individual defendant Robert B. Bregman, the present chief executive officer of such corporation, embarked on a course of action which resulted in the disposal of several unprofitable subsidiaries of the corporate defendant located in the United States, namely Louisiana Foliage Inc., a horticultural business, Sunaid Food Products, Inc., a Florida packaging business, and Plant Industries (Texas), Inc., a business concerned with the manufacture of woven synthetic cloth. As a result of these sales Plant Industries, Inc. by the end of 1980 had disposed of a significant part of its unprofitable assets.

According to the complaint, Mr. Bregman thereupon proceeded on a course of action designed to dispose of a subsidiary of the corporate defendant known as Plant National (Quebec) Ltd., a business which constitutes Plant Industries, Inc.'s entire business operation in Canada and has allegedly constituted Plant's only income producing facility during the past four years. The professed principal purpose of such proposed sale is to raise needed cash and thus improve Plant's balance sheets. And while interest in purchasing the corporate defendant's

Canadian plant was thereafter evinced not only by Vulcan Industrial Packaging, Ltd. but also by Universal Drum Reconditioning Co., which latter corporation originally undertook to match or approximate and recently to top Vulcan's bid, a formal contract was entered into between Plant Industries, Inc. and Vulcan on April 2, 1981 for the purchase and sale of Plant National (Quebec) despite the constantly increasing bids for the same property being made by Universal. ***

In seeking injunctive relief, as prayed for, plaintiff relies on two principles, one that found in [Section 271 of the Delaware General Corporation Law] to the effect that a decision of a Delaware corporation to sell "*** all or substantially all of its property and assets ***" requires not only the approval of such corporation's board of directors but also a resolution adopted by a majority of the outstanding stockholders of the corporation entitled to vote thereon at a meeting duly called upon at least twenty days' notice.

Support for the other principle relied on by plaintiff for the relief sought, namely an alleged breach of fiduciary duty on the part of the board of directors of Plant Industries, Inc., is allegedly found in such board's studied refusal to consider a potentially higher bid for the assets in question which is being advanced by Universal [citation omitted].

Turning to the possible application of [Section 271] to the proposed sale of substantial corporate assets of National to Vulcan, it is stated in *Gimbel v. Signal Companies, Inc.*, [316 A.2d 599 (Del. Ch. 1974)], as follows:

> "If the sale is of assets quantitatively vital to the operation of the corporation and is out of the ordinary and substantially affects the existence and purpose of the corporation then it is beyond the power of the Board of Directors."

According to Plant's 1980 [Annual Report on Form 10-K], it appears that at the end of 1980, Plant's Canadian operations represented 51% of Plant's remaining assets. Defendants also concede that National represents 44.9% of Plant's sales' revenues and 52.4% of its pre-tax net operating income. Furthermore, such report by Plant discloses, in rough figures, that while National made a profit in 1978 of $2,900,000, the profit from the United States businesses in that year was only $770,000. In 1979, the Canadian business profit was $3,500,000 while the loss of the United States businesses was $344,000. Furthermore, in 1980, while the Canadian business profit was $5,300,000, the corporate loss in the United States was $4,500,000. And while these figures may be somewhat distorted by the allocation of overhead expenses and taxes, they are significant. In any event, defendants concede that "*** National accounted for 34.9% of Plant's pre-tax income in 1976, 36.9% in 1977, 42% in 1978, 51% in 1979 and 52.4% in 1980."

While in [a prior case] the question of whether or not there had been a proposed sale of substantially all corporate assets was tested by provisions of an indenture agreement covering subordinated debentures, the result was the same as if the provisions of [Section 271] had been applicable, the trial Court stating:

> "While no pertinent Pennsylvania case is cited, the critical factor in determining the character of a sale of assets is generally considered not the amount of property sold but whether the sale is in fact an unusual transaction or one made in the regular course of business of the seller ***".

***

In the case at bar, I am first of all satisfied that historically the principal business of Plant Industries, Inc. has not been to buy and sell industrial facilities but rather to manufacture steel drums for use in bulk shipping as well as for the storage of petroleum products, chemicals, food, paint, adhesives and cleaning agents, a business which has been profitably performed by National of Quebec. Furthermore, the proposal, after the sale of National, to embark on the manufacture of plastic drums represents a radical departure from Plant's historically successful line of business, namely steel drums. I therefore conclude that the proposed sale of Plant's Canadian operations, which constitute over 51% of Plant's total assets and in which are generated approximately 45% of Plant's 1980 net sales, would, if consummated, constitute a sale of substantially all of Plant's assets. By way of contrast, the proposed sale of Signal Oil in *Gimbel v. Signal Companies, Inc., supra*, represented only about 26% of the total assets of Signal Companies, Inc. And while Signal Oil represented 41% of Signal Companies, Inc. total net worth, it generated only about 15% of Signal Companies, Inc. revenue and earnings.

I conclude that because the proposed sale of Plant National (Quebec) Ltd. would, if consummated, constitute a sale of substantially all of the assets of Plant Industries, Inc., as presently constituted, that an injunction should issue preventing the consummation of such sale at least until it has been approved by a majority of the outstanding stockholders of Plant Industries, Inc., entitled to vote at a meeting duly called on at least twenty days' notice. [Citation omitted.]

In light of this conclusion it will be unnecessary to consider whether or not the sale here under attack, as proposed to be made, is for such an inadequate consideration, viewed in light of the competing bid of Universal, as to constitute a breach of [fiduciary duties] on the part of the directors of Plant Industries, Inc.. [Citation omitted.]

Being persuaded for the reasons stated that plaintiff has demonstrated a reasonable probability of ultimate success on final hearing in the absence of stockholder approval of the proposed sale of the corporate assets here in issue to Vulcan, a preliminary injunction against the consummation of such transaction, at least until stockholder approval is obtained, will be granted.

***

For a more recent treatment of this issue by Delaware courts, see *Hollinger, Inc. v. Hollinger International, Inc.*, 858 A.2d 342 (Del. 2004).

B.   SUCCESSOR LIABILITY

As noted above, and as you will see in much more detail when you study mergers in Section 12.05 below, the Acquiring (or surviving) corporation in a merger assumes not only all of the Target corporation's assets but also all of the Target corporation's liabilities. By contrast, in an asset transaction, the general rule is that the buyer is only buying assets; the buyer does not assume any of the seller's liabilities unless it expressly agrees to do so. Setting aside some possible tax reasons (which we will not consider in this textbook) or other reasons to favor a merger over an asset purchase, it should immediately be clear why an Acquirer would prefer to acquire a Target company by buying its assets. (Of course, the selling corporation would remain liable for its own liabilities following an asset sale; however, the issue of successor liability may arise if the seller does not actually pay these liabilities.)

On the other hand, this is a distinction between mergers and asset transactions that could be abused by buyers. If a given transaction, while technically an asset transaction, has the same effects as a merger, this has led some courts to treat the transaction as if it actually had been a merger and make the buyer liable for the seller's unpaid liabilities—particularly liabilities that were unknown at the time of the transaction—just as it would have been in a merger. This concept of "successor liability," while not followed by all courts, is illustrated in the following case.

Cargo Partner AG v. Albatrans, Inc.
United States Court of Appeals, Second Circuit
352 F.3d 41 (2003)

SACK, Circuit Judge. The Plaintiff-appellant Cargo Partner AG appeals from a decision *** dismissing Cargo Partner's claims against the defendant-appellee Albatrans, Inc. Cargo Partner brought this diversity action against the defendant-appellee Chase, Leavitt (Customhouse Brokers) Inc. ("Chase-Leavitt") seeking to recover on a trade debt owed by Chase-Leavitt to Cargo Partner. Cargo Partner also brought suit against Albatrans, alleging by purchasing all of Chase-Leavitt's assets, Albatrans became liable for Chase-Leavitt's debts, including its debt to Cargo Partner. ***

BACKGROUND

Cargo Partner, Albatrans, and Chase-Leavitt are in the shipping business. Between 1999 and 2001, Chase-Leavitt incurred a debt to Cargo Partner of approximately $240,000 for services rendered by Cargo Partner to Chase-Leavitt. On February 7, 2001, Albatrans entered into an agreement with Chase-Leavitt and its sole shareholder, Alison Leavitt, to purchase all of Chase-Leavitt's assets.

In connection with the acquisition, Chase-Leavitt, which holds a federal customs brokerage license allowing it to perform customs services for clients, agreed to provide its customs brokerage services exclusively to Albatrans until Albatrans (or one of its subsidiaries) acquired such a license. During this interim period, apparently to allow Albatrans to use Chase-Leavitt's license while Albatrans was seeking one of its own, Chase-Leavitt was to operate as a distinct "profit center" within Albatrans, using the assets it sold to Albatrans for that purpose. Chase-Leavitt was required to "accept the advice and direction" of managers hired by Albatrans in this pursuit. After Albatrans acquired a customs brokerage license, it would have the option of causing Chase-Leavitt to discontinue operations, or "conduct[ing Chase-Leavitt's b]usiness in its own or under a subsidiary's name." [Citations omitted throughout this paragraph.]

The acquisition agreement also required [Ms.] Leavitt to continue in Chase-Leavitt's employ until Albatrans obtained the license and gave Albatrans the option of continuing her employment for an additional five years on specified terms. *** In exchange, Chase-Leavitt was to be paid a declining percentage of profits generated by the "profit center" over the ensuing five years, with $250,000 paid in advance immediately upon the close of the transaction.

In March 2001, Cargo Partner commenced a diversity action against Chase-Leavitt and Albatrans in the United States District Court for the Southern District of New York asserting that Albatrans was liable for Chase-Leavitt's debt to Cargo Partner. One of Cargo's theories of recovery—which underlies the only issue on this appeal—was based upon the common-law "de facto merger" doctrine. Albatrans moved to dismiss or, in the alternative, for summary judgment. The district court referred the motion to Magistrate Judge Douglas F. Eaton.

In due course, the magistrate judge issued a report and recommendation to the district court concluding that all claims against Albatrans should be dismissed. The magistrate judge decided that Cargo Partner had not pled facts sufficient to support a finding that there had been a de facto merger between Albatrans and Chase-Leavitt because Cargo Partner had not alleged that [Ms.] Leavitt received any ownership interest in Albatrans after the asset sale. The magistrate judge concluded that the doctrine of de facto merger applies only when a merger of corporate entities is disguised as some other transaction, and that a necessary factor is continuity of ownership between the predecessor and successor entities. Because [Ms.] Leavitt received no ownership interest in Albatrans, there was no de facto merger. [Citations omitted throughout this paragraph.]

The district court adopted the magistrate judge's report and recommendation in its entirety, dismissed Cargo Partner's complaint with respect to Albatrans, and certified the following question for interlocutory appeal to this Court ***:

> Whether the New York State Court of Appeals would apply the weighing of four factors recognized by the Courts of the State of New York as potentially applicable to whether the "de facto merger" exception applies to a transaction styled as a sale of assets, or whether that Court would adopt a definition of the "de facto merger" exception as requiring that a plaintiff must plead and prove all four of those four factors.

[Citation omitted.] We agreed to hear the appeal. [Citation omitted.]

DISCUSSION

***

It is undisputed that New York law applies to this case. Under New York law, there are at least three ways in which a corporation can acquire the business of another: The purchaser can buy the seller's capital stock, it can buy the seller's assets, or it can merge with the seller to form a single corporation. In the first case, the purchaser does not become liable for the seller's debts unless the stringent requirements for piercing the corporate veil are met. Likewise, the purchaser of a corporation's assets does not, as a result of the purchase, ordinarily become liable for the seller's debts. The amount paid for the assets would ordinarily be available to satisfy those debts, at least in part. So long as the buyer pays a bona fide, arms-length price for the assets, there is no unfairness to creditors in thus limiting recovery to the proceeds of the sale—cash or other consideration roughly equal to the value of the purchased assets would take the place of the purchased assets as a resource for satisfying the seller's debts. Moreover, as the magistrate judge observed, allowing creditors to collect against the purchasers of insolvent debtors' assets would "give the creditors a windfall by increasing the funds available compared to what would have been available if no sale had taken place." Only in the third case, when two corporations merge to become a single entity, is the successor corporation automatically liable for the debts of both predecessors ***. [Citations omitted throughout this paragraph.]

New York recognizes four common-law exceptions to the rule that an asset purchaser is not liable for the seller's debts, applying to: (1) a buyer who formally assumes a seller's debts; (2) transactions undertaken to defraud creditors; (3) a buyer who de facto merged with a seller; and (4) a buyer that is a mere continuation of a seller. [Citations omitted.] Only the third exception, the doctrine of de facto merger, is relevant to this appeal.

A de facto merger occurs when a transaction, although not in form a merger, is in substance "a consolidation or merger of seller and purchaser." [Citation omitted.] Applying New York law, we have observed that:

> [T]o find that a de facto merger has occurred there must be [1] a continuity of the selling corporation, evidenced by the same management, personnel, assets and physical location; [2] a continuity of stockholders, accomplished by paying for the acquired corporation with shares of stock; [3] a dissolution of the selling corporation[;] and [4] the assumption of liabilities by the purchaser.

[*Arnold Graphics Industries v. Independent Agent Center, Inc.*, 775 F.2d 38, 42 (2d Cir. 1985).]*

Cargo Partner concedes that it lacks "any factual basis," *** on which to plead continuity of ownership between Chase-Leavitt and Albatrans. It argues

---

* [Footnote by court]: For example, a transaction in which a corporation acquires the assets of another corporation by (1) purchasing the assets of the seller with its stock; (2) assuming the liabilities of the seller; and (3) continuing the operations of the seller through itself but dissolving the seller would likely be treated as a de facto merger. *Cf. Beck v. Roper Whitney, Inc.*, 190 F. Supp.2d 524, 535 (W.D.N.Y. 2001) ("The classic example of a de facto merger is a transaction in which the purchasing corporation pays for the acquired assets with shares of its own stock." (internal quotation marks omitted)).

instead that the New York courts have adopted a more relaxed standard for determining that a sale of assets was a de facto merger since our decision in Arnold.

In *Fitzgerald v. Fahnestock & Co.*, [730 N.Y.S.2d 70 (2001), the court] concluded that the

> hallmarks of a de facto merger include: [1] continuity of owner-ship; [2] cessation of ordinary business and dissolution of the acquired corporation as soon as possible; [3] assumption by the successor of the liabilities ordinarily necessary for the uninterrupted continuation of the business of the acquired corp-oration; and, [4] continuity of management, personnel, physical location, assets and general business operation.

[Citation omitted.] But the court noted that "[n]ot all of these elements are necessary to find a de facto merger." [Citation omitted.] Cargo Partner argues that *Fitzgerald*, not *Arnold*, states the present law of New York and that, under *Fitzgerald*, a de facto merger may be found without fulfillment of the [first] factor, continuity of ownership.

We have no need to resolve the asserted conflict between *Arnold* and *Fitzgerald* or determine whether all four factors must be present for there to be a de facto merger. Whichever test applies, we are confident that the doctrine of de facto merger in New York does not make a corporation that purchases assets liable for the seller's contract debts absent continuity of ownership.

The purpose of the doctrine of de facto merger is to "avoid [the] patent injustice which might befall a party simply because a merger has been called something else." While each of the four factors in *Fitzgerald* (and their similar counterparts in *Arnold*) distinguish mergers from asset sales, continuity of ownership is the essence of a merger. It is, by contrast, the nature of an asset sale that the seller's ownership interest in the entity is given up in exchange for consideration; the parties do not become owners together of what formerly belonged to each. Continuity of ownership might not alone establish a de facto merger, but as the magistrate judge correctly observed, it "is the 'substance'" of a merger. Because there is no continuity of ownership here, the asset purchase was not "a merger ... called something else." [Citations omitted throughout this paragraph.]

To be sure, *Fitzgerald* speaks of "continuity of ownership," [citation omitted], while *Arnold* talks in terms of "continuity of stockholders," [citation omitted]. But the former is simply a more general way to state the latter. And, for our purposes, it is a distinction without a difference. [Ms.] Leavitt's unsecured contractual interest (through her ownership of equity in Chase-Leavitt) in limited future profits generated using Chase-Leavitt's former assets establishes neither continued "ownership" nor "stockholdings."

***

It is true that a number of states, beginning with Michigan in *Turner v. Bituminous Casualty Co.*, [244 N.W.2d 873 (Mich. 1976)], and California in *Ray v. Alad Corp.*, [560 P.2d 3 (Cal. 1977)], have relaxed the requirement of continuity of ownership in products-liability cases. Although some New York courts have applied this rule, the New York Court of Appeals declined to adopt it. As far as we know it has never been applied, in this state or elsewhere, outside of the products-liability context. This apparently reflects its use, specific to that area of law, to maintain strict liability for products despite the transfer of the assets that were used to produce them. [Citations omitted throughout this paragraph.]

CONCLUSION

For the foregoing reasons, the decision and order of the district court dismissing the plaintiff's complaint with respect to Cargo Partner's assertion of the de facto merger doctrine is affirmed.

The *Cargo Partner* court applied the de facto merger doctrine in the context of whether a creditor could recover from the buyer of assets a debt that the seller of assets owed to a creditor. However, the de facto merger doctrine has also been applied in the context of whether shareholders of the selling corporation are entitled to vote on an asset sale and/or whether they are entitled to "dissenters' rights" with respect to the transaction (which is an issue that you will read about in Section 12.06 of this chapter).

As we saw above, in some situations the shareholders of the selling corporation must approve an asset sale—but not always. Moreover, some state statutes do not require shareholder approval for any asset sales. By contrast, nearly all mergers will require approve by the shareholders of the Target corporation. Thus, if a board of directors wishes to avoid submitting a transaction to a shareholder vote (or engaging in a transaction that will give shareholder dissenters' rights), it might attempt to characterize the transaction as an asset sale, rather than a merger. It is possible that a court might view such a transaction as a de facto merger and require shareholder approval. *See, e.g., Farris v. Glen Alden Corp.*, 143 A.2d 25 (Pa. 1958). *But see Terry v. Penn Central Corp.*, 668 F.2d 188 (3d Cir. 1981) (applying Pennsylvania law). Delaware, however, has rejected this doctrine due to concerns that it would lead to too much uncertainty when planning business transactions. *See Hariton v. Arco Electronics, Inc.*, 188 A.2d 123 (Del. Ch. 1963). In other words, in Delaware an asset sale is an asset sale and a merger is a merger and never the twain shall meet.

Another important point made in the *Cargo Partner* case is that some (albeit not New York) courts are willing to "stretch" the *de facto* merger doctrine a bit in the context of products liability cases. In other words, if the creditor of the (now defunct) seller of assets is a victim of a product manufactured by the seller, the plaintiff may have a better chance of imposing successor liability on the buyer of the assets than would an "ordinary" creditor of the seller. This is especially likely if the buyer has continued manufacturing the product that caused the injury. Two of the leading cases on this issue are *Ray v. Alad Corp.*, 560 P.2d 3 (Cal. 1977), and *Turner v. Bituminous Casualty Co.*, 244 N.W.2d 873 (Mich. 1976). You might learn more about this issue in a course on Products Liability, but that is all that we will say about it here.

§ 12.04   DISSOLUTION OF A CORPORATION

Objectives: You should be able to explain to a corporate client that wishes to dissolve: (1) whose approval is necessary and what procedures must be followed to do so; (2) what must happen during the winding up process; (3) how the corporation can discharge its debts or make provision for the discharge of its debts; and (4) how any remaining funds will be distributed to the corporation's shareholders.

Subsidiary Objectives: You should also be able to:

• ***Board and Shareholder Approval.*** *Given a fact pattern, determine if a corporation's dissolution was properly approved by its board of directors and its shareholders.*

• ***Discharging Creditor Claims.*** *Explain to a corporate client how it may discharge both "known" and "unknown" claims against the corporation during dissolution, as well as the advantages and disadvantages of doing so.*

• ***Distributing Amounts to Shareholders.*** *Given a fact pattern in which a corporation has completed its winding up process and has fully paid or provided for all of its debts, which fact pattern specifies (1) the amount of cash that the corporation has remaining, (2) the number of shares of common stock and the* *number (if any) of shares of preferred stock outstanding, and (3) the nature of the liquidation preferences (if any) of the preferred shares, determine how much will be payable with respect to each share of common stock and each share of preferred stock (if any).*

As noted at the beginning of this chapter, a corporation theoretically could last forever. In practice, however, corporations often "end." One way that a corporation could cease to exist is if it merged into another corporation. Another way in which a corporation could cease to exist is if it **dissolved.**

To some degree, you already know a fair amount about dissolving a business from what you learned about partnership dissolutions in Chapter 4. In many ways, corporate dissolutions are similar: after the dissolution is properly approved, the corporation will go through a period of "winding up" during which it will finish uncompleted work and liquidate the assets that it does not intend to distribute "in kind" to its shareholders. The next major step is to pay creditors (or make provision to pay debts, as discussed below). Assuming that some assets remain after paying creditors, then the final step is to determine how these remaining assets will be divided among the shareholders. However, while a corporate dissolution may bear some superficial similarities to a partnership dissolution, there are many important differences.

But first, consider *why* a business would want to dissolve. One obvious reason that should occur to you after having read Section 12.03 above is that perhaps the corporation has just sold all of its assets and is now sitting on a pile of cash or other consideration. In such a situation, the likely next step would be to dissolve the corporation (unless the corporation decides to use the cash to go into a new line of business, which is probably unlikely). Another possible reason to dissolve is that the corporation's business is losing money and appears to be a dead end. For example, imagine a corporation that manufactures typewriters or pay telephones. (While it would have been a good idea for such corporations to diversify into other lines of business long ago, let's assume that they did not.) Because the future of typewriters and payphones does not appear very bright, it probably would not be possible to find a buyer to purchase all of the corporation's assets and then continue running the business. In a case like this, the logical thing to do may be to dissolve the corporation and sell off its assets piece by piece.

MBCA §§ 14.01 through 14.09 concern voluntary[*] dissolutions as opposed to other types of dissolution.

---

[*]   You learned about *involuntary* dissolutions for oppression or other reasons under MBCA § 14.34 in Chapter 9. In addition, MBCA §§ 14.20 to 14.23 concern *administrative* dissolutions, that is, situations where the corporation is dissolved due to reasons such as failing

The first step in a voluntary dissolution is to obtain the requisite approval. MBCA § 14.02 is the applicable section for this issue. Once the dissolution has been properly approved, the corporation remains in existence, "but may not carry on any business except that appropriate to wind up and liquidate its business and affairs." MBCA § 14.05(a). During the winding up process, the corporation (typically overseen by the board) must take several steps, including:

- It must file articles of dissolution with the state government pursuant to MBCA § 14.03 (although it may be advantageous to delay filing this document until the liquidation process is well under way). According to the official comment to Section 14.03, this filing "makes the decision to dissolve a matter of public record and establishes the time when the corporation must begin the process of winding up and cease carrying on its business except to the extent necessary for winding up." (*See also* MBCA § 14.05.)

- It must sell or dispose of the assets[*] that will not be distributed in kind to the shareholders (note that this will convert non-cash assets into cash).

- For debts, it must either discharge (i.e., pay) a debt, take steps to bar a debt under MBCA §§ 14.06 or 14.07 (discussed below), or apply to a court for a determination of the amount that must be set aside for its debts under MBCA § 14.08 (also discussed below).

- Finally, it must distribute any remaining assets to the shareholders according to their interests (i.e., based on how many shares and what type of stock they own).

Discharging or making provision for a corporation's debts may be one of the more complicated issues during winding up. It also will be important from the directors' perspective, because MBCA § 14.09(a) provides that directors must cause the corporation to "discharge or make reasonable provision for the payment of claims ...." Further, MBCA § 14.09(b) provides that directors will not be liable for a breach of subsection (a) with respect to claims that are barred or satisfied under MBCA §§ 14.06, 14.07, or 14.08, as applicable. Obviously, directors will want to get this liability protection, so let's examine these sections.

---

to pay certain taxes or making certain filings. Note that an administratively dissolved corporation can often be reinstated. See MBCA § 14.22.

[*] Note that a corporation's assets include claims that it has against other persons. For example, if the corporation were a plaintiff in a pending lawsuit at the time of its dissolution, it could dispose of this asset (the potential recovery) by assigning it to a third party for a negotiated price. Alternatively, it could continue to pursue the lawsuit. See MBCA §§ 14.05(b)(5), (6).

> **Question**
> Why would a corporation want to bar a creditor's claim in dissolution? Who benefits?

MBCA § 14.06 concerns "known" claims, that is a claim that the corporation is aware that it owes and that is not subject to any contingencies. For example, if a contractor recently installed a new roof for the corporation, the amount owed to the contractor would be considered a "known" claim (even if the exact amount is not currently certain). Section 14.06 establishes a procedure whereby a corporation could end up barring such claims.

MBCA § 14.07, on the other hand, concerns "other" claims, that is, all claims that cannot be considered "known" claims. Obviously, it will be impossible to give actual notice to the holders of claims of which the corporation is unaware. For this reason, MBCA § 14.07 provides that such claims may be barred if the corporation publishes a newspaper notice and meets the other conditions of that section for barring such "unknown" claims. Even so, sometimes it will be difficult for a corporation to estimate how much money it should set aside before it distributes amounts to its shareholders. (After all, shareholders won't want to have to give some or all of these amounts back.) Thus, MBCA § 14.08 allows the corporation (assuming that it has published the newspaper notice contemplated by Section 14.07) to have a court determine how much it should hold back to make provision for contingent claims or unknown claims (or those that arise after dissolution).

But what would happen if the corporation distributes amounts to shareholders without either paying, or taking steps to bar, a creditor's claim? Again, MBCA § 14.09 provides that directors have a duty to discharge or make reasonable provision for debts before allowing distributions to be made to shareholders. However, the official comment to MBCA § 14.09 states that if the directors breach this duty, their liability "should be mediated through the corporation." This is consistent with MBCA § 8.33, which concerns unlawful distributions (and which was covered in Chapter 5), including distributions made in dissolution. *See* MBCA § 8.33(a).

Study MBCA §§ 14.06 through 14.09 and work on the following problems.

Problems

Problem 12-15:   Hockey Corp. has only one class of stock (common stock), of which 500,000 shares are outstanding. Hockey Corp. has dissolved and fully paid all creditors. It has $3 million remaining. *How much will be payable to each share of common stock?*

Problem 12-16: Same facts as Problem 12-15, except that there is also a class of preferred stock, of which 50,000 shares are outstanding. The preferred stock has a liquidation preference of $10 per share but is not participating (i.e., that is the only amount to which it is entitled upon dissolution). *How much will be payable to (1) each share of preferred stock and (2) each share of common stock?*

Problem 12-17: Same facts as Problem 12-16, except that the preferred stock is participating (i.e., it first receives its liquidation preference and then also receives what the common stock receives). *How much will be payable to (1) each share of preferred stock and (2) each share of common stock? Round your answer to the nearest cent.*

Problem 12-18: Basketball Corp. has only one class of stock (common stock), of which 100,000 shares are outstanding. Basketball Corp. wishes to dissolve. After passing a resolution approving the dissolution, Basketball Corp.'s board of directors gives proper notice of a shareholders meeting to approve the dissolution. At the meeting, the holders of 82,000 shares are present in person or by proxy. Of those shares, 45,000 shares are voted in favor of dissolution, 30,000 shares are voted against dissolution, and 7,000 shares abstain. *Was dissolution properly approved? Would your answer be different if the shareholders were voting on a proposal to sell all of Basketball Corp.'s assets?*

Problem 12-19: Tennis Corp. has three shareholders: Ms. Serve owns 500 shares, Mr. Net owns 250 shares, and Ms. Racket owns 250 shares. Tennis Corp. recently dissolved and distributed a total of $100,000 to its shareholders. However, the board of directors took no steps to pay or bar a $10,000 claim held by Joe Creditor. *Assuming that Joe does not attempt to sue the directors, may Joe recover his claim from the shareholders? If so, how would he do so and how much could he recover from each shareholder?*

Problem 12-20: Same facts as Problem 12-19, except that Joe's claim was for $150,000. *May Joe recover his claim from the shareholders? If so, how would he do so and how much could he recover from each shareholder? Is there any way Joe could collect the full $150,000?*

Problem 12-21: Tom's Asbestos Corp. ("TAC") manufactured (as you might expect) asbestos, which it had sold throughout the United States for more than thirty years. TAC has decided to dissolve. *How may TAC bar products liability claims that may be asserted against it in the future? Is this likely to result in many potential claimants knowing that TAC is dissolving? What is the deadline for an asbestos / lung cancer victim to assert a claim against TAC? What is the* statute of limitations *for doing so?*

§ 12.05   MERGERS

Objectives: You should be able to explain to a corporate client that wishes to merge with another corporation, either as the Acquiring corporation or the Target corporation: (1) whose approval is necessary and what procedures must be followed to complete the merger; (2) the effects of the merger on the corporations involved in the merger, their shareholders, and other persons related to the corporation, and (3) what other actions are necessary or advisable in connection with the merger.

Subsidiary Objectives: You should also be able to:

• *"Regular" Mergers and "Triangular" Mergers. Explain a "regular" merger, including naming the constituent corporations (that is, the corporations that are parties to the merger agreement) and explaining the general effects of such a merger. In addition, explain a "triangular" merger (both a forward triangular merger and a reverse triangular merger), including naming the constituent corporations, explaining the general effects of a triangular merger, and explaining why triangular mergers may sometimes be preferable to regular mergers.*

• *Effects of Merger on Constituent Corporations. Explain the general effects of a merger on the constituent corporations, including explaining what happens to the assets, liabilities, articles of incorporation, bylaws, officers and directors of each constituent corporation.*

• *Effects of Merger on Shareholders of Constituent Corporations. Given a copy of a merger agreement (or a description of it), determine what will happen to the shares of stock of each constituent corporation that are outstanding immediately before the merger.*

*   ***Required "Paperwork."*** *Describe the agreements and other documents that are necessary to complete a merger.*

*   ***Board and Shareholder Approval.*** *Given a fact pattern that (1) specifies the number and type of outstanding shares of stock in each constituent corporation and (2) describes the basic terms of the merger agreement, determine—for each constituent corporation—whether (a) its board of directors must adopt the plan of merger (also known as the merger agreement) and (b) its shareholders must approve the plan of merger. Given a fact pattern where a corporation's shareholders are required to approve a plan of merger, determine whether the corporation's shareholders have properly approved the plan of merger.*

As you know, a merger is simply a way for one corporation (or other entity) to acquire another corporation. However, unlike an asset sale, where both the Acquirer and the Target remain in existence following the transaction, in a merger one corporation will cease to exist following the merger.

Let's begin with a simple merger between two corporations, one which we will call the Acquiring or Surviving corporation, and the other which we will call the Target or Disappearing corporation. MBCA § 11.07 lists several effects of such a merger (and, of course, the plan of merger, otherwise known as the merger agreement, could specify additional effects). These effects include:

*   the Acquiring corporation will survive (i.e., remain in existence after) the merger;

*   the separate existence of the Target corporation will end as a result of the merger;

*   all of the assets and other rights of the Target corporation will thereafter belong to the Acquiring corporation;

*   all of the liabilities of the Target corporation will thereafter be liabilities of the Acquiring corporation;

- the Acquiring corporation's articles of incorporation and bylaws[*] are amended only to the extent stated in the plan of merger;

- the Target corporation's shares will be converted into the consideration set forth in the plan of merger (and, if applicable, the Acquiring corporation's shares will be converted as set forth in the plan of merger), except with respect to shares owned by persons who exercise dissenters' rights.

Problems

Problem 12-22:   Target Co. recently merged into Acquire Co. Before the merger, Target Co. (1) owned Blackacre, (2) owned Whiteacre, but subject to a mortgage in favor First Regional Bank, and (3) owed $30,000 to Jane Creditor.   *What effects did the merger have on these three items?*

Problem 12-23: Same facts as Problem 12-22. Target Co. was a manufacturer of industrial machinery. Shortly after the merger, Bob Unlucky was injured by one of the machines that had been manufactured by Target Co. before the merger. *May Bob sue Acquire Co. for his injuries?*

Problem 12-24: Blackacre had been heavily polluted, in violation of state environmental laws that provide for substantial fines for noncompliance. *May the state environmental protection agency fine Acquire Co. for the pre-merger actions of Target Co.? What if in the merger agreement, Target Co. represented and warranted (i.e., promised) to Acquire Co. that it had fully complied with all environmental laws?*

Problem 12-25: *What happened to the shares of Target Co. stock that were outstanding immediately before the merger? If the statute doesn't tell you, where would you look to answer this question?*

At the risk of giving away the answers to Problems 12-23 and 12-24, it may have occurred to you that, from the Acquiring corporation's perspective, a merger is dangerous business because of its assumption of the Target corporation's liabilities. For this reason (and perhaps other reasons), it is common to conduct a merger as a ***triangular merger.*** There actually are two varieties of

---

[*]   MBCA § 11.07 uses the term "organic document."   Meanwhile, MBCA §§ 1.40(15A), (17A), and (17B) define this term to include articles of incorporation and bylaws.

triangular merger: the *forward triangular merger* and, you guessed it, the *reverse triangular merger.* In a forward triangular merger, the Acquiring corporation creates a new subsidiary (or perhaps already had one) and then the Target corporation mergers into the subsidiary, rather than into the Acquiring corporation. A diagram of a forward triangular merger would thus look like this:

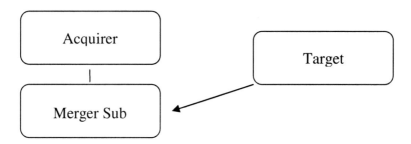

On the other hand, in a reverse triangular merger, the subsidiary of the Acquiring corporation merges into the Target corporation and the Target corporation survives. A diagram of a reverse triangular merger would thus look like this:

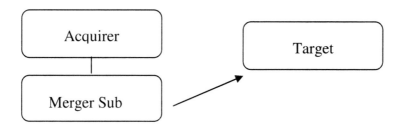

At this point you may be confused by reverse triangular mergers, wondering exactly how the Target corporation can really be the "target" when it actually survives the merger. The answer is that the plan of merger likely will provide that (1) each share of the Acquiring corporation that is outstanding immediately before the merger will remain unchanged; (2) each share of the Target corporation that is outstanding immediately before the merger will be converted into the merger consideration (typically, either cash or new shares of the Acquiring corporation's stock); and (3) each share of the merger subsidiary that is outstanding immediately before the merger will be converted into a share of the *Target* corporation's stock. One reason to select a reverse triangular merger (in which the Target survives) is that sometimes the Target corporation has governmental permits or contracts that could be lost as a result of a merger. For example, contracts sometimes contain anti-assignment clauses, which provide that they may not be assigned to a third party without the consent of the other party.

Further, contracts sometimes defined "assignment" to include mergers. At least one case found such a clause to prevent a contract from being assigned to the surviving corporation in a merger. *See PPG Industries, Inc. v. Guardian Industries Corp.*, 597 F.2d 1090 (6th Cir. 1979). However, the weight of authority is against this case.

In any event, after *either* a forward triangular merger *or* a reverse triangular merger, things will look like this:

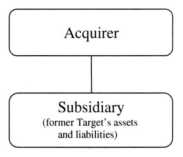

Note that the key advantage of triangular mergers is that, if the Target corporation was subject to enormous, crippling liabilities (which the Acquiring corporation's pre-merger investigation failed to discover) the worst that could happen—outside of a veil-piercing situation—is that the Acquiring corporation "loses" the Target if it files for bankruptcy.

Because "regular" mergers are complicated enough by themselves, for the rest of this chapter we will only consider two-party mergers. However, remember that the "real world" of mergers is more complicated than the following. Not only are you likely to see triangular mergers when you are a lawyer, but mergers could be between two different types of entities, such as an LLC merging with a corporation. In addition, two business entities that are organized under different states' laws could merge.[*] But again, we will keep things relatively simple: in the following discussion we will assume that two corporations, both of which are incorporated under the MBCA, are going to merge.

Unless the merger is between two related companies, such as a parent and subsidiary or two corporations that are owned by the same shareholder(s), there typically is quite a lot of work to do before a merger, particularly if the transaction is very large in terms of dollars. From the Acquiring corporation's perspective,

---

[*]   Generally speaking, if Corporation A, which is incorporated in State A, will merge with Corporation B, which is incorporated in State B, then the parties must comply with the laws of both State A and State B in conducting the merger.

one major pre-merger activity is *due diligence*. Because the Acquiring corporation will, by operation of law, assume all of the Target corporation's liabilities
when the merger becomes effective, it will want to learn as much as possible
about the Target corporation's business and liabilities beforehand. This is
important because the Target corporation's financial statements may not reflect all
of its potential liabilities. For example, the Target corporation could get hit in the
future with a products liability lawsuit if its products have a design or
manufacturing flaw that has not yet come to light. The Target corporation might
be fined or otherwise penalized if it hasn't been conducting its business in
compliance with all applicable laws, particularly if it is in a heavily regulated
industry. Contingencies such as these will not appear on the Target corporation's
financial statements.

Due diligence usually begins with the Acquiring corporation's lawyers
(and perhaps its accountants as well) sending the Target corporation a list of
documents and other information that they would like to examine.[*] The length of
this list is usually a function of two factors: what type of business the Target
corporation is in and how detail-oriented the Acquiring corporation's lawyers are.
While there will be some items that will be on every due diligence request list
(e.g., copies of articles and bylaws, minutes of board and shareholder meetings for
the past several years, financial statements, etc.) some information may be
relevant only to companies in certain industries. For example, if the Target
corporation were in the banking business, then a due diligence request list with
respect to it would look quite a bit different than one with respect to a Target
corporation that, say, manufactures steel.

Due diligence is not really something that can be taught in law school.
Much of it will be done by young associates in the Acquiring corporation's law
firm. (Hey kids: travel to exciting places! And then spend a week in a conference
room reviewing boxes and boxes of documents.) Some due diligence work will be
done by lawyers who specialize in certain areas. For example, it probably would
be a good idea to have a lawyer who specializes in employee benefits law to look
at the Target corporation's employee benefit plans and filings, and a lawyer who
specializes in environmental law look at the Target corporation's environmental-
law compliance information. In any event, the goal of due diligence is much like
kicking tires at a used car lot. If during the due diligence process, the Acquiring
corporation learns that the Target corporation has a great deal of additional
liabilities or other legal problems, it could then negotiate a lower price or even
walk away from the deal.

Another major task will be to negotiate and draft the *plan of merger*, also
known as the *merger agreement*. For a simple two-party merger MBCA §

---

[*]   In addition, it is customary for the Acquiring corporation to sign a confidentiality
agreement concerning its use or disclosure of the information it receives from the Target.

11.02(c) states that the merger agreement must contain, at a minimum, only five items:

- the name of each corporation that is involved in the merger, including the name of the surviving corporation;

- the "terms and conditions" of the merger;

- a description of how the shares of the Target corporation will be converted "into shares or other securities, eligible interests, obligations, rights to acquire shares, other securities or eligible interests, cash, other property or any combination of the foregoing";

- any amendments to the Acquiring corporation's articles of incorporation that will be made as a result of the merger (which are relatively rare); and

- any other provisions required by the laws under which any party to the merger is organized or governed, or by its articles of incorporation.

This is actually a very short list and a merger agreement between two related companies could very well fit onto a single page. However, as you might imagine, a merger agreement for a large transaction between two unrelated parties will almost certainly be much more complicated. In fact, it could be a hundred or more pages. While you probably will not learn how to draft a merger agreement in law school, there are some important parts of a merger agreement of which you should be aware.

One such part is called *representations and warranties.* Without delving into too much detail here, representations and warranties are essentially promises about facts that the parties make to each other. Typically, the representations and warranties that the Target corporation makes to the Acquiring corporation are much more extensive than those that the Acquiring corporation makes to the Target corporation. For example, the Target corporation might represent and warrant that, except as it may disclose on a "disclosure schedule," its business and operations have been conducted in compliance with all applicable laws, rules, and regulations in all material (i.e., significant) respects. If it turns out that this representation and warranty was in fact not true (i.e., that the Target corporation had one or more material legal violations), then the Acquiring corporation would have the remedies specified in the merger agreement. For example, the merger agreement might permit it to terminate the agreement or, if the merger has already happened, to recover compensation from the former shareholders of the Target corporation.*

---

* If the Target corporation is closely held, recovering damages from its former shareholders is relatively easy; it is fairly customary to hold a portion of the merger consider-

Another important part of the merger agreement contains *covenants*. Covenants are essentially promises that the parties make to each other about things that they will do—and things they will refrain from doing—between the time that the merger agreement is signed and the merger occurs. (This gap could be several weeks or even months, due to the need to solicit shareholder approval of the merger, as discussed below. SEC approval may also be required in some cases, such as where the Acquiring corporation will be issuing new shares of stock to the soon-to-be-former Target shareholders.) For example, the Target corporation typically will be required to covenant that it will conduct its business consistently in all material respects with its past practices. In other words, after the merger agreement its signed, it may only do things that are outside the ordinary course of business if the Acquiring corporation consents. This is important from the Acquiring corporation's perspective so that the Target corporation does not "change" in some manner before the merger occurs. For example, the Acquiring corporation probably doesn't want the Target corporation to pay dividends before the merger, thus reducing the amount of its assets. Depending on the Target corporation's business and the things that the Acquiring corporation may be worried about, the covenants section of a merger agreement can be quite extensive.

Several other agreements may be necessary or advisable in a given situation. For example, if the Target corporation has certain key employees that the Acquiring corporation wants to ensure will remain "on board," it may want them to agree to sign employment agreements at the closing of the merger. Conversely, if the Acquiring corporation is worried that key employees of the Target corporation (perhaps the founders of the Target) will compete with it following the merger, it may want those persons to agree to sign noncompetition agreements (also known as covenants not to compete). To make sure that the merger will be approved by the Target corporation's shareholders, it may also be advisable to have major shareholders of the Target corporation agree beforehand to vote in favor of the merger.

Once the merger agreement and any related agreements have been negotiated and drafted to each party's satisfaction, the next step will be to obtain the requisite approvals of the merger. Again keeping in mind that we are assuming a two-party merger, there are *four* groups of people that may be required to approve the merger: both the Target corporation and the Acquiring corporation have boards of directors, and both corporations have shareholders. We will start

---

ation in escrow for some time following the merger. If the Acquiring corporation discovers during this period that some of the Target corporation's representations and warranties were untrue, it could simply deduct its damages from the escrow fund. However, if the Target corporation was publicly traded, such a "hold back" is almost certainly unworkable. In that case, the Acquiring corporation would essentially have no one to sue if it turned out that some of the Target's representations and warranties were untrue. Buyer beware!

with the assumption that each of these four groups must properly approve the merger. If any one or more of them does not approve the merger, then it will not happen. *See* MBCA §§ 11.04(a) and (b).

In Chapter 5, you learned about the process of obtaining board approval for corporate actions and obtaining shareholder approval of corporate actions. Although a merger may strike you as a "big deal" that should require supermajority or perhaps even unanimous director or shareholder consent, the MBCA treats mergers exactly the same way that it treats anything else that directors or shareholders may consider. In other words, with respect to board approval, unless the directors adopt the merger

> ***Shareholder Approval of Mergers in Other States***
> The MBCA treats mergers like anything else that shareholders may vote on. Thus, the official comment to MBCA § 11.04 provides in part that "[i]f a quorum is present, then under sections 7.25 and 7.26 the plan will be approved if more votes are cast in favor of the plan than against it by the voting group. *** This represents a change from the Act's previous voting rule for mergers and share exchanges, which required approval by a majority of outstanding shares." In contrast, many states, including Delaware, treat mergers as a "big deal." Historically, mergers required unanimous shareholder consent. However, this was unworkable because one shareholder could "veto" a merger. Thus, many states moved away from the unanimity requirement but in exchange gave shareholders dissenters' rights, which you will learn about in the next section. Even so, most states still require that a majority of the *outstanding* shares must vote in favor of a merger. See, e.g., Section 251 of the Delaware General Corporation Law. Some states even require that a super-majority, such as two-thirds of the outstanding shares, must approve mergers.

through a unanimous written consent resolution pursuant to MBCA § 8.21, they will need to hold a meeting and vote on the merger, all as you learned about in Chapter 5. But the vote required for director approval of a merger is simply a majority of the directors who are present at the meeting.

Assuming the respective boards approve the merger, they generally must then submit it for the approval of the corporations' respective shareholders. *See* MBCA § 11.04(b) to (d). If a corporation has only one or a few shareholders, then they could approve the merger using a unanimous consent resolution pursuant to MBCA § 7.04 (also as you learned about in Chapter 5). The more likely scenario, however, is that a shareholder meeting will be held. MBCA § 11.04(d) specifies that certain information about the merger must be contained in the notice of the meeting. (This is in addition to the information required by MBCA § 7.05, such as the date, time, and place of the meeting.) Also, if the Target corporation is publicly traded, it will be required to furnish its shareholders with a detailed proxy statement pursuant to Section 14 of the Securities Exchange Act, as you learned in Chapter 10. Finally, if the Acquiring corporation will be issuing stock to the soon-to-be-former Target corporation shareholders, then a great deal of additional information must be provided, as you will learn in Chapter 13.

In any event, as noted above, we are starting with the assumption that all four groups of decision makers must approve the merger in order for it to occur. But like many things in law school, there are exceptions to this general rule. The two exceptions are MBCA § 11.04(g), which is sometimes said to apply to "small scale" mergers, and MBCA § 11.05, which is sometimes said to apply to "short form" or "parent-subsidiary" mergers.

MBCA § 11.04(g) specifies that if four conditions are met then the shareholders of "the corporation" (query: which one is it—the Target corporation or the Acquiring corporation) need not approve the merger. If any one or more of these conditions is not met, then that group of shareholders must approve the merger in order for it to occur. When you read MBCA § 11.04(g), note that it has a cross-reference to MBCA § 6.21(f). As discussed in Chapter 1, one cardinal rule of reading statutes is that you must go read the cross-referenced section. Don't just wonder what it says.

The other exception is found in MBCA § 11.05, which provides that if a parent corporation owns at least ninety percent of the voting stock of a subsidiary, then it may merge with that subsidiary (or merge two or more 90%-owned subsidiaries together) without needing approval from either the subsidiary's board or its shareholders. This of course makes perfect sense because, were such approval required, it would be a foregone conclusion. After all, the parent owns the vast majority of the subsidiary's stock and almost certainly selected all of the subsidiary's directors.

Before you work on some problems concerning shareholder approval of a merger and the effects that a merger will have, you should understand that if a corporation has more than one class of stock outstanding (for example, common stock and preferred stock), the approval of each class may be required *separately*. This is because MBCA § 11.04(f) provides that:

Separate voting by voting groups [a class of stock is considered a "voting group"] is required:

(1)   on a plan of merger, by each class or series of shares that:

(i)   are to be converted under the plan of merger into other securities, interests, obligations, rights to acquire shares, other securities or interests, cash, other property, or any combination of the foregoing; or

(ii)   would be entitled to vote as a separate group on a provision in the plan that, if contained in a proposed amendment to articles of incorporation, would require action by separate voting groups under section 10.04; [and]

***

(3)   on a plan of merger ***, if the voting group is entitled under the articles of incorporation to vote as a voting group to approve a plan of merger or share exchange.

Thus, even a class of *nonvoting* stock would be required to approve a merger separately if it would be converted into something else as a result of a merger, as well as in certain other situations.

However, we will keep things relatively simple in the following problems and assume not only that the merger involves only two corporations that are both incorporated under the MBCA, but also that each corporation has only a single class of common stock outstanding. With that in mind, study MBCA §§ 11.04 and 11.05 and try your hand at the following problems.

Problems

Problem 12-26:   Burger Bell Corp. (which as the Acquiring corporation will be referred to as "A") has 100 million shares of common stock outstanding. Joe's Hamburgers, Inc. (which as the Target corporation will be referred to as "T") has 10,000 shares of common stock outstanding. The boards of directors of A and T have adopted a plan of merger that provides that T will merge into A. A will survive the merger. A's articles of incorporation will not be changed as a result of the merger, nor will there be any change to its currently outstanding shares of common stock. In the merger, each share of T common stock will be converted into the right to receive two shares of A common stock.

A.   *Must the shareholders of T approve the plan of merger?*
B.   *Must the shareholders of A approve the plan of merger?*
C.   *If you owned 10 shares of T common stock immediately before the merger, what will happen to those shares if the merger occurs?*
D.   *If you owned 10 shares of A common stock immediately before the merger, what will happen to those shares if the merger occurs?*
E.   *Immediately after the merger, how many outstanding shares of A common stock will there be?*

Problem 12-27: Cage Corp. ("A") has 100 million shares of its common stock outstanding. Tiger Corp. ("T") has 50 million shares of common stock outstanding. The boards of directors of A and T have adopted a plan of merger that provides that T will merge into A. A will survive the merger. A's articles of incorporation will not be changed as a result of the merger, nor will there be any change to its currently outstanding shares of common stock. In the merger, each share of T common stock will be converted into the right to receive $10 in cash.

A.   *Must the shareholders of T approve the plan of merger?*
B.   *Must the shareholders of A approve the plan of merger?*
C.   *If you owned 10 shares of T common stock immediately before the merger, what will happen to those shares if the merger occurs?*
D.   *If you owned 10 shares of A common stock immediately before the merger, what will happen to those shares if the merger occurs?*
E.   *Immediately after the merger, how many outstanding shares of A common stock will there be?*

Problem 12-28: Shark Corp. ("A") has 100 million shares of common stock outstanding. Guppy Corp. ("T") has 25 million shares of common stock outstanding. The boards of directors of A and T have adopted a plan of merger that provides that T will merge into A. A will survive the merger. A's articles of incorporation will not be changed as a result of the merger, nor will there be any change to its currently outstanding shares of common stock. In the merger, each share of T common stock will be converted into the right to receive a coupon worth $30 toward the purchase of a new fish tank.

A.   *Must the shareholders of T approve the plan of merger?*
B.   *Must the shareholders of A approve the plan of merger?*
C.   *If you owned 10 shares of T common stock immediately before the merger, what will happen to those shares if the merger occurs?*
D.   *If you owned 10 shares of A common stock immediately before the merger, what will happen to those shares if the merger occurs?*
E.   *Immediately after the merger, how many outstanding shares of A common stock will there be?*

Problem 12-29:   Horse Corp. ("A") has 100 million shares of common stock outstanding. Hay Corp. ("T") has 50 million shares of common stock outstanding. The boards of directors of A and T have adopted a plan of merger that provides that T will merge into A. A will survive the merger. A's articles of incorporation will not be changed as a result of the merger, nor will there be any change to its currently outstanding shares of common stock. In the merger, each share of T common stock will be converted into the right to receive one share of A common stock.

A.   *Must the shareholders of T approve the plan of merger?*
B.   *Must the shareholders of A approve the plan of merger?*
C.   *If you owned 10 shares of T common stock immediately before the merger, what will happen to those shares if the merger occurs?*
D.   *If you owned 10 shares of A common stock immediately before the merger, what will happen to those shares if the merger occurs?*
E.   *Immediately after the merger, how many outstanding shares of A common stock will there be?*

Problem 12-30:   Stereo Corp. ("A") has 100 million shares of common stock outstanding.   Component Corp. ("T") has 50 million shares of common stock outstanding.   The boards of directors of A and T have adopted a plan of merger that provides that T will merge into A.   At a properly held meeting of T's shareholders at which 40 million shares were present in person or by proxy, 19 million shares were voted in favor of the merger, 17 million shares were voted against the merger, and 4 million shares abstained.   *Was the merger properly approved by T's shareholders? Would your answer change if T was incorporated under Delaware law?*

Problem 12-31: Bottom Corp. has 50 million shares of common stock outstanding. Of these shares, 46 million are owned by Top Corp. Top Corp. wishes to merge Bottom Corp. into Top Corp. *Is the approval of Bottom Corp.'s board required for this merger? Is the approval of Bottom Corp.'s shareholders required for this merger? Is the approval of Top Corp.'s shareholders required for this merger? Would your answers to any of these question change if Top Corp. is merging into Bottom Corp.?*

§ 12.06   DISSENTERS' RIGHTS

Objectives: You should be able to:

• *Do Shareholders Have Dissenters' Rights in a Merger?
Given a fact pattern that (1) specifies the number and type of outstanding shares of stock in each constituent corporation in a merger, (2) describes the basic terms of the merger agreement, and (3) allows you to determine whether a corporation's stock is publicly traded, determine—for each constituent corporation—whether the shareholders have dissenters' rights with respect to the merger.*

• *Other Transactions.* *List the other transactions that result in a shareholder having dissenters' rights.*

• *How Do Shareholders Assert Dissenters' Rights?
Describe generally the procedural steps that a shareholder must take to assert her dissenters' rights.*

• *How is the "Fair Value" of Dissenting Shares Determined?* *Where a shareholder assets her dissenters' rights, describe generally what factors a court will, or will not, examine to determine the "fair value" of the dissenting shareholders' shares.*

• *Are Dissenters' Rights a Shareholder's Exclusive Remedy?* *With respect to a transaction as to which a shareholder has dissenters' rights, explain whether asserting dissenters' rights is the shareholder's exclusive (i.e., only) remedy.*

Let's assume that you are a shareholder of the Target corporation in a merger but you are unhappy, perhaps even incensed, at the amount, or the type, of consideration that you will receive in the merger. In other words, you think that your Target corporation stock is worth more than what is being offered to you. Or maybe the merger provides that your shares of Target corporation stock would be converted into shares of Acquiring corporation stock and you do not want Acquiring corporation stock (or want *more* of it). What can you do to express your displeasure?

One obvious thing that springs to mind is that you may vote against the merger. Clearly, the requirement that shareholders approve the merger serves as a check or "escape valve" to ensure that the board of directors has done a satisfactory job negotiating the merger. However, as discussed above, even if you vote your shares against the merger the merger will still occur if enough other shareholders vote their shares in favor of it (unless, of course, you happen to own a majority of the outstanding shares).

In previous chapters, we saw a few other possibilities. You could attempt to sue your board of directors for breaching its duty of care in negotiating and adopting the merger agreement and then recommending that the shareholders approve it. Of course, the major hurdle in this route is overcoming the business judgment rule, not to mention the requirements of MBCA §§ 8.30 and 8.31, as you learned about in Chapter 6. Nonetheless, the shareholder-plaintiffs in *Smith v. Van Gorkom* won the case, as you should recall from Chapter 6. Another possibility would be to sue for a breach of the duty of loyalty. *Weinberger v. UOP, Inc.*, which you read in Chapter 11, is one example of this possibility. Of course, this will only be a viable approach if the merger involves a controlling shareholder or you could show that the directors of your corporation had an undisclosed conflict of interest in approving the merger.

There is another possibility for the unhappy shareholder: assert ***dissenters' rights*** (also known as ***appraisal rights***), if they are available to you. Although we will discuss the procedural aspects of asserting dissenters' rights in some detail below, suffice it to say for now that asserting dissenters' rights allows you to have a court—which, of course, is a neutral, disinterested forum—determine the "fair value" of your shares. When the lawsuit is over, the surviving corporation would be required to pay you this amount in exchange for your shares. Thus, your ability to assert dissenters' rights serves as another check or escape valve to ensure that your board of directors does a good job negotiating the merger agreement. If enough shareholders assert dissenters' rights, the merger may be called off. (Merger agreements often contain a condition precedent that if dissenters' rights are asserted with respect to more than a certain amount of shares, then the Acquiring corporation could decide to terminate the merger agreement.)

Do You Have Dissenters' Rights?   But we first need to decide whether you have dissenters' rights with respect to a given transaction. This is where the complicated and difficult MBCA § 13.02 comes in. To understand dissenters' rights, you will need to closely study MBCA § 13.02—as well as the cross-referenced statutes in that section. But before doing so, note how that section is structured:

• Subsection (a) of MBCA § 13.02 lists the types of transactions or other events that will result in a shareholder having dissenters' rights. (Mergers are covered in subsection (a)(1).) If a particular event does not give rise to dissenters' rights, then obviously shareholders do not have dissenters' rights. End of story.

- However, if a shareholder has dissenters' rights as a result of subsection (a)(1), that is not the end of the story because subsection (b)(1) "takes away" dissenters' rights for certain types of shares in certain types of transactions (including mergers). If a shareholder has dissenters' rights as a result of subsection (a)(1) but subsection (b)(1) does *not* take them away, then that shareholder has dissenters' rights.

- On the other hand, if a shareholder has dissenters' rights as a result of subsection (a)(1) and subsection (b)(1) *does* take them away, that is not the end of the story. This is because either or both of subsection (b)(3) or (b)(4) could give dissenters' rights *back*. Subsection (b)(3) restores dissenters' rights that had been taken away by subsection (b)(1) if a corporate action such as a merger would require shareholders to accept certain things in exchange for their shares. Subsection (b)(4) restores dissenters' rights that had been taken away by subsection (b)(1) if the transaction is an "interested transaction," as that term is defined in MBCA § 13.02(5.1).[*]

Confused yet? Don't worry too much; Section 13.02 intimidates many people when they first encounter it. But don't let that stop you from putting it under a microscope and then applying it to the following problems (which may seem somewhat familiar to you). Note that none of the problems involve subsection (b)(4) of MBCA § 13.02. (Also, note that the Delaware dissenters' rights statute is substantially different than the MBCA. However, the following problems only concern the MBCA.)

Problems

Problem 12-32: Burger Bell Corp. ("A") has 100 million shares of common stock outstanding, which are listed on the New York Stock Exchange ("NYSE"). Joe's Hamburgers, Inc. ("T") has 10,000 shares of common stock outstanding, which are not listed on any stock exchange or traded in any stock market. The boards of directors of A and T have adopted a plan of merger that provides that T will merge into A. A will survive the merger. A's articles of incorporation will not be changed as a result of the merger, nor will there be any change to its currently outstanding shares of common stock. In the merger, each share of T common

---

_* The citation to MBCA § 13.01(5.1) is not a typographical error. From time to time, drafters of statutes wish to insert new sections *between* existing sections without having to renumber all of the preexisting sections.

stock will be converted into the right to receive two shares of A common stock.

A.   *Which group(s) of shareholders must approve the merger?*
B.   *Do the shareholders of T have dissenters' rights?*
C.   *Do the shareholders of A have dissenters' rights?*

Problem 12-33:   Cage Corp. ("A") has 100 million shares of its common stock outstanding, which are listed on the NYSE. Tiger Corp. ("T") has 50 million shares of common stock outstanding, which are also listed on the NYSE. The boards of directors of A and T have adopted a plan of merger that provides that T will merge into A. A will survive the merger. A's articles of incorporation will not be changed as a result of the merger, nor will there be any change to its currently outstanding shares of common stock. In the merger, each share of T common stock will be converted into the right to receive $10 in cash.

A.   *Which group(s) of shareholders must approve the merger?*
B.   *Do the shareholders of T have dissenters' rights?*
C.   *Do the shareholders of A have dissenters' rights?*

Problem 12-34:   Shark Corp. ("A") has 100 million shares of common stock outstanding, which are listed on the Nasdaq Stock Market. Guppy Corp. ("T") has 25 million shares of common stock outstanding, which are listed on the NYSE. The boards of directors of A and T have adopted a plan of merger that provides that T will merge into A. A will survive the merger. A's articles of incorporation will not be changed as a result of the merger, nor will there be any change to its currently outstanding shares of common stock. In the merger, each share of T common stock will be converted into the right to receive a coupon worth $30 toward the purchase of a new fish tank.

A.   *Which group(s) of shareholders must approve the merger?*
B.   *Do the shareholders of T have dissenters' rights?*
C.   *Do the shareholders of A have dissenters' rights?*

Problem 12-35: Horse Corp. ("A") has 100 million shares of common stock outstanding, which are not currently listed on any stock exchange or traded in any stock market. Hay Corp. ("T") has 50 million shares of common stock outstanding, which are listed on the NYSE, and held by approximately 3,000 persons. The boards of directors of A and T have adopted a plan of merger that provides that T will merge into A. A will survive the merger. A's articles of incorporation will not be changed as a result of the merger, nor will there be any change to its currently outstanding shares of common stock. In the merger, each share of T common stock will be converted into the right to receive one share of A common stock. A intends to have its stock listed on the NYSE simultaneously with the effective date of the merger.

A.   *Which group(s) of shareholders must approve the merger?*
B.   *Do the shareholders of T have dissenters' rights?*
C.   *Do the shareholders of A have dissenters' rights?*

Problem 12-36: *If ABC Corp., a closely held corporation, sells assets in a transaction that requires shareholder approval under MBCA § 12.02, will its shareholders have dissenters' rights?*

Problem 12-37: *If DEF Corp., a closely held corporation, dissolves, will its shareholders have dissenters' rights?*

Problem 12-38: *If GHI Corp., a closely held corporation, amends its articles of incorporation to change its name to JKL Corp., will its shareholders have dissenters' rights?*

Problem 12-39: *Why do you think that MBCA § 13.02(b)(1) "takes away" dissenters' rights for shares that are publicly traded within the meaning of that section?*

Procedures For Asserting Dissenters' Rights. Assuming that a shareholder[*] has dissenters' rights with respect to a given transaction or event, the

---

[*]   Generally, a shareholder who wishes to assert dissenters' rights must do so with respect to all of the shares that she owns. However, MBCA § 13.03 makes clear that a *record* owner, such as a bank or broker, that holds stock on behalf of multiple clients (i.e., *beneficial*

MBCA specifies several procedural steps that must be taken. To keep the following discussion relatively simple, we will assume that (1) the transaction that gave rise to dissenters' rights is a merger, (2) the corporation's shareholders will vote on the merger at a shareholders meeting, and (3) the dissenting shareholder acquired all of her shares of stock *before* the principal terms of the merger were publicly announced. (The MBCA contains several provisions for situations where any of these assumptions is not true, as well as for parent-subsidiary mergers under MBCA § 11.05 where the subsidiary's minority shareholders are not required to vote on the merger.)

First, under MBCA § 13.20, the corporation is required to notify shareholders that they have dissenters' rights when it sends the notice of the shareholders meeting. The corporation must also provide shareholders with certain financial statements and a copy of the MBCA sections concerning dissenters' rights.

Next, a shareholder who wishes to assert dissenters' rights must so notify the corporation *before the vote is taken* at the meeting. Notice how this requirement could easily "trip up" an unwary (or lazy) shareholder. Further, a shareholder who wishes to assert dissenters' rights must not vote in favor of the merger. Voting no is permissible, as is abstaining or not voting at all, but a shareholder who votes in favor of the merger loses her dissenters' rights.

If the merger occurs, the corporation (notice that the "corporation" at this point will be the surviving corporation) must, within ten days, send a notice to all shareholders who have "perfected" their dissenters' rights as described above. Among other things, this notice will require the shareholder to certify that she did not vote in favor of the merger. The notice will also (among other things): inform the shareholder where she must send her stock certificates and the deadline for doing so; set forth the corporation's estimate of the "fair value" of the shares; inform the shareholder that, if she requests, the corporation will inform her how many shareholders have asserted dissenters' rights and how many shares those shareholders own; and inform the shareholder of the deadline for withdrawing her claim of dissenters' rights.

Let's assume that the shareholder complies with the notice described above and does not thereafter decide to withdraw her claim of dissenters' rights. The corporation must then, within thirty days, pay the shareholder the corporation's estimate of the fair value of the shares (which cannot be less than the fair value estimate that was set forth in the notice described above), plus interest. For example, if the corporation had estimated the fair value of the shares to be $20, and the shareholder owned 1,000 shares, the corporation would send the

---

owners), may assert dissenters' rights on behalf of one or more clients, rather than being required to assert dissenters' rights on behalf of all of its clients.

share-holder a check for $20,000, plus interest. Certain additional information is also required to be given to the shareholder. The corporation must also inform the shareholder that she has the right to demand *additional* payment for her shares, but that if she does not do so within the deadline specified in MBCA § 13.26 she will forfeit her right to do so.

Theoretically, the shareholder might be satisfied with the corporation's estimate of the fair value of the shares and the matter could end there. However, it seems more likely that the shareholder will think that the fair value of the shares is higher. After all, the corporation likely will have estimated that the fair value of the shares is equal to the merger consideration. If the shareholder had agreed, then she most likely wouldn't have asserted dissenters' rights in the first place! But notice how the MBCA's procedures will result in the shareholder getting the undisputed portion of the fair value of the shares now (in the example above, that is $20 per share), rather than waiting until the litigation is over. As the official comment to MBCA § 13.24 states, a "difference of opinion over the total amount to be paid [to the shareholder] should not delay payment of the amount that is undisputed."

If the shareholder is unhappy with the corporation's estimate of fair value, MBCA § 13.26 requires her to notify the corporation of her estimate of the fair value of her shares within thirty days. If the parties are unable to settle their differences within the next sixty days, the *corporation* will be required under MBCA § 13.30 to petition the appropriate court to determine the fair value of the shares. (If it does not do so, then it must pay the shareholder *her* estimate of the fair value of the shares, less amounts that it previously paid to her.)

All dissenting shareholders who have not yet settled will be made parties to the proceeding. Interestingly, MBCA § 13.31 provides that the corporation bears court costs, including the compensation and expenses of court-appointed appraisers, unless the court finds that the shareholder "acted arbitrarily, vexatiously, or not in good faith." The parties, however, would bear their other respective expenses including attorney fees, unless the court finds that a party "acted arbitrarily, vexatiously, or not in good faith," in which case that party could be required to pay some or all of another party's expenses.

Eventually, the court will determine the "fair value" of the shares and the corporation will pay the shareholder that amount (less amounts that she previously was paid as described above), plus interest. But note that there is no guarantee that the court will find a fair value that is higher than the corporation's estimate of fair value. In that case, the shareholder would not be entitled to any additional amounts for her shares; she would only keep what the corporation previously paid her as described above.

What is The "Fair Value" of the Shares? But what is "fair value" and how does a court determine it? MBCA § 13.01(4) defines "fair value" as:

> the value of the corporation's shares determined:
>
> (i)   immediately before the effectuation of the corporate action to which the shareholder objects;
>
> (ii)   using customary and current valuation concepts and techniques generally employed for similar businesses in the context of the transaction requiring appraisal; and
>
> (iii)   without discounting for lack of marketability or minority status except, if appropriate ***.

A few things are important to note about this section. First, subsection (ii) essentially states that the court should use "state of the art" valuation techniques to determine the fair value of the shares. Before *Weinberger v. UOP*, which appears in Chapter 11, Delaware courts had used a technique for valuing shares called the "Delaware block method." However, many commentators had criticized the Delaware block method. Moreover, much like a science, financial analysis techniques are always evolving. As the *Weinberger* court explained:

> In this breach of fiduciary duty case, the Chancellor perceived that the approach to valuation was the same as that in an appraisal proceeding. Consistent with precedent, he rejected plaintiff's method of proof and accepted defendants' evidence of value as being in accord with practice under prior case law. This means that the so-called "Delaware block" or weighted average method was employed wherein the elements of value, i.e., assets, market price, earnings, etc., were assigned a particular weight and the resulting amounts added to determine the value per share. This procedure has been in use for decades. [Citation omitted.] However, to the extent it excludes other generally accepted techniques used in the financial community and the courts, it is now clearly outmoded. It is time we recognize this in appraisal and other stock valuation proceedings and bring our law current on the subject.

Thus, the *Weinberger* court held that the Delaware block method was no longer the exclusive method of valuing shares. As the court wrote, "a more liberal approach must include proof of value by any techniques or methods which are generally considered acceptable in the financial community and otherwise admissible in court." Further, "all relevant factors" should be considered in determining fair value. Thus, courts in Delaware and many other states use different techniques to value shares in dissenters' rights proceedings. While it would obviously behoove you to learn more about these techniques if you are ever involved in a dissenters' rights lawsuit when you are in practice, we will not consider them further here. On the other hand, the official comment to MBCA § 13.01 notes that "[a]bsent unusual circumstances, it is expected that the consideration in any arms'-length transaction will fall within the range of 'fair value' for purposes of section 13.01(4)."

Another issue that is relevant to valuation concerns whether it is appropriate to discount (that is, reduce) the value of the shares for certain attributes that they have, such whether they are sufficient in number to exercise control over the corporation, or whether it would be difficult to resell them to someone else. While cases are divided on these issues, the MBCA is clear. Ponder the following problems:

Problems

Problem 12-40: AB Corp. is owned by two shareholders: Ms. A, who owns 51 shares of common stock, and Mr. B, who owns 49 shares. A world-famous business appraiser has determined that AB Corp. is worth exactly $1 million, and no one has any valid reason to dispute this conclusion. Assume that you have a great deal of money and are looking to invest in AB Corp. Both Ms. A and Mr. B have indicated that either—but not both—of them would sell their shares to you. *How much would you pay for Ms. A's shares? How much would you pay for Mr. B's shares?*

Problem 12-41: Assume that AB Corp. is merged into CD Corp. Ms. A voted her 51 shares in favor of the merger, but Mr. B instead asserted dissenters' rights. *What should be the "fair value" of Mr. B's shares in his dissenters' rights proceeding?*

Are Dissenters' Rights Exclusive? A final issue to consider in connection with dissenters' rights is whether they are an unhappy shareholder's exclusive (that is, only) method to challenge a transaction. For various reasons, a shareholder may prefer to challenge a merger, or sue for damages, on grounds such as breach of fiduciary duty, rather than asserting dissenters' rights. May she do so?

MBCA § 13.40 provides, in somewhat ambiguous language:

(a)   The legality of a proposed or completed corporate action described in section 13.02(a) may not be contested, nor may the corporate action be enjoined, set aside or rescinded, in a legal or equitable proceeding by a shareholder after the shareholders have approved the corporate action.

(b)   Subsection (a) does not apply to any corporate action that:

(1)   was not authorized and approved in accordance with the applicable provisions of: (i) chapter 9, 10, 11, or 12, (ii) the articles of incorporation or bylaws, or (iii) the resolution of the board of directors authorizing the corporate action; [or]

(2)   was procured as a result of fraud, a material misrepresentation, or an omission of a material fact necessary to make statements made, in light of the circumstances in which they were made, not misleading; [or]

(3)   is an interested transaction, unless it has been recommended by the board of directors in the same manner as is provided in section 8.62 and has been approved by the shareholders in the same manner as is provided in section 8.63 as if the interested transaction were a director's conflicting interest transaction;

***

The official comment to this section notes that the "limitations are not confined to cases where appraisal is available." Thus, if shareholders do *not* have dissenters' rights with respect to, say, a merger (such as where their stock was publicly traded within the meaning of MBCA § 13.02(b)(1)), they may *not* challenge the legality of the merger unless one or more of the exceptions in subsection (b) applies.

However, the official comment also states that MBCA § 13.40 "addresses challenges only to the corporate action and does not address remedies, if any, that shareholders may have against directors or other persons as a result of the corporate action, even where subsection [(b)] applies." Does this mean that a shareholder who was unhappy with the consideration that she would receive in a merger (or unhappy about other aspects of the merger) may *both* dissent and sue her board of directors for breaching their duty of care and/or their duty of loyalty?

Courts in other states have generally answered this question in the negative. Returning to the ever-popular *Weinberger v. UOP*, the court there held that:

> While a plaintiff's monetary remedy ordinarily should be confined to the more liberalized appraisal proceeding herein established, we do not intend any limitation on the historic powers of the Chancellor to grant such other relief as the facts of a particular case may dictate. The appraisal remedy we approve may not be adequate in certain cases, particularly where fraud, misrepresentation, self-dealing, deliberate waste of corporate assets, or gross and palpable overreaching are involved. [Citation omitted.] Under such circumstances, the Chancellor's powers are complete to fashion any form of equitable and monetary relief as may be appropriate, including rescissory damages. Since it is apparent that this long completed transaction is too involved to undo, and in view of the Chancellor's discretion, the award, if any, should be in the form of monetary damages based upon entire fairness standards, i.e., fair dealing and fair price.

In other words, in Delaware dissenters' rights are a shareholder-plaintiff's exclusive remedy, unless fraud or other exceptions described above are present. *See also Rabkin v. Philip A. Hunt Chemical Corp.*, 498 A.2d 1099 (Del. 1985) (shareholders may sue for damages if they can prove specific acts of unfair dealing that constitute a breach of fiduciary duties). *But see Glassman v. Unocal Exploration Corp.*, 777 A.2d 242 (Del. 2001) (unless fraud or illegality are present, dissenters' rights are the exclusive remedy in a short-form merger, i.e., where parent merges with 90%-owned subsidiary; the parent corporation need not establish the entire fairness of a short-form merger).

In sum, it appears that if the shareholder's sole claim is that the *price* in the merger was inadequate, then asserting dissenters' rights is the sole remedy. Otherwise, appraisal may not be exclusive. If asserting dissenters' rights is not the shareholder's sole remedy, she may attempt to recover rescissory damages, which in some circumstances could be greater than the fair value of her shares at the time the merger occurred.

§ 12.07   TENDER OFFERS

Objectives: You should be able to:

- *What is a Tender Offer?* *Explain what a tender offer is, and why it sometimes is preferable or necessary for an Acquiring*

Corporation that wishes to acquire a Target corporation to conduct a tender offer instead of acquiring the Target through a merger or an asset purchase.

● **Schedule 13D.** *Explain when (or whether) the Acquirer will need to file a Schedule 13D with the Securities and Exchange Commission ("SEC") with respect to the stock of the Target. If the Acquirer must file a Schedule 13D with the SEC, list some of the basic items of information that must be included in that document.*

● **Basic Regulation of Tender Offers.** *Explain to an Acquirer that wishes to acquire a Target corporation via a tender offer the basic requirements of SEC rules governing tender offers. In particular, you should be able to explain how long the tender offer must stay open; whether shareholders who have already tendered their Target stock to the Acquirer may withdraw it; whether the Acquirer can exclude any Target shareholders from the tender offer; what must happen if the Acquirer increases the price that it is offering or otherwise materially changes the terms of the tender offer; and what would happen if more Target stock is tendered to the Acquirer than it wishes to purchase in the tender offer.*

A.   HOSTILE ACQUISITIONS IN GENERAL

If a (potential) Target corporation receives an offer to acquire the corporation, the Target's board of directors has a duty to consider the offer in good faith. This does not mean, however, that the Target's board must accept the offer or even that it must always start negotiations with the (potential) Acquirer. In fact, the Target corporation's board could in some circumstances reject the offer and refuse to communicate with the Acquirer. (We will consider in the following section the legal effects of doing so.)

What is a spurned—but determined—Acquirer to do at that point? Acquiring the Target corporation through a merger or by purchasing all or substantially all of its assets are both out of the question, because each of those methods would require the Target corporation's board, in addition to its shareholders, to approve the transaction. If the Target's board will not negotiate with the Acquirer, then the transaction will become a ***hostile acquisition***. (Note that in this section, we will assume that the Target corporation is a reporting company under Section 12 of the Securities Exchange Act. In other words, it is publicly traded.)

Generally speaking, there are two ways to acquire a Target on a hostile basis. The first is called a **proxy contest.** Basically, in a proxy contest an "insurgent" shareholder, who could have the goal of acquiring the corporation, seeks to replace the current directors with different directors. To do so, the insurgent shareholder will solicit proxies from other shareholders to vote in favor of the insurgent's board nominees. If the insurgent shareholder successfully solicits proxies from enough other shareholders to defeat the incumbent directors at the next annual meeting of shareholders, the insurgent's candidates will be elected to the board. Obviously, these new directors would be more "receptive" to the insurgent's takeover offers than were the ousted directors.

However, there are many serious drawbacks to conducting a proxy contest. First, soliciting proxies is enormously expensive. If you solicit proxies from a shareholder of a publicly traded corporation, you must provide that shareholder with a proxy statement on Schedule 14A, unless one or more exceptions apply (as you learned in Chapter 10). The preparation of a Schedule 14A will require the involvement of expensive attorneys, and printing and mailing a Schedule 14A proxy statement to thousands of shareholders will obviously be expensive. (Note that the Target's incumbent board does not itself bear such expenses—the *corporation* will pay for their proxy solicitation expenses!) Further, the Target's board could sue the insurgent, claiming that the Schedule 14A or other soliciting materials are false and misleading in violation of SEC Rule 14a-9, which could tie up the proxy contest in expensive litigation.

Perhaps worse, there is no guarantee that the other shareholders will be receptive to the insurgent shareholder and give their proxies. They may distrust the insurgent's motives, fearing that it intends to "loot" the Target. Shareholders of public corporations are often called "rationally apathetic," meaning that they will not think it is worth their time to educate themselves about the proxy contest, especially if they only own a small number of shares. Proxy statements sent to such shareholders are likely to end up in the "circular file" (i.e., the garbage can). Moreover, even if the insurgent is successful in the proxy contest, if the Target's board of directors is staggered into three classes (as you learned is possible in Chapter 5 of this book), the insurgent will only have "captured" one-third of the board. A proxy contest in the following year will be needed to capture a majority of the board, if the Target's articles of incorporation provide that cause is necessary to remove a director before the end of her term. And only God knows whether another proxy contest next year will be successful. Finally, even if the proxy contest is successful and the price of the Target's stock increases due to having better management, the insurgent must "share" these gains with all of the other shareholders (whose stock also increased in value). For these reasons, proxy contests are rare and we will not discuss them further.[*]

The second basic method by which to conduct a hostile acquisition is called a ***tender offer*** (although not every tender offer is done on a "hostile" basis). Basically, in a tender offer, an offeror offers to purchase a specified amount of Target stock from the Target's shareholders if certain conditions are met. If the conditions are met, the tender offer will close, and the offeror will purchase the shares that have been tendered to it. In this sense, a tender offer is simply an invitation to all of the Target's shareholders to tender their shares (that is, deposit their shares into escrow) to the offeror and, if the conditions are met, to sell their shares to the offeror at the offered price. Note that the beauty of the tender offer is that it allows the Acquirer to bypass the Target's board and go directly to its shareholders. As the saying goes, everything is for sale. If you offer an attractive enough price in your tender offer, odds are that it will be successful.

What will this offered price be in a tender offer? Again assuming that the Target is publicly traded, its stock will likely be listed on the New York Stock Exchange, NASDAQ, or some other stock market, which means that every day the many buyers and sellers of its stock create a "market price." In that case, consider the following problem.

Problem

Problem 12-42: You represent Acquirer Corp., which wants to acquire Target Corp. via a tender offer. The current market price of Target Corp. stock is $100 per share and there are 1 million shares outstanding. *How many shares should Acquirer Corp. seek to purchase? What should be the offering price in your tender offer—$100 per share or something higher? If higher, should you recommend that Acquirer Corp. start its tender offer now or is there something else you recommend doing first?*

B.   SECTION 13(d) OF THE EXCHANGE ACT

Hopefully, answering Problem 12-42 was easy. Acquirer Corp. should seek at least 500,001 shares, giving it a majority position in Target Corp. stock. (After doing so, it obviously will remove Target Corp.'s board at the next shareholders meeting, elect different directors, and then could merge Target Corp.

---

[*]   However, as discussed in Chapter 10, recent changes to SEC rules may have made it somewhat easier for shareholders to nominate one or more directors, assuming that the shareholder does not intend to gain control of the corporation.

into itself or a subsidiary. Such a merger is sometimes called a "second-step" merger.)

Further, offering $100 per share in Problem 12-42 simply will not result in a successful tender offer; some "control premium" will be needed to convince enough Target Corp. shareholders to tender their shares so that Acquirer Corp. reaches its goal of acquiring at least 500,001 shares. But maybe a thought has occurred to you: why not go out and buy shares of Target Corp. stock at $100 per share *now*, before the tender offer is announced? If Acquirer Corp. is planning on offering, say, $130 per share, for every share it acquires at a price lower than $130 it saves itself money.

But Section 13(d) of the Securities Exchange Act of 1934 provides that, if Acquirer Corp. were to acquire[*] more than a certain amount of Target Corp. shares, it must file a Schedule 13D with the SEC, Target Corp., and any stock exchanges on which Target Corp. stock is listed. (SEC filings are made electronically and are, within minutes, available to the public as well.) Read Section 13(d) and consider the following problems.

Problems

Problem 12-43: Same facts as Problem 12-42. *How many shares of Target Corp. stock may Acquirer Corp. buy before it triggers an obligation to file a Schedule 13D with the SEC? What is the deadline for filing the Schedule 13D? What information must appear in a Schedule 13D? Is a Schedule 13D required if Acquirer Corp. does not have any plans to acquire Target Corp.?*

Problem 12-44: *If five people, acting together, each acquire 1.001% of Target Corp. stock, must they file a Schedule 13D? See Section 13(d)(3) of the Exchange Act and SEC Rule 13d-5(b)(1). What if these persons have not signed a written agreement?*

Problem 12-45: *When must a Schedule 13D be amended to reflect new facts? See SEC Rule 13d-2(a).*

---

[*]   The ownership threshold of Section 13(d) turns on whether a person has beneficial ownership of a certain amount of the equity securities of a publicly traded company. SEC Rule 13d-3(a) defines beneficial ownership as having, directly or indirectly, "voting power" and/or "investment power" over the shares.

C.   FEDERAL TENDER OFFER RULES

Theoretically, Acquirer Corp. could reach its goal of acquiring a majority of Target Corp. stock by continuing to make open-market purchases of Target Corp. stock. However, such an approach is likely to take a great deal of time, perhaps even years depending on the nature of Target Corp. and its stock. A tender offer essentially speeds things up, and if successful can quickly accomplish Acquirer Corp.'s goal of gaining a majority of Target Corp. stock.

As discussed above, to be successful, the tender offer will almost certainly offer a price that is much higher than the current market price. There is no law or SEC rule concerning how high the offering price must (or may) be. Instead, the offeror must make a judgment call and decide what price must it offer to be successful. In addition, once the tender offer is announced, it is possible that other, competing tender offers for the same Target company will be launched. Obviously, the presence of one or more competing tender offers could set off a "bidding war."

Section 14(d) of the Securities Exchange Act essentially provides that any tender offer that would result in an offeror owning more than five percent of the equity securities (that is, stock) of a publicly traded company must comply, not only with the various subsections of Section 14(d), but also with any SEC rules concerning tender offers. While you probably will not become an "expert" on tender offers by reading the following, you should be aware of the basic substantive rules governing tender offers. Generally speaking, these rules seem designed to protect the Target's shareholders.

First, at the time that it commences the tender offer, the offeror must file a document with the SEC called a Schedule TO. The Schedule TO contains much of the same information that is required in Schedule 13D, as well as information about the tender offer, such as the price offered, the number of shares that the offeror is seeking (sometimes expressed as either or both a minimum and a maximum); a description of prior negotiations (if any) between the offeror and the Target; and other information.[*]

In addition, the tender offer must be publicized to the Target's shareholders. Under SEC Rule 14d-4(a)(1), this could be achieved by a "long form" newspaper publication, but the usual route chosen is to (1) publish a

---

[*] Typically, the offeror in a tender offer will offer cash for the Target shares. However, the offeror could instead offer shares of its own stock. As you will learn in Chapter 13, a public offering of securities (such as stock) must be registered by filing a detailed registration statement/prospectus with the SEC. Fortunately, if the tender offeror is offering stock, the SEC will expedite its review of the registration statement/prospectus. To keep things simple, however, we will assume a cash tender offer.

"summary advertisement" of the tender offer in a newspaper of national circulation and also mail the offering materials to the Target shareholders. The could happen in either of two ways. First, the Target could mail the Schedule TO to its shareholders, at the offeror's expense. Alternatively, the Target could give the offer a list of its shareholders' mailing addresses. *See* SEC Rule 14d-5. Typically, the Target will do the mailing itself to keep this "sensitive" information out of the offeror's hands.

Second, within ten business days after the tender offer starts, the *Target* must file a Schedule 14D-9 with the SEC. The purpose of this form is so that the Target's management can present its opinion of the tender offer: they could endorse it (i.e., recommend it to the shareholders), oppose it, or take no position.

Next, there are many substantive rules that come into play governing the conduct of the tender offer. To see these rules in action, we will return to Acquirer Corp. and Target Corp. from the previous set of problems.

Problems

Problem 12-46: Same facts as Problem 12-42, except that Acquirer Corp. previously acquired 50,001 shares of Target Corp. stock. It then filed a Schedule 13D with the SEC disclosing that it planned to conduct a tender offer for a minimum *and* maximum of 450,000 shares of Target Corp. stock for $130 per share and that, if successful, it would then merge Target Corp. into itself, paying all remaining shareholders $130 per share. Acquirer Corp. has asked you the following questions about its planned tender offer:

A. *How long must the tender offer remain open? See SEC Rule 14e-1(a). What if Acquirer Corp. materially changes the terms of the tender offer? See SEC Rule 14e-1(b).*

B. *May any Target Corp. shareholders be excluded from the tender offer? See SEC Rule 14d-10(a)(1).*

C. *May Acquirer Corp. purchase any Target shares "outside" the tender offer, such as in privately negotiated purchases? See Rule 14e-3.*

Problem 12-47: Same facts as Problem 12-46, except that near the end of the tender offer period only 430,000 shares have been tendered and Acquirer Corp. is worried. It learns that Hank Holdout owns 20,000 shares of Target Corp. stock but has not yet tendered them. After a telephone conversation with Hank, the president of Acquirer Corp. agrees to pay Hank $135 per share, but warns him not to "tell anyone else." *What effect does this have on the tender offer? See SEC Rule 14d-10(a)(2).*

Problem 12-48:   Same facts as Problem 12-46, except that the tender offer is wildly successful: 900,000 shares are tendered. (Remember, Acquirer Corp. was only seeking 450,000 shares in this tender offer.) *Does Acquirer Corp. have to purchase all 900,000 shares? If not, how many must it purchase and how would it decide which ones to purchase? See Exchange Act § 14(d)(6).*

Problem 12-49:   *If a competing tender offer is begun while Acquirer Corp.'s tender offer is still open, may Target shareholders who have already tendered their shares to Acquirer Corp. withdraw their shares? See SEC Rule 14d-7. Why would they want to do so?*

Another important SEC rule concerning tender offers is found in the statute.   Section 14(e) of the Securities Exchange Act provides that it is "unlawful" (that is, a possible criminal violation):

for any person to make any untrue statement of a material fact or omit to state any material fact necessary in order to make the statements made, in the light of the circumstances under which they are made, not misleading, or to engage in any fraudulent, deceptive, or manipulative acts or practices, in connection with any tender offer ***.

If a tender offer is particularly "hostile," this provision could easily result in litigation. For example, the Target's management might allege (or complain to the SEC) that the offeror has engaged in one or more fraudulent acts or made material misstatements. Or perhaps the offeror will claim that the Target's management engaged in such acts. While courts generally have held that Target shareholders have standing to sue under Section 14(e), courts have reached differing conclusions as to whether the Target or the offeror themselves do. (You will also learn about one of the anti-fraud rules, Rule 14e-3, in Chapter 14.)

"Self-Tenders"
A corporation may make a tender offer for its own shares. The rules for such "self-tenders" are very similar to the rules that apply to tender offers by third parties. See Section 13(e) of the Exchange Act and SEC Rule 13e-4.

In the end, if the tender offer is successful (that is, all of the offeror's conditions, such as receiving a minimum number of shares, are either met or the offeror waives them), then a closing will occur. At that point, the tendered shares are released from escrow and the offeror purchases them, paying the offering price to the shareholders who tendered their shares. Conversely, if the tender offer was not successful, any tendered shares would be returned to their owners.

The careful reader will have noted that we have not yet discussed the precise definition of "tender offer." Perhaps surprisingly, neither the Exchange Act nor any SEC rule actually defines "tender offer." Usually, however, it's pretty easy to decide whether something is a tender offer: it is a limited-time offer to acquire a substantial amount of Target shares at a substantial premium over current market prices. However, there are several "unorthodox" types of stock acquisitions that could be considered tender offers. The interested reader may wish to consult two of the leading cases on whether an offer is a "tender offer": *Securities and Exchange Commission v. Carter Hawley Hale Stores, Inc.*, 760 F.2d 945 (9th Cir. 1985); and *Hanson Trust PLC v. SCM Corp.*, 774 F.2d 47 (2d Cir. 1985).

§ 12.08   TAKEOVER DEFENSES

Objectives: *You should be able to:*

•   ***Types of Takeover Defenses.*** *Explain in general terms some defenses that a corporation may erect to make a hostile acquisition of the company less likely, both as a "planning" matter and after an attempted hostile acquisition of the company has actually started.*

•   ***Court Evaluation of Takeover Defenses.*** *Explain the standard that a court will employ to decide whether a takeover defense erected by a Target corporation, such as a "poison pill," is permissible. Given a fact pattern concerning a takeover defense, determine the likely outcome of such a lawsuit.*

•   ***"Revlon" Duties.*** *Given a fact pattern, determine whether the board of directors of a corporation has "Revlon" duties to get the best value reasonably available for the its shareholders. Given fact pattern, determine whether the board's conduct was consistent with its "Revlon" duties and, if not, what remedy is appropriate.*

A.   TYPES OF TAKEOVER DEFENSES

As you know, a corporation's board of directors owes fiduciary duties to the corporation, which has traditionally been interpreted to mean that directors should put the interests of shareholders first. Shareholders, of course, are investors and the goal of investors (or at least most of them) is to earn a good return on their investments. Thus, when a third party is interested in acquiring the corporation, the board has a duty to consider the proposal and determine whether it is in the best interests of the corporation and its shareholders (although this does not necessarily mean that the board must accept the proposal or even negotiate with the bidder). If the offer is attractive enough or can be made so through negotiations, the board's fiduciary duties may compel it to accept.

As you learned above, in mergers and asset sales the board serves as a "gatekeeper" for acquisition offers; both mergers and asset sales must first be approved by the board (and afterwards by the shareholders in most cases). But many of the directors may be "inside" directors that earn generous salaries as executive officers of the corporation. Even the "outside" (non-employee) directors of a corporation may earn generous director fees, particularly if the corporation is large. Human nature being human nature, these persons probably enjoy earning this money and having the power to control a corporation and may—correctly—worry that, if the corporation is acquired by a third party, they will lose their jobs and/or director positions and the incomes and power that come with them. Thus, when a corporation's board of directors erects one or more *takeover defenses*, we should perhaps be a bit suspicious. Perhaps the board is doing so to protect the shareholders (or other "constituencies" such as bondholders and employees) from unfair takeovers and force the Acquirer to negotiate with the board. On the other hand, maybe the board is doing adopting takeover defenses to perpetuate itself in office. The cases that you will read below reflect this tension.

But first, let's examine some of the many types of takeover defenses that a corporation may employ. Generally speaking, these fall into two categories. The first are those that the corporation may adopt as a *planning* matter, when no hostile acquisition of the corporation has been attempted or threatened. The second are those that the board may erect *in response* to a pending or threatened hostile acquisition.

To plan against a hostile takeover, we must first think about how a hostile Acquirer would attempt to get control of the Target company. As discussed in the previous section, the two obvious methods are the proxy contest and the tender offer. In both of these methods, the Acquirer will attempt to replace the current members of the Target's board of directors with persons who will abide by the Acquirer's wishes. What can we do to make this more difficult?

A *staggered board* is an obvious idea. As you learned in Chapter 5, the board may be classified into as many as three classes with overlapping terms. If the board has three classes, then every year only one-third of the directors will be "up" for election; directors generally will serve three-year terms. If a staggered board is coupled with an articles provision that directors may only be removed from office before the end of their terms *for cause*, then even an Acquirer who becomes a majority shareholder through a tender offer would need at least two annual shareholder meetings to elect a majority of the Target's board. In addition, to ensure that the hostile Acquirer who acquires a majority of the Target's stock does not expand the size of the board and then "pack" it with its nominees, the size of the board should be set in the articles. As you learned in Section 12.01 above, an amendment to the articles must first be approved by the board. *See* MBCA § 10.03(a).

Another idea to make a hostile Acquirer's task more difficult would be to include *supermajority provisions* in the Target corporation's articles. As you learned in Chapter 5, MBCA § 7.27 allows the corporation's articles to increase the vote requirement for shareholder action above the usual "more yes votes than no votes" rule. If a hostile Acquirer obtains a majority of the Target corporation's stock in a tender offer, it often will then merge the Target into itself in a "second step" merger. Often, the remaining shareholders in the second step merger may not receive as much, or the same type of, consideration that the shareholders who tendered their shares received. (You will see this tactic at work in the *Unocal* case below.) To prevent such an unfair and coercive transaction from taking place, an articles provision could require, say, an 80% shareholder vote to approve a merger with the Acquirer (or any person who has acquired a certain amount of the Target's stock), unless all shareholders will receive the same amount and type of consideration that was offered in a previous tender offer by the Acquirer. Because it is unlikely that a tender offer will result in the Acquirer owning 80% of the Target's stock, this will ensure that all shareholders are treated equally. Nearly endless variations on this theme are possible.

Another takeover defense that may be adopted as a planning tool before any actual takeover attempt has begun is called a *poison pill.* Poison pills come in many varieties and differ in many important respects, but they are all impressive feats of legal engineering. If you find the following description of poison pills difficult to understand, at least make sure that you grasp the main point: a poison pill is designed to make a hostile acquisition of the company too expensive for the Acquirer. However, the Target company's current directors—and only the Target's directors—have the ability to "kill the pill," that is, to redeem it. If they do, the acquisition may proceed. If they don't, the acquisition will almost certainly not occur. In this way, a poison pill forces a would-be hostile Acquirer to negotiate with the Target's board. If a mutually acceptable resolution can be found, then the Target's board can redeem the poison pill and allow the acquisition to occur.

In terms of specifics, again, poison pills vary greatly. But one typical attribute of poison pills is that they distribute "rights" to the Target's current shareholders. When the poison pill (often called a "rights plan," perhaps to make it sound less ominous) is adopted by the board, each shareholder will receive, free of charge, a distribution of one "right" for each share that she owns. Until one of the triggering events described below occurs, (1) rights may not be exercised and (2) rights may not be traded separately from the stock. In other words, until a triggering event occurs, rights have no real value.[*] Also, if a shareholder sells her shares, she also transfers the associated rights to the purchaser.

A typical triggering event that would make rights exercisable is the acquisition of twenty percent of the Target corporation's stock by an Acquirer that was not previously "approved" by the Target's board. If such a triggering event occurs, then the rights may be exercised (and typically may then also be sold separately from the stock to which they initially attached).

So, what rights do "rights" confer on a shareholder? Typically, poison-pill rights give shareholders the right to purchase additional securities (such as new shares of common or preferred stock) at deep, deep discounts. Beyond that, the precise nature of the rights conferred by a given corporation's poison pill will obviously depend on the terms of that corporation's poison pill, but commonly there are two types: *flip-in* rights and *flip-over* rights.

"Flip-in" rights allow shareholders to purchase additional shares of the Target corporation's stock at a steep discount, perhaps half the market price. For example, the rights might allow a shareholder to purchase a share of common stock that was currently trading for $10 per share for a mere $5 per share. Again, however, the rights would only become exercisable if a triggering event occurred. And importantly, the person (such as a hostile Acquirer) who caused the triggering event to occur would not be allowed to exercise rights.

Note how this could dilute a hostile Acquirer's percentage ownership in the Target. For example, assume that (1) there are 1 million shares of Target Corp. stock outstanding, (2) Target's common stock is currently trading at $10 per share, (3) Target's poison pill contains flip-in rights that become exercisable when an unapproved Acquirer acquires twenty percent of Target's stock, and (4) each right would allow a shareholder (other than the triggering person) to buy one additional share of stock for half price. If X Corp., a hostile acquirer, buys

---

[*]   Typically, rights may be exercised before a triggering event occurs, but would at that point only allow shareholders to buy new shares of stock at prices *far above* current market prices. Obviously, no rational shareholder would do so.

200,000 shares of Target stock for $10 per share, the holders of the *other* 800,000 shares would most likely then exercise their rights, paying $5 per share for 800,000 new shares of Target stock. Afterwards, Target Corp. would have 1.8 million shares outstanding. This would reduce X Corp.'s stake in Target Corp. from twenty percent (200,000 out of 1 million) to 11.1% (200,000 out of 1.8 million). Worse from X Corp.'s perspective, the per-share value of Target Corp. stock would have fallen because Target Corp. sold 800,000 shares for less than the $10 current market value. This economic "poison" will make it highly unlikely that X Corp. would purchase enough shares to trigger the poison pill rights.

"Flip-over" rights allow shareholders to purchase shares of *another* corporation at a deep discount. What other corporation, you ask? Most likely the *hostile Acquirer*. For example, flip-over rights often provide that, if the Target is merged into the Acquirer or an affiliate of the Acquirer, the former Target shareholders would then be allowed to purchase new shares of the Acquirer's stock at deep discounts. (Remember that in a merger the surviving corporation becomes liable for all of the obligations of the Target corporation.) This would obviously upset the Acquirer's other shareholders! In *Moran v. Household International, Inc.*, 500 A.2d 1346 (Del. 1985), the Delaware Supreme Court upheld such a flip-over poison pill against certain legal challenges. *Moran* is discussed in Section 12.07(B) below.

Here's the important point about poison pills, though: at any time before the rights become exercisable (or within a certain deadline afterwards), the Target corporation's board may redeem the rights for a minor payment. Further, only the Target corporation's board can redeem the rights and make the pill go away. Again, if there's only one thing that you remember about poison pills after reading the above (admittedly simplified) discussion, it's that the presence of a poison pill is an effective hostile takeover deterrent—it forces would-be hostile Acquirers to negotiate with the Target's board. Only the Target's board has the "antidote" for the poison pill.

If a hostile acquisition has already been "launched," a Target board that wishes to defeat the acquisition has some other options, which may be particularly necessary if the Target does not have a poison pill or other defenses in place already. For example, it could *self-tender*, that is, launch a tender offer for its own shares, typically at a higher price. The advantage of this tactic is that it creates "competition," and may drive up the price that the hostile Acquirer is offering. One major downside of a self-tender is that if it is successful it will likely require the Target corporation to take on a great deal of new debt to pay for the purchased shares. Further, if the Target repurchases shares there obviously will be fewer of them outstanding, which also means that a hostile Acquirer would need to buy fewer shares to get a majority.

Another defense that may be employed is to simply pay the hostile Acquirer to "go away." This typically takes the form of the Target corporation purchasing/redeeming the shares that the hostile Acquirer owns, for a price higher than what the acquirer paid for them. This form of bribery (to put it bluntly) is referred to as *greenmail.*

Often, a Target corporation that is besieged by a hostile and unwanted takeover will search for a *white knight*, that is, a different company that would be willing to acquire the Target on more favorable terms (such as keeping the current management in place). This tactic was employed in the *Revlon* case that you will read below.

Another response to an unwanted takeover is to launch a takeover of the *Acquirer.* Obviously, this will only work if the Acquirer is itself a publicly traded company, making it possible to purchase a large percentage of its shares and/or conduct a tender offer for its shares. This is referred to as the *Pac Man* defense, recognizing that the hunted sometimes may become the hunter. Interestingly, it could turn out that *both* companies end up owning a majority of the stock of the *other company.* (That is, Company A owns a majority of the stock of Company B, which in turn owns a majority of the stock of Company A!) If that happens, MBCA § 7.21(b) provides that neither corporation may vote the shares that it owns in the other corporation.

These are just a few examples of takeover defenses; others exist and new and more sophisticated takeover defenses arise from time to time. However, rather than delving into more and more arcane takeover defenses, we will now examine the *legal* standards that apply to them. Although most takeover defenses can be adopted by the Target board (without requiring shareholder approval) and therefore would seem to be protected from attack by the business judgment rule, we have to remember that the Target board may be adopting a takeover defense not out of a desire to protect the shareholders from abusive takeovers, but to protect themselves. For this reason, courts apply an intermediate level of scrutiny to takeover defenses (that is, stronger scrutiny than the business judgment rule but less demanding scrutiny than the entire fairness standard or intrinsic fairness standard), as you will see in the following cases.

B.   JUDICIAL SCRUTINY OF DEFENSIVE MEASURES

It's probably best to begin this section by jumping right into one of the most important cases on this topic.

Unocal Corporation v. Mesa Petroleum Co.
Supreme Court of Delaware
493 A.2d 946 (1985)

MOORE, Justice.   We confront an issue of first impression in Delaware—the validity of a corporation's self-tender for its own shares which excludes from participation a stockholder making a hostile tender offer for the company's stock.

The Court of Chancery granted a preliminary injunction to the plaintiffs, Mesa Petroleum Co., Mesa Asset Co., Mesa Partners II, and Mesa Eastern, Inc. (collectively, "Mesa")*, enjoining an exchange offer of the defendant, Unocal Corporation (Unocal) for its own stock.   The trial court concluded that a selective exchange offer, excluding Mesa, was legally impermissible.   We cannot agree with such a blanket rule.   The factual findings of the Vice Chancellor, fully supported by the record, establish that Unocal's board, consisting of a majority of independent directors, acted in good faith, and after reasonable investigation found that Mesa's tender offer was both inadequate and coercive.   Under the circumstances the board had both the power and duty to oppose a bid it perceived to be harmful to the corporate enterprise.   On this record we are satisfied that the device Unocal adopted is reasonable in relation to the threat posed, and that the board acted in the proper exercise of sound business judgment.   *** Accordingly, we reverse the decision of the Court of Chancery and order the preliminary injunction vacated.

[I.]   The factual background of this matter bears a significant relationship to its ultimate outcome.

On April 8, 1985, Mesa, the owner of approximately 13% of Unocal's stock, commenced a two-tier "front loaded" cash tender offer for 64 million shares, or approximately 37%, of Unocal's outstanding stock at a price of $54 per share.   The "back-end" was designed to eliminate the remaining publicly held shares by an exchange of securities purportedly worth $54 per share.   However, *** the securities offered in the second-step merger would be highly subordinated ***.   Unocal has rather aptly termed such securities "junk bonds".

Unocal's board consists of eight independent outside directors and six insiders.   It met on April 13, 1985, to consider the Mesa tender offer.   Thirteen directors were present, and the meeting lasted nine and one-half hours.   The directors were given no agenda or written materials prior to the session.   However, detailed presentations were made by legal counsel regarding the board's obligations under both Delaware corporate law and the federal securities laws.   The board then received a presentation from Peter Sachs on behalf of Goldman

---

*   [Footnote by court]: T. Boone Pickens, Jr., is President and Chairman of the Board of Mesa Petroleum and President of Mesa Asset and controls the related Mesa entities.

Sachs & Co. (Goldman Sachs) and Dillon, Read & Co. (Dillon Read) discussing the bases for their opinions that the Mesa proposal was wholly inadequate. Mr. Sachs opined that the minimum cash value that could be expected from a sale or orderly liquidation for 100% of Unocal's stock was in excess of $60 per share. ***

Mr. Sachs also presented various defensive strategies available to the board if it concluded that Mesa's two-step tender offer was inadequate and should be opposed. One of the devices outlined was a self-tender by Unocal for its own stock with a reasonable price range of $70 to $75 per share. The cost of such a proposal would cause the company to incur $6.1-6.5 billion of additional debt, and a presentation was made informing the board of Unocal's ability to handle it. The directors were told that the primary effect of this obligation would be to reduce exploratory drilling, but that the company would nonetheless remain a viable entity.

The eight outside directors, comprising a clear majority of the thirteen members present, then met separately with Unocal's financial advisors and attorneys. Thereafter, they unanimously agreed to advise the board that it should reject Mesa's tender offer as inadequate, and that Unocal should pursue a self-tender to provide the stockholders with a fairly priced alternative to the Mesa proposal. The board then reconvened and unanimously adopted a resolution rejecting as grossly inadequate Mesa's tender offer. Despite the nine and one-half hour length of the meeting, no formal decision was made on the proposed defensive self-tender.

On April 15, the board met again with four of the directors present by telephone and one member still absent. This session lasted two hours. Unocal's Vice President of Finance and its Assistant General Counsel made a detailed presentation of the proposed terms of the exchange offer. A price range between $70 and $80 per share was considered, and ultimately the directors agreed upon $72. The board was also advised about the debt securities that would be issued, and the necessity of placing restrictive covenants upon certain corporate activities until the obligations were paid. The board's decisions were made in reliance on the advice of its investment bankers, including the terms and conditions upon which the securities were to be issued. Based upon this advice, and the board's own deliberations, the directors unanimously approved the exchange offer. Their resolution provided that if Mesa acquired 64 million shares of Unocal stock through its own offer (the Mesa Purchase Condition), Unocal would buy the remaining 49% outstanding for an exchange of debt securities having an aggregate par value of $72 per share. The board resolution also stated that the offer would be subject to other conditions that had been described to the board at the meeting, or which were deemed necessary by Unocal's officers, including the exclusion of Mesa from the proposal (the Mesa exclusion). ***

Unocal's exchange offer was commenced on April 17, 1985, and Mesa promptly challenged it by filing this suit in the Court of Chancery. On April 22, the Unocal board met again and was advised by Goldman Sachs and Dillon Read to waive the Mesa Purchase Condition as to 50 million shares. This recommendation was in response to a perceived concern of the shareholders that, if shares were tendered to Unocal, no shares would be purchased by either offeror. The directors were also advised that they should tender their own Unocal stock into the exchange offer as a mark of their confidence in it.

Another focus of the board was the Mesa exclusion. Legal counsel advised that under Delaware law Mesa could only be excluded for what the directors reasonably believed to be a valid corporate purpose. The directors' discussion centered on the objective of adequately compensating shareholders at the "back-end" of Mesa's proposal, which the latter would finance with "junk bonds". To include Mesa would defeat that goal, because under the proration aspect of the exchange offer (49%) every Mesa share accepted by Unocal would displace one held by another stockholder. Further, if Mesa were permitted to tender to Unocal, the latter would in effect be financing Mesa's own inadequate proposal.

***

Meanwhile, on April 22, 1985, Mesa amended its complaint in this action to challenge the Mesa exclusion. ***

On April 29, 1985, the Vice Chancellor temporarily restrained Unocal from proceeding with the exchange offer unless it included Mesa. The trial court recognized that directors could oppose, and attempt to defeat, a hostile takeover which they considered adverse to the best interests of the corporation. However, the Vice Chancellor decided that in a selective purchase of the company's stock, the corporation bears the burden of showing: (1) a valid corporate purpose, and (2) that the transaction was fair to all of the stockholders, including those excluded. [The trial court later granted Mesa a preliminary injunction, and Unocal appealed.]

***

[II.]   The issues we address involve these fundamental questions: Did the Unocal board have the power and duty to oppose a takeover threat it reasonably perceived to be harmful to the corporate enterprise, and if so, is its action here entitled to the protection of the business judgment rule?

Mesa contends that the discriminatory exchange offer violates the fiduciary duties Unocal owes it. Mesa argues that because of the Mesa exclusion the business judgment rule is inapplicable, because the directors by tendering their own shares will derive a financial benefit that is not available to all Unocal stockholders. Thus, it is Mesa's ultimate contention that Unocal cannot establish that the exchange offer is fair to all shareholders, and argues that the Court of Chancery was correct in concluding that Unocal was unable to meet this burden.

Unocal answers that it does not owe a duty of "fairness" to Mesa, given the facts here. Specifically, Unocal contends that its board of directors reasonably and in good faith concluded that Mesa's $54 two-tier tender offer was coercive and inadequate, and that Mesa sought selective treatment for itself. Furthermore, Unocal argues that the board's approval of the exchange offer was made in good faith, on an informed basis, and in the exercise of due care. Under these circumstances, Unocal contends that its directors properly employed this device to protect the company and its stockholders from Mesa's harmful tactics.

[III.]　　***

When a board addresses a pending takeover bid it has an obligation to determine whether the offer is in the best interests of the corporation and its shareholders. In that respect a board's duty is no different from any other responsibility it shoulders, and its decisions should be no less entitled to the respect they otherwise would be accorded in the realm of business judgment. [Citation omitted.] There are, however, certain caveats to a proper exercise of this function. Because of the omnipresent specter that a board may be acting primarily in its own interests, rather than those of the corporation and its shareholders, there is an enhanced duty which calls for judicial examination at the threshold before the protections of the business judgment rule may be conferred.

This Court has long recognized that:

> We must bear in mind the inherent danger in the purchase of shares with corporate funds to remove a threat to corporate policy when a threat to control is involved. The directors are of necessity confronted with a conflict of interest, and an objective decision is difficult.

In the face of this inherent conflict directors must show that they had reasonable grounds for believing that a danger to corporate policy and effectiveness existed because of another person's stock ownership. However, they satisfy that burden "by showing good faith and reasonable investigation ...." Furthermore, such proof is materially enhanced, as here, by the approval of a board comprised of a majority of outside independent directors who have acted in accordance with the foregoing standards. [Citations omitted throughout this paragraph.]

[IV.A] In the board's exercise of corporate power to forestall a takeover bid our analysis begins with the basic principle that corporate directors have a fiduciary duty to act in the best interests of the corporation's stockholders. [Citation omitted.] As we have noted, their duty of care extends to protecting the corporation and its owners from perceived harm whether a threat originates from third parties or other shareholders. But such powers are not absolute. A corporation does not have unbridled discretion to defeat any perceived threat by any Draconian means available.

The restriction placed upon a selective stock repurchase is that the directors may not have acted solely or primarily out of a desire to perpetuate themselves in office. Of course, to this is added the further caveat that inequitable action may not be taken under the guise of law. The standard of proof established in [a prior case] is designed to ensure that a defensive measure to thwart or impede a takeover is indeed motivated by a good faith concern for the welfare of the corporation and its stockholders, which in all circumstances must be free of any fraud or other misconduct. However, this does not end the inquiry. [Citations omitted throughout this paragraph.]

[IV.B.] A further aspect is the element of balance. If a defensive measure is to come within the ambit of the business judgment rule, it must be reasonable in relation to the threat posed. This entails an analysis by the directors of the nature of the takeover bid and its effect on the corporate enterprise. Examples of such concerns may include: inadequacy of the price offered, nature and timing of the offer, questions of illegality, the impact on "constituencies" other than share-holders (i.e., creditors, customers, employees, and perhaps even the community generally), the risk of nonconsummation, and the quality of securities being offered in the exchange. [Citation omitted.] While not a controlling factor, it also seems to us that a board may reasonably consider the basic stockholder interests at stake, including those of short term speculators, whose actions may have fueled the coercive aspect of the offer at the expense of the long term investor. Here, the threat posed was viewed by the Unocal board as a grossly inadequate two-tier coercive tender offer coupled with the threat of greenmail.

Specifically, the Unocal directors had concluded that the value of Unocal was substantially above the $54 per share offered in cash at the front end. Furthermore, they determined that the subordinated securities to be exchanged in Mesa's announced squeeze out of the remaining shareholders in the "back-end" merger were "junk bonds" worth far less than $54. It is now well recognized that such offers are a classic coercive measure designed to stampede shareholders into tendering at the first tier, even if the price is inadequate, out of fear of what they will receive at the back end of the transaction. Wholly beyond the coercive aspect of an inadequate two-tier tender offer, the threat was posed by a corporate raider with a national reputation as a "greenmailer".[*]

In adopting the selective exchange offer, the board stated that its objective was either to defeat the inadequate Mesa offer or, should the offer still succeed, provide the 49% of its stockholders, who would otherwise be forced to accept "junk bonds", with $72 worth of senior debt. We find that both purposes are valid.

However, such efforts would have been thwarted by Mesa's participation in the exchange offer. First, if Mesa could tender its shares, Unocal would effectively be subsidizing the former's continuing effort to buy Unocal stock at $54 per share. Second, Mesa could not, by definition, fit within the class of shareholders being protected from its own coercive and inadequate tender offer.

Thus, we are satisfied that the selective exchange offer is reasonably related to the threats posed. It is consistent with the principle that "the minority stockholder shall receive the substantial equivalent in value of what he had before." [Citations omitted.] This concept of fairness, while stated in the merger context, is also relevant in the area of tender offer law. Thus, the board's decision to offer what it determined to be the fair value of the corporation to the 49% of its shareholders, who would otherwise be forced to accept highly subordinated "junk bonds", is reasonable and consistent with the directors' duty to ensure that the minority stockholders receive equal value for their shares.

[V.]   Mesa contends that it is unlawful, and the trial court agreed, for a corporation to discriminate in this fashion against one shareholder. It argues correctly that no case has ever sanctioned a device that precludes a raider from sharing in a benefit available to all other stockholders. However, as we have noted earlier, the principle of selective stock repurchases by a Delaware corporation is neither unknown nor unauthorized. [Citations omitted.] The only difference is that heretofore the approved transaction was the payment of "greenmail" to a raider or dissident posing a threat to the corporate enterprise. All other stockholders were denied such favored treatment, and given Mesa's past history of greenmail, its claims here are rather ironic.

---

[*]   [Footnote by court]: The term "greenmail" refers to the practice of buying out a takeover bidder's stock at a premium that is not available to other shareholders in order to prevent the takeover. The Chancery Court noted that "Mesa has made tremendous profits from its takeover activities although in the past few years it has not been successful in acquiring any of the target companies on an unfriendly basis." Moreover, the trial court specifically found that the actions of the Unocal board were taken in good faith to eliminate both the inadequacies of the tender offer and to forestall the payment of "greenmail".

However, our corporate law is not static. It must grow and develop in response to, indeed in anticipation of, evolving concepts and needs. Merely because the General Corporation Law is silent as to a specific matter does not mean that it is prohibited. [Citation omitted.] In the days when [prior cases] were decided, the tender offer, while not an unknown device, was virtually unused, and little was known of such methods as two-tier "front-end" loaded offers with their coercive effects. Then, the favored attack of a raider was stock acquisition followed by a proxy contest. Various defensive tactics, which provided no benefit whatever to the raider, evolved. Thus, the use of corporate funds by management to counter a proxy battle was approved. [Citations omitted.] Litigation, supported by corporate funds, aimed at the raider has long been a popular device.

More recently, as the sophistication of both raiders and targets has developed, a host of other defensive measures to counter such ever mounting threats has evolved and received judicial sanction. These include defensive charter amendments and other devices bearing some rather exotic, but apt, names: Crown Jewel, White Knight, Pac Man, and Golden Parachute. Each has highly selective features, the object of which is to deter or defeat the raider.

Thus, while the exchange offer is a form of selective treatment, given the nature of the threat posed here the response is neither unlawful nor unreasonable. If the board of directors is disinterested, has acted in good faith and with due care, its decision in the absence of an abuse of discretion will be upheld as a proper exercise of business judgment.

To this Mesa responds that the board is not disinterested, because the directors are receiving a benefit from the tender of their own shares, which because of the Mesa exclusion, does not devolve upon all stockholders equally. [Citation omitted.] However, Mesa concedes that if the exclusion is valid, then the directors and all other stockholders share the same benefit. The answer of course is that the exclusion is valid, and the directors' participation in the exchange offer does not rise to the level of a disqualifying interest. ***

Nor does this become an "interested" director transaction merely because certain board members are large stockholders. As this Court has previously noted, that fact alone does not create a disqualifying "personal pecuniary interest" to defeat the operation of the business judgment rule. [Citations omitted.]

Mesa also argues that the exclusion permits the directors to abdicate the fiduciary duties they owe it. However, that is not so. The board continues to owe Mesa the duties of due care and loyalty. But in the face of the destructive threat Mesa's tender offer was perceived to pose, the board had a supervening duty to protect the corporate enterprise, which includes the other shareholders, from threatened harm.

Mesa contends that the basis of this action is punitive, and solely in response to the exercise of its rights of corporate democracy Nothing precludes Mesa, as a stockholder, from acting in its own self-interest. [Citations omitted.] However, Mesa, while pursuing its own interests, has acted in a manner which a board consisting of a majority of independent directors has reasonably determined to be contrary to the best interests of Unocal and its other shareholders. In this situation, there is no support in Delaware law for the proposition that, when responding to a perceived harm, a corporation must guarantee a benefit to a stockholder who is deliberately provoking the danger being addressed. There is no obligation of self-sacrifice by a corporation and its shareholders in the face of such a challenge.

Here, the Court of Chancery specifically found that the "directors' decision [to oppose the Mesa tender offer] was made in the good faith belief that the Mesa tender offer is inadequate." *** [W]e are satisfied that Unocal's board has met its burden of proof. [Citation omitted.]

[VI.] In conclusion, there was directorial power to oppose the Mesa tender offer, and to undertake a selective stock exchange made in good faith and upon a reasonable investigation pursuant to a clear duty to protect the corporate enterprise. Further, the selective stock repurchase plan chosen by Unocal is reasonable in relation to the threat that the board rationally and reasonably believed was posed by Mesa's inadequate and coercive two-tier tender offer. Under those circumstances the board's action is entitled to be measured by the standards of the business judgment rule. Thus, unless it is shown by a preponderance of the evidence that the directors' decisions were primarily based on perpetuating themselves in office, or some other breach of fiduciary duty such as fraud, overreaching, lack of good faith, or being uninformed, a Court will not substitute its judgment for that of the board.

In this case that protection is not lost merely because Unocal's directors have tendered their shares in the exchange offer. Given the validity of the Mesa exclusion, they are receiving a benefit shared generally by all other stockholders except Mesa. ***

With the Court of Chancery's findings that the exchange offer was based on the board's good faith belief that the Mesa offer was inadequate, that the board's action was informed and taken with due care, that Mesa's prior activities justify a reasonable inference that its principle objective was greenmail, and implicitly, that the substance of the offer itself was reasonable and fair to the corporation and its stockholders if Mesa were included, we cannot say that the Unocal directors have acted in such a manner as to have passed an "unintelligent and unadvised judgment". [Citation omitted.] The decision of the Court of Chancery is therefore REVERSED, and the preliminary injunction is VACATED.

Questions About *Unocal*

1.   If you had been a Unocal shareholder, what would you have done after hearing about Mesa Petroleum's tender offer?

2.   Unocal's board responded to Mesa's tender offer by doing a self-tender for Unocal shares—other than those owned by Mesa. Would such a tactic be legal today? (Recall the discussion of tender offers in Section 12.07 above.)

3.   The first part of the *Unocal* test requires the Target's board to show that they had "reasonable grounds for believing that a danger to corporate policy and effectiveness existed because of another person's stock ownership." How do directors satisfy this burden? What are some examples of such "threats"?

As discussed in Section 12.08(D) below, later cases have refined the *Unocal* test. For example, in *Unitrin v. American General Corp.*, 651 A.2d 1361 (Del. 1995), the Delaware Supreme Court stated that *Unocal* is the proper standard by which to evaluate board actions that are "defensive."[*] Under the second part of the *Unocal* test (i.e., the proportionality of the board's response to a perceived threat), a court should examine whether a takeover defense is "draconian, by being either preclusive or coercive." In other words, the focus is on whether the takeover defense(s) prevent(s) a possible takeover of the company or compel(s) shareholders to vote against the takeover. If the defense(s) is (are) not "draconian," then the court should examine whether it was (they were) "within a range of reasonable responses to the threat" posed. *See also Omnicare, Inc. v. NCS Healthcare, Inc.*, 818 A.2d 914 (Del. 2003).

It is important to note that the board in *Unocal* was trying to *prevent* a takeover. But what should a board do if a takeover becomes likely, or even inevitable? In other words, what are the board's duties when the corporation is "for sale"? The next two cases concern this issue. Part D that follows tries to

---

[*]   The *Unitrin* court also observed that the first part of the *Unocal* test requires a target board to "demonstrate that, after a reasonable investigation, it determined in good faith, that [the bidder's offer] presented a threat to [the target] that warranted a defensive response." Interestingly, "the presence of a majority of outside independent directors will materially enhance such evidence."

make sense of *Unocal* and the many Delaware cases that came after it (including those cited in the previous paragraph).

C.   DUTIES OF THE BOARD WHEN THE CORPORATION IS FOR SALE

As before, we will start with one of the most important cases on this topic.

Revlon v. MacAndews & Forbes Holdings, Inc.
Supreme Court of Delaware
506 A.2d 173 (1986)

MOORE, Justice: In this battle for corporate control of Revlon, Inc. (Revlon), the Court of Chancery enjoined certain transactions designed to thwart the efforts of Pantry Pride, Inc. (Pantry Pride) to acquire Revlon. The defendants are Revlon, its board of directors, and Forstmann Little & Co. and the latter's affiliated limited partnership (collectively, Forstmann). The injunction barred consummation of an option granted Forstmann to purchase certain Revlon assets (the lockup option), a promise by Revlon to deal exclusively with Forstmann in the face of a takeover (the no-shop provision), and the payment of a $25 million cancellation fee to Forstmann if the transaction was aborted. The Court of Chancery found that the Revlon directors had breached their duty of care by entering into the foregoing transactions and effectively ending an active auction for the company. The trial court ruled that such arrangements are not illegal per se under Delaware law, but that their use under the circumstances here was impermissible. We agree. [Citation omitted.] Thus, we granted this expedited interlocutory appeal to consider for the first time the validity of such defensive measures in the face of an active bidding contest for corporate control. Additionally, we address for the first time the extent to which a corporation may consider the impact of a takeover threat on constituencies other than shareholders. See *Unocal Corp. v. Mesa Petroleum Co*, [493 A.2d 946 (Del. 1985)].

In our view, lock-ups and related agreements are permitted under Delaware law where their adoption is untainted by director interest or other breaches of fiduciary duty. The actions taken by the Revlon directors, however, did not meet this standard. Moreover, while concern for various corporate constituencies is proper when addressing a takeover threat, that principle is limited by the requirement that there be some rationally related benefit accruing to the stockholders. We find no such benefit here.

Thus, under all the circumstances we must agree with the Court of Chancery that the enjoined Revlon defensive measures were inconsistent with the directors' duties to the stockholders. Accordingly, we affirm.

[I.]   The somewhat complex maneuvers of the parties necessitate a rather detailed examination of the facts. The prelude to this controversy began in June 1985, when Ronald O. Perelman, chairman of the board and chief executive officer of Pantry Pride, met with his counterpart at Revlon, Michel C. Bergerac, to discuss a friendly acquisition of Revlon by Pantry Pride. Perelman suggested a price in the range of $40-50 per share, but the meeting ended with Bergerac dismissing those figures as considerably below Revlon's intrinsic value. All subsequent Pantry Pride overtures were rebuffed, perhaps in part based on Mr. Bergerac's strong personal antipathy to Mr. Perelman.

Thus, on August 14, Pantry Pride's board authorized Perelman to acquire Revlon, either through negotiation in the $42-$43 per share range, or by making a hostile tender offer at $45. Perelman then met with Bergerac and outlined Pantry Pride's alternate approaches. Bergerac remained adamantly opposed to such schemes and conditioned any further discussions of the matter on Pantry Pride executing a standstill agreement prohibiting it from acquiring Revlon without the latter's prior approval.

On August 19, the Revlon board met specially to consider the impending threat of a hostile bid by Pantry Pride.[*] At the meeting, Lazard Freres, Revlon's investment banker, advised the directors that $45 per share was a grossly inadequate price for the company. Felix Rohatyn and William Loomis of Lazard Freres explained to the board that Pantry Pride's financial strategy for acquiring Revlon would be through "junk bond" financing followed by a break-up of Revlon and the disposition of its assets. With proper timing, according to the experts, such transactions could produce a return to Pantry Pride of $60 to $70 per share, while a sale of the company as a whole would be in the "mid 50" dollar range. Martin Lipton, special counsel for Revlon, recommended two defensive measures: first, that the company repurchase up to 5 million of its nearly 30 million outstanding shares; and second, that it adopt a Note Purchase Rights Plan. Under this plan, each Revlon shareholder would receive as a dividend one Note Purchase Right (the Rights) for each share of common stock, with the Rights entitling the holder to exchange one common share for a $65 principal Revlon note at 12% interest with a one-year maturity. The Rights would become effective whenever anyone acquired beneficial ownership of 20% or more of Revlon's shares, unless the purchaser acquired all the company's stock for cash at $65 or more per share. In addition, the Rights would not be available to the acquiror, and prior to the 20%

---

[*]   [Footnote by court]: There were 14 directors on the Revlon board. Six of them held senior management positions with the company, and two others held significant blocks of its stock. Four of the remaining six directors were associated at some point with entities that had various business relationships with Revlon. On the basis of this limited record, however, we cannot conclude that this board is entitled to certain presumptions that generally attach to the decisions of a board whose majority consists of truly outside independent directors. [Citations omitted.]

triggering event the Revlon board could redeem the rights for 10 cents each. Both proposals were unanimously adopted.

Pantry Pride made its first hostile move on August 23 with a cash tender offer for any and all shares of Revlon at $47.50 per common share and $26.67 per preferred share, subject to (1) Pantry Pride's obtaining financing for the purchase, and (2) the Rights being redeemed, rescinded or voided.

The Revlon board met again on August 26. The directors advised the stockholders to reject the offer. Further defensive measures also were planned. On August 29, Revlon commenced its own offer for up to 10 million shares, exchanging for each share of common stock tendered one Senior Subordinated Note (the Notes) of $47.50 principal at 11.75% interest, due 1995, and one-tenth of a share of $9.00 Cumulative Convertible Exchangeable Preferred Stock valued at $100 per share. *** Revlon stockholders tendered 87 percent of the outstanding shares (approximately 33 million), and the company accepted the full 10 million shares on a pro rata basis. The new Notes contained covenants which limited Revlon's ability to incur additional debt, sell assets, or pay dividends unless otherwise approved by the "independent" (nonmanagement) members of the board.

At this point, both the Rights and the Note covenants stymied Pantry Pride's attempted takeover. The next move came on September 16, when Pantry Pride announced a new tender offer at $42 per share, conditioned upon receiving at least 90% of the outstanding stock. Pantry Pride also indicated that it would consider buying less than 90%, and at an increased price, if Revlon removed the impeding Rights. ***

The Revlon board held a regularly scheduled meeting on September 24. The directors rejected the latest Pantry Pride offer and authorized management to negotiate with other parties interested in acquiring Revlon. Pantry Pride remained determined in its efforts and continued to make cash bids for the company, offering $50 per share on September 27, and raising its bid to $53 on October 1, and then to $56.25 on October 7.

In the meantime, Revlon's negotiations with Forstmann and the investment group Adler & Shaykin had produced results. The Revlon directors met on October 3 to consider Pantry Pride's $53 bid and to examine possible alternatives to the offer. Both Forstmann and Adler & Shaykin made certain proposals to the board. As a result, the directors unanimously agreed to a leveraged buyout by Forstmann. The terms of this accord were as follows: each stockholder would get $56 cash per share; management would purchase stock in the new company by the exercise of their Revlon "golden parachutes"; Forstmann would assume Revlon's $475 million debt incurred by the issuance of the Notes;

and Revlon would redeem the Rights and waive the Notes covenants for Forstmann or in connection with any other offer superior to Forstmann's. *** Part of Forstmann's plan was to sell Revlon's Norcliff Thayer and Reheis divisions to American Home Products for $335 million. Before the merger, Revlon was to sell its cosmetics and fragrance division to Adler & Shaykin for $905 million. These transactions would facilitate the purchase by Forstmann or any other acquiror of Revlon.

When the merger, and thus the waiver of the Notes covenants, was announced, the market value of [the Notes] began to fall. The Notes, which originally traded near par, around 100, dropped to 87.50 by October 8. One director later reported (at the October 12 meeting) a "deluge" of telephone calls from irate noteholders, and on October 10 the *Wall Street Journal* reported threats of litigation by these creditors.

Pantry Pride countered with a new proposal on October 7, raising its $53 offer to $56.25, subject to nullification of the Rights, a waiver of the Notes covenants, and the election of three Pantry Pride directors to the Revlon board. On October 9, representatives of Pantry Pride, Forstmann and Revlon conferred in an attempt to negotiate the fate of Revlon, but could not reach agreement. At this meeting Pantry Pride announced that it would *** top any Forstmann offer by a slightly higher one. It is also significant that Forstmann, to Pantry Pride's exclusion, had been made privy to certain Revlon financial data. Thus, the parties were not negotiating on equal terms.

Again privately armed with Revlon data, Forstmann met on October 11 with Revlon's special counsel and investment banker. On October 12, Forstmann made a new $57.25 per share offer, based on several conditions. The principal demand was a lock-up option to purchase Revlon's Vision Care and National Health Laboratories divisions for $525 million, some $100-$175 million below the value ascribed to them by Lazard Freres, if another acquiror got 40% of Revlon's shares. Revlon also was required to accept a no-shop provision. The Rights and Notes covenants had to be removed as in the October 3 agreement. There would be a $25 million cancellation fee to be placed in escrow, and released to Forstmann if the new agreement terminated or if another acquiror got more than 19.9% of Revlon's stock. Finally, there would be no participation by Revlon management in the merger. In return, Forstmann agreed to support the par value of the Notes, which had faltered in the market, by an exchange of new notes. Forstmann also demanded immediate acceptance of its offer, or it would be withdrawn. The board unanimously approved Forstmann's proposal because: (1) it was for a higher price than the Pantry Pride bid, (2) it protected the noteholders, and (3) Forstmann's financing was firmly in place. ***

Pantry Pride [then sued,] *** challenging the lock-up, the cancellation fee, and the exercise of the Rights and the Notes covenants. Pantry Pride also sought a temporary restraining order ***.

On October 15, the Court of Chancery prohibited the further transfer of assets, and eight days later enjoined the lock-up, no-shop, and cancellation fee provisions of the agreement. The trial court concluded that the Revlon directors had breached their duty of loyalty by making concessions to Forstmann, out of concern for their liability to the noteholders, rather than maximizing the sale price of the company for the stockholders' benefit. [Citation omitted.]

***

[II.A]   We turn first to Pantry Pride's probability of success on the merits. The ultimate responsibility for managing the business and affairs of a corporation falls on its board of directors. In discharging this function the directors owe fiduciary duties of care and loyalty to the corporation and its shareholders. These principles apply with equal force when a board approves a corporate merger pursuant *** and of course they are the bedrock of our law regarding corporate takeover issues. While the business judgment rule may be applicable to the actions of corporate directors responding to takeover threats, the principles upon which it is founded—care, loyalty and independence—must first be satisfied. [Citations omitted throughout this paragraph.]

If the business judgment rule applies, there is a "presumption that in making a business decision the directors of a corporation acted on an informed basis, in good faith and in the honest belief that the action taken was in the best interests of the company." [Citation omitted.]   However, when a board implements anti-takeover measures there arises "the omnipresent specter that a board may be acting primarily in its own interests, rather than those of the corporation and its shareholders ..." [Citing *Unocal.*] This potential for conflict places upon the directors the burden of proving that they had reasonable grounds for believing there was a danger to corporate policy and effectiveness, a burden satisfied by a showing of good faith and reasonable investigation. [Citing *Unocal.*] In addition, the directors must analyze the nature of the takeover and its effect on the corporation in order to ensure balance—that the responsive action taken is reasonable in relation to the threat posed. [Citing *Unocal.*]

[II.B.]   The first relevant defensive measure adopted by the Revlon board was the Rights Plan, which would be considered a "poison pill" in the current language of corporate takeovers—a plan by which shareholders receive the right to be bought out by the corporation at a substantial premium on the occurrence of a stated triggering event. [Citation omitted.]   *** [T]he board clearly had the power to adopt the measure. [Citation omitted.] Thus, the focus becomes one of reasonableness and purpose.

The Revlon board approved the Rights Plan in the face of an impending hostile takeover bid by Pantry Pride at $45 per share, a price which Revlon reasonably concluded was grossly inadequate. Lazard Freres had so advised the directors, and had also informed them that Pantry Pride was a small, highly leveraged company bent on a "bust-up" takeover by using "junk bond" financing to buy Revlon cheaply, sell the acquired assets to pay the debts incurred, and retain the profit for itself. In adopting the Plan, the board protected the share-holders from a hostile takeover at a price below the company's intrinsic value, while retaining sufficient flexibility to address any proposal deemed to be in the stockholders' best interests.

To that extent the board acted in good faith and upon reasonable investigation. Under the circumstances it cannot be said that the Rights Plan as employed was unreasonable, considering the threat posed. Indeed, the Plan was a factor in causing Pantry Pride to raise its bids from a low of $42 to an eventual high of $58. ***

Although we consider adoption of the Plan to have been valid under the circumstances, its continued usefulness was rendered moot by the directors' actions on October 3 and October 12. At the October 3 meeting the board redeemed the Rights conditioned upon consummation of a merger with Forstmann, but further acknowledged that they would also be redeemed to facilitate any more favorable offer. On October 12, the board unanimously passed a resolution redeeming the Rights in connection with any cash proposal of $57.25 or more per share. Because all the pertinent offers eventually equaled or surpassed that amount, the Rights clearly were no longer any impediment in the contest for Revlon. This mooted any question of their propriety under *** *Unocal*.

[II.C.] The second defensive measure adopted by Revlon to thwart a Pantry Pride takeover was the company's own exchange offer for 10 million of its shares. The directors' general broad powers to manage the business and affairs of the corporation are augmented by the specific authority conferred under [Section 160(a) of the Delaware General Corporation Law], permitting the company to deal in its own stock. [Citations omitted.] However, when exercising that power in an effort to forestall a hostile takeover, the board's actions are strictly held to the fiduciary standards outlined in *Unocal*. These standards require the directors to determine the best interests of the corporation and its stockholders, and impose an enhanced duty to abjure any action that is motivated by considerations other than a good faith concern for such interests. [Citations omitted.]

The Revlon directors concluded that Pantry Pride's $47.50 offer was grossly inadequate. In that regard the board acted in good faith, and on an informed basis, with reasonable grounds to believe that there existed a harmful threat to the corporate enterprise. The adoption of a defensive measure, reasonable in relation to the threat posed, was proper and fully accorded with the powers, duties, and responsibilities conferred upon directors under our law. [Citing *Unocal*.]

[II.D.] However, when Pantry Pride increased its offer to $50 per share, and then to $53, it became apparent to all that the break-up of the company was inevitable. The Revlon board's authorization permitting management to negotiate a merger or buyout with a third party was a recognition that the company was for sale. The duty of the board had thus changed from the preservation of Revlon as a corporate entity to the maximization of the company's value at a sale for the stockholders' benefit. This significantly altered the board's responsibilities under the *Unocal* standards. It no longer faced threats to corporate policy and effectiveness, or to the stockholders' interests, from a grossly inadequate bid. The whole question of defensive measures became moot. The directors' role changed from defenders of the corporate bastion to auctioneers charged with getting the best price for the stockholders at a sale of the company.

[III.]   This brings us to the lock-up with Forstmann and its emphasis on shoring up the sagging market value of the Notes in the face of threatened litigation by their holders. Such a focus was inconsistent with the changed concept of the directors' responsibilities at this stage of the developments. The impending waiver of the Notes covenants had caused the value of the Notes to fall, and the board was aware of the noteholders' ire as well as their subsequent threats of suit. The directors thus made support of the Notes an integral part of the company's dealings with Forstmann, even though their primary responsibility at this stage was to the [stockholders].

The original threat posed by Pantry Pride—the break-up of the company— had become a reality which even the directors embraced. Selective dealing to fend off a hostile but determined bidder was no longer a proper objective. Instead, obtaining the highest price for the benefit of the stockholders should have been the central theme guiding director action. Thus, the Revlon board could not make the requisite showing of good faith by preferring the noteholders and ignoring its duty of loyalty to the shareholders. The rights of the former already were fixed by contract. [Citations omitted.] The noteholders required no further protection, and when the Revlon board entered into an auction-ending lock-up agreement with Forstmann on the basis of impermissible considerations at the expense of the shareholders, the directors breached their primary duty of loyalty.

The Revlon board argued that it acted in good faith in protecting the noteholders because *Unocal* permits consideration of other corporate constituencies. Although such considerations may be permissible, there are fundamental limitations upon that prerogative. A board may have regard for various constituencies in discharging its responsibilities, provided there are rationally related benefits accruing to the stockholders. [Citing *Unocal*.] However, such concern for non-stockholder interests is inappropriate when an auction among active bidders is in progress, and the object no longer is to protect or maintain the corporate enterprise but to sell it to the highest bidder.

Revlon also contended that *** it had contractual and good faith obligations to consider the noteholders. However, any such duties are limited to the principle that one may not interfere with contractual relationships by improper actions. Here, the rights of the noteholders were fixed by agreement, and there is nothing of substance to suggest that any of those terms were violated. The Notes covenants specifically contemplated a waiver to permit sale of the company at a fair price. The Notes were accepted by the holders on that basis, including the risk of an adverse market effect stemming from a waiver. Thus, nothing remained for Revlon to legitimately protect, and no rationally related benefit thereby accrued to the stockholders. Under such circumstances we must conclude that the merger agreement with Forstmann was unreasonable in relation to the threat posed.

A lock-up is not per se illegal under Delaware law. *** Such options can entice other bidders to enter a contest for control of the corporation, creating an auction for the company and maximizing shareholder profit. *** However, while those lock-ups which draw bidders into the battle benefit shareholders, similar measures which end an active auction and foreclose further bidding operate to the shareholders' detriment. [Citation omitted.]

***

The Forstmann option had a *** destructive effect on the auction process. Forstmann had already been drawn into the contest on a preferred basis, so the result of the lock-up was not to foster bidding, but to destroy it. *** The principal object, contrary to the board's duty of care, appears to have been protection of the noteholders over the shareholders' interests.

While Forstmann's $57.25 offer was objectively higher than Pantry Pride's $56.25 bid, the margin of superiority is less when the Forstmann price is adjusted for the time value of money. In reality, the Revlon board ended the auction in return for very little actual improvement in the final bid. The principal benefit went to the directors, who avoided personal liability to a class of creditors to whom the board owed no further duty under the circumstances. Thus, when a board ends an intense bidding contest on an insubstantial basis, and where a significant by-product of that action is to protect the directors against a perceived threat of personal liability for consequences stemming from the adoption of previous defensive measures, the action cannot withstand the enhanced scrutiny which *Unocal* requires of director conduct. [Citing *Unocal*.]

***   The no-shop provision, like the lock-up option, while not per se illegal, is impermissible under the *Unocal* standards when a board's primary duty becomes that of an auctioneer responsible for selling the company to the highest bidder.   The agreement to negotiate only with Forstmann ended rather than intensified the board's involvement in the bidding contest.

It is ironic that the parties even considered a no-shop agreement when Revlon had dealt preferentially, and almost exclusively, with Forstmann throughout the contest.   After the directors authorized management to negotiate with other parties, Forstmann was given every negotiating advantage that Pantry Pride had been denied: cooperation from management, access to financial data, and the exclusive opportunity to present merger proposals directly to the board of directors.   Favoritism for a white knight to the total exclusion of a hostile bidder might be justifiable when the latter's offer adversely affects shareholder interests, but when bidders make relatively similar offers, or dissolution of the company becomes inevitable, the directors cannot fulfill their enhanced *Unocal* duties by playing favorites with the contending factions.   Market forces must be allowed to operate freely to bring the target's shareholders the best price available for their equity.   Thus, as the trial court ruled, the shareholders' interests necessitated that the board remain free to negotiate in the fulfillment of that duty.

The court below similarly enjoined the payment of the cancellation fee, pending a resolution of the merits, because the fee was part of the overall plan to thwart Pantry Pride's efforts. We find no abuse of discretion in that ruling.

***

[V.]   In conclusion, the Revlon board was confronted with a situation not uncommon in the current wave of corporate takeovers.   A hostile and determined bidder sought the company at a price the board was convinced was inadequate.   The initial defensive tactics worked to the benefit of the shareholders, and thus the board was able to sustain its *Unocal* burdens in justifying those measures.   However, in granting an asset option lock-up to Forstmann, we must conclude that under all the circumstances the directors allowed considerations other than the maximization of shareholder profit to affect their judgment, and followed a course that ended the auction for Revlon, absent court intervention, to the ultimate detriment of its shareholders.   No such defensive measure can be sustained when it represents a breach of the directors' fundamental duty of care. [Citation omitted.]   In that context the board's action is not entitled to the deference accorded it by the business judgment rule. The measures were properly enjoined. The decision of the Court of Chancery, therefore, is [affirmed].

Questions About *Revlon*

1.   Why do you think that Revlon's board favored Forstmann Little & Co. over Pantry Pride?

2.   What, exactly, are the board's duties when Revlon applies? (Note that in *Lyondell Chemical Co. v. Ryan*, 970 A.2d 235 (Del. 2009), the court observed that there is "no single blueprint" to follow when *Revlon* applies.) Should the board focus only on the price that is being offered, or are other factors relevant? What is the time frame for maximizing shareholder value—immediately, or on a long-term basis? Can the board consider the interests of persons other than shareholders?

3.   When, exactly, do *Revlon* duties arise? Is a "break-up" of the company required to trigger *Revlon* duties? By the way, what is a "break-up" of a company? (The following case may help you answer this question.)

Paramount Communications, Inc. v. QVC Network, Inc.
Supreme Court of Delaware
637 A.2d 34 (1994)

VEASEY, Chief Justice. In this appeal we review an order of the Court of Chancery dated November 24, 1993 (the "November 24 Order"), preliminarily enjoining certain defensive measures designed to facilitate a so-called strategic alliance between Viacom Inc. ("Viacom") and Paramount Communications Inc. ("Paramount") approved by the board of directors of Paramount (the "Paramount Board" or the "Paramount directors") and to thwart an unsolicited, more valuable, tender offer by QVC Network Inc. ("QVC"). In affirming, we hold that the sale of control in this case, which is at the heart of the proposed strategic alliance, implicates enhanced judicial scrutiny of the conduct of the Paramount Board under *Unocal Corp. v. Mesa Petroleum Co.*, [493 A.2d 946 (Del. 1985)], and *Revlon, Inc. v. MacAndrews & Forbes Holdings, Inc.*, [506 A.2d 173 (Del. 1986)]. We further hold that the conduct of the Paramount Board was not reasonable as to process or result.

***

The Court of Chancery found that the Paramount directors violated their fiduciary duties by favoring the Paramount-Viacom transaction over the more valuable unsolicited offer of QVC. The Court of Chancery preliminarily enjoined Paramount and the individual defendants (the "Paramount defendants") from amending or modifying Paramount's stockholder rights agreement (the "Rights Agreement"), including the redemption of the Rights, or taking other action to facilitate the consummation of the pending tender offer by Viacom or any proposed second-step merger, including the Merger Agreement between Paramount and Viacom dated September 12, 1993 (the "Original Merger Agreement"), as amended on October 24, 1993 (the "Amended Merger Agreement"). Viacom and the Paramount defendants were enjoined from taking any action to exercise any provision of the Stock Option Agreement between Paramount and Viacom dated September 12, 1993 (the "Stock Option Agreement"), as amended on October 24, 1993. The Court of Chancery did not grant preliminary injunctive relief as to the termination fee provided for the benefit of Viacom in Section 8.05 of the Original Merger Agreement and the Amended Merger Agreement (the "Termination Fee").

Under the circumstances of this case, the pending sale of control implicated in the Paramount-Viacom transaction required the Paramount Board to act on an informed basis to secure the best value reasonably available to the stockholders. Since we agree with the Court of Chancery that the Paramount directors violated their fiduciary duties, we have [affirmed] the *** preliminary injunction and have [remanded] these proceedings to the Court of Chancery for proceedings consistent herewith.

***

[I.]   Paramount is a Delaware corporation with its principal offices in New York City. Approximately 118 million shares of Paramount's common stock are outstanding and traded on the New York Stock Exchange. The majority of Paramount's stock is publicly held by numerous unaffiliated investors. Paramount owns and operates a diverse group of entertainment businesses, including motion picture and television studios, book publishers, professional sports teams, and amusement parks.

There are 15 persons serving on the Paramount Board. Four directors are officer-employees of Paramount ***. Paramount's [eleven] outside directors are distinguished and experienced business persons who are present or former senior executives of public corporations or financial institutions.

Viacom is a Delaware corporation with its headquarters in Massachusetts. Viacom is controlled by Sumner M. Redstone ("Redstone"), its Chairman and Chief Executive Officer, who owns indirectly approximately 85.2 percent of Viacom's voting Class A stock and approximately 69.2 percent of Viacom's nonvoting Class B stock through National Amusements, Inc. ("NAI"), an entity 91.7 percent owned by Redstone. Viacom has a wide range of entertainment operations, including a number of well-known cable television channels such as MTV, Nickelodeon, Showtime, and The Movie Channel. Viacom's equity co-investors in the Paramount-Viacom transaction include NYNEX Corporation and Blockbuster Entertainment Corporation.

QVC is a Delaware corporation with its headquarters in West Chester, Pennsylvania. QVC has several large stockholders, including Liberty Media Corporation, Comcast Corporation, Advance Publications, Inc., and Cox Enterprises Inc. Barry Diller ("Diller"), the Chairman and Chief Executive Officer of QVC, is also a substantial stockholder. QVC sells a variety of merchandise through a televised shopping channel. QVC has several equity co-investors in its proposed combination with Paramount including BellSouth Corporation and Comcast Corporation.

Beginning in the late 1980s, Paramount investigated the possibility of acquiring or merging with other companies in the entertainment, media, or communications industry. Paramount considered such transactions to be desirable, and perhaps necessary, in order to keep pace with competitors in the rapidly evolving field of entertainment and communications. ***

Although Paramount had considered a possible combination of Paramount and Viacom as early as 1990, recent efforts to explore such a transaction began at a dinner meeting between Redstone and [Martin S. Davis, Paramount's Chief Executive Officer] on April 20, 1993. Robert Greenhill ("Greenhill"), Chairman of Smith Barney Shearson Inc. ("Smith Barney"), attended and helped facilitate this meeting. After several more meetings between Redstone and Davis, serious negotiations began taking place in early July.

It was tentatively agreed that Davis would be the chief executive officer and Redstone would be the controlling stockholder of the combined company, but the parties could not reach agreement on the merger price and the terms of a stock option to be granted to Viacom. With respect to price, Viacom offered a package of cash and stock (primarily Viacom Class B nonvoting stock) with a market value of approximately $61 per share, but Paramount wanted at least $70 per share.

Shortly after negotiations broke down in July 1993, two notable events occurred. First, Davis apparently learned of QVC's potential interest in Paramount and told Diller over lunch on July 21, 1993, that Paramount was not for sale. Second, the market value of Viacom's Class B nonvoting stock increased from $46.875 on July 6 to $57.25 on August 20. QVC claims (and Viacom disputes) that this price increase was caused by open market purchases of such stock by Redstone or entities controlled by him.

On August 20, 1993, discussions between Paramount and Viacom resumed when Greenhill arranged another meeting between Davis and Redstone. After a short hiatus, the parties negotiated in earnest in early September, and performed due diligence with the assistance of their financial advisors, Lazard Freres & Co. ("Lazard") for Paramount and Smith Barney for Viacom. On September 9, 1993, the Paramount Board was informed about the status of the negotiations and was provided information by Lazard, including an analysis of the proposed transaction.

On September 12, 1993, the Paramount Board met again and unanimously approved the Original Merger Agreement whereby Paramount would merge with and into Viacom. The terms of the merger provided that each share of Paramount common stock would be converted into 0.10 shares of Viacom Class A voting stock, 0.90 shares of Viacom Class B nonvoting stock, and $9.10 in cash. In addition, the Paramount Board agreed to amend its "poison pill" Rights Agreement to exempt the proposed merger with Viacom. The Original Merger Agreement also contained several provisions designed to make it more difficult for a potential competing bid to succeed. We focus, as did the Court of Chancery, on three of these defensive provisions: a "no-shop" provision (the "No-Shop Provision"), the Termination Fee, and the Stock Option Agreement.

First, under the No-Shop Provision, the Paramount Board agreed that Paramount would not solicit, encourage, discuss, negotiate, or endorse any competing transaction unless: (a) a third party "makes an unsolicited written, bona fide proposal, which is not subject to any material contingencies relating to financing"; and (b) the Paramount Board determines that discussions or negotiations with the third party are necessary for the Paramount Board to comply with its fiduciary duties.

Second, under the Termination Fee provision, Viacom would receive a $100 million termination fee if: (a) Paramount terminated the Original Merger Agreement because of a competing transaction; (b) Paramount's stockholders did not approve the merger; or (c) the Paramount Board recommended a competing transaction.

The third and most significant deterrent device was the Stock Option Agreement, which granted to Viacom an option to purchase approximately 19.9 percent (23,699,000 shares) of Paramount's outstanding common stock at $69.14 per share if any of the triggering events for the Termination Fee occurred. In addition to the customary terms that are normally associated with a stock option, the Stock Option Agreement contained two provisions that were both unusual and highly beneficial to Viacom: (a) Viacom was permitted to pay for the shares with a senior subordinated note of questionable marketability instead of cash, thereby avoiding the need to raise the $1.6 billion purchase price (the "Note Feature"); and (b) Viacom could elect to require Paramount to pay Viacom in cash a sum equal to the difference between the purchase price and the market price of Paramount's stock (the "Put Feature"). Because the Stock Option Agreement was not "capped" to limit its maximum dollar value, it had the potential to reach (and in this case did reach) unreasonable levels.

After the execution of the Original Merger Agreement and the Stock Option Agreement on September 12, 1993, Paramount and Viacom announced their proposed merger. In a number of public statements, the parties indicated that the pending transaction was a virtual certainty. Redstone described it as a "marriage" that would "never be torn asunder" and stated that only a "nuclear attack" could break the deal. Redstone also called Diller and John Malone of Tele-Communications Inc., a major stockholder of QVC, to dissuade them from making a competing bid.

Despite these attempts to discourage a competing bid, Diller sent a letter to Davis on September 20, 1993, proposing a merger in which would acquire Paramount for approximately $80 per share, consisting of 0.893 shares of QVC common stock and $30 in cash. QVC also expressed its eagerness to meet with Paramount to negotiate the details of a transaction. When the Paramount Board met on September 27, it was advised by Davis that the Original Merger Agreement prohibited Paramount from having discussions with QVC (or anyone else) unless certain conditions were satisfied. In particular, QVC had to supply evidence that its proposal was not subject to financing contingencies.[*] The Paramount Board was also provided information from Lazard describing QVC and its proposal.

On October 5, 1993, QVC provided Paramount with evidence of QVC's financing. The Paramount Board then held another meeting on October 11, and decided to authorize management to meet with QVC. Davis also informed the Paramount Board that Booz-Allen & Hamilton ("Booz-Allen"), a management consulting firm, had been retained to assess, *inter alia*, the incremental earnings potential from a Paramount-Viacom merger and a Paramount-QVC merger. Discussions proceeded slowly, however, due to a delay in Paramount signing a confidentiality agreement. In response to Paramount's request for information, QVC provided two binders of documents to Paramount on October 20.

---

[*]   [Footnote by author]: In other words, QVC would need to prove that it had access to enough money to acquire Paramount.

On October 21, 1993, QVC filed this action and publicly announced an $80 cash tender offer for 51 percent of Paramount's outstanding shares (the "QVC tender offer"). Each remaining share of Paramount common stock would be converted into 1.42857 shares of QVC common stock in a second-step merger. The tender offer was conditioned on, among other things, the invalidation of the Stock Option Agreement, which was worth over $200 million by that point.[**] QVC contends that it had to commence a tender offer because of the slow pace of the merger discussions and the need to begin seeking clearance under federal antitrust laws.

Confronted by QVC's hostile bid, which on its face offered over $10 per share more than the consideration provided by the Original Merger Agreement, Viacom realized that it would need to raise its bid in order to remain competitive. Within hours after QVC's tender offer was announced, Viacom entered into discussions with Paramount concerning a revised transaction. These discussions led to serious negotiations concerning a comprehensive amendment to the original Paramount-Viacom transaction. In effect, the opportunity for a "new deal" with Viacom was at hand for the Paramount Board. With the QVC hostile bid offering greater value to the Paramount stockholders, the Paramount Board had considerable leverage with Viacom.

At a special meeting on October 24, 1993, the Paramount Board approved the Amended Merger Agreement and an amendment to the Stock Option Agreement. The Amended Merger Agreement was, however, essentially the same as the Original Merger Agreement, except that it included a few new provisions [one of which was that Viacom would make a tender offer for Paramount]. ***

Although the Amended Merger Agreement offered more consideration to the Paramount stockholders and somewhat more flexibility to the Paramount Board than did the Original Merger Agreement, the defensive measures designed to make a competing bid more difficult were not removed or modified. In particular, there is no evidence in the record that Paramount sought to use its newly-acquired leverage to eliminate or modify the No-Shop Provision, the Termination Fee, or the Stock Option Agreement when the subject of amending the Original Merger Agreement was on the table.

Viacom's tender offer commenced on October 25, 1993, and QVC's tender offer was formally launched on October 27, 1993. Diller sent a letter to the Paramount Board on October 28 requesting an opportunity to negotiate with Paramount, and Oresman responded the following day by agreeing to meet. The meeting, held on November 1, was not very fruitful, however, after QVC's

---

[**]   [Footnote by court]:   By November 15, 1993, the value of the Stock Option Agreement had increased to nearly $500 million based on the QVC bid.   [Citation omitted.]

proposed guidelines for a "fair bidding process" were rejected by Paramount on the ground that "auction procedures" were inappropriate and contrary to Paramount's contractual obligations to Viacom.

On November 6, 1993, Viacom unilaterally raised its tender offer price to $85 per share in cash and offered a comparable increase in the value of the securities being proposed in the second-step merger. At a telephonic meeting held later that day, the Paramount Board agreed to recommend Viacom's higher bid to Paramount's shareholders.

QVC responded to Viacom's higher bid on November 12 by increasing its tender offer to $90 per share and by increasing the securities for its second-step merger by a similar amount. In response to QVC's latest offer, the Paramount Board scheduled a meeting for November 15, 1993. Prior to the meeting, Oresman sent the members of the Paramount Board a document summarizing the "conditions and uncertainties" of QVC's offer. One director testified that this document gave him a very negative impression of the QVC bid.

At its meeting on November 15, 1993, the Paramount Board determined that the new QVC offer was not in the best interests of the stockholders. The purported basis for this conclusion was that QVC's bid was [subject to too many contingencies]. The Paramount Board did not communicate with QVC regarding the status of the conditions because it believed that the No-Shop Provision prevented such communication in the absence of firm financing. ***

The preliminary injunction hearing in this case took place on November 16, 1993. On November 19, Diller wrote to the Paramount Board to inform it that QVC had obtained financing commitments for its tender offer and that there was no antitrust obstacle to the offer. On November 24, 1993, the Court of Chancery issued its decision granting a preliminary injunction in favor of QVC and the plaintiff stockholders. This appeal followed.

[II.] The General Corporation Law of the State of Delaware (the "General Corporation Law") and the decisions of this Court have repeatedly recognized the fundamental principle that the management of the business and affairs of a Delaware corporation is entrusted to its directors, who are the duly elected and authorized representatives of the stockholders. [Citations omitted.] Under normal circumstances, neither the courts nor the stockholders should interfere with the managerial decisions of the directors. The business judgment rule embodies the deference to which such decisions are entitled. [Citation omitted.]

Nevertheless, there are rare situations which mandate that a court take a more direct and active role in overseeing the decisions made and actions taken by directors. In these situations, a court subjects the directors' conduct to enhanced scrutiny to ensure that it is reasonable. The decisions of this Court have clearly established the circumstances where such enhanced scrutiny will be applied. [Citing *Unocal, Revlon,* and other cases.] The case at bar implicates two such circumstances: (1) the approval of a transaction resulting in a sale of control, and (2) the adoption of defensive measures in response to a threat to corporate control.

[II.A]   When a majority of a corporation's voting shares are acquired by a single person or entity, or by a cohesive group acting together, there is a significant diminution in the voting power of those who thereby become minority stockholders.   ***   [M]any of the most fundamental corporate changes [such as mergers] can be implemented only if they are approved by a majority vote of the stockholders.   ***

*** [S]tockholder votes are likely to become mere formalities where there is a majority stockholder. For example, minority stockholders can be deprived of a continuing equity interest in their corporation by means of a cash-out merger. [Citation omitted.]   Absent effective protective provisions, minority stockholders must rely for protection solely on the fiduciary duties owed to them by the directors and the majority stockholder, since the minority stockholders have lost the power to influence corporate direction through the ballot.   The acquisition of majority status and the consequent privilege of exerting the powers of majority ownership come at a price.   That price is usually a control premium which recognizes not only the value of a control block of shares, but also compensates the minority stockholders for their resulting loss of voting power.

In the case before us, the public stockholders (in the aggregate) currently own a majority of Paramount's voting stock.   Control of the corporation is not vested in a single person, entity, or group, but vested in the fluid aggregation of unaffiliated stockholders.   In the event the Paramount-Viacom transaction is consummated, the public stockholders will receive cash and a minority equity voting position in the surviving corporation. Following such consummation, there will be a controlling stockholder [Redstone] who will have the voting power to: (a) elect directors; (b) cause a break-up of the corporation; (c) merge it with another company; (d) cash-out the public stockholders; (e) amend the certificate of incorporation; (f) sell all or substantially all of the corporate assets; or (g) otherwise alter materially the nature of the corporation and the public stockholders' interests.   ***

Because of the intended sale of control, the Paramount-Viacom transaction has economic consequences of considerable significance to the Paramount stockholders.   Once control has shifted, the current Paramount stockholders will have no leverage in the future to demand another control premium. As a result, the Paramount stockholders are entitled to receive, and should receive, a control premium and/or protective devices of significant value.   There being no such protective provisions in the Viacom-Paramount transaction, the Paramount directors had an obligation to take the maximum advantage of the current opportunity to realize for the stockholders the best value reasonably available.

[II.B]   The consequences of a sale of control impose special obligations on the directors of a corporation.   In particular, they have the obligation of acting reasonably to seek the transaction offering the best value reasonably available to the stockholders.   The courts will apply enhanced scrutiny to ensure that the directors have acted reasonably.   ***

In the sale of control context, the directors must focus on one primary objective—to secure the transaction offering the best value reasonably available for the stockholders—and they must exercise their fiduciary duties to further that end.   ***

In pursuing this objective, the directors must be especially diligent [and well-informed].   [Citations omitted.]   ***

[A prior case] teaches some of the methods by which a board can fulfill its obligation to seek the best value reasonably available to the stockholders.   [Citation omitted.]   These methods are designed to determine the existence and viability of possible alternatives.   They include conducting an auction, canvassing the market, etc.   Delaware law recognizes that there is "no single blueprint" that directors must follow.   [Citations omitted.]

In determining which alternative provides the best value for the stockholders, a board of directors is not limited to considering only the amount of cash involved, and is not required to ignore totally its view of the future value of a strategic alliance.   [Citation omitted.]   Instead, the directors should analyze the entire situation and evaluate in a disciplined manner the consideration being offered.   Where stock or other non-cash consideration is involved, the board should try to quantify its value, if feasible, to achieve an objective comparison of the alternatives.   In addition, the board may assess a variety of practical considerations relating to each alternative, including:

> [an offer's] fairness and feasibility; the proposed or actual financing for the offer, and the consequences of that financing; questions of illegality; ... the risk of nonconsum[m]ation;... the bidder's identity, prior background and other business venture experiences; and the bidder's business plans for the corporation and their effects on stockholder interests.

[Citation omitted.]   These considerations are important because the selection of one alternative may permanently foreclose other opportunities.   While the assessment of these factors may be complex, the board's goal is straightforward: Having informed themselves of all material information reasonably available, the directors must decide which alternative is most likely to offer the best value reasonably available to the stockholders.

[II.C] Board action in the circumstances presented here is subject to enhanced scrutiny. ***

***

The key features of an enhanced scrutiny test are: (a) a judicial determination regarding the adequacy of the decisionmaking process employed by the directors, including the information on which the directors based their decision; and (b) a judicial examination of the reasonableness of the directors' action in light of the circumstances then existing. The directors have the burden of proving that they were adequately informed and acted reasonably.

Although an enhanced scrutiny test involves a review of the reasonableness of the substantive merits of a board's actions, a court should not ignore the complexity of the directors' task in a sale of control. There are many business and financial considerations implicated in investigating and selecting the best value reasonably available. The board of directors is the corporate decision-making body best equipped to make these judgments. Accordingly, a court applying enhanced judicial scrutiny should be deciding whether the directors made a reasonable decision, not a perfect decision. If a board selected one of several reasonable alternatives, a court should not second-guess that choice even though it might have decided otherwise or subsequent events may have cast doubt on the board's determination. Thus, courts will not substitute their business judgment for that of the directors, but will determine if the directors' decision was, on balance, within a range of reasonableness. [Citations omitted.]

[II.D] The Paramount defendants and Viacom assert that the fiduciary obligations and the enhanced judicial scrutiny discussed above are not implicated in this case in the absence of a "break-up" of the corporation, and that the order granting the preliminary injunction should be reversed. This argument is based on their erroneous interpretation of our decisions in *Revlon* and [*Paramount Communications, Inc. v. Time, Inc.*, 571 A.2d 1140 (Del. 1989), hereinafter "*Time-Warner.*"].

In *Revlon*, we reviewed the actions of the board of directors of Revlon, Inc. ("Revlon"), which had rebuffed the overtures of Pantry Pride, Inc. and had instead entered into an agreement with Forstmann Little & Co. ("Forstmann") providing for the acquisition of 100 percent of Revlon's outstanding stock by Forstmann and the subsequent break-up of Revlon. Based on the facts and circumstances present in *Revlon*, we held that "[t]he directors' role changed from defenders of the corporate bastion to auctioneers charged with getting the best price for the stockholders at a sale of the company." [Citation omitted.] We further held that "when a board ends an intense bidding contest on an insubstantial basis, ... [that] action cannot withstand the enhanced scrutiny which *Unocal* requires of director conduct." [Citation omitted.]

It is true that one of the circumstances bearing on these holdings was the fact that "the break-up of the company ... had become a reality which even the directors embraced." [Citation omitted.] It does not follow, however, that a "break-up" must be present and "inevitable" before directors are subject to enhanced judicial scrutiny and are required to pursue a transaction that is calculated to produce the best value reasonably available to the stockholders. In fact, we stated in *Revlon* that "when bidders make relatively similar offers, or dissolution of the company becomes inevitable, the directors cannot fulfill their enhanced Unocal duties by playing favorites with the contending factions." [Citation omitted.] *Revlon* thus does not hold that an inevitable dissolution or "break-up" is necessary. The decisions of this Court following *Revlon* reinforced the applicability of enhanced scrutiny and the directors' obligation to seek the best value reasonably available for the stockholders where there is a pending sale of control, regardless of whether or not there is to be a break-up of the corporation. In [a prior case], this Court held:

> We stated in *Revlon*, and again here, that in a sale of corporate control the responsibility of the directors is to get the highest value reasonably attainable for the shareholders.

[Citation omitted.] ***

Although [prior cases] are clear in holding that a change of control imposes on directors the obligation to obtain the best value reasonably available to the stockholders, the Paramount defendants have interpreted our decision in *Time-Warner* as requiring a corporate break-up in order for that obligation to apply. The facts in *Time-Warner*, however, were quite different from the facts of this case, and refute Paramount's position here. In *Time-Warner*, the Chancellor held that there was no change of control in the original stock-for-stock merger between Time and Warner because Time would be owned by a fluid aggregation of unaffiliated stockholders both before and after the merger:

> If the appropriate inquiry is whether a change in control is contemplated, the answer must be sought in the specific circumstances surrounding the transaction. Surely under some circumstances a stock for stock merger could reflect a transfer of corporate control. That would, for example, plainly be the case

here if Warner were a private company. But where, as here, the shares of both constituent corporations are widely held, corporate control can be expected to remain unaffected by a stock for stock merger. This in my judgment was the situation with respect to the original merger agreement. When the specifics of that situation are reviewed, it is seen that, aside from legal technicalities and aside from arrangements thought to enhance the prospect for the ultimate succession of [Nicholas J. Nicholas, Jr., president of Time], neither corporation could be said to be acquiring the other. Control of both remained in a large, fluid, changeable and changing market.

> The existence of a control block of stock in the hands of a single shareholder or a group with loyalty to each other does have real consequences to the financial value of "minority" stock. The law offers some protection to such shares through the imposition of a fiduciary duty upon controlling shareholders. But here, effectuation of the merger would not have subjected Time shareholders to the risks and consequences of holders of minority shares. This is a reflection of the fact that no control passed to anyone in the transaction contemplated. The shareholders of Time would have "suffered" dilution, of course, but they would suffer the same type of dilution upon the public distribution of new stock.

[Citation omitted.] Moreover, the transaction actually consummated in *Time-Warner* was not a merger, as originally planned, but a sale of Warner's stock to Time.

In our affirmance of the Court of Chancery's well-reasoned decision, this Court held that "The Chancellor's findings of fact are supported by the record and his conclusion is correct as a matter of law." [Citation omitted.] Nevertheless, the Paramount defendants here have argued that a break-up is a requirement and have focused on the following language in our *Time-Warner* decision:

> However, we premise our rejection of plaintiffs' Revlon claim on different grounds, namely, the absence of any substantial evidence to conclude that Time's board, in negotiating with Warner, made the dissolution or break-up of the corporate entity inevitable, as was the case in *Revlon.*

> Under Delaware law there are, generally speaking and without excluding other possibilities, two circumstances which may implicate *Revlon* duties. The first, and clearer one, is when a corporation initiates an active bidding process seeking to sell itself

or to effect a business reorganization involving a clear break-up of the company. However, *Revlon* duties may also be triggered where, in response to a bidder's offer, a target abandons its long-term strategy and seeks an alternative transaction involving the breakup of the company.

[Citation omitted.]

The Paramount defendants have misread the holding of *Time-Warner*. Contrary to their argument, our decision in *Time-Warner* expressly states that the two general scenarios discussed in the above-quoted paragraph are not the only instances where "Revlon duties" may be implicated. The Paramount defendants' argument totally ignores the phrase "without excluding other possibilities." Moreover, the instant case is clearly within the first general scenario set forth in *Time-Warner*. The Paramount Board, albeit unintentionally, had "initiate[d] an active bidding process seeking to sell itself" by agreeing to sell control of the corporation to Viacom in circumstances where another potential acquiror (QVC) was equally interested in being a bidder.

The Paramount defendants' position that both a change of control and a break-up are required must be rejected. Such a holding would unduly restrict the application of *Revlon*, is inconsistent with this Court's decisions in [prior cases], and has no basis in policy. There are few events that have a more significant impact on the stockholders than a sale of control or a corporate breakup. Each event represents a fundamental (and perhaps irrevocable) change in the nature of the corporate enterprise from a practical standpoint. It is the significance of each of these events that justifies: (a) focusing on the directors' obligation to seek the best value reasonably available to the stockholders; and (b) requiring a close scrutiny of board action which could be contrary to the stockholders' interests.

Accordingly, when a corporation undertakes a transaction which will cause: (a) a change in corporate control; or (b) a breakup of the corporate entity, the directors' obligation is to seek the best value reasonably available to the stockholders. This obligation arises because the effect of the Viacom-Paramount transaction, if consummated, is to shift control of Paramount from the public stockholders to a controlling stockholder, Viacom. Neither *Time-Warner* nor any other decision of this Court holds that a "break-up" of the company is essential to give rise to this obligation where there is a sale of control.

[III.]   We now turn to duties of the Paramount Board under the facts of this case and our conclusions as to the breaches of those duties which warrant injunctive relief.

[III.A] Under the facts of this case, the Paramount directors had the obligation: (a) to be diligent and vigilant in examining critically the Paramount-Viacom transaction and the QVC tender offers; (b) to act in good faith; (c) to obtain, and act with due care on, all material information reasonably available, including information necessary to compare the two offers to determine which of these transactions, or an alternative course of action, would provide the best value reasonably available to the stockholders; and (d) to negotiate actively and in good faith with both Viacom and QVC to that end.

Having decided to sell control of the corporation, the Paramount directors were required to evaluate critically whether or not all material aspects of the Paramount-Viacom transaction (separately and in the aggregate) were reasonable and in the best interests of the Paramount stockholders in light of current circumstances, including: the change of control premium, the Stock Option Agreement, the Termination Fee, the coercive nature of both the Viacom and QVC tender offers, the No-Shop Provision, and the proposed disparate use of the Rights Agreement as to the Viacom and QVC tender offers, respectively.

These obligations necessarily implicated various issues, including the questions of whether or not those provisions and other aspects of the Paramount-Viacom transaction (separately and in the aggregate): (a) adversely affected the value provided to the Paramount stockholders; (b) inhibited or encouraged alternative bids; (c) were enforceable contractual obligations in light of the directors' fiduciary duties; and (d) in the end would advance or retard the Paramount directors' obligation to secure for the Paramount stockholders the best value reasonably available under the circumstances.

The Paramount defendants contend that they were precluded by certain contractual provisions, including the No-Shop Provision, from negotiating with QVC or seeking alternatives. Such provisions, whether or not they are presumptively valid in the abstract, may not validly define or limit the directors' fiduciary duties under Delaware law or prevent the Paramount directors from carrying out their fiduciary duties under Delaware law. To the extent such provisions are inconsistent with those duties, they are invalid and unenforceable. [Citation omitted.]

Since the Paramount directors had already decided to sell control, they had an obligation to continue their search for the best value reasonably available to the stockholders. This continuing obligation included the responsibility, at the October 24 board meeting and thereafter, to evaluate critically both the QVC tender offers and the Paramount-Viacom transaction to determine if: (a) the QVC tender offer was, or would continue to be, conditional; (b) the QVC tender offer could be improved; (c) the Viacom tender offer or other aspects of the Paramount -Viacom transaction could be improved; (d) each of the respective offers would be reasonably likely to come to closure, and under what circumstances; (e) other material information was reasonably available for consideration by the Paramount directors; (f) there were viable and realistic alternative courses of action; and (g) the timing constraints could be managed so the directors could consider these matters carefully and deliberately.

[III.B] The Paramount directors made the decision on September 12, 1993, that, in their judgment, a strategic merger with Viacom on the economic terms of the Original Merger Agreement was in the best interests of Paramount and its stockholders. Those terms provided a modest change of control premium to the stockholders. The directors also decided at that time that it was appropriate to agree to certain defensive measures (the Stock Option Agreement, the Termination Fee, and the No-Shop Provision) insisted upon by Viacom as part of that economic transaction. Those defensive measures, coupled with the sale of control and subsequent disparate treatment of competing bidders, implicated the judicial scrutiny of [*Unocal, Revlon*, and later cases]. We conclude that the Paramount directors' process was not reasonable, and the result achieved for the stockholders was not reasonable under the circumstances.

When entering into the Original Merger Agreement, and thereafter, the Paramount Board clearly gave insufficient attention to the potential consequences of the defensive measures demanded by Viacom. The Stock Option Agreement had a number of unusual and potentially "draconian" provisions, including the Note Feature and the Put Feature. Furthermore, the Termination Fee, whether or not unreasonable by itself, clearly made Paramount less attractive to other bidders, when coupled with the Stock Option Agreement. Finally, the No-Shop Provision inhibited the Paramount Board's ability to negotiate with other potential bidders, particularly QVC which had already expressed an interest in Paramount.

Throughout the applicable time period, and especially from the first QVC merger proposal on September 20 through the Paramount Board meeting on November 15, QVC's interest in Paramount provided the opportunity for the Paramount Board to seek significantly higher value for the Paramount stock-holders than that being offered by Viacom. QVC persistently demonstrated its intention to meet and exceed the Viacom offers, and frequently expressed its willingness to negotiate possible further increases.

The Paramount directors had the opportunity in the October 23-24 time frame, when the Original Merger Agreement was renegotiated, to take appropriate action to modify the improper defensive measures as well as to improve the economic terms of the Paramount-Viacom transaction. Under the circumstances existing at that time, it should have been clear to the Paramount Board that the Stock Option Agreement, coupled with the Termination Fee and the No-Shop Clause, were impeding the realization of the best value reasonably available to the

Paramount stockholders. Nevertheless, the Paramount Board made no effort to eliminate or modify these counterproductive devices, and instead continued to cling to its vision of a strategic alliance with Viacom. Moreover, based on advice from the Paramount management, the Paramount directors considered the QVC offer to be "conditional" and asserted that they were precluded by the No-Shop Provision from seeking more information from, or negotiating with, QVC.

By November 12, 1993, the value of the revised QVC offer on its face exceeded that of the Viacom offer by over $1 billion at then current values. This significant disparity of value cannot be justified on the basis of the directors' vision of future strategy, primarily because the change of control would supplant the authority of the current Paramount Board to continue to hold and implement their strategic vision in any meaningful way. Moreover, their uninformed process had deprived their strategic vision of much of its credibility. [Citations omitted.]

When the Paramount directors met on November 15 to consider QVC's increased tender offer, they remained prisoners of their own misconceptions and missed opportunities to eliminate the restrictions they had imposed on themselves. Yet, it was not "too late" to reconsider negotiating with QVC. The circumstances existing on November 15 made it clear that the defensive measures, taken as a whole, were problematic: (a) the No-Shop Provision could not define or limit their fiduciary duties; (b) the Stock Option Agreement had become "draconian"; and (c) the Termination Fee, in context with all the circumstances, was similarly deterring the realization of possibly higher bids. Nevertheless, the Paramount directors remained paralyzed by their uninformed belief that the QVC offer was "illusory." This final opportunity to negotiate on the stockholders' behalf and to fulfill their obligation to seek the best value reasonably available was thereby squandered.

[IV.] Viacom argues that it had certain "vested" contract rights with respect to the No-Shop Provision and the Stock Option Agreement. In effect, Viacom's argument is that the Paramount directors could enter into an agreement in violation of their fiduciary duties and then render Paramount, and ultimately its stockholders, liable for failing to carry out an agreement in violation of those duties. Viacom's protestations about vested rights are without merit. This Court has found that those defensive measures were improperly designed to deter potential bidders, and that such measures do not meet the reasonableness test to which they must be subjected. They are consequently invalid and unenforceable under the facts of this case.

***

[V.] The realization of the best value reasonably available to the stock-holders became the Paramount directors' primary obligation under these facts in light of the change of control. That obligation was not satisfied, and the Paramount Board's process was deficient. The directors' initial hope and expectation for a strategic alliance with Viacom was allowed to dominate their decisionmaking process to the point where the arsenal of defensive measures established at the outset was perpetuated (not modified or eliminated) when the situation was dramatically altered. QVC's unsolicited bid presented the opportunity for significantly greater value for the stockholders and enhanced negotiating leverage for the directors.   Rather than seizing those opportunities, the Paramount directors chose to wall themselves off from material information which was reasonably available and to hide behind the defensive measures as a rationalization for refusing to negotiate with QVC or seeking other alternatives. Their view of the strategic alliance likewise became an empty rationalization as the opportunities for higher value for the stockholders continued to develop.   ***   [Affirmed]

***

Questions About *QVC*

1.   In *QVC*, the court held that *Revlon* duties apply "when a corporation undertakes a transaction which will cause: (a) a change in corporate control; or (b) a breakup of the corporate entity." Was a break-up or change of control of Paramount going to occur if it merged with Viacom?

2.   Recall *Smith v. Van Gorkom* from Chapter 6. Why didn't *Revlon* duties apply in that case?

D.   MAKING SENSE OF *UNOCAL* AND *REVLON*

Unocal and *Revlon* appear at first to apply to very different contexts: *Unocal* applies to defensive measures designed to ward off an unwanted takeover, whereas *Revlon* applies where the board undertakes a course of action that will result in a break-up of the company or a change in control of the company. Both of these tests have been applied in numerous contexts following their adoption, including the evaluation of poison pills and various other types of defensive measures, as well as various types of "deal protection" devices (some of which were present in *Revlon* itself). Let's see how Delaware law has evolved over the years.

Unocal *"Threats."* First, what are the sorts of "threats" that are important for purposes of the first part of the *Unocal* test? An offer that is for an "inadequate" price is one obvious example. Another example is an offer that is "coercive," that is, an offer that will cause shareholders to fear how they will be treated if they do not tender their shares or otherwise approve the transaction, thus adversely affecting their decision-making process. Mesa's offer in *Unocal* was coercive, because it could cause shareholders to "stampede" into the tender so that they would receive cash rather than junk bonds.

In *Paramount Communications, Inc. v. Time Inc.*, 571 A.2d 1140 (Del. 1989), the Delaware Supreme Court seemingly recognized another *Unocal* threat. In that case, Time Inc. (which publishes *Time* magazine and owns the HBO cable channel, among other activities) had been looking for other corporations with which to merge, as part of a long-term business strategy. Eventually, Time set its sights on Warner Communications and the two companies agreed to a stock-for-stock merger. Because Warner was a much larger company than Time, the Warner shareholders would end up owing about sixty-two percent of the post-merger Time-Warner company. However, Paramount then launched a tender offer for Time. Not viewing the Paramount tender offer favorably (and wishing to thwart it), Time then revised its transaction with Warner: instead of merging with Warner, Time would borrow between $7 and $10 billion and make a tender offer for Warner's shares. Because Time would pay cash, the approval of Time's shareholders would not be needed for this transaction (unlike the previous structure of the transaction). Certain other "deal protections" were also implemented. This all had the effect of preventing the Paramount offer from occurring, which made some Time shareholders, as well as Paramount, angry. After all, Paramount was offering a lot of money for shares of Time stock.

Although *Revlon* did not apply to the actions of Time's board (more on this below), *Unocal* did. In an important passage in the *Time* opinion, the Delaware Supreme Court wrote that:

> In this case, the Time board reasonably determined that inadequate value was not the only legally cognizable threat that Paramount's all-cash, all-shares offer could present. Time's board concluded that Paramount's eleventh hour offer posed other threats. One concern was that Time shareholders might elect to tender into Paramount's cash offer in ignorance or a mistaken belief of the strategic benefit which a business combination with Warner might produce. Moreover, Time viewed the conditions attached to Paramount's offer as introducing a degree of uncertainty that skewed a comparative analysis. Further, the timing of Paramount's offer to follow issuance of Time's proxy notice was viewed as arguably designed to upset, if not confuse, the Time

> stockholders' vote. Given this record evidence, we cannot conclude that the Time board's decision *** that Paramount's offer posed a threat to corporate policy and effectiveness was lacking in good faith or dominated by motives of either entrenchment or self-interest.[*]

Id. at 1153. Essentially, this passage seems to be saying that the board knows best and should be able to protect shareholders from their own ignorance. Not surprisingly, this rationale was heavily criticized by corporate lawyers and academics. However, following the *QVC* case (which Paramount also lost!) many commentators believe that *Time* represented the "high water mark" of this rationale.

***Evolution of the* Unocal Test.** As noted above, in *Unitrin v. American General Corp.*, 651 A.2d 1361 (Del. 1995), the Delaware Supreme Court stated that *Unocal* is the proper standard by which to evaluate board actions that are "defensive." Further, under the second part of the *Unocal* test (i.e., the proportionality of the board's response to a perceived threat), a court should examine whether a takeover defense is "draconian, by being either preclusive or coercive." If the defense is not draconian, then the court should examine whether it was "within a range of reasonable responses to the threat" posed. If it is within the range of reasonableness, then the defense will be reviewed under the business judgment rule. In that case, the plaintiffs could rebut the business judgment rule by showing that the defense was "primarily based on perpetuating [the directors] in office or some other breach of fiduciary duty such as fraud, overreaching, lack of good faith, or being uninformed." *Id.* at 1390 (quoting *Unocal*).

So, what does "preclusive or coercive" (and therefore "draconian") mean? One case that provides a good illustration is *Omnicare, Inc. v. NCS Healthcare, Inc.*, 818 A.2d 914 (Del. 2003). In that case, NCS Healthcare, Inc. received two acquisition proposals, one from Omnicare, Inc., and the other from Genesis Health Ventures, Inc. NCS's board eventually agreed to a merger with Genesis and the parties entered into various "deal protection" devices, including a "force the vote" provision which would require that the merger be submitted to a shareholder vote even if NCS's board no longer recommended it. In addition, Genesis and two of NCS's shareholders who together owned a majority of the NCS stock entered into a voting agreement under which these shareholders agreed to vote in favor of the merger. Although Omnicare later made a better offer and NCS's directors recommended that shareholders accept Omnicare's offer, this really didn't matter

---

[*] The court also found that the response of Time's board to this threat was reasonable in relation to the threat, thus satisfying the second part of *Unocal*. Importantly, the court observed that the revised Time-Warner transaction "did not preclude Paramount from making an offer for the combined Time-Warner company ...." *Id.* at 1155.

because the voting agreement and the "force the vote" provision effectively ensured that the NCS-Genesis merger would occur.

Applying the *Unocal* test to these deal-protection devices, the Delaware Supreme Court held (in a three-to-two decision) that the second part of the *Unocal* test was not met because the defenses "made it 'mathematically impossible' and 'realistically unattainable' for the Omnicare transaction or any other proposal to succeed, no matter how superior the proposal." *Id.* at 936. In other words, the "defensive devices employed by the NCS board are preclusive and coercive in the sense that they accomplished a *fait accompli*." *Id.* If left in place, they would ensure that there was no possible way that a NCS-Omnicare merger could occur.[*]

For an interesting contrast to *Omnicare*, see *Orman v. Cullman*, 2004 WL 2348395 (Del. Ch., Oct. 20, 2004). That case also involved a voting agreement whereby the holders of a majority of the Target corporation's stock agreed to vote in favor of the merger. However, unlike *Omnicare*, the Target's directors remained free to consider other acquisition proposals (provided that they were unsolicited) and to withdraw their recommendation if a better deal turned up. Moreover, the acquisition proposal required approval by a "majority of the minority," that is, it was conditioned on approval by a majority of the shares that were not subject to the voting agreement. The Court of Chancery held that these provisions were permissible under *Unocal*. As such, perhaps *Omnicare* only prohibits deal protection devices that make it absolutely impossible for a competing acquisition offer to succeed.[**]

---

[*]   However, the Delaware legislature later "overruled" the result in *Omnicare* by adopting Section 146 (a "corporation may agree to submit a matter to a vote of its stockholders whether or not the board of directors determines at any [later] time … that such matter is no longer advisable and recommends that the stockholders reject or vote against the matter.").

[**]   In *Unitrin*, for example, the actions of the target corporation's board made it very difficult—but not impossible—for a hostile acquisition of Unitrin by American General to succeed. In response to American General's unwelcome takeover attempt, Unitrin repurchased enough shares to increase the board's ownership of Unitrin stock to twenty-eight percent. Because Unitrin had a provision in its certificate of incorporation that required a seventy-five percent vote to approve a merger with any person that owned fifteen percent or more of Unitrin's stock, this meant that the Unitrin directors (voting as shareholders) could block a merger with American General if American General owned more than fifteen percent of Unitrin's stock. However, the Delaware Supreme Court pointed out that American General could still attempt to acquire Unitrin by first launching a proxy contest to replace Unitrin's board. If that succeeded, the new directors could then agree to a merger with American General. Moreover, if American General did this *before* it became a fifteen-percent shareholder, then only a majority shareholder vote would be needed, not a seventy-five percent vote. So there: it was still *possible* (albeit unlikely and difficult) that a Unitrin-American General merger could occur!

When Does* Revlon *Apply? As set forth above, the *QVC* opinion clarified when *Revlon* duties apply. Further elaboration can be found in *Arnold v. Society for Savings Bancorp*, 650 A.2d 1270 (Del. 1994), in which the Delaware Supreme Court held that *Revlon* duties do not apply in a stock-for-stock merger (i.e., a merger in which the Target shareholders will receive shares of the acquirer's stock)—*if there is no change in control*. In other words, if the merger will result in a single entity (or group) controlling the surviving corporation, then the Target corporation's board has *Revlon* duties. On the other hand, if the surviving corporation's stock will be owned by a "fluid aggregation of unaffiliated stockholders" after the merger, then a change in control of the Target would not occur and *Revlon* duties would not apply. However, if the merger is a cash merger (i.e., a merger in which the Target shareholders will receive cash and will have no continuing ownership in the Target or the surviving corporation), then a change in control has occurred and *Revlon* duties apply. Based on this, see if you can correctly answer the following problems:

Problems

Problem 12-50: Whale Corp. is a publicly traded corporation that has 10 million shares of stock outstanding. Of these shares, 6 million shares are owned by Jonah. Krill Corp. has 1 million shares of stock outstanding. Assume that Krill Corp. will merge into Whale Corp. in a transaction in which each share of Krill stock would be converted into one share of Whale stock. *Does the Krill Corp. board of directors have* Revlon *duties with respect to this transaction?*

Problem 12-51: Ocean Corp. is a publicly traded corporation that has 10 million shares of stock outstanding. No Ocean shareholder owns more than 100,000 shares. Drop Corp. has 1 million shares of stock outstanding. Assume that Drop Corp. will merge into Ocean Corp. in a transaction in which each share of Drop stock would be converted into one share of Ocean stock. *Does the Drop Corp. board of directors have* Revlon *duties with respect to this transaction?*

Problem 12-52: Frog Corp. is a publicly traded corporation that has 10 million shares of stock outstanding. No Frog shareholder owns more than 100,000 shares. Fly Corp. has 1 million shares of stock outstanding. Assume that Fly Corp. will merge into Frog Corp. in a transaction in which each share of Fly Corp. stock would be converted into $10 in cash. *Does the Fly Corp. board of directors have* Revlon *duties with respect to this transaction?*

The *Revlon* "triggers" continue to evolve. In *Lyondell Chemical Co. v. Ryan*, 970 A.2d 235 (Del. 2009), a potential bidder, Basell AF, filed a Schedule 13D disclosing that it had the right to acquire 8.3 of Lyondell Chemical Co.'s stock and that it was interested in a possible transaction with Lyondell. Lyondell's board met soon afterward, but decided not to do anything at that time. Two months later, however, Lyondell's CEO met with Basell's CEO and negotiated an acquisition agreement. When some shareholders claimed that this agreement did not maximize "shareholder value" as required by *Revlon*, the Delaware Supreme Court found that *Revlon* duties did not apply when Basell filed the Schedule 13D. According to the court:

> *** *Revlon* duties do not arise simply because a company is "in play." The duty to seek the best available price applies only when a company embarks on a transaction—on its own initiative or in response to an unsolicited offer—that will result in a change of control. Basell's Schedule 13D did put the Lyondell directors, and the market in general, on notice that Basell was interested in acquiring Lyondell. The directors responded by promptly holding a special meeting to consider whether Lyondell should take any action. The directors decided that they would neither put the company up for sale nor institute defensive measures to fend off a possible hostile offer. Instead, they decided to take a "wait and see" approach. That decision was an entirely appropriate exercise of the directors' business judgment. The time for action under *Revlon* did not begin until July 10, 2007, when the directors began negotiating the sale of Lyondell.

Id. at 242 (citations omitted).[*]

For an interesting non-application of *Revlon*, see *McMullin v. Beran*, 765 A.2d 910, 919 (Del. 2000). In that case, the court observed that:

> When the entire sale to a third-party is proposed, negotiated and timed by a majority shareholder, *** the board cannot realistically *seek* any alternative because the majority shareholder has the right to vote its shares in favor of the third-party transaction it proposed for the board's consideration. Nevertheless, in such situations, the directors are obliged to make an informed and deliberate judgment, in good faith, about whether

---

[*] *Lyondell* is also notable for its discussion of how to treat *Revlon* claims against directors when the company has a Section 102(b)(7) director-exculpation provision in its certificate of incorporation. As you learned in Chapter 6, such provisions protect directors from claims for monetary damages (unless one of the exceptions set forth in the statute applies) but do not bar claims for injunctions or other equitable relief.

the sale to a third party that is being proposed by the majority shareholder will result in a maximization of value for the minority shareholders.

Id. at 919 (citations omitted). Thus, even though *Revlon* did not apply, the board still had other fiduciary duties.

Poison Pills. As noted above, in *Moran v. Household International, Inc.*, 500 A.2d 1346 (Del. 1985), the Delaware Supreme Court upheld a "flip-over" poison pill against certain legal challenges. However, while the court did uphold the board's ability to implement a poison pill before any attempted takeover had begun, it observed that the poison pill was:

> not absolute. When [and if] the Household [International, Inc.] Board of Directors is faced with a tender offer and a request to redeem the Rights, they will not be able to arbitrarily reject the offer. They will be held to the same fiduciary standards any other board of directors would be held to in deciding to adopt a defensive mechanism, the same standard as they were held to in originally approving the Rights Plan.

Id. at 1354 (citing *Unocal*).

This raises the question of whether a Target board will ever be *required* to redeem a poison pill or whether it could instead "just say no" to a hostile takeover. In other words, must poison pills only be used for their (stated) purpose of forcing the acquirer to negotiate with the board? Once the Target's board has decided it can't get the acquirer to sweeten its offer, must it redeem the poison pill and let the shareholders decide? *Air Products and Chemicals, Inc. v. Airgas, Inc.*, which is set forth below, is the most recent case from Delaware court to address this issue.

To greatly summarize the facts in *Airgas*, in February 2010, Air Products & Chemicals, Inc. ("Air Products") began a "hostile" tender offer for all of the outstanding shares of Airgas, Inc. ("Airgas") stock. Air Products increased its offering price several times during the tender offer but each time Airgas's board, through public statements and SEC filings, argued that the price was too low. Finally, in late 2010 Air Products made its "best and final offer" of $70 per share. Still, the Airgas board—*including three directors who had previously been nominated by Air Products* and then elected to the board—unanimously agreed that this offer was inadequate; the Airgas board thought a share of Airgas stock was worth at least $78.

To fend off an unwanted takeover, Airgas had a poison pill that would be triggered if an unapproved person acquired fifteen percent of Airgas's stock. Not surprisingly, the Airgas left the poison pill in place during the tender offer. Airgas also had a staggered board, which meant that it would take at least two annual stockholder meetings for a determined acquirer to nominate and elect a majority of new directors to Airgas's board who would then cancel the poison pill. (Interestingly, the three Airgas directors who were nominated by Air Products in 2010 ended up arguing that the poison pill should be left in place!) Further, Airgas had not opted out of Section 203 of the Delaware General Corporation Law, which generally prohibits business combinations with any interested stockholder for three years after the time that such a stockholder became an "interested stockholder." Also, Airgas's certificate of incorporation required a supermajority (67%) vote to approve a merger with an "interested stockholder" (defined as one who beneficially owns at least 20% of Airgas's outstanding voting stock), with certain exceptions. In combination, these were powerful defenses that essentially prevented Air Products from continuing with its tender offer.

On December 21, 2010, Airgas's board unanimously rejected Air Products's $70 per-share offer. Because Air Products refused to increase its offer any further, things had reached an impasse and the case ended up in court. Even though it has been heavily edited, the following portion of the court's opinion is very lengthy. (Reasonable persons could argue that even more editing was in order.) However, it contains a very good discussion of the status of Delaware law concerning poison pills and good example of the application of the *Unocal* standard to a poison pill coupled with a staggered board.

Air Products and Chemicals, Inc. v. Airgas, Inc.
Delaware Court of Chancery
2011 WL 519735, February 15, 2011

CHANDLER, Chancellor.

***

This case poses the following fundamental question: Can a board of directors, acting in good faith and with a reasonable factual basis for its decision, when faced with a structurally non-coercive, all-cash, fully financed tender offer directed to the stockholders of the corporation, keep a poison pill in place so as to prevent the stockholders from making their own decision about whether they want to tender their shares—even after the incumbent board has lost one election contest, a full year has gone by since the offer was first made public, and the stockholders are fully informed as to the target board's views on the inadequacy of the offer? If so, does that effectively mean that a board can "just say never" to a hostile tender offer?

The answer to the latter question is "no." A board cannot "just say no" to a tender offer. Under Delaware law, it must first pass through two prongs of exacting judicial scrutiny by a judge who will evaluate the actions taken by, and the motives of, the board. Only a board of directors found to be acting in good faith, after reasonable investigation and reliance on the advice of outside advisors, which articulates and convinces the Court that a hostile tender offer poses a legitimate threat to the corporate enterprise, may address that perceived threat by blocking the tender offer and forcing the bidder to elect a board majority that supports its bid.

In essence, this case brings to the fore one of the most basic questions animating all of corporate law, which relates to the allocation of power between directors and stockholders. That is, "when, if ever, will a board's duty to 'the corporation and its shareholders' require [the board] to abandon concerns for 'long term' values (and other constituencies) and enter a current share value maximizing mode?" [Citation omitted.] More to the point, in the context of a hostile tender offer, who gets to decide when and if the corporation is for sale?

Since the Shareholder Rights Plan (more commonly known as the "poison pill") was first conceived and throughout the development of Delaware corporate takeover jurisprudence during the twenty-five-plus years that followed, the debate over who ultimately decides whether a tender offer is adequate and should be accepted—the shareholders of the corporation or its board of directors—has raged on. Starting with *Moran v. Household International, Inc.* [citation omitted] in 1985, when the Delaware Supreme Court first upheld the adoption of the poison pill as a valid takeover defense, through the hostile takeover years of the 1980s, and in several recent decisions of the Court of Chancery and the Delaware Supreme Court, this fundamental question has engaged practitioners, academics, and members of the judiciary, but it has yet to be confronted head on.

For the reasons much more fully described in the remainder of this Opinion, I conclude that, as Delaware law currently stands, the answer must be that the power to defeat an inadequate hostile tender offer ultimately lies with the board of directors. As such, I find that the Airgas board has met its burden under *Unocal* to articulate a legally cognizable threat (the allegedly inadequate price of Air Products' offer, coupled with the fact that a majority of Airgas's stockholders would likely tender into that inadequate offer) and has taken defensive measures that fall within a range of reasonable responses proportionate to that threat. I thus rule in favor of defendants. ***

INTRODUCTION

***

*** [W]e are at a crossroads. Air Products has made its "best and final" offer—apparently its offer to acquire Airgas has reached an end stage. Meanwhile, the Airgas board believes the offer is clearly inadequate and its value in a sale transaction is at least $78 per share. At this stage, it appears, neither side will budge. Airgas continues to maintain its defenses, blocking the bid and effectively denying shareholders the choice whether to tender their shares. Air Products and Shareholder Plaintiffs now ask this Court to order Airgas to redeem its poison pill and other defenses that are stopping Air Products from moving forward with its hostile offer, and to allow Airgas's stockholders to decide for themselves whether they want to tender into Air Products' (inadequate or not) $70 "best and final" offer.

***

*** I conclude that the Airgas board, in proceeding as it has since October 2009, has not breached its fiduciary duties owed to the Airgas stockholders. I find that the board has acted in good faith and in the honest belief that the Air Products offer, at $70 per share, is inadequate.

Although I have a hard time believing that inadequate price alone (according to the target's board) in the context of a non-discriminatory, all-cash, all-shares, fully financed offer poses any "threat"—particularly given the wealth of information available to Airgas's stockholders at this point in time—under existing Delaware law, it apparently does. Inadequate price has become a form of "substantive coercion" as that concept has been developed by the Delaware Supreme Court in its takeover jurisprudence. That is, the idea that Airgas's stockholders will disbelieve the board's views on value (or in the case of merger arbitrageurs who may have short-term profit goals in mind, they may simply ignore the board's recommendations), and so they may mistakenly tender into an inadequately priced offer. Substantive coercion has been clearly recognized by our Supreme Court as a valid threat.

Trial judges are not free to ignore or rewrite appellate court decisions. Thus, for reasons explained in detail below, I am constrained by Delaware Supreme Court precedent to conclude that defendants have met their burden under *Unocal* to articulate a sufficient threat that justifies the continued maintenance of Airgas's poison pill. That is, assuming defendants have met their burden to articulate a legally cognizable threat (prong 1), Airgas's defenses have been recognized by Delaware law as reasonable responses to the threat posed by an inadequate offer—even an all-shares, all-cash offer (prong 2).

In my personal view, Airgas's poison pill has served its legitimate purpose. Although the "best and final" $70 offer has been on the table for just over two months (since December 9, 2010), Air Products' advances have been ongoing for over sixteen months, and Airgas's use of its poison pill—particularly in combination with its staggered board—has given the Airgas board over a full year to inform its stockholders about its view of Airgas's intrinsic value and Airgas's value in a sale transaction. It has also given the Airgas board a full year to express its views to its stockholders on the purported opportunistic timing of Air Products' repeated advances and to educate its stockholders on the inadequacy of Air Products' offer. It has given Airgas *more time than any litigated poison pill in Delaware history*—enough time to show stockholders four quarters of improving financial results, demonstrating that Airgas is on track to meet its projected goals. And it has helped the Airgas board push Air Products to raise its bid by $10 per share from when it was first publicly announced to what Air Products has now represented is its highest offer. The record *** confirm[s] that Airgas's stockholder base is sophisticated and well-informed, and that essentially all the information they would need to make an informed decision is available to them. In short, there seems to be no threat here—the stockholders know what they need to know (about both the offer and the Airgas board's opinion of the offer) to make an informed decision.

That being said, however, as I understand binding Delaware precedent, I may not substitute my business judgment for that of the Airgas board. The Delaware Supreme Court has recognized inadequate price as a valid threat to corporate policy and effectiveness. The Delaware Supreme Court has also made clear that the "selection of a time frame for achievement of corporate goals ... may not be delegated to the stockholders." [Citation omitted.]   Furthermore, in powerful dictum, the Supreme Court has stated that "[d]irectors are not obliged to abandon a deliberately conceived corporate plan for a short-term shareholder profit unless there is clearly no basis to sustain the corporate strategy." [Citation omitted.]   Although I do not read that dictum as eliminating the applicability of heightened *Unocal* scrutiny to a board's decision to block a non-coercive bid as underpriced, I do read it, along with the actual holding in *Unitrin*, as indicating that a board that has a good faith, reasonable basis to believe a bid is inadequate may block that bid using a poison pill, irrespective of stockholders' desire to accept it.

Here, even using heightened scrutiny, the Airgas board has demonstrated that it has a reasonable basis for sustaining its long term corporate strategy—the Airgas board is independent, and has relied on the advice of three different outside independent financial advisors in concluding that Air Products' offer is inadequate. Air Products' own three nominees who were elected to the Airgas board in September 2010 have joined wholeheartedly in the Airgas board's determination, and when the Airgas board met to consider the $70 "best and final"

offer in December 2010, it was one of those Air Products Nominees who said, "We have to protect the pill." Indeed, one of Air Products' own directors conceded at trial that the Airgas board members had acted within their fiduciary duties in their desire to "hold out for the proper price," and that "if an offer was made for Air Products that [he] considered to be unfair to the stockholders of Air Products ... [he would likewise] use every legal mechanism available" to hold out for the proper price as well. Under Delaware law, the Airgas directors have complied with their fiduciary duties. Thus, as noted above, and for the reasons more fully described in the remainder of this Opinion, I am constrained to deny Air Products' and the Shareholder Plaintiffs' requests for relief.
***

II. STANDARD OF REVIEW

A.   The Unocal Standard

Because of the "omnipresent specter" of entrenchment in takeover situations, it is well-settled that when a poison pill is being maintained as a defensive measure and a board is faced with a request to redeem the rights, the *Unocal* standard of enhanced judicial scrutiny applies. Under that legal framework, to justify its defensive measures, the target board must show (1) that it had "reasonable grounds for believing a danger to corporate policy and effectiveness existed" (i.e., the board must articulate a legally cognizable threat) and (2) that any board action taken in response to that threat is "reasonable in relation to the threat posed." [Citation omitted.]

The first hurdle under *Unocal* is essentially a process-based review: "Directors satisfy the first part of the *Unocal* test by demonstrating good faith and reasonable investigation." [Citation omitted.] Proof of good faith and reasonable investigation is "materially enhanced, as here, by the approval of a board comprised of a majority of outside independent directors." [Citation omitted.]

But the inquiry does not end there; process alone is not sufficient to satisfy the first part of *Unocal* review—"under *Unocal* and *Unitrin* the defendants have the burden of showing the reasonableness of their investigation, the reasonableness of their process and also of the result that they reached." [Citation omitted.] That is, the "process" has to lead to the finding of a threat. Put differently, no matter how exemplary the board's process, or how independent the board, or how reasonable its investigation, to meet their burden under the first prong of *Unocal* defendants must actually articulate some legitimate threat to corporate policy and effectiveness.

Once the board has reasonably perceived a legitimate threat, *Unocal* prong 2 engages the Court in a substantive review of the board's defensive actions: Is the board's action taken in response to that threat proportional to the threat posed? In other words, "[b]ecause of the omnipresent specter that directors could use a rights plan improperly, even when acting subjectively in good faith, *Unocal* and its progeny require that this Court also review the use of a rights plan objectively." [Citation omitted.] This proportionality review asks first whether the board's actions were "draconian, by being either preclusive or coercive." If the board's response was not draconian, the Court must then determine whether it fell "within a range of reasonable responses to the threat" posed.

***

C.   A Brief Poison Pill Primer—Moran *and its Progeny*

This case unavoidably highlights what former-Chancellor Allen has called "an anomaly" in our corporation law. [Citation omitted.] The anomaly is that "[p]ublic tender offers are, or rather can be, change in control transactions that are functionally similar to merger transactions with respect to the critical question of control over the corporate enterprise." [Citation omitted.] Both tender offers and mergers are "extraordinary" transactions that "threaten[] equivalent impacts upon the corporation and all of its constituencies including existing shareholders." [Citation omitted.] But our corporation law statutorily views the two differently— under DGCL § 251, board approval and recommendation is required before stockholders have the opportunity to vote on or even consider a merger proposal, while traditionally the board has been given no statutory role in responding to a public tender offer. The poison pill was born "as an attempt to address the flaw (as some would see it) in the corporation law" giving boards a critical role to play in the merger context but no role to play in tender offers.

These "functionally similar forms of change in control transactions," however, have received disparate legal treatment—on the one hand, a decision not to pursue a merger proposal (or even a decision not to engage in negotiations at all) is reviewed under the deferential business judgment standard, while on the other hand, a decision not to redeem a poison pill in the face of a hostile tender offer is reviewed under "intermediate scrutiny" and must be "reasonable in relation to the threat posed" by such offer.

In *Moran v. Household International, Inc.*, written shortly after the *Unocal* decision in 1985, the Delaware Supreme Court first upheld the legality of the poison pill as a valid takeover defense. Specifically, in *Moran*, the Household board of directors "react[ed] to what it perceived to be the threat in the market place of coercive two-tier tender offers" by adopting a stockholder rights plan that would allow the corporation to protect stockholders by issuing securities as a way to ward off a hostile bidder presenting a structurally coercive offer. The Moran Court held that the adoption of such a rights plan was within the board's statutory authority and thus was not per se illegal under Delaware law. But the Supreme Court cabined the use of the rights plan as follows:

> [T]he Rights Plan is not absolute. When the Household Board of Directors is faced with a tender offer and a request to redeem rights, they will not be able to arbitrarily reject the offer. They will be held to the same fiduciary standards any other board of directors would be held to in deciding to adopt a defensive mechanism, the same standard they were held to in originally approving the Rights Plan. [Citation omitted.]

The Court went on to say that "[t]he Board does not now have unfettered discretion in refusing to redeem the Rights. The Board has no more discretion in refusing to redeem the Rights than it does in enacting any defensive mechanism." [Citation omitted.] Accordingly, while the Household board's adoption of the rights plan was deemed to be made in good faith, and the plan was found to be reasonable in relation to the threat posed by the "coercive acquisition techniques" that were prevalent at the time, the pill at that point was adopted merely as a preventive mechanism to ward off future advances. The "ultimate response to an actual takeover," though, would have to be judged by the directors' actions taken at that time, and the board's "use of the Plan [would] be evaluated when and if the issue [arose]." [Citation omitted.]

Notably, the pill in *Moran* was considered reasonable in part because the Court found that there were many methods by which potential acquirors could get around the pill. One way around the pill was the "proxy out"—bidders could solicit consents to remove the board and redeem the rights. In fact, the Court did "not view the Rights Plan as much of an impediment on the tender offer process" at all. [Citation omitted.] After all, the board in *Moran* was not classified, and so the entire board was up for reelection annually—meaning that all of the directors could be replaced in one fell swoop and the acquiror could presumably remove any impediments to its tender offer fairly easily after that.

So, the Supreme Court made clear in *Moran* that "coercive acquisition techniques" (i.e. the well-known two-tiered front-end-loaded hostile tender offers of the 1980s) were a legally cognizable "threat," and the adoption of a poison pill was a reasonable defensive measure taken in response to that threat. [Citation omitted.] ***

***

Two scholars at the time penned an article suggesting that there were three types of threats that could be recognized under *Unocal*: (1) structural coercion— "the risk that disparate treatment of non-tendering shareholders might distort shareholders' tender decisions" (i.e., the situation involving a two-tiered offer where the back end gets less than the front end); (2) opportunity loss—the "dilemma that a hostile offer might deprive target shareholders of the opportunity to select a superior alternative offered by target management;" and (3) substantive coercion—"the risk that shareholders will mistakenly accept an underpriced offer because they disbelieve management's representations of intrinsic value."[*]

***

Gilson & Kraakman believed that, if used correctly, an effective proportionality test could properly incentivize management, protect stockholders and ultimately increase value for stockholders in the event that management does resist a hostile bid—but only if a real "threat" existed. To demonstrate the existence of such a threat, management must show (in detail) how its plan is better than the alternative (the hostile deal) for the target's stockholders. Only then, if management met that burden, could it use a pill to block a "substantively coercive," but otherwise non-coercive bid.

The test proposed by the professors was taken up, and was more or less adopted, by then-Chancellor Allen in *City Capital Associates v. Interco*. [Citation omitted.] There, the board of Interco had refused to redeem a pill that was in place as a defense against an unsolicited tender offer to purchase all of Interco's shares for $74 per share. The bid was non-coercive (structurally), because the offer was for $74 both on the front and back end, if accepted. As an alternative to the offer, the board of Interco sought to effect a restructuring that it claimed would be worth at least $76 per share.

***   [T]he Chancellor recognized that "[e]ven where an offer is noncoercive, it may represent a 'threat' to shareholder interests" because a board with the power to refuse the proposal and negotiate actively may be able to obtain higher value from the bidder, or present an alternative transaction of higher value to stockholders. [Citation omitted.] Although he declined to apply the term "substantive coercion" to the threat potentially posed by an "inadequate" but noncoercive offer, Chancellor Allen clearly addressed the concept. Consciously eschewing use of the Orwellian term "substantive coercion," the Chancellor determined that, based on the facts presented to him, there was no threat of stockholder "coercion"—instead, the threat was to stockholders' economic interests posed by a "non-coercive" offer that the board deemed to be "inadequate." As Gilson & Kraakman had suggested, the Chancellor then held that, assuming the board's determination was made in good faith, such a determination could justify leaving a poison pill in place for some period of time

---

[*]   [Footnote by author]: The court was citing Ronald Gilson & Reinier Kraakman, *Delaware's Intermediate Standard for Defensive Tactics: Is There Substance to Proportionality Review?*, 44 BUS. LAW. 247, 258 (1989).

while the board protects stockholder interests (either by negotiating with the bidder, or looking for a white knight, or designing an alternative to the offer). But "[o]nce that period has closed ... and [the board] has taken such time as it required in good faith to arrange an alternative value-maximizing transaction, then, in most instances, the legitimate role of the poison pill in the context of a noncoercive offer will have been fully satisfied." [Citation omitted.] The only remaining function for the pill at that point, he concluded, is to preclude a majority of the stockholders from making their own determination about whether they want to tender.

The Chancellor held that the "mild threat" posed by the tender offer (a difference of approximately $2 per share, when the tender offer was for all cash and the value of management's alternative was less certain) did not justify the board's decision to keep the pill in place, effectively precluding stockholders from exercising their own judgment—despite the board's good faith belief that the offer was inadequate and keeping the pill in place was in the best interests of stockholders.

In *Paramount Communications, Inc. v. Time, Inc.*, [citation omitted], however, the Delaware Supreme Court explicitly rejected an approach to *Unocal* analysis that "would involve the court in substituting its judgment as to what is a 'better' deal for that of a corporation's board of directors." Although not a "pill case," the Supreme Court in *Paramount* addressed the concept of substantive coercion head on in determining whether an all-cash, all-shares tender offer posed a legally cognizable threat to the target's stockholders.

[In *Paramount*, Time's board was not subject to *Revlon* duties; instead, the court applied *Unocal*.] In evaluating the Time board's actions under *Unocal*, the Supreme Court embraced the concept of substantive coercion, agreeing with the Time board that its stockholders might have tendered into Paramount's offer "in ignorance or a mistaken belief of the strategic benefit which a business combination with Warner might produce." [Citation omitted.] Stating in no uncertain terms that "in our view, precepts underlying the business judgment rule militate against a court's engaging in the process of attempting to appraise and evaluate the relative merits of a long-term versus a short-term investment goal for shareholders" [citation omitted] (as to do so would be "a distortion of the *Unocal* process"), the Supreme Court held that Time's response was proportionate to the threat of Paramount's offer. Time's defensive actions were not aimed at "cramming down" a management-sponsored alternative to Paramount's offer, but instead, were simply aimed at furthering a pre-existing long-term corporate strategy. This, held the Supreme Court, comported with the board's valid exercise of its fiduciary duties under *Unocal*.

Five years later, the Supreme Court further applied the "substantive coercion" concept in *Unitrin, Inc. v. American General Corp.* [Citation omitted.] There, a hostile acquirer (American General) wanted Unitrin (the target corporation) to be enjoined from implementing a stock repurchase and poison pill adopted in response to American General's "inadequate" all-cash offer. Recognizing that previous cases had held that "inadequate value" of an all-cash offer could be a valid threat [citation omitted], the Court also reiterated its conclusion in *Paramount* that inadequate value is not the only threat posed by a non-coercive, all-cash offer. The *Unitrin* Court recited that "the Time board of directors had reasonably determined that inadequate value was not the only threat that Paramount's all cash for all shares offer presented, but was *also* reasonably concerned that the Time stockholders might tender to Paramount in ignorance or based upon a mistaken belief, i.e., yield to substantive coercion." [Citation omitted.]

Relying on that line of reasoning, the *Unitrin* Court determined that the Unitrin board "reasonably perceived risk of substantive coercion, i.e., that Unitrin's shareholders might accept American General's inadequate Offer because of 'ignorance or mistaken belief' regarding the Board's assessment of the long-term value of Unitrin's stock." [Citation omitted.] Thus, perceiving a valid threat under *Unocal*, the Supreme Court then addressed whether the board of Unitrin's response was proportional to the threat.

Having determined that the Unitrin board reasonably perceived the American General offer to be inadequate, and Unitrin's poison pill adoption to be a proportionate response, the Court of Chancery had found that the Unitrin board's decision to authorize its stock repurchase program was disproportionate because it was "unnecessary" to protect the Unitrin stockholders from an inadequate bid since the board already had a pill in place. The Court of Chancery here was sensitive to how the stock buy back would make it extremely unlikely that American General could win a proxy contest. The Supreme Court, however, held that the Court of Chancery had "erred by substituting its judgment, that the Repurchase Program was unnecessary, for that of the board," [citation omitted], and that such action, if not coercive or preclusive, could be valid if it fell within a range of reasonableness.

***

More recent cases decided by the Court of Chancery have attempted to cut back on the now-broadened concept of "substantive coercion." The concept, after all, was originally (as outlined by Professors Gilson & Kraakman) intended to be a very carefully monitored "threat" requiring close judicial scrutiny of any defensive measures taken in response to such a threat. In *Chesapeake v. Shore*, Vice Chancellor Strine stated:

One might imagine that the response to this particular type of threat might be time-limited and confined to what is necessary to ensure that the board can tell its side of the story effectively. That is, because the threat is defined as one involving the possibility that stockholders might make an erroneous investment or voting decision, the appropriate response would seem to be one that would remedy that problem by providing the stockholders with adequate information. [Citation omitted.]

Once the stockholders have access to such information, the potential for stockholder "confusion" seems substantially lessened. At that point, "[o]ur law should [] hesitate to ascribe rube-like qualities to stockholders. *If the stockholders are presumed competent to buy stock in the first place, why are they not presumed competent to decide when to sell in a tender offer after an adequate time for deliberation has been afforded them?*" [Citation omitted.]

That is essentially how former-Chancellor Allen first attempted to apply the concept of substantive coercion in *Interco*. Chancellor Allen found it "significant" that the question of the board's responsibility to redeem or not to redeem the poison pill in *Interco* arose at the "end-stage" of the takeover contest. [Citation omitted.] He explained:

[T]he negotiating leverage that a poison pill confers upon this company's board will, it is clear, not be further utilized by the board to increase the options available to shareholders or to improve the terms of those options. Rather, at this stage of this contest, the pill now serves the principal purpose of ... precluding the shareholders from choosing an alternative ... that the board finds less valuable to shareholders. [Citation omitted.]

Similarly, here, the takeover battle between Air Products and Airgas seems to have reached an "end stage." Air Products has made its "best and final" offer. Airgas deems that offer to be inadequate. And we're not "talking nickels and quarters here"—an $8 gulf separates the two. The Airgas stockholders know all of this. At this stage, the pill is serving the principal purpose of precluding the shareholders from tendering into Air Products' offer. As noted above, however, the Supreme Court rejected the reasoning of *Interco* in *Paramount*. Thus, while I agree theoretically with former-Chancellor Allen's and Vice Chancellor Strine's conception of substantive coercion and its appropriate application, the Supreme Court's dictum in *Paramount* (which explicitly disapproves of *Interco*) suggests that, unless and until the Supreme Court rules otherwise, that is not the current state of our law.

***

The foregoing legal framework describes what I believe to be the current legal regime in Delaware. With that legal superstructure in mind, I now apply the *Unocal* standard to the specific facts of this case.

III. ANALYSIS

A.   Has the Airgas Board Established That It Reasonably Perceived the Existence of a Legally Cognizable Threat?

1. Process

Under the first prong of *Unocal*, defendants bear the burden of showing that the Airgas board, "after a reasonable investigation ... determined in good faith, that the [Air Products offer] presented a threat ... that warranted a defensive response." [Citation omitted.] I focus my analysis on the defendants' actions in response to Air Products' current $70 offer, but I note here that defendants would have cleared the *Unocal* hurdles with greater ease when the relevant inquiry was with respect to the board's response to the $65.50 offer.

In examining defendants' actions under this first prong of *Unocal*, "the presence of a majority of outside independent directors coupled with a showing of reliance on advice by legal and financial advisors, 'constitute[s] a prima facie showing of good faith and reasonable investigation." [Citation omitted.] Here, it is undeniable that the Airgas board meets this test.

First, it is currently comprised of a majority of outside independent directors—including the three recently-elected insurgent directors who were nominated to the board by Air Products. ***

Second, the Airgas board relied on not one, not two, but three outside independent financial advisors in reaching its conclusion that Air Products' offer is "clearly inadequate." ***

2. What is the "Threat?"

*** In the supplemental evidentiary hearing, Airgas (and its lawyers) attempted to identify numerous threats posed by Air Products' $70 offer: It is coercive. It is opportunistically timed. It presents the stockholders with a "prisoner's dilemma." It undervalues Airgas—it is a "clearly inadequate" price. The merger arbitrageurs who have bought into Airgas need to be "protected from themselves." The arbs are a "threat" to the minority. The list goes on.

The reality is that the Airgas board discussed essentially none of these alleged "threats" in its board meetings, or in its deliberations on whether to accept or reject Air Products' $70 offer, or in its consideration of whether to keep the pill in place. ***

***

In the end, it really is "All About Value." [Citation omitted.] Airgas's directors and Airgas's financial advisors concede that the Airgas stockholder base is sophisticated and well-informed, and that they have all the information necessary to decide whether to tender into Air Products' offer.

a. Structural Coercion

Air Products' offer is not structurally coercive. A structurally coercive offer involves "the risk that disparate treatment of non-tendering shareholders might distort shareholders' tender decisions." [Citation omitted.] *Unocal*, for example, "involved a two-tier, highly coercive tender offer" where stockholders who did not tender into the offer risked getting stuck with junk bonds on the back end. "In such a case, the threat is obvious: shareholders may be compelled to tender *to avoid being treated adversely* in the second stage of the transaction." [Citation omitted; emphasis added by *Airgas* court.]

Air Products' offer poses no such structural threat. It is for all shares of Airgas, with consideration to be paid in all cash. The offer is backed by secured financing. There is regulatory approval. The front end will get the same consideration as the back end, in the same currency, as quickly as practicable. Air Products is committed to promptly paying $70 in cash for each and every share of Airgas and has no interest in owning less than 100% of Airgas. ***

***

b. Opportunity Loss

Opportunity loss is the threat that a "hostile offer might deprive target stockholders of the opportunity to select a superior alternative offered by target management or ... offered by another bidder." [Citation omitted.] As then-Vice Chancellor Berger (who was also one of the Justices in *Unitrin*) explained in *Shamrock Holdings*:

> An inadequate, non-coercive offer may [] constitute a threat for some reasonable period of time after it is announced. The target corporation (or other potential bidders) may be inclined to provide the stockholders with a more attractive alternative, but may need some additional time to formulate and present that option. During the interim, the threat is that the stockholders might choose the

inadequate tender offer only because the superior option has not yet been presented .... However, *where there has been sufficient time for any alternative to be developed and presented* and for the target corporation to inform its stockholders of the benefits of retaining their equity position, the "threat" to the stockholders of an inadequate, non-coercive offer seems, in most circumstances, to be without substance. [Citation omitted.]

As such, Air Products' offer poses no threat of opportunity loss. The Airgas board has had, at this point, over sixteen months to consider Air Products' offer and to explore "strategic alternatives going forward as a company." [Citation omitted.] After all that time, there is no alternative offer currently on the table[.] ***

c. Substantive Coercion

Inadequate price and the concept of substantive coercion are inextricably related. The Delaware Supreme Court has defined substantive coercion, as discussed in Section II.C, as "the risk that [Airgas's] stockholders might accept [Air Products'] inadequate Offer because of 'ignorance or mistaken belief' regarding the Board's assessment of the long-term value of [Airgas's] stock." [Citation omitted.] In other words, if management advises stockholders, in good faith, that it believes Air Products' hostile offer is inadequate because in its view the future earnings potential of the company is greater than the price offered, Airgas's stockholders might nevertheless reject the board's advice and tender.

In the article that gave rise to the concept of "substantive coercion," Professors Gilson and Kraakman argued that, in order for substantive coercion to exist, two elements are necessary: (1) management must actually expect the value of the company to be greater than the offer—and be correct that the offer is in fact inadequate, and (2) the stockholders must reject management's advice or "believe that management will not deliver on its promise." [Citation omitted.] ***

Defendants' argument involves a slightly different take on this threat, based on the particular composition of Airgas's stockholders (namely, its large "short-term" base). In essence, Airgas's argument is that "the substantial ownership of Airgas stock by these short-term, deal-driven investors poses a threat to the company and its shareholders"—the threat that, because it is likely that the arbs would support the $70 offer, "shareholders will be coerced into tendering into an inadequate offer." [Citation omitted.] The threat of "arbs" is a new facet of substantive coercion, different from the substantive coercion claim recognized in *Paramount*. There, the hostile tender offer was purposely timed to confuse the stockholders. The terms of the offer could cause stockholders to mistakenly tender if they did not believe or understand (literally) the value of the merger with

Warner as compared with the value of Paramount's cash offer. The terms of the offer introduced uncertainty. In contrast, here, defendants' claim is not about "confusion" or "mistakenly tendering" (or even "disbelieving" management)—Air Products' offer has been on the table for over a year, Airgas's stockholders have been barraged with information, and there is no alternative offer to choose that might cause stockholders to be confused about the terms of Air Products' offer. Rather, Airgas's claim is that it needs to maintain its defensive measures to prevent control from being surrendered for an unfair or inadequate price. The argument is premised on the fact that a large percentage (almost half) of Airgas's stockholders are merger arbitrageurs—any of whom bought into the stock when Air Products first announced its interest in acquiring Airgas, at a time when the stock was trading much lower than it is today—who would be willing to tender into an inadequate offer because they stand to make a significant return on their investment even if the offer grossly undervalues Airgas in a sale. "They don't care a thing about the fundamental value of Airgas." [Citation omitted.] In short, the risk is that a majority of Airgas's stockholders will tender into Air Products' offer despite its inadequate price tag, leaving the minority "coerced" into taking $70 as well. The defendants do not appear to have come to grips with the fact that the arbs bought their shares from long-term stockholders who viewed the increased market price generated by Air Products' offer as a good time to sell.

The threat that merger arbs will tender into an inadequately priced offer is only a legitimate threat if the offer is indeed inadequate. *** Air Products and Shareholder Plaintiffs attack two main aspects of Airgas's five year plan—(1) the macroeconomic assumptions relied upon by management, and (2) the fact that Airgas did not consider what would happen if the economy had a "double-dip" recession.

Plaintiffs argue that reasonable stockholders may disagree with the board's optimistic macroeconomic assumptions. ***

*** But nothing in the record supported a claim that Airgas fudged any of its numbers, nor was there evidence that the board did not act at all times in good faith and in reasonable reliance on its outside advisors. ***

The next question is, if a majority of stockholders want to tender into an inadequately priced offer, is that substantive coercion? Is that a threat that justifies continued maintenance of the poison pill? Put differently, is there evidence in the record that Airgas stockholders are so "focused on the short-term" that they would "take a smaller harvest in the swelter of August over a larger one in Indian Summer"? [Citation omitted.] Air Products argues that there is none whatsoever. ***

But there is at least some evidence in the record suggesting that this risk may be real. Moreover, both Airgas's expert and well as *Air Products' own expert* testified that a large number—if not all—of the arbitrageurs who bought into Airgas's stock at prices significantly below the $70 offer price would be happy to tender their shares at that price regardless of the potential long-term value of the company. Based on the testimony of both expert witnesses, I find sufficient evidence that a majority of stockholders might be willing to tender their shares regardless of whether the price is adequate or not—thereby ceding control of Airgas to Air Products. This is a clear "risk" under the teachings of *TW Services* and *Paramount* because it would essentially thrust Airgas into *Revlon* mode.

Ultimately, it all seems to come down to the Supreme Court's holdings in *Paramount* and *Unitrin*. In *Unitrin*, the Court held: "[T]he directors of a Delaware corporation have the prerogative to determine that the market undervalues its stock and to protect its stockholders from offers that do not reflect the long-term value of the corporation under its present management plan." [Citation omitted.] When a company is not in *Revlon* mode, a board of directors "is not under any per se duty to maximize shareholder value in the short term, even in the context of a takeover." [Citation omitted.] The Supreme Court has unequivocally "endorse[d the] conclusion that it is not a breach of faith for directors to determine that the present stock market price of shares is not representative of true value or that there may indeed be several market values for any corporation's stock." [Citation omitted.] As noted above, based on all of the facts presented to me, I find that the Airgas board acted in good faith and relied on the advice of its financial and legal advisors in coming to the conclusion that Air Products' offer is inadequate. And as the Supreme Court has held, a board that in good faith believes that a hostile offer is inadequate may "properly employ[] a poison pill as a proportionate defensive response to protect its stockholders from a 'low ball' bid." [Citation omitted.]

> *B.   Is the Continued Maintenance of Airgas's Defensive Measures Proportionate to the "Threat" Posed by Air Products' Offer?*

Turning now to the second part of the *Unocal* test, I must determine whether the Airgas board's defensive measures are a proportionate response to the threat posed by Air Products' offer. Where the defensive measures "are inextricably related, the principles of Unocal require that [they] be scrutinized collectively as a unitary response to the perceived threat." [Citation omitted.] Defendants bear the burden of showing that their defenses are not preclusive or coercive, and if neither, that they fall within a "range of reasonableness." [Citation omitted.]

1. Preclusive or Coercive

A defensive measure is coercive if it is "aimed at 'cramming down' on its shareholders a management-sponsored alternative." [Citation omitted.] Airgas's defensive measures are certainly not coercive in this respect, as Airgas is specifically not trying to cram down a management sponsored alternative, but rather, simply wants to maintain the status quo and manage the company for the long term. A response is preclusive if it "makes a bidder's ability to wage a successful proxy contest and gain control [of the target's board] ... 'realistically unattainable.'" [Citation omitted.]

Air Products and Shareholder Plaintiffs argue that Airgas's defensive measures are preclusive because they render the possibility of an effective proxy contest realistically unattainable. ***

*** [In the recent Delaware Supreme Court case of] *Versata Enterprises, Inc. v. Selectica, Inc.* ***[,] Trilogy (the hostile acquiror) argued that in order for the target's defensive measures not to be preclusive: (1) a successful proxy contest must be realistically attainable, and (2) the successful proxy contest must result in gaining control of the board at the next election. The Delaware Supreme Court rejected this argument, stating that "[i]f that preclusivity argument is correct, then it would apply whenever a corporation has both a classified board and a Rights Plan .... *[W]e hold that the combination of a classified board and a Rights Plan do not constitute a preclusive defense.*" [Citation omitted; emphasis added by *Airgas* court.]

The Supreme Court explained its reasoning as follows:

Classified boards are authorized by statute and are adopted for a variety of business purposes. Any classified board also operates as an antitakeover defense by preventing an insurgent from obtaining control of the board in one election. More than a decade ago, in *Carmody* [v. *Toll Brothers, Inc.*], the Court of Chancery noted "because only one third of a classified board would stand for election each year, a classified board would delay—but not prevent—a hostile acquiror from obtaining control of the board, since a determined acquiror could wage a proxy contest and obtain control of two thirds of the target board over a two year period, as opposed to seizing control in a single election." [Citation and quotations omitted.]

The Court concluded: "The fact that a combination of defensive measures makes it more difficult for an acquirer to obtain control of a board does not make such measures realistically unattainable, i.e., preclusive." [Citation omitted.]

Moreover, citing *Moran*, the Supreme Court noted that pills do not fundamentally restrict proxy contests, explaining that a "Rights Plan will not have a severe impact upon proxy contests and it will not preclude all hostile acquisitions of Household." [Citation omitted.] Arguably the combination of a staggered board plus a pill is at least more preclusive than the use of a rights plan by a company with a pill alone (where all directors are up for election annually, as in *Gaylord Container* and *Moran*, because the stockholders could replace the entire board at once and redeem the pill). In any event, though, the Supreme Court in *Selectica* suggests that this is a distinction without a significant difference, and very clearly held that the combination of a classified board and a Rights Plan is not preclusive, and that the combination may only "delay—but not prevent—a hostile acquiror from obtaining control of the board." [Citation omitted.]

***

I am thus bound by this clear precedent to proceed on the assumption that Airgas's defensive measures are not preclusive if they delay Air Products from obtaining control of the Airgas board (even if that delay is significant) so long as obtaining control at some point in the future is realistically attainable. I now examine whether the ability to obtain control of Airgas's board in the future is realistically attainable.

Air Products has already run one successful slate of insurgents. Their three independent nominees were elected to the Airgas board in September. Airgas's next annual meeting will be held [some time] around September 2011. Accordingly, if Airgas's defensive measures remain in place, Air Products has two options if it wants to continue to pursue Airgas at this time: (1) It can call a special meeting and remove the entire board with a supermajority vote of the outstanding shares, or (2) It can wait until Airgas's 2011 annual meeting to nominate a slate of directors. I will address the viability of each of these options in turn.

a. Call a Special Meeting to Remove the Airgas Board by a 67% Supermajority Vote

Airgas's charter allows for 33% of the outstanding shares to call a special meeting of the stockholders, and to remove the entire board without cause by a vote of 67% of the outstanding shares. ***

The fact that something might be a theoretical possibility does not make it "realistically attainable." In other words, what the Supreme Court in *Unitrin* and *Selectica* meant by "realistically attainable" must be something more than a mere "mathematical possibility" or "hypothetically conceivable chance" of circumventing a poison pill. One would think a sensible understanding of the phrase would be that an insurgent has a reasonably meaningful or real world shot at securing the support of enough stockholders to change the target board's composition and remove the obstructing defenses. It does not mean that the insurgent has a right to win or that the insurgent must have a highly probable chance or even a 50-50 chance of prevailing. But it must be more than just a theoretical possibility, given the required vote, the timing issues, the shareholder profile, the issues presented by the insurgent and the surrounding circumstances.

[Here, the court found that it was not realistically attainable for Air Products to remove the Airgas directors before the next annual stockholders meeting.]

***

b. Run Another Proxy Contest

Even if Air Products is unable to achieve the 67% supermajority vote of the outstanding shares necessary to remove the board in a special meeting, it would only need a simple majority of the voting stockholders to obtain control of the board at next year's annual meeting. Air Products has stated its unwillingness to wait around for another eight months until Airgas's 2011 annual meeting. There are legitimately articulated reasons for this—Air Products' stockholders, after all, have been carrying the burden of a depressed stock price since the announcement of the offer. But that is a business determination by the Air Products board. The reality is that obtaining a simple majority of the voting stock is significantly less burdensome than obtaining a supermajority vote of the outstanding shares, and considering the current composition of Airgas's stockholders (and the fact that, as a result of that shareholder composition, a majority of the voting shares today would likely tender into Air Products' $70 offer), if Air Products and those stockholders choose to stick around, an Air Products victory at the next annual meeting is very realistically attainable.

*** I thus am constrained to conclude that Airgas's defensive measures are not preclusive.

2. Range of Reasonableness

"If a defensive measure is neither coercive nor preclusive, the *Unocal* proportionality test requires the focus of enhanced judicial scrutiny to shift to the range of reasonableness." [Citation omitted.] The reasonableness of a board's response is evaluated in the context of the specific threat identified—the "specific nature of the threat [] 'sets the parameters for the range of permissible defensive tactics' at any given time." [Citation omitted.]

Here, the record demonstrates that Airgas's board, composed of a majority of outside, independent directors, acting in good faith and with numerous outside advisors concluded that Air Products' offer clearly undervalues Airgas in a sale transaction. The board believes in good faith that the offer price is inadequate by no small margin. Thus, the board is responding to a legitimately articulated threat.

***

*** Air Products chose to replace a minority of the Airgas board with three independent directors who promised to take a "fresh look." Air Products ran its nominees expressly premised on that independent slate. It could have put up three nominees premised on the slogan of "shareholder choice." It could have run a slate of nominees who would promise to remove the pill if elected. It could have gotten three directors elected who were resolved to fight back against the rest of the Airgas board. Certainly what occurred here is not what Air Products expected to happen. Air Products ran its slate on the promise that its nominees would "consider without any bias [the Air Products] Offer," and that they would "be willing to be outspoken in the boardroom about their views on these issues." [Citation omitted.] Air Products *got what it wanted.* Its three nominees got elected to the Airgas board and then questioned the directors about their assumptions. (They got answers.) They looked at the numbers themselves. (They were impressed.) They requested outside legal counsel. (They got it.) They requested a third outside financial advisor. (They got it.) And in the end, they *joined in the board's view* that Air Products' offer was inadequate. John Clancey, one of the Air Products Nominees, grabbed the flag and championed Airgas's defensive measures, telling the rest of the board, *"We have to protect the pill."* [Citation omitted.] David DeNunzio, Airgas's new independent financial advisor from Credit Suisse who was brought in to take a "fresh look" at the numbers, concluded in his professional opinion that the fair value of Airgas is in the "mid to high seventies, and well into the mid eighties." [Citation omitted.] In Robert Lumpkins' opinion (one of the Air Products Nominees), "the company on its own, its own business will be worth $78 or more in the not very distant future because of its own earnings and cash flow prospects ... as a standalone company." [Citation omitted.]

The Supreme Court has clearly held that "the 'inadequate value' of an all cash for all shares offer is a 'legally cognizable threat.'" [Citation omitted.] Moreover, "[t]he fiduciary duty to manage a corporate enterprise includes the selection of a time frame for achievement of corporate goals. *That duty may not be delegated to the stockholders.*" [Citation omitted; emphasis added by *Airgas* court.] The Court continued, "Directors are not obligated to abandon a deliberately conceived corporate plan for a short-term shareholder profit unless there is clearly no basis to sustain the corporate strategy." [Citation omitted.] Based on all of the foregoing factual findings, I cannot conclude that there is "clearly no basis" for the Airgas board's belief in the sustainability of its long-term plan.

On the contrary, the maintenance of the board's defensive measures must fall within a range of reasonableness here. The board is not "cramming down" a management-sponsored alternative or any company-changing alternative. Instead, the board is simply maintaining the status quo, running the company for the long-term, and consistently showing improved financial results each passing quarter. The board's actions do not *forever* preclude Air Products, or any bidder, from acquiring Airgas or from getting around Airgas's defensive measures if the price is right. In the meantime, the board is preventing a change of control from occurring at an inadequate price. This course of action has been clearly recognized under Delaware law: "directors, when acting deliberately, in an informed way, and in the good faith pursuit of corporate interests, may follow a course designed to achieve long-term value even at the cost of immediate value maximization." [Citation omitted.]

***

C.   *Pills, Policy and Professors (and Hypotheticals)*

When the Supreme Court first upheld the use of a rights plan in *Moran*, it emphasized that "[t]he Board does not now have unfettered discretion in refusing to redeem the Rights." [Citation omitted.] And in the most recent "pill case" decided just this past year, the Supreme Court reiterated its view that, "[a]s we held in *Moran*, the adoption of a Rights Plan is not absolute." [Citation omitted.] The poison pill's limits, however, still remain to be seen.

***

The contours of the debate have morphed slightly over the years, but the fundamental questions have remained. Can a board "just say no"? If so, when? How should the enhanced judicial standard of review be applied? What are the pill's limits? And the ultimate question: Can a board "just say never"? In a 2002 article entitled Pills, Polls, and Professors Redux, [well-known attorney Martin] Lipton wrote the following:

> As the pill approaches its twentieth birthday, it is under attack from [various] groups of professors, each advocating a different form of shareholder poll, but each intended to eviscerate the protections afforded by the pill .... Upon reflection, I think it fair to conclude that the [] schools of academic opponents of the pill are not really opposed to the idea that the staggered board of the target of a hostile takeover bid may use the pill to "just say no."

Rather, *their fundamental disagreement is with the theoretical possibility that the pill may enable a staggered board to "just say never."* However, as ... almost every [situation] in which a takeover bid was combined with a proxy fight show, the incidence of a target's actually saying "never" is so rare as not to be a real-world problem. While [the various] professors' attempts to undermine the protections of the pill is argued with force and considerable logic, none of their arguments comes close to overcoming the cardinal rule of public policy—particularly applicable to corporate law and corporate finance—"If it ain't broke, don't fix it." [Citation omitted; emphasis added by *Airgas* court.]

Well, in this case, the Airgas board has continued to say "no" even after one proxy fight. So what Lipton has called the "largely theoretical possibility of continued resistance after loss of a proxy fight" is now a real world situation. Vice Chancellor Strine recently posed Professor [Lucian] Bebchuk et al.'s Effective Staggered Board ("ESB") hypothetical in *Yucaipa American Alliance Fund II, L.P. v. Riggio*]:

[T]here is a plausible argument that a rights plan could be considered preclusive, based on an examination of real world market considerations, when a bidder who makes an all shares, structurally non-coercive offer has: (1) won a proxy contest for a third of the seats of a classified board; (2) is not able to proceed with its tender offer for another year because the *incumbent board majority* will not redeem the rights as to the offer; and (3) is required to take all the various economic risks that would come with maintaining the bid for another year. [Citation omitted.]

At that point, it is argued, it may be appropriate for a Court to order redemption of a poison pill. That hypothetical, however, is not exactly the case here for two main reasons. First, Air Products did not run a proxy slate running on a "let the shareholders decide" platform. Instead, they ran a slate committed to taking [an] independent look and deciding for themselves afresh whether to accept the bid. *** Once elected, [the Air Products nominees] got inside and saw for themselves why the Airgas board and its advisors have so passionately and consistently argued that Air Products' offer is too low ***. The incumbents now share in the rest of the board's view that Air Products' offer is inadequate—this is not a case where the insurgents want to redeem the pill but they are unable to convince the majority. This situation is different from the one posited by Vice Chancellor Strine and the three professors in their article, and I need not and do not address that scenario.

Second, Airgas does not have a true "ESB" [effective staggered board] as articulated by the professors. As discussed earlier, Airgas's charter allows for 33% of the stockholders to call a special meeting and remove the board by a 67% vote of the outstanding shares. Thus, according to the professors, no court intervention would be necessary in this case. This factual distinction also further differentiates this case from the *Yucaipa* hypothetical.

CONCLUSION

***

There is no question that poison pills act as potent anti-takeover drugs with the potential to be abused. Counsel for plaintiffs (both Air Products and Shareholder Plaintiffs) make compelling policy arguments in favor of redeeming the pill in this case—to do otherwise, they say, would essentially make all companies with staggered boards and poison pills "takeover proof." The argument is an excellent sound bite, but it is ultimately not the holding of this fact-specific case, although it does bring us one step closer to that result.

As this case demonstrates, in order to have any effectiveness, pills do not—and can not—have a set expiration date. To be clear, though, this case does not endorse "just say never." What it does endorse is Delaware's long-understood respect for reasonably exercised managerial discretion, so long as boards are found to be acting in good faith and in accordance with their fiduciary duties (after rigorous judicial fact-finding and enhanced scrutiny of their defensive actions). The Airgas board serves as a quintessential example.

Directors of a corporation still owe fiduciary duties to *all stockholders*—this undoubtedly includes short-term as well as long-term holders. At the same time, a board cannot be forced into *Revlon* mode any time a hostile bidder makes a tender offer that is at a premium to market value. The mechanisms in place to get around the poison pill—even a poison pill in combination with a staggered board, which no doubt makes the process prohibitively more difficult—have been in place since 1985, when the Delaware Supreme Court first decided to uphold the pill as a legal defense to an unwanted bid. That is the current state of Delaware law until the Supreme Court changes it.

For the foregoing reasons, Air Products' and the Shareholder Plaintiffs' requests for relief are denied, and all claims asserted against defendants are dismissed with prejudice. ***

The Future. Corporate lawyers are nothing if not creative. New takeover tactics, takeover defenses, and deal protection devices will be developed and evolve in the future. Although the cases discussed above go a long way toward helping us understand the legal propriety of these tactics, they certainly will not be the end of the story. Stay tuned.

This was a very long chapter and covered many issues. Now may be a good time to see how well you retained this information by trying your hand at some multiple choice problems. When working on the following problems, keep in mind that, unless otherwise noted, the MBCA applies. In addition, the case law that you learned about in this chapter applies. And, of course, federal law, such as the tender offer rules, applies as well.

PRACTICE QUESTIONS

Multiple Choice Question 12-1: Liquid Corp.'s board of directors decided that business was no longer good and passed a resolution to dissolve the corporation. Subsequently, the holders of all of Liquid Corp.'s 10,000 outstanding shares of common stock approved the dissolution. During its winding up process, Liquid Corp. sold all of its assets for $100,000 in cash and distributed this money to its shareholders, but took no steps to pay or bar creditors' claims. A few months after Liquid Corp. dissolved, Gas Corp. sued the former shareholders of Liquid Corp. to recover $200,000 that Liquid Corp. owed Gas Corp. The court found that the claim was valid and that Gas Corp. had not been notified that Liquid Corp. was dissolving. Mr. Solid owned 1,000 shares of Liquid Corp. common stock. *Assuming that there were no other classes of stock in Liquid Corp. outstanding before the dissolution, what amount, if any, must Mr. Solid pay to Gas Corp.?*

A $1,000.
B. $20,000.
C. $10,000.
D.   Nothing, because shareholders are not liable for the corporation's debts.

Multiple Choice Question 12-2: Record Corp.'s articles of incorporation provide that:

> "The corporation's authorized capital shall consist of 500,000 shares of common stock and 500,000 shares of preferred stock. Each share of preferred stock shall be entitled to a liquidation preference of $10 upon dissolution of the corporation. Following full payment of this liquidation preference, each share of preferred stock shall be entitled to share in any remaining amounts to be distributed to the shareholders of the corporation, with each share of preferred stock and each share of common stock being treated equally for purposes of this sentence."

Record Corp. was properly dissolved. After the winding-up process was completed by paying off all of its creditors in full and selling its remaining assets, Record Corp. had $1,000,000 in cash left over. At that time, there were 90,000 shares of Record Corp. common stock outstanding, and 10,000 shares of Record Corp. preferred stock outstanding. *How will this $1,000,000 be distributed?*

A.   Holders of common stock will receive $1 per share, and holders of preferred stock will receive $1 per share.

B.   Holders of common stock will receive $10 per share, and holders of preferred stock will receive $10 per share.

C.   Holders of common stock will receive $9 per share, and holders of preferred stock will receive $19 per share.

D.   Holders of common stock will receive $11 per share, and holders of preferred stock will receive $19 per share.

Multiple Choice Question 12-3:   The articles of incorporation of Widget Corp. ("Widget") provide that:

> "The corporation's authorized capital consists of 100,000 shares of common stock and 50,000 shares of preferred stock. Each share of preferred stock is entitled to a liquidation preference of $20 upon dissolution of the corporation. Following full payment of this liquidation preference, no share of preferred stock shall be entitled to receive any further amounts upon dissolution of the corporation."

Widget was properly dissolved. Upon dissolution, Widget distributed $1,000,000 to its shareholders. When they caused Widget to distribute this amount to the shareholders, the members of Widget's board of directors were aware that Widget owed $100,000 to a supplier, Raw Materials, Inc., but did not take any steps to pay or otherwise bar this claim. However, none of Widget's shareholders knew about the amount that Widget owed to Raw Materials, Inc. The amount owed to Raw Materials, Inc. was Widget's only debt at the time of dissolution. At the time of dissolution, there were 1,000 shares of Widget common stock outstanding, and 1,000 shares of Widget preferred stock outstanding. *Which of the following statements is incorrect?*

A.   Raw Materials, Inc. may not recover the $100,000 from the shareholders of Widget because they did not know that Widget owed money to Raw Materials, Inc.

B.   Raw Materials, Inc. may recover the $100,000 from the shareholders of Widget even if they did not know that Widget owed money to Raw Materials, Inc.

C.   If Widget had paid the $100,000 owing to Raw Materials, Inc. and then distributed $900,000 to its shareholders, then a holder of one share of Widget common stock would have received $880 upon the dissolution of Widget.

D.   If Widget had paid the $100,000 owing to Raw Materials, Inc. and then distributed $900,000 to its shareholders, then a holder of one share of Widget preferred stock would have received $20 upon the dissolution of Widget.

Multiple Choice Question 12-4: Seller Corp. ("SC") is involved in the food business and has operated a large bakery for many years. It has three lines of business: its cookie division, its bagel division, and its cake division. The percentages of SC's overall business that these three divisions represented as of the end of the most recently completed fiscal year are as follows:

Division	Percentage of SC's Assets	Percentage of SC's Pre-Tax Income	Percentage of SC's Revenues
Cookie Division	25%	51%	33%
Bagel Division	51%	24%	34%
Cake Division	24%	25%	33%

Buyer Corp. and SC entered into an asset purchase agreement whereby SC will sell the assets of its cookie division and its bagel division to Buyer Corp. for $10 million in cash. SC's President calls you to explain the deal and to ask whether SC can complete this transaction without getting the approval of SC's shareholders. *What is your advice?*

A.   Shareholder approval is not required because this transaction is in the ordinary course of business.

B.   Shareholder approval is not required because SC will definitely still have a "significant continuing business activity" after the transaction.

C.   Shareholder approval is required because SC will definitely not have a "significant continuing business activity" after the transaction.

D.   Shareholder approval might not be required because a court could find that SC will still have a "significant continuing business activity" after the transaction.

Multiple Choice Question 12-5:   Your client, T-Bone Perkins, who is the President and sole shareholder of Messy Oil Corp., has informed you that Messy Oil Corp. plans to conduct a tender offer for 51% of the outstanding shares of common stock of Neat Oil Corp. (Neat Oil Corp. common stock is listed on the New York Stock Exchange.) *Which of the following would be <u>incorrect</u> advice to Mr. Perkins?*

A.   While Messy Oil Corp. normally would be required to hold its tender offer open to all shareholders of Neat Oil Corp. for at least 20 business days, if 51% of the shares were tendered by the second day of the tender offer, Messy Oil Corp. could terminate the tender offer and purchase the shares that have been tendered at that point.

B.   Neat Oil Corp. shareholders may have the right to withdraw their shares from the tender offer while it is still open.

C.   Neat Oil Corp. may not pay any shareholder in the tender offer more than it pays any other shareholder in the tender offer.

D.   If 100% of the shares of Neat Oil Corp. common stock are tendered, Messy Oil Corp. would not have to purchase all of those shares.

Multiple Choice Question 12-6:   Snow Corp. ("Snow") seeks to acquire Sleet, Inc. ("Sleet"), a wholly owned subsidiary of Precipitation Corp. ("Precipitation"). Sleet manufactures all of Precipitation's green widgets.   Precipitation's other wholly owned subsidiary, Rain Corp., manufactures blue widgets. Snow will pay $200 million to Precipitation for all of Sleet's stock. Sleet constitutes 70% of Precipitation's total assets, and last year generated 80% of Precipitation's pre-tax income and 75% of its revenues. After the sale of Sleet's stock, Precipitation will continue to manufacture blue widgets. *Is shareholder approval of Precipitation required to effectuate the sale?*

A.   Yes, because Precipitation's sale of Sleet is quantitatively and qualitatively substantial.

B.   Yes, because Precipitation will be left without a significant continuing business activity after the sale.

C.   No, because shareholder vote is never required where the board decides to sell the corporation's assets.

D.   No, because the sale fits within the "safe harbor" rule of the MBCA.

Multiple Choice Question 12-7: The board of Guitar Corp. ("Guitar"), a public corporation whose stock is traded on the New York Stock Exchange, approved and recommended the acquisition of Drum, Inc. ("Drum"), a closely held corporation, by merger. Guitar had 70,000,000 shares of common stock outstanding. In connection with the proposed merger, Guitar would issue 20,000,000 new shares of common stock to Drum's shareholders. At a validly called meeting of the shareholders of Guitar, the holders of 35,100,000 shares attended the meeting or were represented by proxy. Once the vote was taken, 17,125,000 shares were voted in favor of the merger, 17,100,000 shares were voted against the merger, and the remaining 875,000 shares abstained. *Did the merger receive shareholder approval?*

A.   Yes, because the number of shares voted in favor of the merger exceeded the number of shares that voted against it.

B.   Yes, because the affirmative vote of the shareholders of Guitar was unnecessary because the merger would be a "small scale" merger.

C.   No, because a majority of the outstanding shares were not voted in favor of the merger.

D.   No, because quorum was not satisfied and the vote was invalid.

Multiple Choice Question 12-8: The board of Mellow Corp. ("Mellow"), a public corporation whose stock is traded on the New York Stock Exchange, approved and recommended the acquisition of Stressed, Inc. ("Stressed"), a closely held corporation, by merger. Mellow had 70,000,000 shares of common stock out-standing. In connection with the proposed merger, Mellow would issue 20,000,000 new shares of common stock to Stressed's shareholders. The boards and shareholders of both Mellow and Stressed properly approved the merger to the extent that such approvals were required. Mark, a shareholder of Stressed, abstained from voting his shares on the merger proposal. Before the meeting of Stressed's shareholders, Mark provided written notice to Stressed's board of directors of his intent to exercise dissenters' rights (also known as appraisal rights). *Is Mark entitled to dissenters' rights with respect to this transaction?*

A.   Yes, because Mark is entitled to dissenters' rights and he followed the proper procedure in preserving his right to appraisal.

B.   Yes, because Mark is automatically entitled to dissenters' rights, as he was a shareholder of the target corporation.

C.   No, because Mark would be receiving publicly traded shares in the merger.

D.   No, because Mark's abstention from voting on the merger proposal disqualifies him from demanding appraisal rights.

Multiple Choice Question 12-9: Same facts as the previous question. Assume for purposes of this question that Mark is entitled to dissenters' rights. *What will he be paid for his shares?*

A.   The greater of the liquidation value or the pro-rata value based on a sale of the entire business as a going concern.
B.   The fair value of his shares as determined by the public stock markets.
C.   The fair value of his shares as determined by a court.
D.   The fair value of his shares as determined by the price that would be paid by a willing buyer to a willing seller in an arm's length transaction.

Multiple Choice Question 12-10: Under the MBCA, a merger:

A.   Always requires the vote of the shareholders of both constituent corporations.
B.   May never be used to "cash out" or eliminate minority shareholders.
C.   Is an action from which a shareholder of the target corporation may dissent and receive payment for the value of their shares if the corporation's stock is not publicly traded.
D.   All of the above are correct.

Multiple Choice Question 12-11: Under the MBCA, if a corporation has only one class of stock (common stock) outstanding:

A.   All amendments to the corporation's articles of incorporation must be approved by a majority of the outstanding shares of common stock.
B.   All amendments to the corporation's articles of incorporation must be approved by the holders of common stock on a "more yes votes than no votes" basis.
C.   The board of directors may amend the articles, provided that the shareholders do not thereafter object to the amendment.
D.   Only the board of directors may amend the bylaws.
E.   None of the above is correct.

Multiple Choice Question 12-12:   Under the MBCA, which of the following statements concerning asset sales is correct:

A.   The shareholders of the selling corporation must always approve the sale if it is outside the usual and regular course of business.
B.   The shareholders of the selling corporation are not required to approve the sale if it is in the usual and regular course of business.
C.   The shareholders of the buying corporation must approve the purchase if it is outside the usual and regular course of business.
D.   The shareholders of the buying corporation must approve the purchase if the buying corporation will issue any shares of its stock to the selling corporation.

Multiple Choice Question 12-13:   Solar Corp. is a publicly traded corporation whose common stock is listed on the Nasdaq Stock Market. There are 10 million shares of Solar Corp. common stock outstanding, which currently have a market price of $20 per share. Coal Corp. wishes to acquire Solar Corp. but has not yet publicly announced this plan. Coal Corp. recently gave its President, Mr. Lump, $2 million. Mr. Lump used this money to purchase 100,000 shares of Solar Corp. Mr. Lump has agreed to transfer these shares to Coal Corp. whenever he is asked to do so. In addition, Coal Corp. purchased 300,000 shares of Solar Corp. stock. *Which of the following is a correct statement concerning the requirement to file a Schedule 13D with the Securities and Exchange Commission?*

A.   Solar Corp. and Mr. Lump must file a Schedule 13D within ten days after either of them acquires an additional 100,000 shares of Solar Corp. stock.
B.   Solar Corp. and Mr. Lump must file a Schedule 13D within ten days after either of them acquires an additional 100,001 shares of Solar Corp. stock.
C.   Solar Corp. must file a Schedule 13D within ten days after it acquires an additional 200,000 shares of Solar Corp. stock, but would not need to do so if it acquired only 100,001 shares.
D.   Solar Corp. must file a Schedule 13D within ten days after it acquires an additional 200,001 shares of Solar Corp. stock, but would not need to do so if it acquired only 100,001 shares.

Multiple Choice Question 12-14:   Various Sports Corp. ("VSC") has three lines of business: its football division, its soccer division, and its baseball division. The percentages of VSC's overall business that these three divisions represented as of the end of the most recently completed fiscal year are as follows:

Division	Percentage of VSC's Assets	Percentage of VSC's Pre-Tax Income	Percentage of VSC's Revenues
Football Division	24%	19%	10%
Soccer Division	25%	30%	10%
Baseball Division	51%	51%	80%

Buyer Corp. and VSC entered into an asset purchase agreement whereby VSC will sell the assets of its baseball division to Buyer Corp. for 1 million shares of Buyer Corp. common stock. There currently are 10 million shares of Buyer Corp. common stock outstanding. *Which of the following statements concerning this transaction is correct?*

A.   The approval of VSC's shareholders is not required, but the approval of Buyer Corp.'s shareholders is required.

B.   The approval of VSC's shareholders is required, but the approval of Buyer Corp.'s shareholders is not required.

C.   Neither the approval of VSC's shareholders nor the approval of Buyer Corp.'s shareholders is required.

D.   Both the approval of VSC's shareholders and approval of Buyer Corp.'s shareholders is required.

Multiple Choice Question 12-15:   *Which of the following would be the best legal advice to give to a corporation that wishes to purchase the assets of another corporation and continue manufacturing the same products that the selling corporation currently manufactures?   The buying corporation wishes to avoid "successor liability."*

A.   The buying corporation should pay for the assets with shares of its own stock.

B.   The buying corporation should pay for the assets with cash.

C.   The buying corporation should pay for the assets with a combination of cash and shares of its own stock.

D.   The buying corporation need not be concerned about successor liability if it pays for the assets with shares of its stock so long as it does not use the same physical location that the selling corporation used.

QUESTIONS 12-16 AND 12-17 ARE BASED ON THE FOLLOWING FACTS

The common stock of Glass Corporation ("Glass") is listed on the Nasdaq Stock Market. There are approximately 30,000,000 shares of Glass common stock outstanding, which are held by approximately 5,000 shareholders. The common stock of Beverage Corporation ("Beverage") is held by approximately 200 shareholders, but is not listed on either Nasdaq or the New York Stock Exchange. There are 100,000 shares of Beverage common stock outstanding.

The boards of directors of Glass and Beverage have adopted a merger agreement that provides that Beverage will be merged into Glass. Glass will be the surviving corporation in the merger. In the merger, each share of Beverage common stock will be converted into the right to receive 100 shares of Glass common stock. The merger agreement does not contain any provisions that would amend the articles of incorporation of Glass or that would change or affect the Glass common stock that is outstanding immediately before the merger.

Multiple Choice Question 12-16: *Which of the following statements concerning shareholder approval of this merger is correct?*

A.   The merger requires the approval of the shareholders of both corporations.
B.   The merger requires the approval of the shareholders of Beverage. The approval of the shareholders of Glass is not required.
C.   The approval of the shareholders of Beverage is not required because they will receive publicly traded stock in the merger.
D.   The approval of the shareholders of Glass is not required because Glass will survive the merger and the shares of Glass common stock that are outstanding prior to the merger will not be changed in any way.

Multiple Choice Question 12-17: *Which of the following statements concerning dissenters' rights (also known as appraisal rights) is correct?*

A.   The shareholders of Beverage have dissenters' rights with respect to this merger.
B.   The shareholders of Glass do not have dissenters' rights with respect to this merger because Glass common stock is listed on the Nasdaq Stock Market.
C.   The shareholders of Beverage do not have dissenters' rights with respect to this merger because they will receive publicly traded stock in the merger.
D.   The shareholders of Glass do not have dissenters' rights with respect to this merger because their stock will remain outstanding following the merger.
E.   Both A and D are correct.

QUESTIONS 12-18 AND 12-19 ARE BASED ON THE FOLLOWING FACTS

The common stock of Kite Corporation ("Kite") is held by ten persons. However, Kite is a very large corporation, with more than $1 billion in annual revenues. There are 10 million shares of Kite common stock outstanding. The common stock of String Corporation ("String") is held by approximately 500 shareholders, and is listed on the Nasdaq Stock Market. There are 1,000,000 shares of String common stock outstanding.

The boards of directors of Kite and String have adopted a merger agreement that provides that String will be merged into Kite. Kite will be the surviving corporation in the merger. In the merger, each share of String common stock will be converted into the right to receive one share of Kite common stock. The merger agreement does not contain any provisions that would amend the articles of incorporation of Kite or that would change or affect the Kite common stock that is outstanding immediately before the merger. Kite has no plans to have its common stock listed on any stock exchange following the merger.

Multiple Choice Question 12-18: *Which of the following statements concerning shareholder approval of this merger is correct?*

A.   The merger requires the approval of the shareholders of both Kite and String.
B.   The merger requires the approval of the shareholders of String. The approval of the shareholders of Kite is not required.
C.   The approval of the shareholders of String is not required because they own publicly traded stock.
D.   The approval of the shareholders of String is not required because the surviving company will have more than 200 shareholders following the merger.

Multiple Choice Question 12-19: *Which of the following statements concerning dissenters' rights (also known as appraisal rights) is correct?*

A.   The shareholders of String have dissenters' rights with respect to this merger, but the shareholders of Kite do not have dissenters' rights.
B.   The shareholders of String do not have dissenters' rights with respect to this merger, but the shareholders of Kite have dissenters' rights.
C.   The shareholders of both String and Kite have dissenters' rights with respect to this merger.
D.   The shareholders of neither String nor Kite have dissenters' rights with respect to this merger.

Multiple Choice Question 12-20: The board and shareholders of Asbestos & Lead, Inc., a corporation that was headquartered in Chicago, Illinois, properly approved its dissolution on April 1, 2011. Three days later, the company published the following notice in *The Chicago News*, a local newspaper. The notice was published on only one day.

Notice of Dissolution of Asbestos & Lead, Inc.

Please be advised that Asbestos & Lead, Inc. (the Company) has dissolved. Any persons who have claims against the Company are hereby advised to submit such claims to the Company's Secretary, no later than April 4, 2014, at the following address: Asbestos & Lead, Inc., 111 Main Street, Chicago, IL 60643, Attn: Corporate Secretary. Each claim shall describe the claim in reasonable detail, including the name of the creditor and the reason for the alleged claim. A claim against the Company will be barred unless a proceeding to enforce the claim is commenced no later than April 4, 2014.

Will this notice be sufficient to bar a claim against Asbestos & Lead, Inc. if the holder of the claims does not sue Asbestos & Lead, Inc. before April 4, 2014?

A.   No, because the notice must give claimants at least five years to sue Asbestos & Lead, Inc.

B.   No, because the notice was published only one time.

C.   No, because the notice was published in a local newspaper rather than a newspaper that has a national circulation, such as *The New York Times.*

D.   Yes.

Multiple Choice Question 12-21: *Which of the following statements concerning mergers is correct?*

A.   From the acquirer's perspective, a triangular merger is superior to an asset purchase to minimize future liabilities.

B.   From the acquirer's perspective, a triangular merger is superior to a two-party merger to minimize future liabilities.

C.   In a forward triangular merger, the subsidiary of the acquiring corporation merges into the target corporation.

D.   If a parent corporation owns at least ninety percent of the voting shares of a subsidiary, it may merge the subsidiary into itself without needing the approval of the subsidiary's other shareholders; however, the approval of the subsidiary's board of directors is required.

Multiple Choice Question 12-22:   On Monday, October 2, The Gecko Corp. ("<u>TGC</u>") began a tender offer for shares of Rusty Airplane Corp. ("RAC") common stock.   There are 20 million shares of RAC common stock outstanding, which are listed on the Nasdaq Stock Market.   In its tender offer, TGC is offering $20 per share, subject to receiving a minimum of 10,000,001 shares.   As of Thursday, October 19, only 8 million shares had been tendered.   However, the next day, The Lizard Fund Inc. ("LFI") began a tender offer seeking "any and all" shares of RAC stock and offering $23 per share.   TGC is considering how to respond to this development.   To that end it is considering the following actions:

      I.   Immediately terminate the tender offer and purchase all shares that had been tendered at that time.

      II.   Amend the tender offer so that (1) the offering price for all shares is $24 per share and (2) the tender offer will terminate on Wednesday, November 8.

      III.   Amend the tender offer so that (1) the offering price is $24 per share for all shares tendered on or after Monday, October 23, and (2) the tender offer will terminate on Wednesday, November 8.

Which, if any, of these actions would be legal for TGC to take?

A.   I only.
B.   II only.
C.   III only.
D.   II and III only.
E.   None of the above would be legal actions to take.

Multiple Choice Question 12-23: Consider the following transactions:

I.   Book Corp., a publicly traded corporation with no shareholders that own more than 1% of its stock, wishes to acquire Page Corp. through a merger in which Page Corp. shareholders will receive cash.

II.   Book Corp., a publicly traded corporation with no shareholders that own more than 1% of its stock, wishes to acquire Page Corp. through a merger in which Page Corp. shareholders will receive shares of Book Corp. stock.

III.   Book Corp., a publicly traded corporation, wishes to acquire Page Corp. through a merger in which Page Corp. shareholders will receive shares of Book Corp. stock. Currently, Mr. Ink owns a majority of the outstanding shares of Book Corp. stock and it is expected that he will remain a majority shareholder of Book Corp. following the merger.

In which, if any, of these potential transactions would Page Corp.'s directors have "Revlon" duties under Delaware law?

A.   All of them.
B.   None of them.
C.   I only.
D.   II and III only.
E.   I and III only.

CHAPTER 13
THE SECURITIES ACT OF 1933

This chapter primarily concerns the federal Securities Act of 1933 (alternatively called the "Securities Act" or the "1933 Act"). However, it is important to remember that each state also has a securities statute, many of which predate the federal statute. Moreover, federal law only partially pre-empts these state "blue sky" laws. Nonetheless, we will be spending the bulk of our time in this chapter discussing federal law, for two reasons. First, federal law obviously applies everywhere in the United States. Second, with some notable exceptions, most state securities laws are modeled in part on the federal laws. Thus, understanding federal securities laws will give you a good foundation for understanding most of the state securities laws that you may encounter in practice.

§ 13.01   WHAT IS A "SECURITY"?

The logical place to start our discussion of securities law is with the question: what is a "security"? Clearly, if a given instrument is a "security" then the securities laws will apply to it, whereas if something is not a "security" then the securities laws will not apply to it. Certainly that was something that you did not need a textbook to tell you, but it is important because if a lawyer gives advice with respect to something without realizing that it is a "security" then she not only will have an unhappy client (who may be in a great deal of trouble) but she could be looking at malpractice liability as well. In short, the stakes can be high with securities laws; they are very "plaintiff friendly" and noncompliance with them could perhaps even send your client to jail in an extreme case.

What do you think of when you think of a "security"? (No, this has nothing to do with your Secured Transactions course.) The two items that are most likely to spring to mind are found in the common phrase "stocks and bonds." Certainly, stocks and bonds are considered securities, but there is a much longer list of things that are securities. Let's start by taking a look at how the statute defines a "security."

Section 2(a)(1) of the Securities Act provides that, "unless the context otherwise requires,"

> [t]he term "security" means any note, stock, treasury stock, security future, bond, debenture, evidence of indebtedness, certificate of interest or participation in any profit-sharing agreement, collateral-trust certificate, preorganization certificate or subscription, transferable share, investment contract, voting-trust

certificate, certificate of deposit for a security, fractional undivided interest in oil, gas, or other mineral rights, any put, call, straddle, option, or privilege on any security, certificate of deposit, or group or index of securities (including any interest therein or based on the value thereof), or any put, call, straddle, option, or privilege entered into on a national securities exchange relating to foreign currency, or, in general, any interest or instrument commonly known as a "security", or any certificate of interest or participation in, temporary or interim certificate for, receipt for, guarantee of, or warrant or right to subscribe to or purchase, any of the foregoing.

That is a pretty long list, but you should note that, to allow the statute to respond to developments in the financial world, Section 2(a)(1) provides that "any interest or instrument commonly known as a 'security'" will be considered a security. Wall Street is nothing if not inventive; it is continually inventing new financial products, many of which could not have been imagined in 1933.

"Stock." One of the things on the statute's list of securities that should be familiar to you is "stock." After all, we've spent several chapters of this textbook discussing stock and the rights of shareholders. But does the statute's inclusion of "stock" mean that something that is called "stock" is *always* a security? Not necessarily. In *United Housing Foundation, Inc. v. Forman*, 421 U.S. 837 (1975), the Supreme Court considered whether shares of "stock" in a nonprofit housing cooperative in New York City called Co-op City (technically named Riverbay Corporation) were "securities."

As the Court explained the facts of the case:

To acquire an apartment in Co-op City, an eligible prospective purchaser must buy 18 shares of stock in Riverbay for each room desired. The cost per share is $25, making the total cost $450 per room, or $1,800 for a four-room apartment. The sole purpose of acquiring these shares is to enable the purchaser to occupy an apartment in Co-op City; in effect, their purchase is a recoverable deposit on an apartment. The shares are explicitly tied to the apartment: they cannot be transferred to a nontenant; nor can they be pledged or encumbered; and they descend, along with the apartment, only to a surviving spouse. No voting rights attach to the shares as such: participation in the affairs of the cooperative appertains to the apartment, with the residents of each apartment being entitled to one vote irrespective of the number of shares owned.

Id. at 842. The Court found that these characteristics meant that the "stock" in the case was not really "stock" within the meaning of the federal securities laws. As the Court wrote:

> We reject at the outset any suggestion that the present transaction, evidenced by the sale of shares called "stock," must be considered a security transaction simply because the statutory definition of a security includes the words "any ... stock." ***

> ***

> In holding that the name given to an instrument is not dispositive, we do not suggest that the name is wholly irrelevant to the decision whether it is a security. There may be occasions when the use of a traditional name such as "stocks" or "bonds" will lead a purchaser justifiably to assume that the federal securities laws apply. This would clearly be the case when the underlying transaction embodies some of the significant characteristics typically associated with the named instrument.

> In the present case respondents do not contend, nor could they, that they were misled by use of the word "stock" into believing that the federal securities laws governed their purchase. Common sense suggests that people who intend to acquire only a residential apartment in a state-subsidized cooperative, for their personal use, are not likely to believe that in reality they are purchasing investment securities simply because the transaction is evidenced by something called a share of stock. These shares have none of the characteristics "that in our commercial world fall within the ordinary concept of a security." [Citation omitted.] Despite their name, they lack what the Court in [a prior case] deemed the most common feature of stock: the right to receive "dividends contingent upon an apportionment of profits." [Citation omitted.] Nor do they possess the other characteristics traditionally associated with stock: they are not negotiable; they cannot be pledged or hypothecated; they confer no voting rights in proportion to the number of shares owned; and they cannot appreciate in value. In short, the inducement to purchase was solely to acquire subsidized low-cost living space; it was not to invest for profit.

Id. at 848-51.

Admittedly, *Forman* is a very unusual case. As such, it is usually a safe bet that "stock" is "stock" within the meaning of Section 2(a)(1) and therefore something to which the securities laws apply.

"Investment Contracts." One mysterious entry in the list of "securities" in Section 2(a)(1) is the phrase "investment contract." Unfortunately, the Securities Act did not (and still does not) contain a separate definition of "investment contract," which meant that the courts were left with the task of interpreting it. In *Securities and Exchange Commission v. W. J. Howey Co.*, 328 U.S. 293 (1946), the Supreme Court provided a four-part definition that is still used today. Under the *Howey* test, an "investment contract" involves (1) an investment of money, (2) in a common enterprise, (3) with the expectation of profits, (4) solely from the efforts of others (that is, persons other than the investor). All four parts of this definition must be satisfied in order to find that something is an "investment contract." Of course, not all "securities" are "investment contracts." An investment contract is merely one example of a security.

Over the years, the *Howey* test has resulted in a number of unusual things being labeled as "investment contracts" and therefore subject to the federal securities laws. One example that may surprise you is found in the following case, which is the Supreme Court's most recent pronouncement on the *Howey* test.

Securities and Exchange Commission v. Edwards
United States Supreme Court
540 U.S. 389 (2004)

JUSTICE O'CONNOR delivered the opinion of the Court.

"Opportunity doesn't always knock ... sometimes it rings." [Citing ETS Payphones promotional brochure]. And sometimes it hangs up. So it did for the 10,000 people who invested a total of $300 million in the payphone sale-and-leaseback arrangements touted by respondent under that slogan.

The Securities and Exchange Commission (SEC) argues that the arrangements were investment contracts, and thus were subject to regulation under the federal securities laws. In this case, we must decide whether a moneymaking scheme is excluded from the term "investment contract" simply because the scheme offered a contractual entitlement to a fixed, rather than a variable, return.

[I]   Respondent Charles Edwards was the chairman, chief executive officer, and sole shareholder of ETS Payphones, Inc. (ETS). ETS, acting partly through a subsidiary also controlled by respondent, sold payphones to the public via independent distributors. The payphones were offered packaged with a site lease, a [five]-year leaseback and management agreement, and a buyback agreement. All but a tiny fraction of purchasers chose this package, although other management options were offered. The purchase price for the payphone packages was approximately $7,000. Under the leaseback and management agreement, purchasers received $82 per month, a 14% annual return. Purchasers were not involved in the day-to-day operation of the payphones they owned. ETS selected the site for the phone, installed the equipment, arranged for connection and long-distance service, collected coin revenues, and maintained and repaired the phones. Under the buyback agreement, ETS promised to refund the full purchase price of the package at the end of the lease or within 180 days of a purchaser's request.

In its marketing materials and on its website, ETS trumpeted the "incomparable pay phone" as "an exciting business opportunity," in which recent deregulation had "open[ed] the door for profits for individual pay phone owners and operators." According to ETS, "[v]ery few business opportunities can offer the potential for ongoing revenue generation that is available in today's pay telephone industry." [Citations omitted.]

The payphones did not generate enough revenue for ETS to make the payments required by the leaseback agreements, so the company depended on funds from new investors to meet its obligations. In September 2000, ETS filed for bankruptcy protection. The SEC brought this civil enforcement action the same month. It alleged that respondent and ETS had violated the registration requirements of §§ 5(a) and (c) of the Securities Act of 1933, [15 U.S.C. §§ 77e(a), (c)], the antifraud provisions of both § 17(a) of the Securities Act of 1933, [15 U.S.C. § 77q(a)], and § 10(b) of the Securities Exchange Act of 1934, [15 U.S.C. § 78j(b)], and Rule 10b-5 thereunder, [17 C.F.R. § 240.10b-5]. The District Court concluded that the payphone sale-and-leaseback arrangement was an investment contract within the meaning of, and therefore was subject to, the federal securities laws. [Citation omitted.] The Court of Appeals reversed. [Citation omitted.] It held that respondent's scheme was not an investment contract, on two grounds. First, it read this Court's opinions to require that an investment contract offer either capital appreciation or a participation in the earnings of the enterprise, and thus to exclude schemes, such as respondent's, offering a fixed rate of return. [Citation omitted.] Second, it held that our opinions' requirement that the return on the investment be "derived solely from the efforts of others" was not satisfied when the purchasers had a contractual entitlement to the return. [Citation omitted.] We conclude that it erred on both grounds.

[II]   "Congress' purpose in enacting the securities laws was to regulate investments, in whatever form they are made and by whatever name they are called." [Citation omitted.]   To that end, it enacted a broad definition of "security," sufficient "to encompass virtually any instrument that might be sold as an investment." [Citation omitted.] Section 2(a)(1) of the 1933 Act, [15 U.S.C. § 77b(a)(1)], and § 3(a)(10) of the 1934 Act, [15 U.S.C. § 78c(a)(10)], in slightly different formulations which we have treated as essentially identical in meaning, [citation omitted], define "security" to include "any note, stock, treasury stock, security future, bond, debenture, ... investment contract, ... [or any] instrument commonly known as a 'security.'" "Investment contract" is not itself defined.

The test for whether a particular scheme is an investment contract was established in our decision in *SEC v. W. J. Howey Co.*, 328 U.S. 293 (1946). We look to "whether the scheme involves an investment of money in a common enterprise with profits to come solely from the efforts of others." [Citation omitted.] This definition "embodies a flexible rather than a static principle, one that is capable of adaptation to meet the countless and variable schemes devised by those who seek the use of the money of others on the promise of profits." [Citation omitted.]

In reaching that result, we first observed that when Congress included "investment contract" in the definition of security, it "was using a term the meaning of which had been crystallized" by the state courts' interpretation of their "'blue sky'" laws.   [Citation omitted.]   (Those laws were the precursors to federal securities regulation and were so named, it seems, because they were "aimed at promoters who 'would sell building lots in the blue sky in fee simple.'" [Citation omitted.] The state courts had defined an investment contract as "a contract or scheme for 'the placing of capital or laying out of money in a way intended to secure income or profit from its employment,'" and had "uniformly applied" that definition to "a variety of situations where individuals were led to invest money in a common enterprise with the expectation that they would earn a profit solely through the efforts of the promoter or [a third party]." [Citation omitted.] Thus, when we held that "profits" must "come solely from the efforts of others," we were speaking of the profits that investors seek on their investment, not the profits of the scheme in which they invest. We used "profits" in the sense of income or return, to include, for example, dividends, other periodic payments, or the increased value of the investment.

There is no reason to distinguish between promises of fixed returns and promises of variable returns for purposes of the test, so understood. In both cases, the investing public is attracted by representations of investment income, as purchasers were in this case by ETS' invitation to "'watch the profits add up.'" [Citation omitted.]   Moreover, investments pitched as low risk (such as those offering a "guaranteed" fixed return) are particularly attractive to individuals more vulnerable to investment fraud, including older and less sophisticated investors. [Citation omitted.] Under the reading respondent advances, unscrupulous marketers of investments could evade the securities laws by picking a rate of return to promise. We will not read into the securities laws a limitation not compelled by the language that would so undermine the laws' purposes.

Respondent protests that including investment schemes promising a fixed return among investment contracts conflicts with our precedent. We disagree. No distinction between fixed and variable returns was drawn in the blue sky law cases that the *Howey* Court used, in formulating the test, as its evidence of Congress' understanding of the term. [Citation omitted.] Indeed, two of those cases involved an investment contract in which a fixed return was promised. [Citations omitted.]

None of our post-*Howey* decisions is to the contrary. In *United Housing Foundation v. Forman*, 421 U.S. 837 (1975), we considered whether "shares" in a nonprofit housing cooperative were investment contracts under the securities laws. We identified the "touchstone" of an investment contract as "the presence of an investment in a common venture premised on a reasonable expectation of profits to be derived from the entrepreneurial or managerial efforts of others," and then laid out two examples of investor interests that we had previously found to be "profits." [Citation omitted.] Those were "capital appreciation resulting from the development of the initial investment" and "participation in earnings resulting from the use of investors' funds." [Citation omitted.]   We contrasted those examples, in which "the investor is 'attracted solely by the prospects of a return'" on the investment, with housing cooperative shares, regarding which the purchaser "is motivated by a desire to use or consume the item purchased." [Citation omitted.] Thus, *Forman* supports the commonsense understanding of "profits" in the *Howey* test as simply "financial returns on ... investments." [Citation omitted.]

Concededly, *Forman*'s illustrative description of prior decisions on "profits" appears to have been mistaken for an exclusive list in a case considering the scope of a different term in the definition of a security, "note." [Citation omitted.] But that was a misreading of *Forman*, and we will not bind ourselves unnecessarily to passing dictum that would frustrate Congress' intent to regulate all of the "countless and variable schemes devised by those who seek the use of the money of others on the promise of profits." [Citation omitted.]

Given that respondent's position is supported neither by the purposes of the securities laws nor by our precedents, it is no surprise that the SEC has consistently taken the opposite position, and maintained that a promise of a fixed return does not preclude a scheme from being an investment contract. It has done so in formal adjudications, [citations omitted], and in enforcement actions, [citations omitted].

The Eleventh Circuit's perfunctory alternative holding, that respondent's scheme falls outside the definition because purchasers had a contractual entitlement to a return, is incorrect and inconsistent with our precedent. We are considering investment contracts. The fact that investors have bargained for a return on their investment does not mean that the return is not also expected to come solely from the efforts of others. Any other conclusion would conflict with our holding that an investment contract was offered in *Howey* itself. [Citation omitted].

We hold that an investment scheme promising a fixed rate of return can be an "investment contract" and thus a "security" subject to the federal securities laws. The judgment of the United States Court of Appeals for the Eleventh Circuit is reversed, and the case is remanded for further proceedings consistent with this opinion.

It is so ordered.

———————————————————————

Many other cases have fleshed out the meanings of the four parts of the *Howey* test. For example, the word "money" in the first part of the test (an "investment of money") simply means anything that has value, which should not be terribly surprising. An "investment" is basically the opposite of consumption. Thus, the *Forman* Court noted that "when a purchaser is motivated by a desire to use or consume the item purchased—'to occupy the land or to develop it themselves,' as the *Howey* court put it—the securities laws do not apply." *Forman*, 421 U.S. at 852 (citing *Howey*). In *Forman*, residents of Co-op City bought the stock to have an apartment to live in, not as an investment.[*]

The phrase "common enterprise" has resulted in a split of authority in the federal circuit courts. All courts will accept what is called the "horizontal" formulation of the common-enterprise test. In addition, some courts will also accept the "vertical" formulation of the common-enterprise test. (To date, the Supreme Court has not weighed in on this issue.) The horizontal test requires multiple investors who are similarly situated, that is, who are similarly affected by the success or failure of the enterprise. Thus, if there is only one investor, the enterprise will not be considered an investment contract under the horizontal formulation of the test. If a court accepts the vertical version of the test, however, all that would be necessary to prove that a "common enterprise" is present would

———————————————————————

[*]   In addition to arguing that the shares of Co-Op City were "stock," the residents of Co-Op City also argued in the *Forman* case that they were "investment contracts." They lost both arguments.

be to show a link between the investor's fortunes (that is, how much money the investor will make) and the promoter of the program or a third party.[*]

Litigation over the meaning of the phrase "expectation of profits" has centered on what types of "profits" are needed. As discussed in the *Edwards* case, the Supreme Court in *Forman* identified two types of "profits": "capital appreciation resulting from the development of the initial investment" and "participation in earnings resulting from the use of investors' funds." In other words, capital appreciation (the hope that the value of the security will rise) and dividends or other periodic payments are both considered "profits." And of course *Edwards* itself held that a contractually fixed rate of return also qualifies as a "profit" under the *Howey* test.

Finally, lower courts have not interpreted the "solely from the efforts of others" part of the *Howey* test literally. In other words, "solely" doesn't really mean "solely." (If it did, it would be easy to avoid something being an investment contract by having the investors do some nominal work and then arguing that the profits generated by the enterprise arose, at least partly, from their efforts!) Instead, the court in *Securities and Exchange Commission v. Koscot Interplanetary, Inc.*, 497 F.2d 473 (5th Cir. 1974),[**] held that "the critical inquiry is 'whether the efforts made by those other than the investor are the undeniably significant ones, those essential managerial efforts which affect the failure or success of the enterprise.'" *Id.* at 483 (citation omitted).

"Notes" and "Evidences of Indebtedness." Section 2(a)(1) of the Securities Act provides that some other types of securities include notes, bonds, debentures, and evidences of indebtedness. As noted in a footnote in Chapter 5, bonds typically are secured by the corporation's assets as collateral, whereas debentures are typically unsecured. Further, bonds and debentures tend to have a longer duration than notes. Nevertheless, the use of all three terms, as well as "evidence of indebtedness," in Section 2(a)(1) seems like overkill because they are all types of debt instruments.

---

[*]   Some courts have further refined the vertical formulation of the common-enterprise test into two strands: the *strict* version and the *broad* version. Under the strict version, the fortunes of the investor must be linked to the *fortunes* of the promoter or a third party. Under broad vertical commonality, the fortunes of the investor must be linked to the *efforts* of the promoter or a third party (that is, how hard or effectively the promoter or a third party work). To make things even more confusing, it is possible to conceive of examples of investments that would simultaneously satisfy the horizontal, the strict vertical, and the broad vertical versions of the common-enterprise test.

[**]   It is probably not a good idea to invest in a company that has "Interplanetary" in its name.

But more importantly, keep in mind that Section 2(a)(1) states that "any" note can be a security. Does this mean that when your roommate gave you an "IOU" when you paid for her lunch yesterday, that that "note" was a security and, if she doesn't repay it, you can sue her in federal court? Probably not, as you will learn from the following case.

Reves v. Ernst & Young
United States Supreme Court
494 U.S. 56 (1990)

JUSTICE MARSHALL delivered the opinion of the Court.

This case presents the question whether certain demand notes issued by the Farmers Cooperative of Arkansas and Oklahoma (Co-Op) are "securities" within the meaning of § 3(a)(10) of the Securities Exchange Act of 1934. We conclude that they are.

[I]   The Co-Op is an agricultural cooperative that, at the time relevant here, had approximately 23,000 members. In order to raise money to support its general business operations, the Co-Op sold promissory notes payable on demand by the holder. Although the notes were uncollateralized and uninsured, they paid a variable rate of interest that was adjusted monthly to keep it higher than the rate paid by local financial institutions. The Co-Op offered the notes to both members and nonmembers, marketing the scheme as an "Investment Program." Advertisements for the notes, which appeared in each Co-Op newsletter, read in part: "YOUR CO-OP has more than $11,000,000 in assets to stand behind your investments. The Investment is not Federal [sic] insured but it is ... Safe ... Secure ... and available when you need it." [Citation omitted.] Despite these assurances, the Co-Op filed for bankruptcy in 1984. At the time of the filing, over 1,600 people held notes worth a total of $10 million.

After the Co-Op filed for bankruptcy, petitioners, a class of holders of the notes, filed suit against Arthur Young & Co., the firm that had audited the Co-Op's financial statements (and the predecessor to respondent Ernst & Young). Petitioners alleged, *inter alia*, that Arthur Young had intentionally failed to follow generally accepted accounting principles in its audit, specifically with respect to the valuation of one of the Co-Op's major assets, a gasohol plant. Petitioners claimed that Arthur Young violated these principles in an effort to inflate the assets and net worth of the Co-Op. Petitioners maintained that, had Arthur Young properly treated the plant in its audits, they would not have purchased demand notes because the Co-Op's insolvency would have been apparent. On the basis of these allegations, petitioners claimed that Arthur Young had violated the antifraud provisions of the 1934 Act as well as Arkansas'[s] securities laws.

Petitioners prevailed at trial on both their federal and state claims, receiving a $6.1 million judgment. Arthur Young appealed, claiming that the demand notes were not "securities" under either the 1934 Act or Arkansas law, and that the statutes' antifraud provisions therefore did not apply. A panel of the Eighth Circuit, agreeing with Arthur Young on both the state and federal issues, reversed. [Citation omitted.] We granted certiorari to address the federal issue, [citation omitted], and now reverse the judgment of the Court of Appeals.

[II.A]   This case requires us to decide whether the note issued by the Co-Op is a "security" within the meaning of the 1934 Act. Section 3(a)(10) of that Act is our starting point:

> The term "security" means any note, stock, treasury stock, bond, debenture, certificate of interest or participation in any profit-sharing agreement or in any oil, gas, or other mineral royalty or lease, any collateral-trust certificate, preorganization certificate or subscription, transferable share, investment contract, voting-trust certificate, certificate of deposit, for a security, any put, call, straddle, option, or privilege on any security, certificate of deposit, or group or index of securities (including any interest therein or based on the value thereof), or any put, call, straddle, option, or privilege entered into on a national securities exchange relating to foreign currency, or in general, any instrument commonly known as a "security"; or any certificate of interest or participation in, temporary or interim certificate for, receipt for, or warrant or right to subscribe to or purchase, any of the foregoing; but shall not include currency or any note, draft, bill of exchange, or banker's acceptance which has a maturity at the time of issuance of not exceeding nine months, exclusive of days of grace, or any renewal thereof the maturity of which is like-wise limited." [Citation omitted.]

The fundamental purpose undergirding the Securities Acts is "to eliminate serious abuses in a largely unregulated securities market." [Citation omitted.] In defining the scope of the market that it wished to regulate, Congress painted with a broad brush. It recognized the virtually limitless scope of human ingenuity, especially in the creation of "countless and variable schemes devised by those who seek the use of the money of others on the promise of profits," [citation omitted], and determined that the best way to achieve its goal of protecting investors was "to define 'the term "security" in sufficiently broad and general terms so as to include within that definition the many types of instruments that in our commercial world fall within the ordinary concept of a security.'" [Citation omitted.] Congress therefore did not attempt precisely to cabin the scope of the Securities

Acts. Rather, it enacted a definition of "security" sufficiently broad to encompass virtually any instrument that might be sold as an investment.

Congress did not, however, "intend to provide a broad federal remedy for all fraud." [Citation omitted.] Accordingly, "[t]he task has fallen to the Securities and Exchange Commission (SEC), the body charged with administering the Securities Acts, and ultimately to the federal courts to decide which of the myriad financial transactions in our society come within the coverage of these statutes." [Citation omitted.] In discharging our duty, we are not bound by legal formalisms, but instead take account of the economics of the transaction under investigation. [Citation omitted.] Congress' purpose in enacting the securities laws was to regulate investments, in whatever form they are made and by whatever name they are called.

A commitment to an examination of the economic realities of a transaction does not necessarily entail a case-by-case analysis of every instrument, however. Some instruments are obviously within the class Congress intended to regulate because they are by their nature investments. In *Landreth Timber Co. v. Landreth*, 471 U.S. 681 (1985), we held that an instrument bearing the name "stock" that, among other things, is negotiable, offers the possibility of capital appreciation, and carries the right to dividends contingent on the profits of a business enterprise is plainly within the class of instruments Congress intended the securities laws to cover. *Landreth Timber* does not signify a lack of concern with economic reality; rather, it signals a recognition that stock is, as a practical matter, always an investment if it has the economic characteristics traditionally associated with stock. Even if sparse exceptions to this generalization can be found, the public perception of common stock as the paradigm of a security suggests that stock, in whatever context it is sold, should be treated as within the ambit of the Acts. [Citation omitted.]

We made clear in *Landreth Timber* that stock was a special case, explicitly limiting our holding to that sort of instrument. [Citation omitted.] Although we refused finally to rule out a similar per se rule for notes, we intimated that such a rule would be unjustified. Unlike "stock," we said, "'note' may now be viewed as a relatively broad term that encompasses instruments with widely varying characteristics, depending on whether issued in a consumer context, as commercial paper, or in some other investment context." [Citation omitted.] While common stock is the quintessence of a security, [citation omitted], and investors therefore justifiably assume that a sale of stock is covered by the Securities Acts, the same simply cannot be said of notes, which are used in a variety of settings, not all of which involve investments. Thus, the phrase "any note" should not be interpreted to mean literally "any note," but must be understood against the backdrop of what Congress was attempting to accomplish in enacting the Securities Acts.

Because the *Landreth Timber* formula cannot sensibly be applied to notes, some other principle must be developed to define the term "note." A majority of the Courts of Appeals that have considered the issue have adopted, in varying forms, "investment versus commercial" approaches that distinguish, on the basis of all of the circumstances surrounding the transactions, notes issued in an investment context (which are "securities") from notes issued in a commercial or consumer context (which are not). [Citations omitted.]

The Second Circuit's "family resemblance" approach begins with a presumption that any note with a term of more than nine months is a "security." [Citation omitted.] Recognizing that not all notes are securities, however, the Second Circuit has also devised a list of notes that it has decided are obviously not securities. Accordingly, the "family resemblance" test permits an issuer to rebut the presumption that a note is a security if it can show that the note in question "bear[s] a strong family resemblance" to an item on the judicially crafted list of exceptions, [citation omitted], or convinces the court to add a new instrument to the list, [citation omitted].

In contrast, the Eighth and District of Columbia Circuits apply the test we created in *SEC v. W. J. Howey Co.*, 328 U.S. 293 (1946), to determine whether an instrument is an "investment contract" to the determination whether an instrument is a "note." Under this test, a note is a security only if it evidences "(1) an investment; (2) in a common enterprise; (3) with a reasonable expectation of profits; (4) to be derived from the entrepreneurial or managerial efforts of others." [Citation omitted.]

We reject the approaches of those courts that have applied the *Howey* test to notes; *Howey* provides a mechanism for determining whether an instrument is an "investment contract." The demand notes here may well not be "investment contracts," but that does not mean they are not "notes." ***

The other two contenders—the "family resemblance" and "investment versus commercial " tests—are really two ways of formulating the same general approach. Because we think the "family resemblance" test provides a more promising framework for analysis, however, we adopt it. The test begins with the language of the statute; because the Securities Acts define "security" to include "any note," we begin with a presumption that every note is a security.[*] We

---

[*]   [Footnote by court]: The Second Circuit's version of the family resemblance test provided that only notes with a term of more than nine months are presumed to be "securities." [Citation omitted.] No presumption of any kind attached to notes of less than nine months' duration. The Second Circuit's refusal to extend the presumption to all notes was apparently founded on its interpretation of the statutory exception for notes with a maturity of nine months or less. Because we do not reach the question of how to interpret that exception,

nonetheless recognize that this presumption cannot be irrebutable. As we have said, [citation omitted], Congress was concerned with regulating the investment market, not with creating a general federal cause of action for fraud. In an attempt to give more content to that dividing line, the Second Circuit has identified a list of instruments commonly denominated "notes" that nonetheless fall without the "security" category.   See [citation omitted] (types of notes that are not "securities" include "the note delivered in consumer financing, the note secured by a mortgage on a home, the short-term note secured by a lien on a small business or some of its assets, the note evidencing a 'character' loan to a bank customer, short-term notes secured by an assignment of accounts receivable, or a note which simply formalizes an open-account debt incurred in the ordinary course of business (particularly if, as in the case of the customer of a broker, it is collateralized)"); [citation omitted] (adding to list "notes evidencing loans by commercial banks for current operations").

We agree that the items identified by the Second Circuit are not properly viewed as "securities." More guidance, though, is needed. It is impossible to make any meaningful inquiry into whether an instrument bears a "resemblance" to one of the instruments identified by the Second Circuit without specifying what it is about those instruments that makes them non-"securities." Moreover, as the Second Circuit itself has noted, its list is "not graven in stone," [citation omitted], and is therefore capable of expansion. Thus, some standards must be developed for determining when an item should be added to the list.

An examination of the list itself makes clear what those standards should be. In creating its list, the Second Circuit was applying the same factors that this Court has held apply in deciding whether a transaction involves a "security." First, we examine the transaction to assess the motivations that would prompt a reasonable seller and buyer to enter into it. If the seller's purpose is to raise money for the general use of a business enterprise or to finance substantial investments and the buyer is interested primarily in the profit the note is expected to generate, the instrument is likely to be a "security." If the note is exchanged to facilitate the purchase and sale of a minor asset or consumer good, to correct for the seller's cash-flow difficulties, or to advance some other commercial or consumer purpose, on the other hand, the note is less sensibly described as a "security." [Citation omitted.] Second, we examine the "plan of distribution" of the instrument, [citation omitted], to determine whether it is an instrument in which there is "common trading for speculation or investment," [citation omitted]. Third, we examine the reasonable expectations of the investing public: The Court will consider instruments to be "securities" on the basis of such public expectations, even where an economic analysis of the circumstances of the particular transaction might suggest that the instruments are not "securities" as

---

[citation omitted], we likewise express no view on how that exception might affect the presumption that a note is a "security."

used in that transaction. [Citations omitted.] Finally, we examine whether some factor such as the existence of another regulatory scheme significantly reduces the risk of the instrument, thereby rendering application of the Securities Acts unnecessary. [Citation omitted.]

We conclude, then, that in determining whether an instrument denominated a "note" is a "security," courts are to apply the version of the "family resemblance" test that we have articulated here: A note is presumed to be a "security," and that presumption may be rebutted only by a showing that the note bears a strong resemblance (in terms of the four factors we have identified) to one of the enumerated categories of instrument. If an instrument is not sufficiently similar to an item on the list, the decision whether another category should be added is to be made by examining the same factors.

[II.B] Applying the family resemblance approach to this case, we have little difficulty in concluding that the notes at issue here are "securities." Ernst & Young admits that "a demand note does not closely resemble any of the Second Circuit's family resemblance examples." [Citation omitted.] Nor does an examination of the four factors we have identified as being relevant to our inquiry suggest that the demand notes here are not "securities" despite their lack of similarity to any of the enumerated categories. The Co-Op sold the notes in an effort to raise capital for its general business operations, and purchasers bought them in order to earn a profit in the form of interest.[*] Indeed, one of the primary inducements offered purchasers was an interest rate constantly revised to keep it slightly above the rate paid by local banks and savings and loans. From both sides, then, the transaction is most naturally conceived as an investment in a business enterprise rather than as a purely commercial or consumer transaction.

As to the plan of distribution, the Co-Op offered the notes over an extended period to its 23,000 members, as well as to nonmembers, and more than 1,600 people held notes when the Co-Op filed for bankruptcy. To be sure, the notes were not traded on an exchange. They were, however, offered and sold to a broad segment of the public, and that is all we have held to be necessary to establish the requisite "common trading" in an instrument. [Citations omitted.]

---

[*]   [Footnote by court]: We emphasize that by "profit" in the context of notes, we mean "a valuable return on an investment," which undoubtedly includes interest. We have, of course, defined "profit" more restrictively in applying the *Howey* test to what are claimed to be "investment contracts." See, e.g., [*United Housing Foundation v. Forman*, 421 U.S. 837, 852 (1975)] ("[P]rofit" under the *Howey* test means either "capital appreciation" or "a participation in earnings"). To apply this restrictive definition to the determination whether an instrument is a "note" would be to suggest that notes paying a rate of interest not keyed to the earning of the enterprise are not "notes" within the meaning of the Securities Acts. Because the *Howey* test is irrelevant to the issue before us today, [citation omitted], we decline to extend its definition of "profit" beyond the realm in which that definition applies.

The third factor—the public's reasonable perceptions—also supports a finding that the notes in this case are "securities." We have consistently identified the fundamental essence of a "security" to be its character as an "investment." [Citation omitted.] The advertisements for the notes here characterized them as "investments," [citation omitted], and there were no countervailing factors that would have led a reasonable person to question this characterization. In these circumstances, it would be reasonable for a prospective purchaser to take the Co-Op at its word.

Finally, we find no risk-reducing factor to suggest that these instruments are not in fact securities. The notes are uncollateralized and uninsured. Moreover, unlike the certificates of deposit in [citation omitted], which were insured by the Federal Deposit Insurance Corporation and subject to substantial regulation under the federal banking laws, and unlike the pension plan in [citation omitted], which was comprehensively regulated under the Employee Retirement Income Security Act of 1974, [29 U.S.C. § 1001 *et seq.*, also known as "ERISA"], the notes here would escape federal regulation entirely if the Acts were held not to apply.

The court below found that "[t]he demand nature of the notes is very uncharacteristic of a security," [citation omitted], on the theory that the virtually instant liquidity associated with demand notes is inconsistent with the risk ordinarily associated with "securities." This argument is unpersuasive. Common stock traded on a national exchange is the paradigm of a security, and it is as readily convertible into cash as is a demand note. The same is true of publicly traded corporate bonds, debentures, and any number of other instruments that are plainly within the purview of the Acts. The demand feature of a note does permit a holder to eliminate risk quickly by making a demand, but just as with publicly traded stock, the liquidity of the instrument does not eliminate risk altogether. Indeed, publicly traded stock is even more readily liquid than are demand notes, in that a demand only eliminates risk when, and if, payment is made, whereas the sale of a share of stock through a national exchange and the receipt of the proceeds usually occur simultaneously.

We therefore hold that the notes at issue here are within the term "note" in § 3(a)(10).

***

[Opinions of other Justices omitted.]

Problems

Problem 13-1: Was your roommate's "IOU" for lunch yesterday a "note"?

Problem 13-2: Is the mortgage on your house a "note"? What about the note that you signed when you bought your car?

"Unless the Context Otherwise Requires." Don't forget that Section 2(a) of the Securities Act provides that all of the definitions set forth in that section apply "[u]nless the context otherwise requires." This means that a court could find that something that is, in the abstract, a "security" is really not a "security" in the circumstances of the case. Indeed, this has happened from time to time. For example, *Marine Bank v. Weaver*, 455 U.S. 551 (1982), concerned a certificate of deposit, or "CD," that had been issued by a national bank. On its face, a CD certainly looks like either a note or an evidence of indebtedness: if you buy a CD, the bank is promising to repay the principal amount of the CD, plus interest, at the end of CD's term. Nonetheless, the Supreme Court found that the CD at issue in the case was not a "security" because (among other reasons), the bank that issued the CD was subject to federal regulation that was designed to protect purchasers and was also federally insured. As a result, a CD purchaser doesn't really need the extra protection that the securities laws would provide.

However, in *Landreth Timber Co. v. Landreth*, 471 U.S. 681 (1985), the Supreme Court found that "stock" is always "stock" (at least outside an unusual situation like in the *Forman* case). Before *Landreth Timber*, some federal courts of appeals had held that, in the context of the sale of *all* of the stock of a business, stock is not a "security." To understand this, think back to Chapter 12. As you learned in that chapter, two alternative ways to acquire an entire business are (1) to purchase all or substantially all of its assets or (2) to purchase all of its stock from its existing shareholders. Clearly, most business assets are not securities, whereas shares of stock are securities. As such, this would mean that (1) a purchaser of assets would not get the protection of the securities laws if it had been defrauded by the seller, whereas (2) a purchaser of stock would. Because the choice of whether to acquire a business by buying its assets or instead buying its stock is largely driven by tax and other considerations, the lower federal courts developed the "sale of business doctrine." This doctrine held that stock is not a "security" when it is sold in connection with the acquisition of an entire business. This was meant to bring some legal parity to both of the above-described types of transactions: the securities laws would apply to *neither* of them. However, as noted above, *Landreth Timber* overruled these decisions. Again, "stock" is "stock" regardless of the context in which it is sold.

§ 13.02   REGISTRATION REQUIREMENTS OF THE SECURITIES ACT

Assuming that you want to sell something that is a "security," you have two choices: (1) register that security with the Securities and Exchange Commission (the SEC) or (2) find an exemption from the Securities Act's registration requirement, either for the *security itself* or the type of *transaction* in which it is offered and sold. For example, if a corporation wants to issue and sell shares of its stock to persons who will thereupon become shareholders in the corporation, it must either register those shares of stock or comply with an exemption from registration. In Section 13.03 below, you will learn about some commonly used exemptions from registration. But first, let's assume that the issuer has chosen to conduct a registered offering.[*]

Section 6 of the Securities Act provides that one registers securities by filing a **registration statement** for those securities with the SEC. For example, if ABC Corp. wanted to issue and sell 1 million shares of its common stock in a registered offering, it would file a registration statement with the SEC registering those 1 million shares. A Securities Act registration statement registers the shares that are being sold *in that offering* (although there are a few exceptions to this that we will not discuss here), rather than the entire class of those securities. If a year from now ABC Corp. wants to issue and sell more shares of its common stock, it would have to file a new registration statement for those shares (unless an exemption from registration applied).

Although Section 7 of the Securities Act provides that most registration statements must contain the information that is required by "Schedule A," that is largely of historical interest today. Instead, the required contents of the registration forms can be found in the forms themselves. Although you will likely learn more about what is required by these forms if you take a course on Securities Regulation in law school,[**] suffice it to say here that registration statements usually are *extremely* detailed, containing just about all of the information that an investor would (or should) want to know about the issuer of the securities and the

---

[*]   Registered offerings are often referred to as public offerings. In most cases, a "registered" offering will also be a "public" offering (and vice versa) but these two phrases technically concern two different aspects of an offering. Calling a securities offering a "registered" offering simply means that the securities were registered with the SEC, as you will learn about in this section. On the other hand, a "public" offering typically means one in which a large number of potential investors are solicited. As you will learn in Section 13.03, it's possible to do a "public" offering on an exempt basis.

[**]   On the other hand, many law school courses on Securities Regulation do not focus on *how* to draft a registration statement. To paraphrase my favorite professor from law school, you will spend seven years as a law firm associate drafting registration statements. Then you will become a partner and find some other poor sucker to do it.

securities themselves. If you don't believe this statement, you may want to take a look at the registration statement that Google Inc. filed in 2004 for its initial public offering, or "IPO." (I chose to mention Google simply because it is a company that is familiar to all readers of this textbook who do not live under a rock.) Google's IPO registration statement can be found at the following web address:

http://www.sec.gov/Archives/edgar/data/1288776/000119312504142742/ds1a.htm

Note a few things about Google's registration statement. Once you get past the cover page, the **prospectus** portion of the registration statement appears.[**] As you will learn in more detail below, in a registered offering the prospectus must be made available to all prospective investors and must be delivered to all actual purchasers of the registered securities. The main purpose of requiring a prospectus is so that investors may educate themselves about the issuer and the offered security before deciding to invest. Note that the SEC does not "rate" securities offerings or recommend that investors invest or not invest in a given securities offering. Instead, one of the primary goals of the Securities Act is to mandate the *disclosure* of information that investors would deem important and then allow them to make their own educated investment decisions. (The absence of such information was thought to have been one of the contributing factors to the stock market crash of 1929; the Securities Act and the Securities Exchange Act of 1934 were enacted shortly thereafter.)

So, exactly how much information is there about Google in its IPO registration statement? A *lot*—the prospectus is 124 pages long, followed by 62 pages of financial statements, and then several other documents. This length is typical of a registration statement for an IPO. As you might imagine, a great deal of lawyer, accountant, and business-person time went into the preparation of that document. However, if a company is currently a publicly traded company, preparing a Securities Act registration statement is likely to be a much easier process, because much of the information in it could be "incorporated by reference" from the company's filings under the Securities Exchange Act (which you learned about in Chapter 10). Because Google was a privately held company before it conducted its IPO, it would have had to have drafted its registration statement "from scratch."

So much for the preparation of the registration statement, as it is not something that can be taught in much detail in law school. (As the saying goes, it is something that must be learned by doing.) Instead, let's examine some of the legal issues involved in conducting a registered public offering. Our focus here will be Section 5 of the Securities Act.

[**] Following the prospectus is "Part II" of the registration statement, which largely consists of signatures and various exhibits to the registration statement. Part II is typically not given to investors, although they could review it online at the SEC's website.

Section 5 makes very little sense when you first read it. For one thing, even though it divides the registered offering process into three time periods (the pre-filing period, the waiting period, and the post-effective period) and contains three subsections, the subsections do not correspond to the time periods. In other words, Section 5 is not in chronological order; it is a bit of a jumble. For those of you who are keeping score, the subsections that apply during the pre-filing period are subsections (a) and (c); the subsections that apply during the waiting period are subsections (a) and (b)(1); and the subsection that applies during the post-effective period is subsection (b).

But first, let's discuss what these three time periods are. The *pre-filing period* refers to the period of time that ends when the issuer files its registration statement with the SEC.* Once the issuer has filed its registration statement, the *waiting period* begins. What are you waiting for during the waiting period? That's right, the SEC. Once the SEC declares the registration statement to be "effective," the *post-effective period* begins. As noted above, however, the SEC's purpose (or at least its stated purpose) is not to decide whether an investment is a "good" investment. Instead, by reviewing the registration statement during the waiting period, the SEC attempts to ensure that the issuer has disclosed all of the information that is required by the applicable registration statement form (although the SEC does not *verify* the information). When it is satisfied that the issuer has made all of the required disclosures, the SEC will declare the registration statement effective and the post-effective period will begin. How long the waiting period lasts is largely a function of how well the issuer and its lawyers and accountants prepared the registration statement. If they did a poor job, the waiting period can take a long, long time and result in many SEC comment letters.

One of the goals of Section 5 is to *slow down* the offering process, giving investors an opportunity to receive and review information about the securities offering *before* deciding to invest. As such, the three time periods go from most restrictive to least restrictive. In other words, there are fewer things that the issuer is legally allowed to do during the pre-filing period than in the waiting period. Again, the primary goal of the Securities Act can be summarized in three words: disclosure, disclosure, disclosure. While the law obviously cannot ensure that investors will review this information or that they will come to intelligent conclusions about it, it can at least give them the tools to do so. Although a securities law expert would view the following discussion as a bit oversimplified, the general rules during the registration process can be summarized as follows.

---

*   Does that mean that everything back to the dawn of time is part of a given issuer's pre-filing period? Not really. Although authorities are a bit vague on this point, the pre-filing typically is said to begin when the issuer takes some concrete steps toward conducting the offering, such as hiring an underwriter or when its board of directors passes a resolution approving the offering.

The Pre-Filing Period.   During the pre-filing period, the issuer can *neither offer nor sell* the securities that will be registered. To again use Google as an example, it would have been illegal for Google or anyone acting on its behalf merely to offer to sell Google stock before it had filed its registration statement with the SEC.

At first, this prohibition on pre-filing offers may strike you as sort of silly. After all, what harm is there in merely *offering* a security, assuming that the offeree doesn't actually *buy* the security? Again, keep in mind that the goal of Section 5 is to slow down the offering process and allow investors to be able to see all of the "fine print" before they invest. If an issuer were permitted to make offers before it had prepared its registration statement/prospectus, it surely would only tell potential investors the "good" information about itself. As such, investors could be "pre-sold" on the idea of investing, making them less likely to read that detailed prospectus when it became available. To avoid this possibility, Section 5 makes offers illegal during the pre-filing period.

Moreover, the Securities Act takes a very expansive view of what constitutes an "offer." In your Contracts course in law school, you learned that an "offer" must be definite in its terms. Applying that concept to a securities offering, you might think that an "offer" would have to, at a minimum, specify the security and the asking price. But you would be wrong. This is because Section 2(a)(3) of the Securities Act provides in part that the "term 'offer to sell', 'offer for sale', or 'offer' shall include every attempt or offer to dispose of, or solicitation of an offer to buy, a security or interest in a security, for value." This is a very broad definition. Further, note that by including the phrase "shall include" (as opposed to something like "shall mean") the drafters of the Securities Act did not even provide us with a complete definition.

Taking advantage of this opportunity, the SEC has been liberal in finding that pre-filing activities were "offers." For example, in *In re Carl M. Loeb, Rhoades & Co.*, 38 S.E.C. 843 (1959), which was an internal administrative proceeding, the SEC found that two press releases were illegal "offers." Given that press releases are designed to have a wide circulation, this probably isn't terribly surprising. But in the following portion of the opinion, the SEC gave the following guidance about "offers":

> Section 5(c) of the Securities Act, as here pertinent, prohibits offers to sell any security, through the medium of a prospectus or otherwise, unless a registration statement, has been filed. Section [2(a)(3)] defines "offer to sell" to include "every attempt or offer to dispose of, or solicitation of an offer to buy, a security for value." Section [2(a)(10)] defines a "prospectus" to mean "any prospectus, notice, circular, advertisement, letter, or

communication ... which offers any security for sale ...." These are broad definitions, and designedly so. It is apparent that they are not limited to communications which constitute an offer in the common law contract sense, or which on their face purport to offer a security. Rather, as stated by our General Counsel in 1941, they include "any document which is designed to procure orders for a security." [Citation omitted.]

The broad sweep of these definitions is necessary to accomplish the statutory purposes in the light of the process of securities distribution as it exists in the United States. Securities are distributed in this country by a complex and sensitive machinery geared to accomplish nationwide distribution of large quantities of securities with great speed. ***

One of the cardinal purposes of the Securities Act is to slow down this process of rapid distribution of corporate securities, at least in its earlier and crucial stages, in order that dealers and investors might have access to, and an opportunity to consider, the disclosures of the material business and financial facts of the issuer provided in registration statements and prospectuses. Under the practices existing prior to the enactment of the statute in 1933, dealers made blind commitments to purchase securities without adequate information, and in turn, resold the securities to an equally uninformed investing public. The entire distribution process was often stimulated by sales literature designed solely to arouse interest in the securities and not to disclose material facts about the issuer and its securities. ***

***

The Congress *** adopted a carefully worked out procedure to meet the problem. It is essentially as follows: (1) the strict prohibition of offers prior to the filing of a registration statement ***; (2) during the period between the filing of a registration statement and its effective date offers but not sales may be made but written offers could be made only by documents prescribed or processed by the Commission; and (3) sales continued to be prohibited prior to the effective date. ***

We accordingly conclude that publicity, prior to the filing of a registration statement by means of public media of communication, with respect to an issuer or it securities, emanating from broker-dealer firms who as underwriters *** have negotiated or are negotiating for a public offering of the securities of such issuer, must be presumed to set in motion or to be a part of the distribution process and therefore to involve an offer to sell or a solicitation of an offer to buy such securities prohibited by Section 5(c). ***

As a result of *In re Carl M. Loeb, Rhoades & Co.* and other SEC decisions over the years, lawyers advising companies that were contemplating a registered securities offering gave very conservative advice. While it was generally permissible for an issuer to continue its historical advertising and publicity practices, lawyers worried that a sudden change in these practices on the eve of a securities offering might be viewed by the SEC as an illegal offering during the pre-filing period—even if the advertising or publicity did not directly mention the upcoming securities offering. In addition, lawyers warned their clients not to mention upcoming securities offerings, not to make predictions about the company's future performance, and not to give their opinions about the value of the company's securities.

There are two problems with this sort of advice. First, it's very vague; clients (not to mention their lawyers!) often were unsure what could or could not be done during the pre-filing period. As a result, being perhaps overly cautious was the norm. Second, corporate clients don't like being advised that they should curb their public relations activities. After all, part of running a business involves publicity and advertising, and it is the rare business-person that likes to be told that her company should be quiet, even for a short time.

Fortunately, there are a number of things that are specifically excluded from being considered "offers" and therefore may be done during the pre-filing period. One such example is found in Section 2(a)(3) itself, which provides that the word "offer" does not include "preliminary negotiations or agreements between an issuer ... and any underwriter or among underwriters who are or are to be in privity of contract with an issuer ...." Thus, the issuer can enter into contracts with the underwriters on the offering, even during the pre-filing period. (As discussed below, underwriters assist the issuer in selling the securities and receive commissions or other compensation for doing so.)

In addition, although you would certainly learn much more about them in a Securities Regulation course, the following SEC rules specify some communications that will not be considered to be "offers" during the pre-filing period.

Rule 135—This rule basically provides that a notice of a "proposed" offering won't be considered an "offer" if it contains only the very limited amount of information specified in the rule. For example, the communication can contain the name of the issuer; the "title, amount and basic terms of the securities offered"; and a "brief statement of the manner and the purpose of the offering, without naming the underwriters," among other things. In addition, the communication must contain a legend "to the effect that it does not constitute an offer of any securities for sale."

Rule 163A—This rule, which was enacted by the SEC in 2005, provides (with some exceptions not relevant here) that a communication that is made more than thirty days before a registration statement is filed won't be considered an "offer," provided that it "does not reference [the] securities offering that is or will be the subject of [the] registration statement." However, during the thirty days before the registration statement is filed, the issuer must take "reasonable steps within its control to prevent further distribution or publication of [the] communication." At first, this rule doesn't seem very exciting; however, it allows issuers to engage in virtually any sort of communications or advertising as long as they do so more than thirty days before filing the registration statement and don't actually refer to the upcoming securities offering. This removes a lot of the uncertainty about whether such activities would be considered illegal offers in the pre-filing period.

Rules 168 and 169—These two rules, which were also enacted in 2005, are very similar; however, Rule 168 applies only to issuers that are already publicly traded, whereas Rule 169 applies to any issuer, even one that is contemplating an IPO. Basically, these rules provide that an issuer may—consistent with its past practices—continue to release "factual business information" (as defined in the rules) and, in the case of Rule 168 "forward-looking information" (as defined in Rule 168), without the communications being considered "offers." However, any communication made in reliance on these rules must not contain "information about the registered offering" or be "released or disseminated as part of the offering activities in the registered offering." Furthermore, Rule 169 requires that the information must be "released or disseminated for intended use by persons, such as customers and suppliers, other than in their capacities as investors or potential investors ...."

Rule 163—The most generous of the new rules promulgated by the SEC in 2005, Rule 163 basically provides that an offer won't be considered an "offer." Thus, an issuer that was planning a registered offering and is in the pre-filing period could actually offer the securities to potential investors during the pre-filing period! However, there are a few catches. First, Rule 163 only applies to "well-known seasoned issuers," which basically are companies that have been publicly traded for more than twelve months and that meet some stringent "size" tests. Thus, Rule 163 may only be used by a relatively small group of very large, well-known companies. Second, if the offer is in writing, then additional requirements apply, including an obligation to file a copy of the writing with the SEC.

While the above description of the pre-filing period captures the main issues involved, you should keep in mind that there are many qualifications and exceptions to these rules. Again, you will learn much more about these rules if you take a course in Securities Regulation. However, see if you can handle the following problem. Be sure to consider Rules 135, 163A, 168, 169, and 163.

Problem

Problem 13-3: Michigan Widget Corp. (MWC) manufactures widgets. MWC is currently a privately held company, but it has decided to conduct a public offering of 1 million shares of its common stock. To that end, it has engaged Trosty Underwriters, Inc. to act as the underwriter on this offering and has begun, with its legal counsel, preparing a registration statement for eventual filing with the SEC. Before MWC filed its registration statement with the SEC, it placed the following advertisement in *The Wall Street Journal*, which appeared on March 1.

Attention Investors

Michigan Widget Corp., a profitable and growing business, will be offering 1,000,000 shares of its common stock to new investors in an initial public offering in the very near future. The offering price will be $20 per share. The underwriter will be Trosty Underwriters, Inc.

MWC filed its registration statement with the SEC on May 1. *Did this advertisement cause MWC to violate Section 5 of the Securities Act?*

The Waiting Period.   As noted above, the waiting period begins when the issuer files its registration statement for the offering with the SEC, and ends when the SEC declares the registration statement "effective."   Keeping with the theme that the legal restrictions loosen as the registration process goes on, you should not be surprised that there are more things that the issuer (and those working on its behalf, such as underwriters) may do during the waiting period than in the pre-filing period.

Most importantly, the issuer may make offers (although sales are still prohibited).   However, there are two major problems that make the previous sentence an oversimplification.   First, any "offer" that appears in writing (including email) or by radio or television, will be considered a "prospectus" within the meaning of the Securities Act.   The problem with finding that something is a "prospectus" is that Section 10 of the Securities Act provides, in general, that a "prospectus" must contain the information that appears in the registration statement.   As you saw above, a registration statement typically is a very long and detailed document; Google's IPO registration statement was well over 100 pages long.   Thus, typically the only written offer that may be used during the waiting period is a preliminary version of the long prospectus that appears in the registration statement.   Most other written offers would be considered illegal prospectuses.[*]

Second, if the offeree actually *accepts* the offer, then a "sale" has been made—even if no money or securities have yet changed hands!   This is because Section 2(a)(3) of the Securities Act defines a "sale" as including a "contract of sale."   Thus, if an offeree does something that causes her to be contractually bound to purchase the offered securities, a "contract of sale" has arisen and a "sale" has been made.   And as you know, "sales" are illegal during the waiting period (as well as the pre-filing period).   Thus, it is common, when approaching potential investors during the waiting period, to solicit mere "indications of interest" from them.   Doing so avoids a finding that a "sale" has occurred.

The Post-Effective Period.   Once the SEC declares the registration statement effective, the post-effective period begins.   For the first time, the issuer may make sales.   The issuer must deliver a copy of the final prospectus to each purchaser; the issuer may not deliver the securities to the purchaser until it has done so.   Today, this delivery is typically done electronically.

---

[*]   See Securities Act Rule 430.   However, Rule 134 allows the issuer to use certain other writings during the waiting period without them being considered a "prospectus." Further, the issuer may use a "free-writing prospectus" during the waiting period pursuant to Rules 164 and 433, which contain detailed rules governing the use of such documents.

A written offer continues to be considered a "prospectus." During the post-effective period the only legal "prospectus" that may be used is the final version of the prospectus that was contained in the registration statement. The final prospectus must have all of the blanks, such as the offering price of the securities, filled in. (Usually, the offering price is only determined shortly before the effective date, due to changing securities market conditions.) However, during the post-effective period, a writing that is accompanied by, or preceded by, the final statutory prospectus is considered "free-writing" and need not comply with Section 10. Technically, free writing is excluded from the definition of "prospectus." Thus, if an issuer or underwriter were simultaneously to send a prospective investor (1) a copy of the final prospectus that was contained in the registration statement (i.e., the long, detailed document that was discussed above) and (2) a brochure concerning the issuer or some other writing that would ordinarily be considered an "offer" and therefore a "prospectus," the second document will be permissible. In a sense, it is as if Congress said that it is OK for the issuer and/or underwriters to send prospective investors any written document—as long as they are doing so in the post-effective period when the final prospectus (having been reviewed by the SEC as part of the registration statement) is available and is simultaneously (or previously) sent to that investor.

Again, the above discussion of Section 5 is oversimplified and omits many important exceptions and qualifications. If you find this interesting or the prospect of working on a registered public offering exciting, you should take a course in Securities Regulation.

Underwriters. Do you know people who could buy several million, or even billion, dollars worth of securities? Me neither. Most issuers in securities offerings would answer this question similarly, and thus will need some assistance to sell the securities that they wish to sell. After all, even if the issuer is a great company and the registration statement/prospectus is a work of art, the offering will not be successful without actual buyers.

The people who will (for a fee, of course) help the issuer sell the securities are called *underwriters.* Although the statute defines an underwriter in part as someone "who has purchased from an issuer [or an affiliate of the issuer] with a view to, or offers or sells for an issuer [or an affiliate of the issuer] in connection with, the distribution of any security," when one thinks of underwriters in the context of a large public offering of securities one tends to think of large Wall Street investment banking firms. Indeed, if you looked at the cover page of the Google IPO prospectus, you would have seen some of the biggest names on Wall Street (including at least one that is no longer with us following the 2008-2009 financial crisis).

There are two basic kinds of underwriting agreements: *firm commitment* underwritings and *best efforts* underwritings.   In a firm commitment, the underwriter actually purchases the securities from the issuer (at a discount from the anticipated public offering price) and then resells them to the public.   In contrast, in a best efforts underwriting, the underwriter only agrees to use its best efforts to find buyers for the securities, but does not guarantee that they will actually be sold.   Obviously, a firm commitment underwriting is riskier for the underwriter due to possibility that it might not be able to sell the securities quickly (or at all).   Thus, firm commitment underwritings typically involve higher underwriter fees and commissions than do best efforts underwritings and/or are reserved for "good" securities offerings.

§ 13.03   POPULAR EXEMPTIONS FROM REGISTRATION

As you certainly gathered from reading the above discussion, conducting a registered securities offering is a difficult and expensive process. Doing so might be economically efficient in the context of an offering for several tens or hundreds of millions of dollars. But if every securities offering were required to go through the SEC registration process, capital formation (that is, the ability of companies to raise capital) would dry up. Companies would only be able to obtain funds to expand their businesses by getting bank loans. Obviously, the economy could be adversely affected.

Fortunately, there are a number of exemptions from registration. Exemptions come in two categories: exempt *securities* and exempt *transactions*. Exempt securities are those that are always exempt from having to be registered with the SEC prior to sale—regardless of how many are being sold and to how many and what types of purchasers they are sold. These exempt securities are primarily found in Section 3.

On the other hand, there are exempt transactions.   In other words, securities that are sold in an offering that complies with certain requirements need not be registered with the SEC before they are offered and sold *in that offering*. However, if those same securities were to be later publicly offered and sold, they would most likely be required to be registered before such an offering could take place. The exempt transactions are primarily found in Section 4 of the Securities Act, as well as several SEC rules thereunder. (However, one exempt transaction that you will study below, the intra-state exemption, is inexplicably found in Section 3 rather than Section 4.)

There are many exempt securities and transactions found in the Securities Act and SEC rules, but we will consider only some of the most prevalent: the

Section 4(2) exemption for "private" offerings; the three exemptions found in SEC Regulation D; and the Section 3(a)(11) exemption for "intra-state" offerings.

Section 4(2) Private Offerings.   Section 4(2) of the Securities Act is one of the shortest sections that you will encounter in a securities law. It merely provides that securities need not be registered with the SEC when they are sold in "transactions by an issuer not involving any public offering." Thus, if a securities offering is not a "public" offering—that is, if it's a "private" offering—then the securities sold in that private offering need not be registered with the SEC.

Sounds easy, right? Unfortunately, the Securities Act does not actually define the phrase "public offering" (or, for that matter, "private offering"). Thus, the courts were called on to interpret this phrase. The following case is the leading case interpreting Section 4(2).

Securities and Exchange Commission v. Ralston Purina Co.
Supreme Court of United States
346 U.S. 119 (1953)

MR. JUSTICE CLARK delivered the opinion of the Court.

Section [4(2)]* of the Securities Act of 1933 exempts "transactions by an issuer not involving any public offering" from the registration requirements of § 5. We must decide whether Ralston Purina's offerings of treasury stock to its "key employees" are within this exemption. On a complaint brought by the Commission under § 20(b) of the Act seeking to enjoin respondent's unregistered offerings, the District Court held the exemption applicable and dismissed the suit. [Citation omitted.] The Court of Appeals affirmed. [Citation omitted.] The question has arisen many times since the Act was passed; an apparent need to define the scope of the private offering exemption prompted certiorari. [Citation omitted.]

Ralston Purina manufactures and distributes various feed and cereal products. Its processing and distribution facilities are scattered throughout the United States and Canada, staffed by some 7,000 employees. At least since 1911 the company has had a policy of encouraging stock ownership among its employees; more particularly, since 1942 it has made authorized but unissued common shares available to some of them. Between 1947 and 1951, the period covered by the record in this case, Ralston Purina sold nearly $2,000,000 of stock to employees without registration and in so doing made use of the mails.

---

* [Footnote by author]: At the time of this case, what is currently Section 4(2) of the Securities Act was Section 4(1).

In each of these years, a corporate resolution authorized the sale of common stock "to employees ... who shall, without any solicitation by the Company or its officers or employees, inquire of any of them as to how to purchase common stock of Ralston Purina Company." A memorandum sent to branch and store managers after the resolution was adopted advised that "The only employees to whom this stock will be available will be those who take the initiative and are interested in buying stock at present market prices." Among those responding to these offers were employees with the duties of artist, bakeshop foreman, chow loading foreman, clerical assistant, copywriter, electrician, stock clerk, mill office clerk, order credit trainee, production trainee, stenographer, and veterinarian. The buyers lived in over fifty widely separated communities scattered from Garland, Texas, to Nashua, New Hampshire, and Visalia, California. The lowest salary bracket of those purchasing was $2,700 in 1949, $2,435 in 1950 and $3,107 in 1951. The record shows that in 1947, 243 employees bought stock, 20 in 1948, 414 in 1949, 411 in 1950, and the 1951 offer, interrupted by this litigation, produced 165 applications to purchase. No records were kept of those to whom the offers were made; the estimated number in 1951 was 500.

The company bottoms its exemption claim on the classification of all offerees as "key employees" in its organization. Its position on trial was that "A key employee ... is not confined to an organization chart. It would include an individual who is eligible for promotion, an individual who especially influences others or who advises others, a person whom the employees look to in some special way, an individual, of course, who carries some special responsibility, who is sympathetic to management and who is ambitious and who the management feels is likely to be promoted to a greater responsibility." That an offering to all of its employees would be public is conceded.

The Securities Act nowhere defines the scope of § [4(2)]'s private offering exemption. Nor is the legislative history of much help in staking out its boundaries. The problem was first dealt with in § 4(1) of the House Bill, [citation omitted], which exempted "transactions by an issuer not with or through an underwriter; ...." The bill, as reported by the House Committee, added "and not involving any public offering." [Citation omitted.] This was thought to be one of those transactions "where there is no practical need for [the bill's] application or where the public benefits are too remote." [Citation omitted.]* The exemption as

---

* [Footnote by court]: "... the bill does not affect transactions beyond the need of public protection in order to prevent recurrences of demonstrated abuses." [Citation omitted.] In a somewhat different tenor, the report spoke of this as an exemption of "transactions by an issuer unless made by or through an underwriter so as to permit an issuer to make a specific or an isolated sale of its securities to a particular person, but insisting that if a sale of the issuer's securities should be made generally to the public that that transaction shall come within the purview of the Act." [Citation omitted.]

thus delimited became law.[*] It assumed its present shape with the deletion of "not with or through an underwriter" by § 203(a) of the Securities Exchange Act of 1934, a change regarded as the elimination of superfluous language. [Citation omitted.]

Decisions under comparable exemptions in the English Companies Acts and state "blue sky" laws, the statutory antecedents of federal securities legislation, have made one thing clear—to be public an offer need not be open to the whole world. [Citation omitted.]   In *Securities and Exchange Comm'n v. Sunbeam Gold Mines Co.*, 95 F. 2d 699 (9th Cir. 1938), this point was made in dealing with an offering to the stockholders of two corporations about to be merged. Judge Denman observed that:

> In its broadest meaning the term "public" distinguishes the populace at large from groups of individual members of the public segregated because of some common interest or characteristic. Yet such a distinction is inadequate for practical purposes; manifestly, an offering of securities to all red-headed men, to all residents of Chicago or San Francisco, to all existing stockholders of the General Motors Corporation or the American Telephone & Telegraph Company, is no less "public", in every realistic sense of the word, than an unrestricted offering to the world at large. Such an offering, though not open to everyone who may choose to apply, is none the less "public" in character, for the means used to select the particular individuals to whom the offering is to be made bear no sensible relation to the purposes for which the selection is made .... To determine the distinction between "public" and "private" in any particular context, it is essential to examine the circumstances under which the distinction is sought to be established and to consider the purposes sought to be achieved by such distinction. [Citation omitted.]

The courts below purported to apply this test. The District Court held, in the language of the *Sunbeam* decision, that "The purpose of the selection bears a 'sensible relation' to the class chosen," finding that "The sole purpose of the 'selection' is to keep part stock ownership of the business within the operating personnel of the business and to spread ownership throughout all departments and activities of the business." The Court of Appeals treated the case as involving "an offering, without solicitation, of common stock to a selected group of key employees of the issuer, most of whom are already stockholders when the offering

---

[*]   [Footnote by court]:   The only subsequent reference was an oblique one in the statement of the House Managers on the Conference Report: "Sales of stock to stockholders become subject to the act unless the stockholders are so small in number that the sale to them does not constitute a public offering." [Citation omitted.]

is made, with the sole purpose of enabling them to secure a proprietary interest in the company or to increase the interest already held by them."

Exemption from the registration requirements of the Securities Act is the question. The design of the statute is to protect investors by promoting full disclosure of information thought necessary to informed investment decisions. The natural way to interpret the private offering exemption is in light of the statutory purpose. Since exempt transactions are those as to which "there is no practical need for [the bill's] application," the applicability of § [4(2)] should turn on whether the particular class of persons affected needs the protection of the Act. An offering to those who are shown to be able to fend for themselves is a transaction "not involving any public offering."

The Commission would have us go one step further and hold that "an offering to a substantial number of the public" is not exempt under § [4(2)]. We are advised that "whatever the special circumstances, the Commission has consistently interpreted the exemption as being inapplicable when a large number of offerees is involved." But the statute would seem to apply to a "public offering" whether to few or many. It may well be that offerings to a substantial number of persons would rarely be exempt. Indeed nothing prevents the [C]ommission, in enforcing the statute, from using some kind of numerical test in deciding when to investigate particular exemption claims. But there is no warrant for superimposing a quantity limit on private offerings as a matter of statutory interpretation.

The exemption, as we construe it, does not deprive corporate employees, as a class, of the safeguards of the Act. We agree that some employee offerings may come within § [4(2)], e.g., one made to executive personnel who because of their position have access to the same kind of information that the Act would make available in the form of a registration statement. Absent such a showing of special circumstances, employees are just as much members of the investing "public" as any of their neighbors in the community. Although we do not rely on it, the rejection in 1934 of an amendment which would have specifically exempted employee stock offerings supports this conclusion. The House Managers, commenting on the Conference Report, said that "the participants in employees' stock-investment plans may be in as great need of the protection afforded by availability of information concerning the issuer for which they work as are most other members of the public." [Citation omitted.]

Keeping in mind the broadly remedial purposes of federal securities legislation, imposition of the burden of proof on an issuer who would plead the exemption seems to us fair and reasonable. [Citation omitted.] Agreeing, the court below thought the burden met primarily because of the respondent's purpose in singling out its key employees for stock offerings. But once it is seen that the exemption question turns on the knowledge of the offerees, the issuer's motives, laudable though they may be, fade into irrelevance. The focus of inquiry should be on the need of the offerees for the protections afforded by registration. The employees here were not shown to have access to the kind of information which registration would disclose. The obvious opportunities for pressure and imposition make it advisable that they be entitled to compliance with § 5.

Reversed.

[Opinions of other Justices omitted.]

Although *Ralston-Purina* provides a memorable catchphrase (the offerees in a Section 4(2) offering must be able to "fend for themselves"), it isn't terribly helpful in defining the precise contours of Section 4(2) or in giving us examples of people who can fend for themselves. The only example the *Ralston-Purina* Court gave was "executive personnel who because of their position have access to the same kind of information that the [Securities] Act would make available in the form of a registration statement."

Thus, although there are many cases from lower courts interpreting Section 4(2), its exact requirements remain a bit vague. Here is how the SEC has described Section 4(2):

> Section 4(2) of the Securities Act exempts from registration "transactions by an issuer not involving any public offering." To qualify for this exemption, [each of] the purchasers of the securities must:
>
> • have enough knowledge and experience in finance and business matters to evaluate the risks and merits of the investment (the "sophisticated investor"), or be able to bear the investment's economic risk;
>
> • have access to the type of information normally provided in a prospectus; and
>
> • agree not to resell or distribute the securities to the public.
>
> In addition, you may not use any form of public solicitation or general advertising in connection with the offering.

The precise limits of this private offering exemption are uncertain. As the number of purchasers increases and their relationship to the company and its management becomes more remote, it is more difficult to show that the transaction qualifies for the exemption. You should know that if you offer securities to even one person who does not meet the necessary conditions, the entire offering may be in violation of the Securities Act.

Securities and Exchange Commission, *Q&A: Small Business and the SEC; A guide to help you understand how to raise capital and comply with the federal securities laws*, available at: http://www.sec.gov/info/smallbus/qasbsec.htm.

In addition, the Committee on Federal Regulation of Securities of the American Bar Association Section of Business Law recently released a report entitled *Law of Private Placements (Non-Public Offerings) Not Entitled to Benefits of Safe Harbors—A Report.*[*] In this report, the committee concluded that there are four important factors in a Section 4(2) offering: (1) the manner of the offering, (2) the eligibility of the purchasers, (3) the information provided to purchasers, and (4) the absence of non-exempt resales by the initial purchasers.[**] A few words about these are in order here (both as the ABA committee and other authorities have interpreted them).

In terms of the manner of the offering, the ABA committee points out that the purchasers must be found through some private methods, rather than a public process. As the committee pointed out, neither the issuer nor anyone acting on its behalf may use any form of "general advertising" or "general solicitation" to locate purchasers. (As discussed below, this is also a requirement in most offerings under Regulation D.) To use an extreme example, if the issuer put up a billboard on the highway advertising its offering, the offering clearly would not qualify as exempt under Section 4(2).

Second, each offeree—not just actual purchasers—must also be sophisticated in investing matters to some degree. As discussed below, Regulation D imposes a similar requirement, stating that each "non-accredited" investor in a Rule 506 offering must have "such knowledge and experience in financial and business matters that he is capable of evaluating the merits and risks of the prospective investment" or that the issuer must reasonably believe that the

---

[*] 66 BUS. LAW. 85 (2010).

[**] This is not to say that courts have not found other factors to be important. For example, many courts insist on having a small number of purchasers in a Section 4(2) offering. The ABA committee, however, views the number of investors as itself unimportant, as did the *Howey* court. On the other hand, the more purchasers there are, the more likely it is that some of them will not be able to "fend for themselves."

investor meets this standard.   Purchasers can meet this standard either by themselves, or with the assistance of a "purchaser representative" as defined in Regulation D. The ABA committee believes that this standard from Regulation D should also be used in the context of a Section 4(2) offering and some courts have in fact used similar language in opinions interpreting Section 4(2). One troubling aspect of this requirement, however, is that some courts have stated that *every* offeree must be properly qualified and that the presence of even one unqualified offeree will ruin the exemption for the entire offering.   Nonetheless, the ABA committee points out that the presence of one unqualified offeree is unlikely to ruin the entire offering, at least if the issuer believed in good faith (but mistakenly) that the offeree was able to fend for herself under the *Ralston-Purina* standard and otherwise tried to comply with the exemption.

Closely related to the offeree-sophistication requirement is the requirement that the issuer provide offerees with some amount of information about the issuer and the securities that are being offered. Naturally, this begs the question: how much information is needed? Unfortunately, there is no easy answer in the context of a Section 4(2) offering. Obviously, the more information that the issuer discloses, the better its chances of successfully arguing that it has complied with Section 4(2). On the other hand, the information need not be as extensive as that required by the SEC in a registered offering. (After all, what would be the point of an exempt offering if it didn't save the issuer any time and trouble?) Some cases have been interpreted as requiring an amount of information that is on a sliding scale with the sophistication of the offerees. In other words, the more sophisticated the offerees, or the less complex the investment, the less information that is probably required. If the offerees are not extremely sophisticated and/or the securities that are being offered are complex or unusual, the more information that is required. As discussed below, Regulation D solves this uncertainty by listing precise items of information that must be provided to investors in different contexts.   The ABA committee appears to believe that the informational requirements of Regulation D are a good model for compliance with Section 4(2). *See* 66 BUS. LAW. at 111-13.

The final important Section 4(2) factor identified by the ABA committee is the *absence* of non-exempt resales by the initial purchasers. To understand why this is important, assume that an issuer wants to use Section 4(2) to conduct an exempt securities offering and has identified several potential purchasers. Unfortunately, none of these offerees would qualify being able to "fend for themselves" under *Ralston-Purina*. (In other words, these potential investors are not "sophisticated.") To solve this problem, the issuer arranges to have a very sophisticated investor (let's call her Sally Sophisticate) purchase the securities. However, shortly after the offering is complete, Sally resells the securities to the motley crew of investors to whom the issuer had originally wanted to sell the securities.

To be sure, something this blatant would rarely happen, but if it did ask yourself: who *really* bought these securities—Sally Sophisticate or the persons to whom she re-sold? Now, if Sally had resold the securities to some other person or persons who *themselves* would have been "*Ralston-Purina* types," or if her resales took place a year or more after she purchased the securities so that she could show she had "investment intent" when she bought the securities, then this would probably not be a problem. But if the persons to whom Sally sold would not themselves have qualified as initial purchasers in the Section 4(2) offering, then these resales probably ruined the exemption. It is as if Sally was really just a conduit for the securities to reach the later purchasers. Thus, issuers using the Section 4(2) exemption are well-advised to advise purchasers that they may not resell the securities unless they do so either in a registered offering (not likely) or in a manner that would not violate the securities laws. In addition, it may be wise to have purchasers so agree in writing and to place a "legend" on any certificates representing the securities (e.g., stock certificates) referring to these restrictions on resale.

Despite the helpful guidance of the ABA committee and the many other authorities interpreting it, Section 4(2) remains a bit vague. Thus, it's hard to give a client solid legal advice as to its compliance with Section 4(2) in all but the most clear-cut examples. Fortunately, Rule 506 of Regulation D is a "safe harbor" under Section 4(2). Regulation D is discussed immediately below.

> **"Safe Harbors"**
> A "safe harbor" refers to an SEC rule that may be used to ensure compliance with a statute. Although compliance with the rule is optional, if the issuer does comply with the rule, then it will conclusively be deemed to have complied with the statute. For example, SEC Rule 147 is a "safe harbor" under Section 3(a)(11). Thus, an issuer who complies with Rule 147 will be deemed to have a valid intra-state offering under Section 3(a)(11). Conversely, an issuer who did not comply with Rule 147 may still have a valid Section 3(a)(11) exemption—but there is no guarantee of this.

Regulation D. Regulation D, which consists of Rules 501 through 508 under the Securities Act, is a strange amalgamation of three different exemptions: Rule 504, Rule 505, and Rule 506. While Rules 505 and 506 are fairly similar to one another, Rule 504 doesn't seem to "belong." Thus, we will begin our discussion of Regulation D with Rules 505 and 506, leaving Rule 504 until later.

Rule 505 provides an exemption from registration whereby an issuer (assuming that it is not an investment company such as a mutual fund) may sell, in any twelve-month period, a maximum of $5 million worth of securities.[*] However, the issuer may only sell the securities to a maximum of thirty-five persons, or must reasonably believe that there are only thirty-five purchasers. (There is no limitation the number of *offerees*, though.)   But here's an interesting catch: under Rule 501(e)(1)(iv), "accredited investors" are excluded from this calculation, along with some other types of purchasers. This means that the issuer can sell securities in a Rule 505 offering to a maximum of thirty-five *non-*accredited investors, *and* a theoretically unlimited number of accredited investors.

Who is an accredited investor? Rule 501(a) defines them as follows:

• certain banks and savings and loan associations; registered brokers or dealers; certain insurance companies; investment companies registered under the Investment Company Act of 1940; certain business development companies and small business investment companies; any plan established and maintained by a state or local government, or any agency or instrumentality of a state or local government, for the benefit of its employees, if the plan has total assets in excess of $5 million; and certain employee benefit plans;

• any private business development company as defined in the Investment Advisers Act of 1940;

• any organization described in section 501(c)(3) of the Internal Revenue Code (i.e., a nonprofit entity), corporation, Massachusetts or similar business trust, or partnership, not formed for the specific purpose of acquiring the securities offered, with total assets in excess of $5 million;

• any director, executive officer, or general partner of the issuer of the securities, or any director, executive officer, or general partner of a general partner of the issuer;

• any natural person whose individual net worth, or joint net worth with that person's spouse, at the time of his purchase exceeds $1 million;[**]

---

[*]   If the issuer has, within the past twelve months, sold securities under Rule 505, or pursuant to any other SEC exemption under Section 3(b) of the Securities Act, or in violation of Section 5(a) of the Securities Act, these sales would "count against" the $5 million limit. For example, if six months ago the issuer sold $2 million of securities pursuant to Rule 505, it could only use Rule 505 to sell another $3 million of securities in the next six months.

[**]   The Dodd-Frank Wall Street Reform and Consumer Protection Act, which was enacted in 2010, provides that the $1 million net worth figure must be exclusive of the value of the person's primary residence. Further, this section of the Dodd-Frank Act requires that, not earlier than four years after the date of enactment of the Act, and at least once every four years thereafter, the SEC must "undertake a review of the definition, in its entirety, of the term "accredited investor" *** as such term applies to natural persons, to determine whether the

- any natural person who had an individual income in excess of $200,000 in each of the two most recent years or joint income with that person's spouse in excess of $300,000 in each of those years and has a reasonable expectation of reaching the same income level in the current year;

- any trust, with total assets in excess of $5 million, that was not formed for the specific purpose of acquiring the securities offered, whose purchase is directed by a "sophisticated" person as described in Rule 506; and

- any entity in which all of the equity owners are accredited investors.

There are several other requirements that the issuer must observe in a Rule 505 offering. First, the issuer cannot use Rule 505 if it or certain of its officers, directors, or other affiliates have been in the types of legal trouble set forth in Rule 262 under the Securities Act. These are sometimes called the "bad boy disqualification provisions."

Second, the issuer must provide purchasers with the information that is specified in Rule 502(b). Without delving into too much detail about Rule 502(b), which is quite complicated, suffice it to say that if the issuer were to sell *only* to accredited investors, then no specific list of information is required. (Of course, it would be unwise not to give investors any information! Not only would they be unwilling to invest blindly, but the issuer could also be sued for securities fraud if it fails to disclose material information to purchasers.) On the other hand, Rule 502(b) mandates the disclosure of a great deal of information to *non*-accredited investors. The amount of these required disclosures depends in part on whether the issuer is publicly traded, as well as the size of the offering.

Third, the issuer in a Rule 505 offering may not use any form of "general advertising" or "general solicitation" to reach investors. Rule 502(c) defines these terms as including—but not being limited to—(1) "[a]ny advertisement, article, notice or other communication published in any newspaper, magazine, or similar media or broadcast over television or radio; and (2) "[a]ny seminar or meeting whose attendees have been invited by any general solicitation or general advertising." This obviously makes it difficult for an issuer to find potential investors; oftentimes, an investment banking firm will be needed to help find investors, such as clients with whom they have a pre-existing relationship. Over the years, the SEC has also given "no-action letters" to many issuers, allowing them to undertake certain actions to locate investors. (Again, you may learn more about this in a course on Securities Regulation.)

---

requirements of the definition should be adjusted or modified for the protection of investors, in the public interest, and in light of the economy."

Further, investors in a Rule 505 offering will receive "restricted" securities. As discussed below in the section concerning resales, it is more difficult to legally resell "restricted" securities than it is to resell "unrestricted" securities. Rule 502(d) requires the issuer to use "reasonable care" to make sure that investors do not illegally resell the securities, and lists some actions by the issuer that "may" demonstrate this reasonable care.

Finally, Rule 503 requires the issuer to file a Form D with the SEC within fifteen days after the first sale in any Regulation D offering. However, Form D is a relatively short form that can be quickly completed; the SEC mainly uses it for statistical purposes. Depending on the facts, the issuer may also be required to amend a Form D that it previously filed.

Rule 506 is very similar to Rule 505. Rule 506 imposes the same informational and filing requirements and the same prohibition on general advertising and general solicitation as Rule 505. Rule 506 also results in purchasers having restricted securities. Rule 506 also restricts the offering to thirty-five purchasers, but is subject to the same "counting" rules as those discussed above for Rule 505. Obviously, though, there are some differences between Rule 505 and Rule 506. First, *any* issuer may use Rule 506, even investment companies and those who are subject to the "bad boy" provisions of Rule 262.* Second, there is no dollar limitation under Rule 506. Theoretically, an issuer could use Rule 506 to sell $100 trillion or more of securities (although that is obviously not likely!).

So, what's the downside of Rule 506 as compared to Rule 505? It can be found in the following language from Rule 506(b)(2)(ii):

> Each purchaser who is not an accredited investor either alone or with his purchaser representative(s) [as that term is defined in Rule 501] has such knowledge and experience in financial and business matters that he is capable of evaluating the merits and risks of the prospective investment, or the issuer reasonably believes immediately prior to making any sale that such purchaser comes within this description.

This requirement makes sense when you remember that Rule 506 is a "safe harbor" under Section 4(2). As you learned above, offerees in a Section 4(2) offering must be persons who can "fend for themselves" within the meaning of *Ralston-Purina* and later authorities. Rule 506(b)(2)(ii) reflects this requirement.

---

*   However, the Dodd-Frank Act required the SEC to pass a rule within one year after enactment of the statute that would impose similar disqualifications in Rule 506 offerings. In May 2011, the SEC proposed rules to implement this requirement.

Rule 504, as noted above, doesn't seem to "belong" with Rules 505 and 506. First, it's "smaller": the issuer can only sell $1 million of securities in a twelve-month period under Rule 504 (subject to similar "counting" rules as those found in Rule 505). Second, some issuers may *not* use Rule 504, including public companies, investment companies and certain "development stage" companies." *See* Rule 504(a). Third, the issuer is not required to disclose any particular information to investors in a Rule 504 offering, even non-accredited investors (although, as discussed above, it would be unwise not to give investors any information).

Further, there is no limit on the number of investors in a Rule 504 offering. Theoretically, the issuer could sell $1 of securities to 1 million different investors. Moreover, investors in a Rule 504 offering do not need to be accredited or "sophisticated" in any way. Obviously, this makes Rule 504 very different from Rules 505 and 506.

Finally, Rule 504 *ordinarily* prohibits the use of general advertising or general solicitation and *ordinarily* results in investors receiving restricted securities. However, Rule 504(b)(1) describes three situations in which these rules do not apply. In other words, if any of these three situations applies, then the issuer may use general advertising and general solicitation and investors will get unrestricted securities. When you read Rule 504(b)(1)(i) through (iii), note that (i) and (ii) are very similar to one another.

Section (3)(a)(11) and Rule 147—The Intrastate Exemption. Another important exemption from registration is called the "intra-state" exemption, which is found in Section 3(a)(11) of the Securities Act. In addition, Rule 147 acts as a safe harbor to the statute. Let's begin with the text of the statute. Section 3(a)(11) exempts from the Securities Act's registration requirements:

> Any security which is part of an issue offered and sold only to persons resident within a single State or Territory, where the issuer of such security is a person resident and doing business within or, if a corporation, incorporated by and doing business within, such State or Territory.

Like Section 4(2), this is another surprisingly short section for a securities law. But there is a lot of nuance found in it. First, the phrase "part of an issue," should remind us that the concept of *integration* is always a potential problem in a securities offering, but we will defer discussion of integration until later. Second, each offeree in a Section 3(a)(11) must be a "resident" of the same state. Some cases have held that Section 3(a)(11) may not be used as an exemption if a single offer was made, even mistakenly or inadvertently, to a resident of the "wrong" state. In addition, the SEC and other authorities have traditionally interpreted the residence requirement of Section 3(a)(11) as meaning domicile.

Question

For purposes of Section 3(a)(11), are you a "resident" of the state in which you attend law school? Why or why not?

To return to the phrase "part of an issue," another concern in a Section 3(a)(11) offering is whether the securities have "come to rest" in the state of the offering before they are resold outside the state. (This may remind you of the above discussion of non-exempt resales in Section 4(2) offerings.) Assume that a corporation that is incorporated in Michigan and that does business in Michigan offers and sells shares of its stock to several Michigan residents pursuant to Section 3(a)(11). If these Michigan residents shortly thereafter resell the stock to Ohio residents (or, if you don't like Ohio, name any other state), then it doesn't really look like the stock was bought by Michigan residents. Instead, it looks like the Michigan residents were used as funnels to resell the stock out of state, in a way that Section 3(a)(11) would not have permitted.

Most authorities interpreting Section 3(a)(11) state that one year is a good rule of thumb for securities to come to rest in the state before they may be resold outside the state. Note how this largely places the issuer at the mercy of its investors; their actions could ruin the Section 3(a)(11) exemption. Thus, even though there are no limits on the number or types of purchasers that you may have in a Section 3(a)(11) offering, typically they are sold only to a small number of people that the issuer can trust.

Further, if the issuer is a corporation (such as where a corporation is conducting a stock offering or a bond offering), it must be incorporated in the same state in which all of the offerees reside.[*] In addition, it must be "doing business within" that state. This should raise a few questions in your mind. When is a corporation "doing business" within a given state? What sort of activities count as "business"? Must the issuer's business be *confined* to a single state, or may it have activities in more than one state (so long as it is "doing business" in the state of the securities offering)? A few principles seem to have emerged from case law interpreting Section 3(a)(11). First, "doing business" refers to money-making activities, such as manufacturing widgets or performing services. Simply having an office, or a bank account, or owning land, in a given state does not mean that the corporation is "doing business" in that state. Second, while a corp-

---

[*]   Other types of issuers must be "residents" of the state where the offering occurs. As discussed below, Rule 147 contains rules for determining when a non-corporate issuer is a resident of a state.

oration may do business in multiple states, if it does, it must have the predominant amount of its business activities in the state of the securities offering.

Admittedly, the above discussion of many (if not all) aspects of Section 3(a)(11) is not crystal clear, which makes the safe harbor of Rule 147 all the more important. Rule 147 takes some of the uncertainty of the Section 3(a)(11) away. For example, Rule 147 exactly quantifies the "doing business" requirement. Under the rule, an issuer will be considered to be doing business in a state if it meets four requirements: (1) the issuer derives at least 80 percent of its gross revenues from the state;* (2) the issuer had, at the end of the most recent semi-annual period, at least 80 percent of its assets in the state (on a consolidated basis with its subsidiaries), (3) the issuer intends to, and in fact does, use at least 80 percent of the proceeds from the securities offering "in connection with the operation of a business or of real property, the purchase of real property located in, or the rendering of services within" the state, and (4) the issuer's principal office is located in the state.

Another improvement that Rule 147 makes over Section 3(a)(11) is that an individual investor is deemed to be a resident of the state in which her "principal residence" is located. This is an easier determination than domicile. (The rule also specifies how to determine the residency of non-individual investors.)

Further, Rule 147 gives a bright-line rule for how much time must pass before securities are deemed to come to rest in the state; subsection (e) provides that resales of the securities, by any person, may only be made *within* the state for nine months following the last sale of securities by the issuer. Once nine months has elapsed, resales may be made outside the state. Subsection (f) specifies some "precautions" that the issuer must take to prevent the occurrence of resales that violate the rule; however, keep in mind that impermissible resales may still occur despite the issuer's best efforts. As a result, the intra-state exemption, whether one is using Section 3(a)(11) alone or the safe harbor of Rule 147, is a bit "dangerous" because compliance with the exemption is not completely within the issuer's control.

Comparing and Contrasting Exemptions. There is no perfect exemption from Securities Act registration; the choice of an exemption will depend on the characteristics and needs of your client, the issuer of the securities. For example, if the issuer wants to raise, say, $10 million, then you should immediately recognize that some of the exemptions that you learned about above (Rule 504 and

---

*   This is measured on a consolidated basis, that is, including the issuer's subsidiaries (if any). Rule 147 also specifies the time period used to determine if the issuer derived at least 80 percent of its gross revenues from the state, which depends on when during the calendar year the offering occurs.

Rule 505) would not be available for that offering. Alternatively, if the issuer believes that it will need to sell the securities to many dozens or hundreds of persons, many of whom are not "sophisticated" in investment matters, then you should recognize that Section 4(2) would not be a good choice of exemption for that offering.

To test your knowledge, you may want to try you hand at completing the following chart (perhaps on a separate sheet of paper or on your computer):

	Section 4(2)	Rule 504	Rule 505	Rule 506	Section 3(a)(11) and Rule 147
Are there restrictions on what types of issuers may use the exemption?					
Is there a dollar limit on the offering?					
Is there a limit on the number of purchasers?					
Must investors be accredited or sophisticated?					
Any there limits on the residence of investors?					
Are specific items of information required to be disclosed?					

	Section 4(2)	Rule 504	Rule 505	Rule 506	Section 3(a)(11) and Rule 147
Is general advertising or general solicitation allowed?					
Does the exemption result in investors having "restricted" securities?					

Other Things to Note About Exemptions. One issue that may arise if an issuer conducts two or more securities offerings simultaneously or close together in time is the concept of *integration.* If two or more (supposedly) separate securities offerings are integrated, that means that the SEC will view them as really being only one securities offering. As so combined, the offering must either have been registered or comply with an exemption from registration. The SEC has repeatedly stated that there are five factors to consider in determining whether two or more offerings should be integrated (although it has refused to say how many factors are necessary or whether some factors are more important than others):

- Are the offerings part of a single plan of financing?
- Do the offerings involve issuance of the same class of securities?
- Are the offerings made at or about the same time?
- Is the same type of consideration to be received?
- Are the offerings made for the same general purpose?

Consider these factors in the context of the following problem:

Problem

Problem 13-4: ABC-123 Corp., which is incorporated in Michigan and does business in Michigan, wants to conduct an offering of its common stock to raise about $2 million. It plans to use the money from the offering to renovate and expand its manufacturing operations in Michigan. The company has preliminarily determined that there are two groups of potential investors in this offering: (1) several dozen of the company's employees, all of whom reside in Michigan and range in rank from CEO to night-shift janitor, and (2) Bob Moneybags, a wealthy and sophisticated financial analyst who lives in Cincinnati, Ohio. *May the company claim that the offering to the first group of investors is exempt under Section 3(a)(11) and that the offering to Bob Moneybags is exempt under Section 4(2)? Why or why not?*

A few final notes about exemptions from Securities Act registration. First, if the SEC or an investor challenges the validity of the exemption, the issuer has the burden of proving that it complied with the requirements of the exemption. Second, if possible, it often is wise to structure a securities exemption so that it simultaneously complies with two or more exemptions. That way, if the issuer does not meet the requirements of an exemption, a "back-up" may be available. Finally, despite the fact that a securities offering may be exempt from the *registration* requirements of the Securities Act, the issuer (and perhaps others) will remain liable for securities fraud, such as material omissions from offering documents and false or misleading statements. You will learn a bit more about this elsewhere in this book, as well as in a course on Securities Regulation.

A Brief Note About Resales and Rule 144. If you were paying close attention when you read Section 5, you would have noticed that it applies to "any person." Thus, *any* person—not just an issuer—who wants to offer and sell a "security" must either register the security with the SEC or find an exemption for the transaction. Thus, if you happen to own some shares of Apple Corp. stock or The Coca-Cola Company stock and want to resell them, you must either register them (not likely) or find an exemption.

Luckily, for an "ordinary" investor there is a readily available exemption: Section 4(1). This section exempts securities that are sold in "transactions by any person other than an issuer, underwriter, or dealer." In an ordinary stock market transaction, Section 4(1) will easily apply. However, if the person selling the securities (1) is an "affiliate" of the issuer, such as an officer or director of the issuer, or (2) holds "restricted" securities,[*] then compliance with Section 4(1) is more problematic. If either (or both) of these situations apply, the person who wishes to resell the securities would be well-advised to do so in compliance with

---

[*]   Rule 144 defines "restricted" securities in part as those that were "acquired directly or indirectly from the issuer, or from an affiliate of the issuer, in a transaction or chain of transactions not involving any public offering." Some of the exemptions from registration discussed earlier in this chapter will result in purchasers having restricted securities. By contrast, stock purchased through the U.S. stock markets will not be considered restricted.

SEC Rule 144. You will likely learn more about Rule 144 in a course on Securities Regulation.

§ 13.04   OTHER PROVISIONS OF THE SECURITIES ACT

I have said so repeatedly throughout this chapter, but there is much more to learn about the Securities Act. If you are interested in this topic then you should take a course on Securities Regulation. With that disclaimer in mind, we should briefly touch on three other sections of the Securities Act.

Section 11 of the Securities Act provides that if an effective registration statement for a securities offering contained an "untrue statement of a material fact or omitted to state a material fact required to be stated therein or necessary to make the statements therein not misleading," then any person who purchased the registered securities may sue the issuer and various other persons. Section 11 provides defendants with some potential defenses and also specifies how to calculate the plaintiff's recovery if the plaintiff wins the lawsuit.

Section 12 of the Securities Act is another section that creates potential civil liability. It provides that any person who offers or sells a security in violation of Section 5 is liable for damages to the person who purchased the security from her. There are virtually no defenses to a Section 12(a)(1) lawsuit; it basically imposes strict liability for Section 5 violations. Thus, if an issuer conducted a securities offering without having a valid exemption from registration or if the issuer otherwise violated Section 5 during the offering, purchasers would have the right to rescind their purchase or, if applicable, collect other damages. In this sense, Section 5 is self-enforcing (although the SEC of course can impose penalties for Section 5 violations); no issuer would want to have to give investors all of their money back plus interest.

Section 12(a)(2) provides a civil cause of action in the case of any false or misleading "prospectus." Given that the prospectus is the portion of a registration statement that is more likely to be false or misleading (as opposed to the other parts of a registration statement), Section 12(a)(2) overlaps with Section 11 to a large degree. This is particularly so following the Supreme Court's decision in *Gustafson v. Alloyd Co.*, 513 U.S. 561 (1995).[*] Unlike Section 12(a)(1), there are some potential defenses to a Section 12(a)(2) lawsuit.

---

[*] Despite the broad definition given to "prospectus" in Section 2(a)(10) of the Securities Act, the Court in *Gustafson* held that, for purposes of Section 12(a)(2) lawsuits, a "prospectus" means a publicly disseminated document. Many commentators believe that *Gustafson*, which was a 5-4 decision, was mistakenly decided.

Finally, Section 18, which was heavily amended in 1996, *partially* pre-empts some state securities laws. It provides that, with some exceptions discussed below, the securities law of any state do not apply "covered securities," or securities that will be "covered securities" upon completion of the securities offering. Covered securities include those that are listed on the New York Stock Exchange, the American Stock Exchange and the National Market System of the Nasdaq Stock Market (or any successors to those exchanges), as well as any securities of the same issuer that are equal in seniority or senior to such a listed security.

Problem

Problem 13-5: DEF Corp. common stock is listed on the New York Stock Exchange. *What are some securities of the same issuer that would be "senior" to DEF Corp. common stock?*

Another type of "covered securities" are those that are sold in transactions that are exempt from Securities Act registration pursuant to SEC "rules or regulations issued under Section 4(2) ..." *See* Securities Act § 18(b)(4)(D).

Problem

Problem 13-6: *Of the exemptions that you studied in Section 13.03 of this chapter, which result in securities that are "covered securities" within the meaning of Securities Act § 18(b)(4)(D)? (Your list of five possibilities is as follows: Section 4(2), Rule 504, Rule 505, Rule 506, and Section 3(a)(11)/Rule 147.)*

However, Section 18 does preserve states' rights to pursue actions for fraud or deceit, and to require filings and filing fees in some situations. Nonetheless, states may not require the *registration* of an offering of Section 18 "covered securities." Conversely, states *may* require the registration of securities that are not Section 18 "covered securities," as discussed in the next section.

§ 13.05   A NOTE ON STATE SECURITIES LAWS

You should not forget that all of the states have their own securities laws, which are referred to as "blue sky" laws. Thus, just because an issuer registered a securities offering with the SEC, that does not mean that it was registered in any of the states in which the issuer wishes to offer and sell the securities. Similarly, just because the securities offering is exempt at the federal level, that does not mean that it is exempt from any state's securities law. (However, as discussed in the previous section, Section 18 of the Securities Act pre-empts the registration requirements of state securities laws for some types of securities offerings.)

While there is a great deal of diversity among state securities laws, several states have adopted the Uniform Securities Act (or parts of it). The Uniform Securities Act contains many provisions that should be familiar to persons who have previously studied the federal Securities Act. For example, Section 102(28) contains a definition of "security" that is very similar, albeit more detailed, than the definition found in the Securities Act. Section 201 sets forth a list of exempted securities that is somewhat similar to those on the list of exempt securities in Section 3 of the Securities Act. Section 202 also provides for several exemptions from state registration requirements, some of which can be easily coordinated with a federal exemption from registration.

If an issuer does need to register a securities offering in a state that has adopted the Uniform Securities Act, there are three ways to do it: *registration by notice*; *registration by coordination*; and *registration by qualification*. *See* Uniform Securities Act §§ 302-304. Registration by notice is reserved for investment companies (e.g., mutual funds) that are registered under the federal Investment Company Act of 1940. The aptly named registration by coordination refers to a process of simultaneously registering a federally registered offering in one or more states. Essentially, the states rely on the SEC to review the registration statement and, assuming a few conditions are met, will declare the registration statement effective in their states at the same time that the SEC declares it effective at the federal level.

Finally, registration by qualification is the only option left for securities offerings that are not exempt and that cannot qualify for either registration by notice or registration by qualification. Again, diversity is prevalent among state securities laws, and trying to comply with the requirements of several states at the same time can be very challenging. This is particularly so because some states impose "merit" regulation, at least for some types of offerings. That is, unlike the SEC (whose mantra is "Disclosure, disclosure, disclosure"), some states will prohibit securities offerings that they do not "like."

Thus ends your introduction to the Securities Act and related securities laws. To test your knowledge, the following practice problems await you. However, note that none of the following problems concern the pre-filing period, waiting period, or post-effective period under Section 5 of the Securities Act.

PRACTICE QUESTIONS

Multiple Choice Question 13-1:   Tonya Roosevelt owns a large parcel of undeveloped real estate in Michigan. Tonya plans to sub-divide the parcel into ten plots and sell the plots to ten persons. However, instead of selling the plots solely for cash, Tonya will require that each purchaser agree to farm the land for 15 years, growing the kinds of vegetables specified by Tonya. At harvest time each year, the vegetables will be loaded onto a truck and sold at a local farmers' market. The proceeds from the sale will be divided, with Tonya receiving 80%, and the other persons dividing the other 20% equally, regardless of the kind or quality of the vegetables that they grew. At the end of 15 years, Tonya will transfer full title to the plots to these ten persons, for a $20 cash payment. Tonya does not expect to do any work other than driving the truck. *As to whether this idea would be considered a "security" under federal securities laws, which of the following is correct? Choose the best answer.*

A.   It is not a security, because land is not a security.
B.   It is not a security, because the ten purchasers will be required to perform a great deal of work farming the land.
C.   It is not a security, because these transactions will take place solely in one state.
D.   It is not a security, because it is likely to be considered a limited partnership.
E.   It is a security.

Multiple Choice Question 13-2: *Given that Rule 506 allows a company to raise an unlimited amount of money, whereas Rule 505 is limited to $5 million in a 12-month period, why would an issuer choose a Rule 505 offering instead of a Rule 506 offering when it wishes to sell securities in an exempt offering?*

A.   The issuer can sell the stock to a greater number of investors under Rule 505.
B.   Stock sold in a Rule 505 offering is "unrestricted" and may be freely resold.
C.   Rule 505 does not require that non-accredited investors (either alone or with their purchaser representatives) be "sophisticated," but Rule 506 does.
D.   Rule 505 does not require that any information be disclosed to non-accredited investors, but Rule 506 does.
E.   Rule 505 allows general advertising and solicitation, but Rule 506 does not.

Multiple Choice Question 13-3: You represent SuperLarge Corp., a tele-communications company whose common stock is registered under Section 12(g) of the Securities Exchange Act (i.e., it is a publicly traded company). SuperLarge is considering an offering of common stock to raise additional capital for its operations, which are located in five different states. SuperLarge plans to offer the stock to the residents of those five states. SuperLarge has not made any securities offerings in the last 12 months. *Which of the following statements is correct?*

A.   SuperLarge could raise an unlimited amount of money under Rule 147.
B.   SuperLarge could raise up to $1 million in a Rule 504 offering.
C.   SuperLarge could raise $10 million in a Rule 505 offering.
D.   None of the above is correct.

Multiple Choice Question 13-4: *In* SEC v. Ralston Purina, *the Supreme Court found that, for purposes of determining whether an offering is not a "public" offering and is thus exempt from registration pursuant to Section 4(2) of the Securities Act, which of the following is the most important inquiry?*

A.   The number of persons who purchase the securities in the offering.
B.   The number of persons to whom the securities are offered (even if they don't all end up purchasing the securities).
C.   The characteristics of the offerees, e.g., their "sophistication."
D.   How well-established and financially strong the issuer is.
E.   The total dollar value of securities that are offered.

Multiple Choice Question 13-5: Bob Broker, a stockbroker, maintains discretionary trading accounts for several clients. (A discretionary trading account allows Bob to buy and sell securities for the client's account in his discretion, without any pre-approval by the client.) Each of these accounts is operated independently of Bob's other accounts; thus, Bob may decide to buy securities for one of the accounts but not any of the other accounts, and the profitability of an account does not depend on how well the other accounts fare. However, the amount of Bob's commissions depends on how profitable the account is (i.e., how well the investments in the account perform). *In deciding whether the account itself (rather than the securities in it) is a "security" for purposes of the Securities Act, which of the following statements is correct?*

A.   If the court applies the horizontal formulation of the "common enterprise" part of the *Howey* test, it will find that the account is not a "security."
B.   If the court applies the vertical formulation of the "common enterprise" part of the *Howey* test, it will find that the account is not a "security."
C.   To determine whether the account is a "security" the court should apply the "family resemblance" test.
D.   None of the above is correct.

Multiple Choice Question 13-6: Cheese Corp. ("Cheese") is a corporation incorporated under Wisconsin law. As you might guess from its name, Cheese manufactures cheese and sells it to various grocery stores throughout Wisconsin. All of Cheese's assets and operations are located in Wisconsin. However, Cheese common stock is listed on the New York Stock Exchange and is owned by approximately 800 record shareholders who reside throughout the United States. Cheese wishes to raise approximately $5 million to expand its manufacturing facility in Wisconsin by selling additional shares of its common stock in an offering that is exempt from registration under Section 5 of the Securities Act. It believes that it can sell the entire $5 million of stock to wealthy and "sophisticated" persons who reside in Wisconsin. *Which of the following would be correct advice?*

A.   Cheese may not use the intrastate exemption of Section 3(a)(11) and/or Rule 147 for this offering because its current shareholders reside throughout the United States.

B.   Cheese may not use the intrastate exemption of Section 3(a)(11) and/or Rule 147 for this offering because it seeks to sell more than $1 million worth of stock.

C.   Cheese may use Rule 505 for this offering, provided that all of the non-accredited investors are "sophisticated" (able to understand the merits and risks of the investment).

D.   Cheese may use Rule 506 for this offering, provided that it does not use general advertising or general solicitation in connection with the offering.

E.   None of the above is correct.

Multiple Choice Question 13-7: Same facts as the previous question. Assume that Cheese decides to conduct its stock offering under Section 4(2) of the Securities Act <u>and</u> Rule 506, i.e., Cheese wants its offering to comply with <u>both</u> Section 4(2) and Rule 506. Cheese has identified several potential investors that it wishes to approach to see whether they would be interested in purchasing Cheese stock, including Mr. Lucky. Mr. Lucky, who never completed high school and can barely read and write, inherited $1.5 million when his wealthy parents died two weeks ago. Mr. Lucky, who does not have a job and is not married, usually spends his days playing videogames. Cheese hopes that Mr. Lucky will purchase $600,000 worth of Cheese stock in this offering. *Which of the following would be good advice to Cheese? Choose the best answer. Assume that it is not possible to have a "purchaser representative" represent Mr. Lucky.*

A.   Mr. Lucky would <u>not</u> likely be a permissible offeree/purchaser for purposes of Section 4(2), but would be a permissible offeree/purchaser for purposes of Rule 506.

B.   Mr. Lucky would <u>not</u> likely be a permissible offeree/purchaser for purposes of Rule 506, but would be a permissible offeree/purchaser for purposes of Section 4(2).

C.   Cheese should not offer or sell any stock to Mr. Lucky because he would not be a permissible offeree/purchaser under Section 4(2) or Rule 506.

D.   None of the above is correct.

Multiple Choice Question 13-8: Cooley Corp. is a closely held manufacturing company, with all of its assets and operations in Michigan. It is incorporated under Michigan law. Cooley Corp.'s President, Mr. LeDuc, has informed you that Cooley Corp. wishes to raise $5 million in a stock offering so that it can expand its manufacturing plant in Michigan. Mr. LeDuc also said that he believes that a few of his wealthy and financially sophisticated friends would buy enough stock to meet the $5 million offering amount. *Assuming that Cooley Corp. restricts the stock offering only to offerees and purchasers who are Michigan residents and also strictly complies with whatever other advice you give it, which of the following provisions could be relied upon to exempt this stock offering from registration under the Securities Act of 1933?*

> *I.   Section 4(2) of the Securities Act of 1933*
> *II.   Section 3(a)(11) of the Securities Act of 1933*
> *III.   Rule 504 under the Securities Act of 1933*
> *IV.   Rule 506 under the Securities Act of 1933*

A.   All of the above.

B.   II, III, and IV only.

C.   I, II, and III only.

D.   I, II, and IV only.

Multiple Choice Question 13-9: Same facts as in the previous question, except that Cooley Corp. wishes to raise $6 million in the stock offering. *Assuming that Cooley Corp. restricts the offering only to offerees and purchasers who are Michigan residents and also strictly complies with whatever other advice you give it, which of the following provisions could be relied upon to exempt this stock offering from registration under the Securities Act of 1933?*

> I.   *Section 3(a)(11) of the Securities Act of 1933*
> II.   *Rule 504 under the Securities Act of 1933*
> III.   *Rule 505 under the Securities Act of 1933*
> IV.   *Rule 506 under the Securities Act of 1933*

A.   All of the above.
B.   I, II, and III only.
C.   II, III, and IV only.
D.   I and IV only.

Multiple Choice Question 13-10:   Cloning Corp. ("Cloning") is a new biotechnology corporation. It has all of its assets and operations in California, and is incorporated in California. Cloning intends to go into the business of offering rich pet owners in Beverly Hills, California, the opportunity to clone dead pets such as cats and dogs, for the low, low price of $70,000. Unfortunately, Cloning needs a lot of money to develop its cloning technology and is unable to persuade a bank to loan it any money. Cloning's President, Dr. Frankenstein, has informed you that Cloning wishes to raise $35 million in a stock offering so that it can develop its cloning technology. Dr. Frankenstein also said that he believes that it will be possible to sell the entire $35 million worth of stock to wealthy business-people in Los Angeles, California. *Assuming that Cloning Corp. strictly complies with whatever advice you give it, which of the following provisions could be relied upon to exempt this stock offering from registration under the Securities Act of 1933?*

> I.   *Section 3(a)(11) of the Securities Act of 1933*
> II.   *Section 4(2) of the Securities Act of 1933*
> III.   *Rule 504 under the Securities Act of 1933*
> IV.   *Rule 505 under the Securities Act of 1933*

A.   I and II only.
B.   I, II, and III only.
C.   I, II, and IV only.
D.   All of the above.

Multiple Choice Question 13-11: X Corporation sold some of its shares to 100 different shareholders without registration, relying on the intra-state exemption of Section 3(a)(11) of the Securities Act of 1933. *Which of the following factors will not destroy the exemption?*

A.   An immediate resale of some of the shares by the original purchasers to out-of-state residents.

B.   An immediate resale of some of the shares by the original purchasers to in-state residents.

C.   A resale of some of the shares by the original purchasers to out-of-state residents that occurs more than one year later.

D.   Both B and C are correct.

E.   None of the above factors would destroy the exemption.

Multiple Choice Question 13-12: *In order for X Corporation to qualify for the non-public offering exemption of Section 4(2) of the Securities Act:*

A.   Only the actual purchasers of the shares must be able to fend for themselves.

B.   There can be no more than 25 actual purchasers of the shares.

C.   All of the offerees and purchasers of the shares must be able to fend for themselves in that they have access to the same kind of information that a registration statement would provide them.

D.   None of the above.

Multiple Choice Question 13-13: Technology, Inc. ("Technology") is a Delaware corporation engaged in the manufacture of high tech machines. The company wished to raise new funds for research and expansion. In order to do this, Cosmo Gearhead, the company's Chief Executive Officer and George Poindexter, the company's Chief Financial Officer, sent personal letters to 1,000 people in California, Colorado, Wyoming and New Hampshire asking if they were interested in purchasing stock in Technology. Cosmo and George pursued those people who expressed any interest in the proposal. Ultimately, 100 people purchased $1.5 million worth of Technology stock, but only after the company had disclosed all the information these people had asked for regarding the company's management and experience, its financial statements, and other information. None of these shareholders were insiders or employees of Technology or were wealthy or sophisticated investors. Most were elderly, retired school teachers with modest pensions. *Under these circumstances:*

A.   The offering was probably exempt from registration under the Securities Act because the investors received all the information they asked for from the company.

B.   The offering was probably exempt from registration as a private placement under Section 4(2) of the under the Securities Act.

C.   The offering was probably exempt from registration as a Rule 506 offering.

D.   None of the above are correct.

Multiple Choice Question 13-14: Grocery Corp. is a wholesale supplier to approximately 750 independent grocery stores throughout the United States. In 2011, Grocery Corp. decided that it needed to raise money to build a new warehouse. Instead of taking out a loan from a bank, Grocery Corp. offered promissory notes ("Notes") to all 750 of its grocery store customers. These Notes paid 4% interest annually and had a term of 36 months. In other words, Grocery Corp. agreed to pay interest on the Notes for 36 months and then to pay each Note holder the principal balance of the Note at the end of 36 months. During 2011, Grocery Corp. sold Notes to several grocery store customers and raised $8 million to build its new warehouse. However, Grocery Corp. soon ran into financial difficulties and is unable to repay the Notes. Grocery Corp. argues that the Notes are not "securities" under Section 2 of the Securities Act for the following reasons:

I.   The Notes are not securities because they have a term of more than 9 months.

II.   The Notes are not securities because Grocery Corp. used the proceeds ($8 million) to build a new warehouse.

III.   The Notes are not securities because the Note purchasers had a pre-existing relationship with Grocery Corp. (i.e., the Note purchasers are customers).

Which of the above arguments is (are) likely to be successful in convincing a court that the Notes are not "securities" under Section 2 of the Securities Act?

A.   I only.
B.   II only.
C.   I and II only.
D.   III only.
E.   None of the above.

CHAPTER 14

INSIDER TRADING

This chapter concerns what is loosely called "insider trading." When you hear that phrase you probably envision a somewhat common scene on television newscasts: a well-dressed person from a firm on Wall Street doing a "perp walk," that is, being led away by law enforcement officers into a waiting police car. And you probably have the impression that the allegations against that person have to do with (1) the fact that he or she had "inside information" that was unknown to the public but would be important enough to affect the market prices of securities and (2) he or she profited from that information by buying or selling securities before the information became publicly known. This impression is not inaccurate, just a bit incomplete. The goal of this chapter, then, is for you to understand more fully the legal rules surrounding insider trading. You may find yourself surprised to learn that it's *not always* illegal for a person to use material nonpublic to profit in the securities markets. The trick, of course, is to understand what is and what is not illegal insider trading.

The primary federal weapon to combat insider trading, SEC Rule 10b-5 under the Securities Exchange Act of 1934, will be our main focus, although we will also cover Section 16(b) of the statute. We will consider Rule 10b-5 largely in the context of *criminal* insider trading violations. However—and it is very important that practicing attorneys not lose sight of this fact—Rule 10b-5 has many uses beyond criminal cases. Thus, the concluding section of this chapter will briefly discuss the use of Rule 10b-5 in *civil* lawsuits for the many (and ever-evolving) forms of securities fraud.

§ 14.01   A FIRST LOOK AT RULE 10b-5

The SEC promulgated Rule 10b-5 pursuant to the authority that Congress granted to it in Section 10(b) of the Securities Exchange Act of 1934. Section 10(b) provides in part that:

It shall be unlawful for any person, directly or indirectly, by the use of any means or instrumentality of interstate commerce or of the mails, or of any facility of any national securities exchange--

(b)   To use or employ, in connection with the purchase or sale of any security ***, any manipulative or deceptive device or contrivance in contravention of such rules and regulations as the Commission may prescribe as necessary or appropriate in the public interest or for the protection of investors.

As used in the securities laws, the phrase "it shall be unlawful" means that the violation of the statute could result in criminal penalties such as a jail sentence. However, a close reading of Section 10(b) indicates that the statute *itself* does not make anything illegal; it only makes the *violation of SEC rules* promulgated pursuant to Section 10(b) illegal. Thus, you need to look at Rule 10b-5 to see what is made illegal by Section 10(b).

Unfortunately, Rule 10b-5 is not exactly a model of clarity. It provides:

It shall be unlawful for any person, directly or indirectly, by the use of any means or instrumentality of interstate commerce, or of the mails or of any facility of any national securities exchange,

(a)   To employ any device, scheme, or artifice to defraud,

(b)   To make any untrue statement of a material fact or to omit to state a material fact necessary in order to make the statements made, in the light of the circumstances under which they were made, not misleading, or

(c)   To engage in any act, practice, or course of business which operates or would operate as a fraud or deceit upon any person,

in connection with the purchase or sale of any security.

Note a few things about Rule 10b-5. First, it applies to "any security." In Chapter 13, you learned that there are many unusual things that could be considered "securities." Rule 10b-5 applies to all of them—regardless of whether they are traded (that is, bought and sold) on a national securities exchange. Although all of the insider trading cases that you will read in the following section do in fact involve publicly traded securities, this is not a requirement of Rule 10b-5. However, Rule 10b-5 does require the use of "jurisdictional means," that is, the use of "any means or instrumentality of interstate commerce, or of the mails or of any facility of any national securities exchange." It is nearly impossible for a modern-day securities transaction to occur without the use of such jurisdictional means. If someone uses the telephone (even an intra-state telephone call), or sends an e-mail, or writes a check, or wires funds, then the jurisdictional-means requirement will be satisfied.

Second, the language of Rule 10b-5 isn't terribly helpful. In particular, subsections (a) and (c) seem to overlap almost completely, essentially stating that fraud or deceit in connection with the purchase or sale of a security is illegal.

Subsection (b), on the other hand, provides that it is illegal to make a material misstatement in connection with the purchase or sale of a security. Subsection (b) itself does not make silence illegal; it only imposes a duty to speak if doing so is necessary to correct the statements that one has made (if any). But in the typical insider trading case, the person with material nonpublic information typically profits by *remaining silent*. Thus, if you are concerned about the precise subsection of Rule 10b-5 that insider trading would violate, it typically would not be subsection (b). In any event, as you will see in the following section, *case law*, particular the "trilogy" of Supreme Court cases (*Chiarella, Dirks,* and *O'Hagan*) defines the parameters of insider trading, rather than the language of Rule 10b-5 itself. (One could thus argue that this provides an exception to the rule that you should always read statues and administrative rules very carefully.)

While the language of Rule 10b-5 itself may not be overly helpful, two rules that the SEC promulgated in the year 2000 are. The first of these relatively new rules is Rule 10b5-1. This rule contains two subsections that you may find instructive. First, subsection (a) is the SEC's attempt to distill, in a single sentence, the rules of insider trading that have developed through case law through the year 2000. This subsection provides that:

> The "manipulative and deceptive devices" prohibited by Section 10(b) of the [Securities Exchange] Act and Rule 10b-5 thereunder include, among other things, the purchase or sale of a security of any issuer, on the basis of material nonpublic information about that security or issuer, in breach of a duty of trust or confidence that is owed directly, indirectly, or derivatively, to the issuer of that security or the shareholders of that issuer, or to any other person who is the source of the material nonpublic information.

Second, subsection (b) of Rule 10b5-1 deals with the *scienter* required for an insider trading violation. Briefly put, to be guilty of insider trading, one must (among other things) have *used* the material nonpublic information in connection with the securities trade. In other words, the trade must have been "on the basis of" the information. While some older cases have allowed defendants to show that they would have engaged in the transaction even if they had *not* known the material nonpublic information, Rule 10b5-1 essentially establishes a "mere possession" test[*] by defining the phrase "on the basis of" as follows:

---

[*]   Some commentators question whether the SEC has the authority to establish a "mere possession" text in Rule 10b5-1. Also, subsection (c) of Rule 10b5-1, which we will not consider in any detail in this textbook, provides some affirmative defenses to a finding that one's securities trades were "on the basis of" material nonpublic information.

*** a purchase or sale of a security of an issuer is "on the basis of" material nonpublic information about that security or issuer if the person making the purchase or sale was aware of the material nonpublic information when the person made the purchase or sale.

The other relatively new SEC rule that is helpful is Rule 10b5-2. This rule concerns a theory of insider trading called the "misappropriation" theory, which was endorsed by the Supreme Court in the *O'Hagan* case that appears later in this chapter. Briefly put, the misappropriation theory holds that you would violate Rule 10b-5 by trading securities on the basis of material nonpublic information that you learned from a source to whom you owe a "duty of trust and confidence," without disclosing your intentions to the source of the information. A problem with the *O'Hagan* case, however, is that the Supreme Court didn't give much guidance as to how to determine whether you owe such a duty to a source of information. Rule 10b5-2 was the SEC's attempt to give some additional examples. It provides in part that, for purposes of the misappropriation theory:

a "duty of trust or confidence" exists in the following circumstances, among others:

(1)   Whenever a person agrees to maintain information in confidence;

(2)   Whenever the person communicating the material nonpublic information and the person to whom it is communicated have a history, pattern, or practice of sharing confidences, such that the recipient of the information knows or reasonably should know that the person communicating the material nonpublic information expects that the recipient will maintain its confidentiality; or

(3)   Whenever a person receives or obtains material nonpublic information from his or her spouse, parent, child, or sibling; provided, however, that the person receiving or obtaining the information may demonstrate that no duty of trust or confidence existed with respect to the information, by establishing that he or she neither knew nor reasonably should have known that the person who was the source of the information expected that the person would keep the information confidential, because of the parties' history, pattern, or practice of sharing and maintaining confidences, and because there was no agreement or understanding to maintain the confidentiality of the information.

Don't worry if you don't understand the significance of these two new SEC rules right now. *But be sure to come back and re-read them after you have read the following section.*

§ 14.02   INSIDER TRADING UNDER RULE 10b-5

A.   HISTORY

As noted above, Section 10(b) gave the SEC authority to promulgate rules that make certain "manipulative or deceptive device[s] or contrivance[s]" illegal. It took the SEC several years after the Securities Exchange Act of 1934 was enacted to get around to doing; Rule 10b-5 was not "born" until 1942. Although Rule 10b-5 fairly quickly found use in civil lawsuits by defrauded plaintiffs against persons who sold securities to them or purchased securities from them (as discussed in Section 14.04 below), it wasn't until the 1960s that the SEC began using it to combat insider trading.

The* Cady, Roberts & Co. *Case. One of the most famous insider trading cases, which will be mentioned often in the Supreme Court cases below, is *In re Cady, Roberts & Co.*, 40 S.E.C. 907 (1961). In this case, J. Cheever Cowdin was an employee of the brokerage firm Cady, Roberts & Co. In addition, Cowdin was a director of Curtiss-Wright Corporation. On the morning of November 25, 1959, Cowdin attended a meeting of the board of directors of Curtiss-Wright. At this meeting, the board approved a quarterly dividend that was substantially smaller than dividends the company had paid in previous quarters. After making this decision, the board directed the company's secretary to notify the New York Stock Exchange (NYSE) about the dividend by telegram. Although the secretary promptly did so at approximately 11:00 a.m., the telegram did not arrive at the NYSE until around 11:48 a.m.

Shortly after 11:00 a.m., the Curtiss-Wright board took a break from its meeting. During the break, Cowdin telephoned Robert Gintel, who was a partner in Cady, Roberts & Co., and left a message for him about the reduced dividend. When he received the message, Gintel (surely realizing that the price of Curtiss-Wright stock would drop when this bad news was announced), entered "sell" orders for several of his and Cowdin's customers. These orders were entered by 11:18 a.m. These customers thus were able to sell their shares before the news about the reduced dividend became public and the price of Curtiss-Wright stock dropped by approximately fifteen percent.

The SEC later brought an administrative enforcement action against Cady, Roberts & Co. and Gintel for violations of Rule 10b-5 (among other things). In the proceeding, SEC Commissioner Cary found that Gintel had willfully violated Rule 10b-5 and that Cady, Roberts & Co. was responsible for Gintel's actions. In the course of the opinion, the Commissioner wrote:

> *** An affirmative duty to disclose material information has been traditionally imposed on corporate "insiders," particularly officers, directors, or controlling stockholders. We, and the courts have consistently held that insiders must disclose material facts which are known to them by virtue of their position but which are not known to persons with whom they deal and which, if known, would affect their investment judgment. Failure to make disclosure in these circumstances constitutes a violation of [Rule 10b-5]. If, on the other hand, disclosure prior to effecting a purchase or sale would be improper or unrealistic under the circumstances, we believe the alternative is to forego the transaction.

> The ingredients are here and we accordingly find that Gintel willfully violated Sections 17(a) [of the Securities Act] and 10(b) [of the Securities Exchange Act] and Rule 10b-5. *** It was obvious that a reduction in the quarterly dividend by the Board of Directors was a material fact which could be expected to have an adverse impact on the market price of the company's stock. The rapidity with which Gintel acted upon receipt of that information confirms his own recognition of that conclusion.

> We have already noted that the anti-fraud provisions are phrased in terms of "any person" and that a special obligation has been traditionally required of corporate insiders, e.g., officers, directors and controlling stockholders. These three groups, however, do not exhaust the classes of persons upon whom there is such an obligation. Analytically, the obligation rests on two principal elements; first, the existence of a relationship giving access, directly or indirectly, to information intended to be available only for a corporate purpose and not for the personal benefit of anyone, and second, the inherent unfairness involved where a party takes advantage of such information knowing it is unavailable to those with whom he is dealing. *** [O]ur task here is to identify those persons who are in a special relationship with a company and privy to its internal affairs, and thereby suffer correlative duties in trading in its securities. Intimacy demands restraint lest the uninformed be exploited.

The facts here impose on Gintel the responsibilities of those commonly referred to as "insiders." He received the information prior to its public release from a director of Curtiss-Wright, Cowdin, who was associated with [Cady, Roberts & Co.]. Cowdin's relationship to the company clearly prohibited him from selling the securities affected by the information without disclosure. By logical sequence, it should prohibit Gintel, a partner of [Cady, Roberts & Co.]. This prohibition extends not only over his own account, but [also] to selling for [customer] accounts ***. ***

Id. at 911-12.

State Law on Insider Trading. One reason that *Cady, Roberts & Co.* was such an important decision was that state law prohibitions on insider trading were (and still are) notoriously lax. Near the beginning of the twentieth century, the rule in nearly all states was that officers and directors, although owing duties to the corporation, were not prohibited from using "inside" information when they bought or sold the corporation's securities. However, over the years, some states began to adopt what is called a "special circumstances" doctrine, which holds that officers and directors must disclose information in—you guessed it—"special circumstances."

What were these special circumstances? Generally, this meant that the director or officer knew something extremely important about the corporation that the person with whom he was trading did not know. While this sounds like the modern-day requirement in Rule 10b-5 insider trading cases that the insider have material nonpublic information, state courts were somewhat reluctant to find that the undisclosed information was sufficiently important. For example, consider the oft-cited case of *Goodwin v. Agassiz*, 186 N.E. 659 (Mass. 1933). To simplify the facts somewhat, the defendant Aggasiz[*] was the president and a director of Cliff Mining Company. In May 1926, Aggasiz purchased shares of Cliff Mining Company through brokers on the Boston Stock Exchange. The seller of the shares was the plaintiff. Of course, because the transaction took place through a stock exchange, the plaintiff and the defendant never met face to face.

Afterwards, the plaintiff learned that Aggasiz had been the purchaser of the shares. More importantly, he learned that at the time of the transaction Aggasiz was aware that a geologist for Cliff Mining Company "had formulated in writing in March, 1926, a theory as to the possible existence of copper deposits under conditions prevailing in the region where the property of the company was

---

[*]   Only one of the potential defendants in the case, Agassiz, was before the court; the other potential defendant, MacNaughton, had apparently not been served.

located." *Id.* at 659. Now, why did Aggasiz know this information when the plaintiff (and the public at large) did not? Was it because he was smarter than the plaintiff, or worked harder than the plaintiff, or simply had a hunch? Of course not; Aggasiz knew the information because he was the president of Cliff Mining Company. Understandably, the plaintiff was upset when he learned of this information and claimed that, had he known the information, he would not have sold his shares. He then sued Aggasiz, claiming that "the purchase of his stock in the company by the defendants without disclosing to him as a stockholder their knowledge of the geologist's theory, their belief that the theory was true, had value, [and] keeping secret the existence of the theory, *** constitute actionable wrong for which he as stockholder can recover."

Today, this would probably be a good example of "classic" insider trading prohibited by Rule 10b-5. However, Rule 10b-5 did not exist in 1933. Instead, the court stated the following rule(s):

> The directors of a commercial corporation stand in a relation of trust to the corporation and are bound to exercise the strictest good faith in respect to its property and business. [Citations omitted.] The contention that directors also occupy the position of trustee toward individual stockholders in the corporation is plainly contrary to repeated decisions of this court and cannot be supported. ***
>
> ***
>
> While the general principle is as stated, circumstances may exist requiring that transactions between a director and a stockholder as to stock in the corporation be set aside. The knowledge naturally in the possession of a director as to the condition of a corporation places upon him a peculiar obligation to observe every requirement of fair dealing when directly buying or selling its stock. Mere silence does not usually amount to a breach of duty, but parties may stand in such relation to each other that an equitable responsibility arises to communicate facts. [Citation omitted.] Purchases and sales of stock dealt in on the stock exchange are commonly impersonal affairs. An honest director would be in a difficult situation if he could neither buy nor sell on the stock exchange shares of stock in his corporation without first seeking out the other actual ultimate party to the transaction and disclosing to him everything which a court or jury might later find that he then knew affecting the real or speculative value of such shares. Business of that nature is a matter to be governed by practical rules. Fiduciary obligations of directors ought not to be

made so onerous that men of experience and ability will be deterred from accepting such office. Law in its sanctions is not coextensive with morality. It cannot undertake to put all parties to every contract on an equality as to knowledge, experience, skill and shrewdness. It cannot undertake to relieve against hard bargains made between competent parties without fraud. On the other hand, directors cannot rightly be allowed to indulge with impunity in practices which do violence to prevailing standards of upright business men. Therefore, where a director personally seeks a stockholder for the purpose of buying his shares without making disclosure of material facts within his peculiar knowledge and not within reach of the stockholder, the transaction will be closely scrutinized and relief may be granted in appropriate instances. [Citations omitted.]

Id. at 660-61.

Applying these rules, the court found for the defendants. While commentators continue to debate the precise meaning of *Goodwin*, two factors were important to its holding. First, the transaction took place over a stock exchange. Thus, because the defendant director never "personally [sought] a stockholder for the purpose of buying his shares," the transaction was immune from challenge. Second, the court buttressed its conclusion by observing that, at the time of the stock transaction, the geologist's theory was "at most a hope, possibly an expectation" and that it "had not passed the nebulous stage." In other words, perhaps the information wasn't really that important.

The careful reader will have also noted another flaw in the *Goodwin* court's rule: it only applied when an insider was purchasing shares from a current shareholder. It had no application to the situation where the insider "dumped" shares when she knew *bad news* about the corporation that had not yet been disclosed publicly.

Problems

Problem 14-1: *Assume that you are an insider of a corporation and know some important, nonpublic information about it and that only state law applies. How may you legally act on that information if it is "good news"? How may you legally act on that information if it is "bad news"? (You may assume that the corporation's stock is publicly traded.)*

Problem 14-2: *Was Cliff Mining Company harmed when Agassiz purchased shares from Goodwin without disclosing the existence of the geologist's theory?*

Although the common law rules on insider trading continued to develop, sometimes in novel ways (*see, e.g., Diamond v. Oreamuno*, 248 N.E.2d 910 (N.Y. 1969)), the fact remains that it was—and still is—a poor method of policing insider trading. (In fact, the rule in some states remains that insiders are not prohibited from using material nonpublic information to buy or sell the corporation's securities.) In other words, insiders could "get away with murder" if state law were all that governed insider trading. Thus, the federal government entered the fray.

The Texas Gulf Sulphur Case. *In re Cady, Roberts & Co.* was the SEC's first significant step in policing insider trading. Another important case came a few years later in *Securities and Exchange Commission v. Texas Gulf Sulphur Co.*, 401 F.2d 833 (2d Cir. 1968),[*] *cert. denied*, 394 U.S. 976 (1969), which had facts that were very similar to *Godwin v. Agassiz*. Simplifying the facts greatly, during the fall of 1963 and the spring of 1964 Texas Gulf Sulphur (TGS) determined through geophysical surveys and exploratory drilling that an area in Canada had a very high mineral content, including silver, copper, and zinc. Naturally, TGS did not want to disclose this information immediately (nor was it required to), because it wished to buy mineral rights from the landowners beforehand at a much cheaper price than if the landowners knew of the presence of the minerals.

It was not until mid-April 1964 that news of the extent of the mineral discovery became public, although some rumors had begun circulating earlier that month. Importantly, many employees and directors of TGS began buying TGC stock (as well as options to buy shares of TGS stock) in November 1963, at prices as low as approximately $18 per share. Some of them also "tipped" other people, who likewise bought TGS stock. When news of the mineral discovery became public, the market price of TGS stock rose to $37 per share. The SEC sued TGS, as well as the TGS officers, directors, and employees who had engaged in transactions involving TGS stock, for violations of Section 10(b) and Rule 10b-5.

The court found that these defendants had violated Rule 10b-5. Here are some important portions of its opinion:

> *** [Rule 10b-5] is based in policy on the justifiable expectation of the securities marketplace that all investors trading on

---

[*]   The "American" spelling of "sulphur" is "sulfur."

impersonal exchanges have relatively equal access to material information, [citations omitted]. The essence of the Rule is that anyone who, trading for his own account in the securities of a corporation has "access, directly or indirectly, to information intended to be available only for a corporate purpose and not for the personal benefit of anyone" may not take "advantage of such information knowing it is unavailable to those with whom he is dealing," i.e., the investing public. *Matter of Cady, Roberts & Co.*, [40 S.E.C. 907 (1961)]. Insiders, as directors or management officers are, of course, by this Rule, precluded from so unfairly dealing, but the Rule is also applicable to one possessing the information who may not be strictly termed an "insider" within the meaning of [Section] 16(b) of the [Securities Exchange] Act. [Citation omitted.] Thus, anyone in possession of material inside information must either disclose it to the investing public, or, if he is disabled from disclosing it in order to protect a corporate confidence, or he chooses not to do so, must abstain from trading in or recommending the securities concerned while such inside information remains undisclosed. So, it is here no justification for insider activity that disclosure was forbidden by the legitimate corporate objective of acquiring options to purchase the land surrounding the exploration site; if the information was, as the SEC contends, material, its possessors should have kept out of the market until disclosure was accomplished. [Citation omitted.]

***

An insider is not, of course, always foreclosed from investing in his own company merely because he may be more familiar with company operations than are outside investors. An insider's duty to disclose information or his duty to abstain from dealing in his company's securities arises only in "those situations which are essentially extraordinary in nature and which are reasonably certain to have a substantial effect on the market price of the security if [the extraordinary situation is] disclosed." [Citation omitted.]

Nor is an insider obligated to confer upon outside investors the benefit of his superior financial or other expert analysis by disclosing his educated guesses or predictions. [Citation omitted.] The only regulatory objective is that access to material information be enjoyed equally, but this objective requires nothing more than the disclosure of basic facts so that outsiders may draw upon their own evaluative expertise in reaching their own investment decisions with knowledge equal to that of the insiders.

*** As we stated in [citation omitted], "The basic test of materiality *** is whether a *reasonable* man would attach importance *** in determining his choice of action in the transaction in question." [Citation omitted; emphasis added.] This, of course, encompasses any fact "*** which in reasonable and objective contemplation *might* affect the value of the corporation's stock or securities ***." [Citation omitted; emphasis added.] Such a fact is a material fact and must be effectively disclosed to the investing public prior to the commencement of insider trading in the corporation's securities. *** Thus, material facts include not only information disclosing the earnings and distributions of a company but also those facts which affect the probable future of the company and those which may affect the desire of investors to buy, sell, or hold the company's securities.

In each case, then, whether facts are material within Rule 10b-5 when the facts relate to a particular event and are undisclosed by those persons who are knowledgeable thereof will depend at any given time upon a balancing of both the indicated probability that the event will occur and the anticipated magnitude of the event in light of the totality of the company activity. Here, notwithstanding the trial court's conclusion that the results of the first drill core *** were "too 'remote' *** to have had any significant impact on the market, i.e., to be deemed material," [citation omitted], knowledge of the possibility, which surely was more than marginal, of the existence of a mine of the vast magnitude indicated by the remarkably rich drill core located rather close to the surface (suggesting mineability by the less expensive open-pit method) within the confines of a large anomaly (suggesting an extensive region of mineralization) might well have affected the price of TGS stock and would certainly have been an important fact to a reasonable, if speculative, investor in deciding whether he should buy, sell, or hold. After all, this first drill core was "unusually good and *** excited the interest and speculation of those who knew about it." [Citation omitted.]

***

Finally, a major factor in determining whether the K-55-1 [mineral] discovery was a material fact is the importance attached to the drilling results by those who knew about it. In view of other unrelated recent developments favorably affecting TGS, partic-ipation by an informed person in a regular stock-purchase program, or even sporadic trading by an informed person, might lend only nominal support to the inference of the materiality of the K-55-1 discovery; nevertheless, the timing by those who knew of it of their stock purchases and their purchases of short-term calls—purchases in some cases by individuals who had never before purchased calls or even TGS stock—virtually compels the inference that the insiders were influenced by the drilling results. This insider trading activity, which surely constitutes highly pertinent evidence and the only truly objective evidence of the materiality of the K-55-1 discovery, was apparently disregarded by the court below in favor of the testimony of defendants' expert witnesses, all of whom "agreed that one drill core does not establish an ore body, much less a mine," [citation omitted]. Significantly, however, the court below, *** made no finding that the insiders were motivated by any factor other than the extraordinary K-55-1 discovery when they bought their stock and their calls. No reason appears why outside investors, perhaps better acquainted with speculative modes of investment and with, in many cases, perhaps more capital at their disposal for intelligent speculation, would have been less influenced, and would not have been similarly motivated to invest if they had known what the insider investors knew about the K-55-1 discovery.

Id. at 848-51.[*]

Questions About *Texas Gulf Sulphur*

1.   This case is a famous example of the "abstain or disclose" rule, that is, that certain persons who possess material nonpublic information have two choices: (1) abstain from trading securities on the basis of that information or (2) disclose the information. *According to this case, to whom does the abstain or disclose rule apply?*

---

[*]   In *TSC Industries, Inc. v. Northway,* 426 U.S. 438 (1976), the Supreme Court ruled that, in the context of a proxy statement, an omitted fact is material if "there is a substantial likelihood that a reasonable shareholder would consider it important in deciding how to vote." In *Basic, Inc. v. Levinson,* 485 U.S. 224 (1988), the Supreme Court used a "probability/magnitude" balancing test for deciding whether a *contingent* fact is material like the test used in *Texas Gulf Sulphur.*

2.   *Was the information in this case "nonpublic"? What if the defendants had caused TGS to issue a press release about the mineral discovery and then immediately purchased shares of TGS stock?*

3.   *Was the information in this case "material"? What is the test for determining materiality?   Who makes this decision? Doesn't the fact that the TGS insiders bought stock knowing the information about the mineral strike prove that the information was material, or would that just be "bootstrapping"?*

4.   *Why didn't the defendants' actions in this case constitute common law fraud?*

B.   MODERN INSIDER TRADING LAW

As you will shortly see, the Supreme Court in the 1980s began paring back the somewhat expansive rules that had developed in cases like *Texas Gulf Sulphur.* Today, there are, generally speaking, three types of Rule 10b-5 insider trading cases: (1) "classic" insider trading, which is where an "insider" of a corporation (or other issuer) buys or sells securities of *that corporation* (or other issuer); (2) "tipper-tippee" liability; and (3) "misappropriation," which some call "outsider trading." The following three Supreme Court cases supply us with the ground rules for evaluating each of these three scenarios.

> *TERMINOLOGY*
> There are three different ways to find a defendant guilty of illegal insider trading under Rule 10b-5: *"classic" or "traditional" insider trading; tipper-tippee liability;* and *the misappropriation theory.*

Chiarella v. United States
United States Supreme Court
445 U.S. 222 (1980)

Mr. Justice Powell delivered the opinion of the Court.

The question in this case is whether a person who learns from the confidential documents of one corporation that it is planning an attempt to secure control of a second corporation violates § 10(b) of the Securities Exchange Act of

1934 if he fails to disclose the impending takeover before trading in the target company's securities.

[I]   Petitioner is a printer by trade. In 1975 and 1976, he worked as a "markup man" in the New York composing room of Pandick Press, a financial printer. Among documents that petitioner handled were five announcements of corporate takeover bids. When these documents were delivered to the printer, the identities of the acquiring and target corporations were concealed by blank spaces or false names. The true names were sent to the printer on the night of the final printing.

The petitioner, however, was able to deduce the names of the target companies before the final printing from other information contained in the documents. Without disclosing his knowledge, petitioner purchased stock in the target companies and sold the shares immediately after the takeover attempts were made public.[*] By this method, petitioner realized a gain of slightly more than $30,000 in the course of 14 months. Subsequently, the Securities and Exchange Commission (Commission or SEC) began an investigation of his trading activities. In May 1977, petitioner entered into a consent decree with the Commission in which he agreed to return his profits to the sellers of the shares. On the same day, he was discharged by Pandick Press.

In January 1978, petitioner was indicted on 17 counts of violating § 10(b) of the Securities Exchange Act of 1934 (1934 Act) and SEC Rule 10b-5. After petitioner unsuccessfully moved to dismiss the indictment, he was brought to trial and convicted on all counts.

The Court of Appeals for the Second Circuit affirmed petitioner's conviction. [Citation omitted.] We granted certiorari, [citation omitted], and we now reverse.

[II]   Section 10(b) of the 1934 Act, [15 U.S.C. § 78j], prohibits the use "in connection with the purchase or sale of any security ... [of] any manipulative or deceptive device or contrivance in contravention of such rules and regulations as the Commission may prescribe." Pursuant to this section, the SEC promulgated Rule 10b-5 ***.

This case concerns the legal effect of the petitioner's silence. The District Court's charge permitted the jury to convict the petitioner if it found that he willfully failed to inform sellers of target company securities that he knew of a forthcoming takeover bid that would make their shares more valuable. In order to

---

[*]   [Footnote by Court]: Of the five transactions, four involved tender offers and one concerned a merger. [Citation omitted.]

decide whether silence in such circumstances violates § 10(b), it is necessary to review the language and legislative history of that statute as well as its interpretation by the Commission and the federal courts.

Although the starting point of our inquiry is the language of the statute, [citation omitted], § 10(b) does not state whether silence may constitute a manipulative or deceptive device. Section 10(b) was designed as a catchall clause to prevent fraudulent practices. [Citation omitted.] But neither the legislative history nor the statute itself affords specific guidance for the resolution of this case. When Rule 10b-5 was promulgated in 1942, the SEC did not discuss the possibility that failure to provide information might run afoul of § 10(b).

The SEC took an important step in the development of § 10(b) when it held that a broker-dealer and his firm violated that section by selling securities on the basis of undisclosed information obtained from a director of the issuer corporation who was also a registered representative of the brokerage firm. In *Cady, Roberts & Co.*, [40 S.E.C. 907 (1961)], the Commission decided that a corporate insider must abstain from trading in the shares of his corporation unless he has first disclosed all material inside information known to him. The obligation to disclose or abstain derives from

> "[a]n affirmative duty to disclose material information[, which] has been traditionally imposed on corporate 'insiders,' particularly officers, directors, or controlling stockholders. We, and the courts have consistently held that insiders must disclose material facts which are known to them by virtue of their position but which are not known to persons with whom they deal and which, if known, would affect their investment judgment." [Citation omitted.]

The Commission emphasized that the duty arose from (i) the existence of a relationship affording access to inside information intended to be available only for a corporate purpose, and (ii) the unfairness of allowing a corporate insider to take advantage of that information by trading without disclosure. [Citation omitted.]*

---

* [Footnote by Court]: In *Cady, Roberts*, the broker-dealer was liable under § 10(b) because it received nonpublic information from a corporate insider of the issuer. Since the insider could not use the information, neither could the partners in the brokerage firm with which he was associated. *** The Commission embraced the reasoning of Judge Learned Hand that "the director or officer assumed a fiduciary relation to the buyer by the very sale; for it would be a sorry distinction to allow him to use the advantage of his position to induce the buyer into the position of a beneficiary although he was forbidden to do so once the buyer had become one." [Citation omitted.]

That the relationship between a corporate insider and the stockholders of his corporation gives rise to a disclosure obligation is not a novel twist of the law. At common law, misrepresentation made for the purpose of inducing reliance upon the false statement is fraudulent. But one who fails to disclose material information prior to the consummation of a transaction commits fraud only when he is under a duty to do so. And the duty to disclose arises when one party has information "that the other [party] is entitled to know because of a fiduciary or other similar relation of trust and confidence between them." [Citations omitted.] In its *Cady, Roberts* decision, the Commission recognized a relationship of trust and confidence between the shareholders of a corporation and those insiders who have obtained confidential information by reason of their position with that corporation.[*] This relationship gives rise to a duty to disclose because of the "necessity of preventing a corporate insider from ... tak[ing] unfair advantage of the uninformed minority stockholders." [Citation omitted.]

The federal courts have found violations of § 10(b) where corporate insiders used undisclosed information for their own benefit. E.g., *SEC v. Texas Gulf Sulphur Co.*, [401 F.2d 833 (2d Cir. 1968), *cert. denied*, 404 U.S. (1971)]. The cases also have emphasized, in accordance with the common-law rule, that "[t]he party charged with failing to disclose market information must be under a duty to disclose it." [Citation omitted.] Accordingly, a purchaser of stock who has no duty to a prospective seller because he is neither an insider nor a fiduciary has been held to have no obligation to reveal material facts. [Citations omitted.]

This Court followed the same approach in *Affiliated Ute Citizens v. United States*, 406 U.S. 128 (1972). A group of American Indians formed a corporation to manage joint assets derived from tribal holdings. The corporation issued stock to its Indian shareholders and designated a local bank as its transfer agent. Because of the speculative nature of the corporate assets and the difficulty of ascertaining the true value of a share, the corporation requested the bank to stress to its stockholders the importance of retaining the stock. [Citation omitted.] Two of the bank's assistant managers aided the shareholders in disposing of stock which the managers knew was traded in two separate markets—a primary market of Indians selling to non-Indians through the bank and a resale market consisting entirely of non-Indians. Indian sellers charged that the assistant managers had

---

[*]   [Footnote by Court]: *** The dissent of MR. JUSTICE BLACKMUN suggests that the "special facts" doctrine may be applied to find that silence constitutes fraud where one party has superior information to another. [Citation omitted.] This Court has never so held. In *Strong v. Reptide*, 213 U.S. 419, 431-434 (1909), this Court applied the special-facts doctrine to conclude that a corporate insider had a duty to disclose to a shareholder. In that case, the majority shareholder of a corporation secretly purchased the stock of another shareholder without revealing that the corporation, under the insider's direction, was about to sell corporate assets at a price that would greatly enhance the value of the stock. The decision in *Strong v. Reptide* was premised upon the fiduciary duty between the corporate insider and the shareholder. [Citation omitted.]

violated § 10(b) and Rule 10b-5 by failing to inform them of the higher prices prevailing in the resale market. The Court recognized that no duty of disclosure would exist if the bank merely had acted as a transfer agent. But the bank also had assumed a duty to act on behalf of the shareholders, and the Indian sellers had relied upon its personnel when they sold their stock. [Citation omitted.] Because these officers of the bank were charged with a responsibility to the shareholders, they could not act as market makers inducing the Indians to sell their stock without disclosing the existence of the more favorable non-Indian market. [Citation omitted.]

Thus, administrative and judicial interpretations have established that silence in connection with the purchase or sale of securities may operate as a fraud actionable under § 10(b) despite the absence of statutory language or legislative history specifically addressing the legality of nondisclosure. But such liability is premised upon a duty to disclose arising from a relationship of trust and confidence between parties to a transaction. Application of a duty to disclose prior to trading guarantees that corporate insiders, who have an obligation to place the shareholder's welfare before their own, will not benefit personally through fraudulent use of material, nonpublic information.

[III]   In this case, the petitioner was convicted of violating § 10(b) although he was not a corporate insider and he received no confidential information from the target company. Moreover, the "market information" upon which he relied did not concern the earning power or operations of the target company, but only the plans of the acquiring company. Petitioner's use of that information was not a fraud under § 10(b) unless he was subject to an affirmative duty to disclose it before trading. In this case, the jury instructions failed to specify any such duty. In effect, the trial court instructed the jury that petitioner owed a duty to everyone; to all sellers, indeed, to the market as a whole. The jury simply was told to decide whether petitioner used material, nonpublic information at a time when "he knew other people trading in the securities market did not have access to the same information." [Citation omitted.]

The Court of Appeals affirmed the conviction by holding that "*[a]nyone—* corporate insider or not—who regularly receives material nonpublic information may not use that information to trade in securities without incurring an affirmative duty to disclose." [Citation omitted (emphasis in original).] Although the court said that its test would include only persons who regularly receive material, nonpublic information, [citation omitted], its rationale for that limitation is unrelated to the existence of a duty to disclose.[*] The Court of Appeals, like the

---

[*]   [Footnote by Court]: The Court of Appeals said that its "regular access to market information" test would create a workable rule embracing "those who occupy ... strategic places in the market mechanism." [Citation omitted.] These considerations are insufficient to support a duty to disclose. A duty arises from the relationship between parties, [citation

trial court, failed to identify a relationship between petitioner and the sellers that could give rise to a duty. Its decision thus rested solely upon its belief that the federal securities laws have "created a system providing equal access to information necessary for reasoned and intelligent investment decisions." [Citation omitted.] The use by anyone of material information not generally available is fraudulent, this theory suggests, because such information gives certain buyers or sellers an unfair advantage over less informed buyers and sellers.

This reasoning suffers from two defects. First, not every instance of financial unfairness constitutes fraudulent activity under § 10(b). [Citation omitted.] Second, the element required to make silence fraudulent—a duty to disclose—is absent in this case. No duty could arise from petitioner's relationship with the sellers of the target company's securities, for petitioner had no prior dealings with them. He was not their agent, he was not a fiduciary, he was not a person in whom the sellers had placed their trust and confidence. He was, in fact, a complete stranger who dealt with the sellers only through impersonal market transactions.

We cannot affirm petitioner's conviction without recognizing a general duty between all participants in market transactions to forgo actions based on material, nonpublic information. Formulation of such a broad duty, which departs radically from the established doctrine that duty arises from a specific relationship between two parties, [citation omitted], should not be undertaken absent some explicit evidence of congressional intent.

As we have seen, no such evidence emerges from the language or legislative history of § 10(b). Moreover, neither the Congress nor the Commission ever has adopted a parity-of-information rule. Instead the problems caused by misuse of market information have been addressed by detailed and sophisticated regulation that recognizes when use of market information may not harm operation of the securities markets. For example, [Section 14(d) of the Securities Exchange Act] limits but does not completely prohibit a tender offeror's purchases of target corporation stock before public announcement of the offer. Congress' careful action in this and other areas contrasts, and is in some tension, with the broad rule of liability we are asked to adopt in this case.

Indeed, the theory upon which the petitioner was convicted is at odds with the Commission's view of § 10(b) as applied to activity that has the same effect on sellers as the petitioner's purchases. "Warehousing" takes place when a corp-oration gives advance notice of its intention to launch a tender offer to institutional investors who then are able to purchase stock in the target company before the

---

omitted], and not merely from one's ability to acquire information because of his position in the market. ***

tender offer is made public and the price of shares rises. In this case, as in warehousing, a buyer of securities purchases stock in a target corporation on the basis of market information which is unknown to the seller. In both of these situations, the seller's behavior presumably would be altered if he had the nonpublic information. Significantly, however, [by proposing Rule 14e-3 under the Securities Exchange Act,] the Commission has acted to bar warehousing under its authority to regulate tender offers after recognizing that action under § 10(b) would rest on a "somewhat different theory" than that previously used to regulate insider trading as fraudulent activity. [Citation omitted.]

We see no basis for applying such a new and different theory of liability in this case. As we have emphasized before, the 1934 Act cannot be read "'more broadly than its language and the statutory scheme reasonably permit.'" [Citations omitted.] Section 10(b) is aptly described as a catchall provision, but what it catches must be fraud. When an allegation of fraud is based upon nondisclosure, there can be no fraud absent a duty to speak. We hold that a duty to disclose under § 10(b) does not arise from the mere possession of nonpublic market information. The contrary result is without support in the legislative history of § 10(b) and would be inconsistent with the careful plan that Congress has enacted for regulation of the securities markets. [Citation omitted.]

[IV]   In its brief to this Court, the United States offers an alternative theory to support petitioner's conviction. It argues that petitioner breached a duty to the acquiring corporation when he acted upon information that he obtained by virtue of his position as an employee of a printer employed by the corporation. The breach of this duty is said to support a conviction under § 10(b) for fraud perpetrated upon both the acquiring corporation and the sellers.

We need not decide whether this theory has merit for it was not submitted to the jury. The jury was told, in the language of Rule 10b-5, that it could convict the petitioner if it concluded that he either (i) employed a device, scheme, or artifice to defraud or (ii) engaged in an act, practice, or course of business which operated or would operate as a fraud or deceit upon any person. [Citation omitted.] The trial judge stated that a "scheme to defraud" is a plan to obtain money by trick or deceit and that "a failure by Chiarella to disclose material, non-public information in connection with his purchase of stock would constitute deceit." [Citation omitted.] Accordingly, the jury was instructed that the petitioner employed a scheme to defraud if he "did not disclose ... material nonpublic information in connection with the purchases of the stock." [Citation omitted.]

Alternatively, the jury was instructed that it could convict if "Chiarella's alleged conduct of having purchased securities without disclosing material, non-public information would have or did have the effect of operating as a fraud upon a seller." [Citation omitted.] The judge earlier had stated that fraud "embraces all the means which human ingenuity can devise and which are resorted to by one individual to gain an advantage over another by false misrepresentation, suggestions or by suppression of the truth." [Citation omitted.]

The jury instructions demonstrate that petitioner was convicted merely because of his failure to disclose material, non-public information to sellers from whom he bought the stock of target corporations. The jury was not instructed on the nature or elements of a duty owed by petitioner to anyone other than the sellers. Because we cannot affirm a criminal conviction on the basis of a theory not presented to the jury, [citation omitted], we will not speculate upon whether such a duty exists, whether it has been breached or whether such a breach constitutes a violation of § 10(b). [Reversed.]

***

MR. CHIEF JUSTICE BURGER, dissenting.

I believe that the jury instructions in this case properly charged a violation of § 10(b) and Rule 10b-5, and I would affirm the conviction.

[I]   As a general rule, neither party to an arm's-length business transaction has an obligation to disclose information to the other unless the parties stand in some confidential or fiduciary relation. [Citation omitted.] This rule permits a businessman to capitalize on his experience and skill in securing and evaluating relevant information; it provides incentive for hard work, careful analysis, and astute forecasting. But the policies that underlie the rule also should limit its scope. In particular, the rule should give way when an informational

---

[Footnote by Court]: The dissent of THE CHIEF JUSTICE relies upon a single phrase from the jury instructions, which states that the petitioner held a "confidential position" at Pandick Press, to argue that the jury was properly instructed on the theory "that a person who has misappropriated nonpublic information has an absolute duty to disclose that information or to refrain from trading." [Citation omitted.] The few words upon which this thesis is based do not explain to the jury the nature and scope of the petitioner's duty to his employer, the nature and scope of petitioner's duty, if any, to the acquiring corporation, or the elements of the tort of misappropriation. Nor do the jury instructions suggest that a "confidential position" is a necessary element of the offense for which petitioner was charged. Thus, we do not believe that a "misappropriation" theory was included in the jury instructions.

The conviction would have to be reversed even if the jury had been instructed that it could convict the petitioner either (1) because of his failure to disclose material, nonpublic information to sellers or (2) because of a breach of a duty to the acquiring corporation. We may not uphold a criminal conviction if it is impossible to ascertain whether the defendant has been punished for noncriminal conduct. [Citations omitted.]

advantage is obtained, not by superior experience, foresight, or industry, but by some unlawful means. ***

I would read § 10(b) and Rule 10b-5 *** to mean that a person who has misappropriated nonpublic information has an absolute duty to disclose that information or to refrain from trading.

***

[II]   The Court's opinion, as I read it, leaves open the question whether § 10(b) and Rule 10b-5 prohibit trading on misappropriated nonpublic information.[*] Instead, the Court apparently concludes that this theory of the case was not submitted to the jury. In the Court's view, the instructions given the jury were premised on the erroneous notion that the mere failure to disclose nonpublic information, however acquired, is a deceptive practice. And because of this premise, the jury was not instructed that the means by which Chiarella acquired his informational advantage—by violating a duty owed to the acquiring companies—was an element of the offense.

The Court's reading of the District Court's charge is unduly restrictive. Fairly read as a whole and in the context of the trial, the instructions required the jury to find that Chiarella obtained his trading advantage by misappropriating the property of his employer's customers. The jury was charged that "[i]n simple terms, the charge is that Chiarella wrongfully took advantage of information he acquired *in the course of his confidential position at Pandick Press* and secretly used that information when he knew other people trading in the securities market did not have access to the same information that he had at a time when he knew that that information was material to the value of the stock." [Citation omitted (emphasis added).] The language parallels that in the indictment, and the jury had that indictment during its deliberations; it charged that Chiarella had traded "without disclosing the material non-public information he had obtained in connection with his employment." It is underscored by the clarity which the prosecutor exhibited in his opening statement to the jury. No juror could possibly have failed to understand what the case was about after the prosecutor said: "In sum what the indictment charges is that Chiarella misused material non-public information for personal gain and that he took unfair advantage of his position of trust with the full knowledge that it was wrong to do so. That is what the case is

---

[*]   [Footnote by Justice Berger]: There is some language in the Court's opinion to suggest that only "a relationship between petitioner and the sellers ... could give rise to a duty [to disclose]." [Citation omitted.] The Court's holding, however, is much more limited, namely, that mere possession of material, nonpublic information is insufficient to create a duty to disclose or to refrain from trading. [Citation omitted.] Accordingly, it is my understanding that the Court has not rejected the view, advanced above, that an absolute duty to disclose or refrain arises from the very act of misappropriating nonpublic information.

about. It is that simple." [Citation omitted.] Moreover, experienced defense counsel took no exception and uttered no complaint that the instructions were inadequate in this regard.

***

In sum, the evidence shows beyond all doubt that Chiarella, working literally in the shadows of the warning signs in the printshop, misappropriated— stole to put it bluntly—valuable nonpublic information entrusted to him in the utmost confidence. He then exploited his ill-gotten informational advantage by purchasing securities in the market. In my view, such conduct plainly violates § 10(b) and Rule 10b-5. Accordingly, I would affirm the judgment of the Court of Appeals.

[Opinions of other Justices omitted.]

Questions About *Chiarella*

1.   Mr. Chiarella figured out the identities of target corporations in tender offers before the tender offers were announced. Which corporations' stock did he buy—the target corporations or the acquiring corporations?

2.   Mr. Chiarella worked for the Pandick Press, which printed tender offer documents. Which corporations were clients of Pandick Press——the target corporations or the acquiring corporations?

3.   The Supreme Court found that Chiarella didn't have an abstain-or-disclose duty under the circumstances of this case. But when would someone have such a duty?

4.   Is this case consistent with the *Texas Gulf Sulphur* case?

5.   Why didn't the Supreme Court uphold Mr. Chiarella's convictions based on the "misappropriation" theory?

6.   Assume that some of the acquiring corporations in *Chiarella* had purchased shares of the target corporations' stock before the tender offers were announced. Would that have been a Rule 10b-5 violation?

Chiarella can be read as an example of the "classic" theory of insider trading (or, because Mr. Chiarella was not actually guilty of a Rule 10b-5 violation, perhaps a non-example). Under this theory, an "insider" who has a *Cady, Roberts* duty to the corporation (or other issuer) buys or sells securities of that corporation on the basis of material nonpublic information and uses "jurisdictional means" in doing so.

But there are other things that someone may do with material nonpublic information besides buying or selling securities *for herself* on the basis of that information. She could, perhaps, give the information to someone else. At this point, you might be tempted to call these persons a "tipper" and a "tippee," and conclude that they are both guilty of Rule 10b-5 violations. Not so fast. The rules for whether someone is a "tipper" and someone else is a "tippee" are more complicated than that, as you will see in the second of the important trilogy of Supreme Court insider-trading cases set forth below.

Dirks v. Securities and Exchange Commission
United States Supreme Court
463 U.S. 646 (1983)

Justice Powell delivered the opinion of the Court.

Petitioner Raymond Dirks received material nonpublic information from "insiders" of a corporation with which he had no connection. He disclosed this information to investors who relied on it in trading in the shares of the corporation. The question is whether Dirks violated the antifraud provisions of the federal securities laws by this disclosure.

[I]   In 1973, Dirks was an officer of a New York broker-dealer firm who specialized in providing investment analysis of insurance company securities to institutional investors. On March 6, Dirks received information from Ronald Secrist, a former officer of Equity Funding of America. Secrist alleged that the assets of Equity Funding, a diversified corporation primarily engaged in selling life insurance and mutual funds, were vastly overstated as the result of fraudulent corporate practices. Secrist also stated that various regulatory agencies had failed to act on similar charges made by Equity Funding employees. He urged Dirks to verify the fraud and disclose it publicly.

Dirks decided to investigate the allegations. He visited Equity Funding's headquarters in Los Angeles and interviewed several officers and employees of the corporation. The senior management denied any wrongdoing, but certain corporation employees corroborated the charges of fraud. Neither Dirks nor his firm owned or traded any Equity Funding stock, but throughout his investigation he openly discussed the information he had obtained with a number of clients and investors. Some of these persons sold their holdings of Equity Funding securities, including five investment advisers who liquidated holdings of more than $16 million.[*]

While Dirks was in Los Angeles, he was in touch regularly with William Blundell, the *Wall Street Journal*'s Los Angeles bureau chief. Dirks urged Blundell to write a story on the fraud allegations. Blundell did not believe, however, that such a massive fraud could go undetected and declined to write the story. He feared that publishing such damaging hearsay might be libelous.

During the 2-week period in which Dirks pursued his investigation and spread word of Secrist's charges, the price of Equity Funding stock fell from $26 per share to less than $15 per share. This led the New York Stock Exchange to halt trading on March 27. Shortly thereafter California insurance authorities impounded Equity Funding's records and uncovered evidence of the fraud. Only then did the Securities and Exchange Commission (SEC) file a complaint against Equity Funding and only then, on April 2, did the Wall Street Journal publish a front-page story based largely on information assembled by Dirks. Equity Funding immediately went into receivership.

The SEC began an investigation into Dirks' role in the exposure of the fraud. After a hearing by an Administrative Law Judge, the SEC found that Dirks had aided and abetted violations of § 17(a) of the Securities Act of 1933, [15 U.S.C. § 77q(a)], § 10(b) of the Securities Exchange Act of 1934, [15 U.S.C. § 78j(b)], and SEC Rule 10b-5, [17 C.F.R. § 240.10b-5 (1983)], by repeating the allegations of fraud to members of the investment community who later sold their Equity Funding stock. The SEC concluded: "Where 'tippees' —regardless of their motivation or occupation—come into possession of material 'corporate information that they know is confidential and know or should know came from a corporate insider,' they must either publicly disclose that information or refrain from trading." [Citation omitted.] Recognizing, however, that Dirks "played an important role in bringing [Equity Funding's] massive fraud to light," [citation omitted], the SEC only censured him.

Dirks sought review in the Court of Appeals for the District of Columbia Circuit. The court entered judgment against Dirks "for the reasons stated by the Commission in its opinion." [Citation omitted.] ***

---

[*]   [Footnote by Court]: Dirks received from his firm a salary plus a commission for securities transactions above a certain amount that his clients directed through his firm. [Citation omitted.] But "[i]t is not clear how many of those with whom Dirks spoke promised to direct some brokerage business through [Dirks' firm] to compensate Dirks, or how many actually did so." [Citation omitted.] The Boston Company Institutional Investors, Inc., promised Dirks about $25,000 in commissions, but it is unclear whether Boston actually generated any brokerage business for his firm. [Citations omitted.]

In view of the importance to the SEC and to the securities industry of the question presented by this case, we granted a writ of certiorari. [Citation omitted.] We now reverse.

[II]   In the seminal case of *In re Cady, Roberts & Co.*, [40 S.E.C. 907 (1961)], the SEC recognized that the common law in some jurisdictions imposes on "corporate 'insiders,'" particularly officers, directors, or controlling stockholders" an "affirmative duty of disclosure ... when dealing in securities." [Citation omitted.] The SEC found that not only did breach of this common-law duty also establish the elements of a Rule 10b-5 violation, but that individuals other than corporate insiders could be obligated either to disclose material nonpublic information[*] before trading or to abstain from trading altogether. [Citation omitted.] In *Chiarella*, we accepted the two elements set out in *Cady, Roberts* for establishing a Rule 10b-5 violation: "(i) the existence of a relationship affording access to inside information intended to be available only for a corporate purpose, and (ii) the unfairness of allowing a corporate insider to take advantage of that information by trading without disclosure." [Citation omitted.] In examining whether Chiarella had an obligation to disclose or abstain, the Court found that there is no general duty to disclose before trading on material nonpublic information, and held that "a duty to disclose under § 10(b) does not arise from the mere possession of nonpublic market information." [Citation omitted.] Such a duty arises rather from the existence of a fiduciary relationship. [Citation omitted.]

Not "all breaches of fiduciary duty in connection with a securities transaction," however, come within the ambit of Rule 10b-5. [Citation omitted.] There must also be "manipulation or deception." [Citation omitted.] In an inside-trading case this fraud derives from the "inherent unfairness involved where one takes advantage" of "information intended to be available only for a corporate purpose and not for the personal benefit of anyone." [Citation omitted.] Thus, an insider will be liable under Rule 10b-5 for inside trading only where he fails to disclose material nonpublic information before trading on it and thus makes "secret profits." [Citation omitted.]

[III]   We were explicit in *Chiarella* in saying that there can be no duty to disclose where the person who has traded on inside information "was not [the corporation's] agent, ... was not a fiduciary, [or] was not a person in whom the sellers [of the securities] had placed their trust and confidence." [Citation

---

[*]   [Footnote by Court]: The SEC views the disclosure duty as requiring more than disclosure to purchasers or sellers: "Proper and adequate disclosure of significant corporate developments can only be effected by a public release through the appropriate public media, designed to achieve a broad dissemination to the investing public generally and without favoring any special person or group." [Citation omitted.]

omitted.]   Not to require such a fiduciary relationship, we recognized, would "depar[t] radically from the established doctrine that duty arises from a specific relationship between two parties" and would amount to "recognizing a general duty between all participants in market transactions to forgo actions based on material, nonpublic information."   [Citation omitted.]   This requirement of a specific relationship between the shareholders and the individual trading on inside information has created analytical difficulties for the SEC and courts in policing tippees who trade on inside information.   Unlike insiders who have independent fiduciary duties to both the corporation and its shareholders, the typical tippee has no such relationships.[*]   In view of this absence, it has been unclear how a tippee acquires the *Cady, Roberts* duty to refrain from trading on inside information.

[III.A]   The SEC's position, as stated in its opinion in this case, is that a tippee "inherits" the *Cady, Roberts* obligation to shareholders whenever he receives inside information from an insider:

> "In tipping potential traders, Dirks breached a duty which he had assumed as a result of knowingly receiving confidential information from [Equity Funding] insiders.   Tippees such as Dirks who receive non-public, material information from insiders become 'subject to the same duty as [the] insiders.'   [Citation omitted.]   Such a tippee breaches the fiduciary duty which he assumes from the insider when the tippee knowingly transmits the information to someone who will probably trade on the basis thereof. ...   Presumably, Dirks' informants were entitled to disclose the [Equity Funding] fraud in order to bring it to light and its perpetrators to justice.   However, Dirks—standing in their shoes— committed a breach of the fiduciary duty which he had assumed in dealing with them, when he passed the information on to traders."   [Citation omitted.]

This view differs little from the view that we rejected as inconsistent with congressional intent in *Chiarella*.   In that case, the Court of Appeals agreed with the SEC and affirmed Chiarella's conviction, holding that "*[a]nyone*—corporate

---

[*]   [Footnote #14 by Court]:   Under certain circumstances, such as where corporate information is revealed legitimately to an underwriter, accountant, lawyer, or consultant working for the corporation, these outsiders may become fiduciaries of the shareholders.   The basis for recognizing this fiduciary duty is not simply that such persons acquired nonpublic corporate information, but rather that they have entered into a special confidential relationship in the conduct of the business of the enterprise and are given access to information solely for corporate purposes.   [Citations omitted.]   When such a person breaches his fiduciary relationship, he may be treated more properly as a tipper than a tippee.   [Citation omitted.]   For such a duty to be imposed, however, the corporation must expect the outsider to keep the disclosed nonpublic information confidential, and the relationship at least must imply such a duty.

insider or not—who regularly receives material nonpublic information may not use that information to trade in securities without incurring an affirmative duty to disclose." [Citation omitted (emphasis in original).] Here, the SEC maintains that anyone who knowingly receives nonpublic material information from an insider has a fiduciary duty to disclose before trading.[*]

In effect, the SEC's theory of tippee liability in both cases appears rooted in the idea that the antifraud provisions require equal information among all traders. This conflicts with the principle set forth in *Chiarella* that only some persons, under some circumstances, will be barred from trading while in possession of material nonpublic information. Judge Wright [, in the court below,] correctly read our opinion in *Chiarella* as repudiating any notion that all traders must enjoy equal information before trading: "[T]he 'information' theory is rejected. Because the disclose-or-refrain duty is extraordinary, it attaches only when a party has legal obligations other than a mere duty to comply with the general antifraud proscriptions in the federal securities laws." [Citations omitted.] We reaffirm today that "[a] duty [to disclose] arises from the relationship between parties ... and not merely from one's ability to acquire information because of his position in the market." [Citation omitted.]

Imposing a duty to disclose or abstain solely because a person knowingly receives material nonpublic information from an insider and trades on it could have an inhibiting influence on the role of market analysts, which the SEC itself recognizes is necessary to the preservation of a healthy market. It is commonplace for analysts to "ferret out and analyze information," [citation omitted], and this often is done by meeting with and questioning corporate officers and others who are insiders. And information that the analysts obtain normally may be the basis for judgments as to the market worth of a corporation's securities. The analyst's

---

[*] [Footnote by Court]: Apparently, the SEC believes this case differs from *Chiarella* in that Dirks' receipt of inside information from Secrist, an insider, carried Secrist's duties with it, while Chiarella received the information without the direct involvement of an insider and thus inherited no duty to disclose or abstain. The SEC fails to explain, however, why the receipt of nonpublic information from an insider automatically carries with it the fiduciary duty of the insider. As we emphasized in *Chiarella*, mere possession of nonpublic information does not give rise to a duty to disclose or abstain; only a specific relationship does that. And we do not believe that the mere receipt of information from an insider creates such a special relationship between the tippee and the corporation's shareholders.

Apparently recognizing the weakness of its argument in light of *Chiarella*, the SEC attempts to distinguish that case factually as involving not "inside" information, but rather "market" information, i.e., "information originating outside the company and usually about the supply and demand for the company's securities." [Citation omitted.] This Court drew no such distinction in *Chiarella* and, as THE CHIEF JUSTICE noted, "[i]t is clear that § 10(b) and Rule 10b-5 by their terms and by their history make no such distinction." [Citations omitted.]

judgment in this respect is made available in market letters or otherwise to clients of the firm. It is the nature of this type of information, and indeed of the markets themselves, that such information cannot be made simultaneously available to all of the corporation's stockholders or the public generally.

[III.B] The conclusion that recipients of inside information do not invariably acquire a duty to disclose or abstain does not mean that such tippees always are free to trade on the information. The need for a ban on some tippee trading is clear. Not only are insiders forbidden by their fiduciary relationship from personally using undisclosed corporate information to their advantage, but they also may not give such information to an outsider for the same improper purpose of exploiting the information for their personal gain. [Citation omitted.] Similarly, the transactions of those who knowingly participate with the fiduciary in such a breach are "as forbidden" as transactions "on behalf of the trustee himself." [Citations omitted.] *** [A] contrary rule "would open up opportunities for devious dealings in the name of others that the trustee could not conduct in his own." [Citations omitted.] Thus, the tippee's duty to disclose or abstain is derivative from that of the insider's duty. [Citations omitted.] As we noted in *Chiarella*, "[t]he tippee's obligation has been viewed as arising from his role as a participant after the fact in the insider's breach of a fiduciary duty." [Citation omitted.]

Thus, some tippees must assume an insider's duty to the shareholders not because they receive inside information, but rather because it has been made available to them improperly. And for Rule 10b-5 purposes, the insider's disclosure is improper only where it would violate his *Cady, Roberts* duty. Thus, a tippee assumes a fiduciary duty to the shareholders of a corporation not to trade on material nonpublic information only when the insider has breached his fiduciary duty to the shareholders by disclosing the information to the tippee and the tippee knows or should know that there has been a breach. As [SEC] Commissioner Smith perceptively observed [a prior SEC proceeding]: "[T]ippee responsibility must be related back to insider responsibility by a necessary finding that the tippee knew the information was given to him in breach of a duty by a person having a special relationship to the issuer not to disclose the information ...." [Citation omitted.] Tipping thus properly is viewed only as a means of indirectly violating the *Cady, Roberts* disclose-or-abstain rule.

[III.C] In determining whether a tippee is under an obligation to disclose or abstain, it thus is necessary to determine whether the insider's "tip" constituted a breach of the insider's fiduciary duty. All disclosures of confidential corporate information are not inconsistent with the duty insiders owe to shareholders. In contrast to the extraordinary facts of this case, the more typical situation in which there will be a question whether disclosure violates the insider's *Cady, Roberts* duty is when insiders disclose information to analysts. [Citation omitted.] In some situations, the insider will act consistently with his fiduciary duty to share-holders, and yet release of the information may affect the market. For example, it may not be clear—either to the corporate insider or to the recipient analyst—whether the information will be viewed as material nonpublic information. Corporate officials may mistakenly think the information already has been disclosed or that it is not material enough to affect the market. Whether disclosure is a breach of duty therefore depends in large part on the purpose of the disclosure. This standard was identified by the SEC itself in *Cady, Roberts*: a purpose of the securities laws was to eliminate "use of inside information for personal advantage." [Citation omitted.] Thus, the test is whether the insider personally will benefit, directly or indirectly, from his disclosure. Absent some personal gain, there has been no breach of duty to stockholders. And absent a breach by the insider, there is no derivative breach. ***

The SEC argues that, if inside-trading liability does not exist when the information is transmitted for a proper purpose but is used for trading, it would be a rare situation when the parties could not fabricate some ostensibly legitimate business justification for transmitting the information. We think the SEC is unduly concerned. In determining whether the insider's purpose in making a particular disclosure is fraudulent, the SEC and the courts are not required to read the parties' minds. Scienter in some cases is relevant in determining whether the tipper has violated his *Cady, Roberts* duty.* But to determine whether the disclosure itself "deceive[s], manipulate[s], or defraud[s]" shareholders, [citation omitted], the initial inquiry is whether there has been a breach of duty by the insider. This requires courts to focus on objective criteria, i.e., whether the insider receives a direct or indirect personal benefit from the disclosure, such as a pecuniary gain or a reputational benefit that will translate into future earnings. [Citations omitted.] There are objective facts and circumstances that often justify such an inference. For example, there may be a relationship between the insider and the recipient that suggests a quid pro quo from the latter, or an intention to benefit the particular recipient. The elements of fiduciary duty and exploitation of nonpublic information also exist when an insider makes a gift of confidential

---

*   [Footnote by Court]:   Scienter—"a mental state embracing intent to deceive, manipulate, or defraud," [citation omitted]—is an independent element of a Rule 10b-5 violation. [Citation omitted.] *** [M]otivation is not irrelevant to the issue of scienter. It is not enough that an insider's conduct results in harm to investors; rather, a violation may be found only where there is "intentional or willful conduct designed to deceive or defraud investors by controlling or artificially affecting the price of securities." [Citation omitted.] The issue in this case, however, is not whether Secrist or Dirks acted with scienter, but rather whether there was any deceptive or fraudulent conduct at all, i.e., whether Secrist's disclosure constituted a breach of his fiduciary duty and thereby caused injury to shareholders. [Citation omitted.] Only if there was such a breach did Dirks, a tippee, acquire a fiduciary duty to disclose or abstain.

information to a trading relative or friend. The tip and trade resemble trading by the insider himself followed by a gift of the profits to the recipient.

Determining whether an insider personally benefits from a particular disclosure, a question of fact, will not always be easy for courts. But it is essential, we think, to have a guiding principle for those whose daily activities must be limited and instructed by the SEC's inside-trading rules, and we believe that there must be a breach of the insider's fiduciary duty before the tippee inherits the duty to disclose or abstain. In contrast, the rule adopted by the SEC in this case would have no limiting principle.

[IV]   Under the inside-trading and tipping rules set forth above, we find that there was no actionable violation by Dirks.* It is undisputed that Dirks himself was a stranger to Equity Funding, with no pre-existing fiduciary duty to its shareholders. He took no action, directly or indirectly, that induced the shareholders or officers of Equity Funding to repose trust or confidence in him. There was no expectation by Dirks' sources that he would keep their information in confidence. Nor did Dirks misappropriate or illegally obtain the information about Equity Funding. Unless the insiders breached their *Cady, Roberts* duty to shareholders in disclosing the nonpublic information to Dirks, he breached no duty when he passed it on to investors as well as to the *Wall Street Journal*.

It is clear that neither Secrist nor the other Equity Funding employees violated their *Cady, Roberts* duty to the corporation's shareholders by providing information to Dirks. The tippers received no monetary or personal benefit for revealing Equity Funding's secrets, nor was their purpose to make a gift of valuable information to Dirks. As the facts of this case clearly indicate, the tippers were motivated by a desire to expose the fraud. [Citation omitted.] In the absence of a breach of duty to shareholders by the insiders, there was no derivative breach by Dirks. [Citation omitted.] Dirks therefore could not have been "a participant after the fact in [an] insider's breach of a fiduciary duty." [Citation omitted.]

---

*   [Footnote by Court]: Dirks contends that he was not a "tippee" because the information he received constituted unverified allegations of fraud that were denied by management and were not "material facts" under the securities laws that required disclosure before trading. He also argues that the information he received was not truly "inside" information, i.e., intended for a confidential corporate purpose, but was merely evidence of a crime. The Solicitor General agrees. [Citation omitted.] We need not decide, however, whether the information constituted "material facts," or whether information concerning corporate crime is properly characterized as "inside information." For purposes of deciding this case, we assume the correctness of the SEC's findings, accepted by the Court of Appeals, that petitioner was a tippee of material inside information.

[V]   We conclude that Dirks, in the circumstances of this case, had no duty to abstain from use of the inside information that he obtained. The judgment of the Court of Appeals therefore is

Reversed.

JUSTICE BLACKMUN, with whom JUSTICE BRENNAN and JUSTICE MARSHALL join, dissenting. [Omitted.]

Questions About *Dirks*

1.   *Did Secrist have a* Cady, Roberts *duty to Equity Funding? Why or why not?*

2.   *Secrist passed along material nonpublic information to Dirks. Was Secrist a "tipper" for purposes of Rule 10b-5? Why or why not?*

3.   *Dirks received material information from Secrist and then told the information to some of his clients, who then sold Equity Funding Stock. Was Dirks a tippee and then a "sub-tipper"? Why or why not? Would your answer be different if none of Dirks's clients had sold Equity Funding stock? Would your answer be different if an alleged tippee had never heard of insider trading law?*

4.   *Is it possible for a "tipper" to be convicted under Rule 10b-5 but not her "tippee"?*

5.   *Is it possible for a "tipp**ee**" to be convicted under Rule 10b-5 but not her "tipp**er**"?*

Problems

Problem 14-3: Big Pharma Corp. ("BPC") manufactures pre-scripttion drugs and has been developing a new AIDS vaccine for several years. However, BPC's president, Jim Pirotta, recently received notice from the Food and Drug Administration ("FDA") that it would not approve the AIDS vaccine. Shortly thereafter, Jim told his daughter Veronica to sell her BPC stock. Veronica sold 10,000 shares of BPC stock before BPC publicly announced that its AIDS vaccine would not receive FDA approval. *Did Jim violate Rule 10b-5? Did Veronica violate Rule 10b-5?*

Problem 14-4:   Same facts as Problem 14-3.   In addition, Jim telephoned BPC's law firm, Jones Winthrop & McGillicutty, and told a partner there, Samantha Jones, about the bad news and asked her whether BPC could appeal the FDA's decision.   Samantha, who happened to own some BPC stock, then sold 5,000 shares before BPC publicly announced that its AIDS vaccine would not receive FDA approval.   *Did Jim violate Rule 10b-5?   Did Samantha violate Rule 10b-5?*

Problem 14-5:   Same facts as Problem 14-3.   While walking down the street after work that evening, Jim called his wife Pam on his cell phone and told her about the bad news.   (Pam did not sell any BPC shares afterwards.)   Unbeknownst to Jim, a passerby, Steve, heard this conversation.   The next morning, Steve "shorted" 1,000 shares of BPC stock before BPC publicly announced that its AIDS vaccine would not receive FDA approval.   *Did Jim violate Rule 10b-5?   Did Steve violate Rule 10b-5?*

As mentioned above, the third theory of Rule 10b-5 liability is the misappropriation theory.   Before *United States v. O'Hagan*, which is set forth below, the SEC has unsuccessfully attempted to convince courts to adopt this theory.   For example, in *Carpenter v. United States*, 484 U.S. 19 (1987), the Supreme Court upheld the petitioner's convictions under securities laws by a four-to-four vote, and also unanimously upheld his convictions under federal mail fraud statutes.   Because the securities-law-based portion of the opinion produced a "tie," it had no precedential value.   Nonetheless, it is interesting.

Carpenter involved a reporter, R. Foster Winans, who wrote a column for *The Wall Street Journal* called "Heard on the Street."   In this column, he often commented on publicly traded companies (but using only publicly available information).   However, because the column was widely read it could affect companies' stock prices.   For example, if Winans had positive things to say about a given company, that company's stock price might rise as a result.   Here's where things get interesting.   As recounted by the Court:

> official policy and practice at the *[Wall Street Journal]* was that prior to publication, the contents of the column were the Journal's confidential information.   Despite the rule, with which Winans was familiar, he entered into a scheme in October 1983 with Peter

Brant and petitioner [Kenneth] Felis, both connected with the Kidder Peabody brokerage firm in New York City, to give them advance information as to the timing and contents of the "Heard" column. This permitted Brant and Felis and another conspirator, David Clark, a client of Brant, to buy or sell based on the probable impact of the column on the market. Profits were to be shared. The conspirators agreed that the scheme would not affect the journalistic purity of the "Heard" column, and the District Court did not find that the contents of any of the articles were altered to further the profit potential of petitioners' stock-trading scheme. [Citation omitted.] Over a 4-month period, the brokers made prepublication trades on the basis of information given them by Winans about the contents of some 27 "Heard" columns. The net profits from these trades were about $690,000.

Id. at 23. Winans and Carpenter (who was Winans's roommate) then confessed to the SEC and Brant pleaded guilty. Felis and Winans were tried and convicted of violating Rule 10b-5 and federal mail fraud statutes, and Carpenter was found guilty of aiding and abetting the violations.

Now, you may wonder, *how* did the court convict these persons of a Rule 10b-5 violation? Could it have been "classic" insider trading? Were they "tippers" and "tippees"? After reading *Chiarella* and *Dirks* above, you should understand why these arguments would not have worked for the prosecution in the 1980s. Instead:

[t]he District Court found, and the Court of Appeals agreed, that Winans had knowingly breached a duty of confidentiality by misappropriating prepublication information regarding the timing and contents of the "Heard" column, information that had been gained in the course of his employment under the understanding that it would not be revealed in advance of publication and that if it were, he would report it to his employer. *** [T]he courts below held that the deliberate breach of Winans' duty of confidentiality and concealment of the scheme was a fraud and deceit on the Journal. Although the victim of the fraud, the Journal, was not a buyer or seller of the stocks traded in or otherwise a market participant, the fraud was nevertheless considered to be "in connection with" a purchase or sale of securities within the meaning of the statute and the rule. The courts reasoned that the scheme's sole purpose was to buy and sell securities at a profit based on advance information of the column's contents. The courts below rejected petitioners' submission *** that criminal liability could not be imposed on petitioners under Rule 10b-5 because "the

newspaper is the only alleged victim of fraud and has no interest in the securities traded."

Id. at 23-24.

Again, however, because the Supreme Court evenly split on this issue, the misappropriation theory was left in a sort of legal limbo. In the years that followed, some federal courts accepted the misappropriation theory and others rejected it. In 1997, the Supreme Court had an opportunity to consider the misappropriation theory in the following case:

United States v. O'Hagan
United States Supreme Court
521 U.S. 642 (1997)

Justice Ginsburg delivered the opinion of the Court.

***

[I]   Respondent James Herman O'Hagan was a partner in the law firm of Dorsey & Whitney in Minneapolis, Minnesota. In July 1988, Grand Metropolitan PLC (Grand Met), a company based in London, England, retained Dorsey & Whitney as local counsel to represent Grand Met regarding a potential tender offer for the common stock of the Pillsbury Company, headquartered in Minneapolis. Both Grand Met and Dorsey & Whitney took precautions to protect the confidentiality of Grand Met's tender offer plans. O'Hagan did no work on the Grand Met representation. Dorsey & Whitney withdrew from representing Grand Met on September 9, 1988. Less than a month later, on October 4, 1988, Grand Met publicly announced its tender offer for Pillsbury stock.

On August 18, 1988, while Dorsey & Whitney was still representing Grand Met, O'Hagan began purchasing call options for Pillsbury stock. Each option gave him the right to purchase 100 shares of Pillsbury stock by a specified date in September 1988. Later in August and in September, O'Hagan made additional purchases of Pillsbury call options. By the end of September, he owned 2,500 unexpired Pillsbury options, apparently more than any other individual investor. [Citation omitted.] O'Hagan also purchased, in September 1988, some 5,000 shares of Pillsbury common stock, at a price just under $39 per share. When Grand Met announced its tender offer in October, the price of Pillsbury stock rose to nearly $60 per share. O'Hagan then sold his Pillsbury call options and common stock, making a profit of more than $4.3 million.

The Securities and Exchange Commission (SEC or Commission) initiated an investigation into O'Hagan's transactions, culminating in a 57-count indictment. The indictment alleged that O'Hagan defrauded his law firm and its client, Grand Met, by using for his own trading purposes material, nonpublic information regarding Grand Met's planned tender offer.[*] [Citation omitted.] According to the indictment, O'Hagan used the profits he gained through this trading to conceal his previous embezzlement and conversion of unrelated client trust funds [for which he was jailed, fined, and disbarred]. [Citation omitted.] O'Hagan was charged with *** [seventeen] counts of securities fraud, in violation of § 10(b) of the Securities Exchange Act of 1934 (Exchange Act), [15 U.S.C. § 78j(b)], and SEC Rule 10b-5, [17 C.F.R. § 240.10b-5]; [and seventeen] counts of fraudulent trading in connection with a tender offer, in violation of § 14(e) of the Exchange Act, [15 U.S.C. § 78n(e)], and SEC Rule 14e-3(a), [17 C.F.R. § 240.14e-3(a)] [, among other things]. A jury convicted O'Hagan on all [fifty-seven] counts, and he was sentenced to a [forty-one]-month term of imprisonment.

A divided panel of the Court of Appeals for the Eighth Circuit reversed all of O'Hagan's convictions. [Citation omitted.] Liability under § 10(b) and Rule 10b-5, the Eighth Circuit held, may not be grounded on the "misappropriation theory" of securities fraud on which the prosecution relied. [Citation omitted.] The Court of Appeals also held that Rule 14e-3(a)—which prohibits trading while in possession of material, nonpublic information relating to a tender offer—exceeds the SEC's § 14(e) rulemaking authority because the Rule contains no breach of fiduciary duty requirement. [Citation omitted.] ***

*** We granted certiorari, [citation omitted], and now reverse the Eighth Circuit's judgment.

[II]   We address first the Court of Appeals' reversal of O'Hagan's convictions under § 10(b) and Rule 10b-5. Following the Fourth Circuit's lead, [citation omitted], the Eighth Circuit rejected the misappropriation theory as a basis for § 10(b) liability. We hold, in accord with several other Courts of Appeals, that criminal liability under § 10(b) may be predicated on the misappropriation theory.[**]

---

[*]   [Footnote by Court]: As evidence that O'Hagan traded on the basis of nonpublic information misappropriated from his law firm, the Government relied on a conversation between O'Hagan and the Dorsey & Whitney partner heading the firm's Grand Met representation. That conversation allegedly took place shortly before August 26, 1988. [Citation omitted.] O'Hagan urges that the Government's evidence does not show he traded on the basis of nonpublic information. O'Hagan points to news reports on August 18 and 22, 1988, that Grand Met was interested in acquiring Pillsbury, and to an earlier, August 12, 1988, news report that Grand Met had put up its hotel chain for auction to raise funds for an acquisition. [Citation omitted.] O'Hagan's challenge to the sufficiency of the evidence remains open for consideration on remand.

[**]   [Footnote by Court]: Twice before we have been presented with the question whether criminal liability for violation of § 10(b) may be based on a misappropriation theory. In

[II.A]   In pertinent part, § 10(b) of the Exchange Act provides:

"It shall be unlawful for any person, directly or indirectly, by the use of any means or instrumentality of interstate commerce or of the mails, or of any facility of any national securities exchange—

...

   "(b)   To use or employ, in connection with the purchase or sale of any security registered on a national securities exchange or any security not so registered, any manipulative or deceptive device or contrivance in contravention of such rules and regulations as the [Securities and Exchange] Commission may prescribe as necessary or appropriate in the public interest or for the protection of investors." [Citation omitted.]

The statute thus proscribes (1) using any deceptive device (2) in connection with the purchase or sale of securities, in contravention of rules prescribed by the Commission. The provision, as written, does not confine its coverage to deception of a purchaser or seller of securities, [citation omitted]; rather, the statute reaches any deceptive device used "in connection with the purchase or sale of any security."

   Pursuant to its § 10(b) rulemaking authority, the Commission has adopted Rule 10b-5 ***. Liability under Rule 10b-5, our precedent indicates, does not extend beyond conduct encompassed by § 10(b)'s prohibition. [Citations omitted.]

   Under the "traditional" or "classical theory" of insider trading liability, § 10(b) and Rule 10b-5 are violated when a corporate insider trades in the securities of his corporation on the basis of material, nonpublic information. Trading on such information qualifies as a "deceptive device" under § 10(b), we have affirmed, because "a relationship of trust and confidence [exists] between the shareholders of a corporation and those insiders who have obtained confidential information by reason of their position with that corporation." *Chiarella v. United States*, 445 U.S. 222, 228 (1980). That relationship, we recognized, "gives rise to a duty to disclose [or to abstain from trading] because of the 'necessity of preventing a corporate insider from ... tak[ing] unfair advantage of ... uninformed ... stockholders.'" *Id.*, at 228-229 (citation omitted). The classical theory applies not only to officers, directors, and other permanent insiders of a corporation, but

---

Chiarella v. United States, 445 U.S. 222, 235-237 (1980), the jury had received no misappropriation theory instructions, so we declined to address the question. In *Carpenter v. United States*, 484 U.S. 19, 24 (1987), the Court divided evenly on whether, under the circumstances of that case, convictions resting on the misappropriation theory should be affirmed. [Citation omitted.]

also to attorneys, accountants, consultants, and others who temporarily become fiduciaries of a corporation. See *Dirks v. SEC*, 463 U.S. 646, 655 n.14 (1983).

The "misappropriation theory" holds that a person commits fraud "in connection with" a securities transaction, and thereby violates § 10(b) and Rule 10b-5, when he misappropriates confidential information for securities trading purposes, in breach of a duty owed to the source of the information. [Citation omitted.]   Under this theory, a fiduciary's undisclosed, self-serving use of a principal's information to purchase or sell securities, in breach of a duty of loyalty and confidentiality, defrauds the principal of the exclusive use of that information. In lieu of premising liability on a fiduciary relationship between company insider and purchaser or seller of the company's stock, the misappropriation theory premises liability on a fiduciary-turned-trader's deception of those who entrusted him with access to confidential information.

The two theories are complementary, each addressing efforts to capitalize on nonpublic information through the purchase or sale of securities. The classical theory targets a corporate insider's breach of duty to shareholders with whom the insider transacts; the misappropriation theory outlaws trading on the basis of nonpublic information by a corporate "outsider" in breach of a duty owed not to a trading party, but to the source of the information. The misappropriation theory is thus designed to "protec[t] the integrity of the securities markets against abuses by 'outsiders' to a corporation who have access to confidential information that will affect th[e] corporation's security price when revealed, but who owe no fiduciary or other duty to that corporation's shareholders." [Citation omitted.]

In this case, the indictment alleged that O'Hagan, in breach of a duty of trust and confidence he owed to his law firm, Dorsey & Whitney, and to its client, Grand Met, traded on the basis of nonpublic information regarding Grand Met's planned tender offer for Pillsbury common stock. [Citation omitted.]   This conduct, the Government charged, constituted a fraudulent device in connection with the purchase and sale of securities.[*]

[II.B] We agree with the Government that misappropriation, as just defined, satisfies § 10(b)'s requirement that chargeable conduct involve a "deceptive device or contrivance" used "in connection with" the purchase or sale

---

[*]   [Footnote by Court]: The Government could not have prosecuted O'Hagan under the classical theory, for O'Hagan was not an "insider" of Pillsbury, the corporation in whose stock he traded. Although an "outsider" with respect to Pillsbury, O'Hagan had an intimate association with, and was found to have traded on confidential information from, Dorsey & Whitney, counsel to tender offer or Grand Met.   Under the misappropriation theory, O'Hagan's securities trading does not escape Exchange Act sanction *** simply because he was associated with, and gained nonpublic information from, the bidder, rather than the target.

of securities.   We observe, first, that misappropriators, as the Government describes them, deal in deception. A fiduciary who "[pretends] loyalty to the principal while secretly converting the principal's information for personal gain," [citation omitted], "dupes" or defrauds the principal. [Citation omitted.]

We addressed fraud of the same species in *Carpenter v. United States*, 484 U.S. 19 (1987), which involved the mail fraud statute's proscription of "any scheme or artifice to defraud," 18 U.S.C. § 1341. Affirming convictions under that statute, we said in *Carpenter* that an employee's undertaking not to reveal his employer's confidential information "became a sham" when the employee provided the information to his co-conspirators in a scheme to obtain trading profits. [Citation omitted.] A company's confidential information, we recognized in *Carpenter*, qualifies as property to which the company has a right of exclusive use. [Citation omitted.] The undisclosed misappropriation of such information, in violation of a fiduciary duty, the Court said in *Carpenter*, constitutes fraud akin to embezzlement—"'the fraudulent appropriation to one's own use of the money or goods entrusted to one's care by another.'" [Citation omitted.] *Carpenter*'s discussion of the fraudulent misuse of confidential information, the Government notes, "is a particularly apt source of guidance here, because [the mail fraud statute] (like Section 10(b)) has long been held to require deception, not merely the breach of a fiduciary duty." [Citation omitted.]

Deception through nondisclosure is central to the theory of liability for which the Government seeks recognition. As counsel for the Government stated in explanation of the theory at oral argument: "To satisfy the common law rule that a trustee may not use the property that [has] been entrusted [to] him, there would have to be consent. To satisfy the requirement of the Securities Act that there be no deception, there would only have to be disclosure." [Citation omitted.][*]

***   [F]ull disclosure forecloses liability under the misappropriation theory: Because the deception essential to the misappropriation theory involves feigning fidelity to the source of information, if the fiduciary discloses to the source that he plans to trade on the nonpublic information, there is no "deceptive device" and thus no § 10(b) violation—although the fiduciary-turned-trader may remain liable under state law for breach of a duty of loyalty.[**]

---

[*] [Footnote by Court]:   Under the misappropriation theory urged in this case, the disclosure obligation runs to the source of the information, here, Dorsey & Whitney and Grand Met. Chief Justice Burger, dissenting in *Chiarella*, advanced a broader reading of § 10(b) and Rule 10b-5; the disclosure obligation, as he envisioned it, ran to those with whom the misappropriator trades. [Citation omitted.] The Government does not propose that we adopt a misappropriation theory of that breadth.

[**] [Footnote by Court]:   Where, however, a person trading on the basis of material, nonpublic information owes a duty of loyalty and confidentiality to two entities or persons—

We turn next to the § 10(b) requirement that the misappropriator's deceptive use of information be "in connection with the purchase or sale of [a] security." This element is satisfied because the fiduciary's fraud is consummated, not when the fiduciary gains the confidential information, but when, without disclosure to his principal, he uses the information to purchase or sell securities. The securities transaction and the breach of duty thus coincide. This is so even though the person or entity defrauded is not the other party to the trade, but is, instead, the source of the nonpublic information. [Citation omitted.] A misappropriator who trades on the basis of material, nonpublic information, in short, gains his advantageous market position through deception; he deceives the source of the information and simultaneously harms members of the investing public. [Citation omitted.]

The misappropriation theory targets information of a sort that misappropriators ordinarily capitalize upon to gain no risk profits through the purchase or sale of securities. Should a misappropriator put such information to other use, the statute's prohibition would not be implicated. The theory does not catch all conceivable forms of fraud involving confidential information; rather, it catches fraudulent means of capitalizing on such information through securities transactions.

***

The misappropriation theory comports with § 10(b)'s language, which requires deception "in connection with the purchase or sale of any security," not deception of an identifiable purchaser or seller. The theory is also well tuned to an animating purpose of the Exchange Act: to insure honest securities markets and thereby promote investor confidence. [Citation omitted.] Although informational disparity is inevitable in the securities markets, investors likely would hesitate to venture their capital in a market where trading based on misappropriated nonpublic information is unchecked by law. An investor's informational disadvantage vis-à-vis a misappropriator with material, nonpublic information stems from contrivance, not luck; it is a disadvantage that cannot be overcome with research or skill. [Citations omitted.]

In sum, considering the inhibiting impact on market participation of trading on misappropriated information, and the congressional purposes underlying § 10(b), it makes scant sense to hold a lawyer like O'Hagan a § 10(b) violator if he works for a law firm representing the target of a tender offer, but not if he works for a law firm representing the bidder. The text of the statute requires

---

for example, a law firm and its client—but makes disclosure to only one, the trader may still be liable under the misappropriation theory.

no such result.[*] The misappropriation at issue here was properly made the subject of a § 10(b) charge because it meets the statutory requirement that there be "deceptive" conduct "in connection with" securities transactions.

[II.C] The Court of Appeals rejected the misappropriation theory primarily on two grounds. First, as the Eighth Circuit comprehended the theory, it requires neither misrepresentation nor nondisclosure. [Citation omitted.] As we just explained, however, [citation omitted], deceptive nondisclosure is essential to the § 10(b) liability at issue. Concretely, in this case, "it [was O'Hagan's] failure to disclose his personal trading to Grand Met and Dorsey, in breach of his duty to do so, that ma[de] his conduct 'deceptive' within the meaning of [§]10(b)." [Citation omitted.]

Second and "more obvious," the Court of Appeals said, the misappropriation theory is not moored to § 10(b)'s requirement that "the fraud be 'in connection with the purchase or sale of any security.'" [Citation omitted.] According to the Eighth Circuit, three of our decisions reveal that § 10(b) liability cannot be predicated on a duty owed to the source of nonpublic information: *Chiarella v. United States*, 445 U.S. 222 (1980); *Dirks v. SEC*, 463 U.S. 646 (1983); and *Central Bank of Denver, N.A. v. First Interstate Bank of Denver, N.A.*, 511 U.S. 164 (1994). "[O]nly a breach of a duty to parties to the securities transaction," the Court of Appeals concluded, "or, at the most, to other market participants such as investors, will be sufficient to give rise to § 10(b) liability." [Citation omitted.] We read the statute and our precedent differently, and note again that § 10(b) refers to "the purchase or sale of any security," not to identifiable purchasers or sellers of securities.

***

Chiarella involved securities trades by a printer employed at a shop that printed documents announcing corporate takeover bids. [Citation omitted.] Deducing the names of target companies from documents he handled, the printer bought shares of the targets before takeover bids were announced, expecting (correctly) that the share prices would rise upon announcement. In these transactions, the printer did not disclose to the sellers of the securities (the target companies' shareholders) the nonpublic information on which he traded.

---

[*] [Footnote by Court]: *** [T]he textual requirement of deception precludes § 10(b) liability when a person trading on the basis of nonpublic information has disclosed his trading plans to, or obtained authorization from, the principal—even though such conduct may affect the securities markets in the same manner as the conduct reached by the misappropriation theory. *** Moreover, once a disloyal agent discloses his imminent breach of duty, his principal may seek appropriate equitable relief under state law. Furthermore, in the context of a tender offer, the principal who authorizes an agent's trading on confidential information may, in the Commission's view, incur liability for an Exchange Act violation under Rule 14e-3(a).

[Citation omitted.] For that trading, the printer was convicted of violating § 10(b) and Rule 10b-5. We reversed the Court of Appeals judgment that had affirmed the conviction. [Citation omitted.]

The jury in *Chiarella* had been instructed that it could convict the defendant if he willfully failed to inform sellers of target company securities that he knew of a takeover bid that would increase the value of their shares. [Citation omitted.] Emphasizing that the printer had no agency or other fiduciary relationship with the sellers, we held that liability could not be imposed on so broad a theory. [Citation omitted.] There is under § 10(b), we explained, no "general duty between all participants in market transactions to forgo actions based on material, nonpublic information." [Citation omitted.] Under established doctrine, we said, a duty to disclose or abstain from trading "arises from a specific relationship between two parties." [Citation omitted.]

The Court did not hold in *Chiarella* that the only relationship prompting liability for trading on undisclosed information is the relationship between a corporation's insiders and shareholders. That is evident from our response to the Government's argument before this Court that the printer's misappropriation of information from his employer for purposes of securities trading—in violation of a duty of confidentiality owed to the acquiring companies—constituted fraud in connection with the purchase or sale of a security, and thereby satisfied the terms of § 10(b). [Citation omitted.] The Court declined to reach that potential basis for the printer's liability, because the theory had not been submitted to the jury. [Citation omitted.] But four Justices found merit in it. [Citation omitted.] And a fifth Justice stated that the Court "wisely le[ft] the resolution of this issue for another day." [Citation omitted.]

Chiarella thus expressly left open the misappropriation theory before us today. Certain statements in *Chiarella*, however, led the Eighth Circuit in the instant case to conclude that § 10(b) liability hinges exclusively on a breach of duty owed to a purchaser or seller of securities. [Citation omitted.] The Court said in *Chiarella* that § 10(b) liability "is premised upon a duty to disclose arising from a relationship of trust and confidence between parties to a transaction," [citation omitted], and observed that the printshop employee defendant in that case "was not a person in whom the sellers had placed their trust and confidence," [citation omitted]. These statements rejected the notion that § 10(b) stretches so far as to impose "a general duty between all participants in market transactions to forgo actions based on material, nonpublic information," [citation omitted], and we confine them to that context. The statements highlighted by the Eighth Circuit, in short, appear in an opinion carefully leaving for future resolution the validity of the misappropriation theory, and therefore cannot be read to foreclose that theory.

Dirks, too, left room for application of the misappropriation theory in cases like the one we confront. *Dirks* involved an investment analyst who had received information from a former insider of a corporation with which the analyst had no connection. [Citation omitted.] The information indicated that the corporation had engaged in a massive fraud. The analyst investigated the fraud, obtaining corroborating information from employees of the corporation. During his investigation, the analyst discussed his findings with clients and investors, some of whom sold their holdings in the company the analyst suspected of gross wrongdoing. [Citation omitted.]

The SEC censured the analyst for, *inter alia*, aiding and abetting § 10(b) and Rule 10b-5 violations by clients and investors who sold their holdings based on the nonpublic information the analyst passed on. [Citation omitted.] In the SEC's view, the analyst, as a "tippee" of corporation insiders, had a duty under § 10(b) and Rule 10b-5 to refrain from communicating the nonpublic information to persons likely to trade on the basis of it. [Citation omitted.] This Court found no such obligation, [citation omitted], and repeated the key point made in *Chiarella*: There is no "'general duty between all participants in market trans-actions to forgo actions based on material, nonpublic information.'" [Citations omitted].

No showing had been made in *Dirks* that the "tippers" had violated any duty by disclosing to the analyst nonpublic information about their former employer. The insiders had acted not for personal profit, but to expose a massive fraud within the corporation. [Citation omitted.] Absent any violation by the tippers, there could be no derivative liability for the tippee. [Citation omitted.] Most important for purposes of the instant case, the Court observed in *Dirks*: "There was no expectation by [the analyst's] sources that he would keep their information in confidence. Nor did [the analyst] misappropriate or illegally obtain the information …." [Citation omitted.] *Dirks* thus presents no suggestion that a person who gains nonpublic information through misappropriation in breach of a fiduciary duty escapes § 10(b) liability when, without alerting the source, he trades on the information.

Last of the three cases the Eighth Circuit regarded as warranting dis-approval of the misappropriation theory, *Central Bank* held that "a private plaintiff may not maintain an aiding and abetting suit under § 10(b)." [Citation omitted.] We immediately cautioned in *Central Bank* that secondary actors in the securities markets may sometimes be chargeable under the securities Acts: "Any person or entity, including a lawyer, accountant, or bank, who employs a manipulative device or makes a material misstatement (or omission) on which a purchaser or seller of securities relies may be liable as a primary violator under 10b-5, assuming … the requirements for primary liability under Rule 10b-5 are met. [Citation omitted.] The Eighth Circuit isolated the statement just quoted and drew from it the conclusion that § 10(b) covers only deceptive statements or omissions on which purchasers and sellers, and perhaps other market participants, rely. [Citation omitted.] It is evident from the question presented in *Central Bank*, however, that this Court, in the quoted passage, sought only to clarify that secondary actors, although not subject to aiding and abetting liability, remain subject to primary liability under § 10(b) and Rule 10b-5 for certain conduct.

Furthermore, *Central Bank*'s discussion concerned only private civil litigation under § 10(b) and Rule 10b-5, not criminal liability. *Central Bank*'s reference to purchasers or sellers of securities must be read in light of a longstanding limitation on private § 10(b) suits. In *Blue Chip Stamps v. Manor Drug Stores*, 421 U.S. 723 (1975), we held that only actual purchasers or sellers of securities may maintain a private civil action under § 10(b) and Rule 10b-5. *** Criminal prosecutions do not present the dangers the Court addressed in *Blue Chip Stamps*, so that decision is "inapplicable" to indictments for violations of § 10(b) and Rule 10b-5. [Citations omitted.]

***

The Eighth Circuit erred in holding that the misappropriation theory is inconsistent with § 10(b). The Court of Appeals may address on remand O'Hagan's other challenges to his convictions under § 10(b) and Rule 10b-5.

[III]   [In Part III, the Court held that the SEC had not exceeded its statutory authority by adopting Rule 14a-3 without requiring a showing that the trading at issue entailed a breach of fiduciary duty.]

***

[Opinions of other Justices omitted].

Questions About *O'Hagan*

1.   Why didn't the prosecution allege that O'Hagan had engaged in "classic" insider trading or that he had been tipped?

2.   To whom did O'Hagan owe a duty of trust and confidence?[*]

---

[*]   Note that Rule 10b5-2 calls it a duty of trust *or* confidence, rather than a duty of trust *and* confidence. Is there a difference?

3.   What are some other examples of situations where a person owes a duty of trust and confidence to another person or entity? If this case does not help answer that question, where would you look for an answer?

4.   Would the case have been decided differently if O'Hagan had informed both Dorsey & Whitney and Grand Met that he planned to buy Pillsbury stock before the tender offer was announced? Why or why not?[*]

5.   If the facts in *Chiarella* had occurred <u>after</u> the *O'Hagan* case, would Mr. Chiarella's convictions have been upheld?

6.   Can a misappropriator become a tipper? If so, how?

Problems

Problem 14-6: Big Corp. and Little Corp., both publicly traded corporations, are engaged in confidential merger negotiations. The current market price of Little Corp. stock is $25, but Big Corp. may agree to pay as much as $35 per share in the merger. On April 10, Little Corp.'s president, Mr. Little, had an appointment with his psychiatrist, Dr. Freud. When Dr. Freud asked Mr. Little why he was under so much stress, Mr. Little told him about the planned merger with Big Corp. The next day, Dr. Freud purchased 5,000 shares of Little Corp. stock and options to purchase an additional 20,000 shares. The merger was not announced to the public until April 27. *Did Mr. Little violate Rule 10b-5? Did Dr. Freud violate Rule 10b-5? If so, on what theory? See United States v. Willis*, 737 F. Supp. 269 (S.D.N.Y. 1990).

Problem 14-7: Same facts as Problem 14-6. Little Corp.'s law firm is Sunshine & Rain, P.C. Most of the Little Corp. legal work is done by Mr. Rain, a partner in Sunshine & Rain, P.C. Mr. Rain, who was involved in the merger negotiations, purchased 10,000 shares of Little Corp. stock on April 20. *Did Mr. Rain violate Rule 10b-5? If so, on what theory?*

Problem 14-8: Craig Hustler is a master criminal. On April 21, he broke into the offices of Sunshine & Rain. While rummaging through Mr. Rain's office for things to steal, Craig found some

---

[*]   For a more recent case considering this question, see *SEC v. Rocklage*, 470 F.3d 1 (1st Cir. 2006).

drafts of the merger agreement between Big Corp. and Little Corp. The next day, Craig bought 1,000 shares of Little Corp. stock. *Did Craig violate Rule 10b-5? If so, on what theory?*

Problem 14-9: *Would your answer to Problem 14-8 change if Big Corp. were planning a tender offer for Little Corp. and the question concerned Rule 14e-3 rather than Rule 10b-5?*

What's So Bad About Insider Trading? So far, we have discussed the various insider-trading rules that have arisen under Rule 10b-5 without really considering *why* the federal government should be concerned about insider trading. In other words, is insider trading really an evil that should be prosecuted? Before you answer that question, consider the following hypothetical.

Joe Schmo is an "ordinary" investor who happens to own some stock in Conglomo Corp. Joe has owned Conglomo stock for several years, during which time the market value of the stock has steadily risen. However, unbeknownst to Joe, Conglomo is in secret negotiations with the United States Army to build a new weapons system. If Conglomo receives this contract, its earnings will materially increase, which would likely lead to a significant increase in the price of its stock. While the contract has not yet been awarded, the negotiations are going well and Conglomo's president, Ms. Conglomo, is confident that Conglomo will receive the contract. Meanwhile, Joe (who is not associated with Conglomo other than as a small shareholder) is facing two unexpected expenses. First, he has significant uninsured medical expenses. Second, his daughter is getting married and is planning a very extravagant wedding. Needing funds to pay for these expenses, Joe decides to sell his Conglomo stock and calls his stockbroker to do so.

Now let's consider two different scenarios. In the first scenario, the person who ends up purchasing Joe's Conglomo stock is Ms. Conglomo. Of course, Joe does not know this at the time because stock market transactions like this are essentially "anonymous." Given these facts, there is a strong inference that Ms. Conglomo purchased the stock because she knew that the price was likely to rise when Conglomo receives the Army contract. In other words, it looks like she purchased the stock on the basis of material nonpublic information in violation of her *Cady, Roberts* duty. In the second scenario, the person who ends up buying Joe's Conglomo stock is Jane Plain, another "ordinary" investor who is not associated with Conglomo. Jane decided to buy some Conglomo stock because her research, based entirely on publicly available information, led her to believe that Conglomo stock was a good investment.

Based on what you have learned in this chapter, the first scenario likely involves a Rule 10b-5 violation whereas the second scenario clearly does not. Yet, whether the first scenario or second scenario is the one that actually occurs is essentially random. Is Joe worse off in the first scenario than in the second scenario? Either way, he was planning to sell his Conglomo stock. Either way, he received the same price for it. (In fact, Ms. Conglomo may have been willing to pay a little more than Jane.) Either way, he is going to be upset when, some time later, Conglomo announces that it has been awarded the big new Army contract and the price of its stock rises. So, let's reconsider the question: what's so bad about insider trading? For a good discussion of the arguments on this issue, see STEPHEN M. BAINBRIDGE, SECURITIES LAW: INSIDER TRADING 133-81 (2d ed. 2007).

How Does Anyone Get Caught and What Are the Consequences? Given that insider trading takes place in relative secrecy, you may wonder how anyone actually gets caught violating Rule 10b-5 (or Rule 14e-3). Certainly, a great deal of insider trading goes undetected. But the SEC and the stock exchanges are remarkably adept at detecting it. Using sophisticated computer programs and databases, the exchanges can analyze trading in a given company's securities and detect patterns that fall outside of predetermined norms. For example, assume that ABC Corp. just announced that it would be acquired in a merger by DEF Corp., at a price substantially above the current market price of ABC stock. The SEC and whatever exchange ABC Corp. stock is listed on may examine the trading in ABC stock that occurred in the weeks leading up to this announcement. If this examination shows that a great deal of trades originated in, say, Kansas City, or through a particular brokerage firm, more questions may be asked and the SEC and/or the stock exchange may ask the brokerage firm to turn over its trading records.[*] If something looks "suspicious," the SEC may issue subpoenas and take depositions. In addition, Section 21A(e) of the Securities Exchange Act allows the SEC to pay a "bounty" to any person who reports illegal insider trading. This reward, which could be as high as ten percent of any civil recovery by the SEC or the attorney general, may encourage people to "tattle" on others.

A person who is found guilty of violating Rule 10b-5 may face serious consequences, including (but not limited to) the following. First, a jail sentence is a possibility. (The SEC itself does not have criminal enforcement authority; however, it could refer any case that it believes warrants criminal prosecution to the Department of Justice for prosecution.) Following the Sarbanes-Oxley Act of 2002, "willful" violations of the Exchange Act or rules thereunder could result in up to twenty years in jail and up to $5 million in fines ($25 million for non-individual entities, such as corporations). Next, Section 21A of the Exchange Act

---

[*]   As discussed in Chapter 10, most publicly traded stock is held in "street name," which can make it difficult to readily determine the ultimate "beneficial" owner of the stock.

allows the SEC to bring a civil lawsuit against an inside-trader to recover a penalty of up to three times the "profit gained or loss avoided" as a result of a Rule 10b-5 violation or a Rule 14e-3 violation. In addition, persons who "control" the violator may also be subject to fines under this section, ranging up to $1 million or three times the profit gained or loss avoided, whichever is greater. Further, "contemporaneous" traders could sue to have the Rule 10b-5 violator disgorge her ill-gotten profits (or avoided losses), less any disgorgement ordered under Section 21(d) of the Exchange Act (which also allows the SEC to seek injunctions against securities law violations). *See* Section 20A of the Exchange Act.

Other Issues. The more that one thinks about cases like *Chiarella*, *Dirks*, and *O'Hagan*, the more questions that arise.

Who Is An "Insider"? One issue is whether *every* employee or agent of a company can be considered an "insider" (that is, someone who owes *Cady, Roberts* duties) of the company for purposes of "classic" insider trading or to owe a duty of trust and confidence for purposes of the misappropriation theory. In *Cady, Roberts* and *Chiarella*, the focus was on people who receive information "by virtue of their position" and have a relationship with the company "affording access to inside information intended to be available only for a corporate purpose." Clearly, directors, officers, and "key" employees are covered by this definition, but what about an employee who sees something at work that she wasn't "supposed" to see?

Does Rule 10b-5 Apply to Bonds? Another issue is whether Rule 10b-5 applies to nonconvertible *debt* securities, that is, debt securities that cannot be converted into equity. In *Chiarella* and other cases, the Supreme Court talked about insiders owing duties to the corporation's shareholders. But keep in mind that, as you learned in Chapter 5, most state laws provide that directors and officers do not owe fiduciary duties to the corporation's bondholders. As such, it is perhaps an open question whether an "insider" of a corporation violates Rule 10b-5 if she trades the corporation's bonds on the basis of material nonpublic information.

Evolution of the Misappropriation Theory. A recent misappropriation case that is interesting—if only because of the identity of the defendant—is *Securities Exchange Commission v. Cuban*, 634 F. Supp.2d 713 (N.D. Tex. 2009), *rev'd on other grounds*, 620 F.3d 551 (5th Cir. 2010), which involves the billionaire owner of the Dallas Mavericks basketball team, Mark Cuban. In 2004, Mr. Cuban acquired 6.3% of the stock of an internet search engine company called

Mamma.com (which is now known as Copernic Inc.). Although Mr. Cuban was not a director or officer of Mamma.com, as the company's largest shareholder he was considered important. Thus, when Mamma.com decided to pursue a stock offering (which would likely drive the price of its stock down in the short term but hopefully benefit the company in the long term), it telephoned Mr. Cuban to inform him. According to the complaint in the case:

> The CEO [of Mamma.com] prefaced the call by informing Cuban that he had confidential information to convey to him, and Cuban agreed that he would keep whatever information the CEO intended to share with him confidential. The CEO, in reliance on Cuban's agreement to keep the information confidential, proceeded to tell Cuban about the [stock] offering.

Id. at 717.

Mr. Cuban was angered by the news because he believed that the type of stock offering contemplated by the company would harm current shareholders. Further, "[a]t the end of the call Cuban said: "Well, now I'm screwed. I can't sell." *Id.* Nonetheless, Mr. Cuban *did* sell all of his Mamma.com shares before the company announced the stock offering. Mr. Cuban avoided a loss of more than $750,000 on his investment, because the price of Mamma.com stock dropped substantially in the days after the company announced its plans.

The SEC charged Mr. Cuban with insider trading, based solely on the misappropriation theory. In support of its position, the SEC cited Rule 10b5-2(b)(1) which, as noted earlier in this chapter, provides that a person owes a duty of trust or confidence under the misappropriation theory whenever he "agrees to maintain information in confidence." The court agreed that a duty sufficient to support liability under the misappropriation theory *could* arise (even in the absence of a pre-existing fiduciary or "fiduciary-like" relationship) by an agreement "not to use another's information for personal benefit." However, under the facts of the case Mr. Cuban had never actually agreed *not to trade on the basis of the information.* Even if all of the facts in the complaint were true, Mr. Cuban had merely agreed to *keep the information confidential*, which he had done. As the court put it:

> The agreement, however, must consist of more than an express or implied promise merely to keep information confidential [to support misappropriation liability]. It must also impose on the party who receives the information the legal duty to refrain from trading on or otherwise using the information for personal gain. *** Where misappropriation theory liability is predicated [only] on an agreement, however, a person must undertake, either

expressly or implicitly, both obligations. He must agree to maintain the confidentiality of the information *and* not to trade on or otherwise use it. Absent a duty not to use the information for personal benefit, there is no deception in doing so.

Id. at 725. Although Rule 10b5-2(b)(1) itself does not require that the alleged misappropriator agree not to trade, the court found the SEC had exceeded its authority in promulgating such a rule. In other words,

> [b]ecause Rule 10b5-2(b)(1) attempts to predicate mis-appropriation theory liability on a mere confidentiality agreement lacking a non-use component, the SEC cannot rely on it to establish Cuban's liability under the misappropriation theory. To permit liability based on Rule 10b-5(b)(1) would exceed the SEC's authority [under Section 10(b) of the Exchange Act] to proscribe conduct that is deceptive.

Id. at 730-31. Thus, the district court dismissed the complaint.[*] Whether other courts will follow this line of reasoning remains to be seen.

Where Do Abstain-or-Disclose Duties Come From? Finally, consider one last question. Where, exactly, did the federal courts "find" the abstain-or-disclose duty—in state law or in federal law? As you saw earlier in this chapter, many states have not made insider trading illegal or a breach of fiduciary duty. This suggests that the source of the abstain-or-disclose duty must be in federal law, particularly given the many references in the cases to "*Cady, Roberts* duties." But doesn't imposing fiduciary duties in situations where states have refused to do so raise federalism concerns? *Cf. Santa Fe Industries, Inc. v. Green*, 430 U.S. 462 (1977) (claim for breach of fiduciary duty arising under state law insufficient to support Rule 10b-5 claim, without a showing of deception or manipulation; Rule 10b-5 does not regulate the "fairness" of securities transactions).

These and other issues under Rule 10b-5 await clarification from the courts and/or Congress. Fortunately, Section 16(b) of the Exchange Act, which is discussed in the following section, is more clear-cut than Rule 10b-5.

---

[*] However, the Fifth Circuit Court of Appeals reversed. 620 F.3d 551 (5th Cir. 2010). Reading all of the allegations in the complaint (not just those recounted above) in a light most favorable to the SEC, the court of appeals found that "the allegations, taken in their entirety, provide more than a plausible basis to find that the understanding between the CEO and Cuban was that he was not to trade, that it was more than a simple confidentiality agreement."

§ 14.03   SHORT-SWING PROFITS UNDER
SECTION 16(b)

Section 16(b) of the Securities Exchange Act is another provision that appears to have been intended to combat insider trading.[*] However, unlike Rule 10b-5, it is *completely irrelevant* under Section 16(b) whether the person who was engaged in the securities trades possessed material nonpublic information at the time. Instead, Section 16(b) is largely "mechanical"; if a fact pattern runs afoul of its prohibitions, then there will be liability. There are virtually no defenses that may be asserted to a Section 16(b) lawsuit.

Let's begin by taking a close look at the statute. Section 16(a) provides that it applies to persons who are any of the following: (1) a beneficial owner of more than 10 percent of any class of any equity security (other than an exempted security) which is registered pursuant to section 12 of the Exchange Act, or (2) a director of an issuer of such a security, or (3) an officer of an issuer of such a security. Thus, Section 16 only applies to *some* people and only with respect to *some* securities.

Section 16(b) then provides in part that:

> For the purpose of preventing the unfair use of information which may have been obtained by such beneficial owner, director, or officer by reason of his relationship to the issuer, any profit realized by him from any purchase and sale, or any sale and purchase, of any equity security of such issuer (other than an exempted security) or a security-based swap agreement (as defined in section 206B of the Gramm-Leach-Bliley Act) involving any such equity security within any period of less than six months, *** shall inure to and be recoverable by the issuer, irrespective of any intention on the part of such beneficial owner, director, or officer ***. Suit to recover such profit may be instituted at law or in equity in any court of competent jurisdiction by the issuer, or by the owner of any security of the issuer in the name and in behalf of the issuer if the issuer shall fail or refuse to bring such suit within sixty days after request or shall fail diligently to prosecute the same thereafter; but no such suit shall be brought more than two years after the date such profit was realized. This subsection shall not be construed to cover any transaction where such beneficial

---

[*]   There are a few problems with this statement. First, many scholars dispute whether Section 10(b) and Rule 10b-5 were, when enacted, aimed at insider trading. Second, some scholars argue that Section 16(b) was intended more to combat stock market manipulation than insider trading. Nonetheless, it is fairly safe to say that the effects of Section 16(b) take away potential insider trading profits for certain persons, as you will learn in this section.

owner was not such both at the time of the purchase and sale, or the sale and purchase, of the security or security based swap agreement (as defined in section 206B of the Gramm-Leach Bliley Act) involved, or any transaction or transactions which the Commission by rules and regulations may exempt as not comprehended within the purpose of this subsection.

At first, this looks like a pretty intimidating statute, but let's break it down into its components. First, we have already established that Section 16(b) only applies to the equity securities (in the case of a corporation, that means stock or securities that can be converted into stock) of publicly traded companies.

Second, we have already established that Section 16(b) only applies to the persons who are either officers,[*] directors or ten-percent shareholders of such companies. (Technically, Section 16 applies to persons who own *more* than ten percent of the equity securities of a publicly traded company, but for purposes of convenience we will call them "ten percent shareholders" in this section.)

Third, Section 16(b) applies where one of these persons buys and then sells, or sells and then buys, the securities and the transactions are within six months of each other. If two transactions occur more than six months apart, they cannot be "matched" for purposes of Section 16(b).

Fourth, Section 16(b) only applies where two (or more) "matched" transactions (that is, transactions that occur within six months of each other) produce a "profit." How do you know that they have produced a profit? Check to make sure that the sales price of the securities was higher than the purchase price. If this is not the case, then these two transactions did not, when matched with one another, produce a profit.

Finally, note a couple nuances about the statute. First, Section 16(b) applies to "any" profit resulting from matched transactions. Second, the last sentence provides in part that Section 16(b) does not apply to "any transaction where such beneficial owner was not such both at the time of the purchase and sale, or the sale and purchase, of the security ...." Query: what types of "Section 16(b) persons" were *not* described in this sentence?

Thus, to sum up, when approaching a Section 16(b) problem, you should (1) determine that the corporation whose stock is being traded is a public company, (2) determine that the person who is buying and selling (or selling and buying) that corporation's stock is a "Section 16(b) person" with respect to that corporation, (3) determine whether there were two or more "opposite way" transactions that occurred within six months of each other, (4) determine that these

---

[*]   See SEC Rule 16a-1(f) for the definition of "officer."

"matching" transactions resulted in a profit, and (5) keep in mind the two nuances noted in the previous paragraph.

Confused yet? The only way to really learn and understand Section 16(b) is to work on some hypothetical problems, so try your hand at the following problems. When working on Section 16(b) problems, it is a good idea to make a "chart" of the various transactions involved, including the date, whether the transaction was a "buy" or a "sell," the number of shares that were purchased or sold, and the per-share price.

Problems

Basic Facts for Problems 14-10 through 14-22: Alphabet Corp. is a publicly traded corporation that has 1 million shares of common stock outstanding. Abe has been the president of Alphabet Corp. for the past five years. Bill, Carol, Diane, Ernie, Francisco, Glenda, Hank, and Irene have been directors of Alphabet Corp. for the past two years. The Big Hedge Fund, Inc. is an institutional investor that currently owns no shares of Alphabet Corp. stock.

Problem 14-10: On February 1, Abe buys 1,000 shares of DEF Corp. stock for $10 per share. On March 1, Abe sells 1,000 shares of DEF Corp. stock for $11 per share. Abe is not an officer, director, or ten-percent shareholder of DEF Corp. *What, if anything, is Abe's Section 16(b) liability from these transactions?*

Problem 14-11: On February 1, Abe buys 1,000 shares of Alphabet Corp. stock for $10 per share. On March 1, Abe sells 1,000 shares of Alphabet Corp. stock for $11 per share. *What, if anything, is Abe's Section 16(b) liability from these transactions?*

Problem 14-12: On February 2, Bill sells 1,000 shares of Alphabet Corp. stock for $11 per share. On March 2, Bill buys 1,000 shares of Alphabet Corp. stock for $10 per share. *What, if anything, is Bill's Section 16(b) liability from these transactions?*

Problem 14-13: On February 3, Carol buys 1,000 shares of Alphabet Corp. stock for $10 per share. On March 3, Carol sells 1,000 shares of Alphabet Corp. stock for $9 per share. *What, if anything, is Carol's Section 16(b) liability from these transactions?*

Problem 14-14: On April 1, Diane buys 2,000 shares of Alphabet Corp. stock for $10 per share. On May 1, Diane sells 1,000 shares of Alphabet Corp. stock for $11 per share. *What, if anything, is Diane's Section 16(b) liability from these transactions?*

Problem 14-15: On April 1, Ernie buys 1,000 shares of Alphabet Corp. stock for $10 per share. On May 1, Ernie sells 2,000 shares of Alphabet Corp. stock for $11 per share. *What, if anything, is Ernie's Section 16(b) liability from these transactions?*

Problem 14-16: On April 1, Francisco buys 1,000 shares of Alphabet Corp. stock for $10 per share. On April 2, Francisco buys 1,000 shares of Alphabet Corp. stock for $9 per share. On May 1, Francisco sells 1,000 shares of Alphabet Corp. stock for $11 per share. *What, if anything, is Francisco's Section 16(b) liability from these transactions?*

Problem 14-17: On April 1, Glenda buys 1,000 shares of Alphabet Corp. stock for $10 per share. On April 2, Glenda buys 1,000 shares of Alphabet Corp. stock for $9 per share. On May 1, Glenda sells 1,000 shares of Alphabet Corp. stock for $11 per share. On May 2, Glenda sells 1,000 shares of Alphabet Corp. stock for $12 per share. *What, if anything, is Glenda's Section 16(b) liability from these transactions?*

Problem 14-18: On April 1, Hank buys 1,000 shares of Alphabet Corp. stock for $10 per share. On April 2, Hank buys 1,000 shares of Alphabet Corp. stock for $9 per share. On May 1, Hank sells 1,000 shares of Alphabet Corp. stock for $11 per share. On December 2, Hank sells 1,000 shares of Alphabet Corp. stock for $12 per share. *What, if anything, is Hank's Section 16(b) liability from these transactions?*

Problem 14-19: On April 1, Irene buys 1,000 shares of Alphabet Corp. stock for $10 per share. On April 2, Irene buys 1,000 shares of Alphabet Corp. stock for $9 per share. On April 3, Irene buys 1,000 shares of Alphabet Corp. stock for $8 per share. On May 1, Irene sells 1,000 shares of Alphabet Corp. stock for $11 per share. On May 2, Irene sells 1,000 shares of Alphabet Corp. stock for $12 per share. On May 3, Irene sells 1,000 shares of Alphabet Corp. stock for $13 per share. *What, if anything, is Irene's Section 16(b) liability from these transactions?*

Problem 14-20: *Would your answer to Problem 14-20 change if Irene had resigned as a director of Alphabet Corp. on April 3? What if she resigned on April 1? See SEC Rule 16a-2(a) and (b).*

Problem 14-21: On April 1, Jenny buys 1,000 shares of Alphabet Corp. stock for $10 per share. On April 2, Jenny is elected to the board of directors of Alphabet Corp. On May 1, Jenny sells 1,000 shares of Alphabet Corp. stock for $11 per share. *What, if anything, is Jenny's Section 16(b) liability from these transactions? See SEC Rule 16a-2(a) and (b)..*

Problem 14-22: On April 1, The Big Hedge Fund ("TBHF") buys 90,000 shares of Alphabet Corp. stock for $10 per share. On April 2, TBHF buys 11,000 shares of Alphabet Corp. stock for $9 per share. On April 3, TBHF buys 9,000 shares of Alphabet Corp. stock for $8 per share. On May 1, TBHF sells 80,000 shares of Alphabet Corp. stock for $11 per share. On May 2, TBHF sells 20,000 shares of Alphabet Corp. stock for $12 per share. On May 3, TBHF sells 10,000 shares of Alphabet Corp. stock for $13 per share. *What, if anything, is TBHF's Section 16(b) liability from these transactions?*

Although it may not have seemed like it, the above problems are actually fairly simple, because they mostly involve *individuals* buying and selling relatively small amounts of *stock*. The "real world" is much more complicated. For example, oftentimes officers and directors of publicly traded companies do not themselves own securities; instead, they may be the beneficiaries of trusts or other estate-planning devices or employee benefit plans that own the securities. Their family members may own company stock. They may receive and exercise stock options or types of derivative securities. Fortunately for practitioners, there are several SEC rules under Section 16 that address these and other situations, but they are outside the scope of this textbook.

You might be wondering how a Section 16(b) violation would be detected. Section 16(a) and SEC rules thereunder require persons who are subject to Section 16(b) to file various reports. Within 10 days after becoming subject to Section 16(b), such as by having been elected as a director of a public corporation, a person must file a Form 3 with the SEC to report the amount (if any) of the corporation's equity securities that she owns. Thereafter, with a few exceptions that can be filed on an annual Form 5, a Section 16(b) person must report all of her transactions in company stock within two business days after they occur. These reports are publicly available on the SEC's website and must also be posted on the company's website.

If the reports show a recoverable Section 16(b) profit, it is recoverable by the company. As the statute provides, if the company fails or refuses to recover the profit from the Section 16(b), then a shareholder may bring a derivative suit to do so. And, as you saw in Chapter 8, one of the attractive features of a derivative suit for attorneys is the ability to have the corporation pay the plaintiff's expenses, including attorney fees, if the suit is successful. Thus, Section 16(b) is largely "self-enforcing."

§ 14.04   A NOTE ON OTHER USES OF RULE 10b-5

As noted above, Rule 10b-5 is not just a criminal-law provision. Only four years after it was enacted, federal courts allowed a *private* cause of action under Rule 10b-5. *See Kardon v. National Gypsum Co.*, 69 F. Supp. 512 (E.D. Pa. 1946); *see also Superintendent of Insurance v. Bankers Life & Casualty Co.*, 404 U.S. 6 (1971). In the many decades since then, there have been a plethora of cases in which plaintiffs have sued defendants based on Rule 10b-5. These cases are surprisingly diverse in their fact patterns; this may be because any time some (allegedly) fraudulent or deceptive conduct occurs in connection with a securities transaction, a Rule 10b-5 lawsuit is a possibility. While no attempt is made in this section to describe these cases comprehensively, a short summary is in order. You may learn more about these cases in a course on Securities Regulation.

General Requirements. First, there are some things that you learned in the context of criminal insider trading cases that also apply to private Rule 10b-5 lawsuits. For example, the same definition of materiality applies in both. Also, keep in mind that the purchase or sale of *any* security could support a civil lawsuit under Rule 10b-5. The fact that a security is exempt from registration in a securities offering under Section 5 of the Securities Act (as discussed in Chapter 13) or is privately held does not matter. In addition, there must have been some use of "jurisdictional means" to support a Rule 10b-5 lawsuit, but as you saw above in the discussion of insider trading that is a relatively easy requirement to satisfy.

Plaintiffs and Defendants. Standing in a private Rule 10b-5 lawsuit is limited to persons who actually bought or sold a security. While this seems to follow from the last clause of Rule 10b-5 ("... in connection with the purchase or sale of any security"), consider the following scenario. You own stock of ABC Corp. and are considering selling it at today's market price of $10 per share because the future looks bad for the industry in which ABC operates. However, in an attempt to "prop up" the market price of ABC stock, the company's president makes optimistic statements that are materially false and misleading and does so knowing that her statements are false and misleading. These statements, when heard by the "market," cause the price to rise to $12 per share. Because of these statements and the subsequent increase in the price of ABC stock, you decide not

CHAPTER 14 INSIDER TRADING

to sell your ABC stock. However, the truth eventually comes out, and the price of ABC stock plummets to $8 per share. While you have certainly been harmed by this turn of events because you could have sold your ABC stock back when the market price was $10, you do not have a cause of action under Rule 10b-5 against ABC or ABC's president. *See Blue Chips Stamps v. Manor Drug Stores*, 421 U.S. 723 (1975). To have a different rule would invite an unacceptable amount of litigation—everyone and her brother would claim that they *would have* bought or sold securities if they had known the truth.[*]

However, the defendant(s) in a Rule 10b-5 lawsuit need not have been the person(s) that was (were) on the other side of the transaction from the plaintiff. For example, if the plaintiff bought a security on the basis of a materially false or misleading statement, the defendant need not have been the actual seller of that security. Instead, the defendant's actions must have "touched and concerned" the securities transaction. In other words, the defendant's actions must have somehow affected the transaction. To return to the example in the prior paragraph, suppose that you had bought more ABC stock on the basis of the materially false and misleading statements of ABC's president. In that case, both the president of ABC and (due to agency-law rules such as *respondeat superior*) ABC Corp. can be defendants even though neither of them sold you that stock.[**] As you might guess, the issue of whether the defendant's actions were sufficiently "in connection with" the plaintiff's purchase or sale of a security is very heavily litigated and intensely fact-specific. But note that in *Central Bank of Denver, N.A. v. First Interstate Bank of Denver, N.A.*, 511 U.S. 164 (1994), the Supreme Court held that a plaintiff in a private Rule 10b-5 lawsuit may not sue a person for *aiding and abetting* the "primary" violator. (However, under Section 20(e) of the Exchange Act, the SEC may still bring civil enforcement actions against those who provide "substantial assistance" to violators of the Exchange Act or SEC rules under the Exchange Act.)

Defendant's Fraudulent Actions. In addition, the plaintiff in a Rule 10b-5 lawsuit must prove that the defendant (1) made a material misstatement, (2) omitted a material fact that rendered her statements misleading, or (3) did not disclose a material fact when the defendant was under a duty to do so. Thus, if a defendant made a statement that is materially false, or that is a "half truth" in that

---

[*]   In *Merrill Lynch, Pierce, Fenner & Smith, Inc. v. Dabit*, 547 U.S. 71 (2006), the Supreme Court held that, under the Securities Litigation Uniform Standards Act of 1998, fraud-based lawsuits by "holders" of securities, that is persons who did not buy or sell securities, could not be brought in state court. Instead, such lawsuits must be brought in federal court—even though they would be barred there by the requirement that the plaintiff in a Rule 10b-5 lawsuit must have actually bought or sold securities.

[**]   Remember, when you buy stock in the stock market, you are buying from an existing shareholder; you are not buying newly issued shares from the company.

it was materially misleading because it omitted important information, a Rule 10b-5 lawsuit against her may be viable.

With respect to "omission" cases, that is, cases where the allegation is that the defendant failed to reveal material information, the defendant must have been under a duty to do so. Thus, if Person A sells a security to Person B but does not reveal a material fact, Person B will not have a Rule 10b-5 cause of action against Person A unless Person A owed a fiduciary or fiduciary-like duty to Person B. After all, *silence* is generally only actionable if the defendant had a duty to speak.

Applying this general rule to a corporation, let's revisit the *Texas Gulf Sulphur* case. As you recall, TGS knew about its major mineral strike long before it announced it to the public and had valid business reasons for delaying the release of this information. If the facts of the case had ended there, TGS itself (as opposed to the insiders of the TGS that were buying its stock on the basis of this material nonpublic information) would have had no liability.[*] However, had TGS been buying its own stock, or had it failed to *correct* information that it had issued and that was still "circulating" or "alive" in the market (meaning that investors were still assuming the accuracy of the information), a court would likely have imposed on TGS a "duty to speak." Note, however, that there is no duty to update information that was *as of a specific date*, such as financial statements.

Scienter.   Further, the defendant must have acted with the requisite amount of scienter. The Supreme Court in *Ernst & Ernst v. Hochfelder*, 425 U.S. 185 (1976), held that an "intent to deceive, manipulate, or defraud" was sufficient, but left open the question of whether recklessness would suffice (although it did hold that negligence was not a sufficient level of scienter). Since then, lower federal courts have held that recklessness is a sufficient level scienter for a Rule 10b-5 lawsuit.

Reliance or "Transaction Causation."   The plaintiff in a private Rule 10b-5 lawsuit must also prove reliance (sometimes called "transaction causation"), that is, that she relied on the defendant's material misstatement or material omission in deciding to buy or sell a security. Wait a minute, you might say—how can a plaintiff possibly prove that she relied on an *omission*? Luckily for plaintiffs, in situations where the defendant owed a "duty to speak" to the plaintiff but did not reveal a material fact, courts presume reliance.

---

[*]   In a portion of the case that is omitted from this textbook, the court found that TGS had violated Rule 10b-5 by issuing a materially misleading press release, in which is essentially denied the existence of the mineral discovery.

Another time when reliance is presumed is known as "fraud on the market," which is the situation where the defendant makes a material misstatement with respect to a *publicly traded* security that affects the price of the security.[*] The theory is that, because the securities markets are efficient (or at least most economists believe them to be efficient under the "semi-strong" formulation of the efficient capital markets hypothesis, which you may have learned about in business school), market forces "accurately" price securities by digesting all of the publicly available information about them and then factoring that information into the price. To take a simple example, if a company announces good news, the price of its stock will increase, with the precise amount of the price increase depending on how good the news is. But what if the news is not accurate? In the example a few pages ago, if the president of ABC Corp. makes optimistic statements that are materially false, the market will likely react to this news by assuming that it is true and then increasing the market price of ABC stock. Persons who bought ABC stock at the current (but artificially inflated) price can be said to have relied on the market as a whole to price ABC stock accurately and would not need to show reliance on the misstatement in a Rule 10b-5 lawsuit.

"Loss Causation" and Damages. Finally, the plaintiff must also show that the defendant's actions affected the price of the security (known as "loss causation"). *See also* Section 21D(b)(4) of the Exchange Act. In a face-to-face transaction where the defendant made material misrepresentations, this may be relatively easy to show, but difficult to quantify. In the case of materially false statements made by a corporate official or other person, if there was no change in the price of the security as a result (or if the price of the security did not change when the "real" news was made public), then the plaintiff would be unable to show loss causation. With respect to damages, suffice it to say that there are many different formulas, depending on the facts. However, rescission typically would only be appropriate with respect to a face-to-face transaction.

Other Situations. Rule 10b-5 has been used as the legal authority for suing in many situations that may surprise you. For example, if you suspect that your stockbroker is "churning" your account, that is, engaging in excessive amounts of trading so as to generate greater commissions (and can satisfy certain other requirements), you may have a Rule 10b-5 cause of action against her. *See, e.g., Mihara v. Dean Witter & Co.*, 619 F.2d 814 (9th Cir. 1980). Similarly, if your broker recommended investments that are "unsuitable" in light of the investment objectives that you communicated to her (and certain other requirements are met), you may also have a valid Rule 10b-5 cause of action. *See,*

---

[*] In *Stoneridge Investment Partners, LLC v. Scientific-Atlanta, Inc.*, 552 U.S. 148 (2008), the Supreme Court made it clear that the fraud-on-the-market theory requires that the defendant's misstatements were communicated publicly.

e.g., O'Connor v. R.F. Lafferty & Co., Inc., 965 F.2d 893 (10th Cir. 1992). The list goes on, and will almost certainly continue to evolve.

Final Notes. Finally, the Private Securities Litigation Reform Act of 1995 and other federal legislation made things substantially more difficult for plaintiffs in Rule 10b-5 lawsuits, such as by requiring the plaintiff to meet stringent pleading requirements and imposing new rules on class action lawsuits. Again, you might learn more about this, and other aspects of Rule 10b-5, in a course on Securities Regulation.

Thus concludes our chapter on Rule 10b-5 and Section 16(b). Set forth below are some practice multiple choice questions. As always, the answers appear in the Appendix.

PRACTICE QUESTIONS

Multiple Choice Question 14-1: Elvis Ronson was the CEO of Drugs 'n' Stuff, Inc., a biotechnology company whose stock was traded on the New York Stock Exchange. In June, Drugs 'n' Stuff publicly announced that it was working on developing a drug that would cure colon cancer. By July, the press and several independent medical experts publicly touted this drug as the next "wonder drug." From June to December, the price of Drugs 'n' Stuff stock increased from $30 per share to $60 per share, based primarily on the promising news about this drug. In August, Drugs 'n' Stuff submitted the drug for approval with the U.S. Food and Drug Administration ("FDA"). On December 1, the FDA informed Elvis that it would not approve the drug for use in the United States because it had many adverse side effects. The FDA made its public announcement of their non-approval of the drug at 9:00 a.m. on December 2. By 11:00 a.m., several TV news networks broadcast reports of the FDA's non-approval of the drug. By 11:45 a.m., the price of Drugs 'n' Stuff stock fell from $60 per share to $50 share. At 12:15 p.m. on December 2, Elvis sold 10,000 shares of Drugs 'n' Stuff stock for $45 per share. Elvis had previously purchased his 10,000 shares of Drugs 'n' Stuff stock for $33 per share on July 15. *Based on the foregoing, which of the following statements is correct?*

A.   Elvis has violated Rule 10b-5 and Section 16(b).
B.   Elvis has violated Rule 10b-5, but he has not violated Section 16(b).
C.   Elvis has violated Section 16(b), but he has not violated Rule 10b-5.
D.   Elvis has violated neither Rule 10b-5 nor Section 16(b).

QUESTIONS 14-2 TO 14-4 ARE BASED ON THE FOLLOWING FACTS

Bill Beancounter worked in the accounting department of Large Corp., a publicly traded corporation whose common stock was listed on the New York Stock Exchange. On a Friday afternoon in March, while working on the audit of Large Corp.'s financial statements for the previous year, Bill discovered that financial statements that Large Corp. had included in previous filings with the Securities and Exchange Commission (the SEC) grossly overstated the amounts of Large Corp.'s revenues. For example, in its quarterly report to the SEC for the quarter ended September 30 of the previous year Large Corp. had stated that its revenues were $100 million. In fact, Bill discovered that the correct number was closer to $30 million. Depressed, Bill went to a St. Patrick's Day party with his friend Andy that evening where Bill proceeded to consume several bottles of beer. The alcohol deepened his depression. When Andy asked Bill what was wrong, Bill, now severely intoxicated, told Andy what he had discovered. Another guest at the party, Tom, overheard this conversation, but neither Bill nor Andy knew that Tom heard what Bill said to Andy. Tom owned 500 shares of Large Corp.

common stock, but had no other relationship to Large Corp. On the following Monday morning, while Large Corp. common stock was trading at $10 per share, Tom sold all of his shares of Large Corp. stock through his stockbroker. That same day, Bill remembered that his friend Angie (whom Bill had been trying unsuccessfully to date) owned more than 1,000 shares of Large Corp. common stock. Bill telephoned Angie and had the following conversation:

BILL: "Hi Angie, it's Bill."

ANGIE: "Hi Bill. How are things at Large Corp.?"

BILL: "Well, not so good. Say, do you still own Large Corp. stock?"

ANGIE: "Yes I do."

BILL: "Well, you probably should sell it pretty soon."

ANGIE: "Why?"

BILL: "Well, I can't really tell you, but let's just say that a little birdie told me that there's going to be some bad news about the company coming out soon."

ANGIE: "Thanks for the advice."

BILL: "No problem. Maybe we can go on a date some time."

ANGIE: "It's a deal. Meet me at the Black Rose Pub on Friday after work. Bye."

Angie, who had no relationship to Large Corp. other than as a shareholder, then called her stockbroker and arranged to sell all of her shares of Large Corp. stock. Three weeks later, Bill persuaded Large Corp. to file corrected versions of its financial statements with the SEC. After these financial statements were filed, the trading price of Large Corp. stock plummeted to $4 per share.

Questions appear on the following page

Multiple Choice Question 14-2: Which of the following is a correct statement as to whether Bill has violated any provision of or rule under the Securities Exchange Act of 1934? Please choose the best answer.

A. Bill violated Rule 10b-5 by "tipping" both Tom and Angie about material nonpublic information.
B. Bill violated Rule 10b-5 by "tipping" Angie about material nonpublic information.
C. Bill did not violate Rule 10b-5, but he did violate Section 16(b).
D. Bill did not violate Rule 10b-5 because he did not purchase or sell any shares of Large Corp. stock on the basis of material nonpublic information.

Multiple Choice Question 14-3: Which of the following is a correct statement as to whether Angie has violated Rule 10b-5 under the Securities Exchange Act of 1934? Please choose the best answer.

A. Angie violated Rule 10b-5 because she misappropriated material nonpublic information from Bill.
B. Angie violated Rule 10b-5 because she was an insider of the company and traded on the basis of material nonpublic information.
C. Angie did not violate Rule 10b-5 because she owed no duty of trust or confidence to Large Corp.
D. Angie violated Rule 10b-5 because she was a "tippee" who traded on the basis of material nonpublic information.

Multiple Choice Question 14-4: Which of the following is a correct statement as to whether Tom has violated Rule 10b-5 under the Securities Exchange Act of 1934? Please choose the best answer.

A. Tom violated Rule 10b-5 because he traded on the basis of material nonpublic information that he knew came from a source (Bill) that owned a duty of confidentiality to Large Corp.
B. Tom violated Rule 10b-5 because he misappropriated material nonpublic information from Bill.
C. Tom violated Rule 10b-5 because he should have known that Bill was intoxicated.
D. Tom did not violate Rule 10b-5.

QUESTIONS 14-5 TO 14-8 ARE BASED ON THE FOLLOWING FACTS

Potato Chip Corp. ("PCC") common stock is traded on the Nasdaq Stock Market. In early June, the board of directors of a privately held competitor, Nacho Corp. ("Nacho"), decided to investigate the possibility of making a cash tender offer of $40 per share for 100% of PCC's stock. However, before making a formal tender offer or discussing it with PCC, Nacho purchased 4% of PCC's outstanding stock secretly through several different stockbrokers, without publicly disclosing its identity or intentions, for an average price of $26 per share.

Carrie Cruncher was employed as an accountant by PCC. On Friday, July 11, Paul Potato, who is PCC's President, asked Carrie to prepare a binder of financial statements and other financial information concerning PCC. When Carrie asked why, Paul told her: "Well, I shouldn't tell you this, but I trust you to keep this top secret. We've been negotiating to be acquired by Nacho Corp. It looks like Nacho is going to make a tender offer for PCC stock for $40 per share, but Nacho wants some more information about PCC before it makes a final decision." Carrie then asked: "That's great for our shareholders, but what will happen to employees like me?" Paul replied: "I suppose that Nacho will keep some of our employees, but I suspect that many will be laid off. But I promise to recommend that they keep you."

When she came home from work that day, Carrie was very upset and told her husband, Chuck (who is not employed by PCC), about Nacho's possible tender offer, but reminded him that it was a "top secret" situation and that he couldn't tell anyone about it. Later that night, however, after Carrie had fallen asleep, Chuck called his mother, Grace, and told her: "Go buy some PCC Corp. stock on Monday. Something big is happening—PCC is going to be sold." The following Monday, Grace purchased 1,000 shares of PCC common stock for $26 per share.

Meanwhile, around midnight on Friday, July 11, a janitor, Cletus Clean, was cleaning Carrie's office and happened to see a three-ring binder entitled "Confidential Financial Information For Tender Offer by Nacho Corp. for Potato Chip Corp. Stock." Cletus was not employed by PCC, but instead worked for Cleaning Crew, Inc., a firm that cleans office buildings. Seven years ago, Cletus had signed Cleaning Crew's standard employment contract, which prohibited him from using any client information he might come across while on the job. He also signed a similar confidentiality agreement with PCC. Nonetheless, the following Monday, Cletus purchased 100 shares of PCC common stock for $26 per share. In early August, Nacho started its tender offer for PCC stock at $40 per share. Assume for purposes of the following questions that the information about Nacho's proposed tender offer was material nonpublic information before the tender offer started, within the meaning of Rule 10b-5 under the Securities Exchange Act of 1934.

Multiple Choice Question 14-5: *Did Nacho's secret purchase of 4% of PCC's stock in June violate federal securities laws?*

A. Yes, because Nacho was required to disclose these secret purchases to the Securities and Exchange Commission (the "SEC") by filing a Schedule 13D.
B. Yes, because Nacho's secret purchases were a manipulative and deceptive device
    under Rule 10b-5, which acted as a fraud upon PCC's shareholders.
C. Yes, Nacho violated Rule 14e-3.
D. No, because Nacho had no reporting requirements to the SEC under the above facts.
E. No, because the SEC only regulates stock purchases that constitute insider trading under Rule 10b-5.

Multiple Choice Question 14-6: *Did Carrie violate Rule 10b-5? Choose the best answer.*

A. Yes. Carrie had a *Cady, Roberts* duty to PCC and violated Rule 10b-5 by "tipping" Chuck about material nonpublic information in violation of that duty.
B. Yes. Carrie violated Rule 10b-5 by "misappropriating" material nonpublic information from PCC.
C. Yes. Chuck violated Rule 10b-5; this means that Carrie also violated Rule 10b-5.
D. No, Carrie did not violate Rule 10b-5.

Multiple Choice Question 14-7: *Did Chuck violate Rule 10b-5? Choose the best answer.*

A. Yes. Chuck violated Rule 10b-5 because he was a "tippee" of Carrie and was also a "tipper" of Grace.
B. Yes. Chuck violated Rule 10b-5 because he misappropriated material nonpublic
    information from Carrie and then "tipped" Grace.
C. Yes. Chuck violated Rule 10b-5 because, as Carrie's husband, he owed a *Cady, Roberts* duty to PCC and thus could not "tip" Grace.
D. No. Chuck did not violate Rule 10b-5 because he owed no duties to PCC or Carrie.

Multiple Choice Question 14-8: *Did Cletus violate Rule 10b-5? Choose the best answer.*

A.   Yes. Cletus violated Rule 10b-5 because he traded on the basis of material nonpublic information when he knew or should have known that Carrie would be violating her *Cady, Roberts* duty to PCC by disclosing the information to him.

B.   Yes. Cletus violated Rule 10b-5 because he misappropriated material nonpublic information from PCC and/or Cleaning Crew.

C.   No. Cletus did not violate Rule 10b-5 because he owed no duty of trust or confidence to Carrie or PCC.

D.   No. Cletus did not violate Rule 10b-5 because Carrie did not receive any personal benefit when Cletus learned of the information.

QUESTIONS 14-9 TO 14-11 ARE BASED ON THE FOLLOWING FACTS

Mr. Yellow is the President of Yellow Corp., whose stock is listed on the New York Stock Exchange. Yellow Corp. is engaged in negotiations to be acquired by Orange Corp. in a merger. Although Yellow's shareholders will be paid handsomely for their shares in this merger, Mr. Yellow will be out of a job afterwards, which has made him depressed. On April 15, Mr. Yellow attended a college basketball game with his wife. When she thought that he looked sad, Mrs. Yellow asked Mr. Yellow what was wrong. Mr. Yellow then told her about the planned merger. Sitting a few rows behind them was Fred Fan, who overheard their conversation. Fred is not an employee of Yellow Corp. and has never met Mr. Yellow. On April 20, Fred bought 200 shares of Yellow Corp. stock. The merger was announced on April 30.

Multiple Choice Question 14-9: *Did Fred violate Rule 10b-5? Choose the best answer.*

A.   No, because Fred does not owe any duties to Yellow Corp. or Mr. Yellow.

B.   No, because the information was not material.

C.   Yes, because Fred misappropriated material nonpublic information from Yellow Corp.

D.   Yes, because Fred misappropriated material nonpublic information from Mr. Yellow.

Multiple Choice Question 14-10: In addition, Mr. Yellow called his stockbroker and bought 150,000 shares of Yellow Corp. several days before the merger was publicly announced. *Did Mr. Yellow violate state-law prohibitions on insider trading? Choose the best answer.*

A.   No, because the information was not "material."
B.   No, because Mr. Yellow owed no duties to Yellow Corp. or its shareholders in this fact pattern.
C.   No, because Mr. Yellow did not purchase Yellow Corp. stock in a face-to-face transaction.
D.   Mr. Yellow is liable for insider trading based on state law in this fact pattern.

Multiple Choice Question 14-11: In addition, the president of Orange Corp., Mr. Orange, called his stockbroker and bought 10,000 shares of Yellow Corp. several days before the merger was publicly announced. *Did Mr. Orange violate Rule 10b-5? Choose the best answer.*

A.   No, because Mr. Orange owed no duties to Yellow Corp. or its shareholders in this fact pattern.
B.   No, because no one in the fact pattern "tipped" Mr. Orange.
C.   Yes, this is an example of "classic" insider trading.
D.   Yes, this is an example of misappropriation.

Multiple Choice Question 14-12: Baby Food Corp. common stock is listed on the New York Stock Exchange. On September 1, 2011, Mr. Toddler, who is a director of Baby Food Corp., purchased 10,000 shares of Baby Food Corp. common stock for $20 per share. On November 23, 2011, Mr. Toddler purchased an additional 5,000 shares of Baby Food Corp. common stock for $21 per share. On April 1, 2012, Mr. Toddler sold 15,000 shares of Baby Food Corp. common stock for $22 per share. *What is Mr. Toddler's liability to Baby Food Corp. under Section 16(b) of the Securities Exchange Act of 1934?*

A. $5,000.
B. $10,000.
C. $25,000.
D. $30,000.

Multiple Choice Question 14-13: Baby Food Corp. common stock is listed on the New York Stock Exchange.   There are 1,000,000 shares of Baby Food Corp. common stock outstanding. On June 30, Mr. Crier did not own any Baby Food Corp. common stock. However, on July 1, Mr. Crier purchased 200,000 shares of Baby Food Corp. common stock for $20 per share. On August 17, Mr. Crier purchased an additional 50,000 shares of Baby Food Corp. common stock for $21 per share. On September 30, Mr. Crier sold 60,000 shares of Baby Food Corp. common stock for $22 per share. On October 31, Mr. Crier sold 190,000 shares of Baby Food Corp. common stock for $22 per share, thereby reducing his holdings of Baby Food common stock to zero.   At no time during these events was Mr. Crier an officer or director of Baby Food Corp. *What, if anything, is Mr. Crier's liability to Baby Food Corp. under Section 16(b) of the Securities Exchange Act of 1934?*

A. $50,000.
B. $60,000.
C. $120,000.
D. $500,000.

Multiple Choice Question 14-14:   Cop Corp. common stock is listed on the Nasdaq Stock Market. On January 23, Mr. Robber, who is a director of Cop Corp., purchased 1,000 shares of Cop Corp. common stock for $10 per share. On May 3, Mr. Robber purchased 2,000 shares of Cop Corp. common stock for $11 per share. On August 10, Mr. Robber sold 2,000 shares of Cop Corp. common stock for $14 per share. On December 10, Mr. Robber purchased 1,000 shares of Cop Corp. common stock for $9 per share. *What, if anything, is Mr. Robber's liability to Cop Corp. under Section 16(b) of the Securities Exchange Act of 1934?*

A. $5,000.
B. $6,000.
C. $8,000.
D. $9,000.

Multiple Choice Question 14-15: Mondo Corp. common stock is listed on the New York Stock Exchange. Mr. Bondo has been a director of Mondo Corp. for many years, but only shows up to board meetings about once a year (if he's lucky). Mr. Bondo decided to buy some Mondo Corp. stock, because he hadn't yet bought any. Thus, on April 13, Mr. Bondo purchased 3,000 shares of Mondo Corp. stock for $10 per share. On July 7, Mr. Bondo attended a meeting of the board of directors of Mondo Corp. and was surprised to learn that Mondo Corp.'s business was not doing very well. As a result, Mr. Bondo sold all 3,000 of his shares of Mondo stock the next day, for $8 per share. On October 28, Mr. Bondo read in the paper that Mondo Corp.'s business was starting to recover, so he purchased 1,000 shares for $7 per share. *What, if anything, is Mr. Bondo's liability to Mondo Corp. under Section 16(b) of the Securities Exchange Act of 1934?*

A. $1,000.
B. $3,000.
C. $9,000.
D.   Nothing, because the first transaction was more than six months before the last transaction.

Multiple Choice Question 14-16: Sharp Corp. common stock is listed on the New York Stock Exchange. There are 1,000,000 shares of Sharp Corp. common stock outstanding. On March 13, Mr. Dull, who is neither an officer nor a director of Sharp Corp., owned 99,000 shares of Sharp Corp. common stock. On March 13, Mr. Dull purchased 2,000 shares of Sharp Corp. common stock for $6 per share. On April 13, Mr. Dull purchased an additional 2,000 shares of Sharp Corp. common stock for $7 per share. On August 7, Mr. Dull sold 10,000 shares of Sharp Corp. common stock for $8 per share. *What, if anything, is Mr. Dull's liability to Sharp Corp. under Section 16(b) of the Securities Exchange Act?*

A. $2,000.
B. $4,000.
C. $6,000.
D.   Nothing.

Multiple Choice Question 14-17:   Radio Corp. common stock is listed on the Nasdaq Stock Market. There are 5,000,000 shares of Radio Corp. common stock outstanding. On May 7, Mr. Video, who is a director of Radio Corp., purchased 12,000 shares of Radio Corp. common stock for $17 per share. On October 10, Mr. Video sold 10,000 shares of Radio Corp. common stock for $15 per share. On December 3, Mr. Video sold 2,000 shares of Radio Corp. common stock for $20 per share. *What, if anything, is Mr. Video's liability to Radio Corp. under Section 16(b) of the Securities Exchange Act?*

A. $36,000.
B. $20,000.
C. $6,000.
D.   Nothing.

CHAPTER 15
LIMITED PARTNERSHIPS

In Chapter 1, you learned a little about limited partnerships and limited liability companies (LLCs), among other things. In this chapter, you will learn a great deal more about limited partnerships. In the following chapter, you will learn a great deal more about LLCs. In addition, both chapters will give you an opportunity to review some of the many things that you learned about partnerships and corporations in the preceding chapters. This is because, in many ways, both limited partnerships and LLCs combine attributes of partnerships and corporations; some call limited partnerships and LLCs "hybrid" business organizations. For example, LLCs combine the centralized management and limited liability features of corporations with the flow-through taxation and contractual flexibility features of partnerships. To a large extent, limited partnerships do the same. Of course, both limited partnerships and LLCs are in many ways unique "creatures," as you will see in this chapter and the next.

§ 15.01   CHAPTER OVERVIEW

Limited Partnerships v. General Partnerships. To get a sense of the basic attributes of a limited partnership, perhaps it is best to begin with a review of the characteristics of *general* partnerships and then compare and contrast them with limited partnerships. As you recall from Chapters 3 and 4, a partnership is an association of two or more persons to carry on as co-owners a business for profit. Under RUPA, a partnership is a separate entity from its partners. The same is true of a limited partnership; Section 104(a) of ULPA (defined below) provides that a "limited partnership is an entity distinct from its partners." Moreover, Section 105 provides that a limited partnership "has the power to do all things necessary or convenient to carry on its activities," such as the ability to sue and be sued.

Unlike a corporation, a general partnership can be formed accidentally; no filings with the state are necessary to begin the existence of a general partnership. However, a limited partnership *does* require that a certificate of limited partnership be filed with the state. Until that filing is made, a limited partnership does not exist. This issue is explored in more detail in Section 15.02 below.

As you undoubtedly recall from Chapter 3, RUPA allows partners a great deal of flexibility in structuring their relationship. In other words, RUPA is largely a collection of "default" rules that apply in the absence of contrary rules in the partnership's partnership agreement (assuming those rules do not run afoul of

RUPA § 103(b)). As explored in more detail in Section 15.02 below, the limited partnership statute takes a similar approach.

Another characteristic of general partnerships is that (unless the partnership agreement provides otherwise), partners are "equal" in terms of voting rights and profit-sharing. Here, there are some serious differences with a limited partnership. In a limited partnership, there are *two kinds of partners*; there must be at least one general partner and there must be at least one limited partner. (Usually, a limited partnership will have one general partner and several limited partners.) Typically, the general partner has control over the business, that is, the right to make all of the business decisions affecting the limited partnership, whereas the limited partners have none. Because of this, limited partners are sometimes called "passive" investors. To a degree, this may remind you of a corporation, with the general partner resembling the board of directors and the limited partners resembling the shareholders.

But why would anyone in her right mind want to be a limited partner with virtually no control over the business, as opposed a general partner, which has full control? The answer lies in the rules concerning liability. Although there are some exceptions to this statement that you will learn about in Section 15.04 below, a general partner is personally liable for the debts and obligations of the limited partnership (much like a partner in a general partnership is liable for the partnership's debts and obligations), whereas limited partners are not. As such, the worst-case scenario for a limited partner if the limited partnership files for bankruptcy is that she will lose her investment in the limited partnership. But— much like a shareholder with respect to a corporation—at least her personal assets will not be seized by the limited partnership's creditors. Thus, the trade-off for limited partners giving up control is that they gain a liability "shield."

Under RUPA, partners in a general partnership share profits (and losses) equally, unless there is a different rule in the partnership agreement. Things are quite different in a limited partnership—usually, the partners share profits and losses proportionally based on the capital contributions that they have made to the limited partnership. (In addition, the general partner often is paid a fee for managing the limited partnership.)

As you also learned in Chapter 3, a partner in a general partnership owes fiduciary duties of care and loyalty to the partnership and her fellow partners. However, in a limited partnership, only the general partner is deemed to owe fiduciary duties; limited partners do not. This, of course, is a consequence of the fact that the general partner has control over the limited partnership whereas the limited partners do not.

Finally, another major difference is that the rules governing dissociation and dissolution are very different in limited partnerships than they are in general partnerships. Generally speaking, if a general partner dissociates, the limited partnership *might* dissolve. However, if a limited partner dissociates, dissolution of the limited partnership will not occur.

What Statute to Use? Before exploring these issues in the following sections, a few words about limited partnership statutes are in order. It was a difficult decision to choose which statute to discuss in this textbook. Here's why.

The first uniform limited partnership statute "on the books" was the Uniform Limited Partnership Act, which the National Conference of Commissioners on Uniform State Laws (NCCUSL) promulgated in 1916. However, in 1976, a new uniform statute called the Revised Uniform Limited Partnership Act, variously called "RULPA" or "RULPA (1976)," was passed. RULPA was substantially amended in 1985, and is now sometimes called "RULPA (1985)."

RULPA (1985) is not a "stand alone" statute. That is, RULPA "links" to the Uniform Partnership Act (1914), otherwise known as "UPA." For example, Section 1105 of RULPA (1985) states that "[i]n any case not provided for in this [Act] the provisions of the Uniform Partnership Act govern." However, as discussed in Chapter 1 of this textbook, approximately 35 states now use some version of *RUPA* (as opposed to UPA). For that reason, Chapters 3 and 4 of this textbook discussed RUPA, and only mentioned UPA in passing. Thus, focusing on RULPA (1985) in this chapter would present some practical difficulties because this textbook has not previously covered UPA in any depth.

Fortunately, in 2001 the NCCUSL promulgated an entirely new, "stand alone" limited partnership statute, called the Uniform Limited Partnership Act (2001), or "ULPA (2001)." As the NCCUSL explained in the prefatory note to ULPA (2001):

> The linkage question was the first major issue considered and decided by this Act's Drafting Committee. Since the [NCCUSL] has recommended the repeal of the UPA, it made no sense to recommend retaining the UPA as the base and link for a revised or new limited partnership act. The drafting Committee therefore had to choose between recommending linkage to the new general partnership act (i.e., RUPA) or recommending de-linking and a stand alone act.

The Committee saw several substantial advantages to de-linking. A stand alone statute would:

- be more convenient, providing a single, self-contained source of statutory authority for issues pertaining to limited partnerships;

- eliminate confusion as to which issues were solely subject to the limited partnership act and which required reference (i.e., linkage) to the general partnership act; and

- rationalize future case law, by ending the automatic link between the cases concerning partners in a general partnership and issues pertaining to general partners in a limited partnership.

Thus, a stand alone act seemed likely to promote efficiency, clarity, and coherence in the law of limited partnerships.

For the above reasons, this chapter will cover ULPA (2001). As of early 2011, however, only sixteen states (as well as Washington D.C.) had adopted ULPA (2001) and three other states had introduced bills to adopt it. Most other states continue to use RULPA (1985), making it likely that you will encounter RULPA (1985) in practice if you deal with limited partnerships. For this reason, as well as the fact that there are a few major differences between ULPA (2001) and RULPA (1985), this chapter will also cover the relevant rule from RULPA (1985) in a few places.

Why Use a Limited Partnership? The primary advantages of a limited partnership are that it combines the contractual flexibility and flow-through taxation attributes of a general partnership with the limited liability (at least for the limited partners) and centralized management features of a corporation. But this same combination of benefits could also be achieved with an LLC, an LLP, or even an "S" corporation. Why, then, are there still so many limited partnerships out there? Perhaps a portion of the prefatory note to ULPA can help answer this question:

The new Act has been drafted for a world in which limited liability partnerships and limited liability companies can meet many of the needs formerly met by limited partnerships. This Act therefore targets two types of enterprises that seem largely beyond the scope of LLPs and LLCs: (i) sophisticated, manager-entrenched commercial deals whose participants commit for the long term, and (ii) estate planning arrangements (family limited partnerships).

This Act accordingly assumes that, more often than not, people utilizing [a limited partnership] will want:

- strong centralized management, strongly entrenched, and

- passive investors with little control over or right to exit the entity.

The Act's rules, and particularly its default rules, have been designed to reflect these assumptions.

§ 15.02   FORMING A LIMITED PARTNERSHIP

Objectives: *You should be able to explain to a client who wants to start a business as a limited partnership (1) what steps are necessary to form a limited partnership and (2) some issues the client should consider in drafting a limited partnership agreement. You should also be able to explain what the limited partnership must do if it intends to transact business in a state other than the state in which it is organized.*

Section 201(a) of ULPA[*] provides that "[i]n order for a limited partnership to be formed, a certificate of limited partnership must be delivered to" the appropriate governmental office in the state, such as the secretary of state. In this way, a limited partnership is similar to a corporation: it does not legally exist until the appropriate document is filed with the state. (*But see* subsection (c) of Section 201.) Fortunately, the required contents of a certificate of limited partnership are minimal; they are set forth in subsections (a)(1) through (5) of Section 201.

Problems

Problem 15-1: Assume that a general partner and several limited partners begin running a business as a limited partnership but the general partner neglects to file a certificate of limited partnership. *If the business is not a limited partnership, then what is it?*

---

*   For ease of reading, ULPA (2001) will simply be called "ULPA" for the remainder of this chapter.

Problem 15-2: Your client, Pam McGillicutty, wants to form a limited partnership that will run a restaurant and has hired you to draft the certificate of limited partnership. Pam plans to be the general partner, with her husband and two daughters as the limited partners. Pam plans to name the limited partnership "The McGillicutty Restaurant." *Is this a proper name to appear in the certificate of limited partnership? See* ULPA § 108.

Problem 15-3: *Could Pam be both a general partner and a limited partner? See* ULPA § 113.

Problem 15-4: *Instead of Pam herself being the general partner of the limited partnership, could she form a corporation and have that corporation serve as the general partner? If so, would that be a good idea?*

Problem 15-5: *How may a certificate of limited partnership be amended? See* ULPA § 202.

Typically, a limited partnership will organize in (that is, file its certificate of limited partnership in) the state in which it plans to conduct most of its business. But this does not have to be the case. Much like forming a corporation, you could form your limited partnership under any state's limited partnership statute. The law of that state will then govern the "internal affairs" of the limited partnership, i.e., the relations among the partners and the relations between the partners and the limited partnership. *See* ULPA §§ 106, 901(a).

In addition, much like a corporation, if a limited partnership that is organized under the law of, say, State A "transacts business" in State B, then State B will consider the limited partnership to be a "foreign" limited partnership and require it to obtain a certificate of authority to transact business in State B. *See* ULPA § 902. Note here that ULPA § 903 contains a list of activities that, by themselves, do not constitute "transacting business" in a given state. (All of this should remind you of the discussion of foreign corporations in Section 5.02(A) of Chapter 5.)

The other charter document of a limited partnership, which in most ways is more important than the certificate of limited partnership, is the limited partnership agreement. Much like a partnership agreement may modify most of the default rules of RUPA, a limited partnership agreement may modify many— but not all—of the rules of ULPA. To this end, Section 110 of ULPA provides that:

Except as otherwise provided in subsection (b), the partnership agreement governs relations among the partners and between the partners and the partnership.   To the extent the partnership agreement does not otherwise provide, this [Act] governs relations among the partners and between the partners and the partnership.

Problems

Problem 15-6: *May a limited partnership agreement modify or eliminate a general partner's duty of care?*

Problem 15-7: *May a limited partnership agreement modify or eliminate a general partner's duty of loyalty?*

Problem 15-8: *Must a limited partnership agreement be in writing? See* ULPA § 102(13).

Problem 15-9: *How may a limited partnership agreement be amended? See* ULPA § 406(b).

Problem 15-10: *What happens if there is a conflict between the certificate of limited partnership and the limited partnership agreement? See* ULPA § 201(d). (The answer may surprise you.)

§ 15.03   DECISION-MAKING AND FIDUCIARY DUTIES

Objectives: You should be able to explain to the partners of a limited partnership (1) how business decisions affecting the limited partnership may be made; (2) whether any decisions will require approval by the limited partners; (3) whether the actions of a partner (whether a general partner or a limited partner) may bind the limited partnership and, if so, how; and (4) whether partners owe fiduciary duties to the limited partnership and, if so, the nature of those fiduciary duties. In addition, you should be able to explain how the general partner is chosen and whether the general partner may be removed and replaced by the limited partners.

As stated above, limited partners have no power to manage the limited partnership. As such, ULPA § 302 puts it plainly: "A limited partner does not have the right or the power as a limited partner to act for or bind the limited partnership." This does not mean, however, that a limited partner could not be an employee of the limited partnership and have *agency* authority (that is, apparent or actual authority) to bind the limited partnership to contracts. It simply means that, *in her capacity as a limited partner*, she has no power to bind the limited partnership. A logical consequence of the fact that limited partners have no power to manage the business is that they do not owe fiduciary duties of care and loyalty to the limited partnership or to the other partners simply as a result of being limited partners. *See* ULPA § 305.

The rules for the general partner(s) are exactly the opposite. ULPA § 406(a) states that, except as ULPA may expressly provide in a different section, "any matter relating to the activities [i.e., business] of the limited partnership may be exclusively decided by the general partner or, if there is more than one general partner, by a majority of the general partners." However, a few things do require limited partner consent, such as amending the limited partnership agreement or the certificate of limited partnership, or selling all or

---

How is the General Partner Chosen or Replaced?
Typically, the general partner will be the founder of the limited partnership and will seek out the limited partners, rather than vice versa. However, even though the general partner owes fiduciary duties to the limited partners, ULPA only allows the limited partners to remove the general partner into two situations: unanimously, if one of the conditions in ULPA § 603(4) is present; or though a court order under ULPA § 603(5). For this reason, limited partners may want the partnership agreement to give them the right to remove the general partner in additional situations.

---

substantially all of the limited partnership's assets "other than in the usual and regular course of the limited partnership's activities." *See* RULPA § 406(b). And, of course, you should not forget that the limited partnership agreement could give the limited partners additional rights to approve certain actions.

ULPA § 402 provides that each general partner is an agent of the limited partnership and has apparent authority to bind the limited partnership to actions that are in the ordinary course of business, "unless the general partner did not have authority to act for the limited partnership in the particular matter and the person with which the general partner was dealing knew, had received a notification, or had notice under Section 103(d) that the general partner lacked authority." (This should remind you of RUPA § 301.)

Furthermore, the general partner may have actual authority to do acts that are outside the ordinary course of business. (This also should remind you of RUPA § 301.) The most likely source of such actual authority would be the limited partnership agreement. *See* ULPA § 402(b). Not surprisingly, ULPA § 403(a) makes the limited partnership liable for the general partner's "wrongful act[s] or omission[s], or other actionable conduct ... in the ordinary course of activities of the limited partnership or with authority of the limited partnership."

> **_Derivative Lawsuits_**
> What if a general partner breaches her fiduciary
> duties, thereby injuring the limited partnership,
> but refuses to cause the limited partnership to
> sue? Article 10 of ULPA allows a limited partner
> to bring a derivative action behalf of the limited
> partnership. ULPA's provisions are similar to,
> but much less complex than, the rules for
> derivative actions that you studied in Chapter 8.

Problem

Problem 15-11: *Is the general partner entitled to remuneration for its services? If ULPA does not so state, is there any way for the general partner to be compensated? See ULPA § 406(f).*

With power comes responsibility, or so the saying goes. Thus, ULPA § 408 imposes fiduciary duties on the general partner. Read that section closely and consider the following problems.

Problems

Problem 15-12: You represent Greg Jones, a wealthy real estate developer in Big City. Greg is considering becoming a general partner in a limited partnership to build and operate a large shopping mall. However, Greg is concerned that, if he becomes the general partner, the limited partners will try to prevent him from continuing to operate and invest in other real estate projects, particularly those that feature retail outlets. *What provisions would you suggest adding to the limited partnership agreement to alleviate Greg's concerns? See ULPA § 110(b)(5).*

Problem 15-13: Assume that Greg becomes the general partner, but negligently performs construction work. *Has Greg violated his duty of care to the partnership? See ULPA § 408(c).*

Problem 15-14: *Would your answer to Problem 15-13 change if the partnership agreement had provided that the general partner's duty of care is to avoid engaging in negligence, gross negligence, reckless conduct, intentional misconduct, or a knowing violation of law? See ULPA § 110(b)(6).*

<u>Problem 15-15</u>: *Would your answer to Problem 15-13 change if the partnership agreement had provided that the general partner's only duty of care is to avoid engaging in reckless conduct or intentional misconduct? See ULPA § 110(b)(6).*

§ 15.04   LIABILITY ISSUES

Objectives: Given a fact pattern in which a limited partnership incurs a liability to a third party, either contractually (such as in a loan from a bank) or by a tort (such as where the general partner or an employee of the limited partnership commits negligence in the course of partnership business), you should be able to (1) determine which person(s) are liable for this obligation and (2) explain how the creditor may recover against the assets that belong to the person(s) who are liable.

As noted above, the general partner of a limited partnership is personally liable for the debts and obligations of the limited partnership, but the limited partners are not. At least, this is the general rule. Of course, there is more to it than that.

Liability of the General Partner(s). First, assume that a creditor has a valid, but unpaid, claim against a limited partnership. Well, so far you know that the claim could be recovered from (1) the assets of the limited partnership and (2) the assets of the general partner, but that the claim could not be paid out of the personal assets of any *limited* partner. But as you learned in Chapter 3, if the debtor were a *general* partnership, the creditor could not simply start collecting the claim out of the partners' personal assets. ("Hey, I like that speed boat that Partner A owns. I think I'll take that in satisfaction of my claim against the partnership.") Instead, the creditor typically must attempt to collect from the *partnership* first. If the partnership cannot pay (or if one of the other conditions set forth in RUPA § 307(d) applies), then the creditor can proceed against a partner's personal assets (assuming that the creditor has a judgment against that partner).

How does this work in the context of a limited partnership? Sections 404 and 405 of ULPA provide the rules. Study them closely, see if they remind you of RUPA, and then try your hand at the following problems:

Problems

Problem 15-16: One year ago, Last National Bank (the Bank) made a substantial loan to ABC, L.P., a limited partnership, which has three partners: General Partner A and Limited Partners B and C. ABC, L.P. has defaulted on its loan and now only has assets equal to roughly half of the unpaid loan amount. *From which entities may the Bank potentially recover the loan?*

Problem 15-17: Same facts as Problem 15-16. Assume that the bank sues only ABC, L.P. and wins its lawsuit. *From which entities may the Bank recover the loan?*

Problem 15-18: Same facts as Problem 15-16. Assume that the bank sues only ABC, L.P. and General Partner A, and wins its lawsuit. *From which entities may the Bank potentially recover the loan? How would the Bank go about collecting the unpaid amounts? Would your answer change if there were two general partners?*

Problem 15-19: Same facts as Problem 15-18, except that General Partner A became the general partner of ABC, L.P. after the loan agreement was signed. (General Partner X was the general partner of ABC, L.P. at that time.) *From which entities may the Bank potentially recover the loan? How would the Bank go about collecting the unpaid amounts?*

Problem 15-20: *If you had been the Bank's lawyer at the time of the loan, what would you have recommended that it do in addition to having General Partner X sign the loan agreement on behalf of ABC, L.P.?*

Problem 15-21: Assume that General Partner A negligently injures a pedestrian while on partnership business. *Which entities are liable for this tort? How should the injured pedestrian go about suing (and collecting) on this claim?*

Liability of the Limited Partners. On the issue of limited partner liability, ULPA § 303 is clear:

An obligation of a limited partnership *** is not the obligation of a limited partner. A limited partner is not personally liable, directly or indirectly, by way of contribution or otherwise, for an obligation of the limited partnership solely by reason of being a limited partner, even if the limited partner participates in the management and control of the limited partnership.

As such, there's not much more to say about ULPA § 303. Limited partners are not liable for the limited partnership's obligations simply because they are limited partners. (However, under ULPA § 306, a person who *erroneously* believed that she was a limited partner may, in some circumstances, be liable to the same extent as a general partner.)

By contrast, RULPA contained a very different rule (although the official comment to ULPA § 303 calls it an "anachronism"). Because the RULPA rule is still in effect in some states, let's take a look at Section 303 of RULPA. First, subsection (a) provides that:

Except as provided in subsection (d)[*], a limited partner is not liable for the obligations of a limited partnership unless he [or she] is also a general partner or, in addition to the exercise of his [or her] rights and powers as a limited partner, he [or she] participates in the control of the business. However, if the limited partner participates in the control of the business, he [or she] is liable only to persons who transact business with the limited partnership reasonably believing, based upon the limited partner's conduct, that the limited partner is a general partner.

Because whether a limited partner's actions constituted "control" of the limited partnership was a heavily litigated issue, subsection (b) went on to provide in part that:

A limited partner does not participate in the control of the business within the meaning of subsection (a) solely by doing one or more of the following:

(1)   being a contractor for or an agent or employee of the limited partnership or of a general partner or being an officer, director, or shareholder of a general partner that is a corporation;

(2)   consulting with and advising a general partner with respect to the business of the limited partnership;

---

*   Subsection (d) provides that a "limited partner who knowingly permits his [or her] name to be used in the name of the limited partnership *** is liable to creditors who extend credit to the limited partnership without actual knowledge that the limited partner is not a general partner."

***

(6)   proposing, approving, or disapproving, by voting or otherwise, one or more of the following matters: ***

(7)   winding up the limited partnership pursuant to Section 803; or

(8)   exercising any right or power permitted to limited partners under this [Act] and not specifically enumerated in this subsection (b).

Further, subsection (c) provided that the "[e]numeration in subsection (b) does not mean that the possession or exercise of any other powers by a limited partner constitutes participation by him [or her] in the business of the limited partnership."

Problems

Problem 15-22: Vacation Paradise, L.P., a limited partnership ("VPLP"), runs a beach resort hotel and has three partners: Tom, who is the general partner; Sally, who is a limited partner and is also employed as the manager of the hotel; and Carlie, who is a limited partner and periodically consults with Tom on business matters. VPLP is governed by the 1976 version of RULPA. One day, a traveling salesman, Joe Holiday, visited the hotel and agreed with Sally that VPLP would buy all of its cleaning products from the supplier that Joe represented for the next two years. Sally signed the contract as "Manager of Vacation Paradise, L.P." *Is VPLP liable on this contract? If VPLP does not perform the contract, is Tom liable for damages? If VPLP does not perform the contract, are either Sally or Carlie liable for damages?*

Problem 15-23: After extensive research, Carlie advised Tom that she thought that VPLP should purchase a parcel of property that is adjacent to the hotel from Hector. After additional research, Tom agreed. Later, Tom and Hector signed a contract whereby VPLP would purchase the property from Hector. Tom signed the contract as "General Partner of Vacation Paradise, L.P." *Is VPLP liable on this contract? If VPLP does not perform the contract, is Tom liable for damages? If VPLP does not perform the contract, are either Sally or Carlie liable for damages?*

§ 15.05   FINANCIAL ISSUES

In terms of economics, limited partnerships are quite a bit different than general partnerships. As you surely remember from Chapter 3, in a general partnership the partners share profits (and losses) equally, unless otherwise agreed in the partnership agreement. Moreover, simply being allocated a share of the profits does not result in a partner actually receiving any money. Instead, a distribution must be approved before partners will receive money from the partnership.

ULPA, by contrast, focuses on *distributions* rather than profits and losses.[*] ULPA § 503 provides in part that:

> A distribution by a limited partnership must be shared among the partners on the basis of the value ... of the contributions the limited partnership has received from each partner.

Thus, a partner (whether general or limited) who has made, say, 10% of the overall contributions that partners have made to the limited partnership would receive 10% of the overall amount that the partnership distributes. (In this way, limited partnership distributions are somewhat similar to dividends payable by a corporation.)

But this is not the end of the story. Partners have no right to receive distributions before the limited partnership is dissolved. ULPA § 504. Of course, the limited partnership could decide to pay distributions periodically during its life, and the partnership agreement might even require distributions in some situations.

If the limited partnership does pay distributions before its dissolution, ULPA § 508 imposes some limitations on its ability to do so. Read that section, see if it reminds you of anything that you learned when you studied *corporations* in Chapter 5, and try your hand at the following problems:

Problems

Problem 15-24: Table and Chairs, L.P. ("TCLP") has one general partner (Mr. Table) and five limited partners (the Chair brothers). When TCLP was formed, Mr. Table contributed $10,000 to TCLP

---

[*]   The comment to ULPA § 503 states that "[t]his Act has no provision allocating profits and losses among the partners. Instead, the Act directly apportions the right to receive distributions." However, the comment continues: "Nearly all limited partnerships will choose to allocate profits and losses in order to comply with applicable tax, accounting and other regulatory requirements."

and each Chair brother contributed $1,000. TCLP's most recent balance sheet shows that it has $100,000 of assets, $70,000 of liabilities, and owners' equity of $30,000. *What is the maximum amount of distributions that TCLP could pay to its partners and pass the "balance sheet test" of ULPA § 508(b)(2)? If TCLP distributes the maximum that it may, how will that amount be divided among the five partners?*

Problem 15-25: *What would happen if TCLP decided to distribute more that it legally may? See ULPA § 509.*

In addition, note that if a partner is unhappy with the amount of distributions that she is receiving or some other aspect of the limited partnership's business, she can sell or otherwise transfer her "transferable interest" (defined in ULPA § 101(22) as the partner's right to receive distributions) to a third party, in much the same way that a partner in a general partnership may transfer her transferable interest to a third party. *See* Article 7 of ULPA. The transferee would not become a partner in the limited partnership, but would have the right to receive (1) any distributions that the transferor would otherwise be entitled to receive, as well as the net amount that would otherwise be distributed to the transferor upon dissolution of the limited partnership.

§ 15.06   DISSOCIATION AND DISSOLUTION

Objectives: You should be able to list the events that cause (1) a general partner to be dissociated from a limited partnership and (2) a limited partner to be dissociated from a limited partnership. Given a fact pattern, you should be able to determine whether a partner (whether a general partner or a limited partner) has dissociated from the limited partnership and, if so, the consequences of the dissociation. In addition, you should be able to list the events that will cause a limited partnership to be dissolved and, given a fact pattern, determine whether an event has caused the limited partnership to dissolve. If a partner has dissociated but the limited partnership does not dissolve, you should be able to explain the effects of the partner's dissociation. Finally, given a fact pattern in which a limited partnership dissolves, you should be able to determine how the limited partnership's assets will be distributed to creditors and partners.

ULPA has complex provisions concerning partner dissociation in Article 6 and complex provisions concerning partnership dissolution in Article 8. In many ways, these provisions mirror RUPA's provisions concerning dissociation and dissolution in a general partnership, which you learned about in Chapter 4. Of course, there are also many important differences, which you will learn about in this section.

Limited Partner Dissociation. ULPA § 601 lists the many causes of limited partner dissociation. First, you should note that limited partners do not have the right (as opposed to the power) to dissociate from the limited partnership before its termination. ULPA § 601(a). However, subsection (b) goes on to list many causes of a limited partner's dissociation including, under subsection (b)(1), dissociation by express will.[*] As you read this section, you will see that it bears a very strong (but not identical) resemblance to RUPA § 601.

So, what happens when a limited partner dissociates? As you should recall from Chapter 4, if a partner dissociates from a *general* partnership, there are two possibilities: either the partnership will continue in existence, in which case Article 7 of RUPA will apply, or the partnership will dissolve, in which case Article 8 of RUPA will apply. But given that limited partners are less "important" than general partners (or, for that matter, any partner in a general partnership), the dissociation of a limited partner—for any reason—will not cause the dissolution of a limited partnership.[**] Instead, the limited partnership will continue in existence.

Following her dissociation, a limited partner has the statues of a "mere transferee" of her transferable interest (described in Section 15.05 above). *See* ULPA § 602(a)(3). She is no longer a partner and can no longer vote on any matters that would be decided by the limited partners. Further, any distributions that would have been paid to her as a limited partner (including those upon dissolution of the limited partnership) will be paid to her in her capacity as a former limited partner. This is very different from the situation where a partner dissociates from a general partnership without triggering a dissolution of the partnership. As you learned in Chapter 4, when that happens, the partner is entitled to payment for her interest in the partnership. Not so under ULPA; limited partners are more "locked in" for the duration of the limited partnership's existence. *See also* ULPA § 505 ("A person does not have a right to receive a

---

[*]   The official comment to ULPA § 601 states that subsection (b)(1) "gives a person the power to dissociate as a limited partner even though the dissociation is wrongful under subsection (a)."

[**]   However, if there are no limited partners remaining a dissolution may occur if at least one limited partner is not admitted within the following ninety days, as discussed below.

distribution on account of dissociation."). For example, if a limited partner dies, her heirs would not receive any payout. Instead, her heirs would inherit the deceased partner's transferable interest.

General Partner Dissociation. ULPA § 603—which also bears a strong resemblance to RUPA § 601—lists the causes of general partner dissociation. In addition, ULPA § 604 concerns whether a general partner's dissociation is "wrongful" and, if so, the consequences of a wrongful dissociation. ULPA § 605 concerns the effects of a dissociation (whether or not wrongful) by a general partner. Study those sections, as well as Section 601, and consider the following problems:

Problems

Problem 15-26: Trashcan, L.P. has one general partner (Ms. Rubbish) and forty-seven limited partners, including Mr. Garbage. It does not have a limited partnership agreement that changes any of the default provisions of ULPA. Both Ms. Rubbish and Mr. Garbage died earlier today. *Have these partners dissociated from Trashcan, L.P.? If so, was either dissociation "wrongful"?*

Problem 15-27: Same facts as Problem 15-26, except neither Ms. Rubbish nor Mr. Garbage died. Instead, a guardian and conservator was appointed for each of them. *Have these partners dissociated from Trashcan, L.P.? If so, was either dissociation "wrongful"?*

Problem 15-28: Same facts as Problem 15-26, except neither Ms. Rubbish nor Mr. Garbage died. Instead, they each filed bankruptcy. *Have these partners dissociated from Trashcan, L.P.? If so, was either dissociation "wrongful"?*

Problem 15-29: *What are the effects of a wrongful dissociation?*

ULPA §§ 606 and 607 deal with a general partner's "lingering" authority to bind the limited partnership following dissociation, and her liability for the obligations of the limited partnership following her dissociation, respectively. Read those two sections and try the following problems.

Problems

Problem 15-30: Dog Sitters, L.P. has two general partners (Mr. Shar Pei and Mr. Mutt). Last week, Mr. Shar Pei informed Mr. Mutt that he resigned as general partner, effective immediately. Two weeks ago, Dog Sitters, L.P. ordered $1,000 worth of dog biscuits from Bark Brothers, Inc., a long-time supplier of Dog Sitters, L.P. *If Dog Sitters, L.P. does not pay this bill, may Bark Brothers seek recovery from Mr. Shar Pei? (Do not worry about how it would go about doing so.)*

Problem 15-31: Same facts as Problem 15-30. Today, Mr. Mutt ordered $500 worth of dog biscuits from Bark Brothers, Inc., a long-time supplier of Dog Sitters, L.P. *If the partnership does not pay for these supplies, may Bark Brothers seek recovery from Mr. Shar Pei?*

Problem 15-32: Same facts as Problem 15-31, except that Mr. Shar Pei (not Mr. Mutt) ordered the supplies from Bark Brothers, Inc. *Is the partnership obligated to pay for the supplies? If so, may it seek recovery from Mr. Shar Pei?*

Causes of Dissolution. There are two types of dissolution under Article 8 of ULPA: judicial and nonjudicial. Judicial dissolution under Section 802 is somewhat rare, being limited to situations where "it is not reasonably practicable to carry on the activities of the limited partnership in conformity with the partnership agreement." Thus, we will instead focus our attention on ULPA § 801.

Subsection (1) Section 801 is relatively straightforward, providing that a limited partnership will be dissolved upon the "happening of an event specified in the partnership agreement." Thus, for example, if the limited partnership agreement specified a ten-year term, then the limited partnership would dissolve after ten years.

Subsection (2) is a little trickier. It provides that a limited partnership may be dissolved if (1) all of the general partners consent and (2) "limited partners owning a majority of the rights to receive distributions as limited partners" also consent. To understand this fully, we need to return to the discussion about distributions in Section 15.05 above. As stated there, distributions are shared among partners based on the respective contributions that they have made. Thus, a partner who has made 10% of the overall contributions that partners have made to the limited partnership would receive 10% any distributions. *However*, note that ULPA § 801(2) requires approval by "limited partners owning a majority of the rights to receive distributions *as limited partners*." (Emphasis added.) See if you can correctly apply this rule to the following problem.

Problem

Problem 15-33:   Jumble, L.P. has two general partners and five limited partners.   The partners' respective rights to receive distributions are allocated as follows:

- General partner A: 5%
- General partner B: 6%
- Limited partner A: 10%
- Limited partner B: 15%
- Limited partner C: 15%
- Limited partner D: 15%
- Limited partner E: 5%

In addition, some former limited partners had transferred their transferable interests to various transferees.   These transferees collectively hold rights to receive 29% of any distributions that Jumble, L.P. makes. *Assuming that both general partners consent, what combination(s) of limited partners would need to consent to dissolve Jumble, L.P. under ULPA § 801(2)?*

ULPA § 801(3) features two alternatives: Subsection (A) concerns the situation where a general partner dissociates, but there is at least one remaining general partner; subsection (B) concerns the situation where the *only* general partner dissociates. These sections require careful reading.

Problems

Problem 15-34:   Same facts as Problem 15-33, to wit: The partners' respective rights to receive distributions are allocated as follows:

- General partner A: 5%
- General partner B: 6%
- Limited partner A: 10%
- Limited partner B: 15%
- Limited partner C: 15%
- Limited partner D: 15%
- Limited partner E: 5%

In addition, some former limited partners had transferred their transferable interests to various transferees. These transferees collectively hold rights to receive 29% of any distributions that Jumble, L.P. makes.

General Partner A dissociates, but General Partner B does not. Sixty days later, General Partner A, along with Limited Partners B and C vote to dissolve the limited partnership. The other partners vote against dissolution. *Is Jumble, L.P. dissolved?*

Problem 15-35:   Same facts as Problem 15-34, except that *both* general partners dissociate. Sixty days later, Limited Partners B, C, and E vote to continue the limited partnership and admit a new general partner. The other partners vote against this proposal. *Is Jumble, L.P. dissolved?*

To round out the discussion of dissolution causes, ULPA § 801(4) provides that a limited partnership will be dissolved ninety days after it no longer has any limited partners, unless within that period at least one new limited partner is admitted. Finally, subsection (5) provides that a limited partnership may be administratively dissolved pursuant to Section 809 (which will not be discussed here).

Dissolution Procedures. Assuming that a limited partnership has dissolved, it will begin a period of winding up. Typically, the general partner(s) will handle the winding-up process, although ULPA § 803(c) allows the limited partners to appoint a person to do so if there is no general partner.

During winding up, the limited partnership must marshal its assets, pay or make arrangements for paying its creditors, and then distribute any remaining amounts to the partners according to their distribution percentages (as discussed earlier in this chapter). In general, the process is much the same as the process for winding up a general partnership.

However, there are some notable differences, which should remind us that a limited partnership is a "hybrid" entity. First, borrowing from MBCA §§ 14.06 and 14.07 (which you studied in Chapter 12), ULPA §§ 806 and 807 allow a limited partnership to take steps to bar certain creditors' claims. Section 806 deals with "known" claims and Section 807 deals with all other claims. A description of these sections would sound eerily similar to Chapter 12's description of MBCA §§ 14.06 and 14.07, so instead here are some problems designed to make sure you understand these sections.

Problems

Problem 15-35:   Asbestos, L.P. ("ALP") manufactured (as you might expect) asbestos, which it had sold throughout the United States for more than thirty years. The general partner of ALP is Rufus, who has the right to receive 10% of any distributions that ALP makes. There are three limited partners: Sam, Ally, and Jennifer. Sam has the right to receive 50% of any distributions that ALP makes, and Ally and Jennifer each have the right to receive 20% of the distributions. The partners voted to dissolve ALP. *How may ALP bar products liability claims that may be asserted against it in the future?   What is the deadline for an asbestos / lung cancer victim to assert a claim against ALP?*

Problem 15-36: Same facts as Problem 15-35. In addition, Joe Contractor recently completed some work on a building that ALP owns, but has not yet sent a bill for his services. *What steps, if any, can ALP take to bar Joe's claim?*

Problem 15-37: Same facts as Problems 15-35 and 15-36, except that ALP takes no steps whatsoever to bar Joe's claim. Instead, it distributes a total of $100,000 to the four partners. *May Joe recover his claim from the partners? If so, how would he do so and how much could he recover from each partner?* (Don't neglect to read the cross-reference to ULPA § 404 that appears in ULPA § 807(d)(3).)

Problem 15-38: Same facts as the prior problems, except that ALP had no creditors' claims and had $100,000 to distribute to its partners. *How should this $100,000 be divided among the partners? See* ULPA § 812.

Problem 15-39: *Who, if anyone, would be liable if a dissolved limited partnership did not have enough assets to pay all of its debts?*

§ 15.07   LIMITED LIABILITY LIMITED PARTNERSHIPS

One other major difference between ULPA and RULPA (1985) is that ULPA authorizes a new type of limited partnership: the limited liability limited partnership, or LLLP. Briefly put, an LLLP is the same as a limited partnership, except that *no partner, not even a general partner*, will be personally liable for the LLLP's debts and obligations simply as a result of being a partner. As ULPA § 404(c) explains:

> An obligation of a limited partnership incurred while the limited partnership is a limited liability limited partnership, whether arising in contract, tort, or otherwise, is solely the obligation of the limited partnership. A general partner is not personally liable, directly or indirectly, by way of contribution or otherwise, for such an obligation solely by reason of being or acting as a general partner. ***

Thus, the LLLP is to the limited partnership as the LLP is the general partnership.

Moreover, it is easy to form a limited partnership as an LLLP: all that is required is a statement in the certificate of limited partnership that the entity is an LLLP. Even existing limited partnerships can convert to LLLPs. In fact, there seems little reason not to do so.

PRACTICE QUESTIONS

NOTE: In each of the following problems, unless otherwise noted: (1) ULPA applies and (2) the limited partnership does not have a partnership agreement that changes the applicable rules of ULPA.

Multiple Choice Question 15-1: Blue Crab, L.P., is a limited partnership that runs a seafood restaurant. Karen is the general partner, but due to major surgery has been unable to leave the hospital for several weeks. As a result, Rufus, a limited partner, has "stepped up" and begun managing the restaurant, with Karen's "blessing." (Before this, Rufus worked as the restaurant's main chef and bottle washer.) One day, an employee of Fresh Fish, Inc., the limited partnership's main supplier, made a delivery to the restaurant. Rufus, who was wearing a name tag that said "Rufus Smith, General Partner," signed the receipt. He then told the delivery person that he was "running" the restaurant and that Fresh Fish, Inc. should deliver one hundred pounds of salmon and one hundred pounds of shrimp the following day. *If Blue Crab, L.P. is unable to pay for this order, which of the following is correct?*

A.   Rufus is liable for the order because he breached his implied warranty of authority.

B.   Rufus is liable in his capacity as a limited partner because he participated in the control of the business and, based on his conduct, Fresh Fish, Inc. reasonably believed that he was a general partner.

C.   Blue Crab, L.P. is not liable for this order because limited partners may not conduct business on behalf of a limited partnership.

D.   Karen is liable as a general partner.

E.   Both A and D are correct.

Multiple Choice Question 15-2:   Red Engine, L.P., is a limited partnership that operates an automobile parts supply store. Five months ago, Jessica resigned as general partner and was replaced by Johnny. Today, Jessica was walking down the street when she saw Buford, who was the owner of a sole proprietorship that supplies the spark plugs and carburetors that Red Engine, L.P. sells at its store. Buford and Jessica had known each other for several years, but Buford did not know that Jessica had resigned as the general partner of Red Engine, L.P. Buford asked Jessica whether the limited partnership wanted to continue its supply contract with Buford's business for an additional year. She replied: "Sure." When Johnny found out about the contract, he was very upset and refused to honor it. *Assuming no other facts, and that there are no statutes of frauds issues in this problem, which of the following is correct?*

A.   Red Engine, L.P. is not bound, because Jessica was not a general partner at the time of this contract.

B.   Red Engine, L.P. is not bound, because her conversation with Buford took place more than 90 days after she resigned as the general partner.

C.   Red Engine, L.P. is bound on this contract but may recover damages from Jessica.

D.   Red Engine, L.P. is bound on this contract, but if it does not perform the contract Johnny would not be liable to Buford for damages.

E.   Both C and D are correct.

Multiple Choice Question 15-3: Purple, L.P., is a limited partnership that has the following partners: General Partner 1, General Partner 2, Limited Partner 3, Limited Partner 4 and Limited Partner 5. Each of the partners is an individual. Today, (1) General Partner 1 dissociated by express will; (2) Limited Partner 3 dissociated by express will; and (3) Limited Partner 4 filed bankruptcy. *Which of the following is correct?*

A.   None of the dissociations was "wrongful."

B.   Only General Partner 1's dissociation was "wrongful."

C.   General Partner 1's dissociation was "wrongful" and Limited Partner 3's dissociation was "wrongful."

D.   General Partner 1, Limited Partner 3 and Limited Partner 4 each dissociated and all of these dissociations were "wrongful."

E.   General Partner 1, Limited Partner 3 and Limited Partner 4 each dissociated but only the dissociations of General Partner 1 and Limited Partner 4 were "wrongful."

Multiple Choice Question 15-4: Yellow, L.P., is a limited partnership that has the following partners: General Partner 1, Limited Partner 2, Limited Partner 3, and Limited Partner 4. When Yellow, L.P. was formed, the partners made the following contributions: General Partner 1 ($10,000), Limited Partner 2 ($20,000), Limited Partner 3 ($20,000) and Limited Partner 4 ($50,000). Currently, the balance sheet of Yellow, L.P. shows that it has $300,000 of assets and $170,000 of liabilities. *Which of the following is correct? You may assume that Yellow, L.P. would remain able to pay its debts as they come due in the ordinary course of business.*

A.   Yellow, L.P. may pay a maximum of $130,000 in distributions. If it pays that amount, then General Partner 1 would receive $13,000; Limited Partner 2 would receive $26,000; Limited Partner 3 would receive $26,000; and Limited Partner 4 would receive $65,000.

B.   Yellow, L.P. may pay a maximum of $130,000 in distributions. If it pays that amount, then each partner would receive an equal amount because partners share profits and distributions equally unless otherwise agreed.

C.   Yellow, L.P. may pay a maximum of $170,000 in distributions. If it pays that amount, then General Partner 1 would receive $17,000; Limited Partner 2 would receive $34,000; Limited Partner 3 would receive $34,000; and Limited Partner 4 would receive $85,000.

D.   Yellow, L.P. may pay a maximum of $170,000 in distributions. If it pays that amount, then each partner would receive an equal amount because partners share profits and distributions equally unless otherwise agreed.

E.   None of the above is correct.

Multiple Choice Question 15-5: Brown, L.P., is a limited partnership that has the following partners: General Partner 1, Limited Partner 2, Limited Partner 3 and Limited Partner 4. When Brown, L.P. was formed, the partners made the following contributions: General Partner 1 ($0), Limited Partner 2 ($10,000), Limited Partner 3 ($10,000) and Limited Partner 4 ($10,000). Recently, two of the limited partners voted to dissolve Brown, L.P., but one limited partner, as well as General Partner 1, voted against this proposal. *Which of the following is correct?*

A.   Brown, L.P. will not be dissolved because General Partner 1 did not consent to dissolution.

B.   Brown, L.P. will not be dissolved because all of the partners did not unanimously consent to dissolution.

C.   Brown, L.P. will not be dissolved because the <u>limited</u> partners did not unanimously consent to dissolution.

D.   Brown, L.P. will be dissolved.

Multiple Choice Question 15-6: Same facts as Multiple Choice Question 15-5, except that General Partner 1 dissociated by express will and, 120 days later, two of the limited partners voted to continue the existence of Brown, L.P. and admit a new general partner.   (The other limited partner voted against this proposal.) *Which of the following is correct?*

A.   Brown, L.P. will not be dissolved.
B.   Brown, L.P. will be dissolved because the vote by the limited partners was not unanimous.
C.   Brown, L.P. will be dissolved because the vote by the limited partners did not occur within sixty days.
D.   Brown, L.P. will be dissolved because the vote by the limited partners did not occur within ninety days.

Multiple Choice Question 15-7: Orange, L.P., is a limited partnership that has the following partners: General Partner 1, Limited Partner 2, Limited Partner 3 and Limited Partner 4.   When Orange, L.P. was formed, the partners made the following contributions: General Partner 1 ($5,000), Limited Partner 2 ($10,000), Limited Partner 3 ($20,000) and Limited Partner 4 ($15,000). Upon dissolution, Orange, L.P. distributed all of its assets, consisting of $100,000, to its partners. However, Orange, L.P. did not pay or take any steps to bar a $10,000 claim held by Loan Shark, Inc. *Which of the following is correct?*

A.   Loan Shark, Inc. may recover $2,500 from each partner.
B.   Loan Shark, Inc. may recover $10,000 from General Partner 1 or $1,000 from General Partner 1, $2,000 from Limited Partner 2, $4,000 from Limited Partner 3, and $3,000 from Limited Partner 4.
C.   Loan Shark, Inc. may recover $10,000 from General Partner 1 or $2,500 from each partner.
D.   All four partners are jointly and severally liable to Loan Shark, Inc. for $10,000.
E.   Loan Shark, Inc. may only recover the $10,000 from General Partner 1.

Multiple Choice Question 15-8: Same facts as Multiple Choice Question 15-7, except that Orange was formed as a limited liability limited partnership (LLLP). *Which of the following is correct?*

A.   Loan Shark, Inc. may recover $1,000 from General Partner 1, $2,000 from Limited Partner 2, $4,000 from Limited Partner 3, and $3,000 from Limited Partner 4.
B.   Loan Shark, Inc. may recover $10,000 from General Partner 1 or $2,500 from each partner.
C.   Loan Shark, Inc. may only recover the $10,000 from General Partner 1.
D.   Loan Shark, Inc. may not recover its claim from any of the partners.

CHAPTER 16
LIMITED LIABILITY COMPANIES

As has been stated repeatedly in this book, the primary advantage of operating a one-owner business as a sole proprietorship or a multiple-owner business as a partnership is that they enjoy "flow-through" tax treatment. In other words, if a sole proprietorship or a partnership earns income for a given year, it does not pay taxes on that income. Instead, the business's income (or, for that matter, its loss) is "passed though" to the owner or owners of the business. Usually, this reduces the overall tax burden of the business and its owner(s) because the income is only taxed once. This flow-though tax status comes with a heavy cost, however: the owner(s) face the risk of unlimited personal liability for the debts and other obligations of the business. If the assets of the business are not sufficient to pay the claim and it is not covered by insurance, then creditors of the business can recover against the personal assets of the owner(s).

A corporation has precisely the opposite advantages and disadvantages. As you know, shareholders of a corporation are not personally liable for the corporation's debts or other obligations unless they committed an act that resulted in tort liability or signed a personal guaranty of one or more of the corporation's debts, or if a creditor successfully pierces the "corporate veil." On the other hand, "C" corporations pay taxes on income that they earn. Further, if a "C" corporation pays dividends to its shareholders, the shareholders must pay taxes on that dividend income. There are ways to manage this tax situation, such as by intentionally reducing the corporation's taxable income by paying large salaries to employees, particularly if those employees are also shareholders. Salaries are deductible expenses for the corporation, assuming that they do not run afoul of some rules that you may learn about in a course on corporate taxation. Another possibility is to organize the corporation as an "S" corporation, which—for the most part—results in tax treatment akin to that of a partnership. Nonetheless, these ideas may not be viable for a great many corporations. For example, an "S" corporation is subject to strict requirements on the identities of its shareholders and other matters, as you learned about in Chapter 1. Many businesses will not be able to meet these requirements.

So, wouldn't it be nice to have an entity that is the "best of both worlds," that is, an entity that combines the good attribute of partnerships and sole proprietorships (flow-through tax treatment) with the good attribute of corp-orations (limited liability for owners)? Limited partnerships got us part of the way there: LPs are flow-though tax entities, but eliminate personal liability only for the limited partners, as you learned in Chapter 15.[*] Fortunately, another choice now exists: the ***limited liability company***, or ***LLC***. LLCs are a *new* type of business organization. In other words, instead of arriving at the "best of both worlds" of flow-though taxation and limited liability by modifying the rules applicable to corporations and/or partnerships, state legislatures created LLCs as a different type of entity altogether. Although such a "Frankenstein's Monster" approach perhaps wasn't necessary,[**] that is how things happened.

LLCs combine attributes of partnerships and corporations, thus earning the label of being a "hybrid" business organization. For that reason, you are learning about LLCs at the end of this textbook rather than the beginning, even though LLCs are rapidly becoming the entity of choice for new small businesses. (In fact, many statistics show that LLCs are now being formed at a much greater rate than are corporations or other types of business entities.) You needed first to understand partnerships and corporations before you could be in a good position to study LLCs. This chapter will give you an opportunity to explore LLCs in more detail.

§ 16.01   INTRODUCTION AND CHAPTER OVERVIEW

Basic Characteristics of LLCs. As discussed below, for historical reasons state statutes that govern LLCs are all over the board. In other words, LLC statutes can, and usually do, vary dramatically from state to state. This is remarkably unlike the situation with partnerships and corporations; nearly all states have a partnership statute that is modeled on, or in many cases adopted verbatim from, UPA or RUPA, and most states have corporation statutes that are very similar to the MBCA.

Nonetheless, a few general statements can be made about LLCs with confidence that they are universally true. First, an LLC is not a "default" entity like a partnership; a filing must be made with the state government before an LLC exists. While most states call this document the ***articles of organization***, some states call it the ***certificate of organization***, some states call it the ***certificate of formation*** and other states have other names for it. (However, nearly all LLC

---

[*]   Of course, a limited partnership could have a *corporation* as its general partner, but this may raise other issues. Also, as discussed in Chapters 1 and 15, many states now permit LPs to be organized as limited liability limited partnerships, or LLLPs. *None* of the partners in an LLLP are liable for its debts simply because they are partners.

[**]   As discussed in Chapter 1, the limited liability partnership, or LLP, arrives at a "best of both worlds" result by simply modifying the rules of partner liability. Perhaps unfortunately, the LLP didn't really catch on until long after LLCs had already become popular.

statutes contemplate the existence of another charter document, typically called the *operating agreement*, which is much more important.) In any event, the fact of the matter is that all states require a filing for an LLC to exist. And like a corporation and a partnership under RUPA, upon its formation an LLC becomes an entity that is separate from its owners, who are called the *members*.

Second, as noted above, LLCs are flow-through tax entities. Although for many years the Internal Revenue Service (IRS) struggled to decide whether to treat LLCs as partnerships or corporations for tax purposes, under the IRS's "check the box" regulations (discussed below) an LLC with more than one member can elect to be treated as a partnership for tax purposes. (Single-member LLCs are treated as "disregarded entities.") In almost all situations, it would be wise for an LLC to elect partnership tax treatment.

Third, also as noted above, the members of an LLC enjoy limited liability, like the shareholders of a corporation. Typically, the worst-case outcome for an LLC member will be that the LLC becomes insolvent or files for bankruptcy protection. In that case, the member's investment in the LLC will, for all intents and purposes, become worthless. But at least the member's personal assets can't be reached to satisfy claims of the LLC's creditors. Nonetheless, there is a growing body of case law in which courts have allowed creditors to "pierce the LLC veil" in situations that are analogous to piercing the corporate veil. See Section 16.04 below.

Fourth, there are two basic ways in which the governance of an LLC may be organized: *member-managed* and *manager-managed*. Broadly speaking, the governance of a member-managed LLC resembles the governance of a partnership: all of the owners (members of an LLC or partners of a partnership) have the ability to make, or at least vote on, business decisions and may also have the authority to bind the LLC to contracts and other transactions with third parties. By contrast, the governance of a manager-managed LLC somewhat resembles the centralized management of a corporation, found in the corporation's board of directors, or the management of a limited partnership by its general partner. In a manager-managed LLC, one or more managers—who may, but need not, also be members—is (are) given authority to make business decisions on behalf of the LLC. In such an LLC, the members have only those voting rights reserved to them in the applicable statute or in the LLC's operating agreement.

Finally, LLCs are a very "flexible" type of business entity. As you learned in Chapters 3 and 4, RUPA is largely a series of "default" rules that, with a few exceptions, can be modified by having different provisions in the partnership agreement. So too with LLCs: most LLC statutes make the LLC's operating agreement the most important source of rules governing that LLC.

Beyond this, it is difficult to generalize about LLCs. As noted above, LLC statutes are all over the board, and thus far no "model" LLC statute has been adopted in a majority of the states. How did things end up this way? History provides an answer.

History of LLCs. Wyoming, of all places, was the first state to adopt an LLC statute, which it did in 1977. The IRS regulations in effect at the time identified four characteristics of corporations:

- limited liability for owners;

- continuity of life (that is, the entity would continue to exist despite an owner withdrawing or selling her interest to a third party);

- free transferability of ownership interests; and

- centralized management (such as with a board of directors).

Simplifying things a bit, under these regulations an unincorporated entity (i.e., an entity that is not a corporation) that had *three or more* of these characteristics would be taxed like a corporation. Conversely, an unincorporated entity that had *two or fewer* of these four characteristics would be taxed as a partnership. Importantly, no factor was considered more important than any of the others.

In response to a lobbying effort by a private business, the Wyoming legislature passed a statute creating LLCs. Under this statute, the LLC had a liability "shield," thus making it look like a corporation. However, the Wyoming statute provided for partnership-like effects on the other three characteristics. It provided for decentralized management (as in a partnership); it provided that the entity would dissolve if one of its members ceased to be a member (as in a partnership under UPA and to some degree under RUPA); and it provided that only a member's economic rights were transferable to a third party (as in a partnership). Thus, the Wyoming LLC statute created a new type of entity that had only one "corporate" characteristic (limited liability) and therefore should be treated as a partnership under the IRS regulations.

It worked, although it took many years to know for sure. In 1988, the IRS issued a ruling classifying Wyoming LLCs as partnerships for tax purposes. This led many other state legislatures to pass LLC statutes. For the most part, these statutes were similar to the Wyoming statute, although some of them allowed for manager-managed LLCs. However, beginning in 1989, the IRS, perhaps surprisingly, began to allow for more flexibility in the LLC form. To make a long story short, this gave state legislatures a greater degree of freedom in structuring their LLC statutes, while still ensuring partnership tax treatment to LLCs. This approached reached its zenith in 1997, when the so-called "check the box regulations" took effect. Under these regulations (which are still in effect), an entity formed under a *corporate* statute would be taxable as a corporation, subject to the possibility of electing to be an "S" corporation. However, *any other* business organization with two or more owners would be treated as a partnership *unless* it elected to be treated as a corporation. Similarly, an organization with one owner would be disregarded for tax purposes, unless it elected to be taxed as a corporation.

While the check the box regulations succeeded in making the tax treatment of LLCs much simpler, they ended up complicating the state law picture. Freed from the strictures of the prior IRS regulations governing when LLCs would be treated as partnerships, state statutes began to evolve in different directions. The end result is that LLC statutes today exhibit a great deal of variety from state to state. Because a book like this cannot possibly cover the LLC laws of all fifty states, this leads us to the next question: which LLC statute(s) should we learn about?

What Statute to Use? As with limited partnership statutes in Chapter 15, it was a difficult decision to choose which LLC statute to discuss in this textbook. Because many states began adopting their own LLC statutes before a model LLC statute had been drafted and had gained any "traction," there currently is a great deal of diversity in state LLC statutes. But in the end, I decided to cover two: the Delaware Limited Liability Company Act and the Revised Uniform Limited Liability Company Act (2006), otherwise known as "***Re-ULLCA***."[*] As for the Delaware Limited Liability Company Act, it probably shouldn't surprise you that, as with its corporate statute, Delaware is perceived as being on the vanguard of LLC law. Many "important" transactions involving LLCs use the Delaware LLC statute.

On the other hand, in some respects Delaware's statute is unusual when compared to many other states' LLC statutes. Because of that, I chose to include another LLC statute and Re-ULLCA seemed as good as any. Although Re-ULLCA has so far only been adopted in four states and the District of Columbia, seven other states, including New Jersey and California, are currently considering adopting it. Thus, it seems to have a bit of "momentum." Further, having already studied RUPA and the MBCA, many of the provisions of Re-ULLCA will seem somewhat familiar to you.

---

[*]   In July 2011, a drafting committee of the National Conference of Commissioners on Uniform State Laws proposed some amendments to Re-ULLCA in a project that would "harmonize" statutes concerning unincorporated associations. This chapter does *not* reflect these proposed amendments to Re-ULLCA.

In any event, your professor will likely tell you to focus on one or the other (or perhaps a different LLC statute altogether). But the following sections of this chapter allow you the flexibility to learn both statutes. Keep in mind, however, that the LLC statute in the state where you end up practicing law is likely to be different, perhaps substantially so, from the following discussion. Also keep in mind that there are many court decisions concerning LLCs that are, to put it politely, surprising. This is because for many years courts struggled (and still do) with whether to apply partnership or corporate law concepts to LLCs when LLC statutes were silent on an issue. While this chapter will not, for the most part, discuss such decisions, there may be unusual rules "lurking" in the law of a given state.

§ 16.02   FORMING A LIMITED LIABILITY COMPANY

Objectives: You should be able to explain to a client who wants to start a business as an LLC what steps are necessary to form an LLC and some issues the client should consider in drafting the LLC's certificate of organization and its operating agreement. You should also be able to explain what the LLC must do if it intends to transact business in a state other than the state in which it is organized.

Certificate of Organization (or Certificate of Formation). As noted above, an LLC is not a "default" entity; a filing must be made with the state government before an LLC can exist. Section 18-201(a) of the Delaware LLC statute (hereinafter cited as "*Del.*") provides that "[i]n order to form a limited liability company, [one] or more authorized persons must execute a certificate of formation." *See also* Del. § 18-201(b) (an LLC is "formed at the time of the filing of the initial certificate of formation … [if] there has been substantial compliance with the requirements of this section.").

Similarly, Re-ULLCA § 201(a) provides that "[o]ne or more persons may act as organizers to form a limited liability company by signing and delivering to the [Secretary of State] for filing a certificate of organization." *See also id.* § 201(d) (LLC is formed when the Secretary of State has filed the certificate and LLC has at least one member, unless the certificate states a delayed effective date; filing of the certificate by the Secretary of State is "conclusive proof that the organizer satisfied all conditions to the formation of" an LLC, except in a proceeding by the state to dissolve the LLC).[*]

---

[*]   Similarly, MBCA § 2.03 states that, "[u]nless a delayed effective date is specified, the corporate existence begins when the articles of incorporation are filed," and that the "secretary of state's filing of the articles of incorporation is conclusive proof that the incorporators

As you learned in Chapter 5, the "incorporator" is the person who files a corporation's articles of incorporation with the state. Similarly, Re-ULLCA contemplates that the certificate of organization will be filed by at least one "organizer," which is defined in Re-ULLCA § 102(14) simply as "a person that acts under Section 201 to form a limited liability company." The Delaware statute refers to "authorized persons" filing the certificate of formation in that state, but does not define that term. In any event, as with the formation of a corporation, it is likely, but not required, that the "organizer(s)" of an LLC or the "authorized person(s)" with respect to an LLC will be the (eventual) members of the LLC or an attorney who represents the LLC.

Like articles of incorporation under the MBCA, LLC statutes do not require a great deal of information in a certificate of organization. For example, in Delaware, the certification of formation need only contain the name of the LLC (subject to Del. § 18-102); the address of the registered office and the name and address of the registered agent that the LLC must maintain under Section 18-104; and "[a]ny other matters the members determine to include therein." Del. § 18-201(a). Under Re-ULLCA § 201(b), the certificate of organization must state the LLC's name (subject to Section 108), the address of the LLC's designated office, and the name and address of the LLC's agent for the service of process. Subsection (c) also states that the certificate may contain "statements as to matters other than those required by" the statute, but that such statements are "not effective as a statement of authority." Further, if the LLC will not have any members when the certificate of organization is filed, the certificate must include a statement to that effect.

When is an LLC Formed? (or, "Shelf LLCs"). This brings us to an interesting question: if an LLC does not have any members when its certificate of formation or organization is filed, when does its existence actually begin? This is sort of a chicken-and-egg question: which comes first the LLC or its member(s)? For various reasons, it may be advantageous to have an LLC "on the shelf," that is, already on file with the state, and ready to go if a client needs to form an LLC quickly. In other words, sometimes it is desirable to form an LLC before the identities of the members have been determined. (On the other hand, query whether it's really that difficult or time consuming to form an LLC.)

Under Re-ULLCA § 201(e), if the certificate of organization states that the LLC has no members, then the certificate will lapse *unless*, within ninety days, an organizer of the LLC files a notice stating that the LLC has at least one member and also stating the date on which a member became the LLC's initial member. If that notice is filed, then the LLC's existence is deemed to have begun as of the

---

satisfied all conditions precedent to incorporation except in a proceeding by the state to cancel or revoke the incorporation or involuntarily dissolve the corporation."

"date of initial membership," as opposed to when the certificate of organization was filed.

For example, assume that the organizer of ABC, LLC files a certificate of organization on February 1, and the certificate states that the LLC currently has no members. If the organizer files a notice on, say, March 15, stating that ABC, LLC's initial member became a member on March 10, then the LLC will be deemed to have been formed on March 10. Of course, if ABC, LLC's certificate of organization had stated that it *did* have members at that time, then the LLC would be deemed to have been formed when the certificate of organization was filed, unless the certificate itself specified a delayed effective date.

The Delaware statute does not directly address this issue. However, Del. § 18-101(6) defines a limited liability company as an LLC "formed under the laws of the State of Delaware and having [one] or more members," thus suggesting that an LLC cannot *be* an LLC without at least one member. In addition, Del. § 18-101(11) defines a "member" in part as a "person who is admitted to a limited liability company as a member as provided in § 18-301."

Meanwhile, Del. § 18-301(a) provides in part that:

In connection with the formation of [an LLC], a person is admitted as a member of the [LLC] upon the later to occur of:

(1)   The formation of the [LLC]; or

(2)   The time provided in and upon compliance with the [operating] agreement or, if the [operating] agreement does not so provide, when the person's admission is reflected in the records of the [LLC].

Of course, when it is formed (whenever that may be), an LLC is considered an entity that is separate from its owners, like partnerships, corporations, and other types of business entities. See, e.g., Re-ULLCA § 104(a). In other words, an LLC is a "person" that can sign contracts, own property, sue and be sued, etc. It also has the power to do anything that is "necessary or convenient to carry on its activities." *Id.* § 105.

Operating Agreements. The other charter document that an LLC must[*] have is an **operating agreement** or, as Delaware calls it, a **limited liability company agreement**. (However, Del. § 18-101(7), which defines the term

---

[*]   See, e.g., Del. § 18-201(d).

"limited liability company agreement," observes that such agreements are oftentimes referred to as operating agreements. Thus, and to avoid unnecessary wordiness in this chapter, I will use the term "operating agreement.")

Typically, an LLC's operating agreement will be quite detailed. One reason for this is that the operating agreement is usually the primary source of the "rules" governing the LLC's internal governance matters.[*] For example, Del. § 18-1101(b) provides that "[i]t is the policy of this [statute] to give the maximum effect to the principle of freedom of contract and to the enforceability of [operating] agreements."

Also, Re-ULLCA § 110(a) provides that, with some exceptions noted below, the operating agreement governs, among other things, the "relations among the members as members and between the members and the [LLC]," the rights and duties of managers under the statute, and the "activities of the company and the conduct of those activities." Further, in a provision that seems modeled on RUPA § 103(a) (which you learned about in Chapter 3), subsection (b) provides that "[t]o the extent that the operating agreement does not otherwise provide for a matter described in subsection (a), [Re-ULLCA] governs the matter." In other words, much like RUPA with respect to partnerships, Re-ULLCA is largely a set of "default" rules that may be varied by the operating agreement. Note here that the certificate of organization does not play the same "starring role" as the operating agreement. Indeed, a comment to Re-ULLCA § 102 notes that the phrase "certificate of organization" was purposely chosen to show that "the certificate merely reflects the existence of an LLC (rather than being the locus of important governance rules)."

There are a couple of caveats to this statement about the Re-ULLCA, however. First, Re-ULLCA § 110(c), which appears based on RUPA § 103(b), lists eleven things that an operating agreement may not do, or that it may only do to a limited extent. For example, subsection (c)(11) provides that the operating agreement may not restrict the rights of a person who is not a member or manager of the LLC, except as provided in Section 112(b) (which is discussed below). Compare this provision to RUPA § 103(b)(10). Second, Re-ULLCA 110(d) provides that an operating agreement may, in specified respects, modify the duties of managers and/or members of the LLC, but only in ways that are not "manifestly unreasonable."[**] *See also* Re-ULLCA §§ 110(e), (f), (g).

---

[*]   In addition, much like the bylaws of a corporation or the partnership agreement of a partnership, the operating agreement is a "private" document that does not need to be filed with the state. Thus, operating agreements are available for reading by the public at large.

[**]   Subsection (h) specifies how a court should go about deciding whether such a clause in an operating agreement is "manifestly unreasonable."

Who must agree to, and who is bound by, an LLC's operating agreement? Re-ULLCA § 102(13) defines an "operating agreement" as the "agreement ... whether oral, in a record, implied, or in any combination thereof, of all of the members of [an LLC], including a sole member ...."* Presumably, this means that an agreement among fewer than all of the members of the LLC will not qualify as an "operating agreement" and thus could not change any of the default rules of Re-ULLCA. Although the LLC itself may not have signed the operating agreement, Re-ULLCA § 111(a) provides that an LLC "is bound by and may enforce the operating agreement, whether or not the [LLC] has itself manifested assent" to it. Finally, note that Re-ULLCA § 111(c) provides that persons who *intend* to become the initial members of an LLC "may make an agreement providing that upon the formation of the [LLC] the agreement will become the operating agreement."

In Delaware, the term "limited liability company agreement" (which, as stated above, we will call the "operating agreement" in this chapter) is defined as "any agreement[,] ... written, oral or implied, of the member or members as to the affairs of [an LLC] and the conduct of its business." Del. § 18-101(7). Further, members and managers of the LLC, as well as assignees of LLC interests (discussed in Section 16.05 below) are bound by the operating agreement whether or not they have signed it. On a related note, the operating agreement may provide that a person can only become a member or assignee if she signs the operating agreement, or that a person can only become a member or assignee if she complies with the conditions for becoming a member or assignee (as those conditions are set forth in the operating agreement). In any event, the operating agreement will not be rendered unenforceable by the failure of a new member or assignee to sign it. Although an LLC need not sign its own operating agreement, it is bound by it whether or not it signs it.

Must an operating agreement be in writing? As noted above, both Re-ULLCA § 102(13) and Del. § 18-101(7) contemplate that operating agreements may be oral. However, the Delaware Supreme Court held, in *Olson v. Halvorsen*, 986 A.2d 1150 (Del. 2009), that the Delaware statute of frauds, which precludes the enforcement of oral contracts that are not to be completed within one year, applies to LLC operating agreements. As the court observed:

> *** The statute of frauds does not conflict with the LLC Act anymore than the statute of frauds generally conflicts with contracts. The LLC Act does not guarantee enforcement of all oral or implied LLC agreements. Rather, the LLC Act, like many other contracts, treats LLC agreements by permitting oral, written, or implied agreements. The LLC Act's explicit recognition of oral

---

*   Also, note that Re-ULLCA § 111(b) provides that any person who becomes a member of an LLC is "deemed to assent" to the operating agreement.

and implied LLC agreements does not preclude the statute of frauds. Rather, such legislative recognition indicates that an LLC agreement operates like any other oral, written, or implied contract, i.e., it requires compliance with the statute of frauds.

> The statute of frauds does not contravene the legislative policy of giving "maximum effect" to LLC agreements. The LLC Act cannot—and has not—rendered LLC agreements impervious to all other rules and laws relating to contract law. In no way does the LLC Act limit the types of substantive agreements that contracting parties may enter. The General Assembly did not clearly indicate any intent to advance this unlikely objective.

Id. at 1161. However, due to some uproar about this decision, in 2010 the Delaware legislature amended Del. § 18-108(17) to specifically state that LLC operating agreements are "not subject to any statute of frauds (including § 2714 of this title)."

Although many early LLC statutes contemplated that there would be at least two members in an LLC, today it is clear that LLCs can have a single member (unlike partnerships, which must have at least two partners). In such a case, is the operating agreement effective, or would this be like saying that a person has a so-called "contract" with herself? Fortunately, the statutes are clear on this point: Del. § 18-101(7) expressly provides that the operating agreement of a single-member LLC "shall not be unenforceable by reason of there being only [one] person who is a party" to the agreement, and Re-ULLCA § 102(13) expressly states that a single-member LLC can have an operating agreement.

What if there is a conflict between an LLC's certificate of organization or formation, and its operating agreement? As you learned in Chapter 5, MBCA § 2.06 provides that if there is any conflict between a corporation's articles of incorporation and its bylaws, the articles will prevail. The answer is somewhat different in LLC statutes, at least under Re-ULLCA. (Many LLC statutes are silent on this point, but some are similar to MBCA § 2.06.) Under Re-ULLCA § 112(d), the operating agreement generally "prevails as to members, dissociated members, transferees, and managers." However, the certificate of organization would prevail "as to other persons to the extent they reasonably rely on" it. Delaware's statute does not expressly address this issue.

Purposes of an LLC. As noted above, neither Delaware nor the Re-ULLCA require that an LLC's certificate of organization or formation state the LLC's purpose. In this way, they are similar to MBCA § 2.02 which likewise does not require that a corporation's articles of incorporation state a purpose (unlike many older corporate statutes). However, while MBCA § 3.01 provides that a corporation "has the purpose of engaging in any lawful *business* unless a more limited purpose is set forth in [its] articles of incorporation" (emphasis added), LLC statutes are broader. For example, Re-ULLCA § 104(b) provides that an LLC "may have any lawful purpose, regardless of whether for profit." Similarly, Del. § 18-106 provides than an LLC "may carry on any lawful business, purpose or activity, whether or not for profit," other than banking. Thus, it would be possible to operate a nonprofit organization as an LLC.

Of course, readers who are interested in such an idea would be well-advised to learn more about nonprofits in a different course in law school. Also, keep in mind in particular that a *nonprofit* entity is not necessarily *tax exempt*. To be tax-exempt, an entity must comply with stringent requirements under the Internal Revenue Code. However, a tax-exempt entity could form a nonprofit LLC as a wholly owned subsidiary and use that subsidiary LLC to conduct certain activities or projects. As you learned in Chapter 5, conducting activities through a subsidiary is beneficial in that it can shield the parent organization's assets from the liabilities of the subsidiary, absent circumstances warranting veil piercing.

Low Profit Limited Liability Companies

A few states, including Michigan, have statutes that authorize the formation of "low profit limited liability companies," or "L3Cs." While an L3C must be *primarily* charitable in nature, it may generate some profits in the conduct of its business and it may distribute after-tax profits to its owners. (And, being a type of LLC, it features flow-through taxation and limited liability for its owners.) An L3C will not qualify as a tax-exempt entity under Section 501(c)(3) of the Internal Revenue Code unless all of its members are tax-exempt entities and it meets certain other requirements. However, because L3Cs may qualify as a "program related investment" under the Internal Revenue Code, private foundations may be able to invest in them.

"Series" LLCs. Some states, including Delaware, permit the formation of "series" LLCs, that is, LLCs that have multiple internal "pools" or "cells" of assets, members, and/or managers. For example, a single LLC could have two different "pools": Series A and Series B. Further, this LLC could structure things so that the members and/or managers of Series A are separate and distinct from the members and/or managers of Series B, and that the assets of Series A are separate from, and immune from the liabilities associated with, the assets of Series

B, and vice versa. In a sense, in this example it is as if *two* LLCs exist within the framework of a *single* LLC. *See* Del. § 18-215.

Generally speaking, series LLCs are used only in very "sophisticated" transactions that you may learn more about in an advanced course on Business Organizations. However, note that the drafters of the Re-ULLCA chose not to include such a concept in that statute, writing in the prefatory note that:

> The Drafting Committee considered a series proposal at its February 2006 meeting, but, after serious discussion, no one was willing to urge adoption of the proposal .... Given the availability of well-established alternate structures (e.g., multiple single member LLCs, an LLC "holding company" with LLC sub-sidiaries), it made no sense for the Act to endorse the complexities and risks of a series approach.

"Foreign" LLC Issues. Typically, an LLC will organize in (that is, file its certificate of organization or certificate of formation in) the state in which it plans to conduct most of its business. But this does not have to be the case. Much like forming a corporation, you could form an LLC under any state's LLC statute. The law of that state will then govern the "internal affairs" of the LLC. For example, Re-ULLCA § 106 states that the "law of this state governs: (1) the internal affairs of [an LLC]; and (2) the liability of a member as member and a manager as manager for the debts, obligations, or other liabilities of [an LLC]." Somewhat similarly, Del. § 18-1101(i) provides that an operating agreement "that provides for the application of Delaware law shall be governed by and construed under the laws of ... [Delaware] in accordance with its terms." *See also id.* § 18-901(a)(1) (the laws of the state under which a foreign LLC is organized "govern its organizational and internal affairs and the liability of its members and managers"); Re-ULLCA § 801(1) (substantially the same).

As discussed in Section 16.04 below, many cases have allowed creditors of insolvent LLCs to pierce the "LLC veil" and recover from the members of the LLC in circumstances that are similar to piercing the corporate veil, which you learned about in Chapter 5. So, suppose that an LLC that is organized under the law of a state that has "defendant-friendly" veil-piercing rules is sued in a state that has "plaintiff-friendly" rules and the subject matter of the lawsuit is an event that occurred in the plaintiff-friendly state. Which state's law should apply—the law of the state of organization, or the law of the state where the event at issue in the case occurred? In other words, is veil-piercing a matter of an LLC's "internal affairs"? As noted above, Re-ULLCA § 106 provides that the law of "this state" (i.e., the state of organization) governs the "internal affairs" of the LLC, *as well as* the "liability of a member as member and a manager as manager" for the debts of the LLC.[*]

In addition, much like a corporation, if an LLC is organized under the law of State A and "transacts business" in State B, then State B will consider the LLC to be a "foreign" LLC and require it to obtain a certificate of authority to transact business in State B. See, e.g., Re-ULLCA § 802(a); Del. § 18-902. Note here that Re-ULLCA § 803(a) contains a list of activities that, by themselves, do not constitute "transacting business" in a given state. Also note that Re-ULLCA § 808 specifies the consequences of a foreign LLC transacting business in a state without having the requisite certificate of authority. See also Del. § 18-907. (This should remind you of the discussion of foreign corporations in Section 5.02(A) of Chapter 5 and foreign limited partnerships in Section 15.02 of Chapter 15.)

To see how well you understood the foregoing material, try your hand at the following problems, considering both Delaware law and the Re-ULLCA, unless otherwise noted.

Problems

Problem 16-1: Your client, Pam McGillicutty, wants to form an LLC that will run a restaurant and has hired you to draft the certificate of organization (or certificate of formation). Pam plans to be a member, as well as the manager of the LLC, with her husband and two daughters as other members. Pam plans to name the LLC "The McGillicutty Restaurant." *Is this a proper name to appear in the certificate?*

Problem 16-2: *Must the LLC have an operating agreement? If so, who must sign it? Must the operating agreement be in writing?*

Problem 16-3: *Can Pam be both a member <u>and</u> a manager of the LLC? Could she be the sole member? If she is a manager, what must the operating agreement state? See* Re-ULLCA §§ 407(a), 407(c)(6) and 102(10); *see also* Del. §§ 18-101(10) and 18-402.

Problem 16-4: *Would you recommend including a "purpose clause" in the certificate of organization?*

Problem 16-5: *What would happen if the LLC's certificate of organization stated that the LLC's purpose was to "operate a*

---

[*]   Note that RUPA § 106(b) is somewhat similar, providing that the "law of this State governs ... the liability of partners for an obligation of [an LLP]."

restaurant and conduct related activities," but the LLC's operating agreement stated that its purpose was to "engage in any lawful activity"?

Problem 16-6: Suppose that The McGillicutty Restaurant needs to obtain a loan to purchase equipment and supplies and that Pam, in her capacity as the manager of the LLC, signs a loan agreement with Big National Bank. Further, the Bank requires Pam to sign a personal guaranty of the loan. *Is the LLC bound by the loan agreement? If the LLC cannot repay the loan, is Pam personally liable to repay the loan? Are the other members of the LLC personally liable?*

Problem 16-7: Assume that the McGillicutty Restaurant, LLC was organized under the law of the State of Ketchup. The restaurant has been a big success and Pam wants the LLC to open a "branch" location in the State of Mustard. *What must the LLC do before it opens a restaurant in the State of Mustard? If a customer slips and falls at the LLC's restaurant in the State of Mustard and sues the LLC, which state's law will apply?*

Problem 16-8: *Under Re-ULLCA, may an operating agreement modify or eliminate a member's or manager's duty of loyalty or duty of care? See* Re-ULLCA § 110(c)(4), (d)(3); *see also* Del. § 18-1101(e).

Problem 16-9: *How may an operating agreement be amended? See* Re-ULLCA §§ 407(b)(5); 407(c)(4)(D); and 110(a)(4).

§ 16.03   DECISION-MAKING AND FIDUCIARY DUTIES

Objectives: You should be able to explain to the member(s) of an LLC: (1) how business decisions affecting the LLC may be made; (2) the difference between a member-managed LLC and a manager-managed LLC; (3) whether the actions of a member or manager may bind the LLC and, if so, how; and (4) whether members and/or managers owe fiduciary duties to the LLC and, if so, the nature of those fiduciary duties. In addition, you should be able to explain how the manager (if any) is chosen and whether the manager may be removed and replaced by the members.

As noted in Section 16.01, there are two basic types of governance structures for LLCs: ***member-managed*** LLCs, which are discussed in Part A below, and ***manager-managed*** LLCs, which are discussed in Part B. (It's unfortunate that these two phrases appear so similar in print. When reading this chapter, make sure that you carefully distinguish between them. By the way, can you say "manager-managed" or "member-managed" ten times quickly?)

Before turning to the characteristics of, and differences between, member-managed and manager-managed LLCs, note that many LLC statutes presume that an LLC will be member-managed *unless* its operating agreement states that it is manager-managed. In other words, member-managed seems to be the default form of governance. For example, Re-ULLCA § 407(a) states that a manager-managed LLC is one whose operating agreement provides the LLC is or will be "manager-managed," or that it "is or will be 'managed by managers,'" or that "management of the [LLC] is or will be 'vested in managers.'" Conversely, Re-ULLCA § 102(12) defines a member-managed LLC as an LLC that is *not* manager-managed.

Meanwhile, Del. § 18-402 provides in part that:

> Unless otherwise provided in [an operating] agreement, the management of [an LLC] shall be vested in its members ***; provided however, that if [an operating] agreement provides for the management, in whole or in part, of [an LLC] by a manager, the management of the [LLC], *to the extent so provided*, shall be vested in the manager who shall be chosen in the manner provided in the [operating] agreement. *** [An LLC] may have more than [one] manager. ***

(Emphasis added.)

Many states take a somewhat different approach, requiring an LLC's certificate of organization (or whatever such a state may call that document) to state either that the LLC is member-managed or that it is manager-managed, rather than allowing the choice to be made in the LLC's operating agreement. This approach at least has the advantage of allowing third parties to somewhat easily determine whether the LLC is member-managed or manager-managed because certificates of organization are publicly available whereas operating agreements are not.

But simply knowing whether a given LLC is member-managed or manager-managed may not be all that helpful or illuminating. As noted above, LLCs are extremely flexible; their operating agreements can vary nearly all of the default rules in Re-ULLCA and perhaps all of the rules in the Delaware LLC statute. While one could argue that this is not any different than, say, partnership agreements under RUPA, it nonetheless is true that LLCs tend to be more "diverse" than other types of business organizations. (The fact that LLC statutes are quite varied from state to state only exacerbates this problem.)

Thus, keep in mind that any given LLC, while ostensibly being a "member-manager" LLC or a "manager-managed" LLC, may have provisions in its operating agreement that are quite different—perhaps even radically different—from the rules that are discussed in the following materials. For example, an LLC could be member-managed with respect to some activities and manager-managed with respect to other activities. On this point, the above-quoted portion of Del. § 18-402 provides that an LLC is managed by a manager only "to the extent so provided" in the operating agreement; to the extent that the operating agreement does *not* so provide, the LLC could be considered member-managed. Further, even if a given LLC was "completely" manager-managed, LLC statutes still require *member* approval for certain transactions, as discussed below. In addition, Del. § 18-302(a) allows for different "classes" or "groups" of members that have different rights, powers, or duties. Del. § 18-404 does the same with respect to managers. However, we will try to keep things as simple as possible below.

A.   MEMBER-MANAGED LLCs

Decision-Making in a Member-Managed LLC. In a member-managed LLC, each member generally may participate in the LLC's management. Thus, the members of such an LLC somewhat resemble the partners of a partnership. Thus, Re-ULLCA § 407(b) provides that, in a member-managed LLC:

- the "management and conduct of the [LLC] are vested in the members";

- "[e]ach member has equal rights in the management and conduct of the [LLC's] activities";

- a "difference arising among members as to a matter in the ordinary course of the activities of the [LLC] may be decided by a majority of the members";

- an "act outside the ordinary course of the activities of the [LLC] may be undertaken only with the consent of all members"; and

- the "operating agreement may be amended only with the consent of all members."[*]

You will, of course, notice the similarity of this section to RUPA §§ 401(f) and (j), which you studied in Chapter 3.

In Delaware, Del. § 18-402 (some of which was quoted above) provides in part that:

> Unless otherwise provided in [an operating] agreement, the management of [an LLC] shall be vested in its members in proportion to the then current percentage or other interest of members in the profits of the [LLC] owned by all of the members, the decision of members owning more than 50 percent of the said percentage or other interest in the profits controlling; ***. *** Unless otherwise provided in [an operating] agreement, each member and manager has the authority to bind the [LLC].

Thus, Re-ULLCA and Delaware take different positions on how to count members' votes. As noted above, Re-ULLCA § 407(b) provides that each member has "equal" rights, which is akin to the "one partner, one vote" rule of RUPA § 401(f). (Of course, nothing in Re-ULLCA prevents an operating agreement from changing this rule.) Delaware, on the other hand, gives members proportional votes depending on their relative rights in the profits of the LLC. (See Section 16.05 below for a discussion of how profits in an LLC are allocated to the members.) This schism between Delaware's approach (called "pro rata") and Re-ULLCA's approach (called "per capita") is reflected in the LLC statutes of the various states; about half of the states use a pro rata voting method as the default choice, and about half of the states take a per capita approach.

Problems

Problem 16-10: MNOPQ, LLC ("MNOPQ"), is a member-managed LLC that runs an automobile repair business. MNOPQ has five members: Mike, Nick, Omar, Peggy, and Quinn. MNOPQ does not have any provisions in its operating agreement that would change the provisions of Re-ULLCA or the Delaware statute discussed above. Mike has a 30% interest in the profits of MNOPQ, Nick has a 10% interest, Omar has a 20% interest, Peggy has a 25% interest, and Quinn has a 15% interest. One day,

---

[*] Note that Re-ULLCA § 112(a) provides that the operating agreement could provide that it may not be amended without the approval of a specified nonmember or the satisfaction of a condition.

Nick told the other members that he thought that the partnership needed to buy a new auto repair diagnostic computer, at a cost of $20,000. *Describe, using both Re-ULLCA and the Delaware statute, what combinations of members' approvals would be necessary to approve this decision.*

Problem 16-11:   Same facts as Problem 16-10, except that the decision the members are considering is whether the LLC should open a coffee shop in a vacant space next to the garage where the LLC runs its auto repair business. *Describe, using both Re-ULLCA and the Delaware statute, what combinations of members' approvals would be necessary to approve this decision.*

Problem 16-12:   *To approve these decisions, must there be a meeting of the members? See* Re-ULLCA § 407(d), Del. §§ 18-302(c), (d).   *If the statutes do not so require, what provisions would you suggest putting in an LLC's operating agreement?*

Although Re-ULLCA § 407(b), quoted above, specifies a few decisions that require unanimous approval by the members of a member-managed LLC, and Del. § 18-402 seems to suggest that *all* decisions in a member-managed LLC may be made upon approval by the member(s) holding a majority of the interests in the profits of the LLC,[*] you should note that *other* sections of these statutes require unanimous member approval for certain transactions. For example, Re-ULLCA § 401(d)(3) requires unanimous member consent to admit a new member (unless the operating agreement requires a lesser vote) and section 701(a)(2) requires unanimous consent to dissolve. *See also* Re-ULLCA §§ 1003(a), and 1007(a) (unanimous approval for mergers or conversions); Del. § 18-502(b) ("Unless otherwise provided in [an operating], agreement the obligation of a member to make a contribution or return money or other property paid or distributed in violation of this chapter may be compromised only by consent of all the members.").

Problem

Problem 16-13:   *In counting members' votes on a matter, should "interested" votes be disregarded? See* Gottsacker v. Monnier, *697 N.W.2d 436 (Wis. 2005). Cf. Re-ULLCA § 409(f).*

---

[*]   This majority-vote approach is reflected in other sections of the Delaware statute. For example, for mergers Del. § 18-209(b) provides that "[u]nless otherwise provided in the [operating] agreement, [a merger agreement] ... shall be approved by each domestic [LLC] which is to merge ... by members who own more than 50 percent of the then current percentage or other interest in the profits of the domestic [LLC] ...."

Agency Authority of Members in a Member-Managed LLC. As you will recall from Chapter 2, an agent (or other actor) may have two main types of authority to bind a principal to a third party: actual authority and apparent authority. Actual authority depends on whether the agent (or other actor) reasonably believed that she was authorized to act on the principal's behalf and whether that belief is traceable to the principal's manifestations (i.e., words or other conduct). Apparent authority, on the other hand, depends on whether the third party reasonably believed that the agent was authorized to act on the principal's behalf and whether that belief is traceable to the principal's manifestations.

Generally speaking, the *actual* authority of both members and managers of an LLC has two sources: the LLC's operating agreement and its governing statute. As we have seen, operating agreements can vary dramatically from LLC to LLC to LLC. Statutes are thus easier to examine in a textbook like this. Many LLC statutes provide that, much like partners of a partnership, members of a *member-managed* LLC have broad authority to bind the LLC to contracts and other transactions with third parties. For example, the last sentence of Del. § 18-402, which was quoted above, provides that "[u]nless otherwise provided in [an operating] agreement, each member and manager has the authority to bind the [LLC]." (Note that this makes the operating agreement control both the actual authority and the apparent authority of members and managers.)[*]

But Re-ULLCA § 301(a), in a major departure from prior law, provides that a "member is not an agent of a limited liability company solely by reason of being a member." In other words, the *statute* does not confer either actual or apparent authority on members. The comment to this section explains:

> Most LLC statutes, including the original ULLCA, provide for what might be termed "statutory apparent authority" for members in a member-managed limited liability company and managers in a manager-managed limited liability company. This approach codifies the common law notion of apparent authority by position and dates back at least to the original, 1914 Uniform Partnership Act. ***

> This Act rejects the statutory apparent authority approach, for reasons summarized in [citation omitted]:

---

[*]   Similarly, most statutes provide that managers—but not members—of a manager-managed LLC have authority to act for the LLC, as discussed in the next section. But query how the "ordinary Joe" will be able to determine whether a given LLC is member-managed or manager-managed.

The concept [of statutory apparent authority] still makes sense both for general and limited partnerships. A third party dealing with either type of partnership can know by the formal name of the entity and by a person's status as general or limited partner whether the person has the power to bind the entity.

Most LLC statutes have attempted to use the same approach but with a fundamentally important (and problematic) distinction. An LLC's status as member-managed or manager-managed determines whether members or managers have the statutory power to bind. But an LLC's status as member- or manager-managed is not apparent from the LLC's name. A third party must check the public record, which may reveal that the LLC is manager-managed, which in turn means a member as member has no power to bind the LLC. As a result, a provision that originated in 1914 as a protection for third parties can, in the LLC context, easily function as a trap for the unwary. The problem is exacerbated by the almost infinite variety of management structures permissible in and used by LLCs.

The new Act cuts through this problem by simply eliminating statutory apparent authority.

[Citation omitted.]

Codifying power to bind according to position makes sense only for organizations that have well-defined, well-known, and almost paradigmatic management structures. ***

However, subsection (b) provides that a "person's status as a member does not prevent or restrict law *other than* [Re-ULLCA] from imposing liability on [an LLC] because of the person's conduct." (Emphasis added.) Thus, agency law (as opposed to LLC law) could determine whether a member had actual or apparent authority to act on behalf of or bind the LLC to a third party. For example if, under Section 2.03 the *Restatement (Third) of Agency* (which you studied in Chapter 2), it was reasonable for a third party to believe that a member was authorized to act for the LLC *and* that belief was traceable to a manifestation made by the LLC, then the third party could successfully argue that the member had apparent authority to bind the LLC, despite the member's lack of authority under *Re-ULLCA itself.*[*]   Of course, the trick for the third party here will be showing that its belief was traceable to a manifestation made by the LLC.

Also, note that some LLCs, perhaps in an effort to seem more "normal" to people used to dealing with corporations, may provide in their operating agreements for officer positions, such as a President or Vice President. While there is nothing in most LLC statutes that requires an LLC to have officers (unlike corporate statutes), if an LLC has officers, such persons may have apparent authority by virtue of their positions, as you learned in Chapter 2.

Because of (or perhaps despite) all of this, Re-ULLCA § 302 allows an LLC to file with the state a "statement of authority" which can, for any position in the LLC (e.g., member or manager) "state the authority, or limitations on the authority, of all persons holding [that] position" to transfer real property owned by the LLC or "enter into other transactions on behalf of, or otherwise act for or bind, the company." Alternatively, the statement of authority could describe the authority of a particular *person*, rather than a particular *position*. (Note that Re-ULLCA § 303, however, provides that a person who was named in a filed statement of authority could file a "statement of denial" that denies that she has the authority described in the statement of authority!)

If such a statement of authority has been filed, then it affects the power of a person to bind the LLC to non-members. Generally, third parties are not deemed to know of a *limitation* on authority contained in the statement, except where real property is involved. However, a *grant* of authority (with respect to transactions other than real estate transfers) that is described in the statement "is conclusive in favor of a person that gives value in reliance on the grant," unless that person has knowledge to the contrary or certain other conditions are met. (Similar provisions with respect to real estate transfers are contained in subsection (f).) Unless they are canceled earlier, statements of authority only "last" for five years from the date that they, or their most recent amendments, were filed.

Before we move on to manager-managed LLCs, one final note about member-managed LLCs is in order. All other things being equal, it sometimes will be preferable for an LLC to be member-managed rather than manager-managed because doing so may make it less likely to be regulated under other laws. For example, as discussed in the case that appears in Section 16.07 below, interests in a member-managed LLC are less likely to be considered "securities" under federal and state securities laws than are membership interests in manager-managed LLCs.

---

[*]   The comment to Re-ULLCA § 301(a) provides in part that members' and managers' apparent authority is to be determined under "other law—most especially the law of agency."

B.   MANAGER-MANAGED LLCs

Who is a "Manager"? How is (are) the Manager(s) Chosen? Before we discuss the attributes of manager-managed LLCs, we might well ask who is a "manager." To the general public, this may not be clear; is the "manager" of a retail location a "manager" of the LLC that owns that location? To this end, Re-ULLCA § 102(9) defines a manager as "a person that under the operating agreement of a manager-managed [LLC] is responsible, alone or in concert with others, for performing the management functions stated in Section 407(c)" (which are described below). Similarly, Del. § 18-101(10) defines a manager as a person who is named as a manager in, or designated as a manager pursuant to, the LLC's operating agreement "or similar instrument under which the [LLC] is formed." And, as you learned earlier in this chapter, remember that the managers of an LLC don't have to be members of the LLC, but they often are.

Another good question to ask is how managers are chosen. Here, Del. §§ 18-401 and 18-101(10) don't provide a default answer; they simply state that the manager or managers will be chosen in the manner provided in the LLC's operating agreement.

Problems

Problem 16-14: You are drafting the operating agreement for a Delaware LLC that will have approximately ten members and two managers (some of whom may be also be members). *How would you recommend that the managers be selected? Should two persons actually be named as managers in the operating agreement? If so, how long should their terms as managers be and how should their replacements be selected? If not, should there be an annual election of managers by the members?*

Problem 16-15: Same facts as Problem 16-14. *What would you recommend as to whether managers can be removed from office? Should cause be required? Should managers be permitted to resign? See Del. § 18-602.*

Meanwhile, Re-ULLCA § 407(c)(5) provides that a:

manager may be chosen at any time by the consent of a majority of the members and remains a manager until a successor has been chosen, unless the manager at an earlier time resigns, is removed, dies, or, in the case of a manager that is not an individual, terminates. A manager may be removed at any time by the consent of a majority of the members without notice or cause.

Of course, don't forget that this rule, like nearly every other Re-ULLCA, is subject to modification in an LLC's operating agreement.

Problems

Problem 16-16: Joe is both a member and manager of ABC123, LLC. *If Joe dissociates as a member of the LLC, is he still a manager? Conversely, if Joe ceases to be a manager, is he still a member of the LLC?* See Re-ULLCA § 407(c)(6).

Problem 16-17: Same facts as Problem 16-16. *Is Joe entitled to compensation from the LLC for his services as its manager?*

Decision-Making in a Manager-Managed LLC. As you may guess, if an LLC is manager-managed, then the manager (or managers) have the power to make decisions for the LLC to the extent provided in the operating agreement, subject to some limitations on their authority in the statute. Thus, Re-ULLCA § 407(c) provides in part that, in a manager-managed LLC:

• "[e]xcept as otherwise expressly provided in [Re-ULLCA], any matter relating to the activities of the company is decided exclusively by the managers";

• "[e]ach manager has equal rights in the management and conduct of the activities of the [LLC]";

• a "difference arising among managers as to a matter in the ordinary course of the activities of the company may be decided by a majority of the managers"; and

• the "consent of all the *members* is required to: (A) sell, lease, exchange, or otherwise dispose of all, or substantially all, of the company's property, ... outside the ordinary course of the company's activities; (B) approve a merger, conversion, or domestication under [Article 10 of Re-ULLCA]; (C) undertake any other act outside the ordinary course of the company's activities; and (D) amend the operating agreement."

(Emphasis added.)

For its part, the Delaware LLC statute is less detailed. Del. § 18-402 (which has already been quoted several times in this chapter) provides in part that:

> [If an operating] agreement provides for the management, in whole or in part, of [an LLC] by a manager, the management of the [LLC], to the extent so provided, shall be vested in the manager who shall be chosen in the manner provided in the [operating] agreement. The manager shall also hold the offices and have the responsibilities accorded to the manager by or in the manner provided in [an operating] agreement. Subject to § 18-602 [which concerns a manager's resignation], a manager shall cease to be a manager as provided in [an operating] agreement. [An LLC] may have more than [one] manager. Unless otherwise provided in [an operating] agreement, each member and manager has the authority to bind the [LLC].

Problems

Problem 16-18: *Under both Re-ULLCA and Delaware law, if there is more than one manager, how many votes does each manager get? How many managers must vote in favor of a decision to approve the decision? See* Del. § 18-404(b).

Problem 16-19: *If there is more than one manager, may a manager act alone (i.e., without approval by the other manager or managers)? Does your answer depend on the nature of the action that the manager wants to take?* See the comment to Re-ULLCA § 407(c).

Problem 16-20: *Must managers act at a meeting? See* Del. §§ 18-404(c), (d). *If the statutes do not so require, what provisions would you suggest putting in an LLC's operating agreement?*

Problem 16-21: *In performing its duties, can a manager delegate tasks to other persons and/or rely on opinions or reports from others? See* Del. §§ 18-406, 18-407; Re-ULLCA § 409(c), (g).

Agency Authority of Members and Managers in a Manager-Managed LLC. Many LLC statutes provide that, if the LLC is manager-managed, the manager(s) of the LLC has (have) authority to bind the LLC to third parties, but the members do not. In a sense, this is similar to the rule in limited partnerships, where general partners have authority to manage the limited partnership and bind it to transactions with third parties, but the limited partners do not. But here again, Delaware and Re-ULLCA are a bit "odd" on this point.

As noted above, the last sentence of Del. § 18-402, which was quoted above, provides that "[u]nless otherwise provided in [an operating] agreement, each member and manager has the authority to bind the [LLC]." Stop and think about this sentence for a minute. Essentially, it says that, even if the LLC is manager-managed, not only do managers have authority to bind the LLC to third parties, *but so do members*. Does this make sense? Of course, an LLC's operating agreement could limit a member's actual and apparent authority (as well as the actual and apparent authority of a manager, for that matter). Generally speaking, if you were drafting the operating for a manager-managed LLC, you would be well-advised to consider putting strict limits on the agency authority of members in the operating agreement.

On the other hand, Re-ULLCA is actually *silent* on the issue of the manager's apparent authority. As we saw in the previous section, Re-ULLCA § 301(a) provides that a "member is not an agent of a limited liability company solely by reason of being a member." What about managers? Re-ULLCA doesn't say. However, a comment to Re-ULLCA § 407 provides that, like a member's apparent authority, "[t]he common law of agency will also determine the apparent authority of an LLC's manager or managers, and in that analysis what the particular third party knows or has reason to know about the management structure and business practices of the particular LLC will always be relevant."

But before we leave the topic of agency authority in LLC, don't forget that most of the above discussion concerned whether members or managers could bind the LLC in their capacities *as members of managers*. It is always possible that a given person could be not only a member and/or manager, but an employee of an LLC as well. And as you learned in Chapter 2, oftentimes employees have either or both of actual authority and apparent authority to bind their employers to third parties.

C.   FIDUCIARY DUTIES IN LLCs

Except for the materials covered in Chapter 9 (which concerns closely held corporations) and Chapter 11 (which concerns controlling shareholders), the rules on fiduciary duties in partnerships and corporations are pretty easily summarized. In partnerships, partners owe strict fiduciary duties to each other and the partnership. In corporations, directors and officers owe fiduciary duties to the corporation, but the shareholders do not. Given that the LLC is a "hybrid" of partnerships and corporations, it should not surprise you to find some confusion on how to address fiduciary duties in LLCs.

Many LLC statutes, when addressing fiduciary duties, essentially take the partnership approach if the LLC is member-managed, and the corporate approach if the LLC is manager-managed. In other words, many LLC statutes provide that if the LLC is member-managed, then all of the members owe duties to the LLC* whereas if the LLC is manager-managed, the managers owe fiduciary duties to the LLC, but the members who are not also managers do not. Indeed, this is what Re-ULLCA provides, as discussed below. However, note that these two different approaches may not be a completely appropriate fit for LLCs. For example, while it is true that member-managed LLCs resemble partnerships to some degree, there is at least one important difference: members of an LLC do not usually face personal liability for the LLC's debts and obligations. Thus, query whether partners in a partnership, whose actions could result in personal liability for their fellow partners, should be held to a "higher" standard than members of a member-managed LLC.

Similarly, while manager-managed LLCs do resemble corporations to some degree, in such an LLC it is typically easier for members to exercise control over the manager or remove them than it would be for shareholders of a publicly traded corporation to remove or otherwise influence the directors. Further, if a shareholder of a publicly traded corporation is upset with management's performance, she can simply follow the "Wall Street rule" and sell her shares. Thus, the market may act as a disciplining force on the management of a publicly traded corporation; in an LLC it is likely the *members* that will play this role and will be able to do so fairly effectively. Comparing manager-managed LLCs to closely held corporations, note that it is somewhat easier for a member of an LLC to "exit" the LLC than it is for a shareholder of a closely held corporation to do so. Given these factors, query whether managers of a manager-managed LLC should be held to a somewhat "lesser" standard than should directors of a corporation. Nonetheless, statutes and case law thus far do not really reflect these somewhat subtle differences between LLCs and other business organizations.

Who Owes Fiduciary Duties and To Whom Do They Owe Them? As stated above, the general rule in most LLC statutes is that members owe fiduciary duties if the LLC is member-managed but only managers owe fiduciary duties if the LLC is manager-managed. (Keep in mind here that in a manager-managed LLC a member may, but need not, also be a manager. Such a person would owe duties in her capacity as a manager, but not in her capacity as a member.)

---

*   Because the LLC is a separate entity from its owners, many LLC statutes provide that members in a member-managed LLC owe duties to the LLC, as opposed to the other members. This issue is also addressed below.

Thus, Re-ULLCA § 409(a) provides that members of a member-managed LLC owe to the LLC and, subject to Section 901(b),[*] the other members of the LLC a fiduciary duty of loyalty and a fiduciary duty of care. (Note that this is a bit different than many states' LLC statues in that it provides members owe duties to other members, not only the LLC itself.) *But see* Re-ULLCA § 110(f).

However, if the LLC is *manager*-managed, then Re-ULLCA § 409(g)(1) provides, by cross-reference, that the managers—but not the members—owe fiduciary duties. If this subsection weren't clear enough, subsection (g)(5) drives the point home, providing that a member of a manager-managed LLC "does not have any fiduciary duty to the [LLC] or to any other member solely by reason of being a member." On the other hand, it is possible that, if a court found that a member who was not a manager nonetheless exercised control over the manager(s), that member may owe the same fiduciary duties as would the manager(s).

For its part, Delaware is less clear about fiduciary duties; Del. § 18-1101(c) is the closest the statute comes to telling us whether there are fiduciary duties, who owes them, and what the duties are. It provides in part that:

> To the extent that, at law or in equity, a member or manager or other person has duties (including fiduciary duties) to [an LLC] or to another member or manager or to another person that is a party to or is otherwise bound by [an operating] agreement, the member's or manager's or other person's duties may be expanded or restricted or eliminated by provisions in the [operating] agreement; provided, that the [operating] agreement may not eliminate the implied contractual covenant of good faith and fair dealing.

See also id. § 18-1101(d) (no liability for breach of fiduciary duty for member or manager who relies in good faith on the provisions of the operating agreement); *id.* § 18-1101(e) (operating agreement may limit or eliminate liabilities for breach of contract or breach of fiduciary duty, other than a "bad faith violation of the implied contractual covenant of good faith and fair dealing"); *id.* § 18-107 (unless prohibited by the operating agreement, a member or manager may lend to, borrow from, or transact business with the LLC and shall have "the same rights and obligations with respect to any such matter as a person who is not a member or manager.").

Note Del. § 18-1101(c) doesn't create any fiduciary duties, let alone define or describe them. However, it does recognize that they might exist "at law or in

---

[*]   Section 901 is discussed in Section 16.08 below.

equity" (and that, to the extent that they do exist, the operating agreement may modify or eliminate the duties). Thus, the Delaware statute essentially left it to the courts to define the contours of fiduciary duties in Delaware LLCs, assuming that an LLC's operating agreement does not define or eliminate them. In some cases, Delaware courts have inferred fiduciary duties, at least for managers. *See VGS, Inc. v. Castiel*, 2000 WL 1277372 (Del. Ch. 2000) (member-managers breached their duty of loyalty to another member when they approved a merger without notice to him, even though the defendants had sufficient voting power to approve the merger without the plaintiff), *aff'd*, 781 A.2d 696 (Del. 2001).

A more recent case in Delaware that addresses the existence of fiduciary duties in LLCs is *Kelly v. Blum*, 2010 WL 629850 (Del. Ch. 2010), another unpublished opinion. In this case, the plaintiff argued, among other things, that the defendants, who were managers and controlling members of the LLC, violated their fiduciary duties to him when they approved an "interested" merger involving the LLC. The defendants argued that they did not owe fiduciary duties because the LLC's operating agreement did not provide for such duties.[*] The court disagreed on this issue, writing that:

> even though contracting parties to an [operating] agreement have the freedom to expand, restrict, or eliminate fiduciary duties owed by managers to the LLC and its members and by members to each other, in the absence of a provision explicitly altering such duties, an LLC's managers and controlling members in a manager-managed LLC owe the traditional fiduciary duties that directors and controlling shareholders in a corporation would. In this case, I find that [the operating] agreement does not explicitly alter those default fiduciary duties and that, consequently, [the LLC's] managers and controlling members owe Plaintiff the traditional duties of loyalty and care.

***

> *** Delaware cases interpreting [Del. § 18-1101(c)] have concluded that, despite the wide latitude of freedom of contract afforded to contracting parties in the LLC context, "in the absence of a contrary provision in the LLC agreement," LLC managers and members owe "traditional fiduciary duties of loyalty and care" to each other and to the company. [Citations omitted.] Thus, unless the LLC agreement in a manager-managed LLC explicitly expands, restricts, or eliminates traditional fiduciary duties, managers owe those duties to the LLC and its members and controlling members owe those duties to minority members.

---

[*] To be fair, the defendants' argument on this point was more complex than this.

If a person owes fiduciary duties in the context of an LLC, the usual rule is that such duties are owed to the LLC itself, rather than the members of the LLC. This rule is thus similar to the general rule in corporate law that directors owe duties to the corporation rather than to its shareholders (or other "stakeholders"), as was discussed in Chapter 6. However, there are some exceptions to this statement. First, as noted above, Re-ULLCA § 409(a) provides that fiduciary duties may be owed to members in some circumstances. Second, the Delaware case discussed above provides that (in the absence of a contrary provision in the LLC's operating agreement), managers of a manager-managed LLC owe duties to the LLC *and* its members, and also that controlling members owe duties to minority members. Third, many LLC statutes have borrowed a page from MBCA § 14.30 (which you studied in Chapter 9) and have included "oppression" provisions. For example, Re-ULLCA § 701(a)(5)(B) provides that a member may sue for involuntary dissolution of an LLC if the "managers or those members in control" of the LLC have acted or are acting in an "oppressive" manner. While it is true that this section doesn't technically create any "fiduciary" duties, as you learned in Chapter 9, such oppression statutes are designed to address "abuse" of minority owners by majority owners in closely held businesses.

Before moving on to discuss the fiduciary duties of care and loyalty, one last note: Re-ULLCA § 409 contemplates that there could be *other* fiduciary duties besides care and loyalty. Unlike RUPA § 404(a), which expressly provides that the "only" fiduciaries that a partner owes are the fiduciary duties of care and loyalty, Re-ULLCA § 409 leaves the door open for courts to create additional fiduciary duties in LLCs. Whether they will do so remains to be seen.

The Duty of Care. Re-ULLCA § 409(c) provides that:

> Subject to the business judgment rule, the duty of care of a member of a member-managed [LLC] in the conduct and winding up of the company's activities is to act with the care that a person in a like position would reasonably exercise under similar circumstances and in a manner the member reasonably believes to be in the best interests of the company. In discharging this duty, a member may rely in good faith upon opinions, reports, statements, or other information provided by another person that the member reasonably believes is a competent and reliable source for the information.

Note a few things about this statute. First, it technically only applies to members in a member-managed LLC. However, Re-ULLCA § 409(g)(1) provides that managers have this same duty of care if the LLC is manager-managed.

Second, it bears a strong resemblance to MBCA § 8.30, which you studied in Chapter 6, but is not identical to it. Also, it adds a reference to the "business judgment rule" (which you also studied in Chapter 6), but does not define it. Thus, the courts will be left with the task of deciding the extent to which the business judgment rule will apply to decisions made by members and/or managers of an LLC.

Finally, it allows a member (or manager) to rely on opinions or other information from other persons. This, of course, should remind you of MBCA § 8.30(e). Similarly, although the Delaware statute makes no attempt to define a duty of care, it does provide that:

> A member, manager, or liquidating trustee of [an LLC] shall be fully protected in relying in good faith upon the records of the [LLC] and upon information, opinions, reports or statements presented by another manager, member or liquidating trustee, an officer or employee of the [LLC], or committees of the [LLC], members or managers, or by any other person as to matters the member, manager or liquidating trustees reasonably believes are within such other person's professional or expert competence ....

Del. § 18-406.

The Duty of Loyalty. As with the duty of care, Delaware's statute makes no attempt to define or describe the duty of loyalty with respect to LLCs. However, in the absence of an operating agreement provision limiting or eliminating the duty of loyalty, a court could impose duty-of-loyalty-based prohibitions on the conduct of an LLC member or manager similar to those imposed in corporations and/or partnerships. Indeed, as discussed above, Delaware courts have held that managers and controlling members owe the "traditional fiduciary duties of loyalty and care." Thus, a common-law duty of loyalty could involve elements such as not usurping "LLC opportunities" and avoiding "interested" transactions that were not fair to the LLC, along the lines discussed in the context of corporations in Chapter 7. *Cf. Solar Cells, Inc. v. True North Partners, LLC*, 2002 WL 749163 (Del. Ch. 2002) (entire fairness test may apply to a merger involving an LLC wherein one member's interest would be reduced from fifty percent to five percent; some specific provisions in the LLC's operating agreement affected the court's analysis).

Re-ULLCA, in a provision that appears modeled on RUPA § 404, provides that members (or, if the LLC is manager-managed, managers) owe a duty of loyalty that "includes" (but is not limited to) three elements. *See* Re-ULLCA § 409(b). However, Re-ULLCA § 409(e) goes on to provide that, with respect to claims under section (b)(2) (i.e., claims that a member or manager dealt with the LLC "as or on behalf of a person having an interest adverse to the company"), as well as any "comparable" claim, a defendant will have a defense if the transaction was "fair" to the LLC. Presumably, this would require the defendant to show that an "interested" transaction was entirely fair (i.e., fair dealing and fair price). Further, subsection (f) provides that the members may *unanimously* approve an act or transaction that would otherwise violate a member's or manager's duty of loyalty if they do so after "full disclosure."

The Obligation of "Good Faith and Fair Dealing"

Re-ULLCA § 409(d) states that a member (in a member-managed LLC) and a manager (in a manager-managed LLC) must discharge her duties, and exercise her rights, "consistently with the contractual obligation of good faith and fair dealing." As noted above, under Delaware law, an operating agreement may not "eliminate the implied contractual covenant of good faith and fair dealing." Del. § 18-1101(c). *See generally Nemec v. Shrader*, 991 A.2d 1120 (Del. 2010). Similarly, this duty cannot be eliminated under Re-ULLCA, although an operating agreement could "prescribe the standards by which to measure the performance" of this obligation, so long as the standards are not "manifestly unreasonable." See Re-ULLCA §§ 110(c)(5); (d)(5).

Limiting Fiduciary Duties in the Operating Agreement. Can the duty of care be modified? As noted above, the answer to this question in Delaware is an emphatic "yes." *See* Del. § 18-1101(c). Re-ULLCA takes a more measured approach. *See* Re-ULLCA §§ 110(c)(4); (d)(3)-(4).

What about the duty of loyalty? Again, Delaware says "yes." *See also Fisk Ventures, LLC v. Segal*, 2008 WL 1961156 (Del. Ch. 2008) (operating agreement could eliminate all fiduciary duties). *But see Abry Partners V, L.P. v. F&W Acquisition LLC*, 891 A.2d 1032 (Del. Ch. 2006) Again, Re-ULLCA takes a more measured approach. *See* Re-ULLCA §§ 110(c)(4); (d)(1)-(2); (d)(4); (e).

As noted in Section 16.08 below, members of an LLC can bring both direct and derivative actions in some circumstances. What if a member or manager is being sued for having breached her duty of care, resulting in damage to the LLC? Is there any way to exculpate the defendant? Note here that Re-

ULLCA § 110(g), in a provision that seems modeled on MBCA § 2.02(b)(4) (which you encountered in Chapter 6), allows an LLC's operating agreement to "alter or eliminate the indemnification for a member or manager provided by [Re-ULLCA § 408(a)]" and/or "eliminate or limit a member or manager's liability to the [LLC] and members for money damages," except for five specified items. Notably, such a provision may not shield a member or manager from liability associated with a breach or her duty of loyalty to the LLC.

The foregoing was a lot of information to digest. To see how well you did so, consider the following problems, applying both Re-ULLCA and Delaware law:

Problems

Problem 16-22: Builders, LLC, is a manager-managed LLC that performs construction work and that has several members. Sam is a member and is also the sole manager of the LLC. Sam, along with one other member (Steve) and a non-member employee of the LLC (Tom), also works for the LLC in its construction projects. No other members of the LLC perform work for the LLC. A client of the LLC has sued the LLC, alleging that construction work was negligently performed. *If a court finds that each of Sam, Steve, and Tom acted negligently while working on the construction project, has any of them breached his duty of care to the LLC?*

Problem 16-23: *Would your answer to Problem 16-22 change if the LLC's operating agreement had provided that no manager or member owes a duty of care to the LLC?*

Problem 16-24: *Would your to Problem 16-22 change if the LLC were member-managed?*

Problem 16-25: Same facts as Problem 16-22. Sam also agreed, on the LLC's behalf, to a construction project that resulted in the LLC losing money because the costs that it incurred in completing the project were far greater than the fees to which it was entitled under its contract with the client. Part of the reason for the loss was that the cost of raw materials for the project unexpectedly increased, but the contract did not allow the LLC to pass along these extra costs to the client. *Has Sam breached his duty of care to the LLC?*

Problem 16-26: *In which, if any, of the foregoing problems will Sam, Steve, or Tom be entitled to the protection of the business judgment rule?*

Problem 16-27:   *May Sam perform some minor construction projects for friends and family members "on the side"? May Sam invest in a coffee shop that his cousin plans to open?*

Problem 16-28:   *Would your answer to Problem 16-27 change if the LLC's operating agreement had provided that no manager or member owes a duty of loyalty to the LLC? Would your answer change if the LLC's operating agreement had a provision authorized by Re-ULLCA § 110(g)?*

Problem 16-29:   *Would your to Problem 16-27 change if the LLC were member-managed?*

§ 16.04   LIABILITY ISSUES

Objectives: *Given a fact pattern in which an LLC incurs a liability to a third party, either contractually (such as in a loan from a bank) or by a tort (such as where a member, manager, or employee of the LLC commits negligence in the course of the LLC's business), you should be able to determine which person(s) are or may be liable for this obligation.*

As noted at the beginning of this chapter, part of the "beauty" of the LLC is that its owners do not face personal liability solely because they are owners. In other words, members of an LLC enjoy a liability "veil" much like shareholders in a corporation. Thus, Re-ULLCA § 304(a) provides that an LLC's liabilities are solely the LLC's liabilities and "do not become the debts, obligations, or other liabilities of a member or manager solely by reason of the member acting as a member or manager acting as a manager." Del. § 18-303 is to the same effect. (Note that these sections pertain to *both* members and managers.[*]) Apply these sections to the following problems, which are adapted from problems that appeared in Chapter 5:

Problems

Problem 16-30:   Simmons Landscaping, LLC is a brand new LLC that is wholly owned by Bob Simmons. Bob also serves as the LLC's sole manager and its sole employee although if the business

---

[*]   However, note that Re-ULLCA § 207 provides that if a "record" that was delivered to the Secretary of State for filing, such as an LLC's certificate of organization, contained inaccurate information, the members or managers of the LLC could in some circumstances be liable to persons who suffer a loss in reliance on the inaccurate record.

does well he plans to hire other employees some day. Although Bob invested $1,000 to get the company started, the company needs to borrow $10,000 to purchase equipment. *If you represent a bank that is considering making this loan, what would you recommend that the bank do to increase its chances of having the loan fully repaid?*

Problem 16-31:   One day, Bob was out mowing lawns when he negligently ran over the foot of a customer, who was horribly injured. *Is Simmons Landscaping, LLC liable for this tort? Is Bob personally liable to this customer/victim if the assets of Simmons Landscaping, LLC are not sufficient to compensate her fully for her injuries?*

Veil-Piercing.   Two other exceptions to this rule of non-liability may apply in a given situation. First, many courts have allowed creditors of an LLC to pierce the "LLC" veil and impose liability on the members (and perhaps managers) of the LLC. As you learned in Chapter 5, there are literally thousands of reported decisions involving piercing the *corporate* veil. (In due time, there will likely be thousands of reported decisions involving piercing the LLC veil.) In many of those cases, such as the *DeWitt Truck Brokers* case in Chapter 5, an important factor was whether the corporation has "observed corporate formalities." However, note that Re-ULLCA § 304(b) provides that:

> The failure of [an LLC] to observe any particular formalities relating to the exercise of its powers or management of its activities is not a ground for imposing liability on the members or managers for the debts, obligations, or other liabilities of the [LLC].

Limitations on Distribution.   In addition, some state LLC statutes impose limitations on distributions (i.e., dividends) in a manner similar to MBCA § 6.40(c), which you studied in Chapter 5. Thus, Re-ULLCA § 405(a) provides in part that an LLC may not make a distribution* if, after the distribution:

- the LLC "would not be able to pay its debts as they become due in the ordinary course of the [LLC's] activities"; or

---

* Subsection (g) provides that a "distribution" does not include "amounts constituting reasonable compensation for present or past services or reasonable payments made in the ordinary course of business under a bona fide retirement plan or other benefits program."

- the LLC's "total assets would be less than the sum of its total liabilities plus the amount that would be needed, if the company were to be dissolved ... at the time of the distribution, to satisfy the preferential rights upon dissolution ... of members whose preferential rights are superior to those of persons receiving the distribution."

In addition, in a manner similar to MBCA § 8.33, Re-ULLCA § 406 provides that a member (in a member-managed LLC) or a manager (in a manager-managed LLC) who consents to a distribution that violates Section 405(a) may be liable to the LLC for the amount by which the actual distribution that was paid exceeded what could have been paid legally. The corresponding section in the Delaware LLC statute is Del. § 18-607.

Both veil-piercing and excessive distributions are addressed in the following recent case from Colorado.

Sheffield Services Company v. Trowbridge
Colorado Court of Appeals
211 P.3d 714 (2009)

HAWTHORNE, J.

Plaintiff, Sheffield Services Company, LLC (Sheffield), appeals the trial court's amended order dismissing its "piercing the corporate veil" and wrongful attempt to deplete assets claims against defendant Charles A. Trowbridge, and its "negligent misrepresentation/ nondisclosure" claim against Trowbridge and co-defendant Roy W. Mason. We affirm in part, vacate in part, and remand with directions.

I.   Facts and Procedural Background

Trowbridge and Mason co-managed Colfax Industrial, LLC (Colfax) and Villas Ventures, LLC (Villas) (collectively LLCs). Each LLC owned residential lots in a subdivision in the City and County of Broomfield that it intended to develop.

In April 1998, Colfax entered into a subdivision agreement with Broomfield. The agreement required the LLCs to complete specific landscaping and infrastructure improvements to receive necessary building permits. When the LLCs did not complete this work, Broomfield declared a breach of the agreement.

Later, on behalf of each LLC, Trowbridge negotiated a separate purchase and sale contract with Sheffield to sell it the lots owned by the LLCs. Both contracts provided that each LLC remained responsible for completing the subdivision agreement's requirements. Prior to closing on either contract, Sheffield was aware that the LLCs had not completed the improvements. Nevertheless, Sheffield closed on the contracts.

After the Villas closing but before the Colfax closing, Trowbridge and Mason received a letter from Broomfield explaining that it would withhold building permits if the LLCs failed to comply with the subdivision agreement. Trowbridge and Mason did not disclose to Sheffield, prior to the Colfax closing, either the contents of the letter or the LLCs' continuing noncompliance with the subdivision agreement.

After the Colfax closing, Sheffield learned of Broomfield's letter. To mitigate its losses, Sheffield assumed the LLCs' obligations under the subdivision agreement. Sheffield then filed this action against the LLCs, Trowbridge, and Mason, asserting four claims for relief: (1) breach of contract, (2) breach of implied covenant of good faith and fair dealing, (3) negligent misrepresentation/ nondisclosure, and (4) wrongful attempt to deplete the LLCs' assets.

The trial court entered judgment against the LLCs jointly and severally on Sheffield's breach of contract and breach of implied covenant of good faith and fair dealing claims (collectively breach of contract claims), and dismissed all remaining claims.

Sheffield now appeals the trial court's order dismissing its piercing the corporate veil claim, which the court concluded had been tried by consent; its wrongful attempt to deplete assets claim against Trowbridge; and its nondisclosure/negligent misrepresentation claim against both Trowbridge and Mason. Because Sheffield concedes that Mason's personal liability is limited to its negligent misrepresentation/nondisclosure claim discussed in Part IV below, we address only Trowbridge's personal liability in Part II. And, because the court made no findings as to Trowbridge's status as a member or manager of Villas, we address his personal liability only as it relates to Colfax, and remand to the trial court to determine his status as to Villas.

II.   Holding LLC Manager Personally Liable

Sheffield contends the trial court erred in relying on section 7-80-107(1), [Colorado Revised Statutes], which recognizes personal liability of members of a limited liability company under certain circumstances, to dismiss its claim against Trowbridge because he was not a member of Colfax. We agree.

Initially, we consider and reject Trowbridge's assertions that (1) no veil piercing claim can be considered in this case because Sheffield's complaint did not allege this theory, and thus he was not put on notice to defend against this claim until Sheffield's closing argument; and (2) the trial court abused its discretion in considering this claim because it was not tried by consent of the parties.

***

Here, the pleadings put Trowbridge on notice that Sheffield sought to hold him personally liable. ***

We agree with the trial court that the complaint need not expressly state that Sheffield sought judgment against Trowbridge for the LLCs' breaches of contract based on a veil piercing theory. [Citation omitted.] In addition, because Trowbridge did not object to the court admitting Sheffield's exhibits that related solely to the issue of personal liability and did present documentary evidence concerning the same issue, he impliedly consented to trial on that issue. [Citations omitted.]

Accordingly, the trial court did not abuse its discretion in concluding that Trowbridge's personal liability was tried by consent of the parties. [Citations omitted.]

Thus, we turn to Sheffield's argument on appeal that it is entitled to pierce the LLC veil and hold Trowbridge personally liable for the improper actions of Colfax.

A.   Effect of Section 7-80-107(1)

The trial court determined that section 7-80-107(1) prohibited it from applying the common law doctrine of piercing the corporate veil to impose personal liability on Trowbridge because, although he was a manager, he was not a member of Colfax. Sheffield contends that the trial court erred because it relied on legislative silence to reach a result inconsistent with longstanding equitable jurisprudence on the doctrine of piercing the corporate veil. We agree that the trial court misconstrued section 7-80-107(1) because the General Assembly did not expressly, or by clear implication, manifest an intent to prohibit courts from using the common law piercing the corporate veil doctrine to hold an LLC manager personally liable for the LLC's improper actions.

***

2.   Analysis

In 1990, the General Assembly enacted the Colorado Limited Liability Company Act, becoming the third state after Wyoming and Florida, to adopt such legislation. [Citation omitted.] In addition to favorable tax treatment and flexibility in management and financing, a limited liability company formed under the Act offers members and managers the limited liability protection of a corporation. [Citations omitted.]

However, section 7-80-107(1) of the Act addresses the "application of corporation case law to set aside limited liability" and provides:

> In any case in which a party seeks to hold the *members* of a limited liability company personally responsible for the alleged improper actions of the limited liability company, the court shall apply the case law which interprets the conditions and circumstances under which the corporate veil of a corporation may be pierced under Colorado law.

(Emphasis added.) Section 7-80-107 is the only section of the Act that addresses applying the common law principle of piercing the corporate veil in the LLC context.

Here, the trial court's analysis assumed that section 7-80-107(1) displaced the common law piercing the corporate veil doctrine, at least insofar as it can be applied in actions by third parties seeking to hold an LLC manager personally liable for the LLC's improper actions. We disagree because section 7-80-107(1) does not expressly preclude a court from applying the common law doctrine to hold a manager personally liable for an LLC's alleged improper actions. [Citations omitted.]

To construe section 7-80-107(1) as precluding application of this common law doctrine to LLC managers, as Trowbridge urges, would open the door to fraud. We presume that in adopting section 7-80-107(1), the General Assembly did not intend to create a safe harbor for LLC managers to perpetrate fraud and deceit. [Citation omitted.]

In addition, to so construe section 7-80-107(1) would be inconsistent with the established common law rule that the doctrine may be applied if equity so requires. [*LaFond v. Basham*, 683 P.2d 367, 369 (Colo. App. 1984)] (if adherence to the corporate fiction would promote injustice, protect fraud, defeat a legitimate claim, or defend crime, the invocation of equitable principles for the imposition of personal liability may occur).

Therefore, we conclude that the plain language of section 7-80-107(1) does not prohibit a court from applying the equitable common law doctrine of piercing the corporate veil to hold an LLC manager personally liable for the LLC's improper actions. Having so concluded, we now examine whether, absent a statutory restriction, the common law piercing doctrine applies to LLC managers, a question of first impression in Colorado.

B.   Extending Common Law Piercing to an LLC Manager

Because the common law doctrine of piercing the corporate veil is most fully developed in cases concerning corporate shareholders, we begin by examining those cases.

Piercing the corporate veil is an equitable, common law doctrine that penetrates the corporate veil of limited liability to impose liability on individual shareholders for the corporation's obligations. [Citation omitted.] Its application is appropriate when a corporation is merely a corporate shareholder's alter ego, and the shareholder uses the corporate structure to perpetrate a wrong. [Citation omitted.]

A corporation is a shareholder's alter ego when it is a "mere instrumentality for the transaction of the shareholder['s] own affairs, and there is such a unity of interest in ownership that the separate personalities of the corporation and the [shareholder] no longer exist." [Citation omitted.] Courts consider various factors in identifying such a unity of interest in ownership so as to disregard the corporate fiction and treat the corporation and shareholder as alter egos, including whether (1) the corporation is operated as a distinct business entity, (2) assets and funds are commingled, (3) adequate corporate records are maintained, (4) the nature and form of the entity's ownership and control facilitate misuse by an insider, (5) the business is thinly capitalized, (6) the corporation is used as a "mere shell," (7) shareholders disregard legal formalities, and (8) corporate funds or assets are used for noncorporate purposes. [Citations omitted.]

After finding an alter ego relationship, the court must determine whether justice requires recognizing the relationship's substance because the corporate fiction was "used to perpetrate a fraud or defeat a rightful claim." [Citation omitted.]

Last, the court must evaluate whether disregarding the corporate form and holding the shareholder personally liable for the corporation's acts will lead to an equitable result. [Citations omitted.] The claimant seeking to pierce the corporate veil must show by clear and convincing evidence that each consideration above has been met. [Citations omitted.]

In [citation omitted], a division of this court extended the piercing the corporate veil doctrine beyond corporate shareholders by concluding that a corporate entity may be disregarded and corporate directors held personally liable if equity so requires. The division reasoned that:

If adherence to the corporate fiction would promote injustice, protect fraud, defeat a legitimate claim, or defend crime, the invocation of equitable principles for the imposition of personal liability may occur.

...

[And] to allow a director to hide behind the cloak of the corporation would promote injustice in that it would allow the actions of a director who used assets of a corporation for his personal gain to defeat the valid claim of a creditor.

[Citation omitted.]

We perceive no basis for declining to extend this reasoning to impose personal liability on LLC managers. See [citation omitted] (quoting Robert B. Thompson, *The Taming of Limited Liability Companies*, 66 U. COLO. L. REV. 921, 945 (1995) ***).

Other courts have recognized that LLC managers are similar to corporate officers or directors and that no reason exists in law or equity for treating an LLC differently from a corporation when considering whether to disregard the legal entity. See *Kaycee Land & Livestock v. Flahive*, 46 P.2d 323, 327 (Wyo. 2002) ("[I]f members *and officers* of an LLC fail to treat it as a separate entity ..., they should not enjoy immunity from individual liability for the LLC's acts. ... No reason exists in law or equity for treating an LLC differently than a corporation when considering whether to disregard the legal entity." (emphasis added)); *Roth v. Voodoo BBQ, LLC*, 964 So.2d 1095, 1097 n.3 (La. Ct. App. 2007) (manager of an LLC is similar to an officer or director of a corporation).

Whether the conduct in question is that of a corporate director *** or an LLC manager, as in this case, the injustice wrought by adherence to the corporate or LLC fiction is the same: the director's or manager's actions in using corporate or LLC assets for personal gain would defeat a creditor's valid claim. Comparing the trial court's findings in [citation omitted] with those of the trial court here supports this conclusion.

In *LaFond*, the [court of appeals] relied on the trial court's findings that the defendant, although not a shareholder of the involved corporations, was a board of directors member and an officer, whereby he (1) clearly dictated all policy and activity for both corporations; (2) ran the corporations, alone determined when he would draw money from them, when he would lend money to them, how and when the money would be repaid to him, and when the corporations would rent office space in a building that he owned and made payments on with corporate funds; and (3) when the corporations were virtually insolvent, demanded payment upon his notes and took over corporate assets to the detriment of other creditors.

Here, the trial court found, with record support, that (1) the complicated, interrelated and commingled financial circumstances of Trowbridge and his various business entities were intended to frustrate the entities' creditors; (2) Trowbridge's overall conduct resulted in a clear financial benefit to him, which was not properly documented because of his elaborate scheme of concealment; and (3) Trowbridge engaged in various transactions and complicit conduct that disregarded the separate LLC entities, intending to keep the "ambulance chasers" from identifying and reaching the LLCs' members' assets at the time of liquidation and provide him and one LLC member "plausible deniability" to insulate preferential distributions to another member.

Because allowing an LLC manager to hide behind the LLC's cloak of limited liability would promote injustice, protect fraud, or defeat legitimate creditors' claims, we conclude that the equitable common law doctrine of piercing the corporate veil may be applied to hold an LLC manager personally liable for the LLC's improper actions.

Accordingly, because the trial court's order dismissing Sheffield's claim to hold Trowbridge personally liable for the LLCs' obligations was based on an erroneous conclusion of law, we vacate the order and remand for the court to determine whether its findings as to Trowbridge's conduct warrant applying the common law doctrine of piercing the corporate veil to hold him personally liable for Colfax's breach of contract. The court shall make specific findings, and determine whether, under the common law, (1) Colfax is Trowbridge's alter ego[,] (2) justice requires recognizing the substance of Trowbridge's relationship with Colfax because he used Colfax to perpetrate a fraud or defeat a rightful claim, and (3) disregarding the relationship's form and holding Trowbridge personally liable would lead to an equitable result.

III.   Wrongful Attempt to Deplete Assets

Sheffield contends that the trial court erred by ruling that (1) section 7-80-606, [Colorado Revised Statutes], does not provide a remedy to an LLC's creditors, and (2) an LLC manager is not subject to the common law duty imposed on corporate officers and directors to avoid favoring personal interests over those of the corporation's creditors. We disagree with the first contention and agree with the second.

A.   Section 7-80-606

Section 7-80-606, entitled "Limitations on distribution," provides in relevant part:

(1)   A limited liability company shall not make a distribution to a member to the extent that at the time of distribution, after giving effect to the distribution, all liabilities of the limited liability company ... exceed the fair value of the assets of the limited liability company. ...

(2)   A *member who receives a distribution* in violation of subsection (1) of this section and who knew at the time of the distribution that the distribution violated subsection (1) of this section, *shall be liable to the limited liability company* for the amount of the distribution.

(Emphasis added.)

This section permits an LLC to recover the amount of a wrongful distribution from a member who received it. Sheffield argues that it should be allowed to pursue a claim against Trowbridge under section 7-80-606 to recover wrongful distributions made by Colfax to one of its members. According to Sheffield, we should extend the analysis in *Ficor, Inc. v. McHugh*, 639 P.2d 385 (Colo. 1982), to this case and interpret section 7-80-606 as allowing an LLC's creditor to seek personal liability of an LLC manager who knowingly violates the terms of the statute.

The statute at issue in *Ficor*, section 7-5-114(3), [Colorado Revised Statutes], provided:

The *directors* of a corporation who vote for or assent to any distribution of assets of a corporation to its shareholders during the liquidation of the corporation without the payment and discharge of, or making adequate provision for, all known debts, obligations, and liabilities *shall be jointly and severally liable to the corporation* for the value of such assets which are distributed, to the extent that such debts, obligations, and liabilities of the corporation are not thereafter paid and discharged.

(Emphasis added.) Cf. § 7-108-403(1), [Colorado Revised Statutes] (director who votes for or assents to distribution made in violation of section 7-106-401, [Colorado Revised Statutes], or articles of incorporation is personally liable to corporation).

Although the statute's plain language expressly provided a remedy only for the corporation, the court in *Ficor*, 639 P.2d at 393, held that "all creditors of a corporation, as a group" may assert the remedy provided by the statute "on behalf of the corporation for their own benefit." Therefore, the creditors as a group could recover the wrongfully distributed assets from the defendant corporate directors because those defendants were the parties expressly made liable for the wrongful distribution by the language of section 7-5-114(3).

Section 7-80-606(2), [Colorado Revised Statutes], expressly provides that LLC members who receive a wrongful distribution are liable to the LLC. Sheffield asserts that two LLC members who are not parties to this action received wrongful distributions. Hence, if we accept Sheffield's invitation to apply the *Ficor* analysis and read into section 7-80-606(2) a remedy for LLC creditors, that remedy would be against one or both of those non-party members. Therefore, even assuming, without deciding, that we would extend the *Ficor* analysis to this case, Sheffield could not prevail because the proper parties against whom Sheffield could claim under section 7-80-606 are not parties to this action.

B.   Common Law Duty

Alternatively, Sheffield argues that the trial court erred in not extending to the LLC setting the common law duty owed by corporate officers and directors to avoid favoring their own interests over creditors' claims. We agree.

Under the common law, an insolvent corporation's directors and officers are "trustees" for corporate creditors. [Citation omitted.] However, as trustees, corporate directors and officers do not owe the corporation's creditors the full set of fiduciary duties owed to a solvent corporation's shareholders. [Citation omitted.] Their duty is limited and requires that, when a corporation becomes insolvent, its directors and officers must avoid favoring their own interests over creditors' claims. [Citations omitted.] If the corporate director breaches this duty, he or she is personally liable to the corporate creditors for such "malfeasance." [Citation omitted.]

We have concluded above that an LLC is a business entity alternative to a corporation, whose managers, like a corporation's shareholders and directors, are subject to the common law piercing doctrine. We perceive no basis for declining to extend our reasoning to impose personal liability on LLC managers under the common law "trustee doctrine" that requires corporate directors to avoid favoring their own interests over the corporation's creditors' claims when the corporation becomes insolvent.

Corporations and LLCs are equally susceptible to becoming insolvent and having a director or manager distribute entity assets in a manner favoring personal interests over the corporation's or LLC's creditors. Not to extend the common law trustee doctrine to LLC managers would open the door to fraud and create a safe harbor for managers to favor personal interests over the LLC's creditors.

Therefore, we conclude that when an LLC becomes insolvent, its manager owes a common law duty to the LLC's creditors to avoid favoring personal interests over those of creditors. Breach of this duty results in the LLC manager's personal liability to those creditors. [Citation omitted.] This personal liability is distinct from the personal liability that may be imposed by applying the piercing the corporate veil doctrine to LLC managers. Here, the trial court found that when Trowbridge distributed LLC assets to one of the non-party members, those distributions were "preferential as to the claims of [Colfax's] creditors, including [Sheffield]." The court further found:

> [The] entire factual pattern demonstrates complicit conduct intended to provide [Trowbridge] and one [non-party] member ... plausible deniability intended to insulate preferential distributions to another [non-party] member. The fair inference to be drawn from the overall conduct is that there was a clear financial benefit to [Trowbridge] although perhaps not documented, from this elaborate scheme of concealment.

However, the trial court made no findings whether Colfax was insolvent or whether Sheffield was its creditor at the time LLC assets were distributed. Therefore, we remand for the trial court to make those findings. If Colfax was or became insolvent when Trowbridge made those distributions, the court can then determine whether Trowbridge breached his common law duty owed to Colfax's creditors to avoid favoring his personal interests over theirs.

***

V.   Conclusion

The trial court's order is affirmed to the extent it dismisses (1) Sheffield's negligent misrepresentation/nondisclosure claim, and (2) Sheffield's claim of wrongful attempt to deplete assets under section 7-80-606. The order is vacated to the extent it dismisses Sheffield's claims against Trowbridge seeking to hold him personally liable for (1) the LLCs' breaches of contract under the equitable common law doctrine of piercing the corporate veil, and (2) wrongful depletion of the LLCs' assets under the common law duty of LLC managers to avoid favoring personal interests over creditors' claims. The case is remanded to the trial court to determine, based on the evidence before it, (1) whether Trowbridge is a member or manager of Villas, (2) whether it is equitable to hold Trowbridge personally liable for the LLCs' improper actions by piercing the corporate veil, and (3) whether the LLCs were or became insolvent when Trowbridge distributed LLC assets to the non-party members, and if so, whether Trowbridge breached the common law duty of an LLC manager to avoid favoring personal interests over the LLCs' creditors' claims.

---

§ 16.05   FINANCIAL ISSUES

> ***Objectives:*** *You should be able to explain to a client who wants to form an LLC: (1) whether members must make contributions to the LLC in order to join the LLC and, if so, what form the contributions may take, (2) how the LLC's profits and losses will be allocated among the members, (3) whether the LLC is required to make distributions, (4) if the LLC pays distributions, how they will be divided among the members, (5) whether a member of the LLC may sell or otherwise transfer her interest in the LLC to a third party and, if so, the consequences of such a transfer, and (6) whether the LLC's operating agreement may—or should—modify the statutory default rules on these issues.*

Although LLCs are a hybrid of partnerships and corporations, in terms of financial issues they more closely resemble partnerships than corporations. In part, this is because LLCs will almost always receive "flow-through" tax treatment, as do partnerships. Thus, many of the provisions of Re-ULLCA and the Delaware statute that we will examine in this section will remind you, at least somewhat, of provisions of RUPA that you studied in Chapters 3 and 4. On the other hand, what you may encounter in "real life" with an LLC might not resemble the following discussion much at all. This is because, as with most other provisions of LLC statutes, the provisions governing financial issues can be modified in an LLC's operating agreement. (Also, financial issues tend to be one of the most heavily negotiated provisions of operating agreements for LLCs with more than one member.) Nonetheless, we will look at four main financial issues in LLCs and how Re-ULLCA and the Delaware statute treat them: contributions, profit and loss allocation, interim distributions to members, and the transferability of membership interests to third parties.

Contributions. How does one become a member in an LLC? Re-ULLCA § 401(d) provides that, with respect to a currently existing LLC, a person will become a member in various ways, such as any methods that are specified in the operating agreement or with the approval of all the members. Del. § 18-301(b) provides similar methods by which a member may be admitted to a currently existing LLC. Typically, a person becomes a member by buying an interest in the LLC from the LLC itself or, in some cases, by buying an interest from a current member and then being admitted to the LLC in accordance with its operating agreement or the applicable statute (which admission typically requires the consent of all of the current members).

Note that neither of the sections described in the above paragraph requires a person to make a contribution to the LLC in order to become a member of it (let alone specify the amount of such a contribution).* Nonetheless, it will be the rare LLC that will admit a person as a member without requiring that person to make a contribution. Obviously, the document that will specify any required contributions will be the LLC's operating agreement. It is also likely that the operating agreement will specify what *form* that contributions must (or may) take, such as cash or other property. However, in the absence of such a provision, note that both Re-ULLCA § 402 and Del. §§ 18-501 and 18-101(3) provide that a contribution may consist of just about any legally recognizable consideration, including agreements to make contributions or perform services *in the future*. This is important for members who agree to contribute services to the LLC but who do not contribute cash or other property; the agreed-upon value of their services "counts" as a contribution, which may affect their financial rights, as discussed below. (Further, note that members are generally not entitled to remuneration for their services to the LLC. *See* Re-ULLCA § 407(f).)

What would happen if a member fails to make a promised contribution or fails to perform the promised services? Well, of course the LLC could sue the member. *See, e.g.*, Del. §§ 18-502(a); 18-111. The operating agreement could also specify penalties for the member's failure. *See id.* § 18-502(c); *see also id.* § 18-306. (Under Del. § 18-405, a manager may be subject to specified penalties for breaching the operating agreement or if other events occur.)

Further, Re-ULLCA § 403(b) provides that a *creditor* of the LLC may be able to enforce a member's obligation to make a contribution, if the creditor had extended credit or otherwise relied on the member's obligation to make the contribution. Del. § 18-502(b) is to the same effect.**

---

*   Also, note that Del. § 18-301(d) provides, among other things, that (1) a person can be admitted as a member of an LLC and receive a "limited liability company interest" (as defined below) in the LLC without making (or being obligated to make) a contribution, and (2) unless the operating agreement provides otherwise, a person can be admitted as a member of an LLC without acquiring a limited liability company interest in it. Re-ULLCA § 401(e) is similar. Further, under Del. § 18-403, a *manager* may make contributions to the LLC and share in its profits and losses and distributions as a member.

**   This section provides that (continued on following page):

Allocations of Profits and Losses. As you learned in Chapter 3, in a partnership, profits are allocated equally among the partners and losses are allocated in the same manner as profits, in both cases unless otherwise provided in the partnership agreement. On the other hand, in an "S" corporation, shareholders would report their proportionate share of corporate income (or loss) on their personal tax returns, with their respective shares typically being determined by the percentage of the shares they own. In turn, the number of shares that a shareholder owns may reflect the amount of capital that she contributed to the "S" corporation (assuming she bought the shares from the corporation itself).

So, how should it work in an LLC—should profits and losses be allocated equally, as is the case in a partnership, or based on the amount that member has contributed to the LLC, as is (arguably at least) the case in an "S" corporation? State statutes exhibit a split of authority on this issue, perhaps reflecting the difficulty of deciding whether to treat an LLC like a corporation or like a partnership. Del. § 18-503, as a default rule, allocates profits and losses based on the *contributions* that the various members have made. Specifically, this section states that, unless the operating agreement specifies otherwise, "profits and losses shall be allocated on the basis of the agreed value (as stated in the records of the [LLC]) of the contributions made by each member to the extent that they have been received by the [LLC] and have not been returned." Thus, if Member A has contributed $10,000 to the LLC, Member B has contributed $5,000, and none of those contributions have been returned, two-thirds of the LLC's profits and losses would be allocated to Member A and one-third would be allocated to Member B.

Re-ULLCA § 404(a) does not quite address this issue. It provides that interim *distributions* made by an LLC "must be in equal shares among members and dissociated members." (Of course, the LLC's operating agreement could provide for a different rule.) However, the comments to this section suggest that the operating agreement will usually provide for the allocation of *profits and losses*, perhaps through capital accounts.

Speaking of capital accounts, it is fairly common for LLC operating agreements to provide that members have capital accounts that are similar to the partnership accounts that are created under RUPA § 401(a). As you learned in Chapter 3, RUPA § 401(a) provides that each partner is deemed, during the time that she is a partner, to have an "account," the value of which is (1) increased by any contributions made by the partner and any profits that are allocated to the

---

Notwithstanding [a] compromise [approved by the members], a creditor of [an LLC] who extends credit, after the entering into of [an operating agreement which] ... reflects the obligation, and before the amendment thereof to reflect the compromise, may enforce the original obligation to the extent that, in extending credit, the creditor reasonably relied on the obligation of a member to make a contribution ....

partner and (2) decreased by any distributions received by the partner and any losses that are allocated to the partner. When a partner dissociates from the partnership, the current balance in the partner's partnership account is the "starting point" for calculating how much that partner will receive upon dissociation. An LLC operating agreement could work in much the same way. However, note that distributions and dissociations are handled much differently in LLCs than they are in partnerships, as discussed below.

Interim Distributions. Here we are talking about "interim" distributions, that is, distributions that the LLC may make during its *existence*, as opposed to distributions made upon its *dissolution*, which are discussed in the following section. Both Re-ULLCA and the Delaware statute provide that members are *not* entitled to any interim distributions. Thus, Re-ULLCA § 404(b) provides that a "person has a right to a distribution before the dissolution and winding up of [an LLC] only if the company decides to make an interim distribution," and that a "person's dissociation does not entitle the person to a distribution." *Cf.* Del. § 18-601. Of course, an LLC's operating agreement could require distributions in some situations or in specified amounts, and/or could allow the members or managers to vote on or otherwise decide whether distributions should be paid.

If an LLC pays distributions to its members, as noted above Re-ULLCA § 404 provides that the distributions "must be in equal shares among members and dissociated members," unless otherwise provided in the operating agreement. On the other hand, Del. § 18-504 provides that distributions are allocated among the members based on the relative values of the contributions that they have made and that have not been returned, unless the operating agreement provides otherwise. However, both statutes contemplate that distributions ordinarily will paid in cash rather than in kind. *See* Re-ULLCA § 404(c); Del. § 18-605.

Finally, don't forget that both Re-ULLCA and the Delaware LLC statute limit the amount of distributions that an LLC may legally pay, so as to protect the LLC's creditors, as discussed in Section 16.04 above.

Transferable Interests. Much like RUPA §§ 502 and 503 with respect to partnerships, Re-ULLCA § 502 provides that a member of an LLC may transfer her "transferable interest" in the LLC to a third party. Re-ULLCA § 102(21) defines a "transferable interest" as "the right, as originally associated with a person's capacity as a member, to receive distributions from [an LLC] in accordance with the operating agreement, whether or not the person remains a member or continues to own any part of the right." As with transferring a partnership interest under RUPA, if a member transfers her transferable interest in an LLC, the transfer does not cause her to be dissociated from the LLC or cause the LLC to dissolve, nor does it allow the transferee to participate in management of the LLC or be entitled to inspect the LLC's books and records. (See Re-ULLCA § 503 for provisions concerning charging orders that are very similar to RUPA § 504.)

Similarly, Del. § 18-702 provides that a member's "limited liability company interest" (which is defined in Del. § 18-101(8) as a member's share of the LLC's profits and losses and the member's right to receive distributions of the LLC's assets) can be assigned to a third party, unless the operating agreement provides otherwise. *See also* Del. § 18-603 (operating agreement may provide that a limited liability company interest may not be assigned before the LLC is dissolved). As with Re-ULLCA, the assignee does not have any rights to participate in the LLC's management, unless otherwise provided in the operating agreement or unless all of the LLC's members agree to give such rights to the assignee (unless the operating agreement does not so allow). Instead, the assignment of the LLC interest merely entitles the assignee "to share in such profits and losses, to receive such distribution or distributions, and to receive such allocation of income, gain, loss, deduction, or credit or similar item to which the assignor was entitled, to the extent assigned." However, unlike Re-ULLCA, if a member assigns *all* of her limited liability company interest, then she "ceases to be a member and to have the power to exercise any rights or powers of a member." See Del. § 18-704 for the circumstances under which an assignee may become a member of the LLC and the resulting consequences of such an admission. (Also, see Del. § 18-703 for provisions concerning charging orders that are similar to Re-ULLCA § 503 and RUPA § 504.)

Problems

Problem 16-32: Adam, Betty, and Cindy wish to form an LLC. Adam plans on investing $10,000 in the LLC, as does Betty. Cindy, on the other hand, will not contribute cash to the LLC but has agreed to perform services for the LLC (unlike Adam and Betty). You represent Cindy. *What advice would you give to Cindy about drafting the provisions of the LLC's operating agreement that concern contributions, profit-allocation, and distributions?*

Problem 16-33: Same facts as Problem 16-32. *What would happen if Cindy is unable to perform the services that she is obligated to perform under the operating agreement?*

Problem 16-34: Domingo, Ernestine, and Fabio are the three members of a Delaware LLC. The LLC's operating agreement does not have any provisions that would change the "default" rules of the statute. When the LLC was formed, Domingo contributed land worth $50,000, Ernestine contributed $30,000 in cash ($20,000 of which was later returned to her), and Fabio contributed $20,000 in cash. *How will the LLC's profits and losses be allocated among the three members?*

Problem 16-35: Same facts as Problem 16-34, except that the LLC was formed under Re-ULLCA. *How will the LLC's profits and losses be allocated among the three members?*

Problem 16-36:   George, Harinder, and Irene are the three members of a Delaware LLC. The LLC's operating agreement does not have any provisions that would change the "default" rules of the statute. When the LLC was formed, George contributed $20,000 in cash, Harinder agreed to perform services that the members agreed were worth $10,000 (but so far Harinder has only performed half of those services), and Irene contributed $25,000 in cash. The LLC has been very profitable since it was formed and has a great deal of cash on hand. *Is any member entitled to a distribution? If the LLC pays distributions, how will they be allocated among the three members?*

Problem 16-37: Same facts as Problem 16-36, except that the LLC was formed under Re-ULLCA. *Is any member entitled to a distribution? If the LLC pays distributions, how will they be allocated among the three members?*

Problem 16-38: Same facts as Problem 16-36, including the fact that the LLC was formed under Delaware law. *May Irene sell her interest in the LLC to a third party? If she does, what are the consequences of that sale?*

Problem 16-39: Same facts as Problem 16-36, except that the LLC was formed under Re-ULLCA. *May Irene sell her interest in the LLC to a third party? If she does, what are the consequences of that sale.*

Problem 16-40: Same facts as Problem 16-36, except that George is not only a member of the LLC, but a manager as well. One Saturday, George was out driving on a personal errand (nothing related to the LLC's business) when he struck and injured Jordan. Jordan sued George and obtained a judgment for $100,000. Unfortunately, George does not have $100,000. His only significant asset is his interest in the LLC. *Explain to Jordan* *whether he may reach the LLC's assets to satisfy this $100,000 judgment. If not, what can he do to satisfy his judgment?*

§ 16.06   DISSOCIATION AND DISSOLUTION

Objectives: You should be able to list the events that cause a member to be dissociated from an LLC. Given a fact pattern, you should be able to determine whether a member has dissociated from the LLC and, if so, the consequences of the dissociation. In addition, you should be able to list the events that will cause an LLC to be dissolved and, given a fact pattern, determine whether an event has caused the LLC to dissolve. If a member has dissociated but the LLC does not dissolve, you should be able to explain the effects of the member's dissociation. Finally, given a fact pattern in which an LLC dissolves, you should be able to determine how the LLC's assets will be distributed to creditors and members.

A.   DISSOCIATION OF MEMBERS UNDER Re-ULLCA

Article 6 of Re-ULLCA contains provisions that determine when a member has dissociated from an LLC. These provisions are modeled on Article 6 of RUPA. For example, Re-ULLCA § 602 lists the events that cause a member to dissociate from an LLC. RUPA's corresponding provision, RUPA § 601, is extremely similar. For that reason, some of the following discussion and problems may remind you of things that you saw in Chapter 4.

Dissociation refers to an event that causes a particular member to cease being a member. Re-ULLCA § 602 contains a complete list of these events of dissociation. Obviously, if one of these events occurs and that event is on the "list" in Section 602, then you know that a member has dissociated; conversely, if an event happens and it's not on the list, then you know that a member has not dissociated from the LLC. Note the following about Re-ULLCA § 602 before you go read it.

Section 602(1) basically provides that a member may "quit" being a member by express will, either immediately or as of a date in the future. Subsection (2) provides that a member will be dissociated from an LLC upon the occurrence of an event specified in the operating agreement and subsection (3) provides that a member may be expelled pursuant to the operating agreement, typically after a specified percent of the other members have voted to expel that member. (Compare these sections to RUPA §§ 601(1), (2), and (3).)

Re-ULLCA § 602(4) allows a member to be expelled by the unanimous vote of the *other* member in four specified situations (subsections (4)(A) through (D)). Similarly, subsection (5) allows the LLC (but not a member) to seek a court order expelling a member from the LLC if the member has committed one or more of the "bad acts" specified in subsections (5)(A) through (C).

Subsection (6) provides that, if a member is an individual, she will be dissociated from the LLC if she (1) dies or (2) *if the LLC is member-managed*, a guardian or conservator is appointed for the member or she is judicially determined to be incompetent. Subsection (7) then provides that a member will be dissociated from the LLC if certain debt-related events occur, but only if the LLC is member-managed. Further, subsections (8) through (10), concern members that are not individuals and basically provide that these types of members will be dissociated when they themselves dissolve or otherwise cease to exist.

Re-ULLCA § 602 then has a few additional subsections that do not have comparable provisions in RUPA § 601. First, Re-ULLCA §§ 602(11) provides that a member would be dissociated from an LLC if the LLC participates in a merger and the LLC is not the "surviving" entity or "otherwise as a result of the merger, the person ceases to be a member." Subsections (12) and (13) provide a similar rule for conversions and domestications (which are discussed in Section 16.08 below). Finally, subsection (14) provides that a member will be dissociated when the LLC "terminates." (More on the concept of termination below.)

After carefully reading Re-ULLCA § 602, work on the following problems:

Problems

Problem 16-41: XYZ, LLC, which is member-managed, has three members: Xavier, Yolanda, and Zeke. For the past several months, Zeke has been unhappy with the behavior of his partners and has been considering quitting and moving to Hawaii. One day, while sitting at home alone watching television, Zeke shouted: "That's it, I quit XYZ, LLC." *Has Zeke dissociated from XYZ, LLC?*

Problem 16-42: Same facts as in Problem 16-41, except that on his way into the office, Zeke was hit by an automobile and died. *Has Zeke dissociated from the XYZ, LLC?*

Problem 16-43: Same facts as in Problem 16-42, except that Zeke did not die. Instead, he is currently in a coma on life support machines. All of the doctors who have examined Zeke have determined that it is extremely unlikely that he will ever regain consciousness. *Is Zeke still a member of XYZ, LLC? Would your answer change if (1) a guardian was appointed for Zeke? Would your answer change if XYZ, LLC was manager-managed?*

Problem 16-44: Same facts as in Problem 16-41, except that earlier today Yolanda filed for protection under Chapter 7 of the Bankruptcy Code. *Is Yolanda still a member of XYZ, LLC? Would your answer change if XYZ, LLC was manager-managed?*

Problem 16-45: A group of twenty doctors has approached you about drafting an operating agreement for a PLLC* that they wish to form. *What sorts of provisions would you suggest including in the operating pursuant to Re-ULLCA § 602(2)?*

Problem 16-46: A group of twenty doctors has approached you about drafting an operating agreement for a PLLC that they wish to form. *What sorts of provisions would you suggest including in the operating pursuant to Re-ULLCA § 602(3)?*

Another issue that must be considered if a member has dissociated from an LLC is whether the dissociation was *wrongful*. Under Re-ULLCA § 601(a), a member "has the power to dissociate as a member at any time, rightfully or wrongfully, by withdrawing as a member by express will under" Re-ULLCA § 602(1). However, subsection (b) makes some types of dissociation "wrongful" and subsection (c) sets forth the consequences of such wrongful dissociations. Read those sections, as well as Re-ULLCA § 603, and consider the following problems:

Problems

Problem 16-47: TUV, LLC has three members: Tom, Ulrich, and Vivian, and is a member-managed LLC. When they formed the LLC three years ago, the three members agreed that the purpose of the LLC would be to operate a coffee shop. However, recently Ulrich and Vivian proposed that the LLC should open a seafood restaurant. Tom, who doesn't like this idea, told Ulrich that he

---

*   Typically, an LLC that is formed to provide professional services or services in a "learned profession" such as medicine or law, must be formed as a "professional" LLC, or PLLC, rather than a regular LLC. See Chapter 1.

was quitting the LLC. *Has Tom dissociated from TUV, LLC? If so, was his dissociation wrongful? If Tom has dissociated, does he have any further right to participate in the management of the LLC? If his dissociation was wrongful, what are the consequences of this? Would any of your answers change if TUV, LLC had been manager-managed?*

Problem 16-48: Same facts as Problem 16-47, except that Tom died. *Has Tom dissociated from TUV, LLC? If so, was his dissociation wrongful?*

Problem 16-49: Same facts as Problem 16-47, except that Tom filed for protection under Chapter 7 of the Bankruptcy Code. *Has Tom dissociated from TUV, LLC? If so, was his dissociation wrongful?*

Problem 16-50: Same facts as Problem 16-47. *Can Tom now compete with the LLC by opening another coffee shop? Would your answer change if TUV, LLC had been manager-managed?*

Again, dissociation concerns whether a member ceases to be a member. However, when you studied dissociations from partnerships in Chapter 4, you saw that under RUPA if a partner dissociates by express will from an at-will partnership, the partnership will dissolve. (It's even "easier" to dissolve a partnership under UPA.) *In contrast—and perhaps remarkably—a member's dissociation will not cause an LLC to dissolve. Indeed, under the statute a member's dissociation does not even trigger a right on the member's part to have her interest in the LLC "bought out."*

Thus, a member, even one who has dissociated, may have to wait until the LLC is dissolved to receive some sort of payout. To this end, note that Re-ULLCA § 603(a)(3) provides that, in most cases, when a member dissociates, "any transferable interest owned by the person immediately before dissociation in the person's capacity as a member is owned by the person solely as a transferee." (For a discussion of the rights of transferees of interests in LLCs, see Section 16.05 above.) In other words, a dissociated member no longer has governance rights with respect to the LLC.

Again, a member's dissociation from an LLC does not, by itself under the statute, mean that the member is entitled to a payout of some sort. Re-ULLCA has no counterpart to Article 7 of RUPA, under which partners who dissociate without dissolving the partnership generally are entitled to a payout. Of course, keep in mind that like pretty much all of the rules from Re-ULLCA, an LLC's operating agreement may change these rules. But without such a provision in the operating agreement, an LLC is more or less "stuck" with her investment unless she sells it to a third party (as discussed in Section 16.05) or the LLC dissolves.

So, what causes an LLC to dissolve? That is the subject of the next section.

B.   DISSOLUTION UNDER Re-ULLCA

Re-ULLCA § 701 lists the following events of dissolution of an LLC:[*]

●   an "event or circumstance that the operating agreement states causes dissolution";

●   the unanimous consent of the members;

●   if the LLC has not had members for ninety consecutive days;

●   if, upon application by a member, a court orders the LLC dissolved because either "the conduct of all or substantially all of the company's activities is unlawful" or "it is not reasonably practicable to carry on the [LLC's] activities in conformity with the certificate of organization and the operating agreement"; or

●   if, upon application by a member, a court orders the LLC dissolved because the managers or the members that control the LLC either "have acted, are acting, or will act in a manner that is illegal or fraudulent" or "have acted or are acting in a manner that is oppressive and was, is, or will be directly harmful to the applicant." (However, in such a proceeding, the statute specifically allows the court to order a remedy different than dissolving the LLC.)

Stop and think about this section for a minute. It is a curious combination of partnership and corporate law, befitting the hybrid nature of an LLC. For example, some of the causes of dissolution are basically "lifted" from RUPA § 801. However, the last cause of dissolution listed above, i.e., "oppression," is a corporate concept that you learned about in Chapter 9.

Whatever the cause, if an LLC has dissolved, it must go into a period of winding up. *See* Re-ULLCA § 702. Much like winding up a partnership, winding up an LLC involves liquidating the LLC's assets, paying creditors (or otherwise

---

[*]   In addition, note that Re-ULLCA §§ 705 to 707 concern *administrative* dissolutions, that is, situations where the LLC is dissolved due to reasons such as failing to pay certain taxes or making certain filings.

discharging the LLC's debts, as discussed below), and distributing the remaining amounts (if any) to the members. Re-ULLCA § 702 also allows the LLC to file a statement of dissolution and, when the winding up process is done, a statement of termination with the Secretary of State. Typically, the members (if the LLC were member-managed) or the managers (if the LLC were manager-managed) control the winding up process. However, Re-ULLCA § 702(c) has provisions concerning the situation where the LLC no longer has any members, and Re-ULLCA § 702(e) provides that a court may order judicial supervision for "good cause" upon application by a member, or for other reasons.

Interestingly, Re-ULLCA §§ 703 and 704, "borrowing a page" from MBCA §§ 14.06 and 14.07, allow an LLC to discharge "known" claims by sending a notice to such creditors, and to discharge other claims ("unknown" claims) by newspaper notice. Read those two sections and consider the following problems:

Problems

Problem 16-51: Tennis, LLC has three members: Ms. Serve has a 50% interest in the LLC's profits, Mr. Net has a 25% interest, and Ms. Racket has a 25% interest, as stated in the operating agreement. Tennis, LLC wishes to dissolve. Currently, it owes money to General Contractors, Inc. ("GCI") for installing a new tennis court, although GCI has not submitted its final invoice for this work. *Are there any steps that Tennis, LLC could take to "trick" GCI into having its claim be barred?*

Problem 16-52: Same facts as Problem 16-53. Assume that GCI's claim is not barred, that GCI's claim is for $10,000, but that Tennis, LLC only has $5,000 of assets. *May GCI recover its claim from the members?*

Problem 16-53: Same facts as Problem 16-54. *Would your answer change if Tennis, LLC had distributed its $5,000 of assets to the three members? If so, how much could GCI recover from each member and how would it go about doing so?*

Problem 16-54: Tom's Asbestos LLC ("TAL") manufactured (as you might expect) asbestos, which it had sold throughout the United States for more than thirty years. TAL has decided to dissolve. *How may TAL bar products liability claims that may be asserted against it in the future? Is this likely to result in many potential claimants knowing that TAL is dissolving? What is the deadline for an asbestos/lung cancer victim to assert a claim against TAL? What is the statute of limitations for doing so?*

Under Re-ULLCA § 708, the LLC's assets are first used to pay creditors (including members who are creditors). Remaining funds are distributed as follows:

● First, persons who own a "transferable interest" (as defined above, both members and, if applicable, transferees own a transferable interest) will receive an amount equal to the value of their *unreturned* contributions to the LLC. If there are not enough funds to do so fully for all holders of transferable interests, then the funds that the LLC does have would be divided among these persons "in proportion to the value of their respective unreturned contributions."

● Second, any remaining funds would be distributed "in equal shares among members and dissociated members, except to the extent necessary to comply with any transfer effective under Section 502."

C.   DISSOCIATION AND DISSOLUTION UNDER DELAWARE LAW

Dissociation. Unlike Re-ULLCA, the Delaware statute has little in the way of provisions that tell us when a member would cease to be a member of an LLC (outside of a merger or other business combination that the LLC does not survive). About the best that can be found is Del. § 18-304, which provides that a person ceases to be a member of an LLC if she files bankruptcy or certain other debt-related events occur, unless the operating agreement provides otherwise or all of the members otherwise agree in writing. Also, as noted above, Del. § 18-702 provides that if a member assigns *all* of her limited liability company interest, then she "ceases to be a member and to have the power to exercise any rights or powers of a member."

Del. § 18-603 provides that a member may "resign" from an LLC, but *only* as provided in (and in accordance with) the operating agreement. Further, "[n]otwithstanding anything to the contrary under applicable law, unless [an operating] agreement provides otherwise, a member may not resign from [an LLC] prior to the dissolution and winding up of the [LLC]."

But if a member does resign (i.e., she is permitted to resign by the operating agreement), Del. § 18-604 then provides that:

[U]pon resignation any resigning member is entitled to receive any distribution to which such member is entitled under [an operating] agreement and, if not otherwise provided in [an operating] agreement, such member is entitled to receive, within a reasonable time after resignation, the fair value of such member's limited liability company interest as of the date of resignation based upon such member's right to share in distributions from the [LLC].

Thus, unless the operating agreement gives them additional ways to "quit" or "resign" being a member of an LLC or they sell their interests to a third party, members are locked into their investment in a Delaware LLC. Of course, this is a very important issue that should be addressed in the operating agreement. If you were to draft such a provision in an operating agreement, obviously one issue that should be addressed is when a member is dissociated from or may withdraw or resign from the LLC. Assuming that such an event would, under the operating agreement, trigger a right on the part of the dissociated member to have her interest in the LLC redeemed, the issues to be addressed in such a provision would be somewhat similar to the issues that should be addressed in a buy-sell agreement for a closely held corporation, as discussed in Chapter 9.

Dissolution.   Under Del. § 18-801(a), five events will cause an LLC to dissolve:

- An LLC will dissolve at the time specified in its operating agreement (but if no such time of dissolution is specified, then the LLC's existence is perpetual);

- An LLC will dissolve upon the occurrence of an event specified in its operating agreement;

- An LLC will dissolve if the dissolution is approved by members who own at least two-thirds of the "then-current percentage or other interest in the profits of the [LLC]," unless otherwise provided by the operating agreement;[*]

- An LLC will dissolve if no longer has any members, unless certain events occur within ninety days thereafter; and

- An LLC will dissolve if a court orders dissolution under Del. § 18-802. That section provides that the Court of Chancery may, upon application by a

---

[*]   If there is more than one class or group of members, then two-thirds (counted the same way) of the members of each class or group must approve the dissolution under this section.

member or manager, dissolve the LLC if "it is not reasonably practicable to carry on the business in conformity with [the operating] agreement."

Notably, subsection (b) specifically provides that a member's death, retirement, resignation, expulsion, bankruptcy, dissolution or termination as a member of the LLC does *not* cause the LLC to dissolve, unless the operating agreement provides otherwise. (Also, Del. § 18-806 provides that any of the first four causes of dissolution listed above could be "undone" in some circumstances. Member approval is typically required to revoke a dissolution under that section.)

If an LLC dissolves, the dissolution process is not terribly different from the dissolution of a partnership, which you studied in Chapter 4, or the dissolution of a corporation, which you studied in Chapter 12. An LLC will generally liquidate its assets, pay creditors, and distribute the remaining funds to the members. *See* Del. § 18-803(b). If the LLC were manager-managed, then the manager(s) will usually be in charge of the winding up process, unless the operating agreement provides otherwise. If the LLC were member-managed or if there are no managers (such as where the managers have all resigned), then the members will be in charge of the winding up process. Alternatively, a person selected by the members holding a majority of the profits interests in the LLC may oversee the winding process. In addition, the Court of Chancery could, upon "cause shown," wind up the LLC, *see id.* § 18-803(a), or appoint receivers or trustees to do so, *see id.* § 18-805.

As with the dissolution of any business, "general" creditors are paid first, including creditors who are members and/or managers. *See* Del. § 18-804(a)(1). The next group in line for the LLC's assets are members and former members, with respect to claim under either section 18-601 or 18-604 for distributions that they are owed pursuant to the operating agreement but that have not yet been paid. (*See also id.* § 18-606.) Finally, members receive the remaining assets (if any). How are these assets divided up? Obviously, the operating agreement could provide a detailed answer. In the absence of an operating agreement provision, Del. § 18-803(a)(3) provides that members are paid "first for the return of their contributions and second respecting their limited liability company interests, the proportions in which the members share in distributions." (As discussed above, the default rule in the Delaware LLC statute is that members share distributions based on the relative values of their contributions to the LLC.)

Again though, creditors must be paid, or a provision for their claims must be made, before members can receive any of the LLC's assets upon dissolution. To this end, subsection (b) contains provisions that require the LLC to pay or "make reasonable provision to pay" all of its known debts and obligations, and to make a reasonable provision for claims that are currently asserted against it in a lawsuit or other proceeding. In addition, subsection (b)(3) requires the LLC to:

make such provision as will be reasonably likely to be sufficient to provide compensation for claims that have not been made known to the [LLC] or that have not arisen but that, based on facts known to the [LLC], are likely to arise or to become known to the [LLC] within 10 years after the date of dissolution.

What if the LLC does not have enough assets to do all of this? In that case, Del. § 18-804(b) states that "claims and obligations shall be paid or provided for according to their priority and, among claims of equal priority, ratably to the extent of assets available therefor." Further, under subsection (c), a member who receives a distribution that the member knew violated section 18-804(a) is liable to return the distribution to the LLC. (Conversely, if the member did not know that the distribution violated Del. § 18-804(a), she is not liable to return it.) *See also id.* § 18-804(d) (three year statute of limitations to recover improper distributions).

Finally, Del. § 18-203 provides that the LLC's certificate of formation (as discussed in Section 16.02 above) shall be canceled upon, among other things, the LLC's dissolution and the completion of its winding up process. At that point, a "certificate of cancellation" is to be filed with the Secretary of State.

Problems

Problem 16-55: Jameel, Kathy, and Lamar formed an LLC two years ago. The LLC's operating agreement does not have any provisions that would change the "default" rules of Re-ULLCA. When the LLC was formed, Jameel contributed land worth $60,000, Kathy contributed $20,000 in cash ($10,000 of which was later returned to her), and Lamar contributed $30,000 in cash. One day, Jameel said to Kathy: "I quit. I want my money out of the LLC." *Has Jameel dissociated from the LLC? If so, was his dissociation wrongful? If Jameel has dissociated, will the LLC dissolve? If the LLC does not dissolve, will Jameel "get his money out"?*

Problem 16-56: Same facts as Problem 16-55, except that you may assume that the LLC dissolved. The LLC's only asset is a bank account that contains $250,000. It owes creditors $50,000, including $10,000 owed to Lamar for a loan that Lamar made to the LLC. *How will this $250,000 be distributed to the creditors and members of the LLC?*

Problem 16-57: Same facts as Problem 16-56, except that the LLC's bank account only contains $100,000.

Problem 16-58:   Same facts and questions as Problem 16-55, except that you should apply Delaware law instead of Re-ULLCA.

Problem 16-59:   Same facts and questions as Problem 16-56, except that you should apply Delaware law instead of Re-ULLCA.

Problem 16-60:   Same facts and questions as Problem 16-57, except that you should apply Delaware law instead of Re-ULLCA.

§ 16.07   ARE LLC INTERESTS "SECURITIES"?

As discussed in Chapter 13, a great many things, some of them perhaps surprising, can be considered "securities" for purposes of federal and state securities laws. As you also learned in that chapter, if an instrument is a security, then a person who wants to offer or sell that security must either register it with the Securities and Exchange Commission or find an exemption from the registration requirement. In addition, the other provisions of the securities laws, including the "plaintiff-friendly" anti-fraud rules, will apply.

Thus, deciding whether something is a "security" is a high-stakes question. But what about LLC interests—are they "securities"? Chapter 13 did not say. Consider the following case.

Great Lakes Chemical Corp. v. Monsanto Co.
United States District Court for the District of Delaware
96 F.Supp.2d 376 (2000)[*]

McKELVIE, District Judge.

This is a securities case. Plaintiff Great Lakes Chemical Corporation is a Delaware corporation with its principal place of business in Indianapolis, Indiana. Defendants Monsanto Company and its wholly owned subsidiary, Sweet Technologies, Inc. ("STI"), are Delaware corporations with their principal places of business in St. Louis, Missouri.

On May 3, 1999, Great Lakes purchased NSC Technologies Company, LLC ("NSC"), from Monsanto and STI. NSC is a Delaware limited liability company with its principal place of business in Mount Prospect, Illinois.

On January 4, 2000, Great Lakes filed the complaint in this action, alleging that Monsanto and STI violated [Section 10(b) of, and Rule 10b-5 under,

---
[*]   [Footnote by author]: Many section and sub-section headings have been removed.

the Securities Exchange Act] by failing to disclose material information in conjunction with the sale of NSC.   *** Great Lakes is seeking compensatory damages, punitive damages, indemnification, costs, fees, and rescission of the purchase agreement. ***

*** This is the court's decision on defendants' motion to dismiss.

I.   FACTUAL AND PROCEDURAL BACKGROUND

***

A.   The Formation of NSC

1.   Creation of the NSC Unit within Monsanto

Monsanto is the world's largest manufacturer and distributor of L-phenylalanine ("L-phe"), an amino acid that is a principal ingredient in the sweetener aspartame. Monsanto manufactures and sells aspartame as the product NutraSweet. L-phe is also useful in the production of numerous pharmaceutical products.

In approximately 1985, Monsanto created the NSC Unit within its NutraSweet division to develop specialized pharmaceutical intermediates and pharmaceutical active compounds derived from L-phe.   In 1995, Monsanto reorganized its NutraSweet division and established the NSC Unit as a separate reporting division of Monsanto Growth Enterprises.   Monsanto retained the commercial rights to manufacture and sell L-phe and aspartame to the sweetener market. Monsanto restricted the NSC Unit's sales of L-phe to the pharmaceutical market and to a single customer in the sweetener market, Enzymologa, a Mexican manufacturer of aspartame.   By 1998, the NSC Unit's principal business was based on the development and sale of L-phe and Tic-D, a pharmaceutical intermediate derived from L-phe.

2.   Creation of NSC as a Limited Liability Company

On September 25, 1998, Monsanto entered into an agreement (the "LLC Agreement") with STI to establish the NSC Unit as a limited liability company called NSC Technologies Company, LLC ("NSC"), pursuant to the Delaware Limited Liability Company Act [citation omitted].   The following terms of the LLC Agreement are relevant to the present dispute.

The LLC Agreement names Monsanto and STI as the Members of NSC, and provides that each Member shall have an Interest in NSC. The LLC Agreement defines "Interest" as "[a] Member's Percentage Interest, right to distributions under Section 4.1 of this Agreement, and any other rights which such Member has in the Company." A Member's Percentage Interest is determined according to the Member's capital contributions to NSC. Pursuant to the LLC Agreement, Monsanto contributed assets to NSC totaling $162.9 million, and STI contributed assets totaling $37.1 million, giving the firms an 81.5% and 18.5% Percentage Interest, respectively, in NSC. The LLC Agreement establishes procedures for Members to adjust their Percentage Interest in NSC.

The Members are entitled to receive distributions of Net Cash Flow and allocations of profits and losses. Net Cash Flow is defined, essentially, as all cash receipts of NSC, excluding members' capital contributions, less all cash expenditures, accrued expenses, and loan payments due. Section 4.1 of the LLC Agreement establishes the allocation mechanism by which Members receive distributions of Net Cash Flow ***. The LLC Agreement also provides that NSC's income, profits, gains, losses, deductions, and credits shall be allocated to the Members pro rata in accordance with their respective Percentage Interests.

The LLC Agreement provides that the business and affairs of NSC shall be managed by a Board of Managers. *** Except as otherwise provided for in the LLC Agreement, the Board of Managers has exclusive authority to bind NSC, and to manage and control NSC's business and affairs. The LLC Agreement states:

> Except as otherwise expressly set forth in this Agreement, the Members shall not have any authority, right, or power to bind the Company, or to manage or control, or to participate in the management or control of, the business and affairs of the Company in any manner whatsoever. Such management shall in every respect be the full and complete responsibility of the Board alone as provided in this Agreement.

The Members of NSC may remove the Managers with or without cause.

The Members of NSC are entitled to vote on certain matters, including on all incurrences of indebtedness or guarantees thereof. The LLC Agreement specifies that a Majority in Interest, which is defined as 51% of the Percentage Interests owned by the Members, is required to constitute a quorum, or to amend the LLC Agreement.

The LLC Agreement restricts the ability of Members to transfer or otherwise dispose of their Interests in NSC absent consent of the Board. Moreover, Members are prohibited from disposing of their Interests in NSC when the disposition would cause NSC to be taxable as a corporation, would violate federal or state securities laws, or would violate other laws or commitments binding on NSC. ***

B.   The Sale of NSC

In October 1998, BancBoston Robertson Stephens, an investment bank, prepared a Confidential Descriptive Memorandum (the "Offering Memorandum") on behalf of Monsanto and STI to promote the sale of NSC. *** The Offering Memorandum recites that NSC's sales increased from $8.3 million in 1995 to $34.5 million in 1997, and projects that NSC's sales would increase to $93.2 million in 1999 and $192.2 million by 2002.

On November 10, 1998, Monsanto and STI presented the Offering Memorandum to Great Lakes, together with a letter from BancBoston Robertson Stephens proposing that final bids be submitted by year end. On November 12, 1998, Great Lakes responded to the solicitation with a letter indicating its interest in submitting a bid.

***

2.   Changes in the Market for L-phe and Tic-D

In early 1999, as negotiations over the sale of NSC continued, a number of events were occurring that may have impacted the business prospects of NSC. Monsanto and other competing producers of L-phe, in particular the Korean firm Daesang, began discounting the sale price of L-phe in the sweetener market. As the price of L-phe dropped, NSC allegedly began experiencing diminished sales of L-phe, particularly to NSC's sole customer in the sweetener market, Enzymologa. Moreover, an Italian firm, Archimica, was producing Tic-D, a pharmaceutical intermediate derived from L-phe, by a manufacturing process that allegedly infringed the claims of a United States patent assigned to NSC. Archimica was allegedly selling Tic-D products to NSC's customers.

3.   Great Lakes' Offer to Purchase NSC, and Monsanto's
        Revision of NSC's Financial Projections

On January 15, 1999, [Ian Wolpert, a Vice-President of Monsanto] provided representatives of Great Lakes with revised sales projections for NSC, reducing the forecast of $93.2 million originally stated in the Offering Memorandum to $78 million.

The following week, Great Lakes offered to acquire defendants' Interests in NSC for approximately $130 million.

During the months of January through April 1999, Great Lakes conducted due diligence concerning NSC's business, intellectual property, its product markets, and its actual and projected sales. ***

***

On March 15, 1999, during a teleconference call with Wolpert, representatives from Great Lakes raised concerns about defendants' sales projections for NSC. Wolpert allegedly replied that the reduced sales in 1999 were the result of temporary reductions in orders and the accelerated posting of 1999 sales in 1998, and that the shortfall in sales in the first quarter of 1999 would benefit Great Lakes because those deferred sales would be realized after Great Lakes acquired NSC.

On March 16, 1999, Monsanto and STI provided Great Lakes with revised financial projections, stating that NSC could realize total sales of approximately $68.2 million in 1999. Defendants allegedly assured Great Lakes that NSC's total sales would increase to $124.1 million in 2000, $149.9 million in 2001, and $184 million in 2002. At a meeting the same week between defendants and Great Lakes, Wolpert allegedly stated to Great Lakes' representative that defendants "stood by" these sales projections. After the meeting, [Fred Beyerlein, the Co-Chief Operating Officer of NSC] allegedly told Wolpert that he, Beyerlein, did not stand behind the projections. Defendants allegedly prohibited Beyerlein from advising Great Lakes of his opinions.

In early April 1999, the parties adjusted the purchase price for NSC from $130 million to $125 million. On April 8, 1999, the parties entered into an Ownership Interest Purchase Agreement (the "Purchase Agreement"). *** The parties closed the transaction on May 3, 1999.

4.   The Purchase Agreement

In setting forth the sellers' representations and warranties, the Purchase Agreement refers to the Ownership Interests in NSC being transferred as "equity securities." ***

In § 4.6 of the Purchase Agreement, Monsanto and STI make the representation and warranty that, except as otherwise provided, the financial statements provided by defendants to Great Lakes "reflect all material items and present fairly in all material respects the financial position of the Company as of the dates thereof and the results of operations for the periods described therein."

In § 4.7(a) of the Purchase Agreement, Monsanto and STI make the representation and warranty that, since December 31, 1998, "there has been no change in the business of the Company," which would have a "negative effect or negative change on the operations, results of operations or condition (financial or otherwise) in an amount equal to $6,500,000 or more."

The Purchase Agreement includes a disclaimer which states that Great Lakes is to take full responsibility for evaluating the accuracy of all estimates and projections furnished to it by Monsanto and STI. ***

***

Section 11.1 of the Purchase Agreement states that, except as otherwise provided, Monsanto and STI "will indemnify and reimburse the Buyer for any and all claims, losses, liabilities, damages, penalties, fines, costs and expenses ... incurred by the Buyer and its Affiliates" as a result of, among other things, any breach or inaccuracy of any representation or warranty made by Monsanto or STI as set forth in the Purchase Agreement.

C.   The Dissolution of NSC

On October 5, 1999, Great Lakes filed a Certificate of Cancellation with the State of Delaware, dissolving NSC as a separate entity. NSC's actual sales for 1999 were approximately $33 million, less than 50% of the projections provided by Monsanto and STI to Great Lakes in March 1999.

D.   The Lawsuit

On January 20, 2000, Great Lakes filed an eight count complaint in this court. Count I asserts that Monsanto and STI violated § 10(b) of the Securities Exchange Act of 1934, [citation omitted], and Rule 10b-5 promulgated thereunder, [citation omitted], by making material misrepresentations and by failing to disclose material facts in connection with the sale of securities. ***

*** Great Lakes seeks compensatory damages in excess of $58 million, plus costs, fees, and prejudgment interest. *** Great Lakes [also] seeks to rescind the Purchase Agreement and to recover $125 million as the full amount paid by Great Lakes for the Interest in NSC, plus costs, fees, and prejudgment interest, or to recover compensatory damages in excess of $58 million plus costs, fees, and prejudgment interest. ***

***

On March 9, 2000, Monsanto and STI moved to dismiss the complaint pursuant *** for failure to plead fraud with specificity and for failure to state a claim upon which relief may be granted. Monsanto and STI assert that Great Lakes' federal and state securities claims fail as a matter of law because the Interests in NSC transferred pursuant to the Purchase Agreement do not constitute "securities" under federal or state law, and because plaintiffs fail to adequately plead fraud. ***

II.   DISCUSSION

A.   What Is an LLC?

In Delaware, LLCs are formed pursuant to the Delaware Limited Liability Company Act, [citation omitted]. LLCs are hybrid entities that combine desirable characteristics of corporations, limited partnerships, and general partnerships. LLCs are entitled to partnership status for federal income tax purposes under certain circumstances, which permits LLC members to avoid double taxation, i.e., taxation of the entity as well as taxation of the members' incomes. [Citation omitted.] Moreover, LLCs members, unlike partners in general partnerships, may have limited liability, such that LLC members who are involved in managing the LLC may avoid becoming personally liable for its debts and obligations. [Citation omitted.] In addition, LLCs have greater flexibility than corporations in terms of organizational structure. The Delaware Limited Liability Company Act, for example, establishes the default rule that management of an LLC shall be vested in its members, but permits members to establish other forms of governance in their LLC agreements. [Citation omitted.]

***

B.   Are the Interests in NSC That Were Transferred Pursuant to the Purchase Agreement "Securities" Under Federal Law?

To prevail in its claim that defendants engaged in securities fraud under § 10(b) of the Securities Exchange Act of 1934, Great Lakes must demonstrate that: (i) defendants made a misstatement or omission; (ii) of a material fact; (iii) with scienter; (iv) in connection with the purchase or sale of securities; (v) upon which plaintiffs relied; and (vi) that reliance proximately caused plaintiffs' losses. [Citation omitted.] A threshold question in this matter is whether defendants' alleged misconduct involved a purchase or sale of securities. Defendants contend that plaintiff's claim fails as a matter of law because the Interests in NSC do not constitute securities.

Section 2(a)(1) of the Securities Act of 1933 lists financial instruments that qualify as securities ***. Among the securities enumerated in § 2(a)(1) of the Securities Act, Great Lakes contends that the Interests in NSC constitute either "stock," an "investment contract," or "any interest or instrument commonly known as a 'security.'"

1.   Key Cases Governing the Characterization of Novel
       Instruments

It is helpful, before determining whether the Interests in NSC constitute "stock," an "investment contract," or "any interest or instrument commonly known as a security," to review a series of cases that provide guidance as to how to characterize novel financial instruments.

The Supreme Court defined the parameters of an "investment contract" for the purposes of federal securities law in the case of *SEC v. W.J. Howey, Co.*, [328 U.S. 293 (1946), which is discussed in Chapter 13]. ***

***   The Court stated that "an investment contract for purposes of the Securities Act means a contract, transaction or scheme whereby a person invests his money in a common enterprise and is led to expect profits solely from the efforts of the promoter or a third party." [Citation omitted.] Thus, the three requirements for establishing an investment contract are: (1) "an investment of money," (2) "in a common enterprise," (3) "with profits to come solely from the efforts of others." [Citation omitted.] ***

The Supreme Court established guidelines for whether non-traditional instruments labeled "stock" constitute securities in *United Housing Foundation, Inc. v. Forman*, [421 U.S. 837 (1975), also discussed in Chapter 13] ***

*** The Supreme Court held that the "stock" issued by the cooperative [in the case] did not constitute a security. The shares, the Court found, lacked the five most common features of stock: (1) the right to receive dividends contingent upon an apportionment of profits; (2) negotiability; (3) the ability to be pledged or hypothecated; (4) voting rights in proportion to the number of shares owned; and (5) the ability to appreciate in value. [Citation omitted.] Finding that the purchasers obtained the shares in order to acquire subsidized low-cost living space, not to invest for profit, the Court ruled that the "stock" issued by the cooperative was not a security. [Citation omitted.]

Following the issuance of *Forman*, a number of lower courts began to apply the *Howey* test to distinguish between investment transactions, which were covered by the securities laws, and commercial transactions, which were not. See, e.g., *Landreth Timber Co. v. Landreth*, 731 F.2d 1348, 1352 (9th Cir. 1984) (citing cases). In *Landreth*, the Ninth Circuit addressed whether a single individual who purchased 100% of the stock in a lumber corporation, and who had the power to actively manage the acquired business, could state a claim under the securities laws for alleged fraud in the sale of the business. The Ninth Circuit found that the purchaser bought full control of the corporation, and that the economic reality of the transaction was the purchase of a business, and not an investment in a security.

The court held that the sale of 100% of the stock of a closely held corporation was not a transaction involving a "security."

Reversing the Ninth Circuit, the Supreme Court reasoned that it would be burdensome to apply the *Howey* test to transactions involving traditional stock. [Citation omitted; *see* Chapter 13.] The Court held that, insofar as a transaction involves the sale of an instrument called "stock," and the stock bears the five common attributes of stock enumerated in Forman, the transaction is governed by the securities laws. The Court noted that stock is specifically enumerated in § 2(a)(1) of the Securities Act as a security, and that stock is so "quintessentially a security" that it is unnecessary to apply the *Howey* test to determine if it is a security. [Citation omitted.] *** The Court stated that the *Howey* test should only be applied to determine whether an instrument is an "investment contract," and should not be applied in the context of other instruments enumerated in § 2(a)(1) of the Securities Act. [Citation omitted.]

***

2.   Prior Cases Concerning Whether Interests in LLCs are Securities

The present case raises novel issues regarding the regulation of transactions involving interests in LLCs. The court has identified three cases in which other courts have determined whether interests in LLCs constitute securities.

In *Keith v. Black Diamond Advisors, Inc.*, 48 F.Supp.2d 326 (S.D.N.Y. 1999), the plaintiff, Keith, founded a sub-prime mortgage lending firm, Eagle Corp., and brought it to profitability. Milton was an original investor in Eagle. Black Diamond, a venture capital firm, proposed a joint venture in which it would contribute $150,000 in cash, and Keith and Milton would each contribute their interests in Eagle, to form a New York limited liability company, Pace LLC. Through this transaction, Black Diamond acquired 50% of the interests in Pace, and Keith and Milton each received a 25% stake. Keith alleged that Black Diamond subsequently used its majority position to strip him of control of Pace. Keith sued Black Diamond for federal securities fraud.

The court applied the *Howey* test, and found that Keith had invested money in a common enterprise. The court, however, found that Keith had retained substantial control over the enterprise, such that he did not have an expectation of profits "solely from the efforts of others." As such, the court concluded that the LLC interests were not investment contracts. ***

SEC v. Parkersburg Wireless LLC, 991 F. Supp. 6 (D.D.C. 1997), involves [an] LLC that was established to provide wireless cable services. The promoters of the company sold "memberships" in the company to over 700 individuals in 43 states. The promoters targeted prospective investors who had Individual Retirement Accounts, and encouraged them to divert funds from their IRAs to buy membership units of the company.

The SEC sought to enjoin the sale of the membership interests. The court found that the interests sold in the LLC "easily satisfy" the *Howey* test for investment contracts. The investors' $10,000 minimum contribution constituted an "investment of money." Because the 700 individuals were to receive a pro rata share of the company's revenues, the court found there was a common enterprise. Moreover, the investors had little, if any, input into the company, so their profits were to come solely from the efforts of others.

SEC v. Shreveport Wireless Cable Television Partnership, 1998 WL 892948 (D.D.C. 1998), involves three entities: Reading Partnership and Shreveport Partnership, which are both general partnerships, and Baton Rouge LLC. All three entities were established to provide wireless cable services. Each entity engaged the services of a corporation to develop the telecommunications services and to solicit public investment in the enterprises. The promoters sold memberships in the three entities to approximately 2000 investors.

The SEC sought to enjoin the sale of interests in the ventures. In ruling upon defendants' motion for summary judgment that the interests were not securities, the court applied the *Howey* test to determine whether the interests were investment contracts. The court found that the purchasers of the interests had invested money in a common enterprise. The court found, however, that there was a question of fact as to whether the investors exercised significant control over the management of the corporation, and denied defendants' motion for summary judgment.

Having reviewed these other cases in which courts have considered whether LLC interests might constitute securities, the court will determine whether the Interests in NSC constitute "stock," an "investment contract," or "any interest or instrument commonly known as a security."

3.   Are the Interests In NSC "Stock"?

Great Lakes contends that NSC is the functional equivalent of a corporation, and that the Interests in NSC should be treated as stock. Great Lakes notes that the LLC Agreement refers to the Interests as "equity securities," and that the LLC Agreement prohibits the transfer of the Interests in such a way as would "violate the provisions of any federal or state securities laws."

Monsanto and STI, on the other hand, contend that the Interests cannot be stock because NSC is not a corporation.

As discussed above, the Supreme Court has described the five most common characteristics of stock as follows: (1) the right to receive dividends contingent upon an apportionment of profit; (2) negotiability; (3) the ability to be pledged or hypothecated; (4) the conferring of voting rights in proportion to the number of shares owned; and (5) the capacity to appreciate in value. [Citation omitted.]

As noted by plaintiffs, these attributes of stock also characterize, at least to some degree, the Interests in NSC. NSC's Members are entitled to share, pro rata, in distributions of Net Cash Flow, contingent upon its distribution by the Board of Managers. The Interests are negotiable and may be pledged or hypothecated, subject to approval by the Board of Managers. [Citation omitted.] Members in NSC have voting rights in proportion to their Percentage Interest in the company. And, the Interests in NSC have the capacity to appreciate in value. The Interests in NSC are undoubtedly stock-like in character, but the question remains if the Interests can be characterized as "stock" for the purposes of the federal securities laws.

The primary goal of the securities laws is to regulate investments, and not commercial ventures. [Citations omitted.] In transactions involving traditional stock, lower courts had attempted to distinguish between investment transactions and commercial transactions. [Citation omitted.] The Supreme Court, as discussed above, held that it is unnecessary to attempt to distinguish between commercial and investment transactions when the financial instrument in question is traditional stock. [Citation omitted.] Because stock is listed in § 2(a)(1) of the Securities Act as a security, and because people trading in traditional stock are likely to have a high expectation that their activities are governed by the securities laws, the Court ruled that all transactions involving traditional stock are covered by the securities laws, regardless if the transaction is of an investment or commercial character. [Citation omitted.] The Court expressly limited this rule to transactions involving traditional stock. [Citation omitted.]

The Supreme Court suggested, prior to the issuance of *Landreth*, that certain stock-like instruments might be construed as "stock" for the purposes of the federal securities laws. In *Tcherepnin v. Knight*, [389 U.S. 332 (1967)], the Court considered whether purchasers of withdrawable capital shares in a savings and loan association could state a claim under the federal securities laws for allegedly misleading statements made in solicitation materials. Holders of the withdrawable capital shares were entitled to be members of the association and were granted voting rights in proportion to the number of shares they owned. The holders were entitled to dividends declared by the association's board of directors and based on the association's profits. Certain restrictions applied to the transfer-ability of the instruments. The Court rejected the lower court's finding that the restrictions on negotiability precluded a finding that the shares were securities. The Court ruled that the instruments constituted "investment contracts" under *Howey*. [Citation omitted.] The Court continued, stating that the instruments could also be characterized as "certificates of interest or participation in any profitsharing agreement," as "transferable shares," or as "stock." [Citation omitted.] The Court held that the holders of withdrawable capital shares were entitled to the protections afforded by the securities laws.

In *Marine Bank v. Weaver*, [455 U.S. 551 (1982)], the Court reaffirmed its holding in *Tcherepnin* that the withdrawable capital shares in that case were "like ordinary shares of stock." This statement arose in the context of a suit brought by holders of certificates of deposit who were allegedly defrauded into pledging their certificates to guaranty a third party loan. The lower court held that the certificates of deposit were securities, as they were deemed to be the functional equivalent of the withdrawable capital shares at issue in *Tcherepnin*. [Citation omitted.] The Court found that the certificates of deposit had different characteristics than withdrawable capital shares, as they conferred upon their holders the right to a fixed rate of interest and did not entitle holders to voting rights. The Court found that the certificates of deposit were not securities.

Although, in *Tcherepnin*, the Supreme Court found that stock-like instruments could be deemed "stock" for the purposes of federal securities law, this court does not find *Tcherepnin* controlling in the present case. *Tcherepnin* preceded *Landreth*, which holds that the per se rule announced in that case should apply only to transactions involving traditional stock, because the name "stock" serves to put parties on notice that the transaction is governed by the securities laws. [Citation omitted.] Moreover, the withdrawable capital shares at issue in *Tcherepnin* were clearly investment instruments, and there is no indication that the holding in that case would apply to stock-like instruments used in commercial ventures. [Citation omitted.] Although the Court subsequently reiterated in *Marine Bank* that the withdrawable capital shares in *Tcherepnin* were "stock-like," [citation omitted], the Court did so in order to distinguish certificates of deposit from other instruments deemed to be securities, and did not appear to hold that all "stock-like" instruments should be regulated as securities.

In the present case, the LLC Interests, although they are "stock-like" in nature, are not traditional stock. *Landreth*, thus, is inapplicable to this case, and the court must determine whether the sale of NSC was essentially an investment transaction, in which case the securities laws apply, or whether it was a commercial transaction, in which case they do not. To make this determination, the court will apply the *Howey* test for investment contracts. [Citations omitted.]

The court will also consider whether the Interests can be characterized as "any interest or instrument commonly known as a security."

4.   Are the Interests in NSC an "Investment Contract"?

*** The parties do not dispute that the first prong of the *Howey* test—an investment of money—is satisfied by the facts of this case. The court will now consider whether Great Lakes invested in a "common enterprise," and whether Great Lakes' profits in NSC were to come "solely from the efforts of others."

[*Common Enterprise*]   Monsanto and STI argue that Great Lakes' purchase of the Interests in NSC fails the second prong of the *Howey* test, which requires that an investor invest its money in a "common enterprise." According to defendants, Great Lakes bought the entirety of NSC without pooling its contributions with those of other investors.

Great Lakes, on the other hand, contends that when Monsanto and STI created NSC, they pooled their resources and established NSC as a common enterprise. At the time of sale of the membership Interests, Great Lakes contends, the Interests were securities, and they did not cease to be securities when they were transferred to Great Lakes.

To determine whether a party has invested funds in a common enterprise, courts look to whether there is horizontal commonality between investors, or vertical commonality between a promoter and an investor. Horizontal commonality requires a pooling of investors' contributions and distribution of profits and losses on a pro-rata basis among investors. [Citation omitted.] The vertical commonality test is less stringent, and requires that an investor and promoter be engaged in a common enterprise, with the "fortunes of the investors linked with those of the promoters." [Citations omitted.] The Third Circuit has applied the horizontal commonality approach, [citation omitted], but has subsequently indicated that the vertical commonality test might be applicable in other cases, [citation omitted].

In this case, Great Lakes bought 100% of the Interests of NSC from Monsanto and STI. Great Lakes, accordingly, did not pool its contributions with those of other investors, as is required for horizontal commonality. After the sale, Monsanto and STI retained no interest in NSC, so it cannot be said that the fortunes of Great Lakes were linked to those of defendants, as is required for vertical commonality.

Great Lakes urges that when the Interests in NSC were created, Monsanto and STI pooled their contributions in a common enterprise. Great Lakes contends that Monsanto's and STI's Interests were securities when they were created, and that they did not cease to be securities when conveyed to Great Lakes. In support of this proposition, Great Lakes relies on *Great Western Bank & Trust v. Kotz*, 532 F.2d 1252 (9th Cir. 1976).

Great Western involves a company, Artko, that obtained a line of credit from a bank and executed an interest-bearing, unsecured promissory note to the bank. The bank allegedly relied on considerable financial data prepared by Artko before extending the line of credit. After the bank did not receive payment on the note, it sought recovery from Artko's president under § 17(a) of the Securities Act, [citation omitted]. The question before the court was whether the promissory note constituted a security. Although "notes" are included in the statutory definition of a security, [citation omitted], the court recognized that not all notes are securities. [Citation omitted.] The court inquired whether the bank had contributed "risk capital" subject to the "entrepreneurial or managerial efforts" of Artko, as would support a finding that the note was a security. [Citation omitted.] The court stated that the circumstances of issuance of the note, rather than how the proceeds of the line of credit were used, were determinative of the character of the note. [Citation omitted.] Great Western reaffirms the principle that the character of a financial instrument is determined by the terms of its offer, the plan of its distribution, and the economic inducements held out to potential purchasers. [Citation omitted.] *Great Western* does not draw into question the principle that courts are to look at the specific transaction at issue to determine whether the interests being transferred are securities. [Citation omitted.]

In this case, the challenged transaction is the sale of NSC by defendants to Great Lakes, and not the formation of NSC. Thus, the fact that Monsanto and STI pooled their contributions in the formation of NSC does not change the character of the sale of NSC to Great Lakes. The court concludes that Great Lakes did not invest in a common enterprise.

[*Solely From the Efforts of Others*] Monsanto and STI argue that the profits in NSC did not come solely from the efforts of others, as would support a finding that the Interests in NSC were securities. [Citation omitted.] Rather, defendants contend that Great Lakes had the power to control NSC through its authority to remove managers with or without cause, and to dissolve the entity.

Great Lakes argues, on the other hand, that it depended solely on the efforts of others to profit from NSC, as the LLC Agreement provides that the Members would retain no authority, right, or power to manage or control the operations of the company. In the alternative, Great Lakes contends that the Howey test does not apply to the sale of 100% of a business over which the purchaser intended to exercise control.

There is little caselaw establishing guidelines for determining whether a member in an LLC is sufficiently passive that he is dependent solely on the efforts of others for profits. In the context of general partnerships and limited partnerships, by contrast, there has been extensive litigation on whether partnership interests may qualify as securities. An analogy to partnership law is convenient for analyzing interests in LLCs, but there are important differences between general partnerships, limited partnerships, and LLCs.

General partnerships in Delaware are formed pursuant to the Delaware Revised Uniform Partnership Act, [citation omitted]. Each partner has equal rights in the management and conduct of the partnership business and affairs. [Citation omitted.] In general, all partners are liable jointly and severally for all obligations of the partnership. [Citation omitted.] Because partners have equal rights in the management of general partnerships, and because they are not protected by limited liability, courts consistently state that partners in general partnerships are unlikely to be passive investors who profit solely on the efforts of others. Some courts have adopted per se rules that partnership interests are not securities. [Citation omitted.] Other courts have adopted a presumption that partnership interests are not securities, but permit a finding that partnership interests are securities when a partner has so little control over the management as to be a passive investor. [Citation omitted.]

*** Limited partnerships are comprised of general partners and limited partners. General partners in limited partnerships have all the powers and duties of general partners in general partnerships, and are liable for the debts of the partnership.   [Citation omitted.]   Limited partners have limited liability, but become liable as general partners if they take part in the control of the business. [Citations omitted.] A limited partner may advise a general partner with respect to the business of the limited partnership, or cause a general partner to take action by voting or otherwise, without losing his limited liability. [Citation omitted.] In cases involving transactions of interests in limited partnerships, wherein the limited partners exercised no managerial role in the partnership's affairs, courts treat the limited partners as passive investors, and find that the membership interests of limited partners constitute securities under federal law. [Citation omitted.] Where, however, a limited partner is found to have exercised substantial control over the management of the partnership, courts find that the limited partner has not profited solely from the efforts of others, and rule that the interest in the partnership is not a security. [Citation omitted.]

Membership interests in LLCs are distinct from interests in general partnerships and limited partnerships. The primary differences between LLCs and general partnerships are that members of LLCs are entitled to limited liability, and, depending on the terms of the operating agreement giving rise to the particular LLC at issue, the members of the LLC may be less involved in the management of the enterprise than partners in a general partnership. As such, the grounds for creating a per se rule, or at least a presumption, that interests in general partnerships are not securities are lacking in the context of LLCs.

In comparison with limited partnerships, the Delaware Limited Liability Company Act permits a member in an LLC to be an active participant in management and still to retain limited liability. [Citation omitted.] Thus, there is no statutory basis, as with limited partnerships, to presume that LLC members are passive investors entitled to protection under the federal securities laws.

The Delaware Limited Liability Company Act grants parties substantial flexibility in determining the character of an LLC. Accordingly, the terms of the operating agreement of each LLC will determine whether its membership interests constitute securities. The presumptions that courts have articulated with respect to general partnerships and limited partnerships do not apply to LLCs. Rather, to determine whether a member's profits are to come solely from the efforts of others, it is necessary to consider the structure of the particular LLC at issue, as provided in its operating agreement.

In the present case, the Members of NSC had no authority to directly manage NSC's business and affairs. Section 5.1(a) of the LLC Agreement states:

> Except as otherwise expressly set forth in this Agreement, the Members shall not have any authority, right or power to bind the Company, or to manage or control, or to participate in the management or control of, the business and affairs of the Company in any manner whatsoever. Such management shall in every respect be the full and complete responsibility of the Board alone as provided in this Agreement.

The Members, however, had the power to remove any Manager with or without cause, and to dissolve the company. Great Lakes exercised this authority on October 5, 1999, when it filed a Certificate of Cancellation with the State of Delaware, dissolving NSC as a separate entity. Moreover, Great Lakes' complaint avers that, prior to selling NSC, Monsanto and STI had the power to control the actions of the Managers, insofar as defendants allegedly prohibited NSC's management from speaking directly with Great Lakes regarding sales, sales forecasts, and customer orders.

The powers held by Great Lakes in NSC are comparable to those discussed in *Steinhardt* [citation omitted], wherein the Third Circuit considered whether a limited partner in a limited partnership could state a claim under the securities laws. The limited partner, Steinhardt, purchased a 98.8% interest in the limited partnership, which acquired title to non-performing mortgage loans. The court noted that limited partners generally are passive investors entitled to protection under federal securities law. Upon analyzing the governance of the limited partnership at issue, however, the court found that Steinhardt alone constituted a "Majority of the Partners," and that Steinhardt was free to remove and replace the general partner without notice if the general partner refused to carry out Steinhardt's proposals. [Citation omitted.] In light of this factor and others, the court found that the limited partnership agreement at issue gave Steinhardt significant powers that directly affected the profits it received from the partnership. Accordingly, the court concluded that Steinhardt was not a passive investor, and that Steinhardt's membership in the partnership did not qualify as an investment contract.

The powers held by Great Lakes were comparable to those of Steinhardt, in that Great Lakes had the authority to remove NSC's managers without cause. Because Great Lakes was the sole owner of NSC, its power to remove managers was not diluted by the presence of other ownership interests. [Citation omitted.] Great Lakes' authority to remove managers gave it the power to directly affect the profits it received from NSC. Thus, the court finds that Great Lakes' profits from NSC did not come solely from the efforts of others. [Citation omitted.]

Alternatively, Great Lakes argues that, even if it did exercise substantial control over NSC, the transfer of Interests in NSC is nonetheless covered by the securities laws, because it bought 100% of the Interests in NSC and intended to operate the business. Great Lakes relies on [*Landreth Timber*] in support of this proposition.

Under *Landreth*, as discussed above, a stock transaction is covered by the securities laws even though the purchaser exercises control over the acquired corporation. [Citation omitted.] *Landreth*, however, is applicable only to those cases involving stock, or other financial instruments which are listed in § 2(a)(1) of the Securities Act. [Citation omitted.] When the financial instrument in question is a less traditional instrument that is not enumerated in the statute, but that might qualify as an "investment contract," then the complainant must demonstrate that the instrument satisfies the *Howey* test. As discussed above, the Interests in NSC do not constitute stock, and so *Landreth* is inapplicable.

The court finds that Great Lakes did not invest in a common enterprise, and did not have an expectation of profits "solely from the efforts of others," as is required by *Howey*. The Interests in NSC, thus, are not investment contracts.

5.   Are the Interests in NSC "Any Interest or Instrument Commonly Known as a Security"?

Great Lakes argues that, even if the Interests in NSC do not otherwise satisfy the *Howey* test for investment contracts, they should be deemed to be "any interest or instrument commonly known as a security," as provided for in § 2(a)(1) of the Securities Act.   Great Lakes notes that the LLC Agreement refers to the Interests at issue as "equity securities," and that the LLC Agreement prohibits the transfer of the Interests in such a way as would "violate the provisions of any federal or state securities laws."   Moreover, Great Lakes contends, ten states have defined interests in LLCs as securities, including Indiana, where NSC has its principal place of business.

Monsanto and STI contend that the Interests cannot be an "interest or instrument commonly known as a security," because the Interests in NSC do not satisfy the *Howey* test.

The Supreme Court has indicated that the term "any interest or instrument commonly known as a security" covers the same financial instruments as referred to by the term "investment contract."   In [*United Housing v. Forman*], the Court stated that "[w]e perceive no distinction, for present purposes, between an 'investment contract' and an 'instrument' commonly known as a 'security.'   In either case, the basic test for distinguishing the transaction from other commercial dealings is 'whether the scheme involves an investment of money in a common enterprise with profits to come solely from the efforts of others.'"   [Citations omitted.]   The *Howey* test, the Court explained, "embodies the essential attributes that run through all of the Court's decisions defining a security."   [Citation omitted.]

When confronted with novel financial instruments, numerous courts have considered whether to distinguish between an "investment contract" and "any interest or instrument commonly known as a security," and have declined to do so. [Citations omitted.]   In this case, too, the court finds that it would be improper to extend the definition of a security by reinterpreting the term "any interest or instrument commonly known as a security."

In sum, the court finds that the Interests in NSC constitute neither "stock," nor an "investment contract," nor "any interest or instrument commonly known as a security." The court will grant defendants' motion to dismiss Count I of Great Lakes' complaint.

***

§ 16.08   MISCELLANEOUS ISSUES IN LLCs

Obviously, there is a lot more to learn about LLCs if you want to practice business law.   If that is the case, you would be well-advised to continue your studies beyond the basic Business Organizations course in law school.   But here are a few more issues to keep in mind as you think about LLCs.

Informational Rights of Members and Managers.   Under Re-ULLCA § 410, members (including dissociated members with respect to periods of time during which they were members) have certain rights to information about the LLC.   Under subsection (a)(1), if the LLC is member-managed, a member may upon reasonable notice inspect and copy any of the LLC's records that concern its "activities, financial condition, and other circumstances, to the extent the information is material to the member's rights and duties under the operating agreement or [Re-ULLCA]."   Further, under subsection (a)(2)(A), the LLC shall, *without demand by a member*, furnish each member with "any information concerning the company's activities, financial condition, and other circumstances which the company knows and is material to proper exercise of the member's rights and duties under the operating agreement or [Re-ULLCA]," unless the company reasonably believes the member already knows the information.   In addition, under subsection (a)(2)(B), the LLC shall, on demand by a member, furnish the member with "any other information concerning the company's activities, financial condition, and other circumstances, except to the extent the demand or information demanded is unreasonable or otherwise improper under the circumstances."

If the LLC is manager-managed, then each *manager* has the same rights described above for members.   *See id.* § 410(b)(1).   Further, members can inspect and copy:

> full information regarding the activities, financial condition, and other circumstances of the company as is just and reasonable if: (A) the member seeks the information for a purpose material to the member's interest as a member; (B) the member makes a demand in a record received by the company, describing with reasonable particularity the information sought and the purpose for seeking the information; and (C) the information sought is directly connected to the member's purpose.

Id. § 410(b)(2).   Within ten days after receiving a member's request for this information, the LLC must inform the member of what information it will provide (and when and where it will do so).   But if the LLC refuses to provide any of the information that was demanded by the member, it must state its reasons for that decision. Finally, if a member in a manager-managed LLC is required to vote on a matter, the LLC must, without demand, provide the member "with all information that is known to the company and is material to the member's decision." Regardless of whether it is member-managed or manager-managed, the LLC can "impose reasonable restrictions and conditions on access to and use of information to be furnished" to members, "including designating information confidential and imposing nondisclosure and safeguarding obligations on the recipient."

Under Del. § 18-305(a), a member has the right, subject to any "reasonable standards (including standards governing what information and documents are to be furnished at what time and location and at whose expense)" that are in the LLC's operating agreement or that are established by the manager (in a manager-managed LLC) or the members (in a member-managed LLC), to certain records and information, for any purpose that is "reasonably related to the member's interest as a member of the [LLC]." Included in the list of such records and information are: (1) "[t]rue and full information regarding the status of the business and financial condition of the [LLC]; (2) copies of the LLC's tax returns; (3) the names and addresses of each member and manager; (4) copies of the certificate of formation and the operating agreement (and all amendments to them); (5) "[t]rue and full information regarding the amount of cash ... [or] other property or services contributed by each member and which each member has agreed to contribute in the future, and the date on which each became a member"; and (6) "[o]ther information regarding the affairs of the [LLC] as is just and reasonable." A member's demand for any of this information must be "reasonable" and, under subsection (e), must be in writing and state the purpose of the demand. Subsection (b) gives these same rights to a manager, "for a purpose reasonably related to the position of manager." If a demand is refused, the member or manager (as the case may be) may bring an action in the Court of Chancery to compel disclosure, as provided in subsection (f).

Note, however, that subsection (c) provides that a manager may keep information confidential from members for a reasonable time, if the manager reasonably believes that the information is "in the nature of trade secrets or [is] other information the disclosure of which the manager in good faith believes is not in the best interest of the [LLC] or [that] could damage the [LLC] or its business or which the [LLC] is required by law or by agreement with a [third] party to keep confidential." Further, subsection (g) provides that the LLC's operating agreement could further restrict these informational rights if the restrictions were contained in either the original operating agreement or in any amendment that was approved by all of the members or was approved in compliance with the operating agreement itself.

Derivative and Direct Lawsuits. Re-ULLCA § 902 allows a member to bring a derivative lawsuit to enforce the LLC's rights. Like the derivative lawsuits involving corporations that you studied in Chapter 8, any recovery in a derivative lawsuit would belong to the LLC. *See* Re-ULLCA § 906. That section also authorizes the court use a portion of the LLC's recovery to pay the plaintiff's expenses (including reasonably attorney fees) if the lawsuit was "successful in whole or in part."

Before filing a derivative lawsuit, the member-plaintiff must make a demand, either on the other members (if the LLC is member-managed) or on the managers (if the LLC is manager-managed). If the members or managers, as the case may be, do not cause the LLC to file suit within a "reasonable time" after the demand is made, then the member-plaintiff may file the derivative lawsuit. However, Re-ULLCA § 902(2) provides that a demand is not necessary if it would be "futile," but does not define that term.[*] Under Re-ULLCA § 903, the member-plaintiff must remain a member of the LLC while the lawsuit continues, although the court could substitute another member if the member-plaintiff dies during the lawsuit.

Under Re-ULLCA § 905, if the LLC is a party in the derivative lawsuit, it may appoint a special litigation committee ("***SLC***") consisting of one or more "disinterested and independent individuals" (who need not be members of the LLC) in order to "determine whether pursuing the action is in the [LLC's] best interests." In a member-managed LLC, an SLC may be appointed a majority of the members that are not named as defendants or plaintiffs in the lawsuit (or, if there are no such members, by a majority of the members that are named as defendants). Similarly, in a manager-managed LLC, an SLC may be appointed by a majority of the managers that are not named as defendants or plaintiffs in the lawsuit (or, if there are no such managers, by a majority of the managers that are named as defendants).

After it completes an "appropriate" investigation, the SLC may determine that it is in the LLC's best interests that the lawsuit (1) continue under the plaintiff's control, (2) continue under the SLC's control, (3) be settled on terms approved by the SLC, or (4) be dismissed. The SLC must then file with the court a report supporting its determination. At that point, the court must determine whether the SLC members were disinterested and independent and whether the SLC acted in "good faith, independently, and with reasonable care." If the court so finds, it must enforce the SLC's decision; if the court does not so find, it shall allow the lawsuit to continue under the member-plaintiff's control.

---

[*]   Re-ULLCA § 904(2) provides that if the member-plaintiff did not make a demand, the complaint must state the reasons the demand would be futile. Alternatively, if a demand was made, subsection (1) provides that the complaint must state the "response to the demand by the managers or other members."

Alternatively, under Re-ULLCA § 901 a member may bring a *direct* action against another member, a manager, or the LLC to "enforce the member's rights and otherwise protect the member's interests, including rights and interests under the operating agreement or [Re-ULLCA] or arising independently of the membership relationship." However, to bring such a direct action, the member must prove injury that "is not solely the result of an injury" to the LLC.

In Delaware, Del. § 18-1001 provides that a member of an LLC, or an assignee of an LLC interest may bring a derivative action (i.e., an action "in the right" of the LLC) if "managers or members with authority to do so have refused to bring the action or if an effort to cause those [persons] to bring the action is not likely to succeed." To have standing, a member must meet a "contemporaneous ownership" rule similar to MBCA § 7.41(1), which you studied in Chapter 8. *See* Del. § 18-1002.

Further, the complaint must describe "with particularity the effort, if any, of the plaintiff to secure initiation of the action by a manager or member or the reasons for not making the effort." In *Wood v. Baum*, 953 A.2d 136 (Del. 2008), a derivative lawsuit involving a Delaware LLC in which the plaintiff did not make a pre-suit demand on the LLC's board of directors* the Delaware Supreme Court applied the same demand "futility" tests that are applied to derivative lawsuits involving corporations, i.e., the tests from *Aronson v. Lewis*, 472 A.2d 805 (Del. 1984), and *Rales v. Blasband*, 634 A.2d 927, 934 (Del. 1993), both of which are discussed in Chapter 8. If the lawsuit is "successful," in whole or in part, the court may award the plaintiff reasonable expenses, including attorney fees, from any recovery in the lawsuit or from the LLC itself. *See* Del. § 18-1004.

Mergers, Conversions, and Domestications. Article 10 of Re-ULLCA contains detailed provisions concerning mergers, conversions, and domestications involving LLCs, as does the Delaware statute. Because these provisions are very complex but in some ways mirror what you learned in Chapter 12 about corporate mergers, we will not discuss them in any depth here. Nonetheless, a few words about these provisions are in order.

1.   Mergers. Under Re-ULLCA § 1002, an LLC may merge with a "constituent organization" (which is defined as including not only other LLCs, but partnerships and LLPs, limited partnerships and LLLPs, business trusts, corporations, "or any other person having a governing statute," even if any of these organizations is a non-profit organization) if the governing statute of the

---

*   Yes, the *LLC* had a *board of directors*. Strange but true. Remember, the Delaware LLC is nothing if not flexible.

constituent organization permits the merger and certain other conditions are met.[*] In such a merger, either the LLC or the other constituent organization—whatever type of entity it may be—may be the surviving entity.   Alternatively, a new surviving organization could be created in the merger.   Section 1003 requires that the plan of merger must be unanimously approved by the members of the LLC. However, the LLC's operating agreement could require a lesser level of member approval.   *But see* Re-ULLCA § 1014.   In Delaware, Del. § 18-209 is largely to the same effect; under that statute, an LLC may merge with or into one or more other Delaware LLCs or "other business entities," including foreign LLCs.[**] However, approval of a plan of merger only requires approval by the holders of a majority of the profits interests in the LLC, unless the operating agreement provides a different rule.   Under Del. § 18-210, the operating agreement or the plan of merger could give the LLC's members dissenters' rights.

Much like the mergers that you studied in Chapter 12, when a merger involving an LLC becomes effective, the "disappearing" entity or entities merge into the "surviving" entity and cease to exist.   At that point, all of the assets and liabilities of the disappearing entity or entities will become the assets and liabilities of the surviving entity.   However, note that it would not be possible for the partners of a partnership to "escape" personal liability for the partnership's pre-merger debts by merging the partnership into an LLC.

2.   *Conversions.*   A conversion is where one type of business entity, say a corporation, converts into a *different type* of business entity, say an LLC. Under Re-ULLCA § 1006, an organization (other than a domestic or foreign LLC) may convert into a domestic LLC, and a domestic LLC may convert into another organization (other than a foreign LLC) if the other organization's governing statute allows the conversion and certain other conditions are met.   (At this point, you may wonder why a domestic LLC couldn't convert into a foreign LLC, or vice versa, under section 1006.   Such a transaction would be considered a *domestication*, rather than a conversion.   Domestications are discussed below.)

---

[*]   As you may recall from Chapter 12, the MBCA contains corresponding provisions allowing corporations to merge with other types of entities as well.   However, in Chapter 12 we decided to "keep it simple" and discuss only mergers involving two or more corporations.

[**]   Del. § 18-209 defines the term "other business entity" as:

a corporation, a statutory trust, a business trust, an association, a real estate investment trust, a common-law trust, or any other unincorporated business or entity, including a partnership (whether general (including a limited liability partnership) or limited (including a limited liability limited partnership)), and a foreign [LLC], but excluding a domestic [LLC].

Re-ULLCA § 1007 requires that the plan of conversion be consented to by all of the LLC's members. *But see* Re-ULLCA § 1014. When the conversion becomes effective, the converted organization (that is, the organization *into which* the "converting" organization converts) *continues to be the same entity after the conversion*; it's simply a *different kind* of organization than it was before the conversion. Thus, Re-ULLCA § 1009(a) provides that an "organization that has been converted ... is for all purposes the same entity that existed before the conversion." Subsection (b) is to the same effect. For example, if ABC Corp. converted into ABC LLC, it is the same entity after the conversion, just a different *type* of entity.

In Delaware, Del. § 18-214 allows an "other entity" (which is defined as "a corporation, a statutory trust, a business trust, an association, a real estate investment trust, a common-law trust or any other unincorporated business or entity, including a partnership (whether general (including a limited liability partnership) or limited (including a limited liability limited partnership)) or a foreign [LLC]") to convert into a Delaware LLC. Similarly, Del. § 18-216, allows a Delaware LLC to convert to any such type of entity, including a foreign LLC. As with mergers, the approval of the holders of a majority of the profits interests in the LLC would be required, unless the operating agreement provides a different rule.

3.   *Domestications.* In a domestication, a *foreign* LLC becomes a *domestic* LLC, or a *domestic* LLC becomes a *foreign* LLC. In other words, an LLC that was organized under the laws of one state becomes an LLC that is organized under the laws of a different state. However, much like a conversion, the LLC *continues to be the same entity after the domestication*; it's simply organized under the laws of a different state than it was before the domestication. Re-ULLCA § 1013(a) confirms this observation by providing that a "domesticated" LLC (that is, the LLC *into which* a "domesticating" LLC domesticates) "is for all purposes the same domesticating [LLC] that existed before the domestication." (*See* also subsection (b).) Obviously, the LLC statute of the state in which the foreign LLC is (or will be) organized must permit domestications in order for one to occur with respect to a domestic LLC.

The careful reader will have noticed that Del. §§ 18-214 and 18-216 contemplate both conversions (as described above) and domestications (also as described above). However, note that under Del. § 18-212, certain *non-United States* entities could be domesticated as Delaware LLCs. *See also id.* § 18-213(a) ("Upon compliance with this section, any [LLC] may transfer to or domesticate or continue in any jurisdiction, other than any state, and, in connection therewith, may elect to continue its existence as [an LLC] in the State of Delaware.").

Now that you understand the basics of LLCs, at least under Re-ULLCA and the Delaware statute, you should try the multiple choice questions that appear below.

PRACTICE QUESTIONS

Multiple Choice Question 16-1: *Which of the following general statements about LLCs is correct?*

A.   An LLC must pay taxes on its income unless it meets the same requirements that are imposed on "S" corporations under the Internal Revenue Code.

B.   Although members of an LLC usually are not personally liable for the LLC's debts, the managers of a manager-managed LLC are personally liable for the LLC's debts.

C.   Unlike a sole proprietorship or a partnership, a filing with the state government is required to form an LLC.

D.   A member of an LLC may be held liable for the LLC's debt to a third party if (1) the member participates in the control of the LLC's business and (2) the third party reasonably believed that the member was a manager of the LLC.

Multiple Choice Question 16-2: *Which of the following statements about the formation of an LLC is correct?*

A.   Under Re-ULLCA, an LLC must have at least one member when it is formed.

B.   Both Delaware and Re-ULLCA require that the LLC's certificate of organization or certificate of formation must state whether the LLC is member-managed or manager-managed.

C.   Both Delaware and Re-ULLCA allow LLCs to be formed for non-business purposes.

D.   In both Delaware and under Re-ULLCA, an LLC is presumed to be manager-managed unless its operating agreement provides that it is member-managed.

Multiple Choice Question 16-3: *Which of the following correctly describes the characteristics of member-managed LLCs and manager-managed LLCs?*

A.   In a member-managed LLC, both the Delaware statute and Re-ULLCA presume that the relative voting power of members will be based on the contributions that they have made to the LLC. However, in a manager-managed LLC both statutes presume that each manager will have equal voting power.

B.   In a manager-managed LLC, a member who is not a manager has no actual or apparent authority to bind the LLC to a contract with a third party.

C.   In a manager-managed LLC, it is permissible for a manager also to be a member.

D.   In a member-managed LLC, the members have the right to vote on all major decisions affecting the LLC. However, in a manager-managed LLC, only the managers have the right to vote on major decisions affecting the LLC.

Multiple Choice Question 16-4: *Which of the following correctly describes fiduciary duties in LLCs?*

    I.   *Under Re-ULLCA, in a manager-managed LLC, a member who is not a manager does not owe fiduciary duties to the LLC.*

    II.   *Cases in Delaware have held that LLC managers and controlling members owe fiduciary duties of loyalty and care, in the absence of a contrary provision in the LLC's operating agreement.*

    III.   *In Delaware, an LLC's operating agreement may completely eliminate the fiduciary duties of loyalty and care.*

    IV.   *Under Re-ULLCA, an LLC's operating agreement may completely eliminate the fiduciary duties of loyalty and care.*

A.   All of the above are correct.
B.   Only I, II, and III are correct.
C.   Only I and II are correct.
D.   Only II and III are correct.
E.   Only III is correct.

Multiple Choice Question 16-5: *Which of the following correctly describes agency authority in LLCs?*

A.   In Delaware, members of a member-managed LLC have authority to bind the LLC to contracts with third parties due to their status as members.

B.   Under Re-ULLCA, members of a member-managed LLC have authority to bind the LLC to contracts with third parties due to their status as members.

C.   In Delaware, members of a manager-managed LLC do <u>not</u> have authority to bind the LLC to contracts with third parties due to their status as members.

D.   Under Re-ULLCA, managers of a manager-managed LLC have authority to bind the LLC to contracts with third parties due to their status as managers.

E.   All of the above are correct.

Multiple Choice Question 16-6: *Which of the following correctly describes the allocation of profits and losses and distributions in LLCs?*

I.   *Under Re-ULLCA, the LLC's profits and losses are presumed to be allocated in equal shares among members, unless the operating agreement provides otherwise.*

II.   *In Delaware, the LLC's profits and losses are presumed to be allocated in equal shares among members, unless the operating agreement provides otherwise.*

III.   *Under Re-ULLCA, distributions from the LLC must be made in equal shares among members, unless the operating agreement provides otherwise.*

IV.   *In Delaware, distributions from the LLC must be allocated among the members based on the relative values of the contributions that they have made to the LLC and that have not been returned, unless the operating agreement provides otherwise.*

A.   All of the above are correct.
B.   Only I, III, and IV are correct.
C.   Only II, III, and IV are correct.
D.   Only III and IV are correct.
E.   Only IV is correct.

Multiple Choice Question 16-7: Three years ago, Maggie, Charlie, and Ivy formed an LLC under Re-ULLCA to run a health food store. The LLC's operating agreement does not have any provisions that would change the "default" rules of Re-ULLCA, but does state that the LLC was to exist for only five years and that the LLC is manager-managed. Charlie has been appointed as the manager of the LLC. *Which of the following statements concerning dissociation and dissolution is correct?*

A.   If a guardian or conservator is appointed for Maggie, then Maggie will have dissociated from the LLC.
B.   If Maggie were to dissociate from the LLC by express will, her dissociation is wrongful but will cause the LLC to dissolve.
C.   If Maggie and Ivy vote to dissolve the LLC before the end of its five-year term, it must dissolve.
D.   A court could order the dissolution of the LLC if Maggie proves that Charlie is "oppressing" her.
E.   None of the above is correct.

Multiple Choice Question 16-8: Andy, Deb, Neil, and Finn formed an LLC three years ago. The LLC's operating agreement does not have any provisions that would change the "default" rules of Re-ULLCA or the Delaware statute (whichever is applicable). When the LLC was formed, Andy contributed equipment worth $30,000, Deb contributed $30,000 in cash, Neil contributed $20,000 in cash, and Finn agreed to contribute $20,000 worth of services. (It took Finn two years after the LLC was formed to complete those services.) None of these contributions has been returned, except that $10,000 has been returned to Neil. *If this LLC dissolves and (1) owes no amounts to creditors and (2) has* either *$45,000* or *$180,000 of assets remaining, which of the following would be correct, applying* Re-ULLCA?

A.   If the LLC has $45,000 of assets remaining, then (1) Andy and Deb would each receive $15,000, (2) Neil would receive $5,000, and (3) Finn would receive $10,000.
B.   If the LLC has $180,000 of assets remaining, then (1) Andy and Deb would each receive $60,000, (2) Neil would receive $20,000, and (3) Finn would receive $40,000.
C.   If the LLC has $180,000 of assets remaining, then (1) Andy and Deb would each receive $52,500, (2) Neil would receive $32,500, and (3) Finn would receive $42,500.
D.   Both A and B are correct.
E.   Both A and C are correct.

Multiple Choice Question 16-9: Same facts as Question 16-8. *If this LLC dissolves and (1) owes no amounts to creditors and (2) has <u>either</u> $45,000 <u>or</u> $180,000 of assets remaining, which of the following would be correct, applying <u>Delaware</u> law?*

A. If the LLC has $45,000 of assets remaining, then (1) Andy and Deb would each receive $15,000, (2) Neil would receive $5,000, and (3) Finn would receive $10,000.
B. If the LLC has $180,000 of assets remaining, then (1) Andy and Deb would each receive $60,000, (2) Neil would receive $20,000, and (3) Finn would receive $40,000.
C. If the LLC has $180,000 of assets remaining, then (1) Andy and Deb would each receive $52,500, (2) Neil would receive $32,500, and (3) Finn would receive $42,500.
D. Both A and B are correct.
E. Both A and C are correct.

Multiple Choice Question 16-10: *Which of the following general statements about LLCs is correct?*

A. If a member of an LLC wishes to bring a derivative lawsuit on behalf of the LLC, she must always make a demand on the managers or other members before doing so.
B. Interests in LLCs are defined as "securities" in federal securities statutes.
C. Under some LLC statutes, an LLC may convert into a different type of business organization; however, unanimous consent of the members is typically required to do so.
D. In a manager-managed LLC, members typically only have the right to inspect the LLC's financial statements and its annual report that the LLC must file with the state.

APPENDIX

ANSWERS AND EXPLANATIONS TO MULTIPLE CHOICE QUESTIONS

CHAPTER 1

Answer Key:

1-1:   C
1-2:   B
1-3:   E

Explanations:

Multiple Choice Question 1-1: The correct answer is C. Answer A is incorrect because in a limited partnership the general partner has control over the business, whereas the limited partner(s) does (do) not. Thus, the first goal would not be met if they chose to run the business as a limited partnership. Answer B is incorrect because in a general partnership the partners are personally liable, on a joint and several basis, for the debts and obligations of the partnership. Thus, the second goal would not be met if they chose to run the business as a general partnership. Answer D is incorrect because a "C" corporation is subject to a "double layer" of taxation: the corporation pays taxes on its income and the shareholders pay taxes on any dividends that they receive. Thus, the third goal would not be met if they chose to run the business as a "C" corporation.

Multiple Choice Question 1-2: The correct answer is B. In a general partnership the partners are personally liable. By contrast, the shareholders of a corporation and the member of an LLC are generally not personally liable for the debts and obligations of the corporation or LLC. Thus, on these facts, only Todd and Rod will be personally liable.

Multiple Choice Question 1-3: The correct answer is E. The key fact to keep in mind is that Miriam personally committed a tort. Thus, regardless of how the business is structured, Miriam will be personally liable. Any answer that states that Miriam will not be personally liable is therefore incorrect, which eliminates Answers A and B. On the other hand, Chloe will only be personally liable if the structure of the business imposes personal liability on owners. Answer C is true because partners in an LLP are not generally not liable for torts committed by other partners. Answer D is also true, because partners are personally liable for all partnership obligations, and here the partnership is liable because the tort occurred in the ordinary course of the partnership's business. *See* RUPA § 305. This makes Answer E the best answer.

CHAPTER 2

Answer Key:

2-1:	D
2-2:	B
2-3:	C
2-4:	C
2-5:	D
2-6:	C
2-7:	D
2-8:	C
2-9:	D
2-10:	D
2-11:	D
2-12:	B

Explanations:

Multiple Choice Question 2-1: The correct answer is D. Even though he did not have *actual* authority to quote prices to fix DVD players, Arthur also had *apparent* authority. Section 2.03 of the *Restatement* provides that:

> Apparent authority is the power held by an agent or other actor to affect a principal's legal relations with third parties when a third party reasonably believes the actor has authority to act on behalf of the principal and that belief is traceable to the principal's manifestations.

Here, the "manifestation" that Suzy made was hiring Arthur and putting him in a position where he could deal with customers. This manifestation reached Matthew when he saw Arthur in that position, and it is almost certainly reasonable to think that someone working in Arthur's position at an electronics store would have the authority to agree to repair an item of electronics (the DVD player). Thus, Answer A is incorrect. Answer B is incorrect; whether Arthur was in the scope of his employment is relevant for tort liability, not contractual liability. Answer C is not correct because detrimental reliance is not a requirement to bind the principal on a contract due to the agent's apparent authority.

Multiple Choice Question 2-2: The "correct" answer is B. Remember, the call of the question is which answer is *not* correct. Mark is an unidentified principal because Katherine is aware that Ned is acting on behalf of a principal but does not know who the principal is (nor has she been given facts sufficient to determine the identity of the principal). Thus, Section 6.02 of the *Restatement* provides that the principal (Mark), as well as the agent (Ned) who was acting with actual or apparent authority, are liable on the contract, unless otherwise agreed. Answer A is true because Ned did have actual authority to bind Mark to this contract; the fact that Mark was an unidentified principal does not matter. Answer C is correct due to Section 6.02 of the *Restatement*, as discussed above. Answer D is correct because Katherine cannot avoid the contract simply because there was an unidentified principal. As discussed in Chapter 2, a third party could only avoid the contract if there were an *undisclosed* principal and certain other conditions were met. This makes Answer B the only incorrect answer.

Multiple Choice Question 2-3: The correct answer is C. Here, Katherine notified Ned (the agent) of a fact. The issue is whether knowledge of this fact will be attributed to Mark and, if so, what effect that will have. Under Section 5.02(1) of the *Restatement*, "a notification given to an agent is effective as notice to the principal if the agent has actual or apparent authority to receive the notification, unless the person who gives the notification knows or has reason to know that the agent is acting adversely to the principal as stated in § 5.04." In this scenario, Ned would likely have apparent authority to receive the notification and it does not appear that Katherine knew or had reason to know that Ned would act adversely to Mark. Thus, the notification to Ned will be imputed to Mark and he will not be able to rescind the contract. *See also* Section 5.04 of the *Restatement.* Answer A is not correct because there are some situations in which facts known by agents will not be attributed to their principals. Answers B and D are incorrect for the reasons discussed above, even though Ned has breached his duty of disclosure. *See* Section 8.11 of the *Restatement.*

Multiple Choice Question 2-4: The correct answer is C. Because this scenario involved a tort, the first inquiry (at least under the *Restatement (Second) of Agency)* is whether Hank is a master and Frank is a servant. For the reasons discussed in Chapter 2, it seems obvious that Hank is a master and Frank is a servant. The next question is whether Frank was acting in the scope of his employment when the tort occurred. Clearly, Frank was—he was stocking groceries at Hank's grocery store. Thus, not only will Frank be liable for this tort, so too will Hank on a *respondeat superior* theory. The mere fact that Frank ignored Hank's instructions does not mean that he was outside the scope of his employment; thus, Answer A is wrong. Answer B is wrong because, as a sole proprietor, Hank will be personally liable for all of the business's debts and obligations even if they are larger than the assets associated with the business.

Answer D is wrong because *respondeat superior* liability can result whenever the two conditions described above are met.

Multiple Choice Question 2-5: The correct answer is D. On these facts, Garth's *actual* authority, as stated in the handbook, is to arrange transportation of Empire's products to customers—but only up to $2,000. Given that Garth works in the shipping department, his *apparent* authority would extend to arranging shipping contracts. As discussed above, Section 2.03 of the *Restatement* provides that if a principal makes a manifestation that reaches a third party and, as a result, the third party reasonably believes that the agent is authorized to act, then the agent has apparent authority. Here, the "manifestation" that the company made was hiring Garth as a shipping clerk and putting him in a position where he could deal with customers. This manifestation reached Rumsfeld (and therefore Axis) when he saw Garth in that position, and it is almost certainly reasonable to think that someone working in the shipping department can agree to shipping contracts. However, due to the sign on the wall, Garth's authority would be limited to $3,000; it would not be reasonable for Rumsfeld to think otherwise. Thus, it does not appear that Garth had actual or apparent authority to agree to Contract #1, given that he works in the shipping department and this contract has to do with purchasing copy/fax machines, which has nothing to do with shipping. However, he does have apparent authority to bind Empire to Contract #2. Rumsfeld did not know that Garth's actual authority had been limited to $2,000. Moreover, the sign on the wall would cause Rumsfeld to reasonably believe that Garth could agree to shipping contracts up to $3,000, and Contract #2 was below that limit.

Multiple Choice Question 2-6: The correct answer is C. As stated above, apparent authority requires a "manifestation" by the principal that reaches the third party and causes the third party to reasonably believe that the agent is authorized. A "manifestation" can be words or any other conduct. In determining whether Drew had a reasonable belief that Brett was authorized to buy the beer and whether that belief was based on something that Nell did, Answers A and B are clearly relevant. However, because Answer C concerns something which Drew did not know, it could not form the basis of a reasonable belief by Drew as to whether Brett was authorized to buy the beer.

Multiple Choice Question 2-7: The correct answer is D. Answer A is incorrect because, to void the contract, Clive would also need to show (in addition to the facts presented) that Zelda misrepresented the agency relationship. There is no indication that she did so. Answer B is wrong because agency relationships do not need to be documented in writing (although they often are). Answer C is incorrect because an agent with actual authority can bind a principal, even an undisclosed principal. Answer D is incorrect because Section 6.03 of the *Restatement* provides that, unless otherwise agreed, an agent for an undisclosed principal is a party to the contract.

Multiple Choice Question 2-8: The correct answer is C. Under Sections 6.01, 6.02, and 6.03 of the *Restatement*, unless otherwise agreed, an agent for a disclosed principal is not liable on a contract when she is acting within the scope of her actual or apparent authority, but an agent for an unidentified or undisclosed principal will be. Moreover, a servant who commits a tort in the scope of her employment will be liable for the tort (although the master will be *as well*).

Multiple Choice Question 2-9: The correct answer is D. Here, Pete is the principal and Annie is his agent, and Pete has given Annie actual express authority to go to France and "scout out" new products for the store and order them from merchants. While Pete never said anything about hiring an interpreter (and therefore Annie would not have actual *express* authority to do so), Section 2.02 of the *Restatement* provides that an agent's actual authority includes the authority to take actions that are "implied in the principal's manifestations ... and acts necessary or incidental to achieving the principal's objectives ...." Given that Pete sent Annie to *France*, it would seem necessary for her to hire an interpreter if she does not speak the language there. Answer A is incorrect because nothing in the facts indicates that Pete should be estopped from denying liability. Answer B is incorrect because nothing in the facts indicates that Pete made a manifestation that *reached Marcel* and caused Marcel to reasonably believe that Annie was authorized to hire him. Answer C is incorrect for the reasons discussed above.

Multiple Choice Question 2-10: The correct answer is D. For the reasons discussed above, Annie had actual authority to order products from French merchants. The issue is when that authority was terminated—when Pete died or when Annie learned that Pete died. Under Section 3.07 of the *Restatement*, the termination of Annie's authority does not occur until she has notice of Pete's death. Because she did not receive notice of Pete's death until May 21, she still had actual authority on May 20. This makes Pete (or, because he was a sole proprietor who is now dead, his estate) liable on the contract. Thus, Answer A is incorrect. Answer B is incorrect because even an undisclosed principal can be liable for her agent's acts if the agent was acting with actual authority, as was Annie. Moreover, an agent who acts within the scope of her actual authority is not liable to the principal, which makes Answer C incorrect.

Multiple Choice Question 2-11: The correct answer is D. Answer A is incorrect because a principal *can* ratify an unauthorized act (after all, that's sort of the whole point of ratification) if the requirements of Chapter 4 of the *Restatement* are met. Answer B is wrong because limitations communicated by the principal *to the agent* are irrelevant to whether the agent has *apparent* authority. Answer C is incorrect. Assuming that the requirements of actual or apparent authority are present (or estoppel or ratification), the principal can be bound by the agent's acts.

Multiple Choice Question 2-12: The correct answer is B. By cashing the check and shipping the order, Jack impliedly ratified Joan's actions, making any discussion of whether Joan had authority irrelevant. Ratification transforms an unauthorized act into an authorized act. Therefore, Jack is bound. If he did not like the discount, he should not have ratified it.

CHAPTER 3

Answer Key:

3-1:   E
3-2:   B
3-3:   C
3-4:   B
3-5:   B
3-6:   D
3-7:   B
3-8:   D
3-9:   D
3-10:   C
3-11:   D
3-12:   D
3-13:   B
3-14:   B
3-15:   D
3-16:   B
3-17:   B
3-18:   A

Explanations:

Multiple Choice Question 3-1: The correct answer is E (motion #3 will be granted; the other two motions will be denied). Motion #1 will be denied because a partnership is responsible for torts committed by its partners in the ordinary course of business (here, performing dental work). *See* RUPA § 305(a). Motion #2 will be denied because it is possible that Dr. Drill will be liable for the injury even though he is not the tortfeasor. Partners are jointly and severally liable for the partnership's debts and obligations. *See* RUPA § 306(a). Motion #3 will be granted because a newly admitted partner is not liable for partnership obligations incurred before he or she became a partner. Dr. Fill joined the partnership in 2010, but the tort occurred earlier, in 2008. *See* RUPA § 306(b).

Multiple Choice Question 3-2: The correct answer is B. RUPA § 503 allows a partner to sell her "transferable interest" (defined in RUPA § 502 as "the partner's share of the profits and losses of the partnership and the partner's right to receive distributions") to a third party. However, by itself this does not result in the transferee becoming a partner, nor does it mean that the transferor ceases to be a partner. Moreover, a transfer of a transferable interest does not require the consent of the other partners. *See* RUPA § 503.

Multiple Choice Question 3-3: The correct answer is C. Under the "exhaustion rule" of RUPA § 307(d)(1), in a situation such as this, the creditor would first have to recover from the partnership's assets before recovering from the partners' assets. Answer A is incorrect because RUPA § 103(b)(10) provides that a partnership agreement may not restrict the rights of third parties (such as the right of National Bank to hold both partners personally liable for the loan). Thus, this clause is ineffective. Answer B is incorrect because, as a partner, Denard may be liable for the unpaid loan. Answer D is incorrect due to the exhaustion rule of RUPA; in this situation, the bank cannot recover from the partners' personal assets until it has first exhausted the partnership's assets. Answer E is wrong because Jason had apparent authority under RUPA § 301(1) (and perhaps actual authority under RUPA § 301(2), as well) to bind the partnership to things that are in the ordinary course of business, such as obtaining loans. Thus, if the partnership is bound to repay the loan, Denard can be held personally liable if it does not do so.

Multiple Choice Question 3-4: The correct answer is B. The payment of distributions is considered a decision that is in the "ordinary course of business." As such, it only requires approval by a majority of the partners. *See* RUPA §§ 401(f) and (j).

Multiple Choice Question 3-5: The correct answer is B. Answer A is incorrect because partners are only liable for the debts and obligations of the *partnership*, not the *personal* debts of other partners. Answer C is incorrect because, if the assets of the partnership are not sufficient to pay partnership creditors in full, the creditors can seek recovery from the partners' personal assets. *See* RUPA §§ 306 and 307.

Multiple Choice Question 3-6: The correct answer is D. Unfortunately for Eric, two of the default rules of RUPA that apply, unless the partnership agreement provides otherwise, are that each partner has equal voting power, and that decisions that are in the "ordinary course of business" are decided by a majority vote. *See* RUPA §§ 401(f) and (j). Thus, Eric will be outvoted by the other partners.

Multiple Choice Question 3-7: The correct answer is B. The partners' respective partnership accounts varied over time pursuant to RUPA § 401(a) as follows:

Partner	Initial Contribution	2010	2011	2012	Distribution	Total
Stu	$5,000	($5,000)	$30,000	$40,000	($50,000)	$20,000
George	$5,000	($5,000)	$30,000	$40,000	($40,000)	$30,000
Pete	$10,000	($5,000)	$30,000	$40,000	($50,000)	$25,000

Multiple Choice Question 3-8: The correct answer is D. The partners' respective partnership accounts varied over time pursuant to RUPA § 401(a) as shown below. Note that because they agreed that Keith would be allocated two-thirds of the profits, they also impliedly agreed that he would be allocated two-thirds of the losses as well.

Partner	Initial Contribution	2010	2011	2012	Distribution	Total
Keith	$20,000	($10,000)	$60,000	$80,000	($50,000)	$100,000
Sally	$10,000	($5,000)	$30,000	$40,000	($30,000)	$45,000

Multiple Choice Question 3-9: The correct answer is D. Generally speaking, RUPA allows the partners to structure the partnership as they see fit. However, RUPA § 103(b) contains a list of things that a partnership agreement may not do; provisions in a partnership agreement that run afoul of RUPA § 103(b) will be treated as if they were deleted from the partnership agreement. Here, clauses I and V are permissible and clause II is no different than the default rule in RUPA concerning this issue. However, clause III violates RUPA § 103(b)(10) and clause IV violates RUPA § 103(b)(6).

Multiple Choice Question 3-10: The correct answer is C. *See* RUPA § 202(c)(3) and the cases that appear in Chapter 3.

Multiple Choice Question 3-11: The correct answer is D. Under RUPA §§ 503 and 504, a partner may transfer her "transferable interest" to a third party, but that transferee does not become a new partner unless the other partners unanimously agree. Thus, each of Answers A, B, and C finds specific support in RUPA §§ 503 and 504, making Answer D ("All of the above are correct") the best answer.

Multiple Choice Question 3-12: The correct answer is D. Note that the facts state that the partnership owns the instruments, not the partners themselves. Thus, Little Joe could not sell "his" bass without approval by the partners. Answer A is wrong because the default rule of RUPA § 401(f) is that the partners have equal voting power. Answer B is incorrect because, as a partner, Jeremy has the apparent authority under RUPA § 301(1) to bind the partnership to things that are in the ordinary course of business (unless (1) he lacked actual authority to do so and (2) the third party knew or had received a notification that he lacked authority). Here, playing concerts is clearly in the ordinary course of business for a rock band. Answer C is wrong because of RUPA §§ 501 and 401(g).

Multiple Choice Question 3-13: The correct answer is B. The best that Little Joe's *personal* creditors could do is obtain a charging order on Little Joe's "transferable interest" in the partnership pursuant to RUPA § 504. This charging order operates in much the same way that a garnishment operates with respect to an employee's wages. Answer A is wrong because the default rule of RUPA § 401(i) is that unanimous partner consent is needed to admit a new partner. Answer C is wrong because under RUPA § 401(b) "[e]ach partner is entitled to an equal share of the partnership profits and is chargeable with a share of the partnership losses in proportion to the partner's share of the profits." Here, the partners agreed that Jeremy would be allocated 10% of the profits and the other partners would each be allocated 18% of the profits. Thus, they impliedly agreed to the same division of losses. Finally, Answer D is wrong because partners will be personally liable for partnership debts even if the partnership itself cannot pay them. *See* RUPA §§ 306 and 307.

Multiple Choice Question 3-14: The correct answer is B. Under RUPA § 404(c), a partner has a duty of care "to the partnership and the other partners in the conduct ... of the partnership business." Here, Brutus was driving the partnership's van. The duty of care is to refrain "from engaging in grossly negligent or reckless conduct, intentional misconduct, or a knowing violation of law." Here, Brutus was found to be reckless. Brutus did not violate his duty of loyalty because breaches of the duty of loyalty involve some conflict of interest between the partner and the partnership. See RUPA § 404(b) for RUPA's list of actions that would violate a partner's duty of loyalty.

Multiple Choice Question 3-15: The correct answer is D. Under RUPA § 404(b)(3), one aspect of a partner's duty of loyalty is to "refrain from competing with the partnership," which is what it looks like Rocco would be doing here because his partners are worried that Rocco's new band would take some gigs away from the Downtown Rockers. However, if Rocco were to quit the Downtown Rockers, he would no longer be a partner. Under RUPA § 603(b)(2), upon a partner's dissociation, her duty to refrain from competing with the partnership ceases.

Multiple Choice Question 3-16: The correct answer is B. Under RUPA § 401(f), "[e]ach partner has equal rights in the management and conduct of the partnership business." Thus, Kate will have an "equal voice" in running the partnership. Answer A is incorrect due to RUPA § 401(f) and Answer C is incorrect due to RUPA § 401(j), which states that actions that are in the ordinary course of business need only be approved by a majority of the partners.

Multiple Choice Question 3-17: The correct answer is B. Under RUPA § 401(h), a "partner is not entitled to remuneration for services performed for the partnership, except for reasonable compensation for services rendered in winding up the business of the partnership." Thus, even though Helen is doing more than her "fair share" of the work, she is not entitled to any extra pay for it (unless the partnership agreement were to so provide, which it did not in this fact pattern).

Multiple Choice Question 3-18: The correct answer is A. Under RUPA § 301(1)

> [a]n act of a partner ... for apparently carrying on in the ordinary course the partnership business or business of the kind carried on by the partnership binds the partnership, unless the partner had no authority to act for the partnership in the particular matter and the person with whom the partner was dealing knew or had received a notification that the partner lacked authority.

However, selling the store's *entire inventory to a single buyer* would not likely be considered in the ordinary course of the partnership's business. Thus, under RUPA § 301(2), the partnership is bound only if Carol's act was authorized by the other partners (that is, if she had actual authority). The facts do not indicate that she had such authority. Moreover, under RUPA § 401(j), an act that is outside the ordinary course of business can be taken only if all of the partners consent. Thus, Carol cannot act alone in this situation. This true despite whatever Dave may have thought about the situation.

CHAPTER 4

Answer Key:

4-1:	D
4-2:	C
4-3:	B
4-4:	C
4-5:	B
4-6:	C
4-7:	C
4-8:	B
4-9:	A
4-10:	D
4-11:	D
4-12:	C
4-13:	D

Explanations:

Multiple Choice Question 4-1: The correct answer is D. Although the partnership was formed "to build and manage a health club," this does not make the partnership a partnership for a term or undertaking. In other words, because the partners did not agree that the partnership would *end* after a task was completed or a period of time had passed, this was an "at will" partnership. RUPA § 601 provides that a partner may dissociate from a partnership by express will, which occurred when Robert told Joni he quit the partnership. Moreover, a dissociation from an at-will partnership is "wrongful" only if the partnership agreement were to make it wrongful (which was not the case here). Thus, Answers B and C are incorrect. In an at-will partnership, one partner's dissociation by express will triggers a dissolution (unless the partnership agreement provides otherwise). *See* RUPA § 801(1). Thus, Answer D is correct. Answer A is incorrect because neither RUPA nor a partnership agreement can *prevent* a partner from dissociating; the most that may be done is to make some types of dissociations "wrongful."

Multiple Choice Question 4-2: The correct answer is C. Under RUPA § 703, a partner remains liable for partnership obligations incurred before she dissociated from the partnership (and, in some cases, partnership obligations incurred after she dissociated). However, under subsection (c), "[b]y agreement with the partnership creditor *and* the partners continuing the business, a dissociated partner may be released from liability for a partnership obligation." (Emphasis added.) Thus, Answers A and B are incorrect because they do not reflect that the consent of both groups (creditors and continuing partners) is required.

Multiple Choice Question 4-3: The correct answer is B. Under RUPA § 601(6)(i), if a partner files a bankruptcy petition, he will be dissociated the partnership. Thus, Devin has dissociated. Moreover, because this partnership had a six-year term, Devin's dissociation was wrongful under RUPA § 602(b)(2)(iii). Thus, Answers A, C, and E can be eliminated. As for Peter, he has been expelled (dissociated) under RUPA § 601(5) by court order. This is also wrongful in the case of a partnership for a term or undertaking. *See* RUPA § 602(b)(2)(ii). This makes Answer D incorrect, leaving Answer B as the only correct answer.

Multiple Choice Question 4-4: The correct answer is C. As noted above, in an at-will partnership, the only time that a dissociation is wrongful is if the partnership agreement makes a particular dissociation wrongful. Here, the partnership agreement did not do so. Thus, even though both Devin and Peter have dissociated, neither dissociation was wrongful.

Multiple Choice Question 4-5: The correct answer is B. This is a partnership for a term, here, ten years. Nancy has dissociated by express will under RUPA § 601(1). Under RUPA § 801(2)(i), if the partnership is a partnership for a term or undertaking, a partner's dissociation by express will does not cause the partnership to dissolve, unless at least half the remaining partners vote, within ninety days, to dissolve the partnership. Answer A is incorrect because the partnership agreement provides that the partnership cannot hire an employee without the unanimous consent of the partners. Here, Nancy did not consent to hiring an employee. Even though the partnership agreement wasn't signed, the fact pattern says that it was an accurate reflection of what the partners had orally agreed. Partnership agreements can be oral under RUPA; they need not be written. Therefore, the partnership agreement changed the default rule of RUPA 401(j), which provides that matters in the ordinary course of business are decided by a majority vote of the partners. Answers C and D are incorrect because this is a partnership for a term. As noted above, Nancy has dissociated by express will under RUPA § 601(1), and RUPA § 801(2)(i) provides that a partner's dissociation by express will does not cause the partnership to dissolve, unless at least half the remaining partners vote, within ninety days, to *dissolve* the partnership. The partners do not have to vote to "save" the partnership; RUPA § 801(2)(i) only speaks about voting to dissolve the partnership.

Multiple Choice Question 4-6: The correct answer is C. After paying creditors (the $100,000 owed to the bank), there will be $400,000 to distribute to the partners. The first use of this $400,000 will be to "zero out" the respective partners' partnership accounts. This requires us to calculate what those amounts are (because the fact pattern doesn't tell us). The partners are sharing profits and losses equally because they haven't agreed otherwise. Also, Paul is the only partner that made a contribution ($100,000), which increases his partnership account under RUPA § 401(a)(1). The partnership incurred a loss of $100,000 in 2009. This would mean that all the partners' accounts are negative $20,000, except for Paul, whose account is $80,000. The partnership had a profit of $150,000 in 2010. This would increase all the partners' accounts by $30,000 to $10,000, except for Paul, whose account is now $110,000. The partnership had a profit of $200,000 in 2011. This would increase all the partners' accounts by $40,000 to $50,000, except for Paul, whose account is now $150,000. The total partnership account values are now $350,000. We use $350,000 of our $400,000 to "zero" out these accounts, and then split the remaining $50,000 (which is profit) equally.

Multiple Choice Question 4-7: The correct answer is C. Note that this is an at-will partnership and that there is no partnership agreement. When the probate court appointed Paul's wife Marie as Paul's guardian and conservator, Paul was dissociated from the partnership. *See* RUPA § 601(7)(ii). To determine what effect this had on the partnership, we need to examine RUPA § 801(1) (which concerns at-will partnerships). Generally, the dissociation of a partner will trigger the dissolution of an at-will partnership; however, RUPA § 801(1) provides that this is *not* the case where a partner dissociates for any of the reasons listed in RUPA § 601(2) through (10). Thus, Paul's dissociation did not dissolve this partnership. Thus, Answers A and B are incorrect. Answer D is incorrect because

Paul *did* dissociate. Further, Marie could only become a partner with the unanimous consent of the other partners.

Multiple Choice Question 4-8: The correct answer is B. If the partnership *had* dissolved, then both it and its partners would remain liable to pay its debts. Because the partnership was liable under these agreements, so too are the partners. *See* RUPA § 306. It does not matter whether they also signed personal guaranties of these agreements.

Multiple Choice Question 4-9: The correct answer is A. To answer this question, we need to track the partners' respective partnership accounts over time.

	Contribution	2009 Loss	2010 Profit	2011 Profit	Distributions	Ending Balance
Don	$5,000	($5,000)	$30,000	$40,000	($50,000)	$20,000
Paul	$5,000	($5,000)	$30,000	$40,000	($40,000)	$30,000
John	$10,000	($5,000)	$30,000	$40,000	($50,000)	$25,000
TOTAL						$75,000

If the partnership has $90,000, we must first use that to "zero out" the partners' respective partnership account balances as of the date of dissolution. This will take $75,000, leaving us with $15,000. This remaining $15,000 is profit. Unless otherwise agreed, profits are split equally among the partners. Thus, Don will get a total of $25,000 ($20,000 plus $5,000); Paul will get a total of $35,000 ($30,000 plus $5,000); and John will get a total of $30,000 ($25,000 plus $5,000). This adds up to $90,000.

Multiple Choice Question 4-10: The correct answer is D. Because there is no indication that the partners have agreed on a task or duration that will limit the partnership's "life," this is an at-will partnership. Under RUPA § 801(1), a partner's dissociation by express will triggers the dissolution of an at-will partnership. Thus, the partnership will dissolve if Sally dissociates by express will. (This may strike you as surprising, but read RUPA § 801(1) carefully.) However, nearly anything in RUPA may be modified in a partnership agreement. *See* RUPA § 103. Thus, because amending a partnership agreement requires the consent of all of the partners (unless the agreement itself provides that it can be amended upon the consent of a smaller percentage of the partners), if Sally and all of the other partners were to agree that the partnership will not dissolve, then it will not dissolve.

Multiple Choice Question 4-11: The correct answer is D. Under RUPA § 702 a partner who has dissociated (but without triggering a dissolution of the partnership) continues to have the authority to bind the partnership as follows:

> For two years after a partner dissociates without resulting in a dissolution and winding up of the partnership business, the partnership ... is bound by an act of the dissociated partner which would have bound the partnership under Section 301 before dissociation only if at the time of entering into the transaction the other party:
>
> (1)   reasonably believed that the dissociated partner was then a partner;
> (2)   did not have notice of the partner's dissociation; and
> (3)   is not deemed to have had ... notice under Section 704(c).

Because (1) this transaction occurred within two years after Sally dissociated; (2) this transaction, being something that is in the ordinary course of the partnership's business, is something that Sally would have had apparent authority for if she were still a partner; and (3) Sam reasonably believed that Sally was still a partner and did not know and had not received actual or constructive notice that Sally was no longer a partner, the partnership is bound on this contract. Thus, Answers A, B, and C are incorrect.

Multiple Choice Question 4-12: The correct answer is C. Under RUPA § 704, either the dissociated partner or the partnership has the option of filing a "statement of dissociation." This document would state that a particular partner is no longer a partner of the partnership. Under subsection (c), a "person not a partner" (that is, everyone else in the world outside the partnership) has constructive knowledge of this document ninety days after it is filed. Thus, if Sally ran into Sam four months (around 120 days) after she dissociated from the partnership, Sam would have constructive knowledge that she was no longer a partner. That being the case, the three requirements of RUPA § 702 set forth in the explanation to Multiple Choice Question 4-11 above would not all be met, and the partnership would *not* be bound on the contract. Answers A and B seem plausible on their face, but are not technically correct under RUPA §§ 702 and 704.

Multiple Choice Question 4-13: The correct answer is D. Because the partners agreed on a five-year term, this was a partnership for a term or undertaking. Glenn may dissociate before the end of the term, but doing so by express will is "wrongful" under RUPA § 602(b)(2)(i). Under RUPA § 801(2), the dissociation of one partner before the end of the partnership's term will not cause the partnership to dissolve. Thus, we will examine Article 7 of RUPA rather than Article 8. Under RUPA § 701(a), the partnership must buy out Glenn's interest for the price determined under subsection (b). Meanwhile, subsection (b) provides that the price is the amount that would have been distributable to the dissociating partner under Section 807(b) if, on the date of dissociation, the assets of the partnership were sold at a price equal to the greater of the liquidation value or the value based on a sale of the entire business as a going concern without the dissociated partner and the partnership were wound up as of that date. Interest must be paid from the date of dissociation to the date of payment.

However, two other subsections of RUPA § 701 are also important. First, (c) allows the partnership to deduct from the buy-out price any damages that it incurred as a result of Glenn's wrongful dissociation. Second, subsection (h) provides that Glenn is not entitled to this payment until the end of the partnership's term unless he "establishes to the satisfaction of the court that earlier payment will not cause undue hardship to the business of the partnership." (Also, any deferred payment "must be adequately secured and bear interest.")

CHAPTER 5

Answer Key:

5-1:	E
5-2:	B
5-3:	B
5-4:	A
5-5:	A
5-6:	B
5-7:	D
5-8:	E
5-9:	C
5-10:	B
5-11:	B
5-12:	D
5-13:	A
5-14:	A
5-15:	C
5-16:	C
5-17:	C
5-18:	C
5-19:	A
5-20:	A
5-21:	D
5-22:	A
5-23:	B
5-24:	A

5-25: D
5-26: A
5-27: A
5-28: C

Explanations:

Multiple Choice Question 5-1: The correct answer is E. Answer A is true, as is Answer C, which makes Answer E the best answer. Answer A is true because MBCA § 7.31(a) provides in part that "[t]wo or more shareholders may provide for the manner in which they will vote their shares *by signing an agreement for that purpose."* Thus, *oral* shareholder voting agreements are not enforceable under the MBCA. Answer C is true because subsection (b) of this section makes a voting agreement—such as the one that Mr. Sleep and Ms. Slumber signed last year—specifically enforceable. Thus, Mr. Sleep must vote his shares according to that agreement, which makes Answer B incorrect. Note that the section only requires that "two or more" shareholders, not all of them, be parties to the agreement. Answer D is wrong because, as discussed above, oral shareholder voting agreements are not enforceable.

Multiple Choice Question 5-2: The correct answer is B. Under MBCA § 16.02(a), a shareholder is entitled to inspect the items listed in MBCA § 16.01(e), including the corporation's bylaws, upon at least five business days' written notice. However, if a shareholder wishes to inspect the documents listed in MBCA § 16.02(b), such as the list of shareholders, she must additionally show a "proper purpose" for doing so. *See* MBCA § 16.02(c). Here, Joe wants to see the shareholder list to advertise his new—and competing—business. This is not likely a "proper purpose."

Multiple Choice Question 5-3: The correct answer is B. As discussed in Chapter 5, the formula to determine the number of shares that a shareholder would need to own to elect a given number of directors under cumulative voting is

$$\frac{N \times S}{D + 1} + "1" = X$$

where "N" is the number of directors that you wish to elect to the board; "S" is the number of shares that will be voted at the shareholder meeting; and "D" is the total number of directors that will be elected to the board at the shareholder meeting. Further, the "1" that is in quotation marks means either to add one, or to round up to the next whole number. Here, the question asks how many shares would it take to elect one director, so "N" is 1. Further, "S" is 10,000 and "D" is 9 because all nine directors are elected annually. Thus, (1 x 10,000) divided by (9 + 1) is 1,000. Because that is a whole number, we add 1, to get 1,001.

Multiple Choice Question 5-4: The correct answer is A. Although the notice of the meeting was required to state the purpose of this special shareholders meeting but did not (*see* MBCA § 7.05), the fact that all of the shareholders attended the meeting without objecting to the holding of the meeting or conduct of any business means that they waived any defect in the notice. *See* MBCA § 7.06(b). Answer B is wrong for this reason, as well as the fact that shareholder meetings only requires a minimum of ten days' notice (and a maximum of sixty days notice). *See* MBCA § 7.05(a). Answer C seems plausible, but as noted above the defect in the notice was waived when all of the shareholders attended the meeting. Answer D is wrong because the mere fact that a majority of the shares were voted in favor of a proposal would not cure defective notice. But again, *all* of the shareholders waived the defective notice in this problem.

Multiple Choice Question 5-5: The correct answer is A. With respect to special board meetings, every director must either receive proper notice of the special board meeting or waive the notice. Here, the notice was not sufficient because it was not given at least two days before the meeting. *See* MBCA § 8.22(b). A director may waive the required notice in any of the ways described in MBCA § 8.23, but here only five directors waived notice (by attending the meeting). Thus, four directors neither received proper notice nor waived the defective notice of the special board meeting, making the approval of any action at the meeting invalid. Answer B is incorrect because special board meetings only requires two days' notice, not ten days' notice. Answer C is incorrect because it is not necessary to state the purpose of a special board meeting, just the date, time, and place. Answer D seems plausible, but is incorrect because, as discussed above, *every* director must either get proper notice of a special board meeting or waive the defective notice.

Multiple Choice Question 5-6: The correct answer is B. The notice of the special board meeting was proper because it was given to every director at least two days before the meeting and specified the date, time, and place of the meeting. MBCA § 8.22(b). However, a quorum of directors (unless otherwise provided in the articles or bylaws, this is a majority) was not present—only three out of seven directors were present. *See* MBCA § 8.24. (Unlike shareholders, directors may not use proxies unless an agreement under MBCA § 7.32 authorizes them to do so.) Thus, no business could be conducted at the meeting. Answer A is wrong because, while it is true that a quorum was not present, notices of special board meetings do not have to be sent at least ten days before the meeting (that is the time period for shareholder meetings). Answer C is wrong because a quorum was not present. In addition, notices for special board meetings do not need to state the purpose of the meeting. Answer D is incorrect because a quorum of directors was not present at the meeting, as discussed above.

Multiple Choice Question 5-7: The correct answer is D. Answer A is wrong because this was a *regular* board meeting and, unless the corporation's articles or bylaws provide otherwise, no notice is required for regular meetings. MBCA § 8.22(a). Answer B is wrong because a quorum is a majority of the directors. Here, that would be at least six of the eleven directors. Five directors were physically present and the sixth director was present through a conference call. *See* MBCA § 8.20(b). Answer C is wrong because since a quorum was present when the vote was taken, we only need a majority of the directors *present* to vote yes for the action to be approved. Here, six were present and four voted yes. *See* MBCA § 8.24(c).

Multiple Choice Question 5-8: The correct answer is E. Under MBCA § 7.22(d), a proxy is revocable unless (1) it states that it is irrevocable and (2) it is "coupled with an interest," meaning that the person who holds the proxy has an interest in the shares that are subject to the proxy. (Some examples of such an interest are given in the statute.) Here, even though Buffy is a shareholder in the same corporation, she has no interest in Allie's shares. Thus, despite the fact that the proxy stated that it was irrevocable, Allie can still revoke it.

Multiple Choice Question 5-9: The correct answer is C. Under MBCA § 6.40(c)(2), a distribution (dividend) may not be paid if, *afterwards*, "the corporation's total assets would be less than the sum of its total liabilities plus … the amount that would be needed, if the corporation were to be dissolved at the time of the distribution, to satisfy the preferential rights upon dissolution of shareholders whose preferential rights are superior to those receiving the distribution [i.e., preferred stock with a liquidation preference]." Here, since there is no preferred stock, we need only make sure that, after the dividend is paid, the corporation's assets will be at least equal to its liabilities. Its liabilities are $70,000, so it must keep at least $70,000 of assets on hand. This means that it lawfully may pay a maximum of $300,000 of dividends.

Multiple Choice Question 5-10: The correct answer is B. Here, the corporation must keep on hand enough assets to cover both (1) its liabilities ($70,000) and the liquidation preference of the preferred stock (which computes to $50,000), because the preferred stock is "superior" to the shares that would receive the distribution (the common stock). Thus, it needs to keep at least $120,000 of assets on hand, which means that it could lawfully pay $250,000 in dividends.

Multiple Choice Question 5-11: The correct answer is B. As discussed above, the formula for cumulative voting is

$$\frac{N \times S}{D + 1} + \text{``1''} = X$$

Applying that formula to the facts here, we have (2 x 300) divided by (9 + 1), which equals 60. Because this is a whole number, we add 1 to get 61. Note that "N" was 2 because the question asked how many shares it would take to elect two directors. Also, note that the reference to the 1,000 *authorized* shares was a "red herring."

Multiple Choice Question 5-12: The correct answer is D. Applying the formula for cumulative voting to the facts here, we have (2 x 300) divided by (10 + 1), which equals 54.5454. Because this is a fraction (rather than a whole number), we round up to the next whole number, which is 55.

Multiple Choice Question 5-13: The correct answer is A. This question concerns two concepts: plurality voting and record dates. As discussed in Chapter 5, under plurality voting, someone who owns a majority of the shares of voting stock of a corporation will be able to elect *every* director. Also as discussed in Chapter 5, for purposes of deciding who gets to vote at a shareholders meeting (and how many shares they get to vote), the corporation looks at the list of shareholders as of the record date. It does not matter who owns shares as of the meeting date. Here, the record date was April 2 and the facts indicate that, as of that date, Mr. Black owned 501 shares and Mr. White owned 499 shares. Thus, Mr. Black will be able to elect all of the directors under plurality voting.

Multiple Choice Question 5-14: The correct answer is A. The meeting notice was proper (*see* MBCA § 7.05), there was a quorum (see MBCA § 7.25(a)), and there were more yes votes than no votes (*see* MBCA 7.25(c)). Answer B is incorrect because the notice was proper: it was mailed at least ten but not more than sixty days before the meeting; it was mailed to all persons who owned stock on the record date; and it is contained information about the date, time, place and (because it was a special meeting) purpose of the shareholders meeting. Answer C is wrong because a majority of the *outstanding* shares is not required; MBCA § 7.25(c) merely requires that a majority of the votes that are *cast* be cast in favor of the resolution. Answer D is wrong for similar reasons.

Multiple Choice Question 5-15: The correct answer is C. Under MBCA § 7.27(b),

> An amendment to the articles of incorporation that adds, changes, or deletes a greater quorum or voting requirement must meet the same quorum requirement and be adopted by the same vote and voting groups required to take action under the quorum and voting

requirements then in effect or proposed to be adopted, *whichever is greater.*

(Emphasis added.) Here, the proposal was to amend the articles to require that at least 66.67% of the outstanding shares of Stereo stock must vote in favor of a merger in order for any merger to occur. Because there are 100,000 shares outstanding, we thus would need 66,667 shares to vote in favor of this "supermajority" articles provision in order for it to be adopted. The proposal did not receive that many votes.

Multiple Choice Question 5-16: The correct answer is C. Because Janice is a *shareholder* and not a director, she has no direct power to overturn this decision. *See* MBCA § 8.01. The only viable way to express her displeasure is to remove the current directors and replace them with new directors that will reverse this decision. Answer A is thus incorrect. Answer B is incorrect for the same reason: shareholders do not have the power to make business decisions for the corporation. Instead, shareholders elect the directors (who then make business decisions). In addition, shareholders may vote on "major" transactions such as mergers, but only after those transactions have been proposed by the board. Answer D is wrong because, unless the shareholder has a "buy-sell" agreement with the corporation, the corporation has no obligation to repurchase shares from a shareholder. Nothing in this fact pattern indicates that Janie and MRC are parties to a buy-sell agreement.

Multiple Choice Question 5-17: The correct answer is C. Because the lease was signed before Two Friends Coffee, Inc. was incorporated, it is a pre-incorporation contract and Hassan was a promoter. MBCA § 2.04 provides that "[a]ll persons purporting to act as or on behalf of a corporation, knowing there was no incorporation under this Act, are jointly and severally liable for all liabilities created while so acting." However, one can "contract around" this rule. Here, Hassan tried to do that but was probably unsuccessful. If there is a way to interpret the contract that is consistent with the general rule, then most courts will do so. Here, the contact only states that the corporation will be liable if it adopts the lease. It does *not* state that Hassan would no longer be liable as well. Thus, Hassan most likely will continue to be liable if the corporation cannot perform. Note that *Pete* probably will not be liable, because he did not know about the lease before Hassan signed it. Answer A is incorrect because veil-piercing is not a prerequisite to imposing liability on a promoter. Answer B is incorrect for the reasons stated above. Answer D is incorrect because Hassan and Pete hadn't yet taken any steps to start running the business. Thus, they probably had not formed a partnership as of the time that the contract was signed; they were merely in the "talking phase."

Multiple Choice Question 5-18: The correct answer is C. While different courts have used different lists of factors that are important in deciding whether to "pierce the corporate veil," options I, III, and IV would likely not be considered important by a court. On the other hand, options II and V would clearly be helpful in arguing to pierce the corporate veil in this case.

Multiple Choice Question 5-19: The correct answer is A. Keep in mind that this fact pattern gives you very limited facts. Based only on these facts, none of options I through IV would be correct. Option I is wrong because shareholders do not have preemptive rights (that is, the right to purchase additional shares if the corporation offers new shares for sale in the future) unless the corporation's articles of incorporation provide for them. *See* MBCA § 6.30. Option II is wrong because owning 25% of the stock would not necessarily allow you to elect 25% of the directors. For example, if plurality voting were used, and the holder(s) of the other 75% of the stock voted to elect different directors, your client would not be able to elect *any* directors. Options III and IV are wrong because, unless the shareholder has agreed to transfer restrictions or has a buy-sell agreement with the corporation and/or other shareholders, shares are freely transferable; conversely, neither the corporation nor the other shareholders are under an obligation to buy your shares from you in the absence of a buy-sell agreement.

Multiple Choice Question 5-20: The correct answer is A. It is likely that Mr. Alpha, the "bad guy" under these facts, will be held personally liable on a veil-piercing claim, whereas Mr. Beta probably will not, because he was a passive shareholder (although not all courts would agree). Answer B is incorrect because it assumes that one can never pierce the corporate veil. Answer C is wrong because being a closely held corporation does not—standing alone—mean that the corporate veil will be pierced. Although it is true that veil piercing does not occur in publicly held corporations, this does not mean that *all* closely held corporations are at risk of veil-piercing. Answer D is wrong because being a closely held corporation does not somehow guarantee that the corporate veil will never be pierced.

Multiple Choice Question 5-21: The correct answer is D. Under MBCA § 7.31, two or more shareholders (not necessarily all of the shareholders) may sign a voting agreement specifying how they will vote their shares. Such an agreement may continue for as long as specified in the agreement; MBCA § 7.31 does not contain a "sunset" clause. Moreover, shareholder voting agreements are specifically enforceable. For these reasons, Answers A and B are incorrect. Under cumulative voting, because there are 3,000 outstanding shares and nine members of the board, it would take 301 shares to elect someone to the board, assuming that are 3,000 shares are voted. (See the formula described in the explanation of Multiple Choice Question 5-11 above.) Ms. Bass only owns 300 shares, so she is not guaranteed of having enough shares to elect herself to the board, thus making Answer C wrong.

Multiple Choice Question 5-22: The correct answer is A. Under MBCA § 7.22(d), a proxy is revocable unless (1) it states that it is irrevocable and (2) it is "coupled with an interest," meaning that the person who holds the proxy has an interest in the shares that are subject to the proxy. Here, Frank was a shareholder on the record date, so he presumably is entitled to vote the shares (even though he no longer owned them on the date of the meeting). As between Frank and Ralph, Frank "wins" because he did not give Ralph a proxy to vote the shares. As between Frank and Arthur, Frank also "wins" because (1) it is unclear from the facts whether the proxy stated that it was irrevocable, and (2) even if the proxy did state that it was irrevocable, Arthur has no interest in the shares that are subject to the proxy.

Multiple Choice Question 5-23: The correct answer is B. Although courts have used a variety of factors to determine whether to pierce the corporate veil, of the choices given in this question, Answer B is clearly the most significant. Unlike Answer B, the other factors, standing alone, would not necessarily be considered important in deciding whether to pierce the corporate veil.

Multiple Choice Question 5-24: The correct answer is A. Hopefully, this question was obvious.

Multiple Choice Question 5-25: The correct answer is D. Answer A is simply wrong; it is very common for individuals to be both officers and directors of a corporation. Answer B is incorrect (unless the corporation's articles of incorporation require directors to own stock in the corporation). Answer C is wrong because MBCA § 8.08(a) provides that the "shareholders may remove one or more directors with or without cause unless the articles of incorporation provide that directors may be removed only for cause."

Multiple Choice Question 5-26: The correct answer is A. Answer B is incorrect because officers can have both actual authority (including actual express and actual implied authority) and apparent authority. Answer C is incorrect because shareholders only elect directors; they have no direct influence over the identities of the corporation's officers.

Multiple Choice Question 5-27: The correct answer is A. The contract with Marcus was a pre-incorporation contract because Interesting Books Corp. did not exist at the time that the contract was signed. After incorporation, Interesting Books Corp. would not automatically liable on the contract, making Answer B incorrect. However, it will be liable if it adopts the contract. A corporation may adopt a pre-incorporation contract either expressly (such as through a board resolution) or impliedly, which makes Answer C incorrect. Note that, even if the corporation does adopt the contract, the promoter (Melina) is still liable on the contract unless there is a novation. This makes Answer D incorrect.

Multiple Choice Question 5-28: The correct answer is C. As discussed in the explanation to Multiple Choice Question 5-27, a promoter will be liable on a pre-incorporation contract unless there is a novation that releases the promoter from liability (or unless the contract itself contains language that clearly states that the promoter is not personally liable on the contract).

CHAPTER 6

Answer Key:

6-1:	B
6-2:	D
6-3:	D
6-4:	C
6-5:	A
6-6:	C
6-7:	B
6-8:	B
6-9:	C
6-10:	D
6-11:	A

Explanations:

Multiple Choice Question 6-1: The correct answer is B because MBCA § 8.31(b) does in fact require that the person suing the directors for a breach of the duty of care and seeking money damages of behalf of the corporation has the burden of proving causation and damages. Answer A is incorrect because directors only have a duty to act *as they reasonably believe to be* in the best interests of the corporation. If the standard were that directors must always act "in the best interests of the corporation," then the directors might be liable for every decision or action that turns out badly. *See* MBCA § 8.30(a)(2). Answer C is wrong as a result of the *Caremark* case that appears in Chapter 6; directors have a duty to implement such a system even before they have actual or constructive notice of illegal activities occurring within the corporation (although the actual design of the system is a matter of business judgment). Finally, Answer D is wrong because directors may, in accordance with MBCA §§ 8.30(e) and (f), rely on the opinions of persons who are not professionals, so long as, depending on the person or persons, she or they are "reliable and competent" or "merit confidence" with respect to the subject matter of the opinion.

Multiple Choice Question 6-2: The correct answer is D. As discussed in Chapter 6, courts ordinarily require a showing of gross negligence before finding that directors breached their duty of care, and the comments to MBCA § 8.30(b) also suggest that negligence is not sufficient to find that a director breached her duty of care. Answer B is wrong due to the *Caremark* case that appears in Chapter 6. Answer C is wrong because a finding that a majority of directors were not interested in a transaction would not necessarily shield them from liability. For example, if the plaintiff could show that the directors were grossly negligent in not informing themselves of all material facts reasonably available to them before making a decision, the plaintiff would be able to overcome the business judgment rule and hold the directors liable for the consequences of that decision.

Multiple Choice Question 6-3: The correct answer is D. Answer A is incorrect because the mere fact that the board made a terrible decision does not result in director liability; the plaintiff must still overcome the business judgment rule by showing that the directors were motivated by a conflict of interest; were grossly negligent in not informing themselves of all material facts reasonably available to them before making the decision; or that the decision was "irrational." While this decision might seem "irrational," it is actually very difficult to show that a decision was irrational; it typically requires a showing that the decision was "removed from the realm of reason" or some similar standard. Here, the board thought that the author's fame would "move" a lot of books. They were wrong, but probably not irrational. Answer B is wrong because "fairness" usually is not an issue when the board is being sued for a breach of the duty of care. (Instead, it may be relevant if the board were being sued for a breach of the duty of loyalty.) Answer C is wrong because it not the board's burden to prove they were properly informed; instead, the plaintiff could make this showing as one way to overcome the business judgment rule.

Multiple Choice Question 6-4: The correct answer is C, because honest errors of judgment that are made with due diligence would be protected by the business judgment rule, as well as MBCA §§ 8.30 and 8.31. On the other hand, diverting corporate opportunities to herself or gross negligence in the performance of her duties as a director could result in personal liability for Shelia.

Multiple Choice Question 6-5: The correct answer is A. MBCA § 2.02(b)(4) would shield the directors from monetary liability unless they received a financial benefit to which they were not entitled; intentionally inflicted harm on the corporation or its shareholders; violated MBCA § 8.33 (which concerns excessive distributions); or intentionally violated a criminal law. None of these four exceptions is present under these facts. Answer B is incorrect because the mere fact that the directors are defendants in a lawsuit does not mean that they have a conflict of interest sufficient for the plaintiff to overcome the business judgment rule. (Also, because the directors are not being sued for a *decision* that they made, the business judgment rule would not be directly applicable. Instead, this would be a *Caremark*-based claim.) Answer C is simply nonsensical. The directors *were unaware* that the illegal bribery was taking place. The standard stated in this answer (the directors were grossly negligent in not reasonably informing themselves) would be an appropriate way to overcome the business judgment rule with respect to a decision that the board made. Remember, this is a *Caremark*-based claim; that court in that case stated that "only a sustained or systematic failure of the board to exercise oversight—such as an utter failure to attempt to assure a reasonable information and reporting system exists—will establish the lack of good faith that is a necessary condition to liability." Finally, Answer D is incorrect because the plaintiff would not need to prove that the directors made a decision; liability could rest on inaction (although, as discussed above, it would be a difficult case for the plaintiff).

Multiple Choice Question 6-6: The correct answer is C. Answer A is incorrect because this question concerns the duty of care (here, an alleged lack of oversight) rather than the duty of loyalty (which involves a conflict of interest). Answer B is wrong because one does not "breach" the business judgment rule. In addition, because this case would be based on lack of oversight, rather than a *decision* that the board made, the business judgment rule would not be applicable. Answer C is correct based on MBCA § 8.31(b).

Multiple Choice Question 6-7: The correct answer is B. This question is (obviously) modeled on the facts in *Barnes v. Andrews*, which appears in Chapter 6. In that case, the director did in fact breach his duty of care by not paying sufficient attention to the corporation's business. But he avoided liability essentially because the plaintiff could not quantify what damages the corporation incurred as a result. Perhaps the company would have been wildly successful if the defendant director had better performed his duties, but perhaps it still would have failed. As such, the plaintiff could not prove causation and damages. *See also* MBCA § 8.31(b). Answer A is incorrect because the business judgment rule does not apply when the allegation is that the director was not devoting sufficient oversight to the corporation. Answer C is incorrect because a finding that the director breached his duty of care is, standing alone, insufficient to impose liability on the director. As discussed above, the plaintiff must still prove causation and damages if it is seeking monetary recovery from the director. Answer D is incorrect for similar reasons.

Multiple Choice Question 6-8: The correct answer is B. Because this would be considered a director's conflicting interest transaction (DCIT) with respect to Mr. Drum, as discussed in Chapter 7, he must either have it approved by the disinterested directors or disinterested shareholders after full disclosure, or show that it was "fair" to BOC. Even if you have not yet read Chapter 7 when working on this problem, you should recognize that demonstrating a conflict of interest is one way for a plaintiff to overcome the business judgment rule. Answer A is incorrect because Mr. Drum had an undisclosed conflict of interest in approving the Eureka design given that his daughter—a "related person" under MBCA § 8.60(5)—is the majority shareholder of Eureka. Answer C is wrong because the mere fact that BOC was fined should not impose liability on a director; generally, directors would only be liable if they knowingly approved an illegal act. Answer D is clearly wrong—Mr. Drum did not act in good faith!

Multiple Choice Question 6-9:   The correct answer is C. Because Ms. Crude had no conflict of interest in the choice of the Eureka design, a suit against her would be based on the duty of care. Even though she did not appear to do much in this fact pattern, the board as a whole appears to have been sufficiently informed to retain the protection of the business judgment rule (or, more precisely, the plaintiff will not be able to overcome the business judgment rule, other than with respect to Mr. Drum.) As noted in Chapter 6, the comment to MBCA § 8.30 provides in part that "[d]eficient performance of section 8.30 duties on the part of a particular director may be overcome, absent unusual circumstances, by acceptable conduct (meeting, for example, subsection (b)'s standard of care) on the part of other directors sufficient in number to perform the function or discharge the duty in question." Answer A seems plausible at first, but remember that she did not vote in favor of the Eureka design *because she was absent*, not because she thought the other design was safer. Answer B is incorrect because directors should not be liable simply as a result of missing a meeting at which a particular decision was made. Answer D is wrong because, even though the plaintiff likely *would* be able to show causation and damages, if the plaintiff cannot overcome the business judgment rule, the plaintiff will lose.

Multiple Choice Question 6-10: The correct answer is D, for reasons explained in the explanation of Multiple Choice Question 6-9 above. Answer A is incorrect because a suit against Mr. Drill would be based on the duty of care, not the duty of loyalty, because he had no conflict of interest in the choice of the Eureka design. Answer B is wrong; below average intelligence and drug addition would be no defense to a claim against a director. Answer C is wrong because, even though *some* experts thought the design was unsafe, other experts thought it was sufficiently safe and the board is allowed to rely on the opinions of experts pursuant to MBCA § 8.30(e) unless it has knowledge that makes such reliance unwarranted, which it did not have in this fact pattern. Finally, Answer E is wrong because (as stated in the explanation of Multiple Choice Question 6-8 above), the mere fact that BOC was fined should not impose liability on a director; generally, directors would only be liable if they knowingly approved an illegal act.

Multiple Choice Question 6-11: The correct answer is A, for the reasons set forth in the explanation to Multiple Choice Questions 6-9 and 6-10. However, a few other words are in order. Answer C is wrong because simply choosing the cheapest design does not mean that you did reasonably believe it was in the best interests of the corporation. What if the risks of the design outweighed the cost savings? Answer D is wrong because the facts specifically state that BOC had no "unusual" provisions in its articles. This was a reference to MBCA § 2.02(b)(4) and Answer D describes some of the situations in which directors would be liable even if the corporation had a 2.02(b)(4) provision in its articles.

CHAPTER 7

Answer Key:

7-1:   C
7-2:   D
7-3:   E
7-4:   D
7-5:   C
7-6:   A
7-7:   B
7-8:   A
7-9:   A
7-10: C
7-11: A
7-12: D
7-13: A
7-14: C

Explanations:

Multiple Choice Question 7-1: The correct answer is C. Answer A is wrong because director's conflicting interest transactions (DCITs) are no longer *automatically* voidable; that was the rule at common law before statutes such as MBCA §§ 8.60 to 8.63 were enacted. Under that statute, a DCIT cannot be challenged because of the director's interest in it if (1) it was properly approved by the qualified directors pursuant to MBCA § 8.62; (2) it was properly approved by the qualified shares pursuant to MBCA § 8.63; *or* (3) it is established to have been "fair" to the corporation at the time it was entered into. Answer B is wrong because MBCA § 8.62 requires *more* than that the interested director not participate in the meeting. For example, the interested director must fully disclose the facts that she knows about the DCIT and the DCIT must be approved by a majority of the qualified directors who vote on the transaction. Answer C is correct, but remember it is only one of the three choices to defend a DCIT.

Multiple Choice Question 7-2: The correct answer is D. As noted in the explanation of Multiple Choice Question 7-1, a DCIT cannot be challenged because of the director's interest in it if (1) it was properly approved by the qualified directors pursuant to MBCA § 8.62; (2) it was properly approved by the qualified shares pursuant to MBCA § 8.63; *or* (3) it is established to have been "fair" to the corporation at the time it was entered into. Thus, there are three ways to defend a DCIT. Answer A is wrong because Duane's shares are not "qualified" shares and therefore do not count under MBCA § 8.63. Answer B is incorrect because "sanitization" under MBCA § 8.63 requires that a "majority of the votes cast by the holders of all qualified shares are [voted] in favor of the transaction ....", not that *all* of the qualified shares at the meeting are voted in favor of the DCIT. Answer C is wrong under MBCA § 8.63(d); that section provides that a majority of the qualified shares entitled to be voted constitutes a quorum for purposes of a meeting at which a DCIT will be considered.

Multiple Choice Question 7-3: The correct answer is E. As noted above, a DCIT cannot be challenged because of the director's interest in it if (1) it was properly approved by the qualified directors pursuant to MBCA § 8.62; (2) it was properly approved by the qualified shares pursuant to MBCA § 8.63; *or* (3) it is established to have been "fair" to the corporation at the time it was entered into. Here, there are three interested (non-qualified) directors, who made full disclosure to the two disinterested (qualified) directors. The two qualified directors then approved the transaction outside the presence of the interested directors. This action meets the requirements of MBCA § 8.62. *In addition*, a majority of the qualified shares that were cast were voted in favor of the DCIT after full disclosure. This action meets the requirements of MBCA § 8.63. Thus, the DCIT was approved two ways, even though only one was necessary to shield it from challenges due to the interest of three of the directors. This makes Answer C and D correct (and Answers A and B incorrect), which makes Answer E the best answer.

Multiple Choice Question 7-4: The correct answer is D. As noted in Chapter 7, MBCA § 8.11 provides that, unless the articles of bylaws provide otherwise, "the board of directors may fix the compensation of directors." However, the official comment to MBCA § 8.61 provides in part that "it must be kept in mind that board action on directors' compensation and benefits would be subject to judicial sanction if they are not favorably acted upon by shareholders pursuant to section 8.63 or if they are not in the circumstances fair to the corporation pursuant to section 8.61(b)(3)." Thus, Answers A and B are incorrect. Answer C is clearly incorrect because directors may receive compensation other than stock options for their service.

Multiple Choice Question 7-5: The correct answer is C. Because the shares owned by the directors *and* the shares owned by the directors' spouses would not be considered qualified (disinterested) shares for purposes of MBCA § 8.63, that means that there are only 560,000 qualified shares (800,000 minus 240,000). MBCA § 8.63 requires that a majority of the qualified shares that are "cast" (i.e., voted) must be voted in favor of the transaction. Answer A is incorrect because MBCA § 8.62 requires that at least two qualified (disinterested) directors approve the transaction, if this is the method that one uses to "sanitize" the transaction. Because there is only one qualified director (Mr. Lion is the only director with no interest in the transaction), that isn't enough. Answer B is incorrect because it does not reflect the fact that the shares owned by the directors' spouses would not be considered qualified (disinterested) shares for purposes of MBCA § 8.63. *See* MBCA § 8.63(c)(2), and note that your spouse would be a "related person" to you within the meaning of MBCA § 8.60(5). Finally, Answer D is incorrect because MBCA § 8.63 requires that a majority of the qualified shares that are *cast* (i.e., voted) must be voted in favor of the transaction. Here, there are 560,000 qualified shares (those not owned by the four disinterested directors or related persons, here their spouses). A majority of the 560,000 shares that are voted must be voted in favor of the transaction.

Multiple Choice Question 7-6: The correct answer is A. As noted above, a DCIT cannot be challenged because of the director's interest in it if (1) it was properly approved by the qualified directors pursuant to MBCA § 8.62; (2) it was properly approved by the qualified shares pursuant to MBCA § 8.63; *or* (3) it is established to have been "fair" to the corporation at the time it was entered into. Under Answer A, if a majority of the disinterested directors approve the DCIT, then Sam would not have to show that the DCIT was fair. (Note that MBCA § 8.62 only requires that a majority, but not fewer than two, of the disinterested directors *who vote* on the DCIT voted in favor of it. This makes Answer D incorrect.) Answer B is incorrect because fairness and loyalty are not issues if the disinterested directors or shareholders approve a DCIT. Answer C is incorrect because both director approval under MBCA § 8.62 and shareholder approval under MBCA § 8.62 require full disclosure; if full disclosure was not made, then Sam would have to show that the DCIT was "fair," not that he was acting in good faith.

Multiple Choice Question 7-7: The correct answer is B. Under the ALI's *Principles of Corporate Governance*, a corporate opportunity is defined as *any* of the following:

• Any opportunity to engage in a business activity of which a director or senior executive becomes aware in connection with the performance of functions as a director or senior executive, or under circumstances that should reasonably lead the director or senior executive to believe that the person offering the opportunity expects it to be offered to the corporation; or

• Any opportunity to engage in a business activity of which a director or senior executive becomes aware through the use of corporate information or property, if the resulting opportunity is one that the director or senior executive should reasonably be expected to believe would be of interest to the corporation; or

- Any opportunity to engage in a business activity of which a senior executive becomes aware and knows is closely related to a business in which the corporation is engaged or expects to engage.

Note that Dave is a director, but not an officer, of Bomb Corp. Thus, the third definition of corporate opportunity set forth above does not apply to him. Option I would be helpful to Dave, because it would show that the opportunity did not come to him in his "official capacity" (see the first bullet point above). Option II is irrelevant to Dave because he is not an officer of Bomb Corp. and thus the third bullet point above (the line of business test) does not apply to him. Option III is irrelevant under the ALI test and therefore would not be helpful to Dave. Finally, option IV would be helpful to Dave because it would show that he did not use "corporate resources" to learn of the opportunity (see the second bullet point above).

Multiple Choice Question 7-8: The correct answer is A. Under the *Guth* test used in Delaware to decide if an opportunity is a "corporate opportunity," four factors are important. To quote the *Broz* case that appears in Chapter 7:

> The corporate opportunity doctrine, as delineated by *Guth* and its progeny, holds that a corporate officer or director may not take a business opportunity for his own if: (1) the corporation is financially able to exploit the opportunity; (2) the opportunity is within the corporation's line of business; (3) the corporation has an interest or expectancy in the opportunity; and (4) by taking the opportunity for his own, the corporate fiduciary will thereby be placed in a position inimicable to his duties to the corporation. The Court in *Guth* also derived a corollary which states that a director or officer may take a corporate opportunity if: (1) the opportunity is presented to the director or officer in his individual and not his corporate capacity; (2) the opportunity is not essential to the corporation; (3) the corporation holds no interest or expectancy in the opportunity; and (4) the director or officer has not wrongfully employed the resources of the corporation in pursuing or exploiting the opportunity. [Citation omitted.]

Each of the four items listed in the question (options I through IV) appear on this list. Thus, each of them would be helpful to Dave in arguing that this is not a "corporate opportunity."

Multiple Choice Question 7-9: The correct answer is A. This is another example of a director's conflicting interest transaction (DCIT) because some of the directors are engaging in a transaction (a loan) with the corporation. As noted above, a DCIT cannot be challenged because of the director's interest in it if (1) it was properly approved by the qualified directors pursuant to MBCA § 8.62; (2) it was properly approved by the qualified shares pursuant to MBCA § 8.63; *or* (3) it is established to have been "fair" to the corporation at the time it was entered into. Here, options 1 and 2 clearly were not met. However, because the loan was at the prime interest rate, it is likely fair to the corporation. The Hatfield directors were not charging an excessive (and unfair) interest rate.

Multiple Choice Question 7-10: The correct answer is C. This is not a director's conflicting interest transaction (DCIT) because neither Steve nor any related person to him is engaging in a transaction with MAC or any of MAC's affiliates. Thus, Answer A is incorrect. Answer B is incorrect because Steve's actions implicate the duty of loyalty rather than the duty of care. Answer C is correct because the opportunity to have Fashionista become a client may have been a "corporate opportunity" with respect to MAC and Steve was a director of MAC.

Multiple Choice Question 7-11: The correct answer is A. Directors A and B properly "sanitized" this transaction by having the disinterested (qualified) directors approve it pursuant to MBCA § 8.62. Directors C, D, and E, however, theoretically could still be sued for breaching their duty of care. (Note that directors A and B could not be sued on *care* grounds because they abstained from voting on the transaction.) However, when you are suing directors with respect to a decision that they made, they will be protected by the business judgment rule (BJR) and the plaintiff must "overcome" the BJR in order to win the case. Here, because directors C, D, and E did not have a conflict interest, appear to be well-informed, and did not make an "irrational" decision, they will be protected by the BJR.

Multiple Choice Question 7-12: The correct answer is D. This transaction was not a director's conflicting interest transaction (DCIT) because it did not take place between MMI (or an affiliate of MMI) and Vince (or a related person to Vince). This eliminates Answer B. However, Answer A is wrong because the mere fact that this is not a DCIT does not insulate Vince from liability; after all, there are other theories of liability. Answer C would be incorrect because the mere fact that the land belonged to his wife rather than himself would not shield Vince from liability. This leaves Answer D. Under these facts, it appears that the opportunity to have Julius purchase land was a corporate opportunity that Vince should have disclosed to MMI.

Multiple Choice Question 7-13: The correct answer is A. Under Delaware law, if the disinterested *directors* approve an interested director transaction after full disclosure, the transaction will be protected by the business judgment rule. As such, the fairness (or lack thereof) of such a transaction would not be relevant. This eliminates Answers C and D. However, under *Lewis v. Vogelstein* and other cases discussed in Chapter 7, if the disinterested *shareholders* approve an interested director transaction after full disclosure, the transaction could still be challenged—but only successfully if the plaintiff proves that the transaction amounted to "waste." Because the plaintiff has the burden of proof on this issue, Answer B is incorrect.

Multiple Choice Question 7-14: The correct answer is C. Here, there was only one "interested" director (Jon) out of a total of eleven. Moreover, Jon did not vote on his compensation nor did he take part in the deliberations concerning his compensation. The board of directors has the power to set the compensation levels of officers. Because this was a board decision, the business judgment rule applies. Unless the shareholder could somehow overcome the business judgment rule (which seems extremely unlikely on these facts), the fairness (or lack thereof) of Jon's compensation is not a matter for a court to review. Note that Answer D seems plausible, due to the comment to MBCA § 8.11 which is discussed in Section 7.04 of Chapter 7. However, that comment pertains to directors setting *their own* compensation. Here, the board is setting the compensation of an officer who just happens to be a director. They were not setting the compensation levels of the entire board for their service as directors.

CHAPTER 8

Answer Key:

8-1:   A
8-2:   A
8-3:   D
8-4:   D
8-5:   D
8-6:   E
8-7:   A
8-8:   A
8-9:   D
8-10: E
8-11: D
8-12: A
8-13: A
8-14: D
8-15: A

Explanations:

Multiple Choice Question 8-1: The correct answer is A. Note that BCC was harmed in 2010, when it incurred the $25 million in costs relating to the recall. Frank, however, did not own any BCC stock until April 2011. Under MBCA § 7.41, to have proper standing to bring a derivative lawsuit, a shareholder must (1) have owned stock at the time of the alleged injury to the corporation (or have acquired stock by operation of law from someone else who owned stock at that time) and (2) be a fair and adequate representative of the corporation. Even if Frank would be a fair and adequate representative of BCC, the fact remains that he did not satisfy the "contemporaneous ownership" requirement.

Multiple Choice Question 8-2: The correct answer is A. The MBCA imposes a "universal demand" requirement. There are no exceptions to the requirement to make a demand. *See* MBCA § 7.42. Thus, Answers C and E can be eliminated. In Delaware, demand would be excused if the plaintiffs can allege particularized facts which create a reasonable doubt that, (1) the directors are disinterested and independent or (2) the challenged transaction was otherwise the product of a valid exercise of business judgment. In New York, demand would be excused if the plaintiff alleges with particularity that (1) that a majority of the board of directors is interested in the challenged transaction, (2) the board of directors did not fully inform themselves about the challenged transaction to the extent reasonably appropriate under the circumstances, or (3) the challenged transaction was so egregious on its face that it could not have been the product of sound business judgment of the directors. None of these grounds are present on these facts. First, there really isn't any "challenged transaction" because the board didn't decide anything. Instead, BCC was merely the victim of Engine Parts's defective parts. Second, there is no indication in the facts that any of BCC's directors have any conflict of interest with respect to the subject matter of this lawsuit.

Multiple Choice Question 8-3: The correct answer is D. Here, Frank's demand has been rejected. If he still wishes to file the lawsuit, he must allege with particularity at least one of the grounds described in MBCA 7.44(d), to wit: either that (1) "a majority of the board of directors did not consist of qualified directors at the time the determination [i.e., the rejection] was made or (2) that the requirements of subsection (a) have not been met." Subsection (a) requires that one of the groups listed in subsection (b) or (f) have "determined in good faith after conducting a reasonable inquiry upon which its conclusions are based that the maintenance of the derivative proceeding is not in the best interests of the corporation." Assuming that the June 1 letter is true, then it does not appear that Frank would be able to allege either of these grounds as a way to "overcome" the rejection. As such, it does not look like he will be able to file the lawsuit, making Answer D correct. Answer A is incorrect because, while it is true that Frank normally must wait ninety days after making the demand to file the lawsuit, he may do so immediately if the board earlier rejects the demand (assuming that he could satisfy one of the requirements discussed above). Answer B is incorrect because Frank must make one of the particularized allegations described above in his complaint and it does not appear that he can do so successfully. Finally, Answer C is incorrect because nothing in the MBCA provides for this result.

Multiple Choice Question 8-4: The correct answer is D. MBCA § 7.44(a) provides that a "derivative proceeding shall be dismissed by the court on motion by the corporation if one of the groups specified in subsections (b) or (f) has determined in good faith after conducting a reasonable inquiry upon which its conclusions are based that the maintenance of the derivative proceeding is not in the best interests of the corporation." One of the groups listed in subsection (b) is a "committee consisting of two or more qualified directors [as defined in MBCA § 1.43] appointed by majority vote of qualified directors present at a meeting of the board of directors, whether or not such independent directors constituted a quorum." Given that none of the BCC directors have a personal interest in this lawsuit, they all would be qualified directors, including Mr. Jones and Ms. Smith. Further, because Mr. Jones and Ms. Smith appear to acted in good faith and to have conducted a reasonable inquiry, the court will dismiss the lawsuit.

Multiple Choice Question 8-5: The correct answer is D. In option I, the shareholder was harmed, not the corporation; therefore, this would be a direct lawsuit. Option II would be a derivative lawsuit because the corporation was harmed by receiving an allegedly inadequate price. For similar reasons, option III would be a derivative lawsuit. Option IV would be a direct lawsuit because the *corporation* would not have been harmed by the allegedly inadequate price that its former shareholders received for their shares.

Multiple Choice Question 8-6: The correct answer is E. While some of the answers partially state the tests for excusing demand under Delaware or New York law, the key is in the application of those tests to the facts. Note that the Bob is only one of six members of the board, and the board obviously did not know about his actions before he took those actions. In other words, there was no *board* decision that is being challenged here, nor are a majority of the directors "interested" in the lawsuit. Thus, to say, for example as in Answer B, that demand should be excused because the board was not reasonably informed is nonsensical.

Multiple Choice Question 8-7: The correct answer is A. This question essentially applies MBCA § 7.44(d) and the explanation of it would be very similar to the explanation of Multiple Choice Question 8-3 above.

Multiple Choice Question 8-8: The correct answer is A. This question essentially applies MBCA § 7.44(a) and the explanation of it would be very similar to the explanation of Multiple Choice Question 8-4 above.

Multiple Choice Question 8-9: The correct answer is D. As stated in the facts, Gator is incorporated in New York. Under New York law, there are three situations in which demand is excused; Answers A, B, and C, respectively, describe these situations. Here, the facts are such that all three grounds for futility are likely present.

Multiple Choice Question 8-10: The correct answer is E. The MBCA imposes a "universal demand" requirement. There are no exceptions to the requirement to make a demand. *See* MBCA § 7.42.

Multiple Choice Question 8-11: The correct answer is D. In Delaware, demand would be excused if the plaintiffs can allege particularized facts which create a reasonable doubt that (1) the directors (a majority of them) are disinterested and independent or (2) the challenged transaction was otherwise the product of a valid exercise of business judgment. Answer A reflects the first option and Answer C reflects the second option; thus, Answer D is the best answer.

Multiple Choice Question 8-12: The correct answer is A. Under the rule from the *Zapata* case, which applies if demand had been excused, if a special litigation committee moves to dismiss the derivative lawsuit:

> First, the Court should inquire into the independence and good faith of the committee and the bases supporting its conclusions. … [If] the Court is satisfied … that the committee was independent and showed reasonable bases for good faith findings and recommendations, the Court may proceed, *in its discretion*, to the next step.

> The second step provides, we believe, the essential key in striking the balance between legitimate corporate claims as expressed in a derivative stockholder suit and a corporation's best interests as expressed by an independent investigating committee. The Court should determine, applying its own independent business judgment, whether the motion should be granted. …

(Emphasis added.)

Multiple Choice Question 8-13: The correct answer is A. MBCA § 7.42 imposes a "universal demand" requirement, thus making all of the other answers incorrect. Also, note that Answer B is incorrect because the "irreparable injury" exception only applies to the 90-day waiting period that normally applies after a demand has been made; it does not excuse a shareholder from having to make a demand at all.

Multiple Choice Question 8-14: The correct answer is D. Under MBCA § 7.44(a), if a special litigation committee that consists of two or more "qualified" (basically, that means independent) directors has "determined in good faith after conducting a reasonable inquiry upon which its conclusions are based that the maintenance of the derivative proceeding is not in the best interests of the corporation," then the court must dismiss the lawsuit. Thus, if Hector could show that any of the required elements (represented in Answers A, B, and C) are *missing*, then the court should deny the motion to dismiss the lawsuit.

Multiple Choice Question 8-15: The correct answer is A. Outside of a few narrow exceptions, monetary recovery in a derivative lawsuit will go to the corporation. After all, the "hallmark" of a derivative lawsuit is that the corporation was harmed.

CHAPTER 9

Answer Key:

9-1:	B
9-2:	D
9-3:	C
9-4:	D
9-5:	C
9-6:	B
9-7:	A
9-8:	D
9-9:	A
9-10:	D
9-11:	B
9-12:	A

Explanations:

Multiple Choice Question 9-1: The correct answer is B. The "call" of the question is which of the ideas would prevent Ted from excluding Michael from participating in the business. They all would, except a classified board. Obviously, an employment agreement would protect Michael's employment with the company. Cumulative voting would ensure that Michael is able to elect someone (probably himself) to the board. A Section 7.32 agreement requiring that Michael be appointed as an officer would also help. However, a classified board will not help—all it would do is have one director elected every year, rather than three directors. This could actually make things worse for Michael—after all, Ted owns 60% of the stock.

Multiple Choice Question 9-2: The correct answer is D. As noted in the question, you are following Massachusetts case law, but not MBCA § 14.30. As such, Answer D, which reflects the test used in the *Wilkes* case, is correct.

Multiple Choice Question 9-3: The correct answer is C. Answer A is incorrect because preemptive rights would prevent a minority shareholder from having her percentage ownership in the company "diluted." Answer B is incorrect because setting a higher quorum requirement could allow a minority shareholder to prevent votes from being taken on certain actions by refusing to attend the meeting. Answer D is incorrect because multiple classes of stock could be used to protect the minority. For example, a class of stock owned only by the minority shareholder could be given rights to elect a set number of persons to the board. However, no par or low par value stock will do nothing to protect a minority shareholder from abuse.

Multiple Choice Question 9-4: The correct answer is D. Note that Hank is a minority shareholder and not a member of the controlling group (in this case, a family). Thus, even though SSI is incorporated in Massachusetts, the "equal opportunity" rule from the *Donahue* case does not apply to any repurchases of Hank's stock. It would only apply if SSI were repurchasing shares from a member of the controlling group. While Answer C is correct in pointing out that this is a director's conflicting interest transaction, it is *not* true that such transactions may *only* be completed if they are "fair." (See Chapter 7.)

Multiple Choice Question 9-5: The answer is C. Remember, the call of the question is which answer is <u>not</u> correct. Answers A, B, and D are all true pursuant to MBCA § 7.32. However, Answer C is incorrect because the failure to note the elimination of the board of directors conspicuously on the front or back of both Abe's and Ben's shares does not render the provision or agreement void. At most, it would allow a purchaser of the shares to rescind the purchase if she did not know about the provision.

Multiple Choice Question 9-6: The correct answer is B. Answer A is incorrect because transfer restrictions are not *per se* impermissible under the MBCA. However, MBCA § 6.27(a) provides in part that a "restriction does not affect shares issued before the restriction was adopted unless the holders of the shares are parties to the restriction agreement or voted in favor of the restriction." Thus, even though this would at first glance appear to be an articles amendment that was properly adopted, because Sven did not vote in favor of it, his shares are not affected by it. Answer C is incorrect because the fairness of the price is irrelevant under these facts.

Multiple Choice Question 9-7: The correct answer is A. This agreement met the requirements of MBCA § 7.32, in that it was signed by all shareholders and "made known" to the corporation (by being placed in the corporate minute book). *See* MBCA § 7.32(b)(1)(B). That being the case, it is enforceable as written, despite the fact that it would seem to violate the rule in *McQuade v. Stoneham*. But that is something that one can do with a Section 7.32 agreement. *See* MBCA § 7.32(a)(1) and (3). Answer C is incorrect because MBCA § 7.32 allows agreements that would restrict the board's discretion in violation of the common law rule from cases like *McQuade v. Stoneham*. Answer D is incorrect because MBCA § 7.32 provides that such agreements are valid for ten years—unless the agreement provides for a different time period. This agreement specifically stated that it was valid for 15 years.

Multiple Choice Question 9-8: The correct answer is D. This question concerns the *Wilkes* case and its two-part test for breach-of-fiduciary claims in closely held corporations under Massachusetts law. If there was no legitimate business reason for firing Courtney, she would win the case, and the court would not need to proceed to part two of the *Wilkes* test. As a technical matter, please note that Courtney did not have the burden to establish that there was no legitimate business purpose for firing her. Instead, Henry and Dave would have the burden to show that they did have a legitimate business purpose to fire her. On these facts, it does not look like Henry and Dave had a legitimate business purpose to fire Courtney, which makes Answer A incorrect. Answer B is incorrect because, under Massachusetts law, shareholders in closely held corporations such as this one do owe fiduciary duties to each other. Answer C is not correct because "cause" is a different standard than the legitimate business purpose part of the *Wilkes* test. Also, this answer neglects to apply the *Wilkes* test in any way.

Multiple Choice Question 9-9: The correct answer is A. This question concerns the "reasonable expectations" test, which the court in the *Kemp & Beatley* case applied in interpreting New York's counterpart to MBCA § 14.30.

Multiple Choice Question 9-10: The correct answer is D. Essentially, this question requires students to correctly apply MBCA § 14.34(a). Although other state statutes explicitly authorize remedies other than dissolution of the corporation (or have been interpreted that way by courts), MBCA § 14.30 seems to provide that dissolution is the only remedy. Nonetheless, MBCA § 14.34 essentially allows the defendants or the corporation to make the lawsuit "go away" by agreeing to buy the plaintiff's shares for fair value. Although MBCA § 14.34(b) does contain a deadline for this election, it may be extended in the court's discretion and, even if a court does find that the plaintiff has been oppressed and order dissolution of the corporation, the order often will be conditioned on allowing the defendants to prevent dissolution by buying the plaintiff's shares for fair value.

Multiple Choice Question 9-11: The correct answer is B. One of the "radical" things that may be done with an agreement under MBCA § 7.32 is to eliminate the board of directors, which makes Answer A, as well as Answer C, incorrect. Answer D is incorrect because nothing in MBCA § 7.32 requires the elimination of officers if the board is eliminated. Finally, Answer B correctly states one of the three ways of documenting a MBCA § 7.32 agreement (the other being amendments to either the articles or the bylaws that are approved by all shareholders).

Multiple Choice Question 9-12: The correct answer is A. With respect to agreement I, because it only concerns how Brian and Harold would vote their *shares*, it is permissible as a shareholder voting agreement under MBCA § 7.31. However, agreement II is not permissible—unless MBCA § 7.32 validates it. (Note that one of the things that may be accomplished with an agreement under MBCA § 7.32(a)(4) is the use of director proxies.) However, because agreement II was not signed by all of the shareholders (or unanimously put in the articles or bylaws), it is invalid.

CHAPTER 10

Answer Key:

10-1:   A
10-2:   A
10-3:   B
10-4:   C
10-5:   B
10-6:   B
10-7:   E
10-8:   B
10-9:   C
10-10: A

Explanations:

Multiple Choice Question 10-1: The correct answer is A. Remember, the call of the question was "[w]hich of the following is <u>not</u> an accurate statement ...." A close reading of the statute, which is set forth in the book, will indicate that each of Answers B, C, and D is correct. Therefore, Answer A is the only answer that is not accurate.

Multiple Choice Question 10-2: The correct answer is A. Note that RCC ended up with only 287 record holders of its common stock. Therefore it will not be required to register its common stock under Section 12(g), which makes Answer C incorrect. Moreover, its stock is not listed on a national securities exchange, which makes Answer D incorrect. Section 15(d) provides in part that the "duty to file under this subsection shall also be automatically suspended as to any fiscal year, *other than the fiscal year within which such registration statement became effective*, if, at the beginning of such fiscal year, the securities of each class to which the registration statement relates are held of record by less than three hundred persons." Thus, RCC can discontinue making Exchange Act filings with respect to years after 2012, which makes Answer B incorrect.

Multiple Choice Question 10-3: The correct answer is B. This question should be self-explanatory given the discussion of Forms 10-Q in the text.

Multiple Choice Question 10-4: The correct answer is C. Public companies are not *required* to solicit proxies (but if they do, they must comply with the proxy rules). A company that has a majority shareholder may not need to actually solicit proxies from shareholders, if the majority shareholder will attend the meeting in person. (But see Section 14(c).) Answer A is incorrect because the correct figures under Rule 14a-8 are $2,000, not $1,000 and one year, not six months. Answer B is clearly incorrect given the many cases that appear in the text that concern private litigation under Rule 14-9. Answer D is incorrect because the *Virginia Bankshares* opinion held that, under certain circumstances at least, statements of opinion can violate Rule 14a-9.

Multiple Choice Question 10-5: The correct answer is B. Remember, the call of the question was "[w]hich of the following is not an accurate statement ...." Nothing would prohibit exchanges from adopted rules that are "tougher" than SEC rules and in some cases they have done so.

Multiple Choice Question 10-6: The correct answer is B. This is known as the "500 going up and 300 coming down" rule. Answer A is incorrect because, although 500 record holders is the threshold for *registering* a class of securities under Section 12(g), 300 is the "floor" for *deregistering* the class. Answer C is incorrect because, although some banking and insurance companies may be exempt from Section 12(g), pharmaceutical companies are not automatically exempt. Answer D is wrong because Section 12(g) does not "care" whether the securities are listed on a national securities exchange; instead, if they are so listed, the correct subsection of Section 12 would be subsection (b), not subsection (g).

Multiple Choice Question 10-7: The correct answer is E. Unfortunately from the perspective of shareholder "activists" none of Answers A, B, C, or D is correct under current law.

Multiple Choice Question 10-8: The correct answer is B, as discussed in the text. Answer A is incorrect because SOX did not require *all* Section 12 companies to have an independent audit company; it merely required the SEC to pass a rule (Rule 10A-3) that prevents a national securities exchange from listing the securities of issuers that do not have independent audit committees. Answer C is incorrect; insiders may buy securities of the company and nothing in SOX remotely comes close to prohibiting them from doing so under any circumstances. Answer D is incorrect because SOX does not actually *require* a code of ethics; it merely directed the SEC to adopt rules requiring public companies to *disclose* whether they have a code of ethics for certain senior officers (and, if not, why they do not have such a code).

Multiple Choice Question 10-9: The correct answer is C. Option I is correct, as discussed in the text, as is Option III. Option II is clearly wrong; being public doesn't somehow give a company better access to information about its competitors. Option IV is also wrong because market activity consists largely of *resales*, not issuances of securities by the company.

Multiple Choice Question 10-10: The correct answer is A. Answer B is incorrect because the SEC has never, to my knowledge, pressured companies to de-stagger their boards; instead, as the text discusses, this pressure has come from shareholders. Answer C is incorrect because many majority systems would allow, in some circumstances, "defeated" directors to continue serving on the board, such as where the board refuses to accept a resignation, as discussed in the text. Finally, Answer D is incorrect because the "say on pay" vote is only an *advisory* vote by the shareholders, which means that it is not binding on the company.

CHAPTER 11

Answer Key:

11-1: B
11-2: D
11-3: B
11-4: E

Explanations:

Multiple Choice Question 11-1: The correct answer is B. Clearly, Gizmo is a controlling shareholder of Omega, owning 90% of its stock. This means that Gizmo owes fiduciary duties to Omega, which makes Answer E wrong. Under *Sinclair Oil*, if this transaction involves "self-dealing," then the intrinsic fairness (which is similar to, but not the same as, the entire fairness test) is appropriate. If not, then the standard of review would be the business judgment rule. Because Gizmo appears to have diverted a corporate opportunity from Omega to itself, it appears that self-dealing was present, which would make B the correct answer.

Multiple Choice Question 11-2: The correct answer is D. According to Delaware case law, even if a self-dealing transaction involving a controlling shareholders is approved by the disinterested shareholders after full disclosure (as was the case here) or by the disinterested directors after full disclosure, the plaintiff could still challenge the transaction. To do so successfully, the plaintiff must show that either fair dealing or fair price (or both) were lacking.

Multiple Choice Question 11-3: The correct answer is B. Clearly, Monkey Corp. is the controlling shareholder of Zoo Corp., as it has the ability to elect a majority of the Zoo Corp. directors. This problem was designed to illustrate the hypothetical described in the *Sinclair Oil* case; because the dividends were paid only on the shares owned by the controlling shareholder, the intrinsic fairness test is appropriate.

Multiple Choice Question 11-4: The correct answer is E. Fizz and his family own 6% of the shares of SPC Stock. Although he is the largest shareholder, he does not appear to be a "controlling" shareholder, particularly since he appears to no longer have any influence over SPC's board. Therefore, any transaction between Mr. Fizz and SPC would not be one that involves a "controlling" shareholder. If the board wishes to redeem his shares, it would be an "ordinary" board decision protected by the business judgment rule. But note that the shareholders are attempting to sue *Mr. Fizz*, not the board. Because he is not a controlling shareholder, he does not owe duties to SPC and the court should dismiss the case.

CHAPTER 12

Answer Key:

12-1:   C
12-2:   C
12-3:   A
12-4:   D
12-5:   A
12-6:   D
12-7:   A
12-8:   A
12-9:   C
12-10: C
12-11: E
12-12: B
12-13: B
12-14: C
12-15: B

12-16: A
12-17: E
12-18: B
12-19: A
12-20: D
12-21: B
12-22: B
12-23: E

Explanations:

Multiple Choice Question 12-1: The correct answer is C. Normally, shareholders are not liable for corporate debts, but here the company distributed to the shareholders money that should have gone its creditor (Gas Corp.) instead. In fact, the $100,000 that the company distributed to shareholders would not have been sufficient to fully pay Gas Corp. Thus, outside of a veil-piercing scenario (which is not present in these facts), each shareholder will have to give back what he or she received. Mr. Solid owned 10% of Liquid Corp.'s stock and therefore received $10,000. He will have to repay this amount. *See* MBCA § 14.09. He would have been liable for 10% of the claim if the amount of the claim had been less that the amount that was distributed to shareholders upon dissolution.

Multiple Choice Question 12-2: The correct answer is C. Because there are 10,000 shares of preferred stock, each with a $10 liquidation preference, it will take $100,000 to pay that amount. This leaves $900,000. Record Corp.'s articles essentially provide that shares of common stock and preferred stock will be lumped together and treated equally in sharing this amount. Thus, there are a total of 100,000 shares (90,000 shares of common and 10,000 shares of preferred) dividing $900,000, which means that each share will receive $9. Thus, the preferred stock got a total of $19 per share and the common stock got $9 per share.

Multiple Choice Question 12-3: The correct answer is A. The unpaid and unbarred creditor can recover from the shareholders amounts that the corporation owed, proportionally but subject to a cap (no shareholder would have to return more than the amount that she received upon dissolution of the corporation). This question asks which answer is <u>incorrect</u>. Answer A is the only answer that is incorrect, because it does not matter whether shareholders knew about the unpaid claim. Answer B is therefore correct. Answers C and D are correct because if $900,000 were distributed to the shareholders, the first $20,000 would go to the 1,000 shares of preferred stock to pay their liquidation preference. Afterwards, there would be $880,000 left, to be divided among 1,000 shares of common stock.

Multiple Choice Question 12-4: The correct answer is D. If SC sells the assets of its cookie division and its bagel division to Buyer Corp., it will left with only the cake division, which represents 24% of SC's overall assets, generates 25% of its pre-tax income, and generates 33% of its revenues. Thus, it does not meet the "safe harbor" of MBCA § 12.02 because SC would not retain at least 25% of its assets. However, this does not mean shareholder approval *is* required, only that we cannot be absolutely sure that shareholder approval is *not* required. Thus, Answer D is correct. Answer A is wrong because this transaction is clearly outside the ordinary course of business. Answer B is wrong because, as discussed above, SC will not meet the "safe harbor" of MBCA § 12.02. Answer C is wrong because, as discussed above, the failure to meet the safe harbor does not necessarily mean that SC would not retain a significant continuing business activity (although, of course, the farther away that one gets from the safe harbor, the less likely this would be).

Multiple Choice Question 12-5: The correct answer is A. Remember that this question is asking which answer is wrong. Answer A is incorrect because a tender offer must be held open for at least twenty business days, regardless of how successful it is. The remaining answers are all correct. Note with respect to Answer D that the facts state that the tender offer only sought 51% of the shares.

Multiple Choice Question 12-6: The correct answer is D. If Precipitation sells Sleet to Snow, it will be left with business activities that constitute 30% of its total assets, generate 20% of its pre-tax income, and generate 25% of its revenues. Because this falls into the "25% and 25% or 25%" safe harbor of MBCA § 12.02, Precipitation does not need to seek shareholder approval before this sale.

Multiple Choice Question 12-7: The correct answer is A. Unlike many state statutes, which require that a majority of the *outstanding* shares vote in favor of a merger, the MBCA treats a merger like anything else that the shareholders would vote on, requiring only more "yes votes" than "no votes" and ignoring abstentions. Here, more shares were voted in favor of than against the merger. Answer B is incorrect because Guitar would be issuing 20 million new shares, increasing the number of its outstanding shares by more than 20%. *See* MBCA §§ 11.04, 6.21(f). Answer C is wrong because, as discussed above, the MBCA does not require a majority of outstanding shares to approve the merger. Finally, a quorum was present because more than half of the outstanding shares attended the meeting, which makes Answer D wrong.

Multiple Choice Question 12-8: The correct answer is A. Mark is a shareholder of Stressed, which is closely held and is the target corporation in this merger. Answer B is incorrect because shareholders are not *automatically* entitled to assert dissenters' rights; they must, among other things, notify the board of their intent to dissent before the vote is taken. Answer C is wrong because MBCA § 13.01(b)(1) would not "take away" Mark's dissenters' rights simply because he would be *receiving* publicly traded stock in the merger.   Answer D is wrong because it is only impermissible for a shareholder who is dissenting from a merger to vote "for" the merger. Abstentions and "no" votes are both acceptable.

Multiple Choice Question 12-9: The correct answer is C. Answer A is incorrect because the language is based on *partnership* law (*see* RUPA § 807(b)). Answer B is incorrect because Stressed is a closely held corporation; therefore, there is no public market for its shares. Moreover, a judge would not be bound to use the market price in deciding the fair value of the stock. Answer D is wrong because it likely would include a "minority discount" and a "marketability discount," neither of which are appropriate in determining the fair value of shares in a dissenters' rights proceeding.

Multiple Choice Question 12-10: The correct answer is C. Answer A is incorrect because MBCA § 11.04(g) or MBCA § 11.05, with respect to a given merger, render shareholder approval of a constituent corporation unnecessary. Answer B is wrong because mergers often are, in fact, used to "cash out" minority shareholders, although such transactions could give rise to oppression claims (see Chapter 9) or claims that a controlling shareholder breached its fiduciary duties (see Chapter 11).

Multiple Choice Question 12-11: The correct answer is E. Answers A and B are incorrect because there are some (minor) amendments that may be approved by the board without shareholder approval. *See* MBCA § 10.05. Answer C is wrong because most articles amendments require shareholder approval. Answer D is wrong because the shareholders may amend the bylaws under MBCA § 10.20.

Multiple Choice Question 12-12: The correct answer is B. *See* MBCA § 12.01. Answer A is incorrect because some asset sales, even if they are outside the usual and regular course of business, need not be approved by the shareholders. *See* MBCA § 12.02. Answers C and D are incorrect because the shareholders of the buying corporation generally are not required to approve an asset purchase. Shareholder approval by the buying corporation would only be necessary if MBCA § 6.21(f) applied, which would be the case if the outstanding voting stock of the buyer would increase by more than 20% as a result of the transaction.

Multiple Choice Question 12-13: The correct answer is B. Because Solar Corp. stock is publicly traded, whenever a person—or group—acquires more than 5% of its outstanding stock, the person or group must file a Schedule 13D with the SEC within ten days. Here, Coal Corp. and Mr. Lump are clearly acting as a group. Thus, the total shares held by each of them (400,000) should be considered as owned by the group. Because there are 10 million shares of Solar Corp. stock outstanding, this means if Mr. Lump and/or Coal Corp. acquire another 100,001 shares, they will own more than 5% and will be required to file a Schedule 13D.

Multiple Choice Question 12-14: The correct answer is C. If VSC sells the assets of its baseball division, it will be left with two divisions that collectively represent 29% of VSC's assets and that generate 49% of its pre-tax income and 20% of its revenues. This clearly falls into the "safe harbor" of MBCA § 12.02, making the approval of VSC's shareholders unnecessary. As for Buyer Corp., its outstanding voting stock would increase by 10% (going from 10 million shares to 11 million shares), but this is below the 20% threshold would require a shareholder vote under MBCA § 6.21(f). Thus, the only correct answer is C.

Multiple Choice Question 12-15: The correct answer is B. Of the choices given, the best way to avoid successor liability is to pay for the assets with cash. Paying with stock or a combination of cash and stock could open the buying corporation up to a "de facto" merger argument. Thus, Answers A and C would not be good advice. Similarly, Answer D would not be good advice; paying with stock could give rise to a "de facto" merger argument even if the buyer does not operate at the same physical location as the selling corporation.

Multiple Choice Question 12-16: The correct answer is A. In the merger, Glass will issue 10 million new shares of its stock (100 multiplied by 100,000) to the soon-to-be-former shareholders of Beverage. This means that Glass will go from having 30 million outstanding shares to 40 million, a 33% increase. This means that one condition of MBCA § 11.04(g) would not be met, and the approval of Glass's shareholders would be needed, making Answer B incorrect. As for Beverage, as the disappearing or target corporation, its shareholders must vote on the merger. Answer C is wrong because the characteristics of the merger consideration is irrelevant to whether shareholder approval is required for the target company's shareholders. Answer D is wrong because MBCA § 11.04(g) has four conditions, each of which must be satisfied to conclude that shareholder approval is not necessary. As discussed above, this merger will result in a greater than 20% increase in the number of voting shares of Glass, meaning that one of the four conditions in MBCA § 11.04(g) is not met.

Multiple Choice Question 12-17: The correct answer is E, because both Answer A and Answer D are correct. Answer B is wrong because Glass's shareholders lack dissenters' rights, not because Glass is publicly traded, but because *their* stock will remain outstanding following the merger. *See* MBCA § 13.02(a)(1). Answer C is incorrect because the target company's shareholders would have dissenters rights unless, per MBCA § 13.02(b)(1), *their* stock was publicly traded. The fact that they would *receive* publicly traded stock would not take away their dissenters' rights under MBCA § 13.02(b)(1).

Multiple Choice Question 12-18: The correct answer is B. In the merger, Kite will issue 1 million new shares of its stock to the soon-to-be-former shareholders of String. This means that Kite will go from having 10 million outstanding shares to 11 million, a 10% increase. The other three conditions of MBCA § 11.04(g) would also be met, because Kite will survive the merger, its articles of incorporation will not be changed, and its currently outstanding shares will not change. Therefore, approval by Kite's shareholders is not necessary. This makes Answer A wrong. As for String, as the disappearing or target corporation, its shareholders must vote on the merger. Whether they have publicly traded stock is irrelevant to whether they must *vote* on the merger, so Answer C is wrong. Answer D is also irrelevant to the question of whether shareholder approval is necessary.

Multiple Choice Question 12-19: The correct answer is A. In this merger, Kite's shareholders will not have dissenters' rights because, not only are they not required to vote on the merger, their stock will remain outstanding immediately after the merger. *See* MBCA § 13.02(a)(1). Thus, Answers B and C are wrong. The tricky question is whether the shareholders of String have dissenters' rights. Initially, MBCA § 13.02(a)(1) gives them dissenters' rights because they have the right to vote on the merger and their String stock will no longer be outstanding following the merger. However, because String stock is publicly traded within the meaning of MBCA § 13.02(b)(1), that section takes away their dissenters' rights. Nonetheless, MBCA § 13.02(b)(3) would "restore" dissenters' rights if the String shareholders would be required to accept anything that is not, as of the effective date of the merger, cash or publicly traded stock within the meaning MBCA §13.02(b)(3). Here, the Kite stock will not "fit the bill," which means that String shareholders *do* have dissenters' right.

Multiple Choice Question 12-20: The correct answer is D. Answer A is incorrect because MBCA § 14.07 only requires three years, not five years. Answer B is incorrect because MBCA § 14.07 only requires that the notice be published once. Answer C is wrong because MBCA § 14.07 only requires that the notice be published in a newspaper of general circulation in the county of the corporation's principal office.

Multiple Choice Question 12-21: The correct answer is B. Answer A isn't correct because a triangular merger still runs the risk that the target corporation's liabilities could bankrupt the subsidiary used in the triangular merger. By contrast, the general rule in an asset transaction is that the buyer does not assume the seller's liabilities. Answer C is incorrect because in a forward triangular merger, the target corporation merges into the subsidiary of the acquiring corporation. Answer D is wrong because if MBCA § 11.05 applies, then the approval of neither the subsidiary's board nor its shareholders is required.

Multiple Choice Question 12-22: The correct answer is B. Option I is not legal because a tender offer must remain open for at least twenty business days (unless it is terminated without purchasing *any* shares). Thus, Answer A can be eliminated. As for Option II, it is now October 19. If a material amendment is made to the terms of the tender offer, then SEC Rule 14e-1(b) would require that the tender offer stay open for at least another ten business days. November 8 would be enough time. Option III would not work because the highest price paid in the tender offer to any shareholder must be paid to all shareholders.

Multiple Choice Question 12-23: The correct answer is E. *Revlon* duties apply if the corporation agrees to a transaction that will result in a "change of control" or a "break-up" of the company. Transaction I will result in a change of control of Page Corp.; after the transaction Book Corp. will control what remains of Page Corp. However, Transaction II will not result in a change of control of Page Corp. because no one will have "control" of the combined company after the merger. Transaction III will result in a change of control of Page Corp. because Mr. Ink will have "control" of the combined company after the merger.

CHAPTER 13

Answer Key:

13-1:   B
13-2:   C
13-3:   D
13-4:   C
13-5:   B
13-6:   D
13-7:   A
13-8:   D
13-9:   D
13-10: A
13-11: D
13-12: C
13-13: D
13-14: E

Explanations:

Multiple Choice Question 13-1: The correct answer is B. Answer A is wrong because this investment opportunity involves more than just land. Answer C is wrong because whether the transactions take place solely in one state is irrelevant to whether the transactions amount to a "security." Answer D is wrong because there is no indication in the facts that a limited partnership has actually been formed. (See Chapters 1 and 15.) Applying the *Howey* test to determine whether this transaction might be an "investment contract," we can see that the fourth element ("solely from the efforts of others") will fail because the investors will need to do a lot of work farming the land.

Multiple Choice Question 13-2: The correct answer is C. Answer A is wrong because an issuer can sell to a maximum of thirty-five nonaccredited investors and an unlimited number of accredited investors under both Rule 505 and Rule 506. Answer B is wrong because securities sold under both Rule 505 and Rule 506 are "restricted." Answer D is wrong because Rule 505 and Rule 506 have identical informational requirements. Finally, Answer E is wrong because both Rule 505 and Rule 506 prohibit general advertising and general solicitation.

Multiple Choice Question 13-3: The correct answer is D. Answer A is wrong because you cannot offer securities to residents of more than one state under that exemption. Answer B is wrong because publicly traded companies are prohibited from using Rule 504. Answer C is wrong because the most than can be raised in a twelve-month period under Rule 505 is $5 million.

Multiple Choice Question 13-4: The correct answer is C. Answers A and B are incorrect because *Ralston Purina* specifically rejected a numerical limit on the number of offerees (or, for that matter, purchasers) in a private offering under Section 4(2) of the Securities Act, although the more offerees there are, the more likely it is that one or more of them will not be appropriately qualified. Answers D and E concern factors that were not considered important (or even discussed) by the *Ralston Purina* Court.

Multiple Choice Question 13-5: The correct answer is B. The issue here is whether the discretionary trading account is an "investment contract" (as no other type of "security" would seem to be present). Under the *Howey* test, an investment contract is an investment of money in a common enterprise with the expectation of profits solely from the efforts of others. Under the "vertical" formulation of the common-enterprise element, there must be a link between the fortunes of the investors and the promoter of the enterprise or a third party. The "horizontal" formulation of the common-enterprise element requires multiple investors who are similarly situated. Thus, Answer A would be incorrect here. Answer B is correct because all of the elements of *Howey* are met in this example. Answer C is wrong because the "family resemblance" test determines whether a "note" is a security. It is irrelevant to whether something is an "investment contract."

Multiple Choice Question 13-6: The correct answer is D. Answer A is incorrect because it does not matter under the intrastate exemption of Section 3(a)(11) and Rule 147 where the company's *current* shareholders reside; what is important is whether the *offerees* reside. Answer B is incorrect because there is no dollar limitation on offerings under the intrastate exemption of Section 3(a)(11) and Rule 147. Answer C is incorrect because it is not a requirement of a Rule 505 offering that non-accredited investors be able to understand the merits and risks of the investment. Instead, that is a requirement in Rule 506 offerings.

Multiple Choice Question 13-7: The correct answer is A. Under Section 4(2), all offerees must be able to "fend for themselves" which has translated in case law as requiring a showing that they are either associated with the issuer or otherwise "sophisticated" in investing matters. Clearly, Mr. Lucky is not "sophisticated." However, the fact that he is a millionaire will suffice to make him an accredited investor for purpose of Regulation D and Regulation D does not require a showing that accredited (as opposed to non-accredited) investors are sophisticated.

Multiple Choice Question 13-8: The correct answer is D. Looking at the options that Cooley Corp. has, option I (Section 4(2)) clearly is possible because the offering would be made only to "wealthy and financial sophisticated" persons. Option II (Section 3(a)(11)) is also possible because Cooley is incorporated in Michigan, clearly "does business" in Michigan, and could restrict the offering to Michigan residents. Option III (Rule 504) would not work because it has a $1 million limit in a twelve-month period. Finally, option IV (Rule 506) would also work. Thus, D is the correct answer.

Multiple Choice Question 13-9: The correct answer is D. Changing the dollar amount to $6 million will eliminate Rule 505 as a possibility. As noted above, Rule 504 was already not viable because it has a $1 million limit. Section 3(a)(11) remains viable, as does Rule 506. Thus, the correct answer is D.

Multiple Choice Question 13-10: The correct answer is A. Given that Cloning Corp. wants to raise $35 million, we can quickly eliminate options III (Rule 504) and IV (Rule 505). Option I (Section 3(a)(11) seems viable, as Closing Corp. is incorporated in California, is "doing business" in California, and could restrict the offering to California residents. Section 4(2) also seems viable, if all of the offerees are sophisticated businesspersons. Thus, on these facts Answer A is correct.

Multiple Choice Question 13-11: The correct answer is D. Answer A is wrong because an immediate sale to out-of-state purchasers will ruin the intrastate exemption; the securities must "come to rest" before they may be resold outside the state. Answer B is true, as is Answer C, which makes Answer D the best answer. In Answer B, reselling to other in-state residents is permissible, even immediately after the offering. In Answer C, one year is sufficient for the securities to "come to rest" in the state.

Multiple Choice Question 13-12: The correct answer is C. Answer A is incorrect because all offerees (not just purchasers) must be properly qualified under Section 4(2). Answer B is incorrect because there is no specific numerical limit on the number of purchasers in a Section 4(2) offering.

Multiple Choice Question 13-13: The correct answer is D. Clearly, this was a very bad way to go about doing a stock offering! Answer A is incorrect because whether the investors received all of the information they *asked for* is irrelevant to whether there was a valid exemption from registration. Answer B is clearly incorrect—the company sent 1,000 letters to potential investors and the facts specifically state that none of these persons were sophisticated investors. Answer C is clearly wrong. Under Rule 506 there is a limit of thirty-five non-accredited investors (but no limit on the number of accredited investors). Here, none of the 100 investors were "wealthy" which likely means that none of them were accredited investors.

Multiple Choice Question 13-14: The correct answer is E. Under the "family resemblance" test adopted by the Supreme Court in *Reves v. Ernst & Young*, notes (or at least those with a term of more than nine months) are presumed to be "securities." However, this presumption could be rebutted by (1) showing that the note at issue bears a strong resemblance (i.e., a "family resemblance") to other types of notes that have previously been found not to be "securities" or (2) creating a new class of notes that are not "securities." If the second option is used, the Court set forth four factors to examine (the parties' motivations in entering into the transaction; the plan of distribution; the reasonable expectations of the investors; and whether there are other factors which reduce the risk of the investment). Here, option I is clearly wrong; if anything, a term longer than nine months makes it *more* likely that the note will be considered a security. Option II is incorrect because the *Reves* Court pointed out that if "the seller's purpose is to raise money for the general use of a business enterprise or to finance substantial investments and the buyer is interested primarily in the profit the note is expected to generate, the instrument is likely to be a 'security.'" Whether the investors had a preexisting relationship with the issuer is irrelevant, which makes option III incorrect as well.

CHAPTER 14

Answer Key:

14-1: C
14-2: B
14-3: D
14-4: D
14-5: D

14-6:   D
14-7:   B
14-8:   B
14-9:   A
14-10: D
14-11: D
14-12: A
14-13: A
14-14: C
14-15: A
14-16: A
14-17: D

Explanations:

Multiple Choice Question 14-1: The correct answer is C. Arguably, the bad news from the FDA was no longer non-public information when Elvis sold his shares. Note how the bad news was already driving the price of the stock down. However, Elvis's sale took place within six months after his purchase of shares, and the sales price was higher than the purchase price. Therefore, Section 16(b) would be applicable.

Multiple Choice Question 14-2: The correct answer is B. Bill did not "tip" Tom because he was unaware that Tom was listening to him. Thus, even though Bill had a *Cady, Roberts* duty to Large Corp., he did not receive any sort of personal benefit when Tom heard him. However, in *Dirks* the Supreme Court stated that a gift of material nonpublic information to a friend or relative who trades on the basis of the information confers a personal benefit on the *tipper*. Here, Bill gave a gift of the information to Angie. Answer C is a red herring, as there is no indication that Bill was a "Section 16 person" with respect to Large Corp., or any information about his previous trades. Answer D is wrong because one *can* violate Rule 10b-5 by being a tipper.

Multiple Choice Question 14-3: The correct answer is D. Answer A is incorrect because there is nothing in the facts that indicates that Angie had a duty of trust and confidence to Bill for purposes of the misappropriation theory of insider trading. Answer B is incorrect because the facts do not indicate that Angie was an "insider" that owed *Cady, Roberts* duties to Large Corp. As for Answer C, it is true that Angie did not owe a duty of trust and confidence to Large Corp.; however, the facts indicate that she was a tippee. As discussed in the prior explanation, Bill was a tipper. Given the facts, it seems clear that Angie knew or should have known that she was receiving an improper tip. Given these two conditions, that makes Angie a tippee under the rule from the *Dirks* case.

Multiple Choice Question 14-4: The correct answer is D. Tom was a bystander who overheard material nonpublic information from Bill. However, in the facts, Tom does not owe any duties to Bill or Large Corp. that would support a "classic" insider trading or a misappropriation theory argument. Thus, Tom did not violate Rule 10b-5 even though he traded a security on the basis of material nonpublic information.

Multiple Choice Question 14-5: The correct answer is D. Answer A is wrong because a Schedule 13D would not be required until Nacho owned more than 5% of PCC's stock. Answer B is wrong because it is not a Rule 10b-5 violation to buy stock before launching a tender offer; Nacho's *own* intentions do not constitute material nonpublic information when *Nacho* is doing the buying. Answer C is wrong because Rule 14e-3 does not prohibit buying stock in a target company before launching a tender offer for it. Answer E is wrong because the SEC does in fact regulate many kinds of stock purchases that do not violate Rule 10b-5. In other words, Rule 10b-5 is not the only rule "in the book."

Multiple Choice Question 14-6: The correct answer is D. Answer A is wrong because Carrie does not appear to have tipped Chuck. While she did tell him material nonpublic information, she did so because she was upset about possibly losing her job and does not appear to have intended that Chuck buy PCC stock. (Similarly, she told him that it was "top secret" information and that he couldn't tell anyone about it.) Answer B is wrong because Carrie did not trade on the basis of the information nor did she tip anyone (although it is true that she owed a duty of trust and confidence to PCC). Answer C is nonsensical; just because your spouse violated the law does not mean that you did.

Multiple Choice Question 14-7: The correct answer is B. As discussed above, Chuck was not "tipped" by Carrie; therefore Answer A is wrong. Answer C is wrong because one does not owe a *Cady, Roberts* duty to a company simply because one's spouse works there. Answer D is wrong because Chuck likely did misappropriate material nonpublic information from *Carrie*. Rule 10b5-2 provides in part that one owes a duty of trust or confidence for purposes of the misappropriation theory "[w]henever a person receives or obtains material nonpublic information from his or her spouse, parent, child, or sibling." Thus, Chuck has misappropriated information from Carrie unless he can:

> demonstrate that no duty of trust or confidence existed with respect to the information, by establishing that he or she neither knew nor reasonably should have known that the person who was the source of the information expected that the person would keep the information confidential, because of the parties' history, pattern, or practice of sharing and maintaining confidences, and

because there was no agreement or understanding to maintain the confidentiality of the information. [Rule 10b5-2.]

Given Carrie's admonition that the information was "top secret," it seems unlikely Chuck can do this.

Multiple Choice Question 14-8: The correct answer is B. Given his employment agreement, as well as the confidentiality agreement that he signed with PCC, Cletus owed a duty of trust and confidence to both Cleaning Crew and PCC. *See* Rule 10b5-2. He violated this duty by secretly using material nonpublic information that he learned from these sources to purchase securities.

Multiple Choice Question 14-9: The correct answer is A. Fred does not owe any duties to Yellow Corp. or Mr. Yellow on these facts. Answer B is incorrect because the information was material. Answers C and D are wrong because Fred does not own a duty of trust and confidence to either Yellow Corp. or Mr. Yellow. Fred is simply a spectator at a basketball game.

Multiple Choice Question 14-10: The correct answer is D. As the president of Yellow Corp., Mr. Yellow clearly owes *Cady, Roberts* duties to Yellow Corp. and its shareholders. He violated these duties by trading in Yellow Corp. stock on the basis of material nonpublic information.

Multiple Choice Question 14-11: The correct answer is D. Although Mr. Orange does not owe *Cady, Roberts* duties to Yellow Corp. because he is not an "insider" of Yellow Corp., he does own a duty of trust and confidence to Orange Corp. He thus violated Rule 10b-5 under the misappropriation theory because he used material nonpublic information that he learned from a source (Orange Corp.) to which he owed a duty of trust and confidence to purchase securities, and did not disclose his intentions to the source beforehand.

Multiple Choice Question 14-12: The correct answer is A. The April 2012 sale cannot be "matched" with the September 2011 purchase because it was more than six months later. But we can match the November 2011 purchase with the April 2012 sale. The profit per share is $1 ($22 minus $21) and we can match 5,000 shares. Thus, the answer is $5,000.

Multiple Choice Question 14-13: The correct answer is A. Note that because Mr. Crier is not an officer or director of Baby Food Corp., he may only be subject to Section 16(b) if he owns more than 10% of its outstanding stock. However, for a transaction to "match" for Section 16(b) purposes for someone who is only a shareholder, the person must have been a ten-percent shareholder immediately before the transaction. Thus, the July 1 purchase does not "count," because Mr. Crier did not own more than 10% of Baby Food Corp.'s stock immediately beforehand. However, the August 17 purchase counts, as does the September 30 sale and the October 31 sale. Because the sales price in both sales was the same ($22), it does not really matter which one we use to match with the August 17 purchase. Matching the August 17 purchase with the September 30 sale results in matching 50,000 shares at a $1 per-share profit, for a total recoverable profit of $50,000.

Multiple Choice Question 14-14: The correct answer is C. Note that there is only one sale in this series of transactions (August 10). Because the January 23 purchase took place more than six months before this sale, we can ignore that purchase. Remember that Section 16(b) makes "any" profit recoverable; thus, if given a choice, we should choose the "match" that results in the greatest profit. Here, we should first match the August 10 sale with the December 10 purchase because that purchase price ($9) was lower than the May 3 purchase price ($11). From these transactions, 1,000 shares can be matched at a $5 per-share profit, for a liability of $5,000. However, we still have 1,000 shares "left over" from the August 10 sale to match with the May 3 purchase. From these transactions, 1,000 shares can be matched at a $3 per-share profit, for a liability of $3,000. Total liability is thus $8,000.

Multiple Choice Question 14-15: The correct answer is A. Note that matching the April 13 purchase with the July 8 sale would produce a loss because the purchase price ($10) was higher than the sale price ($8). However, we can match the July 8 sale with the October 28 purchase. From these transactions, 1,000 shares can be matched at a $1 per-share profit, for total liability of $1,000.

Multiple Choice Question 14-16: The correct answer is A. Note that because Mr. Dull is not an officer or director of Sharp Corp., he may only be subject to Section 16(b) if he owns more than 10% of its outstanding stock. However, for a transaction to "match" for Section 16(b) purposes for someone who is only a shareholder, the person must have been a ten-percent shareholder immediately before the transaction. Thus, the March 13 purchase, which put him *over* the 10% threshold, does not count. By contrast, the April 13 purchase and the August 7 sale can be matched. From these transactions, 2,000 shares can be matched at a $1 per-share profit, for total liability of $2,000.

Multiple Choice Question 14-17: The correct answer is D. Note that the May 7 purchase cannot be matched with the December 3 sale because they are more than six months apart. Thus, we can only match the May 7 purchase with the October 10 sale. However, this results in a loss because the sales price ($15) was lower than the purchase price ($17). Hence, there was no "profit" that is recoverable under Section 16(b).

CHAPTER 15

Answer Key:

15-1: D
15-2: C
15-3: C
15-4: A
15-5: A
15-6: D
15-7: B
15-8: A

Explanations:

Multiple Choice Question 15-1: The correct answer is D. Even though she was not "at" the restaurant at the time, Karen is still liable for the limited partnership's debts and obligations because she is the general partner. Answer A is incorrect because Karen appears to have given Rufus *actual authority* to manage the restaurant, which would include ordering food. (Remember, as a "principal," a limited partnership could hire agents that would have authority under the *Restatement (Third) of Agency*.) Thus, he did not actually breach an implied warranty of authority. This also makes Answer E incorrect. Answer B is incorrect because it reflects the rule from the 1976 version of *RULPA*; under *ULPA* limited partners are not liable in their capacities as limited partners. Answer C sounds plausible, but as noted above, a limited partnership may be bound by its *agents*. Here, even though Rufus was a limited partner, he was also acting as an agent.

Multiple Choice Question 15-2: The correct answer is C. Under ULPA § 606(a) a limited partnership can be bound by the acts of a dissociated (i.e., former) general partner if:

    (1)   the act would have bound the limited partnership under Section 402 before the dissociation; and

    (2)   at the time the other party enters into the transaction:

        (A)   less than two years has passed since the dissociation; and

        (B)   the other party does not have notice of the dissociation and reasonably believes that the person is a general partner.

Here, all of these requirements are met. Thus, Answer A is incorrect. Answer B is incorrect because the relevant time period is two years, not ninety days. Answer D (and therefore Answer E as well) is incorrect because if the limited partnership is liable, then so too is its general partner (Johnny). Note that ULPA § 606(b) will make Jessica liable for any damages that Red Engine, L.P. incurs in this fact pattern.

Multiple Choice Question 15-3: The correct answer is C. Here, when General Partner 1 dissociated by express will, it was wrongful. *See* ULPA § 604(b)(2)(A). Similarly, when Limited Partner 3 dissociated by express will, it was wrongful. ULPA doesn't expressly say so, but the official comment to ULPA § 601(b)(1) does. However, Limited Partner 4 *has not even dissociated. See* ULPA § 601(b).

Multiple Choice Question 15-4: The correct answer is A. Under ULPA § 508(b)(2), a limited partnership may not pay a distribution if, following the distribution, its total assets would be less than its total liabilities (plus other amounts not relevant in this question). Thus, the maximum amount of distributions that Yellow, L.P. could pay would be $130,000, which makes Answers C and D incorrect. Moreover, distributions are paid proportionally based on the contributions that the various partners have made. *See* ULPA § 503. Here, General Partner 1 made 10% of the overall contributions by the partners and so would be entitled to 10% of a $130,000 distribution (i.e., $13,000). And so on.

Multiple Choice Question 15-5: The correct answer is A. Under ULPA § 801(2), the consent of all general partners would be needed to dissolve the limited partnership, even if all of the limited partners wanted to dissolve it. None of the other causes of dissolution set forth in ULPA § 801 would apply here. Answers B and C are incorrect because, if the general *had* consented to dissolution, only a majority in interest of the limited partners would need to approve the dissolution, not all of them.

Multiple Choice Question 15-6: The correct answer is D. Under ULPA § 801(3)(B), if a general partner dissociates and there are no other general partners (as is the case in this fact pattern), then the limited partnership will be dissolved *unless*, within ninety days, "consent to continue the activities of the limited partnership and admit at least one general partner is given by limited partners owning a majority of the rights to receive distributions as limited partners ..." and a new general partner is admitted. Here, because the three limited partners all have equal rights to distributions and two of the three of them voted to continue the limited partnership the requisite vote was achieved, but it was too late because it occurred more than ninety days after the general partner dissociated.

Multiple Choice Question 15-7: The correct answer is B. Under ULPA § 807(d), when a limited partnership dissolves, a claim that is not barred may be enforced:

(1)   against the dissolved limited partnership, to the extent of its undistributed assets;

(2)   if the assets have been distributed in liquidation, against a partner or transferee to the extent of that person's proportionate share of the claim or the limited partnership's assets distributed to the partner or transferee in liquidation, whichever is less, but a person's total liability for all claims under this paragraph does not exceed the total amount of assets distributed to the person as part of the winding up of the dissolved limited partnership; or

(3)   against any person liable on the claim under Section 404.

Here, the limited partnership has distributed all of its assets, so subsection (1) would not be helpful for Loan Shark, Inc. Subsection (2) would make the partners liable for the claim in proportion to the percentages of overall distributions they received (see the discussion of ULPA § 503 above). Also, subsection (3), by referring to ULPA § 404, would make the general partner liable for the full amount of the claim. Thus, Answer B is the only correct answer.

Multiple Choice Question 15-8: If Orange were an LLLP, ULPA § 807(d) would still apply. However, the General Partner would not be liable for the entire claim under ULPA § 404. Thus, Answer A is the only correct answer.

CHAPTER 16

Answer Key:

16-1:   C
16-2:   C
16-3:   C
16-4:   B
16-5:   A
16-6:   D
16-7:   D
16-8:   E
16-9:   D
16-10: C

Explanations:

Multiple Choice Question 16-1: The correct answer is C. Answer A is incorrect because, under the check the box regulations, an LLC will generally be taxed like a partnership, regardless of whether it would meet the requirements to be an S corporation. Answer B is incorrect because neither members nor managers are personally liable for the debts and other obligations of the LLC, unless the LLC's "veil" is pierced. Finally, Answer D is incorrect because it states the standards for when a *limited partner of a limited partnership* may become personally liable for the debts and other obligations of the limited partnership; it has nothing to do with LLCs.

Multiple Choice Question 16-2: The correct answer is C. Answer A is incorrect because Re-ULLCA § 201(e) allows an LLC to be formed before it has any members, as discussed on pages 893-94 of the text. Answer B is incorrect because neither statute requires a statement of whether the LLC is member-managed or manager-managed in its certificate of formation or certificate of organization; instead, this is a matter that would be addressed in the LLC's *operating agreement.* Answer D is incorrect because both statutes presume that the LLC will be member-managed (not manager-managed), unless the operating agreement provides otherwise.

Multiple Choice Question 16-3: The correct answer is C. Answer A is incorrect because Re-ULLCA § 407(b) provides that, in a member-managed LLC, "[e]ach member has equal rights in the management and conduct of the [LLC's] activities." Answer B is incorrect because the last sentence of Del. § 18-402 provides that "[u]nless otherwise provided in [an operating] agreement, each member and manager has the authority to bind the [LLC]," regardless of whether the LLC is member-managed or manager-managed. (However, Re-ULLCA § 301(a) does provides that a "member is not an agent of [an LLC] solely by reason of being a member.") Answer D is incorrect because even in a manager-managed LLC, there are some major decisions upon which members must vote. See page 910 of the text.

Multiple Choice Question 16-4: The correct answer is B. Of the choices, Option I is correct under Re-ULLCA §§ 409(g)(1) and (5). Option II is correct, as discussed on page 915 of the text. Option III is also correct under Del. § 18-1101(c). However, Option IV is incorrect; Re-ULLCA does not allow an operating agreement to *completely* eliminate the fiduciary duties of loyalty and care.

Multiple Choice Question 16-5: The correct answer is A. The last sentence of Del. § 18-402 provides that "[u]nless otherwise provided in [an operating] agreement, each member and manager has the authority to bind the [LLC]." This rule applies regardless of whether the LLC is member-managed or manager-managed. Answer B is incorrect because Re-ULLCA § 301(a) provides that a "member is not an agent of a limited liability company solely by reason of being a member." (Note here that *agency law* could give a member authority to bind the LLC, but Re-ULLCA itself does not do so.) Answer C is incorrect due to Del. §

18-402, as discussed above. Finally, Answer D is incorrect because, as discussed on page 912 of the text, Re-ULLCA is actually *silent* on the issue of a manager's apparent authority.

Multiple Choice Question 16-6: The correct answer is D. Option I is incorrect because Re-ULLCA does not actually provide a default rule with respect to *profits and losses*, as discussed on page 934 of the text. Option II is incorrect because Del. § 18-503 provides that, unless the operating agreement specifies otherwise, "profits and losses shall be allocated on the basis of the agreed value ... of the contributions made by each member to the extent that they have been received by the [LLC] and have not been returned." Option III is correct; *see* Re-ULLCA § 404(a) (interim distributions made by an LLC "must be in equal shares among members and dissociated members"). Finally, Option IV is correct under Del. § 18-504, as discussed on page 935 of the text.

Multiple Choice Question 16-7: The correct answer is D. Answer A is incorrect because having a guardian or conservator appointed for her would only dissociate Maggie from the LLC if it were *member-managed*. *See* Re-ULLCA § 602(6). Answer B is incorrect because a member's dissociation from the LLC would not, under the statute, cause an LLC to dissolve. *See* Re-ULLCA § 701. Answer C is incorrect because dissolution generally requires unanimous member consent. Again, see Re-ULLCA § 701.

Multiple Choice Question 16-8: The correct answer is E. Under Re-ULLCA, when an LLC is dissolved, then (unless the operating agreement provides otherwise) funds remaining after creditors have been paid are distributed as follows:

- First, persons who own a "transferable interest" will receive an amount equal to the value of their *unreturned* contributions to the LLC. If there are not enough funds to do so fully for all holders of transferable interests, then the funds that the LLC does have would be divided among these persons "in proportion to the value of their respective unreturned contributions."

- Second, any remaining funds would be distributed "in equal shares among members and dissociated members ...."

Mathematically, this means that both Answers A and C are correct, thus making Answer E the best choice. Answer A is correct because there are a total of $90,000 of contributions that have been made but not returned, whereas the LLC only has $45,000 on hand; thus, each member gets *half* of his or her unreturned contribution back. On the other hand, if the LLC had $180,000 on hand, then each member would first get his or her contributions back, but the remaining amounts would be divided equally. Answer B is incorrect because it presumed that *all* of the $180,000 would be divided according to the members' relative amounts of unreturned contributions.

Multiple Choice Question 16-9: The correct answer is D. In Delaware, when an LLC is dissolved and creditors have been fully paid, Del. § 18-803(a)(3) provides that members are paid "first for the return of their contributions and second respecting their limited liability company interests, the proportions in which the members share in distributions." (The default rule in the Delaware LLC statute is that members share distributions based on the relative values of their contributions to the LLC.) Further, if there are not sufficient assets to do so, then Del. § 18-804(b) states that "claims and obligations shall be paid or provided for according to their priority and, among claims of equal priority, ratably to the extent of assets available therefor." Mathematically, this makes Answer A and Answer B correct, which makes Answer D the best answer.

Multiple Choice Question 16-10: The correct answer is C. Answer A is incorrect because both the Delaware statute and Re-ULLCA contemplate that a demand may be excused in some situations. See pages 968-69 of the text. Answer B is incorrect because federal securities *statutes* do not address whether interests in an LLC are securities; instead, *courts* (in cases such as *Great Lakes Chemical Corp. v. Monsanto Co.* on page 948) must decide whether an LLC interest is a security. Finally, Answer D is incorrect because members have greater informational rights than those described in this answer; see pages 966-67 of the text.

CPSIA information can be obtained at www.ICGtesting.com
Printed in the USA
BVOW081906301211

279526BV00005B/2/P